LIST OF SECTIONS

Alphabetical

	SECTION
Banking and Lending Institutions	2
Banking Services and Procedures	5
Capital Asset Planning	17
Commodity Trading	23
Corporate Expansion, Combination, and Cooperation	20
Corporate Fiduciaries, Trusts, and Agencies	6
Corporate Stock	13
Corporate Surpluses, Reserves, and Dividends	18
Current Asset Planning	16
Financial Planning	15
Financial Reports	8
Forms of Business Organization	12
Government Obligations	11
Interest Rates and Money Markets	1
International Banking	3
Long-Term and Intermediate-Term Borrowing	14
Mathematics of Finance	27
Negotiable Instruments	24
Pension and Profit-Sharing Plans	19
Real Estate Finance	26
Recapitalizations and Readjustments	21
Reorganizations and Bankruptcy	22
Risk Management and Insurance	25
Savings Institutions	4
Securities Markets	10
Security Analysis	7
Selling Securities	9

THIS VOLUME IS ONE OF AN EXTENSIVE GROUP
OF REFERENCE HANDBOOKS PUBLISHED BY
THE RONALD PRESS COMPANY

FINANCIAL HANDBOOK

Edited by
JULES I. BOGEN, Ph.D.
LATE OF NEW YORK UNIVERSITY
GRADUATE SCHOOL OF BUSINESS ADMINISTRATION

Staff Editor
SAMUEL S. SHIPMAN, D.C.S.
NEW YORK UNIVERSITY
GRADUATE SCHOOL OF BUSINESS ADMINISTRATION

FOURTH EDITION
REVISED PRINTING

NEW YORK
THE RONALD PRESS COMPANY

Copyright © 1968 by
THE RONALD PRESS COMPANY

Copyright 1925, 1927, 1933, 1937, 1948, 1952, and © 1964 by
THE RONALD PRESS COMPANY

All Rights Reserved

No part of this book may be reproduced
in any form without permission in writing
from the publisher.

VR-VR

PRINTED IN THE UNITED STATES OF AMERICA

BOARD OF CONTRIBUTING EDITORS

E. SHERMAN ADAMS, PH.D.
   First National City Bank, New York, N. Y.
LESLIE PAUL ANDERSON, PH.D.
   University of Oregon
WILLIAM L. BENNETT
   International Bank for Reconstruction and Development
ELVIN F. DONALDSON, PH.D.
   The Ohio State University
LORING C. FARWELL, PH.D.
   Northwestern University
WILLIAM C. FREUND, PH.D.
   Prudential Insurance Company of America, Newark, N. J.
MEYER M. GOLDSTEIN
   Late, Pension Planning Company, New York, N. Y.
HENRY HARFIELD
   Attorney at Law, Shearman & Sterling, New York, N. Y.
ROBERT O. HARVEY, D.B.A.
   University of Connecticut
SIPA HELLER, J.D.
   New York University
PAUL L. HOWELL
   Third Deputy Comptroller, City of New York
HENRY KAUFMAN, PH.D.
   Salomon Brothers and Hutzler, New York, N. Y.
WALTER G. KELL, PH.D., C.P.A.
   University of Michigan
CLIFTON H. KREPS, JR., PH.D.
   University of North Carolina
ARNOLD R. LAFORCE
   Central Securities Corporation, New York, N. Y.
THEODORE LANG, C.P.A.
   New York University
DOUGLAS E. MATHEWSON, J.D.
   New York University
Z. LEW MELNYK, PH.D.
   University of Cincinnati
MARCUS NADLER, J.D.
   New York University

BOARD OF CONTRIBUTING EDITORS

THEODORE NESS
  Attorney at Law, Netter Netter Dowd Fox & Rosoff, New York, N. Y.
JOHN K. PFAHL, PH.D.
  The Ohio State University
SIDNEY M. ROBBINS, PH.D.
  Columbia University
DAVID SAPERSTEIN
  Attorney at Law, Silver, Saperstein & Barnett, New York, N. Y.
MICHAEL SCHIFF, PH.D., C.P.A.
  New York University
W. KENNETH SHARKEY
  Purdue University
LEO D. STONE, C.P.A.
  The Ohio State University
J. ROGER WALLACE
  The Journal of Commerce, New York, N. Y.

PUBLISHERS' PREFACE

Ever since the appearance of the First Edition in 1925, the FINANCIAL HANDBOOK has been widely accepted as a useful and authoritative reference by those active in business and finance, and their attorneys, accountants, and other professional advisers. In this Fourth Edition, the HANDBOOK has been thoroughly updated to carry on its long tradition of providing reliable guidance and factual information. Tailored as it is to serve those professionally interested in the subject, the HANDBOOK should also continue to be of use in educational institutions that offer training for careers in business, finance, banking, and law.

Recognized experts—including business executives, economists, accountants, and lawyers—here synthesize the leading literature and latest thinking in their areas to present concise statements of current principles and practice. Throughout, the impact of changes in taxation, government regulation, and law, are fully considered, and the latest techniques are explained and evaluated. Thus, coverage includes the changes brought about by the widespread adoption of the Uniform Commercial Code, and the role of the many new quantitative methods of analysis and control in corporate financial planning made possible by the electronic computer. Ready application of material is facilitated through detailed descriptions of systems and methods, and the inclusion of many illustrative examples. Pertinent tables and illustrative forms further enhance the volume's practicality.

For this edition, editorial direction was again placed in the able hands of Jules I. Bogen, who had in the Third Edition maintained so well the high standards established by the distinguished Editor of the first two editions, the late Colonel Robert H. Montgomery. Dr. Bogen's untimely death occurred as he was completing his work on the present edition. A lifetime of active participation in the financial world made Dr. Bogen ideally suited to his editorial task. A highly regarded economist, scholar, journalist, and financial consultant, he brought to the HANDBOOK a rare combination of skills and an unusually wide range of knowledge. The HANDBOOK benefited greatly from Dr. Bogen's work, and the present edition bears the imprint of his exceptional ability.

From the inception of the Fourth Edition, Samuel S. Shipman, long a colleague of Dr. Bogen's and a distinguished member of the financial community in his own right, has served as Staff Editor. As with past editions, the Editor-in-Chief and the Staff Editor have had the assistance of a large Board of Contributing Editors, whose names and major contributions are listed elsewhere in the HANDBOOK. All of the Contributing Editors are individuals of proven ability in their respective fields. Through them the user of the HANDBOOK has access to seasoned judgment and reliable counsel on a particular problem as reflected in the cumulative authoritative literature of finance. Many of the HANDBOOK's sections are among the very best compact presentations of their topics that can be obtained. In addition to the work of the editors, numerous individuals and organizations contributed material and helpful suggestions, and reviewed all or specific parts of the manuscript for the HANDBOOK.

With this edition, the HANDBOOK is presented in an enlarged format which will, it is hoped, enhance its usefulness. With each edition, every attempt is made to further adapt and develop the contents and manner of presentation to better satisfy the reader's needs. The up-to-date and broadened coverage, as well as the improvements in typography, make the Publishers confident that this Fourth Edition will achieve the popularity of its predecessors.

THE RONALD PRESS COMPANY
Publishers

In this Revised Printing the Publishers have sought to reflect the major developments since publication of the Fourth Edition that have affected Interest Rates and Money Markets, Banking and Lending Institutions, and International Banking. For his help in preparing the Revised Printing, special recognition is gratefully given to Professor Sidney M. Robbins, of the Columbia University Graduate School of Business. Credit is also due to Professor Ricardo A. Halperin, CPA (Argentina), University of Buenos Aires; and Patrick L. McDonald, who assisted Professor Robbins.

ABOUT THE EDITORS

Jules I. Bogen, Professor of Finance at the New York University Graduate School of Business Administration from 1932 until his untimely death, began his distinguished career as an active member of the financial community while still a student at Columbia University, where he completed both his undergraduate and graduate work. Connected with *The Journal of Commerce,* New York, from 1922 on, he served as its Editor from 1933 to 1947. He had also served as a technical adviser to the Banking and Currency Sub-Committee of the U. S. Senate, as economic consultant to the Savings Banks Trust Company, and other institutions, and as a member of the Advisory Council for the Research Committee of the American Bankers Association. Dr. Bogen was a past Vice President of both the American Finance Association and the American Management Association. A prolific writer, he was author or co-author of numerous books, monographs, and studies on finance and banking.

Samuel S. Shipman has taught actively as Professor of Finance at the New York University Graduate School of Business Administration for many years. He has also served at the University as Research Associate with the C. J. Devine Institute of Finance. Various trade associations and business concerns have utilized his talents as a consultant and director of research in economics. Dr. Shipman regularly contributes articles on banking, corporate finance, and international business to numerous trade and professional journals.

The twenty-seven Contributing Editors are all men of extensive experience in the world of finance and are recognized as authorities on their subjects. In addition to their practical skill, virtually every one of them has authored successful books or articles. Many of them also contributed to the Third Edition of the HANDBOOK. The group, aside from being made up of experts on every phase of finance, includes members of all of the professions whose disciplines bear upon the subject, including economists, attorneys, accountants, financial analysts, bankers, brokers, and business consultants. The following list of their names and the sections with which each was primarily concerned is ample proof that the HANDBOOK is indeed the work of experts:

E. Sherman Adams	Banking and Lending Institutions / Government Obligations
Leslie P. Anderson	Capital Asset Planning / Risk Management and Insurance
William L. Bennett	Corporate Fiduciaries, Trusts, and Agencies
Loring C. Farwell	Securities Markets
William C. Freund	Banking and Lending Institutions
Meyer M. Goldstein	Pension and Profit-Sharing Plans
Henry Harfield	Corporate Fiduciaries, Trusts, and Agencies
Robert O. Harvey	Real Estate Finance
Sipa Heller	International Banking
Paul L. Howell	Securities Markets / Pension and Profit-Sharing Plans
Henry Kaufman	Government Obligations

Walter G. Kell .... Corporate Surpluses, Reserves, and Dividends
Clifton H. Kreps, Jr. .... $\begin{cases} \text{Savings Institutions} \\ \text{Banking Services and Procedures} \end{cases}$
Arnold R. LaForce .. $\begin{cases} \text{Long-Term and Intermediate-Term Borrowing} \\ \text{Corporate Expansion, Combination, and Cooperation} \\ \text{Recapitalizations and Readjustments} \end{cases}$
Theodore Lang .... $\begin{cases} \text{Mathematics and Finance} \\ \text{Capital Asset Planning} \end{cases}$
Douglas E. Mathewson .... Negotiable Instruments
Z. Lew Melnyk .... $\begin{cases} \text{Capital Asset Planning} \\ \text{Risk Management and Insurance} \end{cases}$
Marcus Nadler .... Interest Rates and Money Markets
Theodore Ness .... $\begin{cases} \text{Forms of Business Organization} \\ \text{Corporate Stock} \\ \text{Pension and Profit-Sharing Plans} \end{cases}$
John K. Pfahl .... Financial Reports
Sidney M. Robbins .... $\begin{cases} \text{Financial Planning} \\ \text{Current Asset Planning} \\ \text{Capital Asset Planning} \end{cases}$
David Saperstein .... Selling Securities
Michael Schiff .... Capital Asset Planning
W. Kenneth Sharkey .... Risk Management and Insurance
Leo D. Stone .... Security Analysis
J. Roger Wallace .... Commodity Trading

CONTENTS

	SECTION
Interest Rates and Money Markets	1
Banking and Lending Institutions	2
International Banking	3
Savings Institutions	4
Banking Services and Procedures	5
Corporate Fiduciaries, Trusts, and Agencies	6
Security Analysis	7
Financial Reports	8
Selling Securities	9
Securities Markets	10
Government Obligations	11
Forms of Business Organization	12
Corporate Stock	13
Long-Term and Intermediate-Term Borrowing	14
Financial Planning	15
Current Asset Planning	16
Capital Asset Planning	17
Corporate Surpluses, Reserves, and Dividends	18
Pension and Profit-Sharing Plans	19
Corporate Expansion, Combination, and Cooperation	20
Recapitalizations and Readjustments	21
Reorganizations and Bankruptcy	22
Commodity Trading	23
Negotiable Instruments	24
Risk Management and Insurance	25
Real Estate Finance	26
Mathematics of Finance	27
Sources	A
General Index	

SECTION 1

INTEREST RATES AND MONEY MARKETS

CONTENTS

How Interest Rates Are Determined

	Page
The price of money	1
The level of interest rates	1
The interest rate structure	1
A century of interest rate movements. Long-term high grade corporate bond yields, 1867–1967 (f. 1)	2
Short-term or long-term rates	2
Changes in structure	2
Short-term and long-term interest rate movements (f. 2)	3
Quality of bonds	3
Role of credit control	3
Changes in the structure of interest rates, selected years, 1953–67 (f. 3)	4
Role of treasury debt management	5

Measuring the Supply and Demand of Funds

Sources of funds	6
Summary of uses and sources of investment funds (f. 4)	6
Users of funds	7
Sources of information	7
Statement of sources and uses of corporate funds (f. 5)	7

The Money Market

Money market defined	8
Relation to other markets	8
Economic basis of money market	9
Organization and operation of New York money market	9
The market for credit instruments	9
Principal lenders and borrowers	9

Individual Money Markets

Short-term government securities	10
Brokers' loans	10
Lenders and borrowers	11
Statistics on brokers' loans	11
Acceptance market	11
Federal Reserve banks and the acceptance market	12
Commercial paper market	12
Volume of commercial paper outstanding	12
Federal funds market	13
Negotiable time certificates of deposit	13

Interpretation of Banking Statistics

	Page
Significant data	14

1. Federal Reserve Statement

Assets of Federal Reserve banks	14
Gold certificate account	14
Redemption fund for Federal reserve notes	14
Consolidated statement of condition of the twelve Federal Reserve banks (f. 6)	15
Cash	16
Discounts and advances	16
Acceptances—bought outright	16
Acceptances—held under repurchase agreement	16
Federal agency obligations held under repurchase agreement	16
U.S. government securities—bought outright	16
U.S. government securities—held under repurchase agreement	16
Total loans and securities	16
Cash items in process of collection	17
Bank premises	17
Other assets	17
Liabilities of Federal Reserve banks	17
Federal reserve notes	17
Deposits: member bank reserves	17
Deposits: U.S. Treasurer—general account	17
Deposits: foreign	17
Other deposits	17
Total deposits	17
Deferred availability cash items	17
Other liabilities and accrued dividends	17
Capital accounts	17
Capital paid in	17
Surplus	18
Other capital accounts	18
Ratio of gold certificate reserves to Federal Reserve note liability	18
Federal Reserve credit	18
Changes in member bank reserve balances and related items (f. 7)	19
Free reserves	19
Federal Reserve control of credit	20
Instruments of credit control	20

2. Statement of Weekly Condition Report of Large Commercial Banks

Weekly condition report of large commercial banks, H.4.2 (f. 8)	21

INTEREST RATES AND MONEY MARKETS

CONTENTS (Continued)

	PAGE
Assets of member banks	22
Liabilities of member banks	23
Turnover of demand deposits	23
Loanable funds	23
Money supply and time deposits, 1947–67 (f. 9)	24

Relation of the New York Money Market to the Interior

Position of New York	25
Balances with domestic banks and domestic interbank deposits	25
Causes of movement of funds	25
Seasonal influences	25

Treasury Financing and the Money Market

Effect of treasury operations on money market	25
Debt management	26
Advance refunding	26

	PAGE
Other Influence on the Money Market	
Effects of business cycle	26
Prices and bank credit	27

Relation of New York to Foreign Money Markets

International position of New York money market	27
The postwar change: balance of payments deficit	27
Restoration of the international money market	27
Effect on the U.S. money market	28
The London money market	28
The bill market	28
Balance of payments problem	28
Bank of England weekly statement	29
Issue department	29
Banking department	29
Bank of England weekly statement (f. 10)	30

SECTION 1

INTEREST RATES AND MONEY MARKETS

How Interest Rates Are Determined

THE PRICE OF MONEY. Interest rates are the prices paid by borrowers to lenders for the use of money. Like all prices, interest rates reflect the changing forces of supply and demand in the market. When the supply of loanable funds exceeds the demand, interest rates tend to decline. Conversely, when borrowing demands exceed the supply of funds, interest rates tend to rise.

THE LEVEL OF INTEREST RATES. The level of interest rates has undergone sustained advances and declines over extended periods of time. These movements reflect basic economic changes affecting the demand and supply of funds. During the depressed 1930's, the level of interest rates declined sharply with the contraction in private demands for funds. During the war decade of the 1940's, interest rates were pegged at the abnormally low level of the depression by the Federal Reserve System. The Federal Reserve banks made reserves freely available to the banking system by purchasing all government obligations offered them at or above par, thus preventing interest rates from rising. When **pegging** was ended in 1951 and interest rates were freed to respond once again to supply and demand forces, the rapid growth of the economy, combined with price inflation, generated a record demand for funds that lifted interest rates to a much higher level by the end of the decade of the 1950's. Thereafter, as the supply of funds overtook the demand, interest rates declined slightly and then tended to stabilize until about mid-1965. Then the continuing expansion of the economy plus the requirements of hostilities in Southeast Asia augmented the demand for funds and led to a swift upward movement of interest rates. By the latter part of the decade, rates were close to their highest levels of the 20th century.

Interest rates have also been subject to **short cycles,** rising above and falling below the longer term trend in response to alternating periods of recession and recovery in the economy. In recessions, interest rates have tended to fall with the contraction of the demand for funds. In recoveries, interest rates tend to rise as demands for funds expand, unless a larger supply of funds offsets the growth of demand. Fluctuations in long-term bond yields over a century are shown in Fig. 1.

THE INTEREST RATE STRUCTURE. Interest rates vary for loans of different maturities and kinds. Individual interest **rates do not fluctuate uniformly** with changes in the level of rates, and at times particular rates move in divergent directions. The structure of interest rates undergoes constant change in response to shifts in demand and supply for particular maturities and types of credit. As a result, **differentials** between individual interest rates constantly widen or narrow.

1·1

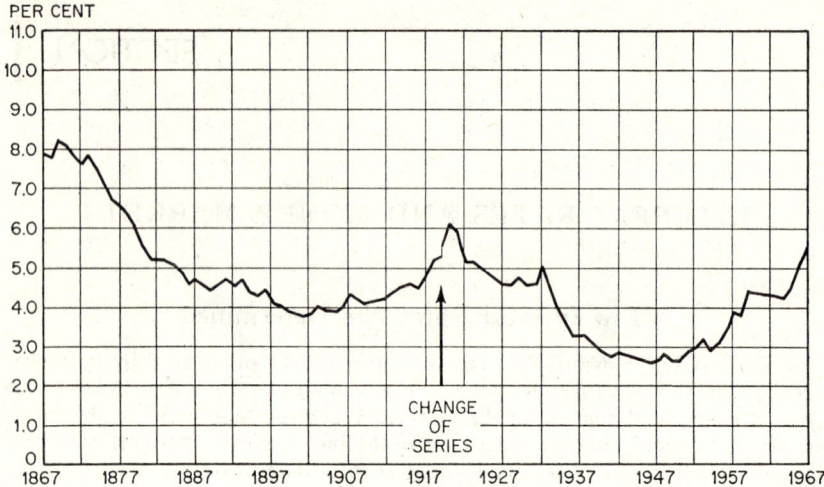

Fig. 1. A century of interest rate movements. Long-term high grade corporate yields, 1867–1967. (Source: 1867–1919, American Railroad Bonds, Macauley; 1919–1967, AAA Corporate Bond Yields, Moody's.)

Short-Term or Long-Term Rates. One major division in the interest rate structure is between short-term rates, that apply to maturities of one year or less, and long-term rates. Because short-term obligations are required in large volume for liquidity purposes, short-term interest rates have usually been lower than long-term rates. However, when the level of interest rates is high and is expected to decline, investors tend to favor long-term obligations to assure themselves a higher rate of return over a longer period, and at such times long-term rates may fall below short-term.

The changing spread between short-term and long-term interest rates is charted by the **Council of Economic Advisors** and published monthly in **Economic Indicators,** a compendium of economic and financial statistics issued each month by the Joint Economic Committee of Congress. Fig. 2 reproduces a chart showing rate movements through the first quarter of 1967. As would be expected, rates on Treasury bills with a maturity of 3 months and prime commercial paper maturing in 4 to 6 months are far more volatile than yields on U.S. government and top quality corporate bonds of long term, because the same change in the prices of long- and short-term obligations produces greater swings in the yields of the issues with nearer maturities. Prices of high-grade, short-term obligations change little, despite wide rate fluctuations, since they will be redeemed at the par value when they mature.

Changes in Structure. Changes in the structure of interest rates between 1953 and 1967 are shown in Fig. 3. Although the level of interest rates rose during this period, the extent of the rise varied greatly. The yield on 3-month Treasury bills rose from 1.90% in 1953 to 4.30% in 1967, an increase of over 125%. However the yield on long-term government bonds rose from 3.16% to 4.85%, an increase of over 50%. The result was a marked narrowing of the yield differential between short-term and long-term rates during this period.

Economists have distinguished between a **pure interest rate,** regarded as the hire for the use of money without considering risk factors, and a **premium for risk**

HOW INTEREST RATES ARE DETERMINED

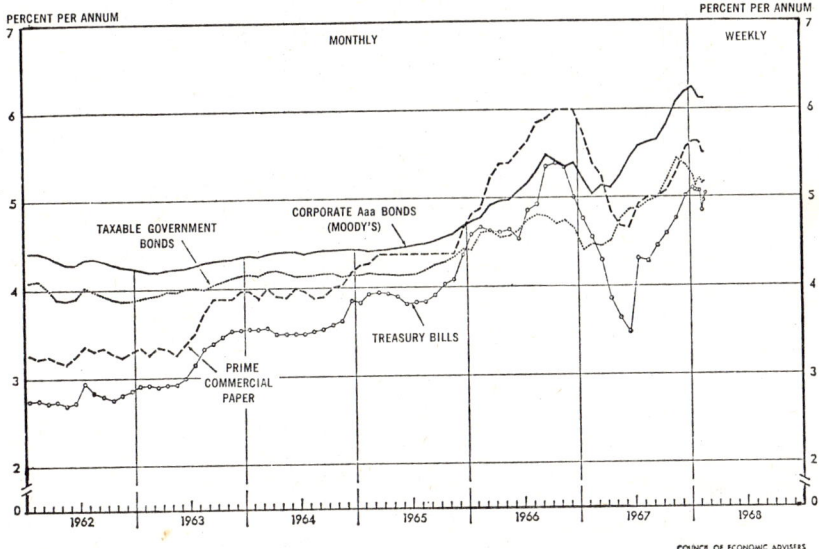

Fig. 2. Short-term and long-term interest rate movements.

that the lender requires because payment on the loan may not be made when due, or because a rise in interest rates may materially depress prices of all but short-term obligations. These risk elements influence the supply of funds for bonds, but other factors also affect the structure of interest rates. All factors of supply and demand must be taken into account in appraising the outlook for each type of interest rate, and in explaining changes that take place in the interest rate structure.

Quality of Bonds. Interest rates also vary for obligations of different quality. The lower the rating on a bond issue, the higher its yield tends to be. Differentials between yields of different ratings of bonds, as between different maturities, reflect **supply and demand** forces. In a period of prosperity, when very few bonds go into default, yield differentials for the several bond ratings tend to narrow as investors bid for lower rated bonds. In a period of economic adversity, when the danger of default looms larger, yield differentials for bonds of different ratings widen, as buying of lower rated bonds slackens and their yields rise.

ROLE OF CREDIT CONTROL. Interest rates are influenced in varying degree by the credit control policies of the **Federal Reserve System** and, to a lesser extent, by actions of **other Federal agencies** whose activities influence the supply and demand of funds.

Federal Reserve policy affects interest rates chiefly through influencing the supply of loanable funds from commercial banks. Under an **easy credit policy**, additional reserves are provided member banks that encourage them to expand loans and investments, and this addition to the supply of loanable funds tends to lower interest rates. Conversely, when the Federal Reserve banks contract member bank reserves through sales of government securities in the open market, they cut down the supply of loanable funds in the hands of commercial banks and so tend to "firm up" interest rates. Since open market operations in government securities by the Federal Reserve banks attain relatively large proportions at

1·4 INTEREST RATES AND MONEY MARKETS

Open-Market Money Rates in New York City

Yearly Average	Prime Commercial Paper, 4-6 Months	Finance Company Paper, Placed Directly, 3-6 Months	Prime Bankers' Acceptances, 90 Days
1953	2.52	2.33	1.87
1962	3.26	3.07	3.01
1967	5.10	4.89	4.75

Bank Rates on Short-term Business Loans

	All Loans	Loans of $200,000 and Over
1953	3.7	3.5
1962	5.0	4.8
1967	6.0	5.9

U.S. Government Security Yields

	3-Month Bills Market Yield	9- to 12-Month Bills Market Yield	3- to 5-Year Issues	Long-Term Bonds
1953	1.90	2.07	2.57	3.16
1962	2.77	3.01	3.57	3.95
1967	4.30	4.71	5.07	4.85

State and Local Governments

Yearly Average	Total	Aaa	Baa
1953	2.82	2.31	3.41
1962	3.30	3.03	3.67
1967	3.99	3.74	4.30

Bond Yields — Corporates (Moody's)

By Selected Rating

	Total	Aaa	Baa
1953	3.43	3.20	3.74
1962	4.61	4.33	5.02
1967	5.82	5.51	6.23

By Groups

	Industrial	Railroad	Public Utility
1953	3.30	3.55	3.45
1962	4.47	4.86	4.51
1967	5.74	5.89	5.81

Fig. 3. Changes in the structure of interest rates, selected years, 1953–67 (per cent per annum).

times, they may have some effect also upon the demand for funds. For example, large sales of short-term government securities by the Federal Reserve banks affect the market for such obligations in much the same way as an increased demand for funds by the U.S. Treasury.

Federal agencies have been particularly active in the mortgage field, and their activities have at times exerted considerable influence upon mortage interest rates. For example, purchases or sales of government-underwritten mortgages by the **Federal National Mortgage Association** (Fanny Mae) affect the supply or demand of funds in the **mortgage market** and, hence, the differential between mortgage and bond interest rates.

Credit control policies are subject to constant change as the Federal Reserve System and other agencies modify their objectives. During the 1950's, the primary aim of Federal Reserve policy was to promote economic stability and to check inflation. In the 1960's, the objective became the stimulation of the rate of growth of the economy by assuring an ample supply of loanable funds at moderate interest rates. During the latter part of this period, increasing attention was given to the problem of the outflow of gold caused by the continuing U.S. international balance of payments deficits. The combined concern with maintaining business expansion and halting the gold outflow was reflected in "Operation Nudge." This program involved support of short-term interest rates at a level high enough to discourage the shifting of short-term balances to foreign financial centers. At the same time, efforts were made to offset the upward movement of long-term interest rates in order to maintain a favorable climate for economic development.

There are times when Federal Reserve policy is the principal influence shaping the course of interest rates, and there are periods when the role of credit policy is minor and other supply and demand factors determine the behavior of interest rates.

The **measures taken by the credit authorities** to influence interest rates and their **effectiveness** also vary from time to time, with changes in the economy and the nation's financial system. Thus, the 1966 limitation that was placed on the rate of interest that could be paid on single and multiple maturity time deposits reversed the flow of funds that had been moving into commercial banks and directed the funds into other specialized thrift institutions, such as savings and loan associations. This shift temporarily alleviated some of the upward pressure on mortgage rates and on the liquidity position of the savings and loan institutions.

ROLE OF TREASURY DEBT MANAGEMENT. Another major factor affecting demand and supply of funds, and thus the course of interest rates, is the debt management policy of the U.S. Treasury. The fact that public debt management decisions are formulated in the **broad public interest,** to promote economic and financial policy objectives of the U.S. government, rather than to raise funds at minimum cost, makes it necessary to give special consideration to Treasury financing decisions in appraising the course of interest rates. This is particularly true because of the coordination of credit control and public debt management policies.

The **Treasury can contribute to a rise in interest rates** by expanding the supply of its long-term bonds through new offerings, refundings, and advance refunding. The Treasury can materially affect the structure of interest rates by shifts in the proportions of short-term, intermediate-term, and long-term obligations that it offers in refundings and in raising needed new money.

Measuring the Supply and Demand of Funds

SOURCES OF FUNDS. The bulk of the supply of funds comes from financial institutions. The most important among these are the institutions that receive **deposit-type savings,** including commercial banks, savings and loan associations, mutual savings banks, and credit unions. **Contractual savings** institutions, which include insurance companies, corporate pension funds, and state and local government retirement funds, are the other major institutional source of funds. Corporations investing their surplus cash, foreigners, and individual investors are less important sources of funds. The limited role of individuals

	1st year	2nd year	3rd year	4th year	5th year	6th year	7th year	(Estimate)	(Projection)
Uses (funds raised)									
Investment funds	29.1	25.6	30.8	34.0	39.8	42.6	45.6	41.3	47.2
Short-term funds	17.1	14.4	11.4	18.7	21.5	25.6	33.4	29.0	25.7
U.S. Government and agency publicly-held securities	10.5	−2.7	5.9	6.0	2.5	3.3	.5	2.6	7.5
Total uses	56.7	37.3	48.1	58.7	63.8	71.5	79.6	72.9	80.4
Sources (funds supplied)									
Savings institutions:									
Life insurance companies	5.2	5.4	5.6	6.4	6.6	7.4	8.3	8.6	8.8
Corporate pension funds	3.2	3.3	3.4	3.5	3.7	3.9	4.7	5.0	5.6
State and local government retirement funds	1.8	2.1	2.2	2.4	2.4	2.7	2.8	3.1	3.9
Fire and casualty insurance companies	1.5	1.1	1.3	1.2	1.3	1.1	.9	.9	1.4
Contractual-type savings institutions	11.7	12.0	12.5	13.6	14.0	15.1	16.7	17.6	19.7
Savings and loan associations	8.4	7.3	9.4	10.3	13.4	11.1	9.5	4.3	7.1
Mutual savings banks	1.4	1.5	2.1	3.1	3.5	4.2	3.9	2.7	3.7
Credit unions	.7	.6	.4	.6	.7	.9	1.1	.9	1.0
Deposit-type savings institutions	10.5	9.4	11.9	14.0	17.6	16.2	14.4	7.9	11.8
Investment companies	1.4	1.1	1.4	1.5	.8	1.1	2.0	2.1	2.5
Total savings institutions	23.5	22.5	25.8	29.0	32.3	32.3	33.2	27.6	34.0
Commercial banks	4.9	8.8	15.8	19.5	19.4	22.2	29.1	18.0	24.0
Business corporations:									
Nonfinancial	10.7	−1.6	3.0	5.5	5.9	7.4	6.8	9.2	5.5
Financial	3.2	2.2	.4	2.6	4.2	4.0	5.1	2.9	3.2
Total business corporations	13.9	.6	3.4	8.1	10.1	11.4	11.9	12.1	8.7
Other investor groups:									
Federal agencies	2.3	1.8	.8	.8	−.8	.4	.2	4.0	2.8
Brokers and dealers	...	−.1	1.0	−.1	1.4	−.4	.4	−.2	...
Other consumer lenders	.2	.3	.2	.4	.4	.4	.4	.3	.3
State and local governments [1]	1.1	1.4	1.0	1.3	1.4	1.2	3.2	3.1	3.6
Foreign investors	4.6	1.8	.6	2.0	.8	.8	−.1	−.9	2.2
Total other investor groups	8.2	5.1	3.6	4.4	3.2	2.4	4.2	6.3	8.9
Residual: Individuals and others [2]	6.2	.3	−.4	−2.3	−1.3	3.2	1.2	8.9	4.8
Total sources	56.7	37.3	48.1	58.7	63.8	71.5	79.6	72.9	80.4

[1] Excluding retirement funds included with savings institutions above.
[2] Includes revaluation of book assets of some holders.

Fig. 4. Summary of uses and sources of investment funds (in billions of dollars).

MEASURING THE SUPPLY AND DEMAND OF FUNDS 1·7

results from the fact that personal savings are lodged, in the first instance, chiefly in deposit-type and contractual savings institutions that derive the bulk of their funds from individuals for whom they act as intermediaries in the investment of personal savings.

USERS OF FUNDS. The demand for funds comes from four major types of users. These are (1) governments, (2) businesses, chiefly corporations, (3) consumers, and (4) mortgage borrowers. Because of the large proportion of the cost of residential and commercial buildings that is borrowed and the long period of time over which such debt is amortized, mortgage borrowing tends to be the largest single use of funds in peacetime. In measuring the demand for funds, only the **net change** in outstanding debt for a given period is important. To the extent that new borrowing is offset by repayments of outstanding debt of the same kind, no net demand for funds results.

SOURCES OF INFORMATION. Statistics of the supply and demand of funds are available regularly. These explain **changes in the level and structure of interest rates.** Projections of the supply and demand of funds for a period ahead, based on prospective developments, provide the basis for appraising the

Sources, total	97.7
Internal sources	60.3
Undistributed profits	24.2
Corporate inventory valuation adjustment	−1.6
Capital consumption allowances	37.7
External sources	37.4
Stocks	1.2
Bonds	10.2
Mortgages	2.1
Bank loans, n.e.c.	7.6
Other loans	2.1
Trade debt	7.7
Profits tax liability	−.4
Other liabilities	6.8
Uses, total	94.9
Purchases of physical assets	75.4
Nonresidential fixed investment	60.4
Residential structures	2.7
Change in business inventories	12.3
Increase in financial assets	19.5
Liquid assets	1.1
Demand deposits and currency	.7
Time deposits	−.7
U.S. Government securities	−1.2
Finance company paper	2.3
Consumer credit	1.1
Trade credit	10.9
Other financial assets	5.6
Discrepancy (uses less sources)	−2.8

Fig. 5. Statement of sources and uses of corporate funds (in billions of dollars).

outlook for interest rates. Figure 4 summarizes supply and demand statistics, with one-year projections, published for each class of borrowers and each major source of funds by the Bankers Trust Co. of New York for a recent period of years. By analyzing supply and demand data for a period of years, trends in these basic forces determining interest rates can be appraised.

Another source of data is the **Flow of Funds/Saving statistics** published quarterly and annually in the Federal Reserve Bulletin. Statistics of the funds raised by the several sectors of the economy, and the sources of such credit, are provided in this series.

In order to project the demand for funds by the government and corporations, use is made of available basic data. The **Federal budget** indicates the amount of deficit financing that the U.S. Treasury will have to undertake, whereas the **schedule of Federal debt maturities** indicates prospective refunding operations. Similarly, a projection of the uses and sources of corporate funds furnishes the basis for estimating corporation borrowing demands. Such a projection can be made in the light of known and expected developments affecting corporate spending. The **Department of Commerce** publishes statistics of the uses and sources of funds by corporations, as shown in Fig. 5 for a recent year, and these can provide a framework for making such projections. In the year covered, internal sources provided the major sources of funds. Among the external sources, the most important were $10.2 billion of net corporate bond financing and $7.7 billion of trade debt. Projections should take into account the recent pattern of fund flows as well as developments that could cause changes in future flows. Thus, high stock prices might induce investors to buy new issues of equities representing an enlarged source of funds while an expected decrease in corporate spending for fixed investment would reduce the overall demand for funds.

The Money Market

MONEY MARKET DEFINED. A money market is a center where the **demand for and supply of short-term funds** meet. It is a clearing center for a large number of financial transactions, both national and international—a place where the loanable funds of the nation and of other nations are held.

The term money market is usually applied only to the market for short-term funds. The market for long-term funds is usually referred to as the **capital market.** However, the market for U.S. government and agency securities and other prime long-term obligations is sometimes included in the "money market," whereas the term "capital market" is used at times to include the market for long-term and short-term funds.

In this Section, the money market is considered to include the market for short-term funds. The market for long-term loans and investments is discussed in the sections on the Securities Markets, Government Obligations, Savings Institutions, and Long-Term and Intermediate-Term Borrowing.

Relation to Other Markets. The money market, even when considered to consist only of the market for short-term funds, is closely related to a number of other markets that rely on it for financial accommodation. The New York money market, for example, is closely related to (1) the capital market for new issues of stocks and bonds; (2) the secondary capital market, including the stock exchanges and brokers and dealers in securities; (3) the foreign exchange market, which embraces international financial transactions between the United States and the rest of the world; (4) the commodity markets, such as the cotton, grains, and sugar exchanges; and (5) the insurance, shipping, and other markets requiring short-term credit accommodation in their operations.

ECONOMIC BASIS OF MONEY MARKET. All these individual markets together provide the economic basis of the money market. Without them there would be little need for a large and well-organized market for short-term funds. Some of them are indispensable, whereas others are not an absolutely necessary part of a monetary center. Thus, an international money market could hardly exist without the support of related bond, stock, and foreign exchange markets.

The great **strength of the New York money market** lies particularly in the city's large and well-organized markets for securities, commodities, etc., that provide a **continuous demand for short-term funds** for financing their operations. Furthermore, from the viewpoint of the lender, these markets provide excellent opportunities for the **safe employment of liquid funds.**

Just as the securities markets cannot function without a money market, so a money market cannot exist without the securities markets; for the money market requires channels through which funds may be invested, whereas the securities markets require sources from which to borrow short-term funds. Similarly, the commodity markets give rise to a considerable volume of loans and bankers' acceptances that help to finance the movement and sale of commodities and at the same time provide a safe and liquid medium for short-term investment. International trade requires **credit,** and thus gives rise to media for the investment of short-term funds. The greater the number of markets included in the monetary center, the greater its absorptive power for credit will be.

ORGANIZATION AND OPERATION OF NEW YORK MONEY MARKET. Although money markets exist in all of the principal cities, the New York money market is by far the most important. It is this market that must be most closely studied in appraising the money and credit situation of the country.

Short-term funds may be invested in New York through either of two channels: (1) **direct loans,** usually collateraled by securities, or (2) purchase of short-term **credit instruments.**

The Market for Credit Instruments. The open market for credit instruments has as its principal subdivisions: (1) **short-term government securities** including Treasury bills and certificates, (2) the **commercial paper** market, (3) the **bankers' acceptance** market, (4) negotiable **certificates of time deposits** issued by commercial banks, and (5) **federal funds** market. The short-term government security market has overshadowed in importance all other markets combined.

Principal Lenders and Borrowers. Those who operate in the money market may be broadly classified into two groups—lenders and borrowers, although sometimes the two functions are combined. The principal lenders in the New York money market are:

1. The Federal Reserve banks.
2. The large commercial banks, which place funds in government and municipal obligations, acceptances, and commercial paper as well as in the call money market.
3. Investing institutions, such as pension funds, insurance companies, and savings banks.
4. Money brokers, who act mainly for out-of-town lenders.

5. Corporations, which are among the largest buyers of short-term Treasury obligations, commercial paper, and bankers' acceptances.
6. Foreign banks, official institutions, and other holders of liquidity reserves in this country.

The borrowers consist principally of:
1. The United States government, which obtains a large volume of funds through the sale of Treasury bills, tax-anticipation bills, and certificates of indebtedness.
2. Brokerage houses and dealers in government securities, which borrow chiefly for the account of their customers or to carry securities purchased pending their resale.
3. Investment banking houses, which utilize the money market for financing new security issues.
4. Individuals who trade in securities.
5. Dealers and traders in commodities they distribute.
6. Importers and exporters, who obtain financial accommodation chiefly through the use of bankers' acceptances.
7. Business concerns and finance companies that issue commercial paper or other short-term obligations to raise funds.

Individual Money Markets

SHORT-TERM GOVERNMENT SECURITIES. Treasury bills and certificates of indebtedness constitute by far the most important media of investment for short-term funds. The volume of such issues available expanded enormously during World War II, dwarfing other short-term investments available by comparison. Since then bills have continued to grow, whereas certificates have been used intermittently in the Federal financing scheme. **Treasury bills** bear no interest and are traded in on a discount basis, whereas **Treasury certificates** are interest-bearing and are quoted on a price basis plus accrued interest like long-term bonds. The financial houses that deal in bankers' acceptances, discussed below, deal also in government securities and, as in the case of the acceptance market, the Federal Reserve banks are among the most important buyers. The rate on short-term Treasury securities is usually lower than the acceptance rate because of the high credit standing of the government.

Commercial banks, large corporations, and foreign governments and central banks are the largest buyers of short-term Treasury obligations. (For further discussion see Sec. 11, Government Obligations.)

BROKERS' LOANS. Although loans on securities are made to various types of borrowers and on varying terms, the great bulk of such loans in the New York money market are call loans to brokers and dealers. Some security loans are also contracted on a time basis, usually for 90 days. Call loans are made on a day-to-day basis and are payable on demand on the day following the day contracted. If not called, they are automatically renewed for another day.

The **volume of brokers' loans** fluctuates widely because of varying conditions in the stock market. One of the major influences on brokers' loans is the degree of speculative activity in the market. When the public is "in the market," the volume of such loans expands greatly, and conversely, when speculation is limited, the volume declines to comparatively small proportions. A second factor affecting brokers' loans is the **level of security prices.** When stock prices are high, a larger amount of loans is required to finance purchases. The **volume of new security issues** is a third factor. Investment bankers underwriting new issues of securities normally have recourse to collateral loans to finance their operations during the period when the securities are being distributed. If new issues are offered on a large scale, there is a tendency for loans on securities to increase.

Margin requirements imposed by the Federal Reserve Board are an important factor in the determination of the volume of brokers' loans. When the Reserve Board raises margin requirements, the inducement to use this form of credit is reduced. Between 1955 and 1968, requirements have been as low as 50%, and as high as 90%, of a security's market value. Regulations T and U govern the amount of credit that may be extended on a security by brokers and banks. A new regulation, Regulation G, limits the amount of credit that may be extended by "other lenders." (For a discussion of margin regulation, see Section 10.)

Lenders and Borrowers. Chief among the lenders in the brokers' loan market are the large New York City banks, although a considerable amount is loaned by banks in other cities through the agency of their New York correspondents. During periods of high levels of speculative activity, persons or firms other than domestic banks and brokers have been active in lending money for the purpose of enabling the borrower to purchase or carry securities. Previously, loans of this nature were not subject to control by the Federal Reserve. Although these loans were small as related to the total volume of security credit, they were characteristically granted on very low initial margins and constituted an unstable and potentially dangerous element in the securities markets. Early in 1968, therefore, the Reserve authorities, through the issuance of Regulation G, extended to these "other lenders" the same margin requirements that applied to banks and brokers.

The brokers and dealers in securities, who constitute the demand element in the market, borrow for two purposes. Firstly, they borrow to **finance the margin accounts** of their customers. Secondly, dealers and underwriters borrow from banks to **finance their securities inventory** pending distribution to investors.

Statistics on Brokers' Loans. Data on security loans are contained in the **Member Bank Call Reports** issued by the Board of Governors for each of the member bank call dates, of which there are usually four a year. For current use more frequent statistics are desirable. The New York Stock Exchange publishes monthly statistics of member firm borrowings on United States government obligations and on other collateral. The most frequent report on brokers' loans is the Weekly Condition Report of Large Commercial Banks. Although this statement includes a smaller number of banks than the reports of the Federal Deposit Insurance Corporation and the member bank call reports, it includes the loans of the largest banks of the country, and indicates weekly changes in the volume of loans.

ACCEPTANCE MARKET. A **banker's acceptance,** or **banker's bill,** is a draft drawn on a bank by an individual or firm ordering the bank to pay to the order of a third person a specified sum of money, either on demand or at some specified future date, and accepted by the bank. The maturity of acceptances is usually from 30 to 180 days. The bank expects the drawer of the draft to provide it with funds to pay the acceptance when due and usually requires that collateral be pledged as security. An acceptance, in effect, substitutes the credit of the bank for that of the drawer.

The market for bankers' acceptances in the United States is **a post-World War I development.** Prior to the passage of the Federal Reserve Act in 1913, national banks were prohibited from creating acceptances. The law establishing the Federal Reserve System permits member banks to create acceptances up to 100% of their combined capital and surplus and, with the permission of the Federal Reserve Board, up to 150%. The provision for an additional 50% applies only to acceptances drawn to create **dollar exchange**. Bankers' acceptances, provided they meet certain requirements, are eligible for discount at the Federal Reserve banks.

The following table shows changes in the volume of acceptances outstanding since the end of 1930.

BANKERS' ACCEPTANCES OUTSTANDING—END OF YEAR
(in millions of dollars)

1930	1,470
1940	209
1950	394
1955	642
1960	2,027
1963	2,890
1967	4,317

The amount of acceptances outstanding at the end of December 1967, classified by transactions that they finance, is shown below:

CLASSIFICATION OF BANKERS' ACCEPTANCE OUTSTANDING—END OF DECEMBER 1967
(in millions of dollars)

Imports into United States	1,086
Exports from United States	989
Dollar Exchange	37
Goods stored in or shipped between points in United States	162
Goods stored in or shipped between points in foreign countries	2,042
Total	4,317

As the above table shows, the volume of bankers' acceptances has increased very rapidly since 1955. This is due not only to the growth of international trade, but also to the spread between the rate of interest on acceptances and the prime bank rate. At the end of 1967 the prime rate was 6%, whereas prime bankers' acceptances with a maturity of 90 days sold at a discount of 5.6%. Under these conditions, many borrowers preferred to finance certain transactions through acceptance credit rather than borrowing directly from the banks.

Federal Reserve Banks and the Acceptance Market. The acceptance market was long under the domination of the Federal Reserve banks, which were the most important buyers of acceptances, both for their own account and for the account of foreign correspondents. However, the Federal Reserve banks now purchase acceptances only in relatively small amounts since the commercial banks prefer to hold them for investment of part of their idle reserves. Insurance companies and other corporations are also large buyers.

COMMERCIAL PAPER MARKET. Commercial paper consists of **promissory notes** of large business concerns of high credit standing, usually maturing in 4 to 6 months, which are bought and sold in the open market. Large companies often prefer this method of raising temporary working capital to direct loans from banks. This type of credit instrument is considered a desirable medium of investment of short-term funds by banks and other lenders.

Volume of Commercial Paper Outstanding. As indicated by the table below, the volume of commercial paper outstanding increased sharply in the postwar period. This reflected in part the widened spread between the commercial paper rate and the prime rate charged by banks, which induced many large corporations to expand the sale of their notes in the open market to supplement their lines of credit with the commercial banks. Another factor in the steep rise has been the rapid **expansion of sales finance companies**, the sales of whose paper directly to investors far exceed those of all other borrowers combined.

The volume of commercial paper outstanding is shown in the following table:

COMMERCIAL PAPER OUTSTANDING—END OF YEAR
(in millions of dollars)

1930	357
1935	172
1940	218
1945	159
1950	333
1955	2,020
1960	4,497
1963	6,747
1967	17,084

Of the commercial paper outstanding at the end of 1967, that placed through dealers amounted to $4,901 million, and finance company paper placed directly, $12,183 million.

Federal Funds Market. This market provides a method whereby member banks may adjust their **reserve balances** with the Federal Reserve banks without borrowing from them. When a member bank's reserves fall below the legal requirement, they must be replenished. The most obvious method of increasing reserve balances is by direct borrowing from the Reserve banks, but member banks are reluctant to do this. It is often possible to obtain temporary additional reserve balances, usually at lower cost, through the Federal funds market.

Federal funds are sight claims on Federal Reserve banks or the United States Treasury. They consist of demand deposits with the Reserve banks, cashiers' checks of the Reserve banks, and checks of the United States Treasury. The Reserve banks give immediate deposit credit for such claims. Thus, a bank that is deficient in reserves may temporarily increase its balances by exchanging its own cashier's check for a check on a Federal Reserve bank drawn by another member bank possessing excess reserves. When the check on the Federal Reserve bank (Federal funds) is deposited with it, the account of the depositing bank is credited immediately, whereas the cashier's check must go through the clearing house and is not debited to the account of the drawer until the next day. Thus, the bank buying the Federal funds obtains an increase in its reserve balances for one day. Interest for one day is added to the cashier's check given in payment for Federal funds.

A **Federal funds market** has been developed in New York by a few money brokers who act as intermediaries in arranging the exchange of checks, charging at times a small commission for their services. The **market rate** on Federal funds is generally lower than the discount rate and is higher only in periods when the Federal Reserve banks are endeavoring to restrict the volume of reserve credit outstanding. A rise in the rate for Federal funds is generally an indication of tighter money and credit conditions.

Negotiable Time Certificates of Deposit. As a result of increasingly competitive money markets in the early 1960's, commercial banks were forced to look elsewhere for sources of funds. In early 1961, the leading New York banks began to issue negotiable interest-bearing time certificates of deposit. Their example was soon followed by banks in other financial centers, and a new open market credit instrument was created. Certificates of Deposit (CD's) have attained considerable importance in recent years as is evidenced by their dramatic growth. Starting from almost nothing in 1961, the amount of CD's had reached a level of over $20 billion by early 1968. The relative attractiveness of CD's lies in that they enable investors to put money to work for a fixed short period of time at a higher rate of interest than prevails in the Treasury bill market. The establishment of a secondary market makes CD's even more attractive since it provides needed liquidity in the event of a pre-maturity sale.

Interpretation of Banking Statistics

SIGNIFICANT DATA. Analysis and forecasting of money market and credit conditions are based primarily upon the interpretation of currently published banking statistics. Significant data are found in the following statements, all of which appear in the principal newspapers on Friday:

1. Consolidated statement of condition of all Federal Reserve banks (H.4.1(a)).
2. Factors affecting bank reserves (H.4.1).
3. Weekly condition report of large commercial banks in New York and Chicago (H.4.3).

1. Federal Reserve Statement

The most important of these statements is the consolidated statement of the Federal Reserve banks (Fig. 6), which reveals changes in the amount of Federal Reserve credit outstanding, the amount of Federal Reserve notes in circulation, the movement of gold, and, above all, the credit policies being pursued by the Federal Reserve System.

An explanation of the details of the Federal Reserve statement follows.

ASSETS OF FEDERAL RESERVE BANKS.

Gold Certificate Account. This shows certificates given by the United States Treasury for the gold taken over from the Reserve banks when the gold content of the dollar was reduced to 59.06% of its former amount on January 31, 1934, under the provisions of the Gold Reserve Act of 1934; together with increases or declines resulting from inflows and outflows of monetary gold.

Until early 1968 the Federal Reserve Act required each Federal Reserve bank to maintain a reserve in gold certificates of 25% against Federal Reserve notes in actual circulation. In March, 1968, this requirement was abolished by Congress to make this country's gold reserves available to help meet the international demand for gold. Since that time, therefore, the amount of the former **Redemption Fund for Federal Reserve notes** has been included in the Gold Certificate Account.

Redemption Fund for Federal Reserve Notes. This was the amount of gold certificates deposited with the U.S. Treasury by the Federal Reserve banks for the redemption of Federal Reserve notes. It was equal to not less than 5% of the amount of notes issued by each Federal Reserve bank and not covered by gold certificates pledged with the Federal Reserve agent. Since the elimination of the gold cover for Federal Reserve notes, this amount has been transferred to the Gold Certificate Account.

Assets	Feb. 7, 1968	Jan. 31, 1968	Feb. 8, 1967
Gold certificate account	9,447	9,547	10,838
Redemption fund for F.R. notes [1]	1,937	1,937	1,834
Total gold certificate reserves	11,384	11,484	12,672
Cash	416	409	347
Discounts and advances	236	843	827
Acceptances:			
Bought outright	63	63	76
Held under repurchase agreement	–	20	50
Federal agency obligations:			
Held under repurchase agreement	5	–	3
U.S. Government securities:			
Bought outright—			
Bills	15,843	15,773	12,135
Certificates	–	–	4,351
Notes	26,952	26,952	21,302
Bonds	6,130	6,130	6,199
Total bought outright	48,925	48,855	43,987
Held under repurchase agreement	397	237	551
Total U.S. Government securities	49,322	49,092	44,538
Total loans and securities	49,626	50,018	45,494
Cash items in process of collection	7,161	7,105	7,151
Bank premises	112	112	107
Other assets [2]	2,221	2,165	1,041
Total Assets	70,920	71,293	66,812
Liabilities			
Federal Reserve notes	40,415	40,277	38,324
Deposits:			
Member bank reserves	21,217	21,838	21,021
U.S. Treasurer—general account	1,019	1,153	489
Foreign	148	160	135
Other [3]	437	463	448
Total deposits	22,821	23,614	22,093
Deferred availability cash items	5,921	5,689	4,809
Other liabilities and accrued dividends	322	318	241
Total Liabilities	69,479	69,898	65,467
Capital Accounts			
Capital paid in	607	606	573
Surplus	598	598	570
Other capital accounts	236	191	202
Total Liabilities and Capital Accounts	70,920	71,293	66,812
Contingent liability on acceptances purchased for foreign correspondents	131	141	181
Ratio of gold certificate reserves to F.R. note liability [4]	27.5%	27.8%	32.3%

[1, 2, 3, 4] For notes, see end of table, p. 16.

Fig. 6. Consolidated statement of condition of the twelve Federal Reserve banks (in millions of dollars) (see continuation).

MATURITY DISTRIBUTION OF LOANS AND SECURITIES, FEBRUARY 7, 1968
(Acceptances and securities held under repurchase agreement are classified as maturing within 15 days in accordance with maximum maturity of the agreements.)

	Discounts and advances	Acceptances	U.S. government securities and Federal Agency obligations Holdings	Changes during week
Within 15 days	235	15	2,379	−339
16 days to 90 days	1	48	8,304	+642
91 days to 1 year	—	—	20,994	− 68
Over 1 year to 5 years	—	—	16,237	—
Over 5 years to 10 years	—	—	853	—
Over 10 years	—	—	560	—
Total	236	63	49,327	+235

[1] Now included in the gold certificate account.
[2] Includes assets denominated in foreign currencies and IMF gold deposited.
[3] Includes IMF gold deposit.
[4] Because of the elimination of the gold cover for Federal Reserve notes, this ratio is no longer reported.

Fig. 6 (Continued)

Cash. This includes coin and currency on hand in the Federal Reserve banks except gold certificates and Federal Reserve notes.

Discounts and Advances. This comprises bills discounted for member banks and advances on their promissory notes secured by U.S. government obligations or similar assets.

Acceptances—Bought Outright. These are prime bankers' acceptances bought by the Federal Reserve Bank of New York for its own account at prevailing interest rates.

Acceptances—Held Under Repurchase Agreement. These are acceptances acquired by the New York Reserve Bank under agreements calling for the seller to buy them back within 15 days or less.

Federal Agency Obligations Held Under Repurchase Agreement. A September, 1966, amendment to the Federal Reserve Act authorized Federal Reserve banks to buy and sell fully guaranteed Federal agency securities. Initial operations in these instruments were restricted to repurchase agreements. This account includes those agreements.

U. S. Government Securities—Bought Outright. These lines give a breakdown on Treasury securities bought by the Federal Reserve in the open market from dealers, dealer banks, or, infrequently, from the Treasury.

U.S. Government Securities—Held Under Repurchase Agreement. This is the amount of securities purchased from nonbank dealers under an agreement calling for the seller to repurchase them in 15 days or less.

Total Loans and Securities. This is the total of discounts and advances, acceptances, Federal agency obligations, and U.S. government obligations.

INTERPRETATION OF BANKING STATISTICS   1·17

Cash Items in Process of Collection. These items are checks, drafts, and other so-called "cash items" deposited with the Federal Reserve banks by commercial banks for collection.

Bank Premises. This shows the book value of bank buildings and building sites owned by the Federal Reserve banks for banking purposes.

Other Assets. Miscellaneous assets such as reimbursable expenses, deferred charges, claims account, interest accrued, overdrafts, premium on securities, and foreign exchange holdings such as those acquired through "swap" agreements and the IMF gold deposit.

LIABILITIES OF FEDERAL RESERVE BANKS.

Federal Reserve Notes. This item shows the amount of Federal Reserve notes of all Federal Reserve banks in circulation.

Deposits: Member Bank Reserves. This total represents the reserves carried by member banks with the Federal Reserve banks. These deposits, although constituting part of the required reserves of member banks, may be drawn upon to meet current requirements, and in fact are actively used by member banks in connection with their check-clearing operations, transfer of funds, currency withdrawals, etc.

Deposits: U.S. Treasurer—General Account. Amounts held on deposit with the Federal Reserve banks by the United States Treasury are entered under this caption. The Federal Reserve banks act as fiscal agents for the Treasury and as such receive government funds on deposit and pay government checks, coupons, and maturing securities.

Deposits: Foreign. Deposits of various foreign central banks and governments, and of the Bank for International Settlements, with the Federal Reserve Bank of New York are recorded under this heading. Each of the other Federal Reserve banks is allotted a participation in these foreign bank deposits.

Other Deposits. Clearing balances of nonmember par collection banks, deposits of the International Bank for Reconstruction and Development, the International Monetary Fund, the International Finance Corporation, the Inter-American Development Bank, the United Nations, the special account of the Treasury (Exchange Stabilization Fund), funds collected for the account of other Federal Reserve banks, and miscellaneous deposits constitute this amount.

Total Deposits. This represents the aggregate deposit liability of the Federal Reserve banks.

Deferred Availability Cash Items. This includes checks, drafts, and other cash items, in process of collection, for which the Federal Reserve banks have given credit to member banks, clearing nonmember banks, and the United States Treasury in a deferred availability account. Final deposit credit subject to actual collection is given for these items in accordance with the Federal Reserve banks' published **time schedule.**

Other Liabilities and Accrued Dividends. This includes: dividends on Federal Reserve Bank stock owned by member banks accrued between the semiannual dividend payment dates and as yet unpaid; unearned discount; unpaid accrued expenses; and sundry payables.

CAPITAL ACCOUNTS.

Capital Paid In. Each member bank is required by the Federal Reserve Act to subscribe to the capital stock of the Federal Reserve bank in a sum equal to

6% of its own paid-in capital and surplus. One-half (3%) of the subscribed capital of the Federal Reserve banks has been paid in and the balance is subject to call if and when deemed necessary by the Federal Reserve Board.

Surplus. The amount of accumulated earnings that has been retained (after payment of an annual 6% dividend on paid-in capital) is considered surplus. (At the end of 1964, the Board of Governors concluded that the growth in the capital and accumulated surplus of the Reserve Banks, as well as in their net earnings, warranted reducing the surplus of the Banks to a level approximately equal to that of paid-in capital instead of subscribed capital.)

Other Capital Accounts. Included are contingency reserves and unallocated net earnings to date after payment of dividends to shareholders and interest paid to the Treasury on Federal Reserve notes outstanding.

Ratio of Gold Certificate Reserves to Federal Reserve Note Liability. This ratio showed the part of Federal Reserve note liability that was backed by gold. With the elimination of the gold cover, this ratio is no longer being reported.

FEDERAL RESERVE CREDIT. Analysis of changes in the volume of Reserve bank credit outstanding, and of the causes for such changes, is greatly facilitated by a brief table (Fig. 7), issued each week along with the regular Reserve bank statement, showing the amount of credit extended by the Reserve banks to the financial system, together with certain other items responsible for increases or decreases in the amount of reserve credit outstanding.

Figure 7 shows that average member bank reserves with the Federal Reserve banks for the week ended February 7, 1968, increased by $667 million over the preceding week, but vault cash (currency and coin) decreased by $425 million, producing a net gain of $242 million in reserves. This gain resulted from substantial offsetting changes in individual items.

Items that reduced reserves were: a $14 million drop in float (reflecting an excess of debits over credits to member-bank accounts with the Reserve banks resulting from check collections for the member banks); a rise of $19 million in currency in circulation; a $28 million reduction in acceptances bought outright and held under repurchase agreements; a $29 million shrinkage in gold stock; and an $11 million drop in government securities bought outright—a total decline in member-bank reserves of $101 million.

Items that increased reserves were: purchases of government securities for the account of the 12 Federal Reserve banks in the amount of $380 million (these securities were bought under repurchase agreements from nonbank government securities dealers); a $5 million increase in Federal Agency obligations held under repurchase agreements; a $2 million rise in Treasury currency outstanding; drops of $184 million in Treasury deposits with Federal Reserve banks and of $35 million in Treasury cash holdings; declines of $19 million in foreign deposits and $17 million in other deposits with Federal Reserve banks; and a shrinkage of $128 million in other Federal Reserve accounts (net)—an aggregate of $770 million. The net result was an increase in member bank reserves of $669 million (the table shows an increase of $667 because of rounding). Since vault cash, which under the July 28, 1959, Act may at the discretion of the Federal Reserve Board be counted as part of the legal reserve, declined by $425 million, while required reserves increased by $238 million (member bank reserves above the required reserves), excess reserves were increased by $4 million. It is the **volume of excess reserves** that determines the ability of the banking system to expand credit.

INTERPRETATION OF BANKING STATISTICS 1·19

Member bank reserves, Reserve Bank credit, and related items	Week ended Feb. 7, 1968	Change from week ended Jan. 31, 1968	Change from week ended Feb. 8, 1967	Wednesday, Feb. 7, 1968
Reserve bank credit:				
U.S. Government securities—				
Bought outright—System account	48,925	− 11	+4,997	48,925
Held under repurchase agreements	414	+380	+ 210	397
Federal Agency obligations—				
Held under repurchase agreements	5	+ 5	+ 4	5
Acceptances—				
Bought outright	63	− 3	− 13	63
Held under repurchase agreements	—	− 25	− 50	—
Discounts and advances—				
Member bank borrowings	241	—	− 112	236
Other	—	—	− 1	—
Float	1,435	− 14	− 582	1,240
Total Reserve bank credit	51,083	+332	+4,453	50,866
Gold stock	11,954	− 29	−1,205	11,884
Treasury currency outstanding	6,788	+ 2	+ 396	6,787
	69,824	+304	+3,643	69,537
Currency in circulation	45,777	+ 19	+2,372	45,933
Treasury cash holdings	1,361	− 35	+ 109	1,352
Treasury deposits with F.R. banks	912	−184	+ 464	1,019
Foreign deposits with F.R. banks	142	− 19	− 3	148
Other deposits with F.R. banks	450	− 17	− 32	437
Other F.R. accounts (net)	−554	−128	− 947	−570
	48,087	−365	+1,962	48,319
Member bank reserves:				
With Federal Reserve banks	21,736	+667	+1,680	21,217
Currency and coin (estimated)	4,198	−425	+ 405	4,464
Total reserves held	25,934	+242	+2,085	25,681
Required reserves (estimated)	25,608	+238	+2,048	25,470
Excess reserves (estimated)	326	+ 4	+ 37	211

On February 7, 1968, U.S. government securities held in custody by the Federal Reserve banks for foreign account were $8,828 million, a decrease of $33 million for the week and an increase of $1,553 million from the comparable date a year ago.

Fig. 7. Changes in member bank reserve balances and related items (in millions of dollars).

Free Reserves. One of the most important clues to prospective interest rate changes, particularly short-term, is the amount of free reserves, which are total excess reserves less member bank borrowings from the Federal Reserve banks. For the week ended February 7, 1968, average free reserves amounted to $85 million ($326 million excess reserves minus $241 million of member bank borrowings). In periods of **active credit ease,** excess reserves are large, whereas borrowings of the member banks from the Federal Reserve banks are small, resulting in large free reserves. In periods of **active credit restraint,** the volume of excess reserves is small, whereas member bank borrowings are large, usually exceeding the amount of excess reserves. Under such circumstances the banks have "negative free reserves." As a general rule, a large part of the excess reserves are held by small country banks since the large tend to be loaned up and invested.

FEDERAL RESERVE CONTROL OF CREDIT. The Federal Reserve can influence the money market in a number of ways: (1) by discounting bills for member banks or making advances to them on their notes secured by government securities; (2) by buying and selling government obligations in the open market; (3) through raising or lowering member bank reserve requirements; (4) through raising or lowering the discount rate, i.e., the rate charged member banks for loans; and (5) through the power of the Federal Reserve Board to permit the member banks to count part or all of their vault cash as legal reserves. In addition, the Treasury can exert considerable influence over the money market.

The basis of Federal Reserve control over credit is the provision of the Federal Reserve Act requiring member banks to maintain deposits with the Federal Reserve banks as reserves against their deposit liabilities. Reserve requirements against deposits may be fixed by the Board of Governors within the ranges:

Against demand deposits	
Reserve cities	10–22%
Country banks	7–14%
Against time deposits (all member banks)	3–10%

When the Board of Governors of the Federal Reserve System raises reserve requirements, the volume of member bank reserves does not undergo change, but excess reserves are converted into required reserves. Similarly, when the Reserve Board lowers requirements, some required reserves are converted into excess.

Instruments of Credit Control. The Federal Reserve System has relied principally on two instruments of credit control—the discount rate, and open market operations. By raising or lowering the **discount rate,** Reserve banks make it more or less expensive for member banks to increase their reserve balances through rediscounting or borrowing. A change in the rediscount rate also signifies to the market that the credit policies of the Reserve authorities are undergoing a change. When the discount rate is raised, it is expected that the Federal Reserve will follow a policy of greater credit restraint, and when the rate is lowered, a policy of credit ease. At times, however, the changes merely reflect an adjustment to prevailing money market conditions. Through buying or selling government securities in the **open market,** the Reserve banks increase or decrease the volume of member bank reserve balances. As a rule, these two instruments of credit control are used together. For example, if the Federal Reserve authorities wish to check the expansion of member bank credit, they may sell government securities. Payment for securities sold is made by checks on commercial banks, which results in debits to accounts of the member banks at the Reserve banks, and thus in a reduction of reserve balances. If, as a result of these transactions, member banks are forced to borrow from the Reserve banks, the latter can make borrowing more expensive by raising the rediscount rate.

In addition to these principal instruments of control, the Federal Reserve System has other means at its disposal through which it can influence the money market. Most important is the **power of the Board of Governors to vary legal reserve requirements** of member banks. By raising reserve requirements, the Board automatically reduces excess reserves that member banks have with the Reserve banks, or actually forces member banks to increase borrowings at the Reserve banks. A reduction in reserve requirements has the opposite effect. A type of qualitative or selective credit control is the **authority to regulate loans on securities** by brokers, banks, and "other lenders" (Regulations T, U, and G).

2. Statement of Weekly Condition Report of Large Commercial Banks

The condition statement of large commercial banks reflects the position of all member and nonmember commercial banks in the United States with deposits in excess of $100 million (see Fig. 8). These banks represent about 60% of the assets of all commercial banks.

	Jan. 31, 1968	Change since Jan. 24, 1968	Change since Feb. 1, 1967
ASSETS			
Total loans and investments	207,142	+1,850	+17,015
Loans (net of valuation Reserves) [1]	145,090	+1,189	+ 8,244
Commercial and industrial loans	64,939	− 120	+ 4,503
Agricultural loans	1,927	− 7	+ 109
Loans to brokers and dealers for purchasing or carrying:			
U.S. govt. securities	1,972	+ 775	− 330
Other securities	3,852	+ 97	+ 886
Other loans for purchasing or carrying:			
U.S. govt. securities	105	+ 8	+ 29
Other securities	2,432	+ 2	+ 357
Loans to nonbank financial institutions:			
Sales finance, personal finance, etc.	5,412	+ 60	− 679
Other	4,267	− 34	+ 73
Real estate loans	29,035	+ 1	+ 1,676
Loans to domestic commercial banks	3,410	+ 116	+ 27
Loans to foreign banks	1,341	− 58	− 94
Consumer instalment loans	16,372	+ 80	+ 407
Loans to for. govts., official insts., etc.	1,063	+ 15	− 76
Other loans	12,156	+ 259	+ 1,589
U.S. government securities—total	28,080	+ 152	+ 2,251
Treasury bills	6,023	+ 182	+ 835
Treasury certificates of indebtedness	—	—	− 338
Treasury notes and U.S. bonds maturing:			
Within 1 year	4,076	+ 12	+ 487
1 year to 5 years	13,627	− 50	+ 3,117
After 5 years	4,354	+ 8	− 1,850
Obligations of states and political subdivisions:			
Tax warrants and short-term notes and bills	3,953	+ 52	+ 1,242
All other	25,489	+ 163	+ 4,335
Other bonds, corporate stocks, and securities:			
Participation certificates in fed. agency loans	1,691	+ 124	+ 641
All other (including corporate stocks)	2,839	+ 170	+ 302
Cash items in process of collection	22,662	+1,986	+ 1,423
Reserves with F.R. banks	17,120	+ 848	+ 2,729
Currency and coin	2,789	− 124	+ 277
Balances with domestic banks	4,167	+ 186	+ 49
Other assets	9,672	+ 484	+ 1,569
Total assets/liabilities	263,552	+5,230	+23,062

[1] Individual loan items are shown gross.

Fig. 8. Weekly condition report of large commercial banks, H.4.2 (in millions of dollars) (see continuation).

	Jan. 31, 1968	Change since Jan. 24 1968	Change since Feb. 1, 1967
LIABILITIES			
Demand deposits—total [2]	119,897	+4,923	+ 7,989
Individuals, partnerships, and corporations	85,948	+1,874	+ 6,610
States and political subdivisions	6,269	+ 934	− 513
U.S. government	5,396	+1,135	+ 2,039
Domestic interbank:			
Commercial	13,310	+ 427	− 171
Mutual savings	589	− 8	− 8
Foreign:			
Govts., off'l insts., etc.	693	− 9	− 27
Commercial banks	1,602	− 55	+ 184
Time and savings deposits—total [3]	104,236	+ 198	+11,069
Individuals, partnerships, and corporations:			
Savings deposits	48,518	− 13	+ 1,925
Other time deposits	39,629	+ 52	+ 7,166
States and political subdivisions	9,693	+ 74	+ 1,145
Domestic interbank	832	+ 6	+ 69
Foreign—govts., official institutions, etc.	5,102	+ 78	+ 674
Borrowings:			
From F.R. banks	733	+ 477	+ 731
From others	5,353	− 647	− 320
Other liabilities	12,690	+ 164	+ 2,320
Total capital accounts	20,643	+ 115	+ 1,273
MEMORANDA			
Total loans net adjusted [4]	141,680	+1,073	+ 8,217
Total loans net adjusted and investments [4]	203,732	+1,734	+16,988
Demand deposits adjusted [5]	78,529	+1,375	+ 4,698
Negotiable time CD's issued in denominations of $100,000 or more included in time and savings deposits—total	20,921	+ 26	+ 2,793
To individuals, partnerships, and corps.	13,699	− 95	+ 1,478
To others	7,222	+ 121	+ 1,315

[2] Includes certified and officers' checks not shown separately.
[3] Includes time deposits of U.S. government and foreign commercial banks not shown separately.
[4] Exclusive of loans to domestic commercial banks.
[5] All demand deposits except U.S. government and domestic commercial banks, less cash items in process of collection.

Fig. 8 (Continued)

ASSETS OF MEMBER BANKS. Loans and investments indicate the total amount of credit extended by the reporting banks. Loans constitute a direct extension of bank credit. The purchase of securities for investment likewise involves expansion of bank credit, since either the seller of securities obtains a deposit credit on the books of the bank or the buying bank's check is deposited in the seller's bank.

Commercial and industrial loans, sometimes termed **business loans,** are by far the principal type of bank loans. **Real estate loans** and **consumer install-**

ment loans now are also important. **Loans to brokers and dealers** and **other security loans** are divided into two categories: loans for purchasing or carrying government securities, and loans on other securities. Separated from other business loans are **loans to nonbank financial institutions**, particularly finance companies. Aside from loans, the principal earning assets of the banks are **U.S. government securities** and **municipal bonds**.

LIABILITIES OF MEMBER BANKS. On the liability side, deposits are divided into various categories. **Demand deposits** have increased rather slowly since 1955, partly because many corporations and individuals have converted demand deposits into time deposits or short-term government obligations on which they receive a relatively high rate of return. On the other hand, **time and savings deposits** have increased sharply.

Domestic interbank deposits represent mainly balances maintained with correspondent banks, particularly in financial centers. **Foreign deposits** represent deposits of foreign banks and government institutions in the United States. Most of these balances are kept in New York City. **Borrowings** represent rediscounts and borrowings by member banks from the Federal Reserve banks and loans made by one commercial bank to another.

TURNOVER OF DEMAND DEPOSITS. The volume of deposits alone does not give a full picture of money supply conditions. It is necessary also to study the turnover or velocity of deposits. The Federal Reserve Bulletin publishes regularly a table showing the amount of checks drawn and deposit turnover, which measures the actual use of deposits. The table below shows debits to demand deposits and the annual rate of turnover of demand deposits in New York and other cities. The figures for New York City are greatly influenced by stock market and other financial transactions. Those in other cities reflect more accurately ordinary business turnover. Both in New York and elsewhere the **turnover of demand deposits has increased sharply,** partly because of the policy of credit restraint followed during periods of prosperity, which dampened the rise in the money supply, and partly because of the increased skill of business concerns in economizing on holdings of cash.

BANK DEBITS AND DEPOSIT TURNOVER

Year[1]	Debits to Demand Deposit Accounts Except Interbank and Government (in billions of dollars)		Annual Rate of Turnover of Demand Deposits Except Interbank and Government	
	New York City	224 Other Reporting Centers	New York City	224 Other Reporting Centers
1964	2,013	2,804	90.7	33.4
1965	2,274	3,250	102.2	37.5
1966	2,845	3,529	120.9	39.7
1967	3,150	3,897[2]	122.1	41.1[2]

[1] Figures are seasonally adjusted annual rates for the month of December.
[2] Revised series includes eight additional reporting centers.

LOANABLE FUNDS. Deposits of member banks in the Federal Reserve banks constitute the basis for the nation's credit system. The larger these reserves, the more investments and loans commercial banks can make. Investments and loans by commercial banks, in turn, provide funds to corporations and individuals.

INTEREST RATES AND MONEY MARKETS

An increase in free reserves of member banks will thus largely determine the loanable funds and the trend of interest rates.

The **nation's money supply** consists of demand deposits and currency in the hands of the public. In recent years a broader measure of the money supply, one including time deposits at commercial banks, has been increasingly used in economic policy considerations.

The reason for counting time deposits in the definition of the money supply is that, in practice, time deposits are almost as readily available for spending as demand deposits or currency. On the other hand, the reason for excluding them is that such deposits must be converted into currency or demand deposits before they can be spent. Moreover, it is argued that if time deposits are included, other highly liquid assets of similar nature, such as short-term government securities and savings and loan shares, should also be included in the money supply.

Year and month	Total money supply and time deposits adjusted	Money supply Total	Currency component [1]	Demand deposit component [2]	Time deposits adjusted [3]
1947 Dec.	148.5	113.1	26.4	86.7	35.4
1948 Dec.	147.5	111.5	25.8	85.8	36.0
1949 Dec.	147.6	111.2	25.1	86.0	36.4
1950 Dec.	152.9	116.2	25.0	91.2	36.7
1951 Dec.	160.9	122.7	26.1	96.5	38.2
1952 Dec.	168.5	127.4	27.3	100.1	41.1
1953 Dec.	173.3	128.8	27.7	101.1	44.5
1954 Dec.	180.6	132.3	27.4	104.9	48.3
1955 Dec.	185.2	135.2	27.8	107.4	50.0
1956 Dec.	188.8	136.9	28.2	108.7	51.9
1957 Dec.	193.3	135.9	28.3	107.6	57.4
1958 Dec.	206.5	141.1	28.6	112.6	65.4
1959 Dec.	209.3	141.9	28.9	113.1	67.4
1960 Dec.	213.9	141.1	28.9	112.1	72.9
1961 Dec.	228.1	145.4	29.6	115.9	82.7
1962 Dec.	245.2	147.4	30.6	116.8	97.8
1963 Dec.	265.2	153.0	32.5	120.5	112.2
1964 Dec.	285.9	159.3	34.2	125.1	126.6
1965 Dec.	313.7	166.8	36.3	130.5	146.9
1966 Dec.	329.0	170.4	38.3	132.1	158.6
1967 Dec.	365.3	181.5	40.4	141.1	183.8

[1] Currency outside the Treasury, the Federal Reserve system, and the vaults of all commercial banks.

[2] Demand deposits at all commercial banks, other than those due to domestic commercial banks and the U.S. government, less cash items in process of collection and Federal Reserve float, plus foreign demand balances at Federal Reserve banks.

[3] Time deposits adjusted are time deposits at all commercial banks other than those due to domestic commercial banks and the U.S. government.

Fig. 9. Money Supply and Time Deposits, 1947–67; Averages of daily figures, seasonally adjusted (in billions of dollars).

Monthly statistics on the money supply as well as on time deposits may be found in the Federal Reserve Bulletin. The volume of demand deposits, currency, and time deposits for a period of years is shown in Fig. 9.

Relation of the New York Money Market to the Interior

POSITION OF NEW YORK. Although the financial importance of other large cities has increased in recent years, the outstanding position of New York in both national and international finance necessitates close financial relationships between New York and interior banks. Many banks establish correspondent connections with New York institutions primarily for the purpose of **facilitating their clearing transactions**; others enter into this relationship to have a larger institution from which they can obtain loans; and still others, particularly smaller banks not members of the Federal Reserve System, maintain their cash reserves with New York banks. Large city banks provide valuable investment advice, and trust, tax, operating, and other services to correspondents. They perform safekeeping functions for out-of-town banks, frequently review investment portfolios, and execute foreign trade transactions. Under ordinary circumstances, therefore, the New York banks have surplus funds of a large number of interior banks.

Businesses all over the country also maintain large deposits in New York banks. Deposits and withdrawals by business depositors are the major factor in the movement of funds from one area to the other.

BALANCES WITH DOMESTIC BANKS AND DOMESTIC INTERBANK DEPOSITS. Changes in the financial relationships between New York banks and the interior banks are reflected in **the statement of New York City member banks.**

An increase in domestic interbank deposits indicates that New York banks have received additional funds from their correspondents, whereas an increase in balances with domestic banks reflects an increase in deposits with correspondent banks and represents a movement of funds to the interior. Decrease in these items have the opposite meaning. Offsetting movements of funds may occur as certain interior banks increase their interbank deposits in New York while other interior banks increase their borrowings.

CAUSES OF MOVEMENT OF FUNDS. A movement of funds between New York and the interior may be caused by a number of factors. If new securities are issued by New York banking houses and these securities are sold throughout the country, the result is a movement of funds from the interior to New York. Payment of principal, interest, and dividends by corporations also leads to a movement of funds between New York and the interior.

Seasonal Influences. Seasonal changes in demand for credit have an important bearing on the financial relationship between New York and the interior. In the winter months, when the banks in the interior have idle funds, they invest in short-term government securities, and this may cause funds to flow to New York, where the larger government security dealers are located.

Treasury Financing and the Money Market

EFFECT OF TREASURY OPERATIONS ON MONEY MARKET. Treasury financing operations involve a larger volume of funds than any other type of operations, reaching on quarterly tax days and new financing periods a volume of several billion dollars. Hence, the effects on the money market are necessarily of considerable importance. Through redemption and refunding of maturing obligations, payments of interest, the call of funds from depository banks, and the collection of income taxes, banking activities are vitally affected at a number of points. Notwithstanding these heavy shiftings of funds, there is usually little disturbance in the money market. This relative stability is due to the efficient mechanism for the handling of the huge volume of government funds.

Treasury operations on the **quarterly tax collection dates,** April 15, June 15, September 15, and January 15, which coincide with **interest payment dates** on many government obligations, reveal the interrelations between the Treasury, the Reserve banks, and the money market. Payment is made by the Treasury by checks drawn on the Reserve banks, which are deposited by recipients with commercial banks and sent by the latter to the Reserve banks for credit to their accounts, thus resulting in an increase in member bank reserve balances. At the same time that these disbursements are made, the Treasury is also receiving checks drawn on commercial banks in payment of taxes and new issues of Treasury securities. As these checks are collected, member banks' balances at the Reserve banks are debited. Collections usually lag several days behind disbursements, and in order to cover the deficit, the Treasury may resort to borrowing from the Reserve banks. This borrowing takes the form of a purchase by the Reserve banks of a **special one-day certificate of indebtedness** that is renewed each day in decreasing amounts as collections come in.

DEBT MANAGEMENT. Treasury borrowing and refunding operations are sometimes used to supplement Federal Reserve measures to influence interest rates. For example, since 1960 debt management has been utilized to keep up short-term interest rates even in periods such as 1961–1962, when the Federal Reserve authorities were following a relatively easy money policy. The aim was to maintain short-term rates at a level comparable with that prevailing in the leading European financial centers, notably London, in order to deter shifting of funds abroad to obtain higher yields. This was achieved primarily through offering large amounts of obligations with maturities up to one year. This policy also shortened the average maturity of the Federal debt.

Advance Refunding. Since June, 1960, the Treasury has been using the device of advance refunding to lengthen the maturity of the public debt with minimum disturbance to the money and capital markets. Under this plan, the Treasury offers to exchange certain issues some months or years prior to maturity for new securities of longer maturity. For example, for obligations maturing within 12 months and for securities with less than 5 years to maturity, new issues in the $3\frac{1}{2}$–16 year maturity range may be offered, while holders of long-term bonds, which, owing to the passage of time, are within the 5–10 year maturity range, may be offered in exchange new bonds with maturities from 12 to 40 years, generally at higher coupon rates. By using advance refunding, instead of offering new long-term securities, the Treasury avoids a sharp rise in medium- and long-term rates and does not compete for new funds with the private sector of the economy.

Other Influence on the Money Market

EFFECTS OF BUSINESS CYCLE. The business cycle strongly influences the money market. During the **upswing** of the business cycle, when trade and industrial activity are increasing, the money and credit situation is usually characterized by an expansion of bank credit and some stiffening of interest rates. Discounts of member banks with the Reserve banks may increase.

In a period of **declining business activity** there is a tendency for bank loans to decrease, and member banks repay their borrowings from the Reserve banks. These factors make for lower interest rates.

PRICES AND BANK CREDIT. The cyclical movement of prices also influences the money market. Rising prices usually reflect better business, which, in turn, requires more bank accommodation, both because of the expanded volume of industry and trade and the higher unit values. Contrariwise, a decline in prices usually accompanies a decrease in business activity and results in a contraction in the volume of bank loans.

Relation of New York to Foreign Money Markets

INTERNATIONAL POSITION OF NEW YORK MONEY MARKET. New York is one of the most important world financial centers, and the New York money market therefore reflects to a considerable extent international as well as domestic financial conditions. Although the United States is a creditor on the international capital market to the extent of billions of dollars, it has become a large debtor on the short-term money market.

THE POSTWAR CHANGE: BALANCE OF PAYMENTS DEFICIT. With the restoration of the economies of the leading countries abroad in the 1950's, the international position of the New York money market underwent a drastic change. Beginning with 1958 the balance of payments deficit of the United States increased sharply, accompanied by a substantial **reduction in the gold stock.** Although there was some improvement in 1961–1962, the situation became so serious as to warrant special measures by the government and the Federal Reserve authorities. To prevent large-scale raids on the dollar, the Federal Reserve Bank of New York began to operate extensively in the foreign exchange markets and made swap arrangements with the leading central banks in Europe. The Treasury sold its obligations in foreign currencies to some governments and central banks in order to increase the supply of foreign exchange that could be used in emergencies. The aim of these operations was to **stabilize the exchange value of the dollar** and thus discourage speculative outflows of funds. During the mid-1960's, the British pound sterling came under increasing financial pressure. In order to meet this pressure, the Bank of England was forced to liquidate large amounts of government-owned long-term assets in the United States. This resulted in a substantial worsening in the U.S. international balance of payments. Further deterioration of the situation resulted when the devaluation of the pound became a reality in late 1967 (see also Section 2, Banking and Lending Institutions).

Restoration of the International Money Market. The return to external convertibility of the leading foreign currencies in 1958 and the restoration of the international money market created a new force in the American money market. Aside from political considerations, short-term funds ordinarily flow from countries with low interest rates to centers where interest rates are higher, particularly when the risk of loss stemming from exchange fluctuation can be eliminated. The resumption of operations in the **forward exchange market,** making it possible to hedge against the foreign exchange risks involved in short-term transactions, removed a major deterrent to the free international flow of funds.

Although the international money markets include all the leading free-world countries whose currencies are freely convertible into dollars, the **largest flow of short-term funds is between New York and London,** since these markets can absorb huge amounts of funds without causing undue disturbances. Paris, Frankfort, Zurich, and Amsterdam are also important money markets, but they lack the breadth and liquidity of New York and London. Hence, in order to prevent large outflows of funds it has been considered necessary during the past few years to coordinate short-term rates of interest in the United States, notably Treasury bill yields, with those prevailing in London, taking into account the cost of hedging in the forward exchange market.

In December, 1967, foreigners (not including international organizations) owned 31.4 billion of short-term dollar assets of which 15.7 billion, or 50%, was held for official accounts. This constituted the **principal international reserve** of many nations, particularly those that prefer to hold mainly short-term dollar assets rather than gold. About $16 billion of U.S. government securities were held by foreign and international accounts, the bulk consisting of short-term obligations. Foreigners are thus in a position to play an important role in the New York money market and to influence the movement of short-term rates.

Effect on the U.S. Money Market. To the extent that a U.S. balance of payments deficit is not financed through export of gold, foreigners build up their dollar deposits or purchase additional short-term Treasury obligations and other money-market instruments. Bidding for these obligations tends to lower short-term rates, and if this trend becomes pronounced, it has to be counteracted by the Federal Reserve through open-market sales or by the Treasury through increasing the supply of short-term obligations. On the other hand, when foreign owners of dollar assets, because of apprehension about the future of the dollar or for other reasons, sell their dollar balances, some of them find their way to their central banks, which can convert them into gold at the fixed price of $35 an ounce (plus ¼% handling charge) in effect since the passage of the Gold Reserve Act in 1934.

Up to 1958 the credit policies of the Reserve authorities were guided entirely by domestic considerations. The differential in short-term rates between New York and European centers did not influence their actions, since practically all European currencies were surrounded by foreign exchange restrictions that impeded the free international movement of funds. **Under present conditions,** however, any appraisal of the probable trend of short-term interest rates must take into consideration not only the domestic economic outlook but also money market conditions in the leading foreign financial centers, and notably London.

THE LONDON MONEY MARKET. Financial London revolves around the **Bank of England,** which has been government-owned since March, 1946, and is the institution of note issue and the central bank. Unlike the Federal Reserve banks, the Bank of England deals with both banks and the public. Commercial banking is largely concentrated in a handful of large **joint stock banks** with headquarters in London and an extensive system of branches throughout the country. **Acceptance houses** specialize in the creation of bankers' acceptances that are dealt in by **bill brokers** and **discount houses.**

The Bill Market. This is the most important section of the money market. Bills are bought and sold by bill brokers and discount houses, which carry their portfolios with funds borrowed from the joint stock banks, chiefly on a day-to-day basis. The joint stock banks do not borrow from the Bank of England directly. When in need of money, they call loans from the bill dealers, who in turn are forced to borrow from the central bank at higher rates.

Balance of Payments Problem. After the return to **external convertibility of the pound sterling** at the end of 1958, Great Britain was confronted with an almost continuous balance of payments problem. To enable the Bank of England to exercise greater power over the money market, it was authorized in that year to require the London Clearing Banks and the Scottish banks to make interest-bearing "special deposits" with it in amounts representing specified percentages of the banks' deposits. Thereafter, the British government tried various other measures, such as raising the discount rate, initiating a program of economic austerity, and eventually, in late 1967, devaluing the pound by 14%. Despite these measures, the payments problem still persisted.

BANK OF ENGLAND WEEKLY STATEMENT. The best indicator of the money and credit situation in London is the weekly statement of the Bank of England, shown in Fig. 10.

The Bank of England, as indicated by the statement, is divided into the Banking Department and the Issue Department. The **Issue Department** has no connection with the public and deals only with the Banking Department. Its function is to issue notes to the Banking Department and to maintain the legal cover for the note issue. Notes issued in excess of the **fiduciary issue,** which is backed by government securities, must be secured 100% by gold. The fiduciary issue may be increased with the consent of the Chancellor of the Exchequer. The **Banking Department** conducts a general banking business. It accepts deposits, makes loans, discounts bills, buys and sells securities, and acts as fiscal agent for the British government.

An explanation of the items of the Bank of England statement is given below.

Issue Department. The liabilities of the Issue Department consist exclusively of **Notes Issued,** which are classified as: (1) notes in circulation and (2) notes in the Banking Department. The Issue Department must maintain the prescribed legal cover for all notes issued regardless of whether they are in the hands of the public or in the Banking Department. The cover for the note issue is shown on the asset side and consists of: (1) **Government debt,** a more or less permanent loan to the State, (2) **Other government securities,** (3) **Other securities,** the nature of which is left entirely to the discretion of the Bank, and (4) **Silver coin.** The total of these four items constitutes the cover for the fiduciary issue, whereas the fifth item, **Gold coin and bullion,** is the cover for notes issued in excess of the fiduciary issue. This amount, as the statement indicates, is an insignificant part of the notes issued. The gold, dollar, and other convertible currency reserves of Great Britain and of the sterling area countries are held by the **Exchange Equalisation Account.**

Banking Department. The liabilities of the Banking Department consist of **Capital, Rest** or surplus, and **Deposits.** Most significant from the standpoint of the money market are the deposit accounts. **Public deposits** represent deposits of the British government, the savings banks, the commissioners of the public debt, and the dividend accounts. **Special deposits** represent the interest-bearing accounts of the London Clearing Banks and the Scottish banks. **Other deposits** are divided into **Bankers' deposits** and **Other accounts.** Although the British commercial banks are not required by law to maintain reserves with the central bank, as in the United States, it is their practice to keep a reserve equivalent to 8% of their total deposits. The reserve consists of 5% in cash and 3% in balances with the Bank of England. Thus, an increase in **Bankers' deposits** has the same significance as an increase in reserves of member banks with the Federal Reserve banks in this country. It means a broadening of the credit base and opens the way for credit expansion. **Other accounts** represent deposits of individuals, business concerns, British banks operating chiefly in the Dominions and foreign countries, foreign central banks, merchant bankers, and financial houses.

BANK OF ENGLAND
December 20, 1967
Issue Department

	£		£
Notes Issued:		Government Debt	11,015,100
In Circulation	3,207,296,134	Other Gov. Securities	3,237,941,721
In Banking Department	43,124,836	Other Securities	781,083
		Coin Other than Gold Coin	262,096
		Amount of Fiduciary Issue	3,250,000,000
		Gold Coin & Bullion *	420,970
	3,250,420,970		3,250,420,970

Banking Department

	£		£
Capital	14,553,000	Gov. Securities	436,028,371
Rest	3,522,854	Other Securities:	
Public Deposits †	14,505,385	Discounts and	
Special Deposits	213,300,000	Advances . 146,969,022	
Other Deposits:		Securities ... 30,875,623	177,844,645
Bankers ... 292,301,020			
Other		Notes	43,124,836
Accounts . 119,503,302	411,804,322	Coin	687,709
	657,685,561		657,685,561

* At 292s. 7d. per fine oz.

† Including Exchequer, Savings Banks, Commissioners of National Debt, and Dividend Accounts.

Fig. 10. Bank of England weekly statement.

On the asset side, **Government securities** represent the government obligations purchased by the Bank of England in the open market. Through the buying and selling of government securities, the Bank exercises a strong influence on the money market, just as do the Federal Reserve banks. An increase in government securities held by the Banking Department means the placing of more funds in the market by the Bank of England, and it is reflected in an increase in bankers' deposits. Similarly, a decrease in the amount of government securities held by the Bank means a decrease in the amount of Bank of England funds in the market.

Other securities are divided into two parts: (1) discounts and advances, and (2) securities. The item **"discounts and advances"** is generally interpreted to represent accommodation extended to the money market on its own initiative; an increase is an indication of more stringent conditions in the money market. Securities consist of miscellaneous items such as: domestic and foreign bills bought by the Bank, deposits kept with foreign central banks and the Bank for International Settlements, and advances made to foreign central banks. **Notes,** and **gold** and **silver** coin constitute the **reserve**—i.e., the ready cash on hand to meet demand for currency by the banks. The **proportion** is the ratio of the "reserve" to total public and other deposits.

SECTION 2

BANKING AND LENDING INSTITUTIONS

CONTENTS

Money and Credit

	PAGE
The role of money	1
Four main functions	1
Definition of money	1
Monetary standards and systems	2
Gold standard	2
Bimetallism	3
Managed monetary systems	3
Types of money	3
The role of credit	4
The value of money	5
Interaction of major factors affecting price level	5
International monetary settlements	5

The United States Money Supply

Early monetary history	6
Federal Reserve currency	6
The new gold standard and devaluation	7
Silver operations	7
Currency in circulation	8
Kinds of U. S. currency outstanding and in circulation, November 30, 1967 (f. 1)	8
Bank credit as money	9
Present monetary system	9

Banking Systems

The evolution of banking	10
The role of commercial banks	10
How commercial banks create deposits	11
The role of central banks	11

Banking System of the United States

Early banking history	12
State and national banks	12
The Federal Reserve System	13
Boundaries of Federal Reserve Districts (f. 2)	14
The Board of Governors	15
Federal Reserve banks	15
Collection of checks and other services	16
Federal Reserve membership	17
Member bank reserves	17
Control of credit through reserves	17
Excess reserves	17
Reserve requirements of member banks (percentage of deposits) (f. 3)	18
The Federal Deposit Insurance Corporation	19

	PAGE
Number of commercial banking offices in the United States according to insurance status, December 31, 1966 (f. 4)	19
Regulatory legislation	19
Mergers and branches	20
Availability and cost of credit	20
Loans and investments	21
Bank supervision and examination	21
Branch and group banking	21
Bank holding companies	21
The branch banking controversy	22
Possibilities in branch banking	23
Interbank relations	23
Proposals for banking unification	23

Banking Trends

From the 1920's to the postwar era	24
Trends in bank loans	25
Postwar changes	25
Total gross loans all commercial banks, June 30, 1967 (f. 5)	25
The growth of bank investments	26
Negotiable certificates of time deposit	26
Bank earnings	27
Banking competition	27

Monetary Policy

Definitions and objectives	28
Exchange stabilization	28
The period following World War II	29
The money supply and the price level	29
Monetary control and bank reserves	30
The instruments of monetary policy	30
Quantitative controls	30
Qualitative controls	30
Federal Reserve policy	31
Postwar policy	31
Limitations of monetary policy	32
Monetary and fiscal policy	32

Other Lending Institutions

Financial intermediaries	33
Suppliers of funds in the financial markets, 1967 (f. 6)	33
Monetary controls over nonbank financial institutions	34
Loans to business	34
Commercial paper	34
Bankers acceptances	35

BANKING AND LENDING INSTITUTIONS

CONTENTS (*Continued*)

	Page
Factors	35
Commercial finance companies	35
Mortgage loans	35
Distribution of mortgage debt	35
Mortgage holdings by financial institutions, June 30, 1967 (*f. 7*)	36
The home mortgage business	36
Types of mortgages	36
Federal agencies in mortgage finance	37
Mortgage loans for non-real estate purposes	37
Consumer lending	38

	Page
Total consumer credit, November 1967 (*f. 8*)	38
Sources of credit	38
Commercial banks	38
Sales finance companies	39
Suppliers of consumer credit, November 1967 (*f. 9*)	39
Credit unions	40
Consumer finance companies	40
Industrial banking	41
Effective rates of interest	41

SECTION 2

BANKING AND LENDING INSTITUTIONS

Money and Credit

THE ROLE OF MONEY. Money is a major element in modern economic life. Without it, or some suitable counterpart, our complex business civilization would be unable to function.

Money has a long and colorful history. Its evolution has been accompanied by, and in many ways has made possible, great advances in trade, in the division of labor, in the specialization of production, in the development of resources, and in the introduction of new machines and techniques. But included in the story of money are panics and periods of catastrophic inflation. Thus, money has contributed immeasurably to mankind's economic progress but when misused has also been responsible for great misery.

The evolution of money and banking systems is not over. Many aspects of the subject are highly controversial today. Further experiments will be tried. For example, the growing use of the computer has generated discussions regarding the possibility of a society that functions largely without money as we currently conceive of it. A survey by the Diebold Group, Inc., suggested that the technology required and the necessity for such a situation may be present by the mid-1970's. Only through a knowledge of past experience and of the present structure of money and banking can a repetition of old fallacies be avoided and real progress achieved.

Four Main Functions. The functions of money are often classified under four headings: (1) As a **medium of exchange**, money facilitates both the production and the distribution of goods and services. Without money, it becomes necessary to rely on direct barter, with all the backwardness such a system entails. (2) As a **standard of value**, money serves as a yardstick or common denominator for the relative value of different goods. (3) As a **standard for deferred payments**, money permits transactions to be undertaken now, with payment due at some specified time in the future. (4) Finally, money acts as an **instrumentality for saving** one's purchasing power until some future date.

Through these uses, money enables men to carry out the complex operations of a modern capitalistic economy, including the division of labor, the transfer of savings into productive enterprise, the making of computations of costs and profits to guide business decisions, and the appraisal of credit as the basis of earning capacity and wealth.

DEFINITION OF MONEY. In modern economies, money is usually considered to consist of **currency** and **demand deposits**, or bank accounts against which checks can be drawn. Only currency and demand deposits are used directly in making payments. Savings accounts are not included in this concept of money, because in paying a bill with a savings account it is first necessary to convert the savings account either into currency or a check. If money ceases to be considered mainly an instrument of exchange but rather an asset fulfilling other functions, the significance of this distinction tends to disappear. Recently, some economists have resorted to a different definition of money that includes time deposits. (For a discussion of the money supply, see Section 1.)

Most transactions in the United States today are settled with bank checks. The amount of currency in circulation reflects primarily the needs of people and of businesses to have sufficient cash for day-to-day operations, for payroll requirements, and for some hoarding and similar purposes.

A theoretical **distinction** is sometimes made between **currency** and **demand deposits**: Currency is universally accepted as money without reference to the credit status of the person who offers it in payment, whereas checks are not. Since the two forms of money are normally interchangeable, this distinction is not significant. During the latter part of the 1960's, some banks began to make available guaranteed checking accounts whereby extensions of credit are automatically granted on checking overdrafts.

Economists today are giving increasing recognition to the growing role in our economy of **"near monies,"** a term denoting highly liquid forms of savings easily convertible into money. Liquidity here refers to the ability of the owner to convert the assets into pure money quickly and without appreciable loss. The principal types of near money are short-term government obligations and savings accounts. It is true that banks can require three months' notice before paying out savings deposits, but in practice this provision is rarely invoked.

MONETARY STANDARDS AND SYSTEMS. Every system of money must have a basic monetary unit, often referred to as **standard money** (see below). Most nations have standard units that are divisible by 100, such as dollars and cents, francs and centimes, pesos and centavos. Great Britain, with its ancient system of pounds, shillings, and pence, is scheduled to adjust fully to a system of decimalization by February 1971.

The standard money, such as the dollar in the United States, may or may not be convertible into some precious metal, depending upon the basic monetary system of the nation. Today, very few countries give their citizens the right to demand gold or silver in exchange for currency or demand deposits.

In early civilizations, widely desired forms of wealth such as cattle, sheep, or oxen were commonly used as **units of value.** These standards were gradually supplanted by precious metals, which were universally prized for purposes of adornment and possessed such advantages as durability, portability, and malleability. As currency systems developed, money units such as the talent, the shekel, and the drachma were defined, consisting of specified quantities of the standard metal of a given fineness. When paper money came into use, it usually bore the promise of a bank or government to redeem the notes or certificates with stated quantities of the standard metal.

The **principal types of monetary systems** developed in modern times have been the gold standard, bimetallism, and fiat or "managed" money.

Gold Standard. Prior to World War I, gold coins were the standard money of most major nations, and other forms of money were freely convertible into gold. However, instead of permitting full-weight gold coins to circulate **(the gold-coin standard)**, some countries preferred to circulate gold certificates that were redeemable with large bars of gold bullion stored by the central bank **(the gold-bullion standard).**

Bimetallism. In the earlier history of the United States, bimetallism prevailed, under which the standard money consisted of both gold and silver. (See discussion of United States Money Supply below.) Currency was convertible into either gold or silver coin at the option of the holder, with the "mint ratio" between the two metals fixed by law.

Managed Monetary Systems. Difficulties arising out of World War I and the great depression of the 1930's forced almost general abandonment of the gold standard, and monetary systems became "managed" by the government. Managed monetary systems do not provide for free convertibility into any metallic standard money so that the value of the currency unit depends largely upon government management. Most of these systems are spoken of as **"fiat,"** because the standard is given value by government fiat or edict, rather than by virtue of any "intrinsic" value that the standard money possesses as a precious metal. The term fiat at times has unsavory connotations because, historically, abandonment of convertibility of currency into gold or silver often led to uncontrolled depreciation. But this was not always true. Moreover, the techniques of managing a fiat standard have been greatly developed during recent years. (Techniques of money management are discussed later in this Section.)

The reasons for the **abandonment of the domestic gold standard** in nearly every country are complex and by no means uniform. History shows that the gold standard was usually abandoned under emergency conditions, particularly during times of war and economic crisis. This phenomenon was virtually universal during the worldwide great depression of the 1930's. Everywhere countries were preoccupied with raising incomes at home and providing more jobs for the unemployed. This required an unprecedented degree of government intervention in the domestic economy and also control over the money supply. Today, governments in many parts of the world have assumed responsibility for maintaining a high level of employment, stimulating domestic economic growth, and maintaining purchasing power. In the United States, the Employment Act of 1946 declared it an objective of public policy to promote maximum production and purchasing power to the end that useful employment opportunities will be available for all those ready, willing, and able to work. (For a discussion of the present monetary system in the United States, see below.) Thus, there is very little prospect of an abandonment of managed money and a return to the domestic gold standard. Gold is now used almost entirely for settling **international balances.**

Types of Money. Money is variously classified, depending upon the purposes in view. Common designations encountered include the following:

1. **Standard money** is the basic money of redemption of a nation's monetary system, which determines the value of all other kinds of money of which the system is composed. Modern standards have been **bullion standards,** consisting of a specified quantity of precious metal (e.g., the gold-bullion standard prevailing in Great Britain between 1925 and 1931); **coin standards** (e.g., the gold-coin standard in the United States until 1933); **exchange standards,** under which a currency is convertible into the currency of some other country at a more or less fixed ratio (e.g., the dollar exchange standard prevailing in Latin American countries); **fiat standards,** consisting of inconvertible paper currency units.

2. **Commodity money** is metallic and other money whose intrinsic value is equal to the denomination it bears. Gold coins that circulated in the United States prior to 1933 were a true example of commodity money.

3. **Token money** is coins whose intrinsic value as metal is less than the denominations they bear. Examples: the United States fractional coinage.

4. **Fractional money** (or **subsidiary coinage**) is metallic or paper money bearing denominations that are fractions of the standard money unit. Examples: quarters, dimes, nickels, and pennies in the United States.

5. **Representative money** is paper money backed 100% by coin or bullion. Example: gold and silver certificates in the United States when they were issued.

6. **Credit or fiduciary money** is paper money backed by promises to pay by the issuer, whether a government or a bank, rather than by coins or bullion. Example: Federal Reserve notes.

7. **Fiat money** is paper or coins whose value is fixed by government edict at a level that bears no relation to redemption or intrinsic commodity value. In the past, fiat money was often repudiated credit money—examples: continental currency of the Revolution or greenbacks issued during the Civil War. With the development of monetary management techniques, however, fiat money has frequently remained stable in value over extended periods of time.

8. **Legal tender** is any money that a debtor is authorized by law to offer in payment of debts. In 1933 Congress gave to all types of money in the United States unlimited legal tender status.

THE ROLE OF CREDIT. The term "credit" has different meanings even in financial usage, but it invariably refers to the use of a **promise to pay** in the future. Credit is thus an invaluable supplement of money in the modern economy—in fact, as has been seen, some types of credit, such as bank deposits and checks drawn against them, are commonly included in the monetary structure of a nation.

Credit is based upon the confidence of the lender that the borrower will fulfill his promise to pay his debt. Confidence in the borrower depends upon his willingness to pay (character) and upon his ability or capacity to pay, which is determined by his present or anticipated future ownership of money or real wealth—i.e., by his capital and his earning power. In government credit, capacity to pay rests upon the taxing power.

Credit is classified in different ways. **Cash credit** arises from loans of money; **merchandise credit,** from sales of goods for future payment. **Installment credit** provides for periodic payment of the sum due over a period of time.

Creditors include banks, business concerns, individuals, and governments, and all of these groups are borrowers as well. Credit extended to business enterprises to finance the production and distribution of goods for sale is classified either as **investment credit** or as **commercial credit.** The former finances the acquisition of plant and equipment—i.e., the means of production—whereas commercial credit is used to pay for current operations: purchases of raw materials and the payment of wages.

Consumer credit, which has acquired great importance in recent decades, refers to credit advances made to individuals to enable them to acquire goods or services for personal consumption. This term does not ordinarily include loans secured by liens on residential property to finance home ownership or improvements.

Real estate credit consists of loans secured by land and buildings, industrial as well as residential.

Bank credit is used with two different meanings: (1) to describe loans or investments made by banks and (2) to refer to bank deposits.

Credit performs the **same cardinal function as money,** serving as a means of payment. Credit greatly facilitates the production and sale of goods and permeates every section of the national economy. It is indispensable to economic progress. Thus, it is through such credit instruments as bonds and mortgage notes that the nation's savings are channeled into industry for capital formation—i.e., for investment in new productive plants and equipment.

THE VALUE OF MONEY. Changes in the commodity price level indicate changes in the value, or the **purchasing power,** of money. For example, in the United States, retail prices on the average (as measured by the Consumers' Price Index, compiled by the U. S. Department of Labor) have increased by about 40% in the twenty years ending in 1967. Thus, during that period, the purchasing power of the dollar was reduced by over one-quarter. Until the mid-1930's, a relatively unsophisticated version of the **quantity theory of money** was in vogue as an explanation of the price level. The theory holds that prices are determined largely or entirely by the volume of money outstanding. This theory has been criticized in that it omits the crucial influence of the velocity of turnover of money and the volume of production. The so-called **"cost-push" theory** has also been offered as an explanation for changes in the price level. This theory gained some prominence as a result of the successive wage increases that occurred during the 1960's.

Interaction of Major Factors Affecting Price Level. The interaction of the major factors affecting the price level has been expressed in the formula $MV + M'V' = PT$, where M is the volume of metallic and paper money outstanding, V its average velocity of turnover, M' the volume of demand deposits, V' its average velocity of turnover, P the price level, and T the volume of goods and services turned over. This formula expresses a truism, since all goods and services exchanged, at the prevailing price level, must be paid for with money. However, it helps to clarify the role played by each of these factors in major changes in the level of prices. Although data on the turnover of currency are unavailable, statistics of the **velocity of turnover** of bank demand deposits, the principal element in the money supply, are compiled by the Federal Reserve System and published monthly as annual rates (see Section 1).

INTERNATIONAL MONETARY SETTLEMENTS. There are two kinds of international money: (1) a national currency unit that is acceptable in a number of other countries as a means of payment, and (2) a medium that is generally acceptable in virtually all countries, namely, gold.

Transactions in international trade are settled in the first instance by means of drafts or other credit instruments drawn in terms of some national monetary unit such as dollars, pounds, or francs. If every nation's trade, service, and capital transactions with every other nation were always in precise balance, there would be no need for any type of international money. The credit instruments drawn between two countries would simply cancel out. But such a situation has never existed. Even if each nation's transactions were balanced with all other nations taken collectively, it would owe money to some nations and be owed money by others. Settlements of such remaining balances between nations could be effected by payment in drafts drawn in terms of the **monetary unit of one nation** that is generally acceptable. Thus, during the nineteenth century the British pound sterling was widely used as the unit of payment between nations, and the London money market acted as a clearing house for a large part of the world's trade. In the post-World War II years, the United States dollar became the principal **international reserve currency** used to settle international balances.

Shipments of **gold** accomplish this same end. However, gold is not as freely used as in the past because many nations with adverse balances of payments do not possess adequate international reserves, and to prevent depletion of gold and foreign exchange reserves they have instituted controls over foreign exchange transactions and foreign trade. International payments are discussed in detail in Section 3 (International Banking).

The United States Money Supply

EARLY MONETARY HISTORY. The first money of the United States consisted of notes issued by the Continental Congress. These became so nearly worthless that the phrase "not worth a Continental" still survives. In 1792 Congress adopted a **bimetallic standard,** defining the dollar in terms of both silver and gold at a mint ratio of 15 to 1 between them. This meant that at the mint gold was valued fifteen times as much as silver. Later, in 1834, the mint ratio was changed to 16 to 1. One problem of the bimetallic standard was that the mint ratio often was not the same as the market ratio. As a result, the metal that was overvalued at the mint tended to drive the other metal out of circulation (Gresham's law). Although bimetallism was not legally abandoned until 1873, silver dollar coins were virtually unknown between 1834 and 1873, since gold tended to be overvalued at the mint during this period. For a time there was a satisfactory circulation of bank notes issued by the **first Bank of the United States,** founded in 1791, and the **second Bank of the United States,** chartered in 1816. State chartered banks also issued notes, but the banking laws of many states were lax and such notes often depreciated in value.

To help finance its needs during the Civil War, the Federal government resorted to the issue of fiat money—United States notes known as **"greenbacks."** The bimetallic standard had been suspended with the suspension of specie payments (redemption of paper money with coin) at the time. Also, to widen the market for government bonds and to end the abuses of state bank notes, the **National Banking System** was set up in 1863. State bank notes were taxed out of existence, and until 1914 national banks had a monopoly of bank-note issue. The bimetallic standard was ended by law in 1873, although currency was not redeemable at the time, and the country returned to an exclusive gold coin standard in 1879.

Expansion of silver production in the West and falling prices caused political agitation for the greater monetary use of silver as money. The Bland-Allison Act of 1878 and the Sherman Silver Purchase Act of 1890 required the Treasury to buy larger quantities of silver for coinage. In 1896 excitement ran high when Bryan campaigned for the presidency on a platform calling for the free coinage of silver at a fixed ratio of 16 to 1. He lost, and the Gold Standard Act affirmed the gold dollar as the standard.

FEDERAL RESERVE CURRENCY. A major defect of the currency system before 1914 was its rigidity. When the public demand for currency increased, as in periods of financial strain, national banks could not issue more notes unless they had government bonds to pledge as collateral. The panic of 1907, when clearing house certificates were used as currency for a time because of a lack of national bank notes, emphasized the gravity of the problem.

One of the express purposes of the Federal Reserve Act of 1913 was to provide an **elastic currency.** Member banks could draw currency from the Federal Reserve banks as needed, and could borrow from these institutions or rediscount eligible commercial paper with them if they did not have sufficient deposit balances to do so. The Federal Reserve banks, in turn, could issue two types of currency: Federal Reserve bank notes and Federal Reserve notes. The former, secured by government obligations, never became a permanent part of the currency because the latter proved to be adequate. Federal Reserve notes were formerly supported by a reserve of 25% in gold certificates held by Federal Reserve banks, the balance of the security being government securities or eligible commercial paper. However, early in 1968 the gold-cover requirement was eliminated.

It was intended that Federal Reserve currency would replace all other types of paper money. National bank notes, however, were not retired until 1935, and silver certificates and greenbacks are still in use as part of our permanent paper currency, although, as mentioned below, silver certificates are gradually being converted into Federal Reserve notes.

The concept of elastic currency was sometimes taken to imply that the volume of money should adapt to the needs of trade. In contrast to this notion, associated with the real-bills doctrine, the modern viewpoint is that the money supply should be used as one of the instruments of control over the economy.

THE NEW GOLD STANDARD AND DEVALUATION. As a result of the worldwide depression of the early 1930's as well as the accompanying hoarding of gold coin and bullion, the United States in 1933 called in from public circulation all gold and gold certificates and prohibited private ownership of gold without license. Thus, the old gold standard, codified by the Gold Standard Act of 1900, was abandoned. Active **control over the money supply** was assumed by the Treasury and the Federal Reserve System. However, the United States remained on the international gold standard for the settlement of international balances. Since 1934 the Treasury has sold gold freely to foreign governments and central banks at the official price of $35 an ounce.

In an effort to raise domestic prices and bring about more employment, the United States in January, 1934, devalued the dollar by raising the price paid for gold by the Treasury from $20.67 to $35 an ounce (and reducing the gold content of the dollar from 23.22 to 13.714 grains of fine gold). It was hoped that by raising the price of gold the United States dollar and goods would become cheaper for foreigners in their own currency. As a result, United States exports would be encouraged and imports reduced. Many foreign countries quickly imitated the United States devaluation, however, and the **chief effect of devaluation** was to stimulate gold production and its flow to the United States. Following the British devaluation of the pound sterling in late 1967, there were rumors that the United States would devalue the dollar. These rumors have been consistently denied by the United States government, although they caused sporadic speculation in the international gold market.

SILVER OPERATIONS. The silver bloc in Congress succeeded in pushing through legislation that for decades required the Treasury to buy substantial amounts of newly mined domestic silver and thereby help support its price. Large stocks of silver were accumulated by the Treasury under Congressional mandate. In 1946 the Treasury's buying price was increased to 90.5¢ an ounce.

During World War II, silver was urgently needed by industry for war purposes, and the Treasury found it necessary to ask Congressional authority to make the metal available from its stocks. Silver was released for war purposes not only to domestic industry but also to allied nations.

In 1946, the Treasury was authorized to sell **"free" silver**—i.e., silver not needed to back silver certificates—to domestic industry. The continued private demand for the metal, however, particularly by the photographic and electronic industries, coupled with a relatively stable world mine output caused a gradual depletion in the Treasury's stock of free silver. Accordingly, in late 1961, the Treasury halted the sale of silver to industrial users and, in an effort to ease the problem, obtained authorization from Congress in 1962 to abandon the silver purchase program. With the cessation of the Treasury sale of silver, its price rose above the prior ceiling and by mid-1963 reached $1.29 an ounce. At about this time, also, new legislation was enacted providing for a gradual program of converting the Treasury's circulating silver certificates (mostly $1 bills) into Federal Reserve notes. In 1967, further legislation was passed that terminated, as of June 24, 1968, the silver redemption feature of the silver certificates. Starting in 1965, the Treasury initiated another silver economy measure by removing all silver from dimes and quarters and reducing the silver content of the half-dollar from 90% to 40%. In May 1967, the Treasury, which had again become a seller of silver, ceased sales to foreigners at $1.29 an ounce and in July of that year halted all sales at that price, thereby freeing the market and resulting in a sharp rise in the price of the metal. The action adopted was to auction two million ounces a week at the going market price.

CURRENCY IN CIRCULATION. Figure 1 shows the composition of the bullion and currency supply of the United States at the end of November 1967.

			Held in the Treasury			
Kind of Currency	Total Outstanding	Currency in Circulation	As Security Against Gold and Silver Certificates	Treasury Cash	For Federal Reserve Banks and Agents	Held by Federal Reserve Banks and Agents
Gold	12,907	...	(12,392)	515	...	...
Gold certificates	(12,392)	...	...	...	12,391	1
Federal Reserve notes	43,278	40,831	...	102	...	2,345
Treasury currency—Total	6,775	5,631	(378)	791 *	...	352
Standard silver dollars	485	482	3	...	...	...
Silver bullion	466	...	375	91	...	...
Silver certificates	(378)	376	...	...	...	2
Fractional coin	5,415	4,383	...	685	...	346
United States notes	323	304	...	14	...	4
In process of retirement	86	86	...	...	...	...
TOTAL †	62,960	46,463 *	(12,770)	1,408	12,391	2,698

* Apparent discrepancy in total due to rounding of figures.
† Does not include all items shown, as some items represent the security for other items; gold certificates are secured by gold, and silver certificates by standard silver dollars and monetized silver bullion. Duplications are shown in parentheses.

Fig. 1. Kinds of United States currency outstanding and in circulation, November 30, 1967 (in millions of dollars). (Source: **Federal Reserve Bulletin,** Washington, D.C.: Board of Governors, Federal Reserve System.)

Gold certificates are not in circulation. These certificates are in effect receipts issued by the Treasury for gold in storage in this country. The difference between the total gold stock shown and the volume of gold certificates represents the overhang from pre-1934 when gold coins and certificates circulated freely.

THE UNITED STATES MONEY SUPPLY

Federal Reserve notes, issued by the Federal Reserve banks, constitute the bulk of the currency. They are obligations of the United States and a first lien on all the assets of the issuing Federal Reserve banks. They are secured by deposit with the Federal Reserve agents of a like amount of eligible paper or Treasury securities. Federal Reserve notes were, until 1968, required to have a minimum reserve of 25% in gold certificates.

The Treasury's outstanding currency consists of the following:

(a) **"Standard" silver dollars** are silver coins favored by some people over silver certificates. Full-weight silver dollars have not been coined since 1873.
(b) **Silver bullion** represents the Treasury's silver stock.
(c) **Silver certificates,** issued by the Treasury and backed by its silver stock, were placed in circulation through the offices of the Federal Reserve banks. These certificates now are being gradually replaced by Federal Reserve notes. In 1967 legislation was passed eliminating the silver redemption of the certificates.
(d) **Fractional coin** constitutes the public's "small change."
(e) **United States notes,** or greenbacks, are a heritage of Civil War days. Although this was originally fiat currency, the Treasury maintains a reserve of gold against them.
(f) In process of retirement are **Federal Reserve bank notes** and **national bank notes.** Deposits of equal value lawful money have been set up to redeem outstanding notes as they are presented.

BANK CREDIT AS MONEY. As previously indicated, demand deposits constitute the bulk of the nation's money supply. Therefore, the Federal Reserve System, because of its influence on the volume of bank deposits, plays a major role in the expansion of the money supply. At the end of 1967, **Federal Reserve credit outstanding,** mainly in the form of United States government obligations, amounted to about $50 billion.

It has been estimated that up to 90% of the nation's business is transacted by means of bank credit. In recent years the volume of bank deposits has been from three to four times greater than the amount of currency in circulation. Prior to 1933, the greater part of commercial bank deposits were created by the making of loans by banks. Since then, bank investments, especially government securities, have become significant in affecting the volume of deposits. The **growth of monetary gold stocks** has also been an important factor at times, although it is not so today.

The Federal Reserve System provides a mechanism whereby bank credit can be expanded in response to demand. When commercial **loans** were the source of most deposits, the volume of bank credit was largely responsive to the demands of business and agriculture. Since 1933, however, and especially during World War II, the volume of bank credit has also reflected the Treasury's credit requirements. In addition, the banks now finance, directly or indirectly, a large amount of credit to consumers.

PRESENT MONETARY SYSTEM. The United States is now on the **conditional gold bullion export standard.** Gold is purchased freely by the Treasury at a fixed price of $35 an ounce, less $\frac{1}{4}$ of 1% as a handling charge, but it is obtainable only for export subject to Treasury license. The international balances of the United States are settled either by gold or by the accumulation of dollar balances by foreigners. However, these dollar balances can be converted into gold only by foreign central banks or governments under a Treasury policy established in 1934.

Domestic ownership of gold is prohibited except for nonmonetary purposes under license from the Treasury. Thus, the United States has abandoned the gold standard domestically, and gold no longer exercises the automatic restraints upon our monetary and credit system that it did before 1933. The United States and other leading countries have, however, adopted numerous techniques of monetary and credit management that are discussed in detail below and in Section 1 (Interest Rates and Money Markets).

Banking Systems

THE EVOLUTION OF BANKING. As early as 2000 B.C., the Babylonian temples were in the banking business, lending at high rates of interest gold and silver that had been left with them for safekeeping. Fifteen hundred years later Greek temples were depositaries and loaned temple funds at interest. Private banking also attained a high state of development in Greek and Roman times.

One of the most famous banks in the modern sense was the **Bank of Amsterdam**, founded in 1609. Essentially a depositary for gold and silver, the bank's income was derived from fees levied on deposits. It also devised a system whereby deposits could be transferred on the books of the bank by written orders that resembled modern bank checks.

The **Bank of England** was granted a charter in 1694, in return for a perpetual loan of £1,200,000 to the government. The bank was successful from the start. Thanks to the prudent temper of the English, it avoided the speculative pitfalls that had wrecked John Law's Royal Bank of France early in the eighteenth century, and has survived as a pillar of strength to this day.

Throughout the eighteenth and nineteenth centuries, banking developed rapidly with the expansion of industry and trade. Each nation evolved distinctive forms reflecting its economic, political, and social structure. **Privately managed banks** predominated. During the nineteenth century, however, the policies of the Bank of England became increasingly public in character, foreshadowing the more recent growth of central and government-controlled banking.

THE ROLE OF COMMERCIAL BANKS. The banking business may be defined briefly as dealing in money and instruments of credit. The term "commercial bank" is usually applied to a lending institution that accepts **demand deposits**. In the United States it is distinguished particularly from mutual savings banks and savings and loan associations, which accept only time deposits or their equivalent.

Note issue was at one time a prime function of most commercial banks. Today paper money is issued in most countries only by the central banks. Note issue has become far less important than demand deposits, which are transferable from one owner to another by means of bank checks or drafts.

Commercial loans constituted the chief business of the banks in most countries until recent years. Funds were advanced to manufacturers or merchants on their own promissory notes, or drafts drawn on customers were discounted. The bank thus substituted its own credit for that of the borrower or his customers. The credit of the bank is transferable and is generally accepted as a means of payment. A bank loan thus transforms the credit of a borrower into money.

In more recent years banks have become department stores of credit for commerce, industry, trade, and consumers. In addition, banks make an important contribution to the nation's economy through investments in public and private securities. During World War II, banks purchased large amounts of United States **government obligations** and thus helped to finance the Treasury's deficits. Since the war the banks have greatly increased their investments in state and local government obligations and mortgages.

Thus, commercial banks play a vital role in modern economic life. They provide the essential mechanism through which most payments are cleared; they create the deposits that are the medium for these payments; and they provide investment funds for the purchase of private and public securities.

How Commercial Banks Create Deposits. Bank deposits increase when commercial banks make loans and decrease when loans are paid off. Similarly, **deposits expand** when banks buy securities from the public and contract when they sell securities to the public.

When a person borrows from a bank, the **normal procedure** is for the bank to credit the borrower's checking account for the amount of the loan. The moment that credit is entered on the borrower's ledger sheet, bank deposits are increased. If the borrower then draws a check on his account for the full amount of the loan, the new deposit is transferred to the ownership of another at the same or more probably at a different bank. But when the loan is paid off, the borrower gives the bank his check for the amount due. This check reduces the borrower's bank balance and thereby diminishes total bank deposits.

Essentially the same thing happens when a commercial bank buys securities. The seller of the securities receives the bank's own cashier's check that he deposits with his bank. The bank that receives this check as a deposit naturally shows an increase in its deposits. Likewise, when a bank sells securities from its portfolio to a nonbank investor, the latter's check in payment for the securities reduces his deposit balance with his bank.

In addition to changes in bank loans and investments, other factors that affect the total volume of bank deposits are changes in (1) interbank deposits, (2) monetary gold stocks, and (3) currency in circulation.

1. **Interbank deposits,** balances of commercial banks with other banks, are affected by a variety of factors, such as the extent to which interior banks prefer to keep excess cash with city correspondents instead of having such funds invested in securities. Interbank balances are frequently excluded from computations of bank deposits, however, because for the banking system as a whole they represent a duplication of bookkeeping credits.

2. **Changes in a nation's monetary gold stocks** normally result in corresponding changes in commercial bank deposits. For example, when gold is imported into the United States, it is sold to the Treasury, which issues a check on its account at the Federal Reserve banks. The seller of the gold deposits this check to the credit of his account in his commercial bank, and total bank deposits are thereby increased.

3. **An increase in the amount of currency** in the hands of the public reflects withdrawals of cash from banks by depositors, which reduces deposits. Conversely, bank deposits increase when the public reduces its holdings of currency by depositing cash with banks.

THE ROLE OF CENTRAL BANKS. Functions of central banks vary, but they usually include a monopoly, or near-monopoly, of note issue, discounting of paper or making direct advances to commercial banks, acting as fiscal agent for the government, open-market operations, foreign exchange dealings, services for foreign central banks, depositary for reserve funds of commercial banks, and controls over the volume of bank credit and bank lending policies.

In the United States, where the central bank consists of the twelve Federal Reserve banks and the unifying Board of Governors of the Federal Reserve System, a distinctive function is the supervision of certain operations of commercial banks and the administration of a great mass of regulations.

The central bank is usually the **basic source of the nation's bank credit,** and as a result exercises great influence upon credit conditions. Through discounting and lending, individual commercial banks can obtain funds to meet demands of depositors or borrowers. **Open-market operations,** usually consisting of the purchase or sale of government securities, create or reduce the banks' deposit balances at the central bank in the same way that commercial bank purchases and sales of securities create and reduce their deposits. Open-market operations are thus an effective instrument for broadening or contracting the credit base of the entire banking system.

The central bank has become the cornerstone of modern banking systems. Although the capital stock is sometimes privately owned, a central bank is in most respects a **government agency.** Its policies are designed to promote the broad public interest.

Banking System of the United States

EARLY BANKING HISTORY. The first bank in the United States was the Bank of North America, established by Robert Morris in Philadelphia in 1782, with a charter from the Continental Congress. Controversy arose over whether the Federal government or the states had authority under the Constitution to charter banks. The Supreme Court upheld the chartering power of the Federal government in 1819 and again in 1824, but in 1837 it upheld the constitutionality of state charters as well.

In 1791 Congress chartered the first **Bank of the United States,** advocated by Alexander Hamilton. Its charter expired in 1811 and was not renewed. Political opposition to the bank sprang partly from fear of domination by foreign interests that held a large part of the stock. A second Bank of the United States was established in 1816, but the renewal of its charter was vetoed by President Jackson in 1836 because of his opposition to eastern financial interests.

Prior to 1838 a bank charter could be obtained only by special legislative act The New York **Free Banking Act of 1838** first provided for granting charters upon compliance with the statutory requirements.

Free banking spread rapidly. But the laws of many states, especially in the Middle West, were lax, and serious abuses developed. Speculators and swindlers founded "wildcat" banks that issued bank notes against little or no security. Depressions brought waves of bank failures. Gradually, state banking laws improved in a number of states, particularly with respect to the reserve required against outstanding bank notes, the chief form of bank credit in those days. The tradition of free banking is today firmly established. Free banking contributed to the rapid growth of industry and trade and encouraged new enterprise, but the price paid by the public through bank failures at times was high. (Trescott, Financing American Enterprise.)

From the standpoint of stability, American banking history makes a sorry comparison with Canada and England. From the standpoint of offering **equality of economic opportunity,** however, the record here compares favorably with that of other nations.

State and National Banks. The **National Bank Act of 1863** provided for a system of banks to be chartered and supervised by the Federal government, rather than the states. These national banks could issue bank notes against government bonds as security, and a prohibitive tax was imposed upon bank notes issued by state banks, which was calculated to eliminate state banking. Most of the banks then in existence did take out national charters, and came under the regulation of the Comptroller of the Currency in place of state bank superintendents.

State banking survived, however, and from 1885 to 1920 expanded rapidly. Inability to issue bank notes became less important with the increasing use of bank checks. Most state banking laws were considerably more "liberal" than the National Bank Act. By 1900, the number of state banks exceeded the number of national banks.

The **McFadden Act of 1927** was intended to equalize the status of national with state banks. It enlarged the powers of national banks to make real estate loans, permitted them to acquire branches where state banks possessed this authority, and relaxed several restrictive features of the National Bank Act.

Today there are nearly 9,000 state-chartered commercial banks and about 4,800 national banks. Many of the state banks, however, are relatively small. National banks hold well over half of the combined assets of both types of institutions. In a sense, therefore, the United States has not a single banking system but fifty-one banking systems. Bankers refer to it as a **"dual system"** of state and national banking.

THE FEDERAL RESERVE SYSTEM. In 1908, following the panic of 1907, Congress created a **National Monetary Commission** to investigate thoroughly the whole field of banking and currency and to recommend legislation. The eventual fruit of its work was the Federal Reserve Act of 1913, a most significant landmark in banking legislation.

A current interpretation of the **Federal Reserve Act,** including later amendments, would state the objectives broadly as: (1) the establishment of an elastic currency and credit system, (2) the inauguration of a nationwide check collection system, (3) improved bank supervision, (4) aid in government financing, and (5) national credit management to achieve a high level of employment, avoidance of inflation, and economic stability with a sustainable rate of economic growth.

The Federal Reserve System consists of (1) the Board of Governors, (2) twelve Federal Reserve banks with twenty-four branches, (3) the Federal Open Market Committee, (4) the Federal Advisory Council, and (5) member banks.

1. **The Board of Governors** is composed of seven members appointed by the President and confirmed by the Senate. It is the directing agency of the system. Members are appointed for 14 years, and a term expires every 2 years. One of the seven governors is appointed as chairman.

2. **The Federal Reserve banks,** one located in each of the twelve Federal Reserve Districts (see Fig. 2), supervise the member banks in each district. Each bank has its own board of directors and officers headed by a President, but its policies are largely determined by the Board of Governors.

3. **The Federal Open Market Committee** consists of the members of the Board of Governors and five Presidents of Federal Reserve banks, elected annually. Assisted by a small advisory staff of economists and specialists, it formulates policies with respect to the purchase and sale of government securities by the Reserve banks.

4. **The Federal Advisory Council** is composed of twelve members, usually commercial bankers, one elected by the directors of each of the Reserve banks. Its function is purely advisory.

5. **Member banks,** numbering over 6,000, include all national banks and those state banks that apply and are accepted for membership.

2·14　　　BANKING AND LENDING INSTITUTIONS

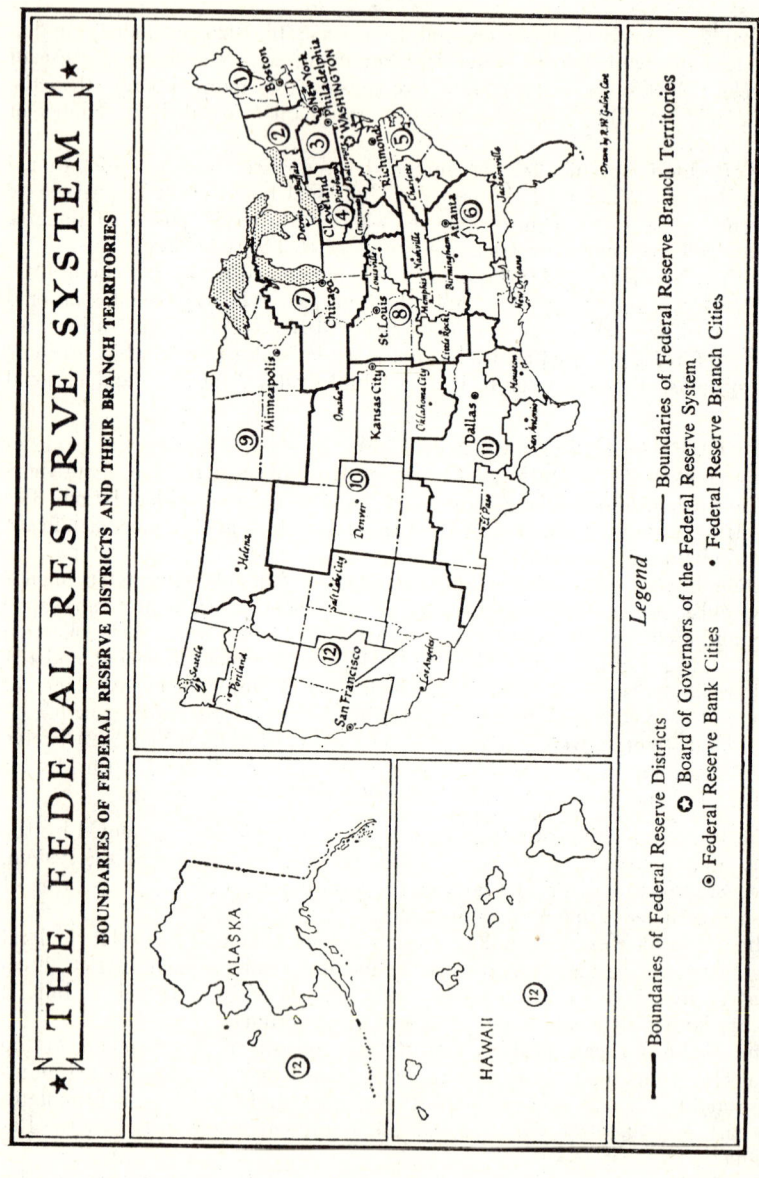

Fig. 2. Boundaries of Federal Reserve Districts. (Source: The Federal Reserve System, Purposes and Functions, Board of Governors, Federal Reserve System.)

The Federal Reserve Act provided for twelve regional banks rather than one central bank. This plan reflected the traditional American distrust of centralized financial control and was intended better to serve the diverse regional requirements of the nation. Such decentralization was, however, found to involve serious disadvantages, and the tendency since 1933 has been to increase greatly the authority of the Board of Governors in Washington.

The Board of Governors. The chief powers of the Board of Governors of the Federal Reserve System include: (1) reviewing discount rates of the Federal Reserve banks; (2) reviewing the decisions of the Federal Open Market Committee, whose membership is numerically dominated by the board in any event; (3) raising or lowering reserve requirements for member banks within a specified range; (4) setting margin requirements on loans made for the purpose of buying or carrying listed securities; (5) defining the types of securities that member banks may purchase; and (6) fixing maximum interest rates payable by banks on time deposits. In addition, the Board has broad discretionary authority that has been used as a basis for **"direct action"** in the shape of advice and instruction to banks to influence credit conditions. The Board also presents recommendations to Congress for new banking legislation.

The board has its offices at the Federal Reserve Building in Washington, where it maintains a permanent research, statistical, legal, administrative, and supervisory staff. It issues a monthly publication, the **Federal Reserve Bulletin,** which is an invaluable source of authoritative data and statistics on money, banking, and business. The annual report of the Board contains an analysis of banking and economic conditions and trends, and summarizes the actions of both the Board and the Open Market Committee. **(Annual Report of the Board of Governors of the Federal Reserve System.)**

Federal Reserve Banks. Each Federal Reserve bank functions under a Federal charter. Its stock is held by member banks, which must subscribe 6% of capital and surplus to the stock of its Federal Reserve bank, of which sum only 50% is paid in, the rest being subject to call. Dividends are limited to 6% on the amount paid in.

Each Reserve bank has nine **directors,** three of whom are known as Class A directors, three as Class B, and three as Class C. Member banks elect Class A and Class B directors, one director in each class being chosen by small banks, one by medium-sized banks, and one by large banks. Class A directors are bankers, whereas Class B directors must be actively engaged in business or agriculture but not connected with a bank. Class C directors are appointed by the Federal Reserve Board and may not be bankers. One of the Class C directors is designated as **Federal Reserve Agent,** whose special duty is to provide close liaison with the Board.

The Federal Reserve banks are primarily bankers' banks, and their deposits consist chiefly of the legally required reserves of member banks. They also hold deposits of the Treasury, of foreign central banks, and of nonmember banks whose checks they collect, but none for individuals or business concerns. Operations include note issuance, investment in government securities, lending to member banks, examination and supervision of member banks, collection of checks, and the performance of a variety of essential services for commercial banks and for the government.

Aside from representation on the **Open Market Committee,** the individual Federal Reserve banks have no major responsibility with respect to the formulation of credit policy. At times, nevertheless, their views have been very influential in shaping decisions of the Board of Governors. Their primary task is the implementation of credit policies formulated by the Board.

One of the functions of the Federal Reserve banks is to make temporary **loans and advances to member banks.** Federal Reserve credit is designed to accommodate banks for a short period only, that is, to help them cope with sudden withdrawals of deposits or seasonal requirements beyond those that can reasonably be met from the bank's own resources. To borrow from a Federal Reserve bank, a member bank may either **rediscount eligible paper** (such as short-term notes obtained by the member bank from commercial, industrial, agricultural, or other business borrowers) or it may issue its own promissory notes secured by eligible paper or government securities. The latter type of member bank borrowings are called advances as distinguished from discounting. In practice, member bank borrowings are mainly secured by United States Treasury securities. The interest charge on either method of borrowing is called the **discount rate.**

The principal means used by the Federal Reserve System to influence the volume of bank reserves is the purchase and sale of United States government securities in the open market. By paying for purchases with a credit to member bank reserves, the nation's credit base is expanded. Sales by the Federal Reserve, on the other hand, lead to a contraction in member bank reserve accounts as these are charged in payment for the securities sold. In addition, the System makes credit available on occasion to dealers in United States government securities through **repurchase agreements.** These agreements provide for a pledge by the dealer to repurchase the securities within 15 days or less. To affect credit conditions, the Federal Reserve also buys bankers' acceptances.

During World War II, the Federal Reserve banks made large-scale purchases of United States government securities. This led to a tremendous **expansion** of member bank reserves and a vast wartime expansion of bank credit and currency in circulation. As shown in Fig. 6 on p. 1·15, in early 1968, all Federal Reserve Banks combined held $49,322,000 in government securities, or roughly 70% of their total assets. Gold certificates and cash items in the process of collection account for the bulk of the remainder. The banks' **principal liabilities** consist of Federal Reserve notes in circulation and the reserve balances of commercial banks.

Collection of Checks and Other Services. A very important service performed for the entire commercial banking system by the Federal Reserve banks is the collection of checks drawn on banks throughout the country, deposited in banks located elsewhere than the towns in which the paying banks are located. The volume of checks handled by the Federal Reserve has grown rapidly over the years, the number today exceeding four billion a year and amounting to over $1¼ trillion. All checks collected and cleared through the Federal Reserve must be **paid at par**—i.e., in full without deduction of any exchange charge by the paying bank. This check clearing service is provided without charge not only for member banks but also for all banks that agree to remit at par. Banks accounting for about 98% of all commercial bank deposits are on the Federal Reserve par list.

Other services of the Federal Reserve banks include the collection of coupons and other items for member banks, telegraphic transfers of funds between members, the safekeeping of securities for banks, supplying currency to banks, receiving and sorting currency returned from circulation, and the performance of certain tasks for foreign central bank correspondents.

A substantial part of the **personnel** of the Federal Reserve banks is engaged in providing fiscal agency, custodianship, and depositary services for the Treasury and other government departments and agencies. Most of this work is connected

THE FEDERAL DEPOSIT INSURANCE CORPORATION. The F.D.I.C. was organized in 1933 to restore public confidence in the banks and to protect bank depositors from losses due to bank failures. To enable it to keep failures to a minimum, the Corporation was given **broad supervisory authority** over all insured banks and discretion with respect to admitting banks to insurance. A new supervisory organization was thus superimposed upon the already complex American banking system.

Membership in the F.D.I.C. is compulsory for all Federal Reserve member banks, but optional for nonmembers. Noninsured commercial banks, numbering a little under 200, hold less than 1% of the nation's banking resources. Statistics on insured and noninsured commercial banks are given in Fig. 4.

	Number of Offices*	Number of Banks*	Number of Branches*
Total	30,795	13,737	17,058
Total insured	30,544	13,541	17,003
Members of Federal Reserve System:			
National	14,436	4,799	9,637
State	4,867	1,350	3,517
Not members of Federal Reserve System	11,241	7,392	3,849
Noninsured	251	196	55

* Excludes non-deposit trust companies.

Fig. 4. **Number of commercial banking offices in the United States according to insurance status, December 31, 1966.**

For a number of years the great majority of the **mutual savings banks** remained aloof from the F.D.I.C. During World War II, however, a considerable number of the larger mutuals, holding well over half of total mutual savings bank deposits, joined the F.D.I.C.

Each deposit account is insured up to $15,000. The assessment funds paid by the banks are invested in government obligations. The very small losses from bank failures since the inception of the F.D.I.C. have enabled it to accumulate a **very large reserve** for future contingencies.

The F.D.I.C. has adopted a strict policy with respect to the admission of newly chartered banks to membership in the insurance fund, and has made diligent efforts to strengthen the banking system through its supervisory activities. It has therefore played an important part in helping to restore the **confidence of the public** in the banks. (See also Section 5, Banking Services and Procedures.)

REGULATORY LEGISLATION. Banking statutes today are the product of an evolutionary process covering more than a century. Congress and the fifty state legislatures have repeatedly amended banking laws. It is not surprising, therefore, that the laws are voluminous and complicated. These laws impose restrictions on banking operations and delegate discretionary powers of regulation to supervisory authorities.

Between 1864 and 1913, Congress passed more than sixty laws amending the National Bank Act, chiefly on matters of detail. Since the establishment of the Federal Reserve System, Federal banking legislation has consisted largely of detailed amendments to both the National Bank and the Federal Reserve Acts.

The **Banking Act of 1933** was a reform measure aimed at correcting specific abuses revealed by the depression. It strengthened the powers of supervisory officials, increased controls over the volume and the use of credit, and provided for temporary insurance of bank deposits.

The **Banking Act of 1935** dealt chiefly with the enlargement of the powers of the Board of Governors of the Federal Reserve System in the field of credit management. It also tightened existing restrictions on several banking operations and established the permanent system of deposit insurance. Some of the major legislation enacted in the post-World War II period is discussed in the following pages.

Inconsistencies in Federal banking laws exist because Congress first legislated only for national banks, later passed some regulations applicable to state member banks as well, then extended some provisions to nonmember insured banks, and finally applied a few restrictions to all banks.

The banking laws of the fifty states also contain diverse provisions, and some have glaring omissions and defects. The more flagrant **weaknesses,** however, have been largely corrected, particularly in the light of the bitter lessons of 1930 to 1933. The banking laws of some states, especially in the East, meet high standards, and in general the tendency has been to strengthen the legislation and to bring it closer to the standards set forth in the Federal laws.

Some of the major types of bank regulations are summarized below.

Mergers and Branches. In the 1960's, the number of banks declined slightly; however, the total number of banking offices (head offices plus branches) has increased greatly. As of Dec. 31, 1966, there were 32,136 banking offices. These changes were largely the result of mergers and the growth of branch banking (see also discussion of Branch and Group Banking, below).

National and state banking authorities exercise extensive supervision over all forms of multiple banking and also regulate bank holding companies. Federal and state laws apply to most types of branch expansion. **State law** determines the status of **branch banking** in each state for national- as well as for state-chartered banks. Most bank **mergers** fall under the Federal **Bank Merger Act of 1960,** as amended in 1966, which requires the approval of three Federal supervisory agencies to assure that mergers are in the public interest. Written approval is required from the Comptroller of the Currency if the proposed remaining bank is a national bank; from the Board of Governors of the Federal Reserve System if it is a state-chartered member bank; and from the F.D.I.C. if it is a nonmember insured bank. Thus, this type of Federal control over mergers extended to all but a very small number of noninsured, nonmember banks in the country. Each of these agencies, in passing upon a proposed merger, is to take into consideration the bank's financial history and condition, the adequacy of its capital structure, its future earnings prospects, the character of its management, the convenience for and needs of the community to be served, and the probable effects of the proposed merger on banking competition. In addition, the one agency required to pass on the merger application must request reports from the other two supervisory agencies and from the Attorney General on the competitive aspects involved.

The standard established in the 1966 amendments was to condone mergers that might lessen competition provided that the anti-competitive effects "are clearly outweighed in the public interest" by benefits to the "convenience and needs of the community."

Availability and Cost of Credit. Control of bank credit is the responsibility primarily of the Federal Reserve System, which exercises this function through its **control over bank reserves** as well as through the **imposition of interest rate ceilings** on time and savings deposits. These regulations have a profound influence on the growth of commercial banks and on their competitive position vis-à-vis other financial institutions.

Loans and Investments. The Federal Reserve System and state laws severely circumscribe the lending and investment practices of commercial banks for the protection of depositors. For example, banks generally cannot lend to any single customer more than 10% of their capital and surplus. Investments in common stock are prohibited, and real estate loans are subject to restrictions. These regulations are discussed in detail in Section 5 (Banking Services and Procedures).

BANK SUPERVISION AND EXAMINATION. Supervision of banks consists chiefly of the **administration, interpretation,** and **enforcement of banking legislation.** It is performed by a number of Federal agencies and by the banking departments of the fifty states. The objective of supervision is the maintenance of a sound banking system.

Commercial banks must also submit to periodic detailed examinations of their condition, operations, and policies. These bank examinations are conducted by the Comptroller of the Currency, by the state banking departments, by the Federal Reserve System for member banks, and the F.D.I.C. for nonmember insured banks. Ordinarily, the overlapping authorities cooperate in order to avoid duplication (see Section 5).

BRANCH AND GROUP BANKING. As we have seen, the status of branch banking is determined by state law, and the establishment, location, and number of bank branches are thoroughly regulated by Federal and state authorities. Branch banking refers to the operation of more than one banking office by a single banking corporation. American banks, like those of most other countries, operated some branches in the early stages of banking development. After the Civil War, however, branch banking was discouraged and for a time almost disappeared. Around 1900 interest in branch banking began to revive in some states, and in 1909 California enacted a statute that permitted statewide branch banking. Since then, branch banking has gained ground. A number of states have followed the example of California. Others have allowed the establishment of branches only on a citywide or regional basis. Others prohibit branches entirely, or the courts hold this to be the case since the statutes are silent on the subject. National banks generally have the same branch banking powers as state-chartered banks in the same state.

Bank Holding Companies. These are corporations organized under the laws of some states to engage in the **acquisition of the stock of subsidiary commercial banks.** Bank holding companies can provide such important **services** to subsidiaries as centralized purchasing; legal, accounting, and tax services; economic and investment advice; and other assistance to improve operations. A holding company is sometimes viewed as a **means of circumventing restrictions on branching,** but holding companies are also found in states with few or no restrictions on branch banking. Holding companies also have the advantage of being able to operate across state lines. During the late 1960's, several important holding companies were formed in New York to circumvent that state's branch-banking restrictions. These companies are regulated by the Federal Reserve Board under the Bank Holding Company Act of 1956, which was amended in 1966.

Chain banking refers to ownership of stock in a number of banks by a single individual or group of individuals, as contrasted with a holding company. It is now relatively unimportant.

THE BRANCH BANKING CONTROVERSY. Branch banking is a highly controversial issue in the field of banking. Vigorous opposition comes, naturally enough, from smaller banks who fear for their existence if large city banks are allowed to establish branches to compete with them. Numerically strong, unit bankers have considerable influence with legislatures. Opinion among city bankers is more evenly divided. Active support for branch banking has come from some economists, supervisory officials, and branch bankers.

The argument is usually restricted to statewide or regional, not nationwide, branch banking. Only a few extremists contend that national branch systems like those of Canada and England should be regarded as models for a country as large and diversified as the United States.

The debate may be summarized as follows:

The Case for Branch Banking

1. **Service:** Many small banks cannot afford to hire good management, whereas branch systems are able to employ and to train competent, experienced personnel. A branch system is better able to institute modern and efficient means of serving depositors and borrowers. For example, at present, small banks may not be able to afford the large-scale computer installations that have made modern banking more efficient.

2. **Competition:** Independent bankers who do provide good service have no reason to fear the competition of a branch bank. Being local men, they have the competitive advantage. The community is entitled to the wholesome competition provided by branch banking, but at present many unit banks have monopolies over credit and other banking services in their localities. Laws prohibiting branch banking simply perpetuate these unjustified monopolies at the expense of the public.

3. **Safety:** Branch systems have greater financial resources, better management, and greater diversification of loans and deposits. During 1930 to 1933, there was not a single failure in Canada or in England where branch banking prevails. California, leader in branch banking, had a far better record than most other states.

New branches, of course, would always require approval of the supervisory authorities.

4. **Effects on economy:** Progress has been achieved in other industries by replacing small and inefficient units with larger and more efficient ones. This is the principle of branch banking.

The Case Against Branch Banking

1. **Service:** Branch banking produces cogs, not bankers. Restricted authority and subservience to a head office stultify initiative. A branch manager is a "hired man" of a distant corporation and does not have the same interest in the welfare of the community as the officer of an independent local bank. He tends to neglect the small depositor and the small borrower.

2. **Competition:** As branch banking expands, unit banks tend to disappear and the community is deprived of the benefits to be expected from normal banking competition.

3. **Safety:** The mere size of a branch system is no guaranty of financial strength: Branch banks in the United States and elsewhere have failed in the past. The adequacy of a bank's capital is entirely relative. In fact, a fundamental weakness of a branch bank is its chronic tendency to expand just for the sake of expansion.

4. **Effects on economy:** Independent bankers have encouraged the growth of new local enterprise. Many a thriving corporation received its initial impetus from

the financial aid of the local banker. Unit banking prevents domination of credit by powerful groups.

Possibilities in Branch Banking. Branch banking is neither panacea nor anathema. Properly regulated, it can be beneficial. Its development, however, should be gradual to assure competent management and to avoid disturbing established sound unit banks. Efficient independent banks can compete successfully against branches, whereas, from the standpoint of public interest, inefficient banks do not deserve to be protected indefinitely against the better-service competition that branch banks can offer. In the long run, the public that is served, rather than the bankers, should be permitted to decide the kind of banking it wants.

INTERBANK RELATIONS. Every commercial bank deals constantly with other banks in the course of its daily operations. It could not otherwise provide the broad banking services that are today required even in the smallest community.

The necessity for interbank transactions has resulted in the evolution of a vast network of **correspondent relations** between banks. The average commercial bank maintains deposit balances with several large city banks. In return for these accounts, the city banks perform a wide variety of services for their correspondents. Some of these services are the same as those rendered by the Federal Reserve banks, such as the collection of checks and coupons and the safekeeping of securities. In addition, however, city banks offer advice regarding investments, credit information, foreign department services, trust services, and assistance in solving bank management problems. Correspondent relations play an important role in the efficient functioning of the banking system.

Another example of interbank relations is the **local clearing house.** This is an association of banks in the same city or county, founded for the primary purpose of exchanging checks among the participating banks to facilitate their prompt collection. Beyond this mechanical function, clearing houses frequently act as an agency for united action on common problems such as service charges.

Bankers have also organized associations along county, state, regional, and national lines. The largest is the **American Bankers Association,** New York, whose membership includes nearly all commercial banks. The A.B.A. maintains a sizable permanent staff of specialists in various fields of banking and functions as a trade association for the entire industry.

The activities of bankers' associations are manifold, including conventions, work with legislative committees, publications, special studies of monetary and banking problems, study conferences, and other educational activities. The **American Institute of Banking,** a section of the A.B.A., has chapters throughout the country that provide study courses for bank employees. The Stonier Graduate School of Banking at Rutgers University, sponsored by the A.B.A., offers an intensive summer curriculum primarily for bank officers. A number of state associations have organized similar study conferences, usually with the cooperation of universities, members of the A.B.A. staff, and supervisory authorities.

PROPOSALS FOR BANKING UNIFICATION. Proposals have been put forward from time to time for greater unification of banking. The **Report of the Commission on Money and Credit,** a privately sponsored study group, recommended in 1961 that all insured commercial banks be required to become members of the Federal Reserve System. Furthermore, the Commission recommended increased coordination of examining and supervisory authorities. At the

Federal level, it stated, there should be only one examining authority for commercial banks. Moreover, the Commission urged the revision of the National Bank Act to enable national banks to establish branches within "trading areas," irrespective of state laws.

A **1962 Report of the Advisory Committee on Banking to the Comptroller of the Currency** also presented the majority view in favor of eliminating much of the present division of responsibilities for the supervision, examination, and regulation of banking operations. It also recommended allowing the establishment of branches by national banks within a 25-mile area even in states where such expansion is now prohibited.

The **Committee on Financial Institutions,** appointed by the President of the United States, recommended in its report dated April 9, 1963, the adoption of compulsory membership for all banks in the Federal Reserve System. It also urged closer cooperation and coordination in the supervision and examination of commercial banks.

Banking Trends

FROM THE 1920's TO THE POSTWAR ERA. From the beginning of the century until about 1920, the pattern of banking did not exhibit very significant changes. In the traditional manner loans were typically on a short-term basis, geared to financing working-capital needs. During the next decade there was a sharp increase in bank holdings of corporate securities as well as in loans on real estate and on the security of common stock, which the Federal Reserve unsuccessfully attempted to arrest. In the depression of the 1930's bank assets declined in volume (to a large extent due to bank failures), and business loans shrank even more.

During that period almost 10,000 banks failed. Far too many banks had been chartered, partly because of mistaken theories as to the virtues of unlimited competition in banking and partly because of the eagerness of state and national supervisors to add to the size and prestige of their respective systems. This had weakened the banking structure, lowered the quality of bank management, and led to unsound methods of competition.

The mortality rate was especially high at first among state banks that had been established with very little capital. But as the depression deepened, banks of all sorts and sizes that a few years before had seemed impregnable buckled under the impact of the unprecedented declines in values and in business activity. Failures generated a vicious spiral of deflation. As more and more banks closed, public hysteria increased. Panic continued to mount until, in March, 1933, President Franklin D. Roosevelt, in his first official act, imposed the **"Bank Holiday"** temporarily closing all banks. This act was made inevitable by the inability of the Federal Reserve banks to provide more currency at the time to meet the hoarding demand. Public confidence was then restored, and a new era in banking was begun with the enactment of the **Emergency Banking Act** of March 9, 1933, providing government capital to reopen banks and assuring adequate currency in the form of Federal Reserve bank notes without gold backing.

At this time, a number of large banks had affiliates incorporated under the general corporation laws of the states to engage in underwriting, selling, and trading of securities. Losses incurred by these affiliates had caused huge losses to many of these banks, leading to some of the worst failures. The Banking Act of 1933 forbade banks to have **security affiliates,** and required the dissolution of those then in existence.

During World War II the government sold a large volume of its obligations to the banking system, and by 1945 the largest proportion of bank assets consisted of U.S. government securities. Since then the composition of bank assets has been marked by the relative reduction of government issues, a relative increase in state and municipal obligations holdings, and a shift in the composition of the loan portfolio. The structure of bank liabilities has also changed as time deposits have become relatively more important as a source of funds.

TRENDS IN BANK LOANS. Up to the end of World War II, commercial and industrial bank loans had been declining in relative importance among bank assets for several decades. A **major decline** in bank lending to business occurred during the depression of the 1930's as a result of sharply curtailed financing needs. The war, together with the official rationing of resources, again curbed private demand for bank funds.

Postwar Changes. Since 1946, there has again been an **upswing** in the utilization of bank loans, but their composition has been changing profoundly. The principal changes have been the diminished relative importance of loans to business and the greatly increased importance of consumer and real estate loans. In the 1920's, **business loans** made up well over half of the total loans, but by 1967 this figure had shrunk to less than 40%. Following in importance were **real estate loans** which at that time comprised about 25% of the loan portfolio. **Consumer loans,** which were insignificant in the prewar period, comprised over one-fifth of the total in 1967. In contrast, because of the imposition of margin requirements, loans for purchasing or carrying securities have declined sharply in importance. Since the end of World War II banks have become veritable "department stores" of credit, offering an unprecedented variety of loans and services. Figure 5 shows the distribution of commercial bank loans in mid-1967.

Purpose of Loan	$ Billions	Percent of Total
Total	$225.1	100.0%
Commercial and industrial	84.5	37.5
Agricultural (except real estate)	9.3	4.1
For carrying or purchasing securities	4.6	2.1
Real estate loans	55.3	24.6
Other loans to individuals	49.5	22.0
To financial institutions	17.9	8.0
All other	4.1	1.7

Fig. 5. Total gross loans of all commercial banks, June 30, 1967. (Source: **Federal Reserve Bulletin.**)

One reason for the relative increase in consumer and real estate loans was, of course, the nature of the postwar economy. Backlogs of huge unfilled consumer demands for cars and other durables had been carried forward from the depression and the war. Housing had been a neglected sector of the economy in the face of a rising population, and the residential mortgage market leaped to the forefront of lending.

The demand for business loans at commercial banks has also been reduced by the increasing amounts of **funds being generated internally by corporations** through undistributed profits and depreciation and other capital consumption allowances. In 1966 these sources provided approximately two-thirds of the requirements of nonfinancial corporations. Another reason large firms have resorted less to bank credit is their **access to open market financing.**

Within business lending, the traditional "self-liquidating" 90-day loan began to decline in importance, and term loans of several years' maturity began to constitute a significant part of the loan portfolios of many banks. The so-called **"real bills" doctrine,** which formerly held sway and maintained that commercial banks ought to make only short-term self-liquidating loans, is in the process of disappearing. Moreover, virtually continuous borrowing through short-term bank loans, which are renewed almost automatically at maturity, has become an accepted practice in commercial banking. Despite the change outlined above, bank loans still provide almost half of the short-term credit requirements of business.

THE GROWTH OF BANK INVESTMENTS. Between 1930 and 1966 there was a considerable increase in the amount of securities held by commercial banks, as the following figures indicate:

Loans and Investments of Member Banks
(End-of-year figures, in billions of dollars)

	1930	1940	1951	1966
Loans	$32	$19	$ 49	$216
United States government securities	5	18	52	56
Other securities	10	7	11	49
Total loans and securities	$47	$44	$112	$321
Securities as percentage of total	31%	57%	56%	33%

The large **deficits of the Federal government,** especially during the war, led to the sale of large amounts of United States Treasury securities to the commercial banks. But with the ending of hostilities, member banks liquidated large amounts of governments to make room in their portfolios for loans to meet the pent-up private demands that had been accumulated over the previous 15 years of depression and war. Since the early 1950's, bank holdings of United States government obligations have remained roughly unchanged. The declining proportion of governments was partly offset by the rise in holdings of other securities, primarily tax-exempt obligations of states and municipalities. Nevertheless, securities declined from 56% of total loans and investments in 1951 to 33% in 1966.

NEGOTIABLE CERTIFICATES OF TIME DEPOSIT. A major development of the postwar period has been the rapid increase in savings and time deposits at commercial banks, reflecting largely the **expansion of individual savings** and the intensive efforts of the banks to attract such savings by offering **higher rates of interest.** Another significant development has been the emergence of negotiable certificates of time deposit issued to large corporate savers.

Time certificates of deposit (C.D.'s) are negotiable receipts issued by large commercial banks evidencing a deposit for a specified length of time, usually under a year. In return for the promise to leave the funds on deposit, C.D.'s carry a stipulated rate of interest for which the Federal Reserve Board sets maximum rates. A **secondary dealer-created market** exists for the certificates of most banks. The typical denomination is $1 million or more, although occasionally trades in lesser amounts take place. The growth of C.D.'s on any significant scale began only in 1961. By December 1967, there were over $20 billion outstanding, and they had become a major money market instrument. Their continued acceptance will depend in large part on the maintenance of an interest rate ceiling that will make these instruments competitive in the open market.

BANK EARNINGS. Although the net profit earned by commercial banks has risen in nearly every postwar year, the return on capital invested has remained roughly stable. **Operating earnings** of commercial banks have risen sharply as a result of four factors:

1. The expansion of earning assets on which income is based.
2. The sharp postwar rise in the level of interest rates.
3. The shift in the composition of assets away from low-yielding governments to more profitable loans and investments.
4. Increased receipts from charges and fees for various services.

Largely offsetting these factors has been the steep increase in **operating expenses** because of the inflationary rise in salaries and other costs, the higher interest rates paid on deposits, and the expansion in the volume of business handled. Banks derive about 60% of their revenues from loans; the second most important source is interest on government securities. In recent years net income after taxes has averaged around 0.6% of total assets for smaller banks to nearly 0.8% for medium-sized banks. On equity, the return is estimated to be roughly between 7% and 10%.

BANKING COMPETITION. Intensity of banking competition varies greatly in different localities. In many small communities there is but one bank that has a virtual monopoly over local credit. Its lending rates are sometimes relatively high. In some cities having a number of banks, competition among them is keen, whereas in other places there is considerable uniformity in such matters as lending rates, service charges, and interest rates paid on savings deposits.

The excessive and uneconomic competition among banks that characterized the 1920's has largely disappeared, partly because of the elimination of thousands of marginal and poorly managed banks that had aggravated that type of competition. Today payment of interest on demand deposits is prohibited, and **maximum rates** have been established by law for interest paid on time deposits. Generally speaking, competition in providing better service has replaced the earlier means of attracting new business.

However, competition from **other types of lending institutions** has been increasing since 1933. In particular, savings and loan associations have been aggressive in competing for real estate mortgages, often lending on terms more lenient than those permitted to commercial banks. They have also bid for savings at higher rates than banks can pay, due to the Federal Reserve interest-rate ceilings.

Other institutions also compete with commercial banks not only in attracting savings deposits but also in making mortgage and business loans. These include mutual savings banks, life insurance companies, and the nonbank-administered pension and trust funds. **Governmental agencies** have been especially active in the field of agricultural credit. As a result, the growth of commercial banks, as measured by the increase in assets, has seriously lagged behind that of most other financial institutions in the postwar period. These trends have also intensified the competition among commercial banks themselves. (The competition to banks from other lending institutions is discussed in detail in the last part of this Section.)

Monetary Policy

DEFINITIONS AND OBJECTIVES. The broad objective of monetary policy is to promote economic stability at a high level of employment and production. To this end, specific measures may be adopted to raise, lower, or stabilize the price level, to curb excessive speculation, to maintain sound banking conditions, to expand foreign trade, to stimulate enterprise, to encourage or restrain consumer buying, to maintain an equitable relationship among various income groups, to maintain an orderly market for government securities, and to influence foreign exchange rates. In wartime, monetary and credit management seeks to assure the success of Treasury borrowing, assist the mobilization of the economy for war, and minimize the harmful aftereffects. Monetary policy as envisioned by many economists operates through a chain of causal factors leading from changes in bank reserves, interest rates, and the stock of money to changes in aggregate demand.

The objectives and criteria of monetary policy depend upon the economic conditions prevailing. "Stability of prices," for example, is usually desirable, but, as the experience of the 1920's proved, steady prices do not always reflect sound economic conditions. Moreover, under given circumstances monetary policy may not, by itself, be fully effective in sustaining a desired level of aggregate demand. Thus, the choice usually available to the economic authorities refers to a policy mix, involving monetary and fiscal measures as well as debt management operations, and sometimes even certain types of direct controls. (See Friedman, A Program for Monetary Stability.)

EXCHANGE STABILIZATION. Monetary policy also embraces such international aspects as the valuation of the nation's money unit in terms of gold or of a foreign currency, foreign exchange controls, policy with respect to the purchase and sale of gold, and regulation of exports and imports of capital.

Monetary depreciation frequently results from a drain on a nation's gold stock, arising either from an adverse balance of trade or from capital outflows. During the early 1930's, frightened capital fled first from one country and then another, causing monetary difficulties in much the same way that runs on banks contributed to bank failures in the United States. Depreciation, or devaluation, has also been carried out as a deliberate policy by many countries, both in the interwar and post-World War II periods, in order to stimulate exports and discourage imports. Members of the **International Monetary Fund** may not depreciate their currencies in excess of 10% without the consent of the Fund.

Upward revaluation of a currency has been far less common. In July, 1946, Canada and Sweden revalued their currencies in terms of the United States dollar to insulate their internal price levels from the effects of sharply rising prices abroad. In March, 1961, the West German mark underwent a 5% upward revaluation, designed to reduce a balance of payments surplus that put inflationary pressures on the domestic economy.

For many years prior to the First World War, England occupied a position of leadership in international finance. After the war, the American dollar emerged as a strong competitor to the pound sterling for international supremacy. During the 1920's and 1930's, however, American policies with respect to war debts, foreign trade, foreign lending, devaluation of the dollar, and silver operations caused difficulties for many foreign currencies. These policies accentuated the tendency for many nations abroad to isolate their internal economies by the adoption of **managed monetary systems** and **trade and exchange controls**.

The Period Following World War II. World War II drastically dislocated trade relations and caused severe currency inflation in most countries. American wartime "lend-lease," relief shipments, and leadership in establishing the International Monetary Fund and the International Bank for Reconstruction and Development marked the adoption of a policy of **closer monetary cooperation** with other countries.

In the period after the Second World War, the United States followed a policy aimed at restoring the devastated productive capacity of Western Europe through the Marshall plan and other **foreign aid programs**. By running a balance of payments surplus, the United States sought deliberately to redistribute international reserves without incurring a drain on its own gold holdings. This period of the "dollar shortage," however, gradually gave way to an uncomfortable **dollar drain** as productive capacities abroad were restored while the United States balance of payments deficit was sharply increased. The reason for this was that the net outflow of private United States capital, together with government aid and military expenditures abroad, exceeded the large positive balance on trade alone. As a result, the United States gold stock declined from $22.9 billion in 1957 to $12.1 billion at the end of 1967, while United States short-term liabilities to foreigners (excluding international organizations) rose from $13½ billion to $31.4 billion.

To deal with this situation, efforts were made to increase the excess of United States exports over imports, to reduce the outflow of capital, especially short-term capital seeking a higher return abroad, and to induce foreign countries to assume more of the burden of foreign aid and the common defense. In addition, steps were taken within the International Monetary Fund to enlarge the supply of international reserves, and to discourage speculative pressure on the leading currencies. These measures were complemented first by voluntary and later by statutory curbs on capital outflows (see Section 3).

THE MONEY SUPPLY AND THE PRICE LEVEL. The relation between the supply of money, including bank deposits, and the price level has been studied for generations by economists and monetary authorities. Although changes in the volume of money outstanding increase or decrease purchasing power, fluctuations in the commodity price level may not, in the short run, correspond in degree, or even in direction, with changes in the quantity of money in circulation. Clearly, other factors than the quantity of money must be taken into account. For example, cash or deposits that lie dormant have no effect upon prices, so that changes in the **velocity of turnover** of money may be more important than variations in quantity. During the postwar period the velocity of turnover of the United States money supply has shown a marked increase and also exhibited marked fluctuations, rising with economic activity and falling during recessions.

The **level of economic activity** is also a paramount influence. When the employment of labor and productive capacity is high, prices tend to rise because of the strong demand for labor and goods pressing against the available supply. In fact, bottlenecks and shortages are likely to develop in some industries even before the full employment of a nation's labor and industrial capacity, thus pushing up prices even in the face of some overall unemployment. Some economists stress the role of built-in economic rigidities and monopoly powers of both management and labor in pushing up prices. These departures from pure competition, it is argued, often result in a cost-push type of inflation, especially at times when overall demands are high. With the restoration of competitive conditions internationally, the view is widely held that price levels will be much more closely related among countries than was true in the decade following World War II.

MONETARY CONTROL AND BANK RESERVES. Changes in member bank reserve balances have a dominant influence upon the banks' **lending and investing policies.** Factors that change the volume of reserves are thus of prime importance in credit management. Reserve balances are expanded or contracted when Federal Reserve banks increase or reduce their advances or investments. When a Federal Reserve bank makes an advance to a member bank, it credits the latter's deposit account and member bank reserve balances are thereby increased. When the member bank repays the advance, its check reduces its reserve account at the Federal Reserve bank.

When a Federal Reserve bank buys government securities in the open market, the dealer who sells the securities receives a check from the Federal that he deposits in his commercial bank. The latter forwards the check to the Federal and its reserve account at the Federal is credited. When the Federal Reserve bank sells securities in the open market, the dealer's check in payment serves to reduce the reserve balance of the member bank where the dealer has his checking account. Federal Reserve banks can thus change the volume of reserve balances at will simply by buying or selling government securities. In addition, purchases raise quotations and thereby lower bond yields, whereas sales have the opposite effects.

Member bank reserve balances are also affected by **changes in monetary gold stocks** and in **currency in circulation.** When currency in circulation increases due to a rise in public demand, member banks withdraw currency from Federal Reserve banks to replenish their vault cash, depleted by depositor withdrawals. Withdrawals of currency from the Federal reduce the reserve balances of member banks. Conversely, when currency returns from circulation, member banks deposit it with Federal Reserve banks and their reserve balances are credited accordingly.

THE INSTRUMENTS OF MONETARY POLICY. The typical instruments of monetary policy are: (1) quantitative controls changing the volume of member bank reserves, and (2) qualitative or selective controls over the uses to which bank credit is put.

Quantitative Controls. Open-market operations have been by far the most important instrument of quantitative control in the United States. Except for a limited period when bankers' acceptances enjoyed a broad market and afforded a medium for open-market operations by the Federal Reserve banks, United States government obligations have been used for this purpose. Under most circumstances, open-market purchases and sales of government securities by the Reserve banks provide a simple and flexible means of regulating the amount of member bank reserve balances.

Another very powerful, though less flexible, instrument of quantitative credit control is the power of the Federal Reserve Board to raise or lower **legal reserve requirements** of member banks. Changes in reserve requirements automatically increase or reduce the quantity of excess reserves, and thereby encourage credit expansion or contraction.

For member banks that do not possess excess reserves, the **discount rate** of the Federal Reserve banks becomes a major instrument of quantitative control, since it determines the cost of obtaining Federal Reserve credit when it is needed. Moreover, changes in the discount rate tend to influence the entire structure of short-term rates and also exercise a psychological effect on the money market.

Qualitative Controls. Qualitative credit controls seek to influence the quality (composition) of credit—i.e., the uses to which credit is put. The synonymous term "selective controls" is more descriptive, because it implies that certain types of credit are selected for special controls. Loans on securities, consumer credit, and home mortgages have been the chief areas in which qualitative controls have been employed in the United States.

The purpose of regulating **loans on securities** by setting minimum margin requirements is to limit credit expansion to finance the purchase of securities and thus to moderate speculation in the stock market. Consumer credit regulation was designed to curb inflationary pressures by restraining consumer buying of durable goods through the setting of **minimum down-payments** and **maximum maturities** on installment purchases. Regulation of real estate credit followed the same general pattern. Control of consumer and real estate credit has not been in effect since 1952.

FEDERAL RESERVE POLICY. Prior to 1928, Federal Reserve policy sought to promote economic stability chiefly by **changes in rediscount rates** and **open-market operations**. In 1928 and 1929, both quantitative and qualitative controls were used to curb the runaway stock market speculation of that time. The Board issued several warnings and attempted other "direct action" to curb the flow of credit into security loans, but its powers then were not adequate to check the expansion of speculative security loans. Adequate powers for this purpose were conferred on the Board in 1933 and 1934.

During the 1930's the Board pursued an **easy money policy** to promote business recovery. However, there is little evidence that low interest rates during this period had a significant effect upon business. The Federal Reserve Board received power to change reserve requirements of member banks, within limitations, in 1935, when the inflow of gold from abroad created excess reserves. The Board raised reserve requirements in 1936 and 1937 to mop up excess reserves, and its action was followed by a decline in government bond prices and a recession.

During World War II, monetary policy was concerned primarily with aiding the **Treasury's financing program.** To keep down the cost of the Treasury's borrowing, the Federal Reserve offered to buy Treasury bills from banks and dealers at a $3/8\%$ yield and certificates of indebtedness at $7/8\%$. These securities thus were made the equivalent of cash, and whenever banks needed additional reserves they sold short-term issues to the Federal Reserve.

Additional reserves were needed chiefly because of the huge expansion in currency circulation and the rapid, persistent increase in the banks' government security portfolios. **Excess reserves** were held around a billion dollars throughout the war period by the Federal's open-market policy, but by the end of the war, United States government security holdings of the Federal Reserve banks had increased by some $22,000,000,000.

Although the Federal Reserve System provided member banks with additional reserves to enable them to subscribe to new Treasury offerings, the Treasury sought to borrow as far as feasible from nonbank lenders, to limit the expansion of bank deposits. Commercial banks could not subscribe for new Treasury issues in the successive War Loan Drives, after the first two, and they could not purchase Treasury bond issues sold at the time until specified dates near their maturity. However, to obtain funds to subscribe to new Treasury issues, other investors, especially insurance companies and savings banks, sold billions of dollars of bank-eligible bonds to the commercial banks, which could readily absorb them, thanks to the open-market policy of the Federal Reserve, and thus expanded bank credit.

Postwar Policy. When the war ended, the expanded money supply, wage increases, and widespread shortages of goods pushed commodity prices higher.

The Federal Reserve System, however, maintained the rigid wartime pattern of low Treasury borrowing rates until the middle of 1947.

The Federal Reserve authorities increasingly chafed under the policy of supporting the prices of Treasury securities. They argued that by constantly stepping into the open market to buy Treasury securities, the Federal Reserve kept increasing bank reserves and became an "engine of inflation." The Treasury, however, favored the pegging arrangement because it resulted in a low interest burden on the debt and simplified the problem of marketing new securities by preventing a drastic decline in bond prices.

In 1951, the Federal Reserve finally succeeded in breaking loose from Treasury domination by reaching the celebrated **"Accord."** Under this agreement, the Federal Reserve was able to withdraw its support of bond prices and to regain use of its full arsenal of credit tools. These have been employed flexibly to promote employment, price stability, and long-run economic growth.

In the recessions of 1953–54 and 1957–58, the Federal supplied considerable amounts of reserves to the commercial banks, largely through open-market purchases of short-term Treasury securities and reductions in reserve requirements. As a result of this policy, short-term rates were driven to very low levels. In the periods of business upswing following recessions the Federal Reserve reversed its policies and reduced bank reserves, primarily through open-market sales of Treasury bills.

Following the onset of a recession in 1960, the Federal Reserve was confronted with a dilemma. Domestic economic conditions called for a decline in interest rates to encourage lending and investing. On the other hand, the deficit in the country's balance of payments was in part attributable to the outflow of short-term capital seeking higher rates of return in foreign countries.

It was this situation that led to the **abandonment of the "bills only" policy** under which the Federal's open-market operations had been confined to Treasury bills. The aim of the Federal Reserve was to hold up short-term rates, because of the adverse balance of payments, but to "nudge" down long-term rates to encourage domestic economic expansion.

LIMITATIONS OF MONETARY POLICY. Monetary policy cannot by itself assure prosperity or economic growth, since other factors, mostly unaffected by monetary policy, frequently have great influence upon economic conditions. These include policies of other government agencies, international conditions, labor-management relations, administered prices, and activities of nonbank financial institutions. Monetary policy operates only within a restricted sphere—i.e., commercial bank portfolios—so that its effects outside this area are difficult to forecast. It is also, as is all economic policy, hampered by lags, both in the recognition and the implementation of measures designed to correct maladjustments in the economy. Moreover, once monetary policies have been adopted there may be a further lag before their influence is felt.

Despite these limitations, it is generally agreed that monetary policy is playing an increasingly important part in promoting **economic stability and growth.** And it does this with less regimentation than many types of economic planning. It does not directly dictate what business and consumers must do, but rather helps to mold the general framework and the financial conditions within which individual choice and judgment may function with comparative freedom. (See Aschheim, Techniques of Monetary Control.)

MONETARY AND FISCAL POLICY. Fiscal policy is the government's policy with respect to raising and spending money. With the great expansion of the financial operations of the government, fiscal policy profoundly influences interest rates and economic conditions in general. It is essential, therefore, that fiscal and monetary policies be coordinated, so that the two work toward common or at least **complementary objectives** rather than at cross-purposes. Thus, for example, Mundell (in Thorn, Monetary Theory and Policy) has stated that:

The practical implication of the theory when stabilization measures are limited to monetary policy and fiscal policy, is that a surplus country experiencing inflationary pressure should ease monetary conditions and raise taxes (or reduce government spending), and that a deficit country suffering from unemployment should tighten interest rates and lower taxes (or increase government spending).

In addition, the Treasury's debt management policies, especially with respect to the amount and types of the securities it issues, strongly influence interest rates, the quantity of bank credit, and the composition of bank investment portfolios.

Other Lending Institutions

FINANCIAL INTERMEDIARIES. One of the most striking facts about the American economy has been the **increasing participation** of institutions in financing business, consumers, and government. Figure 6 shows the estimated net new supply of funds provided by financial institutions and others in the financial markets during 1967. These statistics include only the net annual increase in loans and investments and therefore exclude any funds furnished as the result of refinancing, debt repayments, or amortization. As may be seen, out of a total supply of $80.4 billion, savings institutions provided $34 billion and commercial banks $24 billion.

	Billions of Dollars (est.)
Savings institutions	
Life insurance companies	8.8
Corporate pension funds	5.6
State and local government retirement funds	3.9
Fire and casualty insurance companies	1.4
Savings and loan associations	7.1
Mutual savings banks	3.7
Credit unions	1.0
Investment companies	2.5
Total	34.0
Commercial banks	24.0
Business corporations	8.7
Other investor groups	
Federal agencies	2.8
State and local governments	3.6
Other consumer lenders	.3
Foreign investors	2.2
Residual: Individuals and others	4.8
Total Sources	80.4

Because of rounding, figures may not add to totals.

Fig. 6. **Suppliers of funds in the financial markets, 1967.** (Source: "The Investment Outlook for 1967," Bankers Trust Co., New York.)

MONETARY CONTROLS OVER NONBANK FINANCIAL INSTITUTIONS. Because of the growing importance of nonbank financial institutions, there has been considerable discussion as to whether Federal Reserve controls should be extended to cover their activities. The **advocates of enlarging Federal Reserve powers** usually rest their case on two main propositions:

(1) Nonbank financial institutions are capable of creating **liquid assets** in a manner identical to the demand deposit creation by commercial banks. If a commercial bank demand deposit is shifted to, say, a mutual savings bank, the demand deposit is not destroyed. As soon as the mutual savings bank disburses the funds in the form of a loan or investment, the demand deposit returns to the commercial bank. But because of the original shift of the deposit to the mutual savings bank, there has been added lending or investing by the mutual savings bank that in turn stimulates economic activity. The source of this stimulus, however, does not fall under the monetary controls of the Federal Reserve System. In the illustration, so far as the economy as a whole is concerned, demand deposits (or the money supply) remain unchanged, although the velocity of turnover of the money supply has increased. Moreover, a savings deposit has been created that, although not money in the strict sense, represents a highly liquid asset.

(2) The **asset growth** of nonbank financial intermediaries has greatly outdistanced the asset growth of commercial banks. Since these intermediaries can mobilize liquid assets—that is, can affect the velocity of turnover of the money supply—they weaken the effectiveness of monetary policies and bear some responsibility for the postwar inflation in the United States.

The **opponents of extending Federal Reserve controls** over nonbank financial institutions generally deny that financial intermediaries create credit as do commercial banks, and stress that these institutions are primarily **intermediaries**, acting as conduits for savings—that is, they transfer credit rather than create it. It is also argued that empirical evidence does not offer support for the proposition that monetary policy in the United States has in fact been offset or weakened by the operations of the nonbank financial intermediaries. (See Ketchum and Kendall, Readings in Financial Institutions.)

LOANS TO BUSINESS. In the period since World War II, nonbank sources have become increasingly important as supplementary suppliers of **short-term credit to business.** Such credit is either extended directly by specialized concerns, notably factoring or finance companies, or through the purchase of open-market paper such as commercial paper and bankers' acceptances. The latter markets are discussed briefly below and in greater detail in Section 1 (Interest Rates and Money Markets) and Section 5 (Banking Services and Procedures).

Commercial Paper. Open-market commercial paper consists of the **unsecured promissory notes** of large corporations whose credit rating is so high that their I.O.U.'s are immediately accepted for trading in the money market. Their promissory notes are issued in large denominations, usually for a period of 3 to 6 months, and are sold through commercial paper dealers at a discount plus a small commission. Many concerns tend to favor commercial paper to supplement bank loans because their borrowing needs sometimes exceed the lending capacity of their banks and because the commercial paper rate is usually below the prime rate that the banks charge their best customers. Sales finance companies, by far the largest sellers, place their notes directly with banks and other lenders.

Bankers' Acceptances. Financing by means of bankers' acceptances has also had a rapid growth since 1950. A bankers' acceptance may be considered a predated certified check, payable to the bearer at some future date. It arises primarily from international transactions and is used particularly in conjunction with a commercial letter of credit. Bankers' acceptances are freely traded in dealer-created over-the-counter markets. The essential element making this possible is the **shifting of the credit risk** to the accepting bank (see also Section 3).

Factors. Financial concerns that specialize in advancing funds by outright purchase of accounts receivable are called factors. In this so-called **"nonrecourse"** situation, the factor, after passing on the credit acceptability of each account, assumes complete financial responsibility for the collection. The buyer of the merchandise is notified of the sale of the account and is requested to make his remittance directly to the factor. The **cost of factoring** consists of two parts: a straight interest charge for the cash advanced, which is generally 2 or 3 percentage points above the prime rate at commercial banks, and a commission to cover the cost of investigating credits, bookkeeping, collection of fees, and reserves for losses. The commission is frequently 1% to 2% of the amount of the receivables.

Commercial Finance Companies. These concerns specialize in lending on the pledge of accounts receivable. In this arrangement, termed **"with recourse,"** the borrower retains liability for any delinquent account. Usually, the trade debtors are not notified that their account has been assigned to a finance company since "nonnotification" financing is preferred to avoid giving customers the impression of financial weakness.

Inventory loans can also be arranged with some finance companies on the basis of receipts for goods stored in a bonded warehouse or in a so-called "field warehouse"—i.e., a separate area set aside on the borrower's premises and under the control of an independent warehouseman. The finance company advances a substantial proportion of the value of the inventory. As inventory is withdrawn from stock, either it must be replaced by a satisfactory substitute or the loan reduced. In some instances, stored goods can be withdrawn against a "trust receipt." Banks are the principal source of inventory financing, whereas factors and finance companies are the major purveyors of credit secured by accounts receivable.

MORTGAGE LOANS. Widespread home ownership has made mortgage loans by far the largest single factor in the demand for long-term funds. In 1966, for example, new increases of mortgages outstanding on 1–4-family homes used $10.4 billion, while multifamily, commercial, and industrial mortgages took another $8.5 billion.

Distribution of Mortgage Debt. The total outstanding mortgage debt at the end of 1966 was $356 billion, including $223 billion on 1–4-family houses, $100 billion on multifamily and commercial properties, and $23 billion on farms. As indicated in Fig. 7, **financial institutions** play a dominant role in providing mortgage credit, accounting for $288 billion of the total.

Savings and loan associations typically provide nearly one-third of the total new flow of money into the mortgage market each year. This dominance has been the combined result of the rapid asset growth of these institutions as well as their preference for mortgages. At the end of 1966, over 80% of savings and loan association assets consisted of mortgage loans. Mortgage investments have enabled the associations to pay relatively high dividends on their deposit-shares, which in turn have attracted additional savings.

	Billions of Dollars	Percentage of Total
Total	$356.2	100.0%
Savings and loan associations	116.9	32.5
Life insurance companies	66.4	18.6
Commercial banks	55.7	15.6
Mutual savings banks	48.9	13.8
Individuals and all others	68.3	19.5

Fig. 7. Mortgage holdings by financial institutions, June 30, 1967.

Life insurance companies rank second in terms of mortgage loan holdings and third in the annual supply of new mortgage funds. The percentage of their assets in mortgages has been steadily increasing from 25% in 1950 to 39% in 1966, with most of the balance in corporate bonds.

Mutual savings banks also concentrate heavily in mortgages, now ranking second as annual suppliers of new mortgage loans. Since these banks are found mainly in New England and the Middle Atlantic States their lending activities are also confined mostly to this area.

Commercial banks, as previously indicated, have been rapidly increasing their participation in the mortgage market. This has resulted to a large extent from the notable growth in time deposits and the need to pay interest rates that are competitive with those offered on savings deposits by other institutions.

The Home Mortgage Business. It is estimated that more than 75% of all residential real estate transactions involve the use of mortgage credit. In extending mortgage credit, lenders consider both the asset securing the loan and the credit worthiness of the borrower.

Private **mortgage companies** frequently act as correspondents or intermediaries between mortgage borrowers and institutional lenders. They are usually authorized to act on behalf of the lenders by making stipulated types of mortgage loans in specified amounts. They often also service loans by receiving payments, collecting and remitting real estate taxes and property insurance premiums, and in other ways looking after the loan. Mortgage correspondents typically receive one-half of 1% of the loan balance for these services.

Careful **appraisal** of real estate values is particularly important if the ratio of loan to market value is high. The **percentage of value** extended by any institution depends on law, tradition, and the investment policy of the particular lender. Legal restrictions on the maximum percentage of appraised value vary among different types of institutions as well as among states. For life insurance companies operating in New York State, for example, the maximum ratio permitted on residential dwellings is 75% whereas savings and loan associations are allowed to lend up to 90%. (See also Section 7—Security Analysis.)

Types of Mortgages. The terms of a typical residential mortgage loan require its monthly **amortization**—i.e., the repayment of principal and interest over the life of the loan. The widespread practice of amortizing mortgages has resulted from the dismal experience of the depression of the 1930's when many nonamortized mortgage loans had to be foreclosed at a time of drastically declining real estate values.

An **insured or guaranteed mortgage** is one that has been insured to some extent against loss by a Federal agency (see below).

Conventional mortgages are those made without benefit of any type of government guaranty or insurance. In 1966 out of a total of $224 billion of outstanding mortgage debt on nonfarm 1–4-family homes, $148 billion was conventional, $45 billion Federal Housing Administration-insured, and $31 billion Veterans Administration-guaranteed.

Federal Agencies in Mortgage Finance. In 1947, Congress established the **Housing and Home Finance Agency,** which has under its jurisdiction several agencies. The two most important from the viewpoint of mortgage lending are the **Federal Housing Administration** (F.H.A.) and the **Federal National Mortgage Association** (F.N.M.A., usually called "Fanny Mae"). In early 1968, a reorganization of Fanny Mae was under consideration whereby ownership would become fully private but with sizable Federal influence.

The purpose of the F.H.A. is to add the credit of the Federal government to that of the individual borrowing to buy or build a home. To promote the market for residential mortgages, the F.H.A. insures mortgage loans made for constructing, purchasing, or repairing homes by guaranteeing to pay any loss resulting from defaults in the form of **F.H.A. debenture bonds.** Since these debentures are guaranteed by the United States Treasury, the mortgage loan is in fact underwritten by the Federal government. To be eligible for F.H.A. insurance, the loan and the property securing it must meet detailed specifications. The F.H.A. does not lend money but provides insurance for institutions granting mortgage loans under F.H.A. regulations. The insurance premium is $\frac{1}{2}\%$.

The introduction of F.H.A.-insured mortgages has encouraged lenders to extend some mortgage loans that otherwise would not have been made, to encourage easier credit terms and longer maturities, and to stimulate the demand for mortgage loans during certain periods. The F.H.A. sets **maximum interest rates** on its insured mortgages. Because of the inflexibility of these interest rate ceilings, F.H.A. mortgages may sell at discounts when the market rate exceeds the F.H.A. maximum.

As part of the "G.I. Bill of Rights," Congress authorized the Veterans Administration to guarantee or insure private mortgage loans made to veterans. The V.A. assumes the "first risk" on mortgage loans up to a maximum of $7,500 or 60% of the loan, whichever is less. Under the **V.A. guaranty program,** no insurance premium is paid by either the borrower or lender. However, the V.A. also places a maximum authorization rate on V.A.-guaranteed loans. The permissible rate was 5¾% as of mid-1966. Because of this relatively low rate, V.A.-guaranteed loans have become less attractive to some lenders. [See Robinson (ed.), Financial Institutions.]

Mortgage Loans for Non-Real Estate Purposes. In the postwar period, many home owners increased their equity through amortization payments while market values for residential properties were well maintained or even raised. This set of circumstances was favorable for enlarging mortgage debt on existing properties, with the proceeds of the loans going to other uses, such as financing the college education of children. Thus, the **refinancing of mortgage debt** appears to be playing an increasing role in the mortgage market and consumers are apparently financing more of their needs through mortgage loans.

Mortgages created in connection with **corporate bond issues** are discussed in detail in Section 14 (Long-Term and Intermediate-Term Borrowing).

CONSUMER LENDING. Consumer credit has been playing an increasingly important role in financing consumer expenditures during the postwar years. From a total of $27 billion at the end of 1952, total consumer credit outstanding rose to $97 billion in November 1967. From 1952 to 1966, repayments on installment credit contracts rose from 10.6% to 13.2% of disposable incomes of consumers. The purposes for which consumers incurred this debt are indicated in Fig. 8.

	Billions of Dollars
Total consumer credit outstanding	$96.8
Installment credit	76.7
Automobile paper	31.2
Other consumer goods paper	20.3
Repair and modernization loans	3.7
Personal loans	21.4
Noninstallment credit	20.1
Single-payment loans	8.2
Charge accounts	6.6
Service credit	5.3

Fig. 8. Total consumer credit November 1967.

As noted above, the single most important component of consumer credit consists of automobile paper. Other durable consumer goods, such as dishwashers, refrigerators, and TV sets, are also bought heavily "on time." Personal installment loans, another major category, have increased by over 500% since 1952. Personal services, including doctor bills, travel, and education, are being increasingly financed with installment credit. **Noninstallment credit** accounts for somewhat over 20% of all consumer debt. It is split among single-payment loans, regular retail charge accounts, and service credits.

Sources of Credit. The **Federal Reserve Bulletin** (Board of Governors, Federal Reserve System) contains each month statistical data on the sources and uses of consumer credit. The most important suppliers are commercial banks, sales finance companies, retail stores, credit unions, and consumer finance companies, as shown in Fig. 9.

Commercial Banks. Although it was not until the end of World War II that commercial banks entered the field of consumer credit on a large scale, they are now the largest suppliers. They strive aggressively for this business and occupy a strong competitive position partly because of **local branches**, which make them easily accessible to buyers of consumer durables. Moreover, their rates for installment credit are often lower than those charged by other lending institutions.

Commercial banks not only extend credit directly to consumers but also indirectly by making loans to sales and consumer finance companies. They also provide funds to finance companies through open-market purchases of their commercial paper.

OTHER LENDING INSTITUTIONS 2·39

Sales Finance Companies. The expansion of sales finance companies paralleled the growth of the automobile industry in the United States. Although automobile paper still represents the major portion of their business, installment paper to finance the purchase of other consumer durable goods, especially household appliances, is also handled on a large scale.

	Billions of Dollars	Per Cent of Total
Total installment credit outstanding	$76.7	100.0%
Commercial banks	33.8	44.0
Sales finance companies	16.7	21.7
Credit unions	9.1	11.8
Consumer finance companies	6.1	8.0
Retail stores	8.9	11.6
All others	2.1	2.9
Total noninstallment credit outstanding	20.1	100.0%
Commercial banks	7.0	34.9
Other financial institutions	1.2	5.9
Retail stores	5.6	27.9
Credit cards	1.0	4.9
Service credit	5.3	26.4

Fig. 9. **Suppliers of consumer credit November 1967.**

Sales finance companies specialize in **buying installment contracts from dealers.** They also finance the dealer's inventory of cars and appliances. Such arrangements are usually referred to as "wholesale financing" or "floor planning."

Several very large sales finance companies, such as Commercial Credit Company, C.I.T. Financial Corporation, and General Motors Acceptance Corporation, operate on a national scale. They rank among the world's largest financial institutions and maintain hundreds of offices throughout the country and Canada. Their **capital** is raised in a variety of ways. If the finance company is a subsidiary of a manufacturing concern or some other holding company, the basic source of equity capital is the parent company. Sales finance companies are also **able to borrow heavily** because of the liquidity of most installment contract loans. Aside from obtaining large lines of credit from commercial banks, the large companies are able to tap the open market by selling large amounts of commercial paper and debentures. In addition, sales finance companies borrow long-term funds from insurance companies through direct placements.

The **conditional sale** (or lease in certain states), under which title does not pass to the buyer until final payment has been made, is the basis of sales finance company operation. If payments are not made when due, the finance company simply repossesses its own property. Most states have laws providing for the sale of the repossessed property at auction, and payment of the proceeds, after satisfaction of the debt and all costs, to the delinquent buyer. These laws, because of loopholes and lax enforcement, have proved of limited importance to financially embarrassed purchasers.

Except in those states that have enacted special sales finance legislation, there is **no legal limit on the rate of interest** that can be charged for financing the sale of merchandise on the installment plan. Usury statutes apply only to interest charged for the loan or use of money, and merchandise rather than money is involved in these transactions. Relatively high rates of interest are charged, in part because of high operating expense in such financing.

Sales finance companies operate on either a **recourse** or a **nonrecourse** basis. Under the recourse method, repossessed goods are turned back to the dealer, who reimburses the finance company on a previously arranged basis. Refinements of this method have been evolved, but in essence, it means that the finance company does not assume the credit risk. This method is generally used by large finance companies. Smaller companies nearly all use, for competitive reasons, the nonrecourse method, under which they acquire installment notes unconditionally. In the instance of default, the finance companies assume the responsibility of disposing of repossessed merchandise themselves. The finance company must then rely on the credit of the buyer and the value of the merchandise involved for its protection, rather than on the financial standing of the dealer as under the recourse method.

Credit Unions. Credit union membership is predicated upon a common bond, such as employment, membership in a church or association, or living in the same community. Since passage of the Federal Credit Union Act in 1934, the number of credit unions has increased rapidly, and at the end of 1966, there were over 22,000 with over 18,000,000 members. Their $9 billion of installment credit outstanding at the end of 1966 was nearly 12% of the nation's total. Only members may supply funds to credit unions and borrow from them. Members' deposits are evidenced by passbooks or by certificates of **"savings shares"** on which the credit unions pay dividends. In 1966 about half of the United States credit unions were paying dividends of more than 4½% per annum on their share units.

Most of the loans made by credit unions are **consumer installment loans** extended to members at rates comparable to those charged by commercial banks. It is from the interest received from these loans that the credit unions are able to pay rates of return to their savings members averaging about 4½%. They have thus become increasingly strong competitors for their communities' small liquid savings, and increasingly large consumer installment lenders. Credit unions, especially in their role as competitors for savings, are more extensively treated in Section 4. (Credit Union National Association, Credit Union Yearbook, 1967.)

Consumer Finance Companies. These are the so-called "small loan companies" that at one time were restricted to an upper limit of $300 per loan. With inflation, this limit has been raised by most states, with some now permitting as much as $5,000. Small loan companies make both unsecured loans (based solely on the borrower's income and credit standing) and secured loans, based on a **chattel mortgage** against automobiles, furniture, and other durables. There are a number of very large companies, such as Household Finance Corporation and the Beneficial Finance Company, each of which has hundreds of offices.

Most of the companies operate under the **Uniform Small Loan Act** drawn up by the Russell Sage Foundation and adopted, with various modifications, in some forty states. Designed to drive loan sharks out of business by furnishing small loans at reasonable cost, they are closely regulated. Although personal finance companies are exempted under the usury laws, the rates that they may charge and the amounts they may lend are limited in the Small Loan laws and vary slightly from state to state. Copies of contracts must be given the borrower, and charges are made on a flat basis on the unpaid balance due and collected each month, so that there can be no misunderstanding on the part of the borrower as to what he is paying or what he should pay for the loan. Fees and extra charges of any character are expressly forbidden, as a rule.

The all-inclusive charge varies among the states from 3½% per month on the unpaid balance to as low as 1% on the amount in excess of $200. Although these rates look high compared with the rates on commercial bank loans, they actually are low compared with "loan shark" rates of 520 to 1040% per annum that would be the alternative for many of their borrowers. Because of the very high costs per dollar in lending money in small amounts, these rates are not to be compared with the interest rates of commercial banks, for example, charged on loans of larger sums. These are character loans, co-makers or collateral ordinarily not being required. The borrower and his wife (if married) are required to sign the note. In addition, a **chattel mortgage** may be taken on the household furniture, but it is not filed and is of doubtful legal value. Personal loan companies rarely are willing to take the responsibility for breaking up a home by seizing pledged furniture.

Industrial Banking. The term industrial banking is applied to the lending of money on **co-maker** notes. Starting in Norfolk, Virginia, in 1910, Arthur Morris developed a copyrighted note on which the borrower secured the signatures of two or more persons as co-makers. Accommodation endorsers thus became co-makers with consequent change in their legal and financial responsibilities. Such loans are used both for personal and small business purposes. In this method of lending, investigation fees and discount are deducted in advance. Penalty fees are charged for late payments and other contract infractions specified.

Industrial banks have come more and more to resemble ordinary commercial banks, employing conventional lending methods as well as their characteristic type of loan. Most have now converted to commercial bank charters, in fact, and have dropped the word "industrial" from their names. Many of these, however, continue to specialize in consumer lending.

Effective Rates of Interest. The precise computation of effective interest rates on installment credit is made difficult by the fact that payments not only vary in amount but also in their duration. Moreover, it is often difficult to distinguish between interest and service charges, such as insurance. One formula that provides a close approximation to the effective rate of interest is frequently employed:

$$R = \frac{2 \times M \times I}{P(n + 1)}$$

where

R = rate of interest per annum.
M = number of installment payments per year (if monthly 12; weekly 52).
I = dollar cost of the finance charge.
P = the original balance of the **loan** (principal).
n = number of total installment payments.

Example 1. Assume a commercial bank lends $100 to be repaid over a year with a discount of $6. Find the rate of interest:

$$R = \frac{2 \times 12 \times 6}{\$100 \times (12 + 1)} = 11.1\%$$

Example 2. Assume a small loan company requires monthly payments of $9.90 to repay a $100 loan over one year. This means 12 payments of $9.90 or $118.80 in all. Thus the interest charge is $18.80.

$$R = \frac{2 \times 12 \times 18.80}{\$100 \times (12 + 1)} = 34.7\%$$

SECTION 3

INTERNATIONAL BANKING

CONTENTS

International Payments

	PAGE
The balance of payments	1
Payments transactions	2
Purchase of services	2
The international monetary system	2
Role of gold	2
Total reserves and gold holdings in selected countries (f. 1)	3
Inter-government cooperation	4
U.S. balance of payments program	4
Foreign exchange	4

Foreign Exchange Markets

Nature and functions of foreign exchange markets	5
The New York Market	5
Foreign exchange brokers	6
Quotation of rates of exchange	6
Open market and commercial rates	6
Types of exchange quoted	7
Types of credit instruments	7
Cable transfers	7
Mail transfers	7
Application for foreign check or mail transfer (f. 2)	8
Sight drafts	8
Time drafts	9
Future exchange transactions	9
The forward exchange market	10
Speculation in exchange	10
Arbitrage	11
Free vs. controlled currencies	11
Exchange control	11
Example of controls	12
International financial markets	12
The Euro-dollar market	12
Hard-currency bond issues in Europe	12
Multiple-currency bonds	13

International Departments of Banks

Operations of an international department	13
New accounts section	13
Foreign tellers	14
Foreign exchange traders	14
Commercial credit division	14
Travel section	14
Foreign collections	14

	PAGE
Foreign drawing service	15
Cables	15
Securities	15

Foreign Branches and Affiliates

Foreign operations of American banks	15
Foreign branches	15
Edge Act corporations	15
Agreement corporations	16
Role of the Federal Reserve banks	16
Agencies and branches of foreign banks	16

Financing of Foreign Trade

Risks in foreign trade financing	17
Financing by the exporter	17
Shipment on open book account	17
Consignment	17
Collection drafts	17
Financing by the importer	18
Payment with order	18
Customer's instructions to a bank for the collection of a draft (f. 3)	19, 20
Partial payment in advance	20
Payment on documents	21
Financing by the exporter's bank	21
Advance on drafts	21
Discount of drafts	21
Refinancing bill	21
Financing by the importer's bank	21
Commercial letter of credit	21
Application and agreement for commercial letter of credit (f. 4)	22
Import and export letters of credit	23
A commercial letter of credit (f. 5)	24
Revocable and irrevocable letters of credit	24
Confirmed and unconfirmed letters of credit	25
Revolving letter of credit	25
Assignable letter of credit	25
Authority to purchase	25
Documents attached to draft	26
Traveler's letter of credit	26
A traveler's letter of credit (f. 6)	27
Travelers' checks	28
Traveler's check (f. 7)	28
American Depositary Receipt	28
Foreign securities listings, 1966 (f. 8)	29

CONTENTS (*Continued*)

U.S. Government and International Agencies

	Page
Background	30
The U.S. Export-Import Bank	30
The U.S. Agency for International Development (A.I.D.)	30
The International Monetary Fund and the World Bank	31
International Monetary Fund	31
International Bank for Reconstruction and Development (World Bank)	31
The International Finance Corporation (I.F.C.)	32
The International Development Association (I.D.A.)	32
The Inter-American Development Bank	32

SECTION 3

INTERNATIONAL BANKING

International Payments

THE BALANCE OF PAYMENTS. The accounting balance of payments has been defined by Machlup (in Foreign Trade and Finance, ed. Allen and Allen) as:

> ... a record of all transactions, real and financial, which have taken place over a past period of one or more years between the country's residents and residents of other countries, the record being kept in the form of double entry bookkeeping, with each credit entry balanced by an offsetting debit entry and vice versa.

Total payments or debits of a country must be balanced by an equal amount of receipts or credits. If payments to be made abroad by a country exceed its total receipts, it must cover the difference by drawing on its international liquid reserves, i.e., foreign short-term assets, or by exporting gold, or by borrowing abroad. In the latter case it merely postpones the settlement by promising to pay at some future date.

There are several measures of a country's balance of payments surplus (or deficit). Of these the U.S. Department of Commerce regularly provides two, both adjusted and not adjusted for seasonal factors. The first is the balance on a **liquidity basis,** measured by the increase (or decrease) in United States official reserve assets (gold, convertible currencies, and gold portion of United States subscription to the International Monetary Fund) plus the decrease (or increase) in liquid obligations (deposit accounts, short-term money market paper such as negotiable certificates of deposit with a maturity of one year or less, and U.S. government obligations) held by foreigners, both official and private. The second is the balance on the **official reserve transactions basis,** measured by the increase (or decrease) in United States official reserve assets plus the decrease (or increase) in obligations held by foreign official organizations only.

Items entering into the balance of payments are generally grouped into (1) current items, (2) unilateral transfers, (3) capital movements, and (4) changes in short-term foreign assets and monetary gold movements. **Current accounts** consist of imports and exports of commodities (foreign trade) and services (often called invisible items). **Unilateral transfers** are cash, goods, or services provided to foreigners without a return payment. They are either official, such as reparations or economic aid, or private, such as immigrant remittances to relatives, or contributions to eleemosynary organizations. **Capital movements** are subdivided into short-term and long-term.

The **current items** indicate whether or not a country is paying its way in its commercial transactions with the rest of the world. The **capital accounts** show how, in the absence of monetary gold movements, a favorable current-payments balance has been employed, or how a deficit on current account has been covered through borrowing or sales of securities abroad. (See Kenen, International Economics.)

PAYMENTS TRANSACTIONS. Transactions entering into the balance of payments create the demand for and supply of foreign exchange of a country. At present many of these transactions are subject to legal restrictions. Foreigners buy dollars, for example, to pay for the following current items:

1. Exports of goods from the United States.
2. Services rendered by the United States to foreigners.
3. Interest, dividends, and profits earned by United States capital invested abroad.

Americans buy foreign exchange to pay for:

1. Imports of goods from abroad.
2. Services rendered by foreigners to the United States.
3. Interest, dividends, and profits on foreign capital invested in the United States.

Foreigners buy dollars to finance the following capital and gold movements:

1. Purchases of American securities and investment in real estate and industry.
2. Purchases of foreign securities held in the United States.
3. Amortization and repayment of dollar loans.
4. Gold exports from the United States.

Americans buy foreign exchange to finance:

1. Investment of American capital abroad.
2. Repurchase of American securities held abroad.
3. Amortization and repayment of loans contracted by Americans in other countries.
4. Gold imports into the United States.

Purchase of Services. Payments for services rendered by one country to others include tourist expenditures, bills for freight, travel and communications, insurance premiums, commissions, advertising purchased, rents, royalties, and bills for electric power transmitted across national borders. All these items cause a **demand for and supply of foreign exchange.**

When an American visits Italy, he buys transportation, hotel accommodations, food, amusement, and personal services. These purchases constitute Italian exports (invisible) to the United States. The American tourist pays either with lire purchased in the United States or with American currency, i.e., actual cash or travelers' checks and other dollar credit instruments. In the latter case, the tourist creates a demand for lire and a supply of dollars in Italy when he exchanges his currency or credit instruments into lire.

THE INTERNATIONAL MONETARY SYSTEM. The current structure of the international monetary system dates back to the Bretton Woods agreements (1944), which provided for the creation of the International Monetary Fund (see below). At present most countries hold their foreign exchange reserves basically in three forms: gold (including the gold subscription at the I.M.F.), United States dollars, and, to a much lesser extent, pounds sterling.

By the late 1960's, additions to the free world's gold stock, principally from production (concentrated in South Africa) and Russian sales, were increasingly absorbed by private hoarding. As a result, fears spread that, with the planned reduction in American and British balance of payments deficits, the net additions to world monetary reserves would prove insufficient to support the expanding volume of world trade. To alleviate this problem the governing board of the

International Monetary Fund agreed in 1967 to establish, within the I.M.F., a new facility to supplement existing reserve assets. Creation of these **special drawing rights (S.D.R.'s)**, which would be distributed among all Fund members, requires a favorable vote of 85% of the members. It is planned that the amounts and timing of issuance will be based on the Fund's evaluation of long-run world needs, rather than on short-run, or countercyclical, objectives. Some authorities even feel that the S.D.R.'s could, over the next several decades, eventually replace gold as the key international monetary asset (see Triffin, The World Money Maze).

Role of Gold. Gold still occupies an important role as a reserve asset, as Fig. 1 clearly shows. Under the Emergency Banking Act of 1933, the Gold Reserve Act of 1934, and Treasury regulations, holding of monetary gold by residents of this country is prohibited, and title to all monetary gold is vested in the U.S. government. Since February 1934, the Treasury has followed a policy of buying gold at home and abroad at $35.00 per fine troy ounce (less ¼ of 1% handling charge and the usual mint charges) and selling gold at $35.00 an ounce (plus the

Country	Total Reserves	Gold Holdings
United States	14,830	12,065
Germany	8,155	4,228
France	6,994	5,234
Italy	5,460	2,400
Switzerland	3,555	3,089
United Kingdom	2,695	1,831*

*Third quarter 1967.

Fig. 1. Total reserves and gold holdings in selected countries, December 1967 (in millions of U.S. dollars). (Source: International Monetary Fund, International Financial Statistics, XXI, No. 2, February 1968, 15–16.)

handling and mint charges) to foreign governments and central banks for settlement of international balances and for all legitimate monetary purposes. Because of heavy balance of payments deficits, particularly severe after 1957, the United States not only increased its short-term liabilities to foreigners but also experienced a reduction in its gold holdings from $22.1 billion at the end of 1953 to $12.1 billion at the end of 1967. For this reason Congress eliminated in 1965 the 25% gold reserve requirement against Federal Reserve deposits. In early 1968, Congress also eliminated the 25% gold reserve requirement against Federal Reserve notes.

Though the United States is not committed to sell gold to private parties, it had, beginning October 1961, operated through the London Gold Pool to stabilize the market price of the metal. In March 1968, however, responding to massive speculation in the London gold market, the United States and the six Western European countries constituting the London Gold Pool established dual pricing of gold through shutting off supplies to private buyers. The United States agreed to continue to buy and sell gold at $35 an ounce in transactions with other governments for monetary purposes. The seven nations also agreed not to buy or sell gold in any private market nor to deal with any government that attempted to take advantage of the difference between the free and the fixed price of gold. It was generally agreed that the two-price system for gold was an expedient and that over the long run fundamental modifications would have to take place in internal United States financial policies and in the international monetary system.

INTER-GOVERNMENT COOPERATION. The balance-of-payments problems experienced by some of the leading industrial nations during the decade of the sixties fostered the development of intergovernmental financial cooperation, designed primarily to prevent disorderly situations in the foreign exchange markets. Two features of this cooperation were swap agreements between the Federal Reserve system and the Central Banks of other nations and the placement abroad by the U.S. Treasury of securities denominated in foreign currencies.

The **swap agreements** entitle the participants to obtain foreign currency up to stated amounts so as to meet temporary increases in the demand for these currencies. As of August 1967, the Federal Reserve had entered into swap agreements for an amount exceeding $5 billion, of which it had made net drawings for $0.5 billion. The balance thus represented a supplement to its immediately available reserves.

Also as of August 1967, the U.S. Treasury had over $1.0 billion in **securities denominated in foreign currency** outstanding. By allowing its creditors to maintain their credit balances in their own currencies, the United States contributes to reduction of the pressure on its gold reserves.

U.S. Balance of Payments Program. Because of large balance-of-payments deficits, the United States imposed by the mid-1960's a series of limitations on capital outflows. These consisted of the **interest equalization tax,** designed to restrict American purchases of foreign securities, and various curbs on direct investment abroad and American bank loans abroad. These restrictions were tightened in early 1968. At that time, mandatory rules governing capital transfers were set, including establishment of a zero limit on new capital flows to most Western European countries and more liberal provisions for transfers to underdeveloped countries. Ceilings on profit reinvestments, compulsory repatriation of a portion of foreign affiliates' profits and of liquid assets abroad were also established, with special exemptions for investments below certain amounts.

Restrictions on United States bank lending abroad, as of early 1968 still voluntary, are administered by the Federal Reserve Board and involve over-all ceilings on foreign credits and special curbs on specified lending activities. Nonbank financial institutions, such as savings banks or trust departments, are subject to similar, but in some respects more stringent, regulations, since they have to reduce their holdings of foreign assets by 5% over the December 1967 level. There was some controversy regarding the extent of these controls, and it was generally hoped that they could be alleviated and eventually eliminated as the balance-of-payments situation eased.

FOREIGN EXCHANGE. Trade, travel, and other dealings between nations create the problem of making and receiving payments across political borders. Since one country's currency is not legal tender in another country, a debtor must make payment in the currency of the creditor's country, unless the creditor has agreed to accept payment in the currency of the debtor's country.

Foreign currencies and credit instruments stated in foreign money are called foreign exchange; i.e., bank balances, bank drafts, remittances, telegraphic transfers, checks, and other payment media stated in foreign currencies constitute foreign exchange.

Foreign Exchange Markets

NATURE AND FUNCTIONS OF FOREIGN EXCHANGE MARKETS. A foreign exchange market is a place where foreign exchange is bought and sold in large amounts. In New York and London there is no foreign exchange market place in the literal sense. Business is transacted over the telephone—private wires binding together the important dealers and brokers—and the trading machinery is so efficient that dealers and brokers readily learn demand and supply conditions and quotations for a foreign currency at any time.

The **leading foreign exchange markets** are located in the international financial centers, such as New York, London, Paris, Frankfurt, Amsterdam, and Zurich. In addition, many large cities throughout the world have markets for dealing in foreign exchange. Although widely separated by land and water, these markets are in constant communication with each other by cable, telegraph, telephone, and radio through networks of branches and correspondents maintained by large banks and foreign exchange dealers. Modern communication facilities have practically fused all financial centers into one great foreign exchange market.

The New York Market. The principal foreign exchange market in the United States is in New York. **Quotations for foreign currencies** established there and listed in the daily newspapers provide the basis for foreign exchange transactions in smaller markets throughout the country, such as Boston, Chicago, St. Louis, Houston, Dallas, San Francisco, New Orleans, and Seattle. Because the business day in Europe begins several hours before the American business day, foreign exchange dealers here have the advantage of knowing what developments have taken place in the European markets before they actually begin trading. Rates prevailing in foreign markets have an important bearing on those quoted by New York traders.

The foreign exchange business of the New York market is transacted by the large **commercial banks,** branches, agencies, and subsidiaries of foreign banks, some investment banking firms, and specialized foreign exchange dealers and brokers. By far the most important segment of the market is that comprising the commercial banks. They have the resources, trained personnel, and facilities for carrying out virtually every type of international financial transaction.

When the world is politically and economically at peace and trade between nations is not unduly impeded by governmental regulations, when people are not prohibited or restricted in sending funds abroad, when tourists can travel abroad freely, these banks have a continuous influx and outgo of foreign exchange that increase and decrease, respectively, the balances they maintain with banks in foreign financial centers. They acquire foreign exchange in whatever amount and form offered, such as interest coupons and dividend checks stated in foreign currencies, foreign drafts and remittances, and foreign currency notes, which they forward to branches and correspondents abroad for collection and credit to their accounts. The large commercial banks are continually selling, against their balances abroad, foreign exchange in the amounts and forms demanded, such as drafts, cable transfers, remittances, travelers' and commercial letters of credit, and foreign currency notes. They must thus maintain in practically every country bank balances in amounts commensurate with the volume of business transacted with that country and with due regard to the degree of stability of that country's currency. These balances may fluctuate relatively little from day to day, since purchases and sales of foreign exchange tend to counterbalance each other.

Foreign Exchange Brokers. Brokers act as intermediaries between the bank and dealer buyers or sellers. They are in constant telephonic communication with these participants in foreign exchange, and bring **bids and offers** together. Receiving an offer of exchange at a stated price, the broker seeks a bid at a slightly higher figure; on receiving a bid at a certain rate, he seeks an offer at a slightly lower rate. In either case the seller makes delivery directly to the buyer at the higher rate, and pays the difference to the broker as his commission.

QUOTATION OF RATES OF EXCHANGE. The price of a country's monetary unit, expressed in the currency of another country, is called its rate of exchange. There are two generally used methods of quoting exchange rates: (1) the **direct method,** stating the number of units of domestic currency that will buy a unit, or multiple thereof, of the foreign currency; and (2) the **indirect method,** stating the number of units of the foreign currency that will buy a unit of the domestic currency. The New York exchange market quotes foreign currencies by the direct method, as commodities are quoted, namely, so many dollars or cents per one or 100 units of the foreign currency. In London, most exchange rates are quoted by the indirect method, so many units of the foreign currency for one pound sterling. For example, Swiss exchange may be quoted in New York at 22.9 and in London at 10.45, which would mean that 1 Swiss franc costs 22.9¢ in New York, whereas in London 10.45 Swiss francs would buy £1. Consequently, in London the exchange dealers' rule is "buy high and sell low," the reverse of the principle followed in commodity trading.

London adopted the indirect quotation method because the pound sterling, as the monetary unit of highest value, is exchangeable for multiples of the currency of other countries, and because this method makes possible quick comparison between London exchange rates and foreign rates on London. Thus, when New York quotes £1 = $2.39 and London quotes $2.41 = £1 (instead of the direct method $1 = 8.3 shillings), no calculation is required to compare the two rates.

If several countries use the same monetary unit, as do Great Britain, Ireland, and New Zealand, or the United States and Canada, exchange rates may be quoted in percentage deviations from par.

Open Market and Commercial Rates. The foreign exchange rates quoted daily in the newspapers are the rates at which actual transactions in large, round amounts take place among foreign exchange dealers **("open market trading"),** and not rates at which dealers do business with individual customers **("commercial business").** The rate quoted to customers may be higher or lower than the published rate, and the difference—always in favor of the dealer—reimburses the dealer for his expenses and gives him his profit. The difference between open market and commercial rates varies with the size of the transaction; the larger the amount involved, the smaller is the deviation from the basic rate, and vice versa. When demand for foreign exchange, say for London exchange in the New York market, exceeds the supply, dealers will bid up the price of the pound sterling to induce additional sales by holders of London balances. Should the rate rise above par, it is said that London exchange is quoted at a **"premium."** On the other hand, when the supply of London funds in New York exceeds the demand, dealers will drop the rate to bring out buyers. When the rate goes below par, it is said that the British exchange is at a **"discount."**

In the assessment of tariff duties on imported merchandise, rates of exchange on foreign currencies are used that are gathered at noon daily by the Foreign Department of the Federal Reserve Bank of New York and are certified to the

Treasury Department. These official **noon buying rates** are also released to the public.

Types of Exchange Quoted. The bulk of foreign exchange dealings is in **credit instruments.** Transactions in actual currency notes are only for small amounts across the counter, and are of very little importance in the foreign exchange market.

Rates at which a bank or foreign exchange dealer buys and sells foreign currency notes are based on the quoted rates, but take into account (1) the amount involved, (2) loss of interest while notes remain in the bank or in transit to and from the foreign countries, (3) the cost of shipment and insurance, and (4) a service charge. Since banks and foreign exchange dealers as a rule do not trade among themselves in foreign currency notes, there are no uniform quotations. Rates vary from bank to bank, depending on such considerations as the amounts of foreign currency notes at the disposal of the particular bank. Banks avoid the risk involved in holding large amounts of foreign currency by selling cable transfers or drafts and shipping the notes to the country of origin to cover such sales (see Crump, The ABC of the Foreign Exchanges).

TYPES OF CREDIT INSTRUMENTS. Credit instruments used in foreign exchange transactions may be divided into four main types: (1) cable transfers, (2) mail transfers, (3) sight drafts, and (4) time drafts. Exchange rates quoted in the open market and published in the daily newspapers are, as a rule, rates for cable transfers.

Cable Transfers. A cable transfer (telegraphic transfer or "T.T.") is an order telegraphed by the seller of the exchange to a party abroad (usually a bank located nearest to the recipient of the funds), instructing him to pay immediately out of the seller's account a specified amount of foreign currency to the party named in the order (beneficiary), for account of the buyer. It is essentially a **cash transaction**; the buyer pays to the seller the agreed-upon amount in domestic funds and the seller on the same day, by cable, orders payment abroad. The seller receives domestic funds in cash and the buyer receives the funds abroad, usually on the same day or on the following or second business day if distance, available cable facilities, and time difference occasion some delay. Although the seller often retains the foreign funds for one or two days after he has received the equivalent in domestic funds, interest is not considered in setting the quotation. The cable rate includes the cost of the cable for transactions above a certain minimum amount; for smaller amounts the cost of the cable will be charged to the buyer as a separate item. Cables are sent in prearranged **codes** to reduce the cost, to assure secrecy, and to protect the parties against fraud. All cable transactions for a day with a particular correspondent will be sent in one message at the end of the day. The cable rate is generally slightly higher than the rate for other types of exchange.

Mail Transfers. In a mail transfer, the bank selling the foreign exchange instructs its branch or correspondent abroad by mail to make payment to the beneficiary and obtain a receipt therefor. Since the bank receives the dollar equivalent at the time of the sale, whereas its account abroad is charged only at a later date, depending on the distance, the bank earns **interest** on its foreign currency balance during the time it takes the mail transfer to reach its destination. Consequently, mail transfers sell at lower rates than cable transfers. The use of air mail reduces the time required to transfer funds by mail and so narrows the differences between cable and mail transfer rates. The buyer of a mail or cable transfer receives no written instrument, but merely a **confirmation** of the transaction. Cable and mail transfers are nonnegotiable. (See Fig. 2.)

APPLICATION FOR FOREIGN CHECK OR MAIL TRANSFER

FIRST NATIONAL CITY BANK
NEW YORK

NEW YORK ________ DATE

________ (HEAD OFFICE OR BRANCH)

(PLEASE TYPE OR PRINT ALL DETAILS)

GENTLEMEN:
PLEASE ISSUE YOUR CHECK OR EFFECT A MAIL TRANSFER (AS INDICATED HEREUNDER).

AMOUNT AND KIND OF CURRENCY ________ (AMOUNT IN WORDS)

________ (AMOUNT IN FIGURES) RATE ________ $ ________

AIR MAIL CHARGE $ ________

COMMISSION $ ________

TOTAL $ ________

USE THIS SPACE FOR CHECK	ISSUE CHECK ON ________ (COUNTRY) ________ (CITY) PAYABLE TO ________ (BENEFICIARY) ADVISE THE PAYER BY ☐ AIR MAIL. ☐ SEA MAIL
USE THIS SPACE FOR MAIL TRANSFER	TRANSFER BY: ☐ AIR MAIL. ☐ SEA MAIL TO ________ (BENEFICIARY) ADDRESS ________ (STREET) ________ (CITY OR TOWN) COUNTY OR PROVINCE ________ COUNTRY ________ FILL IN ONLY IF INFORMATION IS TO BE COMMUNICATED WITH TRANSFER: BY ORDER OF ________ FOR ACCOUNT OF ________ OTHER INFORMATION ________

IF THE CHECK OR TRANSFER IS OF OTHER THAN U. S. DOLLARS, THE UNDERSIGNED HEREBY PURCHASES FROM YOU THE AMOUNT AND KIND OF CURRENCY SPECIFIED ABOVE. IN COVER OF THE AMOUNT OF THE ABOVE "TOTAL," THE UNDERSIGNED SUBMITS HEREWITH: ☐ CASH, ☐ CHECK, OR ☐ HEREBY AUTHORIZES YOU TO CHARGE THE ACCOUNT OF THE UNDERSIGNED. THE UNDERSIGNED HEREBY AGREES TO YOUR CONDITIONS AS SET FORTH ON THE REVERSE SIDE HEREOF.

LICENSE No. ________ (IF ANY) TYPE OR PRINT NAME OF APPLICANT ________

SIGNATURE OF APPLICANT ________

STREET ADDRESS ________

CITY AND STATE ________

RECEIVED FROM **FIRST NATIONAL CITY BANK** ________ (SIGNATURE)
THE ABOVE-REQUESTED CHECK.

RESERVED FOR BANK USE

CHECK DRAWN ON
OR
PAYMENT EFFECTED THROUGH ________

CONVERSION ________

COMPUTED BY ________ CHECK No. ________ CHECK OR ORDER SIGNED BY ________

CHECKED BY ________ TRANSFER No. ________ APPROVED FOR FILING ________

OFFSET ________ FUNDS HELD BY ________ (BOOKKEEPER'S NAME) BRANCH COMMISSION ________

SF 1117 (L) REV. 12-60

Fig. 2. Application for foreign check or mail transfer.

Sight Drafts. The most commonly used type of foreign exchange is the bill of exchange or draft. A **draft** is a written order issued by the drawer to a second party (the drawee) to pay to the order of a third party (payee), who may be the drawer, a certain sum of money at sight, or on a specified date, or at a future ascertainable date. **Bills of exchange** are employed in settling foreign obligations mainly because they are negotiable, i.e., their ownership can be readily transferred by endorsement. Bills of exchange are classified on the basis of maturity dates into (1) sight drafts and (2) time drafts. A foreign exchange sight draft is a check, stated in foreign currency, on a foreign bank, drawn against the balance maintained in that bank by the seller of the draft. The buyer of the draft mails it to the payee.

The buyer of a sight draft must arrange his purchase in time to allow the check to reach the payee on or before the date his obligation is due, if he wants to meet it promptly. The rate for sight drafts is lower than that for cable transfers, the spread between the two usually equaling the amount of interest that would be allowed, at the rate prevailing in the country on which the draft is drawn, for the period that the draft is in transit.

Time Drafts. A time draft, also called **long exchange** or a **long bill,** is payable on a specified future date, usually after 30, 60, 90, or 120 days. Normally, the rate for time drafts, the "long rate," is lower than that for sight drafts, since the drawer's account abroad will not be charged until the draft is presented at its maturity date. The long rate is usually equal to the sight rate less interest at the rate prevailing in the center on which the bill is drawn. Time drafts of long tenor are thus quoted lower than those of shorter term.

The demand for and supply of time drafts arise mainly in connection with **foreign trade transactions.** A New York importer of goods from France, obligated by the terms of his contract to pay on receipt of the bill of lading with a 30-day draft on a bank in France, will buy such a draft from his bank. Exporters as a general practice draw drafts on the importer or his bank payable so many days after sight, usually in the currency of the country of the party on whom the draft is drawn. When it is presented to the importer, he accepts it by writing or stamping across the face of the bill the word "Accepted," the date of acceptance, and usually the bank at which it will be paid, followed by his signature. By this act the bill becomes an **acceptance,** and the importer (drawee) assumes liability as acceptor. The exporter, if he elects, may hold the acceptance until maturity, thereby earning the interest it bears. In that event, the acceptance is customarily left for collection with the bank that presented the draft for acceptance (the accepting agent). This is rarely done, however, because of possible loss from a decline in the exchange rate of the currency in which the acceptance is stated. The exporter prefers to sell the draft immediately to a bank or foreign exchange dealer.

FUTURE EXCHANGE TRANSACTIONS. In a **spot** exchange transaction, performance takes place immediately in accordance with the custom of the market. A "future" or **"forward'** exchange transaction is a contract for the purchase or sale of foreign exchange at an agreed rate, delivery and payment to be effected at a stipulated future date. If both parties to the forward exchange contract are banks or exchange dealers, no money passes between them until the date of consummation of the contract. They merely exchange written contracts. If one of the parties is not a bank, or in transactions with financially weak dealers, the bank usually requires a cash margin as security for the performance of the contract.

Forward exchange protects businessmen against the risk of loss from fluctuation in exchange rates, in dealings with foreign countries. An exporter in the United States who sells goods abroad in terms of a foreign currency on 3 months' credit, and calculates the sales price at the current dollar rate for the foreign currency, can guard himself **("hedge")** against loss from a decline in the exchange rate by selling the foreign exchange immediately for delivery 3 months hence. Similarly, an importer in the United States who buys merchandise abroad in terms of a foreign currency on 3 months' credit can determine immediately the dollar cost of the commodities to him by purchasing at once future exchange, for delivery at the time payment will be due. The importer could also protect himself against currency fluctuation by buying a cable transfer for the required amount and lending out the foreign funds for 3 months. He will obviously employ the cheapest method.

Not only exporters and importers but also others dealing with foreign countries and desiring to avoid speculation in foreign exchange hedge by buying or selling forward exchange. Thus, an American who intends to invest funds temporarily in Great Britain can, simultaneously with the purchase of spot sterling, sell future sterling, the delivery to coincide with the date of the liquidation of the investment. This combination of a spot and forward transaction is called a **swap** operation, the spot exchange being "swapped" against forward exchange. Swap operations are double transactions ordinarily consisting of a simultaneous purchase of spot and sale of future exchange, to avoid loss from possible depreciation of the foreign currency in the interim.

The Forward Exchange Market. This is composed of banks and dealers and absorbs the risk of exchange fluctuations in international transactions. Although their purchases and sales tend to cancel out to a large extent, banks and dealers must take a position when the supply of forward exchange in a currency exceeds the demand, or vice versa. The banks and dealers who acquire a net long forward exchange position can hedge it, in turn, by borrowing an equal amount in foreign currency abroad, repayable when the forward contracts mature, and selling the exchange that represents the proceeds of the loan at the spot rate. The foreign exchange to be received from sellers of futures will be used to repay the foreign currency loan. The bank pays interest on the foreign currency loan, but earns interest on the domestic funds realized from the spot sale of the borrowed exchange. Any difference in interest rates in the two financial centers is taken into consideration in quoting the forward exchange rate. By the same token, when a bank sells forward exchange on balance, it can avoid the exchange risk by buying spot exchange simultaneously and lending the money abroad for a period terminating on the delivery date of the forward exchange, when repayment of the loan provides the exchange to cover the net forward commitment.

Banks obtain forward exchange also by buying **time bills** of a maturity coinciding with the delivery date of the forward exchange. When demand for spot exchange of an individual currency increases, the banks can discount time bills in the foreign financial center and sell the proceeds as spot exchange.

Rates for future exchange vary with supply and demand, as in the case of spot exchange. Future exchange may be quoted at a premium over spot. But when foreign exchange dealers and speculators expect a currency to depreciate, the forward rate is quoted below the spot rate, the discount reflecting speculative sales and compensation for the special risk assumed by the buyer. It is obvious that exchange restrictions in a currency that make spot transactions impossible automatically eliminate the forward market in that currency.

SPECULATION IN EXCHANGE. An important factor influencing the foreign exchange market is speculation by dealers and brokers who go **long** of exchange when they expect a rise in the market, and sell **short** when in their judgment rates will go lower. Under normal conditions speculation in the foreign exchange market is very risky, the margin of profit being so small that only expert traders attempt to match their judgment against the trend of the market. When currencies fluctuate more widely, speculation in exchange attracts a large outside public following.

Arbitrage. Banks and others who deal in foreign exchange must keep themselves advised as to **rate fluctuations** in all the money markets of the world. With this information, they are frequently in position to arbitrage; i.e., to buy exchange in one market and sell it in another to profit from price discrepancies. Sharp traders may buy and sell in several money centers simultaneously. They may buy or sell cable exchange in one or more countries against the sale or purchase of a different type of exchange in other countries.

Because of the need for quick action and expert knowledge and the usual small margin of profit, arbitrage operations are generally confined to large banks and foreign exchange dealers having branches or correspondents in all of the principal money centers of the world. The economic effect of arbitrage is to keep the major foreign exchange markets of the world in alignment with each other, where exchange restrictions do not interfere (see Einzig, A Dynamic Theory of Forward Exchange).

FREE VS. CONTROLLED CURRENCIES. When the currency and other media of payments of a country may be used without restriction by residents and foreigners in international transactions, such a currency is termed free or **convertible**. Countries whose international payments and receipts are in approximate equilibrium, or that hold gold or foreign exchange reserves adequate to cover deficits in their international accounts, have an assured ability to maintain free and stable currencies. When a country's total payments to the rest of the world exceed its aggregate receipts, when it has little gold and foreign exchange or does not want to part with gold owned, and when it cannot obtain foreign credits, the exchange value of its currency will tend to decline because the supply of that currency will exceed the demand for it. At this point the government is confronted with the alternatives of permitting its currency to depreciate and retaining a free currency (freedom of transfer), or abandoning the free transfer of currency, i.e., instituting exchange control with the object of maintaining a stable exchange rate.

Exchange Control. Exchange control is exercised either by the government, the central bank, or a specially created authority. It consists of measures designed to limit the demand for and increase the supply of foreign exchange, thus regulating the currency's quotation. It may be provided that no payments can be made abroad without **approval of the controlling authority,** which apportions foreign exchange to make payments for approved imports and certain expenditures abroad that are deemed necessary. Importation and exportation of securities and of domestic and foreign currency may be restricted or prohibited. Residents may be required by law to sell at an official rate all or part of the foreign exchange derived from exports and services performed abroad, and to put at the disposal of the authority bank balances abroad, foreign bills, currencies, and securities held at home and abroad, for which they are paid in domestic currency. Foreigners may be allowed to use balances to buy certain types of commodities for export, or may be limited to purchasing services with them and making specified types of investments within the country.

An **official foreign exchange rate** may be established and maintained by apportioning available exchange in accordance with a scale of relative necessity. Since only a part of the demand for foreign exchange may be satisfied at the official rate, this encourages outside dealings at a **"free" rate,** often of a black market character.

Beginning with the depression of the early 1930's and extending through the decade of the fifties, most countries maintained some form of exchange controls. With the return of the leading free nations to **external convertibility** (applying to foreign exchange acquired by nonresidents in current transactions) and the subsequent relaxation of exchange restrictions, trading in foreign exchange in the financial centers of the free world has increased. Many countries, however, still maintain foreign exchange controls of one kind or another. The most elaborate restrictions are those in force in the less developed countries, which in general have an acute shortage of foreign exchange.

Example of Controls. Venezuela offers an example of a system of exchange controls. The International Monetary Fund (Eighteenth Annual Report on Exchange Restrictions) summarizes restrictions as of the end of 1966 as follows:

Exchange transactions take place at the following rates. The Central Bank of Venezuela purchases proceeds of the petroleum and iron or exporting companies at the rate of Bs. 4.40 per US $1. Most other exchange proceeds are purchased by commercial banks at rates close to Bs. 4.48 per US $1. Proceeds from exports of cacao and coffee may be purchased also by the Central Bank at the rate of Bs. 4.485 per US $1; in certain circumstances they are eligible for special subsidies. The Central Bank sells exchange to the Government and its agencies and to the commercial banks at Bs. 4.485 per US $1. Commercial banks sell exchange to the public at Bs. 4.50 per US $1 for all transactions. The Central Bank, through its Import Subsidy Office, pays a subsidy of Bs. 1.15 per US $1 on exchange purchased to make payments for import of wheat and powdered milk. The Central Bank offers swap facilities under which it buys U.S. dollars at Bs. 4.47 and resells at Bs. 4.50.

Despite these restrictions capital transfers are permitted freely.

INTERNATIONAL FINANCIAL MARKETS. During the late 1950's a market developed in Europe for loans and deposits denominated in hard currencies, distinct from local currencies. Included in the loans were short- and medium-term banking arrangements conducted in the so-called Euro-dollar market and long-term operations in the capital market covering dollar bonds, other hard currency bonds, multiple currency bonds, parallel bonds, and unit of account bonds.

The Euro-Dollar Market. A number of foreign banks (primarily in London and Paris) both accept deposits and make loans in non-local currencies, primarily dollars but also other currencies such as Swiss francs, Deutsche marks, and pounds sterling. These deposit and loan activities constitute the core of the Euro-dollar market. A typical operation may run as follows:

A South American citizen purchases dollars in his own country to be credited to his bank account in New York. After a time he orders his New York bank to transfer the funds to London to obtain a higher interest rate. The New York bank debits his account and simultaneously credits the British bank, which ordinarily (upon the client's instructions) receives the amount transferred in the form of a short-term dollar time deposit. The British bank then uses its dollar assets to make a loan, say to an Italian borrower. Thus the same dollar deposit in New York may support a number of operations abroad.

Euro-dollar loans and deposits are usually short term and in multiples of $1 million. In some cases **"escape" clauses** are provided, by which on payment of a penalty the depositor is able to regain his deposit before it matures. As of mid-1967 the size of this market was about $13 billion.

Hard-Currency Bond Issues in Europe. Though less important in volume than Euro-dollars, the European market for long-term-debt instruments denominated in dollars experienced an impressive development in the 1960's. The main issuing center has been London, but sources of funds have emanated from all over the world. Issuers include governments, private firms, and government-owned enterprises. These bonds are listed on the Luxembourg Stock Exchange as well as the exchanges of the countries participating in the issues. In addition to dollars, typical currencies used have been D. marks, guilders, and Swiss francs. Issues in these currencies, however, have been much less significant than those denominated in dollars.

Multiple-Currency Bonds. The differentiating characteristic of multiple-currency bonds is that they entitle the holder to a choice of currency from a stated set. These bonds have been issued in two forms: in one, the holder elects his currency option at the time of issuance, while in the other he makes his choice when interest and principal are paid. **Parallel issues** involve an extension of the principles underlying the multiple-currency bonds. Essentially, they involve "breaking up" an issue into tranches (parts) to be placed in different markets and denominated in the currency of the market of issuance.

Bond issues in **European units of account** may incorporate various differentiating provisions but generally entitle holders to claim payment of principal and interest in any one of seventeen European currencies. They were first launched in the European capital market in 1961 but have not proved popular (see Einzig, Foreign Dollar Loans in Europe).

International Departments of Banks

OPERATIONS OF AN INTERNATIONAL DEPARTMENT. International or **foreign** departments have been developed principally by banks located in large seaports and financial and manufacturing centers. Most banks in the United States handle foreign business that may come to them through large metropolitan correspondent banks. The latter in turn are represented by their own branches, affiliates, and correspondent banks in every important city of the world.

The international department of a bank transacts three main **types of business**: (1) trading in foreign exchange; (2) financing foreign trade, including collection of drafts, issuance of letters of credit, travelers' letters of credit, and travelers' checks; and (3) services, such as making available to customers economic data on foreign countries, facts about their laws and trade customs, and credit information about foreign firms and individuals. As a rule the banks make no charge for these services, except for actual expense incurred in obtaining specific information.

The **profit** realized on exchange trading usually results from the difference between the prices at which the bank buys and sells foreign exchange, and from arbitrage between different types of exchange or between different markets. Income derived from transactions of the second type is in the form of commissions charged customers. These commissions may be shared with the bank's foreign correspondents.

The **organization of the foreign department** varies from bank to bank, depending on the volume of business and functional and geographical specialization. The international department of a large New York City bank may be composed of the divisions or sections described below.

NEW ACCOUNTS SECTION. This section obtains for the bank accounts of foreign banks and customers and establishes correspondent relations with banks abroad. It keeps records of all account arrangements, including required minimum balances, service charges, and interest; and analyzes the profitability of the accounts. It also determines the routing of collection items payable abroad and passes special instructions received from depositors to the operating divisions of the bank.

FOREIGN TELLERS. All payments and transfers ordered by cable, draft, mail, and over the window are effected by this section. If, for example, a foreign bank orders a payment made out of its credit balance to a firm in the United States, this section will either send its check (cashier's, treasurer's, or manager's check) to the American concern or instruct its correspondent located in the city of the payee to effect payment. If the payee maintains an account with the bank, a foreign teller will credit his account and send him a notice of credit. Foreign tellers also receive and acknowledge payments to the credit of accounts of foreign depositors; and in some banks buy and sell foreign currency notes and coins at rates approved by the Foreign Exchange Traders division.

FOREIGN EXCHANGE TRADERS. This division buys and sells foreign exchange in all forms and keeps a record of the bank's foreign exchange position. It also undertakes arbitrage operations and concludes future exchange contracts and swap transactions.

COMMERCIAL CREDIT DIVISION. This division contains the following sections: (1) foreign credit, (2) import letter of credit, (3) export letter of credit, and (4) loans. The **foreign credit section** maintains up-to-date credit files of foreign accounts; obtains credit information for the bank's customers (mainly for exporters who want to know the credit standing of foreign importers); and submits periodically to the proper officials of the bank credit summaries of borrowing foreign banks and customers. It also answers credit inquiries from other banks regarding foreign accounts.

The **import letter of credit section** opens letters of credit for American importers of goods. It keeps records of legal requirements of the various countries relating to the shipment of goods and making payments. It maintains a **tickler system** to assure payment at maturity of acceptances and other credit instruments under letters of credit.

Exports of American goods to foreign countries are often financed through export letters of credit that originate in the countries of the importers. The **export letter of credit section** examines the shipping documents and drafts presented by American exporters under letters of credit. In many banks import and export letters of credit are handled by one section, which also accepts drafts drawn under letters of credit.

The **loan section** handles loans to foreign customers and also makes advances against commodities stored in the United States for shipment abroad.

TRAVEL SECTION. This section issues travelers' letters of credit in both dollars and foreign currencies, and dollar travelers' checks. It makes arrangements for the purchase of steamship, railroad, and air transportation for customers, and attends to other needs of the traveling public. It supplies domestic correspondent banks with letters of credit, and keeps records of travelers' letters of credit issued on, or for, the account of the bank by foreign and domestic correspondent banks.

FOREIGN COLLECTIONS. This section handles the collection of foreign credit instruments. It is usually divided into incoming and outgoing collections. **Incoming items** are those received by the bank from abroad for collection in the United States; **outgoing items** are sent by the bank to its foreign branches or correspondents for collection abroad. Items that require special treatment, such as documentary bills, and those that cannot be handled conveniently by the foreign tellers are turned over to foreign collections. This section also takes care of consignment shipments to be sold in accordance with the instructions of the foreign customers.

Outgoing collections consist mostly of credit instruments arising from American exports, and to a smaller extent of coupons payable abroad. A careful record is kept of all outgoing items, and nonreceipt of funds in due time is followed up by **tracers**. American exporters occasionally request the banks to make loans to them against the bills forwarded for collection abroad.

FOREIGN DRAWING SERVICE. Some of the larger banks issue foreign checks on their foreign branches or correspondents. Local correspondents desiring to avail themselves of this service are provided special check forms.

CABLES. This section has charge of incoming and outgoing cables, radiograms, and telegrams. It allocates costs of messages to the several divisions of the bank and customer accounts. It traces cables if no confirmation or answer is received within a reasonable time, and repeats mutilated messages.

A subsection of "Cables" is the **Cipher Key**, which transcribes outgoing messages into code form, deciphers incoming code messages, and sets up private codes for use between the bank and its foreign correspondents. It also authenticates cable payment orders and important messages by means of prearranged key words.

Banks that do not maintain a separate translation section have translators in this subsection for translating cables and letters from foreign languages into English, and vice versa.

SECURITIES. This section buys and sells securities for accounts of foreign customers and correspondents. It is also in charge of safekeeping of securities and other important documents entrusted to the bank by foreign clients.

Foreign Branches and Affiliates

FOREIGN OPERATIONS OF AMERICAN BANKS. Prior to World War I, the role of American banks in international transactions was insignificant. London was the financial center of the world, and the sterling bill was generally used in making international payments. A coincidence of two events, the outbreak of World War I and commencement of operations of the Federal Reserve System in 1914, prompted and enabled American banks to enter the field of international finance on a large scale. Of the means chosen by American banks to expand their international operations, the most important have been branches, Edge Act corporations, and agreement corporations.

Foreign Branches. The Federal Reserve Act authorized national banks to establish branches abroad, subject to approval by the Board of Governors of the Federal Reserve System. The only state banks that have opened branches abroad are those of New York. The number of foreign branches of American banks has increased from 26 in 1914 to 280 in 1967.

Edge Act Corporations. A 1919 amendment to the Federal Reserve Act, Section 25 (a), permits the organization of "Edge Act" corporations "for the purpose of engaging in international or foreign financial operations" either directly or through the agency, ownership, or control of local institutions in foreign countries and insular possessions of the United States. Edge Act corporations must have a minimum capital stock, and a majority of the stock must at all times be held and owned by United States citizens. Regulation K of the Board of Governors provides that only United States citizens may serve as directors. The corporations may accept bills up to ten times their capital and surplus. They may not carry on any part of their business in the United States except such as, in the judgment of the Board of Governors, shall be incidental to their international or foreign business. Regulation K stipulates that an Edge Act corporation may be either a **banking corporation** or a **financing corporation** and specifies the activities in which each type of corporation may engage. In 1963, the Board of Governors revised Regulation K providing for substantial liberalization of procedures and elimination of the distinction between banking and financing corporations. At the end of 1966, there were about 50 Edge Act corporations in existence.

In early 1968, in conformance with the U.S. government balance-of-payments program, the Federal Reserve Board, through ruling, curbed further equity investments in banks or other enterprises in Western Europe by Edge Act or agreement corporations (see below). Equity investments elsewhere had to be within the ceilings established for the voluntary foreign credit restraint program.

Agreement Corporations. Section 25 of the Federal Reserve Act authorizes national banks to invest an amount based on their capital and surplus in the stock of one or more banks or corporations federally or state chartered and principally engaged in foreign banking. A national bank is permitted to purchase the stock of such a bank or corporation provided the latter has concluded an agreement with the Board of Governors to the effect that it will conduct its business in such manner and under such limitations as the Board may prescribe. Corporations that have entered into such an agreement are referred to as agreement corporations. At the end of 1966, there were five agreement corporations in existence.

ROLE OF THE FEDERAL RESERVE BANKS. Section 14 of the Federal Reserve Act authorizes the Federal Reserve banks, with the consent or upon the direction of the Board of Governors, to open and maintain accounts, appoint correspondents, and establish agencies in foreign countries. The Reserve banks are also empowered to open and maintain banking accounts for foreign correspondents or agencies, subject to consent of the Board. They have preferred to enter into correspondent relations and special agreements with foreign central banks.

Because the **Federal Reserve Bank of New York** is located in one of the principal financial centers of the world, it acts as the agent of the Treasury in foreign exchange operations. It also acts as agent for the other Federal Reserve banks in their relations and transactions with foreign banks. The New York Reserve Bank holds deposits, earmarked gold, and United States securities for foreign central banks and treasuries. The Federal Reserve Act also granted the Reserve banks power to "purchase and sell in the open market, at home or abroad, either from or to domestic or foreign banks, firms, corporations, or individuals, cable transfers and bankers' acceptances and bills of exchange . . . eligible for rediscount" and to make loans secured by gold.

AGENCIES AND BRANCHES OF FOREIGN BANKS. Since the end of World War I, when the United States assumed a leading role in international finance, many foreign banking institutions have established offices in the United States, mainly in New York City. The business of such offices is **limited by state laws** with which they must comply. Agencies are not permitted to accept deposits and conduct a general banking business, but they may deal in foreign exchange, pay and collect bills of exchange, sell remittances to foreign countries, issue letters of credit, accept drafts, make loans, and transact other business incident to financing foreign trade. Subsidiary banking corporations are organized as domestic corporations under state laws and are not subject to special restrictions because of foreign ownership.

In 1960, the State of New York enacted a law permitting foreign banks, on a reciprocity basis and subject to licensing by the Superintendent and the Banking Board, to open in the state branches with full deposit privileges or to convert their agencies into branches, beginning January 1, 1961.

Financing of Foreign Trade

RISKS IN FOREIGN TRADE FINANCING. Foreign trade involves peculiar risks not encountered in purely domestic business. These risks arise from the use of different currencies, distances between buyers and sellers that are usually greater than in dometic trade, differences in customs and trade usages, tariffs, and governmental regulations. The currency risk can and should be shifted from the importer or exporter to banks. Distances tie up funds for a considerable time, so that financing is often required. Thus, a manufacturer in New York who has sold a quantity of goods to an importer in South Africa or Australia must not only finance the process of production but also carry the financial burden while the goods are in transit to their destination for 3 to 6 weeks. On the other hand, were the contract to stipulate that the importer is to pay on the day the goods are turned over by the manufacturer to the common carrier, the importer would tie up his funds for weeks or months pending their sale. Normally, goods in transit in foreign trade can be financed by the banks by methods usually differing from those in vogue in domestic trade.

FINANCING BY THE EXPORTER. There are various methods by which the exporter may finance his transactions:

Shipment on Open Book Account. If an exporter has maintained business relations with an importer over a number of years and the credit standing and good faith of the importer are unquestionable, the exporter may agree to sell on an open account basis, as in domestic trade. Such an arrangement is extremely advantageous to the importer because it permits him to receive the goods and even sell them before making payment. The exporter runs the risk that in time of stress the importer may give preference to pressing domestic obligations, and efforts to collect by legal proceedings may prove difficult and expensive. Banks may be willing to grant exporters loans on the evidence of the sales contract and shipment of the goods.

Consignment. An exporter may ship goods to his branch, agency, or resident salesman abroad and order sale of the goods while in transit or upon arrival at a fixed or the best obtainable price. Proceeds from the sale are then remitted to the exporter in his currency. The exporter then not only ties up his funds until the goods are sold and paid for, but also assumes the exchange risk.

Collection Drafts. An exporter draws a draft on the importer at the time of shipment. Depending on the credit terms specified in the sales contract, the draft, drawn either in the exporter's or importer's currency as agreed, may be either sight or time, clean, or documentary. A **sight** draft is payable on presentation, whereas a **time** draft is payable either at a specified future date or at a certain period after sight. A **clean** draft is drawn by an exporter to collect an amount due from an importer for a shipment of goods. Such a draft is not accompanied by documents and is used when the exporter has complete confidence in the integrity of the importer. Banks generally do not discount clean drafts unless the credit rating of the exporter warrants it.

A **documentary** draft is accompanied by documents conveying title to the goods and may be either a **D/P draft**, i.e., documents against payment, or a **D/A draft**, that is, documents against acceptance. In a D/P draft the exporter turns over the draft, together with the documents, to his bank for collection, with instructions not to release the documents to the importer until the draft is paid; in a D/A draft the bank is ordered to withhold documents until the importer has accepted the draft. The accepted draft—called **trade acceptance**—becomes a "clean" bill.

The exporter retains control of the goods when he employs a documentary draft, because the importer cannot obtain shipping documents from the collecting bank until he pays or accepts the draft. If a clean draft is used, the importer can secure the merchandise upon arrival of the documents by mail, even though the draft still has a period to run.

If the distance between the exporter and importer is great, and the draft and annexed documents sent by mail steamer or air mail will reach their destination long before the goods arrive, it is customary to allow the importer to postpone payment or acceptance of the draft until the goods have arrived.

A bank that undertakes the service of collection must receive detailed **instructions from the exporter** (drawer) so that it may protect his interests in accordance with the sales contract. The instructions are given on a printed form supplied by the bank (see Fig. 3). The instructions given in each instance are determined by the sales contract, the policy of the exporter, and any special requirements of the moment. Since the bank must follow instructions explicitly, it is advisable that the exporter designate a representative located near the importer (drawee), with instructions "in case of need, refer to." This **local representative** knows the exporter's policies, and reference to him implies that he may be trusted by the bank to modify original instructions to meet emergencies.

The exporter's bank forwards the draft and documents with the exporter's instructions to its branch or correspondent bank in the country of the importer. Upon receipt of payment from the importer the foreign bank remits the funds to the exporter's bank, which in turn makes them available to the exporter. In case of a D/A draft, the correspondent bank will hand over the documents to the importer upon his acceptance of the draft. On the due date, the correspondent bank presents the acceptance to the importer, and when it is paid remits the amount to the exporter's bank. Although the exporter's bank selects the correspondent abroad, the latter acts as the agent of the exporter and not of the bank. Should the correspondent bank become insolvent or bankrupt before it has remitted the collected funds to the exporter's bank, the loss will be borne by the exporter.

FINANCING BY THE IMPORTER. The importer has three principal means for financing his operations.

Payment with Order. This term means that the importer must pay for the goods at the time he places the order with the exporter. He would probably purchase from his bank a draft on a bank located in the city of the exporter, or in the financial center of the exporter's country. In normal times sales on such terms are rarely encountered in foreign trade, except when the credit standing of the importer is unsatisfactory or not known. The exporter receives payment before he ships the goods, often even before he has manufactured them. The importer thus not only finances the entire transaction and assumes the foreign exchange risk involved, but pays over cash without security, except for the credit standing of the exporter. Should the order not be filled, should the goods be unduly delayed or prove to be of inferior quality, the importer's only redress is to bring legal action on the basis of the sales contract unless the exporter makes an adjustment voluntarily.

COLLECTION INSTRUCTION LETTER

Date__________

ACCOUNT NUMBER

From__________

Address__________

To: **MANUFACTURERS HANOVER TRUST COMPANY**, 44 Wall Street, New York, N. Y. 10015

We enclose ☐ For collection ☐ As collateral for an advance — The following described draft(s) **SUBJECT TO THE TERMS AND CONDITIONS PRINTED ON THE REVERSE SIDE HEREOF,** which are hereby agreed to and accepted by us.

Forward through

or through your correspondent.

OUR NO.	DRAWEE AND ADDRESS	MERCHANDISE/VESSEL	TENOR	AMOUNT
		S/S		

Documents	B/L	Inv.	Cons. Inv.	Ins. Ctf.	Ctf. Orig.	VARIOUS

PLEASE NOTE all documents will be dispatched in one airmail unless specifically requested by you to forward them in two separate airmails.

FOR BANK USE ONLY

Please following instructions marked "X"

PROTEST ☐ Non-Payment ☐ Non-Acceptance ☐ No Protest

DOCUMENTS ☐ Deliver against payment ☐ Deliver against Acceptance

FATE* ☐ Cable Advice of { ☐ Non-Acceptance ☐ Non-Payment ☐ Acceptance ☐ Payment

CHARGES ☐ All charges for our account ☐ Airmail documents our expense ☐ Do not waive charges ☐ All charges for account drawee ☐ Airmail documents drawee expense ☐ Waive charges if refused

PROCEEDS* ☐ Remit by cable at ☐ drawees expense ☐ our expense

INTEREST ☐ To be collected at_____% per annum from________until approximate date of arrival of return remittance in New York.

COLLECTION NUMBER

LOCAL CURRENCY ☐ Local Currency Deposit may be accepted (See Over)

IN CASE OF NEED Refer to__________

☐ Who is authorized only to obtain honoring of draft as drawn.

☐ Who is authorized to give instructions which may be followed in every respect.

SPECIAL INSTRUCTIONS

☐ Please credit proceeds to our account at your office

*Our standing instructions to collecting banks request reply and remittance by airmail.

By__________ Authorized Signature

FOR BANK USE ONLY

Documents	B/L	Inv.	Cons. Inv.	Ins. Ctf.	Ctf. Orig.	VARIOUS

O. K. TO FILE

1360 00M 11-65

Fig. 3. Customer's instructions to a bank for the collection of a draft.

CONDITIONS APPLICABLE TO COLLECTIONS

It is understood and agreed that you and your correspondents and their agents or sub-agents shall act as our agents and that you assume no responsibility except for the exercise of ordinary care in the selection of correspondents. You shall not be responsible for any act, error, neglect, or default, omissions, insolvency or failure in business of any correspondent, agent or sub-agent thereof.

Neither you nor any of your correspondents, agents or sub-agents thereof shall be liable for failure to collect, loss of exchange, loss of interest or any other loss or damage due to any of the following events; delay or loss in transmission, delay in arrival of drafts, documents or proceeds thereof or of the underlying goods, or delay in giving notice thereof to us; errors, omissions, interruptions or delay in transmission or delivery of any message by mail, cable, telegram, wireless or otherwise, in cipher or otherwise, or errors in translation or interpretation of technical terms; declared or undeclared war, censorship, blockade, insurrection, civil commotion, breakdown or interruption of communication or because of any law, decree, regulation, control or act of public authority of a domestic or foreign government de jure or de facto or any agency thereof, whether rightfully or wrongfully exercised; or any cause beyond your or your correspondents', their agents' or sub-agents' control. The undersigned agrees that any action taken or omitted by you or your correspondents with respect to the drafts described on the reverse side hereof or the underlying merchandise, if done in good faith, shall be binding on the undersigned and shall not put you or your correspondent under any resulting liability to the undersigned.

If at any time you shall make any advances against or discount any of the drafts described on the reverse side hereof, you shall have all the rights and remedies contained in your letter of hypothecation and general assurance. If there shall be any inconsistency between the terms and conditions of the letter of hypothecation and general assurance and the conditions or instructions appearing on the reverse side hereof, the terms of the letter of hypothecation and general assurance shall be controlling.

At your option, you may instruct your correspondents to advise you by cable, at our expense, of non-acceptance and/or non-payment, as well as payment, of any items discounted by you or against which you have made an advance.

If an "X" appears in box on reverse side reading "Local Currency Deposit May be Accepted", we authorize you as follows:

In the event U. S. dollar cover is not obtainable because of exchange regulations, payment in local currency at the local rate of exchange prevailing at the time of presentment for payment of time or sight draft(s) may be accepted and documents attached to sight draft(s) released, provided drawee agrees in writing to pay on request to collecting bank the difference between the rate of payment and the rate when U. S. dollar cover becomes available.

Fig. 3. (Reverse)

Partial Payment in Advance. To protect himself against the contingency that goods ordered by importers might be rejected on delivery, an exporter may stipulate in the sales contract that importers must remit in advance a partial payment on the order as evidence of good faith and intention to pay the balance as agreed. Such provision is usually made when the order is for specialized equipment, or when the goods involved cannot be satisfactorily disposed of in the country of destination if the importer fails to take them as agreed. The partial payment by the importer should suffice to cover the cost of freight out and back, insurance, and other expenses incident to the shipment of goods abroad.

Payment on Documents. When the contract stipulates payment on documents, the importer must provide funds in the exporter's country to pay for the shipment on the day the exporter turns over to a designated bank documents evidencing shipment of the goods ordered. The importer thus raises the funds, converts them into the currency of the country of the exporter, and carries the financing burden while the commodities are in transit.

FINANCING BY THE EXPORTER'S BANK. The exporter's bank may finance his transactions by the following means:

Advance on Drafts. Under this arrangement, the financing is done jointly by the exporter and his bank. An exporter who is unwilling to have his funds tied up while the goods are en route to the importer may borrow from his bank a percentage of the amount of the draft. The draft on the importer and pertinent shipping documents, turned over by the exporter to his bank for collection, constitute **collateral** for the advance. In case the drawee (importer) fails to pay the draft when due, the bank has recourse against the drawer, whether the draft is made out to the order of the drawer (exporter) and endorsed by him to the bank, or to the order of the bank. Thus the credit risk rests upon the exporter just as when he hands the draft to the bank for collection only. After the draft has been paid by the drawee, the bank retains the amount of the advance plus interest and collection fees, crediting the balance to the exporter.

The amount that an exporter can borrow upon foreign drafts depends upon the financial responsibility of exporter and importer, and the collateral behind the draft. The **character of the merchandise** shipped determines its value as collateral. Staple commodities not subject to rapid deterioration (cotton, wheat, wool) and traded on organized markets are obviously better collateral than perishable goods or manufactured articles requiring expert selling to be disposed of without loss.

Discount of Drafts. The bank may discount the draft drawn by the exporter on the importer when the credit standing of the exporter is high, and particularly if he already has a line of credit. The exporter then receives the face amount of the draft, less interest and collection charges, unless custom requires the drawee to absorb all charges.

Refinancing Bill. Under this arrangement, an exporter hands over to the bank the draft and documents for collection, and the bank allows the exporter to draw upon itself a time draft of a maturity identical with that of the draft upon the importer. The bank accepts the draft on itself, and this refinancing bill becomes a banker's acceptance that the exporter can sell in the open market at a very low rate of discount. When the original draft has been paid by the importer abroad, the bank uses the funds to pay off its own acceptance at maturity.

FINANCING BY THE IMPORTER'S BANK. The importer may finance transactions through his bank in several ways.

Commercial Letter of Credit. This is a device that substitutes a bank's credit for that of the importer by giving the exporter the right to draw drafts upon a designated bank, instead of upon the importer. Such drafts, upon acceptance, become **bankers' acceptances** that command a low rate of discount. A commercial letter of credit may be defined briefly as a notification issued by a bank to an individual or firm authorizing the latter to draw on the bank, its

FR. 171 (4-68)

FOR BANK USE ONLY
L/C No.

APPLICATION FOR COMMERCIAL LETTER OF CREDIT

(IF DELIVERED BY HAND)
DELIVER TO: CHEMICAL BANK NEW YORK TRUST COMPANY,
INTERNATIONAL DIVISION
LETTER OF CREDIT DEPARTMENT
ROOM 805, 20 PINE STREET
NEW YORK, N. Y. 10008

(IF MAILED — ADDRESS AS FOLLOWS:)
MAIL TO: CHEMICAL BANK NEW YORK TRUST COMPANY,
P.O. BOX 1585
NEW YORK, N. Y. 10008

Gentlemen:

..........19.......

Please issue for our account an irrevocable letter of credit substantially according to this application and transmit it:
☐ through your correspondent by: ☐ Airmail ☐ Night Letter / ☐ Full Rate } Cable/Telegram Giving { ☐ Complete Details / ☐ Brief Details
☐ to us for transmission to beneficiary

in favor of..........

for account of.......... at.......... Sight
available by drafts on yourselves (or)..........
for a sum or sums not exceeding in all (..........)
....
(amount in words)

for full invoice value of..........
.......%
(Commodity—State exactly as desired; ELIMINATE DETAILS NOT ESSENTIAL)

☐ CIF.......... ☐ C&F.......... ☐ FOB..........

Drafts must be accompanied by the documents specified below:
☐ Commercial Invoice. ☐ Marine Insurance Certificate/Policy, including War Risk.
☐ Customs Invoice. ☐ Other Risks..........
(specify if any)
☐ Full set clean On Board Ocean Bills of Lading to your order dated not later than..........
(if other than expiry date)
Marked: "Notify..........
☐ Other documents:..........
evidencing shipment from.......... to ....
☐ Partial shipments (not) Delete one (are) permitted ☐ Transshipment (not) Delete one (is) permitted
☐ Drafts must be (drawn and negotiated) Delete one (presented at your office) on or before..........
☐ Marine and War Risk insurance to be effected by us under blanket policy number..........
issued by..........

(Insurance Note—If this Letter of Credit provides for rail or truck shipment or ex-dock or ex-warehouse delivery, please state below (if space provided for remarks) by whom and under what policy insurance is to be covered. If terms are F.A.S., please state by whom and under what policy you will be covered until you receive payment from your buyer.)

REMARKS: ....
You may authorize the negotiating bank abroad to forward all documents in one mail with the relative draft(s) (delete if this clause is not to be included in the Letter of Credit). Please send us..........copies of the Letter of Credit.
Your Correspondent's advising commission, if any, for ☐ Our Account, ☐ Beneficiaries' Account. (Check one).
(If credit is in foreign currency the foreign exchange is to be/ is not to be (Delete one) purchased for our account immediately.)
(If credit is at sight in a foreign currency we do/we do not (Delete one) desire cable advice of payment.)
I/We authorize you, without reference to or approval by us, to set forth the terms of this application in the Letter of Credit in such language as you may deem appropriate, with such variations from such terms as you may in your discretion determine (which determination shall be conclusive) are necessary and are not materially inconsistent with this application.
All rights arising under this agreement shall be determined by the Uniform Customs and Practice for Commercial Documentary Credits fixed by the 13th or by any subsequent Congress of the International Chamber of Commerce and according to the laws of the State of New York.
In consideration of your opening such Credit I/we agree to sign, unless the same shall already have been signed, your current form of continuing Agreement, and I/we agree that the provisions of said Agreement, whether or not signed by us prior to the issue of the Letter of Credit shall apply with respect to all matters relating to the Credit hereby applied for.

Very Truly yours,

....
(Kindly sign with signature(s) authorized to sign such agreements)

S.V.

Fig. 4. Application and agreement for commercial letter of credit.

branch, or a correspondent bank for amounts up to a specified sum, and guaranteeing acceptance and payment of the drafts if drawn in accordance with the terms stipulated in the letter.

A letter-of-credit transaction may be illustrated by the following example. An importer in London purchases from an exporter in New York a quantity of goods, agreeing to make payment by a letter of credit. The importer applies to his bank in London for a letter of credit in favor of the exporter. If his credit standing at the bank is satisfactory the importer is requested by the bank to fill out and sign an "application and agreement for commercial letter of credit." (See Fig. 4. The agreement appears on the reverse side of the application.) In the application the importer asks the bank to open, by cable or mail, a credit for a stipulated amount to be made available to the beneficiary (exporter) by drafts drawn on the bank or its correspondent, upon delivery by the exporter to the drawee bank of specified documents evidencing shipment of goods ordered by the importer.

The agreement usually provides that the importer must put up the funds to meet the acceptances in advance of their maturity. It stipulates that the bank is the owner of the merchandise and documents until the importer has met all his obligations to the bank. It provides that neither the bank nor its correspondents shall be responsible for the existence, character, quality, quantity, condition, packing, value, or delivery of the property purporting to be represented by the documents.

The importer's bank will then instruct its branch or correspondent bank in New York to open a letter of credit in favor of the exporter under the conditions stipulated by the importer in his application. The New York bank, in turn, notifies the exporter that it will accept his drafts if drawn in compliance with the terms of the credit. This notification to the exporter, specifying conditions stipulated by the importer, constitutes the letter of credit. (See Fig. 5.)

If the importer's bank has substantial resources and is well known abroad, such as one of the large London banks, it may send a letter of credit directly to the exporter in New York. The exporter then draws on the importer's bank in London and sells the draft to a New York bank, surrendering to it the letter of credit and the shipping documents specified therein. The New York bank will buy (negotiate) the draft only when the exporter is its customer or known to it, and the documents conform exactly to the stipulations. The New York bank then forwards the draft, letter of credit, and shipping documents to its correspondent in London for collection. The importer's bank must pay or accept the draft, unless the documents do not conform to the provisions of the letter of credit.

A letter of credit not only shifts the burden of financing to a bank or the money market, but also gives the exporter a **bank guaranty** that he will receive cash or a bank acceptance once he has turned over the goods ordered to a common carrier for shipment to the importer in accordance with the letter of credit. An importer supplying a letter of credit is usually able to buy at somewhat lower prices than those quoted to open book account customers, since the exporter neither carries the burden of financing nor assumes the credit risk.

Once a time draft has been "accepted" by a well-known American bank, it becomes a readily negotiable instrument. In recent years the acceptance market has witnessed substantial growth, though only a few more than 100 institutions engage in any significant volume of acceptance financing. New York and San Francisco are the main market centers. Acceptances enjoy a good market among foreign institutions and foreign investors, since these holders are exempt from U.S. Federal income taxes.

Since 1955 the Federal Reserve has maintained a position in acceptances, both to promote the development of the market and to gauge the quality of the paper outstanding (see Cooper, Federal Reserve Bank of New York Monthly Review, vol. 48).

Import and Export Letters of Credit. American banks usually distinguish between and handle separately import and export letters of credit. When an

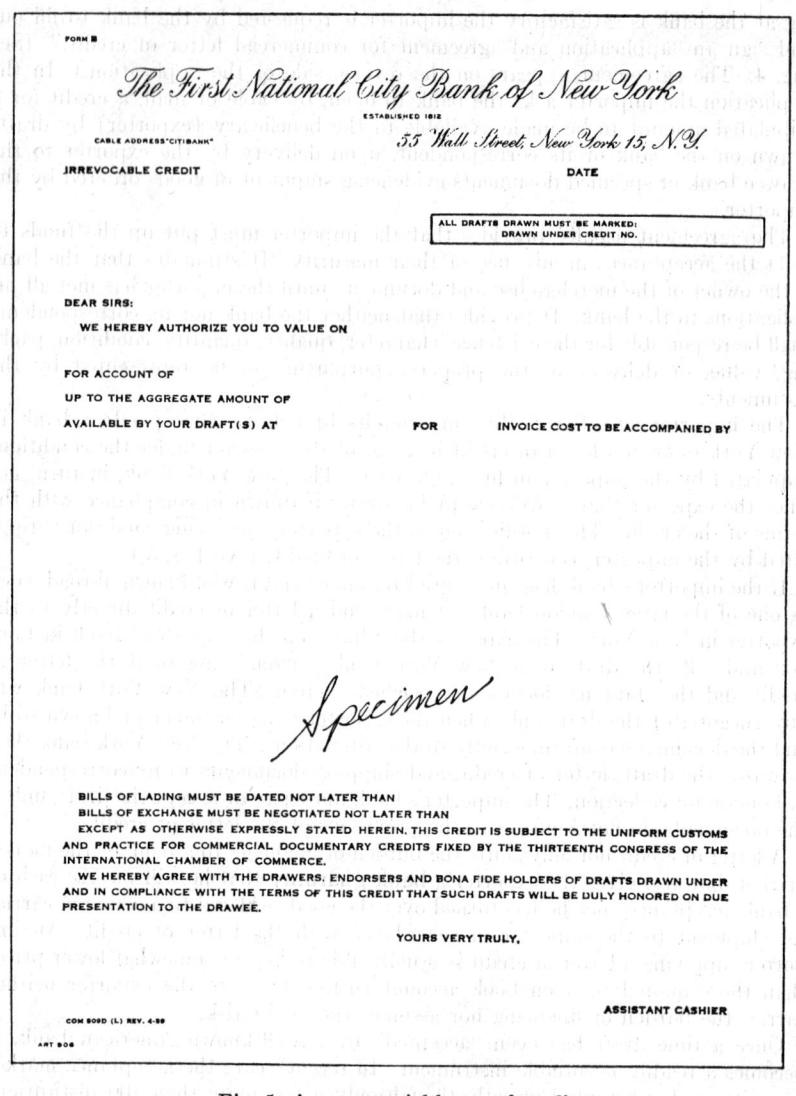

Fig. 5. A commercial letter of credit.

American bank, on the application of an American importer, issues a commercial letter of credit in favor of an exporter located abroad, it is termed an import letter of credit. An export letter of credit is one issued by a foreign bank in favor of an American exporter for the account of an importer abroad buying goods in the United States.

Revocable and Irrevocable Letters of Credit. A revocable letter of credit may be canceled by the importer's bank before drafts drawn by the exporter under the letter of credit have been negotiated by the correspondent bank. Banks do not favor revocable letters of credit, some banks refusing to issue them because they may become involved in resulting litigation. The correspondent bank acting as agent for the importer's bank (credit-issuing bank) assumes no obligation. An irrevocable letter of credit cannot be canceled by the importer's bank for the period specified without the consent of the beneficiary. Exporters generally insist upon irrevocable letters of credit.

Confirmed and Unconfirmed Letters of Credit. When a correspondent bank located in the country of the exporter confirms a letter of credit to the exporter by obligating itself to pay or accept his drafts, it is called a confirmed letter of credit. The confirmation binds the correspondent bank to honor drafts drawn under the credit even if the importer's (issuing) bank should refuse or be unable to meet its obligation. An unconfirmed letter of credit does not give the exporter this additional security. Exporters insist on confirmed letters of credit when the foreign issuing bank is not well known. It is obvious that the correspondent bank will confirm only irrevocable letters of credit, since a bank would not guarantee an agreement that might be canceled at will by the issuing bank.

Revolving Letter of Credit. If an importer maintains continuous business relations with an exporter and receives repeated shipments of goods, a revolving credit in favor of the exporter is often used. A revolving letter of credit assures **automatic renewal of the amount of the credit** when it becomes exhausted. Revolving letters of credit are issued in various forms, of which three types are most frequently employed: (1) The letter of credit provides that when drafts drawn under the letter of credit are paid by the importer, new drafts in equal amounts may again be drawn, so that the stipulated maximum amount may be continually outstanding. Thus, if the letter of credit is for $100,000 and the bank has honored the exporter's draft for $20,000, the credit is reduced to $80,000. But after the importer has paid this draft, the full amount of the credit, or $100,000, again becomes available to the exporter. (2) The exporter draws drafts for the full amount of the credit, and when these drafts have been paid by the importer the original amount again becomes available to the exporter. (3) The exporter is permitted to draw drafts up to a stated amount for a specified period, say a month, corresponding to deliveries of goods forwarded periodically.

Assignable Letter of Credit. A beneficiary may transfer this type of letter of credit to another party. An assignable letter of credit is employed by importers who maintain representatives abroad. It is issued in favor of the **foreign representative,** who is ordered to buy the goods specified by the importer. When the representative has contracted for the goods on the stipulated terms, he assigns the letter of credit to the seller (exporter).

Authority To Purchase. The "authority to purchase" (abbreviated **A/P**), or "authority to negotiate," is a letter or cable sent by the importer's bank to its branch, agent, or correspondent abroad, instructing him to buy an exporter's draft drawn on an importer. The authority to purchase, used mainly in Far Eastern trade, shifts the burden of financing from the exporter to the importer's bank. Its operation is illustrated by the following example:

An importer in Asia has bought goods from an exporter in San Francisco, the contract stipulating payment by a 90-day draft on the importer with an authority to purchase. The importer applies to his bank for an authority to purchase, specifying the amount, expiration date, shipping documents, and other conditions. When the bank approves the application, the importer signs **"a letter of guaranty"** in which he obligates himself to accept and pay the draft, pledging the documents conveying title to the goods as collateral security. The bank then instructs its agent in San Francisco to buy the exporter's draft drawn in compliance with the stated conditions. The San Francisco agent sends a notice (advice of authority to purchase) to the exporter, informing him of the terms upon which the draft on the importer will be purchased. After the exporter has delivered the goods to the shipping company, he presents the draft with the required documents to the agent and receives payment. The authority to purchase thus enables the exporter to sell the draft immediately without using up any of his line of credit with his bank.

In contrast to the letter of credit, which gives rise to banker's acceptances, the authority to purchase gives rise to a **trade acceptance,** with the importer as acceptor. Although under both methods the exporter is only secondarily liable, that is, only if the acceptor should fail to pay, it is obvious that an exporter is less likely to be called upon to pay a dishonored bank acceptance than a trade acceptance. The exporter may, however, be relieved from his liability by being authorized to endorse his draft on the importer with the words **"without recourse."** Thus, if the importer (drawee) refuses to accept or pay the draft, the exporter (drawer) cannot be called upon to refund the money he received from its sale. But authorities to purchase authorizing the exporter to endorse "without recourse" are rarely issued.

The authority to purchase may be **revocable** or **irrevocable.** In a revocable authority to purchase, the issuing bank has the right to cancel the authorization given to its agent to buy the exporter's draft. In such circumstance the **agent's advice of authority to purchase** contains a clause stipulating that the authority may be canceled by giving notice to the exporter.

Documents Attached to Draft. A full set of documents accompanying an exporter's draft under a letter of credit or authority to purchase consists usually of a negotiable bill of lading (two or more copies), an insurance certificate or policy, commercial invoice, consular invoice, certificate of origin, and other documents that may be needed to bring the goods into the foreign country such as an antidumping certificate, inspection certificate, or health certificate. The latter is often required for shipments of agricultural and livestock products. These shipping documents are ordinarily endorsed in blank or to the bank negotiating the exporter's draft. To establish the indisputable legal right of the negotiating bank to the goods represented by the documents, the bank usually requests the exporter to execute a **letter of hypothecation and general assurance.** This instrument contains a number of provisions, of which the most important are those in which the exporter obligates himself to deliver to the bank all the necessary documents, to indemnify the bank against losses and costs arising in connection with the draft, including loss from exchange fluctuations, and to pay the amount of the draft upon notice of protest. It grants the bank discretionary power to dispose at public or private sale, for its own and the exporter's protection and for account and sole risk of the exporter, all or part of the merchandise represented by the title-conveying documents, and to apply the net proceeds toward payment of the draft or drafts secured by these documents.

TRAVELER'S LETTER OF CREDIT. This instrument provides safety and convenience in carrying funds abroad for foreign commercial travelers and tourists. An American tourist planning to visit a number of countries in Latin America could carry dollar currency, exchanging it for currencies of each nation on the spot, but this involves the risk of loss and theft, and actual currency may be quoted at a considerable discount. He could buy separate drafts on banks in each country, but he does not know just how much he will need. By buying a

TRAVELERS IRREVOCABLE LETTER OF CREDIT
APPLICATION AND AGREEMENT

No.________________

FIRST NATIONAL CITY BANK
399 PARK AVENUE, NEW YORK 22, N. Y.

Place________________Date________________

GENTLEMEN:

The undersigned Applicant hereby requests you (as its Agent)* to issue a Travelers Irrevocable Letter of Credit (which, inclusive of any extension, renewal, or partial renewal thereof, is hereinafter referred to as the "Credit") substantially as follows:

A. In favor of:________________; (TYPE or PRINT name(s) of Beneficiary(ies) and prefix Mr., Mrs. or Miss)

B. In the amount of:________________; (Words and Figures)

C. Good until:________________, which date is inclusive; (Month Day Year)

D. To be delivered at the risk of the undersigned to:________________; (TYPE or PRINT name and address)

E. Remarks:

To induce the issuance of the Credit, the undersigned (jointly and severally) agree(s) to the terms and conditions set forth on the reverse side hereof, it being understood (a) that the word "Obligor(s)", wherever appearing therein or herein, shall refer to the undersigned Applicant and to any Client(s) of the Applicant, and (b) that, if this Application and Agreement is signed for and on behalf of a Bank or Trust Company, it shall be the Applicant for the Credit whether or not so designated below, and that the other Obligor(s), if any, will pay to the Applicant, upon demand, each and every amount which the Applicant may disburse and/or for which it may become liable hereunder, and will indemnify and hold the Applicant harmless from and against any and all loss, costs, damages and expenses which it may incur or sustain by reason of being a party hereto.

TO BE COMPLETED BY APPLICANT BANK OR TRUST CO. WHICH ACTS AS ISSUING AGENT

Date of issuance appearing on the Letter of Credit________________

☐ Check enclosed for . . $________________

☐ Debit Applicant's account $________________

SEE "NOTE" BELOW

____
Signature of APPLICANT

____

____
Address of APPLICANT

____
Signature of CLIENT

____
Address of CLIENT

NOTE: If a Bank or Trust Company is a signatory hereto, the Bank or Trust Company should sign as **APPLICANT**, and its client should sign as **CLIENT**. Signature(s) in behalf of Banks, Trust Companies, Corporations and Firms should be official and duly authorized for agreements of this character.

*Words "as its Agent" apply only when this Application and Agreement is signed by a Bank or Trust Company.

PRINTED IN U. S. A.

FIRST NATIONAL CITY BANK	FIRST NATIONAL CITY BANK	FIRST NATIONAL CITY BANK
Signature of Beneficiary(ies):	*Signature of Beneficiary(ies):*	*Signature of Beneficiary(ies):*

Fig. 6. A traveler's letter of credit.

traveler's letter of credit, he obtains a letter addressed by the American bank to listed banks abroad, requesting them to honor drafts drawn by the buyer of the letter up to a stipulated aggregate amount, and not later than a stated date. (See Fig. 6.)

At the time of issue of the traveler's or circular letter of credit, the buyer (beneficiary) is furnished with a **list of the issuing bank's foreign corre-**

spondents who will purchase, at the prevailing rate for sight exchange, drafts drawn in the currency of the country and on the bank named as correspondent. Comparison of the beneficiary's signature on the draft with that forwarded to the correspondent banks serves as **identification.** The beneficiary may in addition present his passport as identification. The bank officers' signatures on the letter of credit are compared with those on file with the correspondent bank, which establishes the genuineness of the letter of credit. As a precaution against overdrafts, the amount of each draft negotiated is entered by the paying correspondent bank on the reverse side of the letter of credit, which is taken away from the beneficiary and returned to the issuing bank by the correspondent paying the final draft that exhausts the amount of credit. The issuing bank charges the buyer a commission ranging from ½% to 1%. In addition, correspondent banks sometimes charge a commission for negotiating the individual drafts.

TRAVELERS' CHECKS. Tourists traveling abroad and at home can protect themselves against the loss of cash by using travelers' checks. These are issued by banks, express companies, and some tourist agencies. They are usually promises to pay on demand even amounts, such as $10, $20, $50, and $100. (See Fig. 7.)

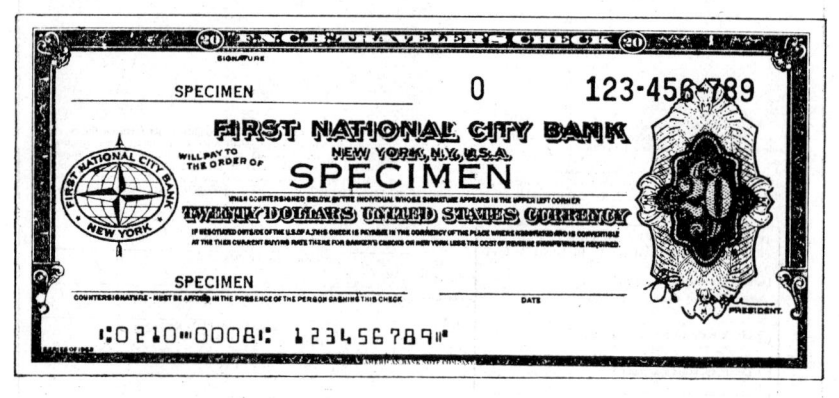

Fig. 7. Traveler's check.

The buyer of the checks signs each check at the time of purchase, and again on presentation for payment. Comparison of the two signatures establishes his identity. Travelers' checks are generally accepted as demand exchange, and in the United States may pass virtually as currency. The checks are usually sold for their face amount plus a commission of 1%.

AMERICAN DEPOSITARY RECEIPT. The international departments of U.S. banks also facilitate purchases by Americans of foreign securities, thus making available dollar exchange for countries abroad. Although the technique of flotation and trading of foreign bond issues stated in U.S. dollars is similar to the procedure followed in the sale of domestic obligations, trading in stocks of foreign corporations differs greatly in its mechanics from the methods involved in this country. Aside from the different laws, regulations, customs, and expenses involved in dealing in foreign equities, the greatest obstacle is the European practice of issuing bearer stock certificates with **annexed dividend coupons.** American investors, used to holding negotiable stock certificates registered in their names and receiving by mail dividend checks, stock dividends, subscription rights, voting proxies, and annual reports, are generally unwilling to hold bearer certificates and to forgo direct contact with the corporation. Moreover, obtaining information about declaration of dividends and their collection and exchange into dollars is a cumbersome procedure.

To overcome these difficulties, the Guaranty Trust Company of New York (now merged into the Morgan Guaranty Trust Co. of N.Y.), in cooperation with a number of leading brokerage firms in New York and abroad and with several stock exchanges, devised in 1927 an American Depositary Receipt (A.D.R.). This instrument is a negotiable receipt, registered in the owner's name, for a **stated number of shares of a foreign corporation** issued by the trust departments of large New York City commercial banks (the Depositaries) upon receipt of notice from their branches or correspondents abroad that a certain number of shares of the foreign corporation has been deposited with them for account of the U.S. resident. The A.D.R. stipulates that the foreign securities will be held in custody as long as the A.D.R. is outstanding. A.D.R.'s are **transferable** at the office of the Depositaries with the same facility as domestic stock certificates. Dividends are disbursed by the Depositaries in dollar checks to the registered holders. When rights for additional stock offerings are issued by the foreign corporations to shareholders, they cannot be exercised by holders of A.D.R.'s unless the foreign corporation has registered the securities with the S.E.C. Consequently, the rights are sold abroad and the dollar proceeds are distributed to holders of the A.D.R.'s.

Region	Number of Listings	Stocks	Corporate Bonds	Government Bonds	Total
Africa	6	139.5	...	15.7	155.2
Asia	21	30.4	2.3	241.4	274.1
Australasia	22	...	...	424.0	424.0
Europe	106	1525.2	200.7	842.3	2568.1
Cent. & S. America	92	...	6.8	131.0	137.8
North America	31	6632.1	143.9	224.7	7000.8
Total	278	8327.2	353.7	1879.1	10560.0

Figures may not add up because of rounding.

Fig. 8. Foreign securities listings, 1966 (market value, millions of dollars). (Source: N.Y.S.E. Fact Book 1967, p. 26.)

Sale of foreign shares in the American market is completed by delivery of the A.D.R. in blank. Holders of A.D.R.'s may at any time demand delivery of the underlying shares or sell the shares in a foreign market, surrender their A.D.R.'s to the Depositaries here, and have the foreign shares delivered to a designated party abroad.

Foreign securities are traded regularly in New York, predominantly in the over-the-counter market, although foreign dollar bonds and stocks of a number of foreign companies are listed on the New York Stock Exchange. As of the end of 1966 the total market value of foreign securities listed on the N.Y.S.E. exceeded $10 billion, distributed as in Fig. 8.

U.S. Government and International Agencies

BACKGROUND. The huge financial resources required to rebuild the war-shattered economics of the belligerent countries and to promote the development of the economically backward areas after World War II could not be supplied by private capital alone. The **postwar problems of foreign trade and investment** were complicated by the lack of currency convertibility and by political instability in many areas. To help solve these problems the U.S. government inaugurated a comprehensive **foreign aid program** and also participated in the establishment of a number of **international financial institutions.** U.S. and international agencies have played an increasingly important part in financing and stimulating foreign trade and investment. Their major functions and operations are summarized below.

THE U.S. EXPORT–IMPORT BANK. In 1934 the United States government entered the field of foreign banking by organizing the Export-Import Bank, which in 1945 was made an independent agency of the Federal government. The Bank is empowered to do a general banking business and to make any type of loan for the purpose of "aiding in the financing and facilitating of exports and imports and the exchange of commodities between the United States or any of its territories or insular possessions and any foreign country or the agencies or nationals thereof."

The Bank makes **long-term loans** to finance purchases of U.S. equipment, goods, and services for projects undertaken by private enterprises or governments abroad and guarantees direct loans extended by financial institutions to overseas buyers. It also finances or guarantees payment of **medium-term commercial export credits** granted by exporters and, in partnership with private insurance companies, offers **short- and medium-term export credit insurance.**

To supplement its capital stock of $1 billion subscribed by the government, the Bank is authorized to borrow from the Treasury on a revolving basis up to $6 billion outstanding at any one time. Although there is a ceiling of $7 billion on its lending operations, the Bank can handle a larger amount of business through participation by private banks in credits advanced and through sales by the Bank of paper from its portfolio without guaranty or endorsement.

In 1966, a new program became operational under which commercial banks are able to borrow from Eximbank against their holdings of certain debt obligations relating to exports. Since September 1967, commercial banks have also been able to borrow on the increase of their total export loan portfolio over that of the preceding year. During the fiscal year ending 1966, total new authorizations for loans, guarantees, and insurance exceeded $2 billion.

THE U.S. AGENCY FOR INTERNATIONAL DEVELOPMENT (A.I.D.) This agency was created in 1961 by combining the International Cooperation Administration (I.C.A.), the Development Loan Fund (D.L.F.), and certain other smaller units. The D.L.F. was incorporated in 1958 by Congress as an independent government operation to serve as an additional source of financing economic development in the free world and "to minimize or eliminate barriers to the flow of private investment capital and international trade." The D.L.F. was authorized to enter into financing arrangements with U.S. and foreign private corporations, governments, or governmental entities and to provide partial or full guaranties to private lenders for approved projects abroad. The I.C.A. insured U.S. private investors abroad against losses resulting from exchange restrictions on transfer of earnings and repatriation of capital and against nationalization, confiscation, or war damage.

At present A.I.D. extends **three forms of insurance:** extended risk guarantees, specific risk guarantees, and Latin American housing guarantees. A.I.D. guarantees cover such risks as loss of investment due to expropriation, nationalization, or confiscation (by a foreign government); damage to investment due to war, insurrection, or revolution; and inability to convert earnings or original investment into dollars due to foreign exchange controls.

THE INTERNATIONAL MONETARY FUND AND THE WORLD BANK. A new approach to the solution of the recurrent troublesome problems of unbalanced international payments, currency depreciation, and exchange restrictions was launched when the **United Nations Monetary Conference at Bretton Woods,** comprising delegates of 44 countries, adopted in 1944 two agreements, to set up an International Monetary Fund (I.M.F.) and an International Bank for Reconstruction and Development (World Bank). These agreements went into effect in 1946.

International Monetary Fund. The Fund was established with an initial capital of $7.7 billion, which was thereafter increased on several occasions. As of April 1967, the Fund's capital was $21 billion. The main **functions of the Fund** are to promote international monetary cooperation, facilitate the expansion of international trade, promote exchange stability, prevent competitive currency depreciation, gradually remove foreign exchange restrictions, and grant member countries foreign exchange loans to correct temporary disequilibria in their balance of payments.

To become a member of the Fund, a country must make a capital subscription and pay 25% in gold. The initial 1947 quotas were based on each country's volume of international trade, which is still the main criterion for quota increases. Each participating country may borrow foreign exchange up to 200% of its quota. An additional facility, established in 1963 and revised and expanded in 1966, provides member countries with financing to meet temporary declines in the value of their exports. This compensatory financing, which may reach 50% of the member's quota, is separate from the other drawing facilities of the Fund.

To supplement its resources in 1962, the Fund entered into borrowing agreements with ten major industrial countries. Under these agreements the Fund is empowered to borrow from these countries a total amount exceeding $5 billion. The present termination date of these agreements is October 1970. As of April 1967, the total outstanding drawings of the 106 member countries from the Fund exceeded $5 billion.

International Bank for Reconstruction and Development (World Bank). The Bank had an initial capital of $9.1 billion. By June 1967, this amount had been increased to almost $23 billion, of which $2.3 billion was paid in.

The Bank grants or guarantees long-term foreign currency loans to member countries facing difficulties to borrow elsewhere on reasonable terms for specific approved productive projects. Its loans are heavily concentrated in areas such as electric power and transportation, which require capital investments of a size underdeveloped nations would find difficulty in raising externally. The Bank is also a major borrower in the world's capital markets. By June 1967, over $3 billion had been raised in this manner, thus supplementing the Bank's own resources to support a loan portfolio of nearly $5 billion. During the fiscal year ended 1967, over $0.8 billion in new commitments were undertaken.

THE INTERNATIONAL FINANCE CORPORATION (I.F.C.). The I.F.C. was organized in 1956 as an affiliate of the World Bank to undertake, in association with private investors, **long-term financing** on an equity basis or through loans to productive private enterprises in member countries, particularly in less developed areas. The I.F.C. was intended to supplement the work of the World Bank by engaging in activities not permitted to the Bank. Unlike the latter, the I.F.C. does not require government guarantees. As of mid-1967, the I.F.C. had 83 members and a capital of $100 million. The scope of its activities is much smaller than that of the World Bank, and as of 1967 total commitments had reached only $220 million. It has also attracted to its projects private capital amounting to several times its own investments.

THE INTERNATIONAL DEVELOPMENT ASSOCIATION (I.D.A.). This second affiliate of the World Bank was created in September 1960 for the primary purpose of making **development loans** to member countries whose balance of payments prospects would not justify their borrowing abroad on conventional terms. The Articles of Agreement stipulate that the forms and terms of the loans shall be such as I.D.A. "may deem appropriate." So far, all development credits have been made to member governments. The loans are repayable in foreign exchange but on very **lenient terms**: over a 50-year period without interest.

The initial capital of I.D.A. was set at $1 billion. By June 1967, $0.5 billion had been added to this account, and $0.2 billion in grants were obtained from the World Bank, bringing total equity to $1.7 billion. Loans outstanding as of the same date amounted to $1 billion.

THE INTER-AMERICAN DEVELOPMENT BANK. The Inter-American Development Bank, of which all American republics except Cuba are members, commenced operations in October 1960. It is a regional bank designed to accelerate economic development in Latin America. The United States is the principal subscriber, and the 19 Latin American countries are both borrowers and lenders. As of December 1966, the Bank's capital amounted to $2.1 billion, of which $0.4 billion was paid in. To supplement these resources, about $0.4 billion had been borrowed in the world's capital markets at competitive interest rates. The Bank makes economic development loans to private enterprises and public bodies that are repayable in the currency in which the loan is made. In 1966, 68 loans totaling $396 million were authorized.

The Bank has a **Fund for Special Operations** with its own capital. Since Fund loans may be extended "on terms and conditions appropriate for dealing with special circumstances arising in specific countries," the terms are usually more liberal than for ordinary loans.

Under an agreement with the United States, the Bank became the administrator of the **Social Progress Trust Fund,** set up to grant loans and technical assistance for social development. As administrator, the Bank is authorized to enter into commitments of up to $525 million, to be drawn from the U.S. Treasury as needed.

SECTION 4

SAVINGS INSTITUTIONS

CONTENTS

Role of Savings Institutions

	PAGE
Direct vs. indirect investment	1
Principal types of savings institutions	1
Purposes of the saver	1
Estimated savings of individuals, in selected media (f. 1)	2
Services and characteristics	3
Change in importance	3

Savings Banking

Function of savings banking	3
Types of savings banks	3
Mutual savings banks	4
Management and ownership	4
Savings accounts	5
Special accounts and services	5
Investments of mutual savings banks	5
Investment problems of mutual savings banks	8
Statement of condition of New York State savings banks (f. 2)	9
The Savings Banks Trust Company	10
The Institutional Securities Corporation	10
Savings bank policy	11
Savings departments of commercial banks	11
Postal savings	12

Savings and Loan Associations

General characteristics	12
Operations	13
Types of accounts	13
Loans and investments	14
Non-real estate loans and investments	14
Federal Home Loan bank system	15
Savings and loan insurance	15

Credit Unions

Functions and operations	16
Organization and membership	16
Loans and charges	17

Taxation of Banks and Mutual Thrift Institutions

Federal tax provisions	17
Allocation of net income before Federal taxes, tax-free additions to reserves, and interest on time and savings deposits, all insured commercial banks	

	PAGE
and all insured mutual savings banks, 1958 (f. 3)	18
Revisions in 1962	19

Trust Companies and Trust Departments

Functions, responsibilities, and services	19

Investment Companies

Nature and purpose	19
Characteristics of investment companies	20
Investment profits	20
The age factor	21
The risk factor	21
The capital market factor	21
The credit cycle factor	21
The government factor	22
Extent of managerial discretion	22
Classification of investment companies	22
Growth of investment company assets since 1940 (f. 4)	23
Management investment companies	23
Closed-end vs. open-end companies	24
Leverage	24
Investment policy	24
Diversified and nondiversified companies	25
Common trust funds	25
Unit or fixed trusts	26
Periodic payment plans	26
Operation	26
Companies issuing face amount installment certificates	27
Accounting problems	27
Annual report	27
Balance sheet of a closed-end investment company (f. 5)	28
Statement of ordinary income of a closed-end management investment company (f. 6)	28
Statement of net assets of an open-end investment company (f. 7)	29
Statement of changes in the net assets of an open-end investment company (f. 8)	29
Taxation	30
State taxes	31
Regulation	31
Investment Company Act	31
Investment Company Institute	33
Investment counsel	33
The Investment Advisers Act of 1940	33

CONTENTS (*Continued*)

Life Insurance Companies

	Page
Savings aspects of life insurance	34
Savings and insurance elements of leading forms of policies (insured at age 35) (*f.* 9)	35
Savings element varies with form of policy	35
Premiums and dividends	36
Participating feature	36
Settlements of policies	36
Ceasing premium payments	36
Policy settlements with beneficiaries	36
Place of life insurance in savings picture	37
Life insurance companies as investors	37
Investment of all United States life insurance companies (*f.* 10)	38

SECTION 4

SAVINGS INSTITUTIONS

Role of Savings Institutions

DIRECT VS. INDIRECT INVESTMENT. Aside from mere hoarding, the saver has two major alternatives in the use of his funds. The first is **direct investment.** He may engage in business alone or with others, acquire real estate, or purchase securities in the open market. If he prefers, he may take a creditor instead of an equity position and purchase mortgages or bonds. These securities he may acquire direct from the issuer, from investment bankers, or through stock brokers. In recent years, government bonds—for the small saver, government savings bonds—have bulked large among available investments.

The other alternative open to the saver, and the principal avenue utilized by small savers, is that of **indirect investment.** The saver may entrust the task of employing his funds to one or more savings institutions designed to serve different types of savers.

Principal Types of Savings Institutions. The principal savings institutions are:

1. Savings banks, and savings departments of commercial banks.
2. Savings and loan associations.
3. Credit unions.
4. Trustees under both living and testamentary trusts, chiefly trust companies and trust departments of banks.
5. Investment companies, including mutual funds.
6. Life insurance companies, which also write annuities.

PURPOSES OF THE SAVER. The saver redistributes his money income over time by restricting present spending for consumption or by utilizing income not required for consumption. In so far as saving is rational, it reflects the saver's realization that his income may become inadequate at some later date in relation to needed expenditures. On the basis of the economic hazards (aside from inflation) that give rise to this uncertainty, the **major purposes** of the saver may be classified as follows:

1. Security
    a. Emergency, whether as added expense (such as maternity), reduced income (such as loss of job), or a planned contingency (such as education).
    b. Either maintenance of one's standard of living by provision of a retirement income for old age or infirmity, or raising the future standard of living by providing a supplementary income.
    c. Provision for dependents after death.
2. Provision of permanent assets, such as a home.
3. Gratification of certain more temporary desires, such as a car, clothes, or a vacation.
4. A large and growing part of saving is compulsory or contractual through pension plans, the social security system, and life insurance premiums.

End of Year	Commercial Banks	Per Cent of Total	Mutual Savings Banks	Per Cent of Total	Savings & Loan Associations	Per Cent of Total	Postal Savings	Per Cent of Total	U.S. Government Savings Bonds	Per Cent of Total	Life Insurance Companies	Per Cent of Total	Credit Unions	Per Cent of Total	Total
					(in millions of dollars)										
1920	$10,546	44.8	$4,806	20.5	$1,741	7.4	$166	0.7	$761	3.2	$5,488	23.4	$7	..	$23,515
1930	18,647	38.6	9,384	19.4	6,296	13.0	250	0.6	..	..	13,690	28.3	37	0.1	48,304
1933	10,979	26.7	9,506	23.1	4,750	11.5	1,229	3.0	..	..	14,613	35.6	40	0.1	41,117
1940	15,403	26.0	10,618	17.9	4,272	7.2	1,342	2.2	2,753	4.6	24,663	41.7	235	0.4	59,286
1945	29,929	22.0	15,332	11.3	7,365	5.4	3,013	2.2	42,900	31.2	37,509	27.5	369	0.3	136,417
1950	35,200	20.0	20,010	11.3	14,038	8.0	3,035	1.7	49,552	28.1	53,630	30.4	892	0.5	176,357
1955	46,331	19.7	28,182	12.0	32,142	13.7	1,985	0.8	50,229	21.4	73,733	31.4	2,442	1.0	235,044
1960	67,079	21.4	36,343	11.6	62,142	19.9	836	0.3	45,642	14.6	95,758	30.6	4,982	1.6	312,782
1961	74,814	22.2	38,277	11.3	70,855	21.0	712	0.2	46,440	14.0	100,300	29.6	5,670	1.7	337,069
1962	88,063	23.9	41,336	11.2	80,422	21.8	591	0.2	46,868	12.7	105,100	28.5	6,300	1.7	368,680

Fig. 1. Estimated savings of individuals, in selected media.

5. Much personal saving—especially that done by the wealthy—is automatic. Income simply exceeds the desired level of consumption expenditure.

Individuals undoubtedly save most frequently to provide **security** for themselves and their families. As noted above, another important motive is to acquire specific durable assets (homes, autos, household appliances, etc.), although individuals of substantial means save almost automatically. **Savings of business concerns** are far larger than individual savings. Business saving occurs through retention of earnings and the cash flow provided by asset depreciation and amortization.

SERVICES AND CHARACTERISTICS. Savings institutions are designed to meet the needs of different classes of savers. The differing characteristics of these institutions frequently reflect differences in the size-classes of the savers that they serve. Thus, the **man of small means** trying to protect himself against an emergency may regard the savings account as safest and most convenient, whereas the **man of larger means**, eager for larger income or appreciation, may seek out an investment company. Again, an **individual desiring retirement income** can turn to an annuity, whereas another, seeking to make financial provision for his dependents after his death, can turn to life insurance. But the exact fields of service of the various institutions, and the lines of demarcation between them, are not clear cut. In addition, over the years changing economic conditions and government activity have caused considerable change in their relative status. For example, mutual savings banks have lost ground to savings and loan associations and credit unions, which operate over a nationwide area, whereas the savings banks are concentrated mainly in the northeastern states; and savings and loan associations and credit unions can usually offer savers higher rates of return on their funds because of their specialization in mortgage and consumer financing. (Kreps and Lapkin, Improving the Competition for Funds Between Commercial Banks and Thrift Institutions.)

Change in Importance. The changing relative importance of leading savings institutions since 1920 is illustrated by the data in Fig. 1 (Facts and Figures—Mutual Savings Banking, National Association of Mutual Savings Banks), showing estimated savings of individuals in selected media in specified years. The figures clearly illustrate the more rapid growth of savings held by savings and loan associations and credit unions as compared with those held by commercial and mutual savings banks. In addition, at year-end 1961, assets of all investment companies totaled almost $26 billion, a nearly fourfold increase over the $7 billion of such assets in 1929. (Arthur Wiesenberger and Company, Investment Companies, 1962.)

Savings Banking

FUNCTION OF SAVINGS BANKING. Savings banks exist primarily to serve savers of moderate means. The savings funds placed with them find outlets mainly in mortgages and United States government securities. Savings banks thus offer a convenient means for accumulating savings and safe-guarding the principal, while providing a modest return and enabling the saver to recall his funds readily.

TYPES OF SAVINGS BANKS. Savings banks are of several types:
1. **Mutual savings banks,** owned by their depositors and operated for their sole benefit by self-perpetuating trustees. This type dates back at least to Rev.

Henry Duncan's "Parish Bank," established in 1810 at Ruthwell, Scotland, and reached the United States in 1816. It is confined to 18 states (and the Virgin Islands)—the six New England states, the five Middle Atlantic states of New York, New Jersey, Pennsylvania, Delaware, and Maryland; Ohio, Indiana, Wisconsin, and Minnesota; and Washington, Oregon, and Alaska. At the end of 1962, there were 512 mutual savings banks with deposits of $41,335,600,000. (National Association of Mutual Savings Banks, Facts and Figures—Mutual Savings Banking.)

2. **Stock savings banks,** which confine themselves to receiving savings deposits but are owned by stockholders and operated for their benefit. Today, few such banks exist.

3. **Savings departments of commercial banks** (both national and state) and trust companies, which were given impetus by the permission granted member banks by the Federal Reserve Act of 1913 to receive savings deposits, and which are now found in the great majority of such institutions. Many small banks have more time than demand deposits. Commercial banks have become strong competitors of mutual savings banks even in the latter's own territory, especially since maximum legal commercial bank rates on time and savings deposits were raised by the Federal Reserve and the F.D.I.C. at the beginning of 1962.

4. **Industrial banks,** typified by the Morris Plan, were akin originally in certain ways to stock savings banks. At their inception around 1910 these institutions extended consumer loans repayable on an installment basis and obtained at least part of their operating funds from the sale of investment certificates or the receipt of time deposits; they thus sought to promote thrift as well as to provide loans to individuals. With the passage of time, however, they tended to enlarge their activities until now most have converted to commercial bank charters.

MUTUAL SAVINGS BANKS. In the mutual savings bank, depositors receive **"interest-dividends"** at a rate fixed or declared by the trustees of the institution from time to time. Retained earnings are carried to surplus accounts, the purpose of which is to protect depositors in the same way as do capital stock, surplus, and undivided profits in the commercial bank. State laws generally require that **surplus** be built up by setting aside a portion of earnings until it equals 10% of deposits. After surplus has reached a specified figure, additional earnings may be used to pay extra dividends. When the bank first opens its doors its sponsors advance funds to cover expenses and initial surplus; these advances are repaid (with or without interest) as earnings rise. Each new depositor shares automatically the protection afforded by the bank's previously accumulated surplus, thereby at once reducing correspondingly the extent or degree of protection enjoyed by each present depositor. Only as earnings are realized on the deposits he makes do his funds contribute to the growth of surplus.

Management and Ownership. Management and ownership are distinct in the mutual savings bank, since the depositors have no voice in its operation. The bank is managed by a **board of trustees** whose rewards consist primarily of honor and prestige. Generally speaking, a high tradition of trusteeship has developed over the years among mutual savings bank trustees; in the older mutual savings bank states, these trustee canons of performance have been crystallized into law. The result is that gainful relationships between a trustee and a mutual savings bank are rarely encountered, in spite of the fact that, in most states, the trustees of a mutual savings bank are a self-perpetuating body that elects new members only to replace those who die, resign, or are removed.

Savings Accounts. In an effort to confine the use of mutual savings banks to small savers and to avoid the disturbance resulting from sudden withdrawals of large accounts, state laws generally fix a **maximum balance** that may stand to the credit of a single depositor. In New York the figure was raised in 1920 from $3,000 to $5,000, in 1926 to $7,500, in 1951 to $10,000, and in 1962 to $15,000, exclusive of accrued dividends. The maximum for joint accounts is $30,000. A person may if he so desires keep accounts in more than one savings bank, or accounts for different members of his family in a single institution. The ownership of savings deposits is generally limited, however, only to individuals and nonprofit organizations.

A savings account is evidenced by a **pass book,** which generally is presented to the bank by the depositor in person or by his assignee when a withdrawal is made. Banking by mail is permitted. The bank must by law reserve the right to require notice of withdrawal, usually 30 or 60 days, but in practice savings banks customarily pay on demand.

According to the National Association of Mutual Savings Banks, New York, at the end of 1962, the average regular deposit account had a balance of $1,838; the dividend rate paid ranged from 2½% to 4¾% annually, with 355 banks paying 4%. The weighted average rate was 4.07%.

Special Accounts and Services. Since World War I, the emphasis in savings has shifted from provision for old age and unforeseen emergencies to more definite and immediate objectives. In part, this is reflected in the attitude of the "regular" savings depositor, but it is also evidenced by the growth of special types of accounts. Thus, many **savings club** plans are now offered to provide, through periodic deposits, funds for vacation, travel, education, Christmas gifts, or the purchase of a home. Under **industrial savings plans,** the employer periodically receives for deposit in a savings bank a specified sum from the wages of those workers who wish to participate. **School savings,** first introduced in 1882, seek to promote habits of thrift among the young. School savings and club plans entail much clerical work, but are encouraged as a potential source of larger regular deposits. At the close of 1962, school and formal club deposits accounted for less than one third of 1% of total deposits.

Since 1907 some Massachusetts savings banks have offered **life insurance and annuities** at moderate rates in limited amounts. At present, savings bank life insurance is restricted to the states of Massachusetts, New York, and Connecticut. The banks writing life insurance are required to invest a minimum amount in their own insurance department and in a central fund. The plan, which has shown steady progress, seeks to eliminate lapses of policies and costly solicitation and other expenses to which ordinary industrial life insurance is subject. At the close of 1961, savings bank life insurance was available through 320 mutual savings banks, and there were 828,000 policies outstanding with a total face value of $1.5 billion. (National Association of Mutual Savings Banks, Facts and Figures —Mutual Savings Banking.)

Incidental services rendered by savings banks include giving advice on family budgets, renting safe deposit boxes, selling savings bank money orders, selling foreign exchange and travelers' checks, and selling and redeeming United States government savings bonds.

Investments of Mutual Savings Banks. Most of the 18 mutual savings bank states have enacted legislation regulating the investments of these banks. Thus they have sought to protect the depositor and, in some instances, also to favor investment within the state. The **New York State law** has served as a model for a number of other states. As of 1958, it authorized the following classes of investments:

1. Bonds of the United States.
2. State and municipal bonds.
    a. Bonds of New York, and bonds of other states that have not defaulted (for more than 90 days) within 10 years or for the payment of principal and interest on which bonds the faith of such state is pledged.
    b. Bonds of municipalities in New York State; in states adjoining New York, provided they have 10,000 population and have not (for more than 120 days) defaulted wtihin 25 years; and in other states whose bonds are legal for investment, provided they are 25 years old, have 30,000 population, and have not defaulted within 25 years. For cities with less than 150,000 population and $200,000,000 of real property as well as for counties in which such cities are located, certain additional requirements exist as to ratio of debt to assessed value of real property (in general for cities 12% and counties 5%) and as to the power to levy taxes on realty without limitation of rate or amount.
    c. Bonds issued by public authorities in New York State.
    d. Canadian bonds; obligations of the Dominion of Canada or any of its provinces or those for which the faith of the Dominion or its provinces is pledged for payment of principal and interest, provided that they are paid in United States funds, have not defaulted for more than 90 days within 10 years, and the issuing governmental unit's debt does not exceed 25% of the assessed value of the property within its jurisdiction.
    e. Obligations of any Canadian city with a population exceeding 150,000, provided such obligations have not defaulted for more than 120 days within 25 years, total indebtedness does not exceed 12% of assessed value, and the principal and interest are payable in United States funds.
3. Railroad bonds, including equipment trusts. Mortgage bonds of railroads that have not defaulted on funded debt within the 5 preceding years and that operate 500 miles of road in the United States or have had operating revenues of $10,000,000 in each of 5 of the last 6 years, and that have covered fixed charges 2½ times in each of 5 of the last 6 years, including the last year. In addition, either dividends equal to one quarter the fixed charges must have been paid in 5 out of the 6 preceding years, or fixed charges must have been earned 1½ times in 9 out of the 10 preceding years, including the last year.

    Assumed and guaranteed bonds are admitted as well as direct obligations. Equipment trust obligations are limited to 80% of the cost of equipment and a 15-year maturity. Collateral trust bonds must be fully secured by other legal rail bonds of no longer maturity. From time to time, restrictions applying to the relation of earnings to fixed charges have been modified, notably since 1931.
4. Public utility bonds.
    a. Mortgage bonds of gas and electric companies that are at least 8 years old and have not defaulted within 8 years. Net earnings must have averaged 2½ times interest charges on funded debt for 5 years, as well as twice for the last year. Gross operating revenues must have averaged $2,000,000 a year for 5 years.
    b. Telephone company bonds are admitted under similar conditions, except that for the 5 preceding years gross operating revenues shall have averaged $5,000,000. Debt must not exceed a prescribed ratio to capital. Debentures are eligible under standards more rigid than for mortgage bonds.
5. Land bank securities.
    a. Bonds of the Federal Land banks and debentures of the Federal Intermediate Credit banks.

b. Bonds of the Savings and Loan Bank of the State of New York and bonds of the Federal Home Loan banks.
6. Real estate mortgages (including construction loans).
    a. First mortgages on real estate in New York State, or in an adjoining state, up to 66⅔% of the appraised value of improved property used for residential, business, manufacturing, or agricultural purposes, up to 60% otherwise.
    b. Loans insured by the F.H.A. or guaranteed by the V.A. Latter guaranty may be as low as 20% if the mortgage is a first lien.
    c. Up to 80% on owner-occupied single family residences, constructed within 2 years and located within 50 miles of the bank. (Limit 50% on value in excess of $15,000. Such mortgages must have monthly amortization and 20-year maximum maturity.)
7. Stock and debentures of a housing company, all of the stock or obligations of which is owned by one or more savings banks, under conditions prescribed by the State Banking Board.
8. Promissory notes payable in 90 days, secured by obligations legal for savings bank investment, or by a savings bank pass book; and promissory notes of a savings and loan association.
9. Bankers' acceptances and bills of exchange of banks or of investment companies, eligible for purchase by Federal Reserve banks.
10. Real estate, both banking house and lot, and that conveyed to the bank in satisfaction of debt, in lieu of foreclosure, or purchased under judgments, decrees, or mortgages.
11. Securities or any other property acquired in settlements or reorganizations.
12. Stock necessary to qualify for membership in the Federal Reserve Bank or the Federal Home Loan Bank, and stock and other securities of the Savings Banks Trust Co. and the Institutional Securities Corp., including participations in F.H.A. mortgages on real property located in New York State or an adjoining state, held by the latter organizations.
13. Obligations issued or guaranteed by the International Bank for Reconstruction and Development.
14. Corporate bonds approved by the State Banking Board upon the application of at least 20 savings banks or the Savings Banks Trust Co.
15. Stocks. Preferred stock, if the earnings over 5 years were 1½ times fixed charges and preferred dividend requirements, and that high in either of the last 2 years. Guaranteed stock, if the earnings of the guaranteeing company were 1½ times fixed charges over 5 years, and in either of last 2 years. Common stock of companies registered on national exchanges, if dividends were paid in each of 10 years and earnings were sufficient over the 10-year period to pay the dividends. Stock of a registered investment company wholly owned by savings banks and limited to investments of types legal for savings banks.
16. Corporate obligations not otherwise legal, but in an amount, together with stock investments, not to exceed surplus and undivided profits.

In order to promote diversification, New York State has also set **maximum limits** for certain classes of investments:

Mortgages and real estate, exclusive of F.H.A. insured loans, the guaranteed portion of G.I. loans, and bank buildings	65% of total assets
Housing company stock and debentures	5% of assets
Railroad bonds	25% of assets (10% in one N.Y corporation, 5% elsewhere)
Public utility bonds	25% of assets (2% in one gas and electric, 3% in one telephone company)

Bank deposits and acceptances	Smaller of 5% of savings bank's deposits or 25% of depositary's capital and surplus
Stock	50% of surplus and undivided profits. (1% of assets in any one company, and 2% of that company's stock.) Common stock of the investment company referred to above, ⅓ of surplus and undivided profits.
Canadian Government and municipal bonds	10% of assets and 2% of assets in any one province or town

In 1946 a new yardstick was introduced in New Jersey for qualifying railroad bonds as legal investments. Bonds could be bought under this law if coverage of fixed charges by the issuing railroad for the 3 preceding years was better than the average for all Class I railroads in the country, and if the percentage of gross revenues remaining after payment of fixed charges was greater than that for Class I roads as a whole. This law sought to permit savings banks to purchase bonds of financially stronger roads in bad times, when earnings and bond prices are low, as well as in good times when they are high. The fixed earnings yardsticks of other states admit to the legal list bonds of inferior quality in periods of large earnings, and force off the list during a depression intrinsically high-grade bonds because of a temporary decline in earnings. A single test of this kind cannot be applied satisfactorily to industrials because of their diverse character or to utilities because of their more uniform performance and wider safety margins.

Investment Problems of Mutual Savings Banks. Long ago the qualities that a mutual savings bank portfolio should possess were stated as safety, liquidity (in the sense of reversibility of the investment, to provide cash through either sale, maturity, or loan), and yield. Different sections of the portfolio provide different qualities, and the relative emphasis shifts as conditions change.

A brief review of developments in New York State since World Wars I and II provides a background for consideration of current investment problems:

1. The 1920's witnessed unprecedented growth in deposits (despite keen competition from other institutions), with high dividend rates and lucrative investments. Government bond holdings and cash fell off, while mortgage loans mounted sharply.

2. During the depression of the 1930's savings bank deposits were swollen at first by an influx of temporary funds. In self defense, banks generally reduced dividend rates, and some limited the sum that they would receive from a single individual. After a drop in 1933, when withdrawals were restricted, deposits showed a small but steady gain. Investments reversed nearly every trend apparent before 1929. Mortgage holdings contracted as a result of drastically reduced lending and the rise of foreclosures; the process of cleaning up the mortgage picture and working off real estate thereby acquired continued until well into the 1940's. Corporate bonds, particularly rails, fell sharply, but governments rose.

3. In the World War II era, government bonds became the most important investment for the large deposit growth.

4. The postwar years show greatly increased competition for savings funds from commercial banks, savings and loan associations, and credit unions. Prior to 1962 the Federal income tax liability on savings banks was almost nil; however, the Revenue Act of 1962 increased the thrift institutions' tax liability moderately. This increase may shift the investments of mutual savings banks

more toward tax-free municipal securities, of which they have previously held relatively small amounts.

Fig. 2 shows the condition of the New York savings banks at the close of 1962.

STATEMENT OF CONDITION OF NEW YORK STATE SAVINGS BANKS
December 31, 1962
(In millions of dollars)

ASSETS

Cash and due from banks	$ 556.3
United States government obligations, direct and guaranteed	2,693.6
Obligations of state and political subdivisions	300.9
Other bonds, notes, and debentures	2,204.5
Corporate stocks	429.7
Real estate mortgage loans	19,804.6
Other loans and discounts	331.5
Bank premises owned	180.1
Other real estate	13.2
Other assets	247.2
Total Assets	$26,761.6

LIABILITIES AND SURPLUS

Regular savings deposits	$23,866.0	
Christmas and other club deposits	16.4	
Industrial (payroll) deposits	50.2	
School savings deposits	51.9	
Other deposits	12.1	$23,996.6
Other liabilities		513.2
Surplus or guaranty fund	$ 1,705.5	
Undivided profits	436.9	
Other general reserve accounts	109.4	2,251.8
Total Liabilities and Surplus		$26,761.6

SUMMARY OF BOND INVESTMENTS
(In millions of dollars)

United States government obligations (direct and guaranteed)	$ 2,694
State and municipals (domestic)	301
Canadian government bonds	108
Railroads	255
Utilities	947
Industrial	237
International Bank	158
Others	499
	$ 5,199

Fig. 2. Statement of condition of New York State savings banks.

Despite increasing economic activity in 1962 and 1963, the general **level of interest rates** changed very little from preceding years. Yields on mortgages and Treasury bonds fell well below the 1959 level but remained above those of most earlier postwar years. Interest rate changes were in accord with the general

Treasury-Federal Reserve objective of maintaining short-term rates high enough to reduce the incentive to shift funds abroad, while fostering reduced long-term rates to encourage domestic economic expansion. This pressure on mortgage rates has given added incentive for mutual savings bankers to press for the application of the **prudent man rule**, which gives the savings institution wider discretion in selecting investments. At present, twelve states have statutes that entitle savings banks to invest a percentage of their deposits at their discretion or provide for supplementing the list of legal investments by action of some administrative agency. (Kreps and Lapkin, Public Regulation and Operating Conventions Affecting Sources of Funds of Commercial Banks and Thrift Institutions.)

The Savings Banks Trust Company. The depression of the early 1930's emphasized to savings banks the benefits of cooperating with one another. Mere amortization of mortgage loans and arrangement of maturities of bond holdings did not suffice, although membership in the Federal Reserve System and in the Federal Home Loan Bank System proved of limited significance. In July, 1933, the New York savings banks organized two institutions, owned entirely by themselves, to provide centralized machinery, the Savings Banks Trust Company, New York, and the Institutional Securities Corporation, New York.

The Savings Banks Trust Company receives deposits from mutual savings banks and can lend to them against suitable collateral, while the Institutional Securities Corp. may buy mortgages from them.

Besides acting as depositary and correspondent, the Trust Co. acts as investment consultant and trustee, as well as a reserve body and clearing house for information on matters of interest to the Savings Banks Association of the State and its members. Its **principal services** are:

1. Banking operations
    Depositary and correspondent.
    Paying agent for money orders.
    Custodian of securities.
    Agent or trustee in connection with readjustment of nonlegal securities, representing members on various institutional group committees.
    Reorganization of mortgages and real estate.
2. Specialized services
    Investment information.
    Analyses of securities proposed for legal list and recommendations to the State Banking Board of those deemed suitable.
    Analyses of bond portfolios for subscribers and rendering of continuous investment service.
    Research on savings bank problems.
    Mortgage and real estate information.
    Agent for banks undertaking housing projects.

The Institutional Securities Corporation. The Institutional Securities Corporation services mortgages and aids in the management, sale, appraisal, and inspection of real estate; through the sale of its debentures to the savings banks it provides an added opportunity for the investment of savings bank funds. **Departmental activities** are:

1. Mortgage and real estate servicing.
2. Appraisal service
    On properties serviced.
    Special appraisals on portfolio analyses and new loan applications. "Screening" of new loan applications for New York savings banks.
3. Mortgage servicing of corporate-owned mortgages.

4. Corporate financing, in sale of debentures and short-term borrowing.
5. Mortgage loans—national market
   Investigation and purchase of insured mortgages.
   Promotional efforts.
   Plans, procedures, and legal studies.
6. Mortgage loans—New York City.

Mutual savings banks in several other states have set up less elaborate organizations of this type. In 1932 Massachusetts set up a Mutual Savings Bank Central Fund, and a year later added deposit insurance. Most mutual savings bank **deposit insurance coverage** today is provided by the F.D.I.C., however. As of July 1960, well over half of all mutual savings banks, holding 85% of total mutual savings bank deposits, were F.D.I.C. insured. (Kreps and Lapkin, Improving the Competition for Funds Between Commercial Banks and Thrift Institutions.)

Savings Bank Policy. The savings bank faces the question whether it properly is merely the holder of the cash reserves that its depositors maintain against the emergencies of life, or whether it should be more completely integrated with the individual's financial plan. Savings bankers themselves differ as to the role their institution should play. Some banks have adopted "split" or **differential dividend rates,** designed to favor the saver as distinguished from the transient. A few, notably the Bowery Savings Bank of New York, have developed a composite plan; **"packaged saving"** as developed by that institution in 1945 applies regular deposits over a specified period to the accumulation of a bank account to be held against emergencies and a block of government bonds, with the protection meanwhile afforded by a savings bank life insurance policy. Much emphasis is now placed, however, on "saving for a specific purpose" plans, such as vacations, taxes, Christmas, education, and large consumer purchases..

SAVINGS DEPARTMENTS OF COMMERCIAL BANKS. Bank failures during the early 30's focused attention upon the position of the savings depositor in the commercial bank. There was, with rare exceptions, no complete departmentalization, nor were savings funds segregated from commercial funds and invested separately. Besides, investments were not restricted as was customary in mutual savings banks. Thus the savings depositors of a commercial bank were ordinarily under a twofold handicap: not only were they without the investment safeguards provided in a mutual savings bank, but their deposits were subject to notice of withdrawal in the event of a run, whereas demand deposits were not.

After the panic of 1907 certain states recognized a right of savings depositors to preferential treatment over commercial depositors and enacted remedial legislation. One state went so far as to require that separate capital and surplus be assigned to the savings department, and restricted the investment of the funds of that department. But in general segregation of assets for savings depositors was criticized as weakening the bank.

The establishment of the **Federal Deposit Insurance Corp.** in 1934 has stilled agitation for special protection to savings depositors. In so far as the Corporation's protection of $10,000 per individual account is regarded as inadequate or incomplete, the attack on the problem has been to emphasize measures to strengthen banks in general so that they will not fail. The Corporation has widespread **powers of examination** and may promote the merger of a weak bank instead of closing it. In order to reduce bank hazards, under the Banking Acts of 1933 and 1935 both the Corporation and the Federal Reserve Board were empowered to regulate rates of interest paid on time deposits, the one for insured nonmember and the other for member banks of the Federal Reserve System. This subject is discussed in greater detail in Section 5 (Banking Services and Procedures).

POSTAL SAVINGS. Government savings banks operated by the post office or by municipalities had long existed in European countries when postal saving was established in the United States in 1910. The system was at first made supplementary to existing banks rather than directly competitive with them, but in the view of bankers this is no longer true. In their view, too, the institution of Federal deposit insurance raises a question as to the justification for continuance of postal savings.

Depositors must be individuals 10 years of age or over and may have but one account. The limit to the credit of one depositor was raised in 1918 to $2,500, exclusive of accumulated interest. Deposits are made in round dollars, and are evidenced by nontransferable certificates in denominations of $1, $2, $5, $10, $20, $50, $100, $200, and $500. Advance notice of withdrawals may be required, as a postmaster may be temporarily short of available funds. Both deposits and withdrawals may be made in person, through a representative, or by mail. A withdrawal by mail involves money order fees.

The **maximum rate of interest** that can be paid on postal savings deposits held for one year or more is 4% per annum, and, on deposits held for less than one year, 3½%. Currently, postal savings deposits are earning 2% per year, compounded semiannually.

The Postal Savings System is administered by the **Postmaster General** and the **Board of Trustees of the System.** The former designates the post offices to act as depositaries, supervises their operations, and manages the Washington office. The Board, composed of the Postmaster General, the Secretary of the Treasury, and the Attorney General, has charge of the investment of deposited funds. A reserve of 5% of deposits in lawful money is maintained with the Treasurer of the United States. A small sum is deposited with qualified depositary banks, but the bulk of the deposits is invested in United States government securities.

At the end of 1962, the Postal Savings System held an estimated $600,000,000 in deposits, which declined steadily for 16 years in a row from a peak of $3,416,-000,000 in 1947 (see data in Fig. 1 on page 2.) Congress has been urged repeatedly in recent years to terminate the Postal Savings System because adequate facilities for the small saver are now provided by banks, savings and loan associations, and United States savings bonds.

Savings and Loan Associations

GENERAL CHARACTERISTICS. Savings and loan associations are mostly cooperative institutions that seek to encourage thrift and to foster home ownership. Dating back in the United States to 1831, they are also known as **building and loan associations** and (in Massachusetts) as **cooperative banks.** Although nationwide in scope and growing rapidly in the newer states, 40% of the associations are found in four states—Pennsylvania, Illinois, New Jersey, and Ohio. They may be chartered and supervised either by the state in which they operate or, since 1933, by the Federal Home Loan Bank Board. Almost one-third of the total number (including the larger associations) possess a Federal charter; more than half of these were organized originally under state law but relinquished their state charters. At the end of 1962, there were about 6,400 associations with assets close to $94,221,000,000. (United States Savings and Loan League, Savings and Loan Fact Book, 1962.)

OPERATIONS. The associations raise their capital chiefly by issuing shares. Under the old **terminating plan,** the shares matured at a specified date and the association was dissolved. Members joining after the association had started paid in the then book value of the shares. The **serial plan** admitted members in groups, each group constituting an independent series of shares that paid no accumulations and had its own maturity date. The **permanent plan** now in general use permits members to join at any time.

Types of Accounts. There is considerable variation in the terminology used by savings and loan associations to describe their accounts; however, there are three basic types: savings accounts, bonus savings accounts, and investment accounts.

A **savings account**—sometimes referred to as a **regular savings account**—of a savings and loan association is very similar to a savings deposit in a commercial or mutual savings bank. A passbook is issued to the savings account holder upon his initial deposit and dividends are added to his book at regular intervals. Additional deposits or withdrawals may be made by the holder of the account at his discretion. Many people make no distinction between a time deposit in a bank and a savings account in a savings and loan association.

Nearly all savings and loan associations offer plans to encourage systematic savings. A **bonus savings account** is a form of systematic saving in which the holder agrees to a definite plan of saving with the understanding that, upon completion of the plan, the savings and loan association will pay a **bonus dividend** in addition to the regular dividend. The holder of the account then either withdraws the funds or transfers them to another form of savings account. The holder may also withdraw from the plan before it is completed. Some savings and loan associations impose a system of fines to encourage holders of systematic savings accounts to stick to their original plans, but this penalty system is used much less often than it was some years ago.

Investment accounts, which are called **paid-up savings certificates** by some savings and loan associations, are designed for investors who have accumulated a sum of money. Certificates or shares are issued, usually in denominations of $100 or $200, to evidence the investment of funds. Dividends on the accounts are either mailed to the registered owners of the certificates or applied directly to other savings accounts that they hold in the association. The certificates are redeemable at the option of the holder.

Legally, savings and loan associations can require written **notice of withdrawal** before making payment to a holder of any one of the three types of accounts; however, in practice, the associations do not impose this requirement. If, in an emergency, an association does require notice of withdrawal, there are technical provisions that are unique to savings and loan associations. These provisions would permit them to stretch out the repayment period so that withdrawals could be paid in an orderly manner. Generally, in a state-chartered savings and loan association, the withdrawal requests are numbered as received, and, after the end of the notice period, the requests are honored in sequence up to a given dollar amount, depending upon the availability of funds. For example, if the limit were set at $1,000, all withdrawal requests would be honored in turn up to $1,000. If a savings account exceeded this amount, the unsatisfied portion would still be subject to withdrawal, but the request for the balance would be placed at the bottom of the list. This procedure would continue for as long as account holders requested additional withdrawals and the association had sufficient funds. **Insurance coverage** would not begin until the association was placed in receivership.

The **one outstanding exception** to this general procedure is found in New York State. A law passed there in 1958 requires that all state-chartered savings and loan associations pay out savings left with them (as requested) on 60 days' notice. If they do not, the associations will be declared insolvent and insurance coverage will take effect immediately.

Members of a mutual savings and loan association may exercise **voting privileges** similar to those of stockholders of a corporation and are permitted to cast one vote for each $100, or fraction thereof, of the participation value of their share accounts. A borrower member is entitled to an additional vote as a borrower, but no member may cast more than 50 votes. The association is governed by a board of from five to fifteen directors (approximately one-third of whom are elected each year for a 3-year term), which in turn elects the officers. In addition to raising funds through share accounts, Federal associations may borrow a sum not exceeding half their share capital, but advances from sources other than a Federal Home Loan bank may not exceed 10%.

LOANS AND INVESTMENTS. Savings and loan associations invest the bulk of their funds in loans on **real estate**. Federal associations are restricted, either by law or the standard charter, to **first mortgage loans** for not more than $35,000 on one- to four-family dwellings (including combined home and business properties), located within 50 miles of their offices; loans running between 5 and 20 years must call for monthly amortization but may be made for as much as 75% of the appraised value of the property, whereas loans running for less than 5 years need not be amortized but may not exceed 50% of the appraised value. However, 15% of the total assets may be placed in loans that do not meet the basic requirements as to size, location of property, or amortization.

The following types of loans are also permitted:

1. Loans authorized under the Servicemen's Readjustment Act of 1944 (G.I. bill of rights) by those associations that have amended their charter to permit such loans.
2. Loans insured by the Federal Housing Administration that do not violate any of the provisions of Sec. 5c of the Home Owners Loan Act. This serves to limit maturities to 20 years and to eliminate improvement loans under Title I, but loans up to 90% of appraised value can be made under item 3 below.
3. Loans under other plans and for greater percentages than the basic 75% and 50% mentioned above, with the approval of the Federal Home Loan Bank Administration. The latter has prepared a list of plans; these are geared to multiple dwellings and include various combinations of maturity, nature of property, amortization, and per cent of appraised value that may be lent. An association may amend its charter so as to permit its directors by resolution to adopt any such Administration plan. The basic purpose is to broaden service to borrowers in metropolitan areas, in which competition for mortgages is keen.

Although V.A.-guaranteed mortgage loans and F.H.A.-insured mortgage loans are permitted, these loans comprised only 11% and 5%, respectively, of total savings and loan association assets in 1962, as compared with 68% for conventional mortgage loans. (United States Savings and Loan League, Savings and Loan Fact Book, 1962.)

Non-Real Estate Loans and Investments. Loans may also be made to members against their shares. The Federal law limits such loans to 90% of their repurchasable value. Finally, Federal associations may invest without limit in direct or fully guaranteed obligations of the United States, obligations of or stock in Federal Home Loan banks, and in other securities approved by the Administration.

The **direct reduction** lending plan is employed by the Federal associations. This plan was initiated about 1910 to replace the earlier system whereby borrowers subscribed to installment shares which, when paid in full, were tendered in payment of the loans.

Savings and loan associations have been strong competitors of both savings banks and commercial banks in mortgage lending and in attracting savings funds. Because of the nature of their earning assets, they are able to pay relatively **high interest rates** to savers.

FEDERAL HOME LOAN BANK SYSTEM. The Federal Home Loan Bank Act provides a **central banking mechanism** for savings and loan associations. Under the Housing and Home Finance Agency, the Home Loan Bank Board supervises the Home Loan Bank System and the Federal Savings and Loan Insurance Corp. There are 12 Federal Home Loan banks; Federal savings and loan associations are required to be members and state chartered building and loan associations, savings banks, and insurance companies may become members or nonmember borrowers. The government provided the bulk of the initial capital of the Home Loan banks, which have issued consolidated debentures to supplement the deposits of their members and their own capital. The Home Loan banks keep an amount equal to their capital and current deposits from members in United States government obligations, in deposits in banks and trust companies, in advances running one year or less, and in securities legal for trust funds in the state in which the bank is located. Chiefly, however, they make either short-term loans to care for the temporary needs of their members or long-term amortized loans to provide funds to supplement their members' home financing program.

Advances are made to member associations against home mortgages, direct or fully guaranteed obligations of the United States, or stock in the Home Loan bank. Loans to one institution may not exceed 12 times its stock holdings in the bank. Acceptable mortgages are restricted as to size ($20,000) and maturity (20 years); 65% of the unpaid balance is lent in the instance of amortized and 50% of unamortized mortgages. The result is to make unavailable as security for loans from the bank mortgages that modify the basic pattern of Federal savings and loan association lending.

SAVINGS AND LOAN INSURANCE. During the 1890's and again in the early 1930's safety and liquidity became major problems for savings and loan associations. In 1934, insurance of savings and loan accounts was adopted to solve these problems. The **Federal Savings and Loan Insurance Corp.** was created (with capital of $100 million subscribed by the Home Owners Loan Corp.), with which Federal savings and loan associations must, and approved state chartered associations may, insure their share accounts. The admission fee is $400 per million; the annual premium is $\frac{1}{12}$ of 1% of aggregate insurable accounts plus other obligations to creditors. One additional annual assessment of equal amount is permitted to cover losses and expenses, but has not been made to date. When the Corporation's reserves reach 5% of its potential liabilities, premium payments cease.

The maximum **amount insurable** per share account is $10,000. Shareholders in an insured association in default are now protected in a manner similar to depositors in closed insured banks. They receive either cash or accounts of equal amount in other insured associations. The Corporation does not insure immediate liquidity of insured accounts, but rather protects shareholders against ultimate loss in the event of insolvency. Only indirectly, by lending to, or purchasing assets from, insolvent associations, or making contributions to them, as well as through careful supervision, does the Corporation seek to prevent defaults and thus to assure liquidity.

On December 31, 1959, the Corporation had assets of $348,650,000 almost entirely composed of United States government obligations. At that time, it insured accounts amounting to approximately $48,128,000,000 in 3,979 insured institutions, both Federal and state chartered, with assets of about $59,550,000,000. (United States Savings and Loan League, Savings and Loan Fact Book, 1962.)

Credit Unions

FUNCTIONS AND OPERATIONS. A credit union is defined by the Bureau of Federal Credit Unions as "a cooperative association organized to promote thrift among its members and to create a source of credit for useful purposes." Its members pool their savings by purchasing shares. Unlike the savings and loan association, however, lending is not for home building but for other personal needs, and closely resembles consumer installment lending by commercial banks.

Credit unions have been common in Europe. The first in the United States was set up in 1892 in Massachusetts, which enacted the first legislation in 1909. In 1921 the Credit Union National Extension Bureau was formed and drew up a standard law for enactment by the states. Credit unions are also, since 1934, **chartered by the Federal government,** successively by the Farm Credit Administration, the Federal Deposit Insurance Corp., the Federal Security Agency, and the Bureau of Federal Credit Unions of the Department of Health, Education, and Welfare. The Federal Act is typical and the description below refers to its provisions.

Organization and Membership. Credit unions are organized chiefly to serve groups of 100 or more persons having a close, common bond of occupation, association, or residence, such as employees of a company, members of a church, or residents of a small community. At the close of 1961, 85% of the 20,047 reporting credit unions were accounted for by groups whose common bond was through employment by the same employer. According to the Credit Union National Association, there were 20,902 active credit unions in the United States at that time, with a reported membership of nearly 12,839,000 and assets of $6,301,000,000.

Members of Federal credit unions are elected by a board of directors and pay a membership fee of 25¢. Each member agrees to save at least 25¢ per month toward the purchase of a $5 share. In most instances savings may be withdrawn at any time, but 60 days' notice may be required if the board deems it necessary. **Dividends** on shares are limited to 6%; they are voted annually by the majority of the members voting at the annual meeting, on recommendation of the board, from the balance of earnings remaining after expenses are paid and a reserve of 20% of net earnings (and all fees and fines) is set aside for bad loans. Dividends are paid only on shares fully paid on December 1 that are outstanding on December 31, in proportion to the number of whole months they are fully paid; they may either be paid or credited to members' accounts, at the board's discretion. In 1961, only 2.9% paid dividends of 2% and below, and 56.6% paid 4% and above. Most credit unions now provide life insurance without extra charge, based on the amounts the member saves and borrows. This has reduced the previously extremely small losses of credit unions to almost nothing. Only about ⅕ of 1%

of the loans prove to be uncollectable. (Credit Union National Association, Credit Union Year Book, 1962.)

The credit union relies heavily for its success upon the **close contact** among and the **interest** of an active membership. Thus each Federal credit union has an **educational committee** to enlist active membership participation, besides a board of five or more directors, officers, a credit committee of three or more members, and a supervisory (auditing) committee of three members. Much of its service is volunteered by the members or provided by the employer. Its importance probably lies more in the training it affords members in business methods, self-government, and prudent management of family finances, than in its accumulation of large amounts of capital.

LOANS AND CHARGES. Loans are confined to members for provident and productive purposes. The **interest charge** may not exceed 1% per month on unpaid balances, but small fines may be assessed for delinquency; the maximum charge on a $100 loan repaid in twelve equal monthly installments is $6.50. The term may not exceed 2 years, and partial repayments are usually required every pay day. The maximum loan is ordinarily $100 if unsecured and $200 if secured, but a credit union with an unimpaired capital and surplus in excess of $2,000 can lend 10% of that sum to one borrower. Funds that are not loaned are either deposited in a bank insured by the F.D.I.C., invested in direct or fully guaranteed obligations of the United States, invested in shares of Federal savings and loan associations, or loaned (up to 25% of unimpaired capital and surplus) to other credit unions. At the close of 1961, 75.6% of the assets of credit unions were in loans to members. Their reserves equaled 6.7% of outstanding loans and 147.7% of delinquent loans. (Credit Union National Association, Credit Union Year Book, 1962.)

"The **object of the credit union** is not profit," says the Bureau of Federal Credit Unions, "but service to its members." It is typically small in size; at the close of 1961, half of all credit unions had less than $100,000 in assets, and 90% had less than $500,000. The median asset holding for all credit unions in the United States was $92,000.

Taxation of Banks and Mutual Thrift Institutions

FEDERAL TAX PROVISIONS. For Federal income tax purposes, commercial banks, as "capital stock" institutions, are treated differently from "mutual" institutions—mutual savings banks, most savings and loan associations, and all credit unions. And one category of mutual institutions—Federal credit unions—is treated differently from the others.

Federal credit unions are fully exempt from **all** Federal, state, and local taxation, except property taxation. Their tax-exempt status derives from §23 of the Federal Credit Union Act of 1934, as amended, which states:

> The Federal credit unions organized hereunder, their property, their franchises, capital, reserves, surpluses, and other funds, and their income shall be exempt from all taxation now or hereafter imposed by the United States or by any State, Territorial, or local taxing authority; except that any real property and any tangible personal property of such Federal credit union shall be subject to Federal, State, Territorial, and local taxation to the same extent as other similar property is taxed. . . .

Mutual savings banks and **savings and loan associations** were also originally exempt from Federal income taxation, on the premise that (like credit unions) they were not operated for profit but were instead mutual, nonprofit, self-help associations. In 1951, however, Congress removed them from the list of tax-exempt organizations under §11 of the Internal Revenue Code and made them, like commercial banks, subject to the regular Federal corporate income tax. By this same revision of the Revenue Code, however, the mutuals were permitted, in computing their income subject to tax, to deduct:

(1) All amounts paid as interest or dividends to depositors or shareholders, or credited to their accounts; and
(2) All amounts added to reserves for bad debts until the amount of such reserves, when added to undivided profits and other reserves, equals 12 percent of the total deposits or withdrawal accounts of its depositors at the close of each year.

Commercial banks were (and still are) likewise permitted, in computing their taxable income, to deduct all amounts paid as interest to depositors; they are not permitted to deduct amounts paid as dividends to shareholders, however. Nor was this the only difference; another lay in the differential treatment for Federal income tax purposes of additions made out of earnings to bad debt reserves. In this respect, a commercial bank is permitted only

(1) To accumulate through deductions from taxable net earnings a bad debt reserve no greater than three times its actual average loss experience over a 20-year period; and
(2) In a given tax year, to deduct from taxable net earnings for addition to its bad debt reserve an amount no greater than is yielded by applying its average 20-year bad debt loss ratio to its outstanding (noninsured or -guaranteed) year-end loans.

This differential Federal income tax treatment was one of several factors that resulted in a strikingly different allocation of income as between commercial banks and mutual savings banks and savings and loan associations. This difference is illustrated in Fig. 3, which compares the 1958 allocation of net income before Federal taxes, tax-free additions to reserves, and interest on time and savings deposits for all insured commercial banks and all insured mutual savings banks. (The picture for mutual savings banks is practically the same as that for savings and loan associations, and for the same reasons.)

	All Insured Commercial Banks	All Insured Mutual Savings Banks
Net income before Federal taxes, tax-free additions to reserves, and interest on time and savings deposits	100%	100%
Tax-free additions to reserves	7%	14%
Interest on deposits	30	86
Taxable net income	63	.001
Federal income tax	25%	.0005%
Dividends to stockholders	17	
Added to surplus from taxable income	21	.0005

(Source: Percentages computed from data in Annual Report of the Federal Deposit Insurance Corporation, Washington, D.C., 1958, pp. 196–197, 218–219.)

Fig. 3. Allocation of net income before Federal taxes, tax-free additions to reserves, and interest on time and savings deposits, all insured commercial banks and all insured mutual savings banks, 1958.

Revisions in 1962. Public and especially commercial banker dissatisfaction with this differential income tax-treatment situation mounted over the years. In the Revenue Act of 1962, Congress again revised the tax treatment of mutual savings banks and savings and loan associations, although it again did nothing about the credit unions. Under the new statute, mutual savings banks and savings and loan associations are, in most instances, able to add only 60% of their net earnings, after interest payments but before reserve allocations, to bad debt reserves, up to the 12% limit; the remaining 40% of net earnings is taxable at regular corporate rates. The result of this **"60-40 rule"** is that mutual savings banks and savings and loan associations now pay a 20% effective tax on their net income after interest payments but before reserve allocations.

In implementing the new "60-40 rule," the 1962 Act distinguished between additions out of current income to (1) reserves for "losses on qualifying real property loans," and (2) reserves for "losses on nonqualifying loans." Additions to the latter class of reserves are now to be made on the basis of past experience with losses on these loans (as in the tax treatment of commercial bank reserves for loan losses). Additions to the reserve for losses on qualifying real property loans are based on the **largest** of: (1) 60% of net income, up to an amount equal to 6% of these loans; (2) the amount necessary to increase the reserve by 3% of these loans; or (3) an amount determined by actual loss experience on these loans. Tax-free allocations of income to loss reserves must cease when the total of both the reserve for losses on qualifying property loans and the reserve for losses on nonqualifying property loans equals 12% of deposits or withdrawable accounts.

Apparently, few mutual savings banks or savings and loan associations have a loss experience bad enough or a reserve for losses on qualifying loans small enough—i.e., less than 3%—to enable them to use the second or third alternative listed above. Thus the "60-40 rule" will apply to almost all the affected mutual financial institutions, giving them a 20% effective rate of tax on net income after interest payments but before reserve allocations.

Trust Companies and Trust Departments

FUNCTIONS, RESPONSIBILITIES, AND SERVICES. Trust companies hold a larger volume of investments for others than any other type of financial institution, but their dominant position is being challenged by the rapid growth of the closed- and open-end investment companies. They operate under strict regulation and will be surcharged by the courts for losses that may result from negligence on their part. Trust companies provide a variety of services ranging from mere custodianship to full management.

Operations of trust companies are discussed at length under Corporate Fiduciaries, Trusts, and Agencies (Section 6).

Investment Companies

NATURE AND PURPOSE. An investment "trust" or "company" is defined by the **Investment Company Act of 1940** as one engaged in the business of investing, reinvesting, owning, holding, or trading in securities (defined to exclude government securities and securities of majority-owned subsidiaries that are not investment companies) having a value exceeding 40% of its total assets (exclusive of government securities and cash items). Exceptions made by the law include security underwriters, distributors and brokers, banks, insurance companies, savings and loan associations, small loan companies, public utility holding companies, and charitable corporations, as well as companies demonstrating to the satisfaction of the S.E.C. that their primary business is of another kind. Popular terminology in many cases has improperly classified as investment companies enterprises that are holding companies or that carry on a finance or security business.

An investment trust or company proper is an agency by which funds of a number of participants are combined and invested in securities so as to **distribute the risk** and **enhance the safety** of the principal and increase the yield to the participants. It also provides **expert management** in order to assure the safe and profitable employment of the funds while avoiding, for the participants, the direct responsibilities of control, finance, and management that they would otherwise bear in connection with investing their funds.

Characteristics of Investment Companies. The investment trust or company has the following general characteristics:

1. It raises capital by issuing shares, frequently preferred as well as common, or, in some instances certificates of beneficial interest. Moreover, the investment trust commonly borrows by issuing bonds within certain well-defined restrictions, and occasionally in other ways.
2. It invests the funds so obtained.
3. It usually avoids controlling interests, which might destroy portfolio diversity, and so limits its participation in any one security that directive and managerial responsibilities are not assumed. It usually votes its shares with management but often does not exercise voting rights at all.
4. Other than in fixed trusts it undertakes continuing supervision of the investment fund on much the same principles as those that any conscientious trustee enjoying discretionary powers should apply in caring for moneyed estates.
5. Although each investment company plans its portfolio with its individual purpose in mind, it usually endeavors to obtain for its shareholders a return in excess of that ordinarily received on investments of comparable safety. This is accomplished in the instance of the typical successful investment trust as the result of most or all of the following:
    a. The favorable average interest and dividend yield that the trust may enjoy through careful selection of securities, which tends to be higher than could be obtained with equal safety if the capital were not sufficient for adequate diversification of risk;
    b. The balance of cash profits on sales of investment securities that normally result from managerial alertness;
    c. The spread between the cost of capital obtained through issuance of bonds or preferred shares and the actual earnings made by investing and reinvesting this capital; and
    d. The consistent accumulation of earning reserves and surplus, built up by regularly appropriating to them a portion of net income.

However, the investment trust cannot be expected to avoid losses in a declining market, since it neither liquidates completely nor sells short. Capital losses in a bear market must, with rare exceptions, be anticipated. Individuals who participate in such investment trust should do so with the thought in mind that participation will continue over a long period in order that they may gain the full realization of yields and growth. This type of investment is **not designed for active trading or speculation.**

INVESTMENT PROFITS. Well-equipped investment companies commonly realize capital gains on their investments, as well as interest and dividends.

These result from taking advantage of broad market movements or from the purchase of particular undervalued securities.

The following circumstances, among others, have been taken advantage of by successful investment trusts in increasing their investment profits:

The Age Factor. Between the intrinsic value of some new issues and estimates of value that an uninformed public puts upon them, there is occasionally a **broad margin.** If the issue is fundamentally sound, the process of "seasoning" that broadens marketability frequently enhances the price of a security out of proportion to any concurrent gain either in safety or income. British investment trusts have long been in the habit of acquiring securities at what proved an economic profit by subscribing at the time of underwriting, or by purchasing at a substantial deduction from even the underwriters' figures in instances when a new issue of merit for some reason is not at first favorably received. The Investment Company Act permits American investment trusts to engage in underwriting as well as reorganizations, and the S.E.C. calls attention to "their potential usefulness in the supply of new capital to industry, particularly to small and promotional ventures," but notes that to date investment companies have not made use of the provision. On the contrary, American trusts have typically bought only seasoned issues for reasons of safety.

The Risk Factor. One reason why new issues are so frequently undervalued when compared with "seasoned" securities is the undue exaggeration of risk in the mind of the average investor by a sense of newness or unfamiliarity. The investment trust, however, will weigh risk more objectively. The result is advantageous purchases when market prices are depreciated out of proportion to the intrinsic value and the degree of risk involved. A well-managed investment trust can avoid losses involved in purchasing overvalued "legals" (eligible for savings bank and trustee investment) and certain classes of "gilt-edged" investments, prices of which have been raised by the artificially concentrated demand to levels unwarranted by their comparative safety.

The Capital Market Factor. The familiar circumstance that general levels of security prices, and the average rates of return on invested capital, vary from market to market and from country to country reflects variations in the demand for and the supply of capital in different centers. To what extent these differences in security prices between markets at any one time are due to varying risk, real or imaginary, and to what extent they may be attributed to comparative scarcity of loanable capital, are the business of the investment trust to fathom out.

Price trends among groups of securities representing different branches of commerce and industry often show wide variations within one country at the same time. This factor of price spread between different classes of commodities and different categories of securities is of the utmost importance in investment trust management.

The Credit Cycle Factor. No institutional investor can afford to neglect the **differences in average yield** on invested capital from time to time in the same country. Such changes in interest rates over a term of years tend to have a periodic character, and are intimately associated with the business cycle. They affect in different ways market values of fixed and variable income securities. In times of business prosperity, rising interest rates have often tended to depress bonds, though the greater safety of underlying assets, the larger earnings of the issuers, and the general buoyancy of the stock exchanges may exert a contrary influence on many issues. Common stocks, on the other hand, benefit markedly from rising earnings and brighter prospects at such times. In times of business recession, the contrary has usually been true, and the relative attractiveness of stocks and bonds is reversed. These movements were especially marked in the recessions of 1957–1958 and 1960–1961 and in the recoveries of 1955–1957 and 1958–1960.

The Government Factor. Since the early 1930's government has played a vastly increased role in business. Price control and allocations of materials during World War II exercised a major influence upon earnings, as have drastic **wartime changes in taxation** that have continued into the postwar period. The alert investment trust can both avoid the pitfalls and seize the opportunities created by the resulting changes in security prices and yields.

EXTENT OF MANAGERIAL DISCRETION. The great majority of investment trusts leave considerable discretion to their directors (within the guidelines provided by the stated objectives of the trust) in investing and reinvesting the capital entrusted to their charge. The **British trusts** place very few restrictions upon directors. General investment restrictions are frequently adopted among American trusts, but in most instances a large degree of freedom prevails.

Distribution of risk ranges from the broadest diversification to a spreading of risk merely within the specific investment field to which a portfolio is limited. In some instances, interests are concentrated in a single industry or in several related industries, while some primarily handle common shares and others fixed yield securities.

The most common stipulation among British investment companies is that not more than 5% or 10% of the issued share and debenture capital shall be invested in any one security or undertaking. Many American trusts follow a similar practice.

CLASSIFICATION OF INVESTMENT COMPANIES. Investment companies in the United States are classified by the S.E.C. as follows:

1. Management investment companies, both closed-end and open-end, usually referred to as **mutual funds.**
2. Unit or fixed and semifixed trusts.
3. Periodic payment plans.
4. Companies issuing face amount installment certificates.

Patterned upon British models, the investment trust has emerged as an important financial institution in the United States only within the last 20 years. The market crash of 1929 brought to an end a period of feverish promotion that had begun in 1927 and was marked by the investment by the American public in all types of investment trusts of almost $7,000,000,000. The substantial losses suffered by closed-end management companies discredited them and accelerated the rise of other types. Both open-end management companies and unit trusts rapidly increased sales of their securities after 1930, and the other two types also attracted some attention. More recently, unit trusts have fallen from favor; their creation was halted and further sales of shares in existing trusts largely ceased, a number having been converted into open-end management companies.

At the end of 1961, according to the Investment Company Institute, New York, the total assets of all investment companies equaled $25,994,089,000, increasing from around $1 billion in 1940. The number of shareholder accounts in 1961 climbed to 5,800,000, involving an estimated 3,000,000 shareholders. Part of this **growth in assets** has been due to the general advance in stock prices; however, more than $11.5 billion of new money has been placed in mutual funds since 1940. Gross sales of these companies were over $2 billion in 1959 and 1960 and almost $3 billion in 1961. In that year there were 169 open-end companies, with total net assets of $22,788,812,000, and 5,319,201 shareholder accounts. The 78 United States and Canadian closed-end companies' assets, including funded debt and bank loans, totaled $3,205,277,000. Figure 4 illustrates the tremendous growth of investment companies since 1940.

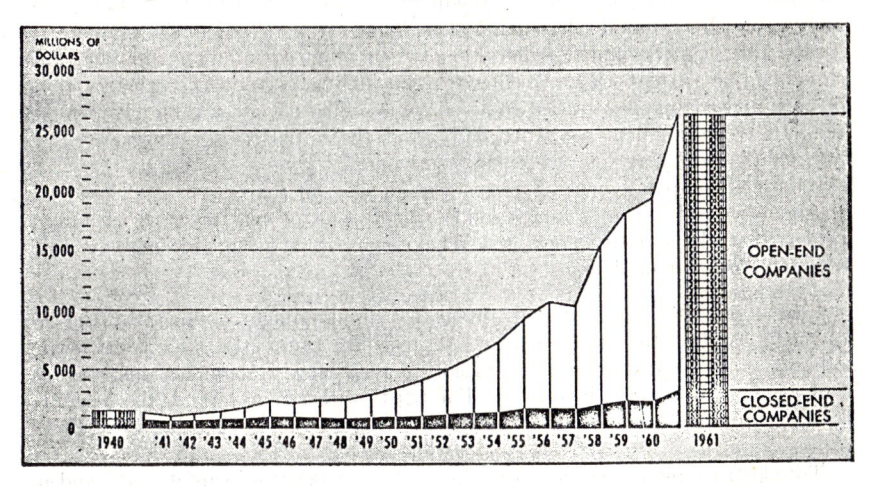

Growth of Investment Company Assets Since 1940

Year	Open-End	Closed-End†	Total
1961	$22,788,812,000	$3,205,277,000	$25,994,089,000
1960	17,025,684,000	2,083,898,000	19,109,582,000
1958	13,242,388,000	1,931,402,000	15,173,790,000
1956	9,046,431,000	1,525,748,000	10,572,179,000
1954	6,109,390,000	1,246,351,000	7,355,741,000
1952	3,931,407,000	1,011,089,000	4,942,496,000
1950	2,530,563,000	871,962,000	3,402,525,000
1948	1,505,762,000	767,028,000	2,272,790,000
1946	1,311,108,000	851,409,000	2,162,517,000
1944	882,191,000	739,021,000	1,621,212,000
1942	486,850,000	557,264,000	1,044,114,000
1940	447,959,000	613,589,000	1,061,548,000

Sources: Open-End—Investment Company Institute.
Closed-End—Investment Company Institute 1940-1946.
Arthur Wiesenberger & Company 1947-1961.

† Including funded debt and bank loans.

Fig. 4. Growth of investment company assets since 1940.

MANAGEMENT INVESTMENT COMPANIES. Management investment companies have no or only limited restrictions on the investments that they may make. They may be classified according to several criteria:

1. Method of operation—closed- vs. open-end companies.
2. Capital structure.
3. Investment policies.

Management trusts are incorporated mostly under general corporation laws and, in a few states, under the banking laws. There are no special provisions governing investment companies under the latter laws. In the early days of investment trust development, a number operated as **common law trusts,** and some continue to be so organized. Especially has this been true of Massachusetts.

Closed-End vs. Open-End Companies. The former have a relatively fixed amount of capital. Their shares are bought and sold in the market through brokers, and are usually listed on a stock exchange. Open-end company shares are sold to investors through investment dealers authorized by the company, at asset value plus a stated sales commission. They can be resold to the company at asset value, less a nominal redemption fee in some cases. Thus the shares of closed-end companies sell at varying relationships to asset values, whereas those of open-end companies are tied to asset values. The net asset value of open-end shares is usually calculated twice daily, and the initial selling charge averages 7%. One concern may sponsor several companies.

Open-end companies generally issue a single class of shares, whereas closed-end companies mostly have senior capital (bonds and/or one or more classes of preferred stock) and are known as **leverage** companies, although some have only common stock outstanding.

Leverage. Leverage is the advantage (or disadvantage) obtained by the use of senior capital. In a rising market, the practice causes the asset value of the common stock to appreciate more rapidly percentagewise than the trust's assets. But leverage also works in reverse. For trusts with senior capital, the declining market after 1929 served to magnify the drop in the asset value of common shares.

To take a simple illustration, a company has $20,000,000 in total assets and its capital is represented by $10,000,000 of preferred stock and $10,000,000 of common (one million shares). If total assets rise in value 50% to $30,000,000, the entire increase of $10,000,000 will accrue to the common stock, whose equity then becomes $20,000,000, a gain of 100%. The asset value per share would rise from $10 to $20. Conversely, if total assets drop 50% in value, the common stock equity is entirely wiped out and a further decrease would impair the preferred also. But if the market should rise again, the common stock can stage a comeback. Strictly speaking, in considering leverage there should be deducted from the working assets of the company static assets such as cash, high-grade bonds, and nonspeculative preferred stocks.

Leverage shares **move faster than the market** for two reasons: first, the leverage, and secondly, the premium or discount at which they usually sell. In prosperous periods, many leverage shares command a premium over asset value, whereas in depressions they mostly go to discounts. In part, the discount reflects the market's appraisal of management and the dividend policy. The premium commanded by high leverage shares with little or even negative asset value reflects its worth as a virtual option on a portfolio of securities above market prices.

The Investment Company Act restricts leverage. Closed-end companies must have assets equal to at least three times debt to borrow more, and/or twice preferred stock to sell additional senior shares. Open-end companies cannot issue senior securities, but may contract bank loans provided their assets equal three times such debt.

Investment Policy. Both closed- and open-end companies approach their **investment problems** in a similar way. The former generally have a more flexible investment policy, since open-end managements are more eager for continuity and regularity of income to facilitate continued sales of their shares. Most closed-end company portfolios consist primarily of common stocks, and turnover of holdings by the twenty-three leading companies in 1961 ranged between 4% and 51%, averaging about 17%. (Arthur Wiesenberger and Company, Investment Companies, 1962.) Although the majority of open-end company portfolios consist entirely or predominantly of common shares, investment policies vary widely. Some concentrate on diversified blue-chip common shares, some on lesser known growth or low-priced common shares, and some on shares in a single favored industry. Others try for a balanced portfolio in which a large proportion of the funds is placed in bonds and preferred stocks of good grade, whereas some concentrate on bonds or preferred stock. Certain trusts seek to remain fully invested at all times, whereas others try to catch the market swings.

Open-end funds are now classified under four main headings. The most important are the **all common stock** funds, which seek to be fully invested in common stocks at all times. These trusts emphasize the **selection** of security purchases more than the **timing**. A second class is the **balanced** funds, which seek to hold bonds and preferred stocks, on the one hand, and common stocks on the other, in varying amounts reflecting the state of the market. Although few undertake to apply any particular formula plan to time purchases and sales of stocks, the pattern of their portfolio policies resembles that of investment managers who utilize formula plans to guide their buying and selling decisions. The objective is to buy stocks on a scale down, and to sell stocks on a scale up.

A third class of open-end funds limits itself to a **particular group** of securities, such as chemicals or natural gas issues. The fourth is limited to **bonds and preferred stocks**. The specialized and fixed income security trusts are relatively small in size as compared with the other two classes of open-end investment companies.

All investment trusts provide the investor with the **advantages** of diversification, selection, and continuous administration of securities. The investor pays for these valuable services ordinarily through a loading charge that is added to the price at the time of purchase and through an annual deduction from the investment income of a sum to defray the cost of operation and of the services of a management or sponsoring organization.

Diversified and Nondiversified Companies. The Investment Company Act distinguishes between these. A diversified company is a management company at least 75% of whose assets are represented by cash and cash items, government securities, securities of other investment companies and other securities, in which holdings of the securities of one issuer do not exceed 10% of the outstanding securities of the issuer or 5% of its own total assets. The nondiversified companies follow a policy of placing all or a considerable part of their assets in special situation investments; however, many variations are found within this group.

COMMON TRUST FUNDS. Similar to open-end management trusts are the commingled or common trust funds administered by some banks and trust companies. Such funds combine a number of small trusts, with each constituent trust participating in both assets and income according to its size. The purpose is to effect diversification, to facilitate efficiency in management, and to secure a greater yield on investment at a lower cost. Use of the device by national banks is regulated by the Board of Governors of the Federal Reserve System (Regulation F), which recognizes **three kinds of funds**—for investment of small amounts, for general investment, and for mortgage investment. Common trust funds have become much more popular in recent years, and many commercial bank trust departments now use them to attract trust investment accounts formerly considered too small to be handled economically.

UNIT OR FIXED TRUSTS. A fixed trust is created under the terms of a trust indenture, contract of custodianship or agency, or similar instrument between a corporation (the "depositor"), a bank or trust company (the "trustee"), and the investors (the "certificate holders") who are the beneficial owners of the trust property. There is no board of directors. The depositor places with the trustee identical units of securities ("underlying property") of specified composition, and against each unit, representing an undivided interest therein, the trustee issues to the depositor a specified number of redeemable trust certificates that are sold to the public. For example, 2,000 certificates may be issued against each unit of four shares of the stocks of 28 corporations and the dividends and other property accumulated thereon. The offering price of a trust share is determined by dividing the total value of the underlying property by the number of trust shares issuable against each unit, and adding to the result a **"load"** averaging 9% for charges and profit. The Investment Company Act requires that the trustee or custodian be an institution having minimum capital, surplus, and undivided profits of $500,000.

Unit or fixed trusts have been replaced by open-end trusts as a vehicle for broad popular investment in equities in recent years. However, the fixed trust idea has been experiencing a revival of popularity as a method of syndicating real estate investment. Under an amendment to the Internal Revenue Code, effective January 1, 1961, **real estate investment trusts** are given the same favorable tax treatment accorded to regulated securities investment companies. Qualifying real estate investment trusts are taxed only on retained earnings; the distributed earnings are taxed only to the shareholder. (For a further discussion of real estate investment trusts, see Forms of Business Organization, Sec. 12, page 9.)

PERIODIC PAYMENT PLANS. Appearing early in 1930, these were in essence devices for selling investment trust securities on a periodic or installment plan basis. Acquiring securities on a regular, budgeted schedule has become, in recent years, an accepted and popular method of putting money aside for the future. This trend has experienced tremendous growth during the past 10 to 15 years. In 1949, many mutual funds initiated informal plans, and, several years later, the New York Stock Exchange supplied somewhat similar facilities in its **Monthly Investment Plan** (M.I.P.). Today, fixed payment plans are growing rapidly. By the end of 1961, about 950,000 investors had contracted to make payments exceeding $4.6 billion into plan accounts. (Arthur Wiesenberger and Company, Investment Companies, 1962.)

Operation. The holder of a periodic payment plan certificate is entitled to receive only the market value of his certificate, which is based on the market value of the securities held by the investment trust underlying the certificate. Most plans provide that payments (in some instances, as low as $5 per month) be made to a trustee bank over a 10-year period, which amounts, less service charges, are used to purchase trust shares (usually fixed or semifixed) to be held for the investor's account by the trustee. **Loading charges** under the plan, which are relatively heavy, are in addition to loading charges on the trust shares and are usually deducted from the payments made in the early months of the contract. During these early months, too, lapses tend to be frequent. The Investment Company Act limits the sales load to 9%, forbids deduction of more than half the first twelve monthly payments to cover the sales load, fixes minimum initial payments at $20 and subsequent payments at $10, and requires that contracts be redeemable.

COMPANIES ISSUING FACE AMOUNT INSTALLMENT CERTIFICATES. Issued only by a few large companies, these certificates, in essence, are unsecured obligations to pay either a stated sum to the holder at a specified future date, provided he makes all payments required by the contract, or a cash surrender value prior to maturity upon surrender of the certificate. Lapses tend to be high, especially during the first and second years when the surrender value is small or nonexistent, although some plans permit reinstatement with credit for the amount paid in. As a result of the variety in regulatory provisions of the many states in which such companies may operate, there is no uniform reserve system required by law. The **Investment Company Act** sets minimum cash capital of companies organized on or after Mar. 15, 1940, at $250,000, requires maintenance of adequate reserves (duly computed in specified ways), and sets cash surrender values and rights of holders in event of default.

ACCOUNTING PROBLEMS. Under the Investment Company Act the S.E.C. is given authority to provide by rule and regulation for a reasonable degree of uniformity in accounting policies and principles followed by registered investment companies in maintaining their records and preparing financial statements required by law.

Every registered investment company is required to file both quarterly and annual reports in prescribed form with the Commission. In addition, the Commission receives copies of the reports made to the stockholders at least semiannually. In practice, many companies make quarterly reports. The annual report must be certified by independent public accountants selected by the directors and approved by the stockholders at the annual meeting.

Annual Report. The annual report must contain the following items:

1. A balance sheet accompanied by a statement of the aggregate value of investments on the given date.
2. A list showing the amounts and values of securities owned on that date.
3. A statement of income, itemized for each category of income and expense exceeding 5% of total income and expense.
4. A statement of surplus, itemized for each charge or credit exceeding 5% of total charges or credits.
5. A statement of aggregate remuneration paid:
   a. To all directors and to all members of any advisory board as regular compensation.
   b. To each director and to each member of an advisory board for special compensation.
   c. To all officers.
   d. To each person of whom any officer or director is an affiliated person.
6. A statement of aggregate dollar purchases and sales of investment securities other than government securities.

Figs. 5 and 6 reproduce the balance sheet (item 1 above) and the statement of ordinary income (item 3) of The Lehman Corporation, New York, a closed-end management company. In lieu of a balance sheet, open-end companies are permitted to show a statement of assets, a statement of changes in net assets, and a

THE LEHMAN CORPORATION
Consolidated Balance Sheet, as of December 31, 1962

ASSETS

Cash and Receivables:			
Cash	$ 1,590,771		
Receivable for securities sold	· 33,586		
Dividends receivable and interest accrued	655,116	$ 2,279,473	
United States Government Obligations (market)		36,241,900	
Other Securities (at market value):			
Bonds	$ 497,125		
Common Stocks	271,172,250	271,669,375	
Miscellaneous Investments		4,061,450	
		$314,252,198	

LIABILITIES

Notes Payable for Securities Purchased		$ 443,138
Depreciation on Stock Loaned		3,177,600
Reserve for Expenses		225,665
Tax Reserve (state and city)		1,420,000
Dividends Payable		14,062,416
Capital Stock and Surplus		
Capital stock		
Authorized:		
14,000,000 shares, $1.00 par value		
Outstanding:		
11,574,005 shares	$ 11,574,005	
Capital surplus and undistributed profits	270,819,550	
Net realized profit on investments and special dividends paid	12,529,824	294,923,379
		$314,252,198

Note: No provision was made for Federal income taxes, as the corporation has elected to be taxed as a "regulated investment company."

Fig. 5. Balance sheet of a closed-end investment company.

THE LEHMAN CORPORATION
Statement of Ordinary Income
for the Year Ended December 31, 1962

Income:		
Interest earned	$1,052,818	
Cash dividends	6,235,171	
Other income	155.203	$7,443,192
Operating Expenses:		
Directors' fees	$ 30,200	
Management compensation	225,000	
General taxes	81,710	
Other expenses	924,647	1,261,557
Net Ordinary Income		$6,181,635
Dividends		5,882,963
Balance		$ 298,672

Fig. 6. Statement of ordinary income of a closed-end management investment company.

statement of net asset values per share and dividends paid for the 3 preceding fiscal years. Fig. 7 reproduces the statement of net assets of the Massachusetts Investors Trust, an open-end company, and Fig. 8 the statement of changes in its net assets. This form has been termed the **"narrative,"** in contrast to the conventional form of report.

MASSACHUSETTS INVESTORS TRUST
Statement of Assets and Liabilities
December 31, 1962

Assets:
Investments at market value	$1,584,994,024
(Average cost per books $783,264,760)	
Short term notes	27,818,899
Cash	12,960,415
Dividends receivable	2,687,427
Receivable for shares sold	923,765
Receivable for investments sold	1,427,385
	$1,630,811,915

Liabilities:
Shares repurchase obligation	$ 1,152,191
Investment purchase obligation	585,850
Capital gains distribution	37,059,490
Accounts payable and other	231,195
Net assets based on carrying investments at market for 119,546,739 shares of $0.33⅓ par value each	1,591,783,189
	$1,630,811,915

Fig. 7. Statement of net assets of an open-end investment company.

MASSACHUSETTS INVESTORS TRUST
Statement of Changes in Net Assets
(On the basis of carrying investments at market value)
Year Ended December 31, 1962

Net assets, January 1, 1962			
Principal		$1,798,937,942	
Undistributed income		937,883	$1,799,875,825
Income:			
Net income for the year per statement	$ 47,662,963		
Equalizing credit	109,534		
	$ 47,772,497		
Less dividends paid		47,851,556	(79,059)
Realized Security Gain	$ 37,343,342		
Less Special Distribution		37,059,527	283,815
Increase in Unrealized Appreciation of Investments			(265,877,427)
Trust Shares Sold and Repurchased			
Receipts from shares sold	$ 113,225,876		
Less shares repurchased		55,645,841	57,580,035
Net Assets December 31, 1962			
Principal		$1,590,924,365	
Undistributed income		858,824	$1,591,783,189

Fig. 8. Statement of changes in the net assets of an open-end investment company.

The following comments may be made on these exhibits:

1. The stated **purpose** of the Massachusetts Investors Trust is "to constitute a conservative medium for that portion of an investor's capital that he may wish to have invested in common stocks believed to be of high or improving investment quality." The Lehman Corporation's broadly diversified list of securities—mainly common stock—emphasizes long-term growth.
2. **Basis** on which investments are carried. Both companies carry investments at market and also note valuation on other bases.
3. **Sources of Surplus.** The Lehman Corp. distinguishes between capital surplus (that may arise from original subscriptions by stockholders, reduction of par or stated value of the stock, or from repurchase of shares at less than book value) and earned surplus (or deficit). It further distinguishes between earned surplus arising from current investment income and that arising from realized capital gains and losses and recoveries on assets charged off, after deducting dividends paid from each source. If one bears in mind the fact that the shares of the Massachusetts Investors Trust were issued continuously at various prices (reflecting changes in net asset values), its statement furnishes comparable information, though arranged in a different manner.
4. **Sources of income and dividends.** British investment companies have traditionally ignored profit and loss on security sales in their income accounts, using profits to reduce the valuation at which the security holdings are carried in the balance sheet. Thus, other than in depression years the portfolio valuation is actually understated. In their earlier years American companies generally avoided such a rigid policy, but as early as 1931 the New York Stock Exchange recommended that profits and losses on security transactions be excluded from the income account and credited instead to a reserve or a special surplus account. A management company is now required to disclose the sources from which dividend payments are made—what portion comes from net income, from net profits on security sales, and from paid in surplus or other capital sources. The date from which the accumulated undistributed income and net security profits must be calculated is either the date of organization, the date of reorganization, the date of write-down of portfolio in connection with corporate readjustment approved by stockholders, or January 1, 1925.

TAXATION. When an investment company is taxed as an ordinary corporation, its shareholders are penalized as compared with investors who invest directly in securities. There is then triple instead of double taxation of income—not only to the corporation originally earning it and to the investment company's stockholders, but also to the investment company. The Internal Revenue Code now enables an investment company to eliminate the added tax burden. It will be observed that both the Lehman Corporation and the Massachusetts Investors Trust have elected to be taxed as "regulated investment companies."

To obtain **tax exemption,** an investment company must meet certain requirements:

1. It must be a domestic corporation—not a personal holding company.
2. It must be registered under the Investment Company Act of 1940, either as a management company or as a unit investment trust.
3. At least 90% of its gross income for any taxable year must be earned in the form of dividends, interest, and capital gains from the sale of securities.
4. No more than 30% of its gross income for any taxable year may be derived from sales of securities held for less than 3 months.
5. It must distribute as taxable dividends not less than 90% of its net income, exclusive of capital gains, for any taxable year. Such dividends may be paid the year following the realization of the earnings, provided they are declared not later than the due date of the company's tax return and are not paid later than the first regular dividend date after declaration.

6. At the close of each quarter of a taxable year:
    (a) At least 50% of its assets must consist of cash, cash items, government securities, securities of other regulated investment companies, and other securities limited to not more than 5% of its assets in securities of any one issuer and not more than 10% of the voting securities of that issuer.
    (b) Not more than 25% of its assets may be invested in any one company, or in two or more controlled companies engaged in the same or a similar line of business.

Investment companies that do not elect to be "registered investment companies" are taxed at the same rate as ordinary corporations.

Only 15% of dividend income is taxable, and distributions to shareholders are tax exempt to the recipient, as a return of capital, to the extent that net income is offset by capital losses (not offset in turn by earned surplus accumulated since organization). Common law or Massachusetts trusts are generally considered corporations for tax purposes.

Most **unit trusts** are so organized as to be classified as pure trusts. The unit trust advises beneficiaries how much of the annual income is taxable to them, and the several tax classifications of that income, including interest, dividends, capital gains, tax exempt income, etc.

State Taxes. In connection with state franchise and income taxes many questions arise, chiefly in allocating income and assets within or without the taxing state or states. Shares of investment companies, even though classified as pure trusts, are subject to original revenue stamp taxes and transfer stamp taxes in the same manner as shares of corporations. The Attorney General of the State of New York has ruled that for the purpose of the New York State stock transfer tax, the tax on the transfer of trust certificates is to be based upon the underlying stocks represented by the certificates.

REGULATION. During the 1920's investment trusts were subject to no special legislation. The **blue sky laws** of the various states covered sale of their securities to the public, while on June 6, 1929, the New York Stock Exchange through its Committee on Stock List issued **tentative requirements** for the listing of investment trust securities of the general or management type, which were revised April 22, 1931. These made certain requirements as to annual reports, accounting methods, and practice. In May, 1931, it further laid down certain requirements with regard to the association of member firms with investment trusts of a fixed or restricted character, whether in connection with organization, management, or distribution of their securities.

Investment Company Act. The S.E.C. undertook an exhaustive study of investment trusts between 1935 and 1941, on the basis of which Congress enacted the Investment Company Act of 1940. This Act regulates companies that do not come under the purview either of the Securities Act of 1933 or the Securities Exchange Act of 1934, and goes beyond these measures that rely upon publicity to correct abuses and deficiencies.

The **general purposes and provisions of the Act** have been stated by the Commission in its 10th Annual Report, 1945, Washington, D.C., as follows:

1. Honest and Unbiased Management. The Act provides for a degree of independence in management personnel by restricting bankers, brokers, commercial bankers, principal underwriters, etc., who may have a possible bias in the management of the company, to a minority of the board of directors. It also requires a minority of the board to be independent of the officers of the company. It prohibits self-dealing and exaction of excessive commissions by affiliated persons of investment

companies. Insider trading in the securities of investment companies is subject to the same regulation as that contained in the Securities Exchange Act of 1934. It enables the Commission to sue in the Courts to prevent gross abuse of trust and gross misconduct and grossly unfair plans of reorganization of investment companies. It makes embezzlement of investment company funds a federal offense, and prevents investment bankers and other affiliated persons from using their investment companies to assist them in their underwriting activities. It provides that an investment company may maintain its portfolio securities and other property in its own custody or in the custody of brokers only under or pursuant to the regulations of the Commission. Otherwise portfolio securities must be maintained in the custody of a bank. The Act also provides for bonding of employees having access to the company's assets.

2. *Greater Participation in Management by Security Holders.* The Act requires investment companies in their registration statements to designate their status as a diversified or non-diversified company as defined in the Act and to set forth therein a precise statement of their investment policies. The status and policies of a company as set forth in its registration statement cannot be changed without an affirmative vote of a majority of the security holders. The Act also requires at least two-thirds of the directors of an investment company to have been elected by the shareholders; restricts the period of effectiveness of management contracts to two years; and requires the approval of such contracts, and therefore in effect of the investment adviser, by the shareholders. The Act also requires ratification of the selection of the accountants of the company by the shareholders; investment company proxy solicitation is subjected to Commission regulation whether or not the company is listed; it is further provided that all shares issued by management companies after the effective date of the Act must be voting shares and requires preferred shares to contain provisions transferring voting power to the holders of such stock in the event of default in the payment of dividends.

3. *Adequate and Feasible Capital Structures.* The Act restricts, in the case of closed-end management companies, the amount of bonds and preferred stock which may be issued, a restriction which, speaking generally, requires closed-end investment companies issuing senior securities to have at least 50% of their assets represented by common stock equity at the time of issuance of such securities. Only one class of bonds and one class of preferred stock may be issued. Open-end companies are not permitted to issue any senior securities but may contract bank loans provided a 300% coverage in assets for such loans is maintained at all times. In the case of face-amount certificate companies the Act requires new companies to have a minimum capital of at least $250,000 and to maintain statutory reserves presumably adequate to mature the certificates. Restrictions are placed on the power of face-amount certificate companies to declare dividends where the effect of such declarations may be to injure the financial stability of such companies. In addition, face-amount certificate companies are not permitted to issue preferred stocks without an order of the Commission.

4. *Financial Statements and Accounting.* The Act requires investment companies to transmit financial reports containing prescribed information to their security holders at least semiannually. Power is given the Commission to obtain annual and periodic reports including financial statements. The Commission is also empowered to enact rules requiring the preservation of books and records which form the basis of such reports; to require financial statements sent to shareholders and the Commission to be certified by independent public accountants; and to promulgate uniform accounting rules.

5. *Selling Practices.* Particularly in the case of open-end companies, periodic payment plans and face-amount certificate companies, numerous abuses in selling practices were disclosed. These the Act remedies in general by requiring investment companies which were not previously required to comply with the registration requirements of the Securities Act to so comply. The Commission is also empowered to correct selling practices of open-end companies which may result in dilution of their shares or in unfair trading profit to insiders and dealers. "Switching" of open-

end investment company securities and those of unit investment trusts and face-amount certificate companies on a basis permitting reloading is prohibited in the absence of an order or rule of the Commission. In addition, sales literature issued by face-amount certificate companies, open-end companies and unit investment trusts, which would include most periodic payment plans, must be filed with the Commission within 10 days after use. Finally, in the case of the Securities Act prospectuses of face-amount certificate companies and periodic payment plans the Commission is empowered by Section 24 (c) of the Act to rearrange the form and items of such documents and to require summaries of information which can be prominently displayed in the prospectus. The Act also regulates the sales load which may be charged on periodic payment plan certificates and prescribes the form of trust indenture to be used and the charges which may be made by trustees and sponsors of unit-investment trusts including those issuing periodic payment plan certificates.

By and large, these objectives are achieved by affirmative statutory requirements or prohibitions, which the Commission's rules and regulations serve to implement. Remedies provided are in part criminal and in part injunctive. The Commission is also authorized to prepare advisory reports upon plans of reorganization of registered companies upon request of the companies or 25% of their stockholders, and to seek to enjoin plans it deems grossly unfair.

Investment Company Institute. Restoration of the investment trust field to public favor has been aided by this trade association (formerly called the National Association of Investment Companies), which embraces practically all the active management investment companies in the country. It works with the S.E.C. on basic rules, forms, and interpretative problems raised by the law; in cooperation with the state securities commissions it has prepared what is in effect a sales literature code for the guidance of investment company security distributors; it has participated in discussion of tax legislation affecting investment companies; and it has undertaken to broaden the scope of the industry's relations with the public. Unit trusts have no similar organizations; their selling practices, however, have been the subject of voluntary action through observance of the code of fair practice of the **National Association of Securities Dealers, Inc.**

INVESTMENT COUNSEL. The investment counsel is engaged in giving continuous advice on the investment of funds in the light of the **individual needs** of each client. It serves both individuals and institutions, normally takes no custody of securities, and rarely assumes sole responsibility for the management of an account. **Fees** are either a fixed sum or a certain percentage of the aggregate value of the accounts managed. The percentage often varies inversely with the size of the account and averages less than one-half of one per cent on large accounts.

The Investment Advisers Act of 1940. This Act was based on a report by the S.E.C., which is authorized by this statute to supervise investment advisers. The Act covers all individuals or organizations who for compensation engage in the business of advising others, either directly or through writings, as to the value of securities or the advisability of investing in, buying, or selling securities, or who for compensation and as part of a regular business disseminate analyses or reports concerning securities. It covers securities services as well as investment counsel, but exempts publications such as newspapers and magazines of general and regular circulation; brokers and dealers who give advice incidentally and gratuitously; banks; certain bank holding company affiliates; those who confine their advice solely to United States government obligations; and attorneys, accountants, engineers, and teachers whose advice is purely incidental. Persons not exempt from the Act must register with the S.E.C. except those who advise solely investment and insurance companies, individuals whose clients are residents of the same state and who give no advice with respect to securities traded on national securities exchanges, and those who have fewer than 15 clients and do not represent themselves to the public generally as investment advisers.

The S.E.C.'s duties with respect to registration of investment advisers are substantially similar to its duties relating to registration of over-the-counter dealers and brokers under the Securities Exchange Act. The registration statement for investment advisers includes, in addition, information regarding the education of the principals of the firm and their business affiliations during the preceding 10 years, although the Commission does not pass upon the qualifications of advisers. Semi-annual reports are required as to any changes in the business conducted.

The investment adviser cannot act as principal for his own account, or as broker for another, in a transaction with his client without first disclosing the fact to his client and obtaining the latter's consent. Use of the term "investment counsel" is confined to registered investment advisers engaged in the work defined above and whose application so states. The S.E.C. is granted authority to investigate **violations of the Act** and to obtain information by subpoena. However, it does not have power to inspect books and records, but it has a rather lengthy and detailed required list of information and records that the investment adviser must establish and retain for at least 5 years. Failure to do so may result in a fine of not more than $1,000 or one year in prison or both if the S.E.C. subpoenas these records and he cannot produce them in court. In the event that violation is disclosed, the S.E.C. may set punitive machinery in motion and may seek to enjoin violators and, under specific conditions, may deny or revoke registration.

Investment advising emerged as an independent occupation only after the first World War. According to the S.E.C., however, there were 1,664 registered investment advisers as of May 31, 1963.

Life Insurance Companies

SAVINGS ASPECTS OF LIFE INSURANCE. Life insurance is commonly regarded by the individual policyholder as a kind of savings. Most life insurance policies combine savings with insurance or protection elements. Here we consider life insurance policies only as an outlet for savings.

The savings aspect of life insurance arises from the use of the **level premium plan**, under which the insured pays the same premium year after year. Mortality risk rises with age; the insurance premium should increase correspondingly. Under the level premium plan, however, during the earlier years the insured pays a larger premium than required for mortality risk alone, the excess going into a reserve that covers a part of the face value of the policy. These excess payments accumulate in the reserve at compound interest, for they are invested in securities or mortgages. This **legal reserve** gives the policy its **cash surrender value** if relinquished by the insured, and its **loan value** if he wishes to borrow against it. Some companies make a deduction from the reserve during the early policy years to cover acquisition expense.

The legal reserve is actually an investment, rather than an insurance, fund. Life insurance may be regarded as:

1. A program to save a specified amount in a specified period of time, to which has been added a supplementary agreement providing that the beneficiary

shall receive that sum even though the insured shall die within the time specified.
2. A sinking fund designed ultimately to replace the economic value of a life.
3. A plan whereby decreasing term insurance (Fig. 9) is combined with increasing savings accumulations to provide a constant sum for the beneficiary. As the savings element—the reserve—mounts, the pure insurance or protection element falls.

Basis—$1,000, 2½% Interest on Reserves Using
Commissioners 1958 Standard Ordinary Mortality Table

	Savings Element (Reserve)			Insurance Protection		
	Whole Life	20-Payment Life	30-Year Endowment	Whole Life	20-Payment Life	30-Year Endowment
Net annual premium	$ 17.67	$ 27.24	$ 25.72	.....	.....	.....
45	167.90	280.22	262.37	$832.10	$719.78	$737.63
50	259.12	442.98	413.77	740.88	557.02	586.23
55	352.54	624.55	581.34	647.46	375.45	418.66
65	535.77	730.81	1000.00	464.23	269.19	0

Fig. 9. Savings and insurance elements of leading forms of policies (insured at age 35) (adapted from The Unique Manual and National Underwriter Life Reports, 1963).

Savings Element Varies with Form of Policy. The savings element differs in the different forms of policy, as follows:

1. **Term insurance.** Policies provide for payment of their face value only if death occurs within a stipulated period, nothing being paid in the event of survival. Although long-term policies (for example, running over 20 years) may have a slight cash value during part of their life, the savings element is negligible. Therefore neither term nor group or industrial insurance will be considered further here.

2. **Whole life insurance.** Policies, whether purchased by premiums payable throughout life (termed ordinary life or straight life policies) or during a limited period or until earlier death (such as 20-payment life policies), promise payment of the face value to the beneficiary if the policyholder dies at any age. The legal reserve under such a policy reaches the face amount at the limiting age of the mortality table—i.e., the age at which the oldest person is presumed to die. Most insurers, therefore, pay the face value to the policyholder if he lives to that age. All such policies involve a large measure of savings.

3. **Endowment insurance.** This differs from whole life in that the maturity is set for some lesser age, ordinarily one that most policyholders hope to attain, such as 60 or 65, or 10 to 25 years after issuance of the policy. Payments are made over a shorter period than in whole life insurance, and they contain a greater—in fact, a major—savings element. Endowment insurance is sometimes called "insured savings" because there is assurance that the goal of the savings program will be reached for the family, whether or not the insured lives to enjoy it.

These differences between the different forms of policy are illustrated in the accompanying table (Fig. 9). The savings element bulks largest in the endowment policy and least in the ordinary life policy.

PREMIUMS AND DIVIDENDS. Obviously, the size of the annual premium, which covers both savings and protection, varies with the type of policy. Because of the shorter period of payments, $1,000 face amount of insurance costs more per annum for an endowment than for an ordinary life policy issued at the same age. Both because of the shorter period of payments and the greater mortality risk, the premium on a policy increases as the age of the insured at time of issue rises. Finally, a 10-year endowment policy costs materially more per annum than does a 30-year endowment issued at the same age, but it makes little difference in the investment, as contrasted with the protection, phase of the contract whether the insured be 25 or 50 years old when he takes out a 10-year endowment policy.

Premium rates are based on careful actuarial computations based on mortality tables, anticipated income from reserves and a **loading charge** for expenses of selling and operation.

Participating Feature. Life insurance policies are ordinarily participating. The **dividends** paid holders of participating policies reflect more favorable mortality experience, larger investment income, and smaller operating expenses than were anticipated in the computation of premiums. These dividends are thus, in a sense, a refund of excess premium collections. Many policyholders take their dividends in cash, regarding them as a reduction in the premium, whereas others use them to buy paid-up additional insurance, thereby purchasing single-premium policies corresponding in type and maturity to the original commitment. A third group of policyholders leaves the dividends with the company to accumulate at interest, which is equivalent to establishing a savings account and does not increase the protection element at all. A final choice is to reduce the age at which the policy becomes paid up or matures, but not its face amount; this is known as an **accelerated option.**

Dividend payments differ among companies. In comparing the relative cost of life insurance in individual companies, average dividends may be deducted from premiums to give the **net cost** of the life insurance policies provided.

SETTLEMENTS OF POLICIES. Insurance policies may be settled by the insured if he wishes to cease premium payments, or with beneficiaries when the policy becomes a claim.

Ceasing Premium Payments. In the event that a policyholder finds it necessary or desirable to cease premium payments, he may either **surrender the policy for its cash value,** continue the **insurance** in a reduced amount with no further premium payments as **"paid-up" insurance,** or continue the insurance in full for a **limited term** at the end of which all protection ceases. If he selects the first alternative and "cashes in" the savings element of his insurance, he in effect treats the insurance as an endowment policy maturing at that time for a reduced amount; if he chooses the second alternative, he treats it as a limited payment life insurance policy for a lesser amount; in the third alternative, he applies the savings element in the policy, represented by the cash value, to the purchase of term insurance for the face amount of the policy.

Policy Settlements with Beneficiaries. Such settlements are of several kinds:

1. **Lump-sum.** A single lump-sum payment in cash to the beneficiary is most common. In some instances, payment may be made to a financial institution for the beneficiary under a trust agreement.

2. **Interest payments.** The company may hold the proceeds as a principal sum payable either at the death of the payee, at the expiration of a designated term of years or, at prior death of the payee, to a designated person or persons, meanwhile paying interest at a fixed rate, or at a minimum guaranteed rate with a higher rate if earned.

3. **Annuities.** The proceeds may be used to purchase a single-premium straight life annuity or an installment refund annuity without participation in excess interest earnings. A joint and two-thirds survivorship annuity provides that, when either beneficiary dies, the survivor receives reduced payments. Whatever the form, as with any annuity, regular periodic payments (usually monthly) are provided sufficient to exhaust the proceeds of the policy and any income accumulating thereon.

4. **Monthly life-income payments.** A life income may be provided, through payment of equal monthly installments for a number of years certain (such as 10 or 20) and as much longer as the payee may live. This option uses part of the proceeds to purchase an income for a fixed period, and part to purchase a deferred life income beginning at the end of that perod and continuing as long as the payee lives thereafter. Usually the fixed period income participates only in excess interest earnings, and often that portion alone is "**commutable**" (can be withdrawn) at any time.

5. **Equal monthly installments.** The company may pay equal periodic installments (usually monthly) of specified size, as long as the proceeds plus interest thereon last, or equal monthly installments for the number of years elected.

PLACE OF LIFE INSURANCE IN SAVINGS PICTURE. During the depression of the 1930's, when adverse economic conditions caused an increase in lapses and forced many policyholders to readjust their life insurance programs, some critics favored divorce of the savings from the insurance elements of life insurance policies. They urged the purchase of **decreasing-term life insurance** from an insurance company, and savings and investment either directly or through an investment institution of the sum thereby saved in premium expense, on the ground that specialized investing agencies would achieve better results. The companies and state supervisory authorities hold that the **need for safety in life insurance** requires investments of the type they make. Moreover, they argue that many persons would not save unless subject to the pressure of meeting fixed periodic premium payments. Furthermore, the average annual premium, they point out, does not exceed $100, which is by no means adequate for profitable investment.

There can be no question that life insurance as now set up causes millions of people to save huge sums that they would otherwise spend upon current consumption. The very effective way in which life insurance is sold and the pressure upon the policyholder for regular payments, and for paying off policy loans, promote personal saving on a large scale. The primary duty of each individual is obviously to secure an adequate amount of insurance to protect his dependents, and if necessary this should be in the lowest-cost types of policies. But over the long run very many persons have benefited by purchasing higher-premium limited payment and endowment policies, thereby utilizing the life insurance companies for the investment of part or all of their savings on a regular, systematic basis.

LIFE INSURANCE COMPANIES AS INVESTORS. Because they gather far larger sums yearly for investment than any other type of savings institution, the life insurance companies exercise a major influence upon the bond and mortgage markets. The bulk of premium income consists of renewal premiums on old policies, and so is relatively stable. Life insurance companies also have large current investment income, and face the need of reinvesting sums received by them in redemption of matured bonds and as amortization payments

	U.S. Government Bonds	Foreign Government Bonds	State, Provincial, and Local Bonds	Railroad Bonds	Public Utility Bonds	Industrial Miscellaneous Bonds
1940	5.8(18.7)*	0.3(1.0)	2.4(7.8)	2.8(9.2)	4.3(13.9)	1.5(5.0)
1945	20.7(45.9)	0.9(2.1)	1.0(2.3)	2.9(6.6)	5.2(11.6)	1.9(4.3)
1950	13.5(21.0)	1.1(1.7)	1.5(2.4)	3.2(5.0)	10.6(16.5)	9.5(14.9)
1955	8.6(9.5)	0.4(0.4)	2.7(3.0)	3.9(4.3)	14.0(15.5)	18.2(20.1)
1960	6.4(5.4)	0.4(0.3)	4.6(3.8)	3.7(3.1)	16.7(14.0)	26.6(22.4)
1961	6.1(4.9)	0.5(0.3)	5.0(4.0)	3.6(2.8)	17.0(13.4)	28.7(22.6)
1962	6.2(4.6)	0.6(0.5)	5.3(4.0)	3.5(2.6)	17.3(13.0)	30.7(23.1)
1963 (est.)	5.7(4.0)	0.9(0.6)	5.5(3.9)	3.4(2.4)	17.5(12.4)	32.9(23.3)

	Total Stocks	Mortgages	Real Estate	Policy Loans	Miscellaneous Assets	Total Admitted Assets
1940	0.6(2.0)	5.9(19.4)	2.1(6.7)	3.1(10.0)	2.0(6.3)	30.8(100.0)
1945	1.0(2.2)	6.6(14.8)	0.9(1.9)	2.0(4.4)	1.7(3.9)	44.8(100.0)
1950	2.1(3.3)	16.1(25.1)	1.4(2.2)	2.4(3.8)	2.6(4.1)	64.0(100.0)
1955	3.6(4.0)	29.4(32.6)	2.6(2.9)	3.3(3.6)	3.7(4.1)	90.4(100.0)
1960	5.0(4.2)	41.8(34.9)	3.8(3.1)	5.3(4.4)	5.3(4.4)	119.6(100.0)
1961	6.3(4.9)	44.2(34.9)	4.0(3.2)	5.7(4.5)	5.7(4.5)	126.8(100.0)
1962	6.3(4.7)	46.9(35.2)	4.1(3.1)	6.2(4.7)	6.0(4.5)	133.2(100.0)
1963 (est.)	7.2(5.1)	50.6(35.9)	4.3(3.1)	6.7(4.8)	6.3(4.5)	141.0(100.0)

(000,000,000 omitted from amounts)

* (Figures in parentheses show percentage ratio to total amount)

Fig. 10. Investments of all United States life insurance companies. (Source: The Institute of Life Insurance, Life Insurance Fact Book, 1963, and Life Insurance Review of 1963.)

on mortgages. After the payment of death benefits and other outlays, there is a large annual addition to reserves that must be invested, for premium rates assume earnings of 2½% or more on reserves. Providing a market for several billion dollars of securities and mortgages annually, for the investment of such additional reserves, the life insurance companies are a major factor in appraisal of the prospective demand for investments.

Laws governing life insurance company investments are generally a good deal more flexible than those regulating investments of savings banks. The bulk of investment funds of life insurance companies has been placed in government obligations, real estate mortgages, and corporate bonds, but they have also acquired considerable amounts of preferred and guaranteed stocks, and small amounts of common stock.

The **Institute of Life Insurance** publishes details yearly on changes in investments of the life insurance companies, as shown in Fig. 10. A study of changes in insurance company holdings from year to year indicates the volume and type of investments being absorbed by these institutions.

For many years prior to the **Life Insurance Company Income Tax Act of 1959,** life insurance companies paid taxes only on income from investments. The new law, however, requires that taxes be paid partly on investment income and partly on income from general operations. The law was first applied to 1958 operations, and, in that year, insurance companies paid an extra $124,000,000 in Federal income taxes, for a total of $445,000,000. For 1960, the total Federal income tax bill for United States life insurance companies was $510,000,000 and, for 1961, about $540,000,000.

As can be seen from the data in Fig. 10, there does not yet appear to be any tax impact on the investment policies of the life insurance companies. This is because the tax still remains in full force on investment income. The tax on general operations is in addition to the tax liabilities that existed prior to 1958; however, life insurance companies may come to depend more heavily on **tax-exempt securities** in the future in order to reduce their total tax bill.

SECTION 5

BANKING SERVICES AND PROCEDURES

CONTENTS

How a Commercial Bank Is Organized
Commercial Banking 1
Securing a Bank Charter 1
   State or national bank? 2
   Capital requirements 2
Regulation of banking 2
   Requirements for directors 2
   Removal of director or officer 3
   Bank examinations 3

Bank Deposits
Kinds of bank deposits 3
Services offered depositors 4
   Checks 4
   Collection services 4
   Payroll services 5
Competition for deposits 5
Restrictions on payment of interest on deposits 5
Federal deposit insurance 6
   The Federal Deposit Insurance Corporation 6
   Insured banks 6
   Insured accounts 7
   Prevention of unsound practices by insured banks 7
   Payment of insured deposits 8
   Payment of dividends and interest by insured banks 8
Deposits are liabilities 9
Right of setoff 9

Checking Accounts
Growing use of demand deposits as money .. 9
   Estimates of the volume of check use in the United States (f. 1) 9
How to select a bank 10
How to open a checking account 10
   Advantages of personal checking account .. 10
Opening a corporate deposit account 11
Partnership accounts 11
Joint accounts 11
   Resolution authorizing opening of corporate checking account (f. 2) 12
Making a deposit 14

When deposited items are available for withdrawal 14
Certification of checks 15
Stop-payment orders 15
Reconciliation of bank account 15
   Federal Reserve bank of Richmond credit for cash items at head office (f. 3)..... 16
Deposit account analysis 17
Service charges 19
Exchange and collection charges 19
   Par clearance system 19
   Nonpar banks 20
Collection service 20

Investments
Growth in importance of investments 21
Securities eligible for bank purchase 21
   Qualification as an "investment security" 22
Preference for government obligations 22
   Types of government securities 23
Valuation of investments 23
   Government classifications 24
   Present reporting practices 24
Portfolio policy 24
   Principle factors 24
   Distribution of investment maturities 25
Profits from sale of securities 25
Tax switching 26
The investment department 26
Real estate mortgages as bank investments .. 26

Loans
Importance of loans 27
Methods of borrowing 27
Uses of bank loans 28
One or more banks? 28
Types of bank loans 28
Secured loans 29
Security loans 30
Single-name vs. two-name paper 31
Accommodation paper 31
Banker's acceptances 31
Term loans 31
Credit analysis 32
The line of credit 33
Consumer loans 34

SECTION 5

BANKING SERVICES AND PROCEDURES

How a Commercial Bank Is Organized

COMMERCIAL BANKING. There are numerous types of so-called "banking" operations—viz., savings banking, mortgage banking, investment banking, etc. This section, however, deals only with **commercial banking**—the business of accepting and holding **demand deposits** (checking accounts) and, on the basis of excess primary reserves provided by these "deposited" deposits, extending credit accommodation to borrowing customers (and creating money in the process, incidentally). Commercial banks also accept and hold time and savings deposits as well as demand deposits, of course, but accepting, holding, and creating demand deposits through lending is the essential and unique business of a commercial bank.

SECURING A BANK CHARTER. Banking is a licensed and regulated business. Many safeguards have been placed around it for the protection of the public. Since prices of most banking services are unregulated and greatly influenced by competition, however, banking differs from public utilities.

The United States has a **free banking system**, which means that it is not necessary to secure a special charter from a legislature to start a bank. It is necessary to secure a charter from the national or state regulatory authorities, however, and this has become quite difficult because excessive chartering of new banks before 1931 has been blamed by some authorities for the many bank failures of the 1931 to 1933 period. In many states, the Superintendent of Banks submits applications for a charter to a **banking commission** composed of outstanding citizens who are familiar with the banking and credit needs of the various communities of the state. Applications that do not receive commission approval are automatically denied.

Securing a bank charter is a lengthy and rather detailed process. Generally, **authority to organize** must be secured from the supervisory authorities before proceeding with the actual steps of organization. An application for permission to organize must clearly indicate that there is a local need for banking service that is not being met by existing institutions. The men proposing to form the new institution must have had banking and business experience, and be residents of good repute of the community where the bank is to be located. The professional promoter is specifically excluded in Instructions of the Comptroller of the Currency Relative to the Organization and Powers of National Banks (Government Printing Office, Washington, D.C.):

The Comptroller of the Currency will refuse to approve any application for the organization of a national bank that contemplates or provides for any promotion fee, or that proposes to set apart or apply any part of the moneys collected from subscribers for the payment of promoters' fees, for the sale of stock, or for service in starting and opening any such bank, whether provided for by contract with proposed bank or by contract with the subscribers to the stock of the proposed bank.

The supervisory authorities (state or national, as the case may be) make a careful investigation to determine whether local conditions warrant approval of the application for a charter. Although this examination varies from state to state, it is quite searching in the financially important states and in the instances of applications for national bank charters. The investigation, at the expense of the applicants, covers the general character and experience of the organizers and proposed officers, the adequacy of existing banking facilities, the need for further banking capital, methods and practices of existing institutions, the interest rates that they charge, the character of the service that as quasi-public institutions they render their community, the economic outlook for the community, and finally, the prospects for success of the new bank if efficiently managed. The examiner is careful to interview personally all those who protest against the organization of a new bank. The advice of the Federal Reserve Bank, the Federal Deposit Insurance Corporation, and other interested agencies is sought by the examiner. Appropriate recommendation is then made to the supervisory authorities, by whom the application is either disapproved or approved.

State or National Bank? In the eastern states, where banking laws have generally been strict and supervision close, state-chartered institutions compare favorably in every way with the national banks. In some southern and western states, minimum capital requirements for state banks have been low and supervision less exacting.

Capital Requirements. Since the rate of earnings on bank assets has been relatively low in recent years, considerably more capital is required for successful bank operation than in the past. **Minimum capital requirements** are set by the law, but they are of little more than academic interest as considerably larger capital funds are usually required for practical reasons. Some states have a minimum requirement as low as $10,000. Minimum capital requirements for national banks, which secure their charters from the Federal government, are: $50,000 in a place of 6,000 population or less; $100,000 for any place with a population of more than 6,000 and not exceeding 50,000; $200,000 for larger towns or cities, except that in the outlying districts of such cities a minimum capital of $100,000 may be permitted if the laws of the state permit the organization of state banks with a capital of $100,000 or less. Higher minimum capital requirements apply to institutions with branches.

REGULATION OF BANKING. Practically every banking activity is regulated by some governmental agency. Primarily banking is regulated for the **protection of depositors,** and to a lesser degree, for the **preservation of competition** among banks.

Requirements for Directors. Special requirements are established for bank directors. They must be citizens of the United States, residents of the local community (or within 50 miles), owners of a substantial amount of stock in the bank (in no event less than $1,000 if the bank is a member of the Federal Reserve System), and of high character and reputation. They must take an oath to well and truly administer the affairs of the bank. They are personally liable when the bank (through its agents) commits any act not in accordance with statutes and legal precedents, and may be held criminally liable for specified acts by their bank, such as loans to bank examiners, fraud, false entries in the books, embezzlement, willful certification of a check in excess of depositor's balance, soliciting or receiving a bonus or commission for making a loan, and contributions to political parties. Directors are liable to creditors, particularly depositors, and to stockholders for failure to examine the bank as required by law, for exceeding the statutory limit on loans, for payments of dividends out of capital, and for mismanagement.

In a long line of decisions, the courts have held that bank directors must be diligent, reasonable, prudent, and possessed of business ability. The position of bank director thus involves substantially more risk than a directorship in a business corporation.

Removal of Director or Officer. Supervisory authorities have the power to remove a member bank director or officer for cause. When, in the opinion of the Comptroller of the Currency, any director or officer of a national bank, or when, in the opinion of the Federal Reserve agent, any director or officer of a state member bank in his district shall have continued to violate any law relating to such bank or trust company or shall have continued unsafe or unsound practices in conducting the business of his bank, after warning to discontinue such violations of law or such unsafe or unsound practices, as the case may be, the Comptroller or Federal Reserve agent may proceed to have him removed The offending officer or director is given a **hearing by the Federal Reserve Board,** which has final authority to require his removal.

Bank Examinations. Historically, the Comptroller of the Currency and state bank supervisory authorities had the sole responsibility for examining the banks under their respective jurisdictions. With the advent of the Federal Reserve System, examination functions were assumed by this agency also. The Board of Governors of the Federal Reserve System maintains a corps of examiners to examine the twelve Federal Reserve banks, while each Federal Reserve bank has an examining staff to examine state-chartered member banks in its district. The reports made by the Comptroller's examiners for national banks are accepted by the Federal Reserve banks, however. One object of the Federal Reserve examiners is to determine whether a member bank is putting Federal Reserve credit to improper use. Examinations by the Federal Reserve banks of state member banks are frequently made jointly with state supervisory authorities, who also have jurisdiction over state nonmember banks.

A particularly searching examination is made by the **Federal Deposit Insurance Corporation** of its members that are not also members of the Federal Reserve System, as well as banks applying for insurance and closed banks. These examiners may, with written permission of the Comptroller of the Currency, examine any national bank and, with permission of the Board of Governors of the Federal Reserve System, any state member bank. Since the F.D.I.C. insures deposits, it is directly involved should an insured bank fail, and so seeks to prevent such an outcome by remedial advance action if weakness is suspected.

It should be noted that bank examiners are not auditors nor is a bank examination an audit, although some auditing must necessarily be performed during the course of the examination. Large banks have an official known as the **bank auditor** or comptroller who heads a department of auditors that functions within the bank.

Bank Deposits

KINDS OF BANK DEPOSITS. Deposits may be **demand** deposits subject to withdrawal by drafts drawn at sight (checks); or **time** deposits withdrawable at a specified future date, after the lapse of a specific period of time, or upon thirty or more days' advance **notice** of withdrawal. Time deposits consist of three classes: (1) time certificates of deposit; (2) time deposits, open account; and (3) savings deposits. **Time certificates of deposit** are deposits evidenced by a certificate that is payable upon presentation at least 30 days after the date of deposit, or upon 30 days' written notice, or that is issued for a fixed and definite term. **Time deposits, open account** involve contracts prohibiting the withdrawal of all or any part of the deposited funds prior to the stipulated maturity date, which must be at least 30 days after the initial date of deposit. Periodic additions to such accounts are permitted, however, as in the case of Christmas Club accounts and vacation savings clubs. **Savings deposits** are time deposits of individuals or nonprofit organizations and must be evidenced by a passbook. Banks have the right to require at least 30 days' notice of withdrawal, but, as a practical matter, funds are available to savings depositors on demand under normal conditions. Payment of funds so deposited is made only on presentation of the passbook, however.

Deposits are also classified according to ownership as United States government, interbank, and "individual, partnership, and corporate"—usually referred to as **I.P.C. deposits.** United States government deposits are called "Treasury tax and loan accounts" because they are used for crediting the government with payments for taxes and purchases of Treasury obligations.

Deposits in a bank take the form of cash, checks on other banks, notes, drafts, and other collection items. They may also arise from credits to depositors' accounts by the various departments of the bank, such as the loan or foreign departments. Such deposits are sometimes called **derivative deposits,** because they are created by a bank's credit-granting activities whereas deposits of cash and claims on other banks are termed **primary deposits** because they supply the bank with its primary reserves—the basis upon which it creates its derivative deposits.

If a bank creates derivative deposits too freely it will lose reserves, and may have to borrow or otherwise recoup them. An individual bank usually gains primary deposits and primary reserves when the banking system as a whole is expanding, and it can then usually expand derivative deposits on its own account. Conversely, a bank must often contract its derivative deposits by calling loans and selling bonds held for investment when other banks are reducing their outstanding credits and causing a shrinkage in the total volume of deposits. Any bank that does not fall in line when credit contraction sets in is likely to lose reserves to other banks that are selling investments or calling loans, and thus drawing reserve balances from banks that do not do so. Each bank is a member of the **banking system,** and must plan its operations with that fact continually in mind.

SERVICES OFFERED DEPOSITORS. Numerous services and inducements are offered to secure primary deposits and borrowing customers.

Checks. The greatest service, which is too often taken for granted, is the privilege of drawing checks on demand deposit accounts. This privilege of payment by check is of enormous convenience, reduces the risk involved in cash payments by mail or personally, furnishes the depositor a receipt in the form of a canceled check for his payments, and, through a monthly statement of account, greatly simplifies the depositor's bookkeeping. (For a detailed discussion of Checking Accounts see page 9 below.)

Collection services. Collection services rendered for a nominal charge by a bank are equally indispensable in modern business. Local items are collected through the **clearing house.** Through its correspondents a bank will collect a draft, note, bill of exchange, or similar item due any place in the United States or abroad. Service charges—usually assessed on a per item basis—are levied by American banks for handling checks and noncash (collection) items. Most depositors, especially those without large collected balances, pay for these services on a monthly basis. Through correspondents and branches a bank may transfer a depositor's funds anywhere in the world. (See also pages 19–21 below.)

Payroll Services. The task of preparing payrolls is another valuable service performed by banks for business depositors. A depositor may advise his bank early in the day, or preferably the day before, as to the amount and denominations of currency (including coin) desired, and the bank will accordingly prepare the payroll and deliver it promptly upon presentation of the depositor's check for the amount. Should the depositor prefer to pay his employees by check, he can file a schedule of their signatures with the bank and arrange for payment upon presentation without identification beyond that afforded by comparison of endorsements with signatures on file.

Banks will either put up the payroll in cash in envelopes (in large cities they will deliver it by armored car), or will furnish special facilities for cashing the payroll checks of employees on some standard identification basis.

Banks also extend **loans** to depositors; in fact, interest on loans is the principal source of most banks' operating income. In times of financial stringency, banks favor depositors over other applicants for credit. But competition for loans has sometimes been so keen in recent years that banks have readily granted loans to all desirable applicants. Whenever a bank can lend, even to a nondepositor, it will usually choose to do so, since borrowing customers are prone to become depositing customers as well.

COMPETITION FOR DEPOSITS. Before 1933, competition for primary deposits through rendering services without charge and the payment of interest on deposit balances allegedly weakened many banks. The great epidemic of bank failures in 1931 to 1933, culminating in the nationwide bank holiday in March 1933, resulted in the adoption of safeguards to prevent competitive practices that weaken banks by destroying earning power, or encouraging speculative loans and investments to recoup losses due to large interest payments and costly services to depositors.

RESTRICTIONS ON PAYMENT OF INTEREST ON DEPOSITS. The Banking Act of 1933 and subsequent legislation amended the Federal Reserve Act as follows:

1. No member bank of the Federal Reserve System "shall, directly or indirectly, by any device whatsoever, pay any interest on any deposit which is payable on demand."
2. "The Board of Governors of the Federal Reserve System shall from time to time limit by regulation the rate of interest which may be paid by member banks on time and savings deposits and shall prescribe different rates for such payment on time and savings deposits having different maturities, or subject to different conditions respecting withdrawal or repayment, or subject to different conditions by reason of different locations, or according to the varying discount rates of member banks in the several Federal Reserve districts." As will be noted, this section is mandatory rather than permissive. The Board is required to set limits on rates paid and also to prescribe different rates. In fact, a literal interpretation of the term "shall prescribe" would require the Board to set the exact rates which might be paid under each set of circum-

stances and not merely promulgate maximum rates. So far, however, the Board has seen fit to fix only maximum rates.
3. "No member bank shall pay any time deposit before its maturity except upon such conditions and in accordance with such rules and regulations as may be prescribed by the said Board, or waive any requirement of notice before payment of any savings deposit except as to all savings deposits having the same requirement."

The Banking Act of 1933 also prohibits any member bank from rendering any free service that is tantamount to payment of interest on demand deposits, or the effect of which is equivalent to the payment of a rate of interest on time or savings deposits in excess of the maximums established by the Board. Absorption by a bank of exchange charges levied on out-of-town checks deposited with it has been barred by the Board of Governors of the Federal Reserve System under this provision.

The Federal Deposit Insurance Corporation imposes similar restrictions on insured nonmember banks under the authority of the Banking Act of 1935; however, the F.D.I.C. has ruled that the **absorption of exchange charges** by insured nonmember banks does not constitute the payment of interest on demand deposits.

FEDERAL DEPOSIT INSURANCE. Six states established deposit insurance plans prior to 1864, but none of these continued to operate after the passage of the **National Banking Act of 1864.** Eight more states adopted similar plans in the period between 1907 and 1917, but none survived the depression of the 1930's. (Annual Reports of the Federal Deposit Insurance Corporation, 1952, 1953, 1956.) All these schemes failed because too many of the banks could not survive depressions, and losses soon exceeded reserves in the guaranty funds. Also, depositors did not discriminate in the choice of state banks when they thought them equally "safe," and reckless banking was allowed to exist because of inadequate bank supervision. Despite unsatisfactory experience with state deposit guaranty plans, political pressure was so great for national legislation to protect depositors from loss due to bank failures that the Banking Act of 1933 set up a system of Federal deposit insurance that the Banking Act of 1935 made permanent.

The Federal Deposit Insurance Corporation. The Federal Deposit Insurance Corporation is managed by three directors, one of whom is the Comptroller of the Currency and the other two appointed by the President of the United States with the advice and consent of the Senate. The Corporation has repaid the capital originally provided by the Treasury and Federal Reserve banks, so that in effect it belongs to its member banks. In addition to the large surplus accumulated from assessments, the Corporation may borrow up to $3,000,000,000 from the Treasury, should an emergency arise.

Insured Banks. All national banks and all state banks that are members of the Federal Reserve System are required to become members of the F.D.I.C. State nonmember banks are also eligible for deposit insurance if they meet the standards of the F.D.I.C. as determined by an examination by the Corporation's examiners.

Any national bank withdrawing from the insurance fund is required to surrender its national charter. Any state-chartered member of the Federal Reserve System withdrawing from the fund forfeits Federal Reserve membership. Any insured bank that is not a member of the Federal Reserve System may withdraw from the insurance plan upon 90 days' written notice to the Corporation and adequate notice, by publication or otherwise, to its depositors. In any instance of withdrawal, deposits at the time are covered for a period of 2 years, and the regular assessments must be paid on them.

Insured Accounts. The Federal Deposit Insurance Corporation insures up to $10,000 of each deposit account in an insured bank. This maximum of $10,000 of insurance applies to a depositor's account in one bank. By **maintaining a deposit in more than one bank,** a depositor may secure $10,000 of deposit insurance in several institutions. Furthermore, funds held by a bank as trustee are insured to the extent of $10,000 for each trust estate. This insurance is in addition to the $10,000 of insurance on the deposit account of the trust department patron in the same bank. The F.D.I.C. at present insures less than half of the total dollar volume of deposits in F.D.I.C.-insured banks, but 98% of the total number of accounts in insured banks is fully covered.

The assessment levied by the F.D.I.C. for this insurance is $\frac{1}{12}$ of 1% per annum on total collected deposits, less the bank's proportionate share of a credit of 60% of the FDIC's **net assessment income** (total assessment income less insurance losses and operating expenses) for the preceding year, which is allowed all insured banks collectively. This assessment or premium is payable to the corporation semiannually at the rate of $\frac{1}{24}$ of 1% of average net deposits during the preceding 6 months. This premium is computed on total deposits, rather than on insured deposits only. Thus, a disproportionate burden is placed on the large city banks, many of whose depositors carry balances far in excess of the insurance limit of $10,000. For example, on a million dollar deposit the F.D.I.C. assessment would be $833.33 or $\frac{1}{12}$ of 1%, but only $10,000 of the deposit would actually be insured. A country bank with most deposit balances under $10,000 may have nearly 100% insurance of its deposits. The argument for this procedure is that an assessment based on insured deposits only would be inadequate, whereas the whole banking system benefits from protection of depositors from the danger of loss due to bank failures, which precipitates "runs" on banks and so exaggerates the evil in depression periods. It is interesting to note, however, that in the banking crisis of the early 1930's, it was frequently the big depositors and not the small ones who precipitated the "runs" on the banks. Thus, it may be argued that since F.D.I.C. deposit insurance assessments are based on a bank's total deposits, then the total deposits should be fully insured. (Kreps and Lapkin, Improving the Competition for Funds Between Commercial Banks and Thrift Institutions.)

Prevention of Unsound Practices by Insured Banks. State experience with deposit guaranty proved that insurance of deposits could be successful only if accompanied by preventive measures to reduce the number of bank failures to a minimum. Provision is made in present Federal legislation for guarding against unsafe and unsound practices on the part of insured banks in conducting their business. Upon the discovery of any such practices the board of directors of the F.D.I.C. is directed to call the attention of the proper authority to such practices— the Comptroller of the Currency, in the case of a national bank; the state supervising banking authority, in the case of a state bank not a member of the Federal Reserve System; and the Board of Governors of the Federal Reserve System in the case of state bank members of the Federal Reserve System. The practices objected to must thereupon be stopped within 120 days or any shorter period as the supervising authority may require. If they are not, 30-day notice is given to the offending bank of the intention to terminate its status as an insured bank. A hearing is thereupon granted to the bank, and if the allegations made against the bank are established, its connection with the deposit insurance system ceases on a date named so far as additional deposits, whether by old or new depositors, are concerned.

Additional capital was provided banks by the **Reconstruction Finance Corporation,** Washington, D.C., following the establishment of deposit insurance, and other legislation was adopted to tighten restrictions on speculative investments. Huge purchases of government obligations by banks, dating from World War II (at the close of which the nation's commercial banks collectively held about $90 billion worth of government securities), have greatly improved the quality of bank investments. Also, the F.D.I.C. has been active in preventing bank failures by sponsoring and aiding mergers of weak banks with stronger institutions. But few banks need even this degree of F.D.I.C. ministration anymore. In fact, banks no longer fail except as a result of defalcation, embezzlement, or loss attributable to other financial irregularities by officers and employees. And, fortunately, such cases are extremely rare. (See, for example, Annual Report of the Federal Deposit Insurance Corporation, 1962.)

Payment of Insured Deposits. Whenever an insured bank is unable to pay its depositors and is closed, insured deposits are made available to depositors at once by the F.D.I.C. Deposits equal to those insured are available in a new bank organized for the purpose, or in an existing insured bank, or by such other method as the Corporation may deem advisable. The Corporation thereupon succeeds to the rights of the depositors in the assets of the failed bank, if it is a **national bank.** In the case of a **state bank** the Corporation will not make payments on insured deposits until the depositors have assigned their claims to the Corporation, or such assignment is effected by state law or otherwise. The Corporation acts as receiver to liquidate the failed bank if it is a national bank, and must accept appointment as receiver in the case of a failed state bank if requested to do so by state authorities. The **new bank** organized to make available insured deposits in the failed bank may within 2 years be converted into a national bank or sold to another bank. Otherwise, it must be liquidated by the F.D.I.C. In this way, it is sought to maintain continuity of banking services in the community where the failed bank is located.

Payment of Dividends and Interest by Insured Banks. No insured bank may pay dividends on its capital stock or interest on any capital notes or debentures outstanding, if such interest is payable only out of net profits, while it remains in default on the payment of any assessment due to the F.D.I.C. Any director or officer of an insured bank who participates in such declaration or payment is subject to fine or imprisonment. However, the prohibition of such dividend or interest payments does not apply if the default in the payment of an assessment is due to a dispute between the insured bank and the Corporation. In that case, the bank need only deposit satisfactory security with the Corporation.

The board of directors of the Corporation may, by regulation, prohibit the payment of interest on demand deposits in insured banks that are not members of the Federal Reserve System, and for such purpose may define the term "demand deposits." It has done both these things, of course. From time to time, the board is also required to limit by regulation the rates of interest or dividends that may be paid by insured nonmember banks on time and savings deposits, but such regulations must be consistent with the contractual obligations of such banks to their depositors. For the purpose of fixing rates of interest or dividends, the board is charged with the duty of prescribing different rates for deposits having different maturities, or subject to different conditions respecting withdrawal or repayment, or subject to different conditions by reason of location or according to the varying discount rates of member banks in the several Federal Reserve districts. The board must also define by regulation what is to constitute time and savings deposits in an insured nonmember bank.

The F.D.I.C. thus has substantially the same authority over interest rates, etc., for insured banks that are not members of the Federal Reserve System that the Board of Governors of the Federal Reserve System has over member banks. This has led to some conflict of authority, particularly with respect to the definition of practices that are to be considered the **equivalent of the payment of interest.** On the absorption of exchange charges on out-of-town checks by a depositor's bank, different rulings have been issued by each agency, for example.

DEPOSITS ARE LIABILITIES. It should be clearly understood that deposits are liabilities of banks. The relationship between the bank and the depositor is that of debtor and creditor. The bank becomes the legal owner of the cash, negotiable instruments, and other items deposited for immediate credit. The depositor is merely a general creditor. In the collection of notes, drafts, and similar items for which immediate credit is not given, however, the bank acts as the depositor's agent and does not become the owner until collection has been effected and credit given.

RIGHT OF SETOFF. In the event of bank failure, a depositor may set off any unsecured debt that he owes the bank against his deposit (which is unsecured), and must pay in cash only the balance due the bank, if any. In setoffs, the claims involved must be of equal character. Thus, if a bank has made a secured loan to a depositor, the latter cannot set off his deposit balance against the loan because the claims are not equally secured. This right of setoff (or offset), and payment of the net balance due, **applies only to the commercial department** of the bank. There can be no setoffs in the savings department or between the savings department and the commercial department, except that a depositor with a savings account who has an obligation due in the commercial department may set off that obligation with his deposit credit even though assets available for distribution to the demand depositors are thereby diminished. This is in conformity with the usual attitude of the courts to favor savings as against commercial depositors. (Yale Law Journal, Vol. 42.)

Checking Accounts

GROWING USE OF DEMAND DEPOSITS AS MONEY. The use of demand deposits as money has been increasing steadily in the United States for over a century. As Fig. 1 shows, from 1939 to 1960 the number of checking accounts in active use at American commercial banks more than doubled, and in

Year	Number of Checking Accounts (millions)	Number of Checks Written (billions)	Dollar Value of Checks Written (trillions)
1939	27	4	1
1952	47	8	2
1957	52	12	3
1959	54	13	3.50
1960	55	14	3.75
1970 (est.)	68	25	6.25

Fig. 1. Estimates of the volume of check use in the United States. (Source: Kreps, Money, Banking, and Monetary Policy.)

1960 totaled over 55 million, or one for almost every other adult in the country. The number of checks written on these accounts is rising at a rate of about 1 billion per year. In 1960, the dollar value of checks written in the United States approximated $3.75 trillion ($3,750,000,000,000), and this magnitude is expected to grow by two thirds by 1970.

To cope with the clearing work generated by present and projected levels of American check use, the Federal Reserve banks, the regional and national city-correspondent banks, and even some of the larger local commercial banks have in recent years gone far in the utilization of large-scale electronic computational and check-processing equipment. These **electronic brains**, controlling check-handling and record-keeping systems geared to process checks in massive volume, are necessary because, even beyond the rapid growth of check use to its present proportions, over three-fourths of all the checks written must be handled in more than one bank. In fact, the **"bank work multiplier"** applied to each check written is now something like 2⅓—the average check being handled by that many banks; and, incidentally, taking the same number of days to get back to the bank on which it was drawn. (Kreps, Money, Banking, and Monetary Policy.)

HOW TO SELECT A BANK. Many banks insist on a personal introduction as a prerequisite to opening a checking account. Such safeguards are not considered imperative in the case of thrift, savings, or other nonchecking accounts.

Before approaching a bank to open an account, the prospective depositor should ascertain the character of the institution and its banking services. He should find out whether the bank welcomes **"regular" checking accounts** of the size that he proposes to maintain. Some banks require minimum balances of $5,000 and more for such accounts, whereas other banks will permit minimum balances as low as $200 or $300 or even lower. Most banks today also provide **"special"** or **"thrift" checking accounts** for depositors who maintain small balances and write relatively few checks. The banks do not require the depositor to maintain a minimum balance in these types of accounts at all, and the service charges are levied on a per check basis by "selling" the depositor his checks. These checks are usually distinctive in design, to distinguish them from the bank's regular checks, and are the only ones the depositor is permitted to use. Some banks have officers who are friendly and helpful and do everything possible to assist even small depositors. Other banks have officers who are uninterested in smaller depositors.

HOW TO OPEN A CHECKING ACCOUNT. Having selected a suitable bank, the prospective depositor arranges for an interview with the officer in charge of new accounts. This officer explains the bank's requirements and regulations. He then asks the prospect to fill in a **new account card** giving personal identification data, such as his occupation, home and business addresses, and similar information. In addition, this card calls for information on previous accounts, present accounts at other banks, etc. If this information indicates to the interviewing officer that the account will be satisfactory, **signature cards** are signed, and the account officially opened with an initial deposit.

Advantages of a Personal Checking Account. Various services, some well known and many little known, are offered to those with checking accounts. One of the most obvious and important is the collecting of checks, notes, drafts, and similar instruments, and crediting of the proceeds to the account of the depositor. The account is frequently used as the basis of **credit reference** given to inquirers by officers of the bank. A bank account avoids the risk of the use of cash. It enables the depositor to secure funds any place where he can "cash" a check. It simplifies personal budgeting and record keeping by furnishing receipts in the form of canceled checks. It furnishes proof of payment and thus avoids duplicate payments and claims.

Maintenance of a satisfactory checking account is the first step in developing a line of credit. Many a young man maintains a savings account on which a small return is realized when it would be more profitable in the long run for him to maintain a checking account. Development of a close and friendly banking relationship may prove a very valuable asset, especially if there is any prospect of his going into business for himself.

OPENING A CORPORATE DEPOSIT ACCOUNT. Banks must exercise particular care in handling a corporation's account. They must be careful in paying money out as it may later be claimed that the money was not used for corporate purposes or that the withdrawal did not have proper authorization.

Before opening an account for a corporation, a bank will require the filing of a **resolution of the board of directors** authorizing the opening and operation of the account, specifying the officers who are authorized to sign checks and other instruments of payment, and clearly indicating what officers have the authority to borrow at the bank and otherwise pledge the credit of the corporation. This resolution must be filed under seal by the secretary of the corporation. In addition, the secretary must certify that there is nothing in the charter or by-laws that limits the authority given in the resolution.

Most banks have printed forms for such a resolution, prepared by their counsel, which the corporation's board of directors must pass and its secretary authenticate and file with them. A typical resolution form is reproduced in Fig. 2.

Throughout the banking relationship, everything is in the name of the corporation and all checks, notes, etc., should be endorsed with the corporate name followed by the name of the officer who authenticates the corporate signature by signing his own name. Thus a typical corporate signature would be "Products, Inc., by John Doakes, Vice President and Treasurer" and not simply "John Doakes, Treasurer."

PARTNERSHIP ACCOUNTS. Partnership accounts are opened on practically the same basis as individual accounts. The bank will, however, require the filing of a copy of the partnership agreement, as all the dealings of the partners with the bank should conform to this agreement.

JOINT ACCOUNTS. A savings, thrift, or checking account may be opened with most banks in the name of two people, either as tenants in common, or as joint tenants. As **tenants in common** either party may make deposits, and endorse checks, drafts, notes, etc., for deposit, but the parties must act jointly when withdrawing funds. In event of the death of one of them, the balance to the credit of the account is divided equally between the survivor and the estate of the deceased. The survivor may withdraw his or her share by furnishing such proof of the death of the other party as the bank may require. The share belonging to the estate of the deceased may be withdrawn upon filing with the bank a surrogate's certificate and a tax waiver.

As **joint tenants** either party, during the lifetime of both, may make deposits and endorse checks, drafts, notes, etc., for deposit, and may at will withdraw or dispose of the whole or any part of the funds deposited. In event of the death of one of them, the survivor may withdraw the balance to the credit of the account upon filing with the bank a tax waiver. Because of the convenience afforded, such accounts are extensively used by husband and wife, and other members of the same family, but they may be opened by any two persons whether or not related to each other.

As to joint tenants, the **New York Banking Law** provides:

When a deposit shall have been made by any person in the name of such depositor and another person and in form to be paid to either, or the survivor of them, such deposit thereupon and any additions thereto made, by either of such persons, upon the making thereof, shall become the property of such persons as joint tenants, and the same, together with all interest thereon, shall be held for the exclusive use of the

RESOLUTION OF BOARD OF DIRECTORS
(Authority to Open Deposit Account)

I HEREBY CERTIFY that I am the duly elected and qualified Secretary of _____ and the keeper of the records and corporate seal of said corporation and that the following is a true and correct copy of a resolution duly adopted at a regular meeting of the Board of Directors of said corporation held in accordance with the By-Laws of said Corporation at its offices at _____ on the _____ day of _____, 19____.

"Be It Resolved, that _____ be, and it is hereby, designated a depository of this Corporation and that funds so deposited may be withdrawn upon a check, draft, note or order of the Corporation.

"Be It Further Resolved, that all checks, drafts, notes or orders drawn against said account be signed by any _____ of the following:
(one, two, three, etc.)

NAME	TITLE
_____	_____
_____	_____
_____	_____
_____	_____

and countersigned by any one of the following:

NAME	TITLE
_____	_____
_____	_____
_____	_____
_____	_____

whose signatures shall be duly certified to said Bank, and that no checks, drafts, notes or orders drawn against said Bank shall be valid unless so signed.

"Be It Further Resolved, that said Bank is hereby authorized and directed to honor and pay any checks, drafts, notes or orders so drawn, whether such checks, drafts, notes or orders be payable to the order of any such person signing and/or countersigning said checks, drafts, notes or orders, or any of such persons in their individual capacities or not, and whether such checks, drafts, notes or orders are deposited to the individual credit of the person so signing and/or countersigning said checks, drafts, notes or orders, or to the individual credit of any of the other officers or not. This resolution shall continue in force and said Bank may consider the facts concerning the holders of said offices, respectively, and their signatures to be and continue as set forth in the certificate of the

CHECKING ACCOUNTS 5·13

Secretary or Assistant Secretary, accompanying a copy of this resolution when delivered to said Bank or in any similar subsequent certificate, until written notice to the contrary is duly served on said Bank.

In Witness Whereof, I have hereunto affixed my name as _____

Secretary and have caused the corporate seal of said Corporation to be hereto affixed this_____

day of_____, 19____

_____
                                                                                 Secretary

IMPRINT
SEAL HERE

I, _____, a Director of said Corporation, do hereby certify that the foregoing is a correct copy of a resolution adopted as above set forth.

_____
                   To be signed by a director other than the secretary

CERTIFIED COPY OF BY-LAWS

of the _____ referring to signing of checks, drafts, etc.
Insert copy of By-Laws here:

TO _____
          Name of Bank   Address

I HEREBY CERTIFY that the foregoing is a true and correct copy of all parts of the By-Laws of_____

_____ a _____ corporation, covering the signing of checks, drafts and orders for the payment of money.

IN WITNESS WHEREOF, I have hereunto affixed my name as Secretary and have caused the corporate seal of said Corporation to be hereto affixed this_____ day of_____ 19____

_____
                                                                                 Secretary

PLACE
SEAL
HERE

                                                          DeLano Service, Allegan, Mich., Form R-2

Fig. 2. Resolution authorizing opening of a corporate checking account.

persons so named, and may be paid to either during the life time of both, or to the survivor after the death of one of them; and such payment and the receipt of acquittance of the one to whom such payment is made, shall be a valid and sufficient release and discharge to said bank, for all payments made on account of such deposit prior to the receipt by said bank of notice in writing signed by any one of such joint tenants, not to pay such deposit in accordance with the terms thereof.

MAKING A DEPOSIT. The bank will accept for deposit checks, sight drafts, matured coupons of United States bonds, and, of course, cash. Immediate credit is given, but immediate withdrawal is permitted only in the instance of deposits of currency and checks drawn on the bank itself. Ordinarily, a **deposit slip** is prepared in duplicate by the depositor and presented with the items deposited. The teller checks the deposit slips and, if everything is in order, he initials one copy and returns it to the depositor as his receipt. The pass book is less commonly used for this purpose.

Banks require depositors to prepare this deposit slip themselves, as it is an original entry and legally binding on the bank after it has been initialed by the teller. Fake claims of mistakes in deposits can be successfully countered with a deposit slip prepared by the depositor himself.

Care should be exercised in preparing this deposit slip. Each check should be listed separately and with it the name of the city on which it is drawn if it is out of town and the name of the bank if it is a local one. Cash should be listed as indicated. Dollar signs should be omitted and all figures should be placed directly under one another, so that additions may be quickly made and easily verified.

All deposits are accepted subject to actual collection and receipt of proceeds. The bank thus reserves the right to charge back to the account **unpaid checks** drawn on other banks. This right is based on the warranty of the endorser as provided in the Uniform Negotiable Instruments Act.

WHEN DEPOSITED ITEMS ARE AVAILABLE FOR WITHDRAWAL. Although the bank gives immediate credit in the deposit account for checks deposited, only the proceeds of those drawn on the bank itself can be withdrawn immediately in cash. Immediate credit to the depositor's account of checks drawn on other banks is for the convenience of the bank itself, but it will not actually receive payment from the drawee banks until some time later. Because of this, depositors are not usually permitted to draw on such a deposit until the bank receives payment and is thus reimbursed for the credit that it has advanced to the customer's account. Until payment is received by the bank, such deposit credits are referred to as **uncollected funds,** which indicates they are unavailable. Many banks, especially small ones in small towns, are pretty "free and easy" in the matter of permitting customers to draw against uncollected funds, however.

Banks may collect these **cash items** through the local clearing house, if they are local items (as about one-third of them are); through their correspondent banks, or through the Federal Reserve banks if they are "out-of-town" items. Large checks and those drawn on banks in certain cities are generally collected by banks, especially larger institutions, through their correspondents, as are all nonpar items. But about half of all nonlocal checks are routed through the Federal Reserve banks for collection under the par clearance system maintained by the Federal Reserve System.

There have been continuous efforts through the years to speed up the check collection process, so as to make funds available to depositors as soon as possible. The air mail and speed-up methods such as maintaining night shift of bank clerks are utilized. As transportation has been speeded up, the time required for collection has been steadily shortened. Credit risks have been reduced as the "uncollected" time has been reduced. A forger has less time to get away before detection.

Each Federal Reserve bank furnishes its district member **banks** and its nonmember clearing banks a schedule giving the time required to **collect checks** anywhere in the country. This schedule is compiled from the banks' records of elapsed time in handling items drawn on the various points. If the forwarding bank is not otherwise notified, it considers items paid at the end of the period indicated in the schedule. The Federal Reserve Bank of Richmond since 1961 has given credit for cash items at its head office on its **time schedule** as shown in Fig. 3.

CERTIFICATION OF CHECKS. To certify a check an officer or teller of the bank stamps or writes upon its face the word "Good," "Accepted," or "Certified," and affixes his signature. By this means the bank signifies that it will honor the check if properly endorsed when presented for payment. Ordinarily, the **contract of certification** extends only to the genuineness of the drawer's signature and the sufficiency of the deposit, endorsements not being guaranteed.

Certification transforms a maker's order into a bank's promise to pay. It is not subject to nonpayment because of stop-payment orders, insufficient or uncollected funds, or other nonapparent defects, if the holder is shown to have given value in reliance on the certification. As against the bank, the demand of the holder of a certified check is sufficient if it is made within the period limited by the statute of limitations, which is usually 6 years.

When a check is **certified at the request of the holder,** the maker is released from all further liability on the check, but when **certification is requested by the maker,** he remains liable to the holder if the bank, for any reason, fails to pay the check. Regardless of payment by the bank, the maker's account is charged with the amount at the time the check is certified. Should the maker of a certified check find that he cannot use it, he can endorse and deposit it in his own account, regardless of who the payee of the check may be. A maker who desires credit for a **destroyed or lost certified check** is required to file with the bank an indemnity bond, usually for twice the amount. Banks are not compelled to certify checks. Some will certify only under special circumstances, or for the maker and never for the payee.

Certified checks are used to a great extent in paying taxes, licenses, and other obligations to the government, deposits required in connection with sealed bids, in real estate and stock and bond transactions, etc. They are not legal tender.

STOP-PAYMENT ORDERS. No legal reason is required of the maker for stopping payment of his check. To be binding on the bank, however, the order must be in writing and accurately describe the check to which it refers. Upon receipt of such an order, the bank as agent of the depositor must refuse payment of the check and is responsible to the depositor for omission to comply with his directions. As the **risk** to the bank is considerable, each of the depositor's checks received must be scrutinized until the check is found or the order is withdrawn. The risk requires that every precaution be taken to prevent the accidental payment of the check. Hence, considerable time is consumed and expense incurred in performing the necessary work. The bank is pleased to cooperate with the depositor when he makes an ethical use of the privilege. The bank has a just complaint, however, when a depositor abuses the privilege by employing it to escape the consequence of drawing against insufficient funds or for petty reasons that could have been otherwise adjusted.

RECONCILIATION OF BANK ACCOUNT. To avoid **overdrafts,** which are criminal offenses in most states, and to detect errors, unauthorized drawing of checks, forgeries, and similar irregularities, the deposit account, as kept by the depositor, should be reconciled with the account on the books of the bank. Banks send a depositor a statement of the transactions that have taken

RICHMOND HEAD OFFICE—TIME SCHEDULE

IMMEDIATE CREDIT
(Monday through Friday Only)

When Received in Time for Clearance on Date of Receipt (10 a.m.):
   Items drawn on other Richmond banks

When Received by 1:30 p.m.:
   Checks drawn on this bank
   Official checks of other Federal Reserve Banks (only when deposited in a separate cash letter)
   Checks drawn on Treasurer of United States
   Postal Money Orders
   Checks bearing Immediate Credit Symbol of Head Office—Thus............ ⟨5C⟩

ONE BUSINESS DAY AFTER RECEIPT

When Received by 1:30 p.m. Monday through Friday or 11 a.m. Saturday:

Items Payable in Cities of—

Atlanta	Ga.	Louisville	Ky.
Baltimore	Md.	Memphis	Tenn.
Birmingham	Ala.	Minneapolis	Minn.
Boston	Mass.	Nashville	Tenn.
Charlotte	N. C.	New Orleans	La.
Chicago	Ill.	New York	N. Y.
Cincinnati	Ohio	Philadelphia	Pa.
Cleveland	Ohio	Pittsburgh	Pa.
Dallas	Tex.	St. Louis	Mo.
Detroit	Mich.	St. Paul	Minn.
Jacksonville	Fla.		

Checks bearing Immediate Credit Symbol of Baltimore Branch—Thus ⟨5AC⟩

Checks bearing Immediate Credit Symbol of Charlotte Branch—Thus ⟨5BC⟩

TWO BUSINESS DAYS AFTER RECEIPT

When Received by 1:30 p.m. Monday through Friday or 11 a.m. Saturday:
   Items Payable Elsewhere in Any Federal Reserve District[1]

Any member bank in the territory of the Richmond Head Office which has for collection a daily average of not more than 300 **immediate credit and deferred credit** cash items, payable outside of the city or town in which such bank is located, may send all items to the Richmond Head Office unassorted in a single cash letter for credit in **one business day** after receipt.

A member bank's own draft on its commercial bank correspondent will be credited on the basis of the actual transit time required to effect collection, and should be listed on a separate cash letter.

---
[1] For the purposes of this circular, any dependency, insular possession or part of the United States outside the States of the United States and the District of Columbia shall be deemed to be in or of such Federal Reserve district as the Board of Governors may designate.

The Board has designated Puerto Rico and the Virgin Islands as being in or of the Second Federal Reserve District and Guam as being in or of the Twelfth Federal Reserve District.

Fig. 3. Federal Reserve bank of Richmond credit for cash items at head office

CHECKING ACCOUNTS 5·17

place in the account, and the remaining balance, upon request or every 3 months, or monthly, depending on the size and activity of the account and the policies of the bank. The larger accounts are always sent monthly statements for the mutual protection of the bank and the depositor.

When this statement is received, the depositor should promptly compare it with his own records (check book or cash book) to see if there have been any errors or improper charges. This comparison and adjustment of the accounts is called a **reconciliation**. It should be done carefully because, if a depositor fails to make such reconciliation after a bank has repeatedly sent him statements of his account, and if subsequently irregularities are disclosed that could have been discovered and avoided by prompt reconciliations, the courts would probably find that the **negligence of the depositor** was a primary, or at least a contributory, cause of the **irregularity**, and that therefore he must suffer the loss occasioned by the irregularity. If there is no negligence on the part of the depositor, the bank as a general rule must bear the full loss caused by irregularities in keeping a depositor's account.

Section 326 of the New York Negotiable Instruments Law provides: "No bank shall be liable to a depositor for the payment by it of a forged or raised check unless within one year after the return to the depositor of the voucher of such payment, such depositor shall notify the bank that the check so paid was forged or raised."

There are **two methods of reconciling the monthly statements** with the balances shown by the depositor's cash book or check book. The one starts with the bank statement as a basis, and the other starts with the depositor's cash or check book balances as a basis. The two methods are illustrated on page 18.

DEPOSIT ACCOUNT ANALYSIS. Analysis of depositors' accounts has become common, as banks have resorted to cost accounting practices to determine the sources of their profits and the cause and incidence of their expenses. They have attempted to determine the cost of handling a deposit, collecting a check, and maintaining an account (overhead, administrative, and other costs). On the income side, they have allowed for the average rate of return realized on earning assets. Armed with this information, they have analyzed depositors'

(Notes for Fig. 3)

In order to obtain the earliest availability as shown in these schedules, cash items should be sorted in accordance with the divisions of the time schedule of the office to which sent and items of each availability should be listed on a separate cash letter; provided, however, any member bank which has for collection a limited daily average number of immediate and deferred cash items, as explained in the schedules, may send all of its items in one cash letter unassorted as to availability for credit in one business day.

Credit for cash items is deferred on a business day basis except that credit for items drawn on banks located in those Federal Reserve cities that are not shown in the one-day division of our time schedules will be deferred on a calendar day basis when received by us on a Saturday or any other day immediately preceding a holiday, provided such items are sent to us listed on a separate cash letter.

When the date of availability of any cash letter falls on a Saturday, Sunday, or a holiday, credit for such letter will be given on the next business day. All cash items are received by this Bank and its Branches under the terms and conditions of our current circular regarding "Collection of Cash Items" and are credited subject to final payment.

Credit for all direct routed cash items that are collectible in one day will be given on the first business day after dispatch by the direct sending member banks; all other direct routed cash items, except the sending member banks' own drafts, will be credited on the second business day following dispatch.

A sending member bank's own drafts on its commercial bank correspondents, when sent direct, should be listed on separate cash letters and reported to us on a separate direct routing advice marked "Transfer Drafts," as credit will be deferred on the basis of the actual transit time required to effect collection.

First Method

First National Bank, December 31, 19—

Balance per statement			$92,415.60
Add—Check of Central Manufacturing Co. protested, now returned, including $2.55 fees			502.55
Deposit of December 31 not credited by bank			1,892.00
Collection charges for December not entered in cash book			4.80
			$94,814.95
Less—Deposit credited by bank not entered in cash book		$ 318.20	
Checks outstanding:			
6319	$ 50.00		
6682	125.00		
6714	73.10		
6716	139.45		
6717	68.25		
6718	1,000.00	1,455.80	1,774.00
Balance per cash book			$93,040.95

Second Method

Balance as per cash book			$93,040.95
Add—Checks outstanding:			
6319	$ 50.00		
6682	125.00		
6714	73.10		
6716	139.45		
6717	68.25		
6718	1,000.00	$1,455.80	
Deposit credited by bank not entered in cash book		318.20	1,774.00
			$94,814.95
Less—Check of Central Manufacturing Co. protested, now returned, including $2.55 fees		$ 502.55	
Deposit of December 31, not credited by bank		1,892.00	
Collection charges for December		4.80	2,399.35
Balance as per bank statement of December 31			$92,415.60

accounts to determine their profitability. Such an analysis is made of large accounts, but on small accounts the banks do not go to the expense of fully analyzing each account. They make studies of typical accounts and then set standards of balance and activity.

In analysis of the **larger accounts**, the average daily balance of collected funds is first calculated. From this are deducted the necessary reserves and till money, which leaves the earning balance. This balance is multiplied by the average rate of return received by the bank to determine the income earned on the free balance for the period under review. The number of items handled is next multiplied by the estimated unit cost for each item, and the product added to the overhead charged to each account. If this total is less than the estimated income, the account is turning in a profit. If it is greater than the income, the account is carried at an indicated loss. In this event, the bank typically charges the amount of indicated loss to the depositor's account as a service charge. A very few Amer-

CHECKING ACCOUNTS 5·19

ican banks may add a **"loading factor"** to these charges in order to allow for profit in their service charge "pricing," but this is far from the common practice.

SERVICE CHARGES. A deposit account may be unprofitable because its balance is less than average, or because the number of deposits made and checks drawn is excessive. Many methods of charging for services greater than warranted by the average balance are in use. For the most part, they are on a **"metered" basis,** increasing with the amount of service required by the depositor.

Most banks imposing service charges allow a specified number of checks and deposits each month without charge, if a stated minimum balance has been maintained. This balance varies from $200 to $300 for neighborhood personal checking accounts to, say, $50,000 for a large corporation account. Permissible activity without charge varies likewise. When the balance falls below the minimum, a service charge is made. Likewise, when the number of items exceeds the maximum, a charge of so much per item is made for the excess. These charges have become an important source of income for small banks. They are less important for large institutions but are certainly not neglected by them, since an adequate system of service charges may well spell the difference between earning profits or incurring losses on checking account operations.

Many city banks offer special personal accounts limited to checking service. Such accounts require no minimum balance, but a charge, usually of 10¢ to 15¢, is made for each blank check given the depositor. A **penalty** is imposed for a check drawn that is not covered with sufficient funds.

Depositors using this plan of payment of service charges should realize that they do not get complete banking service. Bank credit reference, loans, and other valuable services of the bank are ordinarily not available to such depositors. A regular personal checking account, even if it is so small that conventional service charges have to be paid, is of greater value to most depositors, particularly those in business.

EXCHANGE AND COLLECTION CHARGES. Before the Federal Reserve System installed its par clearance system, not only was it customary for banks to impose a collection charge for collecting out-of-town checks, but the paying bank usually deducted a charge for paying checks that were not cashed over its counter. This latter charge was called an **exchange charge.** Theoretically, it was reimbursement to the local bank for the cost of shipping currency or maintaining a balance on which it could draw to pay the sending bank. In small towns with a single bank and no competition, these exchange charges were frequently entirely disproportionate to the cost of rendering the service. In fact, collection and exchange charges became a heavy burden on trade.

Also, since each bank had its own group of correspondents to which out-of-town checks were forwarded for collection, the volume of checks in transit was very large because of circuitous routing. Often a check would travel hundreds of miles out of its way, because of the location of correspondents of the collecting bank.

Par Clearance System. Under the par clearance system, each Federal Reserve bank collects without charge **out-of-town checks** deposited with member banks (and their nonmember correspondent banks) that agree in turn to remit without deduction of exchange charges (i.e., at par) for all checks drawn on them. Since the Federal Reserve banks make no charges for collection services, they collect checks for the great majority of banks. A number of small banks that insist on deducting exchange charges remain outside the system, however. At the end of 1961, 1,630, or over 12% of the nation's banks, were nonpar banks. These banks are largely concentrated in the southeastern and mid-northwestern areas of the United States, and they are typically the only banks in the local communities that they serve. (Kreps, Southern Economic Journal, Vol. XVI.)

About half of all the nonlocal checks deposited in or cashed at banks are initially sent for collection to city correspondent banks that, in turn, often send them on to the Federal Reserve banks. The other half of the nonlocal checks are sent directly to the Federal Reserve banks in the first place. (Joint Committee on Check Collection System of the American Bankers Association, Association of Reserve City Bankers, and Conference of Presidents of the Federal Reserve Banks, Study of Check Collection System.) There the items are sorted by districts, and those drawn on other districts are forwarded to the appropriate Federal Reserve bank or branch. Those that are drawn on member banks or nonmember clearing banks in the Federal Reserve bank's own district are charged directly to the reserve accounts of members or the collection accounts of nonmembers, and the account of the forwarding bank is credited. The Federal Reserve banks thus in effect, either directly or indirectly, constitute clearing houses for all participating banks.

A further development of the Federal Reserve par clearance service is the practice of **direct sending,** whereby a clearing bank, which has received permission, sends items payable in other districts directly to other Federal Reserve banks for the account of its own Federal Reserve bank, and receives credit in turn in its own account.

Whether an item is sent to its own Federal Reserve bank or directly to the Federal Reserve bank in another district, credit is given to the sending bank on the basis of the **deferred availability schedule.** This schedule, which differs for each Federal Reserve bank, states when banks may take credit for out-of-town checks deposited for collection. If advice of nonpayment is not received, the assumption is that checks have been paid.

The sending of checks from one district to another results in debit and credit entries between Federal Reserve banks. These result in debits and credits on the books of the Inter-District Settlement Fund in Washington, which obviates the need for large currency shipments between cities.

Nonpar Banks. Nonmember banks—usually, but not always, small country banks—that refuse to remit at par remain outside the par clearance system. Federal Reserve banks refuse to accept for collection any checks drawn on nonpar banks.

Banks that receive checks drawn on a nonpar bank have to fall back on the **correspondent system** to collect them. Every effort is made to present the check for payment over the window, so that the full amount will be received. This is impossible, however, in the instance of country banks distant from the collecting correspondent. In such circumstances, the exchange charge deduction cannot be avoided. This charge ordinarily ranges from $\frac{1}{10}$ of 1% to $\frac{1}{6}$ of 1% of the face amount of the check. The exchange charge on a $100 check, for example, would be between 10¢ and 17¢. (Wachovia Bank and Trust Company, Par and Rate List for Collecting Checks, Drafts, Notes, Etc.)

COLLECTION SERVICE. Depositors bring many credit instruments to banks for which immediate credit cannot be given. **Cash items** for which immediate credit is given consist almost entirely of checks and government bond coupons. **Collection items,** on the other hand, are (1) credit instruments that are not yet due, or (2) drafts on which the ultimate payer has not yet acknowledged indebtedness, or (3) obligations with documents attached to be delivered upon payment. These are not credited to a depositor's account until the proceeds have actually been received by the bank.

Collection items include:

1. Notes, drafts, acceptances, and coupons that must be presented for payment at the place of business of a firm or corporation, or at a bank, or at the place of business or home of an individual.
2. Drafts and other instruments with documents attached that are surrendered on payment or acceptance of the drafts.
3. Installment contracts and notes secured by mortgages or trust deeds, which call for periodic payments.

In depositing items for collection, the customer should instruct his bank as to what he wishes done in event of nonpayment or nonacceptance. If an item has documents attached, he should specify the manner of handling it and the conditions under which delivery of the documents is to be made. All instruments entered for collection should be endorsed "for collection," as by so doing all holders of the respective items will be given notice of their true character, and the items themselves, or their proceeds, cannot be held against the claim of the true owner.

Inasmuch as the collecting bank acts as the depositor's agent, it cannot be held responsible for loss, provided it and its correspondents follow the instructions of the depositor and use due diligence and care in protecting his rights. A collecting bank is authorized to receive money only, and has no implied power to take a check or anything other than money in payment. If it takes a check and surrenders the item held for collection, it makes the check its own and becomes liable to the principal for the amount of the check as if it had received cash.

Local collections are made by the bank's own messengers or through the city collection department of the clearing house in many of the larger cities. **Out-of-town collections** are generally forwarded to local correspondents directly by the larger banks. The larger banks may, and the other banks usually, collect such items through the country collection department of the Federal Reserve banks. Whatever method is used, a small fee is charged and is deducted from the proceeds collected. These collection charges are little more than nominal. They include any direct expense or disbursements incurred, plus standard charges designed to cover the cost of operating the collection departments of the bank. Most banks view the operation of these departments as a service maintained for the convenience of depositors and correspondents. Collection is a very valuable service rendered business by the banks at cost and often at less than cost.

Investments

GROWTH IN IMPORTANCE OF INVESTMENTS. Bank investments in securities have vastly increased in importance during recent years. During World War II the nation's commercial banks (to facilitate financing the war effort) bought government securities in volumes that would have been regarded as fantastic previously and ended by holding over $90 billion at the end of 1945.

SECURITIES ELIGIBLE FOR BANK PURCHASE. Under the National Bank Act, national banks were permitted to discount and negotiate "promissory notes, drafts, bills of exchange, and **other evidences of debt.**" The Comptroller of the Currency ruled that bonds were "evidences of debt" and were in consequence legal for banks to purchase. The McFadden-Pepper Act of 1927 permitted national banks to buy "bonds, notes, or debentures commonly known as investment securities" and instructed the Comptroller to define "**investment securities**" for the guidance of the banks. This he did in terms of marketability, by ruling that "sales at intrinsic values" must be readily possible on an issue to make it appropriate for bank purchase.

As the law now stands, a national bank may not invest more than 10% of its capital and surplus in the securities "of any one obligor" and it must observe the regulations of the Comptroller with respect to type, quality, and accounting of investments. These regulations, however, do not apply to government securities. Regulations issued under the Banking Act of 1935 set up stricter qualitative standards for bank investments.

Qualification as an "Investment Security." To qualify as an "investment security," a bond must be one in which the investment characteristics predominate. Purchase of bonds convertible into stocks or low-grade bonds, in which the investment characteristics are distinctly or predominantly speculative, is expressly prohibited. **Ratings** by statistical services within the four top rating classifications indicate investment quality, but are not necessarily conclusive. They are used by bank examiners, however, to determine whether the bank's investments conform to the Comptroller's regulations. Responsibility for proper investment of the bank's funds in securities lies with the directors of the bank just as it has in the past.

A bond must also "be salable under ordinary circumstances with reasonable promptness at fair value." It must be either one of a public distribution of securities or issued by an obligor that has other securities with public distribution that would insure the marketability of the issue under consideration. If there is no public distribution it must mature not later than 10 years after issuance and must provide for amortization of at least 75% of the principal before maturity.

Government, state, and municipal bonds are automatically eligible for bank investment, as are issues of the Federal Home Loan banks, the Federal Farm Mortgage Corporation, and securities originating under the Federal Farm Loan Act. All bonds, domestic and foreign, that meet the quality standards may be purchased. But the purchase of stocks is barred, except for stock in the Federal Reserve bank, safe deposit subsidiaries, and others specifically authorized in the banking law. These regulations apply not only to the national banks but also to state banks that are members of the Federal Reserve System.

PREFERENCE FOR GOVERNMENT OBLIGATIONS. The purchase of government securities violates the **"real bills"** or **"productive credit" theory** of maintaining **bank liquidity** through holding short-term, self-liquidating obligations. But in postwar years government securities have been bought and held by banks on the theory that they are readily **marketable**—that is, that they could be sold in the open market (or, if the bank preferred not to sell them, used as collateral on the bank's own promissory notes given to its Federal Reserve or city-correspondent bank) in order to obtain cash as readily as, or more readily than, payment could be secured on short-term (30-, 60-, or 90-day) commercial obligations. Experience has shown that marketability may become impaired in a financial crisis, as during 1930 to 1933. When all banks and other financial institutions as well are attempting to liquidate at the same time, security portfolios become frozen unless there is a "big buyer" who will clear the market at, or close to, the existing level of prices. The Federal Reserve System stands ready to play this role today. In times of crises, therefore, banks now no

INVESTMENTS 5·23

longer anticipate having to shift their investment securities to the market; instead, they expect to shift them through the market and into the central bank.

Government obligations are therefore currently especially favored as bank investments because they can be readily shifted, as necessary, either to the market in usual circumstances or to the Federal Reserve in abnormal times, without much risk of loss in either instance.

Securities issued by the Federal government have always enjoyed a marked preference on the part of the banks from every standpoint except yield. The financing of World War II vastly increased the available supply of government securities. The method of financing the war depressed interest rates generally, and yields on high-grade corporate bonds fell almost as low as those on governments. During World War II, the Federal Reserve banks bought some $22 billion of government obligations, mostly short-term issues. These were bought (1) to expand bank reserves so as to enable commercial banks to buy more government obligations despite a huge rise of currency circulation, and (2) to support the prices of government securities.

The following **features** make government securities especially attractive to banks:

1. The excellent quality of government securities, backed as they are by the unlimited taxing power of the government.
2. Through them, banks can secure access to Federal Reserve credit without paying penalty rates, by pledging them as collateral for a secured advance from the Federal Reserve bank, or by selling them in the open market when the **Federal Open Market Account** is buying.
3. They are preferred over other investments by the bank examiners and the supervisory authorities.
4. The breadth and depth of their market make the shorter-dated issues readily salable at little or no loss to the holder.

Apart from considerations of yield, a bank can properly invest as large a proportion of its resources as it wishes in government securities. But the distribution of maturities must reflect the character of the bank's other assets and its liabilities. Obviously, a bank can have too many long-term bonds, whether government or otherwise.

Types of Government Securities. Subject to the requirements of their portfolios, banks have the option of buying the following types of government securities:

1. **Treasury bills,** which have an initial maturity not exceeding 1 year. Regular bills are currently being issued with maturities of 91, 180, and 360 days. Tax anticipation bills are issued irregularly and for various maturities within one year. The discount yield on bills in mid-1963 ranged from about 3.22% (asked price for 91-day bills) to about 3.50% (asked price for 360-day bills).
2. **Certificates of indebtedness** with a maturity of 1 year and a yield roughly equivalent to the 360-day bill.
3. **Treasury notes** with a maturity of 1 year to 5 years. In mid-1963 they had a market yield of from 3.50% (for 1-year notes) to about 3.90% (for 5-year notes).
4. **Bonds** now outstanding with maturities of up to about 35 years. In mid-1963 these were with coupon rates of between 2.97 and 4.10%.

VALUATION OF INVESTMENTS. Prior to the depression of the 1930's, most banks carried investments at cost, less a reserve for amortization of the premium on bonds bought above par. Further reserves were set up by those banks that were strong enough to do so against future defaults or unusual declines in market prices. This valuation method proved impracticable in the depressed bond markets of 1932 and 1933. If the examiners had forced banks to write down their holdings of securities to the low prices prevailing in the bond market at that time, too many banks would have had their capital impaired. Hence, valuations were based on "intrinsic values," rather than market prices, at that time.

Government Classifications. National and state regulatory authorities in 1938 adopted the following classification of investments for bank examination purposes:

> Group I. This group includes only securities "in which the investment characteristics are not distinctly or predominantly speculative. The group includes general market obligations in the four highest grades, and unrated securities of equivalent value." This entire group is valued at cost. No allowance is made for either appreciation or depreciation, except that premiums paid above par must be amortized.
> Group II. These securities are those "in which the investment characteristics are distinctly or predominantly speculative. This group includes in general market obligations in grades below the four highest, and unrated securities of equivalent value." Securities in this group are valued at the average market price of the 18 months immediately preceding the bank examination and at least 50% of the net depreciation, if any, must immediately be deducted from the capital of the bank in determining its solvency.
> Group III. This comprises securities in default, which must be immediately written down to the market.
> Group IV. This grouping includes stocks and similar holdings. All depreciation on them is considered a loss and must be written off against capital immediately.

Present Reporting Practices. Statements of condition published in the newspapers by banks usually show securities valued on the basis of cost. Such reports may differ from an examiner's report based on the methods outlined above. More conservative banks may value investments at market, if this is below cost, or at cost less a reserve.

PORTFOLIO POLICY. The investment policy of a bank should be fitted to the character of its deposit liabilities, the liquidity and soundness of its other assets, the character and intensity of the loan demand facing it, and its capital structure. If any one of these four is disregarded in policy formulation, difficulties may develop.

Principal Factors. Of these four considerations, the relative **stability of deposits** and the **nature of the bank's loan demand** are the most important. Banks with a large proportion of savings and other time deposits, or with demand deposits that do not fluctuate greatly in volume, do not have to be ready to meet withdrawals as potentially heavy as do banks in the financial centers. A "bankers' bank" must keep especially liquid as wide variations in its deposit totals will occur. Similarly, since it is axiomatic that banks prefer lending to investing, because lending is both more profitable and more constructive, a bank's portfolio policy must always aim at providing, whenever needed, the requisite liquidity to capitalize on good loan opportunities.

The **character of the other assets** of the bank is also of great significance in the selection of securities to be purchased. If other assets are highly liquid, the bank is warranted in purchasing long-term bonds that might be salable at a loss, because deposit withdrawals can be met out of other resources. But if the bank is heavily burdened with long-term bonds, mortgages, term loans, and other relatively "slow" assets, it should confine future purchases to the highest grade short-term commitments until a portfolio better balanced as to maturity has been achieved.

Finally, the **ratio of capital funds to "risk assets"** (especially loans) is important in formulating investment portfolio policy. Since the overriding function of bank capital is to protect depositors from losses arising from shrinkage in the value of the bank's assets, supervisory authorities now tend to believe that a bank should maintain a capital funds to risk assets ratio of at least 1 to 6. Banks approaching this limit must choose, therefore, between issuing additional stock and shifting out of risk assets (loans and municipal and corporate securities) into "riskless" assets (government securities). (Crosse, Management Policies for Commercial Banks.)

With due consideration to the foregoing factors, a bank may seek the maximum income consistent with an appropriate degree of liquidity and solvency. But a bank's investment policy must always be conditioned by considerations of liquidity and solvency, as well as income.

Distribution of Investment Maturities. The market price of a debt security may change because of a **change in the financial condition of the borrower** or a **change in the prevailing rates of interest.** Banks largely avoid the first, or credit, risk by purchasing only securities of such high quality that there is virtually no danger of the debtor's failing to pay interest or principal as due. But they are vulnerable to the second risk, that is, a change in the level of interest rates, because they buy "money bonds," i.e., obligations of such high quality that they fluctuate in price inversely with changes in going rates of interest, and because the banks may have to sell bonds long before their maturity because of losses of deposits, a demand for loans, or Federal Reserve policy changes. To minimize this risk, banks purchase bonds with maturities appropriately distributed among short-term, medium-term, and long-term. They strive to space their maturities on the basis of possible demands that may be made on them by their depositors or borrowers. Banks thus seek liquidity and solvency through a synchronized and conservative distribution of maturities, as well as through the purchase of the highest grades of securities.

The maturity distribution generally reflects to a considerable extent expectations as to the **outlook** for interest rates. When interest rates are high and are expected to rise, banks prefer near maturities to avoid the depreciation expected. They can then buy long-term bonds at the lower prices if and when these materialize. By the same token, banks prefer to buy longer-term bonds when interest rates are expected to decline. (Welfling, Bank Investments, and Lyon, Investment Portfolio Management in the Commercial Bank.)

PROFITS FROM SALE OF SECURITIES. Regulations of the Comptroller of the Currency require national banks to use profits on sales of securities to offset losses. A bank must first write off existing losses and then set up adequate reserves against possible future losses. **All losses must be covered** and adequate provision for future losses must be made before profits from the sale of securities can be used for any other corporate purposes.

Short-term trading profits should not be the aim of bank portfolio management. Banks that have such a trading policy tend to buy securities of poorer quality at times merely because it is felt that they have prospects of appreciation. But if the price does not rise as expected, or if it drops, the security may be frozen in the bond account. Thus, the quality of the portfolio may deteriorate.

This does not mean that every security must be held to maturity. Switches that increase safety or income can frequently be made with changes in economic trends. Likewise, prospective changes in interest rates may warrant shifts from short-term to long-term obligations, or vice versa. But bonds are bought by banks primarily for interest income, not capital gains.

TAX SWITCHING. Even though a bank purchases bonds primarily for interest income, it is perfectly appropriate for it to trade its portfolio for a combination of tax losses and capital gains over a cycle of bond prices. This practice is known as tax switching. It involves the sale, at a loss, of low-coupon bonds that are selling below the price at which they were purchased because of an increase in market rates of interest, and the purchase of dissimilar bonds (i.e., bonds of different maturities but of at least 6 months' remaining maturity) also selling at a discount.

The **advantage** of this portfolio rearrangement is that the bank can deduct the loss incurred on the sale of the bonds from ordinary income in computing its tax liability, while the bonds that were purchased below par to replace those that were sold will, as they near maturity, approach par (reaching par at maturity, of course); hence, a bank subject to a 48% income tax rate bears only 52% of the loss (the government bears the rest), and the increase in value of the newly purchased bonds over their remaining life, treated as a capital gain, is taxed at a maximum rate of 25%. Thus over the full cycle of first falling and then rising securities prices the bank stands to make a net gain of 23% (75% of the capital gain less 52% of the original loss) on the sale of the bonds.

Since losses must for tax purposes be offset against gains if both occur in the same year maximization of the benefits to be derived from tax switching requires that losses and gains be taken in different years. A bank portfolio manager must therefore decide early in each year whether it will be a **"gain year"** or a **"loss year"** in the portfolio. Since gain years (characterized by falling interest rates and rising securities prices) usually occur during economic recessions, when the demand for loans is small, the capital gains then taken tend to offset declines in loan income, thereby tending to stabilize bank income over good and bad years. (Robinson, The Management of Bank Funds.)

THE INVESTMENT DEPARTMENT. Responsibility for investment of the bank's funds rests with its officers and directors. Although they may use ratings of statistical services, they cannot shift the blame if mistakes are made and losses are incurred because of negligence. In addition to investing their own surplus funds, banks select and buy securities for trust funds under their control. They also advise correspondent banks and other customers on the securities that they purchase, and larger institutions maintain facilities for executing security orders for them.

The statistical, analytical, and clerical work involved is often centered in one department, although the trust department frequently has a separate group doing trust investment work. The investment department makes analyses of securities it considers good purchases for the bank to make. It periodically reviews the securities already purchased to see if changes should be made. Although the department is a relatively small one, the work is of tremendous importance to the bank. No department is more closely watched by the senior officers of the bank.

REAL ESTATE MORTGAGES AS BANK INVESTMENTS. Although the experience of banks with real estate mortgage loans was not a happy one during the depression of the 1930's, many institutions are keenly interested in such lending. By following improved practices, such as periodic amortization of a mortgage loan by the borrower through installment payments on account of principal, mortgage lending may be both safe and profitable. Moreover, **Federal Housing Administration** insurance of mortgages and **Veterans Administration** mortgage guarantees have made mortgage lending much less risky for the financial community. Nevertheless, relatively few banks make these types of government guaranteed and insured loans. Most banks prefer, instead, conventional mortgage lending as more profitable and involving fewer complications.

National banks may make conventional first mortgage loans in an amount not exceeding 75% of the appraised value of the property, with a maturity of up to 20 years (provided that such a loan is secured by an amortized mortgage, deed of trust, or other such instrument that provides for periodic payments of sufficient size to amortize the entire principal of the loan within the period ending on the date of maturity); and any mortgage loan insured by the F.H.A. or guaranteed by the V.A. The total amount invested in conventional mortgages by a national bank may not exceed its unimpaired capital and surplus, or 70% of its time and savings deposits, whichever is the greater.

Realistic appraising and periodic amortization can combine to make mortgage lending both a safe and a profitable activity for banks. As evidence of this fact, real estate lending by commercial banks tripled in dollar volume in 20 years, outstanding loans totaling more than $34 billion at the end of 1962. (Federal Reserve Bulletin, June 1963.)

Loans

IMPORTANCE OF LOANS. The volume of bank loans declined sharply during 1929–1933 and remained at a low level during the later 1930's despite some recovery in prices and business activity. Total loans did not change much during World War II and their relative importance among bank earning assets continued to decline as the banks acquired more and more government securities. During the postwar years, however, bank loans have expanded substantially to new record levels, totaling over $140 billion at the end of 1962, as compared with only $26 billion at the end of 1945.

Aside from real estate loans, discussed above, bank loans play a major role in the financing of industry, commerce, and agriculture, both new enterprises and old. They are particularly important to **smaller and medium-sized businesses** that do not have access to the capital funds markets. They also ordinarily provide the most **profitable outlet for the bank's funds,** usually yielding a materially higher rate of return than do investments.

METHODS OF BORROWING. Ordinarily a business man becomes accustomed to borrowing from a bank in one or two ways, and does not consider other methods. There are a number of loan plans with differing interest rates, terms, and security requirements. The cost of borrowing may be reduced by adjusting the method used to the circumstances of each case.

Although, by and large, it is better for most borrowers to confine borrowing to **one bank,** larger concerns frequently prefer to do business with **two or more banks** and are sometimes forced to do so when their financial requirements exceed the lending capacity of their original bank of deposit. Also, the borrower may do business with **more than one department of the bank** to advantage. Thus, exports might be financed through discounting drafts with the foreign department, imports through the commercial credit department, and other operations through over-the-counter loans. Banks make a wide variety of loans, the most important of which are discussed later in this section.

USES OF BANK LOANS. Before 1920, bank loans were used chiefly to finance agriculture and "commerce" (manufacturing and distribution); however, the financing of security distribution and ownership and of consumption has become of great importance in more recent years.

It was once thought economically unsound and socially unwise to use bank credit for other than a fairly narrow range of purposes identified with production or distribution. Loans, it was held, had to be short-term and self-liquidating to be sound. Maturities of more than 90 days were questioned, except for agricultural paper, and a maturity of more than 1 year was considered an improper use of bank credit. In contrast, banks lend nowadays for practically any purpose so long as ultimate repayment is reasonably sure. They make capital loans on a **term** basis, that is, payable in installments, with maturities as long as 10 years.

The **classical function of a commercial bank loan** was to meet seasonal and special working capital needs of a business. It was less expensive for a business man to borrow from the banks to finance an extra volume of business during the months of maximum activity than to expand his permanent capital to carry peak loads, even if he could raise the money on a long-term basis. But many concerns, especially larger ones, prefer to finance entirely on a long-term basis, whereas others now use banks to borrow for long-term, as well as short-term, needs.

ONE OR MORE BANKS? A good banking connection is a valuable asset to every business. Some business men deliberately patronize more than one bank, with the idea that if one bank turns down an application for a loan the other will lend. In an emergency, however, a banker takes care of his good customers first. Customers who have split their banking business among several institutions may then find no one bank gives them preferred treatment. Furthermore, in such circumstances the borrower may find each lending bank trying to secure repayment of its loan on the theory that the other banks would carry the borrower through the period of stringency. Also, a bank may seek repayment of its loan for fear other banks may do so first.

If a local bank is too small to meet the requirements of a larger borrower, the latter has no choice but to look for supplementary banking connections among larger institutions. Likewise, a large enterprise conducting business in more than one town usually finds it desirable to patronize banks in each community, to secure their goodwill and local banking services.

Even in these instances, however, a particularly close relationship with one bank is desirable so that in times of financial stress the bank's officers will have personal knowledge of the business and will feel obligated to take care of its credit needs.

TYPES OF BANK LOANS. Bank credit may be extended through **loans,** interest on which is payable at maturity or at specified dates periodically. Only in rare instances in business lending is interest on loans paid in advance, although in lending to consumers the "discounting" of the borrower's note is common practice. (Credit may also take the form of a **discount** of a note or draft brought in by the borrower as a maker or endorser. Discount is always deducted in advance from the face amount of the obligation.)

The **difference between a loan and discount** is thus technical and of little practical significance. As the amount of the discount is calculated from the face amount of the obligation, the borrower actually pays a somewhat higher rate for the money borrowed. Banking practice determines the use of the loan in certain types of transactions and the discount in others.

As regards maturity, loans may be either **demand** or **time**. The former, also referred to as **call loans**, are payable on demand of either party. Call loans are automatically renewed by mutual assent if notice to the contrary is not given by either party. Time loans have a definite maturity but it is frequently understood that they will be renewed, in whole or in part.

As to obligation of the parties, they may be **single-name** (the ordinary promissory note) or **double-name**. Double-name or two-name paper may take the form of a guaranteed obligation, a receivable (an endorsed note or draft), a bankers' acceptance, or a trade acceptance.

Loans and discounts may be **secured** or **unsecured**. The security may be a pledge of any asset of value, ranging from marketable stocks and bonds and real estate and property to salary and wages in the case of consumer credit.

SECURED LOANS. Although any asset may be pledged to insure repayment of a loan, the collateral ordinarily used may be grouped under the headings of commodities, real estate, securities and, in the instance of consumer credit, salaries, wages, or consumer durable goods.

The suitability of **merchandise** or **commodities** for use as collateral for a bank loan depends upon several factors. The most important of these are standardization of grading, durability, marketability, and stability of demand. A bank can protect itself against adverse price fluctuations by requiring the borrower to hedge his holdings through the sale of future contracts on a commodity exchange. The grains, particularly wheat, rye, and corn, and cotton, have proved to be exceptionally sound collateral for credit extension because they can be hedged, as well as because they meet the tests mentioned.

Bills of lading issued by common carriers are widely used as collateral for loans on commodities in transit, since the document is required to secure possession of goods at the point of destination.

There are two types of bills of lading, the straight bill of lading and the order bill of lading. A **straight bill of lading** is **nonnegotiable,** and thus not acceptable for use as collateral. An **order bill of lading** is **negotiable.** When banks discount drafts secured by bills of lading, they require order bills of lading. If the draft is accompanied by a straight bill, the bank will receive the item for collection only and will not credit the customer's account until the draft has actually been collected.

Enactment of the Federal Bill of Lading Act and adoption of the Uniform Bill of Lading Act by a majority of the states have greatly improved the quality of bills of lading as collateral by safeguarding their legal status.

A **trust receipt** gives the bank title to goods after physical possession has been transferred to the borrower, who holds them as trustee for the lender. In practice, the trust receipt has proved of limited value in many cases because the lender must prove title to specific lots of goods against which a trust receipt has been issued. Other creditors may dispute the lender's assertion that specified goods are not the property of the debtor, and the burden of proof is on the lender to prove his claim and identify the goods beyond question. The safest thing for the lender to do would be to require the borrower to specially label each item, but this is obviously impossible for goods in process and for commodities that cannot be labeled because of their character. Only if the goods bear serial numbers, as in the instance of automobiles, watches, and typewriters, can identification be positive.

Despite these difficulties, trust receipts are used in financing imports where they have served fairly well. They give supplementary protection where credit would be advanced in any case because of the credit standing of the borrower. In domestic trade, field warehousing, described below, has tended to replace the use of trust receipts.

Warehouse receipts, particularly when issued by bonded warehouses, are far superior as collateral to trust receipts. The warehouse receipt acknowledges storage of the goods and sets forth the terms and conditions on which they will be delivered. The receipt may be **nonnegotiable,** that is, the goods will be delivered only to the particular person specified in the receipt, or **negotiable,** in which event the goods will be delivered to the bearer or a person designated by the holder of the receipt. Negotiable receipts pass freely from hand to hand, transferring title to the goods each time.

The states have passed legislation providing for supervision of public warehouses. The Federal Warehouse Act provides for the licensing of agricultural product warehouses that meet minimum standards of financial responsibility and physical safety. The bond deposited by a warehouse protects the lender against theft of the goods.

A warehouse receipt may or may not specify the quality of the goods stored. It generally states the quantity, but this is not absolutely necessary. At times, warehouse receipts specify both quality and quantity, as in the instance of cotton and grain warehouse receipts, which have had a splendid collateral record.

By means of **field warehouse loans,** banks may be given a lien on commodities or merchandise stored on the premises of the borrower with better protection than a trust receipt accords since an outside warehouseman controls the storage space. Warehouse service organizations have worked out methods for the segregation, storage, inspection, and protection of pledged goods, and have demonstrated that they can protect the interests of the lender in such loans. The field warehousing organization receives a fee for its services in supervising and operating the segregated storage space for the pledged goods.

Accounts receivable are sometimes pledged as specific security for credit. Banks usually prefer to make loans on the basis of the general credit of the borrower, however, in which his accounts receivable are given due consideration. Factoring and finance companies require specific assignment of receivables as security for their advances.

Mortgages on real estate may be taken as security for short-term commercial loans, but only as a last resort and rarely. There is too much detail involved in tax and title searches, execution of instruments, recording, appraisal, and insurance. Banks make intermediate- and long-term mortgage loans on real estate and frequently take mortgages as collateral for term loans, but they do not like to go to so much trouble in connection with a short-term commercial loan.

SECURITY LOANS. Loans secured by stocks and bonds constitute the most important type of secured loans. The proceeds of security loans may be used for any business or personal purpose, but they are chiefly incurred for the purpose of carrying securities for distribution or profit.

Most security loans are made against listed securities, so that changes in the value of the collateral may be readily noted and the necessary action taken to protect the bank against loss. Safe margins of collateral value over the amount of a security loan vary from 5 to 10% on government securities to 30 to 50% on unlisted securities. Since 1934, **minimum margin requirements** have been set by the Board of Governors of the Federal Reserve System for listed securities, to regulate the volume of credit granted for this purpose and speculative activity on the security markets In postwar years, these have ranged from 50% upward. In July 1962 they were reduced from 70% to 50%, and in late 1963 they were again raised to 70%.

SINGLE-NAME VS. TWO-NAME PAPER. Under American business practice, most paper acquired by banks is single-name paper. Most manufacturers sell on open-book account, and when they need money they make out their own notes and turn them over to the banks. This differs from the practice of other countries where manufacturers commonly draw drafts to accompany each shipment. When the draft has been accepted, the manufacturer endorses it and discounts it, as two-name paper, at his bank.

The wider use of **domestic trade acceptances** has been advocated in the United States, but they have made little progress in displacing the historic open-book account in financing manufacturers' sales in most industries. In American practice, the domestic trade acceptance has been used at times to secure formal acknowledgment of an overdue open-book account, or as a collection weapon on an overdue account on the assumption that the buyer will be more likely to pay an obligation presented through his local bank. This background adds to the resistance to its wider use.

ACCOMMODATION PAPER. One kind of two-name paper that may be poorer than conventional single-name paper is the so-called **accommodation bill or note** for which the acceptor or maker has received no consideration, but on which he has lent his name and credit to accommodate the drawer, payee, or holder. The accommodating party is usually not identified with the business of the borrower. He is liable to the holder of the paper precisely as if there were a good consideration. But the party he has accommodated is obligated to take up the paper, or to provide the accommodation acceptor, maker, or endorser with funds for doing it, together with expenses legitimately incurred. Litigation sometimes results, however, that may adversely affect the holder of the paper before it is paid.

BANKER'S ACCEPTANCES. Another method of borrowing is through the use of banker's acceptances. These are drafts drawn upon a bank and accepted by it. If banks agree to accept such drafts, under arrangements made in advance, they charge a fee for the service, usually 1½% per annum (i.e., ⅛ of 1% on 30-day drafts, ¼ of 1% on 60-day drafts, ⅜ of 1% on 90-day drafts, etc.). After they have been accepted, these drafts find a ready market on a very low yield basis, since they are then outright obligations of the accepting banks. Naturally, banks will accept drafts only if they feel assured that funds to pay off the drafts will be provided them in advance of the maturities of the acceptances. Such assurance may result from the high credit standing of the customer or the fact that bills of lading or warehouse receipts are attached to the drafts, giving title to marketable goods that could be taken over and sold in the event of default.

Banker's acceptances are widely used in financing **foreign trade**. Their use in domestic trade has been limited, but wider employment of the device has been urged. The suitability of this financing method should be investigated by concerns that sell staple merchandise to a large number of customers, especially if the commodities sold are to be stored in warehouses for considerable periods of time.

TERM LOANS. Since the middle 1930's, banks have made capital loans to businesses, to finance fixed asset acquisition or increase of permanent working capital, for intermediate terms of 1 to 10 years. Such loans usually contain periodic (annual, semi-annual, or quarterly) amortization provisions that either extinguish the loan by maturity or at least reduce it to, say, 25% of the original advance. If only part of the loan is amortized during its life, it is said to have a **balloon maturity.**

Term loans are favored by some banks over the purchase of corporate bonds, since the lending bank negotiates the terms of the loan itself and maintains direct contact with the borrower, which is not the case with investment in bonds. Term loans usually carry a moderately higher interest rate than a short-term credit.

In postwar years, business borrowers have demanded term loans in large volume to finance expansion programs, and, by and large, the banks have willingly met this demand. Consequently, it is now estimated that from 35% to 40% of total bank loans to business is comprised of term credit. (Term loans are discussed in greater detail in Section 14, Long-Term and Intermediate-Term Borrowing.)

CREDIT ANALYSIS. Determination of the amount of credit that can be safely extended to a business enterprise has become a standard procedure. **Statement analysis** is at the base of all credit analysis. Comparison of the financial statements of the applicant with similar companies in the same line and with his own ratios in previous years shows trends and margins of safety. Adequacy of net working capital, sufficiency of quick assets, the size of the inventories and their rate of turnover, the volume of accounts receivable, rate of return realized on invested capital, and other pertinent facts can be gleaned from a study of financial statements.

Further salient information is derived from answers to supplementary questions on points such as the following:

1. Status of the inventory—finished, semifinished, and unfinished; stale, obsolete, or shopworn goods, etc.
2. Method of inventory valuation.
3. Analysis of accounts receivable—average age of the accounts, total of overdue accounts, provision for bad debts, etc.

Bankers prefer **audited statements** prepared by independent certified public accountants. Although not an absolute requirement, bankers place so much more reliance upon audited statements that it is advisable to furnish them if at all possible. In addition to balance sheets and income statements, bank credit men like to see budgets of previous years and comparisons of actual with estimated performance. They also like applicants to submit estimated balance sheets, income statements, cash budgets, and sales forecasts for the coming year or (especially in the instance of term loans) covering the period during which the loan will be outstanding.

Credit files are maintained by banks on each borrowing customer, and on many other business enterprises with which the banks' customers do business from time to time. The credit file is the repository of the credit information collected about each particular "name." The **financial statement section of the credit file** contains the statements discussed above. The **information section** contains reports of interviews by investigators, credit agency reports, trade reports, summaries of the experience of other banks with the subject, and other material gathered by the bank's credit investigators.

The **inquiry section** lists names of those inquiring about the subject of the folder, the credit information given, and the name of the clerk giving that information. Much may be learned about an enterprise by the character of the inquiries made.

The credit file contains details of loans made to the subject in the past and the rates charged. It contains a summary of borrowing limits, guarantors or endorsers required, and similar information.

The **credit department** collects, collates, files, and keeps up to date the information contained in the credit file. It is responsible for the analysis of financial statements, the calculation of ratios, and their interpretation. It is also responsible for the release of credit information to members of the bank's staff and outsiders. Credit files generally contain confidential information that should not get into unauthorized hands. It is the job of the credit department to see that this does not happen. Business men can usually rest assured that the information that they supply the bank will be carefully guarded.

The credit department must be careful in giving out credit information, as it could be liable both to the party to whom the information is given and the one about whom the information is given for resulting damage. Such **liability** for credit information divulged compels bank credit men to be extremely cautious in responding to credit inquiries. Business men who request credit information should realize that bank credit men perforce "damn with faint praise." Because of the liability involved, it is unusual for a bank credit man to give an unequivocal statement, good or bad, regarding the credit standing of an individual or enterprise. A business man must often read between the lines to get the full benefit of a credit report given him by a bank.

THE LINE OF CREDIT. On the basis of the credit analysis, a line of credit is established for customers who desire to borrow seasonally or at short-term. This line of credit is simply a statement by the bank that until further notice it is prepared to lend up to the stated maximum amount, on certain terms and conditions, to the prospective borrower. It is a declaration of intent and not an agreement, **and thus may be canceled or amended by the bank at any time.**

Usually considerable detail is specified in the line of credit regarding terms and conditions of the loans. Amounts that the bank is ready to lend the customer through its foreign department, over-the-counter, on security collateral, and so on may be set forth at length. Varying margins, maturities, and rates on different types of borrowing are usually indicated.

After a line of credit has been passed by the directors, it becomes a guide governing borrowing relations between the bank and the customer. In effect, it is a way of complying with the legal requirement that all loans must be approved by the directors. Officers of the bank can then authorize individual loans under the line of credit as requested by the customer without further action by the board of directors.

A line of credit, once established, is a real protection for the borrower since a banker does not reduce or cancel a line of credit without substantial cause. Bankers who treat lines of credit lightly will quickly lose borrowers. Borrowers agree to notify the bank of any material change in their credit status, and the bank watches new financial statements and industrial and general economic conditions so that changes in credit lines can be made as circumstances require.

Banks may require a minimum deposit balance of a specified percentage, varying from 10 to 20, of the line of credit, but such a **compensating balance** requirement is often waived, especially during periods of monetary ease. It is not necessary to utilize the full amount of a line of credit; in fact, an ample unused margin is considered a sign of financial strength. But if a customer wants to embody a line of credit in a formal agreement, as sometimes happens, a fee may be charged on the unused portion for such a **"stand-by" contract.**

CONSUMER LOANS. Commercial banks have always made small loans, many of which were really consumer loans although not recognized as such. In more recent years, most commercial banks have begun to extend consumer credit as such, and many of them have opened separate departments for handling consumer loans. Many institutions have expanded the operation of these departments to include all phases of consumer credit such as sales financing, personal loans without co-makers, home improvement loans, insurance policy loans, etc. Banks with consumer loan departments are usually prepared to make consumer loans on practically any basis used by any other agency, except pawnbrokers, offering keen competition to other lending agencies in this field. In fact, commercial banks now extend more consumer installment credit than any other class of lending institution. At the end of 1962, for example, commercial banks had extended over 45% of the total of $42 billion of such credit outstanding. (Federal Reserve Bulletin, June 1963.) A more detailed discussion of consumer credit is contained in Section 2, Banking and Lending Institutions.

SECTION 6

CORPORATE FIDUCIARIES, TRUSTS, AND AGENCIES

CONTENTS

	PAGE
Origin and Nature of Corporate Fiduciaries	
Establishment and growth of fiduciaries	1
Definition of fiduciary	1
Trust companies and banks	1
Definitions	1
Trust business	2
Trust	2
Agent	2
Corporate vs. personal trust business	2
Evolution of corporate fiduciaries	2
Economic importance	3
Advantages of corporate fiduciaries	3
Trust department management	4
The Personal Trust Business	
Work of the personal trust department	4
Functions of executor	5
Probate	5
Preparation of inventory	5
Administration	5
Final settlement	6
Work of an administrator	6
Ordinary administrator	6
Administrator cum testamento annexo	6
Administrator de bonis non	6
Ancillary administrator	6
Temporary administrator	6
Guardian of a minor	7
Guardian of an incompetent	7
Assignee	7
Personal Trusts	
Legal concept of a trust	7
Creation of trusts	8
Creating a trust by agreement or deed of trust	8
Creating a trust in a will	8
Living trusts	8
Retirement trusts	8
Life insurance trusts	9
Trusts in contemplation of death	9
Pension and profit-sharing trusts	10
Revocable and irrevocable trusts	10
Special types of personal trusts	10
Sheltering trusts	10
Spendthrift trusts	10
Trusts for incompetent persons	10
Charitable trusts	11
Trusts for emergencies	11

	PAGE
Rewarding trusts	11
Duration of trusts	11
Personal Trust Operation	
Collection of trust assets	11
Relations with the beneficiary	12
Care of trust assets	12
Accumulation of income	12
Trust Instrument Provisions	
Nature of the provisions	13
Provisions affecting income and principal payments	13
Investment provisions	13
Prudent man rule	14
Types of investment most commonly used	14
Absence of express power to sell	14
Restrictions on investment powers	14
Investment duties of a trustee	14
Resignation of a trustee	15
Termination of a trust	15
Management of Trust Investments	
Functions of an officers' investment committee	15
The reviewing department	16
The securities analysis department	16
Department sections	17
Other departments	17
Liabilities of a Fiduciary	
Accountability of the trustee	17
Liability of a trustee dealing with itself	18
Breaches of trust	18
Personal Agency Functions	
Range of functions	18
Services provided by trust companies	18
Agent or depositary for individual executors, administrators, and trustees	18
Custodial accounts for individuals	19
Escrow accounts	19
Personal Trust Fees	
Setting fees and commissions	20
Typical fees	20
Executors, administrators, and guardians	20
Trustees under wills of persons dying after August 31, 1956	20

CONTENTS (*Continued*)

Custodian accounts 21
Investment supervisory services 21

Fiduciary Functions for Corporations

Banks and trust companies as fiduciaries 21
Trustee for bondholders under indenture 22
Individual co-trustee for corporate bonds .. 22
Receiver or trustee 23

Agency Functions for Corporations

Fiscal agent 23
Transfer agent 23
Registrar 23
Subscription agent 24
Depositary under voting trust agreements ... 24
Agent for corporations in process of reorganization, recapitalization, consolidation, or merger 24

SECTION 6

CORPORATE FIDUCIARIES, TRUSTS, AND AGENCIES

Origin and Nature of Corporate Fiduciaries

ESTABLISHMENT AND GROWTH OF FIDUCIARIES. Accumulation of wealth in the hands of individuals and the desire on their part to conserve it for their own and their heirs' benefit were the **basic causes** for the establishment of corporate fiduciaries and their great growth and development in the United States. Until the middle of the nineteenth century, most fortunes primarily represented ownership of land. There was little reason for specialized institutions to assist individuals in the conservation of estates either during their lifetime or after their deaths. The industrial revolution, the development of railroad transportation, and industrial consolidations brought about aggregations of wealth consisting largely of securities, the management of which called for specialized knowledge and judgment. The corporations organized to provide such services are known as corporate fiduciaries.

Definition of Fiduciary. A fiduciary is defined as one who acts in a capacity of trust and confidence for another. No simple definition is sufficiently comprehensive to cover all instances in which an individual or corporate entity acts in a fiduciary capacity. The term is derived from the civil law. It has been held to apply to all persons, individual or corporate, who occupy a position of peculiar confidence toward others; and it implies integrity and fidelity of the person trusted, and it contemplates good faith rather than legal obligation as the dominant basis for transactions.

The term **covers a wide variety of activities and individuals,** including partners when acting one for the other; directors of corporations; public officials; attorneys at law and in fact when performing services for a client or principal; trustees appointed to their position either by will or agreement; executors of estates; receivers in bankruptcy or litigation; and others serving in similar responsible capacities.

At all times the fiduciary is **acting for another party.** The relationship, as a matter of business and law, is that one party places confidence in another party, the fiduciary, to act in good faith and for his best interest. Also the fiduciary is expected to act in the same way as a **prudent man** would act in the conduct of his own affairs.

Trust Companies and Banks. Trust companies and banks act as trustee or agent for the real and personal property of both living and deceased persons, or for the securities of issuing corporations. Such activities are classified as **trust business.**

DEFINITIONS. For a clear understanding of the nature and provisions of the various kinds of trusts, the following terms require definition:

Trust Business. The trust business of corporate fiduciaries was defined by the American Bankers Association in its Statement of Principles as follows:

It is the business of settling estates, administering trusts, and performing agencies in all appropriate cases for individuals, partnerships, associations, business corporations, and public, social, educational, recreational, and charitable institutions and units of government.

Trust. A trust involves the passing of title to property from the creator of the trust to a trustee, with the stipulation that the property be held for the benefit of another. The beneficiary, or **cestui que trust,** as he is sometimes called, may be the creator or another person or persons. (See also Legal Concept of a Trust, p. 7 below.)

Agent. An agent is one who is authorized by another party, known as the **principal,** to represent and act for the latter in making, modifying, or canceling a contract with third parties. (Bergh, Conyngton, and Kassoff, Business Law.) The primary difference between an agent and a trustee is that an agent does not take title to the property involved and usually transacts business under the name of the principal, whereas the trustee takes legal, but not equitable, title to the property and does business in his own name.

CORPORATE VS. PERSONAL TRUST BUSINESS. Trust business in the larger trust companies has, for reasons of efficiency, been divided into two major divisions usually described as the personal trust department and the corporate trust department. The handling of accounts in each of these categories has become highly specialized. Personal trust business is principally confined to settling estates of deceased persons, and the care of the assets included in trust estates. Corporate trust business, on the other hand, comprises primarily the functions of acting as trustee for corporate obligations, fiscal agent for stocks and bonds, and depositary for securities under deposit agreements. Though both types of trust business are usually under the authority of one senior trust officer, for practical purposes personal and corporate trust activities are kept separate from each other and are carried on by personnel who specialize in the different fields.

Evolution of Corporate Fiduciaries. The trust business had its roots in the field of insurance. The first corporations to undertake trust functions were the Massachusetts Hospital Life Insurance Co. of Boston, incorporated in 1818, and the Farmers Fire Insurance and Loan Co., which was authorized to engage in trust business by the New York legislature in 1822. A number of other corporations were founded about the same period to grant insurance and act in a trust capacity.

In time these corporations found the trust business to be **logically allied to banking** rather than to the writing of insurance. They either relinquished the insurance part of their business for banking, or dropped their trust activities to engage exclusively in insurance.

After 1850, many **state-chartered banks** applied to their legislatures for amendments to their charters that would give them the power to act as trustee and engage in other fiduciary activities. In later years, it became no longer necessary for state banks to obtain special charters or amendments to engage in trust business. These powers are now conferred by trust company and banking statutes of the various states.

National banks were not permitted to act as fiduciaries until 1918, when an amendment to the Federal Reserve Act authorized national banks to apply for and receive permission from the Federal Reserve Board to engage in all trust functions exercised by state banks and trust companies in the state in which the national bank is located. The same statute first authorized trust companies to join the Federal Reserve System. Although national banks thus obtained the statutory right to act as fiduciaries, it was not practical for them to do so at first because their charters limited their corporate existence to fifty years, a period of time much shorter than the life of many trusts. National banks were granted perpetual existence in the Banking Act of 1927, which removed the last obstacle to their full participation in trust activities.

Economic Importance. The vast economic importance of trust business may be gauged by the **magnitude of the assets involved.** According to a survey by the American Bankers Association, the holdings in personal trust accounts administered by banks accounting for about 98% of all personal trust department assets in the U.S. were estimated at $57 billion in 1959. In this study, estates, personal agencies, custodial accounts, investment advisory and management accounts, pension and profit-sharing trusts, corporate trusts and agencies, and insurance trusts were not included. In 1961 the assets of noninsured pension funds administered by banks were estimated at $20–25 billion. (See the American Banking Association's publication: The Commercial Banking Industry.)

ADVANTAGES OF CORPORATE FIDUCIARIES. Corporate fiduciaries usually offer the following advantages as compared with individual fiduciaries.

1. **Perpetual existence.** The institutional fiduciary offers continuous administration, which an individual cannot do. It has perpetual existence and a permanent place of business. It provides assurance against interruption of the performance of the duties of trusteeship due to absence, disability, or death, as could happen with an individual trustee. When an individual trustee dies or resigns before the termination of a trust, the appointment of a successor trustee may involve expensive legal proceedings, including an accounting by the previous trustee or his estate, the cost of which is a charge against the principal of the trust fund.

2. **Financial responsibility.** Corporate fiduciaries possess substantial resources. Their operations are constantly under supervision by their own accounting department, by independent auditors engaged by the board of directors, and by government authorities.

Further **protection** is accorded by the fact that assets held in trust are segregated from the assets of the corporate fiduciary. Losses due to fraud, laxity, or failure to live up to the requirements of the law or the trust instrument must be made good to beneficiaries out of the capital and surplus of the corporation.

3. **Legal status.** As a corporation, a trust company can sue and be used in its own name as an entity. Trust companies may also engage in fiduciary activities like any natural person, which other corporations cannot do.

A trust company incorporated in New York, for example, is also subject to restrictions imposed by the Surrogate's Court Act and the Decedents' Estate Act in its handling of trusts and estates of deceased persons, whereas trust activities for living persons are affected by the personal property laws and the law of agency.

In keeping with legal requirements, separate account books and procedures for trust business are maintained. Assets held in trust are completely segregated from trust assets in the banking departments. Assets held in trust do not appear in the statement of condition of a bank or trust company.

   4. **Banking and investing facilities.** The trust department or departments may use the facilities of the banking departments to effect purchases and sales of securities, and deposit accounts may be opened in the same institution for trusts or beneficiaries to receive and hold income from trust assets. Idle funds of trust accounts awaiting reinvestment or distribution may be deposited in a special bank account in the institution. But federal regulations and the laws of New York and some other states require the bank to set aside securities, usually federal or state obligations, as **collateral** for the protection of such deposits.

   TRUST DEPARTMENT MANAGEMENT. Direction of the trust department of a trust company or a bank rests ultimately in the board of directors or trustees of the institution. Under both national and state laws, the board of directors or trustees must set up a **separate department** completely divorced from the institution's banking activities. Direct supervision of the trust department in larger institutions is usually vested in a senior vice-president or trust officer who is responsible only to the president and the board, and who is frequently a member of the board.

The Personal Trust Business

WORK OF THE PERSONAL TRUST DEPARTMENT. The personal trust business includes the performance of trust and agency functions for individuals. **Trust functions** include the settling of estates of deceased individuals and the care and management of trusts created by either deceased or living persons. The major offices that a trust company assumes in this branch of the business are:

1. Executor of estates under a last will and testament of a deceased person.
2. Administrator of decedents' estates as,
   a. Administrator cum testamento annexo, that is, with will attached. (Usually this office is designated as Administrator C.T.A.)
   b. Administrator by appointment of the court of jurisdiction.
   c. Temporary administrator.
   d. Ancillary administrator.
3. Guardian of the estate of a minor, either through appointment in the will of a deceased person or by the court.
4. Guardian of the estate of an incompetent person who has been so adjudged by the court.
5. Testamentary trustee, that is, trustee by appointment in the last will and testament of a deceased person.
6. Inter vivos trustee, through deed or agreement with a living person. Such trusts are known as **living trusts.**
7. Discretionary agencies, combining fiduciary responsibilities with freedom from the formal requirements of the average trust.

Agency functions include:

1. Agent for trustees, executors, and administrators in handling the mechanical phase of their duties.
2. Custodial services such as safekeeping of assets, including the handling of purchases and sales of securities at the direction of the owner. The trust company may collect interest, dividends, and principal and render investment advice in this connection, as well as seek to guard the interests of the owner with respect to changes in the financial structure of issuers.
3. Escrow services, which involve safekeeping something of value that is to be delivered to another party upon the happening of some contingency.

FUNCTIONS OF EXECUTOR. An executor is an individual or corporate fiduciary appointed by a testator in his or her lifetime to carry into effect his or her last will and testament upon his or her decease, and to dispose of the estate according to the will's tenor. The primary function of the executor is to see that the terms of the will are carried out.

The duties of an executor are **usually temporary.** He is to collect all the assets of the estate, pay debts and taxes of the decedent and charges that arise from winding up the estate, and then distribute the remainder to the residuary legatees named in the instrument. Normally an executor does not invest funds of the estate, save in instances where such powers are granted by the testator to the executor during the period of settling the estate. An executor may invest the funds of the estate also if the interested parties consent to his doing so. If such additional powers are granted the executor, he might then be termed a temporary trustee.

In general, an executor's activities are confined to the following duties, as described by a large New York bank in a brochure for the information of its customers:

Probate. This duty involves locating the will and arranging with counsel for probate of the document, or the official proving of the will in the surrogate's court or whatever court has jurisdiction in these matters in the state where the will is to be probated. Upon probate, the will is certified by the court to be the decedent's last will and testament, and the executor is provided with letters testamentary, which empower him to act under the terms of the will and the laws of the state controlling the functions and duties of executors.

Preparation of Inventory. This step includes:
1. Collecting data on the assets and liabilities of the estate from the decedent's records.
2. Opening the decedent's safe deposit box and listing its contents.
3. Attending to appraisal of jewelry, household furniture, and other personal effects of the deceased.
4. Preparing an inventory of all assets, including interests, if any, in close corporations, partnerships, and other private ventures.
5. Tracing insurance policies and ascertaining beneficiaries and the amounts of insurance collectible.

Administration. The manifold administrative duties of an executor after he has ascertained the value and condition of the decedent's estate, to be performed faithfully in keeping with the terms of the will and the various state and federal laws controlling his actions, include:
1. Examining financial statements and other data and preparing reports and comparative figures to appraise interests in close corporations, partnerships, and other private businesses.
2. Paying debts, funeral expenses, and administration expenses.
3. Analyzing investments of the estate and formulating a plan of liquidation when necessary to raise cash for taxes, administration costs, and other expenses.
4. Furnishing counsel with a complete statement of assets and a complete list of debts and expenses in order to prepare estate and inheritance tax returns.
5. Attending to audit and adjustment of estate and inheritance tax returns.
6. Attending to partial distribution of the estate by payments of specific legacies and bequests contained in the will.
7. Attending to the preparation and filing of income tax returns for the decedent and the estate, as well as the audit of such tax returns.
8. Maintaining records of all transactions of the executor with respect to the estate, to facilitate preparation of an accounting to the court and the heirs on completion of the executor's job.

Final Settlement. Final settlement of an estate requires arrangement with counsel to submit to the court a **complete account of the executor** in respect to the management and winding up of the estate, and approval of such accounting either by judicial decree or by receipt and release from the heirs. Payments are then made to the heirs in accordance with the decree and the terms of the will, and proper proof of payment is then filed with the court. Upon filing of the final accounting and proof of payment, the executor is relieved of further responsibility and discharged by the court.

WORK OF AN ADMINISTRATOR. An administrator performs the same functions as an executor, which are to wind up the estate of a deceased person (except in the case of a temporary administrator). Unlike an executor, however, an administrator is appointed by the court having jurisdiction over decedents' estates, rather than by will of the deceased.

Ordinary Administrator. The ordinary administrator is appointed by the court to wind up the estate of a person who has died **intestate**—that is, without making a will. Usually the person with the greatest interest in the proceeds of the estate is named by the court to act as administrator, if in the discretion of the court that person is considered to be competent to act in such capacity. However, if the party with the greatest interest is unable or unfitted to act, or a number of persons having equal interests are unable to agree on who is to administer the estate, the court will usually appoint an outside and disinterested individual or trust company to assume the care and duty of settling the estate under the laws governing estates of intestates.

Administrator cum Testamento Annexo. Also known as administrator C.T.A., this administrator is appointed if the deceased person has made a will but has either failed to name an executor, or the executor so named has refused to or cannot act. The court then names the party who is to administer the estate, but the administrator, in this instance, instead of winding up and distributing the estate according to the dictates of the law governing estates of intestates, is guided by the testator's desires as expressed in the will.

Administrator de Bonis Non. This administrator, designated also as administrator D.B.N., is appointed to succeed a previously appointed administrator who has died before completion of his duties.

Ancillary Administrator. An ancillary administrator is appointed to act for the estate of a decedent who was resident in another state, the assets of whose estate in whole or part are situated in the state where the court appointing the ancillary administrator has jurisdiction.

Temporary Administrator. A temporary administrator takes charge of a decedent's estate if, for some reason or other, an executor cannot immediately assume direction or a permanent administrator cannot be appointed immediately. Almost invariably this situation arises from **litigations,** such as a will contest between heirs dissatisfied with the terms of the will or the entry of claims to the estate by persons not named in the will. Litigation may arise also because the will itself is attacked as fraudulent, or as having been executed under conditions that would invalidate it in the eyes of the law. Under these circumstances, the executor named cannot perform his duties, for the will cannot be probated until the litigation has been settled. A temporary administrator may be appointed also because of a refusal of the heirs, with good cause, to accept the services of the party named as executor, the minority of the executor, a protracted disagreement among heirs of an intestate as to who will assume the duties of administrator, etc.

Temporary administrators have very **few independent powers,** in contrast to executors or other types of administrators. Their duties consist primarily of assembling the assets of the estate. Further activities to settle the estate are usually held in abeyance until the factors preventing permanent administration have been cured. Sales of property or other assets, payment of debts, and other such acts can be effected by a temporary administrator only by special court order. The office of temporary administrator is similar to that of a receiver in bankruptcy or litigation, in that he acts merely as an agent of the court.

GUARDIAN OF A MINOR. A guardian is appointed for a minor either in the will of the deceased or by the court. Usually the guardian is the surviving parent of the minor, a close relative or a close friend of the parents. Under some wills, or in some instances if the guardian named in the will or the surviving parent or close relative is not competent to handle the minor's property, a trust company will be appointed guardian of the minor's estate, whereas an individual will be appointed guardian of the minor's person. A guardian is needed to care for the interests of the minor since under the law a minor is not in a position to manage his own affairs and cannot make a contract. The guardian collects the assets of a minor as speedily as possible. The bank then sets up an accounting for principal and the income from the assets. This it does for its own convenience, as in the estate of a minor the courts do not distinguish between principal and income, all the property belonging to the minor and there being no remaindermen as in a trust account.

The bank requests and receives from the courts a **maintenance order** for the disbursement of funds for the minor's subsistence and education. These funds are paid either to the guardian of the minor's person or to the minor himself if he is old enough to use the money for the purpose for which it is remitted. In rare instances the bank may be appointed the guardian of the minor's person as well as of his property, in which case the bank would pay the minor's bills and give him pocket money. A bank may be appointed to this position if the minor at the time is near his 21st birthday. **Investment of the assets of a minor** in New York State and in many other states is limited to legal investment. If there is no instrument permitting the guardian to do so, a court order may have to be obtained to sell particular property or assets of the minor. Occasionally the guardian is given a **blanket order to make sales** at any time in his discretion, subject to considerations of prudence.

GUARDIAN OF AN INCOMPETENT. The guardian of an incompetent acts in the same manner as the guardian of a minor. He is to apply the property to the well-being of the incompetent. However, if an incompetent has persons dependent upon him, the court will permit application of a part of the incompetent's estate to these dependents.

ASSIGNEE. If a trust company or other fiduciary receives title to the assets of a debtor and holds them for the benefit of the latter's creditors, it functions as assignee. This assignment, like that of receiver that it resembles, is rarely taken by trust companies because of the need for highly specialized business management that is involved.

Personal Trusts

LEGAL CONCEPT OF A TRUST. A trust is a fiduciary relationship with respect to **property,** subjecting the person by whom the title to the property is held to equitable duties to deal with the property for the benefit of another person, which relationship arises as the result of a manifestation of an intention to create it. (American Law Institute, Second Restatement of Trusts.) A trust is created by a transfer of property, either by agreement or deed or by will, in which said property passes to another as trustee. (Scott, on Trusts.)

Actual legal title is given to property by one party to another when a trust is created. The trustee holds title for the benefit of a third party, the **beneficiary.** If title is passed by will, the creator of the trust is known as the **testator**; if title is passed by a living person the creator is known as the settlor, grantor, donor, or trustor. The term used to designate the maker of a living trust is **settlor.**

CREATION OF TRUSTS. A trust may be created to provide income for the support of dependents, the education of children, the maintenance of charitable or educational institutions, or some other desired object. Trusts may be either express or implied. An **express trust** is one created by deed or agreement between the parties, by a declaration or a will. In creating an express trust, the parties involved know and intend at all times that a trust shall arise from their actions. When created by a deed or declaration, it is called a **voluntary, living, or inter vivos trust,** as distinguished from a **testamentary trust,** which is established by will. An **implied trust** is a trust arising by implication from the acts or situation of the parties or from the wording of an instrument, rather than from any direct or expressed declaration to create a trust.

Creating a Trust by Agreement or Deed of Trust. Any competent person may set up a trust under a simple agreement directing how the funds shall be invested, to whom the income from investments shall be paid, and when and to whom the principal shall be paid out upon the termination of the trust. The person named to receive the principal when the trust terminates is known as the remainderman.

When a person has decided upon the amount of a trust he wishes to establish, its terms, and the identity of the trustee, he should have his attorney prepare an agreement of trust setting forth clearly the settlor's intentions and the necessary provisions for putting them into effect. This should preferably be done in conference with the trustee, to assure that the trust will be one the trustee is willing to accept and administer. The trust agreement is signed in duplicate by both the settlor of the trust and the trustee, each of whom retains one of the duplicate originals. The trust is then in existence, and thenceforth it is the duty of the trustee to carry out faithfully the terms of the agreement.

Creating a Trust in a Will. In the creation of a testamentary trust, as of a living trust, it is imperative that a competent and experienced attorney be consulted to advise on the best manner to put the creator's desires into effect. The party to be named trustee should be consulted to insure that he will be willing to act in this capacity under the terms of the will creating the trust, for there may be difficulty in obtaining a substitute if the trustee named should refuse to accept the assignment, as well as added legal expense in applying to the court for a substitute.

LIVING TRUSTS. More important types of trusts that, by their nature, can be created by living persons only are:

Retirement Trusts. These trusts are created to build up an estate during the more fruitful years of an individual's lifetime, while providing relief from the problems of management of the property during the declining period of life. The settlor is both creator and beneficiary in such a trust. If no provision is included for passing on the corpus of the trust to another upon the death of the beneficiary, the courts may construe it as a **naked trust,** that is, one in which no true transfer of property has been made. In the event of a suit against the beneficiary, the trust would then be open to attachment like any other property owned.

Life Insurance Trusts. These consist of the proceeds of life insurance policies on the life of the creator. Policies are made payable to the trustee, and the proceeds are collected by the trustee when due, either during the life of the creator in the case of endowment policies, or at the creator's death with other policies. Life insurance trusts have become increasingly popular in recent years as a means of enabling persons in moderate circumstances to create an estate forthwith without waiting to accumulate savings over a long period of years. Life insurance trusts are divided into three categories, known as funded, partially funded, and unfunded life insurance trusts.

1. Funded life insurance trusts call for the deposit of securities in the trust, and premiums on the life insurance policies are paid from the income received on these investments. The trustee assumes the responsibility not only of caring for the securities, but also of paying the premiums. The creation of an estate is thus assured by the settlor, since payment of the life insurance premiums is made certain. Also, the investment of the proceeds of the insurance policies will be undertaken by the trustee, whether they become due and payable during the lifetime of the settlor or, as is usual, after his decease. Care must be taken in drawing up the agreement creating a funded life insurance trust in New York or any other state that has a rule against the accumulation of income in a trust; provision should be made that, in the event that investment income exceeds the amount of the premiums paid, such excess shall be distributed to some other beneficiary named in the agreement.

2. Partially funded life insurance trusts provide that securities be deposited with the trustee to furnish a part of the premium payments on the life insurance policies making up the trust. The difference between the amount of income accruing from the securities and the total sum needed to pay premiums is provided by the creator of the trust. The trustee is responsible in these trusts for paying the premiums, but he bills the creator for the difference between investment income and premiums payable. To facilitate payment of the difference, an account may be opened in which the creator deposits equal monthly installments to equal his share of the annual premiums due on the life insurance policies.

3. Unfunded life insurance trusts provide that the settlor is entirely responsible for paying the premiums on the policies. No securities are deposited with the trustee. The trustee then assumes no responsibility until the life insurance policies become due and payable, after which the arrangement is the same as under other types of insurance trusts.

Trusts in Contemplation of Death. Trusts of this kind are created by living persons who wish to dispose of a part of their property during their lifetime so that the beneficiaries can enjoy the income without assuming the burden of management, for which they may not be fitted by experience. If a trust is made in contemplation of death, if it takes effect only upon the death of the creator, or if the creator retains control over the property, the trust deed will be **treated as if it were a will** upon the death of the creator.

Trusts in contemplation of death are made if the natural heirs are quite importunate or are actually in need of their share of the estate during the creator's lifetime. The creator establishes a trust for each beneficiary in an amount that is believed to approximate that beneficiary's share of the estate, or what the creator wishes to leave to the individual beneficiary on his death. The creator thus spares himself repeated pleas for the prepayment of funds that his heirs expect to receive at his death.

Pension and Profit-Sharing Trusts. Many businesses have established pension and profit-sharing plans under which trust funds are set up for the payment of retirement and other benefits to employees. (See Sec. 19, Pensions and Profit-Sharing Plans.)

REVOCABLE AND IRREVOCABLE TRUSTS. A voluntary or living trust may be either revocable or irrevocable. The creator may reserve the right to terminate the trust agreement at his pleasure or on the happening of some contingency, or the trust may take the form of an absolute and irrevocable gift. The form to use depends on the circumstances of each individual case, particularly the creator's age. **Younger persons** usually want to retain the right to terminate or alter the agreement as personal and family developments indicate changes in beneficiaries or other terms of the trust, or perhaps make it desirable to terminate the agreement entirely.

Living trusts of **elderly people** should usually be irrevocable. The property in the trust then becomes an absolute gift and gift taxes are paid thereon. A gift tax is not paid if the trust can be revoked, for then the gift is not absolute. Circumstances affecting the lives of older persons are less subject to wide changes as regards beneficiaries or the sizes of their estates. The settlor of an irrevocable trust may retain the right to supervise or to be consulted by the trustee as regards the investment of trust funds during his lifetime, if he so desires.

A **testamentary trust** is revocable only if the testator gives such power to the trustee or some other party.

SPECIAL TYPES OF PERSONAL TRUSTS. Particular requirements of circumstances lead to the establishment of special types of personal trusts, with suitable forms of trust instruments. These arise both in living and testamentary trusts. The more important are:

Sheltering Trusts. It is possible for a husband to provide a separate and certain income for his wife, or for parents to assure the support of their children. At the same time, the settlor or testator may relieve the beneficiaries from investment problems and shield them from the risk of dangerous advisers. This can be done by establishing a sheltering trust, either by agreement or will, with appropriate provisions and conditions to achieve the objectives desired. The next two trusts discussed below are types of sheltering trusts.

Spendthrift Trusts. These are a variety of sheltering trust designed to protect an improvident beneficiary from his or her lack of responsibility in the care and spending of money. Laws of some states permit the placing of both the corpus and the income of a spendthrift trust out of reach of the beneficiary's creditors and do not allow the spendthrift to anticipate income from the trust fund. In New York State, however, many of these advantages of a spendthrift trust are lost because of a statutory provision that corpus and income of a spendthrift trust can be attached under the same contingencies in which this can be done with other personal trusts.

Trusts for Incompetent Persons. Such trusts are created for individuals unable to carry on their affairs because of some physical or mental incapacity. Under this type of sheltering trust, the creator is assured that an incompetent charge will be cared for whether the creator lives or dies. In a living trust of this type, the settlor knows that if he suffers business or investment losses, the incompetent will continue to be provided for.

Charitable Trusts. Trusts for charitable, religious, literary, or scientific purposes may be perpetual in duration, with designated institutions or a class of persons as continuous beneficiaries of the trust income. Beneficiaries may be a church, college, hospital, or other established eleemosynary institution, or a specified activity such as the provision of scholarships and fellowships or the support of the poor of a certain community. When the particular charitable purpose becomes impossible to carry out, an action may be brought in certain cases to apply the trust proceeds to similar purposes.

Trusts for Emergencies. Provision can be made for unforeseen as well as known needs of beneficiaries by authorizing the trustee, in case of emergency, to make use of principal in addition to income from a trust fund. If, for example, a man feels that the income from a trust fund, though adequate for ordinary needs of his beneficiary, may not equal the expenses of higher education, he may give the trustee discretion to use part of the principal for the latter purpose. Likewise, a creator may authorize the trustee to use part of the principal for medical expenses, and other specified contingencies, to relieve beneficiaries of anxiety under circumstances in which income alone may be too small for their needs.

Rewarding Trusts. The creation of such trusts may be motivated by a number of different desires, such as assuring old and faithful servants of an independent income after the employer's death or expressing gratitude to persons who have aided or been kind to the creator during his lifetime.

DURATION OF TRUSTS. Trusts for the benefit of individuals are limited as to duration in all jurisdictions that follow the principles of the English Common Law, as do most of the states of the United States. The courts of England have always opposed the tying up of property for too long a time. The British have laid down two basic rules, widely adopted in the United States, that govern the duration of personal trusts for individual benefit. These are the Rule Againt Perpetuities and the Rule Against Restraints on Alienation. The **Rule Against Perpetuities** requires that full title to property in a trust must be vested in others not later than 21 years after the death of one or more living persons named in the trust instrument. The **Rule Against Restraints on Alienation,** also known as the Rule Against Undue Postponement of Direct Enjoyment or Ownership of Property, holds that vesting in others of title to property placed in trust cannot be postponed pending some unlikely contingency, such as when a specified village will become a city. Under the New York statute, the power to suspend ownership of both personal and real property by means of a trust is limited to a period measured by lives in being at the creation of the trust plus 21 years. The statute further specifies that "lives in being shall include a child begotten before the creation of the estate but born thereafter."

Personal Trust Operation

COLLECTION OF TRUST ASSETS. The settlor under a living trust agreement usually turns over the assets of the trust to the trustee at the time the instrument is drawn, or shortly thereafter. Assets of a testamentary trust, on the other hand, remain under the control of the executor of the estate until it has been settled. The executor may or may not be the trustee named in the will. Upon settlement of the estate by the executor, it is incumbent on the trustee to collect the trust assets **within a reasonable time,** any losses resulting from failure to do so being chargeable to the trustee.

The trustee prepares an inventory of all assets as they are received and appraises them as of the date of receipt. This is done to relieve the trustee of responsibility for losses incurred prior to receipt of the assets and to determine increases or decreases in value following taking of possession, as well as to provide a base for calculating fees.

RELATIONS WITH THE BENEFICIARY. An alert trust company gets in touch with the beneficiary or beneficiaries as soon as it has received and appraised the trust estate. Two considerations impel it to do so. First, establishment of a **friendly relationship with the beneficiaries** is desirable, to make clear to them that the trust company is willing to cooperate with them to the best of its ability within the terms and limitations imposed by the instrument. Secondly, arrangements must be made with the beneficiaries for the **payment of income** and the **rendering of statements** to them by the trustee. In many instances, by mutual agreement between the beneficiaries and the trustee, income is paid in equal monthly or quarterly installments, with any surplus above the regular payments being payable on the anniversary date of the creation of the trust. Statements may be rendered with each income payment, but they are often made quarterly to save the trustee time and trouble and reduce charges against the corpus of the trust.

Once the assets of a trust have been inventoried and appraised, and a personal relationship has been established with the beneficiaries, the trustee begins to administer the trust according to the terms of the will or trust agreement.

CARE OF TRUST ASSETS. Responsibility for the physical care of the assets held in trust accounts is usually placed in one or more persons appointed by the trust department head. These individuals are the only ones permitted to give and take receipts for transfers of securities held in trust.

Index file cards are prepared for each trust, listing the securities and other assets held in the account. The description of bonds held includes first call date, date of maturity, and due date of each issue. Stock descriptions show whether the shares are preferred or common, and dividend dates. Arrearages of interest or dividends due are noted.

Payments of income and principal are listed separately on the cards, partly to avoid accumulations of income in the trust in states where this is banned, and partly to assist in the final accounting required prior to distribution of the corpus on the termination of the trust. If the trust instrument or state laws provide that premiums on bonds purchased above par are to be amortized, a record of such amortization is kept. In New York State, if the settlor or testator does not so direct, the trust company is not required to provide for such amortization.

Machine bookkeeping has modified record keeping practices in important respects, especially in larger trust companies.

Accumulation of Income. Certain states prohibit the accumulation of income in a trust, fearing that excessive amounts of property will thus become impounded in trusts, unless the beneficiary is a minor. In the latter case, when the beneficiary reaches 21 the accumulated income must be paid to him.

During the beneficiary's minority, his share of the income is set aside in a separate account and is excluded from the trust fund proper. The money so set aside for the minor may consist of only part of the income accruing from the trust assets during the beneficiary's minority, if the trustee contributes to the living and educational expenses of the minor from the latter's share of the trust income.

To carry out the donor's purpose to provide an income for the beneficiary, it is proper to include provisions in the trust instrument that the beneficiary shall not anticipate income, and that neither principal nor income shall be assigned or attachable for the beneficiary's debts. In some states, the statute safeguards against alienation of income.

Trust Instrument Provisions

NATURE OF THE PROVISIONS. The provisions of a trust instrument should specify clearly how the trust shall be conducted during its term and the manner in which it is to be distributed on its termination. The most important provisions deal with the disposition of income accruing to the trust, the inviolability of the corpus, investment restrictions, and the final distribution.

PROVISIONS AFFECTING INCOME AND PRINCIPAL PAYMENTS. The simplest arrangement is that the income from the trust shall be payable to one beneficiary and the principal on the latter's death shall be paid to another person or persons. In this instance, no provision is made for payments from principal prior to termination of the trust, and the principal is usually assumed to be inviolable during the life of the trust. But the settlor or testator, to assure beneficiaries adequate income, may provide that they are to receive a specified sum per annum from the trust, and if the income does not provide the amount designated withdrawals may be made from the corpus of the fund. The trust then provides an **annuity**, since beneficiaries are practically guaranteed a fixed income each year.

It is necessary to ascertain the **intent of the creator** before making advances from principal. Counsel should be consulted if the instrument is not clear, to determine the proper course of action. The remaindermen should be requested to agree to any principal payments that are to be made, unless such payments are specifically authorized in the trust terms. If payments are made from the corpus without proper authorization, the trustee is liable for the amount of the payments to the remaindermen upon termination and distribution of the trust.

INVESTMENT PROVISIONS. A trust company is limited in the investment of trust funds by restrictions contained in the instrument under which it acts. Any deviation from limitations laid down by the creator of the trust that results in losses to the trust fund is chargeable to the trustee.

There are three ways in which the creator may define the investment powers of the trustee. These are:

1. Limitation to legal securities, as these are defined by the laws of the state in which the trustee is located. This limitation may be effected either through a clause in the trust agreement or through failure to specify any investment powers. **If no provision for investment is made,** the trustee is held to be bound to securities that are legal investments for trustees.

2. Discretionary investment provisions, which authorize the trustee to use his prudent judgment in selecting securities for the investment of trust funds. Under a discretionary provision, the trustee may invest in any type of security, including stocks as well as bonds and mortgages.

3. Securities may be designated in the trust instrument, consisting of stocks or bonds turned over to the trustee at the inception of the trust, or to be purchased by him. It is commonly provided, however, that the designated securities may be sold if this appears wise to the trustee, which places a measure of responsibility upon him.

Prudent Man Rule. There has been a trend toward liberalizing state laws restricting trust investments. A number of states now use the prudent man rule, first adopted in Massachusetts, which has been defined by the courts as "the exercise of sound judgment and care under the circumstances currently prevailing, which men of prudence, discretion and intelligence would exercise, not in regard to speculation, but in regard to investment, considering income as well as the safety of the principal." No particular groups of securities are specified as legal investments under this rule. Other states designate classes and groups of investments that may be purchased, which then constitute the **legal list** for that state.

Types of Investment Most Commonly Used. The desire to preserve the purchasing power of the corpus of the trust, together with the widespread adoption of the "prudent-man" rule in many states, has resulted in a preponderance of common stock in trust accounts. Of the total market value of asset holdings of personal trusts administered by banks with trust assets of $10 million or more in 1959, common stocks accounted for 61.7%, state and municipal securities 15.7%, U.S. government securities 5.1%, corporate bonds 4.7%, preferred stock 2.6%, and all other assets 10.2%. (Source: The American Bankers Association's publication: The Commercial Banking Industry.)

Absence of Express Power To Sell. If investment powers are not specifically included in the trust instrument, the courts in some states hold that the trustee has no authority to sell assets originally included in the trust. In other decisions, the power of sale is held to be implied even though it is not mentioned. But even if the trust instrument bars the sale of trust assets, there are instances where the courts have permitted liquidation of holdings that constitute a drain on the remainder of the estate, and thereby threaten preservation of the estate as a whole.

Restrictions on Investment Powers. A great variety of restrictions on investment powers are found in individual trusts. The trustee may be authorized to hold assets received, but to reinvest the proceeds from the sale of these assets only in legal investments or government obligations. Rights issued to holders of bonds or preferred stock for the purchase of new common shares may be exercised, it may be provided, even though the trustee is not allowed to invest in common stocks otherwise. The sale of such common shares shortly after their acquisition may be desirable to avoid surcharge due to losses if the shares decline.

It is not wise to restrict the freedom of action of a trustee too closely in matters of investment because of changing economic conditions affecting industries, communities, and individual concerns. Detailed restrictions that seem wise when drawn may work to the disadvantage of a trust later. Efforts to obtain relief from onerous restrictions in the court involve legal costs that may have to come out of the principal of the trust fund. Furthermore, investment instructions should be kept as simple as possible to avoid confusion as to the intent of the creator.

INVESTMENT DUTIES OF A TRUSTEE. Diligence and prudence are required of a trustee at all times, irrespective of the investment provisions of the trust instrument. Even if the instrument limits investment to the legal list, the trustee must select the more desirable investments among these from both a quality and an income standpoint. A trustee is required by law to seek a **reasonable income** from the trust assets, as well as to provide **safety of the principal.** If a legal investment is removed from the legal list by a change in the law or a decline in the issuer's earnings, prudent judgment indicates that it should be sold when a reasonable price can be secured in the market.

A trustee is not expected to have prescience in forecasting long-term business trends or market conditions. If, after considering pertinent factors, a security is purchased and later sold at a loss, a trustee cannot be held liable to surcharge for such loss if it is proved that the transaction was in **good faith** and warranted by conditions at the time. In one instance, a bank sold for a trust securities of a corporation whose earning power had deteriorated over a period of years with recovery prospects quite doubtful. But during World War II, the company enjoyed an unexpected recovery in earnings, and market prices for its securities rose sharply. The beneficiaries sued to surcharge the bank for the difference between the price at which the security had been sold and the high price prevailing at the time of the sale. The court upheld the bank on the ground that it could not be expected to foresee the outbreak of war in the future, let alone the consequences of a war economy upon the operations and earnings of the company.

RESIGNATION OF A TRUSTEE. A trustee may refuse to accept his assignment. But once having accepted the appointment, he may resign only with the permission of the courts, which usually require that a substantial reason be given for requesting relief from the assignment. A trust company or other trustee may resign because of a strong disagreement with a co-trustee appointed to act with it over investment policy or other issues. Resignation may be brought about also because the beneficiary or beneficiaries are constantly at odds with the trustee, and the latter finds it impossible to reach a satisfactory settlement of the difficulties.

The **trust is not terminated** when a trustee is allowed to resign. Rather, another trustee is appointed to carry out the terms of the trust.

TERMINATION OF A TRUST. An accounting of the estate for the entire period of the trust is rendered by a trustee upon termination. After rendering this final accounting, the trustee distributes the corpus of the trust to the named beneficiaries, or those judicially designated by the court as beneficiaries if it is not clear to whom the corpus should be delivered because a beneficiary had died before the termination of the trust. Court approval of the final accounting may be asked, or the beneficiaries may be requested to give a receipt and release. If a minor is involved, it is advisable not to use the receipt and release form of settlement, since a minor cannot give a legally valid release.

Management of Trust Investments

FUNCTIONS OF AN OFFICERS' INVESTMENT COMMITTEE. In most large trust companies, the investment of funds of individual trust accounts is under the care of an officers' investment committee. This committee is usually composed of the senior trust officer, the senior investment officer of the trust department, the head of the securities analysis department, and the junior investment officers who head the several divisions of the reviewing department.

The officers' investment committee is **responsible for the overall investment policy** of the personal trust department. Through the junior officers attached to the reviewing department, it supervises the investments of individual accounts according to their needs and in the light of investment provisions contained in the instruments under which the trusts were created.

The committee is advised by both the **securities analysis department** and the **reviewing department.** The analysis department recommends the purchase, sale, retention, or future liquidation at a specified price of individual securities. The investment committee approves or disapproves these recommendations and submits its findings to the investment committee of the board of directors or trustees of the institution for final approval or disapproval. Ultimate legal responsibility for trust investment rests with the directors.

THE REVIEWING DEPARTMENT. The principal function of the reviewing department is to carry out the decisions of the officers' investment committee in the management of the investments of individual trusts. In a large trust company, the reviewing department comprises the following sections:

1. **Unrestricted accounts.** Trusts in which the company has full powers of investment in all types of securities, without limit as to the amount of each type of security invested in.
2. **Special accounts.** Accounts with special investment provisions such as limitation to bonds, to preferred stocks, or to municipal securities, or where the limitation provides for investment in securities of a specified company or industry.
3. **Legal investment accounts.** Limited to legal securities as defined by the state in which the bank or trust company is located.

The junior officer in charge of each section has a staff that constantly surveys the accounts under his charge. This enables him to keep the investment committee informed as to the investment needs and problems of individual trusts.

A reviewing department of a large institution also has sections that take care of the mechanics of investments for estates or trusts and the setting up of new accounts on a going basis so that they can be assigned to the sections named above. This department makes periodical reviews of custodian accounts.

Reviews of the individual accounts consist of a tabulation showing the current market value of each holding. Securities are classified and totals set down for bonds, preferred stock, common stock, mortgages, and cash. On a summary sheet significant facts concerning the trust's investments and the recommendations of the securities analysis department are listed. This review is signed by the senior reviewer and is presented by him to the officers' investment committee for approval, and for instructions as to the action to be taken.

The reviewing department **watches for calls** of bonds or preferred stock, and brings them to the attention of one of the investment officers, who in turn informs the investment committee. It **notes the issuance of rights** to subscribe for additional securities.

A **diary** of each individual trust account is kept by the reviewing department, which indicates all letters received or sent, telephone calls, etc., and a journal records sales and purchases of securities and additions or withdrawals of assets and cash.

THE SECURITIES ANALYSIS DEPARTMENT. The securities analysis department of a trust company seeks to determine the qualifications of individual issues as trust investments. The department is concerned with **investments for all accounts,** rather than with the needs of individual trusts, though special studies affecting the investments of one account are made from time to time when special circumstances arise. Pertinent industrial, accounting, and financial information is compiled about each issue. This information is embodied in a report, and a recommendation is attached that must be concurred in by the head of the department. Copies of the report and recommendation are sent to each member of the investment committee, who studies them prior to the meeting at which the report is either accepted or rejected. General economic conditions, the movement of interest rates, and trends in individual industries are also studied by this department.

Department Sections. The securities analysis department is divided into specialized sections in the large institution. These are:

1. **Industrial,** the largest group, covering securities of extractive, manufacturing, trade, and miscellaneous enterprises.
2. **Public utility,** concerned with securities of electric light and power, gas, municipal traction, water, and other public service corporations.
3. **Railroad.**
4. **Municipal,** including state, school district, and public authority obligations.
5. **Bank and financial,** including insurance and finance company securities.
6. **Foreign,** comprising government and corporation securities.
7. **Special.** Studies particular situations such as refundings, new financing, reorganizations, proxy statements, and other matters that may affect the position of a security of an issuing company.

OTHER DEPARTMENTS. Other departments that participate in the management of trusts and agencies include:

1. **The Tax Department,** which sees that tax returns are filed and taxes are paid. This department takes care of tax problems that arise in settling an estate, before the final distribution is made. It follows changes in tax laws and regulations affecting fiduciary accounts.
2. **The Accounting Department,** which handles the accounts of each trust and agency and prepares the final accounting prior to termination of the trust company's control of the account.
3. **The Mortgage and Real Estate Department,** handling these important types of investment, which is often placed under the supervision of a separate officers' and directors' committee.

Liabilities of a Fiduciary

ACCOUNTABILITY OF THE TRUSTEE. Fiduciaries are required to act in good faith and with proper diligence, in accordance with the trust instrument and the laws of the state having jurisdiction. Failure to do so is considered a **breach of trust,** and resulting losses are surcharged by the courts against the trustee. The surcharge for breach of trust is designed to return to the beneficiary either the assets that were lost, plus the income thereon, or a sum of money equal to the damage suffered. The beneficiary's interest is thus restored to what it would have been if the trustee had not failed in his duty.

The courts hold a trustee accountable for negligence committed either through positive acts or omissions of duty. [Waterman v. Alden, 144 Ill. 90, 32 N. E. 972 (1893).] Acts of negligence or omissions of duty include:

1. Making any **unauthorized investment** that gives rise to loss. [State v. Washburn, Conn. 187, 34 Atl. 1034 (1896).]
2. **Failure to diversify** investments as authorized by the instrument or law, when this failure results in undue losses to the trust. [Vest v. Bialson, 365 Mo. 1103, 293 S. W. 2d 369 (1956).]
3. **Carelessness** in permitting an agent or co-trustee to breach the trust instrument, which causes losses to the trust fund. [Creed v. McAleer, 275 Mass. 353, N. E. 761 (1931).]
4. **Failure to collect** rents or other income when due, thereby depriving the trust of income.
5. **Retaining securities or other assets for an unreasonable time** after they fall below the standards for trust investment, or holding too long securities that,

when received in the trust, were ineligible for investment of trust funds. [Babbitt v. Fidelity Trust Co., 72 N. J. Eq. 745, 66 Atl. 1076 (1907).]

A large proportion of surcharge suits revolve around the **failure of trustees to sell securities or property** in a trust on some date before these assets suffered sharp declines in value. Counsel for beneficiaries in such cases seek to prove that, with the exercise of due diligence, the trustee would have sold when an annual report appeared showing a loss, or when some other event should have indicated the wisdom of selling. However, since the depression of the 30's, the courts have been less ready to surcharge trustees indiscriminately, recognizing that the decision must be based not on hindsight but upon the situation that existed when the trust company was confronted with the decision whether to hold or sell, and had to weigh the favorable as well as the unfavorable elements in the outlook for the security.

Liability of a Trustee Dealing with Itself. A trustee is liable for losses on all dealings with itself, such as the sale of property to the trust, either directly or indirectly. The beneficiary may approve the transaction and require completion of the sale, recovering the excess, if any, of the selling price over the value of the property to the trust. [Hartman v. Hartle, 95 N. J. Eq. 123, 122 Atl. 615 (1923).] He may also have the sale set aside and all payments for purchase of the property refunded by the trustee. [French v. Westgate, 71 N. H. 510, 53 Atl. 310 (1902).] Profits accruing to a trust, whether from proper or improper management, belong to the beneficiary [Robertson v. Hirsh, 276 Mass. 452, 177 N. E. (1931)], and the trustee is accountable for all profits.

Executors and **administrators** of estates and **guardians** and **committees** of minors and incompetents are liable for the above acts, like trustees.

BREACHES OF TRUST. Breaches of trust for which fiduciaries are always held liable are:

1. Fraud, such as misappropriation of the corpus or income for the benefit of others than the heirs or beneficiaries. This type of breach is not only surchargeable against the fiduciary, but makes him liable also to criminal prosecution.
2. Failure to pay taxes due.
3. Failure to reinvest trust funds for an unreasonable length of time, thereby causing loss of income to the trust.

Personal Agency Functions

RANGE OF FUNCTIONS. Personal agency functions performed by trust companies range from the simple duty of acting as depositary for the assets of individuals, with no other service involved, to the function of fiscal agent. The latter capacity may include possession and complete management of an individual's estate, and can be likened to the function of trustee, save for the fact that legal ownership of the estate remains with the principal and is not vested in the trust company. Not only do trust companies care for the assets of individuals, but they also care for estates under the control of individual executors, administrators, and trustees.

SERVICES PROVIDED BY TRUST COMPANIES. Typical agency services provided by trust companies for individuals include:

Agent or Depositary for Individual Executors, Administrators, and Trustees. Many individuals charged with the care and settlement of an estate or trust find it more convenient to leave the **detail work** and the **custodianship** of the assets to a trust company, while reserving to themselves the making of decisions under the trust instrument. The trust company, as agent, receives the assets from the individual fiduciary and holds them for safekeeping. If requested by the executor or trustee, books recording all transactions affecting the estate are kept by the trust company, including entries of principal accruing from redemption of bonds or preferred stock, income received from coupon payments and dividends, and rents from real property. However, the individual fiduciary may prefer to keep his own books, and the agent then credits all funds received to a bank account or other designated depositary.

The trust company may also **keep the individual fiduciary informed** of redemption of securities, rights to subscribe to additional securities, and steps proposed by an issuer that might affect the position or equity of bonds or outstanding stock. The executor or trustee may direct the institution to make changes in assets from time to time. Investment advisory services are made available by trust companies, as is advice on legal problems connected with performance of fiduciary powers by an individual.

When acting as agent or depositary for an individual fiduciary, the **trust company does not assume the responsibilities** of the former. It acts in a strictly mechanical manner by direction of its client. However, it is advisable for the institution to keep on hand a copy of the instrument under which the client received his powers, to satisfy itself that the principal does not violate the terms of the will or agreement.

Custodial Accounts for Individuals. There are a number of agency services provided individuals by trust departments of banks and trust companies. Three of the chief services of this kind provided are:

1. **Agency accounts,** in which the trust company holds the securities of an individual for safekeeping. Income and principal are collected and remitted to the owner, or the person or institution designated to receive such funds. The trust company renders a periodic statement of transactions affecting the account, differentiating between principal and income.

2. **Agency accounts with investment service** receive the services provided straight agency accounts and the facilities of the trust company's reviewing and security analysis departments for the management of investments, with recommendations for shifts from time to time. Depending on the wishes of the principal and what he wishes to pay for such additional services, **reviews and analyses** may be on a monthly, quarterly, semiannual, annual, or continuous basis. The reviews list securities in the account, comment on their quality, and indicate suggested changes, to be made at the discretion of the principal. In some instances, full discretion to act is vested in the trust company, so that the relationship is essentially that of a trust. This type of service has shown rapid growth in recent years.

3. **Safekeeping accounts** resemble straight agency accounts, except that income and principal, as received, go directly into the principal's bank account. No periodic statements are sent out, but advices of each purchase and sale of securities are sent, the principal keeping his own records of funds received in his bank account.

ESCROW ACCOUNTS. An escrow holds something of value for one person that is to be delivered to another upon the happening of a specified contingency agreed upon between the parties. In this type of account, the trust company does not take title to the property as in a trust. It holds the property as a **depositary** for the parties to the escrow agreement, and protects both in accordance with the contract.

Personal Trust Fees

SETTING FEES AND COMMISSIONS. Fees and commissions on trust and other fiduciary accounts are **set either by law or by the provisions of the instrument,** as in the case of individual fiduciaries. The creator may specify the compensation of the fiduciary as he sees fit, making it either less or more than the fees stated in the state law. Once having accepted a trust, the fiduciary is bound to limit himself to the payment specified. If a trustee is dissatisfied with the fee specified, he must reject the proffered trust, and the court will appoint another trustee. If none will accept the assignment at the fee mentioned, the court will authorize payment of the legal fees to such substitute trustee.

If no payment is specified by the creator, a fiduciary's fees are set by the laws of the state in which he is located. Extra fees, over and above those provided in the instrument or by law, might be permitted by the courts if exceptional demands on the fiduciary's time and ability are necessary to administer the estate or trust properly, so that payment of the usual fees would be inequitable.

TYPICAL FEES. Payments allowed fiduciaries under the laws of the State of **New York,** in most instances, are as follows:

Executors, Administrators, and Guardians. In addition to reasonable and necessary expenses actually paid, the following commissions must be allowed:

1. **Receiving and paying out sums of money.**

    4%   on all sums not exceeding $10,000.
    2½% on additional sums not exceeding $290,000.
    2%   on all sums above $300,000.

2. **Additional commissions** for collecting rents and managing real property.

    5%   of gross rents collected.

Only one commission on principal and income is permitted annually by New York State law, no matter how many trustees there are, if the corpus of the trust is less than $100,000. This commission is usually split up into equal portions for each trustee. If, however, the corpus of a trust is over $100,000, up to three commissions, but no more, may be paid to the several trustees. But there shall be only one 5% commission deducted from rents for the collection thereof and the managing of such properties.

Trustees Under Wills of Persons Dying After August 31, 1956. In addition to reasonable and necessary expenses actually paid, the following commissions must be allowed:

1. **Annual commissions,** payable one-half from income and one-half from principal.

    $5.00 per $1,000 of first $50,000 of principal.
    $2.50 per $1,000 of next $450,000 of principal.
    $2.00 per $1,000 on all additional principal.

2. **Terminal commissions,** at settlement of trustee's account:

    1% on amount of principal paid out.

In most circumstances when the trust corpus is less than $100,000, the payment of **only one commission** is permitted, regardless of the number of acting trustees.

This commission may, of course, be allocated among the various trustees. If, however, the corpus of the trust is $100,000 or more, up to three commissions may be paid. But if the trust at inception is a charitable one existing in perpetuity, the trustee is entitled to no commissions.

Custodian Accounts. These fees differ according to the type of account, the kind of securities involved, and the particular trust company. In general, the leading trust companies in **New York City** charge similar fees for custodial and fiscal services. A typical schedule of fees charged by a major trust company follows:

1. **Fees for custody of securities.**

    Bonds:
    $1.00 per $1,000 par value per annum on first $500,000 in bonds held.
    $.75 per $1,000 par value per annum on the next $500,000 of bonds.
    $.50 per $1,000 par value per annum on all bonds over $1,000,000.

    Stocks:
    $.07 per share per annum on the first 3,000 shares held.
    $.05 per share per annum on the next 2,000 shares held.
    $.03 per share per annum on all shares held in excess of 5,000 shares.

2. **Minimum fee on custodial accounts.** The minimum fee on all custodial accounts will be at least $50 per annum, but not less than $4 per issue per annum.

3. **Fees for receipt and delivery of securities in a custodial account.** For receiving or delivering securities either against payment or receipt, including the transfer thereof if necessary, the charge is $2.50 for each issue or security involved. However, no charge will be made for receiving or delivering securities in connection with the opening or closing of an account.

4. **Statement fees to the owner of a custodial account.** Once in each year the trust company will send a statement of the securities and the transactions affecting them in each custodial account. The cost of this statement is included in the regular charge for the account. Each additional statement will cost $.05 per item listed, the minimum fee being $2.50.

5. **Special statement fees.** For a special statement of yearly income, including profits and losses on security transactions classified for income tax purposes, the charge will be based on the amount of work involved, with a minimum charge of $25.

Investment Supervisory Services. Fees for supervision of investments on custodial accounts vary according to the amount of supervision the owner of the securities desires. Charges for continuous supervision, including custodial charges, imposed by a major bank in New York City are:

½ of 1% of market value of first $500,000 of securities, computed semiannually.
⅜ of 1% of market value of next $500,000 of securities, computed semiannually.
rate for supervision of securities in excess of $1,000,000 subject to negotiation.

The minimum annual fee for such investment supervision is usually $750.

Fiduciary Functions for Corporations

BANKS AND TRUST COMPANIES AS FIDUCIARIES. Banks and trust companies first began to act as fiduciaries for business concerns about 1830. A corporate trustee was first appointed for a corporation bond issue in 1839, when the Beaver Meadow Rail Road Co. appointed the Girard Life Insurance,

Annuity and Trust Co. of Philadelphia trustee under its mortgage. With the development of railroad bond financing in the middle of the nineteenth century, the present form of trusteeship under corporate mortgages was evolved. Trust companies first acted as transfer agent and registrar for corporation stocks about 1860, as the need for safeguards to prevent fraudulent overissuance of shares became apparent. In 1869, the New York Stock Exchange adopted a rule that corporations whose shares are listed on the Exchange must have an independent registrar.

Corporate trust business can be highly mechanized, as a result of which it often proves more profitable to the trust company than personal trust activities.

Corporate trust functions include:

1. Trustee under corporate mortgage or other instrument of indebtedness.
2. Receiver or trustee for corporations involved in reorganization or other litigation.

Corporate agency functions include:

1. Fiscal agent.
2. Transfer agent.
3. Registrar.
4. Agent for corporations in reorganization.
5. Agent for corporations in process of consolidation or merger.
6. Escrow agent.
7. Depositary under voting trust agreements.

TRUSTEE FOR BONDHOLDERS UNDER INDENTURE. The trustee under a corporate indenture functions on behalf of the holders of all the bonds issued under the indenture. At one time, individual trustees were appointed. But individual trustees often died or were incapacitated during the life of a long-term bond issue, and some were inefficient in the performance of their duties. In the interest both of the corporation and the bondholders, the appointment of a qualified fiduciary, with perpetual existence, was logical.

The first duty of a corporate trustee is to **investigate** the issue and the issuer, to assure that all legal requirements have been met. The trust company cooperates in drafting the indenture, under which it will function as trustee.

The trust company **authenticates** each bond to prevent overissuance and to assure that it enjoys the protection of the indenture. Authentication is effected by placing a certifying stamp on the face of the bond, showing that it is covered by the original authorization and indenture.

During the life of the bonds, the trust company watches for any **breach of the agreement** on the part of the issuing corporation. If a breach occurs, it serves notice on the issuer, and if the defect is not remedied it may start an action to protect the bondholders. Upon payment of a part or all of an issue of bonds the trustee receives the paid bonds and either destroys them or officially marks them as paid. Payment of maturing or called bonds may be effected by depositing funds for this purpose with the trustee. In the event bonds are refunded by an exchange for new obligations, the trust company may act as exchange agent.

The exercise of this function by trust companies is greatly influenced by provisions of the **Trust Indenture Act of 1939.** (See Sec. 14, Long-Term and Intermediate-Term Borrowing.)

INDIVIDUAL CO-TRUSTEE FOR CORPORATE BONDS. In addition to the corporate trustee, an individual is often appointed to act as co-trustee with the trust company. This person's responsibilities are theoretically the same as those of the corporate trustee, but he actually plays a passive role until a default or other breach of the indenture occurs. The individual trustee may then bring the action in the courts against the company. This is necessary if the trust company as a **foreign corporation** is barred from bringing suit in the courts of certain states. Under the Constitution, a citizen of one state has all the rights of the citizens of the several states.

RECEIVER OR TRUSTEE. Trust companies have been appointed receiver or trustee for corporations by some courts. This has been opposed by the legal profession, and in New York the trust company law was amended to bar trust companies from accepting such appointments.

Agency Functions for Corporations

FISCAL AGENT. Trust companies act as **coupon-paying** agents for bond interest and as agents for **sinking funds** on bonds and preferred stock. Upon payment of coupons, they are canceled and either returned to the issuing corporation, which pastes them in special coupon books, or destroyed. Trustees require proof, when bonds mature, that coupons have been paid before declaring the indenture satisfied. Trust companies also act as **dividend-paying** agents for equity securities. Through such agency functions, the trust company relieves the issuer of a vast amount of clerical work in keeping records, drawing checks, etc. It also facilitates collection of the funds due them by security holders. Handling many such accounts, a trust company can minimize the cost per item by keeping its staff continuously employed, whereas a corporation would have to hire many people for such work and keep them busy only around the interest or dividend-payment dates.

A further duty of the coupon-paying agent is to **withhold any income taxes** that the corporation is required to withhold or pay on the coupons, and to file with the United States Internal Revenue Service the monthly and annual reports of coupons paid and taxes collected that are required by law. The board of directors of the corporation must give the coupon-paying agent special authorization to withhold and pay income taxes to the government and to make and file the statutory reports.

TRANSFER AGENT. A transfer agent keeps a record of transfers of stock ownership. Either a trust company or an official of the issuing corporation may be named for this function.

The transfer agent is responsible for accurately recording **changes in stock ownership.** He receives certificates for shares sold from the purchaser or his agent, ascertains that they have been properly endorsed by the stockholder of record, and then issues new certificates covering the same number of shares represented by the old certificates, which are canceled by the transfer agent. In addition, a transfer agent must make certain that the seller of shares offered for transfer has the legal power to sell them.

If more than one transfer agent is appointed for a company's stock, it is imperative that they keep each other informed of all transfers. Multiple transfer agents may be appointed for different cities or countries. Transfers of bonds and other securities, as well as stocks, may be effected by a trust company.

Transfer agents are often appointed dividend-paying agents also, since they maintain the stockholders' list in any event.

REGISTRAR. Trust companies as registrars keep a record of the issued and outstanding shares of a corporation to **prevent the issuance of more shares**

than are authorized by the certificate of incorporation. The registrar thus prevents illegal dilution of the equity of shareholders by fraudulent overissue of stock.

It is now a **general rule among stock exchanges** in the United States that shares listed thereon must be registered with an agent not connected with issuer. Certificates transferred by the transfer agent must be countersigned by the registrar, and stock certificates canceled must be recorded as such by the registrar also. The books of both agents must agree, and they provide a constant check on each other in assuring an accurate record of the ownership of issued and outstanding shares and in preventing the issuance of certificates for shares beyond the legally outstanding amount.

SUBSCRIPTION AGENT. Banks and trust companies may act as subscription agents for a new offering of stock by a corporation to its shareholders, through the issuance of rights. In this capacity, they accept subscriptions, issue full- or partly paid receipts or purchase certificates, receive subscriptions from underwriters of the new issue, and deliver the new securities to the subscriber upon surrender of full-paid subscription receipts or purchase certificates.

DEPOSITARY UNDER VOTING TRUST AGREEMENTS. A voting trust agreement calls for the deposit of stock with a trust company under an agreement providing that the shares shall be voted by specified voting trustees. The trust company, acting as agent for voting trustees, issues shares of beneficial interest to stockholders in lieu of their deposited stock certificates. During the duration of the voting trust the **trustees are in effective control of the company.** The depositary trust company also is usually appointed agent to issue and transfer certificates of beneficial interest, and to pay dividends thereon.

AGENT FOR CORPORATIONS IN PROCESS OF REORGANIZATION, RECAPITALIZATION, CONSOLIDATION, OR MERGER. These corporate transactions involve the deposit, transfer, and exchange of securities. Trust companies, with their efficient deposit facilities and their trained organizations, are well qualified to receive and hold the securities involved to effect exchanges and cash payments promptly and smoothly.

SECTION 7

SECURITY ANALYSIS

CONTENTS

Investment Principles

	PAGE
Investment defined	1
Classes of investments	1
Characteristics of investments	1
Safety	1
Forms of safety sought	2
Diversification	2
The timing hazard	2
Return on investment	2
Marketability	3
Liquidity	3
Tax status	3
Legal investments	3
Function of security analysis	4

Bond Analysis

Objective of analysis	4
The credit of the obligor	4
Earnings coverage of interest charges	4
Earnings coverage of junior bond interest	5
Cash flow coverage of debt service requirements	5
Miscellaneous credit factors	5
Protective provisions of bond issue	5
Bond ratings	5
Rating systems	6
The market for bonds	6
Convertible bonds	6
Other fixed-income investments	6
Real estate mortgages	6
Insured and guaranteed mortgages	7
Preferred stocks	7

Common Stock Analysis

Objective of analysis	8
Earnings per share	8
The price-earnings ratio	8
The trend of earnings per share	8
The quality of reported earnings	9
Dividend policy	9
Investor demand	9
Quality of management	10
Analysis procedures	10

Industrial Securities

Nature of the industry	10
Factors of analysis	11
Prospective earnings	11

	PAGE
Sales prospects	11
Selling prices	11
Costs	11
Cash flow	12
Working capital position	12
Accounting peculiarities	12
Capital structure	13
Dividend prospects	13
Other factors	13
Ratio analysis	13
Industry analysis	14

Financial Securities

Distinctive features	14
Bank stocks	15
Analysis ratios	15
Insurance stocks	15
Fire and casualty insurance companies	15
Life insurance companies	15
Other financial stocks	16

Public Utility Securities

Types of enterprises	16
Distinctive features	16
Franchises	16
Utility rates	17
Utility valuation	17
Commission regulation	18
Analysis of a utility company	18
The demand for service	18
Regulatory factors	18
Load factor	19
Character of the plant	19
Capitalization	19
Earning power	20
Operating ratio	20
Classes of public utilities	20
Electric light and power	21
Natural gas	21
Telephone and telegraph companies	21

Railroad Securities

Legal and economic factors	21
Railroad traffic	22
Railroad rates	22
Operating expenses	22
Analysis ratios	23
Railroad financial statements	24
Special analytical factors	24

SECTION 7

SECURITY ANALYSIS

Investment Principles

INVESTMENT DEFINED. The term "investment" has three different meanings in common usage. In the broadest sense, investment refers to the placement of funds in productive assets to earn a return, regardless of whether or not such investment is accompanied by management. In this sense, investment refers to the acquisition by a business of assets for its own use, as well as the purchase of securities in businesses managed by others. A second definition of investment is the acquisition of assets to secure a return in the form of interest, dividends, rents, or capital appreciation, but without assumption of responsibility for management. The third and most narrow definition of investment is the acquisition of assets to secure income where the degree of risk is limited so far as practicable. In this third sense, investment is distinguished from **speculation**, which involves the deliberate assumption of substantial risks to secure capital appreciation or a high rate of return; and **gambling**, which involves the making of wagers rather than the acquisition of interests in property. (Jordan and Dougall, Investments.)

Ownership of **cash** does not constitute investment. Only when cash is used to acquire income-producing assets, whether as creditor or owner, does investment occur.

In this section, the term investment will be used in the second sense stated above, the placement of capital without assuming responsibility for management to obtain a return in the form of interest, dividends, rents, or capital appreciation.

CLASSES OF INVESTMENTS. Investments fall into two main classes, designated in financial, as distinct from legal, terminology as **fixed income** and **equity** investments. Fixed income investments include bonds, real estate mortgages, and preferred stocks. Equity investments include common stocks and ownership of real estate. Convertible bonds and preferred stocks are hybrid forms, acquiring characteristics of equity investments through the holder's option to exchange his fixed income securities for common stocks under specified conditions.

The chief classes of bonds are U.S. government, state and municipal government, and corporate obligations. Common stocks are classified into industrial, financial, public utility, and railroad stocks.

CHARACTERISTICS OF INVESTMENTS. Each investment possesses a number of characteristics that determine its suitability and desirability for individual or institutional investors. The two most important characteristics are **safety** and the **rate of return**. Other significant characteristics are **marketability** and **tax status**.

SAFETY. All investment involves risk. Even the purchase of U.S. government obligations, generally regarded as the highest quality security available, involves two risks, a **decline in price** due to a rise in the level of interest rates and a **decline in the purchasing power** of the dollars received as interest and principal due to a rise in the level of commodity prices. At the other end of the pole, the purchase of common stock in a newly promoted enterprise in a new industry involves manifold risks too numerous to mention.

Each investor is guided by circumstances and temperament in determining **how much risk to assume.** A widow entirely dependent upon the income from her investments should limit the risks she assumes to an absolute minimum. On the other hand, a business man with a large salary may feel justified in assuming considerable risks in order to obtain substantial appreciation on his investments, particularly since long term capital gains are taxed far more favorably than current income. (Graham, Dodd, and Cottle, Security Analysis.)

Safety in investment is thus a relative term, referring to the ability of the investor to assume risk, as well as to the number and character of risks surrounding a particular investment.

Forms of Safety Sought. Safety as an investment objective assumes two forms. **Dollar safety,** which is provided by high-grade bonds, means that the investor who places $1,000 in a bond can expect to receive back substantially the same amount either through its eventual sale or redemption. **Purchasing power safety,** provided best by common stocks, means that the investor who puts $1,000 in equities can expect to recover, say, $2,000 in time should the commodity price level double during the period that stocks are held. Common stocks as a class have proved an effective **inflation hedge** over the long run, but not necessarily over shorter periods. (Clendenin, Introduction to Investments.)

Diversification. Diversification can add to the safety of a portfolio through spreading the risk. In bonds, staggering of maturities lessens the risk of portfolio depreciation due to a rise in interest rates, which causes widest declines in prices of obligations with longer maturities. In common stocks, diversification takes the form of buying equities of companies in different industries and enterprises, so that unfavorable developments affecting a particular industry or enterprise would have only a limited adverse effect upon the performance of the portfolio as a whole. (Hayes, Investments: Analysis and Management)

The Timing Hazard. Wide fluctuation in the level of common stock prices gives rise to a major timing hazard in equity investment. When stocks are bought at a time when prices are substantially higher than will prevail in ensuing years, a portfolio is likely to depreciate in price, and the investor will obtain less in earnings and dividends on his investment than he would if purchases were made at a later date after stock prices had declined. The timing hazard can be minimized by skillful selection of securities based on competent analysis. It can be minimized also by **dollar cost averaging,** which involves periodic investment of a fixed sum in equities over a period of years so as to effect purchases at times of both high and low stock prices. Since more shares will be bought when prices are low than when prices are high, the average cost to the investor over a period of years is lowered. **Formula plans,** which provide for purchases of stocks when the level of prices declines and sales of stocks when prices rise, provide another approach for limiting the timing hazard.

RETURN ON INVESTMENT. Investors seek to obtain the highest return available on investments that provide the kind and degree of safety they desire. The return on fixed income investments like bonds, mortgages, and preferred stocks is limited to the contractual interest or preferred dividend rate.

Common stocks, by contrast, constituting the ownership element in businesses, provide not only a current dividend yield, but also the prospect of future increases in cash dividends, stock dividends, price appreciation, and split-ups that may result from reinvestment of retained earnings and the cash flow from depreciation allowances, research and development outlays, and other management efforts to increase profits. At the same time, however, common stocks are subject to the risk of declines in earnings, dividends, and market price that unfavorable developments affecting the economy or the company may cause.

MARKETABILITY. The ability to readily sell or buy a security is called marketability. When a security can be bought and sold in large amounts without disrupting its price it is said to possess a **broad** market; if only small amounts can be bought or sold at the prevailing price it has a **narrow** or **thin** market. When the bid and asked prices are not far apart, a security is said to enjoy a **close** market. When prices for a security do not fluctuate widely between sales or over a period of time, it has a **stable** market; when prices move over a wide range its market behavior is **volatile**. (See also discussion of **Marketability** in Sec. 10, Securities Markets.)

Liquidity. Liquidity refers to the ability to convert investments into cash at any time without material loss. Short-term U.S. government obligations are a prime source of liquidity, as are commercial paper and deposits in banks. The short maturity and the high quality of these instruments assure their liquidity. In addition, short-term U.S. government securities and commercial paper possess very broad, close, and stable markets, which enhance their liquidity characteristics.

TAX STATUS. High income taxation makes the tax status of investments of major significance to individual investors in the middle and upper income brackets, and to taxed institutional investors. Such investors should be concerned primarily with the **effective return** from an investment after taxes, rather than with the gross return before taxes, in appraising its desirability. Among fixed income investments, tax-exempt obligations hold a particularly favorable position for higher bracket individual investors and taxed institutional investors like commercial banks. Dividend income enjoys an 85% credit when received by corporate investors. Appreciation is taxed only when realized, and long-term capital gains are taxed at only half or less of the rate applicable to ordinary income of individuals.

LEGAL INVESTMENTS. Some classes of investors do not have full freedom of choice in selecting securities for purchase. Laws of a number of states specify "legal" investments for savings banks and insurance companies, whereas commercial banks are required to comply with rating standards specified by supervisory authorities. (Bellemore, Investments.)

Trustees must conform to restrictions laid down by state laws and court decisions. The disadvantages of rigid restrictions on investment powers have been alleviated to a great extent in trust administration by a recent shift in many states away from "legal lists" and to the **"prudent-man" rule.** "Legal" securities customarily are highly rated, fixed-income, fixed-maturity securities to the exclusion of preferred and common stocks. The prudent-man rule permits investment in corporate stocks on a discretionary basis. All but a few states now follow the prudent-man rule on a complete or limited basis. If a **limited-prudent-man rule** is used, from one-third to one-half of the portfolio (depending on the statutory percentage) may be invested under prudent-man standards.

FUNCTION OF SECURITY ANALYSIS. The primary function of security analysis is to appraise the safety, return, and other characteristics of investments in the light of the pertinent facts available to the analyst. The methods of analysis used must be adapted to the security being analyzed.

Basic facts for security analysis are provided in financial manuals, annual reports, and registration statements filed with the Securities and Exchange Commission. Brokerage houses and financial services from time to time publish analyses of particular issues that vary from brief to thorough, in length and character. Data of value to the security analyst appear constantly in newspapers, in trade publications, and in financial periodicals. Professional analysts also rely upon field interviews, addresses by corporate executives before meetings of security analyst associations and elsewhere, and stockholder meetings for facts and insights.

The principles and methods of analysis of **fixed income** investments differ fundamentally from those that govern the analysis of **equity** investments, usually common stocks.

Bond Analysis

OBJECTIVE OF ANALYSIS. Investors in bonds are primarily concerned with the capacity of the obligor to pay interest and principal as they fall due. The chief indices of such capacity are:

1. The credit of the obligor.
2. Protective provisions of the bond issue being analyzed.
3. Bond ratings.

THE CREDIT OF THE OBLIGOR. The credit of the obligor—i.e., his ability to meet all debts as they mature—is the most important factor in bond analysis. A strong credit standing enables the obligor to borrow funds to service outstanding obligations, should available cash resources become inadequate for this purpose. The credit of the obligor is measured by: (1) earnings coverage of interest charges; (2) cash flow coverage of debt service requirements; and (3) miscellaneous credit factors.

Earnings Coverage of Interest Charges. This, in the past the most widely used yardstick for bond quality, is the ratio of earnings available to pay interest (profits before income taxes) to fixed charges. In stable industries, earnings coverage of 2 or more times interest charges may be regarded as adequate; whereas in industries subject to wide fluctuations in earnings coverage of 3, 4, or more times may be required for a good credit rating. In industries sensitive to the business cycle, coverage of fixed charges under recession conditions is the significant ratio.

The **factor of safety** in fixed charge coverage is the percentage by which earnings before taxes may decline before they fail to cover fixed charges. If earnings before taxes are $2,400,000 and fixed charges are $960,000, then such earnings can decline by as much as 60% or $1,440,000 and still cover fixed charges.

If **substantial lease rental obligations** have been incurred, they should be taken into account in computing earnings coverage of fixed charges. However, rentals under long-term leases may include not only a return on the investment of the lessor, but also the return of such investment. In that event, the rentals are equivalent to both the interest and sinking fund payments on a bond issue.

As long-term creditors, bondholders are concerned with future far more than with past or present earnings coverage of fixed charges. Hence the probable **trend of earnings** over a period of years and their **vulnerability to cyclical declines** in business activity and other unfavorable influences are major factors affecting the credit of the issuer.

Earnings Coverage of Junior Bond Interest. If a corporation has both senior and junior debt outstanding, the significant measure of earnings coverage of interest on junior debt is the **ratio to total fixed charges**. Thus, a corporation with a $20,000,000 issue of 4½% debentures and $10,000,000 of 5% subordinated debentures has total interest charges of $1,400,000. If it earns $2,800,000 before income taxes, the coverage of interest on the subordinated debentures would be 2 times, since prior charges of $900,000 must be paid along with $500,000 on the subordinated issue. To say that earnings after deducting $900,000 of interest on the debentures, or $1,900,000, cover interest requirements on the 5% subordinated debentures 3.8 times is patently misleading. But it is accurate to say that interest of $900,000 on the 4½% senior issue is being covered 3.1 times.

Cash Flow Coverage of Debt Service Requirements. The sharp rise in **depreciation allowances** has shifted the emphasis in credit analysis from earnings to cash flow. Since corporate spending for new fixed assets and for inventories tends to decline in recessions, and in any event can ordinarily be curtailed by management, the cash flow from depreciation can be utilized if needed to pay interest and to meet debt maturities. Insurance companies and other institutional investors stress the relation of cash flow to debt service requirements in appraising the credit of companies that seek to borrow through private placements. As with earnings, the future trend of a corporation's cash flow is of primary importance for bond analysis purposes.

Miscellaneous Credit Factors. A number of other factors influence the credit of a corporation. These include its cash and liquid investments, which can be used to service debt even when current earnings and cash flow become inadequate; ownership of securities that can be pledged for borrowing when necessary, and large scale expensing of research, drilling for oil, or other outlays that can be cut back.

PROTECTIVE PROVISIONS OF BOND ISSUE. A bond issue may be given specific protection, over and above that provided by the credit of the obligor, by a mortgage on physical property; pledge of securities under a collateral trust agreement, or a preference over other creditors of the issuer through a covenant of prior or equal coverage or the subordination of other indebtedness (see Sec. 14). As there stated, the chief protection such provisions give, as a practical matter, is **priority** in the event of a future reorganization, should the corporation become unable to meet its interest charges or debt maturities. Because of the specific added protection they have been given, such bond issues sell at lower yields than other obligations of the corporation, unless nearness of maturity may cause an unsecured obligation to sell on a low yield basis.

In some instances, the protection provided by mortgage or pledge of collateral may be so great that the bond issue so protected is considered strong and sells at a relatively low yield even if the credit of the obligor is weak. As a rule, however, delays in interest payments and other uncertainties that accompany a reorganization proceeding will cause investors to expect a materially higher yield from such bonds than from unsecured obligations of issuers with very strong credit.

BOND RATINGS. Widespread use is made of ratings accorded publicly owned bond issues by investment services. These ratings are based on a few broad investment tests, and so do not take the place of a thorough analysis of a bond issue. However, because many investors are guided by ratings in buying and selling bonds, they influence bond yields to a large extent. Institutional investors are particularly influenced by ratings if, as in the case of commercial banks, supervisory authorities use them to determine the **suitability** of bonds for bank investment. Changes in the rating given a bond, therefore, can considerably affect its price and yield.

Rating Systems. The two systems of rating in general use are those of **Moody Investment Service** and **Standard and Poor's.** The rating or rank assigned to a security under each of these systems is customarily denoted by letter. Moody's system uses letters as follows: Aaa; Aa; A; Baa; Ba; B; Caa; Ca; and C. Standard and Poor's ratings are: AAA; AA; A; BBB; BB; B; CCC; CC; C; DDD; DD; and D. The C rating under the Standard and Poor's system, as applied to bonds, is reserved for income bonds on which no interest is being paid. All bonds rated DDD, DD, or D are in default, with the rating indicating the relative salvage value. The **value** of any system of rating is limited by the character and number of tests used, as well as by the fact that the financial statements employed for arriving at the ratings apply to not future, but **past performance.** Hence, ratings tend to follow the market. If the quality of a high-grade bond becomes impaired through loss of earning power by the issuer, ratings are lowered as smaller profits are reported from time to time. But the market quotation for the bond often anticipates such a declining earnings trend some time ahead, or at least reflects smaller profits as they are reported.

Hickman (Corporate Bond Quality and Investor Experience) found that "the agency ratings serve as rough indexes to price and yield stability. On the average, realized yields on low grades were somewhat above those on high grades, but investors seeking price stability should have avoided the low-grade issues."

THE MARKET FOR BONDS. Because the market for bonds is so largely institutional in character, issues favored by insurance companies, pension funds, and other institutions enjoy a wider demand and tend to sell at lower yields than other bonds. For individuals in the **low tax brackets,** savings accounts with their safety and flexibility are favored. U.S. savings bonds, for similar reasons, are the most widely held fixed-income securities. Individuals in the **middle and upper income tax brackets** are large holders of tax-exempt bonds because of the high effective yield, after taxes, that they provide. (See Sec. 11.)

CONVERTIBLE BONDS. These bonds appeal to individual and some institutional investors because they give a call on the stock of the issuer, whereas the **investment value** of the bond limits the extent to which it will decline when the price of the stock falls. This investment value is indicated by yields of similar bonds that do not have the conversion privilege. For example, a 4½% bond convertible into 20 shares of stock would be worth 140 if the stock rose to 70. Should the price of the stock decline by 50% to 35, the bond would decline, not to 70, its conversion value into 20 shares of stock at that time, but to its investment value as a bond, which could be 95 on the basis of the credit of the obligor, the protective provisions, the rating, and the bond's maturity date.

OTHER FIXED-INCOME INVESTMENTS. Analysis of real estate mortgages, leases, and preferred stocks for investment has the same basic objective as bond analysis, but it must be adapted to the special characteristics of these investment media.

Real Estate Mortgages. Real estate mortgages constitute the largest single class of fixed-income investments available. Because of servicing problems and the limited marketability they enjoy as compared with publicly offered bonds, they are held chiefly by **institutional investors,** particularly banks, savings and loan associations, and life insurance companies.

Real estate mortgage loans are now almost always **amortized** by periodic repayments of principal over the life of the loan. In the case of individual house mortgages, uniform monthly payments designed to repay the loan in full at maturity are standard practice.

Mortgages are classified as:

1. **Residential,** including liens on individual homes and multifamily housing.
2. **Commercial,** including office buildings, stores, and shopping centers.
3. **Industrial,** including factories and industrial parks.
4. **Eleemosynary,** such as church loans.

The mortgagee looks to the **value of the pledged property** and the **income of the property** and the **obligor** for assurance that payments will be made as they fall due. In the case of individual home mortgages, both because of the higher ratio of loan to appraised value now commonly loaned and because of uncertainty as to the price at which the pledged property can actually be sold in the market, more stress is placed on income and other resources of the mortgagor than in the past. When a mortgage equals a very high percentage of the market value of the property, the mortgagor has little financial incentive to maintain payments and avoid foreclosure, except for his personal liability on the loan. The **valuation of income-producing property** such as apartments, office buildings, hotels, and motels is largely based on its earning capacity. For that reason, mortgage loans on special purpose property, which may be difficult or impossible to rent to others, are usually a smaller percentage of assessed valuation.

Insured and Guaranteed Mortgages. The attraction of home mortgage loans to investors, even when they equal a high ratio of assessed valuation of pledged property, may be enhanced by insurance or guarantees. A large proportion of residential mortgages is insured by the **Federal Housing Administration.** In the event of default on **F.H.A.** insured mortgages, the institution holding the mortgage forecloses and turns over the property, free of lien, to the F.H.A. in return for debentures on which interest and principal payments are guaranteed by the U.S. Treasury. Since these government-guaranteed bonds will sell close to par, the institutional investor is subject to material loss only from expenses of foreclosure. The **Veterans Administration** guarantees 60% (up to $7,500) of home mortgage loans made to qualified veterans, and in the event of foreclosure and payment of the amount guaranteed the claim of the Veterans Administration is subordinated to that of the mortgagee for the unpaid balance of the loan. **V.A.** guaranteed mortgages, like F.H.A. insured mortgages, have a much broader market than **conventional** mortgages, those lacking insurance or guarantees, because of the protection of government underwriting, their standardized character, and purchases of such loans by the Federal National Mortgage Association under specified conditions.

Preferred Stocks. The investment status of preferred stocks may be adversely affected by large-scale borrowing by the issuer, since debts have priority over preferred stock. Protective provisions that limit the incurring of added debt are important to preferred stocks, therefore, if the financial strength of the issuer is not beyond question. With preferred stocks, as with subordinated debentures and other junior debt, **earnings coverage** of all fixed charges senior and equal to the issue being analyzed is the significant analytical yardstick, rather than coverage of the preferred dividend requirements alone. However, since preferred stock dividends are not a deduction from taxable income, adjustment must be made for the fact that earnings only after payment of income tax are available for paying preferred dividends.

Common Stock Analysis

OBJECTIVE OF ANALYSIS. The objective of common stock analysis is basically different from that of bond analysis, reflecting the fundamental differences between these two classes of securities. The aim of bond analysis is to appraise the ability of the debtor to pay interest and principal as they fall due. But common stock analysis seeks to determine the **probable future value of a share** in the ownership of the corporation. Although numerous factors will affect the value of a common stock, they will do so through:

1. The earnings per share.
2. The price-earnings ratio at which the shares will sell.

EARNINGS PER SHARE. Although the value of a common stock is going to be determined by future, not past or current earnings, **reported profits** provide a basis for projecting what future earnings are likely to be. A record of stable growth of profits indicates that this trend is likely to be maintained in the future, in the absence of developments that would bring about a change. Similarly, a highly volatile or declining trend of profits would presumably persist if no new developments that would improve the trend are in prospect.

Projections of sales volume, selling prices, and costs; planned diversification into new fields; and adjustment for nonrecurring income and costs enable the analyst to estimate the **probable trend** of earnings per share over a period of years in the future. A large part of common stock analysis is the making of such projections, using procedures suited to the industry and corporation being analyzed.

THE PRICE–EARNINGS RATIO. The multiple at which the earnings per share of a common stock are valued in the market reflects chiefly:

1. The trend of earnings per share.
2. The quality of reported earnings.
3. Dividend policy.
4. Demand for the stock among institutional and individual investors.
5. Quality of management.

The **relative importance** of each of these factors varies from time to time with economic conditions and other developments that influence investor attitudes. During the depressed 1930's, stability of dividends as then exemplified by American Telephone & Telegraph was valued highly and given a relatively higher price-earnings ratio. This attitude persisted during the 1940's. The relatively rapid economic growth of the 1950's was accompanied by a pronounced shift in investor preference to growth stocks promising a strong upward trend in earnings per share. Past experience indicates that price-earnings ratios will continue to reflect such shifts in emphasis among the factors that influence the relation of prices of stocks to earnings of the issuers.

The Trend of Earnings Per Share. Earnings growth is highly prized by investors because it results in stock price and dividend increases over a period of years. A higher price-earnings ratio discounts expected profit growth. Conversely, a downward trend in earnings results in a low price-earnings ratio to discount anticipated decreases in profits, price, and dividends. The appreciation in price of a stock with rising earnings per share is beneficial to middle and upper bracket investors especially because appreciation is not taxed to the stockholder until realized, and is taxed at lower rates if the capital gains are long-term. Relative **certainty and stability of growth** may be stressed more than the expected rate of growth, especially by institutional and more conservative individual investors. This explains their willingness to pay relatively high price-earnings ratios for such groups as utilities, life insurance companies, and banks.

Earnings growth is of limited value to an investor if a corporation finances its capital requirements with periodic **offerings of new stock** that tend to **dilute** the growth in earnings per share. Hence, if a corporation finances its expansion from internal sources and borrowing and minimizes dilution of earnings through new stock offerings, a more rapid rise in earnings per share and a higher price-earnings ratio result.

The Quality of Reported Earnings. Accounting practices differ widely among industries and corporations, causing wide differences in the quality of reported earnings that tend to be reflected in price-earnings ratios. The chief factors affecting the quality of reported profits are:

1. **Depreciation allowances.** Depreciation allowances are noncash deductions from earnings that provide funds for the acquisition of productive assets or debt repayment. The larger the deductions for depreciation, therefore, the greater the ability of the corporation to finance profitable expansion that will build up future earnings power without outside financing.
2. **Research and development outlays.** These lead to future increases in sales and profits, and so justify a higher price-earnings ratio.
3. **Inventory and other nonrecurring types of profits.** In periods of rising commodity prices like the 1940's and much of the 1950's, profits were increased by the larger than normal markups on low-cost inventory sold in a rising market, so-called inventory profits. Since such profits disappear when commodity prices stabilize, they are of poor quality and so justify low price-earnings ratios.

Dividend Policy. The proportion of earnings distributed as dividends influenced price-earnings ratios to a greater extent in the past, particularly when income tax rates were lower. However, dividend policy is still significant for low-bracket individual and institutional investors. Higher bracket investors also pay higher price-earnings ratios for stocks expected to benefit from dividend increases, since such issues tend to rise in price as dividend rates are raised. The payment of stock dividends and stock splits also tend to raise the price of a stock, and so the price-earnings ratio. If investors put more stress upon future growth in earnings and dividends and the quality of profits in setting price-earnings ratios, current dividend yields on stocks decline well below that offered by bonds.

Investor Demand. Price-earnings ratios are greatly influenced by investor demand for stocks. Stocks that are popular with individual and larger institutional investors tend to sell at substantially higher price-earnings ratios than those that do not enjoy such a following.

Institutional demand for common stocks has been greatly expanded by the emergence of pension and retirement funds as leading institutional investors. Stock groups that are favored by pension funds, usually those offering prospects of relatively certain, stable earnings growth and consequent appreciation over a long period of years, tend to sell at higher price-earnings ratios. Preferences of individual investors are subject to frequent and erratic changes, resulting in greater volatility of price-earnings ratios for the stocks affected by such shifts in investor attitudes.

Quality of Management. A less tangible but very important analytical consideration is the quality of management. Able management in depth is generally able to cope with problems as they arise, and to take advantage of growth opportunities. Both the **past record** of management and **field studies** will provide a basis for appraising quality of management. However, good managements may become less effective in time, and also managements with a mediocre record may be strengthened, either from within or by bringing in new talent from the outside.

Graham, Dodd, and Cottle (Security Analysis) state that "the appraisal of management is considered an essential—perhaps **the** essential—factor in determining whether an investment should be made in a given business and often whether holdings in a business should be disposed of. Experienced investors and their advisers are greatly influenced in their buy-and-sell decisions by their individual conclusions or by the commonly accepted view as to the caliber of management."

ANALYSIS PROCEDURES. Security analysis procedures must be adapted to the characteristics of individual industries. Methods used in the analysis of industrial, financial, public utility, and railroad securities are surveyed in the remainder of this Section.

Industrial Securities

NATURE OF THE INDUSTRY. Since the category of industrials embraces every type of corporate enterprise except financial corporations, public utilities, and railroads, it comprises a very wide variety of businesses. Although basic principles of investment analysis are the same in each case, their application varies with the character of the business.

The major classes of industrial concerns are:

1. Mining, petroleum, and other extractive enterprises, dependent upon natural resources, the supply of which is usually limited.
2. Manufacturers of industrial materials like metals and chemicals.
3. Manufacturers of producer durable goods and military equipment.
4. Manufacturers of consumer nondurable goods, including textiles, foods, and tobacco.
5. Manufacturers of consumer durable goods and building materials.
6. Wholesale and retail distributors.
7. Service industries like air transport and bus lines that may have public utility characteristics.

Numerous concerns diversify their activities, so that they manufacture and sell products falling in two or more of the classifications given above. Thus, a petroleum company produces chemicals and a company like General Electric manufactures equipment for industry and consumer durable goods.

In analyzing such securities, the investment analyst will consider (1) the long-term trend of the industry; (2) competition within the industry and from other products or services; (3) prospective technological changes and their impact upon earnings; (4) labor factors; and (5) how sensitive the industry is to business fluctuations. Thus, steel is an industry that has long passed its rapid growth phase, meeting competition from other metals and plastics that may be intensified by future technological changes. It is also sensitive to the rate of business activity. On the other hand, steel is so cheap as compared with its competitors and enjoys so wide a variety of uses that for a long time to come an era of business prosperity will necessarily imply a heavy demand for steel products, with corresponding large sales for steel manufacturers. **Wages** constitute a large proportion of the cost of steel, which makes the industry sensitive to wage increases as compared with, say, the petroleum industry, in which the wage element is a much smaller proportion of total cost. **Foreign competition** is another factor that can be quite important, since many steel consumers are concerned only or mainly with price in choosing their sources of supply.

FACTORS OF ANALYSIS. The security analyst is interested in seven major factors in appraising the value of an industrial security. These are:

1. Prospective earnings.
2. Cash flow.
3. Working capital position.
4. Accounting peculiarities.
5. Capital structure.
6. Dividend prospects.
7. Special considerations that may affect the value of the security in the future.

PROSPECTIVE EARNINGS. Prospective earnings are of primary importance, for security prices tend to reflect primarily the future earning power of the enterprise, rather than past or current performance. Prospective earnings in turn reflect:

1. Sales prospects.
2. Selling prices.
3. Costs.

Sales Prospects. Prospects for sales volume will depend upon the company's position in the industry, the outlook for the industry, competition, development of new products, etc. A number of corporations are classified as **"growth companies,"** so far as sales prospects are concerned, because the demand for their product is expanding, giving them gains in sales from year to year interrupted only temporarily, if at all, by business recessions. On the other hand, in older industries the long-term trend may be downward because the demand for the company's products is contracting because of competition from rival products, exhaustion of raw material reserves, or changes in consumer preferences. Industries quite sensitive to the business cycle show wide changes in sales volume from year to year, which makes the stocks of such concerns attractive when bought during recession periods, since sharp gains in sales may be anticipated once the business trend turns upward.

In each industry, there are indications of future sales changes. Thus, an increase in farm income augurs well for mail-order company sales. Greater industrial activity means heavier consumption of fuels and raw materials.

Selling Prices. Prospects for selling prices may be as important as the sales outlook in influencing future earning power. Higher selling prices widen profit margins without adding to costs, whereas price cutting often reduces profits drastically. Competition, antitrust law prosecution, technological changes, marketing policies, and tariff changes can all affect prices charged for a company's products. Thus, a company shifting from direct selling to sales through jobbers may have to reduce its selling prices, although this may be offset by a reduction in marketing expense. Copper mining companies may have to reduce prices if new mines expand the supply on the world market.

Costs. Future earnings may be influenced as much by changes in costs as by any other factor. Changes in raw material prices, in technological processes, in wage rates, and in taxes all affect costs. Periods of rising prices usually mean larger profits, for the higher value of year-end inventories reduces the cost of goods sold, unless last-in–first-out inventory valuation prevents inventory price changes from affecting earnings. Conversely, declines in commodity prices lead to smaller profits because reduced year-end inventories increase the cost of goods sold.

Costs are also affected by **sales volume.** When sales are large, overhead and even direct cost per unit of product tend to be reduced. Conversely, a reduced volume of turnover nearly always indicates higher costs per unit.

The investment analyst must constantly be on the lookout for developments that change costs, and so affect profits. A succession of small tobacco crops, for example, will raise the price of tobacco and so narrow profit margins in the cigarette industry, unless cigarette prices can be raised correspondingly.

In some cases, expenses may be increased in anticipation of larger sales in the future. Thus, an oil or natural gas company may spend large sums of money upon developing new reserves, from which revenue will not be realized for some time to come. Similarly, an aircraft manufacturing company may incur heavy costs in perfecting a new model, sales of which will take place only in the future. When costs increase because heavy development expenses are being incurred for future production, this is not to be considered in the same light as a rise in costs on the existing output.

CASH FLOW. The cash flow is calculated by adding to the net profit figure expenses that have not required an outlay of cash. These are represented so largely by the **depreciation** charge that often a good approximation can be reached by simply adding the depreciation allowance to the net profit figure. Because cash flow can be utilized to acquire new productive assets, to repay debts, or for other corporate purposes, as well as to replace particular assets as they are retired, it must be taken into account along with prospective earnings in analyzing industrial stocks.

WORKING CAPITAL POSITION. The investment value of a security is affected by the working capital position of the issuer, as well as the latter's prospective earning power. With a strong working capital position, the investment status of the stock of a company may be maintained even if earnings decline temporarily. A company may use excess cash to acquire productive assets or other enterprises, or to pay liquidating dividends to stockholders. On the other hand, if working capital is impaired, larger earnings may have to be devoted to replenishing current assets, so that the price of the stock may not discount the increase in earnings.

A large investment in **inventory** may be a factor of weakness, particularly when commodity prices are weak or style changes occur. Heavy **receivables** also may cause loss when commercial failures run high.

The **liability side** of the working capital position is very important where payables run high. Even an enterprise with substantial earning power may be embarrassed by large maturities of bank notes and other debts that cannot be met conveniently, especially during periods of weakness in the security markets.

ACCOUNTING PECULIARITIES. Accounting practices vary greatly among industrial concerns. Some enterprises, particularly those where heavy research or other outlays build up valuable intangible assets, may be said habitually to understate earnings. Others that do not make adequate provision for expenses, taxes, or potential losses may be overstating earnings.

The investment analyst cannot take corporate income accounts and balance sheets at face value. Such statements provide the raw material that he processes to appraise investment values. He must determine the accounting practices pursued in each case and interpret reported figures accordingly. This is particularly so if figures for two or more corporations are to be compared. Thus, results of a company that deducts costs of developing a new product from earnings are not comparable with those of a company that capitalizes such outlays as an asset. **Financial statement analysis** reveals accounting peculiarities.

CAPITAL STRUCTURE. The capital structure of a corporation and its important subsidiaries and affiliates should be analyzed to determine the **prior charges** that have been incurred ahead of the common stock, and **minority stock interests** in subsidiaries. The heavier the senior capitalization of bonds and preferred stock, the less strong is the investment status of the common shares. This is the more true if senior issues are convertible or participating, or have heavy sinking funds and early maturities. Large bank loans or other short-term debts undermine the position of a company's securities if there is any question of the ability of the enterprise to pay such obligations as they fall due.

If corporations have subsidiaries, it is important to learn whether their liabilities are shown in a **consolidated statement**. Practices in consolidating parent and subsidiary corporation statements are not uniform.

DIVIDEND PROSPECTS. The price-earnings ratio of an industrial security may be influenced considerably by the proportion of earnings paid out as dividends, if there is no clear prospect of growth in earnings. A rising trend in cash dividends or periodic stock dividends enhances the **"growth image"** of a stock.

OTHER FACTORS. The competent investment analyst will not be satisfied after he has weighed the six factors mentioned, for other considerations may play a dominant role in determining market values.

In **wasting asset industries** such as mining and petroleum production, proved reserves may be the chief determinant of value. Even large current earnings and a strong working capital position may be of limited significance if the ore reserves of a mining company will be exhausted in the near future. On the other hand, huge ore reserves may make the stock of a mining company quite attractive even if current profits are meager.

A company that possesses a **new patent or process** of value to an industry may be in position to secure large royalty income, even if its own operations are not profitable. There have been a number of instances where such patents constituted the chief asset of the business, and where the value of the stock issue depended upon the outcome of litigation arising from these patents. Needless to say, such stocks are quite speculative at best until the patent uncertainties have been resolved.

A **change in the accounting methods** employed may affect earnings, and therefore stock values. When air transport companies were unable to secure new planes during World War II, after their equipment had been written off entirely, depreciation charges tended to disappear and profits to rise sharply. But this was clearly a nonrecurring advantage. Later, heavy expenditures for jet aircraft sharply reduced earnings and many companies reported net losses after the greatly increased depreciation allowances on this costly new equipment.

A **new statute or government regulation** may become a major investment factor at times. Shifts in defense procurement may have a major impact on corporations receiving a great deal of such business. **Antitrust proceedings** can strongly influence the stocks of the companies affected.

RATIO ANALYSIS. Ratios helpful to the security analyst can be worked out for each industry, primarily for comparative analysis. Examples are sales per $100 of market value of common stock of each company in an industry, and for oil companies oil and gas output and reserves per $100 of market value of common stock.

Such ratios must be used with great care, especially if selling prices or production costs may be more important than the volume of output in determining profits. If the cost of producing a barrel of oil is half as large for one company as for another, the fact that it turns out fewer barrels per share will not prevent it from showing larger profits.

INDUSTRY ANALYSIS. In the analysis of industrial securities, an essential step is to identify and study dominant influences that affect earnings and other elements of value of companies in each industry. These influences not only vary from industry to industry, but also from time to time within the same industry. Examples of such key analytical factors are given in the following summary:

Oil stock values are largely affected by the location of crude reserves and other properties, the proportion of its crude requirements produced by the company, and the relation of product to crude prices. **International petroleum companies,** with a large part of their operations outside the United States, benefit from low-cost crude reserves and more rapid growth rates, but are subject to political risks that do not apply to companies operating mainly within this country. For domestic companies, close regulation of crude production and imports will result in relatively high crude oil costs if a large part of the company's crude requirements must be purchased from others.

Automobile stocks are very much influenced by cyclical fluctuations in demand, as well as by the ability of car manufacturers to adapt their products to changing public tastes. The latter factor has accounted for wide variations in the percentage of the market captured by individual companies in particular years.

Chemical and drug stock values may be very much influenced by development of new products. Staple chemicals and drugs are subject to intense price competition, but new products and those sold under brand names to consumers and having a wide acceptance often give quite satisfactory profit margins. The record of each company's research program is thus a major analytical consideration.

Retail stocks are greatly influenced by a company's adaptability to shifting population patterns and buying habits. In the mail order field, the success of a company in establishing stores and in competing with discount house operations has been of great importance. In grocery chains, the shift from small stores to supermarkets has played a similar role. Widespread automobile ownership and suburbanization were the underlying forces that made such adaptation important.

Tobacco stock values have been affected by the success of managements in adapting their product to consumer concern with health considerations. Shifts in demand to filter cigarettes and consumer response to advertising stressing health factors have favored some companies at the expense of others.

After analyzing financial statements and other pertinent data, the security analyst will want to identify and appraise such key industry influences, and the management's ability to cope with them, to arrive at a realistic appraisal of future earning power and of the value of an industrial stock.

Financial Securities

DISTINCTIVE FEATURES. Securities of financial enterprises are peculiar in that assets of these institutions consist mainly of loans and securities.

FINANCIAL SECURITIES 7·15

The methods of analysis differ, therefore, from those applicable to industrial companies. Quality of assets and effective cost of funds, for example, may be quite significant analytical factors.

BANK STOCKS. The most important group of financial securities are bank stocks. Analysis is made more difficult because of the limited information provided by annual and other reports in many cases. When assets are understated or left out of the balance sheet entirely, the regulatory authorities interpose no objections. They do not regard it as their function to require accurate accounting for investors—they are concerned primarily with the safety of the funds of depositors.

Because of the highly liquid character of bank assets, book value is of more importance than for industrial companies. **Reported book value** is readily determined from the condition statement, as the bank's balance sheet is called. However, **asset value** may vary considerably from the figure shown on the books. Securities are usually carried at cost less a reserve built up through sales of investments at a profit. Loans are shown net of reserves for possible losses. Real estate may be carried at figures varying widely above or below current market values. Many bank managements like to accumulate **hidden reserves**, usually by carrying assets taken over when loans go into default far below their true worth.

Banks derive their **earnings** mainly from interest on loans and investments. Fees and charges for services are a relatively small part of income for most banks. Banks customarily report operating earnings from these two sources and deduct expenses and taxes attributable to such operating income to show **net operating income.** Gains and losses on securities and additions to reserves are then listed, to arrive at net income.

Analysis Ratios. Ratios commonly used in analyzing bank stocks are net operating earnings after applicable taxes per share, market price as a percent of book value, earning assets per share, and the ratio of time to total deposits. When relatively high rates of interest are paid on time deposits, the time deposit ratio may be significant. The rate of growth of deposits and earning assets and the average return on assets, allowing for the tax advantage of tax-exempt securities, are also important indicators of investment value.

INSURANCE STOCKS. Analysis of insurance stocks involves an appraisal of both underwriting and investment results. The investment funds of most insurance companies are derived chiefly from reserves that belong to policy-holders. In **fire and casualty insurance companies,** these are the unearned premium reserves and the loss reserves. In **life insurance companies,** they are the reserves against policies outstanding.

Fire and Casualty Insurance Companies. These companies report underwriting and investment results separately. Some companies rely mainly on underwriting for their earnings, and others chiefly on investment income, including appreciation of the stock portfolio that accounts for a large percentage of the assets of most of these companies. The analyst must recognize this and stress the underwriting or investment outlook accordingly in appraising such stocks.

Life Insurance Companies. Life insurance stock analysis stresses the rate of growth of the company and the types of policies outstanding, as well as such general factors as the trend of interest rates, life expectancy, and taxation of life insurance companies. Although life insurance companies invest mainly in fixed income securities, some have put a material percentage of their funds in common stocks. Because of the high degree of **leverage** in life insurance stocks, this can substantially affect investment values.

OTHER FINANCIAL STOCKS. Analysis of stocks of **finance companies,** including installment finance, business finance, and personal loan companies, stresses profitability and quality of assets, cost of funds, and rate of growth. Similar considerations affect stocks of **savings and loan holding companies,** as well as the impact of special tax law provisions to which they are subject.

Investment company stocks are subject to different considerations. With **closed end** companies, the investment record and the ratio of market price to net asset value at prevailing market prices are important. **Mutual fund** shares are pegged in price by the ability to redeem the shares at the current asset value. The investment record of a mutual fund and the suitability of its portfolio policy to the objectives of the investor are major analytical considerations in the selection of such shares by the investor.

Public Utility Securities

TYPES OF ENTERPRISES. Securities of electric, gas, telephone and telegraph, water, and transit companies are classified as public utilities. Railroads are public utilities in the legal sense, but their securities are classified separately because of economic, regulatory, and other peculiarities.

DISTINCTIVE FEATURES. From an investment viewpoint, public utility companies are distinguished from other corporations in the following respects:

1. Public utilities must generally obtain from a regulatory authority a franchise to provide the specified service.
2. The franchise is, as a rule, exclusive, giving them a **"legal monopoly"** to serve the area specified.
3. Rates charged, financing, and other aspects of operation are subject to regulation in the public interest.

FRANCHISES. The chief provisions of a public utility franchise, affecting directly or indirectly the investment standing of the utility securities, are:

1. The kind of service to be performed.
2. The duration of the franchise.
3. The exclusiveness of the right to perform the service permitted.
4. Territorial limitations in the performance of the service.
5. Restrictions and regulations regarding rates and charges.

A franchise may limit a utility company to a single **service,** such as supplying electricity, operating a telephone system, or running a transit company. As a rule, however, it is permitted to furnish the services that its equipment renders economically possible, even though the franchise does not specify some services. Thus, a telephone company may make its wires available for the transmission of messages by telegraph.

A franchise may be limited as to **duration,** it may be perpetual, or it may be of indeterminate duration. Under a limited franchise a renewal by the political authority is required at the time the franchise expires. A perpetual franchise cannot be revoked, except for some breach of the franchise agreement. Under the "indeterminate permit," the political authority reserves the right to revoke the franchise under specified conditions. It is frequently provided that in the event of revocation the utility company is to receive compensation for its property, either from the municipality or from a successor corporation.

When a franchise is **exclusive,** the utility company receives a monopoly to perform the specified service within a prescribed territory. This eliminates direct competition and duplication of equipment, but it does not exclude indirect competition such as exists between a gas and an electric company. The present-day tendency of public authorities is to avoid duplication of services and wasteful competition by granting exclusive franchises or by refusing to grant additional franchises for the performance of a service that is or can be adequately supplied by existing public utility facilities.

A franchise is usually limited to a **specified area,** although in some cases the area is not definitely outlined. Thus, it may be limited to a single municipality or to a county. Gas and electric companies often operate under a number of different franchises acquired by merger or acquisition, each confined to a limited area.

Early franchises sometimes fixed rates that a utility could charge for its service. But rates are now set by either state regulatory agencies or local authorities.

UTILITY RATES. Utility rates reflect (1) the value of the service, and (2) the cost of the service. The value of the service is what consumers can afford to pay for it; the cost of service is the cost of furnishing it, including a fair return on invested capital. Neither principle can be applied independently of the other. The cost basis of rate-making is impracticable if, under it, rates would be higher than the consumers can afford to pay. On the other hand, rates based on the "value of service" may be so high as to yield unreasonable profits at the public's expense. Utility rates, under judicial precedents, are generally set at levels that give a reasonable return on the capital invested and provide the public with service at rates consumers can readily afford to pay.

UTILITY VALUATION. Adjustment of public utility rates is closely linked to the valuation of property used in performing the service. Courts have sought to define a **"fair value"** for utility property as a base upon which a fair rate of return could be computed. In a number of decisions in the 1920's, fair value was held to be chiefly present-day cost of reproduction, less depreciation, irrespective of original cost. This formula linked earning power of utility enterprises to the fluctuating purchasing power of the dollar, rather than to a return on the dollars invested.

Subsequently the **original cost basis of utility valuation** has come into the ascendancy. This valuation basis would limit the rate base of public utilities to the dollars "prudently" invested in their property. This view has prevailed in rulings of the Federal Power Commission in rate cases affecting companies subject to its jurisdiction, decisions of the Securities and Exchange Commission on issues of securities under the Public Utility Holding Company Act, and rulings by a number of state regulatory commissions that have been influenced by these federal agencies and the Uniform Classification of Accounts issued by the National Association of Railway and Public Utility Commissioners.

The United States Supreme Court, in the **Hope Natural Gas case** (320 U.S. 591), decided in 1944, virtually discarded the "fair value" rule for rate making. Instead of any rigid rate formula, the highest court ruled that "rates which enable the company to operate successfully, to maintain its financial integrity, to attract capital, and to compensate its investors for the risk assumed certainly cannot be condemned as invalid, even though they might produce only a meagre return on the so-called fair value rate base." Thus, the Supreme Court greatly widened the discretion given regulatory commissions in setting rates. This epoch-making decision said further: "From the investor or company point of view, it is important that there be enough revenue not only for operating expenses but also for the capital costs of the business. These include services on the debt and dividends on the stock. . . . By that standard the return to the equity owner should be commensurate with returns on investments in other enterprises having corresponding risks. The return, moreover, should be sufficient to assure confidence in the financial integrity of the enterprise, so as to maintain its credit and to attract capital."

This view was reiterated by the Supreme Court in 1953 in the Northern Natural Gas Co. case (206 F. 2d 690). Numerous state commissions have used prudent investment in one guise or another as a basis of rate rulings following these Supreme Court decisions.

COMMISSION REGULATION. The Federal Power Commission, the Securities and Exchange Commission, and, in the case of communications companies, the Federal Communications Commission have limited regulatory authority over public utilities, though the Federal Power Commission does have power to directly regulate natural gas transmission companies. State commissions set up in most states have the widest powers of regulation. The commission's authority differs from state to state. It usually embraces (1) franchises, (2) rates and services, (3) security issues, and (4) accounts and reports.

When the earnings of a public utility company rise to a level that is believed to yield substantially more than 6% upon the prudent value of its investment, a number of commissions, or municipal authorities in the states where statewide regulation is not provided, will order a rate investigation or require rates to be reduced forthwith. If the demand for service is expanding at a rapid pace, however, a rate reduction may not immediately lower earnings, for the expansion of sales may offset the cuts in rates.

The attitude of the state commission is particularly important in the investment analysis of utility securities, now that the courts are disinclined to overrule their rate decisions, as we have seen above.

ANALYSIS OF A UTILITY COMPANY. In the investment analysis of public utility stocks, prospective earning power and cash flow are primary considerations, as with other securities. The chief items to be taken into account are:

1. Present and future demand for the service.
2. Franchise, rates, and other regulatory factors.
3. The load factor.
4. Character of the physical plant.
5. Capitalization.
6. Reported earning power.

The Demand for Service. The rate of growth in the demand for service in the area served is the major point for analysts. Competition from other services and other fuels must be taken into account in appraising potential demands for utility service.

Throughout their history, with very few exceptions, public utilities other than transit companies have enjoyed an expanding demand for their services. But growth rates vary greatly with population, employment, industrial, and living-standard trends.

Regulatory Factors. Details about the **franchises and rates** charged by public utility companies are available in the financial services. The fact that a franchise expires within the near future may or may not be a serious matter, depending upon the attitude of the franchise-granting authority. Expiration of a franchise may give an occasion for agitation for public ownership. If voters approve the acquisition of a utility by a municipality or power district, payment equal to original cost or better can normally be expected, but this may mean a loss to common stockholders if the shares have been quoted at higher levels.

The fact that the rates charged, especially for residential service, are higher than those charged by neighboring companies may make a company vulnerable to rate reductions. However, relative rates must be checked against the return realized on the rate base. Certain communities share operating economies achieved between consumers and utility companies, which may result in a high rate of return.

Competition from public power projects and the **attitude** of public authorities toward the sale of their power for private distribution largely affect the position of utilities in adjacent areas. The attitude of the community toward municipal or district ownership is also quite important.

Load Factor. This may affect earning power substantially. A utility is required to have capacity adequate to meet the maximum demand for its service at any time. This maximum is the **peak load.** Actual output in a given period, such as a month or year, divided by what would have been produced at continuous peak load operation, is the load factor. The higher the load factor, other things being equal, the more profitable the operation, for plant capacity is idle a lesser percentage of the time.

Character of the Plant. This is important as an indication of its adequacy for future expansion and the need for replacements. An engineering study of the character and condition of plant and equipment, usually prepared by engineers in connection with a new security offering, offers valuable guidance to investors. The Federal Power Commission, under its uniform system of accounts for utilities, has required public utilities subject to its jurisdiction to report **write-ups** of property values, both direct and those resulting from the purchase of property above its original cost. Direct write-ups (Account 107) are to be written off directly against surplus, whereas purchase write-ups (Account 100.5) are to be amortized in most cases over a 15-year period against earnings. State commissions have varying requirements as to eliminating write-ups of property values. In some states, part of the write-ups may be retained in the rate base. Although write-ups are relatively unimportant today, the actual age of the plant is important. Because greater efficiencies have been built into new equipment, the larger the proportion of the plant that is comparatively new, five to ten years, the lower will be the operating costs to the company.

Generally speaking, the investment in plant and equipment of an electric, gas, or telephone company should not exceed 5 times the annual operating revenues. Utilities should have a retirement reserve of over 15% to cover replacements, with a moderately lower percentage for hydroelectric properties.

Capitalization. Regulatory authorities, both Federal and state, have sought to maintain a reasonable balance between bond and stock capitalization of public utilities, to avoid the excessive fixed charges that have plagued railroads. The S.E.C. has favored a capital structure for an operating company that comprises 50% debt, 20–25% preferred stock, and the balance common stock, though the commonly accepted ratio for an electric utility is 50% debt, 15% preferred stock, and 35% common stock. If the common stock equity is less than 20% of total capitalization, the Commission has restricted dividend payments by operating companies being separated from parent holding companies to 50% of available earnings. If the common equity is less than 25%, dividends have been restricted to 75% of earnings available. Such restrictions lapse, needless to say, when the common stock equity reaches the specified percentage of total capitalization through reinvestment of earnings or through the sale of new common stock.

Difference of opinion exists whether the **"reserve for deferred Federal income tax,"** which is built up as a utility uses rapid depreciation methods for tax purposes while retaining straight-line depreciation for reporting and rate regulation, should appear on the balance sheet as a deferred liability or a surplus item constituting part of the common equity. The latter position is based on the view that in an expanding utility a stream of capital expenditures will defer taxes in constant or increasing amounts. The Federal Power Commission, the Securities and Exchange Commission, and the American Institute of Certified Public Accountants have taken an opposite view, holding that this account should not appear in the equity section of the balance sheet. A number of state public utility commissions have required that this item be shown as "restricted surplus."

Earning Power. Analysis of the earning power of a public utility must take into account both regulatory and economic factors. If earnings are substantially above the fair return rate on the rate base, they are vulnerable. Conversely, if earnings fall below a fair return level, rate increases may be obtainable if they are economically feasible.

The **basic economic factors** governing utility earning power are the demand for service and the cost of providing it. Industrial and commercial demand reflects business conditions, whereas residential demand is largely influenced by employment and national income. The cost of providing service is affected by wage changes, fuel costs, and taxes.

Reported earnings of a utility are affected by the accounting treatment of the tax credit from the use of more rapid depreciation methods for tax purposes. A number of jurisdictions require that only taxes actually paid be deducted from earnings, so that tax reductions **flow through** to net income, thereby increasing the reported amount, and could become an argument for lower rates. Elsewhere, the tax reductions go into a "reserve for deferred Federal income tax" and so are kept out of net income, which is then said to be **normalized.** The cash flow is the same in each case, but the investment quality of reported profits is affected by the accounting procedure employed.

Operating Ratio. The operating ratio in public utility analysis is computed by adding operating expenses (including depreciation and amortization) and Federal income taxes and dividing by operating revenues. For a company producing electric power from steam this ratio usually runs around 80%, and for hydroelectric companies, 70%. For natural gas companies and for telephone companies the operating ratio should be about 85%. If Federal income taxes are removed from the numerator of the ratio, the normal ratio for the above companies will tend to run about ten percentage points lower. A more significant result may be obtained if depreciation, amortization, and Federal income taxes are all eliminated from the computation, thus permitting comparison of directly controllable expenses with operating revenues. A well-run, well-capitalized electric utility will have fixed charges equal to less than 12% of operating revenues, and these charges should be earned twice. Gas companies' fixed charges should not exceed 15% of operating revenues, and similarly should be earned twice. Low interest rates have greatly helped utilities to reduce fixed charges and strengthen coverage of interest charges.

CLASSES OF PUBLIC UTILITIES. Public utilities are usually classified by the services performed. The principal classes are: (1) electric companies, (2) natural gas transmission and distribution companies, (3) telephone and telegraph companies. Local transit companies and water works are relatively minor groups. Some utilities own franchises for the operation of two or more services. Most prevalent are combination gas and electric companies. The **Public Utility Holding Company Act of 1935** has tended to limit operations to one type of service.

Electric Light and Power. The electric utility industry has provided a classic example of stable, certain growth, qualities especially appreciated by institutional and many individual investors. Competition from public power projects and those financed by the Rural Electrification Administration has been significant in some areas, but it has represented no serious threat to date. Existence of public projects is not cherished by the privately owned companies, for, being government owned, they do not have to earn a profit and are in position to charge relatively low rates.

Increasing reliance upon atomic power plants as a source of electricty in the future may help the industry to hold down unit generating costs over the long run.

Natural Gas. The growth of gas utilities has been enormously accelerated by the wholesale substitution for manufactured gas of natural gas brought by pipeline companies from producing areas, particularly the great oil fields of the Southwest. Regulation of natural gas companies has largely affected investment values. Because of the high debt ratios of pipeline companies, protected as they are by long-term contracts to buy and sell gas, the Federal Power Commission has favored rates that cover interest charges and yield what it regards as an adequate return on the equity, rather than rates that yield an overall fair return on investments, regardless of how such investment has been financed.

Telephone and Telegraph Companies. The telephone industry has enjoyed particularly rapid, stable growth. Because of its nature, it is largely under single ownership.

The American Telephone and Telegraph Co. is the dominant enterprise in the telephone business in the United States. The A.T.&T., or Bell System, composed of operating telephone and associated companies, does about 90% of the nation's telephone business and owns about 80% of the phones in use. The largest independent telephone system is General Telephone and Electronics Corporation. There are several thousand other independent telephone companies, mostly small local companies. A.T.&T. has by far the largest number of stockholders of any American corporation.

The telegraph business, confronted by severe competition from the telephone and radio, has turned to such newer services as telex, carrier equipment microwave beams, and AUTODIN (automatic digital network).

Municipal ownership has greatly reduced the number and importance of **transit and water works securities.**

Railroad Securities

LEGAL AND ECONOMIC FACTORS. The railroad industry is subject to comprehensive regulation by the **Intrstate Commerce Commission**, a Federal agency, and to a limited degree of regulation by state commissions also. Under the **Interstate Commerce Act**, the Interstate Commerce Commission has the power to fix freight and passenger rates; to pass upon the issuance of new securities; to regulate accounting; to pass upon proposed mergers, consolidations, and leases; and to supervise other phases of railway operation. Relatively rigid regulation and working rules insisted on by railway labor unions have severely handicapped railroads in meeting keen competition from highway, water, pipeline, and air carriers. The investment position of railroad securities in the future will be largely dependent on the extent to which they can become more adaptable to changing competitive conditions in transportation.

RAILROAD TRAFFIC. The bulk of railroad operating revenue is derived from **freight traffic.** The volume of traffic handled depends to a large extent on the location and economic character of the territory served, competing transport facilities available, and the traffic connections developed by the particular railroad.

Density of traffic is very important for earning power. Although it is usually more profitable to carry freight over long distances than for short hauls, a small compact road may be more profitable than transcontinental lines if it carries a sufficiently large volume of traffic. Density is measured by the revenue ton-miles carried per mile of line per annum. A density of less than 1,000,000 ton-miles per annum on an ordinary railroad main line raises the question whether the traffic volume is sufficient for regular profitable operation.

Passenger traffic revenue has suffered heavy losses as volume has dwindled because of automobile and air line competition.

RAILROAD RATES. The Interstate Commerce Commission has the authority to change railroad rates, on its own initiative or on the application of carriers or shippers. The Commission's authority is quite broad under the law, and it may consider the effect of rate changes upon the movement of traffic, as well as upon earning power. The effort to retain traffic eagerly sought by competitors has been a more significant influence on rates than the I.C.C. in many instances, resulting in a gradual erosion of the railway rate structure.

The **level of rates** is measured by revenue received per ton-mile, both for all freight and for particular classes of freight traffic.

OPERATING EXPENSES. Railway accounting is peculiar in that depreciation of fixed assets has a limited role, except for tax purposes. Current maintenance looms large, especially in connection with way and structures, the theory being that a property well maintained does not in fact depreciate. This accounting practice permits heavier maintenance outlays in good times and smaller outlays when revenues fall off.

Maintenance of way and structures includes the cost of replacing rails, ties, ballast, and other parts of roadway and terminals, as well as the wages of labor necessary to maintain tracks, terminals, bridges, and other structures in proper condition. Topography, the proportion of branch mileage, and the severity of the climate play an important part in determining what proportion of operating revenues must be spent for maintenance of way and structures. Effects of maintenance expenditures are cumulative, so that a road that has been overmaintained for a number of years can afford to cut maintenance sharply for a time to counteract a period of low business activity, but an undermaintained road must step up such outlays sooner or later or safe operation will be jeopardized.

Since 1943, the I.C.C. has required annual deductions for depreciation of certain ways and structures, which are included in maintenance.

Maintenance of equipment, comprising the cost of labor and materials used for the upkeep of locomotives, cars, and other rolling stock, is less subject to variation from year to year. However, when traffic declines substantially, a railroad may leave in bad order part of its rolling stock not currently required, to be repaired when traffic volume expands again. The character of equipment, its age, and the extent to which existing rolling stock is to be replaced in the near future will all affect the amount of equipment maintenance outlays of a railroad.

Charges for depreciation and retirement of rolling stock are included with maintenance of equipment. These are considerably larger than for way and structures, and were liberalized for tax purposes by the Guidelines issued in 1962.

Transportation expense constitutes the largest single group of railway operating expenses. This group includes train and station labor, train and station supplies, and fuel. Unlike maintenance, it cannot be deferred but varies directly with the volume of traffic. Because transportation costs may not be deferred, the trend of such costs over a period of years gives a measure of efficiency of management.

Traffic expense includes the cost of obtaining traffic, both personnel and advertising. It corresponds to selling and advertising expense in other industries. **General expense** comprises main office salaries, including accounting, insurance and other departments, and legal costs.

ANALYSIS RATIOS. With the plethora of statistics of railway operation that has been made available by the I.C.C., numerous ratios are available for measuring the efficiency and economy of operation of one railroad over a period of years, as against others in its area, or the nation's railroads as a whole. It should be remembered, however, that the **location** and **character of traffic** of a railroad may be the dominant factors in determining these ratios, rather than management policy. Thus, the Pocahontas coal carriers, Chesapeake & Ohio and Norfolk & Western, carrying solid trainloads of coal on downgrades from the West Virginia mountains to tidewater, have exceptionally favorable ratios because of the nature of their traffic, the small number of branches, the limited passenger business, and, to a lesser extent, because their grades are with, rather than against, the traffic.

The **operating ratio**, most widely used, gives the ratio of all railway operating expenses to railway operating revenues. The **maintenance ratio** shows the percentage of railway operating revenues that is devoted to maintenance, including depreciation. The **transportation ratio** is the percentage of transportation expenses to railway operating revenues. Each of these ratios is usually compared for a given railroad over a period of years, and for similarly situated railroads.

A more thorough analysis of the operations of a particular railroad my be made by performance ratios. The most widely used are **average tons per loaded freight car, freight cars per freight train,** and **train-miles per train-hour,** the latter measuring the average speed of freight trains. These three performance ratios are combined in what is sometimes called the key ratio of efficiency of railway operation—**ton-miles per train-hour.** Since the revenues of a railroad vary with ton-miles carried, whereas expenses are incurred mostly in proportion with train-hours operated, this ratio reflects the key operating factors affecting railroad earning power. Adequacy of maintenance of way expenditures can be measured by **maintenance outlay per equated track mile** and miles of track replaced with new or used rail, and the weight of rail placed. **Equated track miles** are computed by counting the first main track as 1, double and other multiple track as .8, and other track, including sidings and spurs, as .5. Adequacy of maintenance of equipment is measured by repair outlays per locomotive and per freight or passenger car, and by the percentage of locomotives and cars that are in bad order awaiting repairs. Overall efficiency of freight operation is indicated by the ratio of **car-miles per car-day,** which measures the extent to which cars are kept moving and so contributing to revenue. Pounds of fuel used per locomotive-mile and average cost of fuel used measure efficiency of fuel utilization.

RAILROAD FINANCIAL STATEMENTS. Railroad accounting has been subject to detailed regulation by the Interstate Commerce Commission since 1914. At first, such regulation made for more complete and detailed reporting. With the passage of time, however, railway financial accounting fell behind standards established in other industries, particularly with regard to consolidation of parent and subsidiary statements, depreciation, and so on. It should be remembered, however, that the I.C.C. is primarily concerned with accounting to facilitate regulation, rather than with accounting for investors, which is the primary concern of the S.E.C.

In railroad statements, income **taxes**, as well as other taxes, are deducted before computing railway operating income. This tends to understate fixed charge coverage, as against the more common practice of deducting income taxes after interest deductions.

Railroads use each other's rolling stock for through shipments, resulting in **hire of equipment** debits and credits. A line with a large car supply, and one that originates a large part of its traffic, will usually have a credit from this source, but most railroads report debits. Railroads as a whole report debits because they use refrigerator, tank, and other cars belonging to industrial companies and specialized operators of such cars.

A most important consideration in analyzing the investment position of a railroad is its forthcoming **funded debt maturities**. If these are large and net working capital is meager, ability to pay off maturing obligations will depend upon the ability to refund. Should earnings be insufficient or the security markets disturbed, refunding may not be possible, so that reorganization or readjustment becomes necessary.

Some railroad balance sheets may prove misleading for financial analysis purposes because they do not list **contingent obligations**. These should be taken into account by the financial analyst in measuring the burden of fixed charges and debt maturities of a railroad system.

SPECIAL ANALYTICAL FACTORS. In such as the railroad industry, confronted with the need for adapting itself to major technological and economic changes, security analysis must direct itself to appraisal of the progress of individual companies in making such adaptation. The most significant expedients for doing this, other than through better service and more economical operation, are mergers; abandonment of unprofitable lines and services; sale of excess real estate and other property to retire debt and modernize facilities; development of new services like piggybacking and expansion of income from nonrailroad sources such as pipelines, oil, and mineral production on railroad lands; and diversification through acquisitions of other kinds of enterprises that prove profitable.

SECTION 8

FINANCIAL REPORTS

CONTENTS

Evolution of Financial Reporting
Early corporate reports 1
Requirements of the New York Stock Exchange 1
Accounting requirements of the Securities and Exchange Commission 2
Regulation by the Interstate Commerce Commission 3
The trend toward "humanizing" reports 3

Sources of Financial Data
Variability of material 4
Information from the company 4
   The annual report 4
   Quarterly and other interim reports 5
   Statements by corporate executives or spokesmen 5
   Annual meetings 5
Securities and Exchange Commission information 5
Financial reporting services 6
Other secondary sources 6
Short-term credit information 6
   Dun & Bradstreet, Inc. 6
   The National Credit Office 7
   The Robert Morris Associates 7

The Income Statement
Contents 7
Form of statement 8
   Model income statement (f. 1) 8
Sales or revenues 9
Installment sales and deferred income 9
Cost of goods sold 9
Inventory valuation 9
   Effects of price changes 9
   Methods of valuation 10
Depreciation policies 10
Depletion 11
Other operating expenses 12
Nonoperating items 12
Federal income taxes 12
Charges to surplus 12
Nonrecurring items 13

Statement of Financial Position: Balance Sheet
Definitions 13
Classification of accounts 14
   Model form of balance sheet (f. 2) .. 14–15

Current assets 16
   Cash and cash items 16
   Marketable securities 16
   Notes and accounts receivable (trade) 16
   Notes and accounts receivable from officers and affiliates 16
   Inventories 17
Investments 17
Property, plant, and equipment 18
Intangibles 18
Deferred charges 19
Current liabilities 19
   Two main classifications 20
Long-term (fixed) liabilities 20
Contingent liabilities 20
Preferred stock 21
Contributed capital 21
Retained earnings (earned surplus) 22
Additional information 22

Consolidated Statements
Purpose of consolidated statements 22
Advantages and limitations 22
Inclusion and exclusion of subsidiaries 23
Investment in consolidated subsidiaries 24
Reconciliation of dividends received from and earnings of unconsolidated subsidiaries 24
Minority interests 24
Intercompany items and transactions 25

Other Reports
Statement of retained earnings 25
   Statement of retained earnings (f. 3) ... 25
The funds statement 25
   Combined statement of income and retained earnings (f. 4) 26
   Other statements 27

Certification of Reports
Role of certification 27
Standards for certification 27
Form of report 28

Analysis of Financial Statements
Need for critical analysis 28
   Cash or accrual accounting 29
   Expenses subject to managerial discretion .. 29
Purposes of statement analysis 29

CONTENTS (*Continued*)

	Page
Investment analysis	30
Credit analysis	30
Analysis for financial management	31

Ratio Analysis

Use of financial ratios	31
Significant ratios	31
Limitations	32
Balance sheet ratios	32
Current ratio	32
Acid-test ratio	32
Current liabilities to owners' equity	33
Fixed assets to owners' equity	33
Funded debt to net working capital	33
Inventory to net working capital	33
Owners' equity to total assets	34
Funded debt to total capitalization	34
Fixed assets to funded debt	35
Income statement ratios	35
Operating ratio	35
Net profit margin	35
Number of times fixed charges earned	35
Interstatement ratios	36
Receivables turnover	36
Merchandise turnover	36
Turnover of owners' equity	37
Turnover of net working capital	38
Return on investment	38
Per share ratios	38

Proper Use of Ratios

Standards for comparison	39
Selective uses of ratios	39
Short-term creditors	39
Long-term creditors	40
Management	40
Stockholders	40

Comparative Statement Analysis

Comparative statements	40
Comparative balance sheet analysis	40
Application of funds—working papers (*f.* 5)	41
Statement of application of funds (*f.* 6)	42
Comparative income statement analysis	42
Comparison of income statements (*f.* 7)	43
Percentage analysis of income statement (*f.* 8)	44
Projection of financial statements	44

SECTION 8

FINANCIAL REPORTS

Evolution of Financial Reporting

EARLY CORPORATE REPORTS. Little or no financial information was submitted by management to stockholders in a formal report even up to the latter part of the nineteenth century. With stock ownership quite limited, the necessity for giving an account of the management's stewardship of corporate affairs to a large body of owners was not apparent.

Ripley (Main Street and Wall Street) cites innumerable cases illustrative of the "public be damned" attitude of corporate officials toward stockholders prevalent at the time. In its annual report for 1901, one corporation included the following statement:

> The settled plan of the directors has been to withhold all information from stockholders and others that is not called for by the stockholders in a body. So far no request for information has been made in the manner prescribed by the directors. Distribution of stock has not meant distribution of control.

A number of large corporations dispensed with annual meetings and many published no financial reports to stockholders or issued statements containing a minimum of information.

The **first really modern type of annual report** was published by the United States Steel Corp. in 1902. This example was followed by the comprehensive report of the General Motors Corp., which in 1916 was the first to announce formally that it would publish **semi-annual balance sheets and profit and loss statements** in addition to its regular annual report.

Other corporations began to issue reports that were simple, understandable, and as informative as their structure would permit. In contrast, the reports of many companies continued to be skimpy, uninformative, and misleading. This situation was an important factor leading to the demand for corrective legislation by the Federal government and stricter control by the securities exchanges.

REQUIREMENTS OF THE NEW YORK STOCK EXCHANGE. As far back as 1866, the New York Stock Exchange attempted to collect financial statements from listed companies. Since 1900, all companies applying for listing on the Exchange must agree to publish **annual reports of their financial condition and operating results.** This agreement was later expanded so that by 1926 a listed corporation was required to publish, and submit to stockholders at least 15 days in advance of its annual meeting, an annual report containing its financial statements. If a corporation had subsidiaries, it had to publish consolidated statements of the parent and its subsidiaries, or separate statements of the parent and each of the majority-owned subsidiaries. In addition, companies were requested to publish semi-annual or quarterly earnings statements.

But examination of the reports filed with it convinced the New York Stock Exchange that frequent reporting could be confusing and misleading if the statements failed to make a full and fair disclosure of the financial and operating data essential for appraisal of the value of the corporate securities. Accordingly, the Exchange has intensified its efforts, particularly since the passage of the securities laws in the 1930's, to secure adequately informative financial reports from listed companies.

ACCOUNTING REQUIREMENTS OF THE SECURITIES AND EXCHANGE COMMISSION. The heavy losses incurred by investors in the 1931–1933 era resulted in **Federal regulation of security issues and trading.** The Securities Act of 1933, the Securities Exchange Act of 1934, the Public Utility Holding Company Act of 1935, and the Investment Company Act of 1940 gave regulatory authority over financial reporting to the Securities and Exchange Commission. The second annual report of the Commission stated that one of the major purposes of the Securities Act of 1933 was "to place adequate and true information before the investor." A key objective of the Securities Exchange Act of 1934 was "to make available to the average investor honest and reliable information sufficiently complete to acquaint him with the current business conditions of the company, the securities of which he may desire to buy or sell."

Rappaport states (S.E.C. Accounting Practice and Procedure):

Many of the reports or documents required to be filed with the Commission contain financial data, mostly in the form of financial statements and related schedules. These are always a vital, often the most significant, element of the information upon which the investor predicates investment decisions. Because Congress recognized that accounting and accountants performed such an important role in achieving the statutory purpose of disclosure, and because financial statements lend themselves readily to misleading inferences or even deception, whether or not consciously intended, the statutes administered by the Commission deal extensively with accounting.

The Commission is authorized "to prescribe the form or forms in which the required information shall be set forth, the items or details to be shown in the balance sheet and income statements, and the methods to be followed in the preparation of accounts, in the appraisal or valuation of assets and liabilities, in the determination of depreciation and depletion, in the differentiation of recurring and non-recurring income, in the differentiation of investment and operating income, and in the preparation, where the Commission deems it necessary or desirable, of consolidated balance sheets or income accounts of any person directly or indirectly controlling or controlled by the issuer, or any person under direct or indirect common control with the issuer." (Section 19a, Securities Act of 1933, and Section 13b, Securities and Exchange Act of 1934.)

Each registered company, under both the 1933 and 1934 acts, is required to include as part of its registration statement and annual reports a set of financial statements for (1) the registrant, (2) the registrant and subsidiaries consolidated, and (3) unconsolidated subsidiaries. Preparation of these statements is governed by Regulation SX, which prescribes the form and content of the balance sheets, profit and loss statements, schedules, footnotes, and the certificate of the independent public accountant. As a further guide, the Commission from time to time publishes **opinions of its Chief Accountant** on major accounting questions and administrative policy with respect to financial statements.

Unlike the Interstate Commerce Commission, however, the Securities and Exchange Commission has prescribed neither a uniform system of accounts nor a uniform method for the preparation of the financial reports required. Consistent with the rules prescribed in Regulation SX, the registrant is permitted to report its financial statements in such form and order, and may use such generally accepted terminology as will best indicate their significance and character in the light of the statute. To assure proper disclosure, however, the statements filed are **examined by the Commission's staff** to determine whether they have been prepared in accordance with "recognized and accepted principles of accounting" and whether they comply with the rules and regulations prescribed by the Commission. Those statements that do not meet these standards are cited deficient and returned for correction. Unless the financial statements are amended in accordance with principles of accounting acceptable to the Commission, that body may, under Section 8(b)(d) of the Securities Act, and Section 19(a) of the Securities and Exchange Act, refuse to permit the registration statement to become effective or suspend the effectiveness of a registration already effective. Since Section 5(a) of the 1933 Act and Section 12(a) of the 1934 Act make it unlawful to sell or trade in such securities unless a registration statement is in effect, the Commission actually has the power to determine what shall and what shall not be considered **recognized and accepted accounting practices**. This power has had a profound effect on the accounting profession and in many instances has resulted in more comprehensive and informative reports to stockholders. The registration statements and annual reports filed with the Securities and Exchange Commission are available for public inspection.

REGULATION BY THE INTERSTATE COMMERCE COMMISSION. One of the earliest government attempts to compel disclosure of the financial condition and operating results of corporations was Section 20 of the Interstate Commerce Act of 1887, which required common carriers to file annual reports with the Commission on forms prescribed by that body. Examination of these reports disclosed, however, that they were not comparable since each railroad maintained its own system of accounts. To remedy this condition, the **Hepburn Act of 1906** extended the power of the I.C.C. over accounting, specifically authorizing that body to prescribe a uniform system of accounts and to employ inspectors to examine the books of railroads subject to its jurisdiction.

The **uniform system of accounts** prescribed for common carriers by the I.C.C. differs in few essentials from accounting systems employed by industrial corporations. The primary aim of railroad accounting regulation is to facilitate regulation, rather than to enlighten investors in railroad securities. Hence, the instructions emphasize the separation of outlays for additions and betterments from expenses. This tends to result in an understatement of expenses and overstatement of earnings. Depreciation of way and structures is required only to a very limited extent, and consolidation of parent and subsidiary statements is not compulsory.

THE TREND TOWARD "HUMANIZING" REPORTS. The formal, dry annual report to stockholders long in vogue is giving way to more colorful, interesting, and "humanized" annual reports. In the preparation of annual reports, there are **two major groups of readers** to be taken into account, those who are technically trained in understanding financial statements and those who are not. The former includes investment analysts, accountants, controllers, treasurers, credit men, top management personnel, economists, and so on, many of whom also use other sources of information like statements filed with the S.E.C. The latter includes the vast majority of stockholders who are neither trained nor experienced in financial statement analysis and whose primary, and often only, source of information on corporate affairs is the annual report. The need for securing and retaining the goodwill of this group has become increasingly apparent to alert managements. Accordingly, more and more annual reports in the last decade have been prepared so as to appeal primarily to this vast group of stockholders. Pictures, graphs, and other popular features have been included to make the financial statements more interesting and informative.

Sources of Financial Data

VARIABILITY OF MATERIAL. Graham, Dodd, and Cottle (Security Analysis) state:

Most of the corporate data used by the security analyst will have come originally from **two parallel sources.** The first is information sent by the company to stockholders or the press; the second is material filed with a regulatory body—most often the S.E.C. Nearly all this information is reproduced or condensed by the financial services as it becomes available. For many analytical purposes it is sufficient to take the material at second hand, from the various manuals, supplements, or the current information services of Moody's and Standard & Poor's. But for a full-scale analysis the practitioners will generally find it advisable to consult the original sources to make sure that nothing of importance is overlooked.

The amount of material available varies to an extraordinary degree when the entire body of quoted securities is surveyed. At one extreme we have unlisted issues which are subject to no regulatory controls, and for which the published data can range from a complete story down to literally nothing at all. At the other extreme we have the Class I railroads, which include all lines of any importance. These file quarterly with the I.C.C. a large eight-page form that presents statistics in the greatest profusion about nearly every phase of their physical operations and finances. In addition they supply weekly figures of cars loaded on their lines and received from connections.

The **credit analyst** is more often in a position to obtain material directly from the company and to demand data that the company does not present publicly. An important creditor can insist upon financial statements if the company is interested in obtaining funds from the creditor even though the company may not publish financial statements for the general public.

INFORMATION FROM THE COMPANY. The most important source of financial information is the company itself. Even when data coming through other bodies are used, it must be recognized that the initial source of data for the S.E.C., the I.C.C., Dun & Bradstreet, etc., has been the company itself. No regulatory or reporting body assures the complete accuracy of the data that it obtains from the company.

The major source of data coming from the company is the corporation's annual report. Other sources are quarterly and other interim reports, statements by corporate spokesmen, and reports given out by the company under special circumstances, such as financial statements in connection with applications for loans.

The Annual Report. Current annual reports of publicly held companies range all the way from 3 by 5 cards printed on one side to four-color bound publications in excess of 100 pages. Most reports of the leading companies consist of 20 to 40 pages of which a significant portion consists of illustrative graphs and diagrams and pictures of various company operations.

Most reports contain at least a **condensed consolidated balance sheet** and an **income statement.** An increasing number also include a statement of reconciliation of retained earnings and a flow of funds statement. It is becoming increasingly popular to include financial data for a number of years as well as for the current year, to facilitate comparisons. There have even been examples of the inclusion of financial data on competing firms.

Some annual reports include a number of supporting schedules of financial data as well as quantitative data on units produced, physical facilities, employees, stockholders, etc. In addition, most annual reports of leading companies contain a substantial amount of nonfinancial data describing various operations, expectations for the future, list of affiliates, etc.

Quarterly and Other Interim Reports. Many corporations send to stockholders interim reports in addition to the annual report. These may be (a) quarterly statements—some with dividend checks, others under separate cover, and still others through news releases; (b) semi-annual statements; (c) dividend stuffers or inserts other than quarterly reports; and (d) reports of business transacted at annual meetings of stockholders. Some firms send a complete transcript of the annual meetings whereas others send a condensation of the proceedings.

Statements by Corporate Executives or Spokesmen. Additional sources of financial information are statements of corporate officials to the press or contained in public addresses. Such statements may provide information about financial condition and policies, plans for future expansion, labor relations, government controls, dividend payments, contemplated new financing, etc. In some cases these may be reprinted and mailed to stockholders, security analysts, and others.

Many corporate spokesmen appear before the **Society of Financial Analysts** in leading financial centers across the country. Their remarks are reported in leading newspapers and many companies reproduce them and send them to members of the society and, in some cases, also to stockholders.

Annual Meetings. In a further effort to give stockholders a more intimate picture of corporate affairs and thereby cement better relations between stockholders and management, certain corporations have attempted to attract larger numbers of stockholders to annual meetings. Some firms have gone so far as to hold the annual meetings in places where the largest numbers of stockholders are concentrated. Free lunches, tours, souvenirs, etc., are sometimes offered to those who attend. Generally, a fair amount of important data is made available at the annual meeting. Because of the large number of stockholders who cannot attend the meeting, the information presented is sometimes published and sent to all interested parties.

SECURITIES AND EXCHANGE COMMISSION INFORMATION. The majority of large companies with publicly held stock come under the jurisdiction of the Securities and Exchange Commission. The basic purpose of the Securities Act of 1933, the Securities and Exchange Act of 1934, and subsequent legislation is to make more accurate and reliable data available to investors. A substantial amount of financial information is available in the **prospectus** issued in connection with the sale of new securities by a covered company. The prospectus provides a detailed description of the company's business and normally gives much more complete financial information than that contained in annual reports. Prospectuses, however, are available only at the time of the issuance of new securities by the company, and for most companies this is at infrequent intervals.

Annual data are also available through the S.E.C. All companies whose stock is listed on organized securities exchanges must file an annual report with the

S.E.C. These reports bring financial data about the corporation up-to-date from the time of the last prospectus or the original registration statement. They are available for inspection at the offices of the S.E.C. or at the securities exchanges. Financial reporting services collect data from these reports and in turn distribute them to the general public. In addition, most companies make much of the information available in their published annual reports.

FINANCIAL REPORTING SERVICES. The investor seeking information about the finances, operations, and management of a corporation will find valuable material in the data published by such services as Moody's Investors Service and Standard & Poor's Corporation. These investment services present information and opinions from the **point of view of the investor** and provide a factual basis for reaching a judgment about security values. Many other more personalized advisory services are available but their coverage is usually less comprehensive.

Moody's Investors Service publishes five manuals: Industrials, Municipals and Governments, Transportation, Public Utilities, and Banks and Finance. The manual of basic information is published once a year and semiweekly supplements keep the material up-to-date. A **dividend record** provides a continuous record of dividend payments and other pertinent information. A **bond survey** shows coupon rates, maturity, interest dates, Moody's rating, market price, maturity yield, etc.

Standard & Poor's Corporation service includes the **Standard Corporation Record,** the **Dividend Record,** and the **Bond Guide.** In addition, this company publishes analytical and advisory data including **Industry Surveys, Trade and Securities Statistics, Trends and Projections,** and **The Outlook.** The **Standard Corporation Record,** furnishing financial information on American and Canadian corporations and their securities, consists of six loose-leaf alphabetical volumes revised monthly, with a daily news section. The **Dividend Record** prints details on dividend announcements, rights, stock redemption and tenders, etc. The **Bond Guide** reports daily bond calls and tenders, sinking fund proposals, defaulted bond data, etc.

OTHER SECONDARY SOURCES. The **Interstate Commerce Commission** publishes a wealth of data about railroad corporations. Complete annual reports are filed with the commission by all regulated companies. Much of the data is reproduced in an annual publication, "Statistics of Railways in the United States." The **Federal Power Commission** obtains substantial information about various public utility corporations, much of which is also published in an annual statistical report. Other regulatory bodies providing information about corporations include the Federal Reserve Board, the Comptroller of the Currency and state banking departments (concerning **banks**), state insurance departments (concerning **insurance companies**), and the I.C.C. (concerning **pipe lines, trucking companies, express companies,** etc.).

Another source of information is **trade associations.** Some of these organizations publish data about specific companies and others about the industry as a whole. The trade journals and general business publications also contain useful financial information about corporations and industries.

SHORT-TERM CREDIT INFORMATION. Data upon which to base short-term analyses are available from the following sources:

Dun & Bradstreet, Inc. This mercantile agency is a nationwide and international organization for the collection, analysis, and dissemination of credit information. Such information is contained in the Reference Book and the Analytical Report.

The **Reference Book** was first published in 1859 with 20,000 names. It now lists more than 2,000,000 names of business enterprises in the United States and Canada. Trade classifications are identified by symbols on the left, whereas financial and credit ratings are indicated on the right of the company's name. The Reference Book is revised six times a year and is issued in January, March, May, July, September, and November. Changes reflect new names entering the field of business, deletions of defunct concerns, revisions in rating upward or downward, changes in name styles, etc. The **Analytical Reports** are uniform in style, facts being presented in the order of their credit importance. Each report is divided into the following sections: summary, trade, banking, current, finance, management, history, and operation.

The National Credit Office. This agency secures financial statements from thousands of firms and verifies the contents directly with the independent public accountants. Photostatic copies of the statements and verifications are available to the credit grantor immediately on request.

The Robert Morris Associates. This is a national association of bank credit men. Its credit service is a highly specialized one, designed almost exclusively for member banks.

The Income Statement

CONTENTS. The income statement is also called **statement of operations** or **profit and loss statement** but the term "income statement" is generally preferred. This statement reflects the results of operations during a stated accounting period. It presents the revenue for the period, the applicable expenses, and the net income or loss. Data concerning sales, returns and allowances, cost of goods sold, selling and administrative expenses, other income and expenses, income taxes, and net income are normally presented in the income statement.

The American Accounting Association (Accounting and Reporting Standards for Corporate Financial Statements) states:

The income of an accounting period should be reported in a statement providing an exhibit of all revenue and expenses (including losses) given accounting recognition during that period. This practice assures that the income statements for a period of years will disclose completely the entire income history of that period.

The income statement should be arranged to report consistently and in reasonable detail the particulars of revenue and the expense pertaining to the operation of the current periods measured as accurately as is possible at the time the statement is prepared and also any items of revenue or expense not associated with the operations of the current period. Such arrangement of data in a single statement discloses both the earning performance and the entire income history of the enterprise during a given income period.

The income statement should reveal the amount of cost assigned to expense by reason of any reduction of an inventory to its recoverable cost.

In published reports, the usual emphasis is on **return to stockholders**. The income statement is a connecting link between the equity accounts of the balance sheet at the beginning of the period and the balance sheet at the end of the period. It accounts for the change in the proprietorship resulting from operations during the period. In the statement, nonoperating income and expenses (such as interest on borrowed funds) are separated from income and expenses directly related to operations. Operating income, or income before interest and certain other charges, may be a more meaningful figure for studying the efficiency of management and making comparisons between different companies over a period of time than total corporate income. The American Accounting Association (Accounting and Reporting Standards for Corporate Financial Statements) states:

> The realized net income of an enterprise measures its effectiveness as an operating unit and is the change in its net assets arising out of (a) the excess or deficiency of revenue compared with related expired costs and (b) other gains or losses to the enterprise from sales, exchanges, and other conversion of assets. Interest charges, income taxes, and true profit-sharing distributions are not determinants of **enterprise net income.**

In determining **net income to shareholders,** however, interest charges, income taxes, profit-sharing distributions, and credits or charges arising from such events as forgiveness of indebtedness and contributions are properly included. In financial reports and discussions alike, care should be exercised to indicate whether enterprise net income or net income to the shareholders is at issue.

FORM OF STATEMENT. The Income Statement is presented in a number of different ways in published reports. A model condensed income statement from the Accountants' Handbook is presented in Fig. 1.

.... CORPORATION
INCOME STATEMENT
Year Ending December 31, 19—

OPERATING REVENUE
    Gross Sales (or other gross revenue) .... $xxx
    Less Gross Revenue Adjustments (returns, allowances, discounts, etc.).... xxx
    Net Sales (or other adjusted revenue) .... $xxx
    Minor Activity Revenues xxx
    Ancillary Revenues (rent, interest, dividends, etc.) xxx
        Net Operating Revenue .... $xxx

OPERATING EXPENSES *
    Cost of Sales .... $xxx
    Selling Expenses xxx
    General and Administrative Expenses xxx
        Total Operating Expenses xxx

OPERATING INCOME .... $xxx

NONOPERATING CHARGES AND CREDITS
    Extraordinary and Nonrecurring Gains and Losses .... $xxx
    Corrections of Prior Years' Income xxx   xxx
        Total Corporate Income Before Taxes .... $xxx

INCOME TAXES xxx
        Total Corporate Income .... $xxx

DISPOSITION OF INCOME
    Interest xxx
        Net Income to Stockholders (net income) .... $xxx
    Dividends on Preferred Stock xxx
        Net Income to Common Stockholders .... $xxx

    * Depreciation, depletion, and amortization should be disclosed separately or in a footnote.

Fig. 1. Model income statement.

SALES OR REVENUES. The first item on the profit and loss statement is usually sales or operating revenues. If **other sources than sales** of merchandise are important, disclosure of the amount from each of these sources is essential to proper analysis of income. (10% or more of the combined total for either source is considered significant under Rule 5–03 of Regulation SX of the S.E.C.)

Installment Sales and Deferred Income. Several methods of taking up income on installment sales are generally recognized and have received substantial support. The two most commonly employed are (1) taking up total income in the period of sale, and (2) taking up income in proportion to payments received. The latter is the more conservative policy. As the uncertainty of collection without loss or large expense increases, the propriety of taking up income immediately becomes more and more doubtful. And if total income is taken up in the income account in the period in which the sale is made or contract entered into, good accounting practice dictates that ample provision be made for prospective collection losses. The possible variation in current earnings under these circumstances is obvious.

COST OF GOODS SOLD. A reasonably detailed disclosure of the composition of cost of goods sold, including opening and closing inventories, together with an explanation of the basis used in inventory valuation, is essential to any revealing analysis of the operating results of the business enterprise. The S.E.C. has considered this information of such importance to the investor that it has consistently disapproved requests of registered companies to keep confidential the composition of cost of sales unless compelling reasons are presented to prove that such a disclosure would adversely affect the company's financial and operating position.

INVENTORY VALUATION. The cost of goods sold is computed by deducting inventories at the close of the period from the total cost of merchandise available for sale. Hence, the method used to value inventories may profoundly affect the income shown. The higher the closing inventory, the lower the cost of goods sold, and the larger the income. Inventories may be valued at cost, the lower of cost or market, or some other acceptable basis. In determining cost, the method employed might be average cost, first-in first-out, last-in first-out, or some other recognized method. Under the circumstances, a **disclosure of the basis used,** together with a statement as to whether such basis is consistent with that of the preceding accounting period, is very important information for the analyst.

Effects of Price Changes. With rising prices of materials and labor in recent decades, significant problems have been raised relative to inventory valuation. Although the accounting profession has been unwilling to deviate from its acceptance of **lower of cost or market** as the standard way for valuing inventory, considerable leeway is allowed in accepted accounting practice in determining cost of the inventory on hand. Thus, an important management decision in most businesses is the choice of an inventory valuation method. Each of the generally followed techniques has a different effect on the valuation on the balance sheet and on the cost of goods sold amount on the income statement. If the ending inventory is overvalued, the cost of goods manufactured or sold will be less by the amount of the **overvaluation** and the gross profit will be higher. A higher gross profit results in higher income taxes. **Undervaluation** has the opposite effect on profits and taxes. Because of the increasing importance of income tax in recent decades, if a choice is possible many businessmen have chosen to prefer undervaluation, which results in lower income taxes.

Methods of Valuation. Many businesses find it difficult to determine the actual cost of the inventory on hand. When purchases of the same item were made at different times at varying prices, it is difficult to tell which cost items are still on hand at the end of the period. One common practice is to assume that the first items purchased were the first ones used in production or sale. This is the **first-in, first-out** inventory valuation method, which in practice is called **FIFO**. The result is that the book value of the inventory is close to the existing market price. In periods of rising prices, this means that the closing inventory is stated at higher prices than under other methods and that profits also are higher, with correspondingly higher income taxes.

Under the **average cost method,** the weighted average of the varying costs of an item is used as a basis of the inventory valuation. In periods of rising prices, this method results in a lower valuation of balance sheet inventory and lower profits and income taxes than the FIFO method.

The **last-in, first-out** method of valuation is particularly popular in periods of rising prices because it results in a still lower value for balance sheet inventory and lower profits and income taxes. Under this system, which is called **LIFO**, it is assumed that the last item purchased is the first item used or sold. Thus, the balance sheet inventory reflects earlier prices than the latest market prices. The valuation of the closing inventory is lower, the cost of goods sold is increased, and profits and taxes are reduced. Many firms changed to the LIFO method of valuation for tax purposes during and after World War II, when prices were rising sharply. This technique results in lower taxes during inflation and higher taxes during deflation. It also tends to **stabilize income** by minimizing the effect on profits of inventory price changes.

Because of the possible loss or reduction in profits that may come from a drop in inventory prices, many companies carry on their books an allowance or **reserve for decline in inventory values.** This allowance has the effect of decreasing inventory values on the balance sheet, and if the corresponding charge is made against income it also has the effect of decreasing stated income.

It is thus clear that the choice of inventory valuation method may strongly influence the stated income for the company during the period under consideration. It is important that the method of valuation be clearly indicated in the income statement and that some basis be given for adjusting the stated income results at times when the statement shifts from one form of valuation to another between accounting periods. It should also be recognized that it is not possible to compare the incomes of two different companies that use different inventory valuation methods unless the necessary adjustment is made.

DEPRECIATION POLICIES. A major element in cost of manufactured goods that is influenced greatly by management decisions is depreciation expense. Moreover, in most manufacturing and public utility enterprises, depreciation expense is a very significant item of cost.

Depreciation is a decline or **loss in value** caused by a variety of factors, including physical deterioration, market action, and obsolescence. In business and accounting circles, the term is, however, usually restricted to loss in value of nondepletable **fixed assets** due to physical deterioration. Despite proper maintenance and repairs, practically all fixed assets, except land, will eventually wear out. Therefore, proper depreciation charges should be made in order to **allocate the cost** of fixed assets to individual accounting periods during their useful life.

If an asset were entirely expensed at the time of its purchase, the year of purchase would absorb unreasonably high expenses, and income for that year would be understated. The later years would include no charge for use of the asset on the income statement and, therefore, income would be overstated. The opposite extreme would be to capitalize total cost of the asset and to make no charge against it until its useful life expired. Under this approach, profits would be overstated during all the years of use of the fixed asset until the final year, when income would be sharply understated. Neither of these approaches is reasonable from the standpoint of making an accurate determination of current income. Thus, the **standard approach** to absorbing the cost of fixed assets is to allocate it in some manner over their estimated useful life.

The **allocation of cost** of a long-lived asset to individual accounting periods should accomplish two objectives: (1) it should reflect the cost of the benefit that the current period receives from the use of the asset, and (2) it should result in carrying forward as an asset at the end of the current period only that part of the original cost that corresponds to service benefits expected from the asset in the future. In times of changing prices, it is often not possible to have both reasonable depreciation charges against income and reasonable values on the remaining service potential of assets unused and carried on the balance sheet. This is due to the standard accounting practice that accepts depreciation only on the **original cost** of the asset, regardless of its **current market** or **replacement** value.

The **specific charge** against income selected by the firm for use in its accounting statements is of a highly subjective nature. Donaldson and Pfahl (Corporate Finance) state:

The use of original cost presents particular problems when the value of the dollar is changing. In times of inflation, original cost tends to be substantially below current replacement cost or market value and also below a value based on future earning power of the asset to the firm. . . .

The choice of original cost itself is subjective and many more subjective decisions must be made in determining the annual charge for depreciation. One of these subjective decisions regards the residual value of the asset. If an asset has a scrap value at the time of its disposal, the amount obtained from disposal should not be charged as depreciation expense during the useful life of the asset. . . .

A more important subjective decision is the number of years of useful life. . . . The very subjective nature of this decision has caused the Internal Revenue Service to establish average or reasonable lives for specific items under certain uses. . . .

The combinations of future decisions required in determining the depreciation expense for an accounting period is such as to make the actual value chosen subject to substantial question. . . .

In addition to problems of acceptance of original cost, estimate of scrap value, and determination of useful life, there remains the problem of selection of a **method of charging off** the amount of depreciation over the life of the asset. A variety of methods are accepted today (see Sec. 17 for a description of the methods used). Because of the high income tax rates in recent years, business has tended to use those methods of depreciation accounting that result in the lowest income tax payment. By charging more for depreciation less is paid in income taxes. The firm has, therefore, more cash on hand on which it can earn a return. Even though the Internal Revenue Service allows only **total cost** to be charged as depreciation over the life of the asset, it accepts a number of different **methods of spreading** this charge out so that the **timing** of payments of income taxes may be significantly influenced even though the total tax may eventually be the same.

DEPLETION. Depletion is the charge for the **exhaustion of wasting assets** such as timberlands, oil and gas wells, mines, and quarries. When these wasting assets are sold, the remaining physical property has substantially reduced value.

Consequently, as the products are removed from the land and sold, a depletion charge should be made against the income equivalent to the decline in value of the property or the cost of acquiring other natural resources to replace those used up. If this were not done, the shareholder or the analyst would be given a distorted view of profits since part of what were stated as profits would really be a return on the original capital.

For **Federal income tax purposes,** the Internal Revenue Service allows a number of arbitrary approaches to the determination of depletion. In general, these have caused firms to understate rather than overstate profits for income tax purposes. An analyst should determine whether a given income statement uses the Internal Revenue Service allowable depletion, or a depletion figure computed by the company for public statements, or no depletion allowance at all.

OTHER OPERATING EXPENSES. Other operating expenses include such items as selling, general, and administrative expenses. **Selling expenses** include salaries and commissions paid to salesmen, salesmen's traveling expenses, advertising, sales promotion, and other expenses allocated in the sales department. **General and administrative expenses** include salaries of the company's officers and other administrative employees, insurance, stationery, postage, rent, light, and heat expense allocated to the administration, etc. Depreciation on office building and equipment and on assets utilized by the sales department is included in selling, general, and administrative expenses.

The analyst should pay particular attention to compensation of officers included in other operating expenses. Compensation for services, if in a form other than cash, for example, can be so reflected in the account as either to understate or overstate the expense, with a reverse effect on current earnings. In closely held owner-managed companies particularly, the amount paid to management as salary may be strongly influenced by the owner-managers' tax position. In many cases, they pay themselves less in salary than would have to be paid if the firm were publicly owned. In other cases, management compensation in closely held companies might be significantly greater than would normally be expected in a publicly held company. In the first case the profit is overstated whereas in the latter case part of the extra compensation to management is really the equivalent of a dividend.

NONOPERATING ITEMS. Nonoperating income is that income of the company that is not directly related to operations. Ordinarily it is derived from its financial activities rather than from its production and distribution activities. Dividends received on stock and interest received on bonds held by the company are included in this item. Profits from sales other than from "stock in trade" and rental income are also normally included.

Expenses not related to operations are placed under **"nonoperating expenses."** Interest paid on bank loans or bonds outstanding is included in this section, as are losses from sales of assets other than "stock in trade."

FEDERAL INCOME TAXES. Federal income taxes are truly an expense and should be shown as such on the income statement. But since the income tax is based on income before taxes, the latter figure is shown separately on the income statement before the taxes are deducted to give "net income." Thus, profits are commonly shown "before" and "after" Federal income taxes.

CHARGES TO SURPLUS. Many corporations in the 1930's wrote down the value of their fixed assets by charges against capital or paid-in surplus. By decreasing the book value of fixed assets, depreciation charges for subsequent periods were reduced and profits increased. Similarly, some concerns create reserves out of retained earnings for the full amount of amortized bond discount, estimated future pensions payable, or unamortized improvements to leaseholds. In other cases, note and bond discount expense, development expenses, and scrapped and demolished equipment are charged directly to paid-in capital. Sometimes, loss in value of inventory is charged directly to retained earnings. The practical effect of not charging expenses and losses to current operations or to any operating year is that the **net income for the current year is overstated** and that income in future years may also be overstated by reducing future depreciation or other charges.

NONRECURRING ITEMS. Stated net income consists of profit from ordinary operations of the business enterprise plus any nonrecurring profits or losses that may have occurred during the period. The security analyst, however, is interested in current net income chiefly as an **indication of prospective earnings.** Hence the analyst is interested in knowing what part of income represents ordinary profits, what part nonrecurring profits or losses, how likely are nonrecurring items to recur in the future, and whether the treatment of nonrecurring items is sound and consistent. Nonrecurring items include payments of back taxes or tax refunds not previously provided for, the results of litigation or other claims relating to prior years, profits or losses on sale of fixed assets or investments, adjustments of investments to market value, write-downs or recoveries of foreign assets, proceeds of life insurance policies collected, and charge-offs in connection with bond retirements and new financing. Graham, Dodd, and Cottle (Security Analysis) suggest the following rules for the analyst's treatment of nonrecurring items in the income account:

1. Small items should be accepted as reported. For convenience we may define "small" as affecting the net result by less than 10% in the aggregate.
2. When a large item is excluded, a corresponding adjustment must be allowed for in the income tax deduction.
3. Most nonrecurrent items excluded from the single year's analysis must nevertheless be included in a statement of long-term or average results.

Statement of Financial Position: Balance Sheet

DEFINITIONS. The statement of financial position or the balance sheet is a statement of assets, liabilities, and equity at the close of business on the date indicated.

Assets represent all things owned by the business that have a money value. The American Institute of Certified Public Accountants (A.I.C.P.A.) (Accounting Terminology Bulletin No. 1) defines the term as "something represented by a debit balance that is or would be properly carried forward upon a closing of books of account . . . (provided such debit balance is not in effect a negative balance applicable to a liability), on the basis that it represents either a property right or value acquired, or an expenditure made which has created a property right or is properly applicable to the future. Thus, plant, accounts receivable, inventory, and a deferred charge are all assets in balance-sheet classification."

Liabilities and **equity** represent the claims of the creditors and owners (stockholders) against the assets. Frequently, the term "liabilities" is used to include both creditors' and owners' claims. The A.I.C.P.A. (Accounting Terminology Bulletin No. 1) uses the term in that sense in its definition of liabilities as "something represented by a credit balance that is or would be properly carried forward upon a closing of books of account . . . . provided such credit balance is not in effect a negative balance applicable to an asset. Thus the word is used broadly to comprise not only items which constitute liabilities in the popular sense of debts or obligations (including provision for those that are unascertained), but also credit balances to be accounted for which do not involve the debtor and creditor relation. For example, capital stock and related or similar elements of proprietorship are balance-sheet liabilities in that they represent balances to be accounted for, though these are not liabilities in the ordinary sense of debts owed to legal creditors."

Total assets, therefore, should always be equal to the total of the liabilities (including equity). The balance sheet equation, simply stated, is **assets equals liabilities plus equity** $(A = L + E)$. Since the claims of creditors take preference over those of owners or stockholders, the interest of the latter is determined by subtracting the liabilities from the assets. Another common way of stating the balance sheet equation, therefore, is assets minus liabilities equals equity $(A - L = E)$.

CLASSIFICATION OF ACCOUNTS. Assets are usually classified as current, fixed, or deferred. The S.E.C. classification for commercial and industrial corporations includes the following more detailed classifications: Current Assets, Investments, Fixed Assets, Intangible Assets, Deferred Charges, and Other Assets. The classification of liabilities ordinarily is consistent with that of the assets. Frequently, liabilities and equity are shown under one major caption with appropriate classifications thereunder. The S.E.C. follows this practice with the caption "Liabilities, Capital Shares and Surplus" supported by the following classifications: Current Liabilities, Deferred Income, Long-Term Debt, Other Liabilities, Reserves Not Shown Elsewhere, Capital Shares and Surplus.

The **order** in which the different classes of items in the balance sheet are listed will depend in great part upon the custom and practice in the industry. For commercial and industrial enterprises, if the **current assets** represent the greater portion of the company's resources, items usually are listed in order of liquidity with current assets first, followed by **fixed** and **deferred** assets. The liabilities are listed in the same order for comparative purposes. For railroads and public utilities, the greater portion of whose resources is invested in fixed property, the usual order is for the fixed assets to appear first, followed by current assets and deferred charges. For comparative purposes in such companies the liability side usually presents capital stock, long-term debt, current liabilities, and deferred income, in the order mentioned. Whatever the order followed, the grouping on the liability side ordinarily is consistent with that on the asset side. Fig. 2, from the Accountants' Handbook, illustrates a model form of balance sheet.

.... CORPORATION
BALANCE SHEET
December 31, 19X1
ASSETS

CURRENT
Cash on hand and on deposit (except special or restricted deposits)........ $xxx
Temporary investments (market value indicated) xxx
Notes and accounts receivable (trade) .... $xxx
Less allowances for probable bad debts, etc. .... xxx $xxx
Other receivables (including accruals) .... xxx xxx
Inventories (by principal classes, with indication of bases on which stated).. xxx
Prepayments of insurance, rent, salaries, etc. xxx
Total current assets .... $xxx

Fig. 2. Model form of balance sheet.

STATEMENT OF FINANCIAL POSITION: BALANCE SHEET   8·15

INVESTMENTS
  Investments, long-term receivables, funds, and deposits (separately and with indication of bases on which investments and all large items are stated)... xxx

PROPERTY, PLANT AND EQUIPMENT
  Land (basis indicated) .... $xxx
  Natural resources, buildings, and equipment (principal classes listed separately, with indication of bases on which stated) ... $xxx
  Less allowances for depletion and depreciation (separately)   xxx   xxx   xxx

INTANGIBLES
  Goodwill (indication of basis on which stated) .... $xxx
  Patents, franchises, copyrights, etc. (amortized cost—net, or with allowance for amortization shown as a contra) xxx
  Long-term prepayments or deferred charges (separately) xxx
  Organization costs xxx   xxx

    TOTAL ASSETS .... $xxx

LIABILITIES AND STOCKHOLDERS' EQUITY

LIABILITIES
  Current:
    Notes payable (to banks) .... $xxx
    Notes and accounts payable (trade) xxx
    Taxes payable xxx
    Other payables (including accruals) xxx
    Deferred revenue or income xxx
      Total current liabilities .... $xxx
  Long-term:
    Bonds, mortgages, equipment trust certificates, etc. (showing deductions for treasury bonds and unaccumulated discount and addition of unamortized premium) xxx
      TOTAL LIABILITIES .... $xxx

STOCKHOLDERS' EQUITY
  Preferred stock (details):
    Par or stated value .... $xxx
    Contributed in excess of par or stated value .... xxx $xxx
  Common stock (details):
    Par or stated value .... $xxx
    Contributed in excess of par or stated value xxx   xxx
  Contributed capital—other xxx
    Total .... $xxx
  Appropriated retained earnings (supporting schedule) ...... $xxx
  Unappropriated retained earnings (to agree with balance shown on income statement or supporting schedule) xxx   xxx
      TOTAL STOCKHOLDERS' EQUITY xxx
      TOTAL LIABILITIES AND STOCKHOLDERS' EQUITY .... $xxx

Fig. 2. (Continued.)

Although **uniform reporting** has been prescribed for railroads and public utilities by Federal and state regulatory bodies, no such uniformity exists for the preparation of financial statements for the thousands of industrial and commercial organizations engaged in varying types of businesses throughout the country. Recognizing the impracticability of prescribing any one standard form for the many diverse industries, and with a view toward having statements prepared in a manner that will most clearly reflect the financial condition and operating results of each enterprise, the S.E.C. allows a company-wide latitude in such matters, as is evidenced by Rule 3–01 (a) of Regulation SX:

Financial statements may be filed in such form and order, and may use such generally accepted terminology, as will best indicate their significance and character in the light of the provisions applicable thereto.

CURRENT ASSETS. The American Institute of Certified Public Accountants (A.I.C.P.A.) (Accounting Research Bulletin No. 43) defines current assets as follows:

The term current assets is used to designate cash and other assets or resources commonly identified as those which are reasonably expected to be realized in cash or sold or consumed during the normal operating cycle of the business. Thus the term comprehends in general such resources as (a) cash available for current operations and items which are the equivalent of cash; (b) inventories of merchandise, raw materials, goods in process, finished goods, operating supplies, and ordinary maintenance material and parts; (c) trade accounts, notes, and acceptances receivable; (d) receivables from officers, employees, affiliates, and others, if collectible in the ordinary course of business within a year; (e) instalment or deferred accounts and notes receivable if they conform generally to normal trade practices and terms within the business; (f) marketable securities representing the investment of cash available for current operations; and (g) prepaid expenses such as insurance, interest, rents, taxes, unused royalties, current paid advertising service not yet received, and operating supplies. Prepaid expenses are not current assets in the sense that they will be converted into cash but in the sense that, if not paid in advance, they would require the use of current assets during that operating cycle.

Cash and Cash Items. Cash on hand, demand deposits, and time deposits ordinarily are included under this caption. The inclusion of funds other than those freely available for withdrawal to meet ordinary current obligations results in an overstatement of both the working capital and current ratio position of the company. Such noncurrent funds include deposits in foreign banks the withdrawal of which is subject to government restrictions and regulations, funds earmarked for retirement of preferred stock, pension funds, sinking funds, etc.

Marketable Securities. Ordinarily all securities that have a ready market and have been acquired for temporary investment only, except those acquired for purposes of control, are included under this caption. Securities of affiliates, even though of a marketable nature, are normally not included. The basis used in arriving at the value of marketable securities may be cost, book value, or market value.

Notes and Accounts Receivable (Trade). These receivables represent amounts due from trade customers within the period of one year or less on notes and open accounts known to be collectible. Failure to exclude bad debts and provide an adequate allowance for doubtful accounts and notes receivable results in an overstatement of both assets and current earnings.

Notes receivable discounted or transferred represent a contingent liability until honored by the maker at date of maturity. Since the indorser is liable if the maker refuses payment at maturity, disclosure of this information is essential to a fair appraisal of the current position of the company and its ability to pay short-term debts, including those of a contingent nature. Of equal importance to the analyst is the disclosure of the amount of receivables hypothecated or pledged as collateral.

Notes and Accounts Receivable from Officers and Affiliates. A study by the S.E.C. disclosed that, although substantial amounts due from officers and directors were shown separately in balance sheets filed with the Commission, such amounts were included in several cases without disclosure under the caption "Accounts and notes receivable, less allowance," in annual reports to stockholders. In its Accounting Series Release No. 27, the S.E.C. strongly disapproved of this practice and placed upon the certifying accountants the responsibility for disclosing this information in published reports in these words:

Where an indebtedness results from a transaction between the company and one or more of the management, as individuals, the certifying accountants should employ every means at their disposal to insist upon full disclosure by the company and, failing persuasion of the company, should as a minimum qualify their certificate or disclose therein the information not set forth in the statements.

Inventories. The term "inventory" is used to designate the total of those items of tangible personal property that (1) are held for sale in the ordinary course of business or (2) are in process of production for such sale or (3) are to be currently consumed in the production of goods or services to be available for sale.

A primary objective of accounting for inventories is the **proper determination of income** and the process of **matching appropriate costs against revenues.** That portion of purchases or inventory costs not charged against income is left in the asset "inventory" on the Statement of Financial Position. In a manufacturing process, cost includes raw material costs, direct labor costs, and overhead. In a distribution firm, cost of inventory would be purchase cost plus freight.

Determination of cost involves a number of problems in situations where similar items of inventory are acquired at different times and at different prices. Cost for inventory purposes may be determined under any one of several assumptions, including first-in first-out, average, last-in first-out, normal stock, etc. (see previous discussion of inventory valuation on page 10). A departure from cost in pricing of inventory is generally taken when the market value of such goods is less than cost. Thus, inventory is normally priced at **lower of cost or market.** It is only in exceptional cases that inventories may be priced above cost. The general tendency in times of rising prices is for inventory values on the balance sheet to be considerably less than replacement costs.

INVESTMENTS. Investments may be classified as current assets or noncurrent assets. Inclusion of investments in current assets is warranted when the assets consist of **readily marketable securities** that the company intends to convert into cash during the next operating cycle. These types of investments are used as a means of earning a return on temporarily idle cash. Valuation is generally at the lower of cost or market. The valuation is usually applied to the portfolio in its entirety rather than to individual items. The S.E.C. requires that the aggregate cost and aggregate amount on the basis of current market "shall be stated parenthetically or otherwise."

Investments of a more permanent nature, or short-term investments that are not readily marketable, or marketable short-term investments that it is not the intention of the company to liquidate are classified as **noncurrent** assets and are usually included in a separate section in the balance sheet between current and fixed assets. The major item for most manufacturing and distribution firms is securities of affiliates and accounts and notes receivable from affiliates. The affiliates could be controlled subsidiaries in nonconsolidated situations or related enterprises in which the company does not have a more than 50% control. The subdivision "investments" normally also includes noncurrent claims, special deposits, sinking funds, life insurance, investments in other companies, and other real and personal property.

Valuation of long-term investments may be at cost, amortized cost, or book value. Minor market variations are not normally recorded and the lower of cost or market approach is seldom used. If the investment is in an affiliated company, it is likely that there is no market price that can be used for comparison. In this case, the most common practice is to carry investments at cost, but in certain circumstances the book value on the books of the affiliate may be substituted on the parent company's balance sheet.

If the **parent company controls the policies of subsidiaries and affiliates,** the possibilities for over- or understating the value of these assets are substantial. It is necessary for the analyst studying the parent corporation's balance sheet to determine the reasonableness of the valuation.

PROPERTY, PLANT, AND EQUIPMENT. For most industrial concerns and public utilities, land, buildings, structures, machinery, and equipment are a significant portion of total assets. These items are often shown on the balance sheet under a single figure, with a single deduction of allowances (reserves) for depreciation and depletion. Sometimes the value of land is stated separately.

Land is normally carried on the books at cost. **Other tangible fixed assets** are usually carried at book value (cost less depreciation). However, fixed assets are occasionally carried at appraised value, replacement value, replacement less depreciation, or some other recognized valuation. The analyst starts with the balance sheet valuation and adjusts it to suit his particular purpose, such as estimating resale value of property pledged to secure a bond issue.

In some instances, costs have been written up to **appraised values** because of increased values or to adjust cost in the case of bargain purchases. However, such write-ups have been relatively uncommon in recent years. A large number of write-downs of fixed assets took place in the early 1930's but relatively few in recent years. In Accounting Research Bulletin No. 43, the American Institute of Certified Public Accountants reaffirmed its acceptance of the cost approach to fixed asset valuation, in spite of the inflation of the post-World War II years. However, the accounting profession accepts a variety of approaches to determination of the amount of depreciation or depletion.

Net property values can be substantially affected through liberal or conservative **allowances for depreciation.** They may also be affected by charging to operations expenditures for property, equipment, and major repairs that should be capitalized. This practice not only reduces the net property account in the balance sheet but also affects the income account through increased expenses in the year in which the charge was made and decreased expenses in future years when depreciation or other amortization would be included had the property originally been capitalized. Because of the **wide variation** in accepted approaches to capitalization of assets and depreciation accounting policies, special care must be exercised in examining the fixed asset account. Most authorities agree that accepted accounting practice in recent years has led to undervaluation rather than overvaluation of property accounts.

INTANGIBLES. The American Institute of Certified Public Accountants (A.I.C.P.A., Accounting Research Bulletin No. 43), includes **two types of assets** under the heading of "intangibles": (a) those having a **term of existence limited** by law, regulation, agreement, or by their nature (such as patents, copyrights, leases, licenses, franchises for a fixed term, and good will as to which there is evidence of limited duration), and (b) those having **no such limited term of existence** and as to which there is, at the time of acquisition, no indication of limited life (such as good will generally, going value, trade names, secret processes, subscription lists, perpetual franchises, and organization costs). The A.I.C.P.A. further states: "The initial amount assigned to all types of intangibles **should be cost,** in accordance with the generally accepted accounting principle that assets should be stated at cost when they are acquired. In the case of non-cash acquisitions as, for example, where intangibles are acquired in exchange for securities, cost may be considered as being either the fair value of the consideration given or the fair value of the property or right acquired, whichever is the more clearly evident."

According to the A.I.C.P.A., the cost of type (a) intangibles should be amortized by systematic charges in the income statement over the period benefited, as in the case of other assets having a limited period of usefulness. When it becomes reasonably evident that the term of existence of a type (b) intangible has become limited and that it has therefore become a type (a) intangible, its cost should be amortized by systematic charges in the income statement over the estimated remaining period of usefulness. The total cost of type (b) intangibles should be written off when it becomes reasonably evident that they have become worthless.

Although in the past intangibles have frequently been shown in the balance sheet at arbitrary values established by management, more standardized accounting principles are generally followed by larger firms today. It can generally be assumed that the above recommended approach has been used in statements certified by independent public accountants. However, although the normal valuation process is cost or amortized cost, the time period over which amortization should take place must often be determined subjectively, and in many cases the original determination of cost of the intangible is also highly subjective.

DEFERRED CHARGES. Included under this caption on the asset side of the balance sheet are such items as unamortized debt discounts and expenses, experimental costs, development expenditures, and other deferred expenses. Ordinarily, these items are unimportant and are written off to current operations. If they are legitimately chargeable to future periods, they are generally amortized over their estimated useful life.

CURRENT LIABILITIES. The American Institute of Certified Public Accountants (A.I.C.P.A., Research Bulletin No. 43) **defines current liabilities** as follows:

The term current liabilities is used principally to designate obligations whose liquidation is reasonably expected to require the use of existing resources properly classifiable as current assets, or the creation of other current liabilities. As a balance-sheet category, the classification is intended to include obligations for items which have entered into the operating cycle, such as payables incurred in the acquisition of materials and supplies to be used in the production of goods or in providing services to be offered for sale; collections received in advance of the delivery of goods or the performance of services; and debts which arise from operations directly related to the operating cycle, such as accruals for wages, salaries, commissions, rentals, royalties, and income and other taxes, Other liabilities whose regular and ordinary liquidation is expected to occur within a relatively short period of time, usually twelve months, are also intended for inclusion, such as short-term debts arising from the acquisition of capital assets, serial maturities of long-term obligations, amounts required to be expended within one year under sinking fund provisions, and agency obligations arising from the collection or acceptance of cash or other assets for the account of third persons.

This concept of current liabilities would **include estimated** or **accrued amounts** which are expected to be required to cover expenditures within the year for known obligations (a) the amount of which can be determined only approximately (as in the case of provisions for accruing bonus payments) or (b) where the specific person or persons to whom payment will be made cannot as yet be designated (as in the case of estimated cost to be incurred in connection with guaranteed servicing or repair of products already sold). The current liability classification, however, is not intended to include a contractual obligation falling due at an early date which is expected to be refunded, or debts to be liquidated by funds which have been accumulated in accounts of a type not properly classified as current assets, or long-term obligations incurred to provide increased amounts of working capital for long periods. When the amounts of the periodic payments of an obligation are, by contract, measured by current transactions, as for example by rents or revenues received in the case of equipment trust certificates or by the depletion of natural resources in the case of property obligations, the portion of the total obligation to be included as a current liability should be that representing the amount accrued at the balance-sheet date.

Two Main Classifications. Current liabilities consist of two main classifications, **payables** and deferred income. Generally, notes and accounts payable other than regular trade payables are normally stated separately. Also, estimated payables (accrued expenses), such as provision for income taxes, are commonly listed separately. The accrual system of accounting calls for estimating liabilities of the firm as of the balance-sheet date and recording these among expenses even though payments are not yet due. In many firms, accrued expenses such as wages, payroll taxes, corporate taxes, etc., are the most important current liability items. Dividends declared by the board of directors represent a liability of the corporation and should be shown among current liabilities as an accrued payable.

Deferred revenue or income represents monies received but not yet earned. Ordinarily, that portion of the income that has been earned is included in the income statement and the unearned portion is shown as an item of deferred income in the current liability section of the balance sheet or in a separate section of liabilities apart from current or fixed.

LONG-TERM (FIXED) LIABILITIES. The category "long-term liabilities" is used to include all obligations not classified as current. Although this section is sometimes called **funded debt**, use of this term is not recommended since it does not cover all long-term obligations. The most important items included in long-term liabilities are notes and bonds payable with maturities of over one year. Notes and bonds payable are generally valued at face value, no adjustment being made for changes in market value. Ordinarily, treasury bonds are deducted from bonds shown on the liability side of the balance sheet, the difference representing the amount due on bonds outstanding. Frequently, however, bonds acquired by purchase in the open market—for example, for pension funds—are listed among assets.

It is desirable to disclose in financial statements the amounts due on long-term obligations, year by year. Also included should be the amount of bonds authorized in the indenture, the amount issued and not retired or canceled, the amount in sinking funds and other special funds, the amount pledged, the amount held by parent or subsidiary companies, and any facts concerning default in the principal, interest, sinking fund, or redemption provisions. A description of the bond or note issue on the balance sheet invariably includes the interest rate and the maturity date.

CONTINGENT LIABILITIES. Disclosure of contingent liabilities—for example, on lawsuits, and claims—is essential in determining the prospective financial condition and current position of a company. Discovery of contingent liabilities not disclosed is usually quite difficult. If such amounts are substantial, failure to give due consideration to them in any credit or investment analysis may well result in a distorted picture.

PREFERRED STOCK. If the capital stock of a corporation includes preferred stock, the latter's characteristics will affect both its position and that of the common. In listing preferred stock on the balance sheet, the following disclosure is required in all financial statements filed with the S.E.C. (Rule 3-19d, Regulation SX):

1. If callable, the date or dates and the amount per share and in total at which such shares are callable shall be stated.
2. Arrears in cumulative dividends per share and in total for each class of shares shall be stated.
3. Preferences on involuntary liquidation, if other than the par or stated value, shall be shown. When the excess involved is significant there shall be shown (i) the difference between the aggregate preference on involuntary liquidation and the aggregate par or stated value; (ii) a statement that this difference, plus any arrears in dividends, exceeds the sum of the par or stated value of the junior capital share and the surplus, if such is the case; and (iii) a statement as to the existence, or absence, of any restrictions upon surplus growing out of the fact that upon involuntary liquidation the preference of the preferred shares exceeds its par or stated value.

CONTRIBUTED CAPITAL. Par value common stock is normally carried on the balance sheet at par value per share times the number of shares outstanding. The number of shares outstanding is usually determined after deducting treasury shares. If the stock is of no par value, it is generally carried at a stated value. Amounts paid by stockholders to the company in excess of par or stated value are generally carried as **paid-in surplus** or **capital contributed over par.** The American Institute of Certified Public Accountants (A.I.C.P.A., Accounting Terminology Bulletin No. 1) suggests that the contributed portion of proprietary capital be shown as:

(a) Capital contributed for, or assigned to, shares, to the extent of the par or stated value of each class of shares presently outstanding.
(b) (i) Capital contributed for, or assigned to shares in excess of such par or stated value (whether as a result of original issue of shares at amounts in excess of their then par or stated value, or of a reduction in par or stated value of shares after issuance, or of transactions by the corporation in its own shares); and
(ii) Capital received other than for shares, whether from shareholders or from others.

Item (a) is the **capital stock** account. Item (b), capital in excess of par value, has usually been called **capital surplus** or **paid-in surplus**, but the A.I.C.P.A. recommends that these terms be discontinued. This capital arises from a number of sources, including amounts paid in by stockholders in excess of par or stated value, donations of capital stock, write-up of assets, reorganization, recapitalization, profit on sales of the company's own stock, etc. The A.I.C.P.A. recommends that any appreciation included in the stockholders' equity other than as a result of a quasi-reorganization should be designated by more descriptive terms, such as, for example, "excess of appraised or fair value of fixed assets over costs of fixed assets." This implies that capital arising from such appreciation in value be separately stated from other contributed capital. (See also Sec. 18.)

RETAINED EARNINGS (EARNED SURPLUS). The American Institute of Certified Public Accountants (A.I.C.P.A., Accounting Terminology Bulletin No. 1) defines retained earnings as: "the balance of net profits, income, gains and losses of a corporation from the date of incorporation (or from the latest date when a deficit was eliminated in a quasi-reorganization) after deducting distributions therefrom to shareholders and transfers therefrom to capital stock or capital surplus accounts." The A.I.C.P.A. recommends that the use of the term **surplus** be discontinued and that the term **earned surplus** be replaced by terms that will indicate the source, such as retained income, retained earnings, accumulated earnings, or earnings retained for use in the business.

In connection with retained earnings, there should, so far as practicable, be an indication of the extent to which the amounts have been appropriated or are restricted as to withdrawal. Unless specific information to the contrary is disclosed, it is ordinarily assumed that the total amount of retained earnings is freely available for dividends. If there is any legal impediment to declaring dividends from the full amount of retained earnings shown, either under state statutes or otherwise, this fact is of great importance to the analyst and should be disclosed. If retained earnings are **restricted for a specified purpose** such as plant expansion, contingenies, redemption of funded debt, or additions to working capital, the amounts so designated are listed separately as retained earnings reserves. Retained earnings earmarked for these purposes would not be used for dividend distribution, as otherwise no purpose is accomplished by segregating part of the retained earnings in this way. In computing the book value of a share of stock, such reserves are included along with other retained earnings.

ADDITIONAL INFORMATION. The analyst should seek additional information about the items listed in financial statements in the supporting schedules, footnotes, and the certificate of the independent public accountant. Failure to study these critically may lead to oversight of valuable information.

Consolidated Statements

PURPOSE OF CONSOLIDATED STATEMENTS. The American Institute of Certified Public Accountants (A.I.C.P.A., Accounting Research Bulletin No. 51) states:

> The purpose of consolidated statements is to present, primarily for the benefit of the shareholders and creditors of the parent company, the results of operations and the financial position of a parent company and its subsidiaries essentially **as if the group were a single company** with one or more branches or divisions. There is a presumption that consolidated statements are more meaningful than separate statements and that they are usually necessary for a fair presentation when one of the companies in the group directly or indirectly has a controlling financial interest in the other companies.

ADVANTAGES AND LIMITATIONS. The analysis of financial statements of a corporation owning stock of one or more subsidiaries is greatly facilitated by consolidation of the parent company balance sheet and income account with those of the subsidiaries. The S.E.C. requires, if a corporation owns, directly or indirectly, over 50% of the stock of others, not only parent company statements but also consolidated statements and separate or group statements of majority-owned subsidiaries not included in the consolidated report. But consolidated statements can be misleading, unless they are supplemented by separate statements of the parent and major subsidiaries.

The status of bond issues and other creditor claims against the parent and each of its subsidiaries often cannot be determined from a consolidated statement. Earnings for common stock shown by a consolidated statement may mean little, especially if a large part of the profits are earned by one or more subsidiaries unable to pay dividends to the parent because of accumulations of unpaid dividends on publicly held preferred stock, lack of cash, or other reasons.

The American Institute of Certified Public Accountants has emphasized "the necessity of giving further statements for the parent alone, and possibly for certain subsidiaries," in addition to the consolidated statements. For a complete picture investment analysts usually need separate statements of all included subsidiaries and unconsolidated subsidiaries.

INCLUSION AND EXCLUSION OF SUBSIDIARIES. Control over the management of subsidiary companies is usually considered a prerequisite to consolidated statements. Based upon this principle, many parent companies consolidate only subsidiaries in which the parent company owns directly or indirectly more than 50% of the voting stock. The American Institute of Certified Public Accountants has expressed the view that a company of which less than 50% of the voting stock is owned should ordinarily not be included in the consolidation. For companies filing statements with the S.E.C., Rule 4–02(a) of Regulation SX prescribes that "the registrant shall not consolidate any subsidiary which is not a majority-owned subsidiary." Subject to this limitation, that principle of inclusion or exclusion should be followed that will most clearly reflect the financial condition and operating results of the parent company and its subsidiaries.

There are certain exceptions to the general rule on majority ownership. For example, a subsidiary should not be consolidated if control is likely to be temporary or if it does not rest with the majority owners, as in the case of legal reorganizations or in bankruptcy.

The most common exclusions of controlled subsidiaries is in connection with **foreign subsidiaries.** The American Institute of Certified Public Accountants (A.I.C.P.A., Accounting Research Bulletin No. 43) states:

... in view of the uncertain values and availability of the assets and net income of foreign subsidiaries subject to controls and exchange restrictions and the consequent unrealistic statements of income that may result from the translation of many foreign currencies into dollars, careful consideration should be given to the fundamental question of whether it is proper to consolidate statements of foreign subsidiaries with the statements of the United States companies. Whether consolidation of foreign subsidiaries is decided upon or not, adequate disclosure of foreign operation should be made.

For analysis purposes, it is of primary importance that there be disclosed, in a footnote to the statements or otherwise, the **principle followed by the company** in determining inclusion and exclusion of subsidiaries in consolidation, and whether the principle followed in the preparation of the current statements is consistent with the principle of inclusion and exclusion followed in the preparation of the statements of the preceding periods. Varying practices followed are:

1. Inclusion of only 100% owned subsidiaries.
2. Inclusion of only domestic subsidiaries.
3. Inclusion of all subsidiaries in which, directly or indirectly, more than 60% of the outstanding voting stock is owned.
4. Exclusion of subsidiaries in which, for whatever reason, the parent does not exercise control over distribution of earnings.
5. In lieu of consolidation the parent's share in the undistributed earnings of nonconsolidated subsidiaries is shown in its income statement.

INVESTMENT IN CONSOLIDATED SUBSIDIARIES. In acquiring the stock of a subsidiary the parent company may pay a price that is equal to, greater than, or less than its book value. The **difference between the book value and the price paid** for acquired stock of the subsidiary ordinarily is eliminated in consolidation. Although it is a common practice to charge this difference to the consolidated goodwill account if one exists, this is by no means uniform practice. If a company has paid less than book value for the stock of a subsidiary, this discount has been variously treated in consolidated statements as negative goodwill, capital surplus, and as an addition to the depreciation reserve, depending upon the facts in the case.

Retained earnings and losses of subsidiaries cause a discrepancy to develop between the cost and book value of stocks of subsidiaries in any event. In this connection, Rule 4–05(a) of Regulation SX of the SEC prescribes:

> There shall be set forth, in a note to each consolidated balance sheet filed, a statement of any difference between the investment in subsidiaries consolidated, as shown by the parent's books, and the parent's equity in the net assets of such subsidiaries as shown by the books of the latter. If any such difference exists, there shall be set forth the disposition made thereof in preparing the consolidated statements, naming the balance sheet captions and stating the amounts included in each.

RECONCILIATION OF DIVIDENDS RECEIVED FROM AND EARNINGS OF UNCONSOLIDATED SUBSIDIARIES. The parent company's proportionate share of the undistributed earnings or losses of its majority-owned unconsolidated subsidiaries for the period under review is of vital importance for two reasons. First, the consolidated earnings plus or minus the parent's share of the net profit or net loss of the unconsolidated subsidiaries will reveal the **combined profits of the parent and all of its majority-owned subsidiaries.** The significance of this information was brought out in the following case cited by the executive assistant to the Committee of Stock List of the New York Stock Exchange:

> A very large corporation formerly published consolidated statements including only its wholly-owned subsidiaries. These statements apparently justified the dividends which were regularly paid. It also held from 75% to 85% of the stock of certain large unconsolidated subsidiaries. When asked to publish either fully consolidated statements or separate statements of the subsidiaries, it developed that the companies' proportion of the current losses of the unconsolidated subsidiaries had for years been larger than the total profits of the rest of the system as shown by the unconsolidated statements. Certainly, in this case, however unintentionally, the stockholders had been misled.

Secondly, the difference between current earnings accruing to the parent, less dividends declared, will determine the **net increase or decrease in the parent's equity** in its unconsolidated subsidiaries. If the investment account of the company in its unconsolidated subsidiaries has been kept at cost, such information, if available annually from date of acquisition to the date of the latest financial report, would permit the reader to determine the present equity of the company in the net assets of its unconsolidated subsidiaries.

Minority Interests. The size of minority interests in the capital stock of subsidiaries indicates how large a share of their earnings and assets belongs to others than the parent corporation. The amount of such minority interests must be stated separately in consolidated statements filed with the S.E.C. This is desirable since it is only after earnings due the minority interests have been deducted that profits accruing to the parent can be determined.

OTHER REPORTS 8·25

INTERCOMPANY ITEMS AND TRANSACTIONS. Since consolidated statements are designed to show the financial condition and earnings of the entire group of corporations as a unit, intercompany sales, profits, dividends, loans, etc., are eliminated, if significant in amount. Practical considerations may at times necessitate minor exceptions to this rule. In such cases, Rule 4–08 of Regulation SX of the S.E.C. requires the following disclosure:

> In general, intercompany items and transactions, if significant in amount, shall be eliminated; if not eliminated, a statement of the reasons and the method shall be made.

Other Reports

STATEMENT OF RETAINED EARNINGS. This statement shows the balance of retained earnings at the beginning of the accounting period and the items that have resulted in the retained earnings figure at the end of the period. These may include the net income for the period, dividends paid, adjustments in retained earnings relating to prior years, reductions or increases resulting from the sale or reacquisition of the corporation's own stock, transfers to and from appropriated retained earnings, and other nonoperating charges or credits made directly to retained earnings. Fig. 3, adapted by the Accountants'

.... COMPANY
STATEMENT OF RETAINED EARNINGS
Year Ended December 31, 19—

Balance at January 1, 19—, unappropriated		$xxx
Transfer from amount previously appropriated for contingencies (no longer required)		xxx
		$xxx
Deduct:		
Net loss for the year	$xxx	
Cash dividends declared—$0.20 a share	xxx	xxx
Balance at December 21, 19—		$xxx

Fig. 3. Statement of retained earnings.

Handbook from an actual annual report, illustrates a typical statement of retained earnings.

The statement of retained earnings **ties together** the net income figure on the income statement with the final retained earnings figure on the balance sheet. In many cases, the statement is shown as a continuation of the income statement. Fig. 4, adapted by the Accountants' Handbook from an annual report of the Radio Corp. of America, illustrates a combined statement of income and retained earnings.

THE FUNDS STATEMENT. The funds statement is widely used by financial analysts. If such a statement is not prepared by the company, the analyst often attempts to prepare one from information obtained from other reports and supplementary data.

The American Institute of Certified Public Accountants (Perry Mason, Cash Flow Analysis and the Funds Statement) describes the funds statement as follows:

> The funds statement, as a part of the annual report of the corporation, can be characterized as a condensed report of how the activities of the business have been

.... COMPANY
CONSOLIDATED EARNINGS

	Year Ended Dec. 31, 19X2	Year Ended Dec. 31, 19X1
PRODUCTS AND SERVICES SOLD	$xxx	$xxx
COST OF OPERATIONS:		
Wages and salaries	$xxx	$xxx
Pensions, social security taxes, insurance and other benefits	xxx	xxx
TOTAL EMPLOYMENT COSTS	$xxx	$xxx
MATERIALS AND SERVICES BOUGHT FROM OTHERS	xxx	xxx
DEPRECIATION AND PATENT AMORTIZATION	xxx	xxx
INTEREST ON BORROWED MONEY	xxx	xxx
STATE, LOCAL AND MISCELLANEOUS TAXES	xxx	xxx
	$xxx	$xxx
PROFIT BEFORE FEDERAL TAXES ON INCOME	$xxx	$xxx
Federal income tax	$xxx	$xxx
Federal excess profits tax (applicable to a subsidiary)	xxx	xxx
TOTAL FEDERAL TAXES ON INCOME	$xxx	$xxx
NET PROFIT FOR YEAR	$xxx	$xxx
REINVESTED EARNINGS AT BEGINNING OF YEAR	xxx	xxx
	$xxx	$xxx
DIVIDENDS DECLARED:		
For current year:		
Preferred stock, $3.50 per share	$xxx	$xxx
Common stock:		
Regular dividend—$1.00 per share	xxx	xxx
Extra dividend for 19X2—20 cents per share	xxx	—
Total current year	$xxx	$xxx
For first quarter 19X3:		
Preferred stock, 87½ cents per share	xxx	—
Common stock, 25 cents per share	xxx	—
Total dividends declared	$xxx	$xxx
REINVESTED EARNINGS AT END OF YEAR	$xxx	$xxx

Fig. 4. Combined statement of income and retained earnings.

financed, and how the financial resources have been used, during the period covered by the statement. . . .

The principal raw material used in the preparation of a funds statement ordinarily consists of a comparative balance sheet, with the net changes which have taken place in the various items during the period being indicated. Also needed are analyses of certain accounts, especially the retained earnings, where the differences between the beginning and ending balance sheet figures need adjustment for satisfactory reporting, or where a difference is the result of a combination of several items which must be separated. . . .

The statement organizes this material, after some eliminations, combinations, and additional analysis and reclassification, into two principal groups—(1) sources of funds and (2) application, disposition, or use of funds. Broadly speaking, sources of funds are indicated by decreases in assets and increases in liabilities or in the stockholders' equity, while applications of funds are associated with increases in assets and decreases in liabilities or in the stockholders' equity.

Comparative funds statements, covering several years of operations, enable the reader to obtain useful information such as the financing methods used in the past, dividend policies which have been followed, and the contribution of funds derived from operations to the growth of the company. They may also provide reliable clues as to the future financial requirements.

. . . This statement is often more comparable with those of other companies than are the balance sheet and the income statements since . . . some of the major variations in accounting procedure are eliminated in the calculation of the "cash flow" or funds provided from operations. . . .

The A.I.C.P.A. concludes that the funds statement should be treated as a major financial statement and presented in all annual reports of corporations and be covered by the auditors in the short-form report. It should be broad enough to cover **all financial management operations** rather than merely a **reconciliation of cash or working capital.** A typical funds statement also known as a **statement of application of funds,** is shown in Fig. 6, p. 42. (See further discussion below under Comparative Statement Analysis.)

Other Statements. Many other types of financial data are also available on occasion, ranging from simple supporting schedules to explain certain items in the statement of financial position and the income statement to complex reports prescribed by various supervisory credit agencies in which the firm may present its data in a manner significantly different from the formal statements and various kinds of financial summaries and graphic presentations. Of particular interest to some users of financial statements are **estimated statements.** These are generally in one of two forms—"budgets" or "pro forma statements." **Budgets** are not generally made available outside the firm. They are a description of the planned financial results for the firm for a coming period and can be extremely useful management tools. Because of the subjective nature of the estimates in budgets, outside analysts cannot assume exact reliability, nor is the auditing profession prepared to "audit" budgets. The **pro forma** statements give effect to planned or proposed transactions. They are commonly used in connection with the receipt and disposition of funds to be derived from the sale of securities. They may also be used in presenting a balance sheet for the end of the coming year based on the expected changes resulting from operations.

Certification of Reports

ROLE OF CERTIFICATION. The certification of financial statements by independent and public accountants gives added assurance that the information has been presented **in accordance with accepted principles of accounting,** except if otherwise expressly indicated. Statements filed with the S.E.C. and other regulatory bodies must be certified by independent public accountants. The auditor's report that must accompany the financial statements required by the S.E.C. must contain a brief explanation of the scope of the audit, the accountant's opinion of the financial statements covered by the certificate and the accounting principles and practices reflected therein, together with any matters in the statement to which the independent accountant takes exception.

STANDARDS FOR CERTIFICATION. The American Institute of Certified Public Accountants has attempted to establish accepted standards for auditing and certification. There is general agreement in the profession that the audit examination should be performed by persons having adequate technical training and proficiency as auditors. Furthermore, in all matters relating to the assignment, independence in mental attitude should be maintained by the auditors. A further requirement is for due professional care in the performance of the examination and preparation of the report.

The American Institute of Certified Public Accountants (Accounting Research and Terminology Bulletins) states: "The responsibility of the auditor is to express his opinion concerning the financial statements and to state clearly such explanations, amplifications, disagreement, or disapproval as he deems appropriate." Although this is the responsibility of the **independent auditor**, the A.I.C.P.A. recognizes that the accounts of a company are primarily the responsibility of the management. However, it recommends application of similar principles and procedures for those who prepare the financial statements as for the independent auditors.

FORM OF REPORT. A short-form, two-paragraph accounting report recommended by the A.I.C.P.A. is given below. Limitations as to the scope of the examination may be included in the first paragraph and qualifications of the opinion are usually expressed in the second paragraph. In some cases, the two paragraphs are put in reverse order and combined into a single paragraph.

Date

Addressee:

We have examined the balance sheet of X company as of December 31, 19—, and the related statement(s) of income and surplus for the year then ended. Our examination was made in accordance with generally accepted auditing standards, and accordingly included such tests of the accounting records and such other auditing procedures as we considered necessary under the circumstances.

In our opinion, the accompanying balance sheet and statement(s) of income and surplus present fairly the financial position of X company at December 31, 19—, and the results of its operations for the year then ended, in conformity with generally accepted accounting principles applied on a basis consistent with that of the preceding year.

Signature of accountant

Formerly, a variety of forms were used. Accounting Trends and Techniques (A.I.C.P.A.) reported, however, that a survey of six hundred annual reports for the year 1961 indicated that all of the reports contained the recommended short-form auditors' report or its modified version. Thus, uniformity has been achieved in this respect.

Analysis of Financial Statements

NEED FOR CRITICAL ANALYSIS. Because financial statements are not ordinarily prepared for special purposes, such as investment analysis, and because there will necessarily be differences of opinion in appraising many items in the earnings statement and the balance sheet, there is need for critical analysis of even the most detailed and elaborate financial statements. The elements of opinion and accounting convention that enter into the preparation of financial statements make it necessary, in particular, to examine the principal items and practices that may tend to distort reported earnings.

Reported earnings can be distorted through (1) overstatement or understatement of major items of income or expense; (2) estimates for depreciation, depletion, and contingencies; and (3) treatment of nonrecurring and nonoperating gains and losses. The analyst's task may also be greatly complicated by lack of sufficient detail and clarity in the data presented.

Cash or Accrual Accounting. One of the major concerns of the analyst is to note whether the income statement is prepared on a cash or an accrual basis. The **cash basis** reflects only income and expenditures resulting from actual cash receipts and cash disbursements. Such a statement ordinarily is known as a statement of cash receipts and disbursements, and is not a true reflection of income earned and costs and expenses incurred during the period. Since most business is conducted on a credit basis, a statement that portrays only cash transactions usually fails to reflect all of the transactions affecting gains and losses for the period under review.

The **accrual basis** takes into account **all transactions** during the period under review, whether on a cash or credit basis. For example, on the accrual basis a $5,000 sale to a customer on December 15, delivered that date, payment to be received 30 days later, would be included in the income statement as part of gross revenue for December, notwithstanding the fact that the receipt of cash would not occur until the following month. On the cash basis this amount would be excluded from December income and included in January, when the cash is actually received. Unless it is **specifically stated to the contrary,** an income statement is presumed to have been prepared on the accrual basis.

When the company closes its books at the end of the year, there invariably exists certain unrecorded items of income and expenses. Unless these items are reflected in the accounts, income for the current and subsequent years will be distorted. Such items include **accrued income and expense** and **deferred income and expense.** Omission of accrued income and deferred expense will understate current income, whereas omission of accrued expenses and deferred income will overstate earnings.

Expenses Subject to Managerial Discretion. There is room for very wide differences of opinion and practice in handling charges against income that are determined by management rather than by actual obligations incurred or cash expended. Included in this group are provision for depreciation, depletion, amortization, doubtful accounts and notes receivable, and contingencies. Also subject to a wide range of managerial discretion are maintenance and repairs, rents, royalties, management and service contract fees, reserves for taxes other than federal income and excess profits taxes, and bonuses to officers and directors based upon sales or net profit. The S.E.C. considers the disclosures of these items of such major importance that the submission of schedule XVI, entitled "Supplementary profit and loss information," which contains a listing of these items, is mandatory for all financial statements filed with the Commission.

Since the determination of amounts charged against income in any one operating period for such expenses rests with management, net income can obviously be manipulated to show a greater or lesser amount depending upon the objective sought. The analyst requires disclosure in the financial statements of **pertinent information** relating to these items, together with an **explanation of the policy followed,** if he is to be able to interpret the results satisfactorily.

PURPOSES OF STATEMENT ANALYSIS. Generally speaking, there are at least three groups who are interested in the financial statements of a business enterprise. These are: (1) owners or investors, (2) creditors, and (3) management. Although all are interested in the financial condition and operating results of the organization, the primary information that each seeks to obtain from these statements differs materially, reflecting the purpose that the statement is to serve. **Management** is primarily interested in a tool that will measure costs and efficiency and facilitate intelligent decisions. **Investors** desire primarily a basis for estimating earning power. And **credit men** and **commercial banks**

are concerned primarily with liquidity and ability to pay debts within the early future. Yet, with few exceptions, the same balance sheet and income statement are presented for all these purposes. This has caused many students of the subject to suggest the preparation of separate or **single-purpose statements** in such form and detail as will best serve the primary interests of each of the three groups specified.

On the other hand, it has been pointed out that there is no substantial difference in the form of financial statements that serve the needs of all the various interested groups and that the practice of preparing one set of statements is too deep-rooted to be easily abandoned. Consequently, it has been suggested that financial statements be prepared in such a manner as will reveal to the statement analyst all essential financial and operating data ordinarily required to form an intelligent judgment of the condition of the business, whether it be for investment, credit, or management purposes. Along these lines, Bonbright (The Valuation of Property) offers the following suggestion:

> Further research would consider the question whether a workable multiple-purpose scheme of accounts might not be so devised that, by the aid of a pencil and paper, a reader could reconstruct the accounts to fit his own requirements. (For example, such a multiple-purpose balance sheet might report a valuation of current assets at the lower of "cost or market," but with a footnote indicating the cost on one hand and the current market price on the other hand.)

This procedure has been favored by the S.E.C. (particularly in Regulation SX).

INVESTMENT ANALYSIS. The primary objective of most investment analysis is to appraise prospective earning power. Broadly speaking, an analysis to determine bond quality takes into consideration (1) earning power, (2) working capital position, and (3) property protection. Principal emphasis is placed upon the **trend of near and long-term earnings,** which in turn calls for consideration of conditions and prospects in the industry, caliber of management, and other related factors. Working capital position is highly important as a measure of solvency. It indicates the ability of a company to meet debt maturities in times of reduced earnings, and to finance improvements and expanding business without heavy borrowing. Property protection is important chiefly as an indication of relative treatment in the event of reorganization. (See Sec. 7 on **Security Analysis** for detailed discussion.)

Reported earnings can only be interpreted intelligently in the light of accounting policies pursued, particularly as regards such matters as nonrecurring profits and losses, depreciation and depletion, reserves for contingencies, inventory valuations, etc. Accounting conventions may present a picture that could be misleading to the unwary investor.

CREDIT ANALYSIS. Credit men and commercial bankers are primarily concerned with liquidity and a borrower's ability to meet his short-term obligations. Therefore, the ratio of current assets to current liabilities and the adequacy of working capital are most carefully scrutinized. Balance sheet analysis tends to take precedence over the income statement.

Balance sheets prepared or certified by independent public accountants for credit purposes do not purport to reflect **market values,** but are presented as values in use or **going concern values.** Public accountants do not hold themselves out as appraisers of fixed asset or inventory values. However, the National Credit Office and representatives of the New York State Society of Certified Public Accountants have agreed that all assets and liabilities susceptible of verification by direct correspondence should be so verified by independent public accountants.

Fixed assets and **noncurrent indebtedness** are given less attention by the short-term credit grantor than by the long-term creditor, although that portion of the long-term debt that matures in the early future may profoundly affect the current position and should be included therein. Equally, the need for replacement of obsolete or fully depreciated machinery may drastically alter the current asset position of the company.

Until more recent years, the income statement was neither requested by, nor submitted to, the credit grantor. The balance sheet, reflecting the current position and net worth, was considered adequate. The depression of the 1930's, with its accompanying increase in business failures, demonstrated the need for **analyzing operating statements of the borrower** if the credit grantor was to judge risks intelligently. Since that time, the practice of securing the borrower's income statement has become general, for lack of earning power may cause losses to creditors even if a strong working capital position exists. Under such conditions liquid assets can be dissipated rapidly. Conversely, large earnings may make the credit risk small even if the current position is weak.

ANALYSIS FOR FINANCIAL MANAGEMENT. Management seeks information that will promote efficiency and increase profits, and provide a basis for intelligent decisions in the conduct of the business. Balance sheet analysis helps to measure efficiency of utilization of assets. The income statement, however, is most valuable for control purposes, indicating operating efficiency of the enterprise as a whole and individual departments, results of expansion, etc.

Analysis by comparisons is common procedure. Comparison of a company's financial statements with those of other companies in the same industry measures its relative efficiency. Comparisons of current monthly operating figures with those of related months in previous accounting periods, and comparisons of the current annual report with previous annual reports, reveals sales, cost, and profit trends.

Another common form of analysis is a statement that presents details of operations in comparison with planned and budgeted figures. These analyses help management to enforce its policies, to locate strong and weak points in the operating organization, and to maintain a running control over expenditures.

Ratio Analysis

USE OF FINANCIAL RATIOS. Ratio analysis is the process of determining and interpreting numerical relationships based on financial statements. Presentation of these ratios enables the user to better understand financial statements than by looking at the absolute quantities alone. **Major classes** of financial ratios include balance sheet ratios, income statement ratios, interstatement ratios, and per share ratios.

SIGNIFICANT RATIOS. Significant ratios are those that express relationships that are important for the purpose of the analysis. A prospective purchaser of stock might be very much interested in earnings per share, whereas this ratio might have little meaning to the supplier considering selling to the company on an open line of credit. Since management has the responsibility for administering the assets, its primary concern should be operating return relative to total assets. Stockholders, on the other hand, are primarily interested in net profit relative to stockholders' equity or, perhaps, even more so, in the profit per share relative to the market price of the stock.

A widely accepted group of ratios for credit analysis are those published by Dun & Bradstreet, Inc. (Foulke, Twenty-Five Years of the Fourteen Important Ratios). These ratios, along with a number of other commonly used ratios, are discussed in the following pages.

Limitations. In using ratios the analyst must keep a few general limitations in mind. One is that a ratio is no better than the specific absolute figures from which it is derived. Consequently, **awareness of the approach used** in preparing the financial statements is important in determining the usefulness of the ratios developed from them. The analyst must also be sure of the **accounting definitions** of the items included in the ratios. For example, some firms may classify certain prepayments as current assets whereas others may include them in another section of the balance sheet.

A second limitation is that the ratios are not meaningful in and of themselves. They are **useful only when compared** to some standard, such as the ratios of previous periods or those of other companies. It is up to the analyst to select good standards since the conclusions drawn from the ratios can be no better than the standards against which they are compared.

BALANCE SHEET RATIOS. The ratios discussed below are derived from the balance sheet. There are many other balance sheet ratios suggested by some authors, but most are merely rearrangements of the ones here described. Examples are current liabilities to total capitalization, current liabilities to total assets, fixed assets to net working capital, etc.

Balance sheet ratios are used mainly in **analyzing the financial position of the company.** They deal with relationships between owners and short-term and long-term creditors, sources and uses of funds, and degrees of liquidity of the assets. These ratios are of particular importance to analysts mainly interested in the company's ability to meet its obligations, whereas the income statement ratios subsequently discussed are of primary importance to those whose main concern is the degree of profitability of the firm.

Current Ratio. The current ratio is computed by dividing the current liabilities into current assets. Thus, company A, with current assets of $500,000 and current liabilities of $250,000, shows a current ratio of 2:1. For every $1 of current debt the borrower has $2 of current assets on hand. This relationship is of prime importance to the short-term creditor as it gives some indication of a **borrower's ability to meet his current obligations.** It must be kept in mind, however, that current assets are not the only source of funds to meet current liabilities. For example, the firm may borrow from new creditors to repay old.

A current ratio of 2:1 has long been considered generally satisfactory but indiscriminate use of this standard is unsound. The electric utility operating companies have operated successfully for many years with current ratios averaging much nearer 1:1 than 2:1. On the other hand, many manufacturing enterprises would be in rather difficult shape if their current ratios were as low as 2:1. It is necessary to recognize, therefore, that the current ratio varies from industry to industry and, within the same industry, from season to season.

Acid-Test Ratio. The acid-test ratio is computed by dividing current liabilities into current assets exclusive of inventory. The remaining current assets, consisting of cash, marketable securities, and accounts and notes receivable, are sometimes called "quick" assets, and this ratio is sometimes called the **"quick" ratio.**

The acid-test ratio is a supplementary measure of liquidity that places more emphasis on **immediate** conversion of assets into cash than does the current ratio since, in the event of difficulty, most of the "quick" assets could be converted into cash fairly quickly to meet maturing liabilities. In the past, a "quick" ratio of 1:1 has been considered favorable since for every dollar of current liabilities there is a dollar of "quick" assets. However, accounts and notes receivable are not necessarily convertible at face value into cash on very short notice. Furthermore, additional cash needs may arise beyond the amount of the current liabilities at any given time. Thus, like the current ratio, a reasonable standard for the acid-test ratio will vary from season to season and industry to industry.

Current Liabilities to Owners' Equity. This ratio has also been expressed as current liabilities to tangible net worth, which equals capital stock and surplus less intangible assets. Since it is uncommon today to find companies with substantial amounts of **intangible assets,** in practice the two ratios are essentially the same. In the past, intangible fixed assets were excluded on the theory that in liquidation they brought little if any cash. However, it is recognized that in liquidation many other assets may also sell for amounts considerably less than the values carried on the books. Furthermore, conservative accounting practice in recent years has accepted valuation of intangible fixed assets only in connection with a **market sale of these assets,** which would result in a valuation regarded as reasonable.

A company with current liabilities of $250,000 and net worth of $750,000 (capital stock $300,000 and surplus $450,000) has a ratio of 1:3, which means that current liabilities are 33% of owners' equity. In many cases, this would appear to be an ample margin of safety since for every dollar contributed by short-term creditors, stockholders have supplied $3.

This ratio is a measure of the degree of protection to short-term creditors provided by the owners. The higher the ratio, the lower the protection to the short-term creditors. If the company also has long-term debt, the ratio of **total** liabilities to owners' equity should also be considered.

Fixed Assets to Owners' Equity. This ratio gives an indication of the extent to which owner-contributed capital has been invested in fixed assets. The more of the owners' contribution that is tied up in fixed assets, the less is their contribution to current assets, which may mean that creditors have contributed a large proportion of the total. In difficult times, **overinvestment** in fixed assets adds to the difficulties by increasing depreciation, maintenance, and taxes and thus reducing profits.

The higher this ratio, the less the protection for creditors. If it exceeds 100%, which is standard practice for utilities and railroads, it would be a mark of weakness for many industrial operations and would indicate a need for additional equity capital.

Funded Debt to Net Working Capital. Relating funded (long-term) debt to net working capital (current assets minus current liabilities) is one way of examining creditor contribution to the more liquid assets of the firm. For most industrial concerns, funded debt should not exceed net working capital—in fact, for many firms it should be less. If net working capital is less than funded debt, there may be difficulty over the long run in meeting financial obligations, including maturities on the funded debt.

Inventory to Net Working Capital. This ratio is determined by dividing the inventory by the amount of the net working capital (current assets minus current liabilities). Foulke (Practical Financial Statement Analysis) points out that this relationship has unusual significance since net working capital changes moderately from one year to another whereas inventory may fluctuate substantially. He suggests that inventory should be no greater than 75 to 100% of net working capital. The standard obviously depends upon the specific situation. Because inventory is the least liquid of the current asset items, it would be desirable for current assets other than inventory to at least equal current liabilities.

Owners' Equity to Total Assets. The ratio of stockholders' to total assets is sometimes called the **equity** or the **proprietary** ratio. Generally speaking, the higher the ratio the stronger the financial condition of the firm, since a larger proportion of the borrower's resources will have been obtained from owners' contribution. Economic upheavals may bring severe financial losses that will affect particularly those who depend heavily on borrowed funds. By many credit analysts this ratio is ranked in importance with the current ratio. It is of special interest to long-term creditors and is of greater value than the current ratio in analyzing the capital structure for the long-run solvency of the firm.

Proper proportions of debt to net worth vary from industry to industry. The **important criterion** is for total debt to be kept within manageable limits. The more stable the industry, the greater the amount of liabilities that may be incurred with safety. However, there is a point for any firm beyond which additional borrowing may indicate potential future difficulty.

The temptation to **trade on the equity** is great since the smaller the amount of contributed capital, the larger the return to stockholders, assuming a satisfactory profit margin on sales. The danger lies in the need for meeting interest charges and debt maturities in depressions as well as in profitable periods. Heavy fixed charges in a period when profits are abnormally low are a common cause of financial difficulty.

Funded Debt to Total Capitalization. In many larger corporations capitalization comprises long-term bonded debt as well as capital stock and "surplus." Although some writers use the term "capitalization" to include only the par value of bonds and capital stock outstanding, for many purposes it is desirable to include surplus as well. Particularly is this true for corporations with low par or no-par stock carried in the balance sheet at a relatively small amount, so that surplus represents the bulk of the stockholders' equity. Exclusion of surplus would then misrepresent the amount of capital in the business.

The **ratio** of funded debt to total capitalization, expressed as percentage of the total, reflects the relationship between long-term borrowed capital and permanent contributed capital. It is computed by dividing total capitalization, usually less book value of intangibles, into the amount of the funded debt. Thus a corporation with a bonded indebtedness of $600,000, preferred stock outstanding of $300,000, common stock $150,000, surplus $100,000, and intangible assets $150,000 has a capitalization of $1,000,000 (for computation of this ratio it is common practice to eliminate from net worth the book value of intangible assets). Of this total 60% represents long-term borrowed capital and 40% the stockholders' equity or contributed capital. Although no hard and fast rule can be set down as to what a proper relationship should be in such cases, one rough rule of thumb is that the **maximum percentage** of funded debt for public utilities and railroads should not be in excess of 50% of capital structure and for industrials 33⅓%. Earning power may justify a higher or make desirable a lower maximum percentage in each case.

A too-heavy debt burden reduces the margin of safety to bondholders, increases fixed charges upon earnings, decreases earnings available for dividends to stockholders, and, in the case of a sudden depression, may bring on insolvency and force reorganization.

Fixed Assets to Funded Debt. A ratio of 2:1 in this case would mean that for every dollar of bonded indebtedness there are available two dollars of book value of fixed assets to meet the obligation. But since book value and actual liquidating value may be greatly at variance, this ratio can at best be considered only an indication of relative security. In computing book value of fixed assets, depreciation should be deducted. Earning power is the ultimate test of bond values, and this property ratio is therefore only a supplementary measure.

INCOME STATEMENT RATIOS. The following ratios are determined from figures taken from the income statement. A number of other ratios based on the income statement are also commonly used. Frequently, for example, each item on the statement is expressed as percentage of net sales. These ratios are used primarily to analyze the profitability of a company's operations.

Operating Ratio. This ratio is determined by dividing net sales into total operating expenses and is expressed as a percentage. Total operating expenses include virtually all costs except financing costs and income taxes. They include cost of goods sold and selling, general, and administrative expenses. This ratio is the most general measure of operating efficiency and is therefore particularly important to management in judging its operations. The difference between the operating ratio and 100 gives the ratio of operating income to net sales, or **operating profit**. Obviously, the lower the ratio, the higher the margin of profit. According to Donaldson and Pfahl (Corporate Finance) the ratio measures the efficiency of operations but not the efficiency or profitability of all activities of the firm, since it does not take into account nonoperating items such as bond interest and profit from sale of fixed assets.

Net Profit Margin. This ratio is also sometimes called net profit to sales, return on sales, or the profit ratio. It is determined by relating the net income after taxes to the net sales for the period and measures the profit per dollar of sales. Because of changing tax situations, this ratio is also often determined by using income before taxes rather than after taxes. If operating profit is used instead of net profit, the ratio becomes the complement to the operating ratio discussed above.

Number of Times Fixed Charges Earned. This ratio is commonly determined by dividing bond interest charges (and sometimes certain portions of fixed rentals) into the firm's net profit before taxes and fixed charges for the period. This is stated: $\dfrac{\text{Net income + income taxes + fixed charges}}{\text{fixed charges}}$. The numerator indicates the earnings available for payment of interest and other fixed charges that are deductible as business expenses in determining taxable income. This ratio is used mainly as a measure of the ability of the firm to meet interest charges to bondholders. Graham, Dodd, and Cottle (Security Analysis) state that the present-day investor is probably accustomed to regarding the ratio of earnings to fixed charges as the most important specific test of safety of bond investment.

It is generally recommended that this ratio be **determined before income taxes** rather than after and that correspondingly higher standards be used. It is also recommended that for an individual bond issue the ratio be determined on a **"total-deductions" method.** This means that regardless of the priority of the specific bond issue, all bond interest charges of that company should be included in the fixed charges used to determine the ratio. Thus, under the "total-deductions" method all bond issues of the company would have the same "number of times fixed charges earned" ratio.

INTERSTATEMENT RATIOS. The five ratios discussed below are interstatement ratios. That is, they relate to quantitative measures of which one is taken from the balance sheet and one from the income statement. In using interstatement ratios, it is necessary to use **average balance sheet figures** for the period of time covered by the income statement under consideration. Many other interstatement ratios could be developed but the five described below are the most common.

Receivables Turnover. The receivables turnover measures the relationship between credit sales during the accounting period and average receivables outstanding during the period. This ratio is also called the **collection ratio** or the **receivables to sales ratio** and is sometimes expressed as the average number of days receivables are outstanding. The average number of days that uncollected sales are outstanding is computed by multiplying the ratio of outstanding receivables to net sales by the number of days in the business year. For this purpose 360 is ordinarily used instead of 365 days. Thus, in the case of a company that had average outstanding accounts and notes receivable from customers of $120,000 and credit sales for the year of $720,000, the receivables to sales ratio would be ⅙, the receivables turnover would be 6, and the average receivable would be outstanding for $\frac{\$120,000}{\$720,000} \times 360 = 60$ days. If normal terms of sale are 30 days, then one-half of the receivables would seem to be past due.

The collection ratio is a valuable **measure of the collectibility of receivables** and a good **supplementary test of the validity of the current ratio.** If the collection period is substantially in excess of the usual trade terms in the industry, it is probable that many of the receivables will never be collected. Moreover, difficulty may be caused by the excessive amount of working capital tied up in receivables. In such cases, the analyst should obtain **detailed schedules** of the accounts receivable showing amounts not yet due, amounts due, and amounts past due, broken down into classifications such as 30 days past due, 60 days past due, etc. Care should be taken that all cash sales are excluded and only credit sales are included in this computation.

Merchandise Turnover. Ordinarily, the greater the merchandise turnover, the larger the amount of profit, the smaller the amount of capital tied up in inventory, and the more current the merchandise stock. In addition, the concern with the more frequent turnover, other things being equal, has a great competitive advantage in that it can afford to sell its merchandise at a lower price, for increased sales volume may yield a larger total profit even though the margin of profit per unit is slightly less.

Merchandise turnover, therefore, is a valuable **measure of merchandising efficiency** and **inventory quality,** especially of style and perishable goods. It is computed by dividing average inventory into the cost of goods sold. If an income statement gives opening and closing inventories, the average inventory is arrived at by adding these figures and dividing the total by two. If monthly inventories can be obtained, a more accurate average would be arrived at by adding together the monthly inventories and dividing by the number of months involved. The following example illustrates the computation of merchandise turnover:

Inventory at beginning of year	$ 650,000
Inventory at end of year	350,000
Total	$1,000,000
Average Inventory ($1,000,000 divided by two)	$ 500,000

$$\frac{\text{Cost of Goods Sold}}{\text{Average Inventory}} \quad \frac{\$2,500,000}{\$ 500,000} = 5 \text{ Times for Merchandise Turnover}$$

In the above case, the merchandise turnover is 5 times a year or, on the basis of 360 days, it may be stated that, on the average, the total stock is sold out every 72 days (360 divided by 5). If the average turnover in the industry is less than 5, the rate of turnover in the above case would be considered a favorable turnover. If, on the other hand, the average in the industry is 6 times a year, so that inventory is turned over approximately every 60 days, then this turnover might be considered too slow.

If the turnover of the firm is materially at variance with the average turnover in the industry, further investigation is desirable. A **low turnover** may be due to a variety of reasons, including poor merchandise, overvaluation of closing inventory, overbuying, a large stock of old, unsalable merchandise still carried at cost, an anticipated future increase in sales, or a planned policy of substantial stock to meet unusual requests. If the latter is the case, the low inventory turnover may still be desirable in terms of its effect on sales and profits. A **substantially higher rate of turnover** than industry average might indicate superior merchandising but it might also disclose conservative pricing of closing inventory, a real shortage of inventory for needed sales, inventory taking at a point when inventory was unusually low, a contemplated reduction in sales, etc. It should therefore not be concluded that a high inventory turnover is in and of itself desirable.

Turnover of Owners' Equity. This is a measure of the efficiency of the employment of the net worth in the operations of the business. The ratio is computed by dividing tangible net worth into net sales. A comparison with the standard ratio for the industry will serve to indicate whether the borrower is overtrading or undertrading. **Overtrading** refers to an excessively large volume of sales in proportion to capital invested, and **undertrading** is the reverse. The danger of overtrading lies in the fact that the borrower must have recourse to larger amounts of credit, to a point where creditors may contribute a larger amount of funds for current operations than the owners. As the ratio of debts to owners' investment increases, the creditors' margin of safety decreases. If earnings fall off, the borrower may find himself unable to meet his obligations and be forced into bankruptcy, with resulting losses to creditors. Overtrading may be remedied by the investment of additional equity capital. A high ratio could, however, also indicate unusually high efficiency in operations.

Undertrading affects management adversely in that the failure to make full and efficient use of invested capital results in decreased profits and, if permitted to continue, may eventually result in operating losses. Undertrading may be remedied by a more vigorous sales policy, improved methods of merchandising, etc. In any event, owners and creditors alike are interested in this ratio and should study carefully the underlying factors where the ratio is either too high or too low.

Turnover of Net Working Capital. This ratio, which complements the ratio of turnover of net worth, measures the efficiency of the employment of working capital in the operation of the business. It is computed by dividing average net current assets into net sales. When compared with past performances and the standard ratio in the industry for comparable companies, the ratio lends itself to the same sort of interpretation as the turnover of tangible net worth. Generally speaking, the higher the turnover the greater the efficiency and the larger the rate of profits. Too high a turnover may, however, indicate a potentially dangerous shortage of working capital.

Return on Investment. The rate of return on owners' investment is, of course, of primary importance to management and stockholders. Hunt, Williams, and Donaldson (Basic Business Finance) state:

The validity and usefulness of return on investment as a basic business objective for the owners and as a prime measure of performance of the steward—management—is gaining increasing acceptance. The increasing acceptance rests on solid grounds. First, the return-on-investment objective inherently recognizes the value of capital—the fact that its owners could use their funds to advantage in other ventures—and that capital is seldom available for an enterprise in unlimited amount. Second, it puts a premium on economical use of capital in the firm. Third, use of this performance criterion and objective points to broad avenues for improvement of performance.

Return on investment can be **computed in a number of ways** in relation to either total assets, capitalization (equity capital plus long-term debt), or owners' equity. A common ratio for management's use is income before interest payments and income taxes divided by **total assets.** This ratio provides a good indication of the productivity of the capital employed in the business. A variation in this ratio is derived from the earnings (before interest and income taxes) divided by **capitalization.** This refinement emphasizes the earnings on the **permanent** capital as distinguished from the capital supplied by short-term creditors.

The other major way of determining return on investment is to relate the net income to the **stockholders' equity,** or net worth. In this case the cost of borrowed capital and income taxes are deducted before determining net income. This ratio is most significant when the stockholders' equity, as stated on the books of the corporation, is realistically close to the market value of the stock. Stockholders in publicly owned corporations frequently relate the earnings available to them to the **market value** rather than to the **book value** of their shares.

PER SHARE RATIOS. A convenient tool for investors and analysts is **earnings per share,** which are obtained by dividing the total earnings for the period by the number of shares outstanding. If preferred stock is also outstanding, preferred dividends are first deducted in calculating earnings per share of common stock. Earnings per share, in turn, are often related to the market price of the stock to obtain the **price-earnings ratio.**

The owners' equity in the corporation is measured by the **book value per share,** which is obtained by dividing net worth by the number of shares outstanding. Book value represents the amount of going-concern value on the books of the company rather than market value or liquidation value. Many stockholders tend to ignore book value entirely. Graham, Dodd, and Cottle (Security Analysis) state that in the majority of companies the book value per share figure plays so small a part as to warrant its being excluded in the process of valuation. However, they point out that there are a number of situations in which **asset** values (book value per share) can be and often are a major consideration in the appraisal of concerns.

Proper Use of Ratios

STANDARDS FOR COMPARISON. A ratio, in and of itself, has very little real meaning unless it is compared to some appropriate standard. Selection of proper standards for comparison is therefore a most important element in ratio analysis. Donaldson and Pfahl (Corporate Finance) state:

> The four most common types of standards used in ratio analysis in financial management are (1) absolute, (2) past record, (3) other companies' or industry average, and (4) budget or plan.

Absolute standards are those which become generally recognized as being desirable regardless of the type of company, the time, stage of the business cycle, or the objectives of the analyst. An example would be a standard of 2-to-1 for a current ratio. However, . . . absolute standards are not very meaningful. The authors do not believe that there is an independent absolute standard which is desirable in all cases.

The company's own **past performance** can be used as a standard for the present or future. . . . Past standards are useful in so far as the past is indicative of the future. If conditions are constant, past standards become very meaningful. The variance of present conditions from past conditions determines the reliability level in using past performance ratios as standards for current or future operations.

Other companies' or industry average ratios are commonly used in financial analysis as standards. . . . The problem in utilizing industry ratios or making up ratios for similar companies is that no two companies are exactly the same. Variations in accounting method could lead to significant differences in ratios. In addition, variability of product mix, geographc location, corporate objectives, and of most other conditions under which business operates leads to a lack of comparability. . . . Standards developed from other companies' data or from industry data are useful only in indicating areas whether further analysis and study should be made.

A standard commonly used by management is the **planned** or **budgeted standard**. . . . The budget is the statement of what the company intends to do during a stated period of time. Ratios developed from actual performance can be compared to planned ratios in the budget in order to determine the degree of accomplishment of the budgeted or planned objectives of the firm. Budgeted or planned standards determined in advance, taking into account the conditions of the times and the specific company situation, can be very useful in financial analysis.

The discussion in the last paragraph applies primarily to financial managements' use of ratio analysis. Outsiders have difficulty using planned or budgeted standards and must place more reliance on analysis of present versus past performance and comparisons with other similar companies or with the industry. A number of industry standards are compiled by various organizations. Many trade associations collect accounting data from their members from which they prepare average industry ratios. These industry standards are available to the members of the organization and may also be made available to certain outside creditors and others. Dun & Bradstreet, Inc., and Robert Morris Associates are also sources of industry average ratios that provide standards by which creditors are helped to judge conditions in a particular company.

SELECTIVE USES OF RATIOS. Although the ratios discussed above and certain other ratios are all of value in the interpretation of the financial condition and operating results of the company, certain of them are of much greater importance for particular purposes than others.

Short-Term Creditors. Commercial bankers and trade creditors and other short-term creditors are primarily concerned with the ability of a borrower to meet his current obligations promptly. As a result, they are more interested in such ratios as the current ratio, the acid-test ratio, and the turnover of inventory and receivables.

Long-Term Creditors. Long-term creditors are likewise keenly interested in the working capital position of the borrower as an indication of ability to pay interest and principal even if earnings decline. They also find valuable the ratios of total liabilities to owners' equity, owners' equity to total assets, funded debt to net working capital, fixed assets to owners' equity, fixed debt to total capitalization, and fixed assets to fixed debt. Of particular interest is the number of times fixed charges are earned.

Management. All of the above ratios, with comparisons covering a period of years and the situation of competing companies in the same industry, are helpful to management in indicating if improvements in performance are possible. Percentage and trend relationships in the income statement—including operating ratios, profit ratios, the percentages that major classes of expenses bear to sales, and the percentages individual items in the major expense groups bear to the total of that group—are valuable in this connection. Management is also vitally concerned with **efficiency in the use of assets,** as indicated by the various turnover ratios. Its major use of balance sheet ratios (those of particular interest to creditors) is in **judging creditor reaction** to the company's financial position.

Stockholders. Present and prospective shareholders are primarily interested in per share ratios. Those whose major objective in holding the stock in a company is future return place principal emphasis on rate of return and yield (dividends) on their investment. Others are primarily interested in capital appreciation, particularly as measured by market value.

Comparative Statement Analysis

COMPARATIVE STATEMENTS. In analyzing the financial condition of a business, management frequently compares the balance sheet from one year with others and notes changes in each major group of assets, liabilities, and equity, as well as the changes of the individual items within each group. It carries out this process also for income statements. It may also be useful, under certain conditions, to project balance sheets and income statements into the future.

COMPARATIVE BALANCE SHEET ANALYSIS. A comparative study of balance sheets at the beginning and end of a period, or between any two fixed dates, will disclose the changes that have taken place in the assets, liabilities, and equity between those dates. Such changes also indicate the sources from which funds were derived during the period and how these funds were applied. With some additional information, the **statement of balance sheet changes** may be called a **statement of application of funds,** a source and use of funds statement, or a funds statement (see previous discussion on page 26). All of these statements contain the same major sections as the balance sheet itself. The working capital section shows the changes in the company's current position and the fixed capital section the changes in fixed assets and long-term borrowings and contributed capital.

The **funds statement** should also include analysis of changes of certain accounts, such as retained earnings, gross fixed assets, and reserve for depreciation, for which some data may be drawn from the income statement. For example, it may be more meaningful to state that earnings contributed $100,000 to the busi-

THE APEX COMPANY
Application of Funds—Working Papers

	Dec. 31 19X1	Dec. 31 19X2	Year's Excess Debits	Year's Excess Credits	Working Capital Increase	Working Capital Decrease	Funds Applied	Funds Provided
ASSETS								
Cash	$ 4,000.00	$ 5,500.00	$ 1,500.00	....	$1,500.00	....	....	....
Notes Receivable	2,000.00	2,500.00	500.00	....	500.00	....	....	....
Accounts Receivable	3,100.00	2,650.00	....	$ 450.00	....	$ 450.00	....	....
Merchandise	7,000.00	8,800.00	1,800.00	....	1,800.00	....	....	....
Stock of OR Company	10,000.00	....	....	10,000.00	....	....	....	$10,000.00
Land	30,000.00	20,000.00	....	10,000.00	....	....	....	10,000.00
Buildings	60,000.00	80,000.00	20,000.00	....	....	....	$20,000.00	....
	$116,100.00	$119,450.00						
LIABILITIES								
Notes Payable	$ 4,000.00	$ 5,000.00	....	1,000.00	....	1,000.00	....	....
Accounts Payable	2,500.00	2,300.00	200.00	....	200.00	....	....	....
6% Bonds Payable	15,000.00	....	15,000.00	....	....	....	15,000.00	....
5% Bonds Payable	....	10,000.00	....	10,000.00	....	....	....	10,000.00
Capital Stock, Preferred	25,000.00	....	25,000.00	....	....	....	25,000.00	....
Capital Stock, Common	50,000.00	80,000.00	....	30,000.00	....	....	....	30,000.00
Surplus	19,600.00	22,150.00	....	2,550.00	....	....	....	2,550.00
	$116,100.00	$119,450.00	$64,000.00	$64,000.00				
Increase in Working Capital	....					2,550.00	2,550.00	....
					$4,000.00	$4,000.00	$62,550.00	$62,550.00

Fig. 5. Application of funds—working papers.

ness and dividends withdrew $20,000, leaving a net gain of $80,000 in retained earnings, than merely to indicate retained earnings as a source of $80,000 in value.

The examples in Figs. 5 and 6 illustrate one approach to the development of a statement of change in balance sheets. Fig. 5 is a simple work sheet used in analyzing changes and Fig. 6 is a summary statement that presents: (1) amount of funds provided and the source; (2) how these funds were applied; (3) the changes in working capital.

THE APEX COMPANY
Statement of Application of Funds
Year Ending December 31, 19X2

FUNDS PROVIDED:

By Sale of Land	$10,000.00
By Sale of Stock of OR Company	10,000.00
By Issue of Common Stock	30,000.00
By Issue of 5% Bonds	10,000.00
By Profits	2,550.00
Total Funds Provided	$62,550.00

FUNDS APPLIED:

To Purchase of Buildings	$20,000.00
To Retirement of Preferred Stock	25,000.00
To Retirement of 6% Bonds	15,000.00
To Increase in Working Capital (per Schedule)	2,550.00
Total Funds Applied	$62,550.00

THE APEX COMPANY
Schedule of Working Capital

	Dec. 31 19X1	Dec. 31 19X2	Changes in Working Capital Decrease	Changes in Working Capital Increase
CURRENT ASSETS:				
Merchandise	$ 7,000.00	$ 8,800.00		$1,800.00
Accounts Receivable	3,100.00	2,650.00	$ 450.00	
Notes Receivable	2,000.00	2,500.00		500.00
Cash	4,000.00	5,500.00		1,500.00
Total Current Assets	$16,100.00	$19,450.00		
CURRENT LIABILITIES:				
Accounts Payable	$ 2,500.00	$ 2,300.00		200.00
Notes Payable	4,000.00	5,000.00	1,000.00	
Total Current Liabilities	$ 6,500.00	$ 7,300.00		
WORKING CAPITAL	$ 9,600.00	$12,150.00		
INCREASE IN WORKING CAPITAL				2,550.00
			$4,000.00	$4,000.00

Fig. 6. Statement of application of funds.

COMPARATIVE INCOME STATEMENT ANALYSIS. A detailed comparison of two income statements of a company will reveal the changes in the particular income and expense items. Properly interpreted, causes of increases or decreases in sales, the cost of sales, and major expense items may be determinable from such comparisons.

COMPARATIVE STATEMENT ANALYSIS

The example below (Fig. 7) illustrates the use of the **Statement of Variation of Net Income** for the analysis and interpretation of operating data.

J. MARSHALL & COMPANY
Income Statements
For Year Ending December 31

	19X1	19X2	Increase or Decrease *
Net Sales	$200,000.00	$252,000.00	$52,000.00
Less Cost of Goods Sold	150,000.00	180,000.00	30,000.00
Gross Profit on Sales	$ 50,000.00	$ 72,000.00	$22,000.00
Less Selling Expenses	20,000.00	25,000.00	5,000.00
Net Profit on Sales	$ 30,000.00	$ 47,000.00	$17,000.00
Less General Expenses	10,000.00	12,000.00	2,000.00
Net Profit on Operations	$ 20,000.00	$ 35,000.00	$15,000.00
Less Net Financial Expense	5,000.00	4,000.00	1,000.00*
Net Income for the Year	$ 15,000.00	$ 31,000.00	$16,000.00

J. MARSHALL & COMPANY
Statement Accounting for Increase in Net Profit

Net Income—19X1	$31,000
Net Income—19X2	15,000
Increase in Net Income	$16,000

Accounted for as follows:

ITEMS INCREASING NET INCOME:
  (A) Increase in Gross Profits, caused by:
    (1) Increase in volume of sales:
      Sales—19X2 .... $252,000
      Sales—19X1 200,000
      25% (1963 rate of profit) of .... $ 52,000 $13,000

    (2) Increase in rate of gross profit:

Year	Gross Profit	Sales	%
19X2	$72,000 ÷	$252,000 =	28.57+
19X1	50,000 ÷	200,000 =	25.00
Increase in rate of gross profit			3.57+

    $252,000 × 3.57% 9,000
                                                                                          $22,000

  (B) Decrease in Net Financial Expense:
      19X1 .... $ 5,000
      19X2   4,000   1,000 $23,000

ITEMS DECREASING NET INCOME:
  (C) Increase in Selling Expenses:
      19X2 .... $25,000
      19X1 .... 20,000 $ 5,000

  (D) Increase in General Expenses:
      19X2 .... $12,000
      19X1 10,000   2,000   7,000

INCREASE IN NET INCOME (as above) $16,000

Fig. 7. Comparison of income statements.

The items in the income statement reduced to a percentage of sales offer a valuable means of interpreting results. Percentage comparisons highlight elements of strength and weakness often overlooked in a comparison of absolute amounts of difference. In the above case, for example, the profit and loss statement for the year 19x1, reduced to percentages of sales, might be interpreted on a **dollar basis** as follows:

J. MARSHALL & COMPANY
Income Statement for Year Ended December 31, 19X1

For every sale of		$1.00
The cost of that sale was		.75
Leaving a gross profit of		$ .25
to cover following expenses for each one-dollar sale:		
Selling Expenses	$.10	
General Expenses	.05	
Financial Expenses	.025	.175
The net income on each one-dollar sale		$ .075

Fig. 8. Percentage analysis of income statement.

Comparisons of such percentages in successive income statements may reveal trends which management will find quite useful in the formulation of operating and financial policies.

PROJECTION OF FINANCIAL STATEMENTS. A comparison of financial statements discloses changes that took place in the past. The important thing for management, creditors, and investors is to use this information as a basis for projecting financial and operating trends into the future, as a guide for intelligent action.

SECTION 9

SELLING SECURITIES

CONTENTS

	PAGE
The Demand for Capital	
Need for investment funds	1
Factors influencing the demand	1
The Supply of Capital	
Investment of savings	2
Factors influencing disposition of savings	2
Raising capital for the small enterprise	2
Public offering through an investment banker	3
Private offering	4
Direct public offering	4
Small business investment companies	4
Capital	5
Permissible investments	5
Investment policies	5
Exemption of S.B.I.C. offerings from registration	5
Classes of Security Buyers	
Adaptation of securities to buyers	6
Institutional buyers	6
Individual buyers	6
Alternatives for individual buyers	6
Investors and speculators	7
Special groups	7
Investment Banking	
Nature of investment banking	8
Responsibilities to issuer and investor	8
Role of Securities Act of 1933	9
Classes of investment bankers	10
Wholesalers	10
Retailers	10
Internal organization of an investment banking house	10
Purchase of New Issues	
Importance of sound purchasing policies	11
Sources of new financing proposals	11
Pre-existing relations with issuers	11
Finders	11
Traveling representatives and branch offices	12
Commercial banks	12
Other investment banking houses	12
Direct applications	12
Competitive bidding	13
Investigation of financing proposals	13

	PAGE
The underwriting contract	14
Authorization of the contract	14
Types of commitments	15
"Market-out" clause	15
Summary of typical firm commitment contract	16
The purchase group	16
Spreading the risk	16
Increasing the distributing power	17
Size of the purchase group	17
Duration of the purchase group	17
The purchase group contract	18
Pricing of issues and compensation of underwriters	18
Underwriters' "spread"	18
Sale of New Issues	
The selling problem	19
The sales department	19
The selling group	20
Selection of group members	20
Preferential treatment for members of N.A.S.D.	21
Formation of the group	21
Types of selling groups	21
The selling group agreement	21
The public offering	22
Announcing the offer	22
Opening and closing the books	23
Price cutting	23
Security salesmen	24
Standards for salesmen	24
Other Functions of Investment Banking	
Market stabilization	24
Legal restrictions on stabilizing	25
S.E.C. rules	25
Other market activities	26
Statistical and advisory activities	26
Accounting and record-keeping	26
Miscellaneous activities	27
The Securities Act of 1933	
The disclosure principle	27
General description of the 1933 Act	28
Persons and transactions covered	28
"Issuer," "dealer," and "underwriter" defined	28

SELLING SECURITIES

CONTENTS (*Continued*)

	Page
"Distribution" explained	29
Purchase for distribution or "investment"	29
Controlling persons	30
Prohibitions and required acts	30
The prefiling period	31
The waiting period	31
The preliminary prospectus	31
Acceleration of waiting period	32
The summary prospectus	32
Communications not deemed a prospectus	33
The posteffective period	34
Registration procedure	35
Amendment of statement	36
Withdrawal of statement	37
Preparation of the prospectus	38
Age of information	38
Exempted securities	38
Regulation A	39
Exempted transactions	39
Transactions by persons other than issuers, underwriters, and dealers	39
Private offerings	40
Transactions by dealers	41
Brokers' transactions	41
Sanctions	42
Stop orders	42
Injunctions and criminal proceedings	42
Civil liabilities	43

Blue Sky Laws

	Page
Historical background	43
Types of blue sky laws	44
Common provisions and the Uniform Securities Act	45
Antifraud provisions	45
Investment advisory activities	45
Investigations	46
Registration of broker-dealers, agents, and investment advisers	46
Registration of securities	47
Exemptions under blue sky laws	50

SECTION 9

SELLING SECURITIES

The Demand for Capital

NEED FOR INVESTMENT FUNDS. Investment or capital funds are essential to the establishment, maintenance, and expansion of modern industry. Such funds are most frequently required (1) to finance the acquisition, replacement, or expansion of plant, machinery, and other capital assets; (2) to finance the acquisition of control over other businesses; and (3) to refinance or refund maturing long-term indebtedness. (See also, Section 17 on Capital Asset Planning.) At any stage in the development of an enterprise, a need may arise for more capital.

Investment funds are ordinarily utilized for the acquisition of **capital or production goods** rather than consumer goods. True investment involves, on the one side, the commitment of funds to the managers of the enterprise, and, on the other, an agreement to return the funds at a specified date or upon the liquidation of the enterprise, with interim payments for their use in the form of interest or dividends. Hence, the funds committed should be used not for consumption but for the production and distribution of goods and services that can be sold at a profit sufficient, at least, to pay such interest or dividends. Unless an enterprise is in a position to utilize investment funds profitably, it has no genuine economic need for such funds.

Investment funds, as their designation implies, are normally sought on a **long-term** basis. In this respect they differ from funds obtained through commercial borrowing. Commercial loans from banks are deemed more suitable to finance seasonal or short-term working capital requirements than for investment in fixed, long-term assets. (For a detailed discussion of long-term debt financing, see Section 14.) Under ordinary circumstances, if fixed assets are to be acquired, the enterprise will seek investment funds. A demand for such funds may arise also when permanent working capital is required or when commercial loans, originally designed to be retired within a brief period, become more or less permanent in character, and the borrower desires to eliminate chronic reliance upon short-term borrowing.

FACTORS INFLUENCING THE DEMAND. The intensity of the demand for investment funds varies from time to time. It is profoundly influenced by **economic conditions**. The demand is intensified by such factors as the opening up of new industries, inventions and improvements, harmonious relations between capital and labor, harmonious relations between government and industry, active new corporate promotions, and cyclical upswings in business or prices. Conversely, it tends to diminish during periods of business stagnation or depression, falling prices, protracted labor disputes, confusion or uncertainty in governmental policies, strained international relations, and lack of initiative on the part of corporate management, promoters, and investment bankers. Government financing may add largely to the demand for capital at certain times.

Demand for capital is also affected by **conditions in individual enterprises.** A going concern may possess alternative methods of financing the acquisition of capital assets. Capital assets that have outlived their usefulness may be replaced in whole or in part through funds generated by the business. Expansion may be financed through reinvested earnings. Funds for capital purposes are sometimes obtained through liquidation of excess inventories or marketable securities.

These and other factors cause **wide fluctuations** in the private demand for investment funds. Theoretically, such demand should be limited to the funds required for the production and distribution of useful goods and services that can be sold at a profit. In practice, demands for capital are distorted by errors in judgment, unexpected inventions and improvements, overproduction of goods, and other contingencies. It is a basic function of the capital market to equate demands for investment funds with the available supply.

The Supply of Capital

INVESTMENT OF SAVINGS. The supply of investment funds flows chiefly from the savings of the community. Persons who refrain from consuming all their income are the main suppliers of investment capital. The supply of capital thus is affected in large measure by national habits in regard to the accumulation and use of savings. Current savings can be supplemented with funds borrowed from banks, expansion of bank credit playing a role similar to savings.

Factors Influencing Disposition of Savings. The direction in which savings are invested will be influenced by the relative attractiveness of available opportunities and the initiative of corporate management, promoters, and investment bankers in bringing such opportunities home to potential investors. In the United States, where a considerable segment of the population and many financial and business enterprises normally have a surplus of income for investment, where attractive opportunities are plentiful, and where the investment banking organization has achieved a high degree of development, there is a more or less **continuous movement** of private savings into new investments via the capital markets.

Only a part of the accumulated savings of the community is invested in securities. A portion of current savings flows directly into the purchase of real estate, the construction of homes, individual mortgage loans, life insurance policies, and other forms of investment not involving the securities markets. A portion is invested directly by the owners in their own, closely held businesses. A portion takes the form of bank deposits or currency, pending determination of the use to which it will ultimately be put by the owners.

Furthermore, that portion of community savings that is available for investment cannot always be profitably absorbed by industry. Periods occur in which the supply of investment funds exceeds the demand. During such periods persons with surplus funds to invest may have difficulty in finding a satisfactory outlet in the capital markets. On the other hand, if a security does not comply with the standards adopted by investors for their own guidance, or if the return offered does not appear to be adequate compensation for the hazards to be assumed, investment funds may not be forthcoming to meet a particular demand.

RAISING CAPITAL FOR THE SMALL ENTERPRISE. Small businesses seeking capital are often confronted with difficulties that the larger and better known companies do not share. Investors are hesitant to entrust their savings to companies of minor size. **High selling cost per dollar raised** deters many investment banking firms from selling security issues for such companies.

(For a discussion of the cost to an enterprise of raising capital through a security issue, see Section 17.)

Reluctance of investors to purchase securities of small enterprises is attributable to several causes. Firstly, the average investor, in choosing an investment medium, inclines toward a business of which he has some **previous knowledge**. If a corporation is national in scope, if its products are well known to the public, and if information concerning its operations is obtainable from financial manuals and other sources, its securities will be accepted by investors more readily than the securities of a concern known only in its immediate locality. Secondly, an important consideration for the average investor is **marketability**. Wide distribution and a large number of security holders are essential to a broad market, and these are not afforded by securities of a small corporation. Thirdly, a small company may be quite vulnerable to unexpected happenings, technological changes, competitive conditions, and seasonal and cyclical factors. A seasoned enterprise of substantial size with strong banking connections, adequate reserves, and extensive technical resources is better equipped to meet emergencies than one that has not achieved significant stature. Risk is a built-in factor in every investment; and, from the viewpoint of most investors, the size of the **risk factor** varies inversely with the size of the enterprise. This attitude is widespread not only among individuals but among institutional investors as well.

Public Offering Through an Investment Banker. Occasionally, a small enterprise can secure access to investment funds through the securities markets, when its own condition and general market conditions are favorable. If a company offers **unusual promise of future expansion** by reason of the fact that it has developed a new or improved process or product, or has established itself in a vigorous new industry, or has acquired valuable patents or has otherwise shown well-defined growth potential, an investment banking firm may be willing to make an offering of securities on its behalf. Two major considerations may prompt the investment banking firm to undertake the financing under such circumstances, namely: its belief that the general prejudice of investors against the securities of small companies can be overcome by emphasis upon the favorable prospects in the particular instance; and its expectation that the handling of a small issue will pave the way to large-scale financing at a later date.

Exemptions for public sales under certain conditions from the registration requirements of the Securities Act of 1933 have to some extent facilitated financing by smaller concerns. These exemptions, however, are limited to $300,000 for the issuing corporation during a twelve-month period, and they are hedged in with conditions that have become more burdensome in recent years. (See also, discussion of Exempted Securities, page 38.) Compliance with the **blue sky laws** (see page 43) of the states in which the offering is to be made is also necessary. Moreover, the underwriting, printing, legal, accounting, and other expenses involved in a $300,000 public offering are likely to be disproportionately high; and seldom, if ever, can an investment banker be found who is willing to do more than use his best efforts to sell the issue. Thus, the issuer is in the position of risking the expenditures with no assurance that the net proceeds realized will be sufficient even to cover its costs.

For the vast majority of small companies access to the investing public through investment bankers is difficult to achieve. Such companies usually have to look elsewhere for sources of long-term capital funds. Several courses are open to small corporations as alternatives to marketing securities through investment banking channels.

Private Offering. A company may be in a position to attract capital from sources close to the management. Friends, business associates, and others having special knowledge of the business and the management may be receptive to an invitation to invest in the enterprise, particularly if they are offered a participation in the equity on favorable terms. Employees may have sufficient confidence in the business to be willing to purchase securities outright or on an installment basis. Creditors, suppliers, and customers may be agreeable to the purchase of senior securities in order to cement trade relations. The company's lawyers and accountants may be successful in placing its securities with clients willing to forgo marketability in return for a higher yield. Occasionally, an investor or group of investors may be found who are prepared to supply **venture capital** to a small company with unusual growth prospects, in consideration of a **substantial proportion of the equity** in the company.

A private offering of securities is not subject to the requirements of the Securities Act of 1933, but it should be borne in mind that an offering must be within certain limits in order to qualify as a private offering. These limits are considered under Private Offerings, page 40.

Direct Public Offering. A smaller corporation may consider it feasible to make a direct public offering of its securities and not use an investment banking firm. Such an offering may be made through the officers and employees of the company or through salesmen hired on a commission basis to sell the issue. Of course, the offering will be **subject to the Securities Act** unless it comes within one of the exemptions such as the one for small offerings under Regulation A (see page 39). Under the Act an offering is also exempt, except from the fraud provisions, if the securities are sold only to residents of the state in which the issuer is incorporated and is doing business. The exemption is defeated, however, if any part of the issue is sold or offered to nonresidents.

Direct public offerings by issuers of their own securities **may prove unsatisfactory** for several reasons. A certain amount of suspicion may attach to such offerings because doubtful or fraudulent issues have been sold by this method in the past. The cost of this type of financing is often relatively high. Receipt of the proceeds is slow and uncertain, particularly if it is necessary to allow purchasers to make payments in installments. Distribution is often of poor quality, since sophisticated investors will not generally purchase securities that have not been subjected to scrutiny by a reputable investment banking firm. Finally, when officers and employees are called upon to solicit subscriptions they are diverted from their normal duties and the operating efficiency of the business may be impaired.

SMALL BUSINESS INVESTMENT COMPANIES. A study sponsored by the Federal Reserve Board in 1957 estimated the shortage of capital funds for small companies at $500 million a year. Impressed by the magnitude of the problem, Congress enacted the **Small Business Investment Act of 1958,** which was designed to induce venture capitalists to make long-term investments in small businesses. As subsequently amended, this Act authorizes the **Small Business Administration (S.B.A.)** to license small business investment companies **(S.B.I.C.'s)** that are organized under state law to provide long-term capital to small business enterprises.

In order to encourage the organization and financing of S.B.I.C.'s by private investors, **favorable tax treatment** is provided for investors when they sell their securities in the S.B.I.C., and for the S.B.I.C. when it sells its holdings in a small business enterprise.

By October 1962 approximately 630 S.B.I.C.'s were in operation; total capital invested in the program exceeded $500 million; and the S.B.A. reported that about 60% of this amount had been invested in small businesses. Public offerings of securities were made by a number of S.B.I.C.'s during the 1959–1961 period. Local S.B.A. offices serve as a clearinghouse for information on S.B.I.C.'s, and there is a commercial directory that also provides much information, the S.B.I.C. National Directory, contained in Kelley's S.B.I.C.'s—Suppliers of Venture Capital.

Capital. An S.B.I.C must have capital and surplus of not less than $300,000. The S.B.A. is authorized to purchase **subordinated debentures** of the S.B.I.C. in an amount equivalent to its paid-in capital and surplus from other sources, but not in excess of $400,000; and these funds are considered as part of the S.B.I.C.'s capital and surplus and as a base for further loans from the S.B.A. The S.B.I.C. may then borrow from the S.B.A. up to 50% of its capital and surplus, with a limit of $4 million.

Permissible Investments. The capital provided to small business enterprises by the S.B.I.C. may take the form of equity securities or of loans having maturities of at least 5 and not more than 20 years. To be eligible, a small business concern must be independently owned and operated; must not be dominant in its field of operation; and must have assets not exceeding $5 million, net worth not exceeding $2.5 million, and average net pretax income for the preceding two years not exceeding $250,000. Without the approval of the S.B.A., the aggregate amount that an S.B.I.C. may invest in any single small business concern is 20% of the capital and surplus of the S.B.I.C. or $500,000, whichever is less.

Investment Policies. The investment policies of the S.B.I.C.'s have been the subject of both criticism and praise. In October 1962 a study of S.B.I.C.'s was undertaken by Samuel L. Hayes and Donald H. Woods, with the cooperation of the Small Business Committee of the House of Representatives and the Harvard Business Review. (The results of the study were published in the Harvard Business Review for March–April, 1963.) Some of the specific findings were that the independent, equity-oriented, "minimum capital" S.B.I.C. will soon be a thing of the past; that about half of the S.B.I.C.'s have become affiliated with organizations in related fields, such as banks and real estate and construction companies; that many are seeking mergers with other S.B.I.C.'s; that many believe that efficient operations in the field require substantially larger capital structures than they now have; that because of the approximate two-year lag between the time of the S.B.I.C.'s capital acquisition and the placement of its funds, the S.B.I.C.'s may become an important source of funds for growing businesses during downswing cycles when the more conventional sources dry up; that some S.B.I.C.'s specialize in equity financing of small companies, whereas others specialize in straight term loans with no equity features; and that in some quarters there is a ground swell of disenchantment with the program. "The general conclusion of the study," according to the authors, "is that S.B.I.C.'s are definitely **moving away from financing smaller small businesses.** For good or for bad, S.B.I.C.'s appear to be taking on some of the more conservative aspects of financial institutions in their efforts to operate efficiently and to reduce risks. And these tendencies raise some question whether S.B.I.C.'s are effectively accomplishing the task of helping to finance the long-run capital needs of the U.S. small-business community."

Exemption of S.B.I.C. Offerings from Registration. As noted elsewhere in this Section (page 39) the S.E.C. has adopted a regulation (Regulation E) that affords a conditional exemption from registration for securities of S.B.I.C.'s licensed under the Small Business Investment Act of 1958 or approved for licensing by the S.B.A. The amount of such securities exempted is limited to $300,000 during a twelve-month period.

Classes of Security Buyers

ADAPTATION OF SECURITIES TO BUYERS. Successful offerings of securities require a recognition of the several classes of security buyers. Certain types of securities may be suitable for one class and entirely unsuitable for another. In seeking capital for an enterprise, management and the investment banker must keep in mind the necessity of adapting the security to the needs and desires of the class of buyers to which it is to be offered. Such buyers fall into the groups described below.

INSTITUTIONAL BUYERS. Institutional buyers of securities include organizations formed primarily to invest in securities, and those formed primarily for other purposes but that have large sums for investment. Certain types of institutions make investments for their own account and risk; other types make investments for the account and risk of others. The institutional buyer, in selecting investments, is subject to restrictions imposed, as the case may be, by its charter, by "legal investment" laws, by court decisions, by tradition, or by its own peculiar requirements.

Three major types of institutions have been developed in this country to gather together and invest the savings of small investors. These are the **savings bank** and the **savings and loan association,** which receive deposits and share capital and invest them in high-grade securities and mortgages; the **trust company,** which manages the funds of others and makes investments on their behalf; and **financial organizations,** such as the investment company and the mortgage bank, which sell their own securities to the public and invest the proceeds within the limits prescribed by their charters and by statute.

There are several **other classes of institutions** that purchase securities in large volume as an incident to their primary functions. Largest of these are the **insurance companies,** which, in the course of their business, accumulate reserves on so vast a scale that they have become major investors in high-grade securities. A second class consists of the **commercial banks,** which invest part of their deposits in securities and mortgages. A third class, constantly increasing in importance, are the **pension and profit-sharing trusts,** which invest in securities as well as in various types of insurance and annuity plans. (See Leffler and Farwell, The Stock Market.) A fourth class includes **educational, religious,** and **charitable institutions,** which together constitute important buyers of securities.

INDIVIDUAL BUYERS. Individual buyers of securities include those persons who utilize surplus income to purchase securities, as distinguished from those who place their savings with financial institutions that, in turn, invest in securities. There may be included in the category of individual investors firms and corporations that invest surplus funds in securities, instead of keeping such funds on deposit in banks.

Alternatives for Individual Buyers. The individual who has accumulated surplus funds is confronted, at the outset, with the necessity of deciding whether he will select his own investments or relinquish this function to a financial institution such as a savings bank, trust company, or investment company. In the former instance, he may purchase newly issued securities being distributed by an underwriting group; he may exercise rights to subscribe for additional shares in an enterprise in which he already has an interest; or he may purchase from others previously issued and outstanding securities. The individual investor is free to buy any security, from bonds of the highest grade to the most speculative equities. In this respect he has more latitude than the financial institution that, as noted above, is subject to restrictions upon its choice of investments. But whether the individual makes his own selection of investments or permits an institution to make the choice, the ultimate effect is to incorporate his savings into the mainstream of funds flowing into the capital market.

Investors and Speculators. Individual buyers of securities may be classified roughly as investors or speculators. From the standpoint of the capital market, all commitments of funds for capital purposes are investments. From the standpoint of the buyer, however, "**investment**" may be defined as the purchase of securities with the intention of avoiding substantial risk. The investor is primarily concerned with safety of principal and stability of income. "Speculation" may be defined as the conscious assumption of risk to secure a profit expected to result from the favorable outcome of the enterprise in which the risk is assumed. The emphasis in the calculations of the speculator is upon enhancement in value and profitable resale.

Variations in the two basic types of securities—the bond and the share of stock—have been devised to attract funds of investors and speculators. Sales appeal has been increased on occasion by combining investment and speculative features in the same offering. The devices employed include:

1. The **convertible bond,** which entitles the holder to convert his bond into shares of stock at a predetermined conversion rate; and the **convertible preferred stock,** which entitles the holder to convert preferred shares into common at a predetermined rate.
2. The grant of a **common stock bonus** to purchasers of bonds or preferred stock.
3. The grant of **option warrants** to purchasers of bonds or preferred stock, entitling the holder to purchase common stock within a fixed time at a specified price.
4. The **sale of units** consisting of a senior security and common stock, at a fixed price per unit.
5. The grant to a senior security of a **participation with the common stock in earnings** of the enterprise, in addition to the fixed rate of return.

Special Groups. Included in the category of individual buyers of securities are several special groups having pre-existing relationships with the issuers. Among these are stockholders, employees, customers, and suppliers of the enterprise.

Stockholders have a right under some state corporation laws or corporate charters to subscribe to additional issues of stock offered for sale by a corporation, before they are offered to others. This **pre-emptive right** is designed to permit the stockholder to maintain his proportionate interest in the corporate assets, earnings, and voting power. Some corporation laws provide, however, that the stockholder shall have no pre-emptive right unless specifically granted by the charter, or that he may be deprived of this right by provisions of the charter. Even if the legal pre-emptive right does not exist, an issuer may, as a matter of policy, grant to existing stockholders the prior right to subscribe to a new issue of stock. The price at which subscription rights may be exercised is usually at least 5% below the prevailing market price. Subscription rights are generally transferable, so that a stockholder who prefers not to exercise the privilege may sell his rights to others.

Securities are sometimes offered to the **employees** of an issuer with the objective of promoting loyalty, decreasing labor turnover, and improving efficiency. Before 1964, the "restricted stock option plan" was a popular incentive for key employees. The plan offered stock at a price below market value without any Federal income tax on the employee at the time an option was granted or exercised. Under the Revenue Act of 1964, however, options issued to key employees after 1963, known as "qualified stock options," are subject to stricter rules than were "restricted stock options." Thus, an option will generally not qualify for favorable tax treatment if the option price is below the market value of the stock when the option is granted, if the stock is held for less than 3 years (2 years were required for "restricted stock options"), or if the option is exercisable more than 5 (instead of 10) years after it is granted. The less restrictive rules in effect before enactment of the Revenue Act of 1964 will continue to apply to options issued before 1964 and to options granted after 1964 pursuant to a binding contract between employer and employee executed before 1964.

Customer ownership is designed to secure goodwill for an enterprise among buyers of its goods and services. The sale of securities to customers has been especially favored in the past by public utilities. A consumer who is also a shareholder is likely to be more critical of rate reduction agitation or adverse legislation directed against public utilities. Manufacturers have sometimes sought to expand sales by selling stock to wholesale and retail distributors, thus giving the latter a direct interest in the business. Some enterprises unable to raise capital elsewhere have sold securities to customers requiring their output, or to **suppliers** desiring to see their customer remain in business.

Investment Banking

NATURE OF INVESTMENT BANKING. The investment banker is the principal medium for bringing securities to the investing public. His functions include the purchase of whole issues of securities from public bodies or corporate issuers and their distribution to institutional and individual investors, commonly called **"primary distributions"**; and the distribution of blocks of outstanding securities from large holders to the investing public, commonly called **"secondary distributions."** The investment banker may also underwrite the sale of stock to existing stockholders through subscription rights in which event he agrees to take up and distribute whatever portion of the issue is not purchased through the exercise of the rights. This is commonly known as **"stand-by underwriting."**

New capital for corporations and governments is obtained in large volume through investment bankers. The bulk of new bond issues, except United States government obligations, is distributed through them. During the decade following the end of World War I, there was a marked increase in financing by means of stock issues, and it has since become common practice for investment banking houses to engage in the distribution of stock issues as well.

The functions of investment banking houses are different from those of securities exchanges. The exchanges facilitate transfer of ownership after an issue of securities has been distributed to the investing public. But the main burden of originating and selling issues to supply new capital rests upon investment bankers. (Fundamentals of Investment Banking, a study sponsored by the Investment Bankers Association of America.)

RESPONSIBILITIES TO ISSUER AND INVESTOR. In relation to the **issuer**, the investment banker often assumes greater responsibilities than are involved in the mere purchase of securities for resale. He may act as financial adviser, passing upon such questions as the type of security to be offered, the collateral to be furnished, the pricing and timing of the offering, etc. Through stock ownership or representation on the board of directors, he may participate in the management of the issuer. His relation to the issuer, once established, is usually respected by other investment bankers.

As respects the **investing public,** the investment banker also takes a position involving more responsibility than that of the ordinary merchant. The sponsor of an issue is presumably in a superior position to appraise its merits. The name of an important banking firm attached to a prospectus is a potent factor in inducing the public to invest in the security. The public assumes that a reputable firm will not lend its name to a piece of financing without adequate investigation and the exercise of informed judgment. Many banking houses recognize that in sponsoring an issue they assume a **quasi-fiduciary relation** toward the investing public, which survives the initial distribution and may endure for a considerable time after the security is marketed.

The responsibilities that the investment banker assumes toward the issuer are sometimes difficult to reconcile with those that he assumes toward the investing public. The problem is further complicated by considerations of self interest—the natural desire of the investment banker to realize a profit. The 1920's witnessed a radical change in the public taste for securities. Common stocks replaced bonds as the popular medium of investment and were sold to individual buyers with far greater ease. Responding to popular taste during this period, many investment banking firms laid aside their conservative policies in the origination of new issues. Unsound and unseasoned securities were sponsored by reputable houses. Issues were originated without adequate investigation, without the application of proper standards of investment appraisal, and without the most elementary safeguards for the investor. Distribution was facilitated by the misstatement or concealment of material facts in the offering circulars and other selling literature. Purchasers of many issues marketed during this period suffered heavy losses, and public confidence in the investment banking machinery of the nation was impaired for several years thereafter.

Role of Securities Act of 1933. The practices that prevailed in the investment banking business during the 1920's laid the foundation for the passage of the Securities Act of 1933. The primary purpose of the Act is to require **full disclosure** of material facts in connection with the marketing of a security and to impose penalties for violations of that requirement. But the Act does not authorize any Federal agency to pass judgment upon the merits of a security. The Securities and Exchange Commission, which administers the Act, neither approves nor disapproves a security, and it is a criminal offense for any person to make a representation to the contrary. Thus, the chief burden of appraising the soundness of a security continues to rest with the investment banker. (See detailed discussion of the Act starting at page 27.)

Unfortunately, even since the passage of the Act investment bankers have not always discharged this burden with due regard to the interests of investors. This is particularly true in relation to **common stock financing.** During periods when speculative fervor has been rampant, some investment bankers have shown a willingness to sponsor shares of poorly established or highly uncertain enterprises entirely on the basis of conjectural future earnings. From time to time since the end of World War II, there have been recurrences of the ill-considered offerings of prior boom years, and during such periods a segment of the investment banking industry has been exposed to the criticism of having sacrificed the welfare of the investor to opportunities for quick profits.

CLASSES OF INVESTMENT BANKERS. On the basis of function, investment houses may be divided into three classes: (1) wholesalers; (2) combined wholesalers and large retailers; and (3) small retailers.

Firms may be found in each class that specialize in one or more specific types of securities. The tendency of a firm to specialize may originate in the fact that it has acquired special skill, knowledge, and experience in the handling of a particular type of security, such as municipal bonds or public utility securities; the fact that its clientele has a special interest in certain types of investment, such as securities sanctioned by law for institutional investment; or the fact that its relations with issuers are firmly intrenched in one field of enterprise. **Specialization** enables a firm to concentrate more intensively upon one group of securities and to gain a reputation for expert knowledge in its field. On the other hand, a specializing firm may be handicapped by inability to supply its clientele with a diversified list of issues or to keep its sales organization occupied continuously.

Wholesalers. The term "wholesalers" is derived from the commodity markets and applies to firms engaged in the origination and purchase of new issues of securities. The wholesaler purchases new issues, usually in conjunction with other wholesalers, and markets them through retail groups in which the wholesalers themselves may also be participants. A wholesale firm may act as **originator,** in which event it negotiates with the issuer and heads the purchase group organized to underwrite the issue, or it may merely be a **participant** in the purchase group headed by the originating firm.

There are few exclusively wholesale investment houses in the United States. Most wholesalers combine their buying or originating activities with retail selling, and they also engage in other types of activities, as broker-dealers, for example. The combined wholesale and retail houses purchase issues of securities and themselves account for the sale of substantial portions of the issues to institutional and individual investors.

Retailers. Retailers obtain new securities to distribute either by joining a selling group, which undertakes distribution, or by purchasing from members of the selling group at a **discount** from the public offering price. This discount, usually fixed by the selling group agreement, varies from a fraction of 1% to a larger amount, depending upon the quality of the issue, the state of the market, and other factors. Retailers operate chiefly through salesmen who make contact with institutional and individual investors, and who are compensated, directly or indirectly, in proportion to the volume of their sales.

INTERNAL ORGANIZATION OF AN INVESTMENT BANKING HOUSE. There is considerable **variance** in the internal organization of investment banking houses. The typical firm combining the business of wholesaling and retailing is organized to carry on the following operations:

1. Purchase of new issues.
2. Sale of new issues.
3. Stabilizing and other market activities.
4. Statistical and advisory activities.
5. Accounting, record keeping, and miscellaneous.

Some houses are thoroughly **departmentalized,** with each department exercising its own separate and well-defined function. Thus, the functions of negotiating, investigating, buying, selling, trading, statistical analysis, accounting, record keeping, and general management may each be carried on by separate departments. In other houses, some of these functions may be combined in a single department or even in a single individual.

Each of the foregoing functions is discussed below.

Purchase of New Issues

IMPORTANCE OF SOUND PURCHASING POLICIES. The origination of new issues is a major economic function of investment banking. Out of the assortment of financing proposals that are presented to the investment banker, he must choose those to be offered to the public. By virtue of this strategic position, he is a potent factor in determining the channels into which savings are directed.

The investment banker's purchasing policies are of vital importance to the investor. The average individual has a limited ability at best to investigate the merits of a new security. His **chief reliance** is upon the integrity, judgment, and reputation of the sponsoring banker. A recommendation for the purchase of a security made to investors by an investment banking house of standing is frequently all that is necessary to induce immediate absorption of a new issue. The confidence imposed in the investment banker by his clientele begets a responsibility on his part to exercise a high degree of care in the origination of issues.

From the viewpoint of the investment banker himself, adherence to sound purchasing policies is essential. His success in marketing securities is dependent upon **public confidence** to a greater degree than in most other businesses; and public confidence, in turn, depends upon the record of his past offerings. If previous issues have been soundly conceived and have done well marketwise, the sale of subsequent issues is facilitated. Moreover, it is widely recognized in investment banking circles that an issue well bought is at least half sold.

SOURCES OF NEW FINANCING PROPOSALS. New financing proposals reach investment bankers from many sources. The most important of these are discussed below.

Pre-existing Relations with Issuers. As a rule, relations between an investment banking firm and an issuer are continuing in character. Once a firm has successfully distributed the securities of an issuer or has otherwise established itself as financial adviser to the issuer, the association tends to continue, except in instances where the sale of new issues must be effected by competitive bidding. Sometimes the relationship is **informal** and rests entirely upon mutual goodwill. Sometimes it is cemented through the ownership of a stock interest by the investment banking house or through the election to the issuer's board of directors of a representative of the banking house, although the latter course has been discouraged to some extent by the additional liabilities imposed on directors by the Securities Act of 1933 and the Securities Exchange Act of 1934. Occasionally, the relationship is **formalized** through an arrangement between the issuer and the banking house whereby the latter is granted a prior right to purchase future issues during a specified period. It is customary among investment bankers to respect established connections of a firm with a particular issuer and to refrain from considering financing proposals received from such an issuer.

Finders. Many financing proposals are brought to the attention of investment banking firms by independent intermediaries, known as "finders." The finder establishes **initial contact with the issuer** and is expected to make a **preliminary investigation** before presenting a proposal. His compensation, usually paid by the investment banking house, may be a flat sum or a percentage of the underwriting profit. If option warrants or "cheap stock" is received by the underwriter, some may go to the finder.

Under the Securities Act of 1933, one who receives a **finder's fee** from the underwriter is not himself an underwriter if he does not participate directly or indirectly in the distribution of the issue. On the other hand, a finder may become an underwriter within the meaning of the Act if he undertakes for a consideration to perform functions ordinarily within the province of the underwriters, such as handling negotiations looking toward the formation of a selling group, or if securities constituting part of his finder's fee are distributed in the offering.

Traveling Representatives and Branch Offices. The services of the traveling representative of an investment banking firm are of special importance in connection with the origination of **foreign issues**. Like the finder, he is expected to contact the issuer and to make a preliminary investigation before submitting a proposal. The branch offices of an investment banking house bring to the attention of the buying department at the main office enterprises in their area that may be suitable prospects for financing.

A number of large brokerage houses that are not themselves engaged in the underwriting business maintain branch offices throughout the country, and these branches frequently have knowledge of local enterprises in need of financing. When this knowledge is passed along to an investment banking firm, it may prove to be the origin of new underwriting business for the firm.

Commercial Banks. New financing prospects may be referred to an investment banking firm by commercial banks. The commercial banker is often in a position to recommend the services of an investment banker to clients needing long-term capital.

Other Investment Banking Houses. A considerable volume of **new issue business** of an investment banking firm is derived from other banking houses. The channeling of business between investment banking houses is accomplished in two ways. In the first place, a firm known to specialize in a particular type of security will be called in by other firms when they are presented with a security of this type; and the specialist firm may be asked to head the purchasing syndicate formed in connection with the origination of the issue. In the second place, the great majority of investment banking houses obtain participations in new issues by joining with other houses in purchase and selling groups. The size of these participations depends upon such factors as the resources, prestige, and distributing power of the respective participants and their previous relations with the originator of the business. If a highly desirable issue is involved, the proportion allotted to a participant may be influenced by its success in distributing previous offerings originating from the same source.

Direct Applications. New financing proposals reach investment banking houses through direct application by executives or other representatives of corporations. Many houses will not consider an application for financing in an amount of less than $1,000,000, but this standard is by no means universal. Some will not consider an application from a corporation that has never previously offered any securities to the public; others welcome such applications. If applications pertain to enterprises unfamiliar to the investment banker, they may receive little consideration, although some firms maintain facilities for investigating such applications.

If a proposal is presented to an investment banking house, considerable time and expense may be involved in the preliminary investigation, so that it is deemed to be a breach of faith for the issuer to take the proposal elsewhere before it has been acted upon. The more widely a proposal is "shopped around," the more remote are its eventual chances of a favorable reception. If direct application is made, it is helpful to have an accurate, concise, and readable outline of the proposal, with data on operations, past record, and management of the enterprise.

Competitive Bidding. Although most types of issues reach the underwriting stage as a result of negotiation between the investment banker and the issuer, competitive bidding has assumed importance in certain types. For many years, financing by states and municipalities has been regularly conducted on the basis of competitive bids. Competitive bidding is **required by the Interstate Commerce Commission** in the sale of railroad securities except stock issues and several other special types; the **Federal Power Commission** has adopted a **competitive bidding rule** for companies under its jurisdiction, paralleling the Securities and Exchange Commission's rule described below; and the **Treasury Department** requires bids in disposing of weekly bill offerings.

Under authority of the Public Utility Holding Company Act of 1935, the Securities and Exchange Commission has required competitive bidding in the sale of new securities by registered public utility holding companies and their operating subsidiaries and in the sale of utility securities from holding company portfolios. Several categories of transactions are exempted by the Commission from this competitive bidding requirement, including the issuance of securities pro rata to existing security holders pursuant to any pre-emptive right or privilege or in connection with any liquidation or reorganization; the issuance of debt securities having a maturity of not more than 10 years to financial institutions, if the securities are not to be resold to the public and if no finder's fee is paid to any third person; the issuance of securities to a registered holding company or subsidiary.

In general, the investment banking group that has been the successful bidder follows the same procedure in distributing the issue as in the instance of the negotiated type of underwriting.

INVESTIGATION OF FINANCING PROPOSALS. The investigation of a new financing proposal is conducted by the buying department of the originating firm, with such assistance from the issuer and outside experts as it may require. The extent of this investigation varies. The bonds of a large municipality require less investigation than those of a small community. In the instance of a corporate issue, the problem is usually more complicated, although the difficulties are relieved to some extent if requisite information is already in the possession of the banking house by reason of prior relations with the issuer.

The inquiry may be made in two stages. The first stage comprises a quick **preliminary study** of the industry in which the issuer operates, its position in the industry, such other statistical data as are readily available, and the purpose of the proposed financing. On the basis of this survey, members of the investment banking firm determine whether the proposal holds sufficient interest to warrant a more complete investigation.

If the decision is favorable, it is advisable for the firm to have a clear understanding with the issuer that the proposal will not be taken elsewhere while the extended investigation is in progress. By the same token, it is advisable for the issuer to obtain from the investment banking firm a **"letter of intent,"** embodying the proposed terms of the offering. This document, though disclaiming any binding commitment, gives the issuer a sufficient indication of interest to warrant the large expenditure of time and money it will be required to risk in connection with the comprehensive investigation and the ensuing steps.

The second stage of the investigation ordinarily includes a **general examination** of the affairs of the corporation, conducted by the buying department; and engineering, legal, and auditing examinations conducted by experts retained by the firm. For purposes of these examinations the issuer's staff and its attorneys and accountants are usually required to be available to supply information.

The general examination of the issuer covers such factors as ownership and management; credit position; property and products; pricing policies; principal customers; competitive position; labor relations, and general labor conditions in the area of operations; availability of sources of supply of raw materials; public relations; and the financial statements.

The **engineering examination** may cover a description of the products; a valuation of property, tangible and intangible; the physical condition, operating efficiency, and accessibility of properties; the issuer's policies with respect to additions, improvements, and maintenance; present and potential sources of competition; relationship between management and employees; comparison of the issuer's earnings and operating costs with those of other companies in the industry; and the issuer's probable requirements for future improvements.

The **legal examination** relates to such questions as the legality of the issuer's organization; its authorization to do business in the states in which it is operating; the scope of its permissible activities under the articles of incorporation; title to and incumbrances upon properties, leaseholds and franchises; the validity of the proposed issue; and the problems to be encountered in registration under the Securities Act of 1933 and in qualifying under the blue sky laws.

The **auditing examination** covers comparative earning statements and balance sheets for several years; comparative statements of charges to maintenance and depreciation; a review of the internal accounting system and its adequacy; and a detailed audit of accounts.

THE UNDERWRITING CONTRACT. Upon completion of the investigation, the members of the originating firm supervising the activities of the buying department make a decision as to the firm's willingness to handle the business. If the decision is in the affirmative, an offer of purchase is made to the issuer, and upon the acceptance of the offer, the terms agreed upon are embodied in an underwriting or purchase contract. In modern practice, however, seldom is the **contract actually signed** until the morning of the day upon which the registration statement under the Securities Act of 1933 becomes effective.

Authorization of the Contract. Execution of the underwriting contract by the issuer must be authorized by **appropriate corporate action**. In most instances, the issuer's board of directors has sufficient authority to enter into the contract without action by the stockholders. If a charter change is involved or stockholder approval is required for other reasons, a meeting of shareholders must be called. The steps necessary for the validation of an underwriting contract are governed by the law of incorporation, the charter, and the bylaws of the issuer.

Before the passage of the Securities Act of 1933, the originating firm usually acted alone in the execution of the underwriting contract, reserving the **formation of the purchase group** until after the contract had been executed. Since the passage of the Act, the more usual course is for the originating firm to obtain from all the members of the purchase group authorization to execute the contract on their behalf. Under this procedure the formation of the purchase group precedes the signing of the underwriting contract.

Types of Commitments. Originally, an underwriting commitment was an agreement to take up the unsold portion of a security issue that was to be offered, in the first instance, to others. The term has been extended, however, to designate **various methods of guaranteeing or facilitating the flotation of a security issue,** whether or not a financial obligation is imposed on the underwriters. The underwriting commitment may take any of the following forms: (1) an agreement by the underwriters to purchase the entire issue outright and to resell it to the public; (2) an agreement by the underwriters to purchase and distribute publicly any portion of the issue not absorbed by existing security holders; (3) an agreement by the underwriters to obtain purchasers for the entire issue if any part is to be sold by them; or (4) an agreement by the underwriters to use their best efforts to sell the issue publicly, coupled with an authorization to act as selling agents of the issuer or an option to purchase the issue.

Agreements in the first three categories impose upon the underwriters a binding financial obligation to take up and pay for the whole or part of the issue, as the case may be, subject to certain conditions that usually include a "market-out" clause (see below). Agreements in the first and second categories are known as **"firm commitments";** those in the second category being also referred to as **"stand-by commitments."** The third category covers those agreements where the securities will be sold only if the entire issue is sold—such agreements are commonly referred to as **"all or none" commitments.** The underwriter is usually given about 30 days to dispose of the entire issue. Agreements in the fourth category impose no binding financial obligation upon the underwriters to take up any part of the issue but merely require them to use their best efforts to dispose of the securities. Hence, they are known as **"best efforts commitments."**

Most underwriting contracts prior to enactment of the Securities Act of 1933 provided for a firm commitment by the underwriters that guaranteed to the issuer receipt of the entire net proceeds of the financing, except upon the happening of certain remote and catastrophic events. With the introduction under the Act of the 20-day waiting period before a registration statement can become effective, some investment banking firms have tended to veer away from the firm commitment in the strict sense of the term, and in practice there may be little significant distinction between the various types of agreements. Under the Securities Act, offers can be made during the waiting period and underwriters usually take advantage of this even though the underwriting contract is not signed and does not become binding until the effective date of the registration statement. Thus, though a firm commitment contract was originally contemplated, the underwriters may refuse to sign that form of contract unless they find customers for the entire issue during the waiting period.

"Market-Out" Clause. Even if the underwriting assumes the outward form of a firm commitment, the contract usually includes a "market-out" clause permitting the underwriters to cancel their obligations upon the happening of contingencies so broad in scope as to limit substantially the firm nature of the commitment. The **contingencies usually specified** as grounds for cancellation include any substantial change, prior to the public offering, in the financial position of the issuer or its subsidiaries or in political, economic, or market conditions, that, in the judgment of the underwriters, would render it impracticable or inadvisable to market the security. In extreme instances, it is provided that the underwriters may withdraw from their commitment upon the happening of any such contingency at any time before the closing date fixed in the underwriting contract for delivery and payment.

Summary of Typical Firm Commitment Contract. A brief digest of the contents of a typical "firm commitment" contract is set forth below. The digest does not purport to be complete, and additional provisions are necessary to adapt the contract to the circumstances of the particular case.

- A full description of the securities to be issued;
- The issuer's representations and warranties to the effect that a registration statement under the Securities Act of 1933 has been filed, that such registration statement, when effective, will contain no untrue or misleading statement or omission of a material fact, that the accountants certifying the financial statements will be independent public or certified accountants as required by the Act, that the most recent financial statements fairly present the condition and operating results of the issuer, that no substantial adverse change in the issuer's condition has occurred since the date of such financial statements, that no material litigation is pending against the issuer, that the entire net proceeds of the issue will be used for the purposes expressed in the prospectus, and that the issuer will cooperate in qualifying the securities for sale under the blue sky laws of the states designated by the underwriter;
- The agreement of the issuer to sell and the underwriters to purchase the issue, the obligation of the respective underwriters being several and not joint;
- The price at which the securities are to be offered;
- The underwriting discount or commission, the net amount of the proceeds to be received by the issuer, and the method and time of payment and delivery;
- The underwriters' agreement to make a public offering after the effective date of the registration statement at the designated public offering price;
- The issuer's agreement to endeavor to cause the registration statement to become and remain effective;
- The expenses to be borne by the issuer;
- The issuer's agreement to supply the underwriters with copies of the registration statement and amendments thereto and with preliminary and full prospectuses in reasonable quantities;
- The agreement by each of the parties to indemnify the others against certain liabilities;
- The conditions of the underwriters' obligations, including the effectiveness of the registration statement, appropriate opinions from the attorneys and accountants, and appropriate certificates from the issuer's executive officers;
- The issuer's agreement for a specified number of years to furnish the underwriters with financial reports; and
- The "market-out" clause.

THE PURCHASE GROUP. The originating firm will ordinarily invite other investment bankers to join with it in the underwriting. The group organized in this fashion is commonly known as the "purchase group," or the "purchase syndicate." Although the creation of such a group by the originating firm involves a **sharing of the underwriting commissions** or discounts, it provides the advantages of spreading the underwriting risks and increasing distributing power.

Spreading the Risk. The process of originating and distributing securities entails the assumption of a certain measure of risk and the aim of each middleman in the process is to pass the risk along as rapidly as possible until the securities come to rest in the hands of the ultimate investor. A sudden change in the condition of the issuer or in general market conditions may necessitate **postponement** of the public offering or, if the offering has commenced, may render it "sticky" or unsuccessful in whole or in part. The **unsold securities** must either be disposed of at a sacrifice or carried until conditions are more favorable for their disposal. The loss or freezing of the capital of an investment banking firm in an unsuccessful underwriting may interfere with its ability to take on other commitments.

Moreover, a rule of the S.E.C. (Rule X-15C3-1) prohibits any broker-dealer firm from permitting its **aggregate indebtedness** to exceed 2,000% of its net capital. In its **Report of the Special Study of Securities Markets** submitted to Congress in 1963, the Commission recommended that a firm engaged in underwriting be required to have a minimum net capital of $50,000 plus 2% of the aggregate amount of its underwriting commitments or undertakings in the last 12-month period. In view of the existing rule, and the increased emphasis being placed upon capital requirements for underwriters, it has become a matter of prime importance for an originating firm to avoid excessive strain on its own financial resources by bringing in other investment bankers to share the risk.

Increasing the Distributing Power. Inclusion of other firms in an underwriting venture has the further advantage of increasing the distributing power behind the marketing effort. A combined wholesale and retail firm, with its own retail sales organization and its own clientele, is a valuable ally in the selling campaign. When several such firms join forces, the list of potential buyers of the issue is greatly expanded, facilities for reaching potential investors are strengthened, and the time required for distribution is reduced. Thus, there is less chance that adverse conditions may intervene to impede the offering.

Size of the Purchase Group. The size of the purchase group ranges from as few as two members to upward of 100 in the instance of very large issues. The originating firm acts as **manager** of the group, except when it is deemed advisable to substitute a better-known firm or one specializing in the particular type of security involved. The manager is ordinarily authorized to represent each member of the group in the execution and closing of the underwriting contract, organization of the selling group, qualification of the securities for sale under blue sky laws, public offering, market stabilization, and other matters. For these services the manager receives a **stipulated compensation** that is charged against the accounts of the several underwriters in proportion to their respective participations.

Duration of the Purchase Group. The duration of the purchase group is generally fixed by the purchase group contract. This group is maintained at least during the life of the selling group and for as long thereafter as support of the market price is considered necessary. If an issue is quickly and thoroughly absorbed and the market price remains at or above the public offering price, the purchase group may be dissolved in a relatively short time. If the issue is "sticky" and it becomes necessary to repurchase a substantial amount of the securities in order to maintain the price, the life of the purchase group may be prolonged. Many purchase group contracts provide for termination of the purchase group from 20 to 30 days after termination of the selling group, or on such earlier date as the manager may fix. The selling group agreement usually vests the manager with discretion to extend the life of that group for limited periods of time.

THE PURCHASE GROUP CONTRACT. The purchase group contract, otherwise known as the "agreement among underwriters," is the agreement fixing the **rights and liabilities of the underwriters** among themselves. It usually takes the form of a letter addressed to the originating firm from the other members of the group. The following is a digest of the contents of a typical purchase group contract. It does not purport to be complete. As in the instance of the underwriting contract previously summarized, circumstances of the individual case may necessitate the inclusion of other provisions.

Each member of the group agrees to purchase and pay for his proportionate share of the issue and to pay his proportionate share of the manager's fee and of all expenses incurred by the manager in connection with the underwriting. Each member authorizes the originating firm to enter into the underwriting contract with the issuer, to act as manager of the offering and as agent of the respective members, to advance funds or arrange loans for the account of the respective members in connection with the purchase, distribution or resale of the securities, to stabilize the market price of the securities after the effective date of the registration statement, to dispose of securities repurchased in the open market, and to take all steps necessary to qualify the securities under the blue sky laws. Each member confirms that he has examined the registration statement and prospectus and is willing to assume the responsibilities of underwriter under the Securities Act of 1933. The contract generally disclaims that the several underwriters are to be deemed partners or under any joint obligation with the manager or each other. The termination date of the purchase group contract is fixed usually as 20 to 30 days after termination of the selling group but the manager may be authorized to accelerate the termination of the entire agreement or portions thereof. Upon termination, the manager agrees to account to each member for his proportionate share of the profits or losses.

PRICING OF ISSUES AND COMPENSATION OF UNDERWRITERS. One of the managing underwriter's functions is to negotiate the offering price of the issue and the cost of the financing to the issuer. In negotiating the price of a stock issue, the manager is guided by prevailing market conditions, by market quotations on other outstanding securities of the same issuer, and by market quotations on comparable securities of other issuers. Sound practice requires that the offering price should bear a relationship to current or well-defined prospective earnings that is in line with the price-earnings ratio of comparable stocks.

In the instance of **bonds,** the most important factor to be considered is the yield or rate of return offered by comparable bonds, as reflected in prevailing market quotations. The yield is usually expressed in a percentage and is designed to reflect every pertinent factor, such as the safety, stability, and marketability of the bonds. The maturity date is largely governed by custom in the particular industry—10 to 20 years for ordinary industrial issues, and 30 to 40 years for utility issues.

Underwriters' "Spread." The amount to be paid by the underwriters to the issuer is reduced by the underwriters' commission or "spread." Spreads vary with the size and type of the issue, the state of the market, and other factors. In the instance of readily marketable investment issues, such as high-grade municipal bonds, the spread may be less than one point, or a fraction of 1% of the face value of the issue. In the instance of more speculative bond offerings, the spread may range between 4 and 6% of the face value.

The average spread in the case of stock issues is considerably larger than in the case of bond issues. The underwriting of an unseasoned stock issue, requiring an intensive selling campaign for successful placement, may command as much as 20%, or even 25%, of the aggregate proceeds of the offering, although the blue sky laws of a number of states are a limiting factor on the spreads and other expenses of the financing. The New York Stock Exchange, with respect to its members, and the National Association of Securities Dealers also keep watch over underwriters' compensation, the latter group attempting to directly review the fairness of the compensation for offerings in which its members are involved. For a large issue of common stock of a well-known company the spread is frequently under 5%. A portion of the underwriters' compensation is sometimes paid in the form of stock or warrants to purchase stock in the future at fixed or graduated prices. On occasion, payments in stock or warrants are made by controlling stockholders instead of the issuer itself.

Stand-by underwriters may receive a flat commission on the whole issue, regardless of the amount that they are required to take up; or they may receive a small rate of commission on the entire issue plus a higher rate on any portion which they take up. For example, if 100,000 shares of stock are offered to stockholders, the underwriters' commission may be $1 per share on the entire issue and $2 additional for each share not subscribed for by stockholders. If any substantial portion of the issue is taken up by the underwriters, they may organize a retail selling group to complete the distribution.

Under the Securities Act of 1933 **full disclosure** must be made in the registration statement and prospectus of all commissions or discounts (including cash, securities, contracts, or anything else of value) to be paid, directly or indirectly, to the underwriters by the issuer or by any person in a controlling relationship with the issuer. [Securities Act of 1933, Schedule A, paragraph (17).]

Sale of New Issues

THE SELLING PROBLEM. The **objectives** sought by investment bankers in the marketing of new issues are profit, speed, and placement. From the banker's point of view, an offering is successful: (1) if it yields sufficient profit to compensate the purchase group participants for their underwriting risks and the selling group members for their distributing efforts; (2) if it is completed with sufficient dispatch to avoid the risk of unforeseen developments that may hamper the distribution and prolong the underwriting liability; and (3) if it results in securing a wide and permanent placement of the issue, thereby promoting price stability to the satisfaction of investors and issuer.

These objectives are not always consistent with one another. In particular, undue stress upon the necessity for speed may defeat the other objectives. Although too much deliberation in the pace of a distribution presents certain dangers, it is equally true that too much haste has its perils. If dealers and investors are not afforded adequate opportunity to appraise the merits of an issue but are rushed into taking commitments that they quickly regret, substantial amounts of the securities will be "dumped back" on the market and the underwriters may be compelled to effect repurchases on a large scale. This can prove to be a costly operation that may whittle down or wipe out the profit of an underwriting.

THE SALES DEPARTMENT. A highly developed sales organization, with the distributing power that it provides, attracts to the investment banking firm invitations to participate in both purchase and selling groups.

The sales department may consist of a sales manager and a staff of individual salesmen ranging in number from less than a handful to several hundred. The sales manager supervises the staff and usually has an important voice in determining selling prices and policies. The office salesmen maintain contact with customers personally and through correspondence. The outside salesmen or traveling representatives usually sell by personal solicitation.

The salesmen compile, through the years, **customer lists** that constitute a valuable asset to the firm. The direct personal relationship established between salesman and customer is a characteristic of modern investment banking. The strength of an investment banking firm lies not alone in its financial resources, but in a vigorous and adequately trained sales force.

In addition to the selling power generated through the sales force, partners and executives of the firm frequently maintain contacts with insurance companies, investment companies, savings banks, commercial banks, trust companies, and other institutional investors that are large purchasers of securities. Such contacts serve to augment materially the distributing power of a firm.

THE SELLING GROUP. The principal vehicle for the actual distribution of new issues to investors is the selling group. As heretofore indicated, the purchase group contract usually authorizes the originating firm to act as manager of the selling group. The manager handles all the details in connection with the formation and operations of the selling group. In the performance of these functions the manager acts as agent for the members of both the purchase and selling groups.

Selection of Group Members. The first step in setting up a selling group is the choice of dealers to receive invitations to become members. This step is of prime importance, since even the best of issues may fail of acceptance if offered by a group with inadequate distributing facilities. The chief criterion for the selection of selling group members is their ability to obtain permanent placement of the securities.

The large originating firms maintain **records of the past performances** of dealers who have been invited to join their selling groups. They are thus in a position to eliminate those dealers who have been consistently unsuccessful in placing securities allotted to them, and to increase the allotments of those who have been successful. For the small dealer, a regular place on the selling group lists of large originating firms may be a valuable asset. Such a place can be won, however, only by demonstrating a consistent willingness to accept invitations to join selling groups and a consistent ability to place the securities allotted to him.

But indiscriminate acceptance of selling group invitations is not without disadvantages. In the first place, it curtails the exercise of independent judgment by the dealer as to the merits of an issue. Secondly, a dealer recommending a security to a customer should have reasonable grounds to believe that the recommendation is suitable for the customer in the light of his other holdings, his financial situation and his needs, and this obligation cannot be properly discharged by the dealer who feels constrained to accept every selling group invitation that comes his way. Thirdly, an issue with little appeal for investors may require so much selling effort and expense as to render its marketing unprofitable.

The **number of firms to be included** in the selling group depends upon the reception investors are likely to accord the issue that, in turn, depends upon the merits and price of the issue and the general state of the market. If there is uncertainty as to its reception, the number of dealers is increased, so that their aggregate allotments will exceed the total amount to be offered. In this way the entire issue may be disposed of, notwithstanding the inability of some participants to place their allotments. In the instance of large issues, the number of firms invited to participate in the selling group may run to several hundred.

Preferential Treatment for Members of N.A.S.D. The rules of the **National Association of Securities Dealers, Inc.,** provide for preferential treatment to members of the Association in the allowance of concessions or discounts and exclude nonmembers from selling groups in which members participate. Since virtually all the large originating houses are members of the Association, membership has become a prerequisite to an invitation to join any important selling group. Such membership has also become a prerequisite for dealers who do not join the selling group but desire to obtain the benefit of the selling discount usually allowed dealers by selling group participants. It is now customary to provide in both the purchase group contract and the selling group agreement that discounts may be allowed only to members of the Association.

Formation of the Group. When the list of prospective members of the selling group is complete, the manager sends out letters of invitation to dealers on the list. The actual formation of the selling group, however, must be delayed until the registration statement has been filed. This is due to the provision of the Securities Act of 1933 prohibiting offers to sell or offers to buy prior to the **filing date.** Although the preliminary negotiations between the issuer and the underwriters are specifically excepted from this prohibition, the exception extends no further.

In the discussion of the Securities Act of 1933, later in this Section, are described the prohibitions and restrictions on offers to buy and sell, and the various devices that may lawfully be used to acquaint dealers with the issue during the waiting period between the filing of the registration statement and its effective date. Immediately after the registration statement becomes effective, the manager notifies the selling group members of the public offering price, the selling group concession, and the amount offered for subscription or allotted to each member.

Types of Selling Groups. There are two main types of selling groups. In one type the participant receives the right to make a **firm subscription** on the offering date for a fixed amount of the securities. He is informed in advance of the amount reserved for him, and this amount is not ordinarily subject to allotment. He may make additional subscriptions, but these are subject to allotment by the manager. In the second type of selling group the participant is invited to subscribe for any amount he desires, all **subject to allotment** by the manager. In this type, a participant may receive the full amount that he applies for or a lesser amount. If a readily marketable issue is involved, participants are likely to request larger amounts than they actually expect to receive upon allotment.

The **life** of a retail selling group is fixed by the selling group agreement. Normally it is provided that the existence of the group shall extend over a period of 20 or 30 days, subject to earlier termination by the manager or to extension for limited periods by the manager with the consent of at least a majority in interest of the members of the purchase group. Quick termination of the selling group is usually favored by the underwriters, to relieve them of the necessity for maintaining the market price as soon as possible.

THE SELLING GROUP AGREEMENT. Management and operation of the selling group are governed by an agreement in the form of a letter from the manager to the members of the group, sometimes called the "Selected Dealers Agreement." Although the basic outlines of the agreement are relatively simple, special provisions may be inserted for the purpose of preventing abuses in the course of the selling operation. A typical selling group agreement in which the participants are offered the right to make firm subscriptions covers the following points:

- A description of the issue and the underwriting arrangements;
- The offer by underwriters of part of the issue to dealers who are members of the National Association of Securities Dealers, Inc., at the public offering price less a specified discount;
- The reservation of a specified amount for purchase by the dealer to whom the letter is addressed;
- The authorization to the dealer to offer the securities to the public in conformity with the agreement and the terms of offering set forth in the prospectus;
- The agreement of the dealer not to resell at a price below the public offering price nor to allow any concessions to anyone other than members of the N.A.S.D.;
- The time and place of payment for and delivery of the securities;
- The termination date of the agreement, usually 20 to 30 days after the effective date of the registration statement, with authorization in the manager to accelerate the termination of the entire agreement or portions thereof;
- The confirmation by the dealer of his agreement to purchase the specified number of shares; and
- The acknowledgment by the dealer that he has received the statutory prospectus and that in agreeing to purchase the shares, he has relied on the prospectus and not on any other statements whatsoever.

THE PUBLIC OFFERING. Under the 1954 amendments to the Securities Act of 1933, described at a later point, the underwriters and dealers may begin to make offers to sell and to solicit offers to buy the security after the registration statement is filed and before it becomes effective, although no sale or contract of sale can lawfully be made until the registration statement has become effective.

Announcing the Offer. The offers may be made orally or through written communications in the form prescribed by the Act and the rules of the Securities and Exchange Commission. The most important written medium is the **preliminary prospectus** filed as part of the registration statement. This document must contain substantially all the information required to be included in the complete **statutory prospectus,** except that it may omit information respecting the offering price and other matters dependent upon the offering price. (See page 31.) Quantities of the preliminary prospectus are furnished to all underwriters and dealers who are expected to participate in the distribution and they, in turn, distribute the prospectuses to others who may be interested. All persons who receive a preliminary prospectus must later receive the complete statutory prospectus. In the case of certain issues that meet the standards prescribed by the Commission's rules, attention may also be drawn to the offering by means of **summary prospectuses** conforming with the rules. (See page 32.)

Among the communication devices not deemed to be prospectuses is the so-called **"tombstone ad,"** which traditionally merely states from whom a prospectus may be obtained, identifies the security, states the price, and states by whom orders will be executed. (See page 33.) The main function of the "tombstone ad" is to call the issue to the attention of persons who may be sufficiently interested to request a prospectus. It may be published at any time after the registration statement is filed. When the registration statement becomes effective, the manager notifies the other underwriters and the dealers that the securities are released for public sale. A public announcement of the issue is generally made at this point through a "tombstone ad." The underwriters and dealers are furnished with quantities of the complete statutory prospectus for distribution to prospective buyers, including all those who have previously received the preliminary prospectus. If the offering involves an additional issue of a security listed on an exchange, a quantity of prospectuses is also delivered to the exchange for redelivery, on request, to exchange members executing orders in the security.

Opening and Closing the Books. Upon the registration statement becoming effective, the manager "opens the books" to receive subscriptions from selling group members and from outside dealers. Except where subscriptions are firm, he retains the privilege of rejecting them in whole or in part.

The manager is authorized to close the books at his discretion. If the demand for the issue is great, the books are usually closed almost immediately after they are opened. A **public announcement** may then be made to the effect that the issue has been oversubscribed. Such an announcement is not intended to indicate that the entire issue has been placed with investors, for subscribing dealers may not have had opportunity to investigate the actual demand among their customers. Hence, oversubscription generally means oversubscription by dealers, who may still be left with the task of placing the securities with their customers. For this reason a public announcement to the effect that "orders have been received from dealers and others for an amount in excess of the offering" usually reflects the true situation more accurately than one to the effect that the entire issue has been sold.

If an issue is "sticky," the books may remain open for a considerable period. If the offering does not result in placement of the entire issue, the unsold portion is distributed among the members of the purchase group at its expiration.

Price Cutting. The selling group agreement usually provides for the forfeiture of a participant's discount on any securities that the manager repurchases in the open market at or below the public offering price, during the life of the selling group. The manager keeps a record of all securities subscribed for by the respective selling group members in order that securities repurchased in the market can be traced back to the member who sold them in the first instance. These precautions are designed, among other things, to discourage price cutting.

Nevertheless, under stress, or if the rate of distribution is slow, a selling group member may endeavor to stimulate buying through various devices that have the effect of reducing the public offering price and are contrary to the letter or spirit of the selling group agreement and to fair trade practice. The simplest method is to allow the dealers' discount to persons who are not eligible to receive it. As heretofore noted, the dealers' discount may not be allowed by a member of the National Association of Securities Dealers, Inc., to a nonmember of the Association, and the selling group agreement usually contains a prohibition to that effect. Consequently, allowance of the discount to a public buyer or a nonmember dealer is in contravention of the rules of the Association and the selling group agreement.

A more subtle method of price-cutting is found in the practice of **"switching" customers** out of old securities into the new issues. Here, the price-cutting is accomplished by accepting the old securities at a premium above their market prices, in exchange for the new security at the public offering price. Although technically the public offering price is maintained in the transaction, the payment of a premium for the securities accepted in exchange constitutes an indirect rebate to the customer.

A third method is to sell the new security to a customer at the public offering price while simultaneously selling another security to the same customer at a discount from its market price. Here again, the public offering price of the new security is technically maintained, but the customer receives a rebate in the form of a discount on the other security.

Effective means for combating indirect price-cutting practices have been difficult to devise, since new variations on price-cutting methods are constantly being conceived.

SECURITY SALESMEN. New issues are sold in substantial measure through direct solicitation by salesmen in the employ of investment banking firms. These salesmen, usually college educated, receive a training course in the elements of investment and the principles of security selling. They are then supplied with lists of prospective customers and sent out to interview prospects and to obtain orders for the securities offered by their employers. The practice of employing salesmen grew out of the desire of investment bankers to place securities with a large number of individual investors, as distinguished from a relatively small number of institutional investors. This type of placement is designed to obtain a broader market for the offered security and to expand the number of potential buyers of future issues.

In recent years, salesmen have shown a tendency to add some of the functions of investment advisers to their chief function of supplying data concerning the particular issue being offered. Many salesmen, with or without solicitation on the part of their customers, maintain records of the customers' portfolios and suggest the advisability of making changes therein. Often, unfortunately, a salesman is not equipped by training or experience to furnish investment advice. To stimulate sales he is likely to emphasize possible rapid price appreciation and to ignore basic questions pertaining to safety of principal, stability of income, adequacy of return, and similar elements bearing upon the investment merit of a security.

Standards for Salesmen. The problem of elevating the standards for securities salesmen is receiving considerable attention from the Federal and state regulatory agencies, the exchanges, and the National Association of Securities Dealers, Inc. In its 1963 **Report to Congress on the Special Study of Securities Markets,** the Securities and Exchange Commission urged adequate, effective controls over persons who may enter the industry as salesmen, based on standards encompassing competence, character, and integrity. The Report pointed out that during the bull market of 1961 more than one-fourth of all salesmen registered with the N.A.S.D. had less than one year's experience in the securities industry; and at the end of 1962, the year of a severe market break, one salesman out of seven was similarly inexperienced. The Report called for a system of direct individual licensing of salesmen, as well as other categories of personnel, and procedures under which disciplinary action can relate directly to individuals without necessarily involving their employers.

Other Functions of Investment Banking

MARKET STABILIZATION. Stabilizing may be broadly defined as the buying of a security for the purpose of preventing or retarding a decline in its open market price in order to facilitate its distribution to the public. (Stabilizing may also be involved in overallotting or short selling to prevent sharp increases in the open market price, and to cushion later declines by providing the support of covering purchases.) Stabilizing is closely related to the process of underwriting and distributing new issues and, in the eyes of most investment bankers, is an essential feature of that process.

OTHER FUNCTIONS OF INVESTMENT BANKING

Some proportion of an issue, even though initially it may be completely sold by the underwriters to the selling group dealers, will quickly find its way back to the open market. This is due to the fact that some purchasers change their minds and almost immediately resell, and some—the so-called **"free riders"**—purchase in the first instance with the intention of selling out as soon as possible. Many subscriptions are placed in the expectation that the price will advance and a profit can be realized before the date of payment. Again, the temporary oversupply of the security being offered may exert pressure on the market price. Underwriters contend that stabilization is necessary to neutralize the effects of these and other abnormal situations, as well as to provide a fair market price for investors who may not be "free riders" but who consider it necessary or advisable to liquidate their holdings.

If re-offerings are not readily absorbed in the market, they will tend to force the market price below the public offering price of the issue. To prevent such a drop in price, the manager of the underwriting syndicate enters a **syndicate bid** for the securities that may be offered in the open market. The syndicate bid is designed to take up the securities offered for which no other buyers are available, and thus to stabilize the market price at the level of the bid price. Normally, the agreement among the underwriters limits the maximum position resulting from stabilizing to 10 to 15% of the amount of securities underwritten.

Stabilizing is regarded as most useful in the instance of issues that are neither notable successes nor notable failures. In the former, the market for the issue usually takes care of itself. In the latter, where the selling pressure in the open market is too great, the underwriters cannot afford to support the market at or near the issue's original offering price. For the same reason, stabilizing cannot as a practical matter be used to stem a market or economic trend of any major significance.

LEGAL RESTRICTIONS ON STABILIZING. The Securities Exchange Act of 1934 contains a general prohibition against manipulation of security prices up or down. It does not, however, prohibit transactions for the purpose of "pegging, fixing, or stabilizing" security prices, except to the extent that these transactions may be in contravention of the Commission's rules.

S.E.C. Rules. The Commission has prescribed several rules (Rules 426, X-10B-6, X-10B-7, X-10B-8, and X-17A-2) that endeavor to reconcile, as far as possible, the often conflicting objectives of protecting purchasers of securities, on the one hand, and of facilitating the flow of capital into industry, on the other. Among other things, these rules limit the purposes for which and the types of offerings in which stabilizing transactions may be effected; require the filing with the Commission of reports with respect to stabilizing transactions; prescribe strict limits upon the price levels at which stabilization bids may be entered or maintained; prohibit certain trading activities during the period of stabilization; and provide special restrictions upon stabilization in connection with rights offerings.

If the registrant or any of the underwriters knows or has reasonable grounds to believe that there is an intention to overallot or that the price of any security may be stabilized to facilitate the offering of the registered securities, there must be set forth, either on the outside front cover page or on the inside front cover page of the prospectus, in bold letters, a statement substantially as follows:

IN CONNECTION WITH THIS OFFERING, THE UNDERWRITERS MAY OVER-ALLOT OR EFFECT TRANSACTIONS WHICH STABILIZE OR MAINTAIN THE MARKET PRICE OF
....
(Identify each class of securities in which such transactions may be effected.)

AT A LEVEL ABOVE THAT WHICH MIGHT OTHERWISE PREVAIL IN THE OPEN MARKET. SUCH TRANSACTIONS MAY BE EFFECTED ON ....
(Identify each exchange on which stabilizing transactions may be effected. If none, omit this sentence.)
SUCH STABILIZING, IF COMMENCED, MAY BE DISCONTINUED AT ANY TIME.

If the stabilizing began prior to the effective date of the **registration statement**, the prospectus must set forth the amount of securities bought, the prices at which they were bought, and the period within which they were bought.

OTHER MARKET ACTIVITIES. The **trading department** of an investment banking firm buys and sells outstanding securities that present opportunities for profitable trading. It may also be called upon to dispose of securities received from customers in exchange for new issues offered by the firm. The salesman endeavoring to promote the sale of a new issue frequently is told by the customer that he has no cash available for investment. In many instances he meets this problem by reviewing the customer's existing holdings and suggesting **"switches."** When securities are taken in exchange, it becomes the function of the trading department to dispose of them in the open market or to other customers of the firm.

Additional functions performed by the trading department include the making of secondary markets in issues originally offered by the firm, and the execution of commission orders for customers desiring to purchase or sell securities in the open market.

STATISTICAL AND ADVISORY ACTIVITIES. The **statistical department** of an investment banking firm facilitates the work of the other departments by supplying them with analyses and reports on securities and with material that enables them to answer inquiries. When a new financing proposal is received by the firm, the statistical department compiles for the buying department data required for the preliminary investigation of the issuer and for the more comprehensive later investigation. It also furnishes the buying department with information upon the basis of which the latter may advise the issuer as to the most appropriate form of security to be issued and the most favorable time and conditions for the public offering. The statistical department further assists in compiling the material required to be included in the registration statement and prospectus.

The statistical department aids the selling department by equipping salesmen with the information they need to respond to inquiries from prospective buyers. It aids the trading department by supplying analyses on securities that offer profitable trading opportunities. If the firm offers investment advisory service, the statistical department bears the brunt of this work, preparing special studies, circulars, and bulletins for dissemination among customers of the firm.

Many firms invite customers and prospects to submit lists of their holdings for analysis. These lists are reviewed by the statistical department and recommendations are made from time to time for changes into new offerings.

ACCOUNTING AND RECORD-KEEPING. The **accounting department** of the investment banking house keeps records of security and money transactions. Cost accounting, auditing, budgeting, and statistical analysis of records have not been thoroughly developed in this field. Many houses restrict their bookkeeping activities to the **"cage routine"** for keeping records of cash and securities, keeping customers' accounts, preparation of the firm's income account and balance sheet, and the other records required by the rules of the

Securities and Exchange Commission. Few have an auditor permanently attached to the organization, and the budgeting of expenses is rarely encountered.

MISCELLANEOUS ACTIVITIES. Although the basic function of the investment banking firm is to act as middleman in the distribution of new issues, these organizations have branched out into other related activities to increase their revenues. Since the volume of new financing is subject to considerable fluctuation, other activities are often necessary to lend greater stability to income and to aid in meeting overhead expense at all times. The most important related activity is the business of **dealing in securities already outstanding,** as broker or dealer. A number of houses primarily engaged in the investment banking business are member firms of securities exchanges, and such membership enables them to handle a substantial volume of commission orders for customers. Investment banking houses also do an extensive business in unlisted securities, acting as over-the-counter dealers.

On the other hand, many firms primarily engaged in brokerage business have ventured into the business of underwriting, thus swelling the ranks of investment houses. The efforts of brokerage firms to establish profitable underwriting departments have not been universally successful. If the brokerage firm is one of high repute, with a list of institutional and wealthy individual customers, the underwriting department may become a profitable and important adjunct to the firm's business. But if the customers of a stock exchange house have a more speculative outlook or are chiefly concerned with market appreciation, the firm may encounter difficulty in selling them conservative bonds and preferred stocks on a low-yield basis. In some brokerage houses, the management may be satisfied if the underwriting department "breaks even," regarding it as a source of prestige rather than profit.

A number of investment houses act as **managers of portfolios** for individual or institutional investors. This involves the creation of organizations similar to those of the specialized investment counsel concerns; and such organizations are sometimes operated on a virtually autonomous basis to insure independence of judgment. Some investment houses have organized and manage **investment trusts.** Some maintain departments to deal in government securities, foreign exchange, bankers' acceptances, and commercial paper, and to engage in other specialized financial transactions.

The Securities Act of 1933

THE DISCLOSURE PRINCIPLE. President Franklin D. Roosevelt, in his message to Congress of March 29, 1933, recommending legislation for Federal supervision of interstate traffic in securities, said: "There is, however, an obligation upon us to insist that every issue of new securities to be sold in interstate commerce shall be accompanied by full publicity and information, and that no essentially important element attending the issue shall be concealed from the buying public. This proposal adds to the ancient rule of caveat emptor, the further doctrine 'let the seller also beware.' It puts the burden of telling the whole truth on the seller."

This disclosure principle pervades the six statutes subsequently enacted by Congress to regulate interstate dealings in securities—the Securities Act of 1933, the Securities Exchange Act of 1934, the Public Utility Holding Company Act of 1935, the Trust Indenture Act of 1939, the Investment Company Act of 1940, and the Investment Advisers Act of 1940. All these statutes are administered by the Securities and Exchange Commission, which was created by the Securities

Exchange Act of 1934. The Commission holds to the philosophy that disclosure and publicity are the most effective of regulatory devices, that the most important safeguard for the investor is to make available to him all the facts necessary to an intelligent appraisal of the value of a security. In its Report of the Special Study of Securities Markets submitted to Congress in 1963, the Commission stated: "Disclosure is the cornerstone of federal securities legislation; it is the sine qua non of investment analysis and decision; it is the great safeguard that governs conduct of corporate managements in many of their activities; it is the best bulwark against reckless corporate publicity and irresponsible recommendation and sale of securities."

GENERAL DESCRIPTION OF THE 1933 ACT. The Securities Act of 1933 is mainly concerned with the **distribution** of securities, as distinguished from trading activities after they have been distributed. If the mails or the channels of interstate commerce are involved in a distribution by the issuer or by a person controlling the issuer, the securities must be registered with the Commission. The **registration statement** is designed to make available to the investing public comprehensive information concerning the securities offered, the issuer, its management, promoters, and underwriters, the proposed application of the proceeds of the offering, and other pertinent matters. The registration statement becomes effective automatically on the twentieth day after it is filed unless the Commission declares it effective at an earlier date or unless, as usually happens, the issuer delays effectiveness by filing an amendment that starts the 20-day period running anew. A **prospectus** containing the information prescribed by the statute and the rules of the Commission must be furnished to every prospective investor. Criminal and civil liabilities are imposed for material misstatements or omissions in the registration statement or prospectus. The Act also **outlaws fraud** in the sale of securities through the use of the mails or the facilities of interstate commerce, and the antifraud prohibitions apply to sales made not only in the course of distribution but at any other time. The Act **exempts** certain types of securities and transactions from the registration and prospectus requirements but not from the antifraud provisions.

The Commission has no power under the Act to approve or pass upon the merits of any security or to guarantee the accuracy of information contained in a registration statement or prospectus. Every prospectus is required to set forth in bold face on the front page a legend to the effect that the securities have not been approved or disapproved by the Commission, that the Commission has not passed upon the accuracy or adequacy of the prospectus, and that any representation to the contrary is a criminal offense.

PERSONS AND TRANSACTIONS COVERED. Apart from the antifraud provisions, the requirements and prohibitions of the Act apply in general to three classes of persons—issuers, dealers, and underwriters, as those terms are defined in the Act.

"Issuer," "Dealer," and "Underwriter" Defined. An issuer is defined as any person who issues or proposes to issue any security. There are certain exceptions to this definition that need not be mentioned here. It should be noted, however, that an issuer is not always a corporation; in a proper case the issuer may be an individual, a committee, a trust, an unincorporated association, or other legal entity.

A dealer is defined as any person who engages either for all or part of his time as agent, broker, or principal, in the business of offering, buying, selling, or otherwise dealing or trading in securities issued by another person. The definition includes a broker, although an exemption is provided for certain unsolicited brokerage transactions.

An underwriter is defined as a person who has purchased from an issuer with a view to, or offers or sells for an issuer in connection with, the distribution of any security, or who participates directly or indirectly in the undertaking or the underwriting of the undertaking. The definition does not include a person whose interest is limited to a commission from an underwriter or dealer not exceeding the usual and customary distributors' or sellers' commission. For the purpose of defining an underwriter, the definition of issuer includes a person controlling, controlled by, or under common control with the issuer.

As stated by Professor Loss in his authoritative work on "Securities Regulation" (Loss, Securities Regulation):

The term "underwriter" is defined not with reference to the particular person's general business but on the basis of his relationship to the particular offering. No distinction is made between professional investment bankers and rank amateurs. Any person who performs one of the specified functions in relation to the offering is a statutory underwriter even though he is not a broker or dealer. Conversely, even a professional investment banker is not a statutory underwriter in effecting a distribution on behalf of a person not in a control relationship with the issuer, or in arranging a private placement on behalf of the issuer or a person in a control relationship with the issuer.

"Distribution" Explained. The question of what constitutes "distribution" for the purpose of defining an underwriter sometimes presents difficulties. The word "distribution" is not defined in the Act, although two of the Commission's rules (Rules 133 and 154) fix a quantitative standard for determining whether a distribution exists under certain special circumstances. In general, however, "distribution" is construed as more or less synonymous with the term "public offering" used in other provisions of the Act. If the offering is private, no distribution is involved within the meaning of the Act, the purchaser is not deemed to be an underwriter, and the registration requirements are not applicable. Criteria for distinguishing between a public offering and a private offering are discussed at a later point.

Distribution has been held to comprise the entire process by which a block of securities is dispersed and ultimately comes to rest in the hands of the investing public. Hence, in determining whether a distribution is involved, it is necessary to consider not merely the specific transaction between the issuer and its immediate purchaser, but also the extent to which a later public offering of the same securities is likely. A predetermination of the precise amount to be publicly dispersed is not, however, an essential element of distribution. If the total amount publicly dispersed is substantial, a distribution may be involved notwithstanding that the securities are sold in relatively small lots over an extended period of time.

Purchase for Distribution or "Investment." Whether a purchase is made with a view to distribution or investment must be ascertained in any given case by reference to the **intention of the purchaser.** What his intention was at the time of purchase is a question of fact. A state of mind can ordinarily be ascertained only by weighing the evidence, and a person's actions may be of far greater weight than his statements in illuminating his state of mind. The Commission has said that "a statement by the initial purchaser, at the time of his acquisition, that the securities are taken for investment and not for distribution is necessarily self-serving and not conclusive as to his actual intent." (Securities Act Release No. 4552.)

An important factor to be weighed in ascertaining the purchaser's intention is the **length of time elapsing** between acquisition of the securities and their resale. Although retention of securities for any length of time is not conclusive, the longer they are held, the more persuasive would be the argument that their resale is not at variance with an original investment intent. If they are retained for as long a period as 2 years, that fact would create a strong inference that they were originally purchased for investment. On the other hand, a predetermined limitation upon resale for a stated period of time or until the happening of a stated event may create doubts as to the original investment intent.

An **unforeseen change of circumstances** since the date of purchase may also support the argument that resale of the securities would not be inconsistent with an investment representation. But the change must ordinarily relate to the purchaser's own circumstances, not to an advance or decline in the market price or a change in the issuer's operating results.

A further factor that may be of importance in determining whether a purchase is made with a view to distribution or for investment is the **nature of the purchaser's business**. If the purchase is made by an institutional investor or by an individual or firm not engaged in the securities business, the purchaser is in a stronger position to contend that he has purchased for investment than if he is engaged in underwriting or dealing in securities. If the purchaser is an investment banker or dealer, he would be required to show by the clearest kind of evidence that the scope and character of his business is consistent with the purchase of large blocks of securities for investment rather than with a view to distribution.

Controlling Persons. As has been noted, the term "underwriter" includes not only one who purchases from a corporate issuer with a view to distribution, but also one who purchases from a controlling person with a view to distribution. The policy of the Act, to provide for full disclosure of every material element attending a distribution, extends not only to the distribution of a new issue but to a redistribution of outstanding securities that takes on the characteristics of a new offering by reason of the control of the issuer possessed by the person making the offering. In order fully to effectuate this policy, the Act adopts the principle that a controlling person is an issuer for the purpose of defining an underwriter and that anyone who effects a distribution for a controlling person is an underwriter. The result is to require **registration** in connection with secondary distributions through underwriters by controlling persons.

It should be noted, however, that a controlling person is not an issuer, within the meaning of the Act, for any purpose except to define an underwriter. For example, he cannot satisfy the requirement that the registration statement be signed by the issuer.

The concept of control does not depend upon a mathematical formula of 51% of voting power. The Commission has defined the term "control" to mean the possession of the power to direct or cause the direction of the management and policies of a corporation, whether through ownership of voting securities, by contract, or otherwise. This power may reside in a single person or in a group of persons united by business, social, or other ties. A **practical test for control**, as the term is used in the section defining an underwriter, is whether the person in question has power to obtain registration, either alone or acting in concert with other related persons.

PROHIBITIONS AND REQUIRED ACTS. The Act, as amended in 1954, contains several sweeping prohibitions, but these must be read in conjunction with the exemptions. The prohibitions should be considered in the light of their impact (1) before the registration statement is filed; (2) after the registration statement is filed but before it becomes effective; and (3) after the registration statement becomes effective.

The Prefiling Period. Before a registration statement has been filed with respect to a security, the Act makes unlawful the use of the mails or the facilities of interstate commerce to sell the security or to offer to buy or sell it through the medium of a prospectus or otherwise. Although these prohibitions, by their terms, apply to any person, transactions by persons other than issuers, underwriters, or dealers are exempt. Thus, the ordinary investor may lawfully offer to buy a security from the issuer or from an underwriter or dealer before the filing date, but his offer cannot be solicited or accepted by the offeree until the filing date and cannot be accepted until the effective date of the registration statement. The Commission has interpreted these provisions to mean that, prior to the filing of a registration statement, an issuer, controlling stockholder, underwriter, or dealer cannot legally offer a nonexempt security to the public, nor engage in a publicity campaign having for its purpose the sale of the security to the public. **"Conditioning the market"** for a prospective offering before the filing of a registration statement or even before it becomes effective is not permitted.

The Waiting Period. During the period between the filing of a registration statement and its effective date, commonly referred to as the "waiting" or "cooling" period, the Act prohibits the making of sales, contracts of sale, or contracts to sell the security. Under the 1954 amendments, however, issuers and underwriters are permitted, immediately after the filing of a registration statement, to make offers to sell and to solicit offers to buy either orally or by means of preliminary prospectuses or other written communications in the form authorized by the statute and the Commission's rules. Although such offers may now be made or solicited during the waiting period (except in States where they would violate the blue sky laws), the security cannot be sold and offers to buy cannot be accepted so as to make them binding contracts until the registration statement has become effective; nor can the sale be consummated after the effective date without the delivery to the purchaser of a complete statutory prospectus.

The Preliminary Prospectus. The intent of Congress in prescribing a compulsory waiting period between the filing date and the effective date was twofold: to slow down the process of distribution and to afford opportunity for public and professional scrutiny of the proposed issue. It was contemplated that during the waiting period there would be widespread dissemination of information among dealers and the public generally with respect to the issue, but that no contracts or sales would be made until the effective date. Obviously, public and professional scrutiny cannot be stimulated merely by the filing of a registration statement, even though the statement is open to public inspection. Only a relatively few dealers and a small segment of the public can avail themselves of the opportunity to inspect the statement.

In order to promote the dissemination of information during the waiting period, the Commission has by rule (Rule 433) authorized the use of a preliminary prospectus filed as part of the registration statement. This document replaced the old **"red herring prospectus,"** which was similar in many respects but was required expressly to negate any intent to solicit orders. The conditions that must be met to qualify a preliminary prospectus for use are as follows:

(a) The preliminary prospectus must contain substantially the information required to be included in the complete statutory prospectus, except that it may omit information with respect to the offering price, underwriting and dealer discounts or commissions, amount of proceeds, conversion rates, call prices, or other matters dependent upon the offering price; and

(b) The outside front cover page of the preliminary prospectus must bear, in red ink, the caption "Preliminary Prospectus," the date of its issuance, and the following statement:

> A registration statement relating to these securities has been filed with the Securities and Exchange Commission but has not yet become effective. Information contained herein is subject to completion or amendment. These securities may not be sold nor may offers to buy be accepted prior to the time the registration statement becomes effective. This prospectus shall not constitute an offer to sell or the solicitation of an offer to buy nor shall there be any sale of these securities in any State in which such offer, solicitation or sale would be unlawful prior to registration or qualification under the securities laws of any such State.

Acceleration of Waiting Period. When a registration statement has been cleared except for the offering price, underwriting arrangements, and other matters dependent upon the offering price, the necessity for waiting 20 days after the **"price amendment"** is filed would work hardship, particularly where a firm commitment is involved. To avoid such hardship, the Securities and Exchange Commission early adopted the practice of granting requests for acceleration of the effectiveness of the registration statement to the day the "price amendment" is filed or the next day. This makes it possible for underwriters to sign a firm commitment contract on the same day the registration statement becomes effective and thus to avoid the dangers inherent in a 20-day delay. The granting of a request for acceleration, however, depends upon whether the Commission finds that certain preliminary conditions have been fulfilled.

By a rule (Rule 460), the Commission has codified its pre-existing policy with respect to the acceleration of registration statements. The rule provides in substance that the Commission will consider whether the persons making the offering have taken reasonable steps to make the information contained in the registration statement conveniently available to underwriters and dealers who are expected to participate in the distribution of the security. As a minimum this involves the distribution to each such underwriter and dealer, a reasonable time before the anticipated effective date, of as many **copies of the preliminary prospectus** as may be necessary to secure its adequate distribution. If the form of preliminary prospectus that has been distributed is found to be inaccurate or inadequate in material respects, acceleration of the effective date will not be granted until the Commission has received satisfactory assurance that appropriate correcting material has been sent to all underwriters and dealers who received the preliminary prospectus in quantities sufficient for the information of all persons to whom the inaccurate or inadequate material was sent. The granting of acceleration, however, will not be conditioned upon the distribution of a preliminary prospectus in any State where such distribution would be illegal. In addition, in passing upon requests for acceleration, the Commission will consider whether there has been a bona fide effort to make the prospectus reasonably concise and readable, so as to facilitate an understanding of the information contained therein.

The Summary Prospectus. In the case of issuers that meet the standards prescribed by the Commission's rules (Rules 434 and 434A), the use of summary prospectuses conforming with the rules is also permitted during the waiting period. A summary prospectus may be **prepared by an independent organization** primarily engaged in preparing statistical and financial manuals with respect to securities generally and in circulating to subscribers statistical and financial information and summaries. The organization must not receive any payment from the issuer, or from any underwriter or dealer participating in the distribution, for preparing the summary. The summary prospectus may be prepared on a bulletin, card, or other document that summarizes information contained in the preliminary prospectus. Such a summary prospectus may be used only during the waiting period.

A somewhat different form of summary prospectus may be **prepared by the issuer or underwriters.** These must be filed as part of the registration statement and may be used either during the waiting period or after the effective date of the registration statement. When used prior to the effective date they must be captioned "Preliminary Summary Prospectus," must contain the red ink legend appearing on every preliminary prospectus, and must state from whom copies of a more complete prospectus can be obtained.

Communications Not Deemed a Prospectus. The term "prospectus" is defined by the Act generally to include any communication in writing or by radio or television that offers a security for sale or confirms the sale of a security. The Act, however, has always excepted from the general definition a notice, circular, advertisement, letter, or communication in respect of a security that states from whom a written prospectus meeting the requirements of the Act may be obtained and, in addition, does no more than identify the security, state the price thereof, and state by whom orders will be executed.

This exception is the basis of the so-called **"tombstone ad,"** which traditionally is limited in content to the items specified above, although, as will be seen, the Commission's rules have permitted several additional items since 1955. The "tombstone ad" may be used at any time after the registration statement has been filed. Its primary function is to call the issue to the attention of persons who might be sufficiently interested to request a preliminary prospectus before the effective date and a full prospectus thereafter.

By an amendment to the Act in 1954, the Commission was authorized to **expand the information that may be contained in a written communication,** including a "tombstone ad," without bringing it within the definition of a prospectus. Following the amendment, the Commission adopted a rule (Rule 134) that permits a written communication to include any one or more of the following items of information without being deemed to be a prospectus:

. . . the name of the issuer of the security; the full title of the security and the amount being offered; a brief indication of the general type of business of the issuer, limited as provided in the rule; the price of the security, or if the price is not known, the method of its determination or the probable price range; the yield of a debt security or, if the yield is not known, the probable yield range; the name and address of the sender of the communication and the fact that he is participating or expects to participate in the distribution; the names of the managing underwriters; the approximate date upon which it is anticipated the public offering will commence; whether, in the opinion of counsel, the security is a legal investment for savings banks, fiduciaries, insurance companies, or similar investors; whether in the opinion of counsel the security is exempt from specified taxes or the extent to which the issuer has agreed to pay any tax with respect to the security or measured by the income therefrom; whether the security is being offered through rights issued to security holders and, if so, a description of the rights; and any statement or legend required by any state law or administrative authority.

Unless a written communication used under this rule is limited to the form of "tombstone ad" permitted before the 1954 amendment, or is accompanied or preceded by a proper prospectus or summary prospectus, the communication must also contain the following:

(i) a statement whether the security is being offered in connection with a distribution by the issuer or by a security holder, or both, and whether the issue represents new financing or refunding or both; (ii) the name and address of a person or persons from whom a written prospectus meeting the requirements of the Act may be obtained; and (iii) if the registration statement has not yet become effective a statement to the effect that it has not become effective; that the securities may not be sold nor may offers to buy be accepted prior to the effective date; and that the communication does not constitute an offer to sell or the solicitation of an offer to buy nor shall there be any sale of the securities in any State in which such offer, solicitation or sale would be unlawful prior to registration or qualification in such State.

A communication sent or delivered to any person pursuant to the rule, which is accompanied or preceded by a proper prospectus, may solicit from the recipient an offer to buy the security or an indication of the recipient's interest, if the communication contains a statement to the effect that no offer to buy can be accepted and no part of the purchase price can be received until the registration statement has become effective, that any such offer may be withdrawn or revoked without obligation at any time prior to notice of its acceptance given after the effective date, and that an indication of interest will involve no obligation or commitment of any kind.

Within the limits above described, the "tombstone ad" and other written communications may be used at any time after the filing of the registration statement.

Summarizing the results of the 1954 amendments and the Commission's rules promulgated thereunder, it is now permissible during the waiting period to make offers to sell and to solicit offers to buy orally and to use the mails and the facilities of interstate commerce to make offers to sell and to solicit offers to buy through the medium of the preliminary prospectus, the summary prospectus, the "tombstone ad," and other written communications limited in conformity with the Commission's rules. It is not permissible, however, to make any sales, contracts of sale, or contracts to sell until after the registration statement becomes effective.

The Posteffective Period. After the registration statement has become effective, the Act makes unlawful the use of the mails or the facilities of interstate commerce to carry the security for the purpose of sale or for delivery after sale, unless accompanied or preceded by a prospectus that meets the requirements of the Act. Similarly, it is unlawful to use the mails or the facilities of interstate commerce to carry or transmit a prospectus that fails to meet the requirements of the Act. Once the registration statement becomes effective, the prohibition against using the mails or interstate facilities to sell or deliver the security is terminated, but a proper prospectus must precede or accompany the delivery of the security or the confirmation of the sale, whichever first occurs. The reference here is to the complete and **final prospectus**, which must be delivered to the buyer notwithstanding that he may previously have received a preliminary or summary prospectus.

The Act permits the use of **supplementary selling literature** after the effective date if it accompanies or follows, but not if it precedes, the full statutory prospectus. The supplementary literature is subject to the antifraud prohibitions.

Every dealer is required to furnish a prospective purchaser with a copy of the statutory prospectus for a period of at least 40 days after the effective date or the date the public offering begins, whichever is later, and, if he was a participant in the distribution, for as long thereafter as his allotments or subscriptions remain unsold. If securities are those of a company offering an issue to the public for the first time, the 40-day period becomes 90 days or such shorter period as the Commission shall order.

REGISTRATION PROCEDURE. Any security may be registered with the Commission by filing a **registration statement** in triplicate, one copy of which must be signed by the issuer, its principal executive officers, its principal financial officer, its comptroller or principal accounting officer, and the majority of its board of directors or persons performing similar functions. All registration statements must be filed at the Commission's principal office in Washington, D. C.

A registration statement must be on the form prescribed by the Commission; but a statement is deemed to be on the proper form unless objection is made by the Commission prior to the effective date. Since its creation, the Commission has consistently sought to simplify registration forms. The evolution of these forms has been such as to indicate a desire to achieve the fairest possible balance between a maximum of protection to investors and a minimum of difficulty to issuers. The Commission has promulgated a series of optional forms—the "S" **series**—designed to simplify the preparation of registration statements and cut down the expense involved, without sacrificing any information that an investor should have.

Registration forms require information only as to the registrant, unless the context clearly shows otherwise. Information need be given only insofar as known or reasonably available to the registrant. If any required information is unknown and not reasonably available, either because the obtaining thereof would involve unreasonable effort or expense or because it rests peculiarly within the knowledge of another person not in a controlling relationship with the registrant, such information may be omitted as long as the registrant gives whatever information it possesses or can readily obtain on the subject. If a summary or an outline of the provisions of any document is required, the answer must be brief. It is not intended that a statement shall be made as to all the provisions of the document, but only as to the most important provisions in condensed form.

Confidential treatment will be accorded to the provisions of any material contract, or portion thereof, if the Commission determines that its disclosure would impair the value of the contract and is not necessary for the protection of investors. No registration statement or document filed with the Commission or used in connection with an offering may contain information that an appropriate government agency has classified or determined to require protection in the interests of national defense.

At the time of filing a registration statement, the registrant must pay to the Commission a fee of one-hundredth of 1% of the maximum aggregate price at which the securities are proposed to be offered, but such fee may not be less than $25. A Commission rule (Rule 457) specifies the respective methods of calculating the **filing fee** when the securities are to be offered at varying prices based upon fluctuating market prices or fluctuating values of underlying assets, or are to be offered to existing security holders and the unsubscribed portion reoffered to the general public, or are to be offered in exchange for other securities. A filing date is not obtained unless the registration statement is accompanied by the required fee; but an insignificant deficiency based on a bona fide error does not affect the date of filing.

The information contained in a registration statement is available for **public inspection,** and photocopies are furnished to anyone upon the payment of prescribed charges, which are moderate. Contents of the registration statement are available to the public prior to the effective date, as well as thereafter.

The **effective date** of a registration statement is the twentieth day after the filing date, but the Commission is authorized to shorten this 20-day period if it determines that acceleration may be granted with due regard to the adequacy of information respecting the issuer previously available to the public; to the ease with which prospective investors can understand the nature of the securities to be registered, their relationship to the capital structure of the issuer, and the rights of holders; and to the public interest and investor protection.

Amendment of Statement. Amendments to the registration statement may be filed by the registrant at any time, either prior to or after the effective date. Filing of a pre-effective amendment automatically changes the filing date of the registration statement to the filing date of the amendment, and this starts the 20-day period running anew, unless the amendment is filed with the consent of the Commission or pursuant to its order.

The power of **accelerating** or **refusing to accelerate** the effective date has been developed by the Commission into an important administrative device. Although the Commission has no authority to pass upon the merits of any security, it can, by calling for amendments, put off the effective date more or less indefinitely. Moreover, the authority to deny acceleration has been used by the Commission to promote adequate circulation of preliminary prospectuses, to improve the readability of prospectuses, to impose conditions upon indemnification by the issuer of its officers, directors, and controlling persons against liabilities under the Act, and for other purposes. If a statement no longer contains any deficiencies, however, it is mandatory on the Commission to permit it to become effective.

Few, if any, registration statements are in final form when they are filed, and one or more amendments are customarily necessary. After the statement is filed, it is reviewed by the Commission's Division of Corporation Finance where a **Letter of Comment** is prepared, specifying the respects in which the Division considers the statement to require amendment. This is furnished to the registrant, which then files an amendment designed to cover the points raised in the Letter of Comment. The amendment, in turn, may be the subject of a further Letter of Comment requiring additional amendments. In practice, the **"price amendment,"** which supplies information regarding the offering price, underwriting arrangements, and related matters, is not filed until the rest of the statement has been reviewed and informally cleared by the Division.

If the registration statement cannot be appropriately amended within the statutory 20-day period, the registrant generally takes steps to prevent it from becoming effective in deficient form, which would give the Commission grounds for instituting stop order proceedings. Under the former practice, the registrant found it necessary, if unusual delays were encountered, to file **"delaying amendments"** by telegram or letter prior to the expiration of each 20-day period. This is no longer necessary. A rule of the Commission (Rule 473) now permits the registrant, simultaneously with the filing of the registration statement or later, to file a single amendment that indefinitely delays the effective date until a subsequent amendment is filed stating in effect that the registration statement shall become effective within 20 days thereafter or upon acceleration of the effective date by the Commission.

When the registrant believes that its amendments are adequate to cure all deficiencies it may make application, in which the managing underwriters and any selling stockholders must join, for acceleration of the effective date, specifying the date upon which they desire the statement to become effective. If no further deficiencies are found by the Division of Corporation Finance, the application is usually granted by the Commission and an order is entered making the statement effective on the date requested, at an hour designated in the order.

Posteffective amendments are generally filed to correct deficiencies that existed in the registration statement at the effective date but were not discovered until afterward. Theoretically, a posteffective amendment is not filed in order to correct a statement that reflected the truth on the effective date but is no longer true. In practice, however, the Commission sometimes permits the filing of a posteffective amendment to the registration statement to cover matters arising after the effective date. Under the Act, the truth of a statement is tested as of the effective date. If the statement was deficient at the effective date, the registrant is under an obligation to correct the deficiency regardless of when the deficiency is discovered. But if the statement was not deficient at the effective date, no subsequent change in circumstances will make it compulsory for the registrant to file a posteffective amendment. On the other hand, a subsequent change in circumstances that renders the information no longer true in a material respect does require an amendment or supplement to the prospectus. The offering of a security cannot be continued on the basis of a prospectus that contains representations that are no longer true in a material respect.

The Act, in § 10(a)3, requires that a prospectus that is used after 9 months may not contain information that is more than 16 months old. Thus, issues extending beyond 9 months, such as offerings of mutual funds, which are continuous, must periodically file posteffective amendments to bring their financial statements up to date.

An important use of posteffective amendments concerns the **offering of securities not offered at the time the Registration Statement became effective,** which are included within the scope of the Registration Statement. Most significant in this respect are warrants and options issued to underwriters as additional compensation, which are frequently resold by the underwriter shortly after the completion of the public distribution. If the options or warrants were included in the Registration Statement they may be **re-offered** by means of a prospectus included in a posteffective amendment, which prospectus changes only the description of the person who is selling the securities, in this instance the underwriter, as a selling shareholder. If this resale is made shortly after completion of the distribution, the prospectus is sometimes changed only by attaching a sticker to the original prospectus.

Since posteffective amendments do not become effective until the Commission declares them effective, it is usually advisable that no sales be confirmed until the Commission so declares, or if the offering has begun, that it be stopped immediately. The purpose of the posteffective amendment being to correct a deficiency that existed at the effective date, any sales made before the Commission's order is entered may lead to stop orders and civil suits.

Withdrawal of Statement. Any registration statement, amendment, or exhibit may be withdrawn upon application if the Commission, upon finding such withdrawal consistent with the public interest and the protection of investors, consents thereto. The **application for withdrawal** must state fully the grounds upon which it is made. The fee paid upon the filing of the registration statement will not be returned. The registration statement or amendment is not removed from the Commission's files but is marked "Withdrawn upon the request of the registrant, the Commission consenting thereto," with the date of such consent. (Rule 477.) If securities have been offered or sold to the general public through a prospectus that was materially deficient, the Commission usually takes the position that it will not permit withdrawal but will enter a stop order, since the latter course gives the widest possible publicity to the deficiencies.

PREPARATION OF THE PROSPECTUS. Because the prospectus is the part of the registration statement that is most generally furnished to investors, the Commission has repeatedly urged the use of a concise and readable document. It has also implemented this policy in its acceleration rule (Rule 460), which provides that the Commission will consider in passing upon requests for acceleration, whether there has been a bona fide effort to make the prospectus reasonably concise and readable. The registration forms specify material that may be omitted from or condensed in the prospectus, and the Commission has published opinions specifically illustrating what it regards as excessively detailed prospectuses. The prospectus is meant to be an epitome or summary, and obviously should not be as discursive as the longer registration statement.

The Act specifically states that no provision imposing any liability shall apply to any acts done or omitted in **good faith** in conformity with any rule or regulation of the Commission. Consequently, the condensation and simplification of the prospectus in good faith, in accordance with the Commission's rules, should prevent any civil liabilities from arising.

The privilege of condensation and simplification does not extend to **financial statements.** Such financial statements as are set forth in the prospectus must conform with the corresponding financial statements, including footnotes, in the registration statement. The supporting schedules may be omitted from the prospectus, with a few exceptions specified in the Commission's rules and instructions.

The **accountants certifying** the financial statements in the registration statement and prospectus must be independent in the fullest sense of the word. The Commission has frequently held that an accountant lacks independence if he has any relationships with the registrant or its management that create a reasonable doubt whether he can exercise an impartial and objective judgment on questions confronting him.

In the event that the registrant or any of the underwriters knows or has reasonable grounds to believe that it is intended to stabilize the price of any security to facilitate the offering of the registered security, the first or second page of the prospectus must set forth in bold type a legend to that effect.

Age of Information. When a prospectus is used more than 9 months after the effective date, the information must be as of a date not more than 16 months prior to such use, so far as such information is known to the user of the prospectus or can be furnished by such user without unreasonable effort or expense.

EXEMPTED SECURITIES. The Act provides for two general types of exemptions—exemption of certain types of securities from all except the fraud provisions, and exemption of certain types of transactions from the registration and prospectus requirements.

Types of securities exempted from all the provisions of the Act, **except the fraud provisions,** include:

> Securities issued or guaranteed by the United States or any State or Territory thereof or any political subdivision of a State or Territory or any public instrumentality of one or more States or Territories or any National or State bank.

Commercial paper arising out of current transactions and having a maturity at the time of issuance of not more than nine months.
Securities issued by certain nonprofit organizations.
Securities issued by building and loan associations and similar institutions provided that the issuer does not take more than 3% of the face value of the security as a withdrawal fee.
Securities issued by common carriers which are subject to the Interstate Commerce Act.
Certificates issued by a receiver or by a trustee in bankruptcy with court approval.
Insurance policies and annuity contracts.
Securities issued in reorganizations approved by a court or governmental authority.
Securities exchanged by the issuer with its existing security holders exclusively where no commission or other remuneration is paid or given directly or indirectly for soliciting the exchange.
Securities which are part of an issue sold only to residents of the State in which the issuer is incorporated and is doing business.

Though the last three types of securities listed are exempt, it is the **particular transaction** of which they are a part that exempts them rather than the nature of the securities themselves. Thus, it is possible that upon a subsequent reoffering of these securities, other than under one of the specified sets of circumstances, the securities will not be exempt. (They are listed here rather than under Exempted Transactions below because this is the manner in which they are listed in the Act.) The other securities listed are by their very nature exempt and remain exempt regardless of the circumstances under which they are offered.

In addition, the Commission is authorized by the Act to exempt securities if the aggregate amount at which the issue is offered to the public does not exceed $300,000. These **exemptions for small offerings** are not unconditional but are available only if regulations prescribed by the Commission are complied with.

Regulation A. The Commission has adopted several regulations pursuant to this authorization, the most important being Regulation A. This regulation provides a general exemption from the registration requirements for certain classes of domestic and Canadian securities whose aggregate offering price to the public during a 12-month period does not exceed $300,000. In the case of a controlling person of the issuer, the aggregate offering price over the 12-month period is limited to $100,000, except that the full amount of $300,000 may be offered on behalf of the estate of a controlling person within 2 years after his death. The aggregate of all offerings made by the issuer and its controlling persons may not exceed $300,000 during any 12-month period. In every case the conditions of the exemption must be strictly observed. Pursuant to an amendment of the Act passed in 1958, the Commission has also adopted **Regulation E**, which affords a conditional exemption from registration for securities of **small business investment companies** licensed under the Small Business Investment Act of 1958 or approved for licensing by the Small Business Administration. The amount of such securities exempted is limited as in Regulation A.

EXEMPTED TRANSACTIONS. The provisions of the Act exempting certain types of transactions from the registration and prospectus requirements broadly draw the line between the distribution of securities and trading in securities, indicating that the Act is, in the main, concerned with the problem of **distribution** as distinguished from **trading**.

Transactions by Persons Other Than Issuers, Underwriters, and Dealers. An exemption is provided for transactions by any person other than an issuer, underwriter, or dealer. The holder of securities who is not an issuer, underwriter, or dealer is free to make a public offering of his holdings without regard to the registration or prospectus provisions. It should be remembered, however, that the term "issuer" includes a controlling person of the corporation for the purpose of defining an underwriter. If a controlling person desires to liquidate his holdings through an underwriter, neither can rely upon this exemption. Even if a controlling person desires to distribute directly to the public without using an underwriter, the exemption is not available if he acquired the securities from the issuer with a view to distribution, for in that event he would himself be an underwriter.

Private Offerings. A further exemption is afforded to transactions by an issuer not involving any public offering. Whether a particular transaction involves a public offering depends not on any single factor but on all the surrounding circumstances. Among the factors to be considered in determining whether a public or a private offering is involved are:

1. The number of offerees and their relationship to each other and to the issuer.
2. The number of units offered.
3. The size of the offering.
4. The manner of offering.

1. The **number of offerees** does not mean the number of actual purchasers, but rather the number of persons to whom the security is offered for sale. Any attempt to dispose of a security is regarded as an offer. Even preliminary negotiations or conversations with a substantial number of prospective purchasers may cause the offering to be a public offering, although the number of actual purchasers is relatively few.

In the view of the courts, as well as the Commission, the number of buyers is of little significance. With respect to the number of offerees, the Commission's rule of thumb has been that an offering to not more than approximately 25 persons would not involve a public offering under ordinary circumstances. This, of course, assumes that the securities are to be purchased for investment and not with a view to distribution.

Again, the **relationship of the offerees** to each other and to the issuer must be considered. An offering to a given number of persons chosen from the general public may be a public offering, whereas an offering to a larger number of persons having special knowledge of the issuer may be a private offering. For instance, when the offering is limited to institutional investors, they are more likely to have special knowledge of the issuer than the general public. Other groups that may fall within the category of persons having special knowledge of the issuer include its key executives, substantial stockholders, underwriters, bankers, and promoters.

The fact that an offering is limited to the issuer's employees, however, does not assure the availability of the exemption. In S.E.C. v. Ralston Purina Co., 346 U.S. 119 (1953), the Supreme Court said (p. 125): "The exemption, as we construe it, does not deprive corporate employees, as a class, of the safeguards of the Act. We agree that some employee offerings may come within §4(1), e.g., one made to executive personnel who because of their position have access to the same kind of information that the Act would make available in the form of a registration statement. Absent such a showing of special circumstances, employees are just as much members of the investing 'public' as any of their neighbors in the community." The Court held that the applicability of the private offering exemption should turn on whether the particular class of persons affected need the protection of the Act; and that an offering to those who are shown to be able to fend for themselves is a transaction not involving any public offering.

2. The second factor to be considered in determining whether a public offering is involved is the **number of units** offered. If the denominations of the units are

such that only a small number of units are offered, presumably no public offering would be involved. But if many units are offered in small denominations, there is some indication that the issuer recognizes the possibility, if not the probability, of a general public distribution.

3. The third factor is the **size of the offering.** The exemption was intended to be applied chiefly to small offerings. The sale of a small issue is less likely to involve a public offering than the sale of an issue of substantial size.

4. The fourth factor is the **manner of offering.** Transactions effected by direct negotiation between the issuer and the prospective purchasers are much more likely to be nonpublic than those effected through the use of the machinery of public distribution. An offering on the floor of a stock exchange is a public offering, as is any offering addressed to the public generally.

Transactions by Dealers. An exemption from the registration and prospectus requirements, not available to issuers or underwriters, is applicable to dealers' transactions with certain exceptions. The transactions of a dealer that are **not exempt** are as follows:

(a) Transactions in a registered security taking place within 40 days after the effective date of the registration statement or within 40 days after the first date upon which the security was bona fide offered to the public by the issuer or an underwriter after such effective date, whichever is later (the period may be 90 days in some instances if securities are offered to the public for the first time);

(b) Transactions in an unregistered security taking place within 40 days after the first date upon which the security was bona fide offered to the public by the issuer or an underwriter; and

(c) Transactions as to securities constituting the whole or a part of an unsold allotment to or subscription by the dealer as a participant in the distribution of such securities by the issuer or an underwriter.

In the computation of the 40- or **90-day** periods any time during which a stop order is in effect is excluded.

The effect of these exceptions is to require **all dealers,** whether or not they participated in the distribution of a registered security as members of the selling group, to **deliver the statutory prospectus** in connection with all their sales during the periods indicated. A dealer who was not a member of the selling group is relieved of the obligation to deliver a prospectus after the lapse of 40 days from the effective date of the registration statement or 40 days from the commencement of the offering, whichever is later. A dealer who was a member of the selling group must continue to deliver a prospectus for as long after the expiration of the 40-day period as any part of his allotments or subscriptions remain unsold. An underwriter who is no longer acting as such in the distribution is entitled to the same exemption as a dealer. In the case of a distribution of a security that has not been registered and hence may subject the issuer and underwriter to penalties, dealers may lawfully begin to trade after the lapse of 40 days from the first date upon which the security was bona fide offered to the public by the issuer or underwriter.

Brokers' Transactions. The last category of transactions for which an exemption is provided consists of brokers' transactions executed upon customers' orders, but not the solicitation of such orders. The term "brokers' transactions" has been strictly limited to transactions in which no more than the ordinary brokerage function is performed and no more than the ordinary commission is paid. Thus, if the broker forms a selling group to distribute the security, advertises the security for sale, prepares a selling circular, or does any of the other things that are normally associated with the underwriting function, he loses the benefit of the exemption. Moreover, this exemption applies only if the order is unsolicited. Any direct or indirect solicitation of the order prevents the exemption from becoming applicable. The exemption does not apply to the customer's part of the transaction; it protects only the broker who receives an unsolicited commission order.

A rule of the Commission (Rule 154) defines the extent to which a broker may effect **sales for a controlling person**, without forfeiting the exemption for brokers' transactions. Under this rule, a broker may act as agent for a controlling person if the following conditions are met: (1) the broker performs no more than the usual and customary broker's functions; (2) the broker does no more than execute an order or orders to sell as a broker and receives no more than the usual or customary broker's commission, and, to his knowledge, his principal makes no payment in connection with the execution of such transactions to any other person; (3) neither the broker, nor to his knowledge, his principal, solicits or arranges for the solicitation of orders to buy in anticipation of or in connection with the transactions; and (4) the broker is not aware of circumstances indicating that his principal is an underwriter in respect of the securities or that the transactions are part of a distribution of securities on behalf of the principal.

Under the rule, the term **"distribution"** does not apply to transactions involving an amount not substantial in relation to the number of shares or units outstanding and the aggregate volume of trading in the security. As a guide for distinguishing trading from distributing transactions, the rule states in effect that there is not deemed to be a distribution if the transaction in question and all other sales of the same class of securities by or on behalf of the same principal within the preceding 6 months do not exceed the following: (1) in the case of an over-the-counter security, approximately 1% of the total shares or units outstanding or (2) in the case of a listed security, the lesser of that amount or the largest aggregate reported volume of exchange trading during any 1 week within the preceding 4 weeks.

SANCTIONS. There are four main types of sanctions that supply the Act with teeth. These are the provisions for stop orders, injunctions, criminal penalties, and civil liabilities.

Stop Orders. Whenever it appears to the Commission that the registration statement includes any untrue statement of a material fact or any misleading omission of a material fact, the Commission may, after an opportunity for hearing, enter a stop order suspending its effectiveness. The purpose of a stop order is to prevent the use of the mails and the channels of interstate commerce in the distribution of a security on the basis of false, untrue, or misleading information; and also to warn the investing public of the false or misleading character of the representations on the basis of which the security is or has been offered for sale. Jurisdiction to issue a stop order arises only if deficiencies relate to material facts. A **material fact** is one concerning which an average prudent investor ought reasonably to be informed before purchasing the security. In a stop-order proceeding, only the truth or falsity of a statement and its materiality alone are in issue, regardless of the good faith of the parties, except when information is called for only if known. Willfulness is not essential to the issuance of a stop order.

Injunctions and Criminal Proceedings. Whenever it appears to the Commission that any person is engaged or about to engage in a **violation of the Act**, or of any rule of the Commission thereunder, it may apply to the Federal courts for an injunction against such violation. In addition, the Commission may transmit the evidence of any violation to the Attorney General, who is authorized, in his discretion, to institute criminal proceedings against the violators. Any person who willfully violates the Act or the rules of the Commission, or who willfully makes any untrue statement or omission in a registration statement is guilty of a crime and may, upon conviction, be fined not more than $5,000 or imprisoned not more than 5 years, or both.

Civil Liabilities. False or misleading statements or omissions as to material facts in the registration statement give rise to civil liabilities under the Act. Any purchaser of the security, who, at the time of his purchase, was unaware of the untruth or omission, has the right to sue any of the following persons:

Every signer of the registration statement;
Every director who was serving as such when the registration statement was filed or who was named in the registration statement as about to become a director with his consent;
Every accountant, engineer, appraiser, or other expert who has consented to be named as having prepared or certified any part of the registration statement or any report or valuation used in connection with the statement; and
Every underwriter.

Any person so sued, except the issuer, may exonerate himself from liability by proving the following:

That before the effective date he resigned from the position described in the registration statement and advised the Commission and the issuer that he had taken such action; or
That he advised the Commission that the registration statement had become effective without his knowledge and also gave reasonable public notice to that effect; or
That as regards any part of the registration statement not purporting to be made on the authority of an expert, he made reasonable investigation and had reasonable grounds to believe, when the statement became effective, that such part was truthful and not misleading; or
That as an expert, he believed that the part of the registration statement prepared or certified by him was truthful and not misleading at the effective date, or that the registration statement did not fairly represent his statement as an expert.

The damages in such a suit may not exceed the price at which the security was offered to the public.

Finally, civil liabilities may arise in connection with prospectuses and other communications. Any person becomes liable in a civil suit if, through the mails or in interstate commerce, he sells or offers to sell an unregistered nonexempted security, or uses a defective prospectus relating to a registered security, or fails to deliver a prospectus prior to the sale of a registered security, or sells any security, registered or unregistered, exempt or not exempt, except government securities and bank stocks, by a false or misleading prospectus or oral communication. Any such person is liable to the purchaser for the full amount of the purchase price of the security or, if the purchaser no longer owns the security, for damages.

Blue Sky Laws

HISTORICAL BACKGROUND. The term "blue sky laws" is popularly applied to state statutes regulating the offering and sale of securities within the jurisdiction of the respective states. "The name that is given to the law," said Justice McKenna in Hall v. Geiger-Jones Co., 242 U.S. 539, 550 (1917), "indicates the evil at which it is aimed; that is, to use the language of a cited case, 'speculative schemes which have no more basis than so many feet of blue sky.'" Prior to 1911, no American state had adopted a general law on the subject, although railroad and public utility issues were regulated in some cases. The first blue sky law was enacted in Kansas in 1911. It required issuers—designated as "investment companies"—to file a full description of their business, and prohibited their selling securities in the state until and unless authorized by the bank commissioner. During the first year of its operation approximately 1,500 applications for permits were filed, of which about 75% were rejected as fraudulent and about 11% as too speculative. In rapid succession, 18 other states adopted similar statutes. Steps were taken to test the constitutionality of the laws in some states. Courts in Michigan, Iowa, and West Virginia declared their respective blue sky laws unconstitutional, largely because the statutes were impractical or crudely drafted. In 1917, however, the United States Supreme Court in a series of decisions held the blue sky laws of Ohio, South Dakota, and Michigan constitutional as a proper exercise of the police powers of the states.

Today, some type of blue sky law is in force in 48 of the 50 states. The exceptions are Nevada, which requires only the licensing of investment companies registered under the Federal Investment Company Act of 1940 and the licensing of persons selling securities of such companies; and Delaware, which eliminated an antifraud provision from its Code in 1953. The District of Columbia has no local blue sky law, securities transactions in the District being governed by the Federal statutes.

Although the United States Supreme Court sustained the constitutionality of blue sky laws enacted by the several states, there were **limits** upon the ability of a state to regulate the sale of securities within its borders from a point outside the state through use of the mails or instrumentalities of interstate commerce. As a consequence, fraudulent promoters during the 1920's resorted to the device of establishing a base in one state from which telephone and telegraph communications and letters were transmitted to prospective victims residing in other states. The inability of state enforcement agencies to cope with fraudulent interstate transactions was a major factor leading to adoption of the Federal statutes—the Securities Act of 1933 and the Securities Exchange Act of 1934.

The **Federal statutes** were not designed to interfere, in any way, with the operations of state blue sky laws. Each state has police power that it may exercise for the protection of its people and that, but only incidentally and indirectly, may impose burdens on interstate commerce. The Federal government, within the scope of its authority, has police power over interstate commerce, which may, but only incidentally and indirectly, impose burdens on state commerce. The Securities Act of 1933 specifically provides that nothing in the Act shall affect the jurisdiction of the securities commission of any state over any security or any person. The Securities Exchange Act of 1934 provides that nothing in the Act shall affect the jurisdiction of any state securities commission over any security or any person insofar as it does not conflict with the provisions of the Act or the rules and regulations thereunder.

TYPES OF BLUE SKY LAWS. The 48 blue sky laws in effect at the present time may be classified with respect to registration or licensing requirements as follows:

1. Forty-seven states require some form of registration or licensing of **broker-dealers and salesmen,** the exception being Wyoming, which requires registration of securities but not broker-dealers or salesmen other than agents of an issuer.

2. Forty-seven states require some form of registration of **nonexempt securities** or the filing of information by broker-dealers concerning securities they sell or propose to sell, the exception being New Jersey, which requires registration of broker-dealers and salesmen but not securities. The Connecticut statute requires registration of mining issues only. The New York statute is more exacting in respect of real estate syndicate issues than other types.

3. Twenty-five states require some form of registration or licensing of **investment advisers**.

In former years a few state statutes merely authorized a state agency to investigate fraud or suspected fraud in the sale of securities and to enjoin or prosecute the wrongdoers. Statutes of such limited scope are no longer found in any state, and the modern trend is to combine **antifraud** provisions with other regulatory devices. At the present time 40 blue sky laws contain assorted provisions designed to prevent, expose, and penalize fraud.

COMMON PROVISIONS AND THE UNIFORM SECURITIES ACT.
Substantial progress has been made since 1956 in promoting uniformity among state securities laws. The Uniform Securities Act, as approved by the National Conference of Commissioners on Uniform State Laws in August 1956, has served as a model for the streamlining of the state statutes. The Act is in four parts: Part I outlaws fraudulent practices in connection with the sale or purchase of securities and in connection with the furnishing of investment advice, and restricts certain other undesirable investment advisory activities; Part II provides for the registration of broker-dealers, agents, and investment advisers; Part III provides for the registration of securities; and Part IV contains provisions implementing the first three parts and prescribing sanctions against violations of the Act. The Uniform Act, with modifications necessitated by diverse regulatory philosophies, has been adopted in whole or in part by about a third of the states down to the present time; and there is strong sentiment for its adoption in other states.

Nevertheless, the **state statutes still vary widely** in their procedures, substantive standards, and exemptions, and they must be individually scrutinized and complied with before a public offering of securities may be made within their respective jurisdictions. Some provisions found in a growing number of blue sky laws are described below.

Antifraud Provisions. The streamlined antifraud provision patterned after the Uniform Securities Act makes it unlawful for any person, in connection with the offer, sale, or purchase of any security: (1) to employ any device, scheme, or artifice to defraud; (2) to make any untrue statement of a material fact or to omit to state a material fact necessary in order to make the statements made, in the light of the circumstances under which they are made, not misleading; or (3) to engage in any act, practice, or course of business that operates or would operate as a fraud or deceit upon any person.

Although, as noted above, antifraud provisions are included in modern blue sky laws along with other regulatory devices, such provisions operate independently of the registration or licensing systems. They apply to **all persons**, whether or not required to be registered or licensed, and to **all securities and transactions**, whether or not exempted from other sections of the law.

Investment Advisory Activities. Further provisions in the Uniform Act are specifically addressed to investment advisory activities. Investment advisers are prohibited from employing any device, scheme, or artifice to defraud clients or from engaging in any act, practice, or course of business that operates or would operate as a fraud or deceit upon clients. In addition, investment advisory contracts must contain certain clauses, including a prohibition against basing the investment adviser's compensation upon capital gains or capital appreciation; and the investment adviser may have custody of clients' securities or funds only if the rules of the regulatory agency do not prohibit custody and, in the absence of such prohibition, the regulatory agency must be notified that the investment adviser may have custody.

Investigations. The administrator under the Uniform Act is generally authorized to make investigations to determine whether any person has violated or is about to violate the statute or regulations thereunder; to obtain statements as to all facts concerning the subject matter of the investigation; to subpoena witnesses, compel their attendance, take evidence, and require the production of all records deemed relevant or material to the inquiry; and to publish information concerning any violation. No person is excused from testifying in any such proceeding on the ground of self-incrimination, but no individual may be prosecuted for any transaction concerning which he is compelled to testify after claiming his privilege against self-incrimination, except that he is not exempt from prosecution for perjury or contempt committed in testifying.

The **sanctions** for violations of the antifraud provisions include criminal prosecution for a willful violation; injunction; and administrative proceedings to deny, suspend, or revoke registration if the violator is a broker-dealer, an agent of a broker-dealer or issuer, or an investment adviser. Provision is also usually made for civil liability in cases of sales induced by fraud or misrepresentation.

Registration of Broker-Dealers, Agents, and Investment Advisers. The 47 blue sky laws requiring registration or licensing of broker-dealers and salesmen are diversified in their standards for granting or denying the privilege of engaging in the securities business. A measure of uniformity is found only in those states that have adopted the standards of the Uniform Securities Act.

If the state statute follows the pattern of the Uniform Act, it prohibits any person from transacting business in the state as a broker-dealer or agent unless he is registered. A broker-dealer or issuer may not employ an agent to effect nonexempt transactions or transactions in nonexempt securities unless the agent is registered; and the agent's registration is effective only while he is associated with a registered broker-dealer or a particular issuer. No person may transact business as an investment adviser unless he is registered as such, or unless he is registered as a broker-dealer without the imposition of a condition precluding his acting as an investment adviser, or unless his only clients are investment or insurance companies.

Under the Uniform Act a broker-dealer, agent, or investment adviser may obtain registration by filing with the administrator an **application,** together with an irrevocable consent to the service of process upon a designated state official in any non-criminal suit or proceeding brought against the applicant under the state statute. The application must contain information prescribed by rule of the administrator concerning such matters as the applicant's form and place of organization; his proposed method of doing business; the qualifications and business history of the applicant and, in the instance of a broker-dealer or investment adviser, of any partner, officer, director, or controlling person, and, in the instance of an investment adviser, of any employee; any injunction or administrative order or conviction of a misdemeanor involving any aspect of the securities business and any conviction of a felony; and the applicant's financial condition and history. If no proceeding is brought to deny registration, it normally becomes effective on the thirtieth day after the application is filed.

In nearly all blue sky states **registration must be renewed annually.** The present exceptions are Idaho, where the initial registration is permanent for broker-dealers, although the registration of agents must be renewed annually; New Jersey, where registration expires every 2 years for broker-dealers, agents, and investment advisers; and New York, where registration expires every 4 years for broker-dealers and agents, although the registration of investment advisers must be renewed annually.

At present the **fees** for initial registration range generally from $25 to $250 for broker-dealers, from $2 to $25 for agents, and from $25 to $150 for investment advisers. The renewal fee is the same as the initial fee in most states but somewhat less in a few states.

In a growing number of states investor protection is implemented by provisions requiring broker-dealers, agents, and investment advisers to post **surety bonds** in amounts fixed by statute or by the administrator. There is also a strong trend in favor of empowering the administrator to require broker-dealers and investment advisers to maintain a minimum capital and, in the case of broker-dealers, to limit their aggregate indebtedness to not more than 2,000% of their net capital. Most states require registered broker-dealers and investment advisers to file **periodic reports** of their financial condition; and to keep, preserve, and make available for inspection such books and records as are prescribed by the administrator.

The administrator is generally vested with authority by order to deny, revoke, **suspend, or cancel registration** for proper cause after reasonable notice and opportunity for hearing. Under the Uniform Act such an order may be entered if the administrator finds that it is in the public interest and that the applicant or registrant or, in the case of a broker-dealer or investment adviser, any partner, officer, director, or controlling person, has violated any of 12 standards enumerated in the Act. One ground for denial or revocation heretofore existing in some states but not generally enforced has been revitalized by the Uniform Act, namely, a broker-dealer's or investment adviser's **lack of qualification** on the basis of training, experience, and knowledge of the securities business. In a number of states the administrator is authorized by rule to provide for written and oral examinations to be taken by any or all applicants for registration.

Registration of Securities. Each of the 47 blue sky laws that now require some form of registration of securities must be separately examined to determine whether the particular offering is exempted from the registration requirements. If no exemption is available, a variety of documents must be filed with the several administrators in order to qualify the offering in their respective states. In a few instances some type of filing may be necessary even if a particular exemption is available.

Under several statutes the burden is upon the broker-dealer to supply the administrator with information regarding the securities he is selling or proposes to sell. In the great majority of states, however, the statutes contemplate that the issuer or selling security holder will qualify the offering by filing the prescribed information.

The Uniform Securities Act has established guidelines for unifying the heterogeneous registration systems and for coordinating them with the Federal system.

As more and more states follow these guidelines in modernizing their blue sky laws, the countless problems involved in registering and synchronizing an offering for nationwide distribution under the state and Federal statutes will be ameliorated and unnecessary impediments to the flow of capital into industry will be eliminated, with no sacrifice of protection to investors.

Under the Uniform Act it is unlawful for any person to offer or sell any security unless it is registered or the security or transaction is exempted. The Act provides for **three types of registration**: by notification, by coordination, and by qualification.

In all three types of registration under the Uniform Act, the registrant is required to file a consent to the service of process upon the designated state official; to pay the prescribed registration fee; and, in addition to the information described below, to specify the amount of securities to be offered in the state, name the other states in which a registration statement or similar document in connection with the same offering has been or is to be filed, and disclose any adverse order, judgment, or decree entered in connection with the offering by the regulatory authorities in any state or by any court or by the S.E.C.

Registration by notification under the Uniform Act is available only to certain classes of securities. These include: (1) any security whose issuer (including predecessors) has been in continuous operation for at least 5 years if there has been no default during the past 3 years in the payments due on any senior security and the issuer during the 3-year period has had average earnings of 5% on the value of its outstanding common stock; and (2) any security (other than a certificate of interest or participation in an oil, gas, or mining title or lease or in payments out of production under such a title or lease) registered for the benefit of a person other than the issuer if a security of the same class has ever been registered or the security being registered was originally issued pursuant to an exemption under the Act.

The procedure for obtaining registration by notification requires the filing of the following information: a statement demonstrating eligibility for registration by notification; with respect to the issuer and each significant subsidiary, its name, address, and form of organization, the state and date of its organization, and the general character and location of its business; with respect to any person on whose behalf any part of the offering is to be made in a nonissuer distribution, his name and address, the amount of securities of the issuer held by him, and a statement of his reasons for making the offering; a description of the security being registered; information regarding the proposed offering price, underwriting arrangements, and expenses of the offering; a description of any outstanding options; and copies of all sales literature to be used in the offering.

Registration by notification automatically becomes effective, in the absence of any stop order proceeding, on the second full business day after the filing of the registration statement or the last amendment. The administrator has power to accelerate the effective date in emergency situations. For the most part it is expected that this type of registration will be useful for distributions that qualify for exemption under the Federal Securities Act of 1933 as intrastate offerings, private offerings, or interstate offerings of $300,000 or less.

Registration by coordination under the Uniform Act is available to any security for which a registration statement has been filed under the Federal Securities Act of 1933 in connection with the same offering. This type of registration requires the filing of the following information: three copies of the latest form of prospectus filed under the Securities Act of 1933; if the administrator requires, a copy of the issuer's articles of incorporation and by-laws, a copy of any agreements with or among underwriters, a copy of any indenture or other instrument governing issuance of the security to be registered, and a specimen or copy of the security; if the administrator requests, any other information or documents filed under the Securities Act of 1933; and an undertaking to forward all future substantive amendments to the Federal registration statement promptly after they are filed with the S.E.C.

Registration by coordination automatically becomes effective at the moment the Federal registration statement becomes effective if (i) no stop order proceeding is pending, (ii) the registration statement has been on file with the administrator for at least 10 days, and (iii) a statement of maximum and minimum offering prices and maximum underwriting discounts and commissions has been on file for two full business days (or such shorter period as the administrator permits) and the offering is made within those limits. The registrant is further required promptly to notify the administrator of the date and time when the Federal registration statement became effective and the content of the price amendment (which includes the offering price, underwriting and selling discounts or commissions, amount of proceeds, and other matters dependent upon the offering price), and to file a posteffective amendment containing such information. If the Federal registration statement becomes effective before all the foregoing conditions are satisfied and they are not waived by the administrator, the state registration statement automatically becomes effective as soon as all the conditions are satisfied. These provisions are designed to achieve simultaneous effectiveness at the Federal and state levels, without impinging upon the administrator's duty to test the registration statement under the substantive standards of his own state.

Registration by qualification under the Uniform Act is available to any security, whether or not one or both of the other types of registration are available. Presumably, however, it will be used only by the residual cases—the promotional issue that is offered in a single state; the local offering by a company that, though beyond the promotional stage, is not eligible for registration by notification; and interstate offerings of $300,000 or less. The information required is far more detailed and extensive for registration by qualification than for either of the other types. On the whole it is similar in scope to the information called for by the S.E.C.'s Form S-1, the basic registration form under the Federal Securities Act of 1933.

Unlike the other types of registration, registration by qualification does not become effective automatically but becomes effective only when the administrator so orders. The administrator may require, as a condition of such registration, that a prospectus containing any part of the information filed be sent or given to each person to whom an offer is made.

The **fees for registration** of securities vary widely. Some statutes that permit more than one type of registration fix different fees for each type. Some require examination fees in addition. Under most blue sky laws registration fees depend mainly upon the amount of securities to be offered in the state. The Uniform Act contemplates a filing fee equivalent to a fractional percentage of the maximum aggregate price at which the registered securities are to be offered in the state, with provision for minimum and maximum amounts. If the Uniform Act has been followed, the fees generally range from $\frac{1}{20}$ to $\frac{1}{10}$ of 1% of the aggregate offering price, with minimums ranging from $20 to $500 and maximums from $100 to $1,000.

The Uniform Act embodies provisions previously in force in many states that authorize the administrator to require, as a condition of registration by qualification or coordination, that any security issued within 3 years or to be issued to a promoter for a consideration different from the public offering price or to any person for a consideration other than cash, be **deposited in escrow**; and that the proceeds from the sale of the registered security be impounded until the issuer receives a specified amount. The administrator is empowered to determine the conditions of any such escrow or impounding.

A registration statement under the Uniform Act is **effective for at least 1 year** and for any longer period during which the security is being distributed. As long as it remains effective, no matter who has filed it, all outstanding securities of the same class are considered to be registered and can legally be traded by anyone. While the statement continues in effect, the administrator may require the registrant to file quarterly reports to keep current the information contained in the statement and to disclose the progress of the offering.

The **administrator may issue an order** summarily postponing or suspending the effectiveness of any registration statement and may issue a stop order denying or revoking registration after notice and opportunity for hearing, if he finds that the order is in the public interest and that any of the specified grounds for such order exist. The grounds include, among others, failure to make full and accurate disclosure in the registration statement; violation of the statute by the person filing the registration statement, by the issuer or any of its partners, officers, directors, or controlling persons, or by an underwriter; entry of a stop order or injunction in any other jurisdiction; a finding that the offering tends to work a fraud on purchasers; and a finding that the offering involves unreasonable underwriters' and sellers' discounts, commissions, or other compensation, unreasonable promoters' profits, or unreasonable amounts or kinds of options.

In many states, **selling costs** are limited to a fixed percentage of the offering price or the administrator is authorized to fix a maximum percentage. The statutory percentages range from 10% to 25%, but in practice the commissions or discounts permitted by the administrators are lower, varying with the type of security involved.

Every statute requiring registration of securities contains language disclaiming governmental approval or recommendation of the securities. Any representation to the contrary is generally declared to be fraud or a criminal offense.

Prior to the drafting of the Uniform Act, the **North American Securities Administrators** (formerly known as The National Association of Securities Commissioners), an organization of officials administering securities laws in the United States and Canada, had made constructive contributions to the unification of policies under blue sky laws. Among these were the drafting of a uniform application form for qualification of certain securities; a statement of policy to the effect that warrants and stock purchase options other than to the purchasers of securities would be looked upon with great disfavor and would be considered as a basis for denial of registration except where the applicant could justify their issuance; and a similar statement of policy with respect to sales to underwriters or promoters at prices below the public offering price.

EXEMPTIONS UNDER BLUE SKY LAWS. Most blue sky laws, including the Uniform Securities Act, exempt certain types of securities and transactions from the statutory requirements for registration but not from the anti-fraud provisions. Such exemptions are generally provided where, by reason of the nature of the security or the type of transaction, registration is not necessary or appropriate for the protection of investors.

The securities most frequently exempted from registration by the various blue sky laws may be classified as follows:

Securities issued or guaranteed by
- The United States, any state or political subdivision, or any Federal or state agency;
- Any foreign government with which the United States maintains diplomatic relations;
- Banks, savings institutions, or trust companies;
- Savings and loan or building and loan associations authorized to do business in the particular state;
- Insurance companies authorized to do business in the particular state;
- Federal credit unions or credit unions and industrial loan associations organized and supervised under the laws of the particular state; and
- Railroads, other common carriers, public utilities, or carrier or utility holding companies subject to the jurisdiction of certain other governmental agencies.

Securities listed on the New York Stock Exchange, the American Stock Exchange, the Midwest Stock Exchange, and certain regional exchanges.

Securities issued by nonprofit organizations.

Commercial paper arising out of current transactions.

Securities issued by certain cooperative associations.

Securities listed in standard manuals.

Although all these exemptions are not found in the blue sky laws of every state, all except the exemption for securities listed in standard manuals are invariably found in the laws modeled on the Uniform Act. In order to determine whether a particular security is exempt from registration, it is necessary to consult the blue sky law of each state in which the security is to be offered.

Types of **transactions** most commonly exempted from the registration requirements are:

- Isolated transactions by a nonissuer, whether effected through a broker-dealer or not.
- Distribution by a nonissuer of an outstanding security which is either listed in a standard manual or which has a fixed maturity or a fixed interest or dividend rate and on which there has been no default within 3 years in the payment of principal, interest, or dividends.
- Transactions for the account of a nonissuer effected by or through a registered broker-dealer pursuant to the unsolicited order or offer to buy.
- Any transaction between the issuer or selling security holder and an underwriter, or among underwriters.
- Any transaction in a fund or other evidence of indebtedness secured by a mortgage if the entire mortgage is offered and sold as a unit.
- Any transaction by an executor, administrator, sheriff, marshal, receiver, trustee in bankruptcy, guardian, or conservator.
- Any transaction executed by a bona fide pledgee without any purpose of evading the statute.
- Any offers or sales to institutional buyers or to broker-dealers, whether the buyer is acting for itself or in some fiduciary capacity.
- Offerings or sales during a 12-month period to a limited number of persons who purchase for investment, the number varying among the states, but most frequently limited to 25, and some states imposing the condition that the transactions involve strictly limited selling commissions or none at all.

Offers or sales of pre-organization certificates or subscriptions if no commission is paid for soliciting subscriptions and the number of subscribers does not exceed ten.

Offers of additional stock to existing security holders of the issuer if no commission is paid for soliciting purchases.

Offers, but not sales, of a security for which registration statements have been filed under both the state act and the Securities Act of 1933 that have not yet become effective and are not the subject of any stop order proceeding.

The administrator is generally authorized to deny or revoke certain of the exemptions for securities and any of the exemptions for transactions after notice and opportunity for hearing, except that he may by order summarily deny or revoke any of such exemptions pending final determination of the proceedings. The **burden of proving an exemption** is upon the person claiming it.

SECTION 10

SECURITIES MARKETS

CONTENTS

Organization and Functions

	PAGE
Nature of securities markets	1
Classification of securities	1
Functions of securities markets	1
Auction vs. negotiated markets	1
Suitability of market for particular security	2
Organized securities exchanges	2
National stock exchanges	2
Over-the-counter markets	3
Marketability of securities	3
Closeness of a market	4
Breadth of the market	4
Continuity of the market	4
Market stability	4
Brokers and dealers	4
Distinction between roles	4

The New York Stock Exchange

Organization	5
Board of Governors	5
President	6
Membership	7
Securing a seat	7
Types of Exchange members	7
Listing securities on the Exchange	9
Disclosure requirements	9
Listing statements	9
Listing policy	10
Motives for listing	10
Delisting and withdrawal of registration	10
Unlisted trading on exchanges	11
Trading facilities	12
Methods of trading	12
The auction process	12
Publicity for quotations—ticker service	13
Sections of New York Stock Exchange stock ticker tape (f. 1)	13

Securities Trading on Exchanges

Securities transactions	13
Types of orders	14
Market orders	14
Limited orders	14
Stop-loss orders	15
Stopping stock	15
Execution of orders on the Exchange	15
Brokerage commissions on stocks	16
Transfer taxes and registration fees	17

	PAGE
Stocks selling ex-dividend or ex-rights	18
Trading in rights and stock purchase warrants	18
When-issued trading	19
Permissible transactions	19
Limitations imposed by Securities Exchange Act	20
Special procedures for large blocks	20
Short sales	22
Operation of a short sale	22
Loaning rates	23
Margins deposited against short sales	23
Economic effects of short selling	23
Corners and manipulation	24
Control of corners	24
Federal regulation of short selling	24
Odd-lot trading	25
Options or privileges	25
Purpose of privileges	27
Settlement of Exchange transactions	27
The clearing process	28
Steps in settlement	28
Clearance and settlement of the money values of security deliveries	28
What constitutes good delivery	28
Consequences of failure to deliver	29

Speculation in Securities

Differentiation of speculation from investment	29
Advantages and disadvantages of security speculation	29
Advantages	29
Disadvantages	30
Manipulation	30
Market indicators	30
The Dow, Jones averages	31
Other indices	31
Charting	31
The Dow theory of stock price movements	31
Stock market charts and tape readers	32
Security services and ratings	32

Trading on Margin

Margin purchase of securities	32
Opening a margin account	33
Customers' margin requirements	33
Regulation of security credit	33
Relations between broker and customer	34
Brokers' interest charges	34

CONTENTS (*Continued*)

The Brokerage House

	PAGE
Organization of a brokerage house	35
Registered representatives	35
Employment standards	35
Customers' statements	35
Typical form of customer's statement (*f.* 2)	36
Financing the brokerage business	37
Balance sheet of a brokerage house (*f.* 3)	37
Sources of funds for brokers	38
The hypothecation agreement	38
Other methods of obtaining brokerage funds	38
Restrictions on broker borrowing	38
Examination of member firms	39

Bond Trading on the Exchange

The bond room	39
Quotations	39
Sections of New York Stock Exchange bond ticker tape (*f.* 4)	40
What constitutes good delivery	40
Commissions and taxes on bond transactions	41

Over-the-Counter Markets

Functions and importance	41
Classes of securities traded	42

	PAGE
Method of trading—negotiation	42
An actual transaction	43
Clearing transactions	43
The unlisted bond market	44
Self-regulation and the National Association of Securities Dealers	44
Rules of fair practice	45
Other N.A.S.D. activities	45

Federal Regulation of Securities Trading

The Securities Exchange Act of 1934	46
Objectives	46
Chief provisions of the Act	46
Administration of the Exchange Act	47
Registration of securities	47
Regulation of trading—fair and orderly markets	51
Regulation of brokers and dealers	54

International Dealings in Securities

Investment in foreign securities	56
The interest equalization tax	56
International security trading	57
Distribution of blocks of foreign issues	57
American depositary receipts	57
Markets for foreign equities	58
Arbitrage in securities	58

SECTION 10

SECURITIES MARKETS

Organization and Functions

NATURE OF SECURITIES MARKETS. Securities are stocks, preferred and common, certificates of beneficial interest in trusts, and debt obligations or bonds. Securities markets are places where stocks and bonds of all types are bought and sold. Here the constantly changing forces of supply and demand, reflecting ever-shifting appraisals of the worth of securities and requirements of investors, set quotations for bond and stock issues.

Classification of Securities. The issuance and distribution of **new offerings** of securities is covered in Section 9 on Security Selling. The present section deals with trading in all types of **outstanding securities.** These may be classified according to issuer. **Governments** include in the main obligations of the United States. **Tax exempts** are the obligations of states and municipalities, and smaller political subdivisions such as school districts and highway and other "authorities," the interest on which is not subject to Federal income taxation. **Corporates** include stocks and bonds of industrial, financial, utility, and railroad enterprises.

Functions of Securities Markets. The primary function of a securities market is to provide a meeting place for buyers and sellers to effect transactions. More important than the mere mechanical facilities for trading is the creation of an effective market in which securities can be bought and sold promptly and in quantity. There must be substantial demand or buying power on one side, and on the other a considerable supply of securities before a market in which **prices are set in an orderly manner** may be said to exist. To fulfill this most important function, adequate information must be provided to enable participants to appraise values with reasonable accuracy, if they have the intelligence and skill to do so. Misleading practices of buyers and sellers, or other influences that prevent the unimpeded play of the forces of demand and supply, must be minimized.

The broad economic function of the securities market is to aid in the mobilization of savings so as to make them available to enterprises and governmental entities that require funds. Moreover, capital can be shifted readily from one long-term use into another when owners of securities can dispose of them readily and so obtain funds for other commitments.

AUCTION VS. NEGOTIATED MARKETS. The most widely publicized securities markets are the organized exchanges that do business on a **double auction basis.** Here prices are determined in a highly organized market that brings bids and offers together at one place. The balancing of bids against offers at ever-changing quotations produces a continuously moving equilibrium between demand and supply for a particular security.

A **securities exchange** is one of the few examples of a true auction market. Here there are auctions on both sides of the market—competing buyers and competing sellers. The auction method of operation, together with a highly organized publicity system, makes an active securities exchange one of the most sensitive and at the same time one of the most orderly markets of any. Through the stock and news tickers actual sales and information concerning issuing corporations and related matters are broadcast promptly all over the nation. This does much to promote a free and open market for securities listed on exchanges.

In contrast to this public market are the **over-the-counter** markets, where prices are determined by **negotiation** between individual customers and securities dealers or among securities dealers. Here there may be much or little **shopping around** for the best price, and there may be considerable haggling before a price is agreed upon. There is no central market place, and actual sales prices are unknown. **Bid and asked quotations** receive a limited amount of publicity.

Suitability of Market for Particular Security. Whether a security is more suitable for exchange or over-the-counter trading is determined by the volume available for trading, the number of potential sellers and buyers, and the information available about it. A security outstanding in small amount or closely held is generally not suited for active exchange trading. Sales then can be negotiated in the over-the-counter markets, where dealers "make markets" and seek out buyers and sellers. This may hold true also of quite large blocks of listed securities such as bonds, for which an adequate demand may not be available even in a well-organized auction market.

Organized Securities Exchanges. An organized market is one where a **formal mechanism** exists for bringing buyers and sellers together directly or through their representatives. Among the most highly organized markets in existence are the principal securities exchanges, which provide a central trading place at which groups of brokers and dealers meet regularly and transact business with one another for their customers and their own account. Securities exchanges not only offer far more efficient markets in some issues, but also provide arrangements for the settlement of transactions, set up rules and regulations governing the conduct and finances of their members, provide publicity for transactions in securities, and, through rules governing listing and filing of information, establish standards for issuers of the securities that are traded.

Exchanges were established early in history for trading in commodities and slaves. A number of **commodity exchanges** continue to function actively. Securities were first traded on European exchanges several centuries ago. The New York Stock Exchange, the organization of which as an outdoor market has been traced back to 1792, was among the first of its kind in this country.

National Stock Exchanges. As reported by the Securities and Exchange Commission (Statistical Bulletin, February, 1963), there were 14 national stock exchanges registered with the S.E.C. under the provisions of §6 of the Securities Exchange Act of 1934. As a result of changing economic conditions, small trading volume, and Federal regulations, some exchanges have closed or merged with others in recent years. The two largest markets are the New York Stock Exchange and the American Stock Exchange in New York. Other exchanges are located in Boston, Chicago, Cincinnati, Detroit, Salt Lake City, San Francisco, Los Angeles, Philadelphia, Pittsburgh, and Spokane. In addition, there are four small exempt exchanges that are not registered, located in Honolulu, Richmond, Wheeling, and Colorado Springs. Some of these exchanges specialize in certain types of securities such as mining shares.

Practices on these exchanges differ, reflecting volume of trading and types of securities traded. The **New York Stock Exchange,** by far the most important stock market in the world from the viewpoint of volume of securities traded and value of transactions, sets standards that the others tend to emulate. Because of its importance and more highly developed organization and procedures, the New York Stock Exchange is discussed in detail below.

Over-The-Counter Markets. In addition to the organized exchanges with their auction markets there are the negotiated markets, usually referred to as "over-the-counter" or **unlisted** markets (for more detailed discussion of these markets, see p. 41 below). The chief differences between the two are (1) the character of organization, and (2) the method of doing business, though it is also true that securities traded over-the-counter are usually those of smaller companies whose outstanding shares are fewer in number and less widely held than those of listed companies. Because bonds are traded for the most part in large blocks by institutional investors, the bulk of the trading is over-the-counter. In fact, the market for **United States Treasury obligations** is an over-the-counter market and is the most efficient and sensitive in the world. Over-the-counter markets also provide exclusive trading facilities for municipal bonds, railroad equipment trust obligations, most newly issued securities, and thousands of stock and bond issues not listed on exchanges.

The work of the over-the-counter markets is greatly facilitated by the telephone, leased telegraph wire, and teletype. Little business is transacted by direct personal contact. Brokers and dealers may participate actively in both organized exchanges and over-the-counter markets.

Publicity is given quotations of important unlisted securities through a central organization of over-the-counter dealers known as the National Association of Securities Dealers, Inc., which furnishes quotations daily to the newspapers. Published quotations of unlisted securities differ from those of listed issues, however, in that they are restricted to **bid and asked quotations** rather than actual sales prices.

MARKETABILITY OF SECURITIES. A high degree of **convertibility** between money and securities is an important investment characteristic and it is provided by an active market for the particular security. It is of great value to long-term investors as well as short-term traders. Personal and institutional needs or ever-changing business and market conditions may make it highly desirable or imperative that securities be bought or sold promptly. A security is said to have a high degree of marketability when it is possible to convert it into cash or buy it at the current price without perceptible effect on prevailing market prices.

In view of the fact that the bulk of the bonds sold to investors mature in the distant future, whereas preferred and common stocks are without maturity, the characteristic of marketability is of particular importance to security owners. Marketability has been provided by the establishment of efficient securities markets, but mere listing of a security on an exchange does not assure a high degree of marketability. An exchange is a highly publicized auction market with varying degrees of activity among issues traded on it. A post on the New York Stock Exchange floor (Post 30), where about 200 issues are traded, is devoted to trading in relatively inactive issues on a **"cabinet" basis,** with bid and asked prices filed for reference and a substantial part of trading accomplished on a dealer basis.

Too much emphasis should not be placed on the investor's ability to convert securities into cash or cash into securities on a few minutes' notice. Long-term investments or divestments should be based on an analysis of values and of investor requirements. The ability to effect transactions quickly at prevailing prices is only one of several major considerations.

Securities other than short-term United States government and other very high-grade and highly marketable obligations do not provide **liquidity**—i.e., the ability to convert into cash at all times without material loss. They provide **shiftability** among investors. In times of concerted selling, substantial price declines are to be expected because so many more buyers must be attracted.

Marketability has four major aspects. These are:

Closeness of a Market. The more narrow the spread between bid and asked prices, the closer the market a security enjoys. When an issue is quoted in the market at 40 bid, 60 asked, it clearly has very limited marketability due to this wide spread. On the other hand, a close market exists if an issue is quoted 50 bid, 50¼ asked, and it is likely to possess the quality of marketability. A close market indicates that the security can be sold very close to the level at which it can be bought at a given time.

Breadth of the Market. The breadth of a market is measured by its ability to absorb a large volume of either buying or selling orders in a given security without a substantial change in price. Markets are said to be **thin** when a small amount of selling or buying produces relatively large fluctuations in the price of the security.

Market breadth results from a number of factors: the size of the outstanding issue, the character of its distribution among security holders, the size and standing among investors of the issuer, and general security market conditions.

Continuity of the Market. Another factor of importance to the holder of securities is the continuity of a market, measured by the amount of price changes between successive sales. Great emphasis has been placed by spokesmen for the auction markets on the continuity of the market, as reflected in the reports of sales on the ticker tape. From the points of view of the in-and-out trader and the person who borrows heavily on his securities, a continuous market is of the utmost importance. Wide, erratic fluctuations between sales may cause losses and disturb creditors. Some issues traded over-the-counter enjoy a continuous market, although a number of listed securities do not possess this quality.

Market Stability. Stability of a market refers to its price behavior over a longer period of time, rather than between sales. Since security prices are bound to reflect changing economic and political conditions and prospects, technological developments, etc., stability is relative at best. A security can be said to enjoy a stable market when the fluctuation of its price over a year or longer is a smaller percentage of the prevailing price than is the case with stock price averages.

BROKERS AND DEALERS. Professional participants in securities markets may act as brokers or as dealers. As brokers, they execute orders as agents for their customers, and receive commissions for their efforts. As dealers, they buy and sell for their own account or for the account of their organizations with the expectation of profit from their transactions. Most customer orders are executed on stock exchanges by members acting as brokers. Other members on the exchanges, notably the specialists and those who handle odd lots, act as dealers at least part of the time. In the over-the-counter market, the dealer function is particularly important for the existence of a market in particular issues. The willingness of at least one organization to act as a dealer, to buy from and sell to others for its own account, is almost essential for this market to exist.

Distinction Between Roles. There is a legal distinction between the roles of broker and dealer that can be significant. A broker is an agent acting on behalf of a customer, who is the principal in the transaction, and can bind the customer and hold him liable, as principal, even on the basis of an oral order. On the other hand, a transaction between a customer and a dealer is a transaction between two principals and is therefore subject to the law of contracts, including the **statute of frauds** that requires that contracts above a certain amount must be in writing. (**In New York,** the Uniform Commercial Code applies and it provides that an oral contract for the sale of securities, regardless of the amount, is unenforceable **except** if certain things subsequently occur, e.g., if confirmation of the sale is sent the customer and he does not object in writing within ten days, the sale is enforceable.)

It is important to note that the label "broker" or "dealer" is not determinative of the role played in a particular transaction as individuals or firms bearing either label can act in the other capacity. The determining factor is whether they are trading for their own account or are agents representing another on a commission basis. Federal regulation requires that the customer be informed as to whether the dealer is acting as principal or agent in any given transaction. Despite the distinction between their roles, both the courts and the S.E.C. have emphasized that a broker or dealer, in whatever capacity he acts, must observe the standards of a fiduciary in his relations with customers.

The New York Stock Exchange

ORGANIZATION. The New York Stock Exchange, by far the largest of the security exchanges in the United States and Canada, is a voluntary, unincorporated membership association. A directory of the exchange, its constitution and rules, and related laws and regulations are published in the **New York Stock Exchange Guide.**

Among the **objectives** of the New York Stock Exchange, as set forth in Article I of its constitution, are:

. . . to furnish exchange rooms for the convenient transaction of their business by its members; to furnish other facilities for its members and allied members; to maintain high standards of commercial honor and integrity among its members and allied members; and to promote and inculcate just and equitable principles of trade and business.

The constitution of the Exchange sets forth the organic law governing its operations. It is supplemented by rules covering trading practices and relations among members, including such topics as ethical standards of dealing, uniform commissions, regulations of disputes among members, listing of securities, and, most important of all, trading practices on the floor and relations with customers.

Board of Governors. The legislative and judicial powers of the Exchange are invested in a Board of Governors of 33 men. The **composition** of the board provides representation for major member groups. It includes:

- 1 member of the Exchange elected for a one-year term as chairman.
- 1 President of the Exchange, who may not be a member of the Exchange and is elected by the other Governors.
- 13 members who live and work in New York City. Not less than seven of them must be in organizations doing business directly with the public, and not less than ten of them must customarily spend a substantial part of their time on the floor of the Exchange. Three-year terms.
- 6 members or allied members of the Exchange, who live and work in New York City and are partners or stockholders in organizations doing business directly

with the public. Five are allied members and one is an Exchange member. Three-year terms.

9 members or allied members of the Exchange, who live and work outside New York City and are partners or stockholders in organizations doing business directly with the public. At least two are to be members. Three-year terms.

3 public members, who are not engaged in the securities business. They are elected by the other Governors to three-year terms.

The Report of the S.E.C. Special Study of Securities Markets in 1963 was of the opinion that the Exchange was governed to a disproportionate degree by its floor professionals who ". . . are not necessarily the most talented for administration or regulation or the most responsive to public needs, even though the nature of their operations requires them to own seats and to be at the Exchange during the working day." The report recommended that greater voice be given to partners or voting stockholders of member firms who may be more cognizant of the public needs.

The **duties** of the Board of Governors are primarily to determine policies. For the formulation of policies, a revolving **Advisory Committee** of Governors has been created to aid the president. The board has wide disciplinary powers over members of the Exchange. Among other things, Article XIV provides:

Section 6. A member or allied member who shall be adjudged guilty, by the affirmative vote of a majority of the Governors then in office, of a violation of the Constitution of the Exchange or of a violation of a rule adopted pursuant to the Constitution or of the violation of a resolution of the Board of Governors regulating the conduct or business of members or allied members or of conduct or proceeding inconsistent with just and equitable principles of trade may be suspended or expelled as the Board may determine.

The Constitution makes expulsion mandatory for fraudulent conduct, and subjects to **suspension or expulsion** members who are adjudged guilty of violations of the Rules, conduct inconsistent with just and equitable principles of trade, fictitious transactions, activities that have the purpose of upsetting the equilibrium of the market and bring about a condition of demoralization in which prices do not fairly reflect market values, or making misstatements to Exchange officials.

Section 10. A member or allied member who shall be adjudged guilty, by the affirmative vote of a majority of the Governors then in office, of any act which may be determined by the Board of Governors to be detrimental to the interest or welfare of the Exchange may be suspended for a period not exceeding five years.

These disciplinary provisions, backed up by the Securities Exchange Act of 1934 and rules promulgated by the S.E.C. thereunder, give the New York Stock Exchange wide power to secure adherence to "principles of just and equitable trade" for the benefit of securities buyers and sellers.

President. The Exchange became subject, as did all exchanges, to Federal regulation by the Securities and Exchange Commission under the Securities Exchange Act of 1934. Pressure from the Commission led to drastic changes in the Exchange's constitution. These affected administrative organization, and included a provision for the election of a full-time, salaried president, who would act as chief administrative officer. The president was not to be an active member of the Exchange, so that he would not represent any faction among Exchange members or have personal interests to protect in the conduct of his office. The president is the chief executive of the Exchange. He acts as its official representative in all public matters. Administrative duties, performed before the reorganization by standing committees of the Board of Governors, are carried out by salaried officers and employees on the staffs of the departments (Stock List, Public Relations, Member Firms, etc.) functioning under the president.

MEMBERSHIP. The New York Stock Exchange is **limited** to a total membership of 1,366. Only individuals may be members of the Exchange. Members may be or become partners or stockholders in organizations devoted either to the handling of orders on the Exchange, so-called commission houses, or to the business of investment banking, or both. Member organizations may be proprietorships, partnerships, or corporations. Several hundred of the members of the Exchange are partners or stockholders in commission houses doing business with the public; others are floor brokers, traders, specialists, or odd-lot brokers or dealers.

Securing a Seat. Individuals seeking to acquire membership on the New York Stock Exchange arrange for the purchase of a seat from an existing member, or from the estate of a deceased one. Having made such arrangements, they must apply formally for admittance. The past career, the financial standing, and other pertinent matters about an applicant are investigated. Each applicant must be at least 21 years of age, an American citizen, and be sponsored by two Exchange members. The applicant must also pass a test administered by the Exchange, indicating his knowledge of the securities industry. If found satisfactory, the **application** is approved and the sale of the seat is duly consummated.

The **price of a seat** may be determined by private negotiation or by auction in the instance of the sale of a seat of a deceased member. It reflects the estimated profitability of a membership that, in turn, is determined largely by the volume of trading.

Types of Exchange Members. Members of the Exchange may be classified in several clearly defined groups. A large number of member organizations devote themselves to the execution of orders received from nonmember customers for the purchase or sale of stocks and bonds. These are known as **commission houses.** They maintain offices designed to serve the public. Many of these commission houses have branch or even their main offices in distant cities, and contact is maintained between the branches, the main office, and the Exchange by means of leased telegraph and telephone facilities. Commission houses that obtain a large part of their business from outside communities over leased wires are known as **wire houses.**

The **floor broker** executes orders on the floor for other Stock Exchange members. Since only members of the Exchange are allowed to engage in buying and selling on the floor, it is frequently necessary for commission house members who are not able or willing to spend their time on the Exchange floor, or who have too much business to transact there to manage it alone, to have other members execute orders for them. This is done at a reduced rate of commission that varies with the price of the stock. For example, on a stock selling at $45, the customer pays a total commission of $41.50 per 100 shares of which $3.85 goes to the floor broker for executing the order on the floor of the Exchange. (For detailed discussion of Brokerage Commissions see page 16.) The name **"two-dollar" broker,** which once applied to these brokers, was a carry-over from the time a uniform commission of $2 per 100 shares was charged as a fee for their services on the floor of the Exchange.

Floor traders buy and sell on the floor of the Exchange for their own account. They seek to profit from short-term price fluctuations. They have the advantage, as members of the Exchange, of avoiding the payment of commissions and of having direct access to the floor, which gives them a first-hand opportunity to observe the character, technical position, and trend of the market. Floor traders frequently operate for small fractional profits. Their activity tends to broaden the market on the Exchange and provide bids and offers at times when they may be lacking from other sources. In 1945, the staff of the S.E.C. recommended adoption of a rule designed to prohibit or restrict floor trading on the grounds that it may accentuate price movements, and that floor traders possess an inequitable advantage over public traders. After consideration of the rules of the Exchange governing floor trading, however, the S.E.C. refrained from action on this recommendation. Again, in 1963 the Report of the S.E.C. Special Study of Securities Markets recommended that floor trading be abolished. Floor trading as it has been practiced may disappear, but if it does the transition period is likely to last for several years.

Specialists are broker-dealers who concentrate their activity in one or a few stocks at a single trading post on the Exchange. They are able to devote all their time to watching the market and executing orders in these specific issues. As brokers, specialists receive orders in issues in which they specialize from other brokers, performing a function similar to that of floor brokers and for the same rate of commission. Orders placed by customers for future execution, orders placed with a definite price limit away from the market, or orders otherwise unsuitable for immediate execution are generally turned over by commission houses to the specialists, who have the time and facilities for watching for opportunities to execute them. In addition to his functions as a broker's broker, the specialist also acts as dealer on his own account in the particular issues assigned to him. He may buy and sell for his own account, subject to certain restrictions established by the Exchange and the S.E.C. for the protection of outside customers, to make a better market in his stocks. The S.E.C. has indicated that it intends to devote increased attention to the activities of specialists to see that they are properly discharging their responsibilities.

The specialist keeps a record of unfilled buying and selling orders placed with him in his **book,** which is kept at his post on the floor of the Exchange. Similar information concerning prospective demand and supply is not available to other traders in the same form. Authorized persons are permitted to inspect this book, but the information is not generally available. Restraints have been placed on specialists' actions to prevent profit from the "inside" knowledge of the market given by the book.

The S.E.C. has considered but rejected the notion that the functions of brokers and dealers should be fully segregated. Making an effective market for listed issues has involved transactions by specialists both as brokers and as dealers.

Odd-lot dealers fill orders for fewer shares than the unit of trading on the floor of the New York Stock Exchange. Commission houses turn over nearly all customer odd-lot orders to two odd-lot dealer firms. Each of these firms uses a large number of **associate brokers,** located at the trading posts, to assign prices at which odd-lot orders are filled on the basis of the next round lot transactions, and to sell or buy round lots to hold long and short positions of the odd-lot firm within prescribed limits. Odd-lot dealers derive their earnings from the differential from the round lot price at which each order is filled, and normally seek to avoid trading profits and losses. The Report of the S.E.C.'s Special Study of Securities Markets in 1963 questioned the way differentials were being fixed and expressed the feeling that costs charged were not always justified and even where justified could be lowered by increased automation.

Bond brokers and **bond dealers** execute orders or trade in listed bonds in a separate portion of the Exchange floor known as the bond room.

LISTING SECURITIES ON THE EXCHANGE. Securities traded on the floor of the New York Stock Exchange have been listed, i.e., admitted to trading. As a condition precedent to listing, securities must be registered with the S.E.C. in accordance with the provisions of the Securities Exchange Act of 1934 and approved for listing by the Exchange itself.

Issuers must initiate the action for listing. Duplicate originals of the application for listing are filed with the S.E.C. The registration or listing does not become effective until the Exchange has informed the Commission of its approval of the security for listing. Ordinarily, registration becomes effective automatically 30 days after receipt by the S.E.C. of the Stock Exchange's certification, but may become effective within a shorter period by an accelerating order of the S.E.C. (Security registration requirements are outlined under Federal Regulation of Securities Trading below.)

The **listing application** serves the dual purpose of placing before the Stock Exchange information essential to a determination of the suitability of the security for trading on the Exchange and, equally important, of providing the investing public with information to aid its appraisal of the merits of the security.

The listing privilege is granted securities by the New York Stock Exchange under rules promulgated by the **Department of Stock List.** These rules provide that applications may be filed by corporations or foreign governments wishing to have their issues admitted to the list. The Exchange's examiners aid in the preparation of applications, of which the applicant furnishes 650 copies. Such listing application must be accompanied by a check to cover the **initial listing fee,** and by an agreement to pay a **continuing annual fee** for 15 years.

Disclosure Requirements. Applicants who seek to list their issues must file with the Department of Stock List a mass of information concerning the nature of their business, its charter, its capitalization, audited financial statements for the past 2 years, depreciation policy, and many other factors of interest in determining the investment merits of the securities. In addition, the corporation must make agreements with the Exchange covering regular publication of financial statements in the future; maintenance of a transfer agency and a registrar in the Borough of Manhattan, New York City; advice to the Exchange of any vital future change in the business, capitalization, or policy of the enterprise, etc. A **distribution statement** is required indicating the number of holders of various sized blocks of the stock, or bond, issue. Wide distribution of a substantial amount of stock is a basis for expecting a broad market for the issue, not subject to manipulation or corners, intended or unintended.

To protect against forgeries, certificates must be prepared by an approved engraving company and samples submitted to the Exchange.

Accounting standards for companies whose stocks are listed have been raised to a high level through the joint efforts of the Exchange, the S.E.C., and the accounting profession. In general, the accounting and disclosure requirements of the New York Stock Exchange have been adopted but expanded in the registration requirements of the S.E.C.

Listing Statements. The Department of Stock List makes public the listing statements of issues approved for trading on the floor. These listing statements contain much pertinent information about the applicant corporation, its business, and its financial status. Since the advent of the Securities Exchange Act, listing statements have been largely supplanted as information sources by the comprehensive registration statements required by the S.E.C. on its **form 10.** Registration statements are on file at the Exchange and the Public Reference Room of the S.E.C. Listing statements are available at the Exchange.

Although not readily available to the average individual investor, information from these statements is disseminated through the statistical services and brokerage houses.

In listing additional securities and in the alteration of provisions of outstanding issues, an **abbreviated listing statement** may be filed. Much of the data may be "incorporated" in the main registration by reference to statements already filed.

Listing Policy. The general policy of the New York Stock Exchange has been to list only issues of larger and stronger corporations, and to avoid highly speculative promotions. In the instance of the latter, a **period of "seasoning"** on the over-the-counter or other securities markets is considered desirable. Bonds of domestic and foreign corporations and foreign governments are listed when the requirements are met.

To be listed on the "Big Board" an issue must also meet other requirements such as adequate public distribution and trading interest. It will be listed only if its issuer has an established position in the industry. Since 1926, it has been the policy of the Exchange not to list common stocks that do not have voting power. In 1940 the Committee on Stock List decided, as a matter of policy, it would not list new preferred stocks that did not provide at least minimum voting rights.

Other requirements for listing securities refer to the size and character of the enterprise. Formerly, issues of limited size were not listed by the New York Stock Exchange because they could be more readily manipulated or "cornered," but manipulative practices are prohibited or regulated by the Securities Exchange Act of 1934. Adequate size for an issue and adequate distribution of the securities remain, however, prerequisites for an effective national market. Minimum standards of the Exchange are $2 million annually in earnings before tax, $10 million of net tangible assets or aggregate market value of stock publicly held, and distribution of 600 thousand shares in round lots among 1,500 stockholders.

Subject to special restrictions, the Department of Stock List will recommend the listing of general management investment company shares and **American Depositary Receipts,** which represent the deposit of shares of foreign companies with branches of American banks abroad (see discussion in Section 3).

Motives for Listing. A corporation lists its securities because of the more efficient market thereby made available to present or prospective stockholders. **Marketability** and the flow of information are an advantage to the owners. Marketability also facilitates the sale of new issues and the acceptability of shares in transactions—for example, mergers. **Broader distribution of the shares** that may follow from greater public interest in listed issues will provide wider ownership and lessen the prospect of concentration of stock holdings that might lead to a challenge of management. Only listed securities, other than government obligations, can be carried on margin with brokerage houses.

Delisting and Withdrawal of Registration. §12(d) of the Securities Exchange Act provides:

> A security registered with a national securities exchange may be withdrawn or stricken from listing and registration in accordance with the rules of the exchange and upon such terms as the Commission may deem necessary to impose for the protection of investors, upon application by the issuer or the exchange to the Commission. . . .

Securities listed on the New York Stock Exchange may be removed from the list, or dealing therein may be suspended, at any time in accordance with its constitution and rules (New York Stock Exchange Guide, 2498A–2501A). It is an established rule of the Exchange that, in the absence of special circumstances, a security that, in the Exchange's opinion, is eligible for continued listing will not be removed from the list upon request or application of the issuer, unless the proposed delisting has been approved by the stockholders at a meeting at which a substantial percentage of the outstanding amount of the particular security was represented. In the absence of special circumstances, the Exchange will consider approval of delisting by over two-thirds of the outstanding stock, together with failure of 10% of the bona fide individual holders to object, as the minimum requirement.

Since 1934 a frequent **reason for delisting** has been the failure or refusal of the company to comply with requirements covering financial statements. Delisting occurs frequently also because the issue has been redeemed, or because there has been a decline in trading activity due to acquisition of the bulk of the issue by a parent company.

UNLISTED TRADING ON EXCHANGES. Trading on the floor of an exchange in securities that are not formally listed occurs when a corporation does not seek listing but, because of trading interest in the shares, members of the exchange nevertheless execute orders in it. Since 1910, no unlisted securities have been traded on the New York Stock Exchange. On the American Stock Exchange and the regional exchanges, however, trading in unlisted issues constitutes a large part of the activity.

The Securities Exchange Act directed the S.E.C. to make a special study of unlisted trading and report thereon to Congress. Under amendments to the law that resulted, unlisted trading on exchanges has been **subjected to restrictive rules.** The aim of these rules, which continue and extend unlisted trading privileges, is to foster decentralization of trading by expanding the business of regional stock exchanges and, at the same time, to maintain trading facilities for unlisted issues that were traded before 1934. Issues admitted to unlisted trading privileges on the effective date of the Act have retained this status. Their number has been substantially reduced by refundings, mergers, failures, and registration for listing.

Unlisted trading privileges on one exchange may be accorded securities that are listed and registered on at least one other national exchange, on application to, and approval by, the S.E.C. This approval is usually accorded securities listed and registered elsewhere if the applicant exchange shows (1) adequate public distribution, and (2) sufficient public trading activity within its vicinity in the particular stock to justify the extension of unlisted trading privileges. In deciding whether these requirements are met, the S.E.C. considers the distribution of the issue represented by holdings of member firms and banks in the vicinity of the exchange and the volume of trading originating in such "vicinity." The S.E.C. must find that extension of such unlisted trading privileges is necessary or appropriate in the public interest or for the protection of investors. In so doing it considers the exchange's trading machinery, the extent of the auction market, round- and odd-lot trading, and other technical factors. The statutory requirement that there be a "sufficiently widespread public distribution" is to make certain that the applicant exchange will provide a market adequate to cope with transactions of normal size.

A third, but unused, basis for the unlisted trading privilege is provided for securities of companies for which a registration statement is on file under the Securities

Act of 1933 and for which periodic reports are filed under §15(d) of the Securities Exchange Act.

TRADING FACILITIES. Trading on the New York Stock Exchange is carried on in the **trading room,** which occupies the main floor of the Exchange building. Along the sides of this room are the telephone booths having direct connections with the offices of members, where buying and selling orders and messages for the floor members are received. Members can be called from the floor to their telephones by flashing their numbers on two large black annunciator boards located on the two opposite walls of the room.

On the trading floor are found 19 **stock posts,** at each of which the markets for a number of listed stock issues are located. In a wing of the Exchange building is the **bond room,** devoted to facilities for buying and selling listed bonds.

At the posts on the floor of the Exchange are transmitting stations from which reports of sales are sent by electrical devices over the **stock exchange ticker system.** Nearly instantaneous publicity is thus given sales made on the floor of the New York Stock Exchange all over the United States and Canada. In the basement beneath the trading floor are located safe deposit vaults of members and the headquarters of the **Stock Clearing Corporation,** which handles the clearing of transactions after they are made. Nonmembers may view the trading from visitors' galleries. The **Public Relations Department** invites visitors and explains the workings of the Exchange and its economic functions in regularly scheduled lecture-tours.

METHODS OF TRADING. Transactions are executed on the floor of the New York Stock Exchange each business day, Monday through Friday, from 10 A.M. to 3:30 P.M.

Admittance to the Exchange floor during trading hours is limited to members, their clerks, and uniformed employees of the Exchange. The members' clerks and Exchange personnel aid in carrying on transactions and in making the necessary reports of trading. Other employees of members or their firms must remain at their telephone stations during trading hours.

Trading on the floor of the Exchange is restricted, except for about 200 issues of inactive stocks, to buying and selling of 100 share units known as **round lots.** Members at each trading post bid for and offer units of 100 shares or multiples thereof. Prices are negotiated at $\frac{1}{8}$-point variations or multiples thereof, except for United States Government bonds, which are quoted in thirty-seconds, and a few low-priced issues in which smaller price changes are specifically permitted.

The Auction Process. A broker seeking to execute a sell order for a customer goes to the post on the floor of the Exchange where trading in the security wanted is carried on and asks, "How's Steel?", that is, he requests a **"quote."** Usually, the specialists at the post quote the **bids and offers.** Let us say that the **market** is $91\frac{1}{4}$ bid, $91\frac{1}{2}$ asked at the moment. The highest bid and lowest asked prices constitute the market for a security. Our broker having an order to sell "at the market" then offers the stock at $91\frac{3}{8}$. Law, and rules of the Exchange, require the broker to attempt to secure the best available price in executing orders. If there are no takers, he may sell at $91\frac{1}{4}$, the best bid. If, however, one of the bidders says, "Take a 100 at $91\frac{3}{8}$", that then is the agreed-upon price. Whenever brokers agree upon a price through this auction process, a sale is effected. Memoranda are made of the sale by the two brokers, and it is immediately recorded by Exchange employees, reported, and put on the ticker tape. All of this is done with amazing speed, frequently within the space of a few seconds.

SECURITIES TRADING ON EXCHANGES 10·13

PUBLICITY FOR QUOTATIONS—TICKER SERVICE. The stock ticker, providing a record of all round-lot transactions on the floor of the Exchange, plays a very important role in securities trading. The ticker is operated by the Exchange. The Exchange also operates the stock tickers in the lower portion of Manhattan Island, New York City. The Western Union Telegraph Co. transmits quotations, as rapidly as they appear, to other tickers all over the United States and Canada. Under the rules of the S.E.C., the tape must differentiate between unlisted and listed securities on exchanges where issues are admitted to unlisted trading privileges. This is usually done by placing the letter "U" just after the symbol designating the unlisted stock.

To save time and effort, listed issues are designated on the ticker by symbols. Lists of symbols are readily obtainable at brokerage houses. Fig. 1 shows a specimen of the stock tape. The abbreviations represent sales as follows:

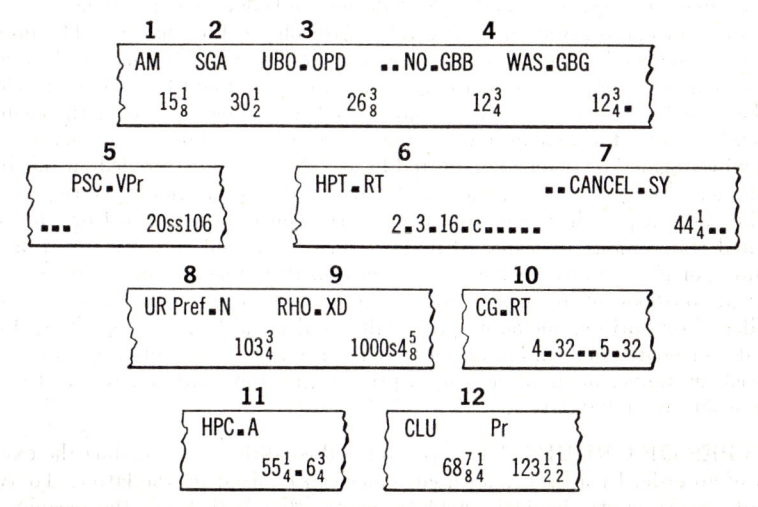

```
 1      2        3             4
AM    SGA   UBO.OPD    ..NO.GBB   WAS.GBG
 15 1/8   30 1/2    26 3/8        12 3/4      12 3/4 .

 5                    6                     7
PSC.VPr             HPT.RT             ..CANCEL.SY
 ...   20ss106       2.3.16.c.....            44 1/4 ..

        8            9                 10
    UR Pref.N     RHO.XD            CG.RT
      103 3/4    1000s4 5/8       4..32..5.32

       11                12
     HPC.A          CLU      Pr
      55 1/4 . 6 3/4       68 7 1/8 4    123 1 1/2 2
```

Fig. 1. Sections of New York Stock Exchange Stock Ticker Tape.

Meaning of symbols in ticker tape illustration

1. Armour & Co.—100 shares at 15⅛.
2. Southern Natural Gas—100 shares at 30½.
3. Delayed report of opening sale of 100 shares of U. S. Tobacco Co., at 26⅜ or an opening sale of U. S. Tobacco Co. representing a price change of two or more points.
4. Error in symbol—100 shares of General Baking Co. common stock was actually sold.
5. Pittsburgh Steel Co.—$5 preferred, 20 shares sold at 106.
6. American Home Products Corp. rights—200 sold at 3/16 for cash delivery.
7. Delete last reported sale of Sperry Rand Corp. at 44¼.
8. United Aircraft Corp. (new) 4% cumulative convertible preferred stock—100 shares sold at 103¾.
9. Rhodesian Selection Trust—ex-dividend 1,000 shares sold at 4⅝.
10. Columbia Gas System, Inc.—rights, 100 sold at 4/32 followed by another sale of 100 at 5/32.
11. Hercules Powder Co., cumulative convertible Class A stock closing quotation, 55¼ bid, 56¾ offered (appears after the closing).
12. Cluett, Peabody & Co., Inc.—common stock high and low prices for the day. 68⅞–68¼—preferred stock high 123½, low 123½ (appears after the closing).

Securities Trading on Exchanges

SECURITIES TRANSACTIONS. The simplest and most common type of transaction on an organized exchange is the ordinary contract to buy or sell a security. Such orders are placed by the public through commission houses or by dealers for their own account. This type of trade is done in units of trading, which consist of 100 shares in the case of most stocks on the "Big Board." Some higher-priced and inactive stocks are traded in ten-share units.

Buying or selling in other than the established unit or round lots is referred to as **odd-lot trading.** A moderate proportion of the trading done on the New York Stock Exchange consists of odd-lot trading. This type of transaction is of particular value to small investors and traders.

Short selling consists of selling securities that are not owned by the seller. (For a full discussion of short sales see page 22.) Settlement of the contract obligation is effected by borrowing the security sold short from **"street" holders,** usually brokers holding the security for the account of their customers, and delivering such borrowed securities to the buyer. Short selling is done for a number of reasons, the most common being a belief that the market is going to decline and the borrowed securities can then be replaced at a lower price. Short sales are also made by specialists and odd-lot dealers to hedge their positions.

Trading in **listed bonds** may also take place on stock exchanges. The unit of trading is one bond of the principal amount of $1,000. Bond trading on the organized exchanges is less important than stock trading, no doubt because of the closer market usually available for larger blocks of listed obligations over-the-counter.

In addition to transactions in outstanding securities, trading goes on in securities on a **when-issued** or **when-distributed** basis. New issues are traded on this basis before delivery of actual securities can be made. Reorganizations give rise to such trading, once a plan has been approved by the court. When-issued or when-distributed transactions are canceled if the securities are not actually issued or distributed, or if substantial changes take place in their terms before issuance.

As an offshoot of regular security purchases and sales are transactions in **privileges or options,** including **puts, calls, and straddles** (see page 25). From a dealer or **writer** of such options, a trader can purchase an option to buy or sell a specified number of shares at a fixed price at any time within a specified period such as 30, 90, or 190 days.

TYPES OF ORDERS. The terms for and conditions surrounding the **execution** of an order by a broker for a customer can be fixed by the latter. To avoid dispute, every effort should be made to assure that both know the meanings of the terms used and the trade practices involved.

Market Orders. Orders to buy and sell at the market provide for execution as soon as feasible, at the most advantageous price obtainable by the broker on the floor, but without limitation as to price. In the event of disrupted or inactive markets, brokers sometimes use their discretion and delay execution for a time, but this is unusual.

Limited Orders. Customers may limit the execution of the order as to price. A limited buying order to purchase New York Central at, say, 20, must be executed at a price of 20 or less. Similarly, a selling order limited at 20 must be executed at 20 or more.

Orders may be limited by the customer also as to the **time** during which they may be executed. Market orders are to be executed as soon as possible, and so are not limited in this way. **Day orders** are automatically canceled if not executed the same day in which given. **Open,** or **"GTC,"** orders are "good till canceled." They remain on the books of the broker until executed or specifically countermanded by the customer. It is, however, a rule of the New York Stock Exchange that brokers must reconfirm these GTC orders with the specialists at least once every six months, on April and October 30. Brokers may check with customers at shorter intervals, say, each month, for confirmation. This is done to avoid errors and forgetfulness on the part of customers.

It frequently happens that numerous orders come into the market for a stock to be executed at a fixed price. Thus, ten different brokers may place limit orders with a specialist to buy varying amounts of Steel at 80. When this price is reached on a decline, the amount of stock available for sale at 80 may be only a fraction of the total of the buying orders. The rule of **"first come, first served"** applies as far as orders on the specialist's book are concerned. Such orders are filled on the basis of priority of receipt. A customer may then be told that there is **stock ahead** that prevents the execution of his order. Under some conditions, if two or more brokers indicate at the same time that they wish to purchase a given block of stock that is offered, they match coins to see which should "get the sale." This gives rise on occasion to a report to a customer, **"Matched and lost."**

Stop-Loss Orders. When buyers wish to limit their losses, they may place stop-loss orders to buy or sell. These are orders that become market orders when the price of a stock reaches a specified quotation. Thus, suppose the buyer of 100 shares of stock at 50 would like to limit his loss to approximately 3 points. He places an order to sell at 47 **"stop."** Whenever a round-lot of stock is sold on the exchange at 47 or less, his 100 shares are offered at market. If market conditions are unsettled, he may not be able to get 47 for his stock, but will get the best price obtainable by his broker at that time. Similarly, short sellers may seek to limit their loss from a rise in the price by placing **stop-loss buying orders.** Thus, a short seller may sell at 48 and place an order to buy "on stop" at 50. Whenever a round-lot sells at 50 or higher on the exchange, this order becomes a market order to buy.

Stop-loss orders also may be used to enter the market. If a trader believed that a rise in price of a stock to, say, 34 would forecast a further rise, he might enter a buy order at 34 stop. If the price rose to, or above, 34, his buy order would then become a market order. A short seller may use the stop order in this way to protect a profit on a short sale. Stop-limit orders may be used in this case. When the stop price is reached, a limit, rather than market, order is entered in the market. It will be executed, if it can be, at the limit or better.

Stopping Stock. A special arrangement may be made by a broker with the specialist in a stock, or with another member, to assure that an order will be executed for a block of stock at a certain price, if better execution cannot be obtained first. A broker may, for example, ask the specialist to "stop" 100 shares of Allied Chemical for him at 80, the best offer in the market at the time. He will then await offers at a lower price. If the next transaction occurs at 80, however, the original order will be executed automatically. The specialist sells the stock, either from his book or for his own account. The "stopped" transaction may not appear on the ticker tape, since its appearance might give a misleading impression of price action in the market.

EXECUTION OF ORDERS ON THE EXCHANGE. Orders to buy and sell securities generally reach a brokerage house over the telephone or by mail from customers, or over its **private leased wire system** from out-of-town branches and correspondents. Large brokerage houses gather in orders from all over the country over such leased wire systems. These orders are transmitted to the floor of the Exchange over a private wire to the member's booth, where an attendant receives them and routes them to the floor member, a floor broker, a specialist, or an odd-lot broker, as the circumstances may require.

Transactions between brokers on the floor of the Exchange are verbal, but a **sales report** is sent by each broker to his telephone clerk. Word of execution is then phoned back to the member's office, and the sales report is later sent there to constitute the basis for subsequent recording and handling of the transaction. The customer will receive in the mails the following day a **confirmation** of his purchase or sale, with the sum to be paid by him or due to him. This confirmation will specify the **transaction date** when the order was executed on the floor, and the **settlement date** when the account of the customer will be debited or credited, as the case may be, following settlement of the transaction. Often, as a courtesy service to the customer, a telephonic confirmation of the transaction is given the customer a few minutes after execution of the order by the broker on the Exchange floor.

BROKERAGE COMMISSIONS ON STOCKS. For many years customers of members of the New York Stock Exchange were charged commissions for executing orders based on the selling price of shares. After some debate the members voted to alter the basis upon which minimum commissions were computed in order to alter the incidence of the commissions to accord more realistically with the costs of executing the transaction. Effective March 30, 1959, the schedule of minimum commissions became (New York Stock Exchange Guide, 1702):

1. On stocks, rights and warrants selling at **$1 per share and above,** commissions are based on the amount of money involved in a single transaction. They are to be not less than the following on a round-lot transaction in a 100-share unit stock or on a transaction involving one or a combination of round-lots in ten-share unit stocks and odd-lots in these stocks if the total involves 100 shares or less:

Money value	Commission
$ 100 to $ 399	2% plus $ 3.00
$ 400 to $2,399	1% plus $ 7.00
$2,400 to $4,999	½% plus $19.00
$5,000 and over	1/10% plus $39.00

If the amount involved in a transaction is **less than $100,** as it might be if ten-share units or odd-lots are involved, the minimum commission is to be mutually agreed.

The minimum commission shall not exceed $1.50 per share or $75 per single transaction, but in any event shall not be less than $6 per single transaction involving $100 or more. Note that the minimum commissions may be exceeded. They are a floor under charges, not a ceiling on them. Competition generally requires that the minimum commission is the one charged.

On **odd-lots** in stock selling at $1 per share or more the commissions are the same as those above minus $2.

2. On stocks, rights, and warrants selling at **less than $1 per** share, commissions are based on fractions of cents per share. A few of the rates are as follows:

Price per share	Commission
1/256 of $1	0.1 cent
1/64 of $1	0.5
½ of $1	3.0
7/8 of $1	5.25

The establishment of minimum commissions or charges has a twofold purpose; it puts competition between members on a service basis, and eliminates what is known as "price competition." The elimination of the latter is especially significant because cut-throat competition could endanger the financial stability of commission houses. Members of the Exchange may, in no event, under the Rules of the New York Stock Exchange, split their commissions with others or charge less than the schedule of charges indicated above.

Floor brokers and specialists currently receive, on orders executed for fellow members of the New York Stock Exchange, a fixed schedule of commissions, which likewise varies with the price of the security. For example, on an order involving 100 shares of stock selling at $45, the commission to a nonmember customer would be $41.50, whereas the floor brokerage, or commission charged a member, would be $3.85.

When nonmembers of the Exchange, such as banks, trust companies, or nonmember investment houses, receive orders that are executed on an exchange, they frequently add a commission of their own to that charged by the broker.

TRANSFER TAXES AND REGISTRATION FEES. An **excise tax is levied by the State of New York** (wherein all sales on the New York Stock Exchange are legally consummated) on all transfers of beneficial ownership of securities taking place within the state. This tax is payable regardless of whether any transfer is made on the books of the issuing corporation, which, like the buyer and seller, may be physically located outside of the state.

§ 270 of Article 12 of the New York Tax Law, effective July 1, 1945, imposes a tax of 2¢ on the transfer of each share, except if the shares or certificates are sold, in which instance the tax rate is as follows:

  1¢ for each share where the selling price is less than $5 per share;
  2¢ for each share where the selling price is $5 or more per share and less than $10 per share;
  3¢ for each share where the selling price is $10 or more per share and less than $20 per share;
  4¢ for each share where the selling price is more than $20 per share.

A few other states also levy an excise tax on the transfer of enumerated classes of securities.

As the tax is levied but once on each transfer, it is paid by the seller and is deducted from the sales proceeds due him.

The **Federal government** levies an **excise tax** of $0.04 per $100 (or major fraction thereof) of the market value of stocks, rights, or warrants sold. There is a minimum tax of $0.04 **per transaction,** and a maximum tax of $0.08 **per share** on transfers involving items priced at $200 per unit or more.

Thus, on a stock selling for $24, the New York State tax would be $4 and the Federal tax, $0.96 on the transfer of 100 shares.

The Federal tax is levied on all transfers. It is, for example, levied on the loan of shares, whether made within one brokerage office or by one broker to another. The return of borrowed stock is not taxed.

A national securities exchange registration fee is likewise charged. § 31 of the Securities Exchange Act assesses a registration fee on exchanges for the privilege of doing business as a national securities exchange. This fee, due March 15, amounts to 1/500 of 1% of the aggregate dollar value of sales of nonexempted securities on the Exchange during the preceding calendar year. In turn, the fee is charged against individual members on the basis of their sales volume. On sales made for the account of customers, the 1/500 of 1% fee is deducted from the gross proceeds due. If a sale is very small, the amount may be forgiven by the commission house.

The combined commission, transfer tax, and registration fee incurred in the sale of 100 shares of stock selling at 30 would be as follows:

100 shares at 30		$3,000.00
Deduct:		
Brokerage commission	$34.00	
New York State tax	4.00	
Federal tax	1.20	
SEC registration fee	.06	39.26
Net proceeds		$2,960.74

STOCKS SELLING EX-DIVIDEND OR EX-RIGHTS. When a dividend has been declared on a stock it is necessary to adjust the basis of its quotation because buyers who have the stock transferred to their names after the closing of stock transfer books on the **date of record** do not receive a dividend. Because of the time required to deliver the stock and record buyer's name on stock ledger the New York Stock Exchange advances the date when stocks shall be quoted and sold on an **ex-dividend basis** to the **third** full business day before date of record.

A dividend declared May 20, payable July 1 to stockholders of record June 10, will go only to holders whose names are recorded on the company books at close of business on the record day. The stock will be quoted and traded on the exchange on an ex-dividend basis June 7, or, if a week end or holiday intervenes, the next preceding business day. Beneficial owners of stock held in street or other names on the record day are entitled to have dividends credited to their account though the stock is never actually transferred to their names.

Similarly, whenever a distribution of **rights to subscribe** to new stock or other distribution is to be made to shareholders, the stock will ordinarily be quoted **ex-rights or ex-whatever else is being given** 3 days before the day of record. The Exchange authorities may fix the date on which securities sell **ex-dividend** or **ex-rights** at their discretion, if circumstances make this desirable. When dividends or rights go to brokers not entitled to them, as where stock certificates are not transferred promptly to the buyer, they are passed on to the right parties through **due bills** accompanying the stock at the time of transfer. If stocks are borrowed for delivery against short sales, the broker will charge the customer for whose account he has borrowed the shares the amount of the dividend, which will go to the lender of the stock as the owner.

TRADING IN RIGHTS AND STOCK PURCHASE WARRANTS. Subscription rights to listed securities are normally traded in on the Exchange. They may become the subject of lively trading on a **when-issued** basis between the time when a new offering of stock to existing shareholders is announced by the board of directors and the date of their issue. Thereafter they are traded in the regular way. Because of the small investment that they require and the speculative opportunities that they present, their price may rise above their mathematical value that is based on the difference between the subscription and the market price of the security. (Leffler and Farwell, The Stock Market.)

Stock purchase warrants, also known as **option warrants,** are commonly attached to other securities at the time of their issue or given to promoters or bankers upon organization of the corporation as compensation for services. These warrants entitle the holder to purchase shares of (usually) common stock at a specified price per share, either within a given period or for an indefinite time. Warrants may be issued separately or attached to other securities, and in the latter instance may be detachable or nondetachable. If warrants are not attached to listed issues, separate listing is required. In some instances, warrants to buy stock listed on the New York Stock Exchange are listed on the American Stock Exchange.

WHEN-ISSUED TRADING. Federal legislation has substantially altered the character of all when, as, and if issued or distributed trading in securities. Section 5 of the Securities Act of 1933 prohibits the sale by issuer, underwriter, or dealer of any security, by the use of the mails or in interstate commerce, unless a registration statement is in effect. Such a statement contains prescribed information about the issuing company and its security, for the benefit of interested investors. Furthermore, a prospectus summarizing this information must be delivered to the buyer before all sales made within 40 days by the company, its agents, or investment bankers (or within 90 days if the securities have never before been offered publicly). When the securities are debt instruments, the **indenture must also be qualified** under the Trust Indenture Act of 1939.

The S.E.C. considers a **when-issued contract** not as a separate security, but as one that represents the security to be delivered and subject to the same requirements as it would be. Thus brokers and dealers, along with issuers and underwriters, are prohibited from dealing in when-issued contracts in advance of the effective date of registration.

§ 4(1) of the Securities Act, it is true, exempts transactions by any person other than an issuer, underwriter, or dealer (which includes a broker). From a practical standpoint, however, one cannot trade readily in when-issued contracts without a broker or dealer.

Permissible Transactions. Under the statute, the following types of when-issued trading are practicable:

1. When-issued transactions executed by brokers upon customers' orders without solicitation may take place at any time. In actual practice this exemption is not important.
2. Brokers and dealers are entirely free to conduct when-issued trading at any time in classes of securities that, because of the character of the issuers, are exempted from the registration and qualification provisions of the Securities Act and its related Trust Indenture Act. These include government obligations, bank stocks, and railroad securities subject to regulation by the Interstate Commerce Commission.
3. Most of the when-issued and all of the when-distributed trading occurs as a result of the **statutory exemptions granted** particular types of transactions: (a) exchanges or distributions of securities arising under Section 11 of the Public Utility Holding Company Act of 1935; (b) securities issued in corporate reorganizations under Chapter X of the Bankruptcy Act; and (c) securities issued in railroad reorganizations under Section 77 of the Bankruptcy Act. These exemptions are available only upon the occurrence of certain administrative or judicial action such as approval of a plan of reorganization or exchange by the S.E.C., a court of appropriate jurisdiction, or the Interstate Commerce Commission.

When-issued or when-distributed trading is permissible without affirmative judicial or administrative action in securities arising out of certain corporate actions approved by stockholders that are held not to constitute a "sale"—e.g., the distribution of a dividend in kind or the declaration of a stock dividend.

When-issued or when-distributed trading, apart from the above exemptions, is **prohibited prior to effective registration.** Such trading after registration is strictly limited by the fact that securities are registered only for immediate offering and sale. The one situation that commonly occurs in which there is an opportunity for when-issued trading after effective registration is the instance where a security is registered for offering to existing security holders for subscription or exchange, to be followed after a lapse of time by an offering of any unsubscribed balance to the public. In this kind of situation there may be when-issued trading of two kinds: (1) in the security that is the subject of the rights during the period after effective registration when it is being offered solely to security holders; and (2) in the rights themselves (or in the warrants evidencing these rights) during the period between the effective date of registration and the date of actual issuance of the rights. Any dealer or broker who sells a registered security on a when-issued basis must make available the formal prospectus to each buyer.

Limitations Imposed by Securities Exchange Act. In addition to restrictions on when-issued trading imposed by the Securities Act and the Trust Indenture Act, which apply to over-the-counter trading of this character, **another set of restrictions** is imposed by the Securities Exchange Act. When-issued trading can take place only on an unlisted trading basis, since the full listing requirements cannot be satisfied. As a practical matter, only corporations with securities already listed or about which substantial public information is available may be admitted to unlisted when-issued trading.

Registration of securities for when-issued trading on exchanges must meet the requirements of S.E.C. Rule X-12D3. To be eligible for unlisted trading: (1) such securities must be issuable only in exchange for a security previously admitted to dealing; (2) the unissued security must be "in the process of admission to dealing" on the exchange; (3) the issuer must have made formal and official announcement specifying the terms of the plan or offer pursuant to which the security is to be issued, the record date, and the approximate date of issuance; (4) the issuer or the exchange must file a simple form with the S.E.C. to show compliance with the when-issued rules.

When-issued transactions appear on the stock ticker tape with the abbreviation "W.I." printed thereafter. These transactions are not cleared until the issue date, or such date as the New York Stock Exchange may fix as the settlement date. The transactions may, however, be **marked to the market** in a manner similar to the practice in short sales described below. Since the New York Stock Exchange does not encourage it, when-issued trading may take place on the American Stock Exchange and over-the-counter markets even though it is intended ultimately to list the actual securities on the Big Board.

With respect to **when-distributed trading**, the New York Stock Exchange requires, as a condition precedent to admission for trading, (1) that a definitive plan for distribution of the security pro rata to holders of outstanding securities of the distributor, without payment of any consideration, be approved by the appropriate court or governmental body; (2) that no possibility of an appeal exist; (3) that the distribution, when completed, be sufficiently broad to meet the Stock Exchange's usual requirements; and (4) that the distributor authorize the distribution to holders of record as of a specified date.

SPECIAL PROCEDURES FOR LARGE BLOCKS. Large blocks of securities are sometimes offered for sale by estates, investment companies and other institutional holders, private individuals, business executives, corporate holders, and others who desire to liquidate or shift their holdings. The auction market is geared to moderate amounts of securities at any one time. It is not usually broad enough to absorb, without substantial price declines, large blocks which exceed the available demand and throw the market out of equilibrium. If such liquidation is pushed, the price of the security is depressed below its intrinsic worth, at least temporarily until this block has been "digested." Such sales entail a sacrifice to the seller.

Prior to the enactment of the Securities Exchange Act of 1934, distributions to the public of large blocks of stocks that were listed on exchanges were frequently accompanied by **manipulation** (1) to raise the price of the security, and (2) to stimulate activity to the point where a demand large enough to absorb the offered security would be created. After passage of the Act, a procedure was developed and widely used whereby larger blocks of listed stocks were distributed to the public over the counter. These offerings were almost invariably made at 3:30 P.M., immediately after the close of the exchange market, to permit stock exchange members to participate in such "off-the-board" offerings. The securities involved were offered at or about the closing exchange quotation of that day. Most of these offerings were completed prior to the opening of the market on the succeeding day, and if not completed by that time they were usually withdrawn to avoid conflict with trading on the floor. These **secondary distributions** could be underwritten, as with new offerings of securities.

These offerings became especially heavy after the start of World War II, when foreign governments sought to liquidate in this country the holdings of American corporate securities that they had sequestered from their own nationals. The New York exchanges became concerned with the loss of trading volume from "off-the-board" offerings of listed securities. Accordingly, they devised means to facilitate offerings of comparatively large blocks of stock directly on the floors of these exchanges.

A **special offering plan** was evolved in 1942. The S.E.C. amended its Rule 12b-2 to permit special offerings of blocks of securities on national securities exchanges pursuant to a plan filed with and declared effective by the S.E.C. This plan provides that a special offering may be made when it has been determined that the auction market on the floor of the exchange cannot absorb a particular block of a security within a reasonable time without undue disturbance of the current price. The offering is made at a **fixed price** set within the framework of the existing auction market.

Members, acting as brokers for public buyers, are **paid a special commisssion by the seller** that ordinarily exceeds considerably the regular rate of commission. This special commission is to compensate for the greater trouble and expense involved in finding buyers, and is a stimulus to make a substantial selling effort. Buyers pay only the fixed offering price, without commission. Full disclosure is made to the buyer of all the details relating to his purchase, including the commission paid to his broker by the seller. A special offering usually gets under way in mid-morning by an announcement on the ticker tape as follows:

NOTICE SPECIAL OFFERING BY RITER & CO 4100 MDE 22¾ COMM ¾

This means that Riter & Co. is handling a special offering of 4,100 shares of stock of McDermott & Co. at 22¾, with a commission of ¾ points, or $0.75, paid to brokers who send in orders for the stock that are accepted by Riter & Co. Owing to advance soundings of the market, the offering may be subscribed within a few minutes. Rules of the New York Stock Exchange require, however, that the books remain open for at least 15 minutes unless the announcement was made well ahead of the time of the offering, and that oversubscriptions be prorated. While special offerings are under way, brokers are obligated to take other stock that may be offered on the floor in the regular way. To prevent the market quotation from "sagging" under the weight of a special offering, **stabilizing purchases** may be made if notice of intention to stabilize the market is given in advance, and such transactions must be reported to the S.E.C.

Special bids may be made for large blocks of stock in similar fashion.

Exchange distribution procedures were introduced in 1953 as another means for selling large blocks of stock. An exchange distribution, as described by the New York Stock Exchange (New York Stock Exchange Guide, 2392) is accomplished by obtaining sufficient buy orders from customers beforehand to permit a cross of the buy and sell orders on the floor in the usual auction market. The stock is offered within the current quotations free of commission to the buyers. The seller may, and does, pay a special commission to the selling brokers as an incentive for their efforts in obtaining buy orders. The success of this procedure depends upon the ability of member organizations to secure sufficient buy orders in a fairly short period of time. Exchange acquisitions may be made when a purchase of a substantial block of stock is desired.

Notice of execution of an exchange distribution or acquisition is given on the tape only after sufficient orders have been received to permit a crossing of them on the floor.

Specialist block purchase, or **sale,** may provide a procedure for selling, or buying, a fairly large block of stock quickly. The specialist in an issue, when asked to bid on a block of stock too large for prompt sale in the usual way, may make a bid after considering his position, the current quotation in the market, and his estimate of near-term future prospects. The bid almost certainly will be somewhat below the best bid in the regular market. The seller will pay the usual commission to his broker. In practice, the cost to the seller of a fairly large block to the specialist under this procedure is likely to be about two to three times the normal commission when compared with the best bid in the regular auction market. The transaction is not reported on the ticker: It is considered a private transaction. The specialist probably expects to be able to sell the stock in the regular auction market within a few days at some profit to himself.

Similarly, the specialist may be willing to offer a fairly large block at a price somewhat above the best offer in the regular auction market. He would sell from inventory or on the expectation that he would be able to cover a temporary short position within a few days in the regular auction market.

SHORT SALES. A short sale is a sale of securities that the seller does not intend to deliver from his own portfolio. A short sale may be one where the seller does not possess the securities sold, or a **"sale against the box,"** if he does own the securities sold but does not intend at the time of sale to deliver them. The short seller expects the price of the security sold short to decline, and he expects in the future to be able to buy back or "cover" his short sale at a lower price, so as to secure a profit. Sellers for the decline are popularly known as **"bears,"** whereas buyers for the rise are known as **"bull"** speculators.

The total volume of short selling that goes on in normal times is only a small fraction of the speculative buying or **"long"** position that prevails. However, in periods of unsettled markets, short selling, by increasing the volume of securities offered for sale in the market at one time, could tend to unsettle trading further. The New York Stock Exchange and other exchanges guard against concentrated short selling by the rules and restrictions applicable to such activity.

Operation of a Short Sale. When a customer wishes to sell a stock short, he gives a selling order to his broker in the usual way. He will specify that the transaction is a short sale. As the broker has to deliver the stock sold the fourth day following, under the settlement rules of the exchange, he must arrange to obtain such stock for delivery. This can be done by arranging to **borrow** the stock from some other broker. Most borrowing of securities is arranged after trading hours.

To provide **security** for the loan of stock, the borrowing broker deposits with the lender a sum of money equal to the market price of the borrowed shares. This money is obtained from the short sale of the issue. Thus, if a brokerage house customer sells 100 shares of Steel at 65, his account is credited on account of a short sale to the extent of approximately $6,500. After the sale, his broker will borrow a certificate for 100 shares of Steel from some broker who is carrying it in a long account. The borrowing broker will deposit with the lending broker the $6,500 received from the sale as security for the loan of stock. The borrowed stock is then delivered at the regular time by the borrowing broker to the buyer of the 100 shares of Steel.

Loaning Rates. Stock is usually loaned **flat.** No interest is paid on the money put up as collateral on the borrowed stock, and a premium is not usually collected by the lender of stock. In earlier years, interest was paid by the lending broker on the money pledged. Ordinarily, however, the use of the money is adequate compensation to the lender of the stock. On occasions when keen demand for loans of a particular stock developed, lenders have received **premiums** for lending stock at the rates of $1 or $2 per round lot per day.

The Securities Exchange Act requires that customers of brokerage houses give specific permission to have their stock loaned before their brokers are permitted to do so. This permission is a standard part of the agreement signed by a customer opening a general account.

As prices of loaned stock fluctuate, the amount of money put up as collateral will be increased or reduced as the interested parties ask that it be **"marked to the market."** If the price rises, the lender wishes more money deposited as collateral; if the stock falls, the borrower wishes to have some of the deposited cash released to him. Loans of stock, like call loans of money, may be called at the option of either party on 24 hours' notice. A Federal transfer tax is levied on loans of stock.

Margins Deposited Against Short Sales. To protect themselves in the event of a rise in price of a stock sold short, brokers require margins to be deposited by short sellers just as in the case of long purchases. Margin requirements on "short" accounts are subject to regulation by the Board of Governors of the Federal Reserve System, just as with "long" accounts. In a **"mixed account,"** in which long and short items are mixed, the margin is figured separately on the long stocks and the additional margin requirement added for short commitments. When premiums are quoted on stocks borrowed, they are charged by the broker to the customer selling short. To some extent, brokers can avoid paying such premiums themselves by intraoffice borrowing of stocks.

ECONOMIC EFFECTS OF SHORT SELLING. There is some diversity of opinion as to the effects of short selling on security markets. Although undoubtedly short selling tends to stabilize the market, since short sellers have to sell on rises and repurchase later when demand for the stock may dwindle, in a period of general liquidation the short seller may unsettle trading to some extent by adding to the current volume of offerings in an already overloaded market.

The major **advantages** claimed for short selling are:

1. Short sellers supply stocks when prices rise, thus tending to retard excessive advances.

2. Short sellers buy in on the decline, thus tending to reduce the extent of the fall in price.
3. Those holding real estate or other less marketable assets can protect themselves against a general decline in the price level by selling standard stocks short.
4. Short selling is necessary on the part of odd-lot dealers, floor traders, and specialists to perform their essential functions.

The chief **arguments against** short selling are:

1. The practice may cause unwarranted declines in security prices, especially when insufficient buying orders in the market weaken the "technical position" of the issue.
2. Short selling by floor members and specialists, who can get an intimate picture of the state of the market, may permit them to profit at the cost of the outside public when it tries to liquidate securities.
3. Short selling may exaggerate security price advances as well as declines, as shorts who sell on a rising market may find it difficult to cover and will have to bid against themselves to obtain stock for this purpose.

CORNERS AND MANIPULATION. Corners arise when the short sellers in a stock find it impossible to borrow shares to deliver against their commitments. A **"technical corner"** is one where the amount of stock sold short exceeds the floating supply. Corners sometimes arise when the stock of a company is being bought up for control, unknown to the shorts. At other times, heavy investment buying of stock may eliminate the floating supply and disclose an unwieldy short interest. In some instances, a condition approaching a corner may arise accidentally, through excessive short selling of an issue with a small floating supply.

Control of Corners. The New York Stock Exchange has sought to avoid corners by refusing to list small issues of stock in which such a condition could readily arise. Also, the Exchange investigates the market position of a stock when it is feared the borrowing supply is becoming inadequate, and it may require members to report at once their positions and commitments in such an issue. When conditions approaching corners do develop, the Exchange under its constitution can order deliveries against short sales deferred, or order that outstanding contracts be **settled at a fixed price** to avoid spectacular price gyrations that tend to unsettle confidence in the remainder of the market and attract unfavorable publicity to the Exchange. In extreme instances, the Exchange has stricken from its list issues in which corners have developed on the ground that a "free and open market" for the issue, the primary objective of the Exchange, has been destroyed. This drastic action is resorted to when the corner has been intentionally created, and especially when the management of the enterprise is involved in the operation.

Corners are not likely to occur in present-day markets because of surveillance by the S.E.C.; weekly reports that members must make as to their short position; publication of trading by directors, officers, and principal holders; power of the S.E.C. to suspend trading; and, finally, statutory prohibitions of manipulative practices.

FEDERAL REGULATION OF SHORT SELLING. In 1930 the New York Stock Exchange promulgated a rule that prohibited short sales at less than the previous sale price, to prevent bear raiding and demoralization of the markets. This rule, however, did not cover several types of transactions that are now considered "short sales."

§10(a) of the Securities Exchange Act of 1934 makes it unlawful for any person to effect a short sale of any security registered on a national securities exchange in contravention of any rules or regulations that the S.E.C. may prescribe as necessary or appropriate in the public interest or for the protection of investors. Under this authority, the S.E.C. promulgated Rules X-10A-1, X-10A-2, and X-3B-3, effective February 8, 1938. The effect of these was to prohibit the short sale of a security except at a price above the last preceding sale price. Odd-lot transactions and certain round-lot transactions of odd-lot dealers were exempted from the rules. Following study of the effect of its rules, and upon the recommendation of the New York Stock Exchange, the S.E.C. modified these rules in 1939 to permit short sales at the price of the last sale, instead of above the last sale price, provided that the last sale price was itself higher than the last different price that preceded it.

In addition to the **exemptions** granted to odd-lot dealers, exemptions are extended to certain short sales on a domestic exchange effected for the purpose of equalizing prices between that exchange and another national securities exchange, short sales effected in arbitrage transactions between securities, and certain short sales made in the course of international arbitrage.

ODD-LOT TRADING. Odd-lot dealers have developed a specialized, highly efficient mechanism for the execution of orders in listed stocks for lots less than the unit of trading: 100 shares, except for specified inactive issues of which the unit of trading on the floor is ten shares.

Odd-lot dealers on the New York Stock Exchange stand ready at all times to buy or sell for their own account from 1 to 99 shares of stock in any listed issue for which a round lot is 100 shares, and from 1 to 9 shares of stock in issues traded in ten-share round lots. The odd-lot dealer charges a **differential** on buy orders of $\frac{1}{8}$ point (on stocks selling for less than $40 a share) or $\frac{1}{4}$ point (on stocks selling at $40 a share or more) above the next price at which a round-lot transaction takes place in the stock market after the odd-lot order has been received on the floor. If instructed to do so, the odd-lot dealer will execute a sale at the appropriate differential away from the prevailing bid in the round-lot market without waiting for a sale in that market. Similar differentials on sale orders are subtracted from the price paid to the customer. The odd-lot seller also pays transfer taxes.

Since the odd-lot dealer automatically buys and sells stock for his own account **on the basis of prices established in the round-lot transactions,** he must be very nimble to limit his long or short position in each issue. This is done by selling or buying round lots on the floor.

In placing orders for odd lots of securities, it is important to keep in mind that it takes about 4 minutes to transmit such an order from a Wall Street brokerage office to the floor of the Exchange. Therefore, on an issue in which the odd-lot differentials is $\frac{1}{4}$, orders to buy at, say, 90 will not be executed until a full lot at $89\frac{3}{4}$ appears on the tape, unless permission is given to buy at the asked price and sell at the bid price and this is satisfactory to the odd-lot dealer.

The commission broker receiving the odd-lot order from the public charges the usual rate of commission for its execution.

OPTIONS OR PRIVILEGES. An important adjunct to stock speculation, described by Filer (Understanding Put and Call Options), is the market in options or privileges, including "puts," "calls," and "straddles." Members of the New York Stock Exchange are forbidden to trade in options on the floor of the Exchange, but they may guarantee these privileges and so assure that they will be honored. **Put and call brokers** issue lists of prices on options from time to time.

A "**put**" is a contract giving the holder the privilege of delivering a stated number of shares of a given stock to the maker within a certain time and at a certain price. It may be purchased by those who hope to make a profit from a decline in the stock.

A "**call**" is a contract whereby the holder gets the privilege of purchasing a given number of shares of a given stock from the maker within a certain time and at a certain price. It is purchased by those who hope to profit from a rise in the shares.

A "**straddle**" or "**spread**" and a "**strip**" or "**strap**" are combinations of puts and calls. Straddles and spreads represent combinations of one put and one call. They differ in that the option prices of the put and call in a straddle are at the market when the options are written; prices are so many points below the market for the put and above the market for a call in a spread. A strap combines two calls with one put; a strip, two puts with one call. The option prices in these instances are at the market when the options are written. These combinations are of importance to the writers of options, but are seldom sold as such. Few speculators are sufficiently ambivalent to seek to profit from both rise and fall in the price of a stock within a short period of time.

Federal and state **tax stamps** are required by law to be affixed to all call contracts. These taxes must be paid by the buyer of the call contract. Maximum Federal and state taxes are $12 per 100 shares. There is no tax on put contracts.

Dividends and distributions on shares that sell "ex" during the life of the option go with the stock. Thus, the holder of a put that sells "ex" must pay to the endorser such dividend or distribution if he decides to deliver the stock; and the holder of a call receives such dividends or distributions if he calls the stock. As regards rights, the **Put and Call Brokers and Dealers Assn., Inc.,** has ruled that the opening sale of the rights, when stock sells ex-rights on the exchange, is automatically the agreed price between the owner and the seller of the option, and this price is the settlement price when either a put or call contract is exercised.

Puts and calls may be purchased for 30, 60, 90, and 190 days' or longer duration, as agreed by the parties to the contract. They are usually written **at the market price** of the stock for an agreed premium. In the past, they were written at so many points above or below the market as fixed by negotiation between the buyer and the seller.

Privileges become valueless if not exercised within the specified time. When exercised, the stock is bought or sold in the regular way, commission being paid on the transaction. Options may be sold as securities in their own right rather than exercised.

The manner in which **speculation** may be carried on with options may be seen by an illustration. Suppose a call on 100 shares of Steel is available when the market price is 70 at a premium of $4.00, plus tax, a share for a 90-day period, the usual price of a one-way option. If during this period Steel should rise to 76, the profit of the option holder by exercising it is computed as follows:

Cost of option	$ 400.00
Cost of 100 shares of Steel at 70 under the option, plus commission	7,046.00
Total cost of stock	7,446.00
Proceeds of sale of 100 Steel at 76, less commission, taxes, and fees	$7,546.22
Profit on transaction	100.22

SECURITIES TRADING ON EXCHANGES   10·27

Purpose of Privileges. Privileges have two chief uses. First, they permit speculators to take positions with a **small amount at risk.** In the instance above described, the maximum amount at risk of the holder of the privilege is $400, plus tax, for if Steel had not risen he would merely have resold the option at a loss or permitted it to expire. If there had been a major rise in the price of the stock, his profit would have been many times the amount invested. By comparison, the outright purchase of Steel at 70 would require an investment of more than $7,000.

In the second place, options may be used as a means of **limiting losses on other commitments.** Thus, suppose a speculator has accumulated 1,000 shares of a stock selling at 80, involving a total investment of $80,000. He wishes to hold the stock for an extended rise but at the same time wishes to guard against a sharp reaction in the stock. This he can do by buying a put, which will allow him to deliver the stock at his option at a stated price in the event of a decline.

The following example contrasts the value of a put privilege with a stop-loss order:

A and B each buy 100 shares XYZ at 50.
A buys a put contract at 50.
B, who does not buy a put contract, enters a stop-loss order at 48½.
XYZ declines to 47.
B is stopped out at or near 48½ since a sale at 48½ or lower causes his stop-loss order to become a **market order,** and the broker must then sell his stock at the best possible price obtainable.
A, protected by his put option contract, knows that he can sell at any time during the life of his contract 100 XYZ at 50.
XYZ rallies to 53 and A can sell his stock at a profit because his put contract caused him to hold his stock until its expiration. B, who sold his stock at a loss on account of the stop-loss order, does not benefit from this upturn in the market price. A, however, pays an option premium substantially greater than any cost incurred by B. To some investors, at some times, this may be worthwhile.

In addition to the two chief uses just mentioned, options may be used as a method of **entering the market** at a future date. This is desired by a trader who is uncertain as to the market outlook or who is awaiting the occurrence of some event, e.g., a court decision. With a call or put, he may buy or sell at a fixed price after he knows the course of events.

Privileges originate to a large extent with large stockholders who seek to earn additional income on their holdings by writing puts and calls which they hope will not be exercised. Sometimes a block of stock can be liquidated by a large holder through the sale of calls. Additional income is earned from the sale of the options until such time as they are exercised, when the sale is finally consummated.

SETTLEMENT OF EXCHANGE TRANSACTIONS. The New York Stock Exchange operates on the principle of **daily settlement.** Every transaction on the Exchange, except where specific exception is made by agreement between the parties, must be settled by 12:30 P.M., so-called **delivery time,** of the fourth following full business day.

Under special circumstances, parties to a security transaction may provide for settlement on a different basis. Thus, "cash" transactions involve settlement by delivery of securities and payment of money on the same day. These are resorted to when it is desired to make the sale that day a matter of record, as in connection with the establishment of security losses for tax or statement purposes on the last day of the year. In other instances, sales may be made for future delivery at **seller's option** up to 60 days. Some sales in this category are really short sales, whereas others represent securities sold by holders living at a distance from New York or abroad, who wish more time to make delivery.

The Clearing Process. Settlement of security transactions on the Stock Exchange is facilitated by the process of clearing, which seeks to offset transactions so that actual deliveries of securities and money can be reduced as far as possible. The **Stock Clearing Corporation,** a subsidiary corporation whose stock is held by the Board of Governors in trust for all the members of the New York Stock Exchange, effects clearing. Without it, settlement daily for the vast volume of transactions that takes place on the New York Stock Exchange in active trading periods would be more difficult.

Only transactions in stocks, rights, and warrants are "cleared" through the Corporation. Odd lots and bonds are not cleared. Nonclearing securities, however, will be delivered by the **Central Delivery Department.** Not all members of the New York Stock Exchange are members of the Stock Clearing Corporation, but those who are not clear through a clearing member. For this privilege, a small charge is made. Regular clearing members defray expenses by charges that are levied in accordance with the volume of various types of activities transacted. In addition to members of the New York Stock Exchange, some nonmember banks and securities houses have clearing privileges.

Steps in Settlement. Settlement of transactions on the Exchange involves four chief steps. These are:

1. **Comparison of Transactions.** Since purchases and sales are made only orally on the floor of the Exchange, with each member sending written reports only to his own office, it becomes necessary to compare the records of each member who has had business with another to assure that there are no discrepancies.

2. **Security Clearance.** For cleared issues, the Stock Clearing Corporation acts as a clearing agency, transactions of each house being offset against one another, so that only the **net balance** of stock or money due need be delivered to or received from the Clearing Corporation.

3. **Actual Delivery of Securities.** Delivery is accomplished largely through the Central Delivery Department of the Stock Clearing Corporation. Delivery of securities to and from banks in connection with collateral loans is also accomplished by the Central Delivery Department.

Clearance and Settlement of the Money Values of Security Deliveries. This is accomplished by the Stock Clearing Corporation, which keeps a **"record sheet"** for each member on which are entered credit and debit items arising from the delivery or receipt of securities. At the end of the day, each member's account is balanced. If he has a credit, he draws a single draft for the sum of the Stock Clearing Corporation, whereas if there is a debit he sends a single check covering it to the corporation.

The routine clerical work of stock and money clearings has been enormously speeded up and simplified by the installation of electronic data processing equipment.

What Constitutes Good Delivery. To protect buyers of securities, the Board of Governors of the Exchange has promulgated rules covering in detail what constitutes a good delivery of securities against sales. Several of the more important rules are:

1. Stock certificates must be accompanied by **proper assignment** executed either on the certificate itself or on a separate paper. The correctness of the signature

SPECULATION IN SECURITIES 10·29

must be guaranteed by a member or a member firm. Members, in turn, frequently want signatures unknown to them guaranteed by a bank or trust company.
2. When an assignment is filled in with the name of an individual or a firm as attorney, a **power of substitution** must be executed.
3. The **signature** on the assignment or power of substitution must correspond with the name on the certificate "in every particular without alteration or enlargement or any change whatever."
4. If part of an issue of stock has been **called for redemption**, called certificates can be delivered only when they have been sold as such.

To facilitate delivery of securities that are traded actively, it is customary to register some certificates in the names of stock exchange houses, which then endorse them in blank. These **"street" certificates** circulate freely from house to house, but may be transferred only just before dividend record dates.

Consequences of Failure to Deliver. Failure to make good delivery constitutes a breach of the implied conditions of the contract of purchase and sale, for which the seller is liable for damages sustained. Deliberate failure may result in **suspension** or **expulsion** from the Exchange. To avoid failure to deliver, brokers for short sellers occasionally pay a premium to borrow stocks when the available shares are scarce in relation to the demand for loans to cover short sales.

When delivery is not forthcoming the buying broker may, but seldom does, after a "failure" of several days, serve a **"buy-in"** notice upon the selling broker. This buy-in notice states that, if delivery is not made, the broker of the buyer will meet his obligation to his customer by buying the stock in the open market for cash and any resulting loss will be charged to the nondelivering broker and his customer.

Speculation in Securities

DIFFERENTIATION OF SPECULATION FROM INVESTMENT. The fundamental difference between speculation and investment is the **degree of risk** involved in a transaction.

The differentiation between speculation and investment is not hard-and-fast, and it is often difficult to distinguish between the two types of commitments. The degree of knowledge about investment possessed by the security buyer is highly important, for only by being able to identify and appraise risks, or having this done by reliable experts for him, can the buyer avoid them and so invest rather than speculate.

From the point of view of the economy, it does not matter whether a buyer of securities makes a speculative or an investment purchase. In either instance, capital in the form of purchasing power is transferred from the buyer to the seller. Speculation can affect economic conditions when it takes the form of extensive purchasing of securities with bank credit, and so expands credit without reference to business or consumer needs. In recognition of this possibility, the Board of Governors of the Federal Reserve System, by the Securities Exchange Act of 1934, was given authority to regulate security loans.

ADVANTAGES AND DISADVANTAGES OF SECURITY SPECULATION. Like other economic phenomena, speculation has its advantages and disadvantages.

Advantages. The economic advantages of security speculation are:
1. Capital is made available to new and untried enterprises, which could not be started at all if investors had to be appealed to for necessary funds. Newer

industries, particularly, get their start because speculators are willing to buy their securities before they have become seasoned.
2. The credit resources of the nation are mobilized for the financing of enterprises in their promotion stages, or those that are not strong enough financially to have an investment appeal. Through bank loans on securities, speculators are able to purchase such speculative issues, safeguarding the banks against loss by the margin they put up.
3. Speculation acts as a stabilizer, though an imperfect one, of security prices. The speculator may be the only one who cares to buy securities when the outlook is clouded, and conversely, he may sell short and so supply stocks when investors are rampantly optimistic.

Disadvantages. Disadvantages that have been urged against security speculation are:
1. Speculation may exaggerate security price swings by causing excessive buying on the rise and thus excessive liquidation on the decline.
2. Losses due to such price swings can discourage investment of savings in stocks by others.
3. Speculation that involves credit in large amounts may exaggerate economic fluctuations, as in the period preceding and following 1929.

MANIPULATION. Stock prices have, at times, been determined by manipulative, as distinguished from unorganized speculative, activity. The usual method of the **"pool" operators** of the past was to accumulate stock over a period of time, refraining from buying on bulges during the period of accumulation. The second step was the "marking up" process, which was accomplished after the block of stock desired had been accumulated. By that time, the floating supply of the issue had usually been reduced so that a few large buying orders sufficed to advance the price to the desired level. The rise tended to attract a public following, and the stock accumulated was then gradually distributed around the high level of the advance, or after a decline had set in.

Market stabilization, which can play a constructive role in security distributions, and for other purposes, involves a different technique. Buying orders are placed at a fixed price or on a **scale down** under the market, to offer resistance to declines. Conversely, selling orders are placed at a fixed price or on **scale up** above the market, so that the stock purchased on declines is disposed of on advances. Thus, price fluctuations are halted or limited in both directions for a time. When notice is given that stabilization transactions are going on, investors and traders are less likely to be misled by them.

Manipulative practices that were frequent in the decade of the 20's and before are now subject to a number of prohibitions and restrictions. §9(a) of the Securities Exchange Act specifically prohibits any transaction in any security that involves **no change in beneficial ownership.**

§9(a)(6) prohibits a series of transactions for the purpose of **pegging, fixing, or stabilizing the price** of any security except in conformance to rules and regulations of the S.E.C. Regulations covering some types of stabilization have been issued by the Commission. Price manipulation and stabilization are further discussed later in this Section, under Federal Regulation.

MARKET INDICATORS. It is usual for some stocks to rise and others to fall on each trading day. Many listed stocks are not traded every day. One can get only a confused picture of the trend of the market from the high, low, and closing quotations of daily trading, or by following the tape. To indicate the direction of the market, **statistical summaries** are published in the financial press—e.g., the number of stocks traded, the volume and the number which closed higher or lower, or unchanged. A list of ten or more of the most active stocks as shown by the volume of trading, with their price changes, may be given.

The Dow, Jones Averages. To provide another indicator of the market's direction, the financial publishing house of Dow, Jones & Co. started compiling at the end of the last century a simple arithmetic average of the closing prices of 11 active, and then representative, stocks, 9 of which were rails. Averages are now computed by Dow, Jones & Co. for **30 industrials, 20 rails, and 15 utility common stocks**, as well as a composite of the three groups. All of these stocks are listed on the New York Stock Exchange. These averages are widely used as a measure of the trend of common stock prices generally over short or long periods. They are computed and published on the ticker tape at the opening of the Exchange and hourly thereafter.

Other Indices. The Associated Press, the New York Times, the New York Herald Tribune, Moody's, and Standard & Poor's publish stock price averages with broader coverage than the Dow, Jones averages. Averages are computed for **bonds** of railroads, public utilities, and industrials. Yield averages are compiled for United States government, municipal and corporate bonds, preferred stocks, and common stocks.

Charting. Stock price indices or individual stock prices, when charted, give a picture of price behavior over a period of time. Such charts of stock prices have been used by some to provide forecasts of stock prices. Behavior of the Dow, Jones stock price average has been used to project the trend of the stock market by followers of the Dow theory. When both prices and volume of trading are charted for a period, interpretation of market behavior may be facilitated.

The Dow Theory of Stock Price Movements. At the turn of the century, Charles H. Dow advanced a theory, which has been enlarged upon by followers, for forecasting stock price trends by interpreting fluctuations in the two primary stock market averages then in existence, industrials and rails. The market at any given time is the resultant of three forces—day-to-day fluctuations, intermediate short-term movements, and, finally, major trends. The objective of Dow theorists is to forecast only **changes in the major trend of the market.** This they consider of special value because it, in turn, foreshadows changes in business activity.

As long as the top of each intermediate movement of the averages is higher than that of the preceding one, a major bull movement is continuing. A change is indicated, according to these theorists, when the peak of an intermediate movement fails to equal and surpass that of the preceding one; a definite signal of change in direction is given when both the peak and the trough fail to equal preceding ones. The **signal of declining business,** it is held, always comes **after** the change in the trend of stock prices has already taken place.

Lest one average be misinterpreted or be subject to misleading special factors, the two averages, rails and industrials, are used to supplement and corroborate one another. When one gives the same type of signal as the other, this confirms and reinforces the signal. Other factors are given varying degrees of emphasis, such as volume of trading, the degree of "penetration" of a new top or bottom, sidewise movement, and double tops and bottoms.

Many other, more elaborate theories for predicting stock price movements have been evolved in more recent years. As with soothsayers of old, failures of such predictions do not discourage those who make them—they merely modify or change their theories. The basic question raised by all these "systems," of course, is whether a market reflecting the actions of millions of persons, in response to a multitude of considerations, is subject to prediction by any mechanistic formula.

Stock Market Charts and Tape Readers. A number of speculative traders utilize charts as an aid to their activities. Although much of the effort to use charts is based upon empirical analysis of past trends, "chartists" usually claim an underlying logical basis for the use of such graphical devices as a guide to trading.

A chart of price movements of an individual stock had value when a pool operation was going on in that issue. If the price trend was studied in conjunction with the volume of sales, it was frequently possible to trace the processes of gradual accumulation by the pool at one price level, the marking up of the price and the distribution of the issue at a higher level. With the outlawing of organized speculative pools by legislation, this type of "chart reading" has lost most of its significance. However, many traders feel a chart of the past price movements of a stock is helpful to them in appraising its current market position.

Charts based on stock price indices are much less certain of interpretation. Some aid, however, in analyzing the technical state of the market, and the relative eagerness of the public to buy or sell stocks at any one time, may be furnished by an open-minded and cautious interpretation of charts of stock price indices.

Tape readers seek clues to the trend of the market, and of individual issues, by noting individual trades and volume and selecting stocks they believe offer opportunities for trading profits. Tape readers may not expect to "carry a position" overnight. S.E.C. regulations require that such "daylight trading," even though the transactions are closed out the same day, be fully margined.

SECURITY SERVICES AND RATINGS. To aid investors and traders, specialized services assemble and publish a mass of statistical information about individual companies. Services vary in quality from reputable gatherers and interpreters of economic and financial information to mere tipster sheets. The leading services, Moody's, Standard and Poor's, and Fitch, publish financial manuals or loose-leaf card systems of a comprehensive character, obtaining the information mainly from annual reports, data filed by the corporations with the S.E.C., and other official sources. Standard investment analysis ratios are computed from the financial statements for those who wish to make a quick appraisal of security values. (For further discussion, see Section 7, Security Analysis.)

The three leading investment services also undertake to evaluate the quality of securities by rating them. Bonds and stocks may be rated from several points of view. Safety of principal, security and certainty of income, asset values behind the security, earning power, and marketability are the usual tests.

A number of organizations provide an investment advisory service that interprets current conditions and trends affecting the market as a whole and individual securities. They make recommendations of purchases and sales for investment or speculation. A number act as investment counsel and service a portfolio of securities, making specific recommendations to buy, sell, or hold, for a fee. Individuals or corporations that provide this service must conform to the requirements of the **Investment Advisers Act of 1940.**

Trading on Margin

MARGIN PURCHASE OF SECURITIES. A purchase of securities may be for cash or **on margin,** where the customer pays down only a portion of the price of the security. A good part of the business carried on by the average commission house consists of margin transactions, though the volume of margin transactions today does not approach pre-World War II volumes, which made up the greater part of commission house business.

In a margin purchase, the customer is required to deposit with the broker, either in cash or acceptable securities, a fraction of the purchase price to protect the firm against loss. The balance is loaned the customer by the brokerage house, which obtains the funds usually by pledging the purchased securities with a bank for a collateral loan. The brokerage house may advance its own capital or free credit balances of other customers for the balance of the purchase price, or the stock bought may be loaned to other brokers who have sold short for their clients and wish to borrow stock in order to make delivery against the short sale.

The buyer must keep the margin good by depositing additional cash or acceptable securities in the event of a decline in prices below the minimum margin requirements. Conversely, the customer may withdraw cash or securities from his account if an advance in price should increase his margin substantially above requirements.

On the sale of a stock held on margin, the broker applies the proceeds to repayment of the debit balance due him from the customer. The balance left in the account of the customer stands to his credit, and, if he has no debit balance on account of other transactions, may be withdrawn by him or allowed to remain as a credit balance in his account.

Opening a Margin Account. Brokers open margin accounts, as a rule, without much investigation into the credit standing of the customer. A minimum deposit of $1,000 is required by most houses, with some desiring larger amounts for new accounts. Only **listed securities** may be carried in margin accounts, subject to both Federal Reserve and Stock Exchange requirements affecting security credit.

Customers' Margin Requirements. Brokerage houses keep customers' margin requirements under constant surveillance, employing margin clerks for the purpose, to determine any deficiencies promptly so that they can call upon customers to make them good.

The New York Stock Exchange requires that customers must have a **maintenance margin** of not less than 25% of the market value of all securities "long" in the account, plus, usually, 30% for short sales. When the margin in an account becomes inadequate, a **margin call** is sent the customer requesting payment of any deficiency.

REGULATION OF SECURITY CREDIT. The Securities Exchange Act of 1934 provides for the regulation of the **initial margins** that members of national securities exchanges shall require from their customers in the purchase of securities. This section of the law is administered by the Board of Governors of the Federal Reserve System, which sets initial maximum loan values and regulates the withdrawal of funds and securities from margin accounts, substitutions of securities, the transfer of accounts from one member to another and special margin requirements for delayed deliveries, short sales, and arbitrage transactions.

Members of national securities exchanges, and brokers or dealers who do a security business through such members, are not permitted, directly or indirectly, to extend credit to a customer on securities registered on a national securities exchange contrary to the rules laid down by the Board of Governors. This prohibition also extends to banks and other nonmember lenders, who cannot make loans on a registered security except in accordance with the Board's requirements. Certain types of loans, however, are freed from this latter restriction.

Members of national securities exchanges and brokers and dealers transacting business through them may borrow only from member banks and nonmember banks that agree to comply with restrictions applicable to member banks as regards loans extended to finance security transactions. The object of this provision is to assist the Board of Governors in regulating credit extensions on securities.

Regulation T controls the extension of credit on registered securities by members of national securities exchanges and brokers doing business through them. **Regulation U** applies to the extension of credit on registered securities by banks. However, existing regulations leave many areas open where credit may in fact be obtained for the purchase of securities. If a bank loan is not obtained for the ostensible purpose of purchasing securities, the borrower may use securities as collateral to an unlimited extent. A substantial decline in the value of the securities could jeopardize market stability regardless of the stated purpose of the loan. There are also many lenders, such as foreign banks and factors, who are not subject to any regulation of their financing of securities purchases.

RELATIONS BETWEEN BROKER AND CUSTOMER. A number of legal decisions have defined the relations between broker and customer in the ordinary margin transaction. (Markham v. Jaudon, 41 N. Y. 235, is the leading case.) The legal relations are fourfold, as follows:

1. The broker as agent, the customer as principal, covering the execution of the order and the arrangement of the loan to carry it.
2. The broker as creditor, the customer as debtor, in so far as the debit or credit balance of the customer is concerned.
3. The broker as pledgee, the customer as pledgor, in relation to the securities purchased by the customer and held by the broker as collateral for the debit balance.
4. The broker as trustee, the customer as beneficiary. This relationship arises only where the customer pays up his debit balance. In that case, both the law and the rules of the New York Stock Exchange prevent the broker from hypothecating customers' securities. He is expected to hold them earmarked for customers' accounts and, if he fails in business, they are not to be commingled with his own assets.

Rules of the New York Stock Exchange and the S.E.C. limit the extent to which customers' securities may be **hypothecated** for loans to what is regarded as reasonable in relation to the amount of the debit balance, regardless of agreements between broker and customer.

S.E.C. rules prohibit brokers from **risking customers' securities** as collateral to finance their own trading or underwriting ventures, or to pledge customers' securities for amounts in excess of customer indebtedness. These rules apply to business done over-the-counter as well as on an exchange.

A customer is expected to respond to margin calls promptly. If he does not, the broker must give a customer **"reasonable notice"** of his intention to offer pledged securities for sale in the market, any balance left after the sale and payment of the debit balance going to the customer, while the latter remains liable to the broker for any deficiency.

Brokerage houses customarily require customers to sign **waivers of notice**. If this is done, the broker may sell out the account when the margin is impaired without going through the formality of notice to customers.

BROKERS' INTEREST CHARGES. Interest charges are paid by customers on their debit balances. The brokerage house itself pays interest on funds obtained by it for the purpose of carrying customers' securities. The interest rate charged by brokerage houses is usually 1 to 2% or more above the call money rate, with a higher differential in the case of small accounts. Some brokerage houses collect **service charges** quarterly or monthly on inactive accounts or those with less than a stated debit balance. Charges may be collected also for duplicate statements and other special services customers may desire.

The Brokerage House

ORGANIZATION OF A BROKERAGE HOUSE. Four main functions in the operation of a brokerage house are operation of the main and branch offices, customer relations, execution of orders on the floor of the Exchange, and financing. In large organizations individual partners or officers may be given responsibility for the staffs handling these functions and their effective performance. In smaller organizations, one or two individuals may have to oversee all of the work.

The **departmental organization** of a brokerage house will depend largely upon its size and the extent to which it carries on other activities besides trading on the Stock Exchange, such as over-the-counter business, underwriting, commodity trading, and foreign business. The most important departments or groups of departments are:

1. Relations with Customers. The branch offices and registered representatives of the main office are included in this division. It is under the management of a partner or partners specializing in contacts with customers.
2. Handling of Orders and Securities. The order department receives orders, records them, and passes them on to the floor member for execution. The clearing house department is concerned with stock clearing activities, taking care of exchange transactions after orders are executed.
3. Records. The accounting work in the brokerage house is onerous. The accounting department must work in close conjunction with the order department. It also cooperates with the margin clerks, who are engaged in watching customers' accounts to insure that required margins are maintained.
4. Cashier's Department. This department handles all cash transactions, including the important function of arranging security loans.
5. Statistical Department. A considerable volume of analytical and statistical work is required in a brokerage house, in connection with inquiries from customers, the preparation of reviews of market conditions or daily "Market Letters," studies of particular securities or industries that are distributed to present and prospective clients, etc.

REGISTERED REPRESENTATIVES. The registered representative in a brokerage house acts as both salesman and adviser in many cases. He provides a personal service to clients by telephone, mail, or their visits to the "board room." In larger brokerage offices, price changes of more important issues are indicated on an electrical wall board with movable figures.

Employment Standards. The New York Stock Exchange exercises control over its members and their employees, particularly those who deal with the public. To maintain standards of selection and retention of employees, the Exchange requires the filing of a personal history of registered representatives. Employees desiring to become registered representatives must successfully complete a course and examination on stock exchange procedure and related subjects. Failure to observe ethical standards and adhere to the principles of just and equitable trade subjects an employee to **revocation** of his registered status.

CUSTOMERS' STATEMENTS. Customers of brokerage houses receive confirmations from the accounting department for each purchase or sale effected. Monthly statements are mailed showing the transactions during the month, inter-

10·36 SECURITIES MARKETS

MERRILL LYNCH, PIERCE, FENNER & SMITH INC

SOCIAL SECURITY OR IDENTIFYING NUMBER	PAGE NO.	PERIOD ENDING	ACCOUNT NO.
123-45-6789	1	01 31 19—	123 45678 0001

MR ML CUSTOMER
123 ANY STREET
ANY CITY N Y

STATEMENT OF SECURITY ACCOUNT

WHEN MAKING INQUIRIES, PLEASE MENTION YOUR ACCOUNT NUMBER AND ADDRESS ALL CORRESPONDENCE TO THE OFFICE SERVICING YOUR ACCOUNT.

WE URGE YOU TO PRESERVE THIS STATEMENT FOR USE IN PREPARING INCOME TAX RETURNS.

FOR DESCRIPTION OF SYMBOLS IN "PRICE" COLUMN AND OTHER MATTERS - - SEE REVERSE SIDE.

DATE	BOUGHT OR RECEIVED	SOLD OR DELIVERED	DESCRIPTION	PRICE	DEBIT	CREDIT
			BALANCE DECEMBER 31	M		2000 00
1 3			DEPOSIT 1 2			17431 00
1 6	100		SCOTT PAPER CO COM	38 1/2	3888 25	
1 6	200		RADIO CORP	101	20298 20	
1 6	200		MARSHALL FIELD	35 1/2	7173 50	
1 9		200	MARSHALL FIELD	37 3/8		7417 37
1 9		200	CHRYSLER CORP	41		8109 55
			SHORT SALE			
1 9			DEPOSIT 1 8			484 00
1 16	100		CHRYSLER CORP	42	4240 00	
			COVER SHORT			
1 16		200	SPERRY RAND	20		55 00
1 24			100 GENL ELECT CO	* DIV		
1 27			INT TO 01 24 6%		27 46	
			CLOSING BALANCE		4184 49	
			CHRYSLER CORP			
	100		GENL ELECT CO			
	200		RADIO CORP			
	100		SCOTT PAPER CO COM			
	200		SPERRY RAND			

Fig. 2. Typical form of customer's statement.

est charged, dividends received, the customer's debit balance, and the securities held in the account. Fig. 2 shows a sample customer's statement. Many brokerage houses have mechanized their accounting to speed operations and reduce costs. Also, statements may be sent less frequently than once a month, if an account is not active. At least once each year the customer may expect to receive a request from the auditor of the brokerage house asking him to verify, sign, and return the statement. If it is believed that the statement contains an error, the customer should immediately notify both the auditor and the broker.

FINANCING THE BROKERAGE BUSINESS. The capital contributed by the partners or stockholders in a brokerage house assures its ability to meet obligations, including repayment of borrowings, and provides funds for the acquisition of exchange seats, furniture, and fixtures. The Stock Exchange and lending banks expect the brokerage house to have adequate **free capital** over and above the value of exchange seats, as the latter are subject to the prior lien of claims of other exchange members.

A balance sheet of a brokerage house is shown in Fig. 3.

Assets

Current Assets:
Cash on hand and in banks; clearing funds, etc.	$ 5,295,780
Deposits on account of securities borrowed	98,900
Receivable from brokers or dealers:	
Securities sold but not delivered	2,096,767
For securities carried in joint account	218,183
Receivable from customers (secured and cash accounts)	19,512,801
Market value of securities held for firm and partners' accounts	4,168,643
Revenue stamps on hand	5,038

Other Assets:
Memberships in exchanges, at market value	233,300
Office furniture and equipment	12,420
Unsecured accounts receivable (deemed collectible)	10,907
Prepaid expenses	27,427
Total Assets	**$31,680,166**

Liabilities

Current Liabilities:
Money borrowed on securities	$12,500,000
Deposits on account of securities loaned	29,000
Payable to brokers or dealers (securities purchased but not received)	1,905,640
Payable to customers:	
Free credits	9,649,013
Credit balances in fully secured and cash accounts	1,909,064
Other credit balances	93,403
Misc. current liabilities such as compensation, unclaimed dividends, commissions, taxes, etc.	464,998

Net Worth:
Estimated amount to be withdrawn by partners for payment of Federal income taxes	400,000
Balance	4,729,048
	$31,680,166

Fig. 3. Balance sheet of a brokerage house.

The **chief income** of a commission house comes from executing orders in listed securities. Houses may trade on their own account. Over-the-counter business and the distribution of new offerings provide **additional sources of income** to many stock exchange houses. Where such other activities are carried on, additional capital is required to help finance these operations, and because greater risk is involved than in the straight commission business on the exchange.

SOURCES OF FUNDS FOR BROKERS. The most important single source of funds for brokers, as Bogen and Krooss have shown (Security Credit: Its Economic Role and Regulation) is the **collateral loan** at the banks. These loans are arranged directly between the brokerage house and the banks or to some extent through firms of money brokers.

A call loan may be terminated by the service of notice of desire for repayment by either borrower or lender. It is repayable the same day if such notice is served before 12 noon on a business day. A **time loan** is made for a definite period of time, usually from 30 days to 3 or 6 months. When interest rates appear to be rising, lenders prefer to make call loans in order to get the benefit of the higher rates later. On the other hand, when lower interest rates are in prospect, they prefer time loans, even though the rate on the latter is at the time substantially below the call money rate. Brokers balance call and time loans in an effort to obtain their funds from dependable sources at the lowest possible average interest cost.

The Hypothecation Agreement. After a loan is arranged between the bank and the broker, the broker sends to the bank collateral meeting the standard requirements and a **loan agreement.** In view of the fact that brokers frequently shift collateral in loans owing to the purchase and sale of securities by customers, and price changes may require additional collateral or permit the release of part of it, the agreement is in blanket form. This is a short form describing briefly the nature of the transaction, as practice has become so far standardized in connection with stock exchange loans that detailed agreements are found unnecessary.

Other Methods of Obtaining Brokerage Funds. In addition to call and time collateral loans, there are other sources of funds available to the broker. By **lending customers' stocks to short sellers,** he can obtain the full market value of the stock, instead of only the percentage that the bank is allowed to lend under the regulation, and without interest. In fact, on the rare occasions when the demand from shorts is keen, the broker may not only obtain cash against a loan of customers' stocks but may also receive a premium from the borrower. Another type of loan utilized by brokers is the **accommodation** or **day loan,** which is used to meet their financial requirements during the course of the business day, and before the amount of call loans needed can be determined with any degree of accuracy. The New York Clearing House banks charge 1% per annum on such day loans. By 4 P.M., the transactions of the day are all in and the cash position of the house can be determined. If a balance is owed to the bank, a temporary loan is arranged for the net amount of the **overcertification,** or day loan, to carry it "overnight" until a new collateral loan can be arranged the following day or cash is deposited to pay off the "overnight loan."

Since the perfection of the present clearing system of settling transactions on the exchange, the amount of such unsecured day loans required has been quite substantially reduced.

RESTRICTIONS ON BROKER BORROWING. §8 of the Securities Exchange Act of 1934 prohibits a member of a national securities exchange, or any broker or dealer doing business through a member, from borrowing in the ordinary course of business on any registered security except from or through a bank under the jurisdiction of the Board of Governors of the Federal Reserve System. Regulations of the Board, however, permit certain loans between brokers. The Board's Regulation U prohibits a bank from making a collateral loan secured by stock for the purpose of purchasing or carrying any registered stock in an amount exceeding the **maximum loan value** of the collateral as prescribed by the Board.

§8 further restricts a member broker's **aggregate indebtedness** to all other persons, including customers' credit balances, to an amount not more than **twenty times his net capital,** exclusive of fixed assets and the value of exchange memberships. Under §15(c)(3) the S.E.C. has promulgated, by rule, similar standards for over-the-counter broker-dealers. Definitions of what constituted indebtedness and net capital were promulgated. Field investigations are frequently made by accountant-examiners to ascertain compliance.

EXAMINATION OF MEMBER FIRMS. To safeguard the public dealing with member houses, the New York Stock Exchange requires at least two sets of financial statements annually from each member firm, on a form prescribed by it. This is referred to as the **stock exchange "questionnaire,"** and, based upon its showing, insistence may be made by the exchange authorities that additional capital be invested in the house or that it dissolve. Failure to comply with such demands involves suspension.

An important feature of the stock exchange questionnaire is an analysis of customers' accounts, indicating the extent to which they are secured by collateral. Accounts with debit balances must be classified into those secured, those partly secured, and those unsecured, with the value of the securities indicated in each instance. In addition, the firm must be **audited** at least once a year by **independent public accountants,** and this is a surprise audit.

Bond Trading on the Exchange

THE BOND ROOM. The section of the Stock Exchange floor where bond dealers and brokers carry on their trading is called the "bond room." Although some 1,200 bond issues are listed on the Exchange, only a fraction of these are active. Trading in listed bonds over-the-counter between dealers assumes large proportions, and generally the volume of transactions off the Exchange far exceeds that on the floor.

To increase trading on the floor in listed bonds, the New York Stock Exchange adopted the **"Nine Bond Rule."** This requires members receiving orders to buy or sell less than $10,000 par value of a listed bond to endeavor to execute the order on the floor. The transaction may be executed over-the-counter only if a better price is thereby obtained for the customer.

Quotations. The ordinary unit of trading in bonds on the New York Stock Exchange is the single $1,000 bond. Quotations on bonds are in percentage of face value. Thus, if a bond is quoted at 89½, the price will be $895 per $1,000 bond. Bonds on which interest is being paid, unless they are income bonds not ordered to be quoted the **regular way,** are quoted **"and interest,"** which means that an additional sum will be added to the purchase price to represent accrued interest from the last coupon-paying date to the date of purchase. Thus, a 4% bond purchased at 95, where interest is payable January 1 and July 1, if purchased on April 1 will cost the purchaser $950, plus $10 interest for 3 months to April 1, plus commission. Bonds on which interest is in default, and income bonds on which regularity of interest payments has not been established, are quoted "flat," in which event they are bought and sold like stock, that is, without payment of accrued interest by the purchaser.

Bond quotations are sent out over separate tickers by the New York Stock Exchange and the American Stock Exchange. Bonds are designated by their coupon rates, except that if a company or government has two or more issues that bear the same coupon rate, the year of maturity is also indicated. A specimen of bond ticker tape is given in Fig. 4.

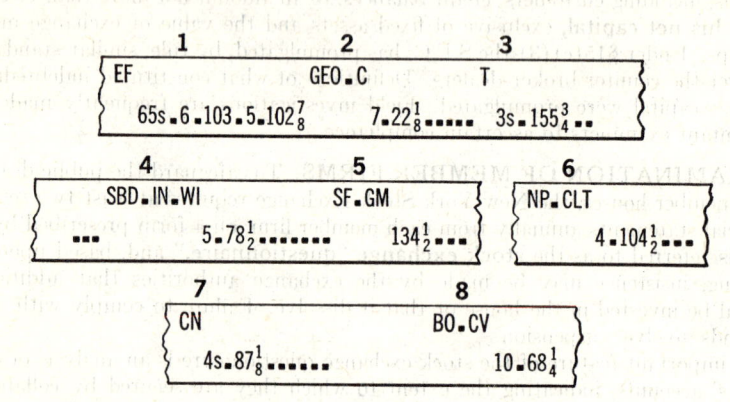

```
   1                  2                3
   EF              GEO.C              T
65s.6.103.5.102⅞   7.22⅛..... 3s.155¾..

   4                  5                6
 SBD.IN.WI          SF.GM           NP.CLT
...  5.78½......   134½...        4.104½...

         7                     8
         CN                  BO.CV
      4s.87⅛......         10.68¼
```

Fig. 4. Sections of New York Stock Exchange bond ticker tape.

Meaning of symbols in bond ticker tape illustration

1. New York Edison Co., Inc.—1965s 6 bonds at 103 followed by 5 bonds at 102⅞.
2. Central of Georgia Ry. Co.—7 bonds at 22⅛.
3. American Telephone and Telegraph Co.—3% bonds, one bond sold at 155¾.
4. Seaboard Air Line R. R. Co.—income bonds, when issued, 5 bonds at 78½.
5. Atchison, Topeka & Santa Fe Ry. Co.—general mortgage bonds, one bond at 134½.
6. Northern Pacific Ry. Co.—collateral trust, 4 bonds at 104½.
7. New York Central R. R. Co.—one 4% bond at 87⅛.
8. Baltimore & Ohio R. R. Co.—convertible, 10 bonds sold at 68¼.

In order to facilitate trading in bonds by those located at a distance from New York, trading in bonds may be made for **deferred delivery up to 7 days**. Since bonds cannot be freely borrowed for delivery on sales made from a distance, this practice has been adopted because of the growing geographical distribution of bond investment. Sales may also be made at seller's option of 30 or 60 days, to cover transactions for European account, and, at times, short sales.

WHAT CONSTITUTES GOOD DELIVERY. Coupon bonds, to be a good delivery, must be accompanied by all unpaid coupons. Coupon bonds that are registered as to principal only will be a good delivery if registered to bearer. **Registered bonds** otherwise are not a good delivery unless sold as such, and a lower price may be bid for registered bonds when efforts are made to sell them.

The rules of the Exchange provide that transactions in coupon bonds may be settled by delivery of either $1,000 or $500 denominations. Denominations below $500 or "small bonds," and those above $1,000 or "large bonds," are to be dealt in specifically as such, except in the case of United States issues. For these, and also for registered bonds, $10,000 denominations are good delivery.

When securities are **stamped** to indicate modification of their terms, they are not a good delivery unless the entire issue has been so marked and the Exchange duly informed of this fact. If part of an issue is stamped, it is necessary to list that part separately. Stamping is far more frequent for bonds than for stock. Efforts to dispose of bonds that are not good deliveries under the rules of the Exchange often involve substantial price concessions from the prevailing market. When bonds are deposited with a trustee under a reorganization agreement or otherwise, separate listing must be obtained for the **certificate of deposit.**

COMMISSIONS AND TAXES ON BOND TRANSACTIONS. The rates of commission established by the New York Stock Exchange on public orders are:

Bonds Selling at	Rate per $1,000 of Principal
Less than $10	$0.75
$10 to $100	1.25
$100 or more	2.50

Since very few bonds of $1,000 principal value sell for less than $100, the commission usually is $2.50. There are **special rates** applicable on some transactions, such as those involving bonds maturing in 6 months to 5 years, bonds maturing or called for redemption within 6 months, and obligations of governments. The commission on transactions between members is substantially lower.

The **Federal transfer tax** on bonds is 5¢ for each $100 of face value or fraction thereof, and applies on all transfers of legal title regardless of whether or not the beneficial interest in the bonds is transferred. This means that a transfer of bonds to a trust account requires the payment of the tax even though the trustee holds the bonds for the benefit of others. Transfers of Federal and municipal bonds, however, are exempt from this tax. There is no New York State levy on bond transfers.

Loans of bonds are regarded as taxable transactions by the Federal tax law. Furthermore, unlike the situation prevailing in connection with loans of stock, the return of borrowed bonds is also held to be a taxable transaction.

Over-the-Counter Markets

FUNCTIONS AND IMPORTANCE. "Over-the-counter markets" is the term used to describe security trading outside organized securities exchanges. This market, though loose and informal in organization, is spread over the entire United States. With the development of better communications and the organization of dealers into associations subject to regulation, the business has gained cohesiveness.

The functions of over-the-counter markets, like those of organized exchanges, are to provide:

1. Facilities for bringing buyers and sellers wishing to trade in securities together.
2. Marketability for the great number of securities that are not actively traded on an organized exchange, and for some that are.

The over-the-counter markets are an integral and important part of American financial markets and perform an indispensable service. From a qualitative point of view, they are as important as organized exchanges, although they furnish a market different in character and mode of operation. From a quantitative point of view, the lack of organization of the over-the-counter markets makes it difficult to measure its importance. There are two aspects to consider: (a) **volume of**

securities available to be traded, and (b) **volume of actual trading** taking place, i.e., turnover. All securities, including corporate and government bonds and stocks, listed and unlisted, are potentially available for over-the-counter trading. But the number of issues actually traded over-the-counter is only a fraction of this vast potential because, for some, trading is done almost exclusively on exchanges whereas, for very many others, the issues are closely held or too small for public trading.

The **market value of all sales** on national securities exchanges in the year ending December 31, 1962, aggregated $54.7 billion for stocks and $1.7 billion for bonds. The Federal debt of over $300 billion gives rise to the largest part of over-the-counter trading. Statistics are not available on the turnover in over-the-counter markets, since transactions are not recorded in a central place.

CLASSES OF SECURITIES TRADED. There are three major classes of securities traded in the over-the-counter markets:

1. Unlisted stocks.
2. Government, municipal, and corporate bonds.
3. New issues.

Each of these has its submarkets and individual characteristics with respect to price determination, degree of organization, local market, and mechanics of trading.

One very important part of the over-the-counter market comprises stocks of banks and trust companies. **Banks** generally do not care to have fluctuations in prices of their stocks given wide publicity, and so practically all bank stocks are unlisted. The nucleus of the over-the-counter market in each city is usually the local bank stocks. **Insurance stocks** are also important, for very few issues in this group are listed on exchanges. Other important groups of stocks quoted on the over-the-counter market are smaller industrials, investment company issues, and preferred stocks of public utility companies.

METHOD OF TRADING—NEGOTIATION. Over-the-counter dealers effect their transactions chiefly over direct telephone conections with other dealers. The increased use of long distance telephones and teletype has expanded the scope of over-the-counter trading to national proportions.

The market for an over-the-counter issue tends to become concentrated in one or a few dealers who specialize in this security and hold themselves out as making a market in it, at any time, either to buy or sell. Issues may be **sponsored** by houses that have underwritten or otherwise helped in their distribution. To establish this market, the dealer will quote regularly bid and asked prices for the security. Often, there may be a considerable spread between bid and asked prices, and the quotations may apply to only small quantities of the issue. A quotation may be good only for the moment and for only a limited quantity; if not immediately accepted, it may be considered to have lapsed. If, after getting "the market" quoted, it is necessary to check with the customer, the dealer may be asked to give a **firm quotation** for, say, 10 or 20 minutes.

Over-the-counter dealers operate in one of two ways. Either they try to avoid taking a position by keeping the volume of buying and selling in each issue in **balance**, or they may be willing to buy more than they sell, or vice versa, and thus take a **long** or **short position**. The policy of the house and the state of the market will largely determine the extent to which positions will be taken. Willingness to maintain a considerable position enables a dealer to **give better service** in executing customers' orders.

Over-the-counter houses operate mainly as dealers, buying and selling as principals rather than agents. This makes it necessary for them to depend upon the good faith of those with whom they deal to a large extent, as **oral orders cannot be enforced** at law when they involve $50 or more under the statute of frauds. If there is doubt concerning the good faith of a customer, **written confirmation** of the order should be obtained. Under Federal regulations it is necessary for firms to disclose to customers in what capacity they are acting.

On an organized exchange, trading is usually done on an auction basis. Brokers representing buyers, along with dealers trading on their own account, crowd about the trading post and **"make a market"** by quoting bids and offers openly. But on the over-the-counter markets, trading is by **private negotiation**. A customer buys directly from a dealer, without recourse to an auction market, or his broker may negotiate for him with one or more over-the-counter dealers. In order to assure the customer a fair price, it is often desirable in an inactive issue to get the **"feel"** of the market by calling several dealers. The best way to check an over-the-counter market is from the daily sheets of the National Quotation Bureau, Inc., which lists bids and offers, or requests for bids and offers, filed with the Bureau by dealers and brokers, along with the name of the house in each case.

The National Quotation Bureau, Inc., makes a business of collecting these quotations and distributing a list to subscribers. These quotation sheets are not generally available to the public, but can be consulted at or through brokerage houses. There are pink stock sheets and yellow bond sheets, divided by geographical area according to trading interest—Eastern, Central, and Pacific. In addition to these daily quotations, which are in some respects advertisements of interest on the part of the dealers making insertions, monthly summaries of over-the-counter quotations are published by the National Quotation Bureau, Inc. Prices at which actual transactions have taken place are not available in the over-the-counter markets, as they are on the organized exchanges.

An Actual Transaction. The manner in which over-the-counter trading operates may be seen from an actual instance. Mr. A or his broker calls up Jones & Co., dealers in unlisted securities, and asks the market in National City Bank stock. Jones's trader knows, or learns from the National Quotation Bureau sheets, what other dealers are quoting. He tells A or the latter's broker that the market is 44 bid, 46 asked. A thereupon puts in an order to buy 50 shares at 45. At the same time, Jones & Co. learns, over the telephone, that Doe & Co. has just offered a block of 50 shares in the market at 44½. The Jones & Co. trader quickly buys these 50 shares at 44½, fills the order of A at 45, and thus makes a half-point profit.

After the execution of the order, the stock must be delivered and cash settlement made. Since there is no stock clearing machinery for over-the-counter trading, comparisons are made by sending reports of purchases and sales by messengers from one house to another. Thereafter stock certificates are delivered against certified checks. Because of the lack of a clearing mechanism, settlement of over-the-counter transactions ties up a much larger volume of funds in proportion to volume than do transactions on the exchanges.

Clearing Transactions. There are several methods by which transactions between houses may be cleared in the over-the-counter markets. The most common, for firms located in the same city, is the **"regular way,"** i.e., the securities must be delivered to the buying house by 12:30 P.M. of the fourth full business day following that on which the trade was made. This follows the procedure of the New York Stock Exchange. Frequently, because of difficulties of physical delivery of the certificates, the sale is closed on a deferred or **delayed delivery** basis, which, according to custom, requires delivery on or before the seventh full business day. In the event that more time is required, the sale may be **seller's option**, and the seller can deliver and receive payment any time within the agreed limit by giving one day's notice. When the seller is unable to make delivery as agreed and the buyer insists, the buyer's broker may **buy in** the securities, charging any loss resulting to the seller. Sales may also be consummated for **cash**, in which instance delivery and payment are to be made the same day. Because of delays in the transfer of stock certificates on the books of the company, delivery may be made of the **receipt** given by the transfer agent in lieu of stock certificates.

THE UNLISTED BOND MARKET. In addition to the large volume of listed bonds that are traded over-the-counter, often on the basis of published prices on the exchanges, a vast number of bond issues are unlisted.

Apart from United States government issues, the most important class of unlisted bonds is **state and municipal issues**. Most of these are traded in on a **yield** rather than a price basis because numerous issues of this kind mature serially and prices would differ for each maturity. Thus, a municipal issue may be quoted 2.45% bid, 2.35% asked, which means that the bid price is such as to give a yield of 2.45% to maturity, whereas the higher asked price will give a yield of 2.35% to maturity. A limited number of such bonds, usually of authorities with a large single maturity, are quoted at a percentage of $1,000 par value, like other bonds, and are referred to as **dollar bonds**. The **Blue List** provides a daily list of offerings by dealers in state and municipal bonds, listed under each state in alphabetical order.

Railroad equipment trust certificates are also traded over-the-counter. Since they have serial maturities, a list of bid and asked prices on a yield basis for each issue is available.

Other unlisted bonds are **quoted on a price basis** on the over-the-counter market. More important groups of issues so quoted are unlisted public utility and industrial bonds and unlisted foreign bonds, including internal currency bonds quoted here.

SELF-REGULATION AND THE NATIONAL ASSOCIATION OF SECURITIES DEALERS. §15A of the Securities Exchange Act provides legal sanction and encouragement of associations of securities dealers for self-regulation. Under this provision, the National Association of Securities Dealers, Inc., a nonprofit membership corporation, has been formed under the joint sponsorship of the industry and the Securities and Exchange Commission. Included in the N.A.S.D. are nearly all investment banking houses and most of the houses dealing in the over-the-counter markets. Membership is required of all registered broker dealers by §15A of the Securities Exchange Act of 1934, as amended.

Among the stated objects of the N.A.S.D., set forth in its Manual are:

1. To promote through cooperative effort the investment banking and securities business, to standardize its principles and practices, to promote therein high standards of commercial honor, and to encourage and promote among members observance of Federal and state securities laws.
2. To provide a medium through which the membership may confer, consult, and cooperate with governmental and other agencies in the solution of problems affecting investors, the public, and the investment banking and securities business.
3. To adopt, administer, and enforce rules of fair practice and rules to prevent fraudulent and manipulative acts and practices, and in general to promote just and equitable principles of trade for the protection of investors.

4. To promote self-discipline among members, and to investigate and adjust grievances between the public and members and between members.

With the organization of the N.A.S.D., there was provided, for the first time, an authority (1) to set standards of conduct not only for dealings between members but also covering relations with the investing public, and (2) to secure adherence to these standards through disciplinary measures—censure, fines, or expulsion. **Expulsion** is a serious matter because the Act provides preferential treatment as regards commissions and allowances. This provision reads:

> The rules of a registered securities association may provide that no member thereof shall deal with any nonmember broker or dealer except at the same prices, for the same commissions or fees, and on the same terms and conditions as are by such member accorded to the general public. [§ 15A (i) (1).]

Rules of Fair Practice. To implement N.A.S.D. objectives, rules of fair practice (N.A.S.D. Manual, D-5, ff) have been adopted to guide members' business practices and to raise standards of the over-the-counter dealers and brokers. Rule 1 provides:

> A member, in the conduct of his business, shall observe high standards of commercial honor and just and equitable principles of trade.

The Board of Governors of the N.A.S.D. has interpreted Rule 1 as follows:

> It shall be deemed conduct inconsistent with just and equitable principles of trade for a member to enter into any transaction with a customer in any security at any price not reasonably related to the current market price of the security.

The Association has sought to keep **mark-ups** of asked over bid prices of its members from exceeding 5%, as tending to be excessive.

The rules provide further:

> ... if a member buys for his own account from his customer, or sells for his own account to his customer, he shall buy or sell at a price which is fair, taking into consideration all relevant circumstances, including market conditions with respect to such security at the time of the transaction, the expense involved, and the fact that he is entitled to a profit; and if he acts as agent for his customer . . . , he shall not charge his customer more than a fair commission or service charge. . . . (Rule 4.)

Other rules impose upon members responsibility for recommendations made to customers; impress upon them the obligations of the fiduciary capacity in which they, at times, serve, and the necessity to disclose the capacity in which they are acting for or with customers; and forbid transactions of a manipulative, deceptive, or fraudulent character.

Other N.A.S.D. Activities. Another phase of the N.A.S.D.'s work has been the preparation of a **Uniform Practice Code** designed to eliminate disputes and misunderstandings between members. For the most part, the Code gives sanction to practice, custom, and usage in technical matters such as deliveries of securities, computation of interest, claims for dividends or interest and similar matters. **Complaints** or requests for arbitration may be filed either by members of the N.A.S.D. or by the public. These will be investigated, heard, and decided by one of the 13 District Business Conduct Committees. The decisions of this Committee are subject to appeal and review by the Board of Governors of the N.A.S.D. and, finally, by the Securities and Exchange Commission.

The N.A.S.D. has, in its own and the public interest, sought to improve over-the-counter market quotations and to assure adequacy of invested capital of its members. Also, the N.A.S.D. requires officers, partners, employees, or other representatives of a member

. . . engaged in the managing, supervision, solicitation, or handling of listed or unlisted business securities; or in the trading of listed or unlisted securities; or in the sale of listed or unlisted securities on an agency or principal basis; or engaged in the solicitation of subscriptions. . . .

from the public to file a detailed personal data sheet and pass an examination in order to become **registered representatives** authorized to deal with the public. Registrants must agree to abide by the Rules of Fair Practice of the N.A.S.D. and, further, to be subject individually to appropriate disciplinary action in the case of violation. This registration is designed to provide a measure of control over the individuals who transact business directly with the public.

Federal Regulation of Securities Trading

THE SECURITIES EXCHANGE ACT OF 1934. The Securities Exchange Act of 1934 (hereinafter referred to as the "Exchange Act") was enacted to improve the functioning of the nation's securities markets and to subject them to a degree of regulation.

Objectives. The Exchange Act is designed to accomplish the following purposes:

1. **Make available to the public reliable information** regarding securities listed on national security exchanges, and their issuers, and the larger issues and issuers of over-the-counter securities, to facilitate appraisal of values by investors and traders.
2. **Prevent and provide remedies for fraud, manipulation, and other abuses** in security trading, both on the organized exchanges and in the over-the-counter markets, to the end that **fair and orderly markets,** free from artificial influences, are maintained.
3. **To regulate the securities markets and brokers and dealers of securities to insure that just and equitable principles of trade are observed** by exchange members and others executing security orders for the public.
4. **Regulate the use of credit** in securities trading.
5. **Regulate trading by "insiders"** in covered securities **and the use of proxies** by corporations whose shares are covered.

Chief Provisions of the Act. These objectives of the Exchange Act are in part implemented by three types of registration: registration of (1) securities, (2) exchanges, and (3) broker-dealers.

1. **Registration of securities** is one of the primary methods used to achieve the objectives of Federal financial legislation. §12 requires issuers of securities listed on national securities exchanges and issuers of certain over-the-counter securities to file extensive data with the S.E.C. for the information of investors and the general public.

2. **Registration of exchanges** and the supervision of their conduct constitute the second method of regulation. Registration includes filing pertinent data with respect to the exchanges' organization, rules of procedure, membership, and other information deemed in the public interest. Among other things, registration includes an agreement by the exchange to comply with the provisions of the Exchange Act and rules and regulations promulgated thereunder, and to enforce, so far as it is within its powers, similar compliance by its members.

3. **Registration of broker-dealers** is the third pillar upon which Federal securities regulation is based. Direct control of the brokers and dealers is attained by denying the use of the mails, or of any instrumentality of interstate commerce, to effect any transaction in securities unless a person is registered with the Securities and Exchange Commission. Registration is accomplished by filing with the S.E.C. detailed information with respect to the business history of the registrant and its officers, directors, and controlling persons. It should be noted that some broker-dealers are also registered as investment advisers and are subject to the additional regulation of the Investment Advisers Act of 1940.

§15(b) makes it mandatory for the Commission to **deny or revoke the registration** of any broker or dealer if it finds that such denial or revocation is in the public interest and that such broker or dealer, or any partner, officer, director, or controlling or controlled person of such broker or dealer

    a. Has willfully made in any document required to be filed or in any proceeding before the S.E.C. a false or misleading statement that was at the time, or in the light of the circumstances under which it was made, false or misleading with respect to any material fact.
    b. Has been convicted, within 10 years, of a felony or misdemeanor involving the securities business.
    c. Is permanently or temporarily enjoined by a court from engaging in the conduct of securities business.
    d. Has willfully violated any provision of the Securities Act of 1933 or of the Exchange Act of 1934 or rules and regulations thereunder.

Through such control and the setting of net capital requirements, the public is to be protected from disreputable or financially irresponsible brokers and dealers.

Authority to **regulate the extension of credit** for the purpose of purchasing and carrying registered securities, and to establish maximum loan values, is lodged in the Board of Governors of the Federal Reserve System. The administration of the regulation as it affects brokers and dealers is in the hands of the staff of the S.E.C.

ADMINISTRATION OF THE EXCHANGE ACT. The Exchange Act is not a self-executing statute. It is administered by a five-man commission, whose members are appointed for five-year terms by the President, and no more than three of whom may be from the same political party. As an adjudicatory tribunal and administrative agency, it is subject to the accepted rules of **administrative law,** including the right to be heard, the weighing of evidence, adherence to legislative directives and **due process.** Orders of the S.E.C. are reviewable by the United States Circuit Court of Appeals.

Administration of the Exchange Act has evolved gradually in the light of experience. The approach of the S.E.C. has been pragmatic. Policies and rules have been flexible and adapted to legitimate business needs. Close liaison has been maintained with those subject to its rules.

Registration of Securities.

1. **Procedure in registration.** §12 of the Securities Exchange Act forbids trading in any security on a national exchange unless the security is either registered or exempt and requires the registration of larger over-the-counter issues. The purpose of this provision is to make available for the investor adequate and current information regarding the affairs of companies whose securities are listed, or are to be listed, on a national securities exchange. §12 specifies the general nature and scope of the information to be furnished.

Registration of a security is effected by the issuing corporation filing an application with the exchange containing such information regarding the security and the company as the statute and its regulations require. A duplicate original must be filed at the same time with the S.E.C. If the exchange authorities approve the security for listing, registration becomes effective 30 days from the date on which the Commission receives certification of the exchange's approval, or within a shorter period if the S.E.C. accelerates the effective date. In practice, most applications are accelerated.

Registered securities include both listed securities and **securities admitted to unlisted trading** on a national securities exchange. Although issuers of securities admitted to unlisted trading do not have to furnish complete data, other provisions of the statute, such as prohibitions against manipulation, etc., are applicable.

A detailed examination is made of applications for registration and supplementary periodical reports to determine whether they provide adequate disclosure of the required information. When it is discovered that material information has been omitted or that sound accounting practices have been violated, the registrant is so informed and correcting amendments are required.

To supply the **information required for registration,** several forms have been developed for basic registration of a security under the Exchange Act. Each registrant is required to file an application on the form appropriate to the particular type of issue or issuer involved. Nonfinancial as well as financial information is required. The data must include all pertinent material facts and must be set forth in such manner as not to be misleading. Detailed information and documents must be filed with respect to:

1. Organization, financial structure, and nature of business.
2. Description of the various classes of securities outstanding.
3. The terms upon which the applicant's securities are to be, and during the preceding 3 years have been, offered to the public or otherwise disposed of.
4. Directors, officers, and underwriters, and each holder of record owning more than 10% of any class of stock or securities convertible into stock or carrying warrants to purchase stock, and independent warrants to purchase stock; also their remuneration and important contracts they have with the issuing company or any company controlling it or controlled by it.
5. Remuneration exceeding $30,000 per annum paid to others than directors and officers in one year.
6. Bonus and profit-sharing arrangements; management and service contracts; and options outstanding on the applicant's securities.
7. Balance sheets and profit and loss statements for not more than the last 3 preceding years, certified by independent public accountants if so required by the Commission; and any further financial statements that the Commission may deem necessary.
8. Copies of such trust indentures, underwriting arrangements, and other similar documents, and voting trust agreements, of both the issuing company and any affiliated company, as the Commission may require.

Continuance of registration upon a national exchange is dependent upon the filing of (1) current reports in the event that certain material changes occur in the affairs of the issuer, and (2) annual reports within 120 days (unless an extension is granted) after the close of the company's fiscal year. These reports are designed to bring up to date the information contained in the application for permanent registration.

A registrant may request **confidential treatment** for information it submits. Objections to disclosure, for the most part, have related to sales figures, an itemized breakdown of the cost of sales, and, in many instances, the publication of salaries and other remuneration paid to officers and directors. If an application for confidential treatment is denied, the issuer has an absolute right to withdraw his listing application. It has been the S.E.C.'s policy to deny confidential treatment other than for trade secrets and processes on the ground that the statute requires a full and complete disclosure of each registrant's financial condition in order to protect public investors against manipulation of securities by "insiders." The courts have upheld the S.E.C. and stated that it properly exercised its discretion by considering the alleged danger of harm and by weighing the request in the scale of public interest. Recently, in conformity with the policy of disclosure, the S.E.C. has required that registrants make **quarterly statements** of sales and earnings if they keep their books on that basis, and a full and prompt disclosure of important developments such as termination of contracts of major importance to the company.

In cases of **withdrawal of registration,** §12(d) of the Exchange Act provides, with respect to applications by an issuer or an exchange to delist securities, that a security may be stricken from listing and registration in accordance with the rules of the exchange and upon such terms as the S.E.C. may deem necessary for the protection of investors.

Applications by an issuer to delist must set forth the reasons for the proposed delisting and material facts relating thereto, as well as any facts it wishes to offer with respect to the advisability of imposing conditions. On occasion the issuer has been required to notify holders of the security of the proposal to delist and of their right to present their views to the S.E.C. with respect to the **imposition of terms.** Conditions have been attached in some instances, usually a requirement that the issuer secure the approval of a majority of the holders of the security in question.

Delisting by the S.E.C. or by an exchange is authorized by the Exchange Act in order to permit eliminating inactively traded securities, or as a means of compelling compliance with the obligations imposed by the Exchange Act. **Suspension of trading** is also authorized upon a finding of violation of the provisions of the Exchange Act.

2. **Accounting requirements and standards.** The heart of the full disclosure requirement is the regulations governing the financial statements. The S.E.C. may prescribe the form and details of the balance sheet and earnings statement, and methods to be followed in the preparation of reports, the valuation of assets and liabilities, the determination of depreciation and depletion, differentiation between recurring and nonrecurring, investment and operating income, and, if the Commission deems it necessary or desirable, the consolidation of statements. The S.E.C. has sought constantly to determine what is desirable and necessary to satisfy the requirements of full and frank disclosure in a nonmisleading fashion.

On April 25, 1938, in its Accounting Series Release No. 4, the S.E.C. stated its **administrative policy on financial statements** as follows:

> In cases where financial statements filed with this Commission pursuant to its rules and regulations under the Securities Act of 1933 or the Securities Exchange Act of 1934 are prepared in accordance with accounting principles for which there is no substantial authoritative support, such financial statements will be presumed to be misleading or inaccurate despite disclosures contained in the certificate of the accountant or in footnotes to the statements provided the matters involved are material. In cases where there is a difference of opinion between the Commission and the registrant as to the proper principles of accounting to be followed, disclosure will be accepted in lieu of correction of the financial statements themselves only if the points involved are such that there is substantial authoritative support for the

practices followed by the registrant and the position of the Commission has not previously been expressed in rules, regulations, or other official releases of the Commission, including the published opinions of its chief accountant.

To supplement this general policy the Commission, in 1940, adopted a comprehensive, basic accounting regulation (Regulation S-X) governing the form and content of most of the financial statements filed under the Securities Act of 1933 and the Exchange Act.

To provide for **auditors' examinations and reports,** Regulation S-X requires that all financial statements be audited by an independent public accountant whose **certificate** shall

1. Contain a reasonably comprehensive statement as to the scope of the audit; and
2. State whether the audit was made in accordance with generally accepted auditing standards.

Furthermore, the certificate must state clearly:

1. The opinion of the accountant in respect of the financial statements covered by the certificate and the accounting principles and practices reflected therein; and
2. The opinion of the accountant as to any changes in the accounting principles or practices or adjustment of the accounts which have been made during the period under review.

In addition to requiring an adequate audit and a clear-cut statement of opinion on the accounting practices, the Commission, to assure reliable financial statements, has insisted that auditors conform to high professional qualifications. In order that auditors have complete impartiality in their review and report, the Commission has required that they be completely **independent of the client** whose financial statements they certify. An auditor having a financial interest in a client, or one who is a director, officer, or employee, is specifically proscribed. One who acts in such manner as to "consistently submerge his preferences or convictions as to accounting principles to the wishes of his client is not in fact independent," it has been ruled.

3. **Ownership reports and insider trading.** §16 of the Exchange Act provides that each officer, director and beneficial owner of more than 10% of any class of registered equity security must file with the S.E.C. and the exchange, if it is a listed security, reports showing his holdings in the company's equity securities, and must report each month thereafter any changes which may occur in his holdings. A monthly summary of such reports is published by the S.E.C. Profits realized by any of these persons from transactions completed within 6 months in equity securities of corporations with which they are so associated may be recovered by the corporation, or by any security holder in its behalf. In practice, the restriction is enforced mainly by private lawsuits instituted by shareholders on behalf of the corporation. This provision is based on the principle that the confidential information that a corporate insider automatically obtains by virtue of his position belongs, in a real sense, to the corporation, since he acquired it confidentially in his capacity as an official or principal stockholder, and should not be used for short-term trading purposes. It has been upheld in the courts. [Smolowe v. Delendo Corp., 136 F. (2d) 231; certiorari denied 320 U. S. 751 (1943); and Upson v. Otis, 152 F. (2d) 606 (1946).]

4. **Proxies, disclosure of policies, and corporate democracy.** Under the Securities Exchange and other Acts that it administers, the S.E.C. prescribes rules

and regulations concerning the solicitation of proxies, consents, and authorizations from holders of securities of companies subject to those Acts.

The essence of the rules now in force is that it is unlawful to make a solicitation that is false or misleading as to any material fact, or that omits to state any material fact necessary to make statements already made not false or misleading. The person solicited is to be furnished information that will enable him to act intelligently upon the matter. (For further discussion see Section 13 on Corporate Stock.)

Regulation of Trading—Fair and Orderly Markets. The second major objective of securities regulation is to secure a **fair and orderly market** wherein prices of securities reflect demand and supply based at least to some extent on informed judgment, unimpeded by artificial manipulative or deceptive devices.

1. **Registration and reorganization of the exchanges.** The first step to secure that objective was the registration and reorganization of the exchanges. §§5 and 6 of the Exchange Act require that national security exchanges register by filing information concerning their constitution, by-laws, and rules and regulations governing memberships, trading procedure, and operations.

§6(b) provides:

No registration shall be granted or remain in force unless the rules of the exchange include provision for the expulsion, suspension, or discipline of a member for conduct or proceeding inconsistent with the just and equitable principles of trade, and declare that the willful violation of any provisions of this title, or any rule or regulation thereunder, shall be considered conduct or proceeding inconsistent with just and equitable principles of trade.

Pursuant to Congressional directive, the S.E.C. made a study of the organization of securities exchanges and submitted a **report on the government of stock exchanges.** It recommended extensive changes in the organization of national securities exchanges to permit more democratic control in conformity with the growing recognition that they are public institutions. In 1937, at the request of the S.E.C., the New York Stock Exchange instituted steps leading to the reorganization referred to above in this Section. Through this reorganization interested groups like customers—through public representatives—and allied and out-of-town firms received substantial representation in the Board of Governors.

2. **Power of the Commission to alter rules and practices of exchanges.** The Commission has broad supervision over the rules, methods, and practices of national securities exchanges. After giving an opportunity to be heard, it can compel the exchange to alter its rules and practices in any manner deemed necessary for the protection of investors and the general public. These powers extend to such matters as the financial responsibility of members, trading hours, methods of soliciting business, reporting of transactions on the exchange, fixing of reasonable rates of commission, minimum units of trading, odd-lot purchases and sales; activities of "specialists" and trading by members on their own account either on or off the floor. Changes ordered by the Commission must be based on the necessity of protecting investors or to assure a **fair and orderly market** or fair administration of the exchange. The Commission can also prescribe the form of accounts which members of the exchanges and those dealing through them shall keep, require reports, and set up a system of examination of their accounts.

In 1936, the S.E.C. reported to Congress on the **feasibility and advisability of the complete segregation of the functions of dealer and broker.** As a result of this study, segregation was not advised but 16 rules for the regulation of trading on exchanges were recommended and substantially adopted by the exchanges. The rules place certain restrictions upon trading for their own account by members and seek to bar transactions that are excessive in view of the financial resources of the member or the state of the market for the security; contain a prohibition against joint accounts in which both members and nonmembers are interested without the prior approval of an exchange; and include a requirement that transactions effected for joint accounts and interests in joint accounts be reported to the exchange. Moreover, members are prohibited from effecting on the floor discretionary transactions in which the discretion exceeds the right to choose the time and the price of the security involved. Other provisions limit the right of a member, while acting as a broker, to effect transactions for his own account in a security for which he holds a customer's order. The rules prohibit members holding options in a security from effecting transactions in that security. Six of the rules deal specifically with specialists and provide that no member should act as a specialist in any security unless registered as such by the exchange; that a specialist's transactions should be limited to those reasonably necessary to permit the specialist to maintain a fair and orderly market; that the specialist should not participate in any joint account except with a partner or another member; that the specialist should keep a legible record of his orders for a period of at least 12 months; and that the specialist should not hold puts, calls, or other options in any security in which he is registered as a specialist. Similar rules govern the conduct of odd-lot dealers.

The **multiple trading** case illustrates the use of the S.E.C.'s power to alter trading rules over the objection of an exchange. Over the years, regional exchanges have developed so-called "multiple trading" practices effecting transactions upon their floors in securities which are also traded on the New York Stock Exchange. By these methods, prices on the regional exchange are determined by New York Stock Exchange quotations reported on the ticker. Members of the New York Stock Exchange who are members also of regional exchanges participate in their "multiple trading" by acting as odd-lot dealers or specialists on the regional exchanges in these issues. The New York Stock Exchange, by an interpretation of its Constitution, sought to bar its members from such activities. After an analysis of the effects of this action, the S.E.C. formally requested the New York Stock Exchange to

... effect such changes in its rules, ... as may be necessary to make it clear that the rules of the exchange, or their enforcement, shall not prevent any member from acting as an odd-lot dealer or specialist or otherwise dealing upon any other exchange outside the City of New York of which he is a member.

Upon the Exchange's refusal to comply with this request, proceedings were instituted and, after weighing all arguments, the S.E.C. found "multiple trading" in the public interest and ordered the change to be made effective.

3. **Prohibition of price manipulation.** §§9, 10, and 15 of the Securities Exchange Act of 1934 prohibit manipulation and fraudulent and deceptive practices, and authorize the promulgation of rules to define certain prohibited practices. §9 prohibits specifically described forms of manipulative activity in connection with listed securities. Transactions that create actual or apparent trading activity or that raise or lower prices, if they are effected for the purpose of inducing others to buy or sell, are declared to be unlawful. **"Wash sales"** or purchases and sales at about the same time by the same party, and **"matched orders"** or transactions between individuals acting in concert to "paint the tape," are declared to be illegal. Persons selling or offering securities for sale are prohibited

from disseminating false information to the effect that the price of the security will, or is likely to, rise or fall because of market operations conducted for the purpose of inducing the purchase or sale of such securities. §§10 and 15 empower the Commission to adopt rules and regulations to define and prohibit the use of new forms of manipulation and other fraudulent or deceptive practices that the Commission may encounter.

In carrying out its duties, the S.E.C. has continuously maintained alert surveillance of trading activity. If there is unusual market activity, a "flying quiz" or preliminary investigation is made to detect and discourage incipient manipulation by prompt determination of the reason for unusual market behavior. If apparent violations are uncovered, formal investigatory proceedings are instituted. These have, on occasion, resulted in suspension and expulsion from the exchange and/or suspension or revocation of broker-dealer registration.

4. Stabilizing security prices. Historically it has been the custom to peg the price of a security offering, whether a primary distribution, a secondary distribution, or a pool liquidation. Almost all distributions—primary, secondary, or special offerings—are at a fixed price. Most of them provide for stabilizing purchases by the managing underwriter or offeror, usually up to 10% of the offering.

§9(a)(6) of the Exchange Act forbids the "pegging, fixing or stabilizing" of security prices in contravention of such rules and regulations as the Commission may prescribe as necessary or appropriate in the public interest or for the protection of investors.

The S.E.C. requires the filing of detailed reports respecting all stabilizing operations conducted to facilitate the distribution of security offerings under the Securities Act of 1933. Abuses have been most prevalent in connection with stabilizing quotations in connection with so-called **"market offerings"** where the price is represented to be at, or based upon, open market prices established by the ebb and flow of supply and demand. Stabilizing of such market offerings is now severely restricted. "Mark-up" of prices is prohibited. §9(a)(6) of the Exchange Act prohibits rigid "pegging" of the market in contravention of S.E.C. rules. Since stabilizers on each day can buy only on a scale-down until the price has dropped by a fixed amount, these rules in effect permit no more than limited stabilization during the distribution.

Regulation requires stabilizers to give notice of their intention to stabilize. If stabilizing has actually been commenced, that fact must also be disclosed. A **"maximum price"** must be set beyond which the stabilizers will not support the market.

5. Control of short selling. Establishing of control over short selling is designed to prevent demoralization of the market, disorderly trading, and bear market raids. These restrictions are discussed above.

6. Margin regulation. The Board of Governors of the Federal Reserve System is charged with prescribing regulations governing the extension and maintenance of credit on registered securities to prevent the excessive use of credit to purchase or carry such securities. Under §7 of the Securities Exchange Act, the Board adopted Regulation T, governing the extension of credit by broker-dealers to customers, and Regulation U to govern loans by banks for the purpose of carrying stocks registered on the Exchange.

Although the Board formulated these rules, the S.E.C. has the responsibility to enforce them. Routine inspections of books and records are made to assure compliance with Regulation T and to explain the meaning and effect of the regulation. In conformity with a policy of having the exchange assume responsibility for the conduct of their own members, inspection by the S.E.C. has been largely confined to over-the-counter firms.

7. Daily statistics of trading. Supplementing the **disclosure required for individual securities,** the S.E.C. has made available data on **trading activity.** These throw light on the technical condition of the market and aid the regulatory authorities in their efforts to maintain a fair and orderly market. Daily reports are issued on the volume of purchases and sales made for their own account by specialists, odd-lot dealers, and other members while on the floor and off the floor. Reports on short sales, securities borrowed, and officer, director, and principal stockholder securities transactions are published in regular statistical releases of the S.E.C.

Regulation of Brokers and Dealers. The third fundamental objective of Federal securities regulation is maintenance of just and equitable principles of trade through regulation of trading activities of broker-dealers. This is important because of the relationship of trust that exists between the customer and the broker-dealer who solicits his business. **Maintenance of solvency** and **protection of customer's funds and securities** from embezzlement or improper hypothecation are the major aims. It is also sought to eliminate overreaching or fraudulent practices and to foster high fiduciary standards among those who do business with the investing public, many of whom are people of small means.

Registration of broker-dealers is the principal method for achieving this objective. Regulation of exchange members and member firms is highly developed. Control of over-the-counter broker-dealers and their activities, because of the decentralized character of their business and the lack of central organization, has not gone so far.

1. Registration of brokers and dealers. Under §15 of the Exchange Act, brokers and dealers, other than those whose business is exclusively intrastate, must register with the S.E.C. in order legally to make use of the mails or instrumentalities of interstate commerce in connection with transactions in any security, except an exempted security or transaction. Registration consists of filing a detailed business history statement of the registrant and its officers, directors, and controlling persons.

§15(b) gives the S.E.C. power to **suspend or revoke registration** (see page 47 above). That section provides that people who have violated the securities acts and/or regulations thereof, or have been convicted of securities fraud, or have made willful misstatements about a material fact to customers or in a filing to the S.E.C. may be denied registration or have their registration revoked.

2. Self-regulation. It has long been the view of the S.E.C. that the securities industry should be responsible, in the first instance, for its own business practices and standards and adherence to them by members of the trade. The already organized stock exchanges have been charged with responsibility to establish such standards and to see that they are observed. A similar program of self-regulation for the over-the-counter markets has been the objective of the specially created **National Association of Securities Dealers, Inc.,** a trade association whose origin is traced to an act of Congress.

As a governmental agency, the S.E.C. stands in the background and is the second line of defense against practices inimical to the public interest. The Commission reviews the actions, or lack of action, of the exchanges and the N.A.S.D. with respect to maintaining just and equitable principles of trade and fair and orderly markets. Upon petition, formal disciplinary action of these business organizations will be reviewed by the S.E.C. To implement this second line of protection, the S.E.C. maintains constant surveillance of trading activities of broker-dealers by inspections, "flying quizzes," and formal investigations. A third line of public protection exists in criminal prosecution by the Department of Justice for fraudulent or other acts violating established law. Such prosecutions are often based upon the findings revealed by investigations of the S.E.C.

3. **Broker-dealer inspection.** A broad program of broker-dealer inspections is carried on by the staff of the S.E.C. to ascertain compliance with the Act and its regulations. Inspections made by accountant-investigators attached to regional offices are designed to educate brokers and dealers in the legal requirements of the Federal securities laws and the rules promulgated thereunder, as well as to check compliance and to detect and prevent fraudulent practices. These investigations also aid in correcting practices that, though not fraudulent, fall short of representing good business standards. Such inspections may afford information useful in appraising the need for new regulations or for changes in existing regulations to protect the public interest.

As a result of its investigations the S.E.C. has frequently found it necessary to invoke the sanctions of the Act to protect the public interest. Fraudulent practices have been enjoined, registration suspended or revoked, and, occasionally, criminal prosecution by the Department of Justice has been instituted.

4. **Transactions at unreasonable prices.** Among the most serious violations of the acceptable business relationships between dealer and customer is the sale of securities by dealers to customers at prices that involve **no reasonable relation to the prevailing market.** The doctrine that it is fraudulent for a dealer to sell securities to customers at prices bearing no reasonable relation to the prevailing market without disclosing the market was established in **Duker & Duker** [6 S.E.C. 386 (1939)], followed by a number of other cases involving similar business conduct. The Commission in one case issued an order revoking registration for violating the Exchange Act, and its application of the fraud doctrine to sales of securities at prices bearing an unreasonable relation to prevailing market quotations was subjected to judicial review for the first time. [Charles Hughes & Co., Inc. v. S.E.C., 139 F. (2d) 434 (C.C.A. 2, 1943), cert. den. 321 U. S. 786 (1944).] The Commission had found that the firm had violated the fraud provisions of the Securities Act and the Securities Exchange Act in dealings with women customers to whom it had sold securities at prices from 16.1% to 40.9% in excess of the prevailing market, without disclosing prevailing market prices to them. The United States Circuit Court of Appeals sustained the Commission's order. In its opinion, the court said:

> An over-the-counter firm which actively solicits customers and then sells them securities at prices as far above the market as were those which petitioner charged here must be deemed to commit a fraud.

This view of the doctrine of fraud has been applied chiefly in cases involving pricing of corporate securities, but with modifications it was applied also in a revocation proceeding in which **sales of oil royalties** were the subject of the Commission's complaint. [Lawrence R. Leeby, 13 S.E.C. 499 (1943), Release No. 34-3450.]

In substance, the Commission holds that a special obligation upon the dealer flows from inherent characteristics of the business of dealing in securities. The dealer holds himself out as one with specialized knowledge and skill in securities markets and investment matters generally. He cultivates his customer's trust and confidence in him and invites reliance on his skill and honesty. That there is an inherent representation that he will deal fairly is plain from his confidential relationship. In the absence of an express representation to the contrary, there is implied the representation that the price is closely related to the current market. The duties of the dealer, under such circumstances, are not measured by the rules that apply to arm's-length bargaining; he is bound to higher standards because of the unique position that he occupies.

Today the problem has been greatly reduced through the **policy of the National Association of Securities Dealers,** which has established clear guidelines in the area. A further check on fraudulent and other practices prohibited by the statutes or regulations is the view of the courts that many of these prohibitions give rise to grounds for civil suit by an injured individual. For example, in several cases, the courts have held that §29 of the Securities Exchange Act gives a purchaser of securities the right to rescind his purchase or recover damages for fraud in over-the-counter transactions. A wrongdoer, therefore, subjects himself not only to the statutory sanctions and penalties but to liability for damages as well. In addition to the increased threat this presents, it provides another means of policing transactions.

International Dealings in Securities

INVESTMENT IN FOREIGN SECURITIES. The American investor may purchase a foreign security in two ways: through buying such security on an American exchange or on the domestic over-the-counter market, or through purchasing it in a foreign market.

Foreign securities available in the American market include a number of dollar bond issues floated here by foreign governments and corporations, shares of leading foreign corporations actively traded in United States markets, and some foreign currency bond issues and less prominent stock issues for which a market has developed in this country.

Those trading in securities issued abroad must keep in mind the following factors:

1. The dollar value of the security and the income therefrom may be affected by currency changes and restrictions.
2. In some countries, income on securities is taxed at the source, so that the holder will not receive the full amount of interest or dividends paid on his holdings. This may be offset by credit for such withholding at the source on the tax return filed in this country.
3. Buying and selling costs and transfer taxes in foreign markets may be higher than prevail here, and, in addition, the cost of shipping the securities and collecting income may be material.
4. Information available may be far less complete and much more difficult to interpret than is the case with domestic securities.
5. S.E.C. regulations in this country and restrictions abroad may affect the ability of American investors to exercise subscription rights given shareholders by foreign corporations.

The Interest Equalization Tax. This tax was proposed in a special message submitted to Congress by President Kennedy in July 1963 outlining the Administration's plans to reduce the balance of payments deficit and was designed to help curb the outflow of long-term capital from the United States. It provided for an "interest equalization tax" on some purchases of new or outstanding foreign issues by Americans, and by foreign residents in the United States, from foreign owners or issuers. The **aim** was to increase the cost of raising capital in the American market in order to discourage borrowing by the leading industrial nations. The tax would not apply to securities of less developed countries, to securities maturing in less than 3 years, to direct investments abroad, or to loans by commercial banks. After the proposal was first made, an **understanding with the Canadian Government** was reached to include a provision permitting the President to exempt new Canadian issues when this was found desirable.

The proposed levy, which was designed to be in effect from July 1963 through the end of 1965, had an appreciable effect even before Congress dealt with it. Because of the uncertainty surrounding the character and timing of congressional action, new issues of foreign bonds in New York came virtually to a halt, while transactions in outstanding issues between foreigners and Americans were slowed down considerably. Partly as a result of this development, the balance of payments deficit declined substantially in the second half of 1963. As of date of publication, no action has been taken by Congress on the proposal.

INTERNATIONAL SECURITY TRADING. Organizations that participate in international dealings in securities in this country include:

1. **Investment banking houses** that offer foreign security issues here and maintain facilities for international security dealings. These houses have played a leading role in the sale of foreign security issues, and also act for foreign correspondents in handling security transactions in the United States market.
2. **Brokerage houses with foreign connections,** including branch offices and correspondents. Many brokerage houses stand ready to accept orders to buy and sell on foreign exchanges as well as on domestic, maintaining relations with member houses of bourses abroad to execute such orders.
3. **Branches and agencies of foreign banks and security houses,** located in the United States and specializing in doing business in their home markets.
4. **Commercial banks** with large foreign departments and branches abroad provide services in connection with international security transactions.

Offerings of blocks of foreign securities can play an important part in international investment. They take securities out of a market in which they are in excess supply, and so sell at depressed prices, and shift them to markets where the demand justifies a higher quotation.

DISTRIBUTION OF BLOCKS OF FOREIGN ISSUES. The origination and distribution of dollar bonds in this country closely resembles the issuance and sale of domestic security issues. Investment banking and brokerage houses with connections abroad may distribute foreign currency obligations and blocks of shares of foreign corporations. One important difference between domestic and foreign shares is that in most foreign markets, stock certificates are **issued to bearer** and carry sheets of coupons against which dividends are paid.

American Depositary Receipts. Frequently arrangements are made to have the foreign shares deposited with a large trust company here or abroad, and to have issued against these deposited shares **depositary certificates or "American shares"** issued in registered form, which can be freely transferred here on the books of a trustee without disturbing the deposited foreign share certificates. The trustee will attend to the collection and distribution of dividends, etc., for the holders of the certificates issued by it, deducting a small fee for the service. When they meet the special requirements of the New York Stock Exchange, such American shares may be listed thereon. American depositary receipts are discussed in Section 3 (International Banking).

Markets for Foreign Equities. Institutional and many individual investors in the United States have become substantial buyers of foreign equities for the following reasons:

1. Such securities may be available at lower price-earnings and price-cash flow ratios than prevail for American securities.
2. Growth rates for foreign corporations may be greater than for corresponding American corporations.
3. Profit margins may be under less competitive pressure if corporations abroad have favored access to expanding markets for their products, as with corporations within the Common Market.
4. Foreign corporations may be subject to lower tax rates and more favorable depreciation regulations.

ARBITRAGE IN SECURITIES. Owing to the fact that discrepancies tend to develop in the prices of securities that are traded in on two or more markets, arbitrage plays an important role in international security dealings.

Arbitrage may be defined as the simultaneous purchase and sale of the same or equivalent things to take advantage of a price discrepancy. By tending to eliminate such discrepancies, the arbitrager performs the economic function of bringing prices into line, thus protecting those who have to buy and sell the things in question. Arbitrage goes on in money and commodities, as well as in securities.

There are three types of arbitrage. **Place arbitrage** seeks to take advantage of price discrepancies in different markets, such as New York and London, or New York and Paris. This is most important in international security arbitrage. **Time arbitrage** seeks to take advantage of price discrepancies between immediate delivery or spot prices and future delivery or future quotations. **Kind arbitrage** seeks to take advantage of discrepancies in price between different things that are or will presently become equivalent to each other, such as convertible securities, split-up shares, and so on.

For effective **international arbitrage in securities,** it is necessary for the arbitrager to be sure that he can obtain execution simultaneously, or nearly so, of his buying and selling orders in different markets, so as to avoid the risk of adverse price fluctuations before completion of the arbitrage. Since he generally seeks a narrow but certain profit, the arbitrager cannot take the risk of being unable to complete the transaction, and so being left with a speculative buying or selling commitment. For this reason, arbitrage is restricted to a large extent to active issues listed on two or more markets. Royal Dutch Petroleum ordinary shares, for example, listed in New York, London, Paris, and several other markets, has been a favorite of arbitragers.

SECTION 11

GOVERNMENT OBLIGATIONS

CONTENTS

The National Debt

	PAGE
Evolution of the debt	1
Magnitude of the debt	1
Public and private debt compared	1
Composition	2
Types of obligations	2
Length of debt maturity	2
Distribution	3
Certainty of payment	3
Cost of the debt	4
The budget	4
Debt management	5

Characteristics of United States Government Securities

General features	6
Selection of government securities	6
Marketable issues	7
Federal agency issues	7
Attractive features	8
United States Savings Bonds	8
Redemption values and investment yields of United States Savings Bonds per $1,000 of bonds (f. 1)	9
Other nonmarketable obligations	9
Tax status of Treasury securities	10
Treasury financing techniques	10

The Market for United States Government Securities

Classes of investors	11
Dealers in government securities	12
Operating funds	13
Operation and size of the market	13
Mechanics of operation	14
The role of the Federal Reserve System in the market	15

	PAGE
Abandonment of "bills only" policy	15
Miscellaneous functions	15
Yield patterns	16
Yield curves of United States securities as of June 15, 1958, and October 11, 1963 (f. 2)	17

Factors Affecting Prices and Yields

Money market obligations	17
Money market supply and demand	18
Money market conditions and bond prices	19
Influence of Federal Reserve policies	19
Effects of Treasury policies	20
"Restricted" issues	20
Deficit financing	21
Nonmanaged factors	21
Major market movements	21
Trends since World War II	22
Annual averages of long-term government bond yields (f. 3)	23
The long-range picture	24

State and Municipal Bonds

Purpose of borrowing	24
Tax status	25
State bonds	25
Taxing power of states	26
Municipal bonds	26
Tax districts	27
Special assessment bonds	27
Revenue bonds	27
Investment factors relating to municipal bonds	27
Marketing of State and local government issues	28
Investors in State and local obligations	28
Methods of payment	29

SECTION 11

GOVERNMENT OBLIGATIONS

The National Debt

EVOLUTION OF THE DEBT. Except for a few years during the early 1830's, the United States has never been out of debt. Wars and slacks in economic activity breed public debts. In 1791 the national debt was about $75 million. The War of 1812 raised the debt to $109 million and the Civil War left a legacy of $2,776 million (including greenbacks) of indebtedness. By 1913 the debt had been reduced to less than $1 billion, but during World War I it soared to over $26 billion. Whittled down to $16 billion by 1930, during the ensuing decade the debt increased substantially for the first time without a war, because of large Treasury expenditures for recovery and relief. Then came the **tremendous debt expansion** of World War II, from $48 billion at the time of the fall of France in 1940 to $279 billion early in 1946. By the end of 1948 the debt had been reduced to $253 billion, which was also the low point in the post-World War II period. The growth in public debt to $304 billion by the end of 1962 was largely due to the Korean War, Treasury deficits during several recessions, and large military and foreign aid commitments.

MAGNITUDE OF THE DEBT. At the end of 1962 the national debt was about 55% of the gross national product. It compared with a market value of all stocks listed on the New York Stock Exchange of $346 billion in December 1962. On a per capita basis, the debt was equivalent to roughly $1,600 for each man, woman, and child.

Public and Private Debt Compared. The net public debt, computed by deducting from gross debt duplicating items, chiefly Federal trust fund holdings, was $257 billion at the end of 1962 and comprised about 26% of the net public and private debt of the nation. As indicated in the table below showing debt aggregates for selected years in billions, the national debt grew more rapidly than other debt between 1929 and 1945, and private debt more rapidly than the national debt from 1945 to 1962.

	1929	1945	1962
National debt	$ 16	$253	$257
State and local government debt	13	14	72
Long-term corporate debt	47	38	156
Short-term corporate debt	42	47	175
Urban real estate mortgages	31	27	211
Farm mortgages	12	7	29
All other private debt	29	20	101
Net debt, public and private	$190	$406	$1,001

A large government debt places a burden on future generations. It requires the **levy of taxes** to cover the interest payment on the debt, which has a significant effect on incentives in the private sector of the economy. The larger the debt the greater the task of debt management.

Equally as important as the size of the debt is the debt structure—maturity and ownership—and the relationship of the debt to national income.

COMPOSITION. The composition of the public debt affects its distribution among various classes of investors, the cost of debt service, and the strength of the Treasury's financial position. The Treasury issues special obligations to government trust accounts and to foreign central banks and governments, and sells as many savings bonds as it can to individual investors. The balance of its borrowing is done in the open market.

Treasury obligations constitute the largest part of the nation's debt structure and are an important investment medium for most financial institutions and individuals. The market for Treasury securities is one of the most important of all financial markets. The way in which the government finances its cash requirements and refinances maturing debt influences the yield on short-term and long-term Treasury issues, as well as that on other money market and capital market instruments. Prices and yields of government securities are a major concern of the Federal Reserve System as well as of the Treasury.

Types of Obligations. Roughly, 15% of the debt consists of special obligations held by trust accounts and foreigners, and 16% of Savings Bonds. Almost all of the remainder, around two-thirds of the total, is represented by **marketable securities**. A tabulation of the debt by types of obligations is published in the Daily Statement of the Treasury (Superintendent of Documents, Government Printing Office) at the end of each month. At the end of 1962, the interest-bearing public debt, in billions, was as follows:

Interest-bearing debt:	
Public issues:	
Marketable obligations:	
Treasury bills	$48.3
Certificates of indebtedness	22.7
Treasury notes	53.7
Treasury bonds	78.4
Total marketable obligations	$ 203.0
Nonmarketable obligations:	
United States Savings Bonds	$ 47.5
Treasury bonds, investment series ...	4.4
Depositary bonds	0.1
Other	0.7
Total nonmarketable obligations ...	$ 52.8
Total public issues	$ 255.8
Special issues	$ 43.4
Total interest-bearing public debt	$ 299.2

Length of Debt Maturity. In recent years the Treasury has intensified its efforts to lengthen the maturity of the debt, which had declined substantially in the post-World War II period. In 1946, the average maturity of the marketable debt was 9 years and 1 month. It fell to as low as 4 years and 4 months in mid-1961 and 4 years and 11 months at the end of 1962. Despite the lengthening of the debt after 1961, a large increase took place in the Treasury's **"floating**

debt," consisting of obligations due within 1 year. The "floating debt" amounted to about 43% of the total marketable debt at the end of 1962. In recent years the increase of this debt has been financed outside the banking system. An important factor contributing to the growth of the "floating debt" has been the need by the Treasury to support short-term rates in order to retard the outflow of gold.

DISTRIBUTION. The widespread distribution of ownership of public debt is shown by the following estimates of holdings by various classes of investors, as published by the Treasury Department for the end of 1962 (figures in billions):

Individuals [1]	$ 65.9
Commercial banks [2]	66.5
Mutual savings banks	6.1
Insurance companies	11.5
Other corporations	20.0
Other firms, institutions, and associations [3]	12.7
State and local governments [4]	19.6
Federal Reserve banks	30.8
U. S. government agencies and trust funds	55.6
Foreign and international [5]	15.3
Total	$304.0

[1] Includes partnerships and personal trust accounts.
[2] Excludes securities held in trust departments.
[3] Includes savings and loan associations, dealers and brokers.
[4] Comprises trust, sinking, and investment funds of state and local governments and their agencies and territories and insular possessions.
[5] Investments of foreign balances and international accounts.

The stake of the public in ownership of the public debt can be appreciated only by considering also its **indirect participation** through millions of bank accounts and life insurance policies. Government trust accounts have acquired large amounts of Treasury obligations for their reserves under Social Security laws. Such holdings increased about $13 billion during the 10 years ended December 31, 1962. The largest of these accounts are the Unemployment Trust Fund, the National Service Life Insurance Fund, and the Federal Old-Age and Survivors Insurance Trust Fund.

CERTAINTY OF PAYMENT. Despite the sharp rise that has taken place in public and private debt since the 1930's, the obligations of the United States Government continue to enjoy the highest confidence of investors. With the ownership of the public debt so widely distributed throughout all segments of the population, default would be inconceivable. Ever since the credit of the United States was established upon a solid foundation under the leadership of Alexander Hamilton, the determination of the American people to honor their obligations has hardly ever even been questioned.

The debt is nearly entirely **internal,** i.e., payable in American dollars rather than in gold or foreign currencies; and the government can never lack dollars with which to pay. At the end of 1962 only $429 million of the Treasury debt was payable in foreign currencies. The government can obtain funds through its virtually unlimited taxing power; it can borrow funds as needed by virtue of its control over the Federal Reserve System; or, should it so desire in an extremity, it could simply print paper money in any denominations and amounts.

In actual practice, the Treasury meets most maturing obligations by **re-borrowing.** The banking system provides a flexible mechanism for supplying the Treasury with any amount that cannot be borrowed on satisfactory terms from other investors. The lending power of the banks can be replenished almost indefinitely by means of reserves provided them through open market operations by the Federal Reserve banks. If commercial banks should ever fail to provide all funds required, the Federal Reserve banks would doubtless provide them. The Treasury is authorized at present to borrow directly from the Reserve banks only to a limited extent. This has been done only as a very temporary expedient, to prevent unsettlement of the money market. Direct borrowing by a government from its central bank in substantial amount is regarded as a long step toward monetary inflation, and it is mentioned here simply to illustrate the ability of the Treasury under all circumstances to secure funds with which to meet its obligations.

There is no real question, therefore, but that all obligations of the United States government will be paid promptly and in full as they fall due. This does not mean the national debt will be paid off; the government can continue indefinitely to meet part of its maturing obligations by re-borrowing. In fact, there are those who recommend that the Treasury should refund some of its debt by issuing perpetual obligations bearing no maturity date, as the British Treasury has done with its "consols."

COST OF THE DEBT. The cost of the public debt depends upon its size, its composition, and the interest rates prevailing at the time obligations are issued.

The average **interest rate** paid by the Treasury on its obligations declined from 4% in 1929 to 2% in 1946, and at the end of 1962 was 3.30%. The amounts of interest payments rose from $5 billion in 1946 to over $9 billion in 1962. This increase reflected not only the increase in Treasury debt but also higher refinancing costs than for the debt incurred during World War II. Annual interest due amounted to less than 1% of the national income in 1929 and to only 1.5% in 1962.

Keeping borrowing costs at a minimum is a major objective of debt management. However, Treasury officials have indicated that **Treasury financing** must also take into consideration the impact of the financing on financial markets and the economy as a whole. For example, excessive issuance of long-term securities in recessions, when interest costs are low, would absorb too large a part of the investment funds needed elsewhere and could even prevent desirable reductions in interest rates. (See The Commission on Money and Credit, The Federal Reserve and The Treasury.)

Although debt service is sometimes referred to as a "burden," the inference should not be drawn that these payments represent a net loss to the economy as a whole. Interest payments are simply transfers of tax revenues to investors. Dollars paid out by the Treasury in interest constitute income to American citizens, corporations, and institutions. As a matter of fact, a goodly proportion of these dollars flows back to the Treasury in the form of income taxes.

There is no formula for determining how large an interest "burden" the nation can support. The answer, if there is one, would have to take into account the level of the national income, the tax structure, and other factors. There is no indication that Federal interest charges threaten to become unsupportable.

THE BUDGET. Fiscal policy is a broad term that embraces the budget policy of the government, i.e., its planned expenditures and anticipated revenues, and the financing policies of the Treasury Department within the budget. It is common practice to use the term **"budget policy"** to refer to the former and **"debt management"** to refer to the latter.

The gross national debt can be reduced, of course, only by means of budgetary surpluses. Without exploring the economic aspects of budget policy in detail, it is pertinent to note that large budgetary surpluses at certain times could be undesirable from the standpoint of economic stability. An overambitious program of high taxes and curtailed government expenditures might plunge the nation into a depression and kill the goose that lays the golden tax eggs. And when employment and production decline substantially, the government is under great political pressure to resort to increased spending, as it did during the 1930's.

It is the Congress, in the last analysis, which enacts the revenue bills and passes upon departmental appropriations. The President, however, usually exercises a major influence over the chief items in the budget, and the Secretary of the Treasury is one of the President's closest advisers. The Treasury's views with respect to fiscal matters are also frequently requested by the Congress.

The annual **Budget Message of the President,** which is delivered early in January soon after the new Congress convenes, is the first official indication of anticipated revenues and expenditures of the Treasury for the fiscal year that will commence the following July 1. Revised budget estimates are made public from time to time at the discretion of the Administration.

Budgetary deficits and surpluses are of special interest to investors because of their effects upon Treasury financing. Up-to-date information is always available as to the status of budgetary receipts and expenditures in the Daily Statement of the Treasury Department.

DEBT MANAGEMENT. The policies and practices of the Treasury in managing the Federal debt include selection of the types and maturities of securities to be offered, terms of new offerings, restrictions as to their eligibility for commercial bank purchase, tax status and redemption features of Treasury issues, payment or refunding of maturing or called obligations, financing of the requirements of governmental agencies, sinking fund operations, and the handling of Treasury cash balances in commercial and Federal Reserve banks. These factors, discussed below, have far-reaching implications for the level of interest rates, the volume of bank deposits, and the composition, distribution, and cost of the national debt.

The **objectives** of debt management were discussed in detail by the Treasury officials in answers to questions posed by the Commission on Money and Credit and published in 1963 in a study entitled The Federal Reserve and the Treasury. The Treasury officials stated:

Debt management policy has three major objectives. First, management of the debt should be conducted in such a way as to contribute to an **orderly growth of the economy** without inflation. In a period of rapid expansion accompanied by inflationary pressures, as much of the debt as is practicable should be placed outside of the commercial banks (apart from temporary bank underwriting) and should include a reasonable volume of intermediate- and longer-term securities. In a recessionary period particular care must be taken to exercise restraint in the amount of long-term securities issued in order not to pre-empt an undue amount of the long-term investment funds needed to support an expansion of the economy. A related aim should be to minimize, as far as possible, the frequency of Treasury borrowings so as to interfere as little as possible with necessary Federal Reserve actions or with corporate, municipal, and mortgage financing.

A second important objective of Treasury debt management is the achievement **of a balanced maturity structure** of the debt, one that is tailored to the needs of our economy for a sizable volume of short-term instruments and also includes a reasonable amount of intermediate- and long-term securities. There must be continuous efforts to issue long-term securities to offset the shortening of maturity caused by the lapse of time, which otherwise results in an excessively large volume of highly liquid short-term debt.

A third objective of debt management relates to **borrowing costs**. While primary weight must be given to the two objectives just noted, the Treasury, like any other borrower, should try to borrow as cheaply as possible. Unlike other borrowers, however, the Treasury must consider the impact of its actions on financial markets and the economy as a whole. Consequently, the aim of keeping borrowing costs at a minimum must be balanced against broader considerations of the public interest.

These several objectives are not easily reconcilable at all times; nor can a priority be assigned to one or another of them under all circumstances.

Not so many years ago, credit management was considered to be the province of the Board of Governors of the Federal Reserve System, and the fiscal requirements of the Treasury were not a major factor in the formulation of credit policy. Today, however, the debt management policies of the Treasury affect credit conditions profoundly.

Characteristics of United States Government Securities

GENERAL FEATURES. United States government obligations enjoy a unique investment status, superior in several respects to that of other classes of securities.

Prompt payment of interest and principal may be considered absolutely certain. The taxing power of the Federal government constitutes a first lien upon all individual and corporate wealth and income of the United States. Since the adoption of the Constitution, the financial integrity of the American government has been unblemished.

There is also a **wide and resilient** market for marketable government issues. This is due partly to their excellent quality, the large number of issues, their broad ownership distribution, and the large volume of outstanding issues. Participating in the marketing of government securities are the Treasury, the Federal Reserve, and dealers. These dealers stand ready at almost all times to buy or sell large or small blocks of all types of Treasury issues with narrow spreads between bid and asked quotations. These features make marketable government securities the most acceptable **collateral** for loans. All types of lenders are willing to lend against them at low rates of interest and up to a very high percentage of the market value. There are no margin restrictions on loans secured by government obligations.

The **two primary investment risks** incurred by investors in government obligations are a **decline in price** due to an increase in the prevailing level of interest rates, and a **decline in purchasing power** of the dollars in which interest and principal are payable.

Government securities afford investors a **wide variety of choice**. Some issues are marketable, others redeemable on demand. Maturities range anywhere from a few days to over 20 years. There are differences as regards tax status, coupon rates and premiums, and eligibility for commercial bank investment. Selection will depend upon the requirements of the individual investor.

SELECTION OF GOVERNMENT SECURITIES. The investor's first decision is between marketable securities and the nonmarketable issues, i.e., savings bonds and notes. Investment features of the latter are discussed below.

CHARACTERISTICS OF UNITED STATES GOVERNMENT SECURITIES 11·7

As compared with marketable issues, they can be purchased only in limited amounts, are redeemable on demand at definite schedules of prices, and, if held to maturity, they often—but not always—yield a better return than marketable issues of comparable maturity. Savings bonds mature either in 7 years and 9 months (Series E Bonds) or 10 years (Series H Bonds).

Among marketable securities, the investor's fundamental problem is to weigh the importance to him of **market stability as against income return.** Generally speaking, these two characteristics vary inversely with each other, depending chiefly upon the maturity of the various issues. An investment in 90-day Treasury bills is, as a practical matter, devoid of the risk of price fluctuation, but the return is usually substantially lower than on obligations of longer maturity. On the other hand, although long-term issues provide a higher return, their market prices are likely to fluctuate over a fairly broad range. The long-term bonds, however, obviously have possibilities for market appreciation as well as depreciation.

Appreciation possibilities are not restricted to the longest maturities. Medium-term issues normally fluctuate less than long-term bonds, to be sure, in response to changes in interest rates, but yields on all maturities tend to decline as they approach maturity, as discussed later under the heading, "Yield Patterns."

Tax status is another investment consideration discussed later on page 10.

MARKETABLE ISSUES. The most important marketable securities issued by the United States Treasury are Treasury bills, certificates of indebtedness, notes, and bonds, all of which are actively traded and are held by many classes of investors.

Treasury bills are noninterest-bearing obligations sold and quoted on a discount basis. They are issued with maturities of 90 days, 180 days, and 1 year. The 90-day and 180-day bills are sold weekly by means of competitive bidding. In August 1963, the Treasury announced that it would place the 1-year bill on a monthly auction basis, instead of the quarterly auction. In 1951 the Treasury introduced a new bill with maturities on tax payment dates to attract the investment of corporation tax reserves.

Certificates of indebtedness have maturities of not more than 1 year. Issues outstanding at year end 1962 had coupons attached to them, although the Treasury has in the past issued certificates without coupons. They enjoy an exceptional degree of market stability and liquidity. Commercial banks hold them in substantial quantities as secondary reserves, and other investors, especially corporations, buy them at times for the temporary employment of excess funds. In recent years the Treasury has relied more on the issuance of longer dated Treasury bills than on certificates.

Treasury notes are issued with maturities of more than 1 year but not more than 5 years. These are also highly liquid, though less so than certificates, and are particularly suitable for commercial bank investment.

Treasury bonds are issued with maturities of more than 5 years. They are usually callable by the Treasury at par at an "option date" several years prior to maturity, and this option date is generally mentioned, in naming an issue, after the maturity date. For example, the 4⅛s, due May 15, 1994-89, are callable at par on May 15, 1989, or on any interest payment date thereafter to maturity on May 15, 1994. When desired, Treasury bonds are issued in registered form.

FEDERAL AGENCY ISSUES. Obligations of Federal Land Banks, Federal Intermediate Credit Banks, Federal Home Loan Banks, the Federal National Mortgage Association, the Bank for Cooperatives, and the Tennesse⌐

Valley Authority are not guaranteed by the Treasury. As of April 30, 1963, these agencies had $9.4 billion in debt issues outstanding, distributed as follows:

Federal Agency Issues Outstanding on April 30, 1963
(In Millions of Dollars)

	Total Outstanding	Within 1 Yr.	1 to 5 Yrs.	5 to 10 Yrs.	10 Yrs. and Over
Bank for Cooperatives	482	482	0	0	0
Federal Home Loan Banks	1,912	1,737	175	0	0
Federal Intermediate Credit Banks	2,021	2,021	0	0	0
Federal Land Banks	2,724	427	1,082	912	303
Federal National Mortgage Association	2,086	171	825	740	350
Tennessee Valley Authority	145	0	0	0	145
Total	9,370	4,838	2,082	1,652	798

Attractive Features. Investors are attracted to Federal Agency issues for the following reasons:

1. Although not guaranteed by the United States Treasury, these issues are regarded as ranking second only to Treasury obligations from the standpoint of **quality**.
2. The Federal Agency market offers excellent **marketability**.
3. Most of these issues are **noncallable** and therefore when the investor makes a commitment he obtains the coupon amount stated in the indenture until maturity.
4. The Federal Agency market at times offers issues with **maturities not otherwise readily available**.
5. At times Federal Agencies sell at very **attractive yield spreads** over Government issues.

UNITED STATES SAVINGS BONDS. These are designed primarily for individual investors who wish assurance against loss of principal in the event they should decide to liquidate their holdings. Savings bonds are not transferable and cannot be used as collateral for bank loans, but they afford a relatively attractive rate of return if held for a number of years.

There are two types of savings bonds now being issued:

1. **Series E bonds** mature in 7 years, 9 months, pay income only at maturity or earlier redemption, and return $100 for every $75 invested if held to maturity, which represents a compound interest rate of 3¾% per year. These bonds are redeemable on demand according to a fixed schedule of prices that returns to the registered holder principal in full plus interest rates that increase with the length of time the bonds have been held, as shown in the accompanying table, Fig. 1. Owners of maturing Series E bonds may extend the maturity date of their holdings for an additional 10 years. There is a special schedule of redemption values for this extended maturity period.

2. **Series H bonds** mature in 10 years, are purchased at par, and bear interest paid semi-annually by Treasury check mailed to the registered owner. Interest payments vary as shown in Fig. 1. The bonds are redeemable on demand at par. An individual can purchase only up to $20,000 maturity value of Series E or H bonds in a calendar year.

CHARACTERISTICS OF UNITED STATES GOVERNMENT SECURITIES 11·9

NEW SERIES E AND H BONDS
Per $1,000 Bond Issued Since June 1, 1959

Years After Issue Date	Series E Bonds Redemption Value	Series E Bonds Yield from Issue	Series E Bonds Yield to Mat.	Interest Check *	Series H Bonds *** Yield from Issue	Series H Bonds *** Yield to Mat.
to ½	$750.00	...	3.75	8.00	1.60	3.75
½ to 1	756.40	1.71	3.89	14.50	2.25	3.88
1 to 1½ ...	767.60	2.33	3.96	16.00	2.56	3.95
1½ to 2 ...	780.40	2.67	4.01	20.00	2.91	4.00
2 to 2½	796.00	3.00	4.01	20.00	3.12	4.00
2½ to 3	811.20	3.16	4.03	20.00	3.26	4.00
3 to 3½	826.40	3.26	4.05	20.00	3.36	4.00
3½ to 4	842.80	3.36	4.06	20.00	3.44	4.00
4 to 4½	860.00	3.45	4.06	20.00	3.49	4.00
4½ to 5	878.00	3.53	4.04	20.00	3.54	4.00
5 to 5½	896.00	3.59	4.03	20.00	3.58	4.00
5½ to 6	914.40	3.64	4.02	20.00	3.61	4.00
6 to 6½	932.80	3.67	4.01	20.00	3.64	4.00
6½ to 7	951.60	3.70	4.01	20.00	3.66	4.00
7 to 7½	970.80	3.72	3.99	20.00	3.68	4.00
7½ to Mat.	990.00	3.74	4.06			
Maturity **	1,000.00	3.75	...			
7½ to 8				20.00	3.70	4.00
8 to 8½				20.00	3.71	4.00
8½ to 9				20.00	3.72	4.00
9 to 9½				20.00	3.74	4.00
9½ to Mat.				20.00	3.75	4.00

* Paid at end of period. H Bonds mature in 10 years.
** E Bonds mature in 7 years and 9 months.
*** Redemption value of $1,000 H Bond is $1,000 at all times.

Fig. 1. Redemption values and investment yields of United States Savings Bonds per $1,000 of bonds.

All series of savings bonds may be registered in the name of one individual, two individuals as co-owners, or one individual as owner and a second as beneficiary.

Series E bonds can be redeemed upon presentation by the owner at any time after 2 months from the date of issue. Series H is redeemable by the owner on 1 month's written notice after 6 months from the date of issue. The redemption check is dated the first day of the second calendar month following presentation of the bond with request for payment, and the redemption value is based upon the month in which the check is dated.

OTHER NONMARKETABLE OBLIGATIONS. These include Treasury bonds—Investment Series A and B, Depositary bonds, Special issues, Treasury bonds—R.E.A. Series, and Foreign Series and Foreign Currency Series.

Treasury bonds, Investment Series A, were issued in 1947 and mature in 1965. Holders of the bonds have the right to redeem the bonds on 1 month's notice. The redemption price changes semi-annually. Interest at 2½% per annum is paid in April and October. At the end of 1962, $453 million of these obligations were outstanding.

Treasury bonds, Investment Series B-1975-80, were issued in 1951 in exchange for U. S. Treasury 2½s of 1967–72 and in 1952 for cash subscription and for part exchange by holders of U. S. Treasury 2½s of 1965–70, 1966–71, and June and December 1967–72. Holders of Treasury bonds, Investment Series B, have the right to exchange them for 1½% 5-year marketable Treasury notes that are issued as of the April 1st or October 1st next preceding the date of the exchange.

Depositary bonds were issued to depositaries and financial agents of the Treasury as a means of compensating these banks for services rendered. There were only $110 million of Depositary bonds outstanding at the end of 1962.

Treasury bonds, R.E.A. Series, were issued starting in 1960 in conjunction with the financing of the Rural Electrification Administration.

Foreign Series and Foreign Currency Series Treasury obligations were issued starting in 1962 to official foreign institutions. The latter series is denominated in foreign currencies, whereas the former series is payable in dollars. The purpose of these issues is to provide a means for investing the dollar reserves accumulated by some European countries and thereby prevent conversion of these dollar holdings into gold.

TAX STATUS OF TREASURY SECURITIES. Interest on most government obligations, including all the marketable securities issued since March 1, 1941, and all series of savings bonds and notes currently being issued, are **fully taxable** under Federal tax laws. All government securities are exempt, however, from state and local taxes except estate, inheritance, gift, or other excise taxes.

In the instance of Series E bonds, the annual increment in value is subject to all Federal taxes and is taxable as interest either (a) from year to year if the holder elects to report on an accrual basis, or otherwise (b) at maturity or prior redemption.

Interest payable on **"partially tax-exempt"** bonds, issued prior to March 1, 1941, is exempt from Federal normal taxes. It is exempt from Federal surtaxes to the extent of $5,000 principal amount of bonds if held by individuals or personal holding companies. There is a similar exemption for such interest from corporation surtaxes, whether upon income or excessive accumulations of surplus.

TREASURY FINANCING TECHNIQUES. The Treasury offers new securities in the following ways:

1. **Treasury bill auctions.** Each Monday the Treasury sells at auction one bill issue maturing in 13 weeks and another in 26 weeks. Frequently, the amount of money raised at these auctions is equal to the amount of maturing bills, but occasionally the Treasury sells bills in excess of the amount coming due. The bills are sold on a discount basis, with allotment made to the highest bidders down to the price at which sufficient subscriptions have been received to cover the amount of bills offered by the Treasury. Those investors who tender for up to $200,000 of 13-week bills and $100,000 of 26-week bills on a noncompetitive basis receive allotments in full at the average competitive bid price. In recent years, the Treasury has also had outstanding issues of 1-year bills. Originally, these matured in the middle of January, April, July, and October, but in 1963 these bills were placed on a monthly auction basis.

2. **Tax-Anticipation Issues.** These are certificates of indebtedness or Treasury bills that mature a week after a quarterly tax payment date but are acceptable at par in payment of taxes on the tax date. These issues are designed to attract the temporarily idle funds of corporations that have been set aside for the payment of taxes.

3. **Coupon Obligations.** This type of financing includes certificates of indebtedness, notes, and bonds. The terms for these issues are usually set by the Treasury after consultation with the Federal Reserve and committees representing institutional investors and are attractive enough to cause the issue to sell in the market at a slight premium. The purpose is to assure that the offering will attract ample subscriptions.

In late 1962, the Treasury announced its intention to periodically sell at auction long-term bonds, with the winning syndicate to reoffer the issues to the public. Several such bond auctions were held in 1963.

4. Exchange Offerings. The Treasury offers the holders of maturing issues the right to exchange them for new issues. If the yield offered on the new issue appears attractive relative to other issues in the same maturity range, a sizeable exchange usually occurs into the new issue.

5. Advance Refundings. These consist of: (1) Prerefundings, in which holders of Treasury issues with a maturity of under 1 year are given the right to exchange their holdings for longer dated issues usually with a maturity from 1 to 5 years; (2) junior advance refundings, in which holders of issues maturing in 1 to 5 years are given the right to exchange into issues usually with a maturity of 5 to 10 years; (3) senior advance refundings, in which holders of issues with a maturity of 5 to 10 years are given the right to exchange into issues with a maturity over 10 years.

Advance refundings have come into prominence in recent years. They have contributed substantially to the improvement in maturity structure of the marketable debt. The Treasury has also stated that advance refunding reduces the reliance on bank financing of the debt, reduces the size and frequency of Treasury financing, and helps to hold down the long-term financing costs. The investor, on the other hand, obtains an immediate income increase on his investment since he accepts in the exchange a long-term issue and in most instances does not have to take a book loss for tax purposes on his original investment.

The Market for United States Government Securities

CLASSES OF INVESTORS. Commercial banks find government securities ideally suited to their investment requirements because of their safety, market stability, ready convertibility into cash, collateral qualities, and diversity of maturities. The average bank maintains a secondary reserve of short-term government securities to enable it to meet possible demands for funds from depositors and borrowers. Other funds are invested in medium- and long-term issues, the distribution depending upon the nature and the bank's appraisal of the likely behavior of its deposits, the character of its other assets, the ratio of capital funds to deposits, its earnings position, and the outlook for the bond market.

Commercial banks are guided by the following basic principles in their investments in government securities. (See Gaines, Techniques of Treasury Debt Management.)

1. Loans have first call on bank assets as long as loan commitments do not jeopardize the bank's liquidity.
2. Banks try to remain fully invested.
3. Investments must be liquid enough to meet all foreseeable cash requirements.

In the aggregate, commercial bank investments in government securities depend upon **loan demand** and the **availability of primary reserves.** Moreover, because other short-term money market investments are available in only a limited supply, banks invest nearly all of their secondary reserves in short-term governments. Commercial banks have reduced their holdings of governments in periods of strong loan demand and monetary restraint, and they have purchased governments in periods of slack in business activity and monetary ease. Thus, banks were net sellers of governments in 1955 and 1959 and net purchasers in 1958, 1960, and 1961.

In recent years the **ratio of governments to total bank investments** has declined steadily as banks have rapidly added to their investments in state and local issues, which are exempt from Federal income taxes. At an increasing number of banks investments in tax-exempt issues equal investments in governments. In 1953, commercial banks held less than 25% of their total portfolio in municipal obligations.

Federal Reserve banks largely hold short-term issues. Their investment operations are determined primarily by considerations of credit policy.

Corporations that find themselves temporarily with excess cash usually invest either in marketable short-term government securities or in savings notes. Concerns that operate pension funds or accumulate their own insurance reserves invest in Treasury bonds, much like insurance companies.

Insurance companies and **savings banks** generally prefer other types of high-grade securities and mortgages that provide a higher return than governments. But when these are not available to absorb investment funds, government obligations are purchased to secure income with a minimum of risk of price depreciation. Because of their marketability, these government securities can be sold readily when other investments become available.

Immediately after World War II and through the early 1950's both insurance companies and savings banks were large investors in governments but since then have liquidated them in order to invest in mortgages and other securities. The **liquidation of governments** has been largely concentrated in issues with a maturity over 5 years.

Savings and loan associations have gradually increased their investments in governments during the post-World War II period. This reflects the growth of the associations and the fact that many of them are required to maintain part of their liquidity in governments.

State and local governments invest sinking funds for debt retirement, civil service pension and disability funds, and other trust funds wholly or in part in Treasury securities. Laws or regulations sometimes restrict the investment of such funds to government securities, or public officials may select them of their own accord to avoid possible criticism.

Foreign investment in government securities has grown appreciably since 1950. It reflects the improvement in the international reserves of foreign countries. Most foreign holdings of governments are in issues due within 1 year.

Individual investors' requirements vary greatly. If safety is the prime consideration, government securities are most desirable. It is generally agreed that a well-rounded investment account should normally contain some proportion of government securities for proper diversification and because of their price stability and marketability. Some individuals operate in government securities on a trading basis partly with borrowed funds, attempting to profit from market fluctuations.

Government trust accounts have a large part of their funds invested in special nonmarketable obligations issued to them by the Treasury because these funds must realize some minimum rate of return in order to meet the actuarial requirements on which the fund is based. Since 1955 market yields have risen enough to satisfy these actuarial requirements and to permit the funds to invest in marketable government debt.

DEALERS IN GOVERNMENT SECURITIES. The great bulk of the transactions in government securities are effected by a few dozen dealers, most of whom have their headquarters in New York City. Larger firms maintain branch offices in principal cities throughout the country.

As the volume of trading in government securities increased after 1932, more and more dealers entered the field. Some are old firms that formerly engaged in general investment banking or dealt in acceptances; others are new concerns organized primarily to deal in government securities. There are also "dealer banks," commercial banks maintaining special departments that transact a government securities business.

The function of the dealer is to act as middleman between those who wish to sell and those who wish to buy securities. The ultimate market for government securities is composed of the several classes of investors described above, dealers providing the essential mechanism to execute buying and selling orders from these investors. Dealers must maintain close contacts with large investors in order to know where large blocks of certain issues might be placed if offered for sale, or where some might be purchased if a customer should wish to buy.

A dealer, by definition, buys and sells for his own account. Under normal market conditions, he stands ready to buy or sell large blocks of Treasury securities at prevailing market quotations. If he is asked to bid on a large block of bonds that he may not be able to dispose of readily, he may bid somewhat under prevailing quotations or offer to take the bonds on a consignment basis.

Operating Funds. Dealers operate with funds far in excess of their own capital, borrowing extensively from commercial banks and business corporations against government securities as collateral. At the end of 1962, borrowings by government securities dealers amounted to $4.4 billion, of which the commercial banks supplied $2.4 billion and the corporations $1.6 billion. Recourse to these credit facilities contributes greatly to the **liquidity and stability of the market** for government obligations.

Some institutions make a practice of **lending securities** from their portfolios to dealers. This enables a dealer to sell and make delivery of almost any Treasury issue, regardless of whether he happens to own some himself. He pledges other securities as collateral for the loan of the issue desired until he acquires these obligations and "repays" the loan.

Dealers watch developments in the market very closely. When they believe that prices may advance they build up their inventory positions through buying more than they sell. They are constantly on the alert to buy or sell issues whose prices get "out of line" with respect to their normal market relationship with other issues. At times, Treasury bonds present opportunities for arbitraging. Some dealers advise customers with respect to the selection of issues, switches from one issue to another, and general investment policy.

OPERATION AND SIZE OF THE MARKET. Almost all transactions in government securities are executed by telephone. The dealer states the best price at which he is willing to buy or to sell a given amount of an issue, and if the investor decides to accept that price the transaction is consummated immediately.

Most substantial investors buy and sell directly from or to dealers. Large **banks,** in addition to buying and selling for their own portfolios, execute transactions with dealers on behalf of their customers, including individuals, corporations, trust accounts, and out-of-town banks. They also hold securities in safekeeping for many of these customers, which facilitates the physical transfer of the securities from sellers to buyers.

Treasury bonds are listed on the New York Stock Exchange and some other exchanges, but notes, certificates, and bills are not. **Dealings on the exchanges,** however, are infrequent and usually in quite small amounts, seldom exceeding a million dollars a day. By contrast, transactions in all types of government securities among dealers amount to a hundred million dollars or more daily even when the market is inactive, and run into several hundred million dollars on a normally active day. On a busy day, trading may exceed half a billion dollars. Thus, the true market at any given time is to be found among the dealers, and not on the exchange.

Dealers buy and sell small quantities of securities as well as large, but the bulk of the trading volume in governments is made up of blocks of a million dollars or more. Among large investors, transactions of only a quarter or half million dollars are considered relatively small. During 1962, the volume of dealer transactions in United States government securities totaled $443 billion, of which $349 billion was in issues with a maturity within 1 year, $56 billion with a maturity within 1 to 5 years, and $39 billion with a maturity after 5 years. Nearly 40% of these dealer transactions were with commercial banks.

Some investors deal through a single dealer whom they have found satisfactory. Large investors, however, frequently "shop around" among dealers in an effort to find one who happens to be able to sell or buy a particular issue at a slightly more favorable price than others. This serves to keep quotations of all dealers for various issues very nearly uniform at all times. Commercial banks usually attempt to **spread their transactions among different dealers** in proportion to the amount of business that they receive from the respective firms in the form of loans and deposit balances.

Mechanics of Operation. Government bonds and notes are quoted on a percentage-of-parity basis. Fractions are quoted usually in 32nds, sometimes in 64ths. Thus a quotation of 101.16 would mean a price of $1,015 for a bond with a par value of $1,000.

Certificates of indebtedness, and sometimes other securities very near to maturity, are quoted on an annual yield basis to maturity. Thus an offering of 3¼% certificates on a 3½% basis would mean a price at which this issue would afford a net return to maturity equal to 3½% on an annual interest basis.

Transactions in government securities are almost always at **net prices.** There is no tax involved and dealers rarely charge commissions as such. They obtain compensation for their services in the form of the spread between bid and asked quotations; i.e., they buy at the bid price and sell at the asked price, the differential usually amounting to ⅜₂nds of a point, sometimes less. In smaller organizations, business may be done on a brokerage or commission basis. Transactions on stock exchanges are subject to fixed commissions. For each transaction, the dealer prepares a "ticket," which is sent to the investor and which confirms the terms of the transaction and presents the computation of the amount due to or from the investor, including accrued interest.

Quotations do not, of course, take into account the amount of **interest accrued** on the current coupons attached to the securities. This sum must be computed and added to the bill of the buyer. Accrued interest on government securities is computed on the basis of the actual number of days in the interest period, not on a uniform 30-day month basis. Bonds and notes bear semi-annual interest coupons, but interest on certificates is paid only at maturity.

Treasury bills bear no interest and are bought and sold at a discount below par. They are quoted on an annual yield basis.

Large dealers issue **daily quotation sheets** for distribution to investors. Each such sheet shows the dealer's closing bid and asked quotations and investment yields for the various issues as of 4 P.M. the previous day. The tabulation usually shows yields to corporations of each issue after making allowance for Federal income tax, the amount of each issue outstanding, its tax status, the price range for the year, and other pertinent data.

THE MARKET FOR UNITED STATES GOVERNMENT SECURITIES 11·15

Delivery of securities and payment by check are normally made on the first business day following the transaction, Friday transactions being cleared on Monday. Arrangement can usually be made with the dealer for delayed delivery if the securities cannot be delivered on the "regular delivery" date. Also, if the seller of securities wishes to be paid in "Federal funds," a check drawn on a Federal Reserve bank, on the regular delivery date or even on the day of the transaction, this can frequently be arranged with the dealer at the time the sale is made.

Dealers in government securities have developed their own trade jargon. A quotation in odd 64ths of a point is usually given in 32nds "plus." For example, a quotation of "101-15 plus" means 101 and $15/32$nds plus $1/64$th, or in other words, 101 and $31/64$ths of a point. A quotation of "101-15, minus to plus" means that the bid price of the issue is 101 and $29/64$ths and the asked price is 101 and $31/64$ths.

Many issues of Treasury bonds have been dubbed with nicknames. For instance, the restricted 2½s, due December 15, 1972-67, are called the "Victories," or more intimately the "Vics," because they were offered during the Victory Loan Drive in December, 1945, and the 3½s of 1990 are called the "Gay Nineties."

THE ROLE OF THE FEDERAL RESERVE SYSTEM IN THE MARKET. The Federal Reserve System plays an important role in the functioning of the government securities market. Very few weeks go by in which the Federal Reserve is not in the market either as a buyer or a seller. In 1962, System holdings of governments increased by $1.9 billion, which represented 25% of the net increase in the Federal debt for that year.

The policy governing Federal Reserve purchases and sales of government securities is formulated by the **Federal Open Market Committee.** Their decisions are influenced by the seasonal flow of bank credit and the need to bring the supply of money into alignment with the flow of goods and services in order to promote sustainable economic growth and full employment. The **Federal Reserve Bank of New York** acts as agent for the Federal Open Market Committee and handles most of the buying and selling of government securities for the twelve Federal Reserve banks. In its open-market operations, the Federal Reserve deals only with a group of so-called **"recognized dealers"**—leading firms selected by the Federal Reserve that have agreed to certain terms in connection with the conduct of their business.

Abandonment of "Bills Only" Policy. Throughout most of the post-World War II period, System open-market operations—the buying and selling of securities for the account of the Federal Reserve banks—were conducted in government securities with a maturity of less than 1 year, primarily in Treasury bills. The "bills only" policy was abandoned in 1961, when the Federal Reserve started to purchase issues with a maturity in excess of 1 year. On June 30, 1963, the Federal Reserve held $21.5 billion of governments with a maturity of less than 1 year, $8.3 billion of from 1 to 5 years and $2.2 billion with a maturity of over 5 years. Even prior to the abandonment of the "bills only" policy the Federal Reserve occasionally purchased longer dated governments. However, this was restricted to those times when such purchases contributed to the restoration of an orderly government securities market.

Miscellaneous Functions. The Federal Reserve is also a source of funds for government securities dealers. To facilitate the smooth functioning of the money market and to help carry out its credit policies, the Federal Reserve often helps nonbank dealers to carry their inventories by making **repurchase agreements** with them and by permitting bank dealers to borrow at the Federal Reserve discount window. These temporary accommodations are particularly prevalent on Fridays, holiday weekends, and at the end of December, when dealer positions are increased in response to year-end balance sheet adjustments.

Moreover, the Federal Reserve Bank of New York acts as agent for government agencies and trust funds, foreign governments and central banks, foreign commercial banks, and some domestic banks in connection with their transactions in government securities. Federal Reserve officials also play an important part in the negotiations involving the sale of **nonmarketable issues** to foreign central banks for the purpose of acquiring foreign currencies in order to retard the outflow of gold. The Federal Reserve banks, as fiscal agents for the Treasury, handle subscriptions for new issues, exchanges, redemptions, and the payment of coupons.

To further the Federal Reserve policy of maintaining "orderly conditions" in the government bond market, the Federal Reserve Bank of New York is in **close touch with the market.** The Securities Department of the Bank is in daily contact with dealers and receives periodic reports from them regarding their operations that are carefully scrutinized, and advice or admonition may be offered from time to time as circumstances dictate. Each week, the Federal Reserve Bank of New York publishes statistics on dealer transactions, dealer inventories, and the financing of government securities dealers.

YIELD PATTERNS. The phrase "yield pattern" refers to the relationship existing at some particular time between the market yields of various maturities of government obligations. The "pattern of rates," the "yield curve," and the "interest curve" are other synonymous terms.

A yield pattern (Fig. 2) is usually portrayed graphically by plotting various market yields on a chart on which years to maturity or call date are marked along the base of the chart. A curve is then drawn that most nearly fits the pattern made by the yields. Curves are sometimes constructed for yields after deductions based upon prevailing rates of Federal corporation taxes. When it is assumed that callable issues will be redeemed on their first option dates, yields are plotted on the basis of these dates rather than maturity dates.

Yield patterns have changed significantly in recent years. As indicated in Fig. 2, the slope of the yield curve was much steeper on June 15, 1958, than on October 11, 1963. Thus, on October 11, 1963, the yield spread between 3-month Treasury bills and governments maturing in 17 years was only 63 basis points compared with 230 basis points on June 15, 1958.

Investors use yield curves in appraising the **relative attractiveness of different maturities.** This involves judgment as to whether the higher yields available for the longer maturities adequately compensate them for the greater risk of possible price declines.

In recent years, bonds have sold to give progressively lower yields as their redemption dates have approached. This causes them to show market appreciation over amortized cost prices even during periods when the pattern of interest rates remains unchanged. The yield curve gives an indication of the extent to which various issues will tend to show market appreciation as they approach maturity, assuming no fundamental changes in the pattern of yields.

Many portfolio managers have found it very profitable to sell bonds several years before they mature and to reinvest in somewhat longer maturities. This is referred to as **"riding the interest curve."** The steeper the curve, of course, the greater are the profit possibilities in this practice of holding bonds for a few years until they sell at the lower yields applicable to shorter-term obligations.

The yield pattern is also used by traders to determine whether an individual issue is selling too high or too low in relation to other issues of comparable maturity, i.e., whether it is "in line" or "out of line" with the market. By consulting the curve to see what an issue of given maturity and characteristics should yield, this can be ascertained at a glance.

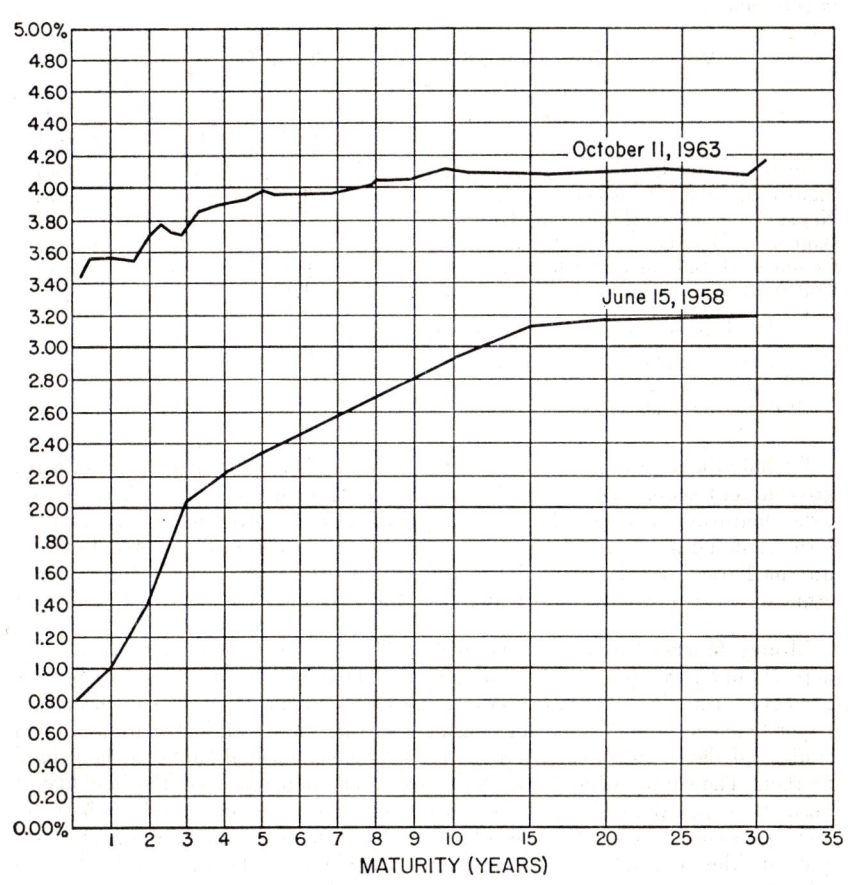

Fig. 2. Yield curves of United States securities as of June 15, 1958, and October 11, 1963.

Factors Affecting Prices and Yields

MONEY MARKET OBLIGATIONS. Separate consideration must be given to determination of yields on short-term, money market Treasury obligations, to how money market conditions in turn affect prices of medium- and long-term bonds, and, thirdly, to how longer-term issues are affected by the policies of the monetary authorities and other factors. (See also discussion in Section 1—Interest Rates and Money Markets.)

The major money market obligations consist of government securities with a maturity of within 1 year, Federal agency issues due within 1 year, commercial paper, bankers' acceptances, commercial bank time certificates of deposit, and repurchase agreements. As indicated in the table below, the volume of these obligations outstanding has grown sharply in recent years, particularly the money market instruments other than United States governments. This is quite different from the money market structure that existed immediately after World War II, when very few money market investments were available other than short-term governments.

Volume of Outstanding Selected Short-Term Investments
(billions of dollars)

	1953	1962	Net Change
Short-term governments	73.2	87.3	+14.1
Short-term Federal agencies	1.3	5.7	+ 4.4
Negotiable time certificates of deposit	0	6.5	+ 6.5
Bankers' acceptances	0.6	2.7	+ 2.1
Commercial and finance company paper	0.6	6.0	+ 5.4
Collateral loans to securities dealers †	1.2*	4.5**	+ 3.3
Total	76.9	112.7	+35.8

† Including repurchase agreements.
* Nonbank dealers.
** Bank and nonbank dealers.

Despite the rapid growth of other money market instruments, **short-term government securities** remain the fulcrum of the money market. These include issues maturing in several days to a year. Short-term governments are a prime form of liquid assets for commercial banks, business corporations, and financial intermediaries. To the Federal Reserve System, the buying and selling of government securities is the principal means for implementing monetary policy.

Money Market Supply and Demand. The demand for money market funds depends upon the amount the Treasury and Federal agencies decide to borrow at short term, the difference between the cost of bank loans and open-market paper financing, the demand for consumer credit, the expansion of international trade, and the extent of the participation by the commercial banks in the capital market. The supply of loanable short-term funds depends upon the liquidity of business corporations, financial intermediaries, and commercial banks, whose reserve position in turn is determined largely by Federal Reserve action. The supply side thus depends largely upon excess reserves of the member banks and other factors that affect member banks' reserve balances.

Prior to 1933, **rediscount rates** of the Federal Reserve banks had considerable influence upon yields of short-term Treasury securities. Thereafter, however, rediscount rates lost their effectiveness as the huge inflow of gold from abroad piled up tremendous excess reserves in the money centers. During the middle 1930's, yields on 90-day Treasury bills declined to the vanishing point. During the early years of World War II, excess reserves declined sharply as currency circulation expanded by leaps and bounds, and at the same time the Treasury adopted a policy of financing a large part of its requirements by means of short-term borrowing. As a result, money market rates began to rise. In 1942, however, the Federal Reserve Board adopted a policy of **pegging** the rates on Treasury bills and certificates of indebtedness at ⅜% and ⅞%, respectively, by means of open market operations, and this step artificially fixed yields on such obligations.

Throughout the war and during the postwar years through 1950 these policies of the Treasury and the Reserve Board completely dominated the money market.

Changes in nonmanaged factors, such as gold movements and currency in circulation, which affect the volume of bank excess reserves, were counteracted by the policy of pegging rates, which was equivalent to engaging in open market purchases of these short-term issues to the extent required to keep yields unchanged.

However, following the **Treasury-Federal Reserve accord** in 1951, cyclical forces began to play a dominant role in the money market. Business expansion and deficit financing by the government resulted in large demands on the money market. This together with Federal Reserve efforts to curb inflationary pressures resulted in sharp increases in short-term rates. In recent years, the monetary authorities have supported short-term rates to retard the outflow of gold, thus substantially reducing the volatility of short-term rates and being in part responsible for reducing the spread between short-term and long-term interest rates.

MONEY MARKET CONDITIONS AND BOND PRICES. Money market conditions have a major influence upon prices and yields of medium- and long-term government securities. Low yields on short-term securities offer a constant inducement to investors to buy longer dated issues to obtain the better return they provide. Commercial banks must keep sufficient funds either as excess cash or invested in short-term obligations to meet their liquidity requirements. Having set aside enough funds in liquid form for this purpose, however, the investment of the remaining funds that banks have available for investment will depend largely upon their appraisal of the relative attractiveness of short-, medium-, and long-term issues. The lower the yields on the short-term money market obligations, the more attractive the longer issues seem by comparison. Also, the volume of funds that banks have available for investment is affected by money market factors that influence deposits and reserve balances.

The expectation that a **differential** will continue to exist between short- and long-term rates adds to the attractiveness of medium and intermediate maturities. If, as anticipated, these issues sell at constantly declining market yields as they approach maturity, market prices will reflect appreciation over amortized book values, giving opportunities for profit from "riding the interest curve," as discussed above.

A reduction in the supply of short-term funds may have repercussions upon the bond market. In the second half of 1958, for example, when the Federal Reserve moved to monetary restraint and reduced the volume of bank reserves, the government bond market had its worst break in years. Banks had to liquidate medium- and long-term bonds in order to meet the demands of borrowers.

INFLUENCE OF FEDERAL RESERVE POLICIES. The Federal Reserve, through open market operations and other monetary instruments, controls the availability of money, and therefore Federal Reserve policy has a significant impact on the prices of government securities. Moreover, the Federal Reserve attempts to maintain an "even keel" in the market during periods of Treasury financing and to prevent disorderly market conditions.

The decline in bond yields during the 1930's was caused chiefly by the great expansion of excess reserves resulting from the inflow of gold, rather than by any positive actions taken by the Reserve authorities. As a matter of fact, although the Board of Governors did not wish to reverse the downward trend of rates, it did seek to reduce the volume of excess reserves to manageable proportions. This was one reason for doubling member bank reserve requirements during 1936–1937. When this cut in excess reserves was followed by a break in bond prices, however, the Reserve banks stepped in to support the market with open market purchases and later reversed in part the increase in reserve requirements.

During World War II, the Reserve banks added more than $20 billion of Treasury obligations to their portfolios. With these huge open market holdings, the Federal Reserve System's control over excess reserves was greatly increased. Sales of a small part of these holdings could quickly wipe out excess reserves and force banks to rediscount heavily.

During the war and in the period immediately after the war, the Federal Reserve also cooperated with the Treasury in pegging interest rates on government issues at low yields, thereby reducing the cost of financing the huge war debt. This policy severely restricted the effectiveness of the Federal Reserve and was abandoned following the Federal Reserve-Treasury accord in 1951.

In order to contain the **inflationary pressures** during the 1954–57 and 1958–60 business expansions, the Federal Reserve sharply slowed down the expansion of bank reserves, forced the commercial banks to liquidate holdings of government securities, and raised the rediscount rate. These measures contributed largely to the substantial rise in interest rates. On the other hand, the Federal Reserve, in order to promote economic recovery during the 1953–54, 1957–58, and 1960–61 recessions, contributed largely to the decline in interest rates during these periods by expanding the volume of bank reserves through open market operations, and by reducing reserve requirements and the rediscount rate.

Until 1961, open market operations had usually been confined to short-term obligations except during the periods of bond market weakness, when buying was extended to medium- and long-term issues in order to strengthen prices directly. Because of the deficit in this country's balance of payments, the Federal Reserve abandoned the "bills only" policy, the conducting of open market operations in short-term government securities. In order to support short-term rates and at times to boost them, the Federal Reserve in 1961 through 1963 frequently made purchases of government securities with maturities above 1 year and sales of issues under 1 year, especially 3-month bills. The Federal Reserve also encouraged **commercial banks** to become active participants in the capital market when it permitted them to pay competitive rates on time and savings deposits in 1961. To offset the cost of these deposits, the commercial banks invested outside the money market—in consumer loans, term loans, mortgage loans, and municipal issues. This practice helped to support short-term rates and hold long-term rates down.

The Reserve Board can affect the government bond market also through making recommendations to the Treasury with respect to financing methods and operations.

EFFECTS OF TREASURY POLICIES. The chief influence of the Treasury on the bond market is exercised by the **choice and timing of new offerings.** In this way, the supply of particular maturities at any one time can be largely influenced. The Treasury competes for funds with other demanders of credit. Depending on debt management objectives and market limitations, the Treasury may finance its requirements in the short-term or the long-term market.

The savings bond program of the Treasury also has important implications for the bond market. The greater the extent to which sales of savings bonds exceed maturities and redemptions, the smaller the volume of funds that the Treasury must borrow in the open market. Also the large amount of savings bonds outstanding makes the Treasury vitally concerned with the bond market because of the fear that a break in bond prices in the market might start a flood of savings bond redemptions.

"Restricted" Issues. During World War II, the Treasury made some efforts to push sales of its securities to **nonbank investors** in order to restrain the inflationary expansion of bank credit. This was a major motive behind the savings bond program and offerings of savings notes, the virtual exclusion of commercial banks from the right to subscribe to new offerings of Treasury bonds, and the handling of these flotations in such a way as to make participation quite profitable for all investors except banks. Some attempt was made to reduce speculative subscriptions, but the restrictions imposed, except on banks, were far from drastic.

Large offerings of "restricted" issues led to the wholesale liquidation of bank eligible bonds by nonbank investors who wished to acquire the new securities at better yields. It also created a large segment of the government bond market that is not controllable by means of the traditional medium of changing the volume of reserves possessed by the commercial banking system through Federal Reserve policy. The offering of "restricted" issues has not been resorted to in recent years.

Deficit Financing. During the 1950's and early 1960's, a large part of the Treasury deficit was financed in the money market. Through 1959 the increase in the volume of short-term governments reflected Treasury difficulty in extending the maturity of the debt and the Treasury's inability to offer long-term bonds at attractive rates during periods of tight money because of the legal maximum coupon of $4\frac{1}{4}\%$ on long-term governments. The increase in Treasury bill sales since 1959 also reflects in part the effort of the Treasury to support short-term rates in order to stop the outflow of gold. Most of the extension in the maturity of the government debt in the early 1960's was brought about through a series of highly successful **advance refunding operations** and a smaller part through cash offerings of intermediate and long-term bonds. These occurred during periods of credit ease and prevented long-term rates from falling more than they actually did.

Because of the large government deficits in the early 1960's, the officials tried to finance a sizable part of the deficit outside the commercial banking system. They were particularly successful in 1962 and 1963, when the entire deficit was financed by nonbank investors, even though these were years of credit ease. During these years, however, the level of interest rates did not fall as low as in previous periods of monetary ease, mainly because of monetary and government debt management policies described above.

If it so desires, the Treasury can purchase outstanding securities in the market for sinking funds. This could become a potential means of supporting prices for its securities.

NONMANAGED FACTORS. Even in periods of full-fledged money management, nonmanaged supply and demand factors at times influence government security market yields and prices. In fact, nonmanaged factors usually determine the direction of interest rate and bond market movements. Monetary policy is usually a matter of deciding how far and how fast to permit interest rates to rise or decline in response to supply and demand factors.

The **available supply of investments** other than government securities is a dominant factor in the bond market. It influences the demand for government securities, especially on the part of financial intermediaries. This supply includes not only the volume of offerings of state, municipal, foreign, and corporate bonds, but also the demand for **mortgage loans,** which has been the largest demand sector in the post-war period. Commercial banks also buy municipal obligations and make mortgage loans, and their buying interest in government securities is influenced by the volume of commercial and consumer loans available, as well as these other longer-term investments.

MAJOR MARKET MOVEMENTS. The first World War was financed by the issuance of Liberty bonds, which bore tax-free coupon rates up to $4\frac{1}{4}\%$. Postwar liquidation of bonds bought for patriotic reasons and other causes drove prices of Liberty bonds into the low 80's and yields to over 5½% in the summer of 1920. Throughout the rest of the 1920's however, the trend of bond prices was generally upward, and at the end of 1929, yields on government bonds were less than 3½%.

Government bond prices declined briefly between September 1931 and January 1932 but rose thereafter. The decline during this period of economic and financial stress was far less than in any other class of bonds. Open market purchases by the Federal Reserve banks in 1932 helped to sustain quotations.

From 1933 until our involvement in hostilities in 1941, the trend of bond yields was steadily downward. Yields for long-term issues declined from an average of about 3½% in 1933 to less than 2½% by the end of 1941. Heavy Treasury deficits were largely financed by selling securities to the banks, which were able to absorb them readily because of rapidly expanding excess reserves resulting from the gold influx.

Throughout World War II, the government bond market was exceptionally stable, reflecting firm control by the monetary authorities and the close cooperation of institutional investors. Colossal offerings in the successive **war loan drives** were absorbed with a minimum of market disruption, although there was greater reliance upon bank credit than in World War I. Although banks could not subscribe directly in the third and later war loans and the Victory loan, they indirectly provided about 40% of the funds raised through absorbing outstanding issues from investors who thereby obtained funds to pay for the new offerings.

Early in 1946 the protracted downward trend of long-term interest rates ended as the Treasury and Board of Governors of the Federal Reserve System indicated they were satisfied with the borrowing rates of ⅜% on bills, ⅞% on certificates, and 2½% on long-term bonds. It was announced, however, that there was no intention of permitting any appreciable increase in these rates. With the public debt so vast and with so large a proportion of it consisting of short- and medium-term maturities, the Treasury wished to maintain low interest rates for its borrowings.

Trends Since World War II. In mid-1947, nevertheless, the Federal Reserve System finally abandoned this rigid wartime pattern of rates and began to permit successive increases in the market yields of short-term Treasury obligations. This **rise in short-term rates,** together with the rapidly increasing demand for long-term credit from private borrowers, led to heavy selling of the longer-term government issues. During the closing months of 1947, the Federal Reserve System gave some market support to these bonds at declining prices. On December 24, 1947, the Federal Reserve sharply reduced the prices at which it would buy government bonds, announcing that these pegs would be maintained "for the foreseeable future."

During the ensuing 11 months, uncertainty as to how long the pegs would be maintained plus the continuing strong demand for credit, resulted in heavy liquidation of government bonds by banks, insurance companies, savings banks, and other investors. A further rise in short-term rates and a boost in member bank reserve requirements contributed to the selling pressure. The Federal Reserve System, however, maintained its fixed buying prices of par on some issues, slightly above par on others.

Toward the end of 1948, it became apparent that the forces of inflation were waning, and prices of government securities rose above the Federal Reserve support prices. The market was generally firm throughout 1949 and the first half of 1950.

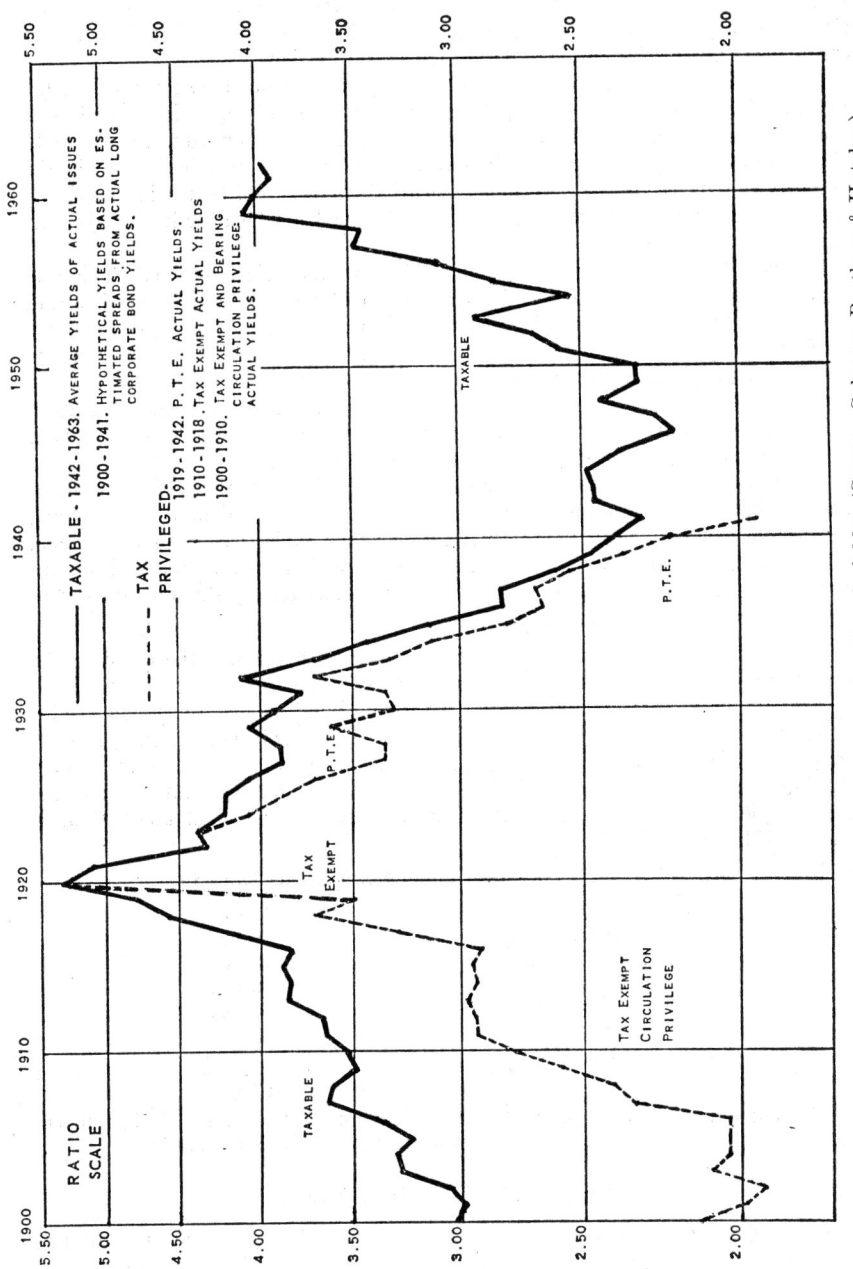

Fig. 3. Annual averages of long-term government bond yields. (Source: Salomon Brothers & Hutzler.)

After the Korean outbreak, however, the demand for credit increased and the Federal Reserve authorities began to adopt measures to **restrain credit expansion**. Again a rise in short-term rates combined with an increasing demand for credit brought renewed pressure on the long-term market.

In March, 1951, as the result of the "accord" worked out between the Federal Reserve Board and the Treasury, the par pegs were finally abandoned and government bonds were permitted to decline several points below par. It was made clear, however, that the Federal Reserve System is still determined to maintain "orderly conditions" in the government securities market and that it has no intention of abandoning its policy of supporting the market whenever it regards such support as desirable.

During the 1950's government bond yields rose, and prices declined. This was partly a consequence of the way in which the Federal debt was financed during and immediately after World War II. It also was due to the large demand for credit by the private sector of the economy throughout the 1950's. These demands together with the need for funds by the Federal government strained the financial resources of the country in several years during the 1950's, especially in 1959, when the annual average yield on 3-month Treasury bills rose to a postwar high of 3.40% and that on long-term governments to 4.07%.

After late 1959, yields on governments fell slightly from their postwar highs. In 1961 both short-term and long-term governments declined in yield. In 1962, short-term yields rose but long-term yields declined somewhat further. In 1963, both short and long-term governments rose in yield, with long-term yields approaching the average annual yields of 1959 and short-term yields remaining substantially below the postwar high.

The Long-Range Picture. Thus, in the twentieth century the trend in the long-term government market falls into three segments: (1) the bear bond market (rising yields) of 1899–1920; (2) the bull bond market (declining yields) of 1920–1946; and (3) the bear bond market of 1946–1960. (See Homer, **A History of Interest Rates.**) These trends are shown in Fig. 3. The mean average yield on long-term governments for the 63 years shown in Fig. 3 is 3.39% and the median yield is 3.49%. A more detailed summary of the yield fluctuations is shown in the table below:

Annual Averages of Government Bond Yields Since 1900

Below 2.50%	12 Years
2.50 to 2.99%	9 Years
3.00 to 3.49%	12 Years
3.50 to 3.99%	16 Years
4.00 to 4.49%	10 Years
4.50 to 4.99%	2 Years
Over 5%	2 Years
	63 Years

Source: Sidney Homer, partner, Salomon Bros & Hutzler, New York, talk entitled, "The Outlook for Long-Term Government Bonds," April 16, 1963.

State and Municipal Bonds

PURPOSE OF BORROWING. State and local governments borrow primarily to finance **capital expenditures**. In fact, some governments are not permitted to borrow for anything except capital expenditures. This is in sharp contrast to the financial needs of business corporations and of the Federal government, which frequently borrow to defray current expenses. Thus, the substantial postwar increase in the debt of State and local governments, which in the period from 1946 to 1962 grew from $14 billion to $81 billion, was due mainly to the large expenditures for highways, schools, sewer and water facilities, residential buildings, veterans' aid, bridges and tunnels, and public health and recreation facilities.

At the end of the fiscal year 1962, State and local long-term debt amounted to $77.3 billion as compared with $3.7 billion of short-term debt. Much of the short-term debt is incurred to tide over the period before tax collections. Despite the substantial expansion in State and local debt, its size is much smaller than that of the Federal debt. State and municipal obligations also differ from Federal issues with respect to the tax treatment on interest income, quality, the magnitude of secondary market activity, and investor following.

TAX STATUS. The investment position of state and municipal bonds is greatly affected by their tax status. Interest on such obligations is exempt from Federal income taxation, a fact that has been of greatly increased value as Federal income tax rates have risen. Most states exempt from taxation their own bonds and those of their political subdivisions.

Although the tax-exempt status of state and municipal bonds has been criticized and proposals have been advanced for its abolition, the consensus is that only a Constitutional amendment could actually bring this about. And since state legislatures are unlikely to give the requisite approval to such an amendment, it is doubtful that the tax status of state and municipal bonds will be modified.

Although the Constitution does not specifically exempt bonds of the states and their political subdivisions from Federal taxation, the United States Supreme Court held long ago in the celebrated case of McCulloch v. Maryland (4 Wheaton 316) that the State of Maryland could not tax the bank notes of the Bank of the United States, an instrumentality of the Federal government, because "the power to tax is the power to destroy." The doctrine of **reciprocal tax exemption**—that the Federal government shall not tax obligations of the states and their subdivisions, and that the states shall not tax Federal obligations, has been evolved from Chief Justice Marshall's decision in McCulloch v. Maryland. But this does not prevent a sovereign government from taxing its own obligations, as the Federal government does, nor does it prevent a state or city from taxing bonds issued by other states, or cities in other states.

The value of the tax exemption enjoyed by bonds of states and their subdivisions varies with prevailing income tax rates. Investors in the high-income brackets are in a position to derive the greatest advantage from such tax exemption. Other investors holding such bonds must remember that they are accepting a lower yield without obtaining the full tax benefit upon which such lower yield is based. Corporate investors can measure the tax benefit that they receive from the corporate income tax rate to which they are subject.

To guide investors in determining whether they are justified in purchasing tax-exempt bonds instead of bonds subject to tax, tables are prepared showing **equivalent taxable yields** at various rates of return. For example, an investor in the 40% income tax bracket who buys a municipal bond on a 3% yield basis obtains a yield comparable to that which he would realize on a 5% corporate bond. Municipal bond houses prepare tables showing equivalent taxable yields derived from municipal bonds at various yield levels for corporations and individual investors in different tax brackets.

STATE BONDS. State bonds are similar to national government bonds in that individuals and corporations are not legally permitted to sue states without their own consent. Bonds of states generally enjoy a high standing, despite this **immunity to suit.** Many states have adopted constitutional provisions regulating the purposes for which indebtedness may be incurred. The use of state credit is now generally prohibited for private benefit. Road construction, parks, welfare institutions, relief, and veterans' bonuses are major purposes for issuing state bonds.

Because of the clause in the Federal Constitution that prohibits a state from passing legislation impairing the obligation of a contract, a state cannot repudiate or alter the character of a debt validly incurred. But this gives no actual protection to bondholders in the absence of the ability to sue a state for repudiation.

TAXING POWER OF STATES. As the credit of a state is based primarily on its tax resources, its taxing powers and the wealth within its territory are of supreme importance in judging the soundness of its obligations. A state cannot tax property without due process of law, nor can it interfere with the taxing powers of the Federal government. With these exceptions, and allowing for tax-rate limitations imposed by their own constitutions, which can of course be removed by amendment, states are free to tax without restriction to service their debts.

Important **ratios** in the analysis of state bonds are per-capita debt, ratio of debt to assessed property value (taking assessment methods into account), and the percentage of state receipts required for debt service. If a state borrows beyond the powers of its citizens to pay, it may default on its debt service. In such situations, it may first apply its revenues to maintain its governmental functions before meeting any of its indebtedness. Hence, **state debt** should bear a reasonable relation to the taxable property and taxable income of the state. A state may tax its own obligations held by its residents, provided the tax is not discriminatory and does not amount to an impairment of the debt contract. Thus, a state cannot levy a tax for the purpose of reducing the interest rate payable on its own obligations.

MUNICIPAL BONDS. Municipal bonds may be classified by the political character of the issuer as (1) county, city, town, or village; (2) special tax district; or (3) authority bonds. More important from the investment standpoint is the distinction between (1) **general obligations** for which the full faith and credit of the municipality are pledged, and (2) **limited obligations,** which comprise special assessment and revenue bonds.

Although judgments may be secured against municipalities that default on their obligations, this is ordinarily of little value to the bondholder because the courts in most states will not permit attachment of municipal property required for the public service. Hence, holders of such obligations must depend upon the ability-to-pay of the municipality, as shown by its budget, taxing power, and the value of the property upon which it may levy taxes, and upon its good faith as reflected in its debt record. It is also important to check upon the validity of the bond issue, for any legal irregularity may result in the inability of the bondholder to obtain payment. Municipalities may file plans for composition of debts under the Municipal Bankruptcy Act.

It must be remembered that municipalities overlap to a large extent. Counties, townships, cities, tax districts, and special assessment districts may embrace the same taxpayers. The financial troubles of Chicago during the early 1930's were accentuated by the multiplicity of taxing authorities formed to cover the same area. Hence, the investment status of a municipal bond is affected by the debt incurred by overlapping political subdivisions, and statistics of debt and tax burdens should include all overlapping tax districts.

The quality of municipal bonds varies widely with the economic character of the community, its population, its wealth and income, and the financial competence of its administration.

TAX DISTRICTS. Special tax districts are generally created for a single governmental purpose, such as school districts, water districts, drainage districts, and road districts. These districts, for purpose of bond analysis, may be classified into two groups: (1) those that are **permanent** and created for a continuous, specialized administrative purpose, and (2) those that are more or less **temporary** and are formed to provide a single public improvement. The most numerous of the first class are the school districts; of the latter, irrigation, drainage, levee, and similar districts. Limitations upon municipal indebtedness imposed by state law have encouraged creation of tax districts.

SPECIAL ASSESSMENT BONDS. Improvements that affect only parts of a municipality are sometimes financed through special assessments upon the property affected, and bonds are issued against these assessments. Such bonds are usually inferior to general obligation municipal bonds, because of the limited source of revenue available to provide debt service. But funds may be provided by the municipality if collections from the special assessments do not suffice to service the bonds, if provision is made for such contributions in the enabling legislation.

REVENUE BONDS. An increasingly important group of bonds that enjoy tax exemption like other state and municipal obligations are revenue bonds. Such obligations are serviced from the revenues of publicly owned facilities rather than taxes. They are issued by states, municipalities, or authorities or districts set up by state law.

Originally issued for bridges and toll highways, large issues of revenue bonds have been put out in recent years to finance public ownership of turnpikes, electric light and power, transit, and other **public utility properties.** Because they are not subject to Federal income taxes, because in most states they can raise rates without approval of regulatory commissions, because interest charges are low owing to their tax-exempt status, and because they operate as a rule without competition, public bodies that issue revenue bonds for the most part enjoy a strong credit position.

Among the factors to be considered in analyzing revenue bonds are (1) sources of revenue, (2) maturity provisions, (3) application of revenue, (4) protective covenants, (5) provisions relating to the issuance of additional bonds, (6) extent to which the facilities fill an economic need, and (7) competing facilities.

An important group of bonds with special characteristics of their own are **obligations of public housing authorities.** They differ from revenue bonds properly so called because they usually depend upon grants from Federal, state, or municipal governments, rather than rents collected, for debt service. These grants, in turn, generally come from tax collections.

INVESTMENT FACTORS RELATING TO MUNICIPAL BONDS. Underlying considerations in the analysis of municipal bonds are:

1. Size and importance of the municipality.
2. Relative permanence and rate of growth of its population and resources, including its geographical location, transportation facilities, industries, commerce, and so on.
3. Co-extensive and overlapping political subdivisions.
4. Percentage of net debt (debt other than obligations sold for self-supporting projects and sinking funds) in relation to assessed valuation of taxable property (making allowance for assessment methods in use).
5. Net debt per capita.
6. State limitation on tax rate levied for debt service.
7. Relative property tax rate.
8. Debt limitations imposed by state law.
9. Legality of the issue.

Since individual, and even institutional, investors are not usually in a position to evaluate properly municipal bonds, certain **credit investigating agencies,** such as Dun and Bradstreet, Inc., New York, compile reports on such bond issues and rate them in relation to the considerations enumerated.

MARKETING OF STATE AND LOCAL GOVERNMENT ISSUES. The process of bringing tax-exempt issues to market is described by Robinson (National Bureau of Economic Research, Post-War Market for State and Local Government Securities) as follows:

Once a state or local governmental unit has completed the necessary legal steps that authorize it to borrow money, the marketing process follows a fairly standardized pattern. If, as is usual, the issue is to be sold by **competitive bidding,**[1] the intention to borrow is announced formally (informal news has already been circulated in most cases) and bids are invited. In the somewhat rarer case of a **negotiated offering,** a consultant or an investment banking house is engaged as a financial adviser. If an investment banking house acts as the adviser, it may also organize the underwriting syndicate. This dual role, however, is frowned on by some critics. In the more common case of a competitive sale, the second phase is that of the organization of groups for the purpose of bidding on the issue. The third stage, which almost always follows hard upon the award of the bid to the group offering the lowest borrowing cost, is the reoffering of the securities by the successful bidders to ultimate investors.

[1] In the year 1957, 86% of the public offerings were sold through public sealed bids, 12% through negotiated sales, and 2% were placed directly—largely with state and local government pension funds. [IBA Statistical Bulletin, No. 6, January 1958, p. 8.]

Municipal bonds are sold primarily over the counter. Commercial banks, as well as many dealers that specialize in making a market for this class of securities, play an important role in the marketing of tax-exempt issues. In a number of markets the full-lot unit of trading is $10,000 par value. Many municipal bond issues, even of larger municipalities, are for relatively small amounts, being issued for a particular improvement.

The **secondary market** for State and local issues is an integral part of the organizational structure of the new issue market. Many of the dealers that underwrite tax-exempt obligations also maintain trading departments. An important source of information on issues available in the secondary market is the Blue List. Other important sources of information are, in addition to the various credit agencies, The Daily Bond Buyer, The Weekly Bond Buyer (these last two being publications of The Bond Buyer, New York), and the Investment Bankers' Association of America (Washington, D.C.).

INVESTORS IN STATE AND LOCAL OBLIGATIONS. The major investors in State and local issues at the end of 1962 were (figures in billions of dollars):

Commercial Banks	24.8
Fire and Casualty Companies	9.7
Life Insurance Companies	4.1
Mutual Savings Banks	0.5
State and Local Retirement Funds	4.0
Nonfinancial Corporations	3.4
Individuals and Others	32.4
	78.9

Commercial banks have become the largest buyers of State and local issues in recent years. During both 1962 and 1963, commercial banks added to their portfolio over 80% of the net yearly increase in State and local obligations. These large investments were due largely to the sizeable inflow of savings deposits to the commercial banks and the pressure on them to invest these deposits in high after-tax yielding assets. Years ago most commercial bank investments in State and local obligations were concentrated in issues with short maturities but in the more recent period banks have invested sizeable amounts in issues with longer maturities.

Fire and casualty insurance companies are also substantial investors in State and local issues. These institutions are subject to the maximum income tax rates so that investment in tax-exempt issues considerably limits their tax liability. Holdings of tax-exempts may also be counted by fire and casualty companies as part of their liquidity position. The yearly takedown by these companies has in recent years been about 20% of the net yearly increase in State and local debt, and they have not restricted their commitments to any maturity category.

Although **individuals,** mainly those in high tax brackets, hold a large part of the State and local debt, their participation in this market has been declining. During the past decade, individuals have been sizeable investors only at times of high interest rates. In 1962–1963 they were virtually eliminated from the market as large buyers because of the aggressive participation of the commercial banks.

Life insurance companies and **mutual savings banks** have not been active participants in the tax-exempt market since they are not in a position to take complete advantage of the tax exemption feature. Both institutions have also been faced with strong demands for credit from the private placement and mortgage markets.

State and local retirement funds were formerly substantial investors in the securities of their own governments. However, the need to place these funds on a sound actuarial basis has forced many of them to liquidate some of their tax-exempt holdings in favor of higher yielding assets.

Business corporations restrict most of their investment in tax-exempt issues to short maturities. Tax-exempt issues do not comprise a significant percentage of the liquid assets held by business corporations.

METHODS OF REPAYMENT. Municipal bonds are generally repaid by one of two methods: (1) through the operation of a sinking fund or (2) by serial, that is, installment repayments. In rare instances payment is made at maturity either from current municipal revenues or by refunding through a sale of a new issue. Most American municipalities use the **serial method** of debt redemption. Under this system, the bonds of a single issue are divided into a number of different maturities, which are paid off out of current revenues. Prevalence of serial maturities explains why these bonds are usually quoted on a yield, rather than a price, basis.

SECTION 12

FORMS OF BUSINESS ORGANIZATION

CONTENTS

Selecting the Proper Form

	Page
Factors in choice of form	1
Financing	1
Taxation	1
Liability	2
Continuity	2
Ease of formation	2
Management	2
Variety of proprietary interests	3
Changing the form	3

Individual Proprietorships and Partnerships

	Page
Individual proprietorships	3
General partnerships	3
Management	4
Sharing of profits and losses	4
Liability of general partners	4
The partnership agreement	5
Advantages and disadvantages	5
Limited partnerships	5
Statutory requirements	6
Operation	6
Taxation	6
Advantages	6

Syndicates, Business Trusts, and Joint Stock Companies

	Page
Syndicates	6
Real estate syndicates	7
Forms of organization	7
Federal and state regulation of public offerings	7
Business trusts	8
Method of formation	8
Trustee and shareholder liability	8
Length of life	8
Tax status	9
Advantages	9
Disadvantages	9
Real estate investment trusts	9
Tax status	9
Joint stock companies	10
Method of formation	10
Tax status	10
Advantages and disadvantages	10

Mutuals, Cooperatives, and Professional Corporations

	Page
Mutuals and cooperatives	10
Forms of cooperative organization	11
Advantages and disadvantages	11
Professional corporations and associations	12

Corporations

	Page
Corporate organization	12
Advantages and disadvantages	13
Promotion	13
Functions of a promoter	13
Compensation	13
Legal status	14
Pre-incorporation contracts	15
Liability of contracting parties	15
Agreements among incorporators	15
Raising capital	16
Choice of state of incorporation	16
State taxes	17
State laws	18
Corporate name	18
The incorporation process	19
Domestic, foreign, and alien corporations	20
Restrictions upon foreign corporations	20
Nature of corporate charter	20
Contents of certificate of incorporation	21
Amendments to charter	21
Bylaws	22
Power to make bylaws	22
Typical provisions	22

Stockholders' Meetings

	Page
Annual meetings	23
Procedure	24
Special meetings	24
Procedure	25
Consent meetings	25
Stockholder consent without a meeting	26
Quorums	26
Voting	26
Protection of minority interests	26

The Board of Directors

	Page
Legal status	27
Statutory provisions	27
Qualifications	27
Number	28
Election	28
Term of office	28
Resignation and removal	28
Liability	29

FORMS OF BUSINESS ORGANIZATION

CONTENTS (*Continued*)

	PAGE
Liabilities imposed by statute	29
Indemnification	30
Compensation	30
Committees	31
Executive and finance	31
Limitations on powers	31
Meetings	32
Quorums	32
Conflict of interest	33

Corporate Officers

	PAGE
Titles and functions	33
Qualifications	33
Powers and duties	34
The treasurer	34
The controller	35
The secretary	35
Compensation	36

SECTION 12

FORMS OF BUSINESS ORGANIZATION

Selecting the Proper Form

FACTORS IN CHOICE OF FORM. A business concern may assume one of the following forms of organization:

Individual or sole proprietorship.
General partnership.
Special or limited partnership.
Syndicate or joint venture.
Business or Massachusetts trust.
Mutual or cooperative.
Joint stock association.
Corporation.

Special forms of business organization that have developed under the influence of Federal income tax law are qualified real estate investment trusts and professional corporations and associations. Business trusts (other than real estate investment trusts) and joint stock associations are largely of historical interest and not apt to be chosen under present statutory procedures that make the corporate form readily available and quite flexible.

There is no single rule to be followed in selecting the most suitable form of organization for a particular enterprise. Each form has advantages and disadvantages that must be weighed in their relation to the business concerned. The following brief discussions of **major factors** to be considered in choosing the most advantageous form of organization will make this apparent.

Financing. Whether a business is to be financed privately or publicly is always important. **Public financing** through the sale of participations in ownership requires a form of organization in which ownership may readily be divided into transferable shares. Freedom from personal liability for shareholders, apart from their initial investment, is also necessary to make the shares marketable. If capital is to be obtained through sale of long-term evidences of debt, the organization should promise a length of life in excess of the maturity of the debt. On the other hand, if the business is one that will be **privately owned** by one or just a few persons, an organization having share capital may be too cumbersome, or be subject to higher taxes than one of the simpler types such as the individual proprietorship or partnership.

Taxation. Because of the high level of Federal individual and corporate income taxes, taxation is often the most important factor. A few basic considerations are touched on here and others in the discussions below dealing with the specific forms of organization.

If the business is to be conducted in corporate form, or in a form that is treated as a corporation, a new **taxable entity** has been created, subject to tax on its net income. Since salaries are tax-deductible, the tax burden can be divided between the corporation and its shareholder-employees. If the amounts involved are large and the individual tax rates of the owners quite high, there may be a substantial advantage in paying a **corporate tax** and retaining a large part of the income in the business instead of incurring **individual tax liability** on the entire income, as in a proprietorship or partnership. To be borne in mind, however, are the **penalty taxes** applicable to the undistributed income of corporations. Moreover, the income of the corporation will be subject to **a second tax** when it is paid out as a dividend or when reflected as a capital gain on the sale of corporate stock at a profit. A collateral benefit of incorporation is the availability to stockholder-employees of various **tax-favored employee benefits,** such as participation in qualified pension and profit-sharing plans and fringe benefits.

Liability. The extent of the personal liability of the proprietors of a concern to its creditors may be a vital consideration. Should a business venture fail and its assets prove insufficient to pay its creditors, the possibility arises of **recourse to personal assets** of the owners. If a business entails great risk, the corporate form, wherein creditors may look for payment to the business assets only, will be favored. However, a corporation without substantial capital may not be able to obtain bank financing without the **personal guaranty** of the stockholders. Such a guaranty is usually limited in amount.

Continuity. To enjoy continuous existence, a business must not be terminated by the transfer of an owner's interest, whether by sale, gift, death, or operation of law. Usually this characteristic is found only in organizations providing for **transferability of shares.** Continuous existence is an outstanding legal characteristic of the corporation. If capital is to be borrowed on long term, this factor is essential. Though a **partnership** usually terminates as a matter of law upon the death or withdrawal of one of the partners, continuity can be achieved through provisions in the partnership agreement. Common provisions are those for continuation of the business by the remaining partners and payment for the former partner's interest. A **closely held corporation,** on the other hand, may in fact lack the continuity it appears to have due to its corporate form; for the death of a major stockholder may require dissolution of the corporation unless some provision has been made for the sale of his interest to the corporation, surviving stockholders, or outsiders.

Ease of Formation. In small concerns with limited capital, or in a business whose duration is expected to be short, ease of organization may be an important factor. Incorporation entails legal procedures which customarily require the services of an attorney. Under modern procedures, however, the formation of a corporation is not usually a complicated task. On the other hand, a partnership agreement relating to a business of any substance should also, as a matter of normal business prudence, be prepared by an attorney.

Management. In business concerns having many co-owners it is not practical for all to exercise direct responsibility in the routine details of management, for bedlam would result. It is necessary, therefore, to choose a form of organization in which management is carried on by representatives of the owners. In a corporation, the stockholders elect a board of directors who have ultimate responsibility for directing the business. The directors, in turn, elect the officers of the company who manage operations subject to policies approved by the board. **Direct management** by owners is usual in partnerships, in smaller corporations whose stockholders are also directors and officers, and, of course, in the individual proprietorship. Such direct management by the owners may be important where risk is great, or where success depends upon the personal contacts or attributes of the owner.

Variety of Proprietary Interests. A major advantage of the corporate form is the ability to create different classes of owners by **classifying the capital stock.** This may involve not only common and preferred stock, but also variations, within each category, in dividend, voting and other rights. This flexibility makes it possible to serve a variety of investor interests in the enterprise.

CHANGING THE FORM. Concerns beginning business as sole proprietorships or partnerships often become corporations when growth or changes in personal situations make it desirable or necessary to obtain the liability, tax, continuity, management or financing advantages of the corporate form. Estate tax problems and the ability to sell stock to pay such taxes when they become payable have led to incorporation of many larger partnerships and proprietorships.

If it is anticipated that a newly organized business may have **initial losses** because of heavy starting-up expenses, it may be desirable to begin as a proprietorship or partnership, so that these losses will be reflected in the individual tax returns of the proprietor or proprietors. On the other hand, the Internal Revenue Code permits certain corporations that can qualify as small business corporations under Subchapter S of the Internal Revenue Code to elect to have their income and operating losses reflected directly in the income of the shareholders. Those making the election are frequently referred to as **Subchapter S Corporations.** This option may be advantageous during a period of initial losses. **Basic requirements** are that the corporation must have not more than 10 stockholders, each of whom must be an individual or an estate of a deceased individual, and must have only one class of stock; not more than 80% of its gross receipts may be derived from sources outside the United States; and not more than 20% of its gross receipts may be from investments.

Individual Proprietorships and Partnerships

INDIVIDUAL PROPRIETORSHIPS. When an individual engages in business as the **sole owner,** the business does not exist apart from the owner. He alone can make ultimate decisions of management, the debts of the business are his debts, and his personal assets are equally subject with those of the business to attachment by creditors.

The proprietor may conduct business and have access to the courts in every state of the union. A proprietor's credit is his **personal credit,** which may limit borrowing except where the loans can be well secured. No formality is associated with the proprietorship's creation, and the nature of its product or service can be changed at the whim of the owner. Although the sole owner suffers all losses he also receives all profits, a powerful incentive for the closest attention to management. An individual proprietor can do business under a trade name, which must, however, be registered in any state in which the business is conducted. As the simplest form of organization, the proprietorship suffers from the defects of instability, lack of continuous management, and financing difficulties.

GENERAL PARTNERSHIPS. A general partnership is an association of two or more individuals as co-owners of a business, with each of the partners having **unlimited liability** for the debts of the business. It is a **contractual** relationship. The contract may be **oral** or **written.** To meet the requirements of the **Statute of Frauds** in most states, a partnership agreement for a term of more than one year must be in writing to be binding as between the parties. An oral partnership agreement on which the parties have acted has been held to be a **partnership at will**. Apart from these technical considerations, it is important, as a matter of business prudence, to reduce the agreement to writing.

A partnership **contract will be implied** to exist where it can be shown that two or more persons share the profits and, in addition, share the losses, or exercise a joint control, or have a common investment. Although the partnership is a **common law** form of organization, many of the states have adopted statutes governing the relationship of partners to one another and to those with whom the partnership may have dealings. The **Uniform Partnership Act** has been adopted by most states and the District of Columbia.

The laws of some states permit partnerships to sue and be sued as firms. The **New York Civil Practice Act and Rules** permits all partnerships to sue or be sued in the firm name, and process to be served upon any one or more partners. In such cases, judgments secured against a partnership may be collected out of property of the firm or of each partner upon whom a summons has been served. **Real estate** is held in the names of the partners, in the name of an individual partner who then holds title in trust for all, or in the firm name. The partnership may operate under a **trade name** not containing the names of any or all the partners. Like the individual proprietorship, a partnership may change the nature of its business activities at the discretion of the partners, and may enforce business contracts in any state without first having obtained a license to do business there.

Management. Each partner is a **general agent** for his partners, and a partnership may be held to contracts executed by one partner. This is true even if a contract is made in violation of the partnership agreement, unless it can be shown that the outside contractor had previous notice of a limitation of the authority of a partner. However, if an unauthorized contract is outside the usual scope of the partnership's business, e.g., borrowing money on the part of a law firm, it will not be enforced against the partnership unless signed by all the partners—the unusual nature of the contract being deemed sufficient to put upon the other party the burden of making inquiry as to the authority of a contracting partner to bind his firm.

Sharing of Profits and Losses. Unless otherwise specified in the partnership agreement, profits and losses of the partnership will be shared equally, regardless of the amount of capital investment by each partner. Disputes among partners as to sharing profits, or any dispute requiring an accounting, are settled in a court of equity.

Each partner is in effect a **trustee of the firm's assets,** including such intangibles as knowledge of opportunities for the firm to make profits. This trusteeship will be strictly enforced by the courts.

Liability of General Partners. Each of the partners is liable for all of the debts of the business. Judgments against the firm that are not satisfied from the firm's assets may be executed against the assets of individual partners. If one partner is required to pay more than his fair share, courts of equity will give him a **right of contribution** against his co-partners for the excess. In equitable proceedings for the final settlement of the accounts of insolvent partnerships, the courts follow a procedure known as the **Rule of Marshaling**. Briefly stated, this rule provides that firm creditors must first exhaust the business assets before they may satisfy their claims out of the personal assets of individual partners, and personal creditors of the partners have a claim against personal assets ahead of firm creditors.

The Partnership Agreement. The features of a general partnership mentioned above prove the need for a written partnership agreement. **A partnership ceases to exist** when any member withdraws, dies, or is legally incapacitated, and immediate dissolution results unless there are agreements to the contrary. Even while a partnership is in existence, disputes may arise over matters that, had pertinent agreement been reduced to writing, would not have caused trouble. Some of the matters that should be included in a partnership agreement follow:

1. Names of partners and the firm name.
2. Kind of business to be conducted.
3. Capital contribution of each partner.
4. Duration of the partnership contract.
5. The time to be devoted to the business by each, and any limitation upon outside business interests.
6. Method of dividing profits and losses.
7. Restrictions upon the agency powers of the partners.
8. Salaries to be paid partners, or limitations upon the withdrawal of profits.
9. Method of admitting new partners.
10. Provision for insurance on lives of partners for benefit of firm.
11. Procedure to be followed in voluntary dissolution.
12. Procedure upon death or withdrawal of partner, including method of valuation of tangible assets and good will, and provision for continuation of the business by the remaining partners.

Advantages and Disadvantages. The partnership form of organization is superior to the proprietorship because it permits several persons to combine their resources and abilities to conduct a business. It is easier to form than a corporation, and retains a personal character making it more suitable in professional fields.

Among smaller and middle-sized businesses, the partnership enjoys considerable vogue. The unlimited liability of partners, the relative instability of the form, and the difficulty of attracting outside capital are, however, important disadvantages to consider.

Partnerships as such pay no Federal income tax, although they are required to file a return; individual partners pay personal income taxes on their shares of the profits. The Internal Revenue Code, however, recognizes the **allocation** among the partners, pursuant to the partnership agreement, of particular items of income or loss, unless the "principal purpose" of making such allocation is the avoidance or evasion of income tax. Partnerships are free from state corporate income and franchise taxes but some states have an unincorporated business tax. The difference in tax burden with the corporate form and with the partnership form must be computed separately for each business. Further, the Internal Revenue Code permits certain unincorporated businesses to elect to be taxed as corporations, and in some instances they may be taxed as such whether or not they make the election, as will be seen in the discussion below of "Taxation of Limited Partnerships"; and on the other hand in a provision much more widely applied, **Subchapter S Corporations,** as mentioned above on page 3, are permitted under the Code to be taxed as partnerships. There are many tax factors that must be considered.

LIMITED PARTNERSHIPS. A limited partnership may be defined as an agreement between one or more general partners, and one or more special or limited partners whose liability is limited to the amount of their capital investment in the firm. A limited partnership, like the general partnership, is a contractual form of organization, but unlike the general partnership it is not a common law form of organization. Statutory authority is required to make the terms of the contract effective against creditors. New York adopted such a statute in 1822, and now all the states have limited partnership statutes. More than forty states and the District of Columbia have adopted the **Uniform Limited Partnership Act.**

Statutory Requirements. The statutes of the various states relative to the formation of limited partnerships differ slightly as to the procedure to be followed. The usual requirement is that a formal agreement be drawn for the signature of all partners. It should show clearly that it is to be a limited partnership, the amount of the contribution to capital of each partner, and a designation of each partner as "limited" or "general." The statutes require that the agreement be filed with a designated public officer, usually the county clerk or recorder of the county where the principal office is to be located. There may also be a requirement that the agreement or a notice be published in newspapers.

Operation. In a limited partnership the limited partner or partners may exercise no voice in the management. If they could do so, creditors might be misled to assume they were general partners. **Limited liability** is enjoyed by special partners only if the firm is registered as a limited partnership. If business is to be conducted in two or more states, therefore, limited partnerships are formed under the statute of each state with the same firm members. It is unwise to use the name of a limited partner in the firm's name unless this is permitted by statute, because those dealing with the firm may infer that he is a general partner and the courts may hold him liable accordingly.

Taxation. According to Federal income tax regulations, an association is **taxable as a corporation** if it has more than two of the following characteristics: continuity of life; centralized management; liability for debts limited to the property of the organization; and free transferability of interests. A limited partnership has centralized management since such rights are given to the general partners. If, however, a limited partnership has a general partner who has substantial assets (other than his interest in the partnership), the income tax regulations recognize that limited liability does not exist. If, in addition, the firm either terminates on the death of a general partner or the interests of the partners are not freely transferable, the organization will be taxed as a partnership.

Advantages. The feature of limited liability may attract capital contributions from persons who would otherwise hesitate to become partners. This form appeals also to persons unable or unwilling to participate in management. The limited partnership provides a method by which an elderly partner may withdraw from active participation in the business but retain an investment without risking his entire estate. A number of New York Stock Exchange firms are limited partnerships for these reasons. Limited partnerships are also frequently used as vehicles for theatrical productions.

Syndicates, Business Trusts, and Joint Stock Companies

SYNDICATES. A variation of the partnership form of organization is the syndicate. It is of short duration if it is formed to carry out a venture that can be completed in a brief period, like the underwriting of a security issue. But it will be of long duration if the purpose requires it.

The **syndicate agreement** usually vests the powers of management in one or two of the members and limits liability of each member to a specific participation. The limitation of liability, whereas binding among the participants, would not be valid as against a creditor without knowledge of it. Since participation in management is not required, the agreement may specify conditions under which a member can withdraw. The syndicate continues after the death of a member, unless his participation proves necessary to the success of the undertaking. Although of ancient origin, the syndicate form is now used principally in connection with security offerings and real estate transactions, the latter being more fully discussed below. Investment bankers form syndicates or groups to divide the risk of purchasing issues of securities from an issuing corporation for resale through a larger selling group to the public.

The majority view of the courts is that a corporation may not become a member of a partnership or syndicate in the absence of authority to do so by statute or charter. Such status is considered to be inconsistent with the management of the corporate affairs by a board of directors chosen by the stockholders. On the other hand, courts have upheld the participation of corporations in joint ventures, which has become common. In most instances, however, corporate joint ventures have taken the form of joint ownership of subsidiary corporations. The New York Business Corporation Law gives New York corporations the general power to become members of partnerships and joint ventures.

REAL ESTATE SYNDICATES. All of the several forms of organization through which one or more promoters and a group of investors join in a real estate venture are commonly referred to as "real estate syndicates." Syndicates with participations of $5,000 or $10,000 or multiples thereof, have been widely utilized. Their relatively high yield has made them interesting to many investors, and the depreciation and other tax deductions that they usually give have made them particularly popular with higher tax bracket investors.

Forms of Organization. "Real estate syndicates" have taken a variety of forms. Most real estate syndicates have been organized as **limited partnerships** with the promoters as general partners and the investors as limited partners. As has been previously noted, the partners of a limited partnership will be taxable upon their shares of the net income of the partnership, if the characteristics of an association taxable as a corporation are avoided. Syndicates that started out as limited partnerships have sometimes been grouped into a **public corporation** by the exchange of partnership interests for stock. Another form of real estate syndicate is that of a **qualified real estate investment trust**, discussed hereafter. Such a trust distributes its net income and a person owning a beneficial interest is taxable as though he were the direct recipient of his share of the net income of the trust. In some instances real estate ventures have been organized in **corporate form** with the promoters receiving stock and the investors receiving stock and instruments of indebtedness, such as debentures. There is, however, a risk that for tax purposes the interest on the instruments of debt will be treated as a dividend.

Federal and State Regulation of Public Offerings. Whatever the form of a real estate syndicate, it is subject to Federal and state statutes regulating the issuance and sale of securities. The Securities Act of 1933 includes as a security a unit of beneficial interest in a trust or a limited partnership interest. The state "blue sky laws" are also applicable to beneficial interests in real estate syndicates. Because of increased public participation in such syndicates, New York State in 1960 passed an amendment to its securities law specifically applicable to the registration of offerings of real estate syndicates.

BUSINESS TRUSTS. This form of organization, also known as a **Massachusetts trust,** was first used in that commonwealth for the purpose of holding and dealing in real estate, a development which came about because the Massachusetts law (prior to 1912) prohibited the formation of a corporation for this purpose. It also is called a **voluntary association, express trust,** or **common law trust.** The last term is more precise because the business trust is an adaptation of the common law trust to business use. In a business trust, legal title to business property is vested in trustees who hold and manage it for beneficiaries **(cestuis que trustent),** who are nominally the contributors or successors to the contributors of the capital used to create the trust. Because of the close analogy to a corporation, and because each beneficiary receives a transferable **certificate of beneficial interest** evidencing his participation, these beneficiaries are popularly called **shareholders,** and the unit of participation is referred to as a **share** or **trust share.**

Method of Formation. A deed of trust should cover the following essentials:
1. Names of trustees.
2. The duration of the trust.
3. Provision for disposition of trust property upon termination.
4. Provision for appointment to vacancies among trustees.
5. Description of property to be transferred to trustees.
6. Directions as to management of trust property.
7. Directions as to sale or transfer of trust property.
8. Provision for the sale of trust shares whereby others may become contributors to the trust capital.
9. Provision for the transfer and registration of trust certificates.
10. Directions for the inclusion of a clause in all contracts stipulating that trustees and shareholders may not be held liable and that creditors may look to the trust property only for payment.
11. Any other provision for the conduct of the trust, such as for limitations on the powers of trustees, remuneration of trustees, distribution of trust income to the shareholders, and limitations upon salaries of employees.

Preparation of a deed of trust requires great care and skill. Close attention must be paid to the common law and statutes of the state in which it is formed.

Trustee and Shareholder Liability. Trustees are liable for business debts unless they expressly disclaim liability at the time of making contracts and provide specifically in the contract that creditors may look to the trust fund only for payment. The execution of a contract "as trustee," even if the name of the trust is added, will generally not suffice to avoid personal liability.

The legal position of **shareholders** is less clear. The courts of the several states are not in agreement as to the legal status of a trust. Some states regard it as a partnership, and some others are inclined to treat it as a de facto corporation, with resultant freedom of shareholders from partnership liability. In the majority of the states in which the question has been decided, the view of the courts is that shareholders are personally liable only if they are entitled to control the management of the business by the trustees but the decisions differ as to what constitutes such control. In any event liability on contracts with third persons can be limited if the limitation is clearly stipulated in the contracts.

Length of Life. The common law and the statutes of most states, with few exceptions, forbid the creation of perpetual trusts or trusts for a term of years, unless the term is limited in the main to the life or lives of specified persons. Exceptions to this rule are commonly provided for pension trusts, insurance trusts and voting trusts, and business trusts. However, some **time limit** should probably be placed on the duration of a business trust to avoid any question as to its legality. The New York statutes provide that such a trust may continue for such time as may be necessary to accomplish its purposes, except that the trust instrument must provide that the trust may be terminated at any time by action of the trustees or by affirmative vote of a specified percentage of its beneficiaries.

The New York statutes, although generally providing that the right to income of a trust is nontransferable, have a specific exception applicable to beneficial interests in a business trust evidenced by transferable certificates.

Tax Status. A business trust will normally be taxed as a corporation for both Federal and state income tax. In some states, including New York, the business trust is subject as a corporation also to a franchise tax.

Advantages.
1. Stability during the life of the trust, since duration is not affected by death of or transfer of the interest of a member.
2. Transferability of ownership and freedom from personal liability, which facilitates aggregation of capital.
3. No limitations upon the type of business in which it may engage.
4. Concentration of management powers in a small board of trustees.

Disadvantages.
1. Possibility of being taxed as a corporation.
2. Uncertainties concerning legal questions, because of the limited number of relevant judicial decisions.
3. Limitations upon the length of life.
4. Possibility of shareholders incurring personal liability.
5. Possibility of being regulated as a corporation, some states requiring qualification as a foreign corporation in order to do business, and the certificate to be treated as a security subject to state **"blue sky laws"** as well as Federal statutes and regulations.

REAL ESTATE INVESTMENT TRUSTS. The Internal Revenue Code gives special tax treatment to a real estate investment trust which elects to qualify for such treatment. **Qualification requirements** cover beneficial ownership, income, assets, and assurance that it be a widely held trust receiving passive real estate income. The trust must be an unincorporated trust or association managed by one or more trustees, having transferable shares or certificates held beneficially by at least 100 persons and holding no property for sale to customers in the ordinary course of its business. Fifty per cent or more of the beneficial interest in the trust may not be held by 5 or fewer individuals. Several additional requirements are designed to assure that the trust's role will be that of an investor as distinguished from an active manager of property. These, of course, do not restrict the trustees in the management of the internal affairs of the trust itself, in such as the selection of tenants, the making and renewal of leases and handling of questions relating to taxes, interest, and insurance.

Tax Status. A **qualified** real estate investment trust's income is subject to corporate tax, except to the extent distributed. The beneficiaries are subject to ordinary income tax on amounts distributed to them, except that distributed capital gains are subject to tax at capital gains rates. Distributions by the trust are not treated as dividends in the hands of the recipient, so that any special credit, exemption, or deduction applicable to dividends is not allowable.

JOINT STOCK COMPANIES. This form of organization resembles a partnership, but ownership is divided into transferable shares and management is vested in a board of directors or managers. It is rarely used, because it possesses few advantages over the corporation, and has the major disadvantage of possible unlimited liability of shareholders. The joint stock company is considered **not a legal entity** and property, unless specifically permitted by a state statute, cannot be held in the firm name but in the names of shareholders. Since that is impracticable, it is customary for the property to be held by the directors as trustees for the benefit of the company.

Method of Formation. Preparation of the **articles of association** is all that is necessary for the organization of a joint stock company. A charter is not needed, although some states, including New York, require the filing of the agreement at a designated public office or offices. The agreement will ordinarily include the following points:

1. Name of the business.
2. Enumeration of purposes, and restrictions upon the type of business.
3. Location of principal office.
4. Capital contribution, and type of shares to be issued.
5. Provision for a board of directors, including term of office, elections, and restrictions upon directors' powers.
6. Provision for stockholders' meetings, and procedures for amendment of articles of association.
7. Duration, and dissolution procedures.
8. Statement that shareholders waive powers of management and general agency.
9. Method of distribution of profits.
10. Provision for unrestricted transferability of shares.

Tax Status. Unless specified by statute, a joint stock company is not subject to state corporation taxes. New York, however, treats it as a corporation for franchise tax, as does the Federal government for income tax.

Advantages and Disadvantages. The tendency of states to pass regulatory statutes and to tax the joint stock company as a corporation, the applicability of Federal and state statutes regulating the issuance of securities, the application by the Federal government of corporate income tax, and the potential unlimited liability attaching to ownership of shares, limit use of this form of organization (the principal example of its use in the United States was the great express companies, which were organized as joint stock companies before the modern corporate era).

Mutuals and Cooperatives, and Professional Corporations

MUTUALS AND COOPERATIVES. The principal examples of mutual organizations are mutual insurance companies and saving banks, which are conducted by trustees for the benefit of policyholders or depositors. The state laws under which mutual insurance companies are organized usually provide for directors to be elected periodically by policyholders. Trustees of mutual savings banks fill vacancies on the board by election. The same practices apply in the conduct of savings and loan associations and other mutual business organizations.

In addition to consumer cooperatives designed to eliminate middlemen and secure the benefits of quantity purchases for individual consumers, there are producer cooperatives which have become an important factor in the marketing and occasionally in the processing of agricultural products. Of importance also are organizations grouping large numbers of cooperatives. Cooperatives have been formed to provide electric and telephone service, especially in rural areas. A number of these have attained substantial size.

Forms of Cooperative Organization. Cooperatives may assume two different forms of organization. One type is a simple unincorporated association similar to a partnership, except that members may be admitted and withdraw without dissolving the organization. Management is vested in a board of directors or in elected officers. The second type is incorporated either as a stock corporation or a nonstock, nonprofit corporation.

Most states have enacted statutes regulating cooperatives. Many of these laws are based upon a **model bill** for the organization of agricultural cooperatives drawn up by the U.S. Department of Agriculture in 1917. The Federal government has promoted formation of agricultural cooperatives and has set up agencies to assist them with financing and in other ways. The board of directors is elected by the members, a limitation of one vote for each member being imposed by most of the statutes.

The Clayton Act and the Capper-Volstead Act exempt farm cooperatives satisfying certain requirements from the **antitrust laws.** However, if agricultural cooperatives act together with nonexempt organizations, they become subject to the antitrust laws. (Packel, The Law of Cooperatives.) Cooperative organizations not specifically exempt from the antitrust laws are subject to such laws. (Associated Press v. United States, 326 U.S. 1 [1945].)

In cooperatives that issue stock, dividends are usually limited by law to from 4% to 8% per year, the statutes of the states varying in this respect. In addition to dividends on stock, there are dividends on patronage. Patronage dividends may go to nonmembers who do business through the cooperative, but at a lower rate than that enjoyed by the members. Cooperatives are financed partly by sale of stock to members or membership dues.

Advantages and Disadvantages. Mutuals and cooperatives differ from other forms of business enterprise in that they are **not conducted for profit.** In mutual insurance companies, excess income over expenses, losses, and reserves is returned as "dividends" to policyholders. In mutual savings banks, the surplus accumulated after the payment of interest-dividends serves as a protection to depositors. In consumer cooperatives, customers ordinarily receive rebates or "dividends" out of earnings, whereas in producer cooperatives the participants share the earnings.

It is contended by business men that cooperatives are being artificially fostered by **preferential tax treatment,** both as to income tax and under the revenue laws. In 1962, legislation reduced the tax advantages of cooperatives and mutuals. Previously, cooperatives, whether or not exempt by statute, could arrange their affairs so that neither the organization nor its members would be taxable on the earnings of the organization. Under the Revenue Act of 1962, however, this freedom from tax is made conditional on the taxability of the members on the pro rata portions of earnings to which they are entitled. That year taxes were also raised on mutual savings banks and savings and loan associations.

Disadvantages of cooperatives are the lack of the profit incentive, limited ability to raise capital as compared with corporations, and the difficulty of attracting top-notch executives to conduct cooperative enterprises that do not pay competitive salaries. Mutual financial institutions for the most part do pay salaries equal to those paid by comparable stock enterprises, so that this difficulty has been overcome by them.

PROFESSIONAL CORPORATIONS AND ASSOCIATIONS. Under the income tax law, a number of employee benefits, such as pensions and profit-sharing plans, are given **favorable tax treatment,** in that the employer obtains a current deduction, whereas the employee is either not taxable on the value of such benefits or else is taxable at a future date and probably at more favorable tax rates (see Sec. 19). The availability of these benefits is one of the advantages of incorporation, since the owners may become corporate employees. State law, however, has required that persons practicing professions, such as lawyers, certified public accountants, doctors, dentists, engineers and architects, do so in an unincorporated form.

In some instances, doctors have organized **unincorporated clinics,** with the members as employees, with a view to obtaining these tax advantages. Moreover, in recent years a number of states have passed statutes permitting the creation of professional associations or corporations. These statutes vary as to provisions and professions covered. In general, however, they enable such an association, if it satisfies the requirements of the Federal income tax law, to provide tax-deductible employee benefits to its members. Furthermore, it will not necessarily be subject to the corporate income tax if it elects, as a small business corporation, to have its income taxed directly to its members.

An example of these statutes is the **"New Jersey Professional Service Corporation Act."** Under this law one or more persons licensed to practice a profession may become shareholders of a professional corporation. However, persons rendering personal services still retain **liability for wrongful acts** committed by them or under their supervision. The corporation is liable up to the amount of its assets for negligent or wrongful acts of those rendering professional services on its behalf, but its assets may not be attached for the individual debts of its shareholders. The shares may be transferred only to another eligible person and with the approval of not less than a majority of the shareholders. The corporation has unlimited existence until dissolved.

Corporations

CORPORATE ORGANIZATION. A corporation is a **statutory** form of organization. It owes its existence to the legislature of the state in which it is organized. Each state has enabling legislation which prescribes the manner in which a corporation may be formed, and strict adherence to these statutes is necessary not only as a prerequisite to its creation but as a continuing obligation during the whole period of its existence.

A corporation is endowed by law with certain characteristics. It is a legal entity, distinct and separate from those who compose it, and as such it may exercise the powers conferred upon it by its charter in the same manner as an individual. It has continuity within the period of life specified in its charter, which in most jurisdictions may be perpetual. The members of the corporation, its shareholders, are not liable for its debts with certain exceptions. A number of states, including New York, Michigan, Massachusetts and Pennsylvania, impose a liability upon shareholders for wages and salaries owed to corporate employees. The shareholders participate only indirectly in its management through their elected representatives, the directors. A corporation is not a citizen under the provision of the constitution which reads that "the citizens of each state shall be entitled to all privileges and immunities of citizens in the several states," and therefore may enjoy corporate privileges in a state other than that of its incorporation only with that state's permission.

Advantages and Disadvantages. Widespread use of the corporation as a form of business organization by the great bulk of all large and medium-sized enterprises results from a number of major advantages that it possesses. These are:
1. Subject to minor exceptions, stockholders are not liable for the debts of the corporation, except to the amount of unpaid subscription on the stock.
2. The division of capital into shares makes it possible to attract both small and large investors.
3. Shares may be classified to vary the degree of risk assumed and to meet the desires of different classes of investors.
4. By the use of voting and nonvoting shares, control may be retained with a relatively small investment.
5. The transferability of shares facilitates the raising of large amounts of capital.
6. A corporation has continuous succession, usually in perpetuity, facilitating borrowing.
7. Its status as a legal entity makes it possible to hold property and maintain legal actions in its own name.
8. Concentration of discretionary powers of management in a board of directors makes for efficiency.

As in the case of each of the unincorporated forms of organization previously discussed, a corporation is subject to disadvantages which should be weighed before the decision to incorporate a business is made. These disadvantages are:
1. The organization tax and other organizational expenses make it somewhat more costly to set up than other forms.
2. A certificate of authority may be required, and usually a fee must be paid to transact business outside the state of incorporation.
3. It is subject to income taxes that may increase the tax burden for smaller enterprises.
4. The business is limited to activities mentioned or implied in the charter, or those incidental thereto, but this difficulty can be minimized by providing for broad corporate powers in the charter.
5. The owners tend to be separated from management.
6. Burdensome reports are required by Federal and state governments.

PROMOTION. Many corporate enterprises are brought into being by one or more promoters. The term **"promoter"** does not have any precise legal meaning. A good nonjudicial definition is: "A promoter is the person conscious of the possibility of transforming an idea into a business capable of yielding a profit, who brings together and holds together the various persons concerned, and who finally superintends the various steps required to bring the new business into existence." (Dewing, Financial Policy of Corporations.)

Functions of a Promoter. The functions of a promoter were long ago defined by a court as follows:

In a comprehensive sense "promoter" includes those who undertake to form a corporation and to procure for it the rights, instrumentalities and capital by which it is to carry out the purposes set forth in its charter, and to establish it as fully able to do its business. Their work may begin long before the organization of the corporation, in seeking the opening for a venture and projecting a plan for its development and may continue after the incorporation by attracting the investment of capital in its securities and providing it with the commercial breath of life. (Old Dominion Copper Mining Co. v. Bigelow, 203 Mass. 159, 177 [1909].)

Compensation. A promoter can be compensated in several ways. He may receive stock; an allowance of 10% of the initial capital stock is not unusual. Thus he shares the risk, for a time at least, of the enterprise he has initiated.

The professional promoter is not always interested in retaining his stock for long, since to realize a cash income from his efforts he must dispose of a large part, if not all, of the stock he receives after a promotion has been completed.

To avoid diluting the stock in the early stages of the enterprise and to secure a possible larger eventual return, promoters may take their compensation in the form of **stock options** carrying the right to buy common stock at a stated price, usually a larger number of shares than they would have received had they accepted stock as compensation.

If the promoter receives stock or a stock option, his **tax treatment** will depend on questions as to fair market value and whether he has income upon the receipt of the option or its exercise. Additional tax questions may involve the treatment of the promoter's income as capital gain or ordinary income.

Compensation may consist also of a contract to manage the business or, in the case of lawyers, engineers, and accountants, of professional retainers for their services.

Promotion may involve large **risks**. There is danger that, after considerable time and money have been expended, the promotion may have to be abandoned because some factor will develop making it inexpedient to go further. This explains why promoters seek large rewards for successful promotions.

Legal Status. The relation of promoters to the corporations they promote has been defined in a long line of court decisions. A promoter of a corporation not yet in existence is not an agent, for there is no principal, nor is he a trustee in the ordinary sense, for he may not hold any property in trust. Nevertheless, the courts have held that a **fiduciary relation** exists between a promoter and the corporation, and many of the rules that apply to a trustee have been applied to his dealings on behalf of the new enterprise and in his final settlement with the corporation after it has been formed. Promoters are bound in their dealings with the new corporation to make a complete **disclosure** of all material facts arising out of the promotional service performed on its behalf. They may make no secret profits at the expense of the corporation. There is no objection to a promoter's making a profit so long as full disclosure is made to a board of directors which is independent and not under the control of the promoter. If it is found that a promoter has made secret profits, the corporation may return property received and sue to rescind the contract, it may retain the property and sue for return of the secret profits, or it may sue for damages.

A separate problem is the legal relationship of promoters to one another. Promoters of a venture may be treated as **joint venturers** as amongst themselves and subject to equitable obligations to one another in dealing with the subject matter of the venture. The relationship may also be that of **principal and agent**, when one or more venturers are active on behalf of others.

The Federal **Securities Act of 1933** may directly affect the liabilities of a promoter if the corporation is being publicly financed and thus comes under the provisions of the act. The act requires statement of the names and addresses of "the promoters in the case of a business to be formed, or formed within two years prior to the registration statement." Rulings of the Securities and Exchange Commission have defined what activities and relationship to the corporation constitute promotion for the purposes of the act. Both **criminal and civil liability** is incurred by one who wilfully violates any provision of the Securities Act or the rules and regulations made thereunder, or who wilfully makes an untrue statement or omits to state a material fact in the registration statement. The activities of a promoter may make him subject to statutory penalties if he participates in the sale of securities without having first complied with the Act, or if he sells securities with the aid of a prospectus or other oral or written communication which contains an untrue statement or omission of a material fact. He may also be held liable to a buyer of the securities if he signs the registration statement or if he is named in the statement as being or is to become a director.

A promoter, even of a closely held corporation, may be liable to a purchaser or seller of stock under the **Securities Exchange Act of 1934.** Specifically, such liability may arise under section 10(b) of that act (and Rule 10B-5 of the S.E.C. promulgated under that section), forbidding the use of the mails or any instrumentality of interstate commerce to defraud or deceive a buyer or seller of a security, whether or not registered on a national securities exchange. This section and the rule promulgated under it have been construed by the courts as applicable to the purchase or sale of shares of closely held corporations. (Loss, Securities Regulation.)

All states except Nevada have so-called **"blue sky laws,"** enacted to protect purchasers of securities. Promoters may be affected by these laws in their efforts to raise money within a state. Thus, filing or registration fees for security dealers, salesmen, and brokers are levied in most states, both as a revenue measure and as a regulatory device. A number require qualification of securities to be offered for sale, particularly those not listed on exchanges, through submission of factual statements to a state officer or commission before the issue can be sold legally in the state. (Loss and Cowett, Blue Sky Law.)

PRE-INCORPORATION CONTRACTS. A new corporation may, once its organization has been completed, accept contracts made on its account before its incorporation. **Acceptance** of such contracts may be expressed or implied. If the corporation accepts the benefits of a contract, it is liable thereon without express recognition or formal acceptance.

Liability of Contracting Parties. Parties who enter into contracts on behalf of a corporation yet to be organized will themselves be personally liable thereon, in the absence of an expressed understanding to the contrary, until assumption of the contract by the corporation. For example, a promoter who makes an agreement that an individual will be employed by a corporation may be liable for failure to organize the corporation. If there is any doubt as to ultimate organization of the corporation or its acceptance of the contracts, the promoters should make their agreements contingent upon such organization and acceptance of the contracts, if they do not want to assume personal responsibility. Otherwise, they may be sued individually for damages that could reach large sums.

Agreements Among Incorporators. A contract among the incorporators of a business may be entered into, defining the nature of the proposed corporation, its purposes, and often details of its organization and management.

Mere **verbal agreement** with regard to incorporation, if not carried out, usually results only in the refusal of the aggrieved party to proceed further. Such agreements often do not furnish sufficient basis for litigation. Even formal agreements between promoters as to the provisions to be inserted into a charter can rarely be specifically enforced, and the only recourse of the aggrieved party is to refuse to participate in the organization of the corporation. If actual damages can be shown, a person damaged may bring suit against the offending parties for breach of contract. If a promoter fails to organize a venture, he may be under an **implied obligation** to return money collected by him.

If the organization of a venture will require contributions by several parties, a **written agreement** may be necessary to delineate the commitments of the various participants, the kinds of stock or other securities to be issued, as well as the state of incorporation and the provisions of the certificate of incorporation and bylaws, which sometimes are annexed in projected form. The period of time over which the commitments to invest in the new venture prior to its incorporation are to extend should be specified.

The statutes of a number of states make this **subscription for shares** of a corporation to be organized irrevocable for a period of time, such as six months or one year, unless the subscription agreement provides otherwise or all the subscribers consent to its revocation. The New York Business Corporation Law provides for a period of irrevocability of three months. In the absence of pertinent statute, the courts are not in agreement as to the irrevocability of subscriptions to the capital stock of corporations to be organized.

RAISING CAPITAL. In smaller promotions, the promoters or their representatives personally seek subscriptions from prospects to stock of the projected corporation. To promote a large enterprise, the procedure frequently followed is to incorporate and then offer the desired number of shares for **public sale** through investment bankers, who are compensated for their services. For issues of $300,000 and more offered for sale publicly, registration under the Securities Act and compliance with the provisions of that statute are required. A prospectus in the form specified by the regulations of the Securities and Exchange Commission must be provided subscribers to the stock, whether it is offered by promoters or by investment bankers. Deliberate misstatements or omissions of material facts subject those responsible to liabilities, both criminal and civil. For public offerings of less than $300,000, a notification must be filed with the S.E.C. and certain information as to the issuer given, including a financial statement, but the S.E.C. requirements are less rigorous for such an offering than for one for which registration must be made. (Loss, Securities Regulation.)

It is not always necessary to wait until the securities of a new enterprise have been sold to the public before acquiring property and beginning business. A block of stock may be sold privately to the promoters or others before the underwriting, to finance initiation of the enterprise. If sold to a small group, such a **private sale** is exempt from the Securities Act registration and other requirements in connection with security selling. (See discussion in Sec. 9.)

The scope of this exemption is not clearly defined. Normally, when a sale is intended to come within the private offering exemption the seller obtains from the purchaser a so-called **"investment letter"** in which the purchaser represents that he is acquiring the securities "for investment and not with a view to distribution or resale thereof." The purchaser must, however, hold the securities for an undefined period of time, which some attorneys have suggested should be two years. Another problem is the number of persons to whom the securities may be offered. A rule of thumb sometimes followed is that the **number of persons approached** with a view to sale should not exceed 20 or 25. It should be noted that if the issue does not qualify as a private sale, the issuer faces not only action by the S.E.C. but possible suits for rescission by the purchaser.

Another exemption under the Securities Act applies to **intrastate** offerings. This, too, may be a difficult exemption to satisfy. It is not available if there is a sale or offering of securities to a person outside the state of incorporation. Additionally, the Act requires for this exemption that the issuer must conduct a substantial part of its business in the state of incorporation.

CHOICE OF STATE OF INCORPORATION. If a corporation is small and expects to own property and operate principally in one state, the advantages of incorporating in that state will normally outweigh possible benefits of incorporating in another state, such as wider powers or lower taxes, and then qualifying in the state of its principal business. If, however, the enterprise is large, business is to be done in a number of states, or ownership of real property is not involved, it would do well to compare the corporation and tax laws of a number of states before choosing a legal domicile.

Organization taxes and fees and annual taxes are important considerations in the choice of the state of incorporation. Other considerations related to corporation laws which should be weighed by the incorporators are:

1. Types of stock permitted; provisions as to cumulative voting; voting trusts.
2. Possible limitations as to the portion of the consideration received for no par stock that may be allocated to capital surplus.
3. Liabilities of stockholders, directors, and officers.
4. Possible restrictions on holding stockholders' and directors' meetings outside the state.
5. Restrictions upon kinds of business in which the corporation may engage.
6. The degree to which the law has been tested and interpreted in the courts.
7. Provision as to residence or stockholding by directors; classification of the board; change in number of directors; removal of directors.
8. Provision as to issuance of stock and stock options to employees.
9. Pre-emptive rights of stockholders as to newly issued stock.
10. Enforceability in closely held corporations of stockholders' agreements.
11. Restrictions upon dividend payments from capital surplus, as distinguished from earned surplus.
12. Procedure for increasing or decreasing capital stock.
13. Ease of entering into mergers and consolidations with domestic and foreign corporations.

The New York Business Corporation Law contains a number of provisions applying to domestic corporations that are applicable also to some foreign corporations. These include provisions relating to dividends or distributions, the purchase of its own shares by the corporation, loans to directors, disclosure to the stockholders of certain corporate actions, voting trusts, and indemnifications of directors and officers. **Foreign corporations** are, however, not subject to New York statutory provisions if either: (1) the shares of such corporation are listed on a national securities exchange, or (2) less than one-half of its total business income for the preceding three years was allocable to New York for state income tax purposes.

State Taxes. The principal state taxes levied specifically on corporations are the organization tax and an annual franchise or income tax. The **organization tax** of **Delaware** is relatively low, and is assessed on a sliding scale favorable to corporations of large capitalization. Starting from a minimum of $10, the Delaware organization tax at this writing is as follows:

Capital Stock	Fee
Shares of stock with par value:	
Up to and including $2,000,000	1¢ per $100
Over $2,000,000 up to and including $20,000,000	$200 plus ½¢ for each $100 over $2,000,000
Over $20,000,000	$1,100 plus ⅕¢ for each $100 over $20,000,000
Shares of stock without par value:	
Up to and including 20,000 shares	½¢ per share
Over 20,000 shares up to and including 2,000,000 shares	$100 plus ¼¢ for each share over 20,000
Over 2,000,000 shares	$5,050 plus ⅕¢ for each share over 2,000,000

A $10,000,000 par value capitalization would require an organization tax of $600 in Delaware, $5,000 in New York (1/20 of 1% of the total), and $2,000 in New Jersey (20 cents per $1,000), at this writing. In Arizona there is no organization tax, merely incorporation fees totaling about $100.

Annual taxes upon corporations in Delaware are low also, and are based on authorized capital with special provisions for an alternative method of computation for corporations having shares with par value below $100. The computation giving the lower tax may be used. In our previous examples of a $10,000,000, $100 par value capitalization, the annual corporation tax in Delaware would be $55. Delaware has also a separate corporate income tax that does not, however, apply to Delaware corporations having only a statutory office in the state. New York's annual or **franchise** tax provides for alternative methods of computation, including a percentage of net income, the corporation to select the method giving the state the largest amount of tax. A large number of other states have a similar method of fixing the annual tax of corporations within their jurisdictions. In some states, a tax must be paid on only the amount of capital employed in the state. If a corporation does business in more than one state, it may be subject to taxation in each state in which it does business. (Beaman, Paying Taxes to Other States.) The District of Columbia and South Dakota have no annual tax.

State Laws. Relatively favorable taxes are a factor to be considered in choosing the state of incorporation, but usually the nature of the state's laws governing corporations has greater bearing. Liberal state statutes will often draw corporations to the state. For this reason, even more than for its low annual taxes, Delaware is a very popular corporate home.

The laws of **Delaware** offer several **advantages.** Incorporators do not have to be residents of Delaware; meetings of stockholders may be held outside the state; dividends may be paid out of current profits, even if a capital deficit exists; very wide powers may be authorized in the charter; and, almost any type of classification of stock is permissible. Furthermore, there has been ample opportunity to test the Delaware laws in the courts, since so many large corporations are incorporated there. The state's legislature, eager to retain the income provided by corporations choosing Delaware as their home, has been quick to enact amendments that are widely desired, and has kept the statute up-to-date as new trends in corporate finance appear.

The principal **disadvantage of Delaware incorporation** results from the fact that most Delaware corporations conduct only a small part of their business in the state. Therefore, they must conform to the licensing laws of other states in which they do business as foreign corporations.

The **Model Business Corporation Act** of the American Bar Association has had a great influence on the statutory law as to corporations. This has resulted in the adoption by many states of new business corporation laws, based in large part on the Model Business Corporation Act, which modernize previous corporation laws. In states in which these changes have been made there will be less reason to incorporate businesses outside the state in which the main office of the business will be located.

CORPORATE NAME. A corporation may choose the name under which it wishes to conduct its business. This name becomes the exclusive property of the corporation, conferred upon the corporation by its charter.

The choice of a name is subject to **restrictions,** which vary from state to state. The restrictions are of three types:

1. The corporation may not use the name of another corporation chartered by the state, or one so similar as to cause confusion.
2. Statutes usually require that the name contain a word or abbreviation indicating that the organization is a corporation.
3. Statutes prohibit the inclusion of words indicative of a banking or insurance business in the name, unless the business is organized for such purposes under pertinent laws.

The above restrictions are found in the statutes or court decisions in most states. In addition, some state laws impose other restrictions. For example, New York specifically prohibits the use of the words "doctor" and "lawyer" by a business corporation. Delaware provides that the name must contain one of the following words—"association," "company," "corporation," "club," "foundation," "incorporated," "institute," "society," "union," "syndicate," or "limited"; or one of the abbreviations—"Co.," "Inc.," or "Ltd." In New York, the Business Corporation Law requires that the name of a corporation (either domestic or foreign) must include the word "corporation," "incorporated," or "limited" or an abbreviation of one of such words. A foreign corporation qualifying in New York is required to add to its name one of such words or abbreviations, if its name does not contain one of them.

In view of the danger of selecting a name that will afterward be found unavailable, it is important to check the desired name against lists on file in the state incorporation office before filing the papers. This may be done by letter or telegram to the Secretary of State. If it is intended that the corporation conduct business in states other than that of its organization, the availability of the corporate name in each such state must also be checked. A corporate name may be reserved for varying periods, ranging from 10 days to 12 months, in a number of states.

A name, once adopted, can be changed only by amending the certificate of incorporation in the manner, and with the consent of stockholders, prescribed by the statutes of the state of incorporation.

THE INCORPORATION PROCESS. Incorporation procedures vary among the several states, and study of the law is necessary in each case. State incorporation laws outline standard procedures, in most states designating the Secretary of State to administer the law and keep records of corporations. The following procedure is typical:

1. Three or more persons indicate a desire to incorporate by filing with the the proper state officer a **certificate of incorporation** in the form prescribed by statute.
2. Filing fees and organization taxes must accompany the certificate.
3. If the Secretary of State finds that the certificate is correct in form, that the business is not against public policy, and that the fees are correct, the certificate is filed in the office of the Secretary.
4. A copy of the certificate is filed in the office of the county in which the principal office of the corporation is to be located. In some states, the corporation must be registered with the tax authorities.
5. Corporate existence begins as specified by the statutes of the state. (In New York, e.g., the corporate existence begins upon the filing of the certificate of incorporation by the Secretary of State.)
6. In a number of states, including New York and Delaware, an organizational meeting of the incorporators is held at which the bylaws are adopted and directors are elected to serve until the first annual meeting of stockholders. In other states, the directors are named in the certificate of incorporation, so that the organizational meeting is that of the directors.

DOMESTIC, FOREIGN, AND ALIEN CORPORATIONS. A corporation within the state in which it is incorporated is referred to as a domestic corporation. In states other than that in which it is incorporated it is termed a foreign corporation. If incorporated outside of the United States, District of Columbia, or the territories of the United States, it is an **alien corporation.** State laws make no distinction between foreign and alien corporations and if the word foreign is used in a state statute, the reference includes alien corporations.

Restrictions upon Foreign Corporations. All states require that a foreign corporation obtain a **certificate of authority** (license to do business) as a prerequisite to doing business within the state. To obtain a certificate of authority, it is usually necessary to file a certified copy of the certificate of incorporation, designate an office within the state, and state the name of an officer or agent upon whom legal process may be served. (In New York the Secretary of State must be designated as a person upon whom valid service of legal process can be made.) Registration with the tax authorities may be required also.

If a foreign corporation **fails to qualify** as required, the consequences vary, depending upon the state law. In a number of states, including New York, it may not maintain a suit in the courts of the state until it has qualified. In other states its contracts are not enforceable by it in the state courts. Still other state statutes make them void or provide that officers and agents and, in some instances, stockholders are personally liable on the corporate contracts. Many states impose fines of varying amounts upon foreign corporations that have failed to qualify.

The question as to what **constitutes doing business** in a foreign state is one which the courts have not treated uniformly. If the transaction is **interstate,** as distinguished from **intrastate,** no license is necessary, for interstate transactions enjoy the protection of the Federal constitution. Difficulty often arises in determining just when a transaction ceases to be interstate and becomes intrastate in character. The result has been a great number of decisions of the state and Federal courts as to whether particular activities constitute intrastate business. (See Eli Lilly Co. v. Sav-On-Drugs, 366 U.S. 276 [1961].) A number of state statutes provide that certain types of activities do not require qualification, such as maintaining bank accounts, holding corporate meetings, owning real estate, making loans secured by real estate, or solicitation of orders by salesmen or through the mail.

If a corporation qualifies to do business in a state, it will be **subject to state income tax** on the portion of its income allocable to the state under the provisions of the state law. The Supreme Court of the United States has held, moreover, that a state has the constitutional power to impose an income tax on the net income of a corporation engaged solely in interstate commerce within the state, if the business activity bears a sufficient "nexus" to the taxing state and the income is fairly apportioned (Northwestern States v. Minnesota, 358 U.S. 450 [1959]). Its decision led to Federal legislation limiting the kinds of activities which could be made the basis of state income taxation. (Beaman, Paying Taxes to Other States.)

NATURE OF CORPORATE CHARTER. The certificate of incorporation is often referred to as the charter of the corporation. It would be more correct to define the corporate charter as the certificate of incorporation read in connection with the corporation laws of the state in which the enterprise is incorporated.

Contents of Certificate of Incorporation. The provisions of the corporation law of the state of New York quoted below are fairly typical.

§ 402. Certificate of incorporation; contents

(a) A certificate, entitled "Certificate of incorporation of .... (name of corporation) under section 402 of the Business Corporation Law", shall be signed by each incorporator, with his name and address stated beneath or opposite his signature, acknowledged and delivered to the department of state. It shall set forth:

(1) The name of the corporation.

(2) The purpose or purposes for which it is formed.

(3) The city, incorporated village or town and the county within this state, in which the office of the corporation is to be located.

(4) The aggregate number of shares which the corporation shall have the authority to issue; if such shares are to consist of one class only, the par value of the shares or a statement that the shares are without par value; or, if the shares are to be divided into classes, the number of shares of each class and the par value of the shares having par value and a statement as to which shares, if any, are without par value.

(5) If the shares are to be divided into classes, the designation of each class and a statement of the relative rights, preferences and limitations of the shares of each class.

(6) If the shares of any preferred class are to be issued in series, the designation of each series and a statement of the variations in the relative rights, preferences and limitations as between series insofar as the same are to be fixed in the certificate of incorporation, and a statement of any authority to be vested in the board to establish and designate series and to fix the variations in the relative rights, preferences and limitations as between series.

(7) A designation of the secretary of state as agent of the corporation upon whom process against it may be served and the post office address within or without this state to which the secretary of state shall mail a copy of any process against it served upon him.

(8) If the corporation is to have a registered agent, his name and address within this state and a statement that the registered agent is to be the agent of the corporation upon whom process against it may be served.

(9) The duration of the corporation if other than perpetual.

(b) The certificate of incorporation may set forth any provision, not inconsistent with this chapter or any other statute of this state, relating to the business of the corporation, its affairs, its rights or powers, or the rights or powers of its shareholders, directors or officers including any provision relating to matters which under this chapter are required or permitted to be set forth in the by-laws. It is not necessary to set forth in the certificate of incorporation any of the powers enumerated in this chapter.

AMENDMENTS TO CHARTER. A charter is, in effect, a contract between the state and the corporation. In theory, therefore, the **consent of the state** must be obtained should the stockholders desire to amend any provision in the charter. Actually, however, the statutes of each state contain provisions permitting the filing of an amendment in the same manner as the original certificate of incorporation.

State laws vary as to procedure in amending a charter, but all are liberal as regards amendment. Generally, a corporation may amend its certificate of incorporation in any respect that would have been permissible as part of its original certificate of incorporation. An amendment must be adopted at an annual or special meeting of the stockholders. In some states a majority vote of the stockholders entitled to vote may adopt an amendment, in others a two-thirds vote is required; in still others, the majority required depends on the nature of the amendment. In most states the certificate of incorporation may require more than a simple majority. Usually, provisions are made for voting by class on amendments that may adversely affect the rights and preferences of some classes of stock.

BYLAWS. Bylaws are rules formally adopted by the stockholders for the government of the corporation. Other persons are not presumed to know the bylaws, since, unlike the certificate of incorporation, they are not filed as a public document. The bylaws may limit but may not extend the powers conferred upon the corporation by its charter; in case of conflict, the provisions of the charter govern. For convenience, bylaws may repeat procedures specifically provided for in the statutes. A bylaw in conflict with statutory provisions, whether adopted before or after the passage of the law, is invalid.

Power to Make Bylaws. The common-law rule vested in the stockholders the power to adopt, amend, and repeal the bylaws. Statutory provisions contain a number of variations. The initial bylaws may be adopted at the organization meeting of the incorporators, as in New York and Delaware. In Indiana, Minnesota, Texas, and Virginia the initial bylaws are adopted by the board of directors. As to **amending** or **repealing** the bylaws, a large number of state statutes provide that this power shall be exercised by the shareholders. Usually, however, in these states the certificate of incorporation or the bylaws may confer this power on the board of directors. A frequent provision of state statutes is that bylaws adopted by the board of directors may be repealed or altered by the stockholders. Several states give the power to alter, amend, or repeal the bylaws to the board of directors, unless reserved by the stockholders in the certificate of incorporation. This is the provision contained in the Model Business Corporation Act.

Typical Provisions. There are no legal requirements covering the arrangement of bylaws, but customary practice is for related provisions to be arranged by subject in a sequence approximating the following:

   I. Stockholders' meetings.
  II. Directors and directors' meetings.
 III. Standing committees.
  IV. Officers.
   V. Capital stock.
  VI. Dividends and finances.
 VII. Sundry provisions.
VIII. Amendments.

Under each of the above headings numerous provisions may be found. The more important items usually included under headings V. through VIII., as listed above, are discussed briefly below. There then follows a more detailed discussion of the subjects of the first four headings, with references throughout to pertinent bylaw provisions.

V. **Capital Stock.** Bylaws respecting capital stock are usually concerned with the form of share certificates, methods of transfer, stock records to be maintained, appointment of stock transfer agent and registrar, and the closing of stock and transfer books for stockholders' meetings and payment of dividends. Stockholders' right to inspect the stock record books is usually set forth in detail even though the statutes of the state may contain detailed provisions on this matter.

VI. **Dividends and Finances.** Bylaws commonly state that accounts will be maintained on a fiscal or calendar year basis; provisions covering the authority to establish bank accounts designating the officers who may sign and countersign checks, and a direction that receipts be deposited promptly in the name of the corporation. Although the payment of dividends is within the discretion of the directors, the bylaws often prescribe dates for dividend payments. Corporations that, by the nature of their business, are likely to come into possession of stocks and bonds of other corporations should have bylaws relative to the handling of such securities.

VII. **Sundry Provisions.** Bylaws providing for profit sharing plans for employees and for the carrying of insurance on the lives of certain executives are illustrations of special matters often found in this section.

VIII. **Amendments.** Provisions relative to amendment of the bylaws will depend on whether they are enacted by the directors or stockholders. Usually, a majority vote is required in each case, with the power reserved to stockholders to amend bylaws made by the directors.

Stockholders' Meetings

ANNUAL MEETINGS. Annual meetings of stockholders are held each year on the date specified in the bylaws. The **time of the meeting** is established, such as "the second Tuesday in January." Mailing of a notice is usually required a specified number of days prior to the meeting. The date is frequently fixed in relation to the corporation's fiscal year, with a sufficient interval to permit the financial report of the year to be available at the time of the meeting.

Although stockholders are presumed to know the bylaws and hence cannot plead lack of **notice** if none is given, the bylaws customarily provide for such notice, and directions as to how and when it is to be given are set forth in detail. Some statutes require the mailing of a notice to each stockholder, and in such states failure to mail the notice may invalidate the meeting. It becomes the duty of the secretary of the corporation in such cases to prepare and mail the notice, and he will retain a copy on which the date of mailing has been entered as proof that the bylaws have been complied with. Occasionally the bylaws require that the secretary shall publish the notice in one or more newspapers. A typical form of notice mailed to stockholders follows:

Notice of Annual Meeting of Stockholders

Notice is hereby given that the annual meeting of the stockholders of the "XZ" Manufacturing Corporation will be held at the office of the Company, 120 Broadway, New York, N. Y., at 2 o'clock P.M. on the 5th day of January 19... for the election of directors and the transaction of such other business as may come before the meeting.

Stockholders entitled to vote at the annual meeting will be stockholders of record at the close of business on the 31st day of December 19...

John Doe
President
Richard Roe
Secretary

New York, N. Y.
Dec. 1, 19...

Meetings must be held within the state of incorporation unless the statute specifies that the corporation bylaws may authorize meetings in another state, and the bylaws have so provided. (Grange-Woodbury, Corporation Law for Officers and Directors.)

In **publicly held corporations,** the notice of the stockholders' meeting will be accompanied by a proxy solicited by the management. If the stock is listed on a national securities exchange, the solicitation of proxies is subject to regulation by the S.E.C. under the Securities Exchange Act of 1934. (See Sec. 13.)

Procedure. A stockholders' meeting is frequently attended by directors and officers. In large, publicly owned enterprises members of the press who are not stockholders may be permitted to attend as a matter of courtesy. But only stockholders entitled to vote, their proxies, and such officers as are designated by the bylaws to be officers of the meeting attend as a matter of right. In addition, legal counsel for the corporation usually is on hand to advise. If there is to be a contest between opposing groups, each group may have its legal counsel present.

The procedure at an annual meeting is usually as follows:

1. Calling the meeting to order.
2. Election of officers (if not designated by the bylaws).
3. Appointment or election of inspectors.
4. Reports of officers.
5. Reports of committees.
6. Election of directors.
7. Unfinished business.
8. New business.

Unless the bylaws prescribe who shall preside at meetings, a **presiding officer** must be elected at each meeting. Usually the bylaws provide that the president of the corporation shall preside at the meeting and that the secretary of the corporation shall act as its recording officer.

A number of statutes provide for **inspectors** or **judges of election** to be appointed at a stockholders' meeting at which directors are to be elected. The manner of appointment of inspectors should be specified in the charter or bylaws. In the absence of such provision, stockholders ordinarily elect inspectors at the start of the meeting. Unless so required in the bylaws, inspectors of election need not be stockholders. In the event of a contest for control, inspectors of election will be called upon to determine the validity of proxies, many of which are likely to be contested. If the statute, charter, or bylaws do not provide for inspectors, they need not be appointed. In that event, the stockholders themselves may pass upon the validity of contested votes, unless the bylaws authorize the chairman or the president to do so.

It is customary at annual meetings for the president to discuss the progress of the business during the year past, and to present plans for the future. Printed statements of the financial condition of the corporation may be distributed to stockholders at the meeting, and the financial status of the corporation may be explained by either the president or the treasurer. If standing committees have been appointed, their reports are received at this time.

SPECIAL MEETINGS. The bylaws outline the method by which a special meeting of stockholders may be called and describe the notice to be given. Usually the right to call such a meeting is vested in the board of directors, the president, or a certain percentage of the voting stockholders. Upon the authority of the call made in the manner prescribed by the bylaws, the secretary will prepare and mail the notice. Such a notice, to be valid, must state the business to come before the meeting, for valid action may be taken at a special meeting only upon the matter for which the meeting was called as set forth in the notice. As for the annual meeting, the notice must be mailed in conformity with the bylaws, which specify the number of days prior to the meeting that a notice shall be mailed.

The statute may set a minimum time for such notice which cannot be shortened by the bylaws. An example of a formal call by the board of directors of a corporation for a special meeting follows:

Call for Special Meeting of Stockholders

We, the directors of the X Corporation do hereby call a special meeting of the stockholders of said corporation to be held at the office, No. 120 Broadway, New York, N. Y., on the 10th day of January 19... at 2 o'clock P.M. for the purpose of considering and acting upon a proposed increase in the capital stock from 240,000 to 350,000 shares and to do all things necessary in connection therewith, and we do hereby authorize the secretary of the corporation to send out notice of said special meeting in the form and manner prescribed by the bylaws of this corporation.

             John Smith
             Will Caster
             Edward McLain

New York, N. Y.
Dec. 1, 19...
To Richard Roe
 Secretary of the X Corporation

A notice to the stockholders mailed by the secretary of the corporation pursuant to the call outlined above might be as follows:

Notice of Special Meeting of Stockholders

Notice is hereby given that a special meeting of the stockholders of the X Corporation has been called by the Board of Directors to be held at the principal office of the corporation, 120 Broadway, New York, N. Y. on the 10th day of January 19... at 2 o'clock P.M. for the following purpose:

 Considering and acting upon a proposed increase in the capital stock from 240,000 to 350,000 shares and to do all things necessary in connection therewith.

 By order of the Board of Directors

             Richard Roe
              Secretary

New York, N. Y.
Dec. 5, 19...

Procedure. Immediately following the calling to order of a special meeting the secretary reads the notice of meeting and an affidavit to the effect that it was mailed in the prescribed manner. His statement is written into the minutes as proof of the validity of the meeting. The purpose of the meeting is then explained and a suitable motion put for vote; after opportunity is afforded for discussion a vote is taken. Although no action may be taken on any other matter, the presiding officer may permit discussion. The meeting normally adjourns as soon as the result of the vote is announced.

CONSENT MEETINGS. Consent meetings are special meetings not properly called, and for which notice in the form prescribed by the bylaws has not been given. They depend for their validity upon the presence of all of the stockholders or upon the willingness of those not present to sign a waiver of the call and notice. It is usual to have the stockholders present sign the minute book as evidence of their presence, and the signed waivers of call and notice are posted in the minute book as a permanent record. Consent meetings are limited to corporations with few stockholders; in the case of such corporations, meetings are usually held upon consent unless there is some disagreement among the stockholders. (Grange-Woodbury, Corporation Law for Officers and Directors.)

STOCKHOLDER CONSENT WITHOUT A MEETING. The statutes of a substantial number of states, including New York and Delaware, provide that any action requiring a vote of the stockholders may be taken on the written consent of all the stockholders without a meeting. Such a provision is part of the Model Business Corporation Act. In other states, unanimous consent of the stockholders, or the consent of a specified percentage of the stockholders, is stated to be a permissible method of approval of particular kinds of acts, such as the sale or lease of property not in the ordinary course of business, or the guarantee of the obligation of another person, or voluntary dissolution.

QUORUMS. Most states have provisions relating to a quorum of shareholders. Usually the statutes provide that a quorum is a **majority of the shares entitled to vote,** unless otherwise provided in the charter or, in some instances, in the bylaws. A large number of states, including New York, provide that a quorum must be not less than one-third of the voting shares. In Delaware and a number of other states, the statute leaves quorum requirements to the charter or bylaws. In a **closely held corporation** where there are several stockholder interests, a useful device to protect minority interests is a provision fixing quorum requirements at more than a majority. The New York Business Corporation Law provides that the certificate of incorporation may contain such a quorum requirement. A quorum requirement of more than a majority is generally allowable but is forbidden in some states, including New Jersey.

VOTING. The statutes of some states prescribe the method of voting, while others leave a choice between one vote per share and the cumulative method. It is usually provided that stockholders may use proxies if they do not wish to attend in person. The **eligibility** of stockholders to vote is determined by ownership of shares on the day of the closing of the transfer books, which the bylaws set as a day sufficiently in advance of the meeting to insure time to prepare lists of those eligible.

Normally the election of directors and other matters is by a majority of the shares represented at a meeting at which a quorum is present or represented. As to matters not in the ordinary course of corporate business or affecting the rights of classes of stockholders, state statutes vary as to the percentage of affirmative votes required and whether or not such vote is by class. A number of states, including New York and Delaware, permit the certificate of incorporation to require a greater proportion of the shares for action on any matter than would otherwise be required. A number of states also permit action by a lesser proportion than would otherwise be required.

PROTECTION OF MINORITY INTERESTS. One of the main characteristics of the corporate form of doing business is the separation of ownership, in the form of capital stock, from management, which is in the hands of the directors elected by the stockholders. As a result, those owning a majority of the voting stock are in a position to control the corporation by electing the members of the board of directors. Various legal devices have been worked out to protect minority interests (a number of which are discussed throughout this section and in Sec. 13). Common devices designed to protect minority interests include the following: **cumulative voting** in electing the board of directors, **stockholder agreements** to vote for certain directors, the creation of **different classes of stock** entitled to vote separately for different members of the board, requirements in the certificate of incorporation that the board of directors be elected by more than a simple majority, **voting trust agreements,** and **provi-**

sions for arbitration or dissolution in case of a deadlock. (O'Neal, Close Corporations.)

In the smaller, closely held corporation, the problem of protecting minority interests and **resolving conflicts between owners** should be thoroughly considered from the start. If there is a falling out between owners in such situations, a minority owner may find his interest rendered practically worthless if sufficient precautions have not been taken in advance. Shares in these corporations usually lack a ready market outside of the existing owners or their transferability is expressly restricted. (O'Neal and Derwin, Expulsion or Oppression of Business Associates: 'Squeeze-Outs' in Small Enterprises.)

The Board of Directors

LEGAL STATUS. The status of the board of directors, considered collectively, is that of **agent** for the corporation. The corporation may act only through the board. But this is no ordinary agency, for the powers exercised by the directors are not specifically granted to them by the corporation. Rather, they are found in all the statutes, charter provisions and bylaws, or they are established by custom. The directors may delegate some of their powers to officers, a privilege not possessed by an ordinary agent. Directors are often referred to as trustees, but here too they are not trustees in the ordinary usage of the word, for they do not hold title to the property of the corporation.

A more accurate statement would be to say that directors occupy a position of trust, or a **fiduciary** relationship toward the corporation and to the stockholders collectively. Some of the rules of law applicable to agents and many of the rules relative to trusteeship are applicable to directors. More important for an understanding of a director's legal status is his well-established responsibility to exercise the utmost **good faith** in dealing with corporate property, and not to seek his own advantage at the expense of the corporation's or its stockholders', together with an obligation to exercise prudence and diligence in the management of the corporation's affairs.

A director does not have to know all the technical details of the operation of a business. He is expected to apply whatever skill and ability he possesses with diligence to the business of the corporation. The rule is stricter in the case of bank directors, courts in some states having held that by accepting a directorship in a bank a person represents that he possesses at least ordinary knowledge and skill. The tendency has been to apply more severe standards to such matters as attention to the affairs of the business and the duty to check on the performance of the officers. (Grange-Woodbury, Corporation Law for Officers and Directors.)

STATUTORY PROVISIONS. The position of directors in governing the affairs of a corporation is so important that state corporation laws contain a number of provisions covering their selection and activities.

Qualifications. The statutes of the state of incorporation, the charter, and in some instances the bylaws may establish qualifications for directors. A few states require that directors be stockholders. If the purpose of imposing such a qualification is to insure that directors have a financial interest in the corporation, the statutes fail to achieve this end, for it has become common practice to transfer by agreement to a nonstockholder whose services are desired as a director a single "qualifying" share to make him a shareholder of record without a bona fide interest. Similarly, statutes occasionally require that the directors, or some of their number, be citizens or residents of the state. Most state statutes either have no provision as to stock ownership or residence, or else state that neither shall be required unless the corporate charter or bylaws provide otherwise. Few large corporations place qualifications for directors in their charter or bylaws.

Number. The statutes usually provide that the charter or bylaws of a corporation shall fix the number of directors at a minimum of three. New York and Delaware provide that if the number of shareholders is less than three, the number of directors may also be less than three but not less than the number of shareholders. Bylaws frequently express the number of directors as a variable between a minimum number and a maximum number, both odd, to avoid deadlocks. Some state statutes, in fixing the minimum number of directors, cover the possibility of a variable number.

Election. Directors are normally elected at the annual meeting of stockholders. If there should be a vacancy due to death, resignation, or a revision of the charter or bylaws providing for additional directors, a special meeting may be called for the election. Pursuant to statutory authority, the bylaws usually provide for the filling of vacancies by the board of directors. A notable exception is Illinois, which has a constitutional requirement that directors be elected by stockholders. The New York statute, although generally permitting such action by the directors, provides that, in the absence of a contrary provision in the certificate of incorporation or in bylaws adopted by the stockholders, a vacancy created by a removal of directors without cause shall be filled only by vote of the stockholders. Delaware and New York and several other states permit the board of directors to fill newly created directorships resulting from an increase in the number of directors. In the absence of such a statutory provision, a right of the directors to fill vacancies on the board for an unexpired term does not include the right to fill newly created directorships. Until a new board of directors is elected, the old board "holds over" even though the term for which its members were elected has expired, and they are considered de facto directors (directors in fact), with all the powers possessed during their regular term.

Term of Office. The bylaws customarily provide that directors will hold office for one year, or until replaced if for some reason the stockholders fail to hold an election. Should it be desired that only part of a board of directors be elected each year, the bylaws may divide the directors into classes and provide for initial terms of, say, 1 year, 2 years, and 3 years, respectively. Thereafter but one-third of the directors will need to be replaced each year, thus providing for continuity of management policies. Authority may be granted in this section of the bylaws for the directors to elect a new member of the board in case a vacancy occurs during a term.

Resignation and Removal. Directors may resign at any time, leaving a vacancy on the board of directors. The best practice is to authorize the remaining directors to fill vacancies created by resignation or death, without a special stockholders' meeting for the purpose. This may be accomplished by a suitable bylaw provision.

It is extremely difficult to remove directors in the **absence of bylaw, charter, or statutory authority,** until the expiration of their term in office. **Misconduct or unfitness** must be proved to the satisfaction of the court. Even though stockholders complain that the management is inefficient and the directors incompetent, the courts ordinarily will not interfere. But stockholders may by court action obtain injunctions against wrongful acts and acts that do not fall within the definition of ordinary prudence.

Under the law of a number of states, bylaws may provide for the removal of one or more directors, with or without cause, by the stockholders at a **special meeting**. Many state statutes, however, do not refer to the removal of directors and a few require that removal be for cause or by court action. If cumulative voting is in effect, statutes permitting removal without cause generally provide against removal of less than the entire board by a vote that would defeat the cumulative voting principle.

LIABILITY. The fiduciary relationship between the directors and the corporation gives rise to liabilities when directors are guilty of a breach of trust. Directors are ordinarily not held liable for honest mistakes of judgment, no matter how costly to the corporation. They are, however, expected to exercise ordinary prudence and diligence in the management of corporate affairs, and if failure to act in this manner results in loss to the corporation, stockholders may hold them liable through a representative action brought in the name of the corporation. But wide differences in court decisions and judicial reluctance to lay down general rules make it difficult to judge in advance whether directors will be held liable for losses caused by their negligence. **Bank directors** have been held liable for not making inquiry into the nature of the loans made by the officers, when it was proved that such loans were made in violation of law or without ordinary care.

Directors who cause their dissent to be entered on the minutes when action is taken by the board are not liable for the losses caused by such action of the majority. Absence from meetings of the board is not in itself **negligence**, but may be so considered in the light of circumstances. For example, absence because of illness or an occasional absence does not ordinarily indicate neglect of duty. But habitual absence may be held tantamount to a disregard of the responsibility assumed by the acceptance of membership on the board.

Directors who deliberately exceed powers granted them in the charter or bylaws are liable to the corporation for losses resulting from such **ultra vires acts**.

Directors are liable for **fraud**. An example of fraud is the use of their position as directors to make contracts unfair to the corporation from which they benefit personally. Also in this category falls the issuance of stock to directors without adequate consideration, loans to directors and officers that are inadequately secured and unpaid, and **unreasonable salaries and bonuses**.

The courts have been reluctant to impose liability on directors who take advantage of intimate knowledge of a corporation's affairs in purchasing stock of the corporation from a stockholder, it having been held that a director (Bowden v. Taylor, 254 Ill. 464, 467) "is not a trustee for such stockholder with respect to his stock. Officers of a corporation may purchase the stock of stockholders on the same terms and as freely as they might purchase of a stranger." There is, however, some authority holding that a director has a fiduciary obligation in this situation. Moreover, transactions in the stock of a registered corporation by officers, directors, and major stockholders are regulated by the Securities Exchange Act of 1934.

Liabilities Imposed by Statute. Many of the liabilities imposed on directors by common law are also found in the statutes. In some instances, statutes provide fines and penalties. For example, a provision in a state statute against issuing false financial reports, or requiring the keeping of certain records may also impose a fine for violations.

Some of the acts for which liability is imposed in statutes are:
1. Payment of dividends, except from earned surplus or other permissible sources under the applicable state law.
2. Accepting promissory notes in payment for stock.
3. Impairing capital through purchase by a corporation of its own shares.
4. Failure to keep certain records.
5. Failure to permit examination of certain record books by stockholders.
6. Issuing stock for inadequate consideration; many state statutes, however, provide that the judgment of the directors as to the value of the consideration received for shares shall be conclusive in the absence of fraud.
7. Transferring property of an insolvent corporation for purposes of defrauding or preferring creditors.
8. Conversion, misapplication, or fraud, in connection with the corporation's property.
9. Issuing false financial statements or reports.
10. Assenting to loans to officers or directors.

Directors of corporations whose securities are offered publicly and those whose securities are listed on stock exchanges are further liable under certain provisions of the Securities Act of 1933 and the Securities Exchange Act of 1934. These liabilities are both civil and criminal. Violation of the Securities Act of 1933 subjects wilful violators to a fine of not more than $5,000 or imprisonment for not more than 5 years, or both. If there is an untrue statement of a material fact or omission of a material fact required to be stated as necessary to make statements made in a registration statement not misleading, directors and others named in the act are liable to the purchaser for the difference between the price (not in excess of the offering price) and the market value at time of suit. If the purchaser has sold the security, the director is liable for the difference between the price paid (not in excess of the offering price) and the price at which sold. The law provides certain exceptions under which directors may escape liability.

Directors are required to refund profits realized from the sale of listed stocks sold within 6 months after purchase, under the Securities Exchange Act of 1934.

Indemnification. Bylaws frequently contain a provision indemnifying any director or officer against expenses incurred in defense of any suit or proceeding, civil or criminal, in which he is made a party by reason of being a director or officer, except in relation to matters as to which he is adjudged liable for negligence or misconduct in the performance of his duties to the corporation. Such indemnification of officers and directors is specifically permitted by numerous state statutes. In the absence of a bylaw provision or an agreement, the cases are in conflict as to the right of indemnification or reimbursement. (Washington and Bishop, Indemnifying the Corporate Executive.) The New York Business Corporation Law imposes limits on permissible indemnification of directors and officers.

COMPENSATION. Directors serve without compensation, unless compensation is fixed by the bylaws or they are empowered by the bylaws to fix their own compensation. This is usually a small fee for each meeting and may sometimes include traveling expenses. If the chairman of the board of directors or a committee of the board is expected to assume duties comparable to those of an officer, he will usually receive a salary that will be authorized by the bylaws.

Directors may serve as officers and be paid the salaries fixed for such posts. As a matter of precaution, directors who are salaried officers of the corporation should not attend meetings of the board when the salaries are being considered or fixed, as the contract may be questioned later.

If a director renders services that are beyond those that he might reasonably be expected to give, as when a lawyer who is a member of the board represents the corporation as its attorney or an engineer who is a director prepares detailed plans, he may expect to be paid the fair value of such services. If, however, there is no express contract made in advance to pay for such services, the director may have difficulty in obtaining payment on the basis of an implied contract.

COMMITTEES. Large boards of directors are unwieldy. If members are drawn from sections of the country remote from the place of meeting, it may be difficult to secure a quorum. Even if it is possible to assemble the board frequently, the transaction of business is slowed down in a large board if more than perfunctory attention is given matters under consideration. The business of a large corporation is complex, and it is not to be expected that all the directors of a large board will be sufficiently familiar with the details to pass intelligently upon them. It is customary, therefore, and legally within the power of the board to establish standing committees to take care of specified matters of the business. Sometimes, these are provided for in the bylaws.

These smaller bodies can assemble as often as necessary. Because of their smaller size, they are able to transact business with dispatch. Committee members are chosen with a view to their knowledge of the type of problems likely to come before the committee.

Executive and Finance. Often there is but one committee, the executive committee. This committee is usually empowered to exercise all the powers of the board during intervals between board meetings. In addition, however, there may be a finance committee which, as is indicated by the name, supervises the corporation's finances. Provisions of the bylaws of a large corporation quoted below indicate powers of these two standing committees:

The Board of Directors shall elect from the Directors an Executive Committee and a Finance Committee, and shall designate for each of these Committees a Chairman of the Committee to serve during the pleasure of the Board of Directors. . . .

During the intervals between meetings of the Board of Directors, the Executive Committee shall possess and may exercise all the powers of the Board of Directors in the management and direction of all the business and affairs of the Company (except the matters hereinafter assigned to the Finance Committee) in such manner as the Executive Committee shall deem best for the interests of the Corporation in all cases in which specific directions shall not have been given by the Board of Directors. . . .

The Finance Committee shall have special and general charge and control of all financial affairs of the Corporation and such other matters as may be assigned to it from time to time by the Board of Directors. The Secretary, Assistant Secretaries, Treasurer, Assistant Treasurers, Comptroller, Assistant Comptrollers, the Accounting Department and their respective offices shall be under the direct control and supervision of the Finance Committee.

During the intervals between the meetings of the Board of Directors, the Finance Committee shall possess and may exercise all the powers of the Board of Directors in the management of the financial affairs of the Corporation and such other matters as may be assigned to it from time to time by the Board of Directors, in such manner as said Committee shall deem to be best for the interests of the Corporation, in all cases in which specific directions have not been given by the Board of Directors.

Limitations on Powers. In spite of apparently sweeping powers given standing committees either in the bylaws or by resolutions of the board of directors, there are limitations upon their powers. They may act only on ordinary matters arising in the usual course of business. Exceptional matters should be passed upon by the whole board, for the validity of actions taken may otherwise be successfully attacked in the courts. The distinction between ordinary and exceptional matters depends on the manner in which the corporation has been conducting business and the nature of the question. Certainly, declarations of dividends, decisions substantially to expand operations of the corporation, new plant and property acquisitions and similar matters greatly affecting the corporation's finances and business should be voted on at meetings of the whole board. However, if a committee's action is ratified formally by the board, or if the board is made aware of such action and takes no step to rescind it, decisions of the committee become those of the board. The board may overrule its committees, unless rights of outsiders acquired by a committee's action will be impaired. The New York Business Corporation Law provides that committees shall have all the authority of the full board as to matters delegated to them, but excepts from this broad provision certain specified kinds of corporate action.

MEETINGS. Directors manage a corporation by **collective action.** Directors as individuals have the right to inspect the corporate books and otherwise to inform themselves of the affairs of the corporation, but can take no action as individuals. Directors must meet and, by concerted action, exercise their powers and perform their duties.

Bylaws prescribe the time and place of the regular meeting of the board, and specify the manner in which special meetings may be called. The bylaws can allow the directors to fix the place of their meetings. It is customary to provide that the president of the company or the chairman of the board may call a meeting upon a specified number of days' notice. **Informal meetings** may be validated even though not called in the manner prescribed in the bylaws, provided the directors sign a call and waiver of notice or, if they are already assembled, sign a written consent that is placed in the minutes. Small corporations frequently dispense with regular meetings where directors are actively engaged in the business and formal meetings are not necessary. However, when the statute requires formal action, a meeting must be held. A number of states, including Delaware, permit action to be taken by the board of directors by **written consent** of all of the directors **without a meeting.** The New York Business Corporation Law, does not, however, permit action of the board of directors without a meeting.

Special meetings of directors, unlike those of stockholders, may act upon any matter brought before them, and no statement of the purpose of the meeting need be included in the notice.

Quorums. Normally, a majority of the board of directors constitutes a quorum for the transaction of business. If a quorum is present at a meeting, an act of its majority binds the corporation. Many state statutes, after defining a quorum as a majority of the board, permit a greater, and in some instances, a lesser percentage to be fixed by the articles of incorporation or bylaws. Frequently, as in Delaware, where less than half of the directors may constitute a quorum, a minimum of one-third of the directors or two directors is specified in the statutes. New York permits a percentage more than one-half (without any limitation) to constitute a quorum by a provision of the certificate of incorporation, but notice of this provision must appear on the stock certificates.

Similarly, with respect to **action by a quorum,** a substantial number of state statutes permit the charter or bylaws to vary the usual role of a majority. This is so in New York (with the same requirement of notice).

To accommodate the corporate law to what is in fact an incorporated partnership, New York and North Carolina permit the shareholders of **closely held**

corporations by agreement to regulate directly the conduct of the corporate business.

Conflict of Interest. The courts have held that if a director who is interested in a particular matter votes on it, so that he forms a necessary part of a majority that acted affirmatively on it, the action taken is **voidable** by the corporation; nor can he be counted toward a **quorum**. A number of state statutes change this rule in various ways. California and North Carolina, for example, provide that a transaction involving **self-dealing** is not invalid if disclosure is made of the director's interest and if the transaction is approved by a sufficient number of disinterested directors or if it is just and reasonable. New York has a similar provision, requiring disclosure and that the transaction either be approved by a sufficient number of disinterested directors or by the stockholders or else be fair and reasonable when approved. Other state statutes provide that self-interest does not make a contract void or voidable, but places the burden of proof of fairness on the director. In some instances, state statutes permit interested directors to vote on particular matters, such as reasonable compensation and pension benefits to directors for services as directors or officers.

The **validity of contracts** between the corporation and the directors may also be affected by charter or bylaw provisions permitting an interested director to be counted toward a quorum or to vote on the matter in which he is interested. Such provisions have been held valid by the courts, although the contract or other arrangement may still be struck down, if it is found to involve unfairness to the corporation. Approval of the transaction by the stockholders may shift the burden of proof of unfairness to the one claiming that it exists. (Washington and Rothschild, Compensating the Corporate Executive.)

Corporate Officers

TITLES AND FUNCTIONS. The proper functioning of a corporation requires a minimum of three officers—a **president, secretary,** and **treasurer.** These offices may be filled, unless contrary to state law, by two persons, for the duties of secretary and treasurer do not conflict and may be combined in one person. Statutes prescribe the requirements either directly or by implication. They may state that there shall be a president, secretary, and treasurer, or they may refer to such officers in other provisions. The officers, their general duties, and any limitations on their powers should usually be prescribed in the bylaws, though provisions for this purpose can be included in the certificate of incorporation.

Frequently, the directors also elect **vice-presidents, assistant treasurers, assistant secretaries,** and a **controller** and, occasionally, an **auditor.** A number of larger organizations dignify heads of departments by making them vice-presidents. New business representatives of banks may be made assistant secretaries to give them more prestige. If there are a number of vice-presidents, one may be designated as first or executive vice-president to indicate that he will act for the president in the latter's absence. It is not unusual to combine the office of vice-president with that of treasurer or secretary.

QUALIFICATIONS. A number of statutes provide that the president must be chosen from among the directors. With the exception of this requirement, they leave the qualifications of officers to the bylaws. If the bylaws are silent, as they frequently are on this matter, the choice of officers is left freely to the directors. In small corporations, directors and officers are often the same persons.

The directors must rely on the officers to carry out their responsibilities faithfully and efficiently. If the officers fail, it is the board of directors who must bear the responsibility, since the officers are their agents in the management of the corporation's business. It is customary for the directors to fix the **officers' salaries**, although these are occasionally set in the bylaws.

POWERS AND DUTIES. Officers of a corporation derive their powers from (1) the statutes, (2) the charter, (3) the bylaws, (4) resolutions of the board of directors, and (5) custom or usage. For example, a statute may require the treasurer to render certain financial reports. The charter defines the type of business the officers are to conduct. Bylaws may require the president to preside at stockholders' meetings, the treasurer to prepare annual financial reports, and the secretary to prepare and mail notices and record the minutes of meetings. The board of directors may by resolution require officers to make certain reports, and may limit their powers or extend them beyond those ordinarily exercised.

Custom and usage, however, are the chief determinants of officers' powers, and define most of their duties. Officers have been found negligent by the courts because they did not perform the duties customarily exercised by corporate officers. Third parties have held corporations to contracts made by officers contrary to instructions in resolutions of the board or bylaws, because by ordinary usage they are considered to have had the right to believe that the officers had the power to make the contracts in question. The situation will vary from one corporation to another. In some corporations the **president** is chosen chiefly for his ability to promote sales, and manufacturing details are left to a technically trained general manager. In others, where the president's job is like that of a general manager, the powers ordinarily exercised by the president are possessed by the **chairman of the board** of directors.

The Treasurer. The treasurer is the **financial officer** of the corporation. Whereas the statutes are usually silent as to the many duties and responsibilities of the treasurer, bylaws frequently treat them in detail because of the importance of the office. The following **bylaw provisions** define the treasurer's duties and responsibilities in a typical manner:

The treasurer shall have custody of and be responsible for all money and securities of the company; shall keep full and accurate records and accounts in books belonging to the company, showing the transactions of the company, its accounts, liabilities, and financial condition, and shall see that all expenditures are duly authorized and are evidenced by proper receipt and vouchers. He shall deposit, in the name of the company, in such depository or depositories as are approved by the directors, all moneys that may come into his hands for the company's account. His books and accounts shall be open at all times during business hours to the inspection of any director of the company.

The treasurer shall also indorse for collection or deposit all bills, notes, checks, and other negotiable instruments of the company; shall pay out money as may be necessary in the transactions of the company, either by special or general direction of the board of directors, and on the checks signed by the president and himself and shall generally together with the president have supervision of the finances of the company.

He shall also make full report of the financial condition of the company for the annual meeting of the stockholders and shall make such other reports and statements as may be required of him by the board of directors or by the laws of the state.

He shall give bond in the sum of $ with sureties satisfactory to the board of directors for the faithful performance of his duties and for the restoration to the company in the event of his death, resignation or removal from office of all books, papers, vouchers, money and other property belonging to the company that may have come into his custody. He shall receive such compensation as may be fixed by the board of directors.

The treasurer of larger corporations may divide the responsibilities set forth in the above bylaw provisions with the **controller.** If there is a controller, the treasurer's primary duty is the custody of monies and securities, and he will have direct charge of the books of account which record changes in cash and securities owned. To this end, he will also maintain the corporation's bank account, probably act as a cosigner of checks, and will carry out the purchase and sale of securities. It is not the treasurer's duty to select the bank at which the corporation's funds are to be deposited, but he may recommend a bank to the directors.

As indicated in the above extract, the bylaws may require the treasurer to give a bond. Some states require the treasurer, and sometimes any corporate officer, to give a bond or other security.

Although the bylaws prescribe the duties of the treasurer he is **subordinate to the president** and the **board of directors,** who may prescribe the manner in which his duties are to be carried out and exercise supervision over him. There is nothing to prevent the directors or the president adding duties or responsibilities to those set forth in the bylaws.

The Controller. Large corporations usually have a controller or comptroller. This officer relieves the treasurer of the duty of keeping the books of account and other records of the corporation, leaving to the treasurer the handling of the corporate funds. The controller usually supervises all types of statistical reports used to control the operations of the corporation, and has direct charge of the **accounting department.** He is usually responsible for approving all vouchers before the treasurer may pay bills. Since his office is independent of the treasurer's, the corporation is thus provided with an additional check over its disbursements. The controller is responsible for the periodical internal audit of accounts and the preparation of unaudited financial reports.

It is to the controller that the president looks for records that measure operating efficiency. His duties go far beyond the determination of profit and loss after operations are complete. His function is dynamic, in that he is expected to establish the data and reports by which control over operations may be maintained at all times. Weaknesses and losses can then be checked before they become serious. Even in an organization of moderate size, the presence of a competent controller or an employee performing similar duties is highly desirable for efficient operation.

The Secretary. The secretary is the **recording officer** of the corporation. A few statutes impose specific duties upon the secretary. More frequently, the statutes impose duties upon the corporation, such as the preparation of an alphabetical list of stockholders, which either devolve upon the secretary under the bylaws or are performed by the secretary as one of the functions customarily undertaken by his office. Charters rarely mention the secretary, but the bylaws almost invariably place upon him such duties as acting as secretary at stockholders' and directors' meetings, mailing notices of meetings, keeping the minute books, and having custody of the corporate seal. Bylaws ordinarily include in the recital of the secretary's duties those specified by statute, in order to assign responsibility definitely and to make sure that these functions will not be overlooked.

Upon the secretary is placed responsibility for keeping the corporate officers informed of reports due governmental agencies. For this function he will keep in close touch with legal counsel for the corporation. The secretary, more than any other officer, is directly concerned with stockholder relations. He is responsible for the preparation of lists of those eligible to vote at meetings, notices of meetings, and the proper recording of resolutions. In many corporations, the secretary is in charge of the stock record books.

In **smaller corporations**, the secretary may be more concerned with the operation of the business than with the recording functions. In such cases, it may be prudent to engage legal counsel to see that corporate meetings are called properly, that the procedure called for by law is followed and that proper records are maintained.

COMPENSATION. Adequate incentive for corporate management has long been recognized as a problem in an economic system where ownership and management of enterprise have become separated to an increasing extent. Unless management has a stake in profits, those who conduct a business do not have the same pecuniary incentive to expand profits as did the entrepreneur of old, who owned as well as managed his business.

Bonuses, profit-sharing, stock ownership plans, and stock options have been widely used through the years to increase the incentives for management, over and above the fixed salaries paid. High personal income taxes, however, have tended to limit the effectiveness of such executive compensation plans. (Washington and Rothschild, Compensating the Corporate Executive.)

Another solution to the problem of adequate incentives for management is offered by Revenue Code provisions authorizing **pension and profit-sharing plans** that furnish benefits that are not taxable to the recipient currently as they are set aside for him. These plans, when approved on the basis of broad coverage and other standards set by law, provide deferred income to executives and other employees of a corporation that is taxable only when received after retirement or severance of employment. Beneficiaries may expect that they will be subject to lower rates of personal income rate taxation at that time because their ordinary income will be lower or will have ceased entirely. Should they not survive, their dependents will participate in death benefits provided.

These plans, which have gained greatly in popularity, may or may not be based on profit-sharing. Employee pension and profit-sharing plans are discussed at length in Sec. 19.

SECTION 13

CORPORATE STOCK

CONTENTS

Nature of Capital Stock

	PAGE
The stockholder's relationship to the corporation	1
Liability of holders	1
Stock certificates	1
Negotiability of stock certificates	2
Stock transfer procedure	3

Par Value of Corporate Stock

Use of par value	4
Legal significance of par value	4
Donated stock fiction	4
Valuation of property or services as payment for stock	5
"Full-paid and nonassessable"	5
Par value stock certificate (f. 1)	6
Low par value	6

No-Par Value Stock

Reasons for adoption	7
Stated value	7
True no-par	7
No-par stock in the balance sheet	8
Objectionable methods of presenting no-par stocks in balance sheet	9
Advantages of no-par stock	9
Disadvantages of no-par stock	9
No-par value stock certificate (f. 2)	10

Stock Terms and Definitions

Authorized stock	10
Reservation of authorized stock	11
Changes of authorized capital stock	11
Issued stock	12
Full-paid stock	12
Part-paid stock	12
Treasury stock	12
Reasons for acquisition	13
Methods of acquisition	13

Voting Power

Voting by stockholders	13
Cumulative voting	14
Contingent voting	15
Proxies	15
Proxy of stockholders (f. 3)	16
S.E.C. proxy regulations	16
Voting trusts	17

Stock Subscriptions

Legal status	18
Form of stock subscription (f. 4)	18

Preferred Stock

	PAGE
Classification of stock	19
Definition of preferred stock	19
Dividend preference	19
Classes of preferred stock	20
Participating preferred stock	20
Asset preference	20
Protective provisions	21
Voting power of preferred stock	21
Redeemable preferred stock	21
Convertible preferred stock	22

Other Classes of Stock

Classified common stocks	22
Voting and nonvoting common stock	23
Variation of dividend rights	23
Guaranteed stock	23
Founders' shares	23

Sale of Stock

Pre-emptive rights	24
Sale to stockholders	24
Sale to the general public	25
Sale of stock to employees	25
Sale of stock to customers	25

Stock Subscription Rights

Action by the board of directors	25
Action by stockholders	26
Letter to stockholders	26
Subscription warrants	26
Value of subscription rights	26
Subscription warrant for common stock (f. 5)	27
Market quotations for rights	28

Bonus Stock

Definition and uses	28
Consideration for bonus stock	28

Stock Purchase Warrants

Nature of stock purchase warrants	29
Detachable and nondetachable warrants	29
Duration of the option	29
Exercise of the option	30
Option warrants and pre-emptive rights	30

Fractional Shares

How fractional shares arise	30
Inconvenience caused by fractional shares	30
Methods of disposing of fractional shares	31

SECTION 13

CORPORATE STOCK

Nature of Capital Stock

THE STOCKHOLDER'S RELATIONSHIP TO THE CORPORATION. Ownership of a corporation is divided into **shares** of capital stock evidenced by **certificates** held by shareholders. A certificate may be issued for any number of shares, it being customary for a stockholder to have his total ownership in a corporation evidenced by one certificate. The owners' **equity,** or the interest of the shares, consists of the value of the assets, less sums due creditors. This equity, divided by the number of shares outstanding, yields a quotient which is the **book value** of each individual share. **Market value,** which usually varies widely from the book value, reflects the demand for, and the supply of, the shares, which are influenced primarily by the prospective earnings of the corporation. Stock may be preferred as to dividends and assets, but preferred shareholders are owners and not creditors. The return received by shareholders is a dividend, not interest, regardless of the terms of the stock issue.

Although some of the rights listed below are occasionally surrendered by shareholders, or exceptions to them are noted in the certificate of incorporation, stockholders of a corporation ordinarily possess the following rights:

1. To hold a proportionate ownership in the assets of the corporation, evidenced by a certificate.
2. To transfer ownership of their shares.
3. To receive dividends on their shares when declared by the board of directors.
4. To inspect the corporate books. However, this does not extend to an examination of the books of account or minutes of directors' meetings except under special circumstances.
5. To subscribe proportionately to any new issue of stock.
6. To vote at stockholders' meetings.
7. To vote on questions affecting the corporation property as a whole.
8. To protect the corporation against wrongful acts of management.
9. To restrain ultra vires acts of the corporation.
10. To share in the proceeds of dissolution.

Liability of Holders. Stockholders are ordinarily liable only for the loss of their interest in the corporation in the event of failure. New York's statute makes stockholders in some instances liable for wages due if not recoverable from the corporation; this liability is limited to corporations the stock of which is not listed or regularly traded in and to the ten largest stockholders of such corporations. Several other states, including Pennsylvania and Massachusetts, impose a liability on shareholders for salaries and wages owed to employees of the corporation. Formerly, stockholders of banks, national and state, were subject to double liability, but this has been generally eliminated.

STOCK CERTIFICATES. Stock certificates are written evidences of ownership of shares of stock. The issue of stock certificates is not necessary either to the existence of the corporation or to make one a stockholder in a corporation. A stockholder becomes a shareholder as soon as his subscription is received by the corporation and related statutory and charter provisions have been fulfilled.

If stock is purchased in the open market, the holder is not entitled to vote it or receive dividends on it from the corporation until the shares have been transferred to his name on the corporation's books. He has, however, a claim against the seller of the stock for dividends that accrue to the owner between the date of purchase and the date of transfer of shares.

The New York Stock Exchange does not permit its members to vote stock bought or sold for customers that is in process of transfer.

Negotiability of Stock Certificates. Stock certificates, being instruments evidencing participation in ownership rather than evidences of debt like promissory notes or bonds, are not inherently negotiable. The quality of negotiability is, however, conferred on stock certificates by the **Uniform Stock Transfer Act.** This Act permits transfer of title to corporate stock represented by certificates:

1. By delivery of the certificate, endorsed, either in blank or to a specified person, by the person appearing on the certificate to be the owner of the shares represented thereby; or
2. By delivery of the certificate and a separate document containing a **written assignment** of the certificate, signed by the person appearing on the certificate to be the owner of the shares represented thereby. Such assignment or power of attorney may be drawn either in blank or to a specified person.

The Uniform Stock Transfer Act was adopted in all the states and the District of Columbia. An increasing number of states, including New York, New Jersey, Illinois, Pennsylvania, and Massachusetts, have, however, replaced the Uniform Stock Transfer Act with the **Uniform Commercial Code,** which provides that investment securities, including stock certificates, are negotiable.

In addition, title to **stock seized by court order** may be transferred by separate instrument.

The usual practice when stock certificates are sold through brokers is to endorse them in blank. They may then pass through many hands before again being transferred on the books of the corporation to a new owner of record.

The negotiable instrument status given stock certificates greatly facilitates transfers. It is unnecessary to make an extensive investigation of the genuineness of the title of owners of stock certificates offered for sale. A purchaser for value of a **stolen certificate,** endorsed by the owner in blank, is secure in his title if he has no knowledge of the theft. It is necessary only that the holder be a **bona fide purchaser,** as defined by the Uniform Stock Transfer Act, "a purchaser for value in good faith, without notice of any facts making the transfer wrongful." The Uniform Commercial Code protects a purchaser who takes delivery "for value in good faith and without notice of any adverse claim."

The Uniform Stock Transfer Act is not applicable to certificates issued prior to the adoption of the Act. Except for Alaska, which adopted the Act in 1959, the latest adoptions of the Act were in the decade prior to 1950. The Uniform Commercial Code is applicable to transactions after its effective date. As to a **stock certificate not governed by the Act or the Code,** one who buys the certificate from a finder or thief acquires no title. But even as to certificates not covered by these statutes a bona fide purchaser, under judicial decisions, may be protected. A transferor cannot rescind a transfer of stock because the transferee obtained the certificate through fraud, duress, by mistake, or without consideration, if the certificate has been transferred to a bona fide purchaser for value.

Under the Uniform Stock Transfer Act assignments and transfers without actual **delivery** of the stock are considered merely promises to transfer. If the vendor does not deliver but instead transfers to another bona fide purchaser for value, the stock certificate cannot be recovered, the first buyer's only remedy being to sue the vendor for damages for breach of contract. This is also the case under the Uniform Commercial Code.

The Code provides that delivery of a certificate without **endorsement** transfers title as between the parties, but the recipient becomes a bona fide purchaser only when an endorsement is supplied. Under the Uniform Stock Transfer Act mere delivery of a certificate does not transfer title.

When **stock certificates are lost or accidentally destroyed,** before issuing new certificates corporation officers usually require that the owner set forth in an affidavit all the facts surrounding the loss, and that a **bond** be posted to secure the corporation against the possibility that the lost shares may be presented later by an innocent purchaser for value. If the corporation does not re-issue a lost certificate, it may be compelled to do so by judicial proceeding, as part of which the owner will be required to post a bond to protect the corporation from liability.

STOCK TRANSFER PROCEDURE. The transfer of stock in large corporations is facilitated by the use of transfer agents and registrars. Trust companies maintain facilities for handling economically large numbers of transfers that occur daily in the shares of corporations whose stocks are traded on the security markets.

A **transfer agent** supervises and certifies transfers of corporate stock. The extent of his supervision depends upon custom or his specific agreement with the corporation. He usually keeps the stock certificate book in his custody. When a transfer is to be made, the certificate of stock, duly assigned, is surrendered to the transfer agent, who thereupon cancels the surrendered certificate, attaches it to its proper stub in the stock transfer book, and then issues a new certificate in the name of the transferee. This certificate is sent to the proper corporate officials who affix their signatures and the corporate seal—unless the corporate seal is entrusted to the transfer agent—make the required entries in the transfer and stock books held by the corporation, and return the signed, or signed and sealed, certificate to the transfer agent. The transfer agent thereupon seals the certificate, if not already sealed by the corporation, certifies it has been duly issued, and delivers it to the transferee.

Occasionally, even though a transfer agent is employed, the stock certificate book is retained in the **custody of the corporation,** and when a certificate is presented for transfer it is cancelled by the transfer agent and turned over to the corporation in exchange for a new certificate issued in the name of the transferee. This certificate is then certified by the transfer agent and delivered to the owner. When the stock certificate book is kept by the corporation, the transfer agent keeps an independent record of stock certificates issued and surrendered, to assure the regularity of each issue or transfer.

A **registrar** supervises transfers of corporate stock to insure that certificates are properly issued. He maintains records of stock certificates issued and of the surrender and reissue of certificates, with the names of the parties involved in each transfer. The registrar passes upon each certificate at the time it is issued and countersigns evidence of due issuance. The duties of registrar and transfer agent are necessarily distinct, and cannot be performed by a single person or institution.

The work of a transfer agent or registrar, to be effective, must be discharged by persons of the highest character and unquestioned standing. Trust companies and banks are best qualified for these functions. Employment of transfer agents and registrars is generally advisable when transfers of stock are likely to be numerous. To effect transfers rapidly and accurately, the employment of a qualified transfer agent and registrar, or a transfer agent alone, is advisable. They relieve corporate officials of much detail and responsibility, reduce the possibility of fraud or error in the issuance of stock to a minimum, and afford safety and convenience not otherwise obtainable. Stock exchanges require that stocks listed by them shall be issued through suitable transfer agents and registrars.

Par Value of Corporate Stock

USE OF PAR VALUE. Capital stock may be assigned a par or fixed value in the certificate of incorporation. This value is printed upon the stock certificate. For many years the customary par value, except for quite speculative ventures, was $100, although $50 was favored by some Pennsylvania corporations. Today, the trend is toward the use of low par value shares.

LEGAL SIGNIFICANCE OF PAR VALUE. The par value of capital stock purports to represent the **minimum original investment** in cash, property, or services behind each share. The New York Business Corporation Law (Sec. 504 c) states: "Shares with par value may be issued for such consideration, not less than the par value thereof, as is fixed from time to time by the board." With regard to payment of dividends, the law states (Sec. 510 a1) that the net assets of the corporation (total assets minus total liabilities) remaining after such payment "shall at least equal the amount of its stated capital." The latter, in turn, is determined as follows (Sec. 506 a): "Upon issue by a corporation of shares with a par value, the consideration received therefor shall constitute stated capital to the extent at least of the par value of such shares."

These restrictions, which are similar to those in statutes of other states, are based on the premise that the par value, subject to the vicissitudes of business, is paid in for the **protection of creditors** and so is not available for dividends to stockholders. If stock is issued for cash at less than its par value, stockholders are liable for the deficiency, the stock being **part-paid and assessable.** If property or services exchanged for stock have been fraudulently overvalued, creditors have in some instances been able to have the stockholders held liable for the deficiency.

Banks and insurance companies under most state laws may issue only stock with par value, and regulatory authorities may require recapitalization or liquidation if the capital becomes impaired. Banks and insurance companies hold the funds of the general public, which is not in position to study the financial position of each institution, as do creditors of ordinary corporations. Hence regulatory authorities seek to protect public creditors by safeguarding the integrity of the capital as a cushion for creditors.

Donated Stock Fiction. A subterfuge, frequently resorted to before the widespread use of no-par and low-par value stock, for avoiding open violation of the rule against issue of stock below par, was for a stockholder to donate a substantial portion of his holding to the company and for the company to resell these shares, usually to raise working capital. As the **donated shares** became treasury stock, they then could be sold at any price, since the par value rule does not apply to the sale of treasury stock. The stock was originally issued to the donors at par for property or services presumably at a proper valuation. However, the very fact that they were ready to make the corporation a gratuitous gift of a considerable portion of their holdings was proof that they had secured the stock very cheaply, that the property or services they gave in exchange were greatly overvalued, and that the stock was actually exchanged at considerably less than par. This is a form of overcapitalization and results in what is referred to as **watered stock.** (Donaldson and Pfahl, Corporate Finance.)

Valuation of Property or Services as Payment for Stock. Such subterfuge as the donated stock fiction is only possible because of the leniency of the courts in placing a valuation on property or services given in payment of subscriptions to stock. Courts use one of two rules in deciding upon such questions of valuation. In some jurisdictions, the **"true value" rule** is employed. Here the motive, intent, and good faith of directors who take property or services in payment of stock subscriptions are disregarded, and the subscriber to stock who has given such property or services, in order to relieve himself of liability, must show that the property or services were actually worth in dollars and cents the face or par value of the shares. However, even here the court will be disposed to give the promoter the benefit of any doubt. In jurisdictions where the **"good faith" rule** prevails, courts will accept whatever valuation the directors have placed on such property or services, provided the parties to the transaction have acted fairly and in good faith. "In the majority of states, where the 'good faith' rule prevails, the creditors must prove not merely that the valuation was excessive, but also that it was fraudulent. Of course, this is a heavy task." (Bonbright, Col. Law Rev., vol. 24.)

The increasing tendency of **state statutes** is to make the **judgment of directors** as to the value of the property, labor, or other services received on stock subscriptions conclusive in the absence of actual fraud.

Trouble not infrequently arises with respect to property or services taken in payment of stock subscriptions because of failure of the management by formal action to place a valuation on the property or services. The valuation should be made by directors or stockholders and a formal record made of it. Some states specifically require this by statute. Many state statutes provide that neither promissory notes nor future services constitute payment or part payment for shares of stock.

"Full-Paid and Nonassessable." Certificates of par value capital stock are designated "full-paid and nonassessable," when a consideration at least equal to the par value has been paid for the shares. If the consideration received is less than the par value, but the certificates are nevertheless designated "full-paid and nonassessable," the corporation is estopped from assessing the stockholders for the deficiency. In a few jurisdictions, even creditors may not enforce payment of the unpaid balance, but the Federal and most state courts have followed the lead of the Supreme Court in holding that creditors not aware of the failure to pay in the full par value when they lent funds may be presumed to have relied on the par value of the shares as representing the capital of the corporation. They can compel **assessment of stockholders in the event of insolvency,** provided they can prove that the stock is in fact partly paid or that property and services received in payment for the shares were fraudulently overvalued. Creditors cannot complain, however, if they extended their loans prior to the issue of the stock and could not therefore be misled by it, or if they had knowledge of the facts about the stock issue when they made their loans. Creditors may waive their rights to enforce payment of the unpaid balance on partly paid stock. Many corporations insert a "no recourse" clause in mortgage indentures for bond issues, by which bondholders surrender the right to seek additional payments on partly paid stock that may be outstanding. State statutes vary as to the circumstances under which corporate creditors may proceed directly against stockholders on unpaid subscriptions. Fig. 1 shows the form of a par value stock certificate.

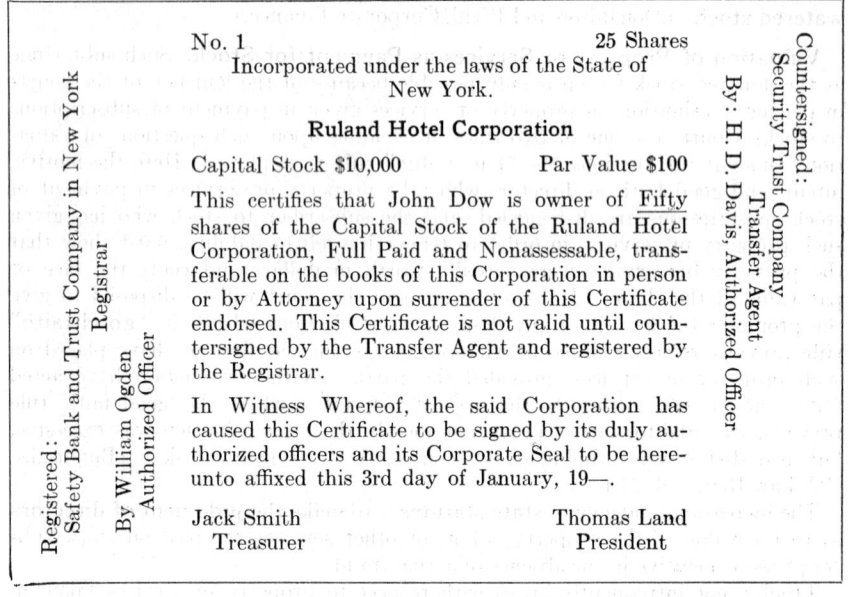

```
┌─────────────────────────────────────────────────────────────────────────┐
│                       No. 1                    25 Shares                │
│                 Incorporated under the laws of the State of             │
│                                 New York.                               │
│                                                                         │
│                           Ruland Hotel Corporation                      │
│                                                                         │
│                 Capital Stock $10,000         Par Value $100            │
│                                                                         │
│                 This certifies that John Dow is owner of Fifty          │
│                 shares of the Capital Stock of the Ruland Hotel         │
│                 Corporation, Full Paid and Nonassessable, trans-        │
│                 ferable on the books of this Corporation in person      │
│                 or by Attorney upon surrender of this Certificate       │
│                 endorsed. This Certificate is not valid until coun-     │
│                 tersigned by the Transfer Agent and registered by       │
│                 the Registrar.                                          │
│                                                                         │
│                 In Witness Whereof, the said Corporation has            │
│                 caused this Certificate to be signed by its duly au-    │
│                 thorized officers and its Corporate Seal to be here-    │
│                 unto affixed this 3rd day of January, 19—.              │
│                                                                         │
│                 Jack Smith                      Thomas Land             │
│                  Treasurer                        President             │
└─────────────────────────────────────────────────────────────────────────┘
```

Registered: Safety Bank and Trust Company in New York — By William Ogden, Authorized Officer — Registrar — Countersigned: Security Trust Company, Transfer Agent — By: H. D. Davis, Authorized Officer

Fig. 1. Par value stock certificate.

Low Par Value. The trend in corporate capitalization has been toward use of low-par value stock. Low-par value shares have frequently been exchanged for stock of a higher par or stated value by corporations desirous of creating a large capital surplus against which to charge asset write-downs or accumulated losses. These reductions in capital are effected with the consent of stockholders. When stock is sold above its par or stated value, it is said to be sold **at a premium**. Widespread use of low-par value shares has made the sale of stock at a premium quite common.

Many states tax no-par value shares as though they had a $100 par value. A tax saving is realized if low-par, rather than no-par, shares are used. Thus, New York levies an **organization tax** of "one-twentieth of one percentum upon the amount of the par value of all the shares with a par value which it is authorized to issue, and a tax of five cents on each share without a par value which it is authorized to issue." (New York Tax Law, section 180.) If 10,000 shares are sold at $5 a share, the corporation raises $50,000. The capital stock tax would be $500 with no-par shares, but only $25 if the shares are given a par value of $5.

The **Federal stock issue and transfer taxes** also formerly favored the use of low-par shares. The Federal issue and transfer taxes since 1959 have, however, been based on **actual value** as to issuance of stock and selling price or actual value as to transfers. The issuance tax is at the rate of 10 cents per share of actual value, with a rate of 4 cents per share applicable to regulated investment companies. On transfers the rate is 8 cents per share if the selling price is over $200 per share and, as to other transfers, 4 cents per $100 of actual value but not less than 4 cents per share.

No-Par Value Stock

REASONS FOR ADOPTION. No-par stock was first authorized in New York in 1912. It may now be issued under the statutes of all states except Nebraska and the District of Columbia.

The principal reason for the authorization of no-par shares was the desire to remove restrictions upon the selling price of newly issued shares. Par value stock cannot be sold below the par value without subjecting the purchaser to liability for the deficiency. But no-par value stock can be sold at any price, unless the statutes or charter establishes a minimum price. If the certificate of incorporation provides a **stated** value for no-par stock, the power to change the stated value may be given the board of directors. Thus, stock can be sold at a low price without resort to the fiction of issuing shares to promoters for overvalued property or services, and then having these shares donated back to the corporation so that they could be sold at a low price without subjecting the buyer to liability.

Some states provide that no-par value stock shall be given a stated value. In the absence of such stated value, the stock is **true no-par,** and all the consideration received from its sale is considered capital.

STATED VALUE. A stated value for no-par stock sets an amount that is entered on the corporation's books as **capital.** Any added consideration received from the sale of stock is designated as **capital surplus.** Some states prescribe a minimum below which the stated valued may not be fixed, usually $1 or $5. Sales of stock below its stated value may subject a buyer to liability. A low stated value permits the creation of a large initial capital surplus.

TRUE NO-PAR. True no-par stock has no stated value, but all the consideration received is considered capital. The New York Business Corporation Law provides that no-par shares may be issued for such consideration as is fixed by the board of directors, unless the **certificate of incorporation** reserves this right to the stockholders; if the right is reserved to the stockholders, they may either fix the price by a vote or delegate this right to the board of directors. This provision is similar to that of a number of states.

Under the **Delaware statute,** the board of directors has power to fix the issue price of no-par stock, unless this power is reserved to stockholders in the certificate of incorporation. In the latter event, exercise of the power is by two-thirds vote of stockholders entitled to vote in the matter—either by consent in writing or at a special meeting of the stockholders. Even if such power is reserved to the stockholders, the directors of a Delaware corporation may fix the consideration for a first issue of stock amounting to not more than 10% of the whole amount of authorized capital.

Some statutes permit the **sale of additional stock at any price to anyone,** in the discretion of the board of directors, if no restrictions are specified in the corporation's charter. However, courts of equity will protect stockholders against dilution of their equity by the sale of new shares to others much below the prevailing market value. (Note, Col. Law Rev., vol. 26.) The fact that the charter or statute gives the board of directors or majority of shareholders the right to issue no-par shares for such consideration as they deem best will not prevent courts of equity from intervening on an application of existing shareholders to enjoin a dilution of their shares by the issuance of new shares below their real value.

The courts also will intervene if no-par stock is sold at **different prices to different parties at the same time,** but such sales may be permissible on the basis of legitimate business considerations.

The use of no-par stock is now firmly fixed in American corporate practice. A number of states do not permit the use of no-par stock by monied corporations, such as banks and insurance companies. The statutes of Delaware, however, do not make this distinction. A holding company registered under the Public Utility Holding Company Act of 1935 is barred from selling no-par shares.

NO-PAR STOCK IN THE BALANCE SHEET. Considerable variation occurs in accounting for no-par stock issues in the balance sheet. The proper method with true no-par shares is to capitalize the entire consideration received from the sale of stock. If, however, there is a division of the consideration between the capital stock and the surplus account, as might not be improper under certain circumstances, that particular surplus account should be designated **Capital Surplus, Paid-in Surplus,** or by some other designation that will distinguish it from **earned surplus.**

Of every class of stock without par value, the number of shares issued as well as the total number authorized should be shown in the balance sheet. This applies as well to par value stock issues, but the par value of issued stock permits a reader to determine the number of shares. It is frequently the practice, however, to indicate the par value only when it is less than $100, particularly in the larger companies whose issues are dealt in on the exchanges. If the par value is not mentioned, it is understood to be $100.

The following examples illustrate actual balance sheet treatments of capital stock and surplus in a no-par stock issue:

CASE 1

6% cumulative preferred stock ($50 par value)	$30,333,900
Common stock (6,497,627 no-par shares)	64,976,270
Capital surplus	31,197,532
Undivided profits	50,212,546

1. The common stock of this company originally had a par value of $10. When exchanged for no-par stock, the shares were assigned a stated value of the same amount, which was retained in subsequent issues of the stock.

2. A considerable capital surplus has been accumulated from sales of common stock above the stated value, and of the preferred above the par value.

3. Earned surplus is designated "Undivided profits." As a matter of usage, the accounting profession now prefers the term "retained earnings" to "earned surplus." (Wixon, Accountants' Handbook.) Other acceptable variations are "retained income," "accumulated undistributed earnings," "earnings retained for use in the business," and "retained earnings reinvested."

CASE 2

Common stock (560,000 no-par shares)	$7,000,000
Surplus	3,651,503

1. Each share of this company represents $12.50 of the capital stock.

2. The surplus may or may not contain a portion of the stockholders' contributions. If it does, good practice requires that that portion be segregated in a separate account and properly labeled.

CASE 3

Preferred stock ($100 par value)	$3,361,300
Common stock (549,546 no-par shares)	9,736,998
Capital surplus	1,548,945
Current surplus	3,999,206

1. No stated value is indicated for the no-par common shares.
2. If the capital surplus is paid-in surplus, then the capital stock represents only a portion of the consideration received for the stock.
3. Current surplus is apparently earned surplus and is properly segregated from capital surplus.

CASE 4

Capital stock, no-par value (stated capital $1 per share). Authorized 400,000 shares, issued and outstanding 209,351 shares .... $ 209,351
Capital in excess of stated capital 3,882,128

In this case the item designated as capital stock is only a small fraction of the total amount paid in by shareholders.

OBJECTIONABLE METHODS OF PRESENTING NO-PAR STOCKS IN BALANCE SHEET. The following methods of setting forth no-par capital stock in the balance sheet are occasionally encountered, though they do not represent approved practice.

1. Failure to differentiate paid-in surplus from earned surplus, and the resulting inability of readers of the balance sheets to know whether dividends are being paid from accumulated earnings or from the previous contributions of stockholders.
2. Lumping capital stock and surplus together in one figure in the case of shares without stated value so that the reader is unable to learn what sum represents the stockholders' permanent investment and what sum represents earnings.
3. If there are two classes of stock—preferred and common—both of no-par value, their amounts may be merged together, and only the number of shares of each class outstanding is shown. There is nothing to indicate whether the preferred shares are carried at their paid-in value or their value in liquidation.

ADVANTAGES OF NO-PAR STOCK. Advantages claimed for no-par stock are:

1. Truthful representation of ownership. Regardless of the par value assigned to a share of stock, it represents fractional ownership in the corporation. A dollar par value may confuse uninformed purchasers, who may believe that because a share has a certain par value it is worth that amount. The buyer of no-par shares acquires only a proportionate share in the assets and earning power of a corporation.
2. Selling price may be adjusted to prevailing market quotations. Corporations may seek to sell stock when prevailing quotations are lower than the par value of the shares. Questionable practices were often used to create "full-paid" par value stock which could then be sold below par. With no-par stock this procedure is unnecessary, for it can ordinarily be sold at a price fixed by the board of directors.
3. Number of shares may be increased easily. If it appears desirable to increase the number of shares to effect wider distribution or prepare for new financing, it may be accomplished by a simple split-up of no-par shares. With par value stock, it would be necessary to reduce the par value or to declare a stock dividend. All that is necessary to split up no-par shares is the authority to issue more stock. If there is sufficient unissued stock available, the directors have the power to issue it; if not, an amendment of the certificate of incorporation is necessary.

DISADVANTAGES OF NO-PAR STOCK. The disadvantages of no-par stock are:

1. The courts insist that the capital of a corporation with no-par stock must be kept intact, which raises a number of problems as to how the amount of such capital shall be determined, and how it can be reduced when necessary.

2. Organization taxes on no-par stock sold below $100 are higher than on low-par stock in some states.

3. Stock transfer taxes may be higher on no-par stock, which is a disadvantage to the stockholder.

4. There is danger of impairment of the equity of old stockholders through the issue of no-par value stock for overvalued property, if the preemptive right to subscribe to new issues has been waived.

Generally speaking, no-par stock has disappointed the expectations of those who sponsored its introduction. It has given rise to legal and accounting complications and difficulties that were not then contemplated. Hence, the trend has been away from its use, and toward substitution of low-par stock, which is simpler and more certain in character. But experience with no-par stock did break down popular attachment to the $100 par value as a standard, and so paved the way for public acceptance of par values of $10, $5, $1, and in certain cases as low as 1 cent. A no-par value certificate is illustrated in Fig. 2.

No. 20   75 shares

Acme Realty Corporation

Incorporated under the Laws of the State of Delaware

Capital Stock

This is to certify that Richard Roe is the owner of ten shares, fully paid and nonassessable shares, without nominal or par value, of the Capital Stock of

Acme Realty Corporation

transferable on the books of the Corporation by the holder hereof in person or by duly authorized attorney upon surrender of this Certificate properly endorsed.

This Certificate is not valid unless countersigned by the Transfer Agent and registered by the Registrar.

In Witness Whereof, the Corporation has caused this Certificate to be executed by its duly authorized officers.

Dated Feb. 19—

Thomas Smith   Elmer Doe
  Secretary   President
              (Corporate Seal)

Registered:
Safety National Bank and Trust Company
New York
Registrar
J. P. Hoskins, Authorized Officer

Countersigned:
Security Trust Company
Transfer Agent
By: H. P. Davis, Authorized Officer

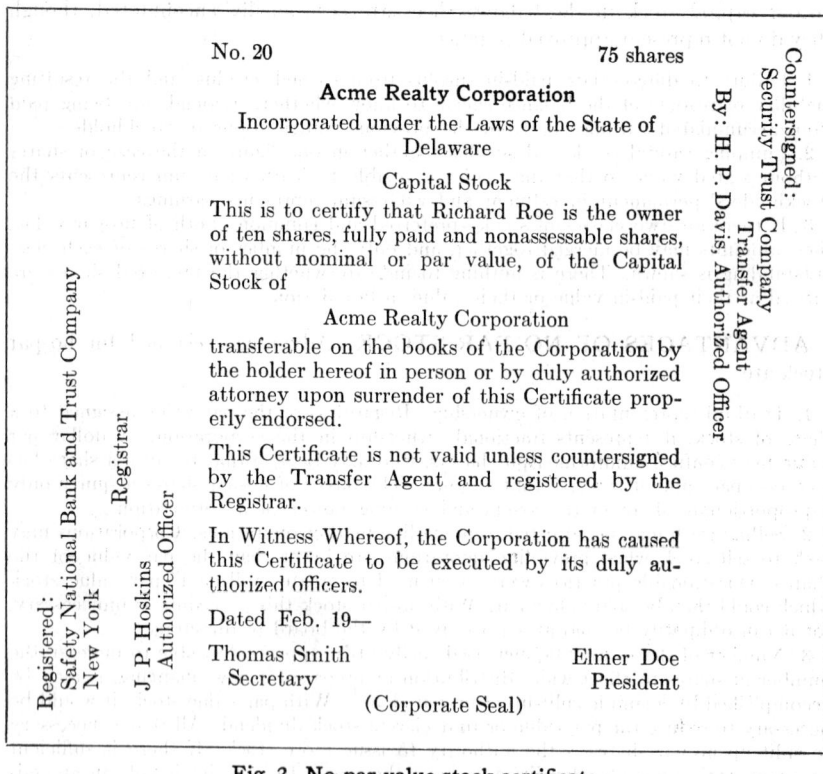

Fig. 2. No-par value stock certificate.

Stock Terms and Definitions

AUTHORIZED STOCK. The authorized stock of a corporation is specified in its certificate of incorporation. It is the maximum number of shares that may be issued. Should the corporation desire to increase or decrease the number of shares or change the par value, it will be necessary to submit the question to the stockholders at a meeting and, if approval is obtained, to file an amendment to the certificate of incorporation in the form and manner provided by the statute. If preferred stock is authorized or any special restrictions or privileges apply to a class of stock, this is set forth in the certificate of incorporation, and these too may be changed thereafter only by formal amendment of the charter.

RESERVATION OF AUTHORIZED STOCK. The authorized capital stock may or may not be issued in its entirety immediately upon the organization of the corporation, depending upon the company's policy. Particularly if it sees opportunities for future expansion by new acquisitions or otherwise, it will fix the authorized stock sufficiently high to have unissued stock constantly on hand.

If a company enters into contracts calling for the issue of stock at some time in the future, it will not only see to it that it has a sufficient amount of unissued stock for the purpose, but it may take the further step of reserving the required amount on its books. Some statutes—that of California, for example—**compel** a corporation to increase the authorized stock sufficiently when stock purchase warrants and convertible securities are issued. The Maryland statute provides, however, that authorization of convertible securities also includes the authorization of the stock into which they are convertible.

Some of the reasons making it desirable for a company to have a supply of authorized but unissued stock on hand are:

1. For **new financing,** whether a sale of additional shares to stockholders through issuance of rights, a sale to bankers, an exchange of shares for property or services, an exchange for securities in other corporations through merger, etc., or in payment of a debt.
2. To declare **stock dividends**—recurring or occasional.
3. For issuance to the management, promoters, bankers, or others to whom **options** to buy stock have been given by way of compensation given on a contingent basis. Such options will not ordinarily be exercised until the market value of the outstanding shares rises above this option price, but the corporation must stand ready to deliver shares to the option holder without delay upon application.
4. For issuance in **exchange** for bonds or preferred stock which is convertible into common stock. If the bonds are convertible into preferred stock, then a sufficient authorized amount of that issue must be held in reserve to meet all conversion requirements.
5. If stock purchase **warrants** are outstanding, carrying the privilege of purchasing the stock at a given price, a sufficient amount of authorized stock must be held available to meet the entire requirements of such options.
6. Shares may be reserved against an employee's stock **subscription plan** or against subscriptions by customers.
7. Shares may be reserved against **scrip dividends** convertible into the stock.

CHANGES OF AUTHORIZED CAPITAL STOCK. The authorized stock, fixed as it is by the charter, cannot be changed, whether in amount or in the classification of the shares, even with the consent of all the stockholders unless the power to change it has been expressly conferred upon corporations by statute. (Fletcher, Cyclopedia of the Law of Private Corporations.) In other words, a corporation has no implied authority to increase or diminish its capital stock. All states, however, by statute have conferred the right upon corporations to change their original capital stock and it is exercised generally by action of the stockholders. A change in the authorized stock necessitates **amending the charter,** and, although the general requirements of the various states are similar, the details vary and the statutes must be consulted in each case to determine just what is required. Usually the consent of a majority or two-thirds of the voting shares is necessary.

The changes in authorized capital stock most commonly made are:

1. Increase or decrease of the amount of authorized capital stock.
2. Increase or decrease of the number of shares.
3. Increase or decrease of the par value of shares with or without a change in the amount of authorized capital stock. If the authorized capital stock is not changed, a change in the par value necessitates the reverse change in the number of shares.
4. Change of par value shares to shares without par value or reverse.
5. Creation of one or more classes with specified preferences.
6. Change of common stock to preferred stock, or of preferred stock to common stock.
7. Change of preferences of existing preferred stock.

ISSUED STOCK. When a corporation sells its stock, the shares sold are termed issued stock. As long as it remains in the hands of stockholders it is known as **outstanding** stock, losing that status only when reacquired by the corporation.

FULL–PAID STOCK. Stock is full paid when the corporation has received payment up to the full par value, or up to the amount established as the selling price of no-par shares. Payment may be in cash, in real, personal, or intangible property, and in services (labor done). If property and services received for stock are overvalued, **watered** stock results. Since the passage of the Federal Securities Act, which requires the filing of a prospectus showing among other information the details of such transactions, it has become increasingly difficult for promoters, incorporators, and directors to issue excessive amounts of stock for property and services.

PART–PAID STOCK. Part-paid stock, as the name indicates, is stock which has been issued for less than the par value or the agreed subscription price. Statutory authority is necessary for the issuance of stock as partly paid and subject to call for additional payments by stockholders. The issuance of partly paid stock, with the amount paid shown on the face or back of the certificate, is authorized by the Delaware statute. The practice is not common in American financial practice, but it is quite common in England and other countries. Stock sold in this country on the installment plan is usually not issued until the final installment has been paid. Often stock offered on the installment plan was previously issued fully paid and was subsequently reacquired by the corporation for the express purpose of making it available to employees through installment purchase agreements. A **public sale** of stock that is only part paid, with the attendant danger of liability to creditors or further call by the board of directors, is normally impracticable. Practice dictates that stock sold to the public be "full paid and nonassessable." Even where **private sale** rather than public is contemplated, the possibility of issuing stock that is not fully paid is seldom considered.

TREASURY STOCK. Treasury stock is stock that has been issued as full paid and nonassessable and has come back into the possession of the issuing company by purchase, gift, or otherwise, and is kept alive in the corporation's treasury. It is issued but no longer outstanding stock. **Unissued stock,** whether or not reserved for a particular purpose, is not treasury stock. The term "treasury stock" is properly used to designate only the shares of its own stock which a company has acquired and which are held subject to disposal by its directors or its stockholders. It is not an asset of the company and should not be included in the current assets. Nor should it be lumped with the company's security investments in other concerns. It should be set out separately on the balance sheet, preferably as a **deduction from outstanding stock** if its reissue within the near future is not contemplated.

Stock once issued for its full par value or otherwise fully paid has a different status from the same stock before issue. It is full-paid stock, and may be resold at any price regardless of par value or previous issue price; or it may be given away as a bonus with preferred stock or bonds, or sold to employees, or be otherwise issued without involving the recipient in liability to the corporation or its creditors; generally such stock may be sold without violating the pre-emptive right of stockholders, but some state statutes make pre-emptive rights applicable to treasury stock. So long as the stock is held by the corporation in its treasury, it is inert and can neither vote nor participate in dividends.

Reasons for Acquisition. Some reasons for a corporation acquiring its own shares are:

1. To acquire shares for mergers, sale to officers or employees, or other corporate purpose, so that outstanding capital stock need not be increased.
2. To reduce outstanding stock when it is felt that the earnings of the corporation may decline.
3. To acquire a block of stock from the estate of a large stockholder or others, if such stock would otherwise be acquired by unfriendly interests or competitors.
4. To buy shares from a stockholder in a closed corporation who is desirous of disposing of his interest, for which there is no market.
5. To declare a dividend in treasury stock.
6. To prepare for the retirement of an issue of stock. This is quite common if an issue of preferred stock is outstanding and the corporation wishes to eliminate it.
7. To have stock available for the exercise of stock options and warrants.

Methods of Acquisition. There are two common methods by which treasury stock may be acquired:

1. By **purchase.** A corporation may in most states purchase its own stock, provided that in so doing it does not impair capital; a number of state statutes require stockholder approval if capital surplus rather than earned surplus is to be used for such a purchase.

2. By **donation.** A corporation's stock may be donated to the corporation for a number of reasons. In the days before no-par stock had been legalized and a low par value was considered inexpedient, promoters were liberally paid for property and expenses in stock and immediately donated some of this stock back to the corporation. As it had been issued as fully paid stock, it could then be sold at a price below the $100 par value. Stock may be donated to the corporation in the same manner to facilitate the sale of preferred stock through giving common with each preferred share as a bonus. Large stockholders may donate stock in a time of stress to help the corporation raise cash. They may donate shares to be used as a bonus for officers or employees. A large stockholder may donate stock to eliminate a profit and loss deficit.

Voting Power

VOTING BY STOCKHOLDERS. The right to vote is a fundamental right of the stockholder. Unless restricted by the charter for certain classes of stock, this right cannot be questioned.

At **common law,** the right to vote was given the individual stockholder, and not his stock. Each stockholder had one vote regardless of the number of shares owned. This is still the rule in England, unless the corporate "regulations" (bylaws) provide otherwise. In the United States, the statutes of the states give to each stockholder as many votes as he has shares of stock. In fact, this practice is so universal that the right can be said to exist by usage, so that even in the absence of statutory provision it has long been enforced by the courts on that ground. (Western Cottage Corp., etc. v. Burrows, 144 Ill. App. 350, 370 [1908].)

Corporations owning stock in other corporations may vote such shares through authorized representatives, as can natural persons. However, it is well established in law that a corporation may not in any manner vote its own stock which it may have acquired and have in its treasury.

The bylaws usually authorize **closing of the transfer books** for some period prior to the meeting, so that ownership of the shares and the names of those entitled to vote may be determined. The same purpose is served by a bylaw permitting the secretary to limit the right to vote to stockholders of record at the close of business on some day prior to the meeting. This is the usual practice of corporations whose stock frequently changes ownership, common among large corporations.

A majority vote of the shares present at a meeting (provided a quorum is present) is necessary to elect a director or pass a resolution if **statutory voting** is used. A mere plurality of the votes would not be sufficient to elect a director. For example, at a stockholders' meeting with 300 voting shares present for the election of a director, the leading candidate received 150 votes. No director is elected, for while the first candidate has a plurality, he lacks one vote of having a majority. Each director is balloted for separately, hence ownership of a majority of the shares will elect all of the directors. As to specified matters, such as merger and consolidation, sale or mortgage of assets not in the regular course of business, amendment of the certificate of incorporation or dissolution, a two-thirds majority may be required. In addition, many state statutes permit the certificate of incorporation to require the affirmative vote of a greater proportion of the stock than would otherwise be required.

Cumulative Voting. Cumulative voting is designed to enable a minority of the stockholders, who under statutory voting would not be able to elect a director, to gain representation on the board. This method of voting is mandatory by constitution or statute in some states; in a large number of other states, the statutes permit the certificate of incorporation to provide for such a method of voting. Courts have disagreed as to whether cumulative voting may be applicable by statute to pre-existing corporations. Under cumulative voting, each stockholder is entitled to as many votes as he has shares of stock, multiplied by the number of directors to be elected. He can then concentrate his votes on one candidate or upon as few as he desires, for in cumulative voting a plurality and not a majority of votes is necessary for election.

If a corporation has 300 shares of voting stock represented at the stockholders' meeting, there are five directors to be elected and the minority owns 148 shares, it would be entitled to 740 votes. If the minority wished to elect two candidates, it would cast 370 votes for each. The majority interest owning 152 shares is entitled to 760 votes, so that if it spreads these votes over five candidates each would receive 152 votes, and over four candidates 190 votes. Thus, it is useless for the majority to spread its votes over more than three candidates who would be unopposed, as the minority would have no votes left after having used its voting power to assure the election of two directors.

To determine how to vote shares with cumulative voting for the election of directors to best advantage, the following formula is used:

$$\text{Minimum number of shares required} = \frac{\text{Total number of shares outstanding} \times \text{Number of directors desired}}{\text{Total number of directors to be elected} + 1} + 1$$

To elect one director in the case of the corporation having 300 shares outstanding, a minority would need $\left(\frac{300 \times 1}{6} + 1\right)$ or 51 shares, with 255 votes, all to be cast for one director. Thus, ownership of 17% of the voting stock would be sufficient to insure representation on the board of directors for the minority.

CONTINGENT VOTING. Ordinary voting privileges are often denied **preferred stockholders.** In exchange for the preferential right to a stipulated rate of dividend before any dividend may be paid on the common stock, the purchaser of preferred stock surrenders his right to vote. However, there is often a provision that, in the event no dividends are paid for a specified period, the preferred stocks shall have voting power. This may consist of a power to elect one or two members to the board of directors, if such directors constitute a minority of the whole board. Some charters go further and give the preferred stockholders exclusive or majority voting rights until dividend arrears have been paid up. The number of dividend payments that must be passed before preferred stockholders receive the voting privilege varies from one corporation to another. Failure to pay a full year's dividend is a common stipulation.

Statutes in a number of states provide that preferred stockholders, even though nonvoting on ordinary matters, have the **right to vote on questions affecting the status of the corporation's property as a whole.** Such questions as mortgaging or selling the corporation's property or franchise, guaranteeing bonds of another corporation, voluntary dissolution, and merger or consolidation with another corporation are in this category. Most state statutes give holders of preferred stock a right to vote as a class on amendments to the certificate of incorporation modifying the rights of their class of stock in relation to other classes of stock. To deny nonvoting stockholders the right to vote in the above contingencies, it must be specifically excluded by charter.

PROXIES. Under the common law, each stockholder had to be present at the meeting. He could not delegate to another the right to attend and cast his vote. The practice of giving a **power of attorney** to another to attend the stockholders' meeting and vote the shares has become so common, however, that it is now accepted usage even where not specifically authorized by statute. State statutes provide in some instances that a proxy is not valid beyond a certain period, such as eleven months, unless otherwise provided in the proxy.

A proxy is a power of attorney to vote corporate stock. It is **revocable** like any other agency, therefore, unless coupled with an interest, such as proxies given to one who holds the stock as security for a loan. Personal attendance by a stockholder at a meeting cancels any proxy that he may have given. A proxy with a later date than one previously given automatically cancels the first proxy. Under the principles of the law of agency, the death of the stockholder also cancels a proxy. Statutes in some states provide that revocation of a proxy is effective only after notice to the secretary of the corporation.

Proxies usually **authorize the holder** not only to vote for directors, but also to vote on other questions that may come up at the meeting. In practice, most proxies are given for a specific meeting and any adjournments thereof.

A proxy is shown in Fig. 3.

```
PROXY                    AMERICAN CAN COMPANY
                    ANNUAL MEETING OF STOCKHOLDERS, APRIL 24, 19—
                         THE CONRAD HILTON, 7th AND 8th STREETS
                       AT SOUTH MICHIGAN BOULEVARD, CHICAGO, ILLINOIS

    The undersigned hereby appoints WILLIAM C. STOLK, WILLIAM E. BUCHANAN, WILLIAM EWING
and JOHN R. HENRY, and each of them, proxies, with full power of substitution, to vote for the
undersigned all shares of stock of AMERICAN CAN COMPANY which the undersigned would be
entitled to vote if personally present at the Annual Meeting of Stockholders to be held on April 24,
1962, at 10:00 A.M., Central Standard Time, and at any adjournment thereof, upon the matters set
forth in the Notice of such meeting. Said proxies are directed to vote pursuant to the Proxy Statement
for the election of the persons nominated therein as directors, as checked below upon the following
matters, and otherwise in their discretion:

Management recommends a vote FOR        ☐ FOR      Proposal 1 — To elect Lybrand, Ross
                                        ☐ AGAINST    Bros. & Montgomery as auditors.

                                        ☐ FOR      Proposal 2 — By two stockholders, con-
Management recommends a vote AGAINST    ☐ AGAINST    cerning stock options.

                                        ☐ FOR      Proposal 3 — By two stockholders, con-
Management recommends a vote AGAINST    ☐ AGAINST    cerning the Company's annual proxy
                                                     statement.

                                        ☐ FOR      Proposal 4 — By two stockholders, con-
Management recommends a vote AGAINST    ☐ AGAINST    cerning cumulative voting.
                                                                                    (over)

        If not otherwise specified on the reverse side, this Proxy will be voted FOR Proposal 1 and
    AGAINST Proposals 2, 3 and 4.

    Dated.................19—.

    Sign exactly as name appears below. For
    joint accounts all co-owners must sign.     Signed..........................................
           THIS PROXY IS SOLICITED ON BEHALF OF THE MANAGEMENT.
```

Fig. 3. Proxy of stockholders.

S.E.C. Proxy Regulations. The Securities and Exchange Commission, acting under section 14 of the Securities Exchange Act of 1934, issued its Regulation X-14, Rules Relating to the Solicitation of Proxies, which requires that substantially the following items of information be provided holders of stock registered on national security exchanges, when they are asked for proxies to be voted at stockholders' meetings:

1. The revocability of the proxy.
2. A dissenter's right of appraisal on any matter to be acted upon, his right to surrender his holdings at an appraised price.
3. Identification of persons making the solicitation, how it will be made, and who will bear the cost.
4. Any substantial interest of certain persons in matters to be acted upon, security holdings or other interest of those soliciting the proxy or of those nominated for election as directors.
5. The number of outstanding shares of voting securities and the principal holders thereof; the existence of cumulative voting rights.
6. If there is to be an election of directors, the nominees and directors presently in office whose terms will continue.
7. The remuneration of interested directors, nominees for director, or officers, if there is to be an election or consideration of any bonus, profit sharing, or

other remuneration plan, or any material transaction in which any director, nominee for election as a director, or officer will participate or has participated during the last fiscal year.
8. Details as to the selection of auditors, identification, and description of any financial interest that they may have in the company.
9. Any bonus, profit sharing, and other remuneration plans that are to be acted upon.
10. Any pension and retirement plans that are to be acted upon.
11. Any options, warrants, or rights that are to be granted or extended.
12. The authorization or issuance of securities otherwise than for exchange for outstanding securities.
13. Any action that will be taken for the modification or exchange of securities.
14. Any plans for mergers, acquisitions, or similar matters.
15. If any matter specified in 12, 13, or 14 above is to be included, certified financial statements.
16. Any acquisition or disposition of property.
17. Any planned restatement of accounts.
18. Action with respect to reports of the company or its directors.
19. Matters not required to be submitted to a vote of security holders but that will be submitted.
20. Any proposed amendment of charter, by-laws, or other documents.
21. Other proposed actions not referred to above must be briefly described.

The **latest amendments** to the Securities Acts and the Regulations and Rules of the Securities and Exchange Commission are published commercially in the form of a looseleaf service. (Federal Securities Law Reports, vol. 2, Commerce Clearing House.)

These regulations are chiefly concerned with the solicitation of proxies by or on behalf of management. Information is, however, also required as to **persons other than the management** soliciting proxies in a proxy contest. The information specified by the regulations must be given in the **letter soliciting the proxy.** Letters soliciting proxies for a meeting for election of directors must also be accompanied ordinarily by a financial statement of the corporation for the preceding fiscal year. The S.E.C. requires that space be provided in proxies for a direction to vote "no," if the stockholder so wishes, on each matter to be acted upon at the meeting. Proposals that minority stockholders intend to bring up at the meeting, and of which they have informed management, must be tersely described in the solicitation.

At the request of any security holder, a management sending out a request for a proxy must disclose the **approximate number of holders** of each class of stock being solicited and the **cost of mailing.** The management must send out proxy solicitations or other communications for other shareholders, upon receipt of their written request to do so, delivery of the material, envelopes, and postage, and "reasonable reimbursement of all expenses incurred in such mailing."

Preliminary copies of the proxies must be filed with the commission at least 10 days prior to mailing to security holders. The commission advises that final printing not take place until its comments have been received.

Stock listed on an exchange may be held by a member firm in a **street name.** Rules of the New York Stock Exchange and the American Stock Exchange require the transmission to customers of proxy material held in street names with a request for instructions and notice that the stock may be voted at the firm's discretion in the absence of instructions.

VOTING TRUSTS. Under a voting trust, stockholders assign legal title to their shares to trustees in return for transferable **voting trust certificates.** The trustees thus acquire the power to vote the stock for the duration of the trust without interference from the beneficiaries. The terms of the agreement require the trustees to distribute any dividends, rights, or benefits which may accrue during the life of the trust. Statutes usually place a definite limitation on the life of a voting trust (10 years in New York and Delaware), or require that a limit be fixed. Some state statutes (as New York and Delaware) provide for extensions or renewals of a voting trust agreement within a specified period prior to its expiration. In the absence of such a statutory provision, a new voting trust may be created only following the expiration of the term of the prior agreement.

A common reason for the creation of a voting trust is to insure **continuity of control** over the business for the life of the trust. Transfer of voting trust certificates does not affect control. A majority of stockholders may thereby insure continuance of control over a long period, even though ownership of their stock should change. Another frequent use is in connection with **corporate reorganizations**, with the voting trustees, usually appointed by the court, controlling the affairs of the reorganized company for a specified period of time.

Stock Subscriptions

LEGAL STATUS. A subscription to capital stock (Fig. 4) is an offer to purchase shares in a corporation. When the subscription is accepted, a binding sale of the stock results. The subscriber then becomes a stockholder at once, with the benefits and liabilities involved, later issuance of the actual certificate merely providing him with evidence of his holdings. A subscription must be dis-

---

Acme Shoe Manufacturing Co., Inc.

Incorporated Under the Laws of the State of Delaware

Authorized issue 5,000 shares common
without par value.

I .... hereby subscribe for .... shares of the Capital stock of the Acme Shoe Manufacturing Company, and, upon the call of the treasurer of said company, agree to pay therefor the sum of .... dollars ($...............).

Subscriber ....

Address ....

Witnessed:
.... Agent

Fig. 4. Form of stock subscription.

tinguished from an **agreement** to subscribe to stock in the future. Failure to fulfill the agreement will not subject the would-be purchaser to liability as a stockholder, but only to damages for breach of his agreement. A subscription agreement should also be distinguished from a **purchase** or an agreement to purchase stock from another stockholder. A subscription is associated with **original issuance** of stock by a corporation. An agreement to purchase or a purchase of treasury stock is a purchase transaction and not a subscription.

Preferred Stock

CLASSIFICATION OF STOCK. The charter of a corporation may provide for the issuance of more than one class of stock. The most common classification is into preferred and common stock. Preferred stock is given a preference over common in the distribution of dividends, and may also be given other preferences. Voting rights may be denied these preferred classes in exchange for the preferences given, or voting rights may be made contingent upon failure to pay dividends on preferred stock for a certain period of time. Within the general definitions of the various types of preferred stock to be subsequently described, there are literally hundreds of possible minor variations in the rights, privileges, and restrictions specified. The impact of the Federal corporate income tax has been to reduce the use of preferred stock paying nondeductible dividends in favor of debentures paying deductible interest. As investments, preferred stocks are attractive to some corporations because dividends received by corporations are taxable at reduced rates whereas interest is fully taxable.

DEFINITION OF PREFERRED STOCK. Preferred stock is stock that, by the certificate of incorporation or the bylaws, has been given a preference over the common stock in respect to **dividends**. It is usually stipulated that the preferred stock will receive a certain rate of dividend before dividends will be paid upon the common stock. Preferred shares may be preferred also as regards **distribution of assets upon dissolution** and have other privileges not enjoyed by the common stockholders, but the dividend preference feature is the most important. If there are no further stipulations, preferred stock will in other respect have all the rights of the common stock.

DIVIDEND PREFERENCE. Dividends on preferred stock with par value are expressed as a **percentage of the par value**. "Preferred as to dividends at the rate of 6% per share" is a typical charter provision. Some issues of preferred stock are **without par value,** and the dividend is then expressed as so many dollars and cents per share, such as "preferred as to dividends in the amount of $5.00 annually." Preferred stockholders, like common stockholders, are entitled to dividends only when declared by the board of directors. The dividend becomes a debt of the corporation only after directors have declared it. Dividend rates vary greatly. Some issues sold in the period from 1920 to 1927 bore rates as high as 8%. Rates of 5% and lower became more common thereafter.

If preferred stock is **cumulative,** dividends not paid in any year will accumulate and must be paid at a later date before dividends can be paid on the common stock. Unless a contrary intent appears, a statement that preferred dividends "will be paid out of the profits of each year," even though the word "cumulative" is not used, may be held to make the stock cumulative. The New Jersey courts developed a "dividend credit" rule as to noncumulative preferred stock, holding that unpaid dividends accumulated to the extent earned in years in which the corporation had profits, and had to be paid before any dividend could be distributed to the common stock. But in the leading case, that of the Wabash Railway, the United States Supreme Court held that dividends do not accumulate on noncumulative preferred stocks, even if earned, provided that the issuing corporation uses the retained earnings for justifiable capital improvements. (Barclay v. Wabash Railway, 250 U.S. 197, decided in 1930.) The court said:

> When the net profits of a corporation out of which a dividend might have been declared for the preferred stock, are justifiably applied by the directors to capital im-

provements, the claim of the stock for that year is gone, if by the terms of the articles of incorporation and the certificates, the preferential dividends are not to be cumulative. The fact that there were profits in that year out of which dividends might have been (but were not) declared does not entitle such stock to a correspondingly greater preference over other stock when the profits of a later year are to be divided.

CLASSES OF PREFERRED STOCK. A corporation may have more than one class of preferred stock. Also, one class of preferred stock may be issued in several **series**, each receiving a different rate of dividends or differing in some other characteristic, but all enjoying the same degree of preference over the common. Each series is usually designated by a **letter**, as Preferred A and Preferred B.

Each class of preferred stock has a different **degree** of preference. For example, there may be a 6% first preferred stock and a second preferred with a preference of 8% that is entitled to dividends only after dividends have been declared on the first preferred. Some companies have put out as many as five different classes of preferred, usually in reorganizations, almost equaling some of the joint stock companies of the sixteenth century that, according to W. R. Scott (Joint Stock Companies to 1720), had as many as seven or eight different classes.

PARTICIPATING PREFERRED STOCK. Participating preferred stock is entitled to dividends in excess of the stipulated preferential rate, under specified conditions. The question whether preferred stock is participating where this feature is not expressly stipulated in the charter has been decided differently in several jurisdictions, but the majority view is to the effect that in such a case the preferred stock is not entitled to dividends beyond its stated preferential rate. (Fletcher, Cyclopedia of the Law of Private Corporations.) The courts that have held preferred stock to be nonparticipating have considered the stated preferential rate to be also a statement of limitation. To avoid the possibility of a preferred stock being held to be participating, the phrase "preferred as to dividends at the rate of ....% per annum, and **no more**" is frequently used.

The most common form of participation is to permit the preferred to share with the common in further dividend distributions, after both have received the preferential rate of dividend on the preferred. There are many types of special participation. It may be provided, for example, that after having been paid a preferential dividend of $3 per share and the common has received $1 per share, the preferred will be entitled to a further distribution of $1 per share before additional dividends are paid on the common stock, or to share *pari passu* with the common up to $1 more. The vast majority of preferred stocks are nonparticipating.

ASSET PREFERENCE. If a preferred stock is, by the terms of the certificate of incorporation, preferred as to dividends only, it will share pro rata with the common stock upon dissolution. However, preferred stock is frequently **preferred as to assets** at dissolution. The preference may be to the amount of the par value or, if the stock is without par value, for a stated amount. A distinction is not infrequently made between **involuntary and voluntary dissolution**, and in the latter case the amount of the asset preference may be higher. Preference as to assets may be of substantial value to stockholders in case of reorganization, establishing a priority for them, or of dissolution required by law, as under the Public Utility Holding Company Act. If the amount of the asset preference of preferred stock in liquidation is not clear, the Securities and Exchange Commission held that the shares should receive their **fair investment value.**

Although the matter is by no means uniformly settled, the weight of authority in the United States is that the inclusion of a preference as to assets in the preferred stock contracts limits holders to the amount of this preference. There is a conflict in court decisions as to whether accrued dividends must be paid if there were no profits even though the contract reads "preferred as to assets up to par value and cumulative dividends." But the great weight of authority is in favor of the payment of accrued dividends to holders of cumulative preferred stock upon dissolution, regardless of the earnings record. (Fletcher, Cyclopedia of the Law of Private Corporations, vol. 12, section 5449.)

PROTECTIVE PROVISIONS. Occasionally provisions are included in the charter to lend protection to the preferred stock. For example, it may be provided that no bond issue and no stock issue with superior preferential rights shall be put out without the consent of two-thirds of the preferred stock, or that the property of the corporation may not be subjected to a mortgage without the consent of the preferred. In some instances, the charter stipulates that a sinking fund will be put aside each year for the redemption of the preferred stock. Sometimes, it is required that common dividends shall not be paid if this will reduce current assets to less than twice current liabilities, or until a reserve for, say, 2 years' preferred dividends has been set aside.

VOTING POWER OF PREFERRED STOCK. The right to vote is a fundamental right of all stockholders, both preferred and common. The terms of the preferred stock contract may deny all voting rights to the preferred, or it may give the preferred the right to vote only under specified conditions, of which the following example is typical:

The holders of the preferred stock shall not be entitled to vote at any meeting of stockholders, provided, however, that if at any time the amount of four quarterly dividend payments on the preferred stock (whether or not consecutive) shall have accumulated and remain unpaid, then the holders of the preferred stock shall have the same right to vote as the holders of the common stock, so long as any accumulated dividends on the preferred stock remain unpaid.

Sometimes preferred stock is given exclusive voting rights if a given number of quarterly dividends remain unpaid. The Securities and Exchange Commission and the stock exchanges oppose the issue of preferred stock without contingent voting privileges. The New York Stock Exchange will not list preferred stock unless the preferred stockholders are given the right to elect at least two directors if as many as six quarterly dividends are passed; also, to approve by at least a two-thirds majority charter or bylaw amendments that may materially affect their position. Illinois does not permit the issuance of nonvoting stock.

The corporation **statutes** of a state may provide that on certain propositions the preferred stock shall have the right to vote. These include the sale or mortgage of assets not in the regular course of business, amendments to the certificate of incorporation changing the priorities of classes of stock, merger or consolidation, and voluntary liquidation.

REDEEMABLE PREFERRED STOCK. Preferred stock, especially if it carries a high dividend rate, is likely to be made redeemable or, as it is more often termed, **callable.** Such a provision in the preferred stock contract gives to the corporation the right to call in the preferred stock at a stated **call or redemption**

price on advance notice of, say, 30 days or so many months. It is customary to set a call price above the par value, to compensate the owner for the involuntary loss of his investment. Redemption provisions may merely establish the right to call in the stock, or may require the corporation to establish a **sinking fund** for the redemption of a stipulated amount of stock each year.

The reason a corporation wants the option to redeem is to enable it at some future date to retire the issue to reduce preferred dividend requirements or because some other provision proves burdensome. The preferred stock may have been sold when the corporation had no other alternative, and the management had no thought of retaining it as a part of the permanent financial structure. Subsequently, the preferred stocks may be retired out of earnings by sale of common stock or with borrowed funds. Should earnings decline or security prices be depressed, corporations with low earnings but strong cash positions may find their preferred stock can be purchased in the market at low prices, and may deem it wise to use some of their surplus cash to buy up the preferred stock. Purchase of the stock below its par value results in an increase in the surplus by the difference between the amount paid and the par value.

The most common **advantage of callable preferred stock** is the ability to refund it with an issue carrying a lower preferential dividend rate or a bond issue, when a decline in the level of interest rates or improvement in the credit standing of the issuer makes this practicable.

CONVERTIBLE PREFERRED STOCK. Preferred stock is sometimes made convertible at the option of the holder into another class of stock. With few exceptions, this privilege permits conversion into common shares. For example, preferred stock may be made convertible into common at $50, which means that for $100 par value of his preferred stock the holder may obtain two shares of common. If the common then sells at $75, the preferred is worth $150 on a converted basis.

The minimum selling price of convertible preferred stock is its investment value as a preferred stock issue. But it will **sell at a premium** to reflect the conversion privilege, especially as the common stock rises to or above the conversion price. When the common stock advances well above the conversion price, a corporation may force conversion by calling in the preferred at its redemption price. Usually, conversion can take place after preferred stock has been called, up to, say, 10 days of the actual redemption date.

The value of a conversion privilege may be **diluted** if there is no provision to protect preferred shareholders from a split-up or a stock dividend on the common shares. A consolidation with another corporation may also reduce the value of the conversion privilege. Provisions are often inserted in the charter to protect preferred stockholders from such dilution by requiring a reduction in the conversion price when additional shares are issued.

The conversion privilege may be **perpetual or limited** to a specified number of years. The ratio at which preferred stock may be converted into common also may vary. For example, preferred may be convertible into common at $20 for the first 2 years, at $25 for the next 2 years, and at $30 thereafter. This is done to stimulate conversion within a few years after issuance.

Other Classes of Stock

CLASSIFIED COMMON STOCKS. The charter of a corporation may classify its capital stock into classes other than preferred and common.

Voting and Nonvoting Common Stock. The most frequently encountered classification of common stock is into Class A and Class B, with only one class having voting power. This division into two classes, one of which is deprived of voting power, and the other of which has exclusive voting power and which is usually a small issue held by one or a few persons, is a device to retain control and to gain the advantages of continuity of management. Its purpose is similar to that of **voting trusts,** for which it may be a substitute.

The disfranchisement of common stock in the hands of the public has **legal sanction.** Practically all statutes permit an issue of stock to be deprived of voting power; a notable exception is Illinois, which does not permit the issuance of nonvoting stock. The issuance of nonvoting common stock, however, has been attacked on the ground of public policy. It is contended that the aggregations of capital represented by modern corporation enterprises should be subjected, at least ultimately, to the control of the rank and file of stockholders, and that to permit them to be controlled by limited groups is a dangerous public policy. To the contention that stockholders by and large are interested only in the safety of income and principal of their investment, and not in the management of the corporation, it is answered that, although they may not exercise their right of management currently, they at least have the latent power to take matters into their own hands and correct abuses whenever the management has been unfaithful to its trust or shown inefficiency. The **New York Stock Exchange** has discountenanced the practice to the extent of refusing to list stocks of companies that do not give full voting power to all their common stock and by requiring the **delisting of stock** when a recapitalization deprives the common shares held by the public of voting rights. Various laws, such as the Public Utility Holding Company Act, prohibit the use of nonvoting common stock in regulated corporations.

Variation of Dividend Rights. Coupled with, or in place of, the voting power distinction may be differences in dividend and other rights. For example, a number of closely held corporations for the purpose of going public establish two classes of stock both with voting rights but one class with full dividend rights and the other with little or no dividend rights for a period of years or indefinitely. The class with dividend rights is then sold to the public while the controlling stockholders, the existing owners of the corporation, retain the class that will receive little or no dividend payments. This reduces the total amount of dividend payments that the corporation will have to make without hampering the sale of shares at attractive prices to the public. Stocks retained by controlling stockholders may be made convertible after a specified year into the class of shares that is bought by the public.

GUARANTEED STOCK. Stock upon which payment of dividends has been guaranteed by another corporation is known as guaranteed stock. It may be either preferred or common. Guaranties were most widely used in the building up of large railway systems, smaller railroads being leased at a rental providing a specified rate of dividend on the stock of the lessor corporation. But industrial and public utility companies also have occasionally guaranteed stocks of subsidiaries and allied enterprises.

A guaranteed stock is, in effect, a **dual security.** Dividend payments are a fixed obligation of the guarantor but the issue remains the stock equity of the issuer.

FOUNDERS' SHARES. Founders' shares or **management shares** are given to promoters or managers. They are usually **deferred stock,** in that dividends cannot be paid until a specified amount has been paid on other classes of stock held by the public. It is seldom used in the United States but is common in England. If given to promoters as compensation, it is intended to demonstrate their faith in the new enterprise. If given to management, it provides an incentive to build up earning power, for if profits are large the founders' shares may become quite valuable.

Sale of Stock

PRE-EMPTIVE RIGHTS. A stockholder has a common law right to subscribe to new issues of stock before it can be offered to outsiders. This pre-emptive right is designed to protect such stockholder's proportional interest in the assets, earnings, and voting power of the business. Before offering new stock to outsiders, a corporation whose stockholders have the pre-emptive right must afford them a reasonable length of time to subscribe pro rata to the issue. Only if they fail to subscribe can the stock be sold to others at the same or a higher price. Pre-emptive rights do not apply to **treasury stock**, except in states where the statutory law changes this rule.

It has been held that stock issued for the **acquisition of property** and in **consolidations** does not give rise to pre-emptive rights for the old stockholders. Pre-emptive rights become complicated where there is more than one issue of stock and one of the issues is nonvoting, or votes only in certain contingencies. The weight of authority denies to **nonvoting preferred stock** a pre-emptive right to subscribe to new issues. Moreover, the uncertainty has been troublesome to corporate lawyers, who are inclined therefore to insert in the certificate of incorporation a clause denying the pre-emptive right to such issues.

The pre-emptive right in most states does not apply to **originally authorized stock** scheduled for sale within a reasonable period after organization. Subscribers to the original issue are then assumed to have purchased their shares with the knowledge that the authorized stock would all be sold, establishing the proportional status of the stockholders. If, by the terms of the original offering, the stockholders could prove that the unissued stock was to be held indefinitely for some future expansion they might present a good case for pre-emptive rights when the stock was subsequently issued. Section 622(e)(5) of the New York Business Corporation Law provides that there will be no pre-emptive right to subscribe to issues of originally authorized stock unless it has remained unissued for 2 years.

A number of statutes now authorize the waiver of the pre-emptive right in the corporate charter. Many corporations have taken advantage of this privilege, so that they do not have to offer new stock issues first to their shareholders. Section 1106 of the California Corporation Code goes further and abolishes the pre-emptive right, unless it is reserved to stockholders in the charter. Pennsylvania, Indiana, and Oklahoma have similar statutory provisions.

SALE TO STOCKHOLDERS. If the pre-emptive right has not been waived, or if it is considered desirable to grant the right even though it has been waived in the charter, new shares are generally offered to old stockholders at a price lower than the market quotation. Shareholders may then either subscribe pro rata for the shares to which they are entitled, or they may sell their subscription rights to others. Stockholders constitute a group already interested in the corporation, and hence are ordinarily better prospects in the sale of stock than prospective buyers who lack a similar personal interest in and knowledge of the corporation's affairs. Sale of a new issue to stockholders can be guaranteed by a **stand-by underwriting agreement.** (See Section on Security Selling.)

SALE TO THE GENERAL PUBLIC. New corporations, those with a small number of stockholders and others seeking a wider market for their shares, sell stock to the general public.

Small corporations ordinarily face a difficult task, because expenses of sale tend to be high in relation to the amount involved. Security dealers find from experience that the selling effort is often greater and the expense no less for a small issue than for a large one. The stock-buying public is slow to buy securities in little-known corporations, especially when the sale is not sponsored by well-known security dealers. Small corporations have therefore depended heavily upon sales of stock to the management and its friends, to existing stockholders, and to local citizens of means.

The methods and problems of selling stock to the general public are discussed in the Section on Security Selling.

SALE OF STOCK TO EMPLOYEES. The sale of stock to executives under stock option and stock purchase plans has been a widespread practice. Many corporations have adopted **employee savings plans,** involving matching employer contributions with all or part of the contributions used to purchase company stock.

Frequently a corporation will buy in outstanding stock in the market for resale to employees on the installment plan. Stock is often sold to employees at a price lower than the market price, perhaps under a contract restricting its resale for a period of time. Such stock certificates should bear a **reference to the restrictive terms,** so that a purchaser from the employee cannot claim to be innocent of the restrictions. Issues of new stock to employees may be subject to the preemptive rights of old stockholders, if these are not waived in the charter. A number of state statutes permit the sale of stock to officers or employees free of preemptive rights by the vote of a majority or two-thirds of the shares entitled to such rights.

SALE OF STOCK TO CUSTOMERS. The practice of selling securities to customers was popular in some fields in the '20's but has since dwindled in importance. Public utilities seeking to win consumer goodwill and to discourage agitation for lower rates sold preferred and common stock to their customers at that time. But the subsequent decline in utility earnings and stock prices in the 1930's showed that customer ownership could produce ill will under adverse conditions, and the practice is no longer usual. Some smaller industrial concerns sell stock to large customers, who thereby seek to assure themselves of future supplies of needed parts or products at attractive prices. A smaller company may unduly sacrifice its independence in this way, however.

Stock Subscription Rights

ACTION BY THE BOARD OF DIRECTORS. The issuance of additional stock must first be approved by the board of directors. The approval takes the form of a **resolution** stating the amount to be sold, the purpose of the issue, and, if authorized but unissued stock is not available, a direction to the officers of the corporation to submit a charter amendment increasing the authorized capital for approval of stockholders, either at a regular meeting or at a special meeting to be called in accordance with the bylaws. The resolution will usually state that, in the event any requisite charter amendment has been approved, the new shares will be offered stockholders at a specified price and transferable warrants evidencing subscription rights issued.

ACTION BY STOCKHOLDERS. An increase in the amount of authorized stock requires **amendment of the certificate of incorporation,** which must first be approved by a vote of stockholders as directed by the statutes. Some require that such matters be submitted to a special meeting of stockholders called for the purpose. In the absence of such a requirement, the proposal can be brought up at the annual meeting, although it should be specifically mentioned in the stockholders' notice of that meeting. Following approval, the charter amendment is filed in the manner provided by law.

LETTER TO STOCKHOLDERS. An officer of the corporation will formally announce the new stock issue to shareholders by means of a letter explaining the subscription rights offered shareholders, specifying the record date for determining who is entitled to the rights, stating how long the offer will remain open, indicating when warrants to evidence the subscription rights will be mailed, and covering the disposition of fractional rights, i.e., rights to subscribe to less than one share.

SUBSCRIPTION WARRANTS. As soon as practicable after the record date, subscription warrants are mailed to stockholders of record on the specified date, to evidence their right to subscribe to the new issue. The warrants usually recite the terms of the issue, state the number of shares to which the stockholder is entitled to subscribe, the subscription price, the office which will receive the subscription, the final date for exercise of the rights, and the date the new stock will be issued. On the back of the warrant there is a subscription agreement to be signed by the subscriber, and a form for the assignment of the warrant in case the shareholder wishes to sell it to someone else.

A similar form is provided for **fractional warrants** if a stockholder is entitled to subscribe to a fractional share. The fractional warrants are the same as the warrants for full shares, except that they usually specify that the warrant must be accompanied by other fractional warrants to make up a right to buy one full share. Occasionally provision will be made for the substitution of **cash** for additional fractional warrants. Copies of the front and back of subscription warrants of the San Diego Gas & Electric Co. are shown in Fig. 5.

VALUE OF SUBSCRIPTION RIGHTS. New stock is usually offered shareholders at a price lower than the current market quotation for the old shares. The subscription rights will then have a market value. The **reason** why rights have a value is indicated by the following example.

Suppose a corporation is increasing its outstanding stock by 50% through an offering to stockholders. To maintain his proportionate interest in the corporation, a stockholder is entitled to subscribe to one-half a new share for each share he owns. If the offering price is $44 and the market price is $50, the stockholder owning two shares worth $50 each may subscribe to one new share for $44. This brings the market price per share down to $48, other things remaining equal. Each old share will have lost $2 of its market value in the averaging process, and the new share will be worth $4 more than its cost. When the rights are issued, the price of the stock ex-rights will decline in the market to $48 (assuming no other factors have affected the quotation). The decline will be caused by the **dilution of the equity** as a result of the sale of new stock below the prevailing market price. The stockholder theoretically is no better off; he lost $2 on each of his old shares but gained $4 on his one new share. Should the stockholder not

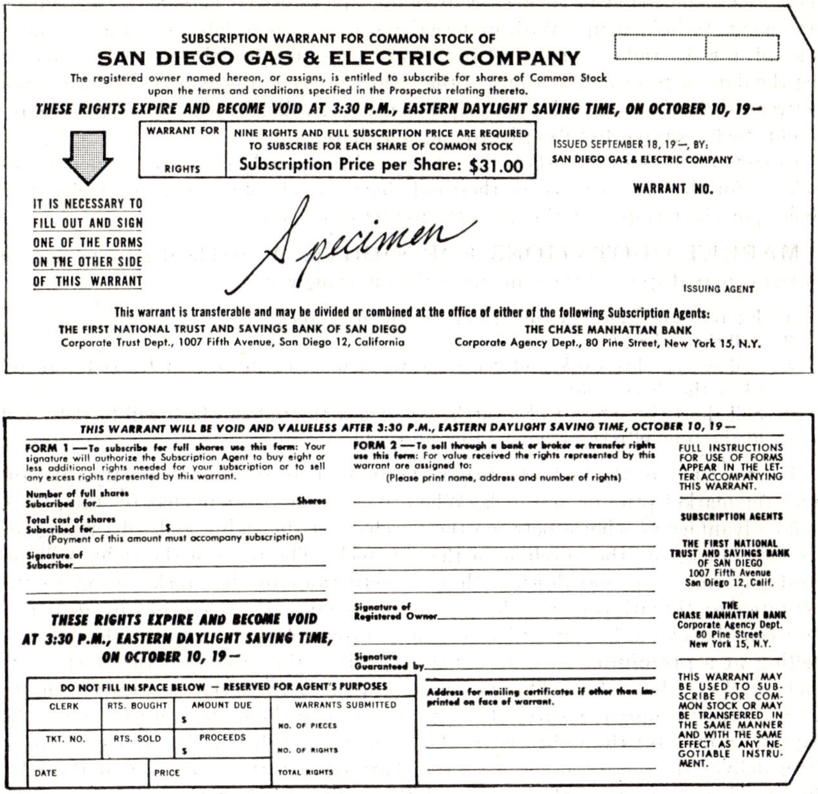

SUBSCRIPTION WARRANT FOR COMMON STOCK OF

SAN DIEGO GAS & ELECTRIC COMPANY

The registered owner named hereon, or assigns, is entitled to subscribe for shares of Common Stock upon the terms and conditions specified in the Prospectus relating thereto.

THESE RIGHTS EXPIRE AND BECOME VOID AT 3:30 P.M., EASTERN DAYLIGHT SAVING TIME, ON OCTOBER 10, 19—

WARRANT FOR RIGHTS	NINE RIGHTS AND FULL SUBSCRIPTION PRICE ARE REQUIRED TO SUBSCRIBE FOR EACH SHARE OF COMMON STOCK Subscription Price per Share: $31.00

ISSUED SEPTEMBER 18, 19—, BY:
SAN DIEGO GAS & ELECTRIC COMPANY

WARRANT NO.

IT IS NECESSARY TO FILL OUT AND SIGN ONE OF THE FORMS ON THE OTHER SIDE OF THIS WARRANT

Specimen

ISSUING AGENT

This warrant is transferable and may be divided or combined at the office of either of the following Subscription Agents:

THE FIRST NATIONAL TRUST AND SAVINGS BANK OF SAN DIEGO
Corporate Trust Dept., 1007 Fifth Avenue, San Diego 12, California

THE CHASE MANHATTAN BANK
Corporate Agency Dept., 80 Pine Street, New York 15, N.Y.

THIS WARRANT WILL BE VOID AND VALUELESS AFTER 3:30 P.M., EASTERN DAYLIGHT SAVING TIME, OCTOBER 10, 19—

FORM 1 —To subscribe for full shares use this form: Your signature will authorize the Subscription Agent to buy eight or less additional rights needed for your subscription or to sell any excess rights represented by this warrant.

Number of full shares Subscribed for ________ **Shares**

Total cost of shares Subscribed for ________ $ ________
(Payment of this amount must accompany subscription)

Signature of Subscriber ________

THESE RIGHTS EXPIRE AND BECOME VOID AT 3:30 P.M., EASTERN DAYLIGHT SAVING TIME, ON OCTOBER 10, 19—

DO NOT FILL IN SPACE BELOW — RESERVED FOR AGENT'S PURPOSES			
CLERK	RTS. BOUGHT	AMOUNT DUE $	WARRANTS SUBMITTED NO. OF PIECES
TKT. NO.	RTS. SOLD	PROCEEDS $	NO. OF RIGHTS
DATE	PRICE		TOTAL RIGHTS

FORM 2 —To sell through a bank or broker or transfer rights use this form: For value received the rights represented by this warrant are assigned to:
(Please print name, address and number of rights)

Signature of Registered Owner ________

Signature Guaranteed by ________

Address for mailing certificates if other than imprinted on face of warrant.

FULL INSTRUCTIONS FOR USE OF FORMS APPEAR IN THE LETTER ACCOMPANYING THIS WARRANT.

SUBSCRIPTION AGENTS

THE FIRST NATIONAL TRUST AND SAVINGS BANK OF SAN DIEGO
1007 Fifth Avenue
San Diego 12, Calif.

THE CHASE MANHATTAN BANK
Corporate Agency Dept.
80 Pine Street
New York 15, N.Y.

THIS WARRANT MAY BE USED TO SUBSCRIBE FOR COMMON STOCK OR MAY BE TRANSFERRED IN THE SAME MANNER AND WITH THE SAME EFFECT AS ANY NEGOTIABLE INSTRUMENT.

Fig. 5. Subscription warrant for common stock.

desire to exercise his rights, he may sell them on the market at or about $2 each. Rights to buy listed issues are usually listed and quoted on stock exchanges.

Trading in the stock itself is continued on a **rights on** or **cum rights** basis so long as the stock carries with it, in the above example, the right to subscribe to one-half of a new share. To ascertain the value of the right during this period, the following formula may be used, R representing the value of the right, M, the market price of the old stock, S, the subscription price of the new shares, and N, the number of old shares required to subscribe to one new share:

$$R = \frac{M - S}{N + 1}$$

Substituting the figures in the above example,

$$R \text{ (the value of the right)} = \frac{\$50 - \$44}{2 + 1} = \$2$$

After the record date the stock will sell **"ex-rights,"** which means that the value of the right has been deducted from the market price because the stock no longer carries rights. Under the rules of the New York Stock Exchange, transactions in shares would be ex-rights on the third business day preceding the record date if there is no contingency, such as waiting for the effective date of a registration statement, to hold it up. With underwritten issues, such delay is common and a due bill for the rights is received by buyers after the third business day preceding the date of record. The value of the right will then approximate the difference between the market and the subscription price, divided by the number of shares of old stock required to subscribe to one new share.

In spite of the fact that the value of the right is merely compensation to stockholders for the loss in value of their old shares, stockholders may be inclined to look upon the receipt of rights as in the nature of a bonus.

MARKET QUOTATIONS FOR RIGHTS. A stockholder in possession of rights may dispose of them in one of the following ways:

1. Exercise the rights by subscribing for the new stock.
2. Sell the rights.
3. Sell part of his stock and subscribe for new shares by use of his rights to replace the shares sold.
4. Sell short the shares to be purchased against the rights, which will be delivered at the time of receipt against the short sale.

The tendency of the market price of the rights is to maintain a **parity relation** with the market price of the stock. When the two prices are in that relation, there is no advantageous choice between the purchase of the rights and subscribing for the new stock, and the purchase of the old stock. The price of the rights will accordingly move up and down with the fluctuations of the stock, owing to the activities of the arbitragers, who are quick to take advantage of any disparity between the two values in order to gain a profit. If, for example, the stock is **selling at a premium** above its parity with the rights, they sell the stock short and purchase the rights. This purchase and sale causes the two quotations to draw closer to mutual parity. The arbitragers may hold this position until the expiration date for the rights, when they will exercise their rights and a few days later deliver the new securities on their short sales of the stock. Or, if the relative market position of the stock and the rights should reverse itself and the stock should be quoted at a discount from parity with the rights or at parity, they will undo their position by covering their short sale in the stock and at the same time sell the rights they hold.

Bonus Stock

DEFINITION AND USES. Bonus stock is issued to aid in the marketing of another class of security. The most frequent instance of its use is in connection with the sale of preferred stock, although it may be issued also in connection with the sale of bonds, usually debentures. The purchaser of the senior security is, through the bonus stock, given an opportunity to realize speculative gains, while enjoying a senior position for his investment.

CONSIDERATION FOR BONUS STOCK. The only kind of stock which may be issued without any consideration is treasury stock. Therefore, stock is sometimes issued for property or services to those interested in financing a new corporation and then donated to the corporation, to create treasury stock which can be used as a bonus to facilitate sales of preferred stock or bonds to the public. Another procedure is to consider part of the price received for the preferred stock or bonds as the consideration for common stock issued as a bonus.

Stock purchase warrants have supplanted bonus stock in corporate financing to a large extent.

Stock Purchase Warrants

NATURE OF STOCK PURCHASE WARRANTS. These warrants, also known as **option warrants,** are commonly issued with or attached to bonds, preferred and at times common stock, and entitle the owners of those securities to purchase usually shares of common stock, in a stated ratio to their holdings, at a certain price per share, and within a stated period or for an indefinite time. Sometimes warrants accompanying bonds or notes give the right to subscribe for preferred stock. The **purpose of the warrants** is to make the bond or stock they are attached to a more attractive purchase to investors. The holders of securities with warrants not only have the greater security that goes with a bond, note, or preferred stock, but will also have an opportunity to benefit from future appreciation of the common stock. They will be able to purchase the common stock at the fixed price after the market price will have risen, or, if they do not desire to subscribe, they will have the advantage of seeing the option-bearing bonds or preferred stocks they hold, or the warrants if detached, rise in value in sympathy with the common stock. Option warrants are frequently issued in reorganizations, in mergers and consolidations, and in promotions, at times in lieu of common stock. They may also be issued as compensation for management. Where the profit realized on their sale is a long-term capital gain, they have a marked tax advantage.

DETACHABLE AND NONDETACHABLE WARRANTS. Option warrants are generally attached to the security with which they are originally issued, and they are subsequently either detachable or nondetachable. If detachable, they are **separately negotiable.** The option-bearing security is then quoted both with and without warrants. The warrants may be detachable immediately upon issuance, or not until some stated date, or upon the redemption or maturity of the option-bearing security if the warrants do not expire with that redemption or maturity.

If the warrants are nondetachable, there can be **no market** for them, and their value remains merged with that of the bond or stock to which they are attached. They are only detached when they are exercised, or upon the redemption or maturity of the option-bearing security. Stockholders presenting them for subscription for the common stock, if they are issued with preferred stock, may either receive back the preferred stock certificate without the warrants, together with a certificate for the new common stock, or they may get a new preferred stock certificate, depending upon the practice adopted by the issuing company. An owner of a stock purchase warrant may care to exercise his option only partially. In that case, he can exchange his preferred stock certificate carrying the warrant for two certificates also with warrants, one of which will call for the number of shares of common stock he wishes to subscribe for.

Option warrants are at times issued as separate certificates delivered simultaneously with bonds or preferred stock, or as entirely independent instruments not connected with any obligation or stock. They have been issued to and retained by banking houses as a part of their compensation for undertaking the flotation of a security or for assisting in the promotion of a new concern, but this practice is subject to restrictions imposed by regulatory authorities.

DURATION OF THE OPTION. Stock purchase warrants extend over periods of varying lengths. The time in which they are exercisable may begin immediately upon the issuance of the securities they are attached to, or not until several years after their issuance. They may then run for a stated number of years within the life of the option-bearing security, anywhere from 1 to 2 years to 20 or more. They may be perpetual.

If the bond or stock is **redeemable,** the warrant may become void with redemption, or void a number of days after redemption, or it may continue in effect for a number of years after redemption. Similarly, it may expire with the maturity of the bond or may extend beyond the bond's maturity. Warrants are sometimes issued that may be exercised only upon the redemption of the stock carrying them. The warrant thus partly offsets the disadvantage to the holder of the preferred stock of having his investment retired.

EXERCISE OF THE OPTION. The subscription price named in warrants is ordinarily fixed above the current market value of the stock subject to the option, with the result that it is not immediately profitable to exercise the warrants. The warrant holder must wait until the market price rises above the subscription price. If the market price should never score this advance before the expiration date of the warrants, they will be **valueless** at that time. If, on the other hand, it should rise above the subscription price, the warrants become **equivalent to stock rights** except that the holders of the option warrants have a longer period in which to exercise them. The option warrants may still have many years to run before they expire; on that account holders may postpone exercising them immediately and may be satisfied to see the value of the warrant rise with the price of the stock to be subscribed for. Their attitude is analogous to that of **holders of convertible bonds,** who do not necessarily convert as soon as the stock into which the bonds are convertible rises above the conversion price, since the bonds will score an approximately equivalent advance. Because a smaller investment is required to hold warrants than the stock that may be purchased with them, and the percentage rise in the price of a warrant exceeds that of the stock, these options provide a favorable medium for speculation in the stock. They usually sell at substantial premiums over their mathematical value.

OPTION WARRANTS AND PRE-EMPTIVE RIGHTS. The issue of stock purchase warrants is subject to the stockholders' pre-emptive right to purchase the new shares called for by the option, except where by charter or bylaw provision the stockholders have given their consent to the sale of the option-bearing securities to others. Stock purchase warrants are instrumental in the **procurement of a higher price** for the securities they are attached to. The common stockholders are, therefore, benefited at the outset by the issue of option warrants to others than themselves. If the options are exercised and the new common stock issued, their equity is diluted proportionately.

Fractional Shares

HOW FRACTIONAL SHARES ARISE. Fractional shares arise out of stock dividend declarations, the issue of stock rights and stock purchase warrants, stock split-ups, stock and bond conversions, recapitalizations, and exchanges of stock in corporate combinations and reorganizations. In the case of a 10% stock dividend, for example, an owner of five shares would be entitled to receive but one-half a share as his portion of the dividend. The problem of how to handle fractional shares has been given considerable thought.

Inconvenience Caused by Fractional Shares. Certificates may be issued for fractional shares. This is satisfactory neither from the standpoint of the corporation nor of the shareholders, since the fractional shares may remain outstanding indefinitely and cause considerable inconvenience. Accounting for great numbers of fractional shares on the books of a corporation will lead to endless complications. Holders of fractional shares, may, under applicable law, be entitled to dividend or voting rights. To eliminate fractional shares, holders may be required to exchange a sufficient number into full shares, by a specified date, after which they are entitled to proceeds of sale of full shares by the company or the fractional shares become valueless.

METHODS OF DISPOSING OF FRACTIONAL SHARES. The issuance of fractional shares can be avoided by one or a combination of the three following methods:

1. A payment in cash by the corporation to the stockholders entitled to fractions, usually at the market price on the day when the fractional shares are issuable to them.
2. The corporation undertakes, or gets a brokerage house to undertake, to buy or sell rights to receive fractions of a share without commission at a fixed price based on the market.
3. **Negotiable scrip certificates,** made out to bearer, are issued in lieu of fractional shares. Holders are given a limited period of months or a few years in which to acquire sufficient scrip to make the exchange for a full share or to sell scrip. After the final date, they are entitled to their share of the proceeds of sale of full shares held against the scrip or the scrip becomes valueless, as specified on its face.

SECTION 14

LONG-TERM AND INTERMEDIATE-TERM BORROWING

CONTENTS

Principles and Forms of Borrowing

	PAGE
Debt vs. equity capital	1
Advantages of debt financing	1
Low cost	1
No dilution of the equity	1
No sharing of voting power	1
Availability of funds	1
Trading on the equity	1
Disadvantages of debt financing	1
Present borrowing undermines ability to borrow in future	2
Trading on the equity may magnify losses.	2
Financial weakening of company	2
Threat to solvency of business	2
Types of borrowing	2
Short-term vs. long-term borrowing	2
Unsecured vs. secured borrowing	2
Bonds and notes	2
Principles of debt financing	3
Business cycle and debt financing	3
Long-term industry trend and debt financing	3
Measuring borrowing capacity	3
Amortization and debt financing	4
Power to incure debt	4
Corporate authorization	4
Public regulation of bond issues	4

General Characteristics of Bonds

	PAGE
Definition	5
Denominations	5
Forms of bonds—coupon bonds	5
Registered bonds	6
Bonds registered only as to principal	6
Terms of payment	7
Bonds payable in gold	7
Interest payments	7

Bond Indentures

	PAGE
The need for the bond indenture	7
Corporate trustees	8
Certification of bonds	8
To enforce the terms of the indenture	9
Administrative duties	9
Trust Indenture Act of 1939	9
Indenture provisions required by the Act	10
Provisions of a bond indenture	11
Summary of contents	11
Names of the parties	11
The preamble	11

	PAGE
Grant or assignment of trust	12
Conditions governing the issue of bonds	12
Particular covenants of the indenture	12
Remedies of trustees and bondholders	13
Period of grace	14
Acceleration of maturity in cases of default	14
Individual action of bondholders	14
Releases of mortgaged property	15
Consolidations and mergers	16
"No recourse" clause	16
Changes in trust indentures	16
Supplemental indentures	17

Mortgage Bonds

	PAGE
Mortgage instruments	17
Purpose of the mortgage	17
Closed mortgages	18
Disadvantages of closed mortgages	18
Open-end and limited open-end mortgages	18
Restrictions on issue of bonds under open-end and limited open-end mortgages	18
Issuance of bonds against deposit of cash with trustee	19
Bonds issued in series	19
Mortgage on after-acquired property	19
Existing liens on subsequently acquired property	20
Avoiding application of after-acquired property clause	20
Scope of lien and mortgage bond titles	20
Terminal bonds	21

Collateral Trust Bonds

	PAGE
Nature of security	21
Types of collateral	21
Pledged securities	22
Payment of principal, interest, and dividends on pledged securities	22
Voting pledged stock	22
Release of pledged securities	23
Consolidation, merger, or sale of assets of subsidiary	23
Pledge of miscellaneous collateral	23

Equipment Obligations

	PAGE
Character of obligation	23
Equipment mortgage plan	24
Conditional sale plan	24
Philadelphia plan	24

CONTENTS (Continued)

Covenants in equipment obligation agreements 24

Debenture Bonds

General character 25
Common provisions 25
Use of debentures 25
Subordinated debentures 26

Guaranteed Bonds

Purpose 26
Forms of guaranty 27
Value of the guaranty 27
Legal position of guaranteed bonds 27

Income Bonds

Nature of obligation 28
Methods of determining income and basis of payments 28
Discretionary payment of interest on income bonds 28
Cumulative and noncumulative income bonds. 28
Reasons for use of income bonds 29
Capital funds 29

Miscellaneous Classes of Bonds

Joint bonds 29
Assumed bonds 29
Trustees' or receivers' certificates 30
Participating bonds 30
Voting bonds 30
Bonds held in the treasury 30

Convertible Bonds

Nature of the conversion right 30
Advantages and disadvantages of convertible bonds 31
Conversion ratio or price 31
Fixing conversion rate 32
Interest and dividend adjustments.......... 32
Time of conversion 32
Subscription privilege 32
Protective features against dilution or destruction of conversion privilege.............. 33
Factors influencing conversion 34
Bonds with warrants 34

Retirement of Bonded Debt

Methods of retirement 35
The call feature 35
Investors and the call feature 35
Method of redemption 35
Amortization through sinking fund 36
Types of sinking funds 36
Fixed annual amounts 36
Percentage of earnings 36
Per unit of output 36
Variable annual amounts 36
Acquisition of bonds for sinking fund...... 37
Deposit of bonds in sinking fund in lieu of cash payments 37
Dangers of excessive sinking fund charges.... 37

Serial Bonds

General characteristics 37
Fixing the size of serial maturities 38
Callable serial bonds 38
Comparison of sinking fund and serial bonds 38

Refunding of Bonds

Nature of operation 39
Refunding before maturity 39
Methods of refunding 39
Factors in refunding before maturity...... 39
Refunding at maturity 40
Extensions 40

Term Loans

Characteristics 40
Purposes and terms 41

Private Placements

Widespread use 41
Principal advantages 41
Disadvantages 42
Services of investment bankers 42

Leasing of Fixed Assets

Alternative to borrowing 42
Sale-and-leaseback financing 43
Advantages to corporation of leasing 43
Disadvantages of leasing 43
Equipment leasing 44
Leasing as junior financing 44

SECTION 14

LONG-TERM AND INTERMEDIATE-TERM BORROWING

Principles and Forms of Borrowing

DEBT VS. EQUITY CAPITAL. Contrasted with the ownership elements in a business corporation is the type of financial interest created by borrowing, which results in a debt by the corporation to the lender. The lender or creditor acquires a **prior claim** to the income of the business for his interest, and, at maturity or default, the principal of the loan is a prior claim to the assets of the corporation, which must be satisfied before the stockholder-owners receive anything. Because creditors receive a claim to earnings and assets that has priority over the equity in the enterprise of the stockholders, borrowing has been described as **trading on the equity.**

ADVANTAGES OF DEBT FINANCING. Corporations favor bond financing because of:

Low Cost. Borrowing gives the double advantage of providing funds at relatively low interest cost to a business in good credit standing and the deductibility of interest from taxable income. A 5% bond issue involves an effective interest cost of only 2½% to a corporation subject to an income tax of approximately 50%, so that preferred stock paying 5% in dividends involves an effective cost of funds that is twice as high since dividend payments are not deductible by the corporation. (See also, Cost of Capital discussion in Sec. 17.)

No Dilution of the Equity. Bondholders are entitled only to the rate of interest specified and the repayment of principal when due. The sale of common stock, by contrast, dilutes the equity of the enterprise for those stockholders who do not or may not subscribe pro rata to a new issue of shares by the corporation.

No Sharing of Voting Power. Bondholders have no voice in the conduct of a business, except to the extent that **restrictive provisions** are included in indentures or if a representative of the bondholders is elected to the board of directors.

Availability of Funds. Major institutional investors such as banks and life insurance companies invest only or mainly in bonds and notes, so that these rich sources of funds can be tapped only through borrowing.

Trading on the Equity. Because earnings on borrowed money usually substantially exceed the net cost of borrowing, stockholders benefit from "trading on the equity" by giving creditors a **prior claim** to earnings and assets.

DISADVANTAGES OF DEBT FINANCING. Arguments against resort to bond financing are in the four following paragraphs.

Present Borrowing Undermines Ability To Borrow in Future. Financial history is replete with examples of corporations that found it advantageous to preserve their borrowing power as a **last recourse** in the event money must be raised for whatever reason.

Trading on the Equity May Magnify Losses. Interest on debt is a **fixed charge** that must be paid even when earnings decline. If a business suffers an operating deficit, its loss will also be increased by the need to pay interest. To a loss corporation, there is no tax benefit from the deductibility of interest payments.

Financial Weakening of Company. The need to meet fixed interest requirements, sinking funds, and principal at maturity weakens the financial position of a concern with limited earning power. Maintenance of property may be neglected and cash resources impaired under the pressure to remain solvent by paying interest and principal as they fall due. Fixed charges limit managerial discretion in formulating business policies, which can be doubly dangerous in an era of rapid economic change.

Threat to Solvency of Business. Many corporations find that their earnings lack the necessary stability to permit successful use of debt in substantial amounts. A sudden decline in earnings may bring default and force reorganization of the business due to inability to meet interest or principal repayments as these fall due. The reorganization often spells loss of control for the management.

TYPES OF BORROWING. These may be classified from two points of view.

Short-Term vs. Long-Term Borrowing. The purpose of the loan will affect its maturity. If money is borrowed for the construction of a new building, the purchase of land, or the acquisition of other capital goods, the term will usually be long enough to give the borrower time to repay at least a portion, if not all, of the loan out of earnings from these capital assets and the cash flow from depreciation. On the other hand, if money is borrowed for the purchase of commodities to be processed and resold, the term will be influenced by the time it takes to sell the processed goods and receive payment therefor. Short-term debt is that coming due within one year. Frequently, the term **intermediate financing** is used to refer to loans for periods of from one to ten years, and long-term borrowing to longer maturities. These designations are, however, not standardized. Short-term debt is discussed in Section 16.

Unsecured vs. Secured Borrowing. The strength of the general promise of the borrower to pay will generally determine whether it will be necessary to pledge specific security for the loan, as by a mortgage on fixed property or the pledging of receivables. The greater the ability to pay, the more likely that the loan will be unsecured. The trend in bond financing by larger and stronger enterprises has been toward unsecured debenture issues. However, some types of lenders must as a matter of law require collateral, at least as regards certain types of loans. Sometimes, instead of security a **negative pledge clause** is used which restricts or prohibits the pledging of assets as security to other borrowers.

Bonds and Notes. Long-term loans are usually made through the use of bonds, whereas for intermediate-term borrowing the debt instruments are usually promissory notes. Publicly offered **corporate notes** are similar to bonds in all respects except maturity.

PRINCIPLES AND FORMS OF BORROWING 14·3

The terms "bonds" and "notes" are often used interchangeably. When notes are given to banks, insurance companies, or other institutional investors in connection with **term loans** or **private placements,** the main differences between them and a bond issue are that usually no trustee is appointed, the instruments are simple note forms rather than engraved certificates, and the terms are set forth in the agreement between the parties rather than in a formal indenture. These are differences in form rather than substance.

PRINCIPLES OF DEBT FINANCING. A corporation that resorts to borrowing should be guided by several basic principles:

Business Cycle and Debt Financing. Past experience has shown that the more vulnerable a company's business is to the business cycle, the greater the need for restraint or caution in the use of debt in financing. Since industrial concerns operate under **competitive conditions,** the demand for most industrial products is less stable than, for example, the demand for electricity. Similarly, the personal equation enters into the management of a manufacturing business to a greater extent than it does in the management of an electric power and light company.

Many corporations find it advantageous to strengthen their financial position during the **prosperity** phase of the business cycle by reducing debt and building up cash resources, so paving the way for future expansion. Conversely, expansion can be effected on more advantageous terms during a **recession.** Some of our most successful corporations have resorted to borrowing to finance expansion during a recession, so that their capacity to produce has been enlarged by the time it is needed to meet prosperity demands.

Long-Term Industry Trend and Debt Financing. Experience has shown the wisdom of taking long-term industry trends into account in debt financing. The **railroads** have suffered from excessive interest charges and debt maturities because they have expanded debt despite uncertainties as to the long-term trend of their earnings. The most favorable condition for borrowing is that of industries whose earnings and cash flow display stable growth trends over the longer run.

Measuring Borrowing Capacity. Both corporate managers and lenders are placing major stress on the relation between cash flow and interest and principal payments due in measuring the capacity of an enterprise to service debt. In the past, the ratio of debt to total capitalization and the ratio of earnings available to pay interest to annual interest charges were stressed. As the cash flow from depreciation and other sources has expanded, and as the ultimate reliance of a business upon its cash flow for funds to service debt has become better recognized, the **prospective cash flow** is regarded widely as the best guide to measuring the extent to which a business may safely incur debt.

Donaldson (Corporate Debt Capacity) suggests that management carefully estimate a **maximum adverse limit** for its cash flow under adverse conditions as a guide to its debt capacity. This maximum adverse limit could be based upon an analysis of probable sales volume and other determinants of cash flow in a recession, and upon the condition of the company immediately preceding the recession. "A well informed management," he states, "can with considerable confidence set finite limits on the expected impact of any future recession period on the business with respect to sales and other elements of net cash flows."

So many factors other than recession can affect cash flows, such as competitive price reductions, overproduction, obsolescence of products, prices or facilities, strikes, etc., that many managements would hesitate to regard a maximum adverse limit for cash flow based solely or mainly on the assumption of a recession as a safe guide to borrowing. A **margin of safety** for an outflow of cash beyond that of any adverse limit based on past experience is usually considered desirable to protect a corporation's credit standing and ability to borrow in the future under unfavorable, as well as favorable, economic conditions.

Amortization and Debt Financing. Corporate managements at times have assumed that the trend of earnings and cash flow will continue upward, or at least stable, indefinitely, so that long-term debt need not be repaid. But experience shows it is wiser to provide for partial if not complete debt retirement through the use of **sinking funds** or **serial maturities**. The Securities and Exchange Commission has used its authority to require public utility companies to amortize funded debt. The Interstate Commerce Commission adopted a similar policy for railroads after the depression of the early thirties. Provision for gradual debt retirement by even the strongest enterprise builds flexibility into its capital structure, so that it can be adapted automatically to less favorable conditions in the future.

POWER TO INCUR DEBT. The power to borrow money is a so-called "general power" given by law to business corporations as incidental to normal operations. As pointed out by Bergh, Conyngton and Kassoff (Business Law), "this power must be exercised only for business purposes. In connection with it the corporation may obligate itself on promissory notes and bills of exchange." The power to issue bonds or to mortgage property may, however, be limited by the certificate of incorporation, the bylaws, or state statutes. Section 518 of the New York Business Corporation Law provides:

Corporate bonds.—(a) No corporation shall issue bonds except for money or other property, tangible or intangible, actually received, or labor or services actually performed for the corporation or for its benefit or in its formation or reorganization, or a combination thereof. In the absence of fraud in the transaction, the judgment of the board of directors as to the value of the consideration received shall be conclusive.

(b) A corporation may, in its certificate of incorporation, confer upon the holders of any bonds issued or to be issued by the corporation, rights to inspect the corporate books and records and to vote in respect of the affairs and management of the corporation and any other rights which shareholders may have.

Corporate Authorization. In the creation of long-term corporate indebtedness, corporations are required to follow the procedure specified in the laws of the state of incorporation, the certificate of incorporation, and the bylaws. This consists of a series of steps and resolutions by the directors and, if necessary, the stockholders of the corporation. They generally comprise the following, in the order of their occurrence:

1. A reference in the minutes of the corporation to the authority of the board of directors to create a bond issue and enter into a mortgage arrangement.
2. A resolution of the board of directors authorizing the proper officers of the corporation to issue the bonds and sign a mortgage indenture, or deed of trust.
3. A stockholders' meeting approving the resolution of the directors, if required by statute or by the charter or bylaws of the corporation.
4. A certified statement that the necessary approval of stockholders and directors has been obtained.

Following these steps, the trust indenture is drafted and the bonds are issued.

PUBLIC REGULATION OF BOND ISSUES. The ordinary business corporation requires no direct sanction of a government authority to create funded debt. The laws of most states require new railroad and public utility issues of funded indebtedness to be sanctioned by public service commissions. The Transportation Act of 1920 has given authority over railroad bond and stock issues to the Interstate Commerce Commission. Similarly, the Public Utility Holding Company Act of 1935 gave authority to the Securities and Exchange Commission to approve or disapprove of bond and stock issues of registered public utility holding companies and their subsidiaries. Under the Trust Indenture Act of 1939, which is discussed in detail below, corporations issuing bonds subject to registration under the Securities Act of 1933 must file an indenture with the S.E.C. as part of the registration statement.

General Characteristics of Bonds

DEFINITION. Bonds are credit instruments that contain a promise to pay a specified amount of money at a fixed date, usually more than 10 years after issuance, and a promise to pay interest periodically at stated dates. A bond is similar to a promissory note, but it is made out in standard denominations and it is usually negotiable. All the bonds of an issue are generally covered by a so-called **deed of trust** or **trust indenture** made out to a trustee, who holds the indenture for the benefit of all the bondholders. Violation of any of the terms of the indenture enables the trustee to take remedial action, in accordance with its terms or pertinent statutes.

The chief characterisitcs of bonds are given below.

DENOMINATIONS. Most bonds are of $1,000 denomination but are also encountered in denominations of $10,000, $500, and $100. Denominations under $1,000 are called small **pieces** or **baby bonds.** Corporations may make provision for the issue of larger denominations in multiples of $1,000, and may make the smaller denominations exchangeable for the larger. The use of larger denomination bonds has been favored by banks to cope with the task of processing the mounting volume of coupon collections. Although the amount of a bond is printed on the certificate, it is common practice to indicate the denomination by a letter prefixed to the serial number of the certificates, as M for $1,000. Corporations do not favor the issuance of denominations smaller than $1,000 because of the expense of providing a greater number of engraved certificates and the fees charged by trust companies for making exchanges when various denominations are interchangeable. Transfer agents for bond issues, in addition to charging a minimum sum for their services, charge under certain conditions a fee for each bond certificate registered or transferred.

To investors the objection to low denominations is the **nonacceptability of small pieces** by purchasers and the rules of the security exchanges or the customs of bond dealers. Under the rules of many stock exchanges, bonds in denominations under $500 are not a "good delivery," and their acceptance may be refused by the purchaser. It is the general practice of corporations to agree in the trust indenture to convert small pieces into larger denominations at the option of investors, but in a number of issues small or unusually large denominations, once issued, are not convertible into other denominations. The **interchangeability** of denominations of any bond issue publicly dealt in can be determined from bond descriptions contained in such reference books as Standard & Poor's and Moody's Manuals.

FORMS OF BONDS—COUPON BONDS. Bonds may be issued in either of two general forms—(1) coupon bonds, and (2) registered bonds.

Coupon bonds are negotiable to bearer, and therefore are also called **bearer bonds.** The attached coupons represent claims for periodical interest on the successive dates indicated. The coupons are promissory notes payable to bearer, and a bona fide purchaser before their maturity is protected in the same way as in other negotiable instruments.

The great bulk of corporation bonds are in coupon form of the denomination of $1,000. Their popularity is due to the ease of negotiating and transferring them, inasmuch as ownership passes by mere delivery. Accordingly, coupon bonds may not be easily recovered if lost. No claim can be made against a corporation if, without receiving previous notice of the loss, it has paid interest or principal on lost bonds to one not entitled to receive them. Corporations will duplicate **lost or destroyed** coupon bonds and the trustee will authenticate them if the bondholder gives satisfactory evidence of the loss or destruction and furnishes a bond of indemnity for the amount the company and trustee may require. Provision for the issuance of bonds to replace lost or destroyed bonds is made in the trust indenture.

REGISTERED BONDS. Registered bonds are bonds payable to the parties whose names appear on the face, and are recorded in the bond register or transfer books kept by the company and its duly authorized transfer agent or registrar. They are transferable only when notation of the transfer has been made on the bonds themselves and entry has been made on the bond register. Because of the marketability factor, registered bonds often sell at a small discount from the price at which bearer bonds sell.

Bonds may be registered as to both principal and interest, in which instance they are called **fully registered** bonds; or they may be registered only as to principal and thus be only **partly registered** bonds. The denomination of fully registered bonds is usually $1,000, $5,000, or $10,000. As they are without coupons, interest is paid to the registered holder by check.

Bonds Registered only as to Principal. These bonds, or as they are at times called, registered bonds **with coupons,** are payable only to the registered holders so far as the principal is concerned, but the interest is paid upon the presentation of the attached coupons. The bond certificate has a form for entering the date of registration, the name of the registered owner, and the signature of the registrar or transfer agent. As transfers of the bond are made, these entries are repeated on the bond certificate as well as on the registration record of the company or its transfer agent. This type of registered bond can be converted into an unregistered coupon bond by simply entering "bearer" and recording it in the bond register. Coupon bonds may be made interchangeable with the fully registered type, in which instance a new certificate may be issued, or the coupons may be detached and the old certificate used. Not infrequently, when a number of coupon bonds are exchanged for fully registered bonds, that fact and the serial numbers of the coupon bonds turned in are noted on the new certificate. **Interchangeability** of bonds is specified in the trust indenture. When indentures authorize fully registered bonds and the exchange of denominations, a small charge may be made for any transfer or exchange involving the issuance of a new certificate.

Wider use of registered bonds is favored by banks because of the vast and rising volume of coupon collections, a procedure that does not lend itself to automation. It has been urged that registered bonds be made exchangeable without charge for coupon bonds, so that holders would not be at a disadvantage in selling them.

TERMS OF PAYMENT. Bonds and interest coupons, in order to be negotiable instruments, must be made unconditionally payable in a fixed sum of money. The type of money may be designated in the bond. It may be made payable in (1) **legal tender currency,** or (2) **foreign currency.** A bond can also be made payable, both as to interest and principal, in two or more currencies either at a **fixed rate** of exchange or at the **prevailing rate** when the interest or principal matures. Foreign currency bonds are issued in foreign countries and are subject to the laws and regulations of the respective governments of these countries.

BONDS PAYABLE IN GOLD. Bonds issued by both governments and business corporations before June, 1933, were generally made payable, both principal and interest, "in gold coin of the present standard weight and fineness." This provision, used since the Civil War era, was designed to protect holders against devaluation or currency depreciation due to abandonment of the gold standard. By joint resolution of Congress approved by the President June 5, 1933, this clause was rendered null and void, not only with respect to future obligations but also with respect to all outstanding obligations, whether issued by public bodies, including the United States government, or by private persons, including corporations. The resolution declared that "every obligation heretofore or hereafter incurred . . . shall be discharged upon payment, dollar for dollar, in any coin or currency which at the time of payment is legal tender for public and private debts." The United States Supreme Court upheld the constitutionality of this joint resolution.

INTEREST PAYMENTS. With relatively few exceptions, interest on bonds is paid **semi-annually,** usually on the first or the fifteenth day of the month. A corporation may make the interest payable at its own office, but when the size of the issue warrants and the bonds bear coupons, it designates one or more paying agents, usually the trustee under the trust indenture of the bonds, at whose office the interest as well as the principal is payable. The name and location of the office of the paying agent or agents appear on the face of the coupon. Interest on bonds that are registered as to both interest and principal may be paid directly by the debtor corporation, but a paying agent may also be employed in such instances.

The New York Stock Exchange requires that the paying agent of bonds listed on the exchange be located in the Borough of Manhattan, New York City. Other stock exchanges also require a local paying agent, which may require a corporation to have paying agents in more than one city. The **paying agents** or **places of payment** may be changed during the life of a bond issue. Coupons are not invalidated by the fact that the interest is made payable at a place other than that designated on their face.

Bond Indentures

THE NEED FOR THE BOND INDENTURE. The corporation bond is legally defined as "a **promise to pay under seal,**" the amount promised being the par value of the bond. As the courts have held that the seal may be represented by the mere signature of the corporation, the essential form of the bond does not differ materially from an ordinary promissory note. Yet the formal document or engraved certificate constituting the bond is something more than a mere promise to pay a definite sum on a fixed or ascertainable date. It is an evidence of "a right to participate in a certain legal contract—the trust indenture which the corporation enters into with a trustee." (Dewing, Financial Policy of Corporations.) The **trust indenture,** also known as the **deed of trust,** is in the form of an agreement between the corporation and a trustee or trustees that represent the bondholders.

Though the bond certificate and the trust indenture are separate documents, the law construes the **two as one** instrument, particularly when there is reference in each instrument to the other, as is generally the case. The face of the bond usually recites that it is issued under the terms of a specific trust indenture and bears, in addition to the signature of the corporation, an authentication or certification by the trustee to the effect that it is one of the series covered by the trust indenture. The text of the bond is in turn reproduced in the trust indenture.

The trust indenture has become a practical necessity in corporate long-term borrowing, largely because of its convenience in fixing the rights and privileges of the bondholders, and the rights, privileges, and liabilities of the debtor corporation. Since the holders of most corporation bonds are unknown to the debtor corporation and to one another, they would, without the indenture and the corporate trustee, be under the necessity of acting individually to enforce their respective rights. The corporation might (in a manner similar to borrowing on a real estate mortgage) issue the mortgage to each of its bondholders, but when one considers the length of the typical corporate mortgage (perhaps as long as 300 pages or more), it is obvious why the corporation does not follow such practice. A more important reason for not following such a procedure is the fact that the corporation would be exposed to the risk of innumerable actions at law due to varying interpretations of the bond and mortgage contract by the different bondholders. When bonds are issued under a trust indenture, the trustee, as one of the parties to the indenture, represents the bondholders collectively and deals directly with the corporation in their behalf. In other words, by use of the indenture device, the corporation is enabled to deal with a large group of persons as if they were one.

CORPORATE TRUSTEES. At present the trustees named in trust indentures under which corporation bonds are issued are generally banks or trust companies. Originally it was common practice for individuals to act in this capacity. Several states still require that at least one individual, a resident of the state, be appointed a trustee if the corporation's property is located there. Thus, a deed of trust may have both an individual and a corporate trustee. In the event of the death of the individual trustee, the corporate trustee may appoint a successor. The corporate trustee is generally selected either by the debtor corporation or by the bankers to whom the bond issue is sold, or jointly by both. Trustees acknowledge in the trust indenture their acceptance of the trust.

If there is an **individual co-trustee,** in order to enable the corporate trustee to transact business in the absence of the individual trustee the latter is usually permitted to appoint the corporate trustee as his **attorney in fact,** and it is not infrequently the practice for him to execute this power of attorney at the very outset, with the result that the bank or trust company may in effect be the sole trustee. Even if the appointment of an individual co-trustee is not provided for in the trust indenture, it is usual to stipulate that such appointment may be made by the joint action of the debtor corporation and the corporate trustee. The need for this may arise in the event that it should be necessary to take action in a state that prohibits the execution of trust functions by foreign corporations.

The **chief duties of the trustee** are the following:

Certification of Bonds. In the absence of default by the debtor corporation in the provisions of a trust indenture, the principal duty of the trustee is the authentication or certification of the bonds, barring certain functions under mortgage deeds and collateral trust indentures. The bonds are delivered to the trustee for authentication after they have been executed by the president or vice-president of the issuing company, under corporate seal attested by the secretary or an assistant secretary of the corporation. **Authentication** consists in affixing its signature under the following statement on the bond certificates:

> "This bond is one of the bonds described in the within mentioned deed of trust.
> .... Trust Company
> by ....
> Trust Officer"

The trustee does not guarantee the validity of the obligation by such authentication or certify that the bond has been issued according to required legal formalities or in accordance with the charter requirements of the corporation. It merely certifies that the bond is one of the issue provided for and described in the trust agreement and entitles the holder to the benefits of the provisions of the trust indenture. Bonds not bearing such authentication by the trustee are not valid under the trust agreement. In this way some protection is afforded against overissue or forgery of the bonds.

Bonds are authenticated whenever they are issued whether at the outset, upon the creation of the debt, or later as transfers or exchanges of denominations or forms of bonds are made. The **indenture provisions** stipulate the circumstances under which the trustee may or must authenticate bonds submitted to it by the corporation. Upon receiving bonds from the company for authentication, the trustee examines them to see if they conform in all particulars, except as otherwise stipulated in the indenture, with the text of the bond reproduced in the indenture.

To Enforce the Terms of the Indenture. The trustee is expected to take action to protect bondholders in the event of default in the payment of interest or principal, or the violation of some other covenants of the indenture. For specified types of **default,** action is compulsory; for others the trustee has discretion. The indenture may provide for reimbursement of outlays incurred in taking protective action. The Trust Indenture Act requires the trustee to see that the corporation performs its obligations and to notify bondholders of any default.

Administrative Duties. Indentures commonly require the trustee to handle the details of sinking fund payments, bond redemptions, and interest payments. Similarly, when the trust indenture contains a mortgage or a pledge of collateral, the trustee is required to attend to the safe custody of the pledged property, handling of insurance proceeds, property substitution, etc.

TRUST INDENTURE ACT OF 1939. This Act was enacted by Congress for the **protection of holders** of corporation bonds. In the past, issuing corporations had failed to provide an independent trustee capable of protecting and enforcing the rights of bondholders. Conflicting interests such as interlocking directorates involving the trustee and the issuing corporation existed in some cases. Also, it was felt that certain trust indentures were not drawn to give adequate protection to bondholders since they contained **exculpatory clauses** relieving the trustee of liability and the need of taking effective action to protect bondholders' interests. The Act bans such clauses and requires that the indenture contain standard protective provisions, that the essential provisions of trust indentures be more completely disclosed to security holders, and that responsible, disinterested trustees be selected in each case.

The Trust Indenture Act provides in substance that if debt securities (bonds, notes, and other evidences of indebtedness) to be issued under an indenture must be registered under the Securities Act of 1933, such registration will not become effective unless (1) the indenture meets the requirements of the Trust Indenture Act, (2) the registration statement contains certain information with respect to the qualifications of the trustee, and (3) the registration statement and the prospectus contain an analysis of the important provisions of the indenture. The Trust Indenture Act also applies to debt securities issued in exchange for other securities of the same corporation under a voluntary readjustment plan or under a reorganization plan approved by a court, even though the securities may not be required to be registered under the Securities Act.

Indenture Provisions Required by the Act. To be **qualified** under the Act, an indenture must contain certain provisions, the most important being the following:

1. A **financially responsible** corporate trustee must be named and the interests of the trustee must not conflict with those of the indenture security holders. One of the trustees must be a corporation with capital and surplus of not less than $150,000 and it cannot be affiliated with the issuer or underwriter.

2. In a situation where certain defined **conflicts of interest** arise, such as would exist if (a) the trustee is acting under another indenture of the same issuer, or (b) the trustee or its officers are affiliated with the issuer or the underwriter, then the trustee must either resign, remove the conflicting interests, or notify security holders and let them exercise their defined powers of removal.

3. The indenture terms must require the corporation to furnish a **list of bondholders** to the trustee at stated intervals, and this list must be made available by the trustee to individual bondholders upon demand.

4. The trustee must be required to submit an **annual report** to bondholders indicating the nature of any advances made by the trustee to the corporation; the condition of the property held in trust—releases, substitutions, etc.; and other relevant matters such as the continued ability of the trustee to function in a disinterested capacity.

5. The indenture must require the corporation to furnish the trustee with (a) evidence of **recording** the indenture, (b) a **certificate of fair value** prepared by an independent engineer, appraiser, or other expert, as to the fair value of property or securities released from the lien of the indenture, and of securities or property to be used as the basis of the issuance of additional securities, the withdrawal of cash, or the release of other property or securities subject to the lien of the indenture, and (c) **annual and special reports.**

6. The indenture must require the trustee to notify the bondholders of all **defaults** within 90 days.

7. The debenture must provide that in the event of default the trustee must exercise his defined powers and rights with the same degree of care and skill that a **prudent man** similarly situated would exercise.

8. The indenture must provide that if a **trustee becomes a creditor** of the obligor within 4 months prior to default or after such default, the trustee must set apart and hold in a special account for his benefit and the benefit of the bondholders any payments or property received in settlement of the account, which amounts will be subject to apportionment by the court of jurisdiction.

The indenture may provide that holders of not less than a majority of the outstanding securities may consent on behalf of all the security holders to the waiver of any past default. It may also provide that holders of not less than 75% of the securities outstanding may consent on behalf of all the security holders to the postponement of any interest payment for a period not exceeding 3 years from its due date. However, it is not standard practice to include such provisions in qualifying indentures under the Trust Indenture Act.

The Trust Indenture Act is **administered by the Securities and Exchange Commission**, but the Commission's only function is to see that the terms of each indenture conform to the prescribed standards. Application for qualification of indentures must be filed with the Securities and Exchange Commission. The Commission has no powers with respect to the enforcement of the provisions of the indenture. After the indenture has been executed it is enforceable only by the parties, like any other contract. However, the Trust Indenture Act widens the basis for action by bondholders against the trustee for negligence and misfeasance, and places additional responsibility, and incidentally expense, on the corporation.

PROVISIONS OF A BOND INDENTURE. The character of the provisions set forth in a trust indenture will depend on (a) whether the bond issue is secured or unsecured, and (b) the circumstances surrounding each individual issuing corporation.

Summary of Contents. The main contents of the typical corporate trust indenture may be summarized as follows:

1. Names of the parties and the preamble.
2. The consideration and grant or the assignment in trust.
3. The conditions governing the issuance of the bonds, including (a) limitations in amount and (b) conditions of (1) certification and delivery, (2) registration, and (3) interchange of the bonds.
4. Definition of terms used in the indenture.
5. Particular covenants of the indenture.
6. Provisions as to pledged bonds and stocks.
7. Provisions relating to redemption of bonds.
8. Remedies of trustee and bondholders.
9. Releases of property.
10. Consolidations, mergers, and purchases affecting the borrowing corporation.
11. Possession prior to default, and defeasance.
12. Provisions concerning the trustee.
13. Miscellaneous provisions.
14. Execution, acknowledgment, recording, affidavits of good faith, etc.

Each of the above provisions not already covered or considered subsequently is discussed immediately below.

Names of the Parties. The parties to an indenture are the debtor corporation and the trustee. The corporate names of the debtor and of the trustee are required to be stated fully. The state of incorporation of the company is mentioned, and whether it was organized under general laws or created by special charter, consolidation or merger, or otherwise. If there is an individual as a co-trustee, his name is mentioned as a party to the agreement.

The Preamble. The preamble sets forth: (1) the purposes of the indenture; (2) the preliminary corporate proceedings that have been taken to meet the legal requirements for entering into the agreement, such, for example, as directors' and stockholders' meetings, the passage of the necessary resolutions, and the like; and (3) the form of the bonds, coupons, and trustee's authentication of the bonds.

Grant or Assignment of Trust. This section of the trust indenture comprises a description of the mortgaged property, if the indenture is a mortgage deed of trust, and other collateral or covenants made for the protection and benefit of the bondholders. The mortgaged property is described in sufficient detail to be identified, and the mortgage is made a record lien. **Stock-in-trade** and other personalty are usually excepted from the mortgage, to permit the debtor corporation to sell, exchange, or otherwise dispose of such assets without hindrance. Statutes in nearly all states disallow the mortgaging of stock-in-trade left in the custody of the mortgagor. Moreover, it is generally impracticable to give a satisfactory lien on movables, if they are liable to pass out of the jurisdiction in which the mortgage is recorded or filed as a chattel mortgage. As to railroads, the statutes of many states declare that rolling stock and other appurtenant chattels are real estate for mortgage purposes. If **future-acquired property** is to be included in the mortgage, this is definitely stated. Likewise, if the company possesses or exercises any franchise, exclusive of its right to be a corporation, this may be brought under the lien. Following the granting clauses, it is usual to list the property excepted from the mortgage and to refer to any prior liens.

Conditions Governing the Issue of Bonds. The authorized amount of the bonds to be issued, if limited to a definite sum, is generally stated in the trust indenture, as well as the amount to be immediately issued. Limitation of the amount of bonds to be issued is usually based on a flexible yardstick, rather than a rigid dollar amount. When additional bonds may be issued under specified restrictions, the trustee must be assured by certified statements of the proper officers of the company that the prescribed conditions for additional issues are present. Moreover, if the proceeds of an issue of bonds have been limited to expenditures of a specified character, such as the acquisition of property or for improvements and betterments, the trustee may hold the funds until certification is made to it that such expenditures have been effected. The purposes for which bonds are authorized for issuance in the future are usually stated in the indenture.

Variations in the forms of bonds, their denominations, interest rates, conversion privileges, sinking fund provisions, rights of redemption, and the like are also specified in the indenture.

Particular Covenants of the Indenture. This section of the trust indenture contains the covenants entered into by the debtor corporation, among which the following are standard:

1. That it will pay the principal and interest of every bond authenticated by the trustee at the dates, places, and in the manner mentioned in the bonds or coupons.
2. That it will designate an office or agency in a particular city or cities where the bonds and coupons may be presented for payment.
3. That it has good title to any mortgaged property and that it will defend the title.
4. That it will keep any mortgaged property in proper repair, making such renewals, replacements, additions, betterments, and improvements as may be necessary for the profitable conduct of the business, and that it will generally do nothing that would impair the lien of the bonds.
5. That it will keep the mortgaged premises properly insured against loss from fire or other cause. (The proceeds of any such insurance, if exceeding in any case of loss a stated figure, as for example, $5,000, are to be paid to the trustee, which will pay it to the company as the destroyed property is replaced or additions or betterments equal in value to the destroyed property are made to

other portions of the mortgaged property. The insurance policies may be deposited with the trustee, as in the case of ordinary real estate mortgages, or the more recent practice may be followed of submitting to the trustee an annual statement of the policies in force.)
6. That it will pay all taxes and assessments levied upon its property, franchises, or income.
7. That it will maintain its corporate existence and its right to do business.
8. That it will properly record the mortgage and pay any necessary fees.

Other covenants contained in this portion of the indenture may require the corporation not to create any debt having priority of lien upon the trust estate; not to increase any outstanding issue of bonds having such priority of lien; and not to extend the time of payment of any such bonds but to pay them at or before their maturity. There may also be a covenant forbidding the corporation to permit any mechanics', laborers', or other **statutory lien** to remain outstanding upon the pledged property that might or could be held to be prior to the lien of the indenture.

Additional covenants may require the company to maintain a **sinking fund** for the retirement of the bonds; to maintain a replacement fund for the protection of the mortgaged property; to meet certain prescribed conditions before paying dividends on capital stock; and to maintain certain minimum working capital requirements.

Remedies of Trustees and Bondholders. The trust indenture provides for the remedies that may be exercised by the trustee and bondholders in the event of a breach or default in any of the conditions laid down in the trust agreement. These "events of default," as they are called, may include any default under a trust indenture having priority of lien to the indenture in question. The remedies under the indenture also become available if the corporation remains adjudged a bankrupt for a stated number of days, or has instituted proceedings to be adjudged a voluntary bankrupt, or has made an assignment for the benefit of creditors, or a receiver has been appointed to liquidate and wind up its affairs, and the court order making the appointment has remained in force undischarged or unstayed for a stated number of days.

Principal remedies that the trust agreement usually provides are:

1. The **right of entry,** or the right of the trustee to take possession of the mortgaged property and operate it for the benefit of the bondholders, applying the net earnings to the payment of the interest or principal. When the default has been made good, the property passes back to the corporation.
2. The **right to sell** the property to the highest bidder without suit.
3. The **right to foreclose** the mortgage and dispose of the property under judicial sale.
4. The **right to bring suit** for the specific performance of any covenant or agreement or for the enforcement of any other legal or equitable remedy.
5. The **right to declare the principal due** before the stipulated maturity date and to recover judgment against the company for the amount due and in the event of the sale of the mortgaged property to recover judgment for any unpaid portion of the debt.

The trustee can exercise the stipulated remedies in its discretion, or it may be forced to take action by the written request of the holders of a stated proportion in amount of the bonds, ranging from 10% upward, provided it is guaranteed indemnity for all expenses it may incur in taking such action. Ordinarily, the trustee does not act unless it is requested by bondholders, usually as represented by a protective committee. The Trust Indenture Act has required more direct action by the trustee under indentures subject to the Act because of the **"prudent business man" test** imposed.

Remedies given the trustee are rarely exercised, however. Thus, the right to enter and take possession of the property of the debtor is avoided by the appointment under the bankruptcy statutes of a trustee to take charge of the assets and business of the corporation. Similarly, the right to dispose of mortgaged or pledged property without a suit of foreclosure is rarely exercised. As a practical matter, these indenture provisions serve primarily to safeguard the priority of the bond issue in the event of reorganization under the Bankruptcy Act or liquidation.

Period of Grace. Except for default in payment of the principal when due, the debtor corporation is granted a period of grace, ranging from 30 days to 6 months, in which no action on the default can be taken by the trustee. In the event of default in payment of interest, the default begins to run from the date the interest is due. In the event of other defaults, it may be provided that the period of grace begins to run from the date the trustee gives the corporation written notice of the default, as stipulated in the indenture. The giving of this notice may be made by the trustee on its own motion or may be requested by holders of a certain proportion in amount of the bonds. A default in the payment of principal or interest automatically comes to the attention of bondholders, but **notice of other defaults** can only be communicated to them by the trustee, as required by the Trust Indenture Act. These other defaults (aside from sinking fund defaults) are in many instances simply technical in nature and not too important from a financial viewpoint.

Acceleration of Maturity in Cases of Default. As the agreements to pay interest periodically and to pay principal when due are regarded as independent covenants, it is generally provided that in the event of any defaults in the covenants by the debtor corporation, the principal of the debt becomes immediately payable. This acceleration of the payment of the principal is necessary in order to afford the bondholders the right of **immediate foreclosure.** Without such right, the only remedy is to foreclose for the installment of interest immediately due.

Individual Action of Bondholders. The indenture provides that suits for the application of remedies in the event of defaults may be brought by individual bondholders only if the trustee, after it has been requested in writing by a stated proportion in amount of the bondholders and has been offered indemnification for any expenses it may have to pay, refuses or neglects to take action.

The courts, however, have generally held that refusal of action on the part of the trustee to enforce remedies in behalf of bondholders because a sufficient proportion of them have not requested the action does not bar them from their equitable rights. Suits may be brought by a bondholder individually. In the case of Hubbard v. Galveston, H. & S. A. R. Railway Co. (U.S. Circuit Court of Appeals, 5th Circuit, 200 Fed. 504), the court made the following statement regarding individual action by bondholders to protect their rights:

It is contended by defendants, in support of their general demurrers, that the remedies provided in the mortgage were embodied therein for the protection of the bondholders as a class, expressly made subject to the control of the holders of a majority in amount, and plaintiffs, being minority bondholders, cannot maintain a suit to foreclose the mortgage. Fairly considering their bill, all they are attempting is to collect the interest past due and have the sinking fund made whole, and in their oral and printed arguments they have disclaimed any other intention. It is well settled that, regardless of such provisions of a mortgage, if the contract has been breached, the minority bondholders cannot be deprived of their right to equitable relief because a majority of the bondholders, whose interests might be adverse, should decline to join with them.

In suits of this character, however, one bondholder cannot obtain judgment against the corporation that would impair similar rights of other bondholders under the same trust indenture. In Watson v. C., R. I. & P. Ry., a bondholder individually sued the corporation to reach property not covered by the mortgage, on the ground that the trustee refused to carry out the obligation to recover judgment for the entire principal of all the bonds outstanding, together with all interest in default, and in the event of the foreclosure of mortgaged property not affording the sum required, to recover the deficiency under a further judgment. The Appellate Division of the New York courts [169 App. Div. (N.Y.) 663] held that "as the trustee had acted, no independent action by a bondholder could be maintained," and one of the judges, in an assenting opinion, maintained that the principle of equality of bondholders under the same indenture would be violated if one bondholder, in his own separate right, recovered a judgment enforceable against property of the mortgagor even though not covered by the mortgage. The same reasoning was applied in Gue v. Canal Co. (24 How. 263), an earlier case decided by the U.S. Supreme Court.

Thus, it will be seen that in voluntary readjustment plans a dissenting bondholder cannot be coerced into accepting any extension or adjustment of maturity or reduction of interest. The bondholder's contract rights with respect to payment of principal and interest are clear cut, and the courts will protect them to an unlimited extent as long as the individual action of one bondholder does not impair similar rights of other bondholders under the same indenture, and so long as the property does not come under the jurisdiction of a court in a **Federal Bankruptcy Act proceeding.**

Releases of Mortgaged Property. Since mortgages cover relatively long periods of time, a debtor corporation may from time to time find it desirable to sell, exchange, or abandon property covered by the deed of trust. To meet this situation, trust indentures, as a rule, contain a clause permitting, under prescribed conditions, partial releases and substitutions of property covered by the mortgage when sanctioned by the trustee. Such releases are recorded in the same jurisdictions in which the mortgage is recorded, namely, in all counties of all states in which the mortgaged property is located. Without the recording of such instrument the property could only be sold or otherwise disposed of subject to the lien of the mortgage.

The provisions concerning releases comprise such matters as: (1) the nature and amount of property subject to release, (2) the identification of the specific parcels of property released, (3) the method or methods of ascertaining its value, (4) the application of the proceeds from its sale, and (5) the extension of the mortgage lien to substituted property or to property acquired with the proceeds from the sale of released property. The prime purpose of the conditions relating to releases is to **protect the equities of the bondholders** from impairment and to maintain the value of the whole property secured by the mortgage.

In applying to the trustee for a release from the mortgage, the company must make the following typical averments:

1. That the property to be released is no longer needed in the operations of the company.

2. That it was sold or exchanged for property of at least equal value.
3. That any cash proceeds will be deposited with the trustee, and that any property acquired in exchange will be placed under the lien of the mortgage. In the instance of the release of any portion of the property subject to a prior mortgage, any cash consideration received will be deposited with the trustee under that mortgage.

The application for release will have to be accompanied by various documents, including a certified copy of the directors' resolutions authorizing the application, opinion of counsel as to the title of the property to be acquired, and, as required by the Trust Indenture Act, a "certificate of fair value" prepared by an independent engineer of the property to be disposed of and of the property to be secured in exchange, if any.

Any **cash proceeds** deposited with the trustee are returned to the company:

1. To reimburse it for the cost of property purchased or constructed under the terms of the indenture.
2. For the redemption of bonds at the option of the company, or for their purchase in the open market or on tender made by holders.

The indenture may stipulate that unless the company uses the cash within one year of its deposit with the trustee, the latter may employ it in redeeming bonds issued under the indenture or in other securities as specified.

Consolidations and Mergers. Provisions relating to the possible consolidation, merger, or sale of the entire assets of the debtor corporation are also found in trust indentures. The principal feature of such provisions is the requirement that in the event of a merger, consolidation, or sale of assets, the rights and equities of the bondholders should in no way be impaired and that the property and other equities covered by the trust indenture as an entirety should remain so subject after the consolidation, merger, or sale of assets, and that the successor corporation shall assume the bonds of the predecessor corporation.

"No Recourse" Clause. Trust indentures generally contain a clause, which may be reproduced in the bond certificate, by virtue of which the bondholders waive their right as creditors to take advantage of the law rendering incorporators, stockholders, officers, and directors personally liable for certain acts or omissions. Under this clause, for example, it is impossible for the trustee or the individual bondholder to sue stockholders for any balance due on their stock. The clause describes the bonds as solely corporate obligations and states that **no personal liability** attaches to the above-mentioned individuals because of these obligations.

Changes in Trust Indentures. A trust indenture, being a contract, cannot be altered without the **consent of the parties** to it, including the bondholders. Unless the instrument contains a provision permitting its modification with the consent of a certain majority in amount of the bondholders—two-thirds, three-fourths, or 85%—usually their unanimous consent must be secured to any proposed change. Such consent may be obtained by requesting the deposit of the bonds under an agreement with a committee having the matter in charge. If all the bonds or the majority required by the indenture are deposited, the change in the indenture becomes effective and is binding in the latter case on any nonassenting minority. When a sufficient amount of the bonds is not deposited to enforce the change upon all, the plan may be abandoned or it may be carried out so far as the assenting bondholders are concerned. In this event, the assenting bonds are stamped with an appropriate notation to indicate their changed status.

An example of a legend that may appear on so-called **stamped bonds** is as follows:

> The owner of the within bond has participated in the plan of readjustment dated . . . . and by such participation the within bond is subject to such plan and modification and is so received by every subsequent holder thereof.

The two classes of bonds into which the original issue has been thus divided—the stamped and the **unstamped**—have distinct market quotations, and the latter may sell at a premium because payment in full is expected by dissenters.

Indentures may provide for bondholders to vote by proxy, as in the instance of corporate stock.

Supplemental Indentures. This is a method of modifying or adding to the provisions of the indenture, and special provision is usually made for it in the indenture itself. The trustee may be authorized to join with the debtor company in the execution of such supplements to the indenture. Supplemental indentures have a variety of purposes, the most common of which are:

1. To subject to the lien of the indenture additional property or additional collateral security, acquired through consolidation, merger, purchase, or otherwise. This is the most common use of supplemental indentures.
2. To have a public record of the terms of a new series of bonds if the bonds are issued under a mortgage, since supplemental indentures are recorded in the same public offices as the mortgage.
3. To evidence the assumption, as the result of a consolidation, merger, or purchase of assets, of bond issues that will have priority of lien on the mortgaged property.
4. To evidence the succession of another corporation to the debtor corporation and its assumption of the latter's bonds.
5. To evidence any change in the indenture that favors the bondholders.
6. To evidence a change in any covenant of the indenture, which will require the consent of the bondholders and the stamping of an appropriate endorsement upon the bonds.

Mortgage Bonds

MORTGAGE INSTRUMENTS. A mortgage bond, the principal type of secured debt instrument, is secured by a mortgage deed of trust containing, in addition to the usual provisions and covenants, a conditional conveyance or **pledge of property.** The mortgage trust indenture contains a detailed legal description of the specific property that is mortgaged. The terms of the conveyance are very similar to those of the ordinary real estate mortgage, the debtor corporation being the mortgagor and the trustee the mortgagee in the interest of the bondholders. Similarly, the debtor corporation retains possession of the mortgaged property although the defeasance clause in the mortgage indenture states that if the corporation pays off the bonds in the manner described in the indenture, the title to the property reverts to the corporation free of any lien that the trustee may have possessed.

Purpose of the Mortgage. The mortgage bond consists of two separate instruments—the bond and the mortgage. The bond proper is an unsecured debt of the issuing corporation. If the bond is additionally secured by a mortgage, the holder's position is thereby strengthened. If a corporation is forced to default in the payment of its bonds, secured obligations possess priority in reorganization or liquidation to the extent of the value of the property pledged. The "absolute priority" doctrine in corporate reorganization cases safeguards the position of secured creditors.

CLOSED MORTGAGES. The maximum amount of bonds that may be issued under the deed of trust is known as the amount authorized. When the total amount authorized has been put out, the issue, or the mortgage, if the bonds are secured, is said to be closed.

Closed mortgages are of **several types**:

1. The typical one by the terms of which the entire authorized amount of bonds is to be issued at once.
2. One that becomes closed only after several issues have been put out under the mortgage and the entire authorized amount sold.
3. One that is closed by the voluntary action of the corporation, through the creation of a supplemental indenture, before the exhaustion of the total authorized amount.

Disadvantages of Closed Mortgages. Under a closed mortgage covering the entire property of a corporation, when the maximum amount of bonds authorized has been issued, **additional borrowing** has to be done under a second or junior mortgage, subordinate in lien to the first. At one time it was customary for corporations, especially railroads and the older public utilities, to limit the authorized amount to the immediate capital requirements, with the consequence that in time they had a number of mortgages on their property of different degrees of priority and each for a relatively small amount. Except in real estate corporations and other special situations, closed mortgages are no longer used in corporate bond financing.

OPEN-END AND LIMITED OPEN-END MORTGAGES. Mortgage bonds that are not limited to specific amounts are known as open-end or indeterminate issues or mortgages. If the authorized amount is specified but is fixed at a figure far in excess of the requirements of the present or the near future, being intended to cover all requirements for an indefinite time, the issue is known as a limited open-end mortgage.

Open-end and limited open-end issues are the usual types of mortgage bonds put out nowadays by railroads, public utilities, and some industrial companies. The advantage of such mortgages lies in the greater **flexibility** they lend to the financial structure of corporations, since the volume of borrowing can be adjusted to the growth of the enterprise. Additional issues may be sold for specific purposes mentioned in the trust deed and for general corporate purposes. These provisions in the trust deed usually provide that additional bonds may be put out from time to time at the discretion of directors to reimburse the company's treasury for a specified percentage of expenditures for capital improvements, additions, and new acquisitions. Likewise, a certain amount may be reserved to refund underlying issues.

Restrictions on Issue of Bonds Under Open-End and Limited Open-End Mortgages. Various restrictions are imposed upon the issue of bonds under open-end and limited open-end mortgages. The trustee is charged with the duty of seeing that these restrictive provisions are properly complied with by the corporation before it authenticates any additional bonds. The following provisions are typical of many issues:

1. Restriction to a stated percentage, say 60%, 65%, or 75% of the lower of actual cost or the fair value of net property additions subsequent to the sale of the original issue of bonds.

2. Limitation of interest payable on the corporation's bonds, including that of the proposed issue, to a stated ratio to the net earnings available for interest payment for a stated period preceding the issuance of the additional bonds. For example, it may be provided that additional bonds may be issued under the mortgage only if interest payments will have been covered twice in each of two preceding years.
3. Restriction of the amount of bonds outstanding to a certain proportion of the net current assets or net quick assets of the corporation.
4. Restriction to a fixed ratio to capital stock outstanding or to the capital stock and surplus.

ISSUANCE OF BONDS AGAINST DEPOSIT OF CASH WITH TRUSTEE. In some mortgages it is provided that the corporation may issue bonds some time in advance of capital expenditures or the acquisition of additional property, provided the proceeds are immediately deposited with the trustee and drawn upon only after certification by the corporation that the proper expenditure has been made or additional property has been acquired. The purpose of this provision is to enable the corporation to take advantage of a favorable market for the bonds.

BONDS ISSUED IN SERIES. The use of the open-end and limited open-end mortgages by the larger companies has led to the practice of issuing under the same trust deed bonds in successive series or installments, the aggregate amount of which, however, must always be within the total authorized by the indenture. The indenture specifies in detail the terms of the **first series,** which is to be issued immediately. The terms of each of the **later series**—their date, amount, maturity, interest rate, dates of interest payments, denominations, and forms of the bonds and their interchangeability, provisions relating to conversion, sinking fund, redemption, and taxes—will be such as the board of directors may in their discretion fix from time to time, and they will be expressed in the bonds of such series. The bonds of the same series must be identical in tenor except as to denomination. Just in what respects one series can be made to differ from the others is governed by the indenture. In some instances, the indenture may, for example, stipulate that every series shall mature not before a certain year and not beyond a stated later year. Each series is designated by a distinctive letter, or by the date of its issue or of its maturity, or by the interest rate it bears. The terms of each successive series are set forth in a supplemental indenture.

Trust deeds permitting the issue of bonds in series impart a desirable element of **flexibility** to mortgage bond financing. The terms of new bond issues can be adapted to **prevailing market conditions** so that the desired amount of new capital can be secured on the most advantageous terms. The corporation is not compelled to seek a revision of its indenture, a procedure that may be attended with difficulties.

Bonds other than mortgage bonds—collateral trust bonds and debentures—may also be issued in series.

MORTGAGE ON AFTER-ACQUIRED PROPERTY. As security for an issue of bonds, a corporation often mortgages not only property that it owns or has an interest in at the date of the mortgage deed, but it also covenants to extend the lien to property acquired in the future. The clause in the trust indenture extending the lien is termed the after-acquired property clause. It is usually expressed thus: ". . . all and singular, its property and franchises of every nature and description whatsoever, whether now owned or hereafter to be acquired." This clause has been interpreted by the courts to include **all real**

property vested in the corporation, whether or not such property is used in its business. However, if the terms of the mortgage clearly indicate that property subsequently acquired, but that does not constitute a part of the plant used in the company's business, is not intended to come under the after-acquired property clause, it will be excluded from the mortgage.

The application of the after-acquired property clause may also be limited by a statement in the mortgage deed that only property that is acquired with the proceeds of the present or subsequent issues is to come under the lien of the mortgage.

Existing Liens on Subsequently Acquired Property. If there are existing liens on property acquired subsequent to the date of the trust indenture containing the after-acquired property clause, the priority of such liens is not disturbed by the clause. But if one corporation is merely a "dummy" of another corporation, a mortgage on the property of the latter attaches to property of the former.

If a corporation has outstanding a prior lien mortgage containing an after-acquired property clause, additional property acquired with the proceeds of **junior lien obligations** is also subject to the lien of the prior mortgage, even though such prior mortgage has been closed and no further bonds can be issued thereunder.

Avoiding Application of After-Acquired Property Clause. The after-acquired property clause in closed mortgage deeds has the effect of preventing the corporation from doing future financing except with junior securities. If the clause in a closed mortgage, or in a limited open-end mortgage with burdensome restrictions, does hamper the financing of new property acquisitions, it may be avoided by:

1. Issuance of a **purchase money mortgage** to the vendor of the property. The purchase money mortgage, as its name implies, is given to the seller as part of the purchase price of the property. The courts have held that when a vendor deeds its property to the buying corporation subject to a purchase money mortgage received in payment, an after-acquired property clause in an outstanding mortgage bond issue of the buying corporation does not affect the lien of the purchase money mortgage. Hence, property transferred subject to a lien for a part of the purchase money, i.e., subject to a purchase money mortgage, remains covered by this encumbrance until the lien is satisfied and extinguished. A mortgage given as part consideration in the purchase of real property thus takes priority over a mortgage with an after-acquired property clause executed previously. The earlier mortgage, however, covers the purchased property as a junior lien, subject to the rights of the holders of the purchase money mortgage.

2. Organization of a **subsidiary** to acquire and finance the property.

3. **Consolidation** with another corporation that then acquires the desired property, except if it is held that the successor corporation assumes the obligations under the after-acquired property clause.

4. Acquisition of the property under **leases or conditional sales agreements**, to avoid taking of title by corporations whose mortgages have after-acquired clauses.

SCOPE OF LIEN AND MORTGAGE BOND TITLES. Mortgage bond titles are not always descriptive of the degree of security or priority provided. The title **first mortgage bond** does not necessarily mean that the issue has a first lien on all company property. The first mortgage lien may be restricted to a small segment of a corporation's property, or it may apply to substantially all its fixed assets. A corporation may have a number of first mortgage bond issues with first mortgages on different properties; or first, second, and third mortgages on the property of the company as a whole. Similarly, a mortgage bond issue might be a first mortgage on the smaller part of the company's properties and a second mortgage on the larger part of the properties. Generally speaking, however, such complex debt structures survive only in some railroads. It is necessary to examine the chief indenture provisions to establish the actual priority of a given mortgage bond issue. Financial manuals summarize such information.

Bond issues variously termed general and refunding, first and refunding, first and consolidated, and so on are put out under open-end or limited open-end mortgages to finance additions, betterments, and acquisitions, already made or to be made in the future, and to refund underlying issues, either those previously put out by the corporation or those assumed by it in consolidations or mergers. They are especially characteristic of the financial structures of railroads and public utilities.

TERMINAL BONDS. In many large cities, railroads making joint use of terminals do not own them directly but through a joint subsidiary especially organized to take title to the properties. The subsidiary issues bonds secured by a mortgage on the property. It is a common practice for the parent railroads to guarantee such bonds jointly and severally, either on their face or through a lease or operating agreement.

Collateral Trust Bonds

NATURE OF SECURITY. Collateral trust bonds are bonds secured solely or for the most part by the pledge of stocks or bonds or both as collateral with the trustee under a **collateral trust indenture.** This indenture empowers the trustee to sell the pledged securities in the event of default, and from the proceeds recover the sum due on the bonds. A pledge of securities is also frequently included as additional security in mortgage deeds on physical property of large companies, especially in refunding issues. Practically the same provisions relative to the pledge are found in these mortgages as in the regular collateral trust agreements. Bonds issued under such an indenture may be known as mortgage and collateral trust bonds.

The **credit position** of a collateral trust bond issue is determined not only by the value of the collateral and the strength of the obligor, but also by its status in reorganization under the **Bankruptcy Act.** Trustees are usually enjoined by the court from selling the collateral in reorganization proceedings, but the treatment of such bonds under the plan will reflect the value of the collateral at the time of reorganization. Moreover, damages have been awarded bondholders in some cases for loss caused them by the delay in selling collateral due to bankruptcy proceedings.

Types of Collateral. The securities pledged under collateral trust agreements may be of the following four general classes:

1. Bonds and stocks of partly or wholly owned subsidiary companies. This is the usual case.
2. Prior lien long-term bonds of the pledgor company deposited to secure short-term notes or a junior issue of bonds. The bonds deposited as collateral must be mortgage bonds, as there would be no purpose in simply duplicating the company's unsecured promises to pay.

3. Bonds and stocks of companies entirely independent of the pledgor or issuing company, held merely for investment. Such bonds are issued by some investment trusts, to take one example.
4. Installment notes or other obligations of a corporation's customers, which may be pledged by a finance company or a manufacturer to secure its obligations.

PLEDGED SECURITIES. The pledged securities **must be deposited** with the trustee, under the typical agreement, as a prerequisite to its authenticating the bonds. Practically the only exception to this rule is when a bond issue has a secondary lien on the pledged securities, which in that case are deposited with the trustee under the prior lien indenture. A trustee may, however, release a sufficient number of pledged shares of stock to qualify directors. Deposited stocks and registered bonds may remain in the name of the debtor company until a default occurs, the trustee having an irrevocable power of attorney to enable it at any time to transfer securities as authorized under the indenture; or the securities may be transferred to the name of the trustee in the first place if this is required by the terms of the indenture. On the other hand, because of the greater difficulty of effecting transfers of securities registered in the name of a corporation or trustee, pledged stocks may first be transferred to the name of a nominee, such as an employee in the trustee's office, who thereupon assigns the securities to and deposits them with the trustee.

Payment of Principal, Interest, and Dividends on Pledged Securities. Upon maturity of any pledged bonds, the principal is to be paid to the trustee. Any dividends or interest payments received by the trustee during the life of the pledged securities are turned over to the pledgor corporation, so long as the latter is not in default. Bond coupons are delivered to the corporation for collection as they mature. But if payments are made from the proceeds of sale of property subject to a mortgage, or if they represent capital distributions, they are usually retained by the trustee. Cash thus received by the trustee, as well as funds received in payment of the principal or pledged bonds, is held as **additional security** for the bonds issued under the collateral trust indenture, and is only paid to the corporation in reimbursement for capital expenditures or against deposit of other securities of equivalent value. In the event of **default,** all pledged securities standing in the corporation's name are immediately transferred to the name of the trustee, which then takes steps at once to collect and retain all dividends and interest.

Voting Pledged Stock. The pledgor corporation is permitted to vote pledged stock unless it defaults in any respect, in which instance the voting power is exercised by the trustee. If stock is registered in a trustee's name, the latter delivers proxies on request before annual or special meetings of the stockholders of the company whose shares have been pledged. If the stock pledged represents a stated proportion of the total outstanding, such as two-thirds, it may not usually be voted so as to authorize any increase in the capital stock of the issuing company unless provision is made for the pledging of the new shares under the indenture, so that the ratio of the stock pledged to the total outstanding will not be decreased. This provision is designed to insure control over the **subsidiary company** for the collateral bondholders.

It may also be stipulated that additional shares or bonds of the subsidiary already outstanding that may be acquired by the pledgor company shall be pledged. This corresponds to the after-acquired property clause in mortgage deeds.

All **stock dividends** declared by a company whose stock is pledged are retained by the trustee, and no steps may be taken by the pledgor company looking to the dissolution of a subsidiary whose shares are pledged without the consent of the trustee. A pledgor company, if it has a controlling interest in a subsidiary, is usually required to covenant to pay the subsidiary's taxes and other assessments if the latter should fail to meet them.

Release of Pledged Securities. A collateral trust indenture may authorize the trustee to release to the pledgor company certain of the pledged securities, provided they are replaced with securities of at least equivalent value. The indenture may specify the **method** by which such equivalent value may be determined. Thus, two arbitrators may be appointed to appraise the collateral, one by the pledgor company and one by the trustee. If the two arbitrators disagree, it may be provided that the value of the substituted securities shall be determined by a member of a stock exchange. The indenture may also state the **principles of valuation** the arbitrators should follow.

CONSOLIDATION, MERGER, OR SALE OF ASSETS OF SUBSIDIARY. Indentures make provision for the possible consolidation or merger of subsidiaries, the securities of which are pledged under an indenture, or for the sale of their assets. In the event that a subsidiary is combined by any one of these three methods with a corporation other than the parent company, securities received by the parent company in exchange for its pledged holdings are to be deposited under the indenture.

In the event of **failure of a subsidiary** whose securities are pledged under an indenture, the trustee may join in a plan of reorganization and accept in exchange for the pledged securities of the old company the securities of the reorganized company.

PLEDGE OF MISCELLANEOUS COLLATERAL. When bonds are secured by the deposit of securities in which the **pledgor corporation does not have the controlling interest,** the provisions of the indenture will differ from those described in the foregoing pages. The income from the securities may be retained by the trustee for the payment of the interest on the bonds issued under the indenture, and there will often be a strict provision for maintaining the market value of the collateral at a certain percentage above the face amount of collateral trust bonds outstanding, by deposit of additional securities when necessary. Free substitution of pledged securities may be permitted, provided the new securities are at least equal in value to those replaced. This type of indenture contains no provisions relating to the automatic pledge of additional issues of stock or bonds by a company whose securities are pledged.

Equipment Obligations

CHARACTER OF OBLIGATION. Equipment obligations have been issued for the most part by railroads and other transportation companies. They constitute in essence a lien on specific equipment with priority over any lien that other obligations of the issuer may possess on such equipment.

Such obligations are known as **equipment trust certificates** or **equipment trusts,** and as **equipment notes** or **bonds,** depending upon the form of the agreement. They may be issued under three plans: (1) the equipment mortgage plan; (2) the conditional sale plan, sometimes referred to as the New York plan; and (3) the so-called Philadelphia plan, which is in the form of a lease agreement.

Equipment Mortgage Plan. This form of obligation is an ordinary bond or note secured by a lien on equipment. The railroad company acquires title to the property and executes a trust agreement by means of which the property is conveyed to a trustee in the same manner as under ordinary mortgage bonds or notes. An obstacle to their wider use has been the presence of after-acquired property clauses in the outstanding mortgages of many of the railroads, by virtue of which equipment becomes subject to these liens as soon as the railroad receives title to it.

Conditional Sale Plan. Under this arrangement, the vendor of the equipment, usually the manufacturer, transfers it to a trustee, which executes an agreement to sell it to the railroad for an **initial cash payment** and a number of **deferred payments.** These deferred payments are represented by equipment notes or bonds, as they are called under this plan. Title to the equipment, it is stipulated, remains with the trustee until all the notes have been paid, when title passes to the railroad.

Philadelphia Plan. This arrangement is generally employed today. It consists of two parts—a **trust** and a **lease agreement**—that are rendered virtually one by means of references in each to the other. Parties to the trust agreement are the vendors of the equipment, a trust company that is to act as trustee under the indenture, and the railroad company. The vendor agrees to deliver the equipment to the trustee and receives from the latter its so-called share certificates, or equipment trusts, which are sold to investors. Thereupon the equipment is leased, under the lease agreement, to the railroad in consideration of the latter paying a **periodic rental** sufficient to defray interest on the trust certificates (the coupons attached are called dividend warrants) and the installments of principal as they fall due. The railroad also pays the trustee an **advance rental** of 20% to 25% of the value of the equipment, so that the trustee is required to issue trust certificates for only 80% to 75% of the purchase price of the equipment. It is stipulated in the lease agreement that when a railroad has paid all rentals, the trustee will execute the proper instrument of conveyance so as to transfer title to the equipment to the railroad.

The main characteristics of this form of equipment obligation are: (1) that the obligations are issued by the trustee, though the railroad may undertake to guarantee their payment by endorsement or otherwise; and (2) that pending the completion of the rental payments by the railroad, complete title to the equipment rests in the trustee on behalf of holders of its trust certificates.

Financial institutions now acquire title to the equipment in many cases and lease it at specified rentals under **long-term leases** without providing for the issuance of equipment trust certificates to other investors. For example, railroad cars may be leased by a financial institution for 15 years at rentals sufficient to return the cost and a specified rate of return, after which the rental drops to a nominal amount. These arrangements, sometimes made by equipment manufacturers too, are similar to other arrangements for substituting long-term leases for borrowing that are discussed at the end of this section.

COVENANTS IN EQUIPMENT OBLIGATION AGREEMENTS. Aside from provisions for payment of interest (or dividends) and principal, the usual covenants establish the railroad's obligation:

1. To maintain the equipment in proper condition and repair, and replace that which is destroyed.
2. To insure the equipment.

3. To pay all taxes.
4. To idemnify the trustee for all claims arising out of the ownership or use of any of the property.
5. To fasten and keep on each piece of equipment a metal plate showing that the trustee is the owner.
6. To file periodically with the trustee a statement of the location and condition of the equipment.

In the event of **default** on any of the covenants, payment of interest and principal becomes due immediately, and the trustee may take possession of the equipment and sell it for the purpose of reimbursing itself for the amount still due on the equipment trust certificates or notes. The railroad covenants that it will at its own expense deliver the equipment at such place or places on its road as the trustee may reasonably designate.

Railroad equipment obligations have a particularly strong legal position because Section 77 of the Bankruptcy Act excepts them from the injunction against taking immediate possession of pledged property that is applicable to other creditors of a railroad undergoing reorganization.

Debenture Bonds

GENERAL CHARACTER. These are direct obligations of the issuing corporation, resting solely on its **general credit** without specific mortgage or pledge, or assignment of property. Debentures are almost invariably issued under trust indentures, with a trustee to supervise the execution of the various covenants contained in the indentures.

COMMON PROVISIONS. Covenants usually used in debenture agreements are:

1. **Acceleration** of the maturity of the debt in the event of default on the debentures or on other outstanding obligations, or in case of receivership, insolvency, or bankruptcy.
2. A **negative pledge clause** restricting or prohibiting the pledging of assets as specific security to other creditors.
3. As an alternative to a negative pledge clause, a covenant may provide that the issue be secured by a prior lien if a subsequent mortgage is placed on the corporation's property, or to be secured equally and ratably with these later mortgage bonds. These clauses are known, respectively, as the **covenant of prior coverage** and the **covenant of equal coverage**.
4. A requirement that the corporation **maintain current assets equal to a certain ratio** of its current liabilities, usually 1½ or 2 to 1. This may act as a brake on the payment of dividends.
5. **Limitations on the total funded debt,** which may be restricted to a certain proportion of the total assets or net tangible assets. Sometimes it is provided that no further debentures may be issued.
6. Protective covenant in the event of merger or consolidation, sale of assets, or other contingencies.

USE OF DEBENTURES. In recent years debentures have supplanted mortgage bonds as the dominant type of debt used by industrial corporations. This trend reflects an increasing tendency of investors to rely on the protective provisions in the debentures, which are designed to **prevent financial difficulties,** rather than on the specific security provided by mortgages, which is useful only after financial difficulties have occurred. (Guthmann and Dougall, Corporate Financial Policy.) The prior position of mortgage bonds has concrete significance only in the event of liquidation or reorganization of the debtor corporation.

Avoidance of the use of mortgages may strengthen the ability of a corporation to obtain trade and bank credit in larger amounts. Some classes of corporations, such as financial concerns, retailers, and holding companies, may not have significant amounts of mortgageable fixed assets to pledge. Debentures have also been issued by utility companies with near-term or serial maturities, to reduce the size of their mortgage debt and thus improve the quality of the mortgage bonds.

SUBORDINATED DEBENTURES. One of the most striking features of long-term corporate financing since World War II has been the increasing use of subordinated debentures. This trend has been characterized as follows by one authority: "If the postwar development of financing with ordinary debentures has been amazing, . . . the multiplication of issues of subordinated debentures has been all the more so. Within the past few years, hundreds of companies have put out such issues, and the number appears to be growing rapidly from year to year." (Kent, Corporate Financial Management.) Although sales finance and consumer finance companies have been the largest issuers, many manufacturing corporations have resorted to subordinated debenture financing, often with **conversion privileges.**

As the name indicates, the subordinated debentures have claims to interest and principal **junior to that of ordinary debentures.** Generally, the indenture agreement makes their claims inferior to all the liabilities for borrowed money, whether short-term or long-term. Thus, in the event of insolvency such debt would rank below other bonds and bank loans, secured or unsecured, but not below amounts due trade creditors.

The use of these bonds, as a substitute for common or preferred stock, has a number of **major advantages.** They increase the future borrowing power of the company by adding to its earning assets without increasing its senior debt. This advantage is of special importance to finance companies, which are heavy borrowers from banks. The protection to other creditors is strengthened by the fact that the claims of the debentures are subordinated not only to already existing senior debt but also that subsequently incurred.

Secondly, the **cost** to the company is much less than that of equity financing since the interest paid is deductible from taxable income. Subordinated debentures have replaced preferred stock in the capital structures of many corporations because of the great tax benefit that attaches to borrowing in an era of very high corporate income tax rates.

Subordinated debentures appeal to investors because they provide a **higher yield than ordinary debentures.** Their investment appeal is often enhanced by relatively shorter maturities and by conversion privileges.

Guaranteed Bonds

PURPOSE. A guaranteed bond is one that is guaranteed by a corporation other than the issuing corporation. The purpose of such a guaranty is to improve the investment character of a bond issue. Typical reasons for the use of the guaranteed bond are:

1. A parent company may desire to improve the credit standing of a subsidiary by putting its own credit behind the latter's bonds.
2. A wealthy controlling stockholder may guarantee obligations of a corporation to facilitate their sale.
3. A corporation may guarantee bonds of another corporation in connection with the lease of its property.

FORMS OF GUARANTY. Bonds of one corporation may be guaranteed by another, which may be the parent company or the lessee of the other company's property. The guaranty may apply to the payment of both principal and interest or of interest alone. A guaranty may be secured by deposit of collateral.

A guaranty may be one of three kinds: (1) a guaranty **by endorsement of the bond;** (2) a guaranty **by special covenant** with the debtor corporation; or (3) a guaranty **under a lease or operating agreement.** Guaranty by endorsement on each individual bond certificate is the most effective form, especially in the event of a reorganization under the Bankruptcy Act.

The other forms of guaranty—by contract and under a lease of the debtor corporation's property—do not usually appear on the face of the bonds.

Bonds may be guaranteed by two or more corporations. Such guaranty may be a **joint** guaranty or a **joint and several** guaranty.

VALUE OF THE GUARANTY. The value of a guaranty depends on (1) the financial standing of the guarantor and (2) the strategic importance of the business and assets of the debtor corporation to the guarantor. If the credit standing of the guaranteeing corporation is higher than that of the direct debtor, the bonds will have a better investment standing as a result of the guaranty. On the other hand, they may not have as high standing as the direct, well-secured obligations of the guarantor. There have been instances, however, in which, because of the strategic value of the debtor corporation's property to the guaranteeing concern, a guaranty has been honored even when the guarantor's own obligations have gone into default. Needless to say, if the debtor's credit or the specific security gives the bond a strong position, the guaranty would not detract from its strength.

LEGAL POSITION OF GUARANTEED BONDS. A guaranty by one corporation of the interest and principal of the bonds of another does not prevent enforcement of the covenants of the debtor corporation; nor is it necessary to make the guarantor a party to a foreclosure suit to enforce the lien of the obligations. If the guarantor pays the interest and principal, no action can be taken by the bondholders against the debtor corporation, unless the bonds are also secured by a mortgage, in which instance the bondholders may sue and foreclose to protect the equity of their lien. If foreclosure proceedings give only partial recovery of principal and accrued interest, the guarantor is subject to suit for recovery of the deficiency.

The legal position of a guaranteed bond with respect to the guaranteeing corporation is not uniform. In the case of a **guaranty by endorsement on each individual bond certificate,** the courts have generally held that the guaranteed bond occupies the same position with respect to the unsatisfied principal as a debenture bond of the guaranteeing corporation. On the other hand, an **indirect guaranty** under a lease arrangement providing for the payment of interest on all outstanding funded debt of the lessor could prove less effective than a direct guaranty by endorsement. In the event of a reorganization and the disaffirmance of the lease by the trustee, the claim of the lessor corporation other than a railroad corporation is limited under Chapter X of the Bankruptcy Act to (a) rent up to the date of disaffirmance that is due and unpaid, (b) damages under the covenants of the lease, and (c) damages for future rents up to a maximum of 3 years less any recovery assured or anticipated during that period. With disaffirmance of a railroad lease, the discounted value of future rentals for the unexpired term of the lease constitutes an unsecured claim against the lessee corporation. If a lease is affirmed, the lessee's reorganization plan will usually make provision for the security holders of the leased line on the basis of relative earning power in the system, if the leased line also is placed in reorganization.

Income Bonds

NATURE OF OBLIGATION. Bonds the payment of interest on which is contingent on the net profits of the issuing corporation are designated as income bonds. They have also been called **adjustment bonds,** from the fact that they have been commonly issued in reorganizations to readjust fixed interest debt. Income bonds have been issued only occasionally to raise funds for new promotions, or for established concerns that want to obtain the tax benefit of borrowing without adding to their fixed charges. However, if an issue bears too many of the characteristics of equity ownership, regardless of its label, the Internal Revenue Service will view the interest payments as "essentially equivalent to a dividend" and taxable as such. The tax benefits of debt would then be lost. (Seghers, Reinhart, Nimaroff, Essentially Equivalent to a Dividend.)

A corporation issuing income bonds undertakes to pay the interest only as and to the extent that net earnings are available. The principal of income bonds, however, is payable like that of other bonds, and may be secured by a mortgage. Income bonds may also be debentures. Bonds may provide both a low fixed rate of interest and additional interest contingent on earnings.

Methods of Determining Income and Basis of Payments. The methods of determining the net earnings applicable to interest payments on income bonds, and the basis of the payment, are set forth in the **trust indenture.** This takes determination of earnings for this purpose out of the hands of the directors, who through manipulation of accounts could make it appear that the corporation is not earning the interest on the income bonds when it is doing so. Even though the indenture specifically requires the payment of interest "whenever earned," accounting questions may arise that make the exact definition of earnings difficult. Thus, the dividing line between ordinary repairs as an expense item and improvements as a capital item is often nebulous. Similarly, allowance of proper depreciation charges is a troublesome point.

It is a general provision in indentures of income bonds that if the entire interest charge is not earned during the designated period, not more than the part earned need be paid to the bondholders. Thus, if the semi-annual interest rate is 2½% and earnings during the last 6 months available for this interest amount to but 1% on the bonds outstanding, bondholders will receive this 1% upon presenting for payment their coupons for the period. It is commonly stipulated that the interest is payable only to the nearest ½% per ¼% earned.

Discretionary Payment of Interest on Income Bonds. Most income bond indentures provide that interest must be declared and paid by the board of directors to the extent that it has been earned in each year, often after specified deductions. Interest may be declared even if not earned, should the board so decide.

In rare instances, payment of interest on income bonds, whether it is earned or not, has been left to the discretion of the board of directors of the debtor corporation. In such instances, payment of interest earned must be made before the company may pay dividends on its capital stock.

CUMULATIVE AND NONCUMULATIVE INCOME BONDS. As in the instance of preferred stock, income bonds may be made cumulative or noncumulative. When cumulative, unpaid interest for each year is considered as a deferred payment, and must be paid eventually before shareholders can receive dividends, or at the maturity of the bonds. In many issues, the **accumulation is limited.** Thus, unpaid contingent interest on a number of railroad income bonds issued in reorganization is cumulative only up to three years' unpaid interest and no more.

Income bonds differ widely in their provisions. The exact character of an income bond is determined wholly by the terms of the indenture under which it has been issued.

REASONS FOR USE OF INCOME BONDS. Income bonds have been issued chiefly under **reorganization plans,** particularly by railroads. They have also been substituted for preferred stock in whole or part by a number of other corporations, because of the substantial tax advantage. Main reasons for their use have been:

1. Uncertainty concerning future earnings, and the consequent desire to reduce fixed interest charges. This practice has been encouraged by the Interstate Commerce Commission.
2. Institutional investors prefer to receive contingent interest obligations to stock in reorganizations, since legal restrictions may limit the ability of institutions such as life insurance companies to hold stock indefinitely.
3. The use of income bonds results in an income tax advantage, since interest paid on income bonds is deductible for income tax purposes whereas preferred stock dividends are not deductible. However, two Supreme Court decisions have created a risk that in certain cases income bonds may be classified as preferred stock for income tax purposes. (Seghers, Reinhart, Nimaroff, Essentially Equivalent to a Dividend.)

CAPITAL FUNDS. A common feature of railroad reorganizations has been the provision of capital funds in connection with the use of income bonds, to prevent siphoning away of all earnings to pay interest, regardless of the needs of the property. Thus, available income for income bonds is usually defined as the earnings available after payment of (a) all fixed charges, (b) all sinking fund payments made under the first mortgage, (c) credit to the capital fund account, and (d) any amount necessary to restore to the capital fund account funds used to pay interest on first mortgage bonds. A percentage of operating revenues must be appropriated to the capital fund, to be used for the purchase of equipment, for making improvements to equipment, or for additions and betterments to other property. **Deductions** for depreciation of way and structures may take the place of appropriations to the capital fund.

Miscellaneous Classes of Bonds

JOINT BONDS. Joint bonds are **obligations issued jointly** by two or more corporations, usually railroads. They are joint and several obligations of the issuers.

ASSUMED BONDS. These are obligations issued by one corporation for which a successor corporation has assumed liability. They usually arise as the result of purchase of assets in their entirety, mergers, consolidations, and reorganizations, in each of which transactions the issuing corporation usually passes out of existence and the new or successor corporation assumes all the obligations under the deed of trust. In the event of a consolidation or merger the assumption of the obligation is by effect of law and is therefore **automatic.** In a purchase of assets and in reorganizations, the assumption by the successor concern is the result of **agreement**.

TRUSTEES' OR RECEIVERS' CERTIFICATES. These are usually short-term obligations issued, under the direction of the court, by a trustee or receiver administering an insolvent corporation. They are used to obtain funds for current operating expenses or other urgent needs during the reorganization proceedings. Their **priority** is determined by the court and frequently they are ranked above all or some of the existing secured claims. The reorganization plan usually provides for paying off the certificates, and they ordinarily have a strong legal and financial position.

PARTICIPATING BONDS. Although bonds as a rule bear a fixed rate of interest, a few corporations, particularly those handicapped by poor credit and those that have been reorganized, have issued bonds that give the holders a participation in surplus earnings accruing during the life of the bonds, **over and above the fixed rate of interest**. These are known as participating bonds. The extent of the participation is defined in the trust indenture, but it may be greatly affected by the accounting methods used by the debtor corporation.

Participation is variously regulated. It may be a specified addition to the fixed rate or it may represent a stated proportion of the earnings of the corporation. When the participation is limited to a maximum rate on the bonds, the additional rate in excess of the fixed interest rate, if not paid as earned, may be made cumulative.

VOTING BONDS. Holders of corporation bonds other than income bonds generally have no voice in management so long as there is no default. There have been a few exceptions, however, usually in connection with reorganizations. The indenture under which income bonds are issued may give holders the right to vote for directors in the event interest on the bonds is not paid for a certain length of time.

BONDS HELD IN THE TREASURY. According to the usual meaning of the term, bonds held in the treasury of a corporation are issued obligations that the corporation has **repurchased** or otherwise reacquired, apart from sinking fund requirements, and that it carries alive and is free to dispose of eventually as it desires. The term is sometimes applied also to **authorized but unissued** bonds that have been duly authenticated by the trustee under the indenture and are therefore ready for issuance.

Obligations that have been reacquired by the issuing corporation may be **shown in the balance sheet** either as an asset or as a deduction from the total issued amount of bonds. Accounting practice sanctions carrying them as an asset, especially if they are being held for the purpose of resale, provided, however, there is or is likely to be a market for the bonds. In this instance they should be valued at cost or resale value, whichever is the lower.

Convertible Bonds

NATURE OF THE CONVERSION RIGHT. The trust indenture may give bondholders the privilege to convert their bonds into another security of the issuing company at a specified price, within a given time, and under stated terms and conditions. Bonds that carry this privilege are most often **debenture issues**, and the securities into which they are convertible are almost always **junior issues**, usually preferred or common stock, or units consisting of both. There **have**

been instances among public utilities and railroads of short-term notes that were convertible into long-term mortgage bonds that were deposited as collateral to secure the notes. There are instances also in which bonds are made convertible into the securities of another company.

The typical convertible bond is one exchangeable for common stock of the same issuer at the option of the holder.

ADVANTAGES AND DISADVANTAGES OF CONVERTIBLE BONDS. Some purposes achieved by a corporation in issuing convertible bonds are:

1. A lower rate of interest need be paid and a higher price is received for the bonds. Bond buyers are willing to pay a premium for the conversion privilege.
2. A substantial demand exists for bonds that are convertible into stock, even if the quality of the bond is not very high. Individual investors in particular are partial to convertible bonds. Convertible bonds are favored by those who want to finance security purchases with bank loans, since margin requirements do not apply to bank security loans on bonds.
3. Upon conversion, a company rids itself of a fixed interest charge and its capital structure is simplified. Convertible bonds thus make for a more flexible financial structure, and reduction of debt through conversion clears the way for new bond financing at a later time.
4. Through conversion of convertible bonds, a corporation obtains a substantially higher price for its stock than by selling shares in the first place.
5. Convertible bond offerings do not have the depressing effect on the market price of the company's stock of new common stock issues of similar size, and bonds are converted only as demand for the stock lifts its price.
6. Convertible bonds do not cause the immediate dilution of earnings per share that stock issues do.

Disadvantages to the corporation in issuing convertible bonds are:

1. Conversion dilutes the equity of the stockholders, whereas borrowing with straight debt securities avoids this.
2. Substantial conversions into voting common stock could shift control of the company.
3. Reduction of debt through conversion reduces the advantage of "trading on the equity."
4. Conversion, by reducing interest charges, increases income taxes to which the corporation is subject.
5. An element of uncertainty is introduced into the capital structure as to when and how many of the bonds will be converted.

CONVERSION RATIO OR PRICE. The conversion ratio expresses the rate at which the bonds are exchangeable for stock. It may be expressed in terms of the number of shares one bond of $1,000 par is convertible into, in which case it is known as the conversion ratio or rate; or it may be expressed in terms of the amount of par value or principal amount of the bonds exchangeable for one share of stock, in which case it is known as the conversion price. Thus, if a bond with a par value of $1,000 is said to be convertible into common at $32.50, it means that $32.50 of bonds at par will be convertible into one share of common, or at a rate of 30.769 common shares per $1,000 bond.

A constant conversion price may be stipulated for the entire life of the privilege, or the price may be increased at the end of each successive period of years. Similarly the **rate of conversion** may change as specified amounts of bonds are converted.

Sometimes conversion involves a cash payment by bondholders. Through this device The American Telephone & Telegraph Co. has raised huge amounts of capital, over and above what was received through sales of convertible bonds, from cash payments made in connection with conversions.

FIXING CONVERSION RATE. The conversion price is usually fixed at the time of issue at a level considerably above the current market value of the stock for which the bond is exchangeable. The conversion privilege becomes attractive only when the market price of the stock rises above the conversion price. The factors to be considered in fixing the conversion price are:

1. The **price** of the stock when the bonds are issued.
2. The **prospects** of the company, earnings, dividend yield, and their probable effect upon the price of the stock into which the bonds are convertible.
3. **Popularity** of the conversion privilege with investors. Convertible bonds are particularly popular in a rising stock market, and a higher conversion price is likely to be acceptable when the market is rising and investors tend to be optimistic.
4. **Length of the period** during which the bondholder may convert. As a rule, the longer the period, the less favorable the conversion rates need be with relation to current prices for the company's stock.

INTEREST AND DIVIDEND ADJUSTMENTS. At the time of conversion usually there is accrued interest on the bonds, to which the holder is entitled. On the other hand, if dividends, cash or stock, are being paid on the shares, there may be accrued dividends to which he is not entitled when he receives the shares. Provision is generally made in **convertible bonds** for the adjustment of such accrued interest, and less often for the adjustment of the accrued dividends as well, at the time of conversion. The company is credited with the accrued dividends and the bondholder with the accrued interest, the difference being settled by cash payment. Regular stock dividends are adjusted on the basis of the market value of all dividend stock in excess of certain permitted dividends. Unless provision is made for such adjustments, the bondholder cannot require payment of accrued interest nor the corporation the payment of the accrued dividends.

TIME OF CONVERSION. The privilege may become exercisable immediately upon issuance of the securities, or after several years. It may not expire until the bonds mature, or it may terminate at an earlier date prior to the maturity of the bonds. If the bonds are redeemable, it is frequently provided that the privilege shall continue up to a certain number of days, ranging from 5 to 30, before the redemption date. Merger, consolidation, or sale of assets may also affect the privilege. Sometimes bondholders are obliged to give a few days' advance notice to the company of their intention to effect conversion.

Stock issued upon conversion is customarily issued as of a **conversion date**, which may be several days prior to the actual date of issuance of the stock certificates. This date is the date of the last act necessary to complete the conversion. It may be the last date upon which surrender notice or payment of fractional adjustments is made. An exact determination of the conversion date is of importance if adjustments of accrued interest and dividends are to be made, or if there is any question as to the voting or subscription rights of the new stock issued in conversion.

SUBSCRIPTION PRIVILEGE. Unless waived by charter provision or otherwise, or there is some statute to the contrary, stockholders have a preemptive right to subscribe ratably to obligations convertible into stock. The privilege of subscription to convertible bonds is then extended to stockholders, and if the price of subscription is less than the market value of the bonds quoted on a "when, as, and if issued" basis, as is usually the case, the rights have a **market value.** A right refers to the privilege to subscribe to the bonds attaching to each share owned, and its value is calculated by dividing the difference between the market value of the new bond and the subscription price by the number of shares it is necessary to own in order to entitle one to subscribe to the bond. When the stock sells **ex-rights,** its price is marked down by the value of the right, and this loss offsets the stockholder's gain in getting the bond at less than market value.

Suppose convertible bonds are offered to stockholders at par, the owner of each 5 shares being entitled to subscribe to $1,000 principal amount, and the bonds are quoted **when, as, and if issued** at 103. The value of the one right is ascertained as follows:

Market value of bond	$1,030
Subscription price of bond	1,000
Value of rights attaching to 5 shares	30
Value of one right	6

This value of the right is its parity value at which a purchase of bonds in the market, on the one hand, and a purchase of rights and subscription to the bonds, on the other, bring equal results. The market price of the rights constantly gravitates toward this parity by reason of the operations of arbitragers who, to reap profits, at one and the same time sell the bonds on a "when, as, and if issued" basis and buy the rights and subscribe for the bonds. The market price of rights fluctuates with the market price of the bonds, and if the latter falls below the subscription price, the rights become valueless. Rights to buy convertible bonds are evidenced by transferable warrants in the same manner as rights to subscribe to stock.

PROTECTIVE FEATURES AGAINST DILUTION OR DESTRUCTION OF CONVERSION PRIVILEGE. Convertible bond issues generally anticipate changes in capitalization that might cause dilution or actually destroy the value of the conversion privilege. The following adjustments and restrictions protect convertible bondholders (Hills, Cal. Law Rev., Vol. 19):

1. If shares issuable upon conversion are split up into a greater number or combined into a lesser number, the number of shares issuable upon conversion will be increased or decreased accordingly.

2. If issuable shares are changed into the same or a different number of shares of any other class or classes, the conversion privilege will apply to the equivalent number of these new shares.

3. Payment of stock dividends reduces the conversion privilege in the same proportion as the total number of shares outstanding immediately after the stock dividend bears to the total number of shares outstanding immediately prior to the stock dividend. Hence, by the conversion instrument, the holder may be entitled to receive upon conversion at any time after payment of the dividend the new stock in addition to that he was entitled to before the dividend.

4. The maximum number of additional shares and the minimum price at which they may be issued without adjusting the conversion rate are fixed in the conversion instrument. There are many rather complicated methods used for adjusting the rate when necessary on account of the issuance of additional shares. As a further protection against dilution from the issue of subscription rights to stock, as well as the declaration of large stock and cash dividends, it may be provided that **advance notice** of such rights or dividends be given so that holders of the

convertible bonds might effect their conversions and take advantage of the offer of stock or payment of dividends.

5. Holders of the conversion privilege have no rights upon the termination of the corporate existence of the company by merger, consolidation, dissolution, or otherwise, except such as are granted by the successor corporation or by existing statute. On this account, the trust indenture will generally require that the successor company recognize the conversion privilege granted by its predecessor or predecessors.

FACTORS INFLUENCING CONVERSION. Holders of convertible bonds are not necessarily influenced to make immediate conversion by the fact that the current market quotation for the stock is above the conversion rate. The price of the bonds will rise in sympathy with the price of the stock, and so far as present market values are concerned there is no advantage in conversion. The rise in the price of the bonds is assured, as the stock advances in price, because of the operations of professional arbitragers who reap profits by purchasing the bonds, selling the stock short, and making delivery on the short contracts after effecting conversion. As a result of these operations, the two securities tend to maintain a **parity relationship,** at which it is immaterial whether the stock is purchased or the bonds are bought and converted into stock. This tendency to parity, however, disappears when the stock falls to a point where the investment value of the bond, apart from the conversion privilege, is higher than its parity with the low-priced stock.

Conversion of the bonds **may be forced** by the issuing corporation by any of the following methods:

1. Increasing the dividend rate on the common stock so that the increased income to the holder upon conversion will more than offset the increased risk due to the exchange of bonds for stock.
2. Calling the bonds for redemption when the market value of the stock into which the bonds are convertible is greater than the redemption price. Bondholders who do not convert then incur a loss by failing to do so.
3. Giving attractive subscription rights or some other benefit to common stockholders, which bondholders can obtain only through conversion.

BONDS WITH WARRANTS. An obligation similar in purpose to the convertible bond is the bond with warrants attached that give the owner the right to purchase a certain amount of stock at specified prices. These prices will be higher than the market price of the common stock at the time the bonds are sold. In effect, a warrant represents a call upon the future prosperity of the company, and its value will depend upon the expectation that the market price of the common stock will rise above the specified subscription price before the warrant expires.

Generally, the **warrants are nondetachable,** that is, they may be separated from the bond only when the bondholder desires to exercise his right to buy stock. **Detachable** warrants may be separated from the bond and sold as separate instruments for what the market will bring. From the viewpoint of the corporation, the nondetachable warrant has the advantage that it may be canceled by redemption of the bond issue, provided the bondholder has not found it to his advantage to exercise the right of purchase prior to redemption.

As compared to convertible bonds, the use of bonds with warrants attached has the **advantage from the corporation's viewpoint** of providing the company, through exercise of the warrants, with a possible source of additional funds to be used for expansion, retirement of debt, or whatever other purpose the management deems wise. Conversion does not of itself provide the company with additional funds if no cash payment is required of bondholders in connection with conversion.

Retirement of Bonded Debt

METHODS OF RETIREMENT. Corporate bonds can be retired before or at maturity. Experience has shown that it is unwise to make no provision for retirement of bonds before they mature, since financial, economic, or corporate conditions may occur before then that could make an earlier refunding or repayment of the issue advantageous. **Flexibility in management** of a corporation's long-term debt requires that the corporation have the right to call bonds for redemption before their maturity.

THE CALL FEATURE. A bond issue may be made redeemable before maturity in whole or in part. If so, redemption is at the option of the issuing corporation, unless there is a provision for a sinking fund that makes a periodical "call" compulsory. The advantage to the debtor corporation of the **optional call** lies in the flexibility that such a provision adds to the company's capital structure. The call privilege has been used advantageously by corporations for the purpose of (a) eliminating bond issues with unfavorable indenture provisions, (b) replacing short-term obligations with long-term obligations, or vice versa, (c) reducing debt, and (d) refunding high coupon bonds with low coupon bonds if interest rates decline. The last-named advantage, **refunding to effect interest savings,** has been of great value in periods of low interest rates like the 1930's. Corporations with noncallable issues deprive themselves of this opportunity to effect substantial interest savings through refunding. Hence, corporations seek to make all bond issues callable at small or no premiums over par.

Investors and the Call Feature. Investors strongly dislike callable bonds, since corporations will exercise the option to call in bonds only when it is advantageous to themselves. When bonds are called in during a period of low interest rates, as is often the case, investors are deprived of higher-yielding issues at a time when these can be replaced only with lower yields.

This conflict of interest between issuer and investor can be **resolved in two ways.** First, investors are given **call protection,** usually by a provision that a bond issue may not be called in for a period of years, such as 5 or 10, immediately after it is put out. Secondly, bonds are made **callable only at premium prices,** to reimburse the investor for the loss of his investment at a time when it cannot be replaced advantageously. Call prices are usually scaled down over a period of years, so that the premium narrows as the bond approaches maturity. For example, a 30-year bond issue may not be callable during the first 5 years of its life; it may be callable at 108 during the second 5 years; at 106 the third 5 years; at 104 the fourth 5 years; at 102 the fifth 5 years, and at 101 during the last 5 years before maturity, when it becomes redeemable at par value. Because investors seek call protection, bonds that enjoy such protection can usually be sold at materially lower yields than those without it.

The indenture may provide **different call prices** for the small amounts of bonds that are being redeemed for a sinking fund and for redemption of the issue as a whole. Sometimes, call protection applies only or mainly to redemption of a whole issue, but not to redemption for a sinking fund.

Method of Redemption. The method of redemption is described in the bond indenture. The usual stipulation is that **notice** of the redemption of callable bonds be given bondholders through publication in the press from 30 to 90 days prior to the redemption date. If the corporation elects to pay off only a portion of the issue, about 10 days or so before first publication of the notice it notifies the trustee of the aggregate amount of bonds to be redeemed. The trustee then proceeds, in the presence of a representative of the corporation, to **draw by lot** the numbers of the bonds to be redeemed. These numbers will appear in the public notice of redemption.

AMORTIZATION THROUGH SINKING FUND. A sinking fund for bond retirement is a periodical appropriation of cash, paid to the trustee for the purpose of purchasing or otherwise redeeming bonds before maturity or retiring them at maturity. It is often provided that bonds may be deposited with the trustee in lieu of cash. Provision for the sinking fund is included in the trust indenture. As a rule its operation is compulsory, the corporation being under contractual obligation to accumulate the funds and effect the redemptions in accordance with the terms of the indenture. The trustee administering the sinking fund usually serves also as the indenture trustee.

Experience has demonstrated both to issuers and lenders that the **orderly retirement** of a bond issue over its life is highly desirable for both. Corporations cannot know in advance that they will be in position to take care of a large bond maturity at a distant date, at least without serious strain. But **gradual redemption** out of the corporate cash flow over the life of the issue, especially when the amounts redeemed each year can be adjusted to changing conditions, avoids such risk. As the sinking fund reduces the size of the bond issue, it becomes less burdensome, its quality tends to improve, and the problem of a burdensome maturity is avoided.

TYPES OF SINKING FUNDS. Sinking funds may be classified by the manner in which the annual amounts are determined. They are:

Fixed Annual Amounts. The fixed amount may be either a fixed face amount of bonds or a fixed amount in dollars, the former being more common. If bonds purchased for the sinking fund are canceled and the interest saved is not paid into the fund (noncumulative sinking fund), this method has the disadvantage of placing the heaviest debt service load upon the earlier years of the issue, since the interest charges decrease as the debt is retired.

Percentage of Earnings. Since the sinking fund is designed to reduce fixed charges, it is quite logical that the obligation to retire debt be governed by the ability to pay. The usual measure of ability is net earnings. In order to provide for a **minimum amount** of debt reduction, a corporation will often provide a fixed annual sinking fund payment below which the fluctuating amount based on a percentage of earnings cannot fall. The percentage of earnings sinking fund is widely favored because of its flexibility.

Per Unit of Output. In wasting asset industries, the sinking fund appropriation may be a certain number of cents per ton of coal mined or per barrel of oil produced. In this way, bonded debt is retired as the assets securing that debt are depleted. If there is no production, no sinking fund payment burdens the business.

Variable Annual Amounts. The sinking fund may take the form of an increasing or a decreasing amount each year. A corporation may desire to increase the annual sinking fund payment each year because (a) it believes the growth of earning power will make it feasible or (b) so as to make the total annual outlay on debt service constant. In (b), sometimes called the **cumulative sinking fund** method, bonds purchased or called are **held alive** in the sinking fund by the trustee, who collects interest on these bonds and applies it to retire additional bonds. Under this plan, the corporation pays out a constant sum yearly for interest and sinking fund.

ACQUISITION OF BONDS FOR SINKING FUND. It is usually provided that bonds may be purchased for the sinking fund in the open market or privately, or as the result of tenders for which the company has advertised, at not more than par plus a premium. If the bonds are **callable,** they may be purchased at the "call" price or less, but if not so available they may be called by lot for the sinking fund. If bonds are **not callable** for the sinking fund and cannot be purchased at the price stipulated, it may be provided that sinking funds shall be invested in United States government securities or the securities of other corporations or in other bond issues of the same corporation, or that the sinking fund is to be returned to the corporation for investment in property to be pledged under the bonds or otherwise.

The indenture may authorize that bonds of the same corporation purchased for the sinking fund shall be kept alive. In this instance they will be held by the trustee and will continue to draw interest, which may be used to reduce the annual periodical sinking fund appropriation or to increase the number of bonds redeemed with the sinking fund. These bonds are sometimes available for reissue if earnings are satisfactory. Usually, if purchased bonds may be kept alive, they are endorsed as being held only for the sinking fund. If the redeemed bonds are canceled, interest on them ceases and the corporation's interest charges are reduced.

When invited by the trustee in a **public announcement** to make tenders or proposals to sell bonds, holders submit sealed offers that are accepted in an amount sufficient to exhaust the stated sum of cash that the trustee has available at the time. Obviously the corporation will accept the lowest offers.

DEPOSIT OF BONDS IN SINKING FUND IN LIEU OF CASH PAYMENTS. Many trust indentures permit corporations to offer bonds that they have purchased in lieu of cash in meeting their sinking fund requirements. The trustees are to accept the bonds at a value fixed in the indenture, which may be the cost of their acquisition in the instance of a sinking fund expressed in dollars or the par value in the instance of a sinking fund of a fixed face amount. Such a provision enables a corporation to take advantage of prevailing low prices for its bonds and to hasten the reduction of fixed charges, or to accumulate a quantity of bonds against the sinking fund requirements of several years.

DANGERS OF EXCESSIVE SINKING FUND CHARGES. Mandatory sinking fund payments become a fixed charge to the issuing corporation like interest on the bonds. Unless covered by cash flow in excess of other necessary outlays, sinking fund appropriations deplete a corporation's cash resources and could become a cause of financial distress. Adaptation of sinking fund requirements to **projections of cash flow and cash needs** of the enterprise over a period of years will minimize this danger.

Serial Bonds

GENERAL CHARACTERISTICS. Serial bonds are issues that mature in installments on successive dates. Their purpose is similar to that of sinking fund bonds. Instead of contributing to a sinking fund to pay off its obligations, how-

14·38 LONG-TERM AND INTERMEDIATE-TERM BORROWING

ever, a corporation agrees to redeem its bonds in serial order, a certain portion coming due and being payable each year or at some other regular period until the whole amount has been retired. A **default** in the payment of the principal of any maturity constitutes a default on the entire issue, thus hastening the maturity of bonds not yet due. The **coupon interest rate** may be the same for all maturities, and in such an instance the several maturities are sold at different prices to return different yields.

Serial maturities are especially **adapted to** the financing of assets of shorter life, and they are universally used in equipment trust financing. They are also favored by investors who want shorter maturities because of their own liquidity requirements, or because they expect a rise in interest rates and so do not want long-term maturities.

There is some **difficulty in listing** serial bonds, since a different quotation will apply to each maturity. On the over-the-counter markets, they are usually quoted on a yield, rather than a price, basis.

FIXING THE SIZE OF SERIAL MATURITIES. Serial maturities may be arranged on an **equal amount basis** or on an **annuity basis.** When the maturities come due in equal amounts, the corporation has a heavier burden of debt service in the earlier years of the issue than in the later years, since as the amount of bonds outstanding is reduced through the maturity of the successive installments, the interest cost is proportionately lessened. This condition is overcome under the annuity method of amortization. Under this plan, the principal amount of each successive installment is increased in proportion as required interest payments are decreased. Principal is amortized and interest is paid by the periodical payment of a uniform amount, usually semi-annually. The amount of each of these installments is determined by the rate of interest and the term of the bond.

CALLABLE SERIAL BONDS. Serial bonds may be made subject to redemption before maturity either as a whole or in part. When callable as a **whole,** a different redemption price may apply to each serial maturity, the more distant maturities generally being redeemable at a higher premium than the nearby maturities. When serial issues are called **in part** through sinking fund operations, the plan may be followed of calling bonds by lot in inverse order of their maturity.

COMPARISON OF SINKING FUND AND SERIAL BONDS. In weighing the choice between sinking fund and serial bonds, the following factors should be taken into account:

1. Serial bonds permit lower cost borrowing when short-term interest rates are substantially lower than long-term.
2. Serial bonds must be paid off at par as they mature, whereas corporations can buy in bonds at a discount if quoted below par in the market to satisfy sinking fund requirements.
3. Debt retirement is inflexible with serial maturities, whereas the use of sinking funds, especially those based on earnings, makes for flexible debt retirement practices. Default on a sinking fund seldom precipitates bankruptcy as does failure to pay principal when due.
4. Debt retirement is more certain in the case of serial issues, since bondholders have shown greater willingness to waive or postpone sinking fund payments than they have to extend maturities.
5. Serial issues have poorer marketability as compared with sinking fund issues, because of the complications arising from varying maturities and yields, and the thin market for some maturities.

Refunding of Bonds

NATURE OF OPERATION. Refunding consists of replacing one security issue with another. It may take the form of a direct exchange. Usually, however, it consists of retiring an outstanding issue with the proceeds from the sale of a new offering. The old issue may be **wholly** or only **partly** refunded. The refunding operation may take place before maturity or at maturity.

REFUNDING BEFORE MATURITY. An outstanding issue of bonds may be refunded into a new issue whenever conditions in the investment market are favorable and the new issue can be floated at a saving in fixed interest charges as compared with the old issue. Refunding before maturity may also be undertaken (a) to eliminate bond issues with unfavorable indenture provisions, such as a closed mortgage issue with an after-acquired clause or an issue with a heavy sinking fund or restrictive dividend covenant; or (b) to replace short-term obligations with long-term, or vice versa.

Methods of Refunding. Refunding before maturity may be accomplished through **negotiation with bondholders** or the **sale of a new bond issue** to replace the existing issue. A holder of a 6% noncallable issue in a period of low money rates will obviously refuse an offer to refund, unless accompanied by a substantial cash bonus. If the refunding is for a purpose other than reducing interest charges, bondholders might be induced to exchange their bonds by (a) improving the security, (b) providing a sinking fund for the new issue, (c) paying the old bondholder a cash bonus, (d) placing a higher interest rate on the new issue, etc.

If a bond issue is callable, refunding can be accomplished through exercise of the company's option to redeem the old bonds when the bond market is receptive to a refunding offering, the proceeds from which will be employed to redeem the old issue.

Factors in Refunding Before Maturity. In considering the advisability of refunding a callable bond issue before maturity so as to effect a **reduction in interest charges**, the following factors should be weighed by the corporation:

1. Will additional restrictive covenants have to be included in the indenture of the new issue, which may offset to some degree the benefit of a reduction in interest charges?
2. Can a more favorable maturity date be secured through refunding?
3. What will the net dollar savings be as a result of the refunding? In this connection the following factors should be considered:
   a. The dollar cost to call the outstanding issue, after allowing for tax savings provided by the call premium paid upon redemption and other deductible expenses.
   b. Expenses of refinancing, such as the cost of registration under the Securities Act if the new issue is to be publicly sold; printing and engraving expenses; fees paid to legal counsel and trustees; and the investment bankers' commission if this issue is to be sold publicly. With direct placements, a fee may be paid an investment banker who acts as intermediary.
   c. The interest rate, maturity, and selling price of the new issue.
   d. The trend of interest rates, which may indicate that the refunding should be delayed if a further decline in rates seems probable.

For an example, take a corporation with a $1,000,000 bond issue outstanding with a 5½% coupon rate, due in 25 years and callable at 105. The corporation has been advised that investment bankers will be able to sell a new 25-year 4½%

issue at a price to net the company par (after registration costs, banking, and counsel commissions). What would the dollar savings amount to? The cost to call the 5½% issue would be $1,050,000 before income taxes, and $1,026,000 after income tax savings based on a 48% tax rate. The corporation would have to sell $1,026,000 principal amount of 4½% bonds and provide for the amortization of the additional principal amount of $26,000 over the 25-year life. This amortization or sinking fund would require an annual payment of $1,040, assuming the sinking fund will retire bonds at par. Average annual interest charges on the new 4½% issue would be $45,608 (4½% of the average amount outstanding, which is found by taking the amount outstanding during the first and last years and dividing by 2, i.e., $1,026,000 plus $1,001,040 divided by 2, which equals $1,013,520). Hence, annual interest and amortization charges on the new 4½% issue would average $46,648. The annual interest requirements on the 5½% issue is $55,000. Thus, annual savings would be $8,352 before income taxes, or $3,844 after allowing for a 52% tax deduction for interest payments. The income tax paid on added net income further reduces the benefit from refunding.

REFUNDING AT MATURITY. Refunding is common at maturity. It may be necessary either because the company lacks the necessary cash to pay off the maturing bond issue, or because it is believed sound financial policy to continue borrowing and conserve cash for other uses.

A corporation unable to sell a new issue on satisfactory terms may ask the bondholders to accept new bonds in lieu of the old. It may be necessary to offer holders of the maturing bonds an inducement to make the exchange. The offer of exchange of new for maturing bonds may be underwritten by an investment banker.

EXTENSIONS. In the event a corporation is unable to refund a maturing obligation and lacks the cash to pay it off, the management may ask bondholders to extend the maturity of the issue. It may be necessary to offer bondholders some **inducement** to have them agree to an extension of maturity. Since it is usually to the interest of the creditors, as well as the corporation, to avoid reorganization proceedings, with all the expense attending them, it is often possible to win agreement of most holders to the extension of a maturing obligation. However, bondholders who do not agree to the extension must be paid in cash. Extensions are discussed in conection with corporate readjustments (Sec. 21.)

In the instance of bond issues that were placed privately with financial institutions, exchange or refunding at maturity is usually more readily arranged by negotiation between issuer and institutional investor.

Term Loans

CHARACTERISTICS. Intermediate term loans from commercial banks repayable over a period of years are an important alternative to bond financing. Commercial banks, recognizing that even working capital loans are renewed indefinitely by many borrowers as new inventories and accounts receivable are acquired to replace those that are liquidated, look upon term loans repaid in installments over a period of years out of the cash flow as a more realistic form of financing for numerous concerns, small as well as large.

A term loan may be fully amortized over its term or a **balloon maturity** equal to a substantial part of the loan may come due on its final date. Term loans are generally unsecured, and the term is usually from 5 to 10 years, but with first class borrowers even longer terms have been agreed to. In some instances, a corporation arranges a term loan from one or more banks and a direct placement with a life insurance company or large pension fund, with payments on the latter starting after the bank term loan has matured.

PURPOSES AND TERMS. The purposes of term loans are too numerous to mention in detail. They may be incurred for (1) the purchase of equipment or the acquisition of other fixed assets, (2) refinancing of funded debt or revamping of capital structures, and (3) replenishment or increasing of working capital. With regard to the second point, a term loan may be used to retire a bond issue in order to reduce interest costs, rearrange maturities, or eliminate restrictive provisions. Or the proceeds of the loan may be used to retire a preferred stock issue, thus substituting tax-deductible interest payments for nondeductible dividends.

In making a term loan, the bank places most emphasis on **cash flow**. It wants to be assured of the ability of the borrower to put aside regularly a sum for the retirement of the debt. As a measure of further protection, the bank may insist on restrictive covenants in the loan, such as (a) protective provisions pertaining to the issuance of additional debt, (b) restrictions on dividend payments, and (c) provisions requiring the maintenance of a certain working capital position. In term loans to smaller business concerns it is not uncommon to find provisions limiting salaries and bonuses to officers and forbidding a merger or consolidation without the consent of the lending bank.

Private Placements

WIDESPREAD USE. In the period since World War II nearly half of the total volume of corporate bond sales has been effected through private placements in which an **entire issue is sold** to one or a few institutional investors, mostly life insurance companies but including pension funds and eleemosynary institutions as well. This development has been especially important in non-regulated industries since most public utility and railroad issues must be sold through public offerings under competitive bidding. To a minor extent, common and preferred stock issues also have been placed privately. Although a major part of the total volume is accounted for by the larger corporations, many of the issues are relatively small, frequently under $1 million.

PRINCIPAL ADVANTAGES. The advantages, both from the standpoint of lender and borrower, that have accounted for the great importance of private placements are:

1. Life insurance companies, and to a lesser extent other institutional investors, are constantly seeking adequate suitable investment outlets for their large investable funds. Through direct negotiations with issuers they can obtain all or a large part of issues tailored to the needs of both borrowers and lenders. In public offerings, the investment bankers might allot insurance companies only limited amounts, particularly of attractive issues that are in strong demand.
2. Flotation costs to the issuer may be reduced, since underwriting commissions need not be paid and privately placed issues need not be registered with the Securities and Exchange Commission. Moreover, delays due to negotiations with bankers and the waiting period before registration becomes effective are avoided.
3. Many corporations of moderate size, particularly those that have previously not made public offerings of their securities, might find it difficult or even im-

possible to negotiate a public offering on reasonable terms when market conditions do not appear favorable. An insurance company, on the other hand, is ready at all times to arrange direct placements if the borrower's statements demonstrate ability to service the debt out of its cash flow.

4. If the issuing corporation should run into financial problems, adjustment of the terms of debt is more readily negotiated with one or a few institutional creditors than with the numerous holders of a bond issue that was publicly distributed.
5. The borrowing company can take down the funds borrowed only as they are needed for its expansion program instead of, as in a public sale, receiving the entire amount at once and thus incurring interest charges on the whole issue. By paying a **commitment fee,** a borrower may obtain assurance that the necessary funds will be forthcoming at some future date under stipulated conditions. Sometimes a **termination fee** may have to be paid the lender for any part of the commitment not taken.

DISADVANTAGES. The chief disadvantages of private placements are:

1. Bonds or notes thus acquired lack marketability. They cannot be resold in the open market, as can publicly offered securities, since a market has not been established through a public offering.
2. The issuer loses the opportunity of purchasing bonds for retirement at a discount in the open market, should interest rates rise or prices decline for other reasons.
3. Future financing may be more difficult since the borrowing corporation loses the benefit of broad distribution of its securities, which makes them known to many investors.
4. Since institutional lenders are sophisticated investors with great bargaining power, they may be able to exact terms that make the supposed economies to the borrower illusory. Furthermore, debt agreements may contain provisions that are more restrictive on the borrower than those in indentures of publicly distributed bonds.

SERVICES OF INVESTMENT BANKERS. Frequently, investment bankers act as "go-betweens" in arranging a private placement and in acting as financial advisors in the transaction. For this service, particularly important to smaller corporations, the banker receives a **finder's fee** that is far smaller than those incurred in a public distribution of securities.

Leasing of Fixed Assets

ALTERNATIVE TO BORROWING. Acquisition of fixed assets by leasing as an alternative to borrowing has long been common in some industries, such as railroads and office equipment. Many railroads acquire other lines, rolling stock, and terminal facilities through leasing. Business machine and shoe machinery manufacturers pioneered in direct leasing of industrial equipment. Since World War II, an enormous expansion of leasing of both buildings and equipment has taken place. The huge needs for funds confronting business, tax benefits, and the eager search by institutional investors, particularly life insurance companies, for investment outlets providing a greater return than high-grade bonds contributed to this development. A notable expansion of the variety as well as the volume of asset leasing has taken place. Trucks and automobiles, airplanes and a great variety of specialized equipment are now being leased by many thousands of enterprises, large and small. Organization of a number of specialized leasing companies has accompanied the great increase in popularity of this alternative to debt financing.

SALE-AND-LEASEBACK FINANCING. In recent years this relatively new method of real estate and industrial financing has become widespread. The usual arrangement is for an institutional investor, such as a life insurance company, to buy a property from a business concern, or to build a new one to specifications, and then lease it back to the company. The standard **primary lease** period is 20 to 30 years, during which rentals are sufficient to return the investment with an agreed upon rate of return. The lessee can then renew the lease for periods of 10 years at a nominal rental. Under **net leases,** maintenance, insurance, taxes, etc., are the obligation of the lessee.

ADVANTAGES TO CORPORATION OF LEASING. The leasing of property offers a number of advantages over ownership to a corporation:

1. Leasing finances 100% of the cost of the assets involved, whereas only a percentage of the cost of owned assets is usually borrowed to finance their acquisition. This conserves funds for working capital requirements, which have been undergoing rapid expansion throughout the economy.
2. When assets are leased instead of being bought with the proceeds of a bond issue, restrictions imposed in bond indentures are avoided, while borrowing capacity is conserved for other needs in the future.
3. To the extent that leasing lessens the need for stock financing, it helps to avoid dilution of the equity of stockholders.
4. Leasing reduces both investment in fixed assets and long-term borrowing, which has been said to "clean up" the balance sheet of a corporation. If prospective creditors take lease rental charges fully into account, however, this advantage is minimized.
5. Modernization and expansion are facilitated when assets can be acquired without down payment and merely by entering into a lease agreement.
6. Leasing may give a tax advantage, although this has become less significant as depreciation allowances have been liberalized. Leases may result in larger rental deductions from taxable income in the early years of the lease, rentals can include the value of land that is not subject to depreciation, and the sale of a building for leaseback may cause a capital loss to the selling corporation.
7. Leasing can help simplify management and collective bargaining problems. When a building is leased, the management of the company stays out of the real estate field to this extent and reduces the number of unions with which it negotiates agreements.
8. The maximum claims of lessors against a corporation undergoing reorganization under Chapter X is for 3 years' future rent.

DISADVANTAGES OF LEASING. Arguments against leasing as a substitute for ownership and borrowing include:

1. Higher cost, both in the form of a higher return on the lessor's investment during the primary lease period and the rentals paid during the renewal periods after the investment has been amortized.
2. The loss of terminal values after the end of the lease, such as appreciation of land and increases in values caused by inflation and lessee improvements. If assets are owned, these terminal values are retained.
3. Need for getting lessor's approval for changes and additions to property, and the difficulty of financing improvements made to the property of a lessor.
4. When assets leased for a long time become obsolete, there may be strong reluctance to abandon them when large rentals are payable for their use.
5. The tax benefit will be challenged when the lessee is given an option to purchase at other than market value at the time of purchase. Some leases have been construed as sales, or have been ignored for tax purposes if they were held to be mere devices for charging off undue amounts against taxable income for depreciation under the guise of rentals.

EQUIPMENT LEASING. Leasing of equipment has experienced particularly rapid growth because it provides **special advantages** to the lessee, such as shifting the risk of obsolescence to the lessor. Lessors of trucks and cars enjoy such advantages as mass purchasing, mass resale of used equipment, and centralized servicing of vehicles that enable them to offer attractive rental rates in their leases.

The choice between leasing and ownership and borrowing involves not only a comparison of the effect of each on cash flow and profits, but also a weighing of other factors such as freeing of management time and effect on efficiency and morale of company employees through such factors as prompt servicing of leased trucks that suffer breakdowns on the road.

LEASING AS JUNIOR FINANCING. One important reason why leasing has expanded persistently despite higher costs and other disadvantages is its basic role as a junior financing medium for many businesses.

Leasing resembles subordinated debentures in that it permits a business to acquire a number of assets without expanding its senior debt. When petroleum companies obtain tankers and service stations through leases rather than borrowing, even at relatively high rentals, they safeguard their ability to resort to bond financing when the need arises.

So long as managements find that leasing helps assure their ability to borrow readily in the future on favorable terms in needed amounts, they are likely to favor the use of leases for many of their asset requirements.

SECTION 15

FINANCIAL PLANNING

CONTENTS

Definition and Scope

	PAGE
Concepts of financial planning	1
Financial planning defined	1
Comprehensive character of financial planning	2
Continuous planning	3
Role of the computer in financial planning	3

Budgeting and Financial Planning

Budgeting defined	5
Budget procedure	6
Use of budgets in financial planning	6
Types of budgets	7
The budget period	7

Planning for Profit

Concepts of profit	8
Measuring profit	8
Profit as a tool of management	9
Objectives of profit planning	9
Scope of profit planning	10
Measuring results against objectives	11
Form of operating report in a profit plan (f. 1)	12
Maintaining interest of all levels of management	13
Rate of return as a gauge of performance	13
Determining earnings	14
The investment base	14
Inclusion of leases in the investment base	15
Components of the rate of return	15
Formula chart. Relationship of factors affecting pattern of investment (f. 2)	16
Using rate of return to evaluate divisions	16
Cost-volume-profit relationships	17
Decomposing costs	18
Choosing a measure of volume	19
Methods employed to decompose costs	19
Break-even analysis in profit planning	20
The break-even chart	20
Using break-even analysis	20
Break-even chart (f. 3)	21
Flexible budgeting in profit planning	22
Interpreting the flexible budget	22
Installing the flexible budget	23
Direct costing in profit planning	23
Direct costing and management	24
Direct costing annual income statement by product class (f. 4)	24
Direct costing in practice	24

Financial Statement Projections

	PAGE
Types of pro-forma statements	25
Profit and loss forecasts	26
Balance sheet projections	26
Period of balance sheet projection	26
Estimated profit and loss statement (f. 5)	27
Projected balance sheet (f. 6)	28
Review of balance sheet projection	29
Retained earnings projection	29

Financial Planning for Long-Term Expansion

Need for planning in expansion	30
Factors entering into expansion planning	30
Long-term goal of the company	30
Forecast of economic conditions	30
Long-term forecasts of demand and selling prices	31
Larger sales without expansion	31
Estimating expansion required	31
Production costs at increased volume	31
Selling and advertising costs	32
Increased working capital requirements	32
Financial requirements of expansion	32
Profitability of contemplated expansion	33

Business Conditions and Financial Planning

Influence of external factors	33
Forecasting business conditions	33
Adjusting the business to economic conditions	34
Size and composition of inventories	34
Accounts receivable and credit policies	34
Provisions for contingencies	34
Amounts and maturity dates of bank loans	34
Fixed charges on long-term obligations	35
Relation of fixed to total costs	35
Purchases of materials and equipment	35

Organization for Financial Planning

Responsibility for financial planning	35
Duties of financial vice-president, treasurer, and controller	35
Financial planning functions of the board of directors	36
Financial executives of the board of directors	37
Reports to the board of directors	38
Board committees	38

SECTION 15

FINANCIAL PLANNING

Definition and Scope

CONCEPTS OF FINANCIAL PLANNING. Financial planning is a term frequently used in financial literature but seldom explicitly defined. Writers use financial planning to mean all or some of the following concepts:

Planning for Profit. Many writers regard financial planning as synonymous with "planning for profit," or analysis of the elements of income and cost with a view to securing a higher return on the capital invested in the enterprise.

Budgeting. Frequently the term financial planning is used interchangeably with budgeting in general.

Projections of Financial Statements to Future Dates. The net outcome of planning may be formulated into projected or "pro-forma" financial statements that enable management to evaluate both the adequacy and the realism of the planning.

Preparation of a Cash Budget or Forecast. This use of the term refers to a projection of the cash requirements of a corporation for a specified future period and the funds likely to become available during the period.

Management of Working Capital. Financial planning is regarded by some as being concerned primarily with efficient administration of current assets and the securing of the working capital of the business on desirable terms (see Section 16).

Management of Fixed Capital. Some regard financial planning as consisting chiefly of the preparation of a capital budget and the administration of fixed assets, including depreciation and replacement policies (see Section 17).

Planning the Capital Structure. When used in this sense, the term refers to the capitalization of a corporation, including a determination of the amount, the proportions, and the characteristics of bonds, preferred stock, and common stock to be issued.

Formulation of Corporate Financial Policies. This use of the term is practically coextensive with financial management of a business in its broadest sense.

Each of these concepts of financial planning covers an important phase of financial management. They are not mutually exclusive, but rather constitute parts of a whole.

FINANCIAL PLANNING DEFINED. For a definition that will embrace all of the aspects mentioned, financial planning may be described as a forward-looking appraisal of the financial aspects of the business program, leading to decisions regarding the most effective course of action to be taken over a future period. Its fundamental objectives are to place the enterprise in a **sound financial**

condition and to earn **satisfactory profits**, both for the immediate future and over the long run. Such planning is a primary responsibility of top management.

Financial planning and **business planning** are interdependent at every stage. A forecast of sales, for example, cannot be made without reference to productive capacity, whereas production cannot be planned ahead without a reliable forecast of sales. But both sales and production must be planned in the light of the financial consequences, whereas production and sales plans will determine the working and fixed capital requirements of the business. Thus, top management may decide that a profitable expansion of sales can be effected provided productive capacity is first enlarged and modernized, but this will call for a large outlay of cash that could not be raised on satisfactory terms until some future period. Therefore, the expansion program may be deferred for purely financial reasons.

The list of **interdependent variables** that enter into overall business and financial planning could be extended at length. Every phase of business planning implies financial considerations, just as every phase of business planning determines what is sought through financial planning. It is a matter of judgment to select the important phases of business operation that bear most directly upon the financial condition and earning power of the enterprise, and practical financial planning will be concerned chiefly with these.

In this Section, budgeting as an overall tool of financial planning, profit planning, financial statement projections, and planning for long-term expansion are the aspects of financial planning that are considered in detail. Because of its importance, special attention is given to profit planning.

COMPREHENSIVE CHARACTER OF FINANCIAL PLANNING. The financial condition of a business is presented in its balance sheet, whereas its earnings are reported in the profit and loss statement. It is logical, therefore, to base financial planning upon the major items appearing in these two financial statements. Financial planning is concerned with the impact of business policies and trends upon every item in the balance sheet and the profit and loss statement. For this purpose, a **condensed version of the balance sheet** could be used, as follows:

Assets	Liabilities
Current Assets	Current Liabilities
Cash and Equivalent	
Inventories	Fixed Liabilities
Finished Goods	
Goods in Process	Net Worth
Raw Material	Capital Stock
Accounts Receivable	
Investments	Retained Earnings
Fixed Assets (Less Allowances)	
Other Assets	

A **condensed profit and loss statement** for financial planning would contain the following items:

    Sales
    Less Cost of Sales
      Gross Profit
    Less Selling and Administrative Expenses
      Operating Profit
    Plus Other Income
    Less Other Charges
    Net Profit Before Federal Income Taxes

If financial planning is thus considered to be a preview of the financial statements of a business as they will appear at a specified future date, full cognizance must be taken of the major influences, external and internal, that will affect these statements at the time. Such preplanning of a corporation's financial condition and earnings will have to be based upon:

1. Forecasting of economic conditions.
2. Sales forecasts.
3. Expected selling prices.
4. Estimates of future operating costs, including material costs and wage rates.
5. The production schedule.
6. Planning of product lines.
7. Planning for profit.
8. Planning for working capital requirements and for the effective use of working capital.
9. Planning for capital expansion program.
10. Planning for new financing and refinancing.
11. Planning for effective use of funds flowing from profits.
12. Providing for contingencies.
13. Adjusting financial planning to economic conditions.

These elements of planning are indicative rather than inclusive. The order given above is merely accidental. Actually, financial planning must either be simultaneous for all the elements involved or the order must be adapted to the specific requirements of each business.

CONTINUOUS PLANNING. Sound financial planning like other business planning must be kept current. It is not enough merely to formulate a good financial plan. The application of the plan will call for constant revisions, both of goals and measures, as circumstances dictate. The complexity and uncertainty of doing business require that financial planning be adaptable not only to a given anticipated level of operations, but to unexpected developments that will arise from time to time. Changing market demands, inventions, changes in labor and materials costs, and the effect of overhead costs upon profit and working capital require continuous revision of projections of the future financial condition of the business and its profits. **Alternative plans** must be formulated so that, in the event unforeseen factors affect the anticipated level of operations, the company will not be faced with an emergency for which it is not prepared. Capital requirements and costs should be estimated for various levels of production and sales. Inventories and receivables applicable to different production and sales schedules should be projected to aid in planning working capital requirements.

ROLE OF THE COMPUTER IN FINANCIAL PLANNING. In business, the initial applications of the computer have been mainly in handling routine office and accounting functions. Although these applications have contributed to a significant cost reduction, they represent only a limited exploitation of the full potential of the computer. In a survey of twenty-seven major companies with extensive computer experience, McKinsey & Company, Inc., found that nine could be considered "lead" companies that had achieved a relatively high degree of success in their computer operations. The "above average" performance of these companies was largely ascribed to their ability to put the computer to work not only on the traditional routine areas but also in helping to resolve the crucial decisions of the business. According to McKinsey, in the above average companies, management ". . . sees the computer-systems effort as a major economic resource to be used in running the business." (Getting the Most Out of Your Computer, McKinsey & Company, Inc.)

As an aid to decision-making, the computer thus far has been primarily useful in areas such as manpower and production scheduling and sales forecasting. With few exceptions, its **application to financial decisions** has been more limited, but continued work is being done in this field, as illustrated below:

1. **Inventory Management.** This is probably one of the more common instances of computer financial application. Inventory simulation, for example, has been employed to determine the interactions of an inventory system, to automatically furnish rules for operating purposes, and to pretest the effectiveness of these rules.

2. **Budget Management.** This is another important financial application of the computer. Its use has provided three principal benefits: It has facilitated obtaining budgetary approval because original estimates may be readily modified to meet the requirements of operating, financial, and management personnel; permitted more realistic estimates by enabling more frequent revisions of approved budgets as new data are obtained; and provided a wider range of information because each expenditure may be classified in a number of different ways.

3. **PERT Cost.** Program Evaluation and Review Technique (PERT) was introduced primarily to control the **time aspect** of a project by improved scheduling. Later, a companion **cost program** was developed. The key element of the Pert System is the **network,** which may be defined as a flow plan representing the sequence and interrelationships of all the activities and events that must be achieved to reach the planned objectives. Through evaluation of the network, improved scheduling results, which is helpful in budget management. In addition, time, cost, and manpower summaries can be prepared for management that show the rate of progress of the project and compare the plan against actual results. To accomplish this, data are collected from the project and processed in a computer, resulting in reports that monitor the program and pinpoint areas that require attention.

4. **Information Analysis.** Work has been done in developing computer programs to trace the flow of financial information from original entries to final presentation. As a result, management can be provided with a summarization of updated financial information leading to the development of reporting systems that minimize duplications, eliminate little-used data, and facilitate retrieval of information on any subject.

5. **Capital Investments.** Time-adjusted techniques are now used by a number of companies to evaluate alternative investment opportunities. Computer programs have been developed for use in these methods. Such a program may employ as inputs earnings, depreciation, salvage values, taxes, interest on borrowed money, and probabilities of economic life. Based upon these input factors, the computer then will determine rates of return for each period of possible economic life and an overall average rate of return. Where it may not be feasible to ascertain the input directly, the computer can calculate year-by-year values to satisfy expressed requirements. For example, the computer could determine the appropriate depreciation input to meet the requirement of any selected depreciation method.

6. **Cost Estimating.** For new product development, cost estimating is indispensable in order to anticipate the price that may be charged, the size of the market that may be captured, and the profit that may be realized. Considerable time often is required to make such estimates, which cuts down upon the experimenting that may be done to obtain more accurate forecasts. To eliminate this difficulty new methods of cost estimating are being developed that involve use of

the computer. It is expected that these methods will lead to the accumulation of a library of formulas and tables that will greatly expand the potentials of cost estimating. As pointed out by Marvin (N.A.A. Bulletin, Vol. 45):

... Once the library of formulas and tables reaches a point at which it covers a significant portion of the estimating problems of the business, the computer can make its contribution to the cost estimating activity with high-speed solution and summarization of estimated costs. The computer contribution can also include, and this is of particular importance in a research and development business, the automatic selection of formulas from electronic storage.

7. Securities Management. Computers have been used to obtain various financial-statement ratios; to determine stocks possessing minimum stipulated characteristics; to calculate and compare yields from a whole series of possible bond transactions, taking into account such variables as interest income, amortization, taxes, and sales proceeds; and to develop optimum portfolios that maximize return and minimize risk. Work is also being done at the University of Chicago to use the computer to make rate of return calculations that could help evaluate the effectiveness of various methods of making investment decisions.

Budgeting and Financial Planning

BUDGETING DEFINED. The terms budget, budgeting, and budgetary control are variously defined. Heiser (Budgeting—Principles and Practice) discusses the looseness of the terminology and suggests several definitions that stress the overall nature of the budget.

... the wider practice of the art has given rise to a loose terminology so that today the terms "budget" and "budgeting" do not mean the same thing to all people. Originally, the budget was understood to be a complete, over-all plan, but now one speaks of "sales budgets," "expense budgets," "capital expenditure budgets," and the like. Similarly, today one speaks of "budgeting one's time" as well as money. Specifically, is a budget a financial document, and can the term "budgeting" be applied in the absence of a complete and comprehensive matching of anticipated revenue with anticipated expenditures? Can a management, for example, claim to practice budgeting if it "budgets" only certain of the company's activities?

The foregoing questions are important for the insight which they give into the subject. Certain definitions, therefore, are in order ...

The author thinks of the budget as an over-all "blueprint" of a comprehensive plan of operations and actions, expressed in financial terms.

Budgeting is conceived to be the preparation of a budget **and** its fullest use, not only as a device for planning and coordinating, but also for control.

In the first definition it should be recognized that while the financial nature of the document is the necessary result of the fact that money is the common denominator of all business transactions, nevertheless, the document is only a financial reflection of transactions with nonmonetary things—man-hours of labor, tons of raw material, units of product, and so on. With reference to the common practice of applying the term "budget" to mere segments of the budget, as mentioned above, the author believes that this practice, while understandable, is unfortunate in that it leads to confused thinking on the subject ...

Heckert and Willson (Business Budgeting and Control) also emphasize the need for including the whole business operation in the budget and point to the forward-looking nature of budgetary control. They define the business budget "as a coordinated plan of financial action for the enterprise. It can thus be distinguished from other accounting controls chiefly because budgetary control, if properly installed, does these things:

"a) Encompasses all the business operations and not merely a given department or certain types of costs.

"b) Relates sales income in total and by segments to the corresponding costs and expenses.

"c) Establishes predetermined operating objectives and is forward looking; and is not restricted merely to a comparison of actual results with standard."

BUDGET PROCEDURE. In the light of the general policies of the enterprise, the separate departments and subdivisions of the business usually prepare individual **departmental budgets**. For this they require statistical and accounting data covering past results, which should be furnished them by the controller. The departmental budgets are then molded into a preliminary budget by the budget director, who in some organizations is also the controller, who submits it to top management for review and approval. Discussions with department heads may cause various sections of the budget to be revised while the overall budget is in preparation.

The form and content of a budget should be adapted to meet the need. Some concerns, because of the nature of their business, require detailed budgets, whereas others find that the ends of planning, coordination, and control are achieved with less detail in their budgets.

A comprehensive budget for a manufacturing company will usually include the following sections:

1. Sales budget.
2. Production budget.
3. Materials budget.
4. Labor budget.
5. Manufacturing expense budget.
6. Research and development budget (frequently covers several years).
7. Distribution cost budget.
8. Administrative expense budget.
9. Plant and equipment budget (usually prepared for several years ahead and revised at least annually).

All of the above budgets are useful in the preparation of the following **financial budgets**:

10. Estimated cash receipts and disbursements for each month of the budget period.
11. Estimated profit and loss statement for each month, or each quarter of the budget period, or for the entire budget period.
12. Estimated balance sheet as at the end of each month, or each quarter, or the end of the budget period.

These budgets are all presented to top management for final approval.

USE OF BUDGETS IN FINANCIAL PLANNING. Financial planning should precede and control the formulation of a budget. A good budget is the result of good planning. It is possible to plan the operations of a business without a budget, but it is inconceivable that a budget could be prepared without prior planning. The budget is an expression in financial terms of the plan of operations.

Prior to adoption of the budget, the following questions must be answered:

1. Will the program produce the maximum profits attainable under the circumstances?

2. Will the program keep the business in sound financial condition?
3. Do the financial resources of the business permit attainment of the contemplated program?
4. Should the plan of operations as expressed in the budget be revised, and in what respects?

TYPES OF BUDGETS. There are three principal types of budgets: the appropriation budget, the fixed or forecast budget, and the variable or flexible budget.

The **appropriation budget** is used primarily by organizations that do not have a complete budget system, but nevertheless desire to place a limit on the amount to be expended upon a particular activity. Appropriation budgets are used most frequently in connection with advertising, research and development, etc. Appropriation budgets have only limited uses in business, though they are very common in governmental budgeting.

Fixed or forecast budgets establish a plan of operations in which the standard of measurement does not vary with actual conditions. Thus, if unit costs have been set at $1 on the assumption that volume of production will be 100,000 units, the budgeted unit costs would not vary if production should actually be only 80,000 units. With fixed budgets, changes in the volume of sales do not alter the budget, but the figures remain "fixed" or "static." They are prepared on the assumption that sales and production volume, production costs, and profits can be forecast with some degree of accuracy. In practice, however, actual results are frequently wide of the mark.

Fixed budgets become of little value when the volume of operations differs materially from forecasts, primarily because of the influence of fixed or overhead expenses upon total costs with changes in the volume of business. Fixed budgets are gradually being replaced by flexible or variable budget systems in which unit costs are related to the volume of production. Gardner (Variable Budget Control), in commenting upon the fixed or static type of budget, states:

> Static budgeting has failed in most enterprises completely to meet its objectives for sustained periods of time, not because looking ahead is not valuable but because the basis for looking ahead has not been expressed in mobile units that keep pace with unpredictable changes.
>
> Under a static budgetary control or any fixed cross-section of expectancies we measure costs at a projected, or anticipated, level of activity. At that point, and that point alone, we know exactly what we should spend or how we stand. Unfortunately, at other points of activity we have no predetermined relationship, or at least not one of a current nature, nor do we have any device to interpolate between known static relationships. Thus we find that when the planned program changes as the result of unpredictable external forces, the control is distorted and uncertain.

Only **flexible budgeting** provides a sound basis for financial planning, because it can readily be adapted to actual experience. For instance, if a forecast is based upon sales of 100,000 units but only 80,000 units are actually sold, total costs of production and of distribution would not decline by 20%. In most instances, the actual reduction would be less because of continuing overhead costs. It can normally be assumed that if sales and production volume vary from the forecasts, unit costs and profits also will be affected. This subject is discussed later in this section as an aspect of cost-volume-profit relationships.

THE BUDGET PERIOD. The bulk of companies probably prepare **annual** budgets covering month by month changes. **Shorter-term** budgets are used when closer review is necessary, such as by companies experiencing sharp seasonal changes, relying heavily upon short-term borrowing, or selling low-margin products. In order to plan for such circumstances as capital expansion, introduction of new products, and crystallizing dividend policies, **longer-term** budgets are often employed, particularly by the larger companies. In these instances, the budgets are apt to show only changes covering longer periods. Heckert and Willson cite typical practices in long-range budgeting as follows (Business Budgeting and Control):

First year	Monthly budgets
Second year	Quarterly or semi-annual budgets
Third year	Semi-annual or annual budgets
Fourth and fifth, etc. years	Annual budgets.

Budgets that are prepared 1 year in advance are likely to be revised at least each quarter. For more accurate budgeting, more frequent revisions are used and some companies budget progressively, such as by dropping and adding 1 month. The budget period also is discussed in Section 16 under cash budgeting and in Section 17 under planning of capital expenditures.

Planning for Profit

CONCEPTS OF PROFIT. Economists have long been concerned with the concept of profit and have formulated theories to explain its existence. In the early nineteenth century, the notion was developed that profits represented the return to the entrepreneur for the services he rendered in coordinating the activities of the other factors of production. With the rise of the large corporation and the separation of ownership and management, the **administrative responsibility** of the enterprise became lodged in the management rather than the ownership group. This shift was accompanied by a decline in the importance of the payment theory of profit and the rise of the concept of profit as a reward for incurring risks or uncertainties, an important aspect of which is the return to entrepreneurs for innovation.

Measuring Profit. Whatever may be the merits of the theories, profit represents an important driving force that underlies the activities of business firms, forms the basis of dividends to stockholders as well as taxes to governments, and is a major factor entering into the valuation of the firm. Accordingly, it becomes important to provide a quantitative dollar measurement of profit. For this purpose, the **economist** views it as a surplus in excess of all costs, which he defines broadly, and measures it by the **increase in the value of an enterprise from period to period,** after allowing for dividend distributions and capital receipts. This gain in value is the result not only of operations but also of changes in asset values, gauged by capitalizing expected future net income. Thus, economic profit emphasizes the balance sheet, expectations, and real dollars adjusted for changes in the value of the price level.

Although the economist's view has influenced business practice in various ways, particularly in capital-investment decisions, management generally determines profit in accordance with the accounting definition, which is oriented toward the income statement. Thus the **accountant** measures profit as the **difference between revenue and the costs used to produce the revenue.** To arrive at a figure for any interval of time, various allocation decisions are necessary. On the revenue side, for example, a construction contract may extend over several periods, requiring a determination of the portion pertaining to the period in question; on the cost side, an allocation must be made of costs applicable to revenues of the current period and costs related to revenues of other periods. For any particular financial period, therefore, the profit reported depends upon the portion of the total revenue flows recognized in the period as well as the costs considered applicable to these revenues and included in the period's financial statement. The difference represents the profit, which reverts to the benefit of the proprietors of the enterprise and is reflected in the change that takes place in their ownership interests, after allowing for any amounts withdrawn.

Profit as a Tool of Management. Because qualitative factors of judgment and objectives are often important in measuring profit, the same accounting conventions may not be appropriate in different instances. Within the framework of accounting consistency, there are many opportunities for allocation decisions to influence the reported profits. Management may report one profit to its stockholders, another to the Internal Revenue Service, and employ still another for internal analysis. Moreover, within certain limits, and depending upon the **objective in view,** management may report either a higher or a lower level of profit. For example, it may desire profits that appear conservative in order to discourage pressure for dividends, or profits that appear liberal to facilitate a new financing.

Along these lines, Bows (N.A.A. Bulletin, Vol. 42) has noted that "Internal accounting must be flexible and geared to the particular management and business, and should be subject to constant changes to meet their needs." Commenting in the same vein, he points out the pressures on a management with a conservative policy, and correspondingly conservative earnings, to match the more liberal policy of a competitor.

. . . Obviously, just looking at the problem from a competitive standpoint, it is completely unfair for one company which is not realistic in its practices to take advantage of its competition by utilizing all the loopholes in the rules to obtain the highest reported earnings. Yet, if we do not shut the door, sound business practice will lose—because realistic management will be criticized if its earnings are not up to its competition. How long can the management of Company A stand by and let B's management make better deals for its shareholders? C.P.A.'s see time and time again examples of companies which have been realistic in their practices forced to adopt less conservative procedures to overcome stockholder or director criticism of reported earnings.

OBJECTIVES OF PROFIT PLANNING. Profit planning is the name given to the use of forecasts of profits for the purpose of

1. Increasing the earnings of the enterprise, while
2. Preserving the integrity of the capital investment.

The chief benefit derived from planning profits usually is the **analysis** that it entails of the financial aspects of the **production and distribution policies** of the business, to measure their impact upon earning power. Planning for profit is successful only when it also assures **preservation of the invested capital** of the business. The earnings reported by the accountant for any given year are, at best, an approximation based upon accounting conventions. **True profitability** can be determined only over a period of years. A business that enjoys a profit of 20% on the investment for 5 years is not successful if it is then forced to liquidate and returns little or nothing to stockholders. It follows, therefore, that adequate maintenance of plant and equipment, and the accumulation of an adequate fund to finance their replacement, are necessary for the preservation of a concern's capital investment. In much the same way, inadequate development of markets for a company's products through advertising may permit competitors to ease out the enterprise and usurp its position in the industry. Failure to carry on essential research that will maintain a company's competitive position also may result not only in reduced profits for later years but in a gradual whittling away of the capital value of the business, which is determined chiefly by its capitalized earning power.

Boosting current profits at the expense of the future is futile. For example, a mining company that extracts only high-grade, low-cost ores from a particular vein might show a very substantial current profit, but over a period of years total profits would be cut should it prove unprofitable to return to that vein for the lower-grade, higher-cost ores. But if both types of ore had been extracted simultaneously, the low-grade ore might have been salable at considerable aggregate profit.

SCOPE OF PROFIT PLANNING. Since profit planning is the expression of a company's methods for achieving its profit objectives, it embraces **all the activities of a firm,** from research through manufacturing to sales. To permit management to evaluate the effort required and to take advance measures to forestall possible blocks, the plan must indicate **all the major steps** necessary to attain the stipulated objectives. Thus, the plan incorporates sales forecasting, budgeting, and asset control procedures. The controller of a large company has described the widespread scope of profit planning as follows (Voller, N.A.A. Bulletin, Vol. 42):

Profit planning includes a complete financial and operational plan for all phases and facets of the business. It therefore encompasses budgeting programs for control of expenses, sales forecasting and sales planning programs, planning and programming additions to or deletions from working capital and plant investment, and a review of all factors which have an impact on return on investment, both from a short-term viewpoint of one year and longer periods of time. The profit planning function must not be merely financial in scope. It must disclose the methods and programs by which the financial goals set forth are to be achieved.

This type of program is usually started by the chief accounting officer because of the multitude of facts that are available to him. Usually, as a starting point, budgetary control programs are installed in some form or another and from this point the planning function evolves.

Once the plan is defined the development of a formal or informal format is the next step. The information necessary to the plan can be rigidly defined or broadly outlined. This must be done whether there is extensive participation or not. A check list and time schedule of some type must be prepared. The format is developed starting with estimated sales, manufacturing costs and capacities, service expenses, administrative, selling and engineering expenses, long-term debt expenses, etc. In addition to these basic profit and loss factors, programs and plans must be established for each individual function.

To develop plans of this scope **careful scheduling is necessary** because often one segment of a plan cannot be undertaken until a preceding one is completed. Moreover, revisions may become necessary as the various portions are put into place and the interaction of the different phases of the company's operations upon each other are evaluated. In effect, therefore, the planning is undertaken on a continuous basis although it is important to observe target dates for the completion of certain phases. One corporation vice-president has described these operations as follows (Keller, N.A.A. Bulletin, Vol. 44):

In February, I received from our controller's office the scheduled dates on which the 1963 sales budget and operating budget for the international operations of the Armstrong Cork Company were to be reviewed with the company forecasting committee. The other operations managers received their schedules on the same date. Thus, it is evident that profit planning is a well-organized and definitely scheduled function in our company. In effect, it is a continuous process.

In the Armstrong Cork Company, the responsibility for profit and return on capital employed is placed with the vice-presidents and general managers of the four operating units of the company (one of which includes international operations) . . .

Obviously, detailed work on profit planning for 1963 did not begin immediately after the February notice from the controller of the budget completion dates. But programming the program did. With the combined sales forecast to be completed on October 19 and the operating budget on December 17, a schedule was set for each of our units so we could meet these dates. These time schedules are detailed for every step, from the completion of process specifications to after-tax profits by product lines. When the budgets of each unit are received in the general office, they must be consolidated, inter-company transactions eliminated, and analyses and interpretations prepared prior to the forecasting committee review. This means that, after allowing for mailing time, each unit must have its work completed about eighteen days before the review dates. . . .

The basic schedules are set by the controller of international operations, and he then has each company controller develop a more detailed schedule for his company. The work begins in August with the finalization of standard process specifications by the manufacturing companies. They follow this with the development of unit material and labor standards and basic data for expense budgets. While this is in process, the marketing managers are working on their unit sales budgets. Unit standard costs and factory expense budgets are completed by the time the sales budgets are approved. The factory cost of sales is established by the budgeted sales volume and selling and administrative expense budgets completed between the date of completion of the sales budget and final operating budget.

Thus, detailed profit planning begins in August, and the work intensifies until the final plans are consolidated and approved as the international operation's operating budget about the middle of December.

MEASURING RESULTS AGAINST OBJECTIVES. The plan is geared to an approved profit objective. The stipulated objective, in turn, is broken down into subobjectives for the various units of the company. In appraising progress of the plan, it is important that results be judged against the profit objective rather than against other standards, such as historic performance. To **pinpoint responsibility** for these results, each unit manager assigned a segment of the plan reports regularly the performance of his unit in meeting plan objectives. To the extent that variances occur, these must be explained so that top management may judge their significance. It is important for top management to know whether the variances were beyond the control of the responsible head, such as those caused by changes in wage rates or material price changes; were within his control, such as higher costs resulting from overtime necessitated by poor scheduling; or were temporary in nature, such as lowered sales caused by unseasonable weather. The Director of Management Services, Westinghouse Electric Corporation, has described this aspect of profit planning (Evans, N.A.A. Bulletin, Vol. 40):

> Reports of actual results for management purposes should first of all be tied to plans and objectives which were previously established. The very best measure of performance in a given period of time is the plan which was established at the beginning of that period of time. Too often we are content to devote hours and days to the development of plans and objectives, then never relate actual results to the objective to determine how good our plan was or how effective we were in carrying it out. We fall back on comparisons of last year against this year or against some long-term arbitrary ratios to measure how well we have done our job. A report of actual results which does not make a comparison with the established objectives for the period in question is almost useless as a control device.

```
To:       PRESIDENT.
Date:
From:     OPERATING DIVISION MANAGER
Subject:  REPORT OF (MONTH) OPERATIONS
```

Copy to: CHAIRMAN OF THE BOARD   OPERATING VICE PRESIDENT
          EXECUTIVE VICE PRESIDENT AND TREASURER   CONTROLLER
          EXECUTIVE VICE PRESIDENT — OPERATIONS

SALES FOR THE MONTH WERE _____ : VARIABLE MARGIN _____ :
OPERATING PROFIT _____ : NET PROFIT AFTER TAXES _____ .

SALES ANALYSIS

PROFIT PLAN   (LIST AND DISCUSS MAJOR VARIANCES
ACTUAL   FROM FORECAST AND EFFECT ON
% CHANGE   INCOME FOR THE MONTH.)

ANALYSIS OF MANUFACTURING AND SERVICE ACTIVITY COSTS

PROFIT PLAN   (LIST AND DISCUSS MAJOR VARIANCES.)
ACTUAL
% CHANGE

ANALYSIS OF CAPACITY COSTS   %
                           PROFIT PLAN   ACTUAL   CHANGE

MANUFACTURING AND SERVICE
SELLING
A & G
ENGINEERING

(MAJOR VARIANCES WITHIN AN EXPENSE GROUP SHOULD BE SET OUT SEPARATELY AND DISCUSSED.)

YEAR-TO-DATE SUMMARY   %
                           PROFIT PLAN   ACTUAL   CHANGE
SALES
VARIABLE MARGIN
OPERATING EARNINGS
PROFIT BEFORE TAX
RETURN ON NET INVESTMENT

GENERAL COMMENTS

BRIEF REVIEW OF CHANGES IN OBJECTIVES, IF ANY: COMMENTS, WHERE APPROPRIATE, ON ORGANIZATION MATTERS, LABOR DEVELOPMENTS, PRODUCT DEVELOPMENT, MANUFACTURING PROGRAMS, ETC.

SUMMARY OF OUTLOOK FOR SUCCEEDING MONTH, NEW ORDERS, BACKLOG AND EVALUATION OF RESULTS YEAR-TO-DATE WITH RESPECT TO THE PROFIT PLAN.

Fig. 1. Form of operating report in a profit plan.

Secondly, reports of actual results should reveal the basic reasons why performance has deviated from objective or from a previous actual level in terms of the major influencing factors at work. These major influencing factors would include such things as wage rate and material price changes, physical volume of sales, realized sales price, mix of product and cost of expense control. In individual situations, other factors may be deemed to be of vital importance and require segregation. It means little or nothing to operating management to know if they have failed to meet a given objective, unless it knows why it failed in terms which can be measured and understood and which can guide the way to future action.

Finally, reports of actual results against plan should be drawn in terms of individual responsibilities. A business firm is an organization of individuals. The president delegates pieces of his over-all responsibility to those members of his management team reporting directly to him. These men further delegate responsibility, naming specific individuals to be responsible for specific results. If the accounting system does not produce reports of actual results against objective in terms of the individuals responsible, top management is at a loss to know how to institute corrective action.

These elements of reporting in a profit plan are illustrated in Fig. 1. In this instance, a division manager is reporting the results of the month's operations to top management; the division manager thus has the responsibility for the effectiveness of the performance and for explaining departures from plan. The report covers an analysis of sales, manufacturing and service activity costs, and capacity costs, as well as a summary of year-to-date results. In each instance actual performance is measured against those called for under the profit plan. Provision also is made to explain major variances. (Voller, N.A.A. Bulletin, Vol. 42.)

Maintaining Interest of All Levels of Management. This means of regular reporting not only permits top management to follow the course of the plan and evaluate its effectiveness but also helps insure the continuous interest and participation of all levels of management. An effective profit-planning program necessitates the interest and cooperation of the entire staff. It is important, therefore, for subordinates to recognize that higher levels of management are vitally interested in the comparison of performance against plan and in the measures being taken to produce better results. Recognition of the significance of profit-improvement achievements as an accepted company philosophy is a helpful stimulant to bring about the continued cooperation necessary to effect a successful program of this type. The importance and means of assuring concern for profit-improvement at every level of management has been summarized as follows (Hoffman, Harvard Business Review, Vol. 41):

... motivation of supervisors and managers toward increased profit improvement efforts requires that bosses down the line be interested, not only in dollars saved and numbers of improvements installed, but also in the **time** and **effort** subordinates are giving to the study of operations and the design of improvements. In both principle and practice it is important that supervisors and managers be held responsible for the profit improvement record of their units, with staff units (if there are any) playing the role not of initiator but of "resource."

A good system of formal controls developed by the managers who use them, and a clear specific statement of profit improvement philosophy developed by top management, can also be helpful if the proper atmosphere of day-to-day emphasis on profit improvement has first been established.

RATE OF RETURN AS A GAUGE OF PERFORMANCE. The magnitude of profit by itself means little unless gauged against some input base. A small profit that is the outcome of a modest investment may reflect a better performance than a large profit flowing from a large dollar input. Accordingly, a widely used measure of managerial effectiveness is the **rate of return on investment**. In its Executive Committee Control Charts (Treasurer's Department, E. I. DuPont de Nemours and Co.), Du Pont states its belief ". . . that a manufacturing enterprise can best measure and judge the effectiveness of its efforts in terms of return on investment." (For purposes of evaluating alternative investment opportunities, the payback or some form of time-adjusted method of determining rate of return is also used. See Section 17.) The return on investment is calculated by dividing earnings for the period by the investment base, but there is substantial disagreement on what profit or investment base to use. The National Association of Accountants has thrown light on industry practice in these respects by means of a survey of 44 field interviews with companies that use rate of return as a management tool (N.A.A. Research Report No. 35).

Determining Earnings. The N.A.A. points out that the definition of earnings should correspond with the definition of investment. As a result, when return on assets is used, only income from the assets comprising the investment base should be included; when return on equity is employed, only income applicable to the equity interest should be counted. In practice, many companies include **dividends and interest** in earnings to measure return on investment; in other cases only operating earnings are used. The exclusion of dividend, interest, and "other" income is justified on the grounds that the resulting figure is more comparable to that used by divisions and better represents operating performance. Similarly, many companies exclude interest expense because it is felt that operating management should not be held responsible for financial expenses. Other firms deduct interest before determining their rate of return, possibly because the practice is more conservative, although the N.A.A. points out that such a rate might better be described as a "return to stockholders on total assets."

The extent of management responsibility also arises in the decision whether to use earnings after or before **income taxes.** Firms employing the pretax figure apparently feel that taxes are beyond the control of management or that extensive tax carry-forwards could make aftertax figures misleading. Companies deducting income taxes point out that taxes are an accepted cost and that investors are more interested in the aftertax figure. Most companies deduct **depreciation** in ascertaining the amount of earnings to use in the calculation, even though they may count assets at gross.

The Investment Base. As a gauge of management performance, companies ordinarily employ **total assets** as the investment base because management has this total at its disposal. As refinements of this approach, some companies use **operating assets** to match operating earnings, or they may go even further and exclude assets that are not expected to earn a return, such as excess cash or assets equivalent to the tax liability. Sometimes, **equity plus long-term debt** serves as the investment base, since this represents permanent capital as contrasted with the assets provided by short-term creditors. If there is reason to stress the equity interest, as in a closely held corporation, the return may be calculated on the amount of stockholders' capital in the business. The same company may use different figures in the investment base for different purposes; for example, total assets may be used when an evaluation of management performance is desired, whereas one of the other bases may appear preferable for comparison with other companies.

When assets are used as the investment base, a major area of disagreement is whether they should be **gross or net of depreciation.** Those favoring **gross assets** contend that depreciation should not enter into a valuation base because its determination often has nothing to do with value; the various methods permissible in determining depreciation could distort comparative results; a fully depreciated asset may still make a contribution toward production, although if the efficiency of the older assets has been deteriorating, this fact would be reflected in reduced earnings; and deducting depreciation could inflate considerably reported rates of return. Those arguing for **net assets** claim that measurement of performance should not be affected by the age of the assets and their value should therefore be adjusted through depreciation; a net figure is also more consistent with reporting practices; depreciation allowances represent charge-offs that already have been reinvested in the business thereby relieving the old assets from the necessity of earning a return; and, in any event, it is inconsistent to relate a profit figure from which depreciation has been deducted to an investment figure from which accumulated depreciation has not been deducted.

Inclusion of Leases in the Investment Base. Accountants disagree on the extent to which leases should be reflected in financial statements. Both the American Institute of Certified Public Accountants and the S.E.C. have indicated that if it is clear that **a transaction is in substance a purchase,** the leased property should be counted among the assets of the lessee, with appropriate accounting for the corresponding liability. Myers (cited by Moonitz, Harvard Business Review, Vol. 41), in a research study made at the instance of the A.I.C.P.A., concluded that "to the extent, then, that the rental payments represent a means of financing the acquisition of property rights which the lessee has in his possession and under his control, the transaction constitutes the acquisition of an asset with a related obligation to pay for it." Cook (Harvard Business Review, Vol. 41), on the other hand, contends that financial statements are not intended to portray every relevant fact about the future of an enterprise and that to capitalize arbitrary amounts in the balance sheet represents a dangerous approach that departs from the cost principle of accounting.

In practice it is uncommon for balance sheets to include leases even when they are substantially a purchase. Regardless of accounting policy, however, in determining the total amount of assets that may serve as the investment base or, correspondingly, in measuring the fixed-charge relative to the equity segment of the liability side of the balance sheet, a number of financial analysts have indicated the need for some adjustment. Gant (Harvard Business Review, Vol. 37) proposes, as one approach being adopted to an increasing extent, the **capitalizing of annual lease rentals at some arbitrary rate**—say about 6% to 8%. Graham, Dodd, and Cottle (Security Analysis: Principles and Techniques) suggest that in the chain-store field, where many enterprises rent while others own their store locations, one-third of the annual rentals for building space paid by chain and department stores be regarded as fixed charges and the capitalized value of these rentals, say at 4½%, should be regarded as funded debt in computing stock-equity ratios.

COMPONENTS OF THE RATE OF RETURN. For purposes of profit planning, the rate of return on investment represents the end-result of the company's activities. This rate, in turn, initially may be broken down into **two basic components,** earnings as a per cent of sales and the turnover of investment. Earnings as a per cent of sales is calculated by dividing earnings by sales whereas capital turnover is calculated by dividing sales by total investment. The product of these two ratios produces the rate of return on investment.

$$ROI = \frac{\text{Earnings}}{\text{Sales}} \times \frac{\text{Sales}}{\text{Total Investment}}$$

Earnings may be decomposed into sales minus cost of sales, and cost of sales into the mill cost of sales plus selling and administrative expenses. Total investment, in turn, may be broken down into working capital plus permanent investment, and working capital into inventories, accounts receivable, and cash. Du Pont has expressed these relationships in chart form, as shown in Fig. 2, and in-

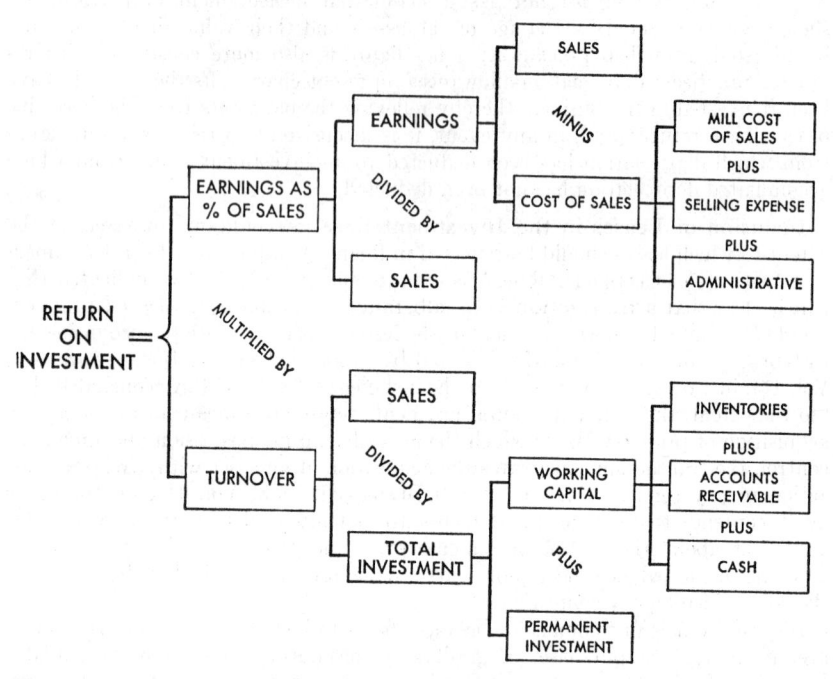

Fig. 2. Formula chart. Relationship of factors affecting pattern of investment.

corporates it into the chart system used by the company's Executive Committee in reviewing with each general manager the results of his department's operations. The company points out that "The formula is set up in this manner so that the separate effects of Earnings as percent of Sales and Turnover upon Return on Investment can be determined. Earnings as percent of Sales reflects the success (or lack of success) in maintaining satisfactory control of costs. Turnover reflects the rapidity with which the capital committed to the operation is being worked. Thus the manager of an operating investment can improve his Return by reducing costs or working existing investment harder, both of which factors are within his control."

USING RATE OF RETURN TO EVALUATE DIVISIONS. The growth of **semi-autonomous divisions** within a broad corporate framework has centered attention on the need to rate the results of these divisions. Management has employed various devices for this purpose, including qualitative judgment, the trend of sales, the percentage of the market captured, and the number of new products introduced. Since each of these factors reflects a different aspect of operations, the firm may use some combination of the factors giving particular stress to the one that appears most significant to its activity. For example, pharmaceutical companies may pay particular attention to the new products emerging from their research efforts. In general, however, these are supplementary devices, and the principal measure ordinarily used is the division's rate of return on investment. As Dearden has stated, ". . . in most decentralized profit-center systems the rate of return earned by a division is the most **influential** factor in evaluating performance. It is doubly important, therefore, that the rate represent the effectiveness of management action as accurately as possible." (Dearden, Harvard Business Review, Vol. 39.)

The effort to give divisional management adequate independence while retaining the division's role as part of an overall corporate effort leads to **special problems** in determining and judging the significance of the division's rate of return. These problems include the method of allocating headquarters' services, how interdivisional transfers of goods and services will be handled, allowing for differences in the economic environment where the various divisions operate, adjusting for difficulties the divisional manager may have inherited from his predecessor, and allowing for the fact that the effectiveness of the division's activities may not be reflected in the current year's operations but may be deferred to the future. The decisions made to resolve these problems depend heavily upon the conditions and characteristics of the individual firm. These decisions, however, must recognize the need for determining and using the divisional rate of return in a way that reduces the possibility that the divisional manager will take steps that improve the division's rate at the expense of that of the corporation. This point has been stressed by Dearden: "It is vital to the effective operation of a decentralized profit-control system . . . that action taken by a local manager to improve the division's rate of return also improve the company's rate of return to a corresponding degree. Otherwise, the system will be motivating the divisional manager to take action that, from a corporation-wide viewpoint, is unprofitable."

COST–VOLUME–PROFIT RELATIONSHIPS. In discussing this subject, the N.A.A. (N.A.A. Research Report No. 37) has stated that, "volume is . . . one of the key factors which must be considered in profit planning." This point of view is reflected in the considerable attention given by business firms to determining the effect on profits of proposed volume changes. In planning the activities of a firm, it is profitable to schedule the production of an additional unit of a product so long as its marginal revenue is positive; that is, as long as the revenue from producing an additional unit exceeds the cost of production. Because the relationship between cost and volume underlies the whole area of profit planning it has been the subject of study by both economists and financial analysts for a long period of time. In their approaches, however, the economist and the financial analyst have taken **different views** of the shape of the marginal cost curve.

By and large, the **economist** has visualized a marginal cost curve that changes over time, depending upon such factors as the length of the period involved and changes in the proportion of variable and fixed costs. Accordingly, his general proposition is that it is profitable to expand output while marginal revenue is greater than marginal cost. As stated by Samuelson, "As long as a step toward extra output gives us more marginal revenue than marginal cost, our profit is increasing and we continue to produce more output. But whenever marginal cost exceeds marginal revenue, we contract output. . . . Best-profit equilibrium is **where marginal cost and marginal revenue are equal.** Here alone is the optimal situation of maximum profits." (Samuelson, Economics—An Introductory Analysis.)

On the other hand, the **financial analyst** generally recognizes that within a given level of capacity, the growth in total costs as a result of an expansion in production is traceable to an increase in variable costs. Variable costs, in turn, tend to move directly and proportionately with production and, therefore, the variable cost per unit, which may be compared with the economist's marginal cost, is constant. Thus, the N.A.A. has defined variable costs as follows (N.A.A. Research Report 37):

Usage of capacity to make and to sell goods or services requires that additional costs be incurred. Such costs of producing and selling tend to vary directly and proportionately with sales. For this reason, the term variable cost is often used as a synonym for direct cost.

The divergence between the two concepts has been noted by Dean (Dean, Managerial Economics), as follows:

Economists have long speculated about the shape of the relationship of cost to output, since it plays a key role in determining the theoretically optimum level of production. The accepted doctrine has been that marginal costs rise continuously as output rate increases above some given level, and that the resulting average cost curve has a U-shaped relation to output. In contrast with this doctrine, businessmen have quite generally supposed that marginal cost is constant, at least over the output range of normal experience.

It is difficult to reconcile these points of view because of the lack of suitable cost studies of a sufficiently large number of cases. But, after considering the problem, at least one writer has concluded that the financial analyst's notion of constant variable costs per unit is more accurate. (Burchard, N.A.A. Bulletin, Vol. 42.)

Are variable costs of the firm constant or increasing? That is the question that causes the basic disagreement between the two analyses. The pursuit of profits takes different paths. If variable costs are increasing, to maximize profit, management must locate the volume where marginal cost and marginal revenue are equal. If variable costs are constant, full capacity automatically provides the maximum profit; the important operating facts for management to know are the break-even volume and the degree of its fixed costs. The difference between the two analyses is fundamental. They are not compatible.

. . . .

Variable costs for the Reliance Company (an actual firm with an assumed name) are constant. Since this is so, the cost of producing an additional unit is the same; that is, marginal cost is also constant . . . This fact of constant marginal cost is borne out in the accounting records examined by this writer over the years.

Whatever may be the theoretical merit of the economist's point of view, in practice firms have found it desirable for purpose of profit planning to define a category of costs that varies directly with volume. As stated by one firm surveyed by the N.A.A. (N.A.A. Research Report No. 37), "this definition was chosen because it fills our need for clear-cut costs in analyzing results of operations and in making short-run decisions on product pricing."

DECOMPOSING COSTS. In studies of cost-volume-profit relationships, costs are generally divided into the following categories:

1. **Variable costs and expenses**—which are almost directly related to volume and include such costs as direct labor, direct material, and compensation insurance.
2. **Fixed expenses**—which remain fixed in amount regardless of volume. Examples of fixed expenses are property taxes, fire insurance, executive salaries, interest on bonds, and depreciation charged on a time basis.

3. **Semivariable expenses**—which vary, but not proportionately, with volume. Examples are light and power and salesmen's commissions paid on a guaranteed minimum basis. Sometimes these expenses vary with policy rather than volume changes.

To provide this type of breakdown, costs generally are analyzed relative to some measure of output.

Choosing a Measure of Volume. The volume unit employed to measure how costs change depends upon the nature of the decision being made and the cost records of the company. The N.A.A. has set up four major criteria to consider in selecting such a unit (N.A.A. Research Series No. 16).

1. The unit must reflect changes in the activity that induces the cost variations. In factory departments, for example, the measure of production might be labor hours, labor dollars, machine hours, or some physical product unit, applied if considered desirable to each department separately. In marketing, different units are needed for different functions and, therefore, such measures might be selected as calls made by salesmen, number of orders or, in the case of warehousing costs, weight of goods handled.

2. To the extent possible, the unit selected should measure only volume changes. In the case of dollar sales, as an illustration, changes in selling price would influence the reported figures as well as changes in physical volume; in the case of labor dollars, wage rates could cause shifts in reported levels rather than the number of hours worked. To obviate such distortions, standard selling prices and standard costs may be employed.

3. The unit should be simple and readily understood. For this reason, sales dollars or labor dollars may prove more satisfactory in the long run than a weighted activity index.

4. The unit selected should emerge from statistics already collected rather than requiring additional clerical expense.

Methods Employed To Decompose Costs. The N.A.A. survey found that companies tended to use **three principal methods** to separate costs into their fixed and variable components.

1. **Inspection of the chart of accounts.** This is usually the starting procedure and if sufficiently detailed records are available many of the accounts may be classified on this basis. The general procedure is first to assign accounts to departments and then to classify them as variable or fixed depending upon the function done by each department. It may be found that an account that is direct in one department is a fixed cost of another.
2. **Statistical analysis** through such methods as scatter charts or regression equations.—Although these methods are often described in the professional literature, the N.A.A. found that they were not widely used in practice. The reason usually mentioned for this is that such methods are more useful for the analysis of historical costs rather than applicable to the current situation. Sometimes, the historical analysis sets the basis for future classifications.
3. **Industrial engineering studies.**—It is not uncommon for plant industrial engineers and plant controllers to work together in determining cost classifications. This method entails a careful study of what physical volume of supplies, employees, or services should be allowed at different output levels.

Once cost breakdowns have been established, they are periodically reviewed to determine if operational or organizational changes require adjustments or shifts in the classifications. The cost breakdowns, in turn, provide the foundation for three major areas of profit planning: break-even analysis, direct costing, and the flexible budget.

BREAK-EVEN ANALYSIS IN PROFIT PLANNING. The break-even volume of sales occurs at that level that produces a margin of income above variable costs that equals the amount of fixed costs incurred during the period. In terms of dollars, the break-even point may be calculated from the following formula:

$$\text{Dollar Sales at Break Even} = \frac{\text{Fixed Costs}}{1 - \dfrac{\text{Variable Costs}}{\text{Sales}}}$$

In terms of units, it may be calculated from the following formula:

$$\text{Unit Sales at Break Even} = \frac{\text{Fixed Costs}}{\text{Sales Price per Unit} - \text{Variable Costs per Unit}}$$

A high break-even point suggests that the base underlying a company's earnings is precarious. To reduce the level, the selling price may be raised, variable costs cut, or fixed costs reduced. **If the gap is wide** between the sales price and variable costs per unit, a change in either of these two factors will have a relatively modest influence on the break-even level, and more efforts might be concentrated on lowering fixed costs. **If the gap is narrow** either raising the sales price or reducing variable costs could have a sharp effect on the break-even level. Which course to adopt in this instance would depend upon such factors as competitive market conditions, the elasticity of consumer demand, and the company's efficiency of operations.

The Break-Even Chart. A break-even chart is often used in profit planning. Fig. 3 is a chart prepared by Brelsford (A.M.A. Fin. Mgt. Ser. No. 87) for this purpose. The break-even point on the chart shows the level of sales at which operations produce neither a profit nor a loss. Break-even charts must be prepared with great care, as an error in estimating fixed and variable costs could greatly distort the break-even point and lead to faulty policy decisions. Break-even charts can be prepared to enlighten management on various phases of profit planning, such as the effect of changes in costs upon profits.

Using Break-Even Analysis. Break-even analysis often is linked with the type of chart presentation shown in Fig. 3. As a **means of chart presentation,** there is considerable difference of opinion as to the usefulness of the device. As a **technique of analysis,** which emphasizes the marginal approach, there is wide agreement on its importance. The controller of one large corporation has stated: "This entire field of 'profit planning' has become associated with the break-even analysis, or the cost-volume-profit interrelationship. . . . If your company is typical, there are many useful ways of putting cost-volume-profit analysis to work" (Willson, N.A.A. Bulletin, Vol. 41).

In discussing the means available to business executives to control overall business costs and maximize earnings, Rucker states that ". . . one of the most helpful means is break-even point control." He cites how one manufacturer of a large line of textiles sold nationally analyzed the cause of the firm's inadequate earnings by classifying the different product lines into those with an operating margin below and those above the company average. It was found that the first group accounted for about two thirds of the physical volume but less than one third of the total dollar operating margin. By shifting the emphasis from the high unit-cost products to those with higher-than-average operating margins, the firm was able to lift its pretax profit about 100% in 9 months even though the physical volume of sales declined slightly (Rucker, Harvard Business Review, Vol. 33). In

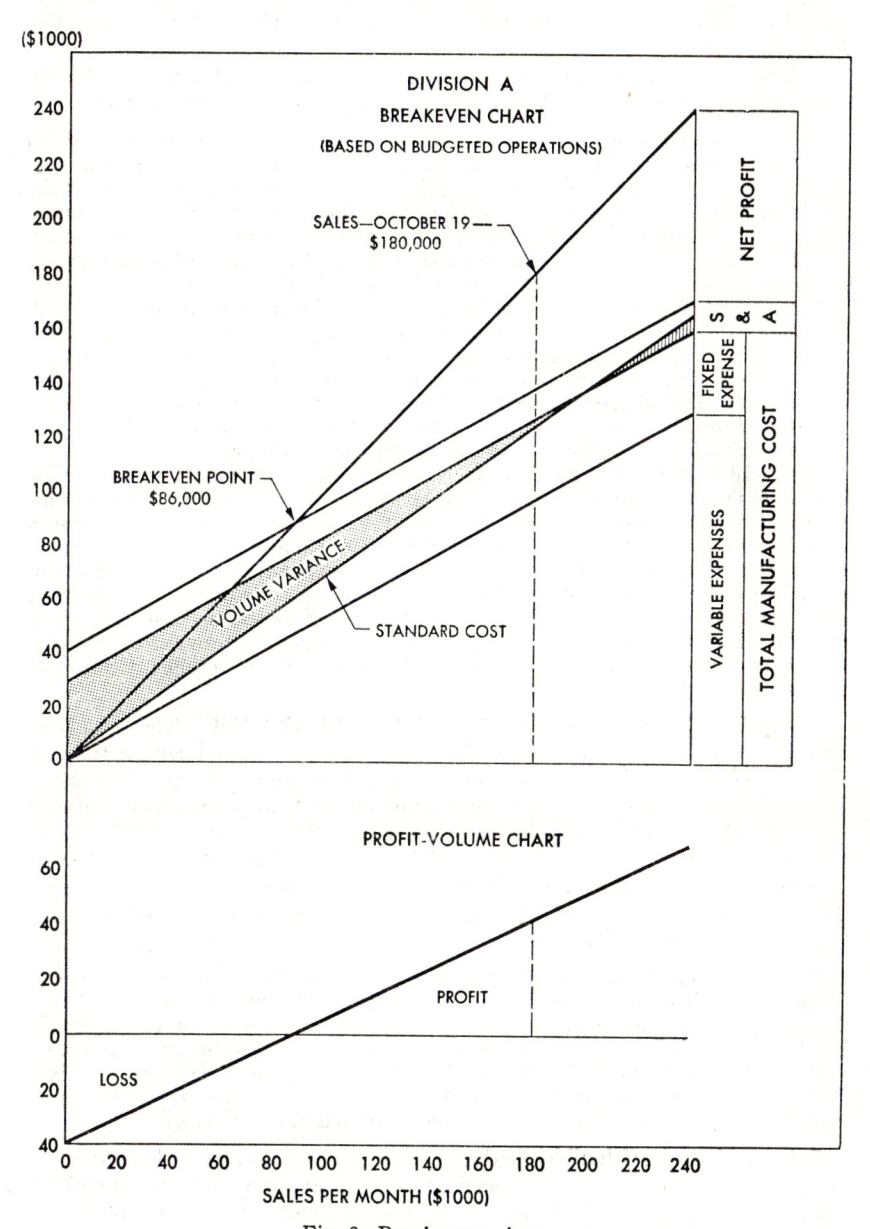

Fig. 3. Break-even chart.

a different context, to analyze the advisability of refunding a bond issue before maturity, Spiller, has suggested a method of calculating a break-even refunding rate that takes into account the timing of cash flows (Financial Executive, Vol. XXXI).

Robbins and Foster have summarized the various uses of the break-even analysis in profit planning as follows (The Journal of Finance, Vol. XII):

As an aid in budgeting, they (financial analysts) show the pre-tax profits generated at various volume levels above the break-even point output base; management may then determine at a glance the expected profits relative to the break-even point at the budgeted volume and the effect of variations from this figure. A **safety factor measure** may be constructed by determining the relationship between actual production and the volume at break-even. Relative efficiency may be checked by comparing the dates during each year when break-even production is reached.

More importantly, however, when the ties that link break-even investigations with the chart form are cut and the traditional emphasis on determining the point of no-return is lifted, the technique is broadened to cover a variety of volume-cost relationships. By directing attention to cost differentials rather than totals, it throws light on the **profitability of product lines.** Decisions to abandon items that show losses on the basis of total costs may be waived so long as they provide income balances over variable costs that contribute toward the recovery of fixed costs.

The variable-fixed cost break-down facilitates translating pricing problems affecting individual products into policy action. In appraising the advisability of introducing price cuts recommended by the sales department, for example, the availability of such data makes it easy to determine the increase in sales volume necessary to compensate for the reduction. With respect to the long-range viewpoint, this information is employed to gauge the influence of physical expansion on costs and profits. In these cases, the changes in plant facilities lead to shifts in the levels of fixed costs which must be taken into account in the analysis. The technique also provides an **administrative tool** to control costs and to establish benchmarks in developing operating policies.

FLEXIBLE BUDGETING IN PROFIT PLANNING. The sales forecast links together the individual budgets of a business. Accordingly, if the estimate is inaccurate, the usefulness of the budget in profit planning is reduced because cost allowances based upon production schedules associated with projected sales might bear little resemblance to those that would have been established based upon output actually achieved. The flexible budget provides the means of overcoming this deficiency by gearing cost allowances to varying volumes of business. The Accountants' Handbook describes this advantage as follows (Wixon, Accountants' Handbook):

The preparation of a flexible budget, in reality, involves the construction of separate budgets for each volume of production ranging from 60 to 100% of capacity. Under flexible budgeting the cost-volume relationship of each element of manufacturing overhead is studied by departments in order to establish allowable expenditures for each level of production. The flexible budget is thus more effective than a fixed budget in controlling costs since it provides a periodic comparison of actual costs incurred with predetermined costs at the **volume of activity** experienced.

Interpreting the Flexible Budget. Although the flexible budget principle pertains to all the component budgets, its widest application is in **controlling manufacturing expenses.** In cost accounting, these expenses are distributed to products during the period by means of predetermined rates representing the relationship between total estimated manufacturing expenses and some measure of normal production. During the course of a period, manufacturing expenses are absorbed into inventory by applying the predetermined rates to actual production. Since the manufacturing expenses experienced by each department are also being recorded, at the close of the period the accounts indicate the extent to which the calculated manufacturing expenses differ from the actual. The calculated expenses are said to be overabsorbed when they are greater and underabsorbed when they are less than the actual expense. In order to evaluate the results of the period, it is important to analyze the composition of this variance. The basic division is into a controllable and volume variance: The controllable variance indicates whether a foreman spent more or less than the budget for the level of activity achieved; the volume variance reveals the degree to which plant capacity was not utilized (Wixon, Accountants' Handbook).

Installing the Flexible Budget. Flexible budgets are prepared so as to permit revision of estimates of operating costs and profits with changes in sales and production volume. Then, failure to attain the volume of sales used in the sales budget, which necessitates alterations in the production schedule, would not vitiate the value of production and distribution cost budgets. This flexibility is obtained by developing for each cost center a formula that shows how costs change with volume; the formula contains a constant cost factor and a variable factor related to the measure of volume selected. By inserting the applicable volume into the formula, costs pertaining to that volume are obtained. The practice of one company in this respect is described as follows by Welsch (N.A.C.A. Bulletin, Vol. 34, now called N.A.A. Bulletin):

The flexible budget consists of a series of formulas, one series for each department. Each series has a formula for each account in the department or cost center. The formula for each account indicates a fixed amount and/or a variable rate. The fixed allowance is a monthly dollar amount independent of activity. The variable portion of the formula is a variable rate carried to three decimal places, being related to a 'base' expressive of volume. Generally speaking, the productive departments use departmental direct labor hours as a base, nonproductive factory departments use total direct labor hours, and selling and administrative departments use net sales dollars.

Applying the formulas to the volume for the department will give the budget allowance for each account in that department.

The Chief of the Variable Budget Group of another company points out that the installation of a broad variable budget program built around a standard of requirements necessitates **considerable time for completion.** Accordingly, at Hughes Aircraft the installation of such a program is divided into three phases for clarity and planning:

PHASE I—Provides for quick control by applying variable budgets to the indirect labor, by functional group, based on existing functions and methods.

PHASE II—Requires a complete evaluation of functions, methods and procedures for the purpose of streamlining operations. It also calls for the application of work-measurement methods to all indirect functions.

PHASE III—Requires variable budgets to be set for all other indirect expenses. In this phase, the variable budgets and burden rates are reconciled, break-even charts prepared, and cost and profit-analysis methods put into effect. (Featherstone, The Controller, now called Financial Executive, Vol. 27.)

DIRECT COSTING IN PROFIT PLANNING. In the conventional income statement **overabsorption** of expenses tends to increase profit whereas **underabsorption** reduces it. Since over- or underabsorption is related to the output attained in this form of statement, profit is influenced not only by the volume of sales and efficiency of operations but also by the rate of factory production. To obviate such difficulties, an increasing number of companies began to adopt direct costing in the early 1950's. This method is described as direct costing because only direct materials, direct labor, and the variable portion of overhead are counted in inventory valuation, whereas the remaining expenses are considered a period or fixed cost. Periodic financial statements developed in this fashion maintain the relation between profit and sales and conform more closely to the marginal-income concept found in break-even analysis and flexible budgeting.

Direct Costing and Management. The income statement is one of the most important statements used by management in evaluating and planning the course of an enterprise. Cost-volume-profit relationships have become a major technique for profit planning. The direct-costing income statement makes use of the cost-volume-profit concept by highlighting marginal income and segregating fixed costs that do not change from period to period. Thus, this form of income statement facilitates managerial planning.

Fig. 4 summarizes a typical direct-costing income statement taken from the Accountants' Cost Handbook (edited by Dickey.)

	Product A (100 sales units)	Product B (250 sales units)	Product C (600 sales units)	Total
Sales	$1,000	$2,000	$3,000	$6,000
Variable Cost of Sales				
Materials	200	300	300	800
Direct labor	300	300	900	1,500
Manufacturing overhead	400	500	600	1,500
Total	$ 900	$1,100	$1,800	$3,800
Variable manufacturing margin	$ 100	$ 900	$1,200	$2,200
Variable selling and G & A costs	200	100	300	600
Marginal income (loss)	$ (100)	$ 800	$ 900	$1,600
Direct Fixed Costs				
Manufacturing	50	150	300	500
Selling and G & A	50	100	150	300
Total	$ 100	$ 250	$ 450	$ 800
Profit (or loss) after direct costs	$ (200)	$ 550	$ 450	$ 800
Apportioned Fixed Costs				
Manufacturing	$ 100	$ 150	$ 150	$ 400
Selling and G and A	50	100	150	300
Total	$ 150	$ 250	$ 300	$ 700
Net operating profit (loss)	$ (350)	$ 300	$ 150	$ 100

Fig. 4. Direct costing annual income statement by product class.

The statement makes clear that Product C contributes the most to company profits, Product B is profitable but makes a smaller contribution, while Product A detracts from profits since it shows a marginal loss of $100. The Accountants' Cost Handbook also contains a detailed discussion of the accounting aspects of direct costing.

Direct Costing in Practice. In its study of 50 companies, the N.A.A. employed depth interviews to determine how direct costing was used, why the specific methods were selected, and the results that took place. (N.A.A. Research

Report No. 37). It obtained numerous examples of the benefits cited by the companies for the application of direct costing to profit planning. Based upon these examples, it grouped the uses of direct costing in profit planning under the following major categories:

Evaluating profit consequences of volume changes
Projecting profit results from change in sales mix
Decision making in the manufacturing area
Make or buy decisions

The N.A.A. study also points out that profits depend upon a suitable balance of selling prices, mix, volume, and costs. It then cites the following list of **pricing problems** to which direct costing was applied by companies participating in the study (p. 45):

1. Pricing individual products.
2. Finding the most profitable products.
3. Identifying products needing attention for profit improvement.
4. Improving sales mix.
5. Evaluating proposals to increase profits by increasing volume.
6. Deciding how far to go in meeting competitive prices.
7. Improving understanding of costs by management responsible for pricing.

The breakdown of costs into their fixed and variable components and the determination of marginal income as part of a regularly prepared income statement focuses management's attention on this form of analysis. As a result, it makes profit analysis more meaningful by revealing the more critical product areas. Davis has summarized these **benefits of direct costing** as follows (N.A.A. Bulletin, Vol. 42):

In addition to specific decisions, direct costing aids profit planning, since the necessary data is readily obtainable from the regular financial statements. It likewise enables management to select objectives realistically and then make decisions with confidence that the objective will be attained. The making of profits is one of the primary objectives of any business. Under direct costing, profit is meticulously planned in advance. It is never thought of as some indeterminate result which arises as a left-over at the end of a fiscal period. The separation of fixed and variable costs furnishes all the requirements for successful profit planning by establishing budgets for period costs and delineating the profit-making power of various products, processes, territories, etc.

Further in this connection the marginal income figure which direct costing provides pinpoints the areas where management efforts should be concentrated and where unprofitable items should be eliminated. This is especially true when output has reached near-capacity levels. Careful selection from among alternate courses of action in these circumstances results in a maximization of profits.

From the managerial point of view, therefore, it is contended that the direct-costing income statement provides the information required for decision-making in a more usable and understandable form. Thus, direct costing, along with break-even analysis and flexible budgeting, stands as a major element in cost-volume-profit determination.

Financial Statement Projections

TYPES OF PRO–FORMA STATEMENTS. Financial statements intended to portray the effects of future circumstances are often described as pro-forma statements. These may be divided into **two general categories:**

In the first, the future circumstances refer to **structural changes** where the effects may be gauged with some degree of certainty. A company that is contemplating a refinancing, for example, may reflect in a pro-forma balance sheet and income statement the results of substituting the new for the old securities. Or a company may want to show its stockholders pro-forma statements as they might appear following a proposed acquisition. Because of their importance, the S.E.C. requires that companies clearly indicate the bases employed in preparing pro-forma statements purporting to give effect to the receipt and application of any part of the proceeds from the sale or exchange of securities.

In the second category of pro-forma statements, the future events involve **economic projections** the influence of which is more difficult to gauge. A company, for example, may reveal the projected results of a future capital expansion program in a pro-forma income statement and balance sheet. Since business decisions are based on management's judgment of the influence of future events on a company's financial condition, such forecasted statements are important aspects of profit planning.

PROFIT AND LOSS FORECASTS. Profit planning for shorter periods is usually based on profit and loss statements by months. Long-term profit forecasts are normally prepared for 6- or 12-month intervals after the first year.

The **form** of the estimated profit and loss statement should correspond to that which the company uses in its regular financial statements, to facilitate the work. It is usually desirable to round off even hundred dollars.

Fig. 5 gives an estimated profit and loss statement or operating forecast prepared by Brelsford. It should be noted that cost of sales has been calculated from standard costs, and variations for material, labor, and manufacturing expenses have been estimated.

Concerns that produce a large number of products prepare estimated profit and loss statements by products or product group. Thus, one large company prepares 20 estimated profit and loss statements by products monthly.

BALANCE SHEET PROJECTIONS. A projection of a concern's balance sheet gives a preview of the company's financial condition on a specified future date, based on the plan of operations adopted. Among **uses** made of balance sheet forecasting are:

1. To note the flow of reinvested profits into current and fixed assets.
2. To aid in adapting operations to seasonal variations.
3. To determine financing requirements and desirable methods of financing, particularly as between short-term borrowing, bond sales, stock flotations, and reinvested earnings.
4. To check on the accuracy of operating budgets.
5. To aid in planning capital expansion.
6. To forecast cash balances and requirements.
7. To facilitate profit planning designed to secure an adequate return on the investment in the enterprise.
8. To determine the effects of financial policies.
9. To maintain the ratio of current assets to current liabilities, and other financial ratios, at a desirable level.

Period of Balance Sheet Projection. Many companies prepare balance sheet projections on a monthly basis. Unless the projection is used to forecast cash balances, it is usually sufficient to project for periods of 2 or 3 months. Some concerns prepare a single balance sheet projection for the whole budget period, at 6-month intervals. If operations are unstable and projections are difficult to make in consequence, some businesses refrain from preparing a projected balance sheet until the forecast period is well under way and the ability to adhere to the budget is demonstrated by actual results.

OPERATING FORECAST
ABC Company—Division A
December, 19X5

(000 omitted)

	Actual October	November	December	Fourth Quarter 19X5	Year 19X5	January	February	March	First Quarter 19X6	Second Quarter 19X6	Third Quarter 19X6
Net Sales	$ 180	$ 185	$ 186	$ 551	$1,720	$ 189	$ 190	$ 198	$ 577	$ 642	$ 660
Cost of Sales at Standard	123	126	127	376	1,076	131	131	137	399	450	476
Gross Profit at Standard	$ 57	$ 59	$ 59	$ 175	$ 644	$ 58	$ 59	$ 61	$ 178	$ 192	$ 184
Variances:											
Material	$ 9	$ 10	$ 10	$ 29	$ 70	$ 10	$ 10	$ 11	$ 31	$ 39	$ 40
Productive Labor	6	6	6	18	74	7	7	8	22	21	18
Manufacturing Expense:											
Volume	3	2	2	7	44	1	1	(1)	1	(9)	(12)
Revision of Standards	1	1	1	3	10	1	1	1	3	3	3
Controllable	9	9	9	27	170	7	7	6	20	9	-0-
	$ 28	$ 28	$ 28	$ 84	$ 368	$ 26	$ 26	$ 25	$ 77	$ 63	$ 49
Gross Profit	$ 29	$ 31	$ 31	$ 91	$ 276	$ 32	$ 33	$ 36	$ 101	$ 129	$ 135
Divisional Selling and Adm. Expense	10	10	10	30	120	10	10	10	30	30	30
Operating Profit	$ 19	$ 21	$ 21	$ 61	$ 156	$ 22	$ 23	$ 26	$ 71	$ 99	$ 105
% of Sales	10.6%	11.4%	11.3%	11.1%	9.1%	11.6%	12.1%	13.1%	12.3%	15.4%	15.9%

Fig. 5. Estimated profit and loss statement.

BALANCE SHEET FORECAST
ABC Company, December, 19X5

(000 omitted)

	Actual October 31, 19X5	November 30, 19X5	December 31, 19X5	January 31, 19X6	March 30, 19X6	June 30, 19X6	September 30, 19X6
Current Assets:							
Cash	$ 550	$ 575	$ 545	$ 595	$ 555	$ 565	$ 700
Accounts Receivable	900	925	930	945	990	1,070	1,100
Inventories	1,800	1,850	1,860	1,890	1,980	2,140	2,200
Total Current Assets	$3,250	$3,350	$3,335	$3,430	$3,525	$3,775	$4,000
Current Liabilities:							
Accounts Payable	$ 250	$ 260	$ 260	$ 265	$ 275	$ 300	$ 310
Accrued Charges	270	280	280	285	295	320	330
Provision for Income Taxes:							
Income Taxes—Current Year	215	255	295	40	135	325	525
Income Taxes—Prior Year	50	50	–0–	295	220	145	70
Total Income Taxes	$ 265	$ 305	$ 295	$ 335	$ 355	$ 470	$ 595
Dividends Payable	–0–	45	–0–	–0–	–0–	–0–	–0–
Total Current Liabilities	$ 785	$ 890	$ 835	$ 885	$ 925	$1,090	$1,235
Net Current Assets	$2,465	$2,460	$2,500	$2,545	$2,600	$2,685	$2,765
Current Ratio	4.1:1	3.8:1	4.0:1	3.9:1	3.8:1	3.5:1	3.2:1
Other Assets:							
Other Assets	$ 15	$ 15	$ 15	$ 15	$ 15	$ 15	$ 15
Property, Plant and Equipment—Net	2,000	2,025	2,050	2,075	2,125	2,300	2,500
Intangible Assets—Net	10	10	10	10	10	10	10
Deferred Charges	25	25	25	25	25	25	25
	$4,515	$4,535	$4,600	$4,670	$4,775	$5,035	$5,315
Stockholders' Equity:							
Capital Stock	$3,000	$3,000	$3,000	$3,000	$3,000	$3,000	$3,000
Capital in Excess of Par Value of Capital Stock	50	50	50	50	50	50	50
Retained Earnings	1,465	1,485	1,550	1,620	1,725	1,985	2,265
	$4,515	$4,535	$4,600	$4,670	$4,775	$5,035	$5,315

Fig. 6. Projected balance sheet.

The projected balance sheet ordinarily has the **same form and content as the regular balance sheet** of the company to facilitate preparation and interpretation, though frequently it is condensed to show only more significant items. Fig. 6 shows a projected balance sheet. If a complete budgetary system is in use, the additional work involved in preparing projected balance sheets is usually slight because most of the projected items are to be found in the several sections of the budget. Only a few, such as deferred charges, must be projected. Accounts receivable, for instance, are estimated by adding to the opening balance of accounts receivable the amount of the estimated sales on account, and deducting therefrom estimated collections during the period. Similarly, the other balance sheet items are projected on the basis of data contained in the sales, cost, and expense budgets.

Inasmuch as the budget, together with a forecast of the balance sheet, will normally be presented to top management prior to the beginning of the period to which it applies, it is usually necessary to estimate also the balance sheet as it will be at the beginning of the period. The actual beginning balance sheet can then be substituted in the forecast at a later date. Since the projected balance sheet is an estimate, it is usually desirable to present all figures in round hundred dollars to ease computations and to emphasize that the figures are only estimates.

To facilitate financial planning, **all liabilities should be shown** on the balance sheet forecast. Thus, Federal income taxes payable on the year's income should be listed among current liabilities as a "provision for Federal income taxes," on the basis of the profit forecast in the Estimated Profit and Loss Statement. If the balance sheet is being prepared a year in advance, the tax liability should be computed on the basis of current rates of taxation. If evidence of change is reasonably clear-cut, a footnote reference as to its effect may be desirable. Establishment of provision for taxes that will not be payable until after the close of the period places a corresponding amount of current assets at the disposal of the business. Adequate allowances should be set up for contingencies that may arise during the forecast period.

Review of Balance Sheet Projection. The basic purpose of predetermining balance sheets for future periods is to test in advance the consequences of the financial program under consideration. Each item of the balance sheet projection should be compared with the beginning balance sheet to uncover unhealthy or undesirable trends, as a guide to financial planning. By applying the same type of ratio and trend analysis to the elements of the balance sheet projection as will be used subsequently by a banker or other creditor, the management can take corrective action in time.

RETAINED EARNINGS PROJECTION. A forecast of retained earnings should accompany the projected balance sheet. Typical of such a forecast is the following:

RETAINED EARNINGS FORECAST
for Year Ending December 31, 19X5

Estimated retained earnings, December 31, 19X4.... $............
Plus estimated profits for 19X5.................... $............
Less:
    Provision for disputed Federal income tax ....
    Dividend on common stock ($2 per share)........ ....
    Dividend on preferred stock ($1.50 per share) ....
Estimated increase in retained earnings............ ....
Estimated retained earnings, December 31, 19X5.... .... $............

Such a forecast is of value in formulating and testing dividend policy, evaluating the capital structure, and measuring the impact of mergers and other developments upon the net worth position of the enterprise.

Financial Planning for Long-Term Expansion

NEED FOR PLANNING IN EXPANSION. Coordinated planning is necessary for expansion on a sound financial basis. The **objective** of such expansion is to increase, or at least to maintain, profits without jeopardizing the financial stability and strength of the enterprise. Expansion proposals that do not further this objective should not be undertaken. (See also discussion in Sections 16, 17, and 20.)

Long-term planning necessarily involves a **wider margin of error** than monthly or annual forecasts. It is the more important, therefore, that they be based on conservative appraisals of the outlook. A sudden spurt in demand is not sufficient basis for expanding productive capacity, unless it is likely to continue. A sales forecast covering several years is a very difficult undertaking, even for staple products. Similarly, estimates of the cost of current and fixed assets required to carry on a larger volume of business may prove wide of the mark. Estimates used in any long-term expansion plan should be revised periodically.

There are exceptional occasions, as in the instance of aircraft manufacturers following World War II, when it became necessary to plan for contraction rather than expansion. Similar techniques are applicable.

FACTORS ENTERING INTO EXPANSION PLANNING. The following factors must be considered in planning long-term expansion:

1. The long-term goal of the company.
2. Forecast of economic conditions over the period.
3. Long-term forecasts of demand and selling prices.
4. Possibility of meeting anticipated larger demands without expansion.
5. Required expansion of plant and equipment to meet estimated sales demands.
6. Cash outlay for such expansion of plant and equipment, by years.
7. Production costs at increased volume.
8. Selling and advertising appropriations required each year to dispose of increased output.
9. Increase in working capital required to finance additional production.
10. Summary of cash required each year for
    a. Plant and equipment outlays.
    b. Increase in working capital.
    c. Selling and advertising expenses.
11. Profits estimates.
12. Ability to finance requirements.

Long-Term Goal of the Company. As an essential guide to planning of expansion, top management should ask itself where it wants to lead the enterprise during the next "X" number of years. What does it hope will be the status of the business at the end of that period? Frequently it will be found that there is wide difference of opinion among executives and directors as to such ultimate goals. It is helpful to put the answers to this question on paper in terms of ultimate desired sales volume, competitive status in the industry, character and quality of products, unit costs, and profits.

Forecast of Economic Conditions. Plant expansion that is started at a peak of business prosperity may not be completed until after a depression has set in, so that increased capacity may become available at a time when sales and prices

FINANCIAL PLANNING FOR LONG-TERM EXPANSION   15·31

are declining. Also, costs of construction are highest during a period of prosperity. Other things being equal, therefore, it is **best to expand in less prosperous periods** when construction costs are low. If conditions are not propitious for the issuance of securities at such times, it may be necessary to use cash on hand or short-term borrowings to finance the expansion, bonds or stock being sold later when the capital markets become more favorable. Businesses whose financial positions are relatively weak obviously should not undertake expansion on this basis, for they may become financially embarrassed if the depression persists and security markets remain unfavorable for new financing by them.

Long-Term Forecasts of Demand and Selling Prices. The **success of expansion** is often dependent mainly upon the accuracy of a long-term sales forecast. To check such a forecast, the management will want to know:

1. Whether increased demand is temporary, or whether it will continue for a longer period of years.
2. If demand can be stimulated further by larger selling and advertising outlays.
3. What will be the probable trend of selling prices? Sales income is the product of volume and prices. A relatively small decline in selling prices may offset a considerable expansion in unit sales.
4. What are competitive conditions? An expanding trend in demand for one concern may be checked by larger output of competitors, the entry of new producers into the business, more imports or inroads by substitute products into total consumption.

Graphic charts may be of considerable assistance in projecting sales as a guide to expansion plans.

Larger Sales Without Expansion. Consideration should be given as a matter of course to the possibility of meeting a larger demand for the company's products by adding another shift, by stepping up efficiency, and by more rapid turnover of working capital. Such expedients are particularly desirable if the stability of demand in the future appears questionable.

Estimating Expansion Required. The need for additional productive capacity should be related to factors such as the number of machines, floor space, or time units required. For example, if a plant has 6,000 machines, each capable of producing 100 units per year, at 80% of capacity (to allow for breakdowns, retooling, etc.) maximum annual output is 480,000 units. If the sales forecasts for the next 3 years are 475,000 units, 525,000 units, and 600,000 units, it is evident that consideration must be given to plant expansion some time in the following year. This is a mere rule-of-thumb procedure, but it is helpful in making expansion requirements more concrete. Such **coordination of plant needs with sales forecasts** is done by top management in close consultation with the production and sales managers, engineers, and market experts.

Whenever possible, expansion of plant and equipment should be **carried on in sections or units.** Thus, expansion of a chemical plant might call for two separate units, each capable of producing 100,000 gallons, rather than a single new unit producing 200,000 gallons. Should demand fall short of expectations later, it is then possible to scale down the expansion program or to operate one unit at capacity and close the other if both are actually constructed. Also, each unit can be put into operation as rapidly as it is completed, so that it can begin to add to profits with a minimum of delay.

Production Costs at Increased Volume. Since the effect on profits is the ultimate guide to expansion, the latter's effect on production costs, including depreciation on new plant and equipment, should be weighed carefully. A larger plant may raise overhead costs so that the break-even point in operations is lifted to a serious extent. Thus, if an increase in capacity of 50% is contemplated, costs might be calculated for actual sales increases of 15%, 30%, and 50%. These computations may indicate that a particular expansion program would add to profits only when a sales rise of almost the full 50% is achieved.

Selling and Advertising Costs. Selling and advertising expenses to dispose of additional production should be projected in advance. Sometimes only a **temporary increase** in such outlays is required. At other times a **permanent expansion** of such expenses is needed, making expansion of dubious wisdom.

Increased Working Capital Requirements. Expansion will add to cash required to finance current operations, as well as to inventories and receivables. Failure to provide for such additional current asset needs could lead to financial embarrassment.

Financial Requirements of Expansion. The financial requirements of a plant expansion program are the total of:

1. Outlays required for expansion of plant and equipment.
2. Increased working capital needs.
3. Special appropriations for selling and advertising campaigns.
4. Operating losses that may be incurred on new facilities pending the time they are placed on a profitable basis.

The board of directors will decide how this sum shall be provided, if the expansion program is approved. It can be financed, at least temporarily, from depreciation and reinvested earnings, as well as by borrowing and the sale of capital stock. If a business has a large cash balance for contingencies, this may be drawn upon for the purpose.

A **typical summary calculation** of the financial requirements of an expansion program follows:

CALCULATION OF FINANCIAL REQUIREMENTS FOR EXPANSION OF PLANT AND EQUIPMENT, 1965–67

Year	Capital Outlay for Plant Expansion	Increased Working Capital Required	Special Selling and Advertising Appropriations	Total Requirements	Less Cash Obtainable from Depreciation Allowances and Estimated Profits	Cash Requirements
1965	$1,500,000	$125,000	$150,000	$1,775,000	$200,000	$1,575,000
1966	1,250,000	100,000	100,000	1,450,000	400,000	1,050,000
1967	1,250,000	75,000	100,000	1,425,000	550,000	875,000

It will be noted from the above table that cash requirements to finance expansion are estimated at $1,575,000 for 1965, $1,050,000 for 1966, and $875,000 in 1967. Arrangements can be made to raise the sums required in time from internal or external sources, on the basis of this computation.

When one considers that the estimates used are at best only intelligent guesses, it is advisable to add a **margin of safety**. But this does not justify indiscriminate use of "10% for the margin of error." Optimists are inclined to add 10% to sales forecasts and to deduct 10% from cost estimates. Pessimists reverse the process, adding 10% to costs and deducting 10% from sales estimates. If estimates have passed through three or four echelons before reaching the top management for final approval, several allowances may have been made for this "10% margin of error," without disclosure thereof on the estimates themselves.

Profitability of Contemplated Expansion. Profit and loss projections can show the effect of contemplated expansion upon earnings. These reflect estimates of sales and costs following expansion, including such items as:

1. Additional depreciation of fixed assets.
2. Repairs and maintenance of new equipment.
3. Property taxes, insurance, etc.
4. General and administrative expenses.
5. Income taxes on the additional profits to result from expansion.

If **bonds** are to be issued to finance the expansion, interest on and retirement of the bonds must be allowed for. If **new stock** is to be sold for this purpose, the resulting additional earnings should be sufficient to pay dividends and leave an extra margin of profit to the old stockholders who, in the final analysis, are assuming a substantial risk in undertaking the expansion of facilities. If expansion is financed by the **reinvestment of earnings,** these ploughed-back profits constitute an additional investment on the part of the stockholders, who should expect a reasonable profit thereon.

Business Conditions and Financial Planning

INFLUENCE OF EXTERNAL FACTORS. Financial planning must be adapted not only to internal factors of the business, but equally to external economic conditions. External conditions may have a more potent influence upon sales at any given time than the ability of management or the quality of the product. It is seldom that management deteriorates rapidly, but economic conditions can violently affect sales and profits.

Financial planning involves:

1. A forecast of economic conditions for a future period.
2. An appraisal of how the business may be affected thereby.
3. Adjustment of financial policies accordingly.

FORECASTING BUSINESS CONDITIONS. Economists recognize **three major types of business fluctuations.** First, there is the long-term trend, which may extend over a period of many years; second, the business cycle; and third, seasonal variations within the year. The first step in planning is to prepare a forecast of economic conditions. The long-term trend is of particular importance for newer "growth" industries and others that have passed their prime and are declining. Cyclical forecasts beyond 2 or 3 years are of limited value, as a rule. But for each forecast an appraisal of the stage of the business cycle, a forecast of its duration, and a prediction of the ensuing phase of the cycle are valuable.

The practice of one large corporation in adjusting its internal planning to a forecast of economic conditions is described as follows (Vaughn, N.A.C.A. Bulletin, Vol. 33):

Our central statistical department constantly follows and analyzes a great many economic indicators related to general domestic business conditions such as: gross national product, personal income, personal consumer expenditures, business expenditures for plant and equipment, Federal Reserve Board Index of industrial production, wholesale and retail price indexes, and a host of others. Their analysis shows how the trends in these values and indexes have been found over the years to correspond with, or vary from, the pattern of our own company's sales, both in the aggregate and by product groups and lines.

In September of each year, the current status of these economic trends, together with other factors and conditions to be reckoned with, are presented to management by the head of our statistical department. Based on his recommendations and after discussion with management, general business assumptions for use in the preparation of the various budgets for the coming year and for the ensuing four years are agreed upon.

ADJUSTING THE BUSINESS TO ECONOMIC CONDITIONS. In adjusting financial planning to the business cycle, particular attention should be given to the following aspects:

   Cash for contingencies.
   Size and composition of inventories.
   Accounts receivable and credit policies.
   Provisions for contingencies.
   Amounts and maturity dates of bank loans.
   Fixed charges for long-term obligations.
   Relation of fixed to total costs.
   Purchases of materials and equipment.

Maintenance of a good current ratio (ratio of current assets to current liabilities) is not sufficient to guard against the effects of adverse business developments. If collections of accounts receivable become slow and inventories cannot be disposed of because of an oncoming depression, a business may find its cash insufficient to meet current obligations. But if cash and government securities are accumulated during prosperity, the enterprise is prepared for unfavorable developments.

Size and Composition of Inventories. A good system of inventory control will assist in relating finished goods inventory to varying sales prospects, and inventories of raw materials and goods in process to shifting production schedules. **Coordination of production to sales** is important at all times, but particularly so during the latter part of a period of prosperity and the period of liquidation that follows, when the risk of inventory losses is greatest.

Accounts Receivable and Credit Policies. Loose credit policies during periods of prosperity will result in poor experience with accounts receivable during the subsequent recession. Credit policies should be tightened during prosperous periods when orders are more plentiful, whereas credit policies can be liberalized to some extent during a depression, when weaker concerns have been weeded out and more orders are needed.

Provisions for Contingencies. During periods of prosperity, provision may be made for contingencies that often arise during a period of liquidation and depression by setting aside reserves out of retained earnings. Such action will restrict the size of the retained earnings available for dividend declarations, and thus conserve the resources of the enterprise. There is a current tendency, however, to avoid use of general purpose contingency reserves. The Accountants' Handbook (Wixon, ed.) states that " . . . segregation of retained earnings to give some recognition to possible losses is warranted—if at all—only where a specific condition exists or is in prospect which may lead to loss, and the amount of the loss may be estimated at least roughly."

Amounts and Maturity Dates of Bank Loans. Every effort should be made to repay bank loans during periods of prosperity, except for borrowing to finance purely seasonal requirements.

Fixed Charges On Long-Term Obligations. Fixed charges must be paid not only during prosperity, when this constitutes no problem, but also during a depression. Refinancing of obligations should be sought when capital markets are favorable to reduce annual interest and sinking fund requirements.

Relation of Fixed to Total Costs. If fixed or overhead costs are high in relation to total costs, the business is vulnerable in a period of declining sales. A relatively small decrease in volume could then result in operating losses. A solution may be found through reductions in overhead. If this requires new facilities, these may be acquired from earnings or stock sales in prosperity.

Purchases of Materials and Equipment. If the financial condition of the enterprise permits, purchases of materials, parts, and equipment should be stepped up **in depression periods** to take advantage of low prices that usually prevail at that time. Needless to say, such a purchasing policy should carefully avoid the risk of acquiring unsalable stock piles of obsolete and out-of-style goods. Conversely, inventories should be held down as far as feasible **when prices are high**, and raw material inventories should be hedged if feasible. Many businesses have found, however, that efforts to forecast commodity price changes involve a high degree of error, and so prefer to adjust purchasing to production schedules, rather than to prognostications of price movements.

Organization for Financial Planning

RESPONSIBILITY FOR FINANCIAL PLANNING. Financial planning is a **function of top management.** Responsibility for such planning must rest with those who have the authority to make major decisions and whose position gives them the overall view of the business that is essential to proper financial planning.

Financial planning may be divided into major and minor planning. Major financial plans are drawn up or approved by top management. These lay down the broad objectives that serve as a guide to lower echelons of managerial authority in the preparation of minor financial plans.

Financial planning may start either at a high level, such as the board of directors or the chief executive, and be turned over to a committee or to an official like the controller for development and completion, or it may begin with the controller or treasurer and travel upward either to the chief executive, the board of directors, or a committee of the board.

Corporate financial planning is a responsibility of:

1. The board of directors.
2. Committees of the board.
3. The chief operating officer.
4. The chief financial officer, who may be a vice-president in charge of finance, or the treasurer, or the controller.

Active operating responsibility for financial planning is frequently placed with the chairman of the finance committee, a vice-president in charge of finance, the treasurer, or the controller. In smaller companies, the president may perform the functions of the chief financial officer.

Duties of Financial Vice-President, Treasurer, and Controller. Duties of the treasurer and the controller vary to a great extent among corporations, one or the other being the superior officer, depending upon the organizational setup, the ramifications of the concern's activities, and the forcefulness and reputation for financial acumen of the individuals concerned. The controller may be appointed by the president or elected by the board of directors. In some instances, the treasurer or the controller may also be the vice-president in charge of finance. Based upon a survey of 278 corporations, the A.M.A. has summarized these functions of the three major finance officers as follows (AMA Research Study 55):

In general, one can conclude from AMA's questionnaire research, the treasurer is largely responsible for obtaining capital from external sources and for possessing and managing the cash, valuables, and property of the firm. This latter is often referred to as his "custodial" function. The controller is charged with maintaining the company's financial health through "inspection" activities—accounting and auditing. The controller "controls" the disbursement of money so that it is used honestly, efficiently, and according to previously determined policy. The vice president of finance (if the firm has one) is most often a policy-making manager who forms a link between other top company managers and the financial activities of the company. One of his principal duties is supervising the treasurer and the controller.

In other words, the treasurer and his organization obtain capital and possess money and valuables; the controller, through his inspection, review, and planning activities, sees that this money is used correctly and honestly. One may say, therefore, that the average corporation employs both a treasurer and a controller as a "check and balance" arrangement. The inspection duties of the controller and the custodial duties of the treasurer are logically separated so that less chance of theft and other irregularities exists. Strangely enough, this idea is not often stated in print, but it is perfectly plain in the responses of many of the participants in this report. The vice president of finance, in a very large corporation, fits in logically as a buffer between the treasurer and the controller. In such large firms accounting and auditing (and many other duties) so occupy the time of the controller that he cannot participate adequately in **general** financial management. The custodial and external financial duties of the treasurer are likewise greatly expanded in the very large firm. In such a case the third financial officer becomes more necessary.

The **director of the budget** in a corporation is usually made responsible to the chief financial officer, although he sometimes reports directly to the president.

FINANCIAL PLANNING FUNCTIONS OF THE BOARD OF DIRECTORS. The functions of the board of directors in financial planning may be specified in the corporate by-laws, but this is not usual. The broad responsibilities that the law places upon the board of directors, however, necessarily imply that they will assume this task. Holden, Fish, and Smith (Top-Management Organization and Control) report:

In substantially all the companies reviewed, the board of directors **establishes broad basic policies, handles major financial matters,** selects the officers and sets their salaries, and takes care of other matters of a similar character. In addition, it receives reports from the management on the company's operation since the last meeting, and passes judgment as to whether, in view of circumstances, the results are satisfactory.

Gordon, in a study published by the Brookings Institution (Business Leadership in the Large Corporation), commented on the above statement as follows:

How much of the activities that these writers attribute to directors represents actual practice in the particular companies that were studied, and how much is merely a summary of what was found in the companies' by-laws, we are not in a position to say. We should suppose, from our own study, that this part of their analysis reflects conditions as they are supposed to be rather than conditions as they actually are.

Gordon, reporting the results of his own study, states:

. . . executives rather than directors make the bulk of decisions which enter into the leadership function in the large corporation. This is particularly true of initiation.

Origination and formulation of proposals almost invariably come from the executive group, and directors, insofar as they participate at all in the decision-making function, do so through their power to veto or approve decisions laid before them by the chief executive. By virtue of this fact, the creative and dynamic elements of business leadership cannot be expected to develop out of the deliberations and activities of the board as a formal group . . . but absence of initiation by the board holds today in the larger corporation even for major financial matters, including investment policy and expansion programs. However real in some cases may be the board's veto power over the chief executive's recommendations in these fields, the initiation—seeing the need for action and formulation of a plan—comes from the executive group, even on the broadest financial questions.

The **extent** to which the board of directors dominates financial planning in practice varies widely. Some boards leave such planning almost entirely to operating officials. In other instances, the board consists in large part of these operating officials. Frequently the board discusses basic long-term objectives of the enterprise, setting financial goals for the officers to achieve.

The board of directors is responsible, in any event, for dividend policies, the establishment of allowances out of retained earnings, and changes in capital structure. The **by-laws** of most corporations provide that appropriations above a specified sum for capital expansion or rehabilitation of plant and equipment must be approved by the board. Holden, Fish, and Smith found that "the determination of the amount and sources of working capital is a board function in approximately one-half of the companies and a management function in the remainder. There are by-law provisions in several cases which stipulate this action as a board function. In one instance a by-law provision even specified the actual amount of money to be reserved as working capital." With reference to subsidiaries, they found that "in only one-fourth of the companies are financial relationships with subsidiary or affiliated companies a matter for board consideration. Where the management has authority for this function, a few companies state that the board sets limits for loans or credits within which management has complete freedom of action."

By-laws may provide that the board of directors should select the banks in which the corporation will maintain its accounts. Pension and profit-sharing plans are almost invariably subject to board approval, as is usually the case with fixing compensation of corporate officers.

Financial Executives on the Board of Directors. Financial executives are frequently included on the board of directors, and so participate in financial planning in a dual capacity.

The National Industrial Conference Board (Business Policy Study No. 103), in a survey of 456 manufacturing companies, found the following representation of financial executives on boards of directors:

Position	Number of Companies
Vice-Presidents, Finance	31
Secretaries	79
Secretary and Treasurers	29
Secretary and Controllers	4
Treasurers	106
Controllers	21
Financial, other	12
	282

If operating financial executives are on the board, the latter keeps in closer touch with financial planning and operations. Financial executives, in turn, are in a better position to implement policies favored by the board, and to integrate their own financial planning with that of higher authority.

Reports to the Board of Directors. To aid the directors **in planning the broader financial phases** of business operation, adequate reports are required. Some companies furnish board members with fairly detailed financial reports at each meeting, supplemented with interim reports as these become available. If the board passes upon the budget, an opportunity should be afforded directors to acquaint themselves with the facts and figures before asking them for formal approval. Budget estimates should be supported by adequate data on past results, current conditions, and estimates of the effect of the plan of operations upon the financial condition and profits of the enterprise. Holden, Fish, and Smith cite an interesting practice followed by one management at its monthly board meetings:

> A set of large wall charts is prepared each month. These charts present financial, production and sales data. Even the balance sheet is drawn up in magnified form. The purpose of these charts is to focus the attention of board members on each item being discussed by the president. Prior to adopting this practice, the directors were provided with reports, and during the president's discussion they were often observed thumbing through the reports and giving their attention to pages or portions not being discussed. Now, after the full presentation by the president, the directors are handed the reports as heretofore.

Board Committees. To conserve the time of board members and to expedite planning and action, the majority of boards of larger corporations have appointed committees of directors for special functions. With respect to financial planning, formal committees probably are still not the common practice, but their use appears to be increasing. For example, a 1962 study by the N.I.C.B. (Business Policy Study No. 105) found that, "the use of formal committees as an aid to the management of financial and accounting affairs is gaining wider acceptance . . . a substantial majority of the 141 committees examined have been created within the past ten years, many within the past five years."

Of the companies that have recently formed financial committees, the study found that most cited the need ". . . for a means of strengthening communications and control, because of their growth, decentralization, and increased complexity of operation." In the instances where corporations do not have financial committees, the executive committee of the board frequently includes in its duties decisions on financial and accounting matters.

The N.I.C.B. study lists the following six **committees commonly employed** as aids to financial planning and management:

> Finance Committee
> Capital Appropriations Committee
> Budget Committee
> Pension or Retirement Committee
> Salary Committee
> General Accounting Committee

With respect to the **finance committee,** the study indicates:

> Of all committees used in financial and accounting management, the finance committee generally has the broadest responsibility and wields the most power. However, only 15 percent of 194 industrial companies studied have a finance committee. Of these, sixteen are committees of the board of directors.

ORGANIZATION FOR FINANCIAL PLANNING

Most finance committees pass on or recommend action on a broad range of financial matters, such as equity financing, capital budgets and expenditures, dividend policy, forecasts and future planning, and expansion programs. Their recommendations are frequently tantamount to board action.

The finance committee, if it exists, is responsible for planning finances. **Duties** of the finance committee vary, but they invariably include consideration of the budget and of the financial policies reflected in the budget. Proposals for capital expenditures above a prescribed minimum, changes in capitalization, new financing, dividend declarations, the setting up of reserves, and salaries of officers and employees above a stated level are passed upon by the finance committee, which recommends action to the board of directors.

SECTION 16

CURRENT ASSET PLANNING

CONTENTS

Nature of Working Capital

	PAGE
Definition of working capital	1
Types of working capital	1
Excess working capital	2
Advantages and disadvantages of large contingency funds	2
Circular flow of working capital	3
The working capital cycle (f. 1)	3

Administration of Current Assets

Cash	4
Investment of surplus cash	4
Time deposits in banks	4
Short-term Treasury obligations	5
Long-term Treasury obligations	5
Federal agency obligations	5
Commercial paper and bankers' acceptances	5
Repurchase agreements	5
Corporate securities	5
Loans to officers or employees	6
Tax considerations	6
Receivables	6
Inventories	7
Objectives of inventory control	7
Factors determining size of inventory investment	7
Inventory control systems	8
Inventory valuation	8

Working Capital Requirements

Factors affecting working capital needs	9
General nature of business	9
Period of manufacture and cost of product	10
Turnover of inventories	10
Turnover of accounts receivable	10
Terms of purchase	10
Terms of sale	10
Expansion of business	11
Seasonal variation	11
Inherent hazards and contingencies	11
Cyclical and secular changes	11
How large a surplus of working capital?	12

Sources of Working Capital

Raising permanent working capital	12
Short-term borrowing	12
Financing the small business	13
Raising variable working capital	13

	PAGE
Bank loans	14
Accounts receivable financing	14
Advantages and disadvantages	15
Inventory financing	15
Depreciation as a source of working capital	16
Tax liabilities	16

Analysis of Working Capital

Statement of variation in working capital	16
Illustrative comparative balance sheet (f. 2)	17
Statement of variation of working capital (f. 3)	17
The working capital budget	18
Working capital ratios	18
Working capital ratios of manufacturers, 1951–1962—Dun & Bradstreet (f. 4)	20–21
Working capital ratios of wholesalers, 1951–1962—Dun & Bradstreet (f. 5)	22
Working capital ratios of retailers, 1951–1962—Dun & Bradstreet (f. 6)	23
Liquidity ratios	19

The Cash Budget

Cash income vs. profit	24
Significance of a cash budget	24
Integrating cash forecasts and the business program	25
Long-term cash forecasts	25
Advantages of long-term cash forecasting	26
Shorter-term forecasts	26
Uses of a cash budget	27
Preparation of a cash budget	27
Cash receipts and disbursements method	27
Receipts and disbursements method of cash forecasting (f. 7)	28
Forecasting collections from sales	28
Form for forecasting sales and receipts for the cash budget (f. 8)	29
Forecasting disbursements	30
Cash forecasts by adjusted earnings method	31
The predetermined balance sheet method of forecasting cash	31
Working capital differentials method of cash forecasting	31
Adjusted earnings method of cash forecasting (f. 9)	32
Cash forecasts and borrowing	32
Utilizing cash more efficiently	32
Three major areas	33

SECTION 16

CURRENT ASSET PLANNING

Nature of Working Capital

DEFINITION OF WORKING CAPITAL. The term working capital is variously defined for different purposes. To the business man, working capital comprises the current assets of the business, however obtained. It is common for a business man to say that he borrows at short term from the bank to increase his working capital. By this he means he increases his current assets, but obviously not the excess of current assets over current liabilities. Economists, also, use the term working capital to mean all current assets in a business, however derived. The credit man, the accountant, and the investment analyst, on the other hand, usually define working capital as only the excess of current assets over current liabilities, or the **net current assets**. To distinguish these two uses of the term, a distinction may be drawn between working capital, comprising the current assets of the business, and **net working capital**, which is the excess of current assets over current liabilities.

As here used, **current assets** comprise cash, readily marketable securities held as investments, other items that are considered equivalent to cash, and assets that in the normal course of business will be converted into cash within a year or less, such as accounts receivable and merchandise inventory. **Current liabilities** comprise debts that will, in the ordinary course of business, be liquidated within a year, such as notes and accounts payable.

Earlier economists used the term **circulating capital** in referring to working capital, to emphasize the fact that such assets constantly change in form. John Stuart Mill defined circulating capital as capital "which fulfills the whole of its office in the production in which it is engaged by a single use," to contrast it with fixed capital. Some economic writers have used the term **operating capital** in referring to working capital.

TYPES OF WORKING CAPITAL. Working capital is often classified as **permanent, regular,** or **normal** on the one hand, and **seasonal** on the other. Permanent working capital constitutes the minimum of current assets required to conduct the business, even during relatively dull seasons. The additional working capital in the form of cash, receivables, and inventory required during the more active business seasons of the year constitutes the additional seasonal working capital that the enterprise needs. In most industries, the amount of permanent and seasonal working capital required by a business will also vary greatly in the several stages of the business cycle. During a depression, the need for both will decline, whereas during periods of prosperity both permanent and seasonal working capital needs expand sharply. Some writers term added seasonal and cyclical working capital requirements as **variable working capital**.

Every business must be prepared to meet additional working capital needs in an emergency, such as a strike, floods, or fire. These **risks** can be minimized by insurance in many, but not all, instances. If such emergencies tend to recur frequently, as in a large, far-flung enterprise, the cash needs arising from them are more properly classified as part of the permanent working capital requirements.

EXCESS WORKING CAPITAL. A distinction should also be drawn between the **true** working capital requirements of the business and the excess working capital retained as a contingency fund to be used for whatever need may arise. At one time it was common for business to rely upon the banks for seasonal and even for part of its regular working capital needs, while few concerns had a surplus of liquid resources available for contingencies. During most of the period since World War II, large earnings and the ease with which money could be raised in the security markets enabled numerous concerns to build up their cash resources. As a result, they could not only finance all their prospective working capital needs but were also able to maintain excess balances, often invested in marketable securities or other liquid assets, that could be used to finance future expansion, to cover operating losses, or to meet other contingencies.

Advantages and Disadvantages of Large Contingency Funds. The advantages of maintaining a large contingency fund over and above the working capital requirements of the business have been summarized as follows (Stillman, Controller (now Financial Executive), Vol. 27):

The executive managers of many major corporations have become increasingly desirous of maintaining a level of cash funds which is in excess of the foreseeable operating needs of business. The extra cash is regarded as a **reserve**, which permits latitude and rapid decision, within limits, in matters involving plant expansion, acquisitions of other companies, acceleration of research or advertising activites, and the like. These excess liquid resources also represent a **hedge** against the vicissitudes of a business slump or other unforeseen emergencies. To a considerable extent, the growing penchant for long-range planning is supported by the confidence which management derives from the availability of substantial quick assets.

The practice of maintaining a surplus of cash resources for unspecified contingencies has been criticized on the ground that it may lead to wasteful outlays, carelessness about costs, delay in adjusting operations to changing business conditions, and a lower average net return on investment in the enterprise. This **critical viewpoint** has been expressed as follows by Guthmann and Dougall (Corporate Financial Policy):

. . . redundant current funds reduce the return on investment and encourage waste and manipulation. Each dollar should do as much work as possible, but idle and unnecessary dollars might better be distributed to the owners of the corporation or be used to reduce debts and save on interest charges.

Reflecting this same notion, the vice-president and treasurer of one large concern has pointed to the fact that his company's financial planning ". . . includes the policy of carrying as little cash as is practical for our operation. Any excess cash over this requirement is automatically used to reduce our short-term debt under the flexible arrangements possible with our type of credit agreement." (Reed, Financial Executive, Vol. XXXI.)

As a result of these diverse attitudes, there has been no striking change in the **overall ratio of current assets to current liabilities of all American corporations** in recent periods. Between 1950 and 1962, the ratio declined somewhat, from 2.02 to 1.79 times, as seen in the following statistics compiled by the Securities and Exchange Commission:

NATURE OF WORKING CAPITAL 16·3

Current Assets and Liabilities of United States Corporations *
December 31, 1950, 1960 and 1962
(In billions of dollars)

	1950†	1960††	1962†††
Current assets, total	161.5	289.0	325.9
Cash on hand and in banks	28.1	37.2	41.0
United States government securities	19.7	20.1	20.1
Receivables from United States government	1.1	3.1	3.6
Notes and accounts receivable	55.7	126.1	146.5
Inventories	55.1	91.8	100.9
Other current assets	1.8	10.7	13.8
Current liabilities, total	79.8	160.4	181.9
Advances and prepayments, United States government	.4	1.8	2.0
Notes and accounts payable	47.9	105.0	119.8
Federal income tax liabilities	16.7	13.5	14.9
Other current liabilities	14.8	40.1	45.2
Net working capital	81.7	128.6	144.0

* Except banks, savings and loan associations and insurance companies.

† 1950 figures from United States S.E.C. Statistical Bulletin, Vol. 13, No. 10, Oct. 1954, p. 14.

†† 1960 figures from United States S.E.C. Statistical Bulletin, Vol. 22, No. 7, July 1963, p. 20.

††† 1962 figures from United States S.E.C. Statistical Bulletin, Vol. 22, No. 10, Oct. 1963, p. 19.

Note: Figures are adjusted to balance.

The slight decline in the current ratio, and more significantly the drop in the percentage of cash to total current assets from 17.4% in 1950 to 12.6% in 1962, probably reflect the techniques that have been developed to utilize cash more efficiently in business operations, as described below.

CIRCULAR FLOW OF WORKING CAPITAL. At the organization of a business, cash is provided by the owners. A part of the cash is invested in

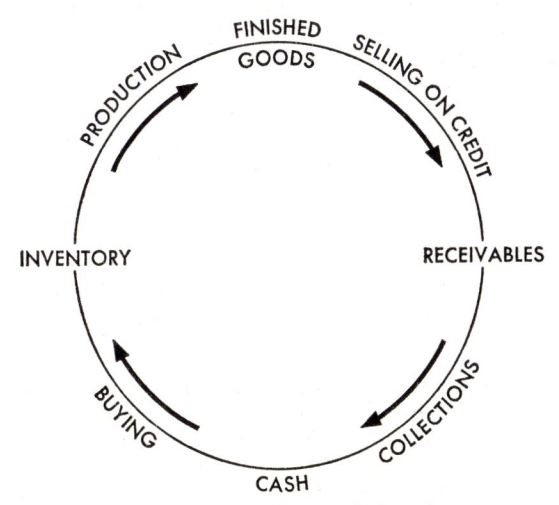

Fig. 1. The working capital cycle.

fixed assets—machinery, plant, furniture, etc.—and the remainder is kept available to meet **current requirements.** Out of this latter sum, merchandise is purchased in either finished form or in the form of raw materials that are then processed into finished goods. These goods are sold and thus converted again from merchandise into accounts and notes receivable. Upon collection of the receivables, cash flows back into the business. The cycle completed, the cash becomes available to repeat the working capital cycle once again. (See Fig. 1.)

To illustrate, assume $50 in cash is used to acquire raw materials. Another $100 is expended for labor and manufacturing expense. The goods costing $150 are then sold for $200, and after a lapse in time are paid for, so that cash in the amount of $200 flows back to the business. With the completion of the cycle, the sum of cash returned is found to exceed the amount paid out by the amount of the gross profit. The continuity and rate of flow from one phase of the cycle to the other are major factors affecting the earning power of the enterprise. In a profitably run business, every completed cycle yields a return. A constant and rapid circulation of working capital provides the enterprise with a stream of cash, the only asset ordinarily acceptable in liquidating the claims on the business made by its creditors, employees, government, and the owners.

Administration of Current Assets

CASH. The most liquid portion of the working capital of a business consists of its cash. This comprises both the cash that is actually to be used in the financing of current operations and the additional sums of cash that are held for other known and possible uses.

The bulk of the cash is customarily **held on deposit in banks,** except for limited sums of money required for petty cash and payrolls, as well as receipts that have not yet been deposited in the bank. Enterprises whose operations cover a wide area may maintain their deposits in a number of banks, both for convenience and to secure the goodwill and guidance of local bankers in each community where they operate. Before 1933, when bank failures were relatively frequent, such a policy involved a risk of loss, but this has been minimized since by Federal deposit insurance and other remedial measures that have been adopted. Deposits up to $10,000 in an insured bank are protected by Federal insurance.

Corporations operating abroad face a special problem because part of their cash consists of foreign currencies subject to the risk of exchange depreciation and transfer restrictions. These risks usually make it desirable to keep foreign cash balances at a minimum, even if some loss is involved in transfers. Cash held abroad may be hedged through sales of foreign exchange for future delivery, or funds may be withdrawn through shipments of goods from the country where exchange controls permit.

INVESTMENT OF SURPLUS CASH. If cash materially exceeds near-term needs of the business, a large part may be invested in order to secure some return on this liquid portion of the assets of the business. Available investments include:

Time Deposits in Banks. A modest rate of return may be obtained by depositing the portion of the cash not immediately required in a bank as a time deposit, which is subject to advance notice of 30 days to 6 months before withdrawal, or against a certificate of deposit with a fixed maturity. Starting in 1961, banks began to issue interest-bearing negotiable and marketable Time

Certificates of Deposit. The banks may pay **interest** on time deposits, although the payment of interest on demand deposits is barred by law.

Short-Term Treasury Obligations. The most common investment for corporate funds is short-term government securities, which give the twin **advantages** of safety and liquidity. Treasury bills, certificates of indebtedness, tax anticipation notes, and Treasury notes and bonds maturing within 5 years are available. Nearness of maturity minimizes risk of price depreciation, should these investments be sold before they mature. (See also discussion of Government Obligations, Section 11.)

Long-Term Treasury Obligations. These involve more **risk of price fluctuation** due to changes in the level of interest rates. Hence, their purchase can be justified only to a limited extent with funds that are unlikely to be required in the business for an indefinite period. As stated by Stillman (Controller, now Financial Executive, Vol. 27):

> Although a good yield on investments is a desirable objective, safety of principal should certainly be the primary aim. During periods of declining interest rates it is easy for the investor to be lured into placing his funds into increasingly longer maturities, with the objective of maintaining the eroding yield on his investments. This practice can prove a snare, as was demonstrated in the aftermath of the speculative government bond market which existed in 1958.

Federal Agency Obligations. Various Federal agencies have been created to help meet specialized financing needs of the public. Although neither the principal nor interest of the bonds and notes issued by these agencies is usually guaranteed by the Federal government, the obligations are considered to be of high quality.

Commercial Paper and Bankers' Acceptances. Commercial paper represents the unsecured promissory notes of large corporations sold at a discount whereas bankers' acceptances are drafts drawn on and accepted by a bank. These are high-grade, money-market instruments that have become more popular in recent years with corporate money managers seeking short-term outlets for their funds. (See discussion of Money Markets in Section 1.)

Repurchase Agreements. These involve the purchase of securities, ordinarily government obligations, by a corporate investor from a dealer and their simultaneous resale to the dealer at a specified future delivery and payment date. Corporate money managers familiar with money-market operations have been attracted to these agreements because they can be tailored to individual cases and afford a relatively good return.

Corporate Securities. Every enterprise incurs numerous risks in the conduct of its own business. The cash retained as a contingency fund should be regarded as an "iron reserve" that should be readily available for any event that may arise. There is no justification, therefore, for a business corporation to invest surplus cash in corporate securities, particularly those of a speculative character. Formerly, it was not uncommon for corporations to invest surplus cash in corporate securities for income and profit, but heavy losses have discouraged this practice. Needless to say, these remarks do not apply to investment in securities of subsidiaries, to the purchase of a corporation's own securities for actual retirement or resale to employees, or to investments in corporate securities by investment companies. Also, they do not apply to the investment of pension, insurance, and other funds that are not in fact part of the cash resources of the business.

Loans to Officers or Employees. Such advances may be justified on a small scale in individual instances. They cannot, however, be regarded as a proper investment for surplus cash. Rather, they should be considered a part of personnel costs, and repayment should be sought as soon as practicable.

TAX CONSIDERATIONS. §§531–7 of the Internal Revenue Code impose a punitive surtax upon corporations that retain earnings beyond the "reasonable anticipated needs" of the business. If excess working capital has been accumulated from earnings, and particularly if the excess has been invested in securities, the corporation should be prepared to state specific business reasons to justify the retention of the earnings rather than their distribution as dividends. If the funds have been accumulated for future expansion, definite plans for such expansion should be available to the Internal Revenue Service. Vague or indefinite plans, or unsupported opinions to the effect that the corporation will eventually need the money, may not be sufficient to avoid the imposition of a surtax.

RECEIVABLES. The volume of credit extended by a business to its customers is measured by its receivables—accounts and notes receivable. The volume of receivables is determined by sales and credit policies, as well as by the effectiveness of collections of outstanding accounts. Since this function involves the final stage in the working capital cycle—the conversion into cash of receivables previously created by sales of merchandise on credit—it is of prime importance. Even if purchasing, production, and sales are efficiently conducted, careless credit and collection policies will result not only in losses due to bad debts, but also in the freezing of a large amount of current assets into slow or doubtful receivables.

The total volume of credit extended to customers must thus be under constant surveillance as one aspect of working capital management. If necessary, selling policies should be adjusted to keep receivables within the desired bounds. This requires, in turn, **customer credit limits**, sometimes referred to as **maximum ledger balances**, for each account. Factors usually considered in setting the maximum of credit to be extended to a customer include his financial condition, character, ability, the nature of his business, age of his enterprise, its net worth, sales volume, margin of profit, and previous ledger experience with him. The greater the profit margin, the higher the credit limit that can safely be extended. Generally speaking, for the group of customers where the anticipated bad debt loss equals the expected net profit on sales, no credit should be extended and only C.O.D. terms should be granted.

Although terms of sale are generally governed by established trade practices, they may be modified in particular instances. Also, strictness of enforcement of sales terms varies. **Cash discounts** are often desirable because they speed up accounts receivable turnover, but they may be a very costly means of raising cash and, if not required by custom, their continued use should be critically reconsidered from the viewpoint of relative cost of working capital. If trade practices demand the allowance of discounts, management should make certain that customers pay within the stipulated time set in the credit terms to secure the discount. The granting of discounts if payment is delayed beyond the specified period results in an even greater cost for the use of cash so obtained.

Management can readily test customer **adherence to credit terms**. For example, in a concern that carries average receivables of $50,000 and has net annual sales of $600,000, the turnover of receivables is 12 times, so that receivables are converted into cash once every 30 days. If the terms of sale are 2% 10 days, net 30 days, it is apparent that either no customers take advantage of the discount and pay within 10 days, or that many customers pay late, beyond the 30-day period. An examination of the ledger experience will focus attention on slow payers, and limitation of further credit extension to them should reduce accounts receivable and free cash for other uses.

Efficient **collection practice,** by reducing the amount of receivables, is a vital part of working capital management. Laxity in this regard may tie up an undue amount of cash, as well as increase credit losses.

INVENTORIES. Measured by dollar value, inventories constitute the major element in the working capital of many businesses. Control of inventories, which for manufacturers comprise raw materials and supplies, goods in process, parts, and finished merchandise suitable for sale, is often the most important problem in the administration of working capital.

Objectives of Inventory Control. Administration of inventory is designed to regulate the size of the investment in goods on hand, the types of goods carried in stock, and turnover rates. Effective inventory control should provide adequate stocks of goods of proper quality to meet the requirements of production and sales, while at the same time keeping the required investment to a minimum. Increases or decreases in the inventory investment must be tested against the effect on the company's return on investment, as well as working capital needs.

Factors Determining Size of Inventory Investment. The investment in **raw materials** inventory by a business depends on the nature of the productive process and, more significantly, on purchasing policies. The minimum inventory is the amount necessary to keep production schedules going. Hand-to-mouth buying policies result in inventories at or near this minimum, whereas much larger stocks on hand result from forward buying or speculative current purchasing.

The investment in **goods-in-process** is usually determined chiefly by the length of the productive process. Industries that have a very short production period, such as canneries and paper mills, have a relatively smaller investment in goods-in-process than, say, manufacturers of heavy electrical generating equipment or shipbuilders. But review of production and sales policies may reduce inventories of goods-in-process in particular instances.

Management usually has more control over the investment in **finished goods** inventories, which are more sensitive to the coordination of production and sales. The nature of the demand for a product affects production planning. If a strong seasonal demand exists, manufacturers have to produce and store goods in large quantities prior to their sale. Even in industries producing staple products enjoying a steady demand through the year, some anticipation of requirements is essential, necessitating maintenance of finished goods inventories. Also, to keep down overhead costs per unit, the rate of operations may exceed orders on hand, especially where production of small quantities is uneconomical. This factor can build up inventories of finished goods rapidly when sales fall off.

Foulke (Practical Financial Statement Analysis) has suggested a rule-of-thumb principle for limiting the **size of inventory:**

> When a manufacturer or a wholesaler is operating on a tangible net worth between $50,000 and $250,000, wide practical experience has indicated that extreme care should be exercised in the analysis, even though the ratio of net sales to inventory is in satisfactory relationship, if the inventory is greater than three-quarters of the net working capital. When the tangible net worth exceeds $250,000, the inventory should be no greater than the net working capital. In a retail business with a tangible net worth in excess of $50,000, the inventory should be no greater than the net working capital.

Inventory Control Systems. Various systems have been developed by business firms to control their inventory. Certain of them may be more suitable for particular products and a multiproduct concern may employ several methods. Hoffman describes the following systems (Inventories—A Guide to Their Control, Costing, and Effect Upon Income and Taxes):

Min-Max System—This is one of the oldest methods and is still widely used. For each item of inventory a **maximum** level is set that demand presumably will not exceed as well as a **minimum** level representing a margin of safety required to prevent out-of-stock conditions. The minimum level governs the ordering point.

The Two-Bin System—In this system, the stock of each item is separated into two piles or bins. In the first is sufficient stock to satisfy demand between the receipt of an order and the placing of the next one. In the second bin is the safety stock. When the first-bin stock has been exhausted reordering occurs, while the stock in the second bin is used to cover requirements.

Order Cycling System—In this system, periodic reviews are made of each item of inventory and orders are placed to restore stocks to a prescribed supply level. The frequency of review generally depends upon the criticalness of the item.

Statistical Inventory Control Systems—Mathematical approaches have been developed to help in inventory management decisions. Despite the interest in this area, stimulated by operations research and the computer, the National Association of Accountants found in a field survey that "relatively few of the companies approached did report the application of these mathematical concepts to their own inventory management." (N.A.A. Res. Rep., No. 40, Feb. 1964.)

Turnover Rates—A desirable inventory-to-sales ratio is employed as a guide for management action to modify procurement so as to bring inventories into line.

The Perpetual Inventory Control System—In this system the removal or receipt of each item of inventory is recorded and new balances are calculated. Information is also kept on maximum, minimum, reorder point, and order quantity for each item. Because of the considerable clerical effort involved, computers may be employed in the operation of such a system.

Budgetary Control Systems—Through budgets, inventory consumption and levels are coordinated with expected usage.

Inventory Valuation. High inventory valuations result in an overstatement of earnings, a false sense of adequacy of working capital, possible overly liberal dividend and bonus distributions, and excessive tax payments. On the other hand, **understatement** of inventory values minimizes financial strength and could lead to eventual heavy tax burdens if the inventory is disposed of and added profits are realized in a period of high tax rates. Avoidance of these extremes is facilitated by adopting a basis of valuation that minimizes the effect of commodity price changes.

The **chief methods** of inventory valuation currently in use are:

1. Specific cost.
2. First-in first-out.
3. Average cost.
4. Last-in first-out.
5. Cost or market, whichever is lower.
6. Inventory valuation allowances.

The first four methods are variations of actual cost. **Specific costs** are employed where physical units can be differentiated and the actual price paid for each unit is known. The **first-in first-out (FIFO)** method uses the most recent price paid for the goods as a basis for valuation, so that it gives inflated inventory values in periods of rising prices and understated values in periods of falling prices. The **average cost**, involving use of simple, weighted, or periodic averages, is merely an attempt at pricing inventory at the average of prices paid over a period of time. The **last-in first-out (LIFO)** method results in a matching of the cost of current purchases against current sales, so that the valuation basis for inventory does not ordinarily change despite fluctuations in prices.

Cost or market, whichever is lower, is a combination of both actual cost and replacement cost. Under conditions of declining prices, the inventory value will be reduced to market price, so that working capital will decline to reflect anticipation of future losses. When prices are rising, the inventory will be valued at cost, which will give smaller working capital and profits than would replacement cost.

Current practice in cost determination for inventories is reflected in published annual reports (Accounting Trends and Techniques, 1963, Reporting on 622 Large Corporations), which show that 195 companies used last-in first-out, 153 average cost, 183 first-in first-out, and the remaining 91 companies a variety of methods.

The use of inventory **revaluation allowances** anticipates future price declines, style or technological changes or other factors that could reduce the value of stocks on hand. They provide protection against overstatement of working capital through the use of inventory valuations that may not stand up in the light of future developments. Such valuation allowances do not ordinarily lessen income taxes payable, as they are not recognized by the Internal Revenue Service as reducing taxable income.

In the selection of a method, consideration should be given to the physical nature of the inventory, the frequency and magnitude of price fluctuations, the rate of inventory turnover, and the average size of the inventory. (See also discussion in Section 8 on Financial Reports.)

Working Capital Requirements

FACTORS AFFECTING WORKING CAPITAL NEEDS. A number of factors affect the working capital requirements of each business. An appraisal of these provides guidance to management in estimating prospective needs. Some students of working capital management have listed the following factors as pertinent:

1. General nature of business.
2. Length of period of manufacture and cost of product.
3. Turnover of inventories.
4. Turnover of accounts receivable.
5. Terms of purchase.
6. Terms of sale.
7. Expansion of business.
8. Seasonal variations.
9. Hazards and contingencies inherent in the particular type of business.

To this list should be added the effects of cyclical changes in business, long-term trends in the industry, and the size of the surplus of liquid resources desired by the management as protection against contingencies of all kinds.

General Nature of Business. A public utility enterprise requires a relatively small inventory of supplies. Payment for its service is received in cash promptly after it is furnished, and sometimes even before. Hence, its working capital requirements are quite limited by comparison with the heavy fixed capital investment that is needed.

At the other extreme is a retail business conducted on leased premises. Its current assets constitute virtually all of the assets of such a business. Generally speaking, trading and financial enterprises require relatively **large amounts of working capital,** public utilities comparatively **small amounts,** whereas manufacturing concerns stand between these two extremes, their needs depending upon the character of the industry of which they are a part.

Period of Manufacture and Cost of Product. The longer it takes to make a product and the greater its cost, the larger the inventory tied up in its manufacture. A company engaged in turning out a product that involves an aging process, such as a distillery, must make a particularly heavy investment in inventory. On the other hand, one engaged in bread baking or meat packing sells the bulk of its output daily and therefore, although the investment in working capital is quite large, it is turned over far more rapidly. Some concerns making heavy machinery and equipment minimize their investment in inventory by requiring advance payments from customers as work proceeds on their orders.

Turnover of Inventories. The ratio of annual sales to working capital or any component thereof (turnover ratios) measures the number of times current assets are converted back into cash during a year. The higher the rate of turnover, the larger is the volume of business that can be conducted with a given amount of such current assets. For inventories also, the higher the rate of turnover the less the risk of loss due to changes in demand, style changes, and price declines. Although **variations in the ratio** of inventory turnover are inevitable as between different industries, frequently encountered differences in turnover rates between companies engaged in the same industry reflect differing sales policies, efficiency, and inventory control methods.

Turnover of Accounts Receivable. The rate at which accounts receivable are converted into cash is primarily a reflection of sales and credit policies. The sale may be but the first step in converting merchandise into cash. **Prompt collection** of accounts receivable is essential to complete the cycle. **Slow collection** of receivables can wipe out the benefit derived from a rapid inventory turnover, since it ties up funds that could otherwise be used to acquire goods for further sales.

Terms of Purchase. The more favorable the terms on which the business does its own purchasing, the less cash is tied up in merchandise. If only a short period of time elapses between delivery and payment dates, accounts payable are smaller and more cash is required to finance a given volume of business. By effective planning, purchases may be self-financed. This may be seen if one takes, as an illustration, a business where 8 days are required for delivery of materials ordered and the terms of purchase are 2% 10 days, 30 days net. A minimum inventory of only 8 days' supply is then needed to assure continuous operation. If raw material deliveries are spaced 10 days apart, the company could take advantage of the cash discount and still have adequate inventories for operations, provided no interruption of delivery is likely to occur. In effect, the vendor of the raw material finances a 10 days' supply for the manufacturer at all times in this case.

Terms of Sale. The more liberal the credit terms offered customers, the larger the funds that will be tied up in accounts receivable. **Discretion of management** in setting credit terms is affected by prevailing trade practices as well as by changing economic conditions. During depression periods, credit terms are often relaxed to stimulate sales, while in a sellers' market credit terms may be shortened and payment on time strictly enforced because buyers are so eager to get goods.

Foulke (Practical Financial Statement Analysis) has observed that "every industry has its own customs, and in practically every industry the recognized terms of sale are constantly being modified by particular concerns so that a process of evolution is always going on."

Expansion of Business. Growth industries require more working capital than those that are static, other things being equal. As a business expands, working capital requirements increase, although not necessarily in proportion. More efficient utilization of working capital is often possible as a business expands to its "optimum size," but efficiency of working capital use decreases when it goes beyond that point.

Seasonal Variation. The wider the seasonal variation in an industry, the more additional working capital is temporarily required in the active season. Thus, almost all of the current assets of a manufacturer of ladies apparel may be temporary in nature. As the manufacturer prepares for his active season, his inventory may rise from practically nothing to a peak reached just as volume deliveries begin. As goods are shipped, accounts receivable replace inventory as the significant element of working capital. Final conversion from accounts receivable to cash, as customers pay their bills, ushers in the low point in working capital requirements.

A business frequently finds itself with excess working capital at its seasonal low point. **Diversification** of products or activities often makes possible a more effective use of working capital throughout the year, reducing fluctuations in its amount from one season to another.

Inherent Hazards and Contingencies. An enterprise operating in an industry subject to wide fluctuations in demand and prices for its products, periodic operating losses, or rapidly changing technology, requires **additional working capital** to cope with these conditions, over and above its permanent and seasonal requirements.

Cyclical and Secular Changes. External factors affecting the working capital needs of all businesses include the cyclical ebb and flow of activity and long-run trends in each industry. Although cyclical and secular economic changes cannot be predicted with precision, effective management of working capital requires that allowance be made for these fluctuations so that the business will be reasonably well prepared for them.

A **contraction** in the volume of business done by an enterprise, whether for seasonal, cyclical, or secular reasons, tends to expand its cash. This results from the reduction in inventory and receivables that usually accompanies a decline in sales and curtailment or cessation of spending upon the acquisition of fixed assets. When new fixed assets are not being acquired, as is common in depressions, the depreciation allowance contributes to the growth of cash, unless the operating profit does not suffice to cover at least part of the depreciation charge. Except where substantial operating losses are incurred, a business may give a misleading appearance of financial strength in a period of reduced activity. As business improves, the cash will dwindle and a shortage of working capital may develop.

Conversely, in **prosperity** working capital requirements expand rapidly and cash resources are used up at great speed. Not only do inventory and receivables expand rapidly under such conditions, but investment in new fixed assets tends largely to exceed the current depreciation deduction.

Commodity price changes that may accompany fluctuations in the business cycle exaggerate the effects on working capital. Expanding volume usually is accompanied by rising prices, and decreasing volume by price declines.

HOW LARGE A SURPLUS OF WORKING CAPITAL?

No rule can be laid down to govern the size of surplus working capital resources, because possible needs for liquid resources are well-nigh infinite. Provided stockholders do not object and penalties are not incurred under Sections 531–7 of the Internal Revenue Code, surplus cash resources retained in the business may constitute quite a large part of the total investment. If surplus working capital has reached excessive proportions, the management may utilize cash to retire its own stock by purchase in the open market or through inviting tenders from holders. A partial liquidation can be effected by using excess working capital to reduce capitalization.

Sources of Working Capital

RAISING PERMANENT WORKING CAPITAL. The portion of the working capital of the business that will be required even in less active periods should not be raised on a temporary basis. Obviously, if the money for this purpose is borrowed at short term so that repayment becomes necessary within a brief period, embarrassment could result.

The logical source of permanent working capital is the proprietors of the business. In the instance of a corporation, this means the **sale of preferred or common stock,** or the **reinvestment of earnings** through the surplus account. In either event, funds so acquired can be retained in the business permanently, so that no problem of repayment arises while the funds are still required in the enterprise. The larger the proportion of permanent working capital obtained through the sale of stock or the reinvestment of earnings, the stronger the credit of the enterprise, and hence the more easily will other working capital needs be obtained through borrowing or otherwise.

Next to the sale of stock and the reinvestment of earnings, **bond financing** provides permanent working capital for the longest period of time. However, since a bond issue has a fixed maturity, provision should be made for ultimate repayment, since this should not be done with current assets that will be required in the business at that time. The soundest procedure is to provide a sinking fund for retirement of bonds issued for permanent working capital. In effect, the bond issue then merely anticipates the retention of earnings to provide the permanent working capital of the business. (See also Section 14, Long-Term and Intermediate-Term Borrowing.)

Similar in character to a bond issue as a source of permanent working capital is a **term loan** from a bank or insurance company. Such a loan is generally of shorter maturity than a bond issue, but gradual repayment is always provided for through regular payments on account of principal.

Short-Term Borrowing. Less desirable than the sources of permanent working capital listed above are short-term borrowing expedients. Smaller concerns and larger enterprises with limited capital and poorer credit are compelled to use shorter-term bank loans, factoring, and other expedients more suitable for raising seasonal and other variable working capital. However, profitable concerns with insufficient capital have often secured their permanent working capital by short-term borrowings that are renewed repeatedly as they fall due. Bank loans in particular have been used in this way, although to a decreasing extent in the last two decades or so.

Financing the Small Business. A small business is often at a handicap compared with a large concern in raising permanent working capital (see also Section 9, Selling Securities). Accordingly, the **Small Business Administration,** which in 1953 became the successor to the Reconstruction Finance Corporation, was created to help small businesses in various ways, particularly granting of financial assistance.

The SBA commented as follows regarding its program (1962 Annual Report to The President and Congress—Small Business Administration):

Difficulty in obtaining adequate financing on reasonable terms continued to be a major problem of small business in 1962. The SBA helped with the problem through counseling on financial matters, assistance in obtaining private financing, loans in participation with banks, and direct Government loans.

During the year SBA approved nearly 6,000 loans to help small firms strengthen their operations, expand and modernize their facilities, and increase job opportunities in their communities. The agency also introduced a new loan plan designed to encourage additional banks to join with SBA in loans to small businesses.

Under authorization granted in 1958, the SBA also extends assistance to privately owned small business investment companies that provide both equity capital and long-term loans to small business concerns. The 1962 report pointed out:

The SBA licensed more than 200 additional small business investment companies to provide long-term loans and equity capital to small firms. By the close of the year, the SBIC's had well over a half billion dollars of capital for use in small business loans and investments, and had stepped up their rate of financing small firms. As of the year end, they had made more than 6,900 small business loans or investments totaling about $360 million.

RAISING VARIABLE WORKING CAPITAL. Working capital required for limited periods of time may be secured from **temporary** sources. Many businesses have found, however, that they prefer to raise seasonal and cyclical working capital also from the more permanent sources such as reinvested earnings or the sale of stock or bonds. In this way, they avoid incurring short-term liabilities that may prove embarrassing should working capital needs be larger or longer-lasting than anticipated.

A part of the variable working capital requirements can be obtained from **trade creditors,** covering the period between the receipt of goods purchased and the date of payment. The longer this period, the less necessary it becomes to seek financing elsewhere to finance inventory and even receivables, if the terms of payment will cover part of the period after the goods have been purchased but before payment is received from the ultimate purchaser.

Working capital requirements may be reduced by offering favorable credit terms to customers. Through allowing a **cash discount** for prompt payment, the volume of outstanding accounts receivable can be reduced sharply. However, a cash discount may be a costly way to finance, since offering terms of 2% 10 days,

30 days net is equivalent to lending money at the rate of approximately 36% per annum (in effect, 2% is charged for the use of funds for a period of only 20 days). Nevertheless, cash discounts are allowed in many trades, both as a matter of custom and because prompt payment of accounts tends to reduce credit costs and risks as well. Efficient credit and collection practice accomplishes the same result.

BANK LOANS. The most widely used source of temporary working capital is the bank loan, particularly the unsecured commercial or industrial loan made by the bank to finance short-term working capital needs. Such loans may run from 30 days to several months, with renewals not uncommon.

If the credit of the borrower is not rated highly enough by the bank to grant a loan requested, if large sums are required, or when the bank has doubts about the purpose of the loan or the conduct of the borrower's business, **collateral** may be sought. This collateral may consist of goods, accounts, and notes receivable, or government obligations or other marketable securities.

Exacting credit standards applied by commercial banks, and pressure by many banks in the past for repayment of loans as unfavorable business conditions developed, caused business managements generally to seek other sources of working capital following the World War I period. Many concerns used large earnings and the proceeds of the sale of securities in the favorable markets of the 20's to become independent of bank borrowing at that time. Others turnsd to specialized lenders or government lending agencies.

Over the past several decades, however, banks have become increasingly aggressive in competing for commercial loans. They have tended to discard the traditional notion of confining their activities largely to short-term, so-called self-liquidating loans. At present, they participate actively in many different kinds of business financing, such as granting loans secured by accounts receivable, commodities and equipment, as well as providing relatively long-term loans. (See discussion in Section 5, Banking Services and Procedures.)

ACCOUNTS RECEIVABLE FINANCING. Accounts receivable may be financed either through the outright sale of such accounts by the business, or through borrowing with the accounts assigned as security. The outright sale of accounts, known as **factoring,** has long been used in the textile industry but factors have extended their operations to other fields as well. Factors usually purchase accounts receivable without recourse and it is common to notify the customer that his account has been sold. If factoring is conducted on a continuing basis, the seller's invoice may note that the sum due is payable directly to the factor.

Installment paper is commonly sold on the same basis to a **sales finance company** by the dealer selling goods on the installment plan. It is more common for the sales finance company to obtain recourse against the dealer, although part of the charge may be set aside as a dealer's reserve out of which the dealer is expected to reimburse himself for losses due to nonpayment of installment notes.

Loans against a pledge of accounts receivable are commonly made on a nonnotification basis, and this arrangement is therefore called **nonnotification financing.** This method is preferred by concerns fearful of antagonizing customers by informing them that their accounts have been pledged. Numerous specialized finance companies, and more recently commercial banks, have made this type of financing of accounts receivable available. The amount of the advance usually ranges from 70 to 90% of the face value of accounts receivable, depending upon their quality. The interest charges may differ widely, depending upon the financial strength of the borrower and his customers.

SOURCES OF WORKING CAPITAL   16·15

Advantages and Disadvantages. Financing working capital requirements through the sale or pledge of accounts receivable offers the following advantages:

1. The credit of the business may not be strong enough to permit financing in any other way.
2. Where accounts receivable constitute a large part of the assets of a business, as in the case of companies selling on the installment plan or those that find they must give relatively long credit terms for competitive reasons, the pledge of accounts receivable is a logical method of financing.
3. Interest is paid only upon funds actually received and used in the business, rather than upon borrowed money that is not required immediately, or that may not be used during the period of a loan because of miscalculation of requirements.
4. When accounts receivable are sold, the factor assumes the credit risk, thereby freeing the client from the necessity of maintaining a credit and collection department.
5. The immediate cash made available permits an increased volume of operations.

Disadvantages of accounts receivable financing may include:

1. The higher rate of interest payable than on bank loans, if the latter are obtainable.
2. Customers may resent the sale or pledge of their accounts, if they are notified that this has been done.
3. Sale or pledging of receivables may restrict the ability of a company to obtain short-term credit from other sources.

INVENTORY FINANCING. Inventories may be pledged for loans in several ways. The bill of lading of a common carrier, a bonded warehouse receipt, or a trust receipt specifying that the goods involved belong to the lender may be used.

As a practical matter, it is often essential that goods be kept on the premises of the borrower. Because of the legal weakness of the trust receipt, **field warehousing** has been developed to protect the lender in such instances. A field warehouse, consisting of a segregated space on the premises of the borrower placed under the control of an outside warehouseman, is designed to give the lender security comparable to that provided by an independent warehouse. The cost of field warehousing ranges from ½ of 1% to 2% of the value of the goods per annum, and interest charged by banks and finance companies for loans secured by field warehouse receipts ranges from 5 to 13%. The amount loaned may run from 65 to 85% of the value of the goods pledged. The amount of the interest charged and the percentage of inventory value loaned reflect the financial responsibility of the field warehouse company, the physical characteristics of the field warehouse, the financial position of the borrower, and the character of the merchandise. The borrower who cannot obtain funds through an ordinary bank loan in the required amount finds a field warehouse arrangement helpful because of the resulting ability to take advantage of cash and quantity discounts, which are often several times as large as the cost of funds obtained in this way.

Loans on the pledge of commodities were at one time largely limited to staple raw materials traded in on commodity futures exchanges. In recent years, this technique has been extended to lending on a wide variety of semimanufactured and finished goods located on the premises of the borrower.

The need for exercising great caution in granting loans on warehouse receipts was dramatically illustrated by the case of the Allied Crude Vegetable Oil Refining Corp. in 1963. Banks, brokerage houses, and other concerns lent many millions of dollars on the strength of warehouse receipts certifying the storage of commodities, particularly soybean oil. When Allied failed and the receipts were looked to, much of the inventories turned out to be nonexistent, causing large losses to the lending concerns.

DEPRECIATION AS A SOURCE OF WORKING CAPITAL. When depreciation deductions from earnings are not balanced by new investment in fixed assets, an increase in working capital will result if such funds are not used to pay off loans or to distribute dividends to stockholders. Under depression conditions, a flow of cash to the business may come not only from the sale of products and the collection of resulting accounts receivable, but also from depreciation, if gross profit is sufficient to cover the depreciation allowance.

Working capital can, however, be obtained only temporarily from deferral of acquisition of fixed assets. Eventually, when additional plant capacity will again be needed, the investment in fixed assets may exceed current depreciation, and inroads will be made into working capital to acquire new fixed assets unless funds are obtained from some other source. Hence, management must prepare for a **conversion of working capital into fixed assets** during a period of expansion.

TAX LIABILITIES. The deferred payment of taxes can be a source of temporary working capital. Taxes are not paid from day to day, but the estimated liability therefor is indicated in the balance sheet. The tendency to place corporations on a **pay-as-you-go basis** has diminished the significance of Federal income tax accruals as a source of working capital.

Federal, state, and local governments require business to perform the task of tax collector. Withheld personal income taxes, old-age benefit taxes, excise taxes, and sales taxes are collected by business and then turned over to government. The period of time during which business holds and may use these funds ranges from a maximum of a month in the instance of withheld income and old age taxes to a maximum of about 3 months in the instance of some state and local sales taxes. A **business acts as a trustee** for these funds, and severe penalties are imposed for failure to turn them over to the government at prescribed dates.

Analysis of Working Capital

STATEMENT OF VARIATION IN WORKING CAPITAL. The comparison of balance sheets for the beginning and the end of a specific period has long been used as a management tool, to check efficiency of the use of funds. The "sources and uses" statement has as its purpose the analysis of how funds have been procured for the business and how they have been employed. The statement of variation in working capital uses this technique to analyze changes in working capital components between two dates. A comparison of current assets and current liabilities, as shown in balance sheets at the beginning and the end of a specific period, shows changes in each type of current asset, as well as the sources from which working capital has been obtained.

A simple illustration is provided in Figs. 2 and 3. After increases and decreases have been tabulated, the change in working capital and the sources supplying these funds can be determined.

More thorough analyses of changes in working capital through a source and application of funds analysis may be made by incorporating some items from the income statement as well. Although a funds statement may also be used to analyze cash, its most common application is to working capital. Indicative of its importance, Mason has stated that, "the funds statement should be treated as a major financial statement. It should be presented in all annual reports of cor-

X Corp.
Comparative Balance Sheets
Dec. 31, 19X5 and Dec. 31, 19X6

	Dec. 31, 19X5	Dec. 31, 19X6	Increases in Assets—Decreases in Liabilities and Net Worth	Decreases in Assets—Increases in Liabilities and Net Worth
Assets:				
Cash	$ 10,000	$ 30,000	$20,000	
Accounts Receivable	35,000	50,000	15,000	
Inventories	50,000	80,000	30,000	
Plant and Equipment (net)	30,000	25,000		$ 5,000
Total Assets	$125,000	$185,000		
Liabilities:				
Accounts Payable	$ 15,000	$ 45,000		30,000
Net Worth:				
Capital Stock	100,000	120,000		20,000
Retained Earnings	10,000	20,000		10,000
Total Liabilities and Capital	$125,000	$185,000	$65,000	$65,000

Fig. 2. Illustrative comparative balance sheet.

X Corp.
Statement of Variation of Working Capital
Dec. 31, 19X5 and Dec. 31, 19X6

Increases in Working Capital:	
Cash	$20,000
Accounts Receivable	15,000
Inventories	30,000
TOTAL	65,000
Sources of Working Capital:	
Increases in Payables (from creditors)	30,000
Increase in Capital Stock (from stockholders)	20,000
Increase in Retained Earnings	10,000
Decrease in Plant and Equipment (from depreciation)	5,000
TOTAL	$65,000

Fig. 3. Statement of variation of working capital.

porations and be covered by the auditor's short-form report." ("Cash Flow" Analysis and the Funds Statement.) The Accounting Principles Board of the A.I.C.P.A. (Opinion Bul. No. 3) substantially agreed, and, early in 1964, the president of the New York Stock Exchange urged such action.

Guthmann and Dougall (Corporate Financial Policy) have summarized the **uses of the funds statement** as follows:

. . . comparison of these sources and applications of working 'funds' may reveal that current funds have been diverted to permanent uses, or that working capital has been drained by operating losses or dividends; or the statement may show that inappropriate means of financing have been used. Another purpose of this exhibit is to reveal why funds (working capital) may have increased or decreased while accounting profits moved in an opposite direction. This statement does not, however, reveal shifts among the items making up current assets or current liabilities nor tell whether any loss of working capital has unduly weakened financial position. Only an examination of the balance sheet at the end of the period will show the end effects of these changes and permit ratio analysis to check solvency.

THE WORKING CAPITAL BUDGET. Efficient management of working capital, as of other phases of business financing, entails careful measurement of future requirements and the formulation of plans for meeting them. The working capital budget is an important phase of overall financial budgeting. This budget is to be distinguished from a cash budget that is designed to insure all the financial requirements of a business, including funds for the acquisition of fixed assets, repayment of long-term loans, and similar items. The working capital budget measures permanent and variable working capital requirements and assures that they are provided for as needed.

Heckert and Willson (Business Budgeting and Control) have described as follows the **objectives** of the working capital budget:

Working capital is subject to budgetary control in the sense that a proper relationship must be determined and planned as between working capital and operations.

The objective of the working capital budget is to secure effective utilization of the investment. Such utilization may be measured by the rate of turnover as measured against sales or cost of sales. This is the key to the method. Scatter charts may be used to learn the behavior of working capital in relation to volume. It is often found desirable to refine the relationship and establish separate standards for each element, particularly cash, receivables, and inventory. The technique then provides the necessary information for any volume of business.

WORKING CAPITAL RATIOS. The ratio analysis of working capital has been evolved primarily for credit analysis. However, it can also be used by management as a means of checking upon the efficiency with which working capital is being used in the enterprise. The most important ratios for working capital management are the turnover of working capital, inventory turnover, and the average collection period for accounts receivable. (See also Section 8, Financial Reports.)

Ratio analysis takes two forms. First, the behavior of the ratios for one business over a period of years reveals trends. Secondly, a ratio for one concern can be compared with the average for other concerns in the same line of business. In making such comparisons, allowance must be made for differences in the character of the enterprise and for special policies each pursues deliberately.

Dun & Bradstreet, Inc., compute regularly, for the preceding 5 years, median working capital ratios for different groups of manufacturers, wholesalers, and retailers. Although compiled primarily for credit analysis purposes, these provide a standard against which a business can check its own ratios. The ratios for the period 1951–62 are shown in Figs. 4, 5, and 6 (pages 20–23).

ANALYSIS OF WORKING CAPITAL

The ratios used in the tables are:

1. **Current Assets to Current Debt.** Frequently referred to as the **current ratio**, it measures the relative ability of a company to pay its short-term debts.

2. **Turnover of Net Working Capital.** Derived by dividing net sales by average net working capital for a period—generally a year—this ratio measures the rate of working capital utilization. A company showing a turnover in excess of industry standards may be in need of additional net working capital, to be supplied by owners through reinvested earnings or the sale of additional stock. A concern with a lower than average ratio may have an excess of investment in net working capital.

3. **Average Collection Period.** The average collection period is equivalent to the average number of days required to convert receivables into cash. It is determined by dividing average receivables on the books during a year by average daily credit sales (net sales ÷ 365). It indicates the extent to which customers are conforming to credit terms, and is thus a reflection of the efficiency of the credit department.

4. **Net Sales to Inventory.** The number of times in any one period that inventory is turned over is computed by dividing net sales for a period, generally a year, by the average inventory carried during the period. The faster the rate of turnover, the greater the profit realized from the investment in inventory, unless the high rate of turnover is due to excessive markdowns.

5. **Current Debt to Tangible Net Worth.** The ratio of current liabilities to tangible net worth shows how much of the capital used in an enterprise has been provided by short-term creditors and how much by the owners. The funds permanently invested by the owners serve as a cushion for credit temporarily extended to the business. Accordingly, the higher the ratio, the greater the risk to short-term creditors.

6. **Inventory to Net Working Capital.** Inventory is the least liquid of the elements in working capital. Its ratio to net working capital shows the extent to which the owners of the business have invested in this asset.

7. **Current Debt to Inventory.** This ratio relates total current liabilities to inventory. This provides another indication of the extent to which the business is relying on funds from disposal of unsold inventory to meet its debts.

LIQUIDITY RATIOS. For some analytic purposes, management, creditors, and financing agencies are concerned primarily with the ability of a business to turn its assets into cash promptly to meet its short-term obligations. The best measure of this is the relationship of cash and United States government securities to current liabilities, termed the liquidity ratio. This ratio has been decreasing in recent years. For all United States corporations, excluding banks, savings and loan associations, and insurance companies (based upon data compiled by the United States Securities and Exchange Commission), the ratio was 60% in 1950 but declined to 34% in 1962.

A somewhat similar ratio, favored by bank credit men, is that of cash, government securities, and accounts receivable to current liabilities. This ratio, sometimes called the **"acid test"** or the **"quick assets"** ratio, assumes that the accounts receivable are collectible when due but that there is no similar assurance that inventory can be liquidated on short notice. For the same corporations mentioned above this ratio also has been declining in recent years and amounted to 1.16:1 at the close of 1962.

CURRENT ASSET PLANNING

Line of Business	Current Assets to Current Debt	Turnover of Net Working Capital	Average Collection Period	Net Sales to Inventory	Current Debt to Tangible Net Worth	Inventory to Net Working Capital	Current Debt to Inventory
	Times	Times	Days	Times	Per Cent	Per Cent	Per Cent
Agricultural Implements and Machinery	3.11	3.47	33	3.6	35.7	89.8	55.6
	3.35	3.05*	39	3.8	29.7	80.3	55.6
Automobile Parts and Accessories	2.64	4.65	33	6.6	38.1	75.5	81.0
	2.97	4.19*	40	5.5	31.3	72.7	77.4
Breweries	2.10	9.30	19	14.9	23.2	62.0	147.2
	2.55	8.68*	17	16.1	20.3	52.0	125.6
Chemicals, Industrial	2.55	4.19	33	6.3	33.4	65.2	101.6
	2.79	4.35*	43	6.7	26.7	64.5	87.5
Coats and Suits, Women's	2.51	5.74	31	10.6	57.0	68.3	105.0
	1.85	8.38*	42	11.5	92.3	75.0	154.3
Confectionery	3.44	6.45	17	8.8	21.8	65.2	62.9
	2.81	6.36*	20	8.4	29.5	72.9	80.6
Cotton Goods, Converters, Non-factored	3.16	4.22	49	5.9	39.2	75.3	66.3
	2.27†	4.78*	49†	8.7†	88.5†	85.6†	92.7†
Dresses, Rayon, Silk, and Acetate	2.13	10.73	31	17.1	74.2	68.7	135.3
	1.70	13.95*	35	14.7	113.6	83.3	184.4
Drugs	3.36	2.88	41	4.8	27.5	61.4	68.4
	3.26	3.19*	43	5.7	26.1	54.7	87.6
Electrical Parts and Supplies	2.54	4.92	36	5.2	45.6	86.3	82.1
	2.86	4.25*	42	5.0	35.9	78.1	70.8
Foundries	2.73	5.73	33	8.1	30.6	62.4	99.1
	3.10	4.60*	38	9.7	23.6	50.4	109.1
Fruits and Vegetables, Canners	2.11	5.05	18	3.6	52.1	143.1	62.6
	2.04	5.56*	22	3.3	57.5	133.4	70.1
Furniture	3.20	4.42	37	6.1	29.5	71.8	65.0
	2.89	4.70*	45	5.8	32.4	74.0	74.2

ANALYSIS OF WORKING CAPITAL 16·21

Hardware and Tools	3.20	3.31	35	4.6	29.9	77.7	59.7
	3.65	3.64*	39	4.6	24.2	72.4	54.1
Hosiery	3.11	4.96	30	6.1	22.9	78.8	59.5
	2.97	4.65*	35	5.5	25.5	80.1	58.4
Machinery, Industrial	2.74	3.81	43	4.6	39.8	78.5	76.9
	3.32	3.38*	49	4.9	28.5	69.4	68.1
Meats and Provisions, Packers	2.16	20.28	11	25.8	37.2	79.4	100.3
	2.55	16.98*	12	27.6	32.0	65.7	107.5
Metal Stampings	2.81	5.25	30	7.3	31.5	71.0	84.8
	2.88	4.50*	36	7.7	28.2	65.0	83.8
Overalls and Work Clothing	3.32	4.40	32	4.6	36.2	91.0	50.8
	2.94	4.38*	38	4.4	42.9	87.0	60.0
Paints, Varnishes, and Lacquers	3.51	4.56	34	6.9	24.3	67.2	68.3
	3.67	4.76*	39	7.1	24.8	64.4	68.6
Paper	2.62	4.61	27	7.1	25.0	72.4	90.6
	2.78	4.72*	30	7.3	18.9	65.8	85.8
Paper Boxes	2.50	5.62	24	9.6	27.7	63.7	103.9
	2.76	5.90*	27	9.6	25.9	70.8	82.9
Shirts, Underwear and Pajamas, Men's	2.16	5.49	46	6.7	69.6	98.7	81.6
	1.92	6.16*	45	5.3	92.5	113.9	90.7
Shoes, Men's, Women's, and Children's	2.68	4.01	39	5.3	46.0	81.0	68.3
	2.39	4.02*	51	5.3	58.7	86.0	85.4
Steel, Structural Fabricators (Sell on Short Terms)	2.80	4.78	41	6.5	35.9	73.2	80.9
	2.86	5.24*	51	6.8	33.8	66.7	83.6
Stoves, Ranges, and Ovens	3.29	4.11	37	4.7	31.1	79.1	61.8
	3.72	4.37*	48	4.9	26.3	69.0	53.8

† 1956–1961 average.
* 1956–1960 average.

Fig. 4. Working capital ratios of manufacturers, 1951–1962—Dun & Bradstreet (First figure 1951–1955 average—second figure 1956–1962 average).

CURRENT ASSET PLANNING

Line of Business	Current Assets to Current Debt (Times)	Turnover of Net Working Capital (Times)	Average Collection Period (Days)	Net Sales to Inventory (Times)	Current Debt to Tangible Net Worth (Per Cent)	Inventory to Net Working Capital (Per Cent)	Current Debt to Inventory (Per Cent)
Automobile Parts and Accessories	3.24	4.68	33	5.2	34.5	85.0	55.8
	2.88	4.37*	37	4.7	42.2	89.2	61.4
Drugs and Drug Sundries	2.60	6.52	30	6.8	54.8	92.9	65.7
	2.64	6.48*	34	6.7	55.7	88.4	69.1
Dry Goods	3.40	4.34	45	6.4	34.0	67.6	61.9
	2.67	5.07*	49	5.8	50.9	74.5	76.1
Electrical Parts and Supplies	2.46	5.90	40	7.2	56.3	82.2	84.7
	2.38	6.12*	44	7.1	56.4	79.3	89.2
Fruits and Produce, Fresh	3.51	18.86	15	48.7	23.7	30.6	139.2
	3.31	14.76*	18	37.1	29.1	40.0	152.5
Furnishings, Men's	3.53	3.76	45	5.7	31.9	66.3	58.3
	2.61	3.27*	59	4.7	49.5	73.8	84.2
Groceries	2.70	9.55	16	9.6	42.7	98.9	53.6
	2.56	10.88*	15	11.2	54.6	101.8	64.0
Hardware	3.23	3.88	32	4.2	35.4	89.3	46.0
	3.58	3.68*	41	4.2	32.9	83.0	48.8
Hosiery and Underwear	3.70	4.87	41	6.8	31.8	67.3	61.2
	3.25†	4.72*	51†	6.0†	37.9†	73.6†	71.2†
Lumber	2.92	9.99	33	9.0	39.7	73.2	78.5
	2.90	6.49*	39	7.3	39.7	70.1	76.8
Meat and Poultry	2.20	16.63	19	39.0	43.4	58.0	145.3
	2.17	23.35*	16	42.4	59.6	45.8	183.9
Paper	2.74	6.49	32	7.5	44.2	76.8	77.5
	2.69	6.43*	36	7.8	47.1	74.9	83.5
Plumbing and Heating Supplies	3.26	4.77	41	5.4	34.1	80.8	56.2
	3.50	4.35*	50	5.2	32.7	75.7	56.9
Shoes, Men's, Women's, and Children's	3.00	5.62	50	6.4	40.9	66.8	82.3
	2.26	4.84*	63	6.5	71.7	77.3	103.6
Wines and Liquors	1.95	9.03	35	7.8	72.5	99.8	106.3
	2.18	9.32*	34	9.5	59.2	89.2	95.1

† 1956–1961 average.
* 1956–1960 average.

Working capital ratios of wholesalers, 1951–1962—Dun & Bradstreet (First figure 1951–1955 average—second figure 1956–

ANALYSIS OF WORKING CAPITAL

Line of Business	Current Assets to Current Debt	Turnover of Net Working Capital	Average Collection Period	Net Sales to Inventory	Current Debt to Tangible Net Worth	Inventory to Net Working Capital	Current Debt to Inventory
	Times	Times	Days	Times	Per Cent	Per Cent	Per Cent
Clothing, Men's and Boys'	3.66	2.89	**	3.6	27.8	85.0	50.3
	2.70	3.07*	**	3.6	44.6	91.6	62.1
Department Stores	3.55	4.02	**	6.0	27.6	66.6	62.1
	3.53	3.90*	**	5.4	28.8	67.2	61.1
Lumber and Building Materials	3.50	3.88	50	5.5	30.3	72.0	58.6
	4.29	3.29*	68	5.0	23.0	62.2	53.5
Shoes	3.15	4.17	**	4.0	33.3	107.5	45.5
	2.68	5.10*	**	3.8	39.6	119.8	51.3
Women's Specialty Shops	2.72	5.18	**	7.3	38.9	66.2	96.7
	2.33	4.74*	**	6.3	53.7	77.9	98.6

* 1956–1961 average.
** Part of the annual sales were for cash and part were on charge account. To obtain an average collection period it would have been necessary to deduct the amount of the cash sales from the annual net sales and then to have determined the average number of days for which the accounts and notes receivable were outstanding based upon the resultant yearly charge sales. This information was available in too few instances to obtain an average collection period that could be used as a broad guide.

Fig. 6. Working capital ratios of retailers, 1951–1962—Dun & Bradstreet (First figure 1951–1955 average—second figure 1956–1962 average).

The Cash Budget

CASH INCOME VS. PROFIT. It is important to bear in mind that the net profit from operations, as shown by the profit and loss statement, is not at all the same as the excess of cash receipts over cash outgo. Many items of cash expenditure are not included as expenses in the profit and loss statement; conversely, some items of expense do not require a cash outlay in the same period. The **difference** between "estimated net profit from operations" and "estimated excess of cash receipts over cash outgo" is not a mere accounting detail, but may be of crucial importance in financial planning. Cash planning based upon adding the estimated profit for a period ahead to the existing cash balance could lead to wholly mistaken conclusions and financial difficulties.

Some **factors that cause a variation** between a statement of estimated profit or loss and a statement of estimated cash receipts and disbursements are:

1. Sales are included in the profit and loss statement, but cash payment may not be received until a subsequent period.
2. Payments to trade creditors for materials and supplies charged to costs of operation may be made in a later period.
3. Many expenses, such as interest or insurance, may actually be paid in a period prior or subsequent to that in which they are applicable.
4. Some items of income may be received in cash in one year, but might be applicable to the operations of another year.
5. Cash receipts from the sale of capital assets are not an element of operating income, but they do increase the availability of cash.
6. Similarly, payments for capital assets are not an element of cost at the time they are purchased and paid for, but do absorb cash.
7. Depreciation of fixed assets is charged to costs of operations, but does not involve a cash outlay as a rule until a later period.
8. Estimated uncollectibles and other asset valuation accounts reduce profits, but not cash.
9. Purchase or sale of investment securities may not affect income, but does affect cash balances.
10. The proceeds from the sale of corporate stock or bonds increase cash, but not income.
11. Repurchase or redemption of a company's bonds or stock decreases cash, but not income.
12. Cash dividends to stockholders decrease the amount of cash on hand.
13. Such book charges against profit as amortization of patents do not require a cash outlay.

SIGNIFICANCE OF A CASH BUDGET. Since changes in income and cash may differ substantially, it is imperative to plan for cash flows. A cash budget is the most effective tool to aid planning for the cash requirements and resources of a business. It is an inclusive forecast of cash income and outgo and of estimated cash balances for a future period. Its **primary purpose** is to utilize existing and anticipated cash resources to finance operations, pay debts as they mature, pay for expansion considered desirable, and maintain a satisfactory liquid position.

Cash planning is more than a mere mechanical assembly of estimates of cash requirements from expense and capital budgets, and the balancing of these requirements against cash balances and anticipated receipts. Sales, production, pricing, financing, and other policies should be critically re-examined in the light of the cash budget, and modified if the latter indicates this to be desirable.

INTEGRATING CASH FORECASTS AND THE BUSINESS PROGRAM. Planning of business operations should be concomitant with planning of cash requirements and resources. Inadequacy of cash for working capital needs is often given as the most common cause of financial embarrassment. A more accurate statement would usually be that the business planning was not coordinated with cash planning. Large cash outlays are needed for wages, materials, overhead expenses, etc., that will not be recovered until collections of accounts receivable occur. Prior to the adoption of a plan of operation, therefore, careful estimates of the availability of cash to finance the program must be prepared, to make sure the company will not find itself forced to borrow on short notice at excessive cost, if indeed funds can be secured at all under such circumstances.

Cash may be likened to an essential lubricant of the business operating machine, and it must be provided in the proper amount and at the proper time for smooth operation. A shortage of the cash lubricant could force a halt in operations; an excess of cash may invite inefficiency.

A comprehensive operating budget will indicate the **sources and amounts of cash** to become available and the requirements for a future period, providing the basic data to be incorporated in the cash budget. Prior to adoption of either the operating or cash budget, the financial desirability of the business program as laid out should be reviewed by top management.

If a cash forecast indicates a **deficit of resources** during all or part of the budget period, the entire plan of operations must be re-examined to see if this deficit can be overcome internally. It may be that the program is too ambitious for the resources available, or that certain budgeted activities can be curtailed or delayed until a later date. For instance, in planning product lines it is common to set manufacturing costs and distribution expenses against anticipated receipts from sales to estimate the profitability of a new product. Consideration should be given also to the cash required to manufacture and sell the product. If a product line requires large sums of cash to finance its manufacture and marketing, the strain placed upon the financial resources of the company may be found to be disproportionate to the anticipated profits. Conversely, a product line may show a relatively small margin of profit, but warrant a larger place in the company's operations because the cash required would be well within the resources of the company as revealed by the cash budget.

LONG-TERM CASH FORECASTS. Long-term cash forecasting normally includes any cash forecast in excess of 1 year. But "long-term" must be given an **elastic interpretation** if fluctuations in sales and a weak financial condition necessitate restricting cash forecasts to a short period such as 1 or 2 months. A 3-month cash forecast might be short-term for one company and long-term for another.

Necessarily, long-term cash forecasts must be tentative, and cannot include the details usually found in a short-term forecast. Some cash forecasts are made for a 5-year period, and occasionally even longer. Cash forecasts in excess of a year are usually broken down by 6 months or yearly totals.

With respect to long-range forecasting, the National Industrial Conference Board (Studies in Business Policy, No. 99), in a study of over 200 companies, found that:

> Five years is the most commonly used period for long-range cash forecasts, and three years the next most frequently used. Occasionally, projections for as long as ten years are made for a specific need; for example, getting an idea of what long-term debt structure will look like as a result of a proposed new product line.

Many companies, however, do not attempt to forecast more than one or two years in the future, because their businesses are unusually sensitive to swings in general business activity. Through experience, such companies have found that forecasts of greater length are so inaccurate that it is not worth the effort to make them.

Long-term cash forecasting can be conducted successfully only as part of coordinated financial planning that includes a long-term forecast of profits, planning for capital expansion, and formulation of an overall financial program for the company.

Advantages of Long-Term Cash Forecasting. Long-term forecasts of cash are of value principally at the executive or finance committee and board of directors levels in the formulation of overall financial policies. They establish a pattern for shorter-term forecasts, and thus tend to minimize the danger of day-to-day cash expenditures based on exaggerated emergencies or optimism.

A long-term cash forecast is valuable in channeling cash resources, so as to avoid reinvestment of a disproportionate share of profits in current or fixed assets, or the incurring of fixed liabilities that are either unnecessary or beyond the financial strength of the company to carry. Long-term cash forecasts are essential to the proper planning of capital expansion and in arranging well in advance for increased working capital requirements and higher operating costs caused by expansion or rising prices. Also, the sale of new securities can be timed to take advantage of favorable markets, and a stable dividend rate can be established based on the cash to become available for this purpose over the period of the forecast.

SHORTER-TERM FORECASTS. The period of the cash budget is largely dependent upon stability of sales and production. If sales volume and prices are erratic, the period of the cash budget must be shortened.

Normally the cash budget is prepared separately for each month of the budget period. If cash balances are low or profit margins narrow, however, it may be advisable to break down the cash budget to a weekly and even to a daily basis. Frequently, it is desirable to prepare the cash budget by weeks for the first month or two, and by months thereafter. Sometimes a budget is prepared by months for the first 3 months, and by quarters thereafter.

A **progressive cash budget** is one that is revised regularly as time elapses. Thus, in a progressive budget prepared for a 3-month period, a month is added as each month expires, figures for the remaining 2 months being revised.

Some concerns with ample reserves of cash prepare the budget by quarters or 6-month periods. A budget prepared for quarters or half-years may obscure temporary sharp declines in cash during the period. Thus, with a cash budget prepared for a 3-month period, total cash receipts for the entire period, when added to the opening balance, may be more than sufficient to meet anticipated requirements. Yet a severe deficiency in cash could occur at some time during the period that will not be revealed by the cash budget.

Length of the shorter-term cash budget period used by the companies studied was described by the N.I.C.B. (Studies in Business Policy, No. 99) as follows:

A cash forecast period of one year is used most frequently by cooperating companies, although short-range forecast periods range from one week to two years, depending on the characteristics of the business and the purpose for which the forecast is used.

In the case of very short-term forecasts, estimated cash flow is usually shown on a daily or weekly basis. In the case of longer forecasts, monthly intervals are more common.

USES OF A CASH BUDGET. A cash budget can assist in:

1. Efficient use of cash. Careful planning permits a business to be run with less working capital. By timing cash disbursements to coincide with cash receipts, it may be possible to avoid having large cash balances one week, and a deficit the next, to be followed by another large cash balance thereafter. Thus, unnecessary borrowing can be avoided.
2. The financing of seasonal business fluctuations. This is particularly important with businesses that have to borrow on accounts receivable or inventories at high cost.
3. Borrowing at short and longer term. By this means advantage can be taken of changing interest-rate patterns to reduce the cost of capital.
4. Making provision for paying maturing obligations. This is particularly important with large payments such as maturing bond issues, interest on indebtedness, and taxes.
5. Providing funds for capital expansion. A cash budget helps to avoid premature borrowing, with consequent unnecessary interest costs, as well as to facilitate arranging loans and stock sales in advance.
6. Financing of hedging operations.
7. Coordination of cash receipts and requirements of subdivisions and operating units.
8. Investment of surplus cash. Because the company can gauge the length of time the cash will not be needed in the business, this money can be invested, thereby providing additional income.
9. Realization of savings from cash discounts, advantageous purchases of materials, etc.
10. Dividend policy formulation. This is important in order to plan for future growth without unduly impairing the current dividend distributions to stockholders.

PREPARATION OF A CASH BUDGET. Cash budget procedures must be adapted to the specific requirements of each enterprise. The **most commonly used methods** of preparing a cash forecast are:

1. Cash Receipts and Disbursements Method.
2. Adjusted Earnings Basis.
3. Predetermination of Balance Sheet.
4. Working Capital Differentials.

Cash Receipts and Disbursements Method. This method of forecasting cash is the most commonly used, but the others, or variations of them, are becoming increasingly popular. The cash receipts and disbursements method is more elastic and can be prepared by weekly, 10-day or monthly periods, whereas the others require longer periods and must be part of forecasting procedures for profit and loss or balance sheet items. For companies with erratic or highly seasonal sales records and irregular earnings, or whose cash balances are low in relation to requirements, the cash receipts and disbursement method usually permits a **more effective control of cash,** since actual receipts by source and actual expenditures for each classification of expense can be compared with the amount that has been forecasted during the period. Also, **greater flexibility** is possible in the control of payments and cash disbursements can more easily be timed to receipts, thereby decreasing the size of cash balances required to support a given volume of business activity.

However, the other methods are simple and satisfactory if earnings are stable and cash reserves ample. The adjusted earnings and predetermination of balance sheet methods have been found quite suitable by companies that have developed a good system of budgetary planning and control.

CURRENT ASSET PLANNING

If a complete budget plan is already in use, the cash receipts and disbursements approach necessitates translating operating and cost budgets into estimates of cash receipts and disbursements. A form for cash receipts and disbursements forecasts is shown in Fig. 7, with separate columns for estimated and actual receipts and

Forecast of Cash Receipts and Disbursements
January to March, 19—

	January		February		March	
	Budget	Actual	Budget	Actual	Budget	Actual
Estimated receipts:						
Cash sales						
Collections from accounts receivable						
Interest income						
Miscellaneous income						
Total receipts						
Estimated disbursements:						
Accounts payable						
Payroll						
Expenses						
Advertising						
Interest expense						
Plant and equipment						
Repayment of bank loan ...						
Total disbursements						
Estimated excess of cash receipts over disbursements..						
Estimated balance beginning of month						
Estimated balance end of month						

Fig. 7. Receipts and disbursements method of cash forecasting.

disbursements by months. It is usually preferable to prepare the cash forecast first without including purely financial items such as proceeds from the sale of securities, bank loans, or dividends. **After completion** of the cash budget without these items, top management can arrive at decisions regarding financing, borrowing and dividend declarations, and it is then a simple matter to alter the cash budget in conformance with these decisions.

Forecasting Collections from Sales. Forecasts of receipts from sales should be based upon past experience and adjusted for the trend of business as it affects the company. Consideration must be given not only to fluctuations in business activity and seasonal trends, but to such specific factors as the date on which Easter occurs, which may greatly affect sales for a particular week or month. A form for forecasting sales and receipts is shown in Fig. 8.

In determining the lag between sales and collections, graphs of sales and collections for several years are helpful. Particular note should be made of the **effect of**

	MAY			JUNE			JULY		
	Unit Price	Quantity	Revenue	Unit Price	Quantity	Revenue	Unit Price	Quantity	Revenue
Gasoline—barrels									
Premium gas—barrels									
Aviation gas—barrels									
3rd grade gas—barrels									
Kerosene—barrels									
Lube oil—barrels									
Grease—pounds									
Fuel and crude—barrels									
Gas oil—barrels									
Asphalt—tons									
All other products									
Other revenue									
Prepaid freight on sales									
TOTAL REVENUE									
Amount of Federal gas taxes									
Amount of Federal lub. taxes included in selling prices									
TOTAL SALES REVENUE									
Less discounts									
Worthless debts, etc.									
NET TOTAL SALES REVENUE									
Cash to be received from said revenue on basis experience									
1. Cash and current credit sales collected during current month									
2. From credit sales previous month									
3. From credit sales prior to previous month									
TOTAL RECEIPTS									

NOTE: Data as indicated on this form are reported by months for the full forecast period, each sheet containing data for three consecutive months. Four sheets are required for forecasts covering 12 months while five sheets are required for forecasts covering 13 and 14 months. (From The Cash Budget, Policyholders Service Bureau, Metropolitan Life Insurance Co.)

Fig. 8. Form for forecasting sales and receipts for the cash budget.

seasonal variations upon collections and of the **effect of general business conditions** upon the length of the collection period. One method of estimating collections from sales is to determine the number of days' sales that are outstanding, as follows:

Sales for December, 19X5	$500,000
Accounts receivable, December 31, 19X5	150,000
Per cent of sales outstanding (150,000 ÷ 500,000)	30%
Multiplied by number of days in month	31
Days' sales outstanding	9.3

ESTIMATING COLLECTIONS FROM CUSTOMERS
January, 1966

Accounts receivable, December 31, 19X5		$150,000
Sales for January, 19X6		600,000
Total		$750,000
Deduct:		
Estimated accounts receivable, January 31, 19X6:		
9.3/31 of $600,000	$180,000	
Bad debts (estimated)	25,000	205,000
Probable collections, before discounts		$545,000
Less probable cash discounts 1%		5,450
Estimated cash collections		$539,550

When accounts receivable remain **overdue** for a long period, the possibility of their becoming uncollectible increases. It is advisable, therefore, to estimate separately collections from accounts receivable overdue 1 month, 2 months, or 3 months, and those that are more than 3 months overdue.

Sometimes the days of uncollected sales are computed as a **standard turnover rate** to provide a basis for forecasting, as well as a test of collection policy. But inasmuch as collections may vary with the season of the year, it may be advisable to compute these rates separately by months or seasons. Individual percentage estimates of collections may be made of each month's sales. For example, experience may show that net charge sales made during January will be collected as follows:

January	15%
February	75%
March	7%
Over	1%
Discounts	.75%
Bad debts	1.25%

In estimating collections from sales, particular attention must given to the:

Terms of sale.
Trend of business.
Seasonal influences.
Discount policy.
Credit policy.

Forecasting Disbursements. Anticipated cash disbursements for operating expenses during the period are estimated from budgets of costs and expenses. The **capital budget** indicates amounts to be disbursed during the period for capital additions. If budgeting methods permit, it is preferable to estimate payments to suppliers from the **purchase budget** rather than from budgets of operating expenses. Since a part of the purchases in a given period may go into materials inventories, the operating expense will not show the total amount of purchases for which the company will have to pay during the forecast period. In one method of estimating cash payments that will be due for materials and supplies, total purchases are added to the accounts payable outstanding at the end of the preceding period, and the accounts payable expected to be outstanding at the end of the period are deducted from the sum of these two. **Probable discounts** to be taken should be deducted to show the net cash payments that will have to be made during the forecast period.

In estimating payments for wages and salaries, necessary calendar adjustments should be made. Thus, if the forecast is on a monthly basis and wages are paid weekly, due allowance must be made for months with five weekly payrolls.

Cash Forecasts by Adjusted Earnings Method. The estimated net income for the forecast period is adjusted, under this method, to a cash basis by adding in all transactions that will affect cash but not profit or loss, and eliminating profit and loss transactions that do not affect cash. Depreciation, for example, is added to the estimate of profit, since it does not in itself involve a cash outlay. The excess of collections over sales is added to estimated earnings, since it represents an increment of cash for the period by reducing the investment in accounts receivable. By the same token, an excess of sales over collections is deducted from estimated earnings because it increases the investment in accounts receivable. Expected reductions in inventories are added to estimated earnings, whereas anticipated increases in inventory are deducted therefrom. Fig. 9 illustrates how this is done.

The Predetermined Balance Sheet Method of Forecasting Cash. If a comprehensive budget system is in use, forecasts of balance sheets for future dates are prepared. Some concerns prepare estimated balance sheets for the last day of each month of the forecast period, and thus have projections of each item in the balance sheet except cash. An estimate for cash can then be obtained by simple subtraction. Concerns that have used this method claim it is far easier to apply than the receipts and disbursements method, since forecasted balance sheets are prepared in any event, and that it is at least as accurate.

Here also, as with the adjusted earnings method, future cash receipts and expenditures are not forecast item by item, so that timing of disbursements to receipts for businesses with meager cash balances is not facilitated. Also, if earnings are erratic, revisions in cash forecasts must await the preparation of revised balance sheet forecasts.

Working Capital Differentials Method of Cash Forecasting. Forecasting cash by the working capital differentials method, used in only a few instances, involves **projecting current assets and liabilities** as of future dates, based upon anticipated levels of sales and production. Heckert and Willson (Business Budgeting and Control) state that:

> By this method the net working capital at the beginning of each month is adjusted by estimated net income and other receipts and disbursements to arrive at the estimated working capital at the end of each month. From this are deducted the required working capital, excluding cash, and the standard cash balance, to arrive at the amount of cash available for deposit and investment.

They further indicate that such an approach has been used ". . . when standard valuations required for receivables, inventories, and other working capital at

16·32   CURRENT ASSET PLANNING

Cash Receipts and Disbursements
Quarter ending March 31, 19—

	January	February	March
1. Estimated net profit for quarter	$	$	$
Add:			
Depreciation			
Prepaid insurance and other expense written off			
Excess collections over sales			
Reductions in inventory			
Increase in accounts payable..................			
Sale of investment securities			
Sale of capital assets			
2. Total			
Less:			
Excess sales over collections...................			
Payment of accrued taxes			
Increase in inventories			
Decrease in accounts payable			
Purchase of investment securities			
Payment to sinking fund			
Interest on bonds			
Plant and equipment			
3. Total			
4. Increase or decrease in cash balance			
(line 1 + line 2 − line 3)			
Add cash balance beginning of month			
Add loans from banks			
Cash balance end of month			

Fig. 9. Adjusted earnings method of cash forecasting.

various sales volumes have been determined; and when the major objective is the reinvestment of surplus funds."

CASH FORECASTS AND BORROWING. If a cash deficiency is indicated for the budget period, arrangements for a bank loan or other credit accommodation should be made without delay. Credit-granting institutions ordinarily are more amenable if accommodation is sought in advance of needs, especially if the application for credit is accompanied by a copy of a cash forecast showing the sum required and the probable date of repayment.

UTILIZING CASH MORE EFFICIENTLY. The cash budget provides the basis for developing a program of utilizing cash more efficiently. By being able to operate with less cash, a company not only reduces its dependence upon outside financing but also permits each dollar to earn more profit. In citing the **benefits** of its program of cash planning and control, one large company pointed to an increase in cash turnover from 28.8 times in 1958 to 52.7 times in 1962 that, in turn, resulted in a reduction in average cash requirements and borrowings of $8.3 million and an interest savings of $500,000 over the year. This gain, it indicated, represented ". . . a major contribution to profits." (Reed, Corporate Cash Management, Vol. XXXI.)

Three Major Areas. A program of more effective cash utilization covers three major areas: (1) accelerating the rate of cash inflow, (2) controlling the rate of cash outflow, and (3) curtailing the amount of cash balances at banks. Companies employ special techniques in each of these areas.

Possibilities for **speeding cash inflows** start at the moment an order is received. The order written by the salesman may be integrated more effectively into the accounting system and may be transmitted more promptly through use of leased teletype wires. Billings may be handled more efficiently and credit and collection methods improved. In recent years, attention has been given to reducing the time between the forwarding of a check by a customer and its conversion into available cash to the company. For this purpose, national firms have made use of **lock-box** techniques under which customers forward payments to lock boxes at post-office stations strategically located throughout the country where local banks pick up the checks, deposit them to the firm's account, and process them for collection.

To **control the rate of cash outflow,** careful planning of disbursements is necessary. For this purpose, control over cash payments may be centralized and cash transferred by wire to local offices for disbursement shortly before actual requirements. Cash movements, both receipts and disbursements, are guided through a carefully integrated network of banks covering local institutions that service branches or divisions, other institutions located at focal geographic spots to which surplus funds may be directed, and one or several control institutions to head up the entire system located in the home-office city of the corporation.

Reduction of bank balances may be brought about through careful analyses of the size and purpose of these balances. Effective planning may reveal that requirements could be met with less cash on hand. Another factor to consider is the amount of balances necessary to compensate banks for the services they render. To determine fair balances, a number of companies periodically analyze their accounts from the point of view of ascertaining the amounts that would provide each bank with a suitable profit based upon indicated item costs and earnings rates.

In a study of the cash-management practices of 42 companies, the N.A.A. found that with only few exceptions such management was done centrally. Whereas the small companies also centralized most cash handling functions, the large companies often decentralized some of these functions, such as disbursing local operating expenses and receiving payments from customers in the area. (N.A.A. Research Report No. 38.)

SECTION 17

CAPITAL ASSET PLANNING

CONTENTS

Nature of Fixed Capital

	PAGE
Fixed capital assets	1
Nature of capital assets	1
Economic nature of fixed capital	2
Components of fixed capital	2
Fixed capital assets in relation to total assets	2
Comparison of investment in net fixed assets to total assets for ten leading industrial companies (f. 1)	3
Recovery of fixed tangible assets	3
Valuation of fixed tangible assets	4

Planning of Capital Expenditures

Importance of controlling capital expenditures	4
Effect on future operating costs	5
A balanced capital investment	5
Purchase of additional equipment	6
Relevant costs in replacement decisions	6
Handling surplus capital assets	7
Insurance on fixed capital assets	7
Necessity for long-range planning	8
Use of long-range forecasts	8
Capital expenditures and financial planning	9
Planning expenditures for anticipated growth	9
Timing of capital expenditures	9
Obsolescence of capital assets	9
Fixed asset turnover	10
Effect of changes in rate of turnover	10
Factors offsetting decrease in turnover	11
Planning for the investment tax credit	11

The Capital Budget

Coverage	12
Advantages	12
Preparation	13
Capital expenditures budget (f. 2)	13
Selection of projects to be included	14
Review	14
The Appropriations Committee	15
Appropriation requests	16
Appropriation request for capital expenditure (f. 3)	17
Divisional appropriation request (f. 4)	17
Approval of appropriation requests	18
Blanket appropriations	18
Capital expenditure control	18
Company organization to control expenditures	19
Capital budget and cash planning	20
Form for connecting budgetary authorization to cash distributions (f. 5)	21

	PAGE
Form for projecting capital expenditure requirements (f. 6)	21

Estimating Profitability of Investments

Evaluating alternative projects	22
Relative use of evaluation methods	22
The payback	22
The accounting or average return method	22
The discounted cash-flow method	23

Depreciation in Financial Management

Objectives of depreciation provision	23
Allocation of cost of capital assets	23
Capital asset valuation	24
Replacement of capital assets	24
Capital asset replacement funds	25
Obsolescence of capital assets	25
Maintenance vs. depreciation	25
Effect of depreciation on working capital	26
Effect of inadequate depreciation	26
Depreciation a cost of operation	27
Impact of changing price levels upon depreciation	27
Appreciation and depreciation	28
Methods of calculating depreciation	28
Straight-line method	28
Declining-balance method	29
Sum-of-the-years-digits method	30
Interest method	30
Depreciation based on production	30
Depreciation based on sales or profits	31
Writing off assets on acquisition	31
Financial effects of depreciation policies	31
Depreciation regulation	32
The 1962 guidelines	32
Other aspects of depreciation regulation	33

Depletion of Wasting Assets

The depletion problem	33
Financial significance of depletion	33
Valuation of wasting assets	34
Methods of calculating depletion	35
Percentage depletion	35
Depletion and financial reporting	35

Special Problems of Capital Planning

Capital investments and cash flows	36
Measures for evaluating investment proposals	36
Payback or payout period	36

CONTENTS (Continued)

	PAGE
The accounting or average rate of return method	37
Time-adjusted methods	38
Discounted cash flow	38
Amortization table (f. 7)	38
Uneven cash flows (f. 8)	39
The excess present value method	40
Excess present value calculation (f. 9)	40
Other factors involved in investment decisions	40
Sunk costs and depreciation	40
Disposal value	41
Incremental costs and savings	41
Capital budgeting and taxes	41
Discounted cash flow return solution (f. 10)	42
Unequal lives	43
Excess present value applied to sum-of-the-years-digits method (f. 11)	44
Ranking projects	46

The Cost of Capital

The general concept	47
Profit vs. wealth maximization	48
Other definitions of cost of capital	48
Borrowing and lending rates	48
Applications of the cost of capital	49
Financial structure vs. capital structure	49
Specific costs of capital	50
Classification of capital funds	50
Cost of borrowed funds	50
Costs incurred in sale of securities	51
Cost of bonds	51
Accurate method	52
Before and after-tax cost of debt	53
Cost of preferred stock	53
Cost of common stock	54
Direct sale of common stock to the public	54
Avoidance of dilution	55
Determination of price per share	55
Computation of cost	55

	PAGE
Sale of common stock under pre-emptive rights	56
Indirect sale of common stock through convertible securities	58
Cost of retained earnings	59
Selecting the tax rate	60
Disagreement as to need for tax adjustment	60
Cost of depreciation funds	61
Combined cost of capital	62
Average cost of capital	62
Selected balance sheet and income data for H. E. Corp. (f. 12)	63
Computation of the market value of H. E. Corp. capital structure (f. 13)	63
Computation of average cost	64
Book values vs. market values	64
Computation of average cost of capital for H. E. Corp. (f. 14)	65
Determining the type of capital structure	66
Lease reporting and the cost of capital	66
Actual vs. market yields	67
Common equity and average costs	68
Dividends vs. earnings	68
Variability of composite cost of capital	70
Business valuation and cost of capital	70
An illustration of the effect of varying financing plans on the cost of capital and the market value of the enterprise (f. 15)	71
Cost of capital to an enterprise (f. 16)	72
The U-shaped cost of capital curve	73
Concluding remarks	73
Computation of the cost of capital of the H. E. Corp., with $75,000,000 (at par) of debt securities (f. 17)	74

Risk and Uncertainty

Risk defined	75
Uncertainty defined	75
Application to investment decisions	76
Comparison of two investment opportunities (f. 18)	77

SECTION 17

CAPITAL ASSET PLANNING

Nature of Fixed Capital

FIXED CAPITAL ASSETS. Fixed capital assets consist of relatively permanent assets acquired for use in the conduct of the business, and not intended for disposal in the ordinary course of events. In clarifying this definition, Finney and Miller (Principles of Accounting: Intermediate) point out that a building used as a factory is a fixed asset because it conforms with these requirements. On the other hand, an unused factory building is not considered a fixed asset because it is no longer involved in the operation of the business. Similarly, they indicate, land held as a prospective site for a future plant is not a fixed asset even though it is a permanent property and is not intended for sale, because it is not used in the operations.

The Accountants' Handbook comments as follows on the **balance sheet classification of land**:

Land and realty are ordinarily reflected in the fixed asset section of the balance sheet when such property does not represent the stock in trade of the accounting entity. A current asset classification is justified for firms who regard land and realty as inventory, and for companies who are not primarily engaged in real estate but who expect to sell such property within the next year. If land and realty are held for speculation and it is expected that a sale will not be accomplished before the end of the next fiscal period, classification as an investment is warranted.

Land held for a future plant site should be classified as investments or other assets. The inclusion of this item in fixed assets . . . is not recommended.

Leaseholds generally are classified as **intangible assets** inasmuch as their value lies exclusively in the right of use accruing from the payment of rents and is irrespective of the value represented by the physical properties to which the right attaches.

Nature of Capital Assets. The capital of a business can be classified as (1) fixed capital, and (2) working capital. The character and use of an asset are important in determining its proper classification. A manufacturer of washing machines will properly regard a washing machine as part of his inventory of finished goods that he hopes to dispose of shortly, whereas a laundry carries a washing machine as fixed capital that produces recurring income. Current assets are relatively liquid, and can and normally will be disposed of in the ordinary course of business, whereas fixed capital, such as buildings and furniture, is not readily convertible into cash. Current assets usually have a short life, but fixed capital is usually of considerable permanency. Tangible current capital, such as inventories, enters into the productive process to emerge in an entirely new form consisting of the finished products of the company. The entire cost of the raw material is at that time an element of cost of production. Fixed capital, on the other hand, is used in the production of finished goods, or in the furnishing of services throughout its useful life, and enters into costs of manufacturing by means of a periodic allocation of its cost by depreciation.

Economic Nature of Fixed Capital. Mill (Principles of Political Economy) has given a lucid explanation of the economic nature of fixed capital:

Another large portion of capital, however, consists in instruments of production, of a more or less permanent character; which produce their effect not by being parted with, but by being kept, and the efficacy of which is not exhausted by a single use. To this class belong buildings, machinery, and all or most things known by the name of implements or tools. The durability of some of these is considerable, and their function as productive instruments is prolonged through many repetitions of the productive operation. In this class must likewise be included capital sunk (as the expression is) in permanent improvements of land. So, also, the capital expended once and for all, in the commencement of an undertaking, to prepare the way for subsequent operations: the expense of opening a mine, for example; of cutting canals; of making roads or docks. Other examples might be added, but these are sufficient. Capital which exists in any of these durable shapes, and the return of which is spread over a period of corresponding duration, is called Fixed Capital.

Components of Fixed Capital. The main elements of fixed capital are:

1. Tangible fixed assets
   a. Plant and equipment.
   b. Land.
   c. Natural resources, such as mining properties, timber lands, and oil fields.
2. Intangible fixed assets.
3. Fixed security investments.

Physical property used in manufacturing, merchandising, or in furnishing services is known as **tangible fixed assets**. Most tangible fixed assets, such as plant and equipment, furniture, trucks, etc., are subject to depreciation, but land is not subject to depreciation. Natural resources are subject to depletion as ore or oil is extracted, or timber is cut.

Intangible fixed assets include goodwill, trademarks, patents, copyrights, franchises, and so on. Some intangible fixed assets, such as patents, are subject to amortization.

Permanent **investments** in allied or subsidiary companies may be regarded as part of the fixed capital of a company. Such investments are frequently made in lieu of outright purchase of tangible or intangible assets and include:

1. Stocks and bonds of allied or subsidiary companies.
2. Long-term advances to subsidiaries.

In addition, a company may set up funds or earmark security investments for the following purposes:

1. Funds for expansion or replacement of facilities.
2. Funds for redemption of bonds or stock.
3. Funds for employees' pensions.
4. Funds for self-insurance.
5. Funds for specified contingencies.

These funds are in effect part of the fixed capital of the business.

FIXED CAPITAL ASSETS IN RELATION TO TOTAL ASSETS. The necessity for careful management of fixed capital assets is evidenced by the large proportion of total assets they constitute in numerous enterprises. Figure 1, for example, shows the relationship between net fixed assets and total assets for

NATURE OF FIXED CAPITAL

the top ten companies representing different fields of activity in Fortune's list of the 500 largest United States industrial corporations ranked by sales. In four cases, the ratio was 50% or over; in three instances, it fell between 40% and 45%; and in another three instances it ranged between 29% and 35%.

Name of Company	Industry	Percentage Net Fixed Assets to Total Assets *
United States Steel Corporation	Steel	63
Standard Oil Company (New Jersey)	Petroleum	60
International Business Machines Corporation	Computers and Office Equipment	59
E. I. du Pont de Nemours & Company	Chemicals	52
Swift & Company	Meat Packing	45
National Dairy Products Corporation	Dairy	44
General Motors Corporation	Automotive	41
General Electric Company	Electrical Equipment	35
International Harvester Company	Agricultural Equipment and Trucks	34
General Dynamics Corporation	Aircraft and Submarines	29

* Data based upon 1962 annual statements. To determine net fixed assets some arbitrary allocations were made, but in no instance was the amount involved very significant relative to the total net fixed assets. Du Pont's investment in General Motors was excluded from its statement. IBM includes its rental machines under the category Factories, Office Building, and Other Property.

Fig. 1. Comparison of investment in net fixed assets to total assets for ten leading industrial companies.

This **variation in the ratio** is to be expected because of the wide differences in the fields of activity covered and the varying dependence of the corporations on fixed assets. In discussing this subject as it pertains to plant property, the Accountants' Handbook states:

Almost all business firms make use of buildings and equipment, but in some cases the portion of the total capital of the enterprise so invested is much greater than in others. In a recent year all corporations filing balance sheets with their federal income tax returns had buildings and equipment amounting to 23% of their total assets. Insurance companies had less than 1% of their funds invested in these assets; for electric and gas utilities, 79% was so invested. For manufacturing corporations depreciable fixed assets made up 31% of the total, with a low of 7% in tobacco manufacturing and a high of 44% in petroleum and coal processing.

RECOVERY OF FIXED TANGIBLE ASSETS. The term "Fixed Tangible Assets" is, in some respects, a misnomer, in that it reinforces the erroneous impression that these assets are a "fixed" or "permanent" investment in the company. Actually, expenditures on such assets are a deferred cost of doing business. If fixed tangible assets (excluding land) have an estimated life of 10 years, then the cost of these assets is spread over a 10-year period through the medium of depreciation or depletion allowances. Recovery of expenditures on capital assets is effected either through an **increase in profitable sales** or a **decrease in costs of operation**. If profit or loss on operations were calculated over a 10-year period, instead of annually, expenditures on capital assets would be treated like any other cost of operation.

The essential nature of fixed tangible assets as an item of cost is not changed by the fact that this cost is spread over a period of years. The **value** of fixed tangible assets as listed on a balance sheet (cost of capital assets less accumulated depreciation) is really that portion of their cost that has not yet been allocated to costs of operation. The **cost** of fixed tangible assets allocated to production costs, through depreciation allowances or otherwise, should be recovered in the sales price of the product.

VALUATION OF FIXED TANGIBLE ASSETS. Fixed tangible assets are normally valued for balance sheet purposes at historical cost less depreciation or depletion. This is in sharp contrast to the practice used in valuing current assets, which are almost invariably valued on a current or liquidating basis. For instance, accounts receivable are brought to a current value basis by providing an estimate of expected uncollectibles, and inventories and temporary investments are most often valued at the lower of cost or market. Thus, the **viewpoint of the banker or short-term creditor** dominates the valuation of current assets. The banker or short-term creditor is interested in the liquid position of the company and its ability to repay short-term obligations. Inasmuch as fixed capital properly should be financed on a long-term basis, an investor or lender does not normally look to the liquidating value of the fixed assets for return of his investment or loan, but rather to the anticipated earnings of the company through the judicious use of its fixed capital.

Planning of Capital Expenditures

IMPORTANCE OF CONTROLLING CAPITAL EXPENDITURES. Financial control over capital expenditures is basic to the proper administration of a business. Effects of decisions regarding capital expenditures are permanent, far-reaching, and frequently the determining factor in the success or failure of an enterprise. Once acquired, capital assets cannot be disposed of except at a substantial loss. If purchased on a **long-term credit** basis, a substantial down payment usually is required, and a continuing liability is incurred for the balance, payable over a long period of time. The issuance of long-term bonds to finance the acquisition of capital assets mortgages the future earnings of the company. If increased earnings do not result from the purchase of the additional capital assets, the ability of the company to discharge its financial obligations may be impaired, with disastrous results. Expansion of capital facilities by means of the sale of stock dilutes ownership of the company, and if not carefully planned and controlled it may result in the loss of voting control by management or in the inability of the company to earn an adequate return upon its invested capital.

The basic principles involved in managing and controlling fixed capital apply to every business, regardless of size or industry. **In a small business,** investment in fixed capital is usually by the owner or manager, who personally supervises all activities of the business. He can control the relative investment in fixed assets and in current assets. **In a large organization** no one man can personally oversee the activities of the entire enterprise. Management must rely upon carefully devised procedures, standards, and the recommendations of individuals and committees to whom authority has been delegated. As a business increases in size, procedures for the control of capital expenditures must be tightened. These procedures and techniques must be adapted to the particular company and industry, although the basic principles remain generally applicable.

EFFECT ON FUTURE OPERATING COSTS. The amount and the wisdom of the initial expenditure on capital assets may have an important effect upon future operating costs. For example, geographical location of plants with relation to markets and sources of raw materials may result in a difference in operating costs of several hundred thousand dollars a year, but the difference in cost of land and buildings at one location as compared with another may be a relatively small sum. The construction of a general purpose factory building may make it more adaptable to new uses the company may have for it later, and the structure will have a higher resale value should disposal of the plant become necessary later. On the other hand, although a special purpose plant may cost considerably more initially and be less salable, it can result in substantial operating economies. The **balancing of initial expenditures against estimated savings** in future operating costs requires careful analysis of both the engineering and financial aspects of the company's operations. For instance, the use of structural steel and reinforced concrete will invariably be more costly than mere brick and timber, but future operating costs may be so much lower in consequence that the added outlay may be well worthwhile. Similarly, wider aisle widths require a higher initial construction outlay, but may result in the more economical use of available floor space, greater flexibility in coping with future changes in production layout, and lower costs in handling materials, parts, or finished products. To produce a maximum return upon the investment involved, the design of a plant should include features that yield substantial savings at reasonable cost, with due regard to the advantages of flexibility as regards future uses of the structure.

Even with respect to physical structure, the least expensive plant in the long run may not be the most desirable. In this connection, Voris (The Management of Production) states:

> The principal objective of factory planning is **to provide physical facilities at a minimum cost consistent with economical operation.** While factory planners strive to construct the most inexpensive factory buildings, they also wish to provide minimum fire insurance rates and heating bills, maximum safety for their employees, and ideal lighting and ventilation. Thus, the cheapest structure may not necessarily provide minimum costs.

A BALANCED CAPITAL INVESTMENT. A careful balancing of facilities at each stage of the productive process is necessary to avoid higher operating costs and delays caused by facility "bottlenecks" and the freezing of capital in idle equipment and partially completed inventories. A lack of balance among productive facilities also burdens the profit and loss account with added depreciation allowances, insurance, and other costs.

Productive facilities at each stage of operations should be sufficient, after providing for anticipated breakdowns and other interruptions in operations, to turn out enough units of product to avoid idle time in succeeding operating departments because of failure to receive adequate work in process. But it is uneconomical for productive facilities in Department A, for example, to have a capacity in excess of that which can be handled by Department B, which processes materials received from Department A, for this creates excessive inventories of partially completed units and unnecessarily increases fixed capital investment.

A balanced capital investment results from **relating capital assets to anticipated production volume** based upon a careful analysis of sales demands. The productive output of each department and process must be dovetailed into the requirements of the next process or operation. In providing capital equipment at each stage of the productive process, due allowance should be made for breakdowns, retooling, and other ordinary and anticipated stoppages in production.

The National Industrial Conference Board (Studies in Business Policy, No. 62), points out that

... to maintain balance in the company's operations, most company managements study each new proposal in relation to the company's over-all operations. For example, as pointed out by one producer: "Each operation in our plant must be held in balance with another so that a similar volume of production can be maintained at each stage."

On an overall basis, the development of such thinking should lead to a statement showing the number of machines, supporting facilities, and floor space, with an evaluation of the costs thereof, and should indicate to management the capital required to attain a balanced investment as related to the volume of business required to warrant the expenditure.

PURCHASE OF ADDITIONAL EQUIPMENT. In order to evaluate the advisability of purchasing additional capital equipment, the reasons for making the expenditures must be carefully analyzed. Dean (Capital Budgeting) has developed a useful classification of investments that may be summarized as follows:

(A) Replacement investments
    (1) like-for-like replacements
    (2) obsolescence replacements
(B) Expansion investments
(C) Product-line investments
    (1) on new products
    (2) on improving old products
(D) Strategic investments

Replacement investments are intended principally to reduce costs. In the case of like-for-like replacements, the reduction comes about because of the influence of equipment age on costs, whereas in the case of obsolescence replacement the reduction is effected through technological improvements. **Expansion** investments are directed toward increasing capacity rather than toward changing the operating process. With respect to **product-line** investments, expenditures may be for purposes of developing new items or for improving those already being produced. Proposals for **strategic** investment are more likely to involve basic policy and therefore to require the approval of top-level management.

Relevant Costs in Replacement Decisions. Cost savings are the underlying basis of replacement decisions, but the relevant costs pertain to the future. Those that already have been made are sunk and irrelevant to the replacement decision. The importance of differentiating between **sunk** and **future costs** is stressed in the literature on the subject. For example, Smith (N.A.A. Bulletin, Vol. 39) makes the following comments:

The particular difficulties connected with the analysis of future costs in replacement decisions involve the determination of the future capital wastage costs. For existing equipment, this involves the future decline in disposal value. The original cost of the old facility is sunk, irrecoverable, and totally irrelevant. The depreciation charges shown on the books are similarly independent of the company's real future costs. These bookkeeping values, though useful for income measurement, have no significance for the replacement decision. The capital wastage cost for the new machine over its lifetime is its prospective acquisition cost, less ultimate resale value. Since the investment commitment has not yet been made this total decline in value is relevant for the decision.

In weighing the financial desirability of replacing capital assets, consideration should be given to the number of years for which the estimated savings will be realized, as well as the time required to pay out the additional investment. A troublesome factor in any such calculation is **estimating the probable life of new equipment,** as obsolescence could start a vicious circle in which successive replacements would make necessary the writing off of undepreciated balances. Some concerns have adopted a rule of thumb that direct savings must be sufficient to pay out the investment in 3, 4, or 5 years. Such a rule of thumb should be based on the company's previous experience with capital asset replacement.

HANDLING SURPLUS CAPITAL ASSETS. Unused capital assets not only represent an unprofitable investment of the capital of a company, but increase costs of operation because of the necessity for insurance, additional storage space, watchmen's salaries, etc. One large company [see Factory Management and Maintenance (now Factory), Vol. 104] installed a system of centralized control over the movement and disposition of all surplus, idle, and obsolete machinery and equipment of its more than 25 manufacturing plants, and reported many benefits such as

1. Saving in capital expenditures through the transfer of unused equipment from one plant to another instead of purchase of similar new equipment.
2. Provision of spare equipment or parts for breakdowns or emergencies.
3. Utilization of inactive equipment for experimentation in new processes or improvement of existing processes.
4. Reduction of idle equipment to a small proportion of investment and prevention of undue accumulation of obsolete equipment.
5. Higher salvage returns.

Basically, this plan involved taking a physical inventory of all machinery. Inactive machinery or equipment was reported by the local plant to the central office and classified as follows:

Class 1 (inactive usable).—Machine is still of possible value to the local plant which has reported it, and is to be kept there for further possible use. Light machinery might be moved inexpensively to storage space, but heavy machinery is left undisturbed to avoid unnecessary handling costs.

Class 2 (inactive unusable).—Machine is of no further value to the local plant, but has a possible value for transfer to allied plants or for sale in the used machinery market. It is moved to storage space, or left in place if removal is difficult, until its final disposition is determined.

Class 3 (scrap).—Machine is unusable and has no resale value. The local plant's salvage department is instructed to remove all good usable parts, and the remainder of the machine is broken up for consignment to the junk pile. Junk is disposed of when economical lots become available.

INSURANCE ON FIXED CAPITAL ASSETS. Consideration should be given to insuring fixed assets against loss resulting from fire, sprinkler damage, explosion, or other hazards (see Sec. 25, Risk Management and Insurance). The adequacy of insurance coverage should be re-examined at regular intervals. A fire may destroy more than the physical assets of a company; the loss of productive facilities may result in inability to supply customers' demands and thus permit competitors to usurp a company's market while plant and equipment are being restored. In some instances, such loss is irreparable.

NECESSITY FOR LONG-RANGE PLANNING. Planning for capital expenditures must be considered from a long-range point of view for the following reasons:

1. Capital expansion and replacement of facilities must be adapted to anticipated sales requirements.
2. Each year's expansion should be fitted into an orderly plan of growth, whenever possible.
3. The profitability of capital expenditures should be tested from a long-term point of view.
4. Construction contracts, plant sites, franchises, water power rights, and so on usually must be contracted for in advance.
5. Capital expenditures must be integrated into the cash planning of the company so that funds may be provided when needed either from internal or external sources.
6. Wherever possible, it is more economical to make large capital expenditures during depression periods, so as to take advantage of low prices and to have full facilities available during the subsequent period of increased business activity.

Use of Long-Range Forecasts. The National Association of Accountants conducted a study of long-range forecasting (N.A.A. Bulletin, Vol. 40). In reporting its findings, the N.A.A. pointed to the need for capital budgets incorporating future programs because of the complexity of modern machinery and the long period required for any substantial construction. In order to insure that facilities will be available when needed, future requirements must be anticipated. Although the study disclosed frequent references to 2-year budgets and 5-year forecasts were quite common, there were also instances of 10- and 20-year surveys. One company described its procedures as follows:

Our program is projected over a period of five years and is based upon a thorough survey of industry trends, processes and methods, new equipment, sales forecasts, production capacities and profit forecasts. This program is divided into two parts: the period covering the next fiscal year and the period covering the succeeding four years. The program is prepared three months prior to the next fiscal year, at which time the next fiscal year is carefully reviewed and broken down into quarters and another year in the future is projected. Revisions in any period or year may be made at this time to reflect changes in trends or methods.

Any substantial capital expenditures will inevitably be reflected in a company's operations, with the change, initially at least, most apparent in either sales or costs, depending upon the nature of the expenditure. Accordingly, even if the capital budget is planned over a long-term period, it should be **integrated with the operating budgets.** This interrelationship, as well as the length of the period covered by the forecast of expenditures, was noted by Matthews, following an intensive study of the capital expenditure policies and procedures of a dozen firms (Harvard Business Review, Vol. 37):

Half of the firms I studied make rough estimates of expenditure needs for periods as long as three years, and, as might be expected, the large firms are the ones most involved in long-range planning. Most of these have instituted long-range planning operations only during the last several years. Five years is the normal planning period, and plans typically integrate sales and cost projections, operating needs, and capital equipment needs. Equipment plans are, understandably, very general (and in no sense firm) beyond a one-year budget.

Matthews mentions as "the most ambitious plan," one covering a 20-year period, undertaken by a large, integrated, multidivisional firm.

CAPITAL EXPENDITURES AND FINANCIAL PLANNING. Capital expenditures cannot be viewed from a narrow or short-term point of view, but must be integrated into the financial and business programs of the company. The economic justification for a capital expenditures program must be based upon a long-term estimate of profits, which in turn requires projection of sales and costs of operation for a period of years.

Capital expenditures may affect operating costs over a long period of time. **Results of unwise planning** of capital expenditures are felt in subsequent years through increased depreciation, insurance, property taxes, handling costs, etc. Unless a capital expenditure is recognized as a total mistake, and therefore written off against surplus in a single year, its effect on earnings is registered year after year. Frequently, higher costs of operation may not be recognized as a result of poor planning for capital expenditures during a previous period, but may be erroneously ascribed to other causes.

PLANNING EXPENDITURES FOR ANTICIPATED GROWTH. Long-range planning must be related to the current activities and progress of a company. In effect, the company develops a series of short-term guidelines that eventually merge into its longer-term objectives. This **interaction between short- and long-term goals** is indispensable in order to provide for orderly growth and eventual profit maximization. In discussing this aspect of planning, James (N.A.A. Bulletin, Vol. 43) states:

> Long-range capital planning is an absolute necessity for any company that is to grow successfully. . . .
>
> Accomplishment of that purpose requires the establishment of objectives and the design and use of a master plan for long-range growth purposes—the road-map required for progress. It is the required guidepost to permit management to compare the future projections of the company with the current progress being made. For growth to become a reality, management must initiate action on a time schedule which will direct capital into the projects that raise the over-all return on investments. . . .

Timing of Capital Expenditures. Whenever possible, capital expenditures should be **made during periods of depression** so as to take advantage of low prices of material and the greater availability of labor. Capital additions during the valley of a business cycle will be available to meet the sales requirements of the succeeding period of prosperity, whereas construction undertaken at the peak of prosperity may not be completed until the subsequent period of depression. Unavailability of funds for capital expansion and rehabilitation during a depression may, of course, require variation in this procedure. Long-range planning of capital construction is thus necessary for the proper timing of capital outlays with relation to the business cycle, so that funds will be on hand when they can be used to best advantage.

Capital expenditures invariably result in an **increase in fixed expenses** that can be taken care of easily during a period of profitable sales, but that may prove burdensome during a business recession. By long-range planning of capital expenditures, their impact upon depreciation and other fixed expenses is known in advance, and allowance can be made for them in projecting operating results.

OBSOLESCENCE OF CAPITAL ASSETS. In long-term planning for replacement of capital assets, a distinction should be made between replacements resulting from normal wear and tear plus foreseeable obsolescence, and those arising from **extraordinary** obsolescence. The former can be estimated with reasonable accuracy over a period of time, whereas the latter are in many instances unpredictable. Extraordinary obsolescence of capital assets frequently is far more important than either normal obsolescence or depreciation in affecting fixed capital requirements of a business. As stated by Dean (Capital Budgeting):

> Guessing the probable economic life of the equipment whose adoption is at issue is one of the most difficult problems of measuring capital productivity. In a sense, obsolescence estimates enter at two levels. First, the test of whether or not the old model should be superseded by the new equipment is in essence a test of whether the old is now obsolete. But to apply this test, the time at which the new equipment will in turn become obsolete must be projected. Only in this way is it possible to determine the economic life of the new and thus compare its average lifetime cost with the marginal cost of keeping the old. Thus, a second level of obsolescence estimates enters, which involves expectations about the unknown new technological developments that may shorten the economic life expectancy of the new equipment. Sometimes this estimate of the life span of the new equipment is easy, as in the new-model investments of automobile companies where the lifetime is clearly no greater than that of the product model. But usually this mortality prediction is quite difficult and necessarily conjectural.

FIXED ASSET TURNOVER. The turnover on fixed property investment represents the relationship between the volume of business and the amount of capital tied up in fixed property. This ratio may be **figured in either of two ways**:

1. As the dollars of sales per year for each dollar of fixed property investment.
2. As the physical units of volume per year (pounds, barrels, cases, etc.) for each dollar of fixed property investment.

Of these methods the latter is the sounder, since it is based on fixed measures that are unaffected by changing price levels.

Computing the turnover **on the basis of money sales** and fixed property investment may be satisfactory in normal times when prices are steady. But prices for products may fluctuate so greatly that changes in this turnover might be misleading unless changing price levels are recognized. If no measure of physical volume is available, it may be approximated by adjusting the sales figures sufficiently to eliminate the effect of changing price levels. This may be done by use of a **price index**. Published price indexes may be used when they are fairly representative of the trend of values of the particular products in question. Oftentimes, an individual price index may be readily prepared on the basis of representative items of products handled.

The value of this ratio also depends upon the basis of fixed asset valuations in the balance sheet. Obviously, these will largely influence the ratio, and affect validity of comparisons.

EFFECT OF CHANGES IN RATE OF TURNOVER. All proposals to increase fixed property investments should take into consideration the effect on this turnover. Additional property investments should be justified by a similar relative and permanent increase in volume of business, in order to protect the turnover. To expand properties on the basis of a temporary increase in the volume of business, or an increase resulting from inflated prices, would not be conservative. The trend of this turnover is an indicator of the trend of **unit fixed property expenses on the volume of business done.**

When a business makes expenditures for added fixed assets, an added burden of expenses in the form of insurance, taxes, and depreciation is incurred, as well as an added financial burden in the form of interest or dividends that should be earned on the increased capital invested. These **fixed expenses** bear a constant relation to the amount of fixed property. Unless an increased volume of production with corresponding increase in income is realized from the added fixed investment or a definite saving is effected in the cost of production, the added expenses become a heavy handicap on the company's finances. As the turnover on fixed property improves, the unit expense decreases; and as the turnover decreases, the unit expense increases.

The results of an increased turnover on fixed property are reflected in the following illustration:

Assume annual volume of business of	$300,000
Fixed property investment of	100,000
Indicating a turnover of	3 times
Fixed property expenses—interest, depreciation, taxes, etc.	20,000
Which figures on sales	6.7%
Assume that by increasing the fixed assets by $25,000 the volume of business could be increased to	$400,000
On the fixed property investment of	$125,000
The turnover would be	3.2 times
Fixed property expenses	$ 25,000
Which figures on sales	6.25%

The percentage of upkeep and carrying charges decreases from 6.7% to 6.25% of sales as a result of the higher turnover. Incidental economies are also likely to result because of the larger percentage increase in volume of production than in investment.

Factors Offsetting Decrease in Turnover. A decrease in the rate of fixed capital turnover may be caused by the addition of labor-saving machinery. Often the savings in labor cost will more than offset the increase in carrying charges of the added fixed investment. Care must therefore be exercised in making deductions from changes in the rate of fixed capital turnover. Unless it is known to what extent the additions to plant have been made to increase output, and to what extent they have been used simply to reduce the labor requirements, the ratio will not possess its full significance.

PLANNING FOR THE INVESTMENT TAX CREDIT. In order to encourage modernization and expansion of the nation's productive facilities, the **Revenue Act of 1962** provided an investment tax credit based upon the useful life of a qualifying piece of property. The maximum credit is 7% for general business and 3% for certain public utilities. A **limit** is placed upon the amount of credit that may be taken in any one year but provision is made for carrying back and forward any unused credit. The law created the need for a number of decisions, such as when the credit should be reflected in income, the advisability of revising depreciation policies in light of the credit restrictions, and the timing of capital expenditures to maximize the benefits that may be obtained. The nature of the planning required has been summarized as follows by Baker (N.A.A. Bulletin, Vol. 44):

It would be well to bring to mind in review a few of the more important aspects of the investment credit, mainly those of a tax planning nature. Taxpayers should review their depreciation practices and replacement policies in view of the applicable percentages of the credit, as the percentage which may be taken depends on the useful life of the property. It should be remembered that a little increase in the useful life of an asset can mean immediate savings of dollars. Timing of purchases should be planned in order to take full advantage of the credit. The carry-forward and carry-back provisions should not be forgotten in tax planning, and the fact that no carry-back is available prior to January 1, 1962. Lastly, if a taxpayer is going to put up a fence he should get some cattle, so that it will qualify for the credit.

According to the 1962 Act, a company taking the 7% credit could depreciate only 93% of the cost of its machinery outlays. This requirement was eliminated in the **Revenue Act of 1964,** which provided that the basis of the property no longer had to be reduced by the amount of the investment credit.

The Capital Budget

COVERAGE. The capital budget covers all proposed outlays for a specified period for:

1. Additions and extensions to plant and equipment.
2. New plant and equipment.
3. Replacement of whole units (the salvage value of old items being deducted from the cost).
4. Cost of land upon which a plant is to be constructed.
5. Furniture, fixtures, and office equipment.

On the other hand, the following items are **current costs of operation,** and should be included in the operating rather than the capital budget:

1. Maintenance and repairs.
2. Small tools.
3. Repair parts.
4. Depreciation of fixed assets.

Some companies include **estimated requirements for maintenance and repairs** in the capital budget. If this is done, separate totals are shown for the amount regarded as capital outlay and the amount that will be considered current operating expense. The latter portion is then transferred to the operating budget for each period involved. The capital budget is known variously as the Construction Budget, Plant and Equipment Budget, Factory Expansion Budget, Plant Additions Budget, Facilities Budget, Capital Outlay Budget, Budget of Capital Expenditures, or other significant designating titles.

ADVANTAGES. Control of capital facilities is difficult without a capital budget. For one thing, preplanning of a company's financial position is impeded, inasmuch as probable capital requirements have not been calculated but each such project is taken up individually as the need presents itself. Since **simultaneous consideration of all capital outlays** proposed is not provided, projects are not selected in the order of essentiality or desirability. Moreover, when integrated planning of expenditures is lacking, **coordination among the different units of a company** is difficult and they may even act at cross-purposes. For example, Matthews (Harvard Business Review, Vol. 37) cites a case of one division basing its expenditure program on the premise that total company sales would grow, while a different division assumed that sales would shrink.

Despite the advantages, many companies do not prepare a capital budget but review each request for capital expenditures individually on its merits. Justification in the form of an engineering analysis usually accompanies the request for authorization to make the purchase or to commit the company. In commenting on the failure, in some instances, of managements to use plans in making capital expenditures, Matthews notes that "Some believe that the uncertainty of the future makes it unwise, if not impossible, to plan even generally in advance. Others are afraid of overcentralization and usurpation by staff planners of responsibilities that should rest on the shoulders of operating executives."

PREPARATION. A request is usually issued by the head office to the operating units of an enterprise for proposals for the capital expenditures budget. Frequently these requests are issued at the same time as are requests for the operating budgets. Figure 2 shows the capital budget form used by one large company.

Company			Date		
\multicolumn{3}{c	}{Capital Projects}	\multicolumn{2}{c	}{Expenditures}	Anticipated Date of New Expenditures
Item Number	For	Amount	Actual to Date	Balance	

Fig. 2. Capital expenditures budget.

Instructions on the reverse of this form are as follows:

List on this form all projects or acquisitions of a capital nature now under construction or for which commitments have been made, and give the anticipated date of completion or fulfillment. Group items by fiscal year periods for the next five years and state the total for each year. If approved appropriations do not already exist, please prepare and submit "Appropriation for Capital Expenditure" forms to cover items in the following categories listed hereon:
    (a) Projects now under way on which further payments are to be made.
    (b) Projects not under way but on which commitments have been made.
    (c) Projects on which no commitments have been made but for which a definite appropriation is desired.
Budgeted expenditures should include only major capital items involved in expansion and improvement plans. Minor capital expenditures necessary for normal operating needs are charged against the blanket appropriation and need not, therefore, be listed and covered by individual appropriations. A blanket appropriation should be included for each fiscal year. "Appropriation for Capital Expenditure" forms are to be prepared at the time commitments are to be made, and no commitment is to be made until approval is granted.

The capital budget is made up of **plant and equipment budgets** of the several departments of the business. General managers of each operating unit or department submit requests for authority to make such outlays as they consider necessary or desirable. These requests are forwarded to the budget director, the controller, or an assistant to the president, according to the organizational setup of the company. The **budget director** or other official entrusted with responsibility for assembling the departmental capital budgets consolidates the requests and reviews them prior to presentation to higher authority, which may be the president, the executive vice-president, or the appropriations committee, who in turn presents the capital budget to the board of directors for final approval.

The capital budget is usually approved by the board of directors only as to the total dollar amount involved. **Individual projects** must be approved by an authorized official or committee after study of the particular project.

Selection of Projects To Be Included. Experience has shown that many projects are recommended for inclusion in the capital budget that, although praiseworthy in themselves, may not be necessary for the enterprise or likely to produce additional earnings commensurate with the capital involved. Frequently department heads place requests for new equipment merely because of a normal human desire to have the finest and most modern equipment available. In many instances, in an effort to anticipate future requirements, requests are made for equipment based upon relatively remote needs. To keep annual fixed capital outlays within reasonable limits, capital budget control procedures must see that more desirable projects get the right of way over others.

Capital expenditures may be essential to the **maintenance of the concern's competitive position.** In such instances, a company has little choice but to include these projects in the capital budget. Replacements of essential capital assets as a result of normal wear and tear or obsolescence also are unavoidable. However, **timing** of such expenditures frequently can be advanced or delayed, depending upon the company's financial position.

Many expenditures find their justification in the increased earnings that will result. Suggested projects of this kind should be listed in the order of their profitability, with due consideration to the effect of postponement or cancellation upon other phases of the company's business. More desirable proposals can then be launched first.

It is good practice to require operating departments to submit proposals for inclusion in the capital budget under the following categories:

1. Essential.
2. Profitable.
3. Desirable.
4. Replacements resulting from normal wear and tear or normal obsolescence.
5. Replacements resulting from extraordinary obsolescence.

Explanations should also be required as to why a particular project is classified under one or another of these headings. Projects classified as profitable, for example, should be supported by computations showing the time within which the investment can be recovered from the net cash receipts, an estimate of the reductions in costs to be expected, and some indication of the expected rate of return. As an example, the budget manual of one large company states:

By November 1st each Divisional Executive will develop within his division and submit to the Appropriations Committee an itemized estimate of all such expenditures for which justifiable need is definitely anticipated during the following year, giving substantiating earnings, payout, or other reasons in each case. Individual projects should be divided into four classifications:
    (a) Essential to satisfactory operations.
    (b) Desirable on an earnings basis (estimated payout .... years).
    (c) Desirable from the standpoint of logical expansion and development, but not urgent.
    (d) Replacement of necessary assets.

REVIEW. The budget manual of one company defines the responsibility of the several authorities reviewing the capital budget as follows:

The **appropriations committee,** consulting if necessary with the divisional executive concerned, will critically review divisional estimates as to urgency, desirability, profitability, cheaper alternatives, and will then consolidate and submit the estimates to the executive committee with its recommendations.

The executive committee will review the consolidated estimate from an overall viewpoint, satisfying itself as to necessity, profitability, justification and urgency of each project, considering the desirability of deferring some projects so that they may be used as fill-in jobs during slack periods to help stabilize employment and so lessen the shock of depression, taking into account proper coordination of divisions, and submitting a final budget estimate with recommendations to the board of directors by ....

The board of directors will consider the proposed budget from the standpoint of overall policy, taking into account the availability and judicious allocation of funds, general business, economic and financial conditions and sales projects, and will finally pass upon the budget in principle.

Some companies appoint a **Facilities Committee** to review the capital budgets of their several divisions. The facilities committee is frequently composed of a chief engineer, the budget director, the purchasing officer, and representatives of the major operating divisions.

The Appropriations Committee. The departmental estimates are often submitted to this committee for review and classification of projects as to urgency and desirability from the overall viewpoint of the company. In this way the final capital budget as submitted to the board of directors or the president represents the considered view of ranking officials who can integrate proposed capital expenditures with the business and financial plans of the company. When individual appropriation requests are then submitted to this committee, a careful analysis can be made of each project in the light of the following:

1. Resulting reduction in cost of operation.
2. Relation to requirements of the sales budget.
3. Improvement in quality and variety of the company's products.
4. Prevailing economic and financial conditions.
5. Funds available for capital investment.
6. Effects upon future earnings.
7. Extraordinary obsolescence of productive facilities.
8. Payout period of the capital expenditure.
9. Relative profitability.

The appropriations committee is usually assigned **limits of authority** within which it can approve smaller appropriation requests included in the approved budget. Projects above the assigned limit are referred by the committee to a higher authority, as are those within the assigned limits but not included in the capital budget.

A survey of a number of large companies by Holden, Fish, and Smith (Top-Management Organization and Control) produced the following recommendations regarding composition of the appropriations committee:

> Membership, as with any committee, should include only those who definitely add to the group judgment. In this case it could appropriately include the chief engineer, because of his ability in judging the soundness of construction plans, costs and alternatives; the controller, for his financial and economic viewpoint, particularly as to the availability of funds and correct time for undertaking the project; the director of organization and cost control, for the benefit of his viewpoint on cost reduction, effects upon the organization and manpower considerations; and the divisional executive concerned, who attends to present his case and see that all factors are given consideration. Others may be requested to attend when necessary, such as the research manager to advise on new developments.

The most important feature of this particular procedure, however, is the analytical agency which reviews all the proposals, and by whose analyses the committee must be very largely guided. A very capable individual—one of the stature of a departmental manager—is required to head the analytical work. Upon the projects presented the company will spend very large sums, and it is therefore essential to have in this position a person able to present consistently high-quality, accurate analyses. This person might also be the chairman of the committee, he and his staff constituting an independent, full-time agency concerned with appropriation analyses. In some companies a section of the engineering department makes the analyses. Others object to this on the ground that the engineering department also works out the designs, methods, and savings, and is therefore not in a position to criticize and reject its own work. For that reason they prefer an independent agency embodying adequate engineering talent.

APPROPRIATION REQUESTS. Individual appropriation requests are required for each item of capital expenditure as it is made, even though it is included in an approved capital budget. The individual appropriation requests are approved after review by an authorized official or committee. The **size of the expenditure** is a determining factor in the rank of the official whose authorization must be secured. If provision for a project has not been made in the capital budget, approval of a higher ranking official is required than if it is covered in the budget.

The appropriation request may be required to specify the reason for the expenditure. One company requires that the reason be specified as:

New business.
Increased needs of present business.
Normal replacements.
Change in manufacturing method.

Another classification used is:

Cost reduction.
Production of a new product.
Additional volume of existing product.
Replacement of existing equipment.

Some companies require the following information to be included in the appropriation request:

1. Purpose of expenditure.
2. Estimated costs of acquisition or construction.
3. Loss on assets retired.
4. Savings resulting from capital expenditure.
5. Fixed costs resulting from new capital asset, such as annual depreciation, insurance, taxes, etc.

Forms of appropriation requests for capital expenditures are shown in Figs. 3 and 4.

Approved appropriations remain valid until the project has been either completed or canceled. Upon completion of the project, should any **unexpended balance** remain, the appropriation for it should be canceled and not be made available for other purposes.

If the original appropriation does not prove adequate to cover the full cost of the project, a **supplemental appropriation** will be needed. Many companies permit deferment of the supplemental appropriation request if the excess expenditure will not be greater than 5% or 10% of the original appropriation. Some

```
                    APPROPRIATION FOR CAPITAL EXPENDITURE
                                                          Appropriation No._____
_____                           Date
            Plant

This appropriation is to cover a Capital Expenditure made necessary by:
        NEW BUSINESS                    [ ]     NORMAL REPLACEMENT              [ ]
        INCREASED NEEDS OF PRESENT BUSINESS [ ] CHANGE IN MANUFACTURING METHOD  [ ]
                   DESCRIPTION OF PROPOSED CAPITAL EXPENDITURE


              (Use reverse side for detailed explanation of necessity for this capital expenditure)
                        DETAILS OF ESTIMATED INSTALLED COST
| Purchase Price | Plant Materials & Supplies | Labor | Overhead | Total |
|                |                             |       |          |       |

Estimated useful life of new installation:_____
Estimated dates expenditures will be made (Specify months and amounts)

Capital Account classification and amount:_____
Expense Account classification and amount:_____
Estimated completion date:
             RECORD OF PREPARATION AND ACTION ON THIS APPROPRIATION
|   Plant Record   | Date |   Parent Company Record   | Date |
| Prepared by:     |      | Received by General Manager: |    |
| Approved by:     |      | Action by General Manager:   |    |
|                  |      | Action recorded and copy returned |    |
|                  |      | to subsidiary company: (Budget Director) |    |
```

Fig. 3. Appropriation request for capital expenditure.

```
                         Appropriation Request
                    .................. DIVISION

                              Appropriation Request No. ..........
        APPROPRIATION REQUEST FOR (Describe in detail): ..............
        ..........................................................
        ..........................................................
        DETAILS OF ESTIMATED COST: ...............................
        ..........................................................
        ..........................................................
        ESTIMATED DELIVERY OR COMPLETION DATE: ....................
        ESTIMATED DATES AND AMOUNTS OF CASH REQUIRED: .............
        ..........................................................
        ESTIMATED FIXED EXPENSES RESULTING FROM ACQUISITION: ......
                (Estimated depreciation, insurance, etc.)
        WAS THIS ITEM INCLUDED IN CAPITAL BUDGET? .................
        ANTICIPATED SAVINGS: ......................................
        INDICATE URGENCY OR DESIRABILITY OF THIS EXPENDITURE: .....

        Approved ................    Approved ................
                  Budget Director              Plant Manager
        Approved ................
                  For Appropriation Committee.
```

Fig. 4. Divisional appropriation request.

companies also have a provision that this deferment of the supplemental request is contingent upon the project being completed within 30 or 60 days. Most companies provide that supplemental appropriations are unnecessary if the amount of the excess expenditure is small, such as $50 or $100.

Approval of Appropriation Requests. It is common practice to require approval of appropriation requests for each specific expenditure on plant or equipment. The authority required for such approval ordinarily is governed by the size of both the request and the company. In many instances, the project request for funds may pass through several levels of management. For example, the N.A.A. Accounting Practice Report No. 7 cites the following case:

The approval of the detailed expenditure request is established so that various levels of management have different approval authority. These are outlined below:

> Plant manager up to $1,000
> Division manager to $5,000
> Group Vice-Pres. to $50,000
> Executive Vice-Pres. to $75,000
> Executive Committee—in excess of $75,000

Special policies delegate authority to the executive vice-president for approval of expenditures in excess of $75,000 or in cases of emergency.

Blanket Appropriations. Most companies set up blanket appropriations to cover minor capital expenditures made necessary by normal operations, as well as those that are not determinable at the time the budget is completed. Usually, a limit is set on the amount of any one purchase. Where there are a number of operating units, the amount of the blanket appropriation is fixed after consideration of the normal replacement requirements of each.

It is a good policy to restrict blanket appropriations so that purchases of major capital items will not be charged to them. In the event of an emergency, however, the blanket appropriation should be available for other purchases, provided an explanation is given at a later date.

Blanket appropriations expire at the end of the fiscal year. A new blanket appropriation should be granted for each year.

CAPITAL EXPENDITURE CONTROL. Control over capital expenditures is facilitated by classification of outlays as:

1. Major projects.
2. Routine expenditures.
3. Replacements.

The line of demarcation between major and routine projects is dependent upon the size of the company and the consequent degree of control of capital expenditures exercised by top management. Sound control of major projects involves careful analysis of the initial cost of each purchase or installation, as well as of the annual cost of maintenance. Maintenance costs necessitated by major capital expenditures include repairs, depreciation, property taxes, insurance, additional labor costs, etc. The effect of proposed capital expenditures upon fixed charges, cash requirements, and prospective earnings should be weighed. Prior to the approval of a request for capital appropriation, careful comparison should be made of the cost of production with existing and with the proposed equipment.

Wherever possible, recommendations for capital expenditures should be forwarded to the plant methods and cost control sections for their review. When a recommendation is approved, estimates of the cost of the facility should be prepared and savings in direct labor, material consumption, and overhead costs estimated.

Routine expenditures require control inasmuch as multiples of small authorizations may in the aggregate exceed a single major project. However, without in any way diminishing the degree of control, it is frequently possible to delegate authority to approve routine capital expenditures to lower echelons of managerial authority. **Major projects** require more careful handling.

As an aid to control over capital expenditures, **monthly reports** should be prepared by each operating unit and forwarded to the budget director or to the official designated to control capital expenditures. In the preparation of these reports, particular stress should be laid upon the sufficiency of the appropriation request. If indications are that the appropriation request will be underrun or overrun, this should be indicated. It is important that the progress in each department be apparent from the report, and that the estimated cost to complete the construction or the purchase of a facility be shown.

It must be borne in mind that additional investment in facilities raises the break-even point of an enterprise. If capital outlays are not carefully integrated with sales efforts and financial resources, an expansion program may have marked adverse effects upon earnings and liquidity.

Company Organization To Control Expenditures. In a recent study, the American Management Association (Curtis, A.M.A. Research Study 55) describes a steel company with three major committees generally concerned with finances—a **finance committee,** a **long-range planning committee,** and an **expenditures planning committee.** The last-mentioned committee, chairmaned by the vice-president, planning and control, with the vice-president, operations, as a member, is directly concerned with controlling capital expenditures. Its purpose is:

. . . To review and report the progress to completion or rejection of each job request estimated to be a major job request, uncovering and reconciling any interdepartmental differences of opinion as to type of equipment and extent of work involved, and expediting to obtain the earliest return on all budgeted dollars. Major job requests include all appropriations over $5,000, all repair jobs over $10,000 . . .

The committee meets bi-weekly to review the progress of jobs and to analyze major job requests. A **capital equipment analysis** normally is required for "aggressive capital expenditures" to produce new products or increase existing capacity and for "optional expenditures on existing facilities for quick return" by reducing costs or increasing productivity. This analysis is performed ". . . at the direction of the committee when the engineering department has completed suitable design and cost estimates. The **capital expenditure analyst** (also on the committee) may consult directly with anyone who can improve the accuracy of the final analysis." The committee need not require a capital equipment analysis for " 'necessary' defensive expenditures" such as required repairs of replacements or unavoidable overhead for safety considerations.

With respect to repair and replacement jobs, the committee may give final authorizations to request forms and forward them to the controller. For appropriation jobs, the chairman submits the recommendations of the committee to the president. Such jobs, covered by capital equipment analysis, are listed in a follow-up section of the minutes when they have been in operation one year. The chairman is instructed to ". . . write the originator of the request, the vice president of operations, requesting a follow-up or 'make good' report comparing actual performance with that originally projected for justification."

As a general policy, preparation of a **performance review**, such as that required by the steel company, is considered very desirable because it enables management to evaluate the adequacy of the original assumptions and analyses leading to the authorization of the project. Yet Matthews (Harvard Business Review, Vol. 37) notes that only half of the companies he studied undertook performance reviews that incorporated revenue as well as cost analyses. The reasons for this resistance included a belief that total profit performance was sufficient to evaluate capital expenditure programs, apprehension that operating personnel would be more reluctant to express ideas if subject to review, and the difficulty in isolating relevant cost and revenue data. However, he stresses the fact that ". . . the managements that **do** use performance reviews are enthusiastic about them."

CAPITAL BUDGET AND CASH PLANNING. The capital budget is a summary of proposed expenditures for the period and should be interrelated with the general cash forecast. In this way, allowance can be made for plant and equipment outlays in cash planning. (See Sec. 16, Current Asset Planning.)

Outlay for capital requirements must be related to the cash forecast for a company. This is particularly necessary when capital replacements or additions are made in whole or in part with reinvested earnings. Unless the amount allocated to capital expenditure is pre-planned, there is danger of diverting cash required for working capital to the acquisition of fixed assets, thereby impairing the ability of the company to discharge its current financial obligations.

When capital expenditure exceeds the annual provision for depreciation, the excess must come either from reinvested profits, borrowing, or the sale of stock, on the one hand, or from existing cash, on the other. If cash is used up for the purpose, it represents a diversion of working capital into fixed capital.

The **maximum funds** available for capital expansion without impairment of working capital are measured by:

1. Reinvested earnings for period.
2. Annual allowance for depreciation and depletion.
3. Proceeds from sale of additional stock.
4. Proceeds of bond issues or term loans.

Failure to purchase capital assets during any year, on the other hand, will result in an increase of working capital to the extent of the provision for depreciation. This can be illustrated by the following:

Sales		$1,000,000
Costs	$700,000	
Depreciation	100,000	800,000
Net profit		$ 200,000

It will be noted that receipts are $1,000,000 and outlay $700,000, so that working capital, and eventually cash, is increased by $300,000, or the sum of net profit and depreciation. But whenever equipment is replaced, the cost of the replacement will then come out of working capital at the time.

Commenting on the importance of the capital expenditure budget in developing the cash budget, the N.A.A. Accounting Practice Report, No. 7, states that "because such capital expenditures are non-recurring and are not spread uniformly over the year, the capital budget must be closely related to the flow of cash. . . . In order to meet the needs for cash budgeting, details of cash outlays by month, quarter and year are necessary." This is illustrated in Fig. 5, where the budgeted unexpended balances of approved authorizations are distributed into the quarterly periods of the year when it is expected that the cash disburse-

THE CAPITAL BUDGET 17·21

BUDGET OF CAPITAL EXPENDITURES FOR THE YEAR ENDING DECEMBER 31

	Status of Authorization For Expenditure	Estimated Amount of Authorization	Approximate Unexpended Balance of Approved Authorizations
Electric Furnace	Approved	$ 50,000	$ 50,000
Warner & Swasey Lathe	Approved	40,000	40,000
Air Condition Building XYZ	Approved	63,000	42,000
Trucks	Approved	25,000	25,000
Welding machines	Not Requested	40,000	
Lift Trucks	Not Requested	15,000	
Other Items	Not Requested	100,000	
		$3,200,000	$450,000

Approval to Be Requested in 19—	DATE OF EXPECTED CASH DISBURSEMENT					Year 19—
	Year 19					
	First Quarter	Second Quarter	Third Quarter	Fourth Quarter	TOTAL	
$	$ 50,000	$	$	$	$ 50,000	
		40,000			40,000	
	21,000	21,000			42,000	
	10,000		15,000		25,000	
40,000	10,000	10,000	10,000	10,000	40,000	
15,000			15,000		15,000	
100,000	20,000	20,000	20,000	20,000	80,000	20,000
$5,000,000	$1,800,000	$1,600,000	$1,000,000	$750,000	$5,150,000	$300,000

Fig. 5. Form for connecting budgetary authorization to cash distributions.

ment will be made. The **timing of the expenditures** may be provided in the budget request, the appropriation request, or in supplemental material. In the event of planned major expansions, **additional outside funds** may be required. Because these amounts are likely to be substantial, suitable advance knowledge of when they will be required is desirable in order that the necessary financial arrangements may be made. In Fig. 6, estimated capital expenditure requirements are projected 5 years ahead.

ESTIMATED CAPITAL EXPENDITURES REQUIREMENTS
Years ----- through -----
Page 1 of 9

PROJECT	DESCRIPTION	2nd. Year	3rd Year	4th Year	5th Year
Cost Reduction Program: Improvements in Refrigerator and Freezer manufacturing facilities	Reduce the cost of draw press operations, resulting in reduction of manpower, scrap and drawing compound. Dry Film Machines with automatic loader and unloader	$100,000.00	$100,000.00	$120,000.00	
	Anodize and plate parts presently farmed out. This would result in a savings on piece part cost. Anodizing Machine Plating Machine				$175,000.00 125,000.00
TOTAL COST REDUCTION PROGRAM		$100,000.00	$100,000.00	$120,000.00	$300,000.00
Replacement Program: Production equipment	Lift trucks, material handling, & misc. small equipment.	$133,200.00	$115,000.00	$129,000.00	$145,000.00
TOTAL REPLACEMENT PROGRAM		$133,200.00	$115,000.00	$129,000.00	$145,000.00

Note: Other items and the other categories of the program are covered in the Estimated Capital Expenditures Requirements, but are not included in this Exhibit. All data is hypothetical.

Fig. 6. Form for projecting capital expenditure requirements.

Estimating Profitability of Investments

EVALUATING ALTERNATIVE PROJECTS. The rapid expansion of American business since World War II has directed management's attention to the need for evaluating the relative profitability of alternative investment opportunities. For this purpose, various measures of rate of return on investment are employed that take into account both the profits expected to flow from a project and the funds that will have to be committed to it. **Three principal methods** are in use to determine the rate of return for evaluating alternative projects: the payback, the financial statement or average return on investment method, and the discounted cash-flow method.

Relative Use of Evaluation Methods. In a survey of the 500 largest industrial corporations, 215 responded to the question, "What method do you use for calculating the rate of return on your investment for each type of capital expenditure?" (Amling, Some Determinants of Capital Expenditure Decision in the Largest Industrial, Public Utility, Transportation and Merchandising Corporations in the United States). Among these corporations, it was found that the payback was the most popular method; approximately 34% indicated that they used it as the sole approach for determining the rate of return, while about 52% used it either alone or in combination with one of the other methods. The second most popular method was the discounted cash flow method, which was used alone by about 19% of the firms and in combination with another method by 28%. The average return on investment method was used solely by 15% of the companies and in combination by 27%.

The survey found that the method used for calculating rate of return **varied with the type of capital-expenditure project.** The payback was used particularly in projects involving routine replacements, short lives, relatively small expenditures, and a prospective quick return on the investment. Industries apparently giving preference to this method included food and beverages, aircraft and parts, and paper and allied products. Companies turned to the discounted cash-flow method if the project was more complex, predictable, and stable. This method was used more widely in the petroleum refining industry, mining, and to a lesser degree in metal manufacturing. It was favored by the bigger companies. The average return on investment method was used principally in the textile, glass, and cement industries. A brief description of each of these methods follows and a more extensive discussion is given in the section below on "Special Problems of Capital Planning."

The Payback. The payback generally is calculated by dividing the total investment by the sum of the net income per year after taxes plus depreciation. Thus, it shows the number of years that are required for the cash-flow income of a project to return the capital invested. It is simple to calculate and important where liquidity is a prime objective. On the other hand, it does not take into account the number of years beyond payback that earnings will continue nor does it consider the rate at which these inflows occur.

The Accounting or Average Return Method. In this method, the average annual earnings over the life of the investment are compared with either the average or the initial investment. Company practices differ rather widely with respect to what should be included in average earnings and investment. Although this method conforms with the determination of the rate of return as a measure of performance, it does not take into account the timing of money flows. It, therefore, provides the same return to projects with the same average earnings and investments even though one may give a much more rapid rate of repayment than the other.

The Discounted Cash-Flow Method. This method takes into account the fact that money received earlier has a greater value than money received at a later time. The return on investment in this method is that rate which equates the sum of the present values of a series of future cash flows to the value of the original investment.

In its study of Return on Capital as a Guide to Managerial Decisions (Research Report No. 35), the N.A.A. summarized the **importance of the time factor** in determining the rate of return as follows:

> Dollars available in the near future are worth more than dollars to be received at a more distant date because money can be invested to earn a return which compounds with time. Consequently, a project which promises an early return is more desirable than one in which the return will be longer delayed, other things being equal. Likewise, a project in which some outlays can be deferred is more desirable than one which requires that expenditures be made at an earlier date. The discounted cash-flow method reflects in rate of return differences in the timing of cash outflows and inflows. This is accomplished by discounting cash flows to the same point in time.

In comparing projects with different life-spans, an assumption underlying the discounted cash-flow method is that funds can be constantly reinvested at the given rate of return. In order to obviate use of such an assumption, other methods employing the present-value concept may be used. For example, in the excess present value method the present value of the cash-flow earnings might be determined at a discount rate equal to the **cost of capital** or the company's **indicated earnings,** and the resulting sum compared with the original cost of the investment. Another factor to be taken into consideration in comparing rates of return is the relative **risks** involved, because the financial manager might decide that the greater risks associated with a higher-return project detracted sufficiently from it to make a poorer-yielding project more desirable.

Depreciation in Financial Management

OBJECTIVES OF DEPRECIATION PROVISION. The functions of depreciation in financial management are to:

1. Provide a means of allocating the cost of capital assets to current costs of operation.
2. Evaluate capital assets.
3. Make financial provision for the replacement of capital assets.

Allocation of Cost of Capital Assets. The large majority of accountants regard depreciation as an allocation of the cost of plant and equipment over the estimated service life of the assets. For example, a plant that cost $100,000 and has an estimated service life of 10 years would be regarded as an element in total cost of production if a single profit and loss statement covering the 10-year period were prepared. Inasmuch as annual statements of profit and loss are issued, the cost of the plant is spread over 10 years. Under the so-called **straight-line method** of providing for depreciation, 1/10 of the cost of the plant, or $10,000, would be charged as a cost of operation each year. At the end of the first year, the balance sheet of the company would show a net value of $90,000 (after deducting the allowance for depreciation) for the plant. In the second year, another $10,000 would be charged to costs of operation and the net asset value would be reduced to $80,000. Under this concept of depreciation, undepreciated values of capital assets assume the nature of deferred costs of operation.

Capital Asset Valuation. Current practice is to deduct the allowance for depreciation from the cost or other valuation of capital assets on the balance sheet. Although an expression may be used such as "the capital assets shown on the balance sheet are worth . . . ," net valuations of capital assets listed on the balance sheet often bear little relation to true worth. Assets that were purchased 10 years ago and that are being depreciated over a 20-year period may be worth considerably more on a reproduction basis than the balance sheet valuations, or they may be of doubtful value because of obsolescence.

Replacement of Capital Assets. For financial planning, the chief function of depreciation is usually its role in financing replacement of plant and equipment. Depreciation allowances provide, out of the operations of the business, resources for replacement of fixed assets. True, funds withheld as depreciation allowances may be devoted to other purposes such as acquiring inventory or accounts receivable, but in that event funds raised in other ways can be devoted to the acquisition of fixed instead of current assets.

If depreciation is regarded as a means of financing replacement of assets, **reproduction** costs, especially in a period of rising prices, become far more suitable than **original or historical** cost as a basis for computing the annual depreciation allowance. Thus, if a plant was constructed 10 years ago at a cost of $1,000,000 and is being depreciated over a 20-year period on a straight line, the yearly depreciation allowance would be $50,000. Should a rise in prices lift the replacement cost of the plant to $2,000,000, it is evident that the accumulated depreciation will be altogether insufficient to provide for the eventual replacement of the plant. Actually, the annual allowance will be only half as large as needed for replacement, and earnings will be overstated to that extent.

Depreciation allowances, in effect, constitute a conversion of fixed capital assets into cash, so that it is available for reinvestment in similar fixed assets. But if the price level changes, the sum thus realized may be too great or too little for the purpose in view. That is because depreciation as ordinarily computed is based on historical cost.

Accountants have advanced rather persuasive practical **objections to the use of replacement cost** in computing annual depreciation allowances. These may be paraphrased as follows:

The function of accounting is to record costs and to allocate them to the periods to which they relate. Replacement costs of fixed assets fluctuate widely and irregularly from year to year. Allowing for technological changes, it may be impossible to estimate such cost accurately. Basing depreciation on reproduction cost would require almost continuous revision of depreciation charges from year to year. The expense involved in revising reproduction costs annually is often prohibitive.

Nevertheless, financial executives may be guided by reproduction costs. The point can be illustrated by the following example:

A company makes a fortunate purchase of some machinery at exceptionally low cost. The equipment has an estimated service life of 5 years. Depreciation calculated on historical cost would result in a very low charge to current cost of operations during this 5-year period. However, replacement of this machinery at a far higher cost is inevitable at the end of the period. Obviously, depreciation based on historical cost will not provide sufficient reserves for the replacement of these machines out of current operations. But depreciation allowances can be supplemented by earnings retained in the business for this purpose, whether or not they are specifically earmarked.

It is not necessary as a practical matter to make continuous revisions of reproduction costs of plant and equipment. As major changes in construction costs of plant and equipment occur, reproduction values can be estimated roughly and provision made for their replacement through sources that supplement depreciation allowances.

Capital Asset Replacement Funds. Provision for depreciation in the earnings statement does not of itself assure funds for the purchase of new capital assets when required. Provision for depreciation is tantamount to conversion of fixed assets into current assets. At any particular moment, however, the current assets of a business may consist of accounts receivable, inventories, or short-term securities. Depreciation allowances limit disbursement of receipts as dividends, but do not assure they will be held in the form of cash until used for replacement of particular assets. A business may thus find it necessary to resort to outside financing to acquire capital assets, despite adequate depreciation allowances for the purpose. Some concerns maintain a replacement fund consisting of cash or securities equal to the amount of the periodic depreciation allowances, to ensure that they will have the means for financing the acquisition of new capital assets.

OBSOLESCENCE OF CAPITAL ASSETS. Obsolescence is of two kinds—**normal obsolescence,** which is at least partially foreseeable and should therefore be included in the amount of the periodic provision for depreciation, and **extraordinary obsolescence,** which is wholly unpredictable. In providing for extraordinary obsolescence, it is good practice to make a special appropriation for this contingency out of current or retained earnings. It is not practicable to include provision for extraordinary obsolescence in current depreciation, since there is no basis for estimating the amount needed.

MAINTENANCE VS. DEPRECIATION. Public utilities formerly charged repairs, replacements, and retirements of capital assets to operating expenses in lieu of depreciation while railroads, in part, still employ such a policy. At one time, it was not uncommon for industrial companies also to regard maintenance and replacement outlays as taking the place of depreciation allowances. The use of actual maintenance and replacement outlays as a substitute for depreciation allowances is unsatisfactory because of the highly irregular character of the former. In times of poor earnings, there is strong temptation to "skimp on maintenance," so as to overstate income.

Adequate maintenance and repairs of fixed assets prolong their life, but do not constitute a substitute for depreciation. As stated by Hatfield in his now classic remark, "All machinery is on an irresistible march to the junk heap and its progress, while it may be delayed, cannot be prevented by repairs."

Efforts have also been made to combine the depreciation charge with estimated maintenance costs into **a single depreciation rate.** Although the procedure has some logic, it is considered unsatisfactory because it does not recognize the separability of the two concepts. In discussing the relation between maintenance and depreciation, Paton and Paton (Asset Accounting) note that:

> ... it is obviously difficult to determine the amount of maintenance for years in advance, particularly in the face of changeable prices for repair service and supplies,

and the calculation of depreciation is subject to sufficient uncertainty without the introduction of an additional estimate. A more satisfactory method of recognizing the close relation between maintenance and depreciation is to accrue the cost of major parts or elements of a plant unit as depreciation, while permitting the cost of routine servicing and minor repairs to be charged to operations as incurred or spread in terms of annual budgets as circumstances dictate.

EFFECT OF DEPRECIATION ON WORKING CAPITAL. The provision for depreciation, it has been said, tends to convert fixed capital assets into working capital to the extent that the annual allowance for depreciation exceeds the year's new capital expenditures. This can be demonstrated by a hypothetical example.

Let us assume that the balance sheet at the beginning of the year shows:

Current Assets	$100,000	Capital Stock	$300,000
Fixed Assets	200,000		$300,000
	$300,000		

and that the results of operations for the year, on a cash basis, are:

Sales	$100,000
Costs	$75,000
Depreciation	25,000
	$100,000
Profit	0

and that no investments are made in capital assets. The balance sheet at the end of the year then would show:

Current Assets	$125,000	Capital Stock	$300,000
Fixed Assets (Net)	175,000		$300,000
	$300,000		

It will thus be seen that though the income statement shows neither a gain nor a loss, the book value of fixed assets has declined $25,000 and the current assets have been increased by the same amount. As a result of the gradual conversion of fixed assets into current assets, businesses have been able to weather periods of adversity by withholding new capital investments. In effect the annual provision for depreciation has been available to cover operating deficits or to provide funds for other purposes, where it has been earned.

EFFECT OF INADEQUATE DEPRECIATION. In the above illustration, if depreciation of only $10,000 had been deducted, a profit of $15,000 would have been reported. The balance sheet at the close of the year would have been as follows in that event:

Current Assets	$125,000	Capital Stock	$300,000
Fixed Assets (Net)	190,000	Retained Earnings	15,000
	$315,000		$315,000

If these results are repeated yearly, at the end of 8 years, when capital assets should have been fully depreciated, the balance sheet would appear as follows:

Current Assets	$300,000	Capital Stock	$300,000
Fixed Assets	120,000	Retained Earnings	120,000
	$420,000		$420,000

It will readily be appreciated that the apparent profit of $15,000 yearly might have tempted the board of directors **to declare dividends,** for stockholders would expect to share the profits. Any dividends that might have been declared during this period would in reality have been distributions of capital. In any event, altogether inadequate provision would have been made for replacing assets. Furthermore, in computing costs, insufficient depreciation would have been included. If 100,000 units of the product were produced each year, for example, costs would have been understated by 15¢ per unit, or $15,000 a year, because of inadequate allowance for depreciation.

The principles involved in the above simple example are equally valid in large enterprises with multiple products and earnings varying widely from year to year.

DEPRECIATION A COST OF OPERATION. It is sometimes suggested that the periodic depreciation allowance is merely a "book" charge against earnings not at all comparable to other expenses of operation. But this is true in any sense only if there is no need for replacing fixed assets for an indefinite period in the future. Otherwise, depreciation is an actual cost of doing business, just like wages, materials, or insurance. If depreciation is based upon historical cost, it is an allocation of part of the original investment in fixed assets to the current period. Depreciation based upon the expected cost of replacement of capital assets recognizes the fact that, in the conduct of business, replacement of capital assets is inevitable and provision should be made for it in advance. Failure to provide for depreciation adequately understates cost just as surely as failure to include any other expense incurred during the accounting period.

IMPACT OF CHANGING PRICE LEVELS UPON DEPRECIATION. During **a period of advancing prices,** a corporation faces the necessity of planning for the replacement of capital assets at a cost considerably in excess of original or historic cost of the acquisition. Thus, a plant constructed during depression years might not be replaceable in a subsequent period of prosperity for less than twice its original cost. Depreciation based on original cost would not be sufficient to safeguard the integrity of the company's capital in that event, and part of the profit reported should be considered earmarked for replacement of assets as required.

Conversely, **in a period of low prices,** replacement is usually far below original cost. During periods of business recession, when the price level has declined sharply, concerns have written down the book value of fixed assets. The primary motive usually was to reduce the annual depreciation charge, thereby increasing reported profits or decreasing operating losses. Such asset write-downs in effect adjust the annual depreciation to a lower expected replacement cost. If reproduction cost of fixed assets should rise again, depreciation deductions become inadequate and earnings are, in effect, overstated.

From the financial point of view, there is good reason to reflect what appears to be a **lasting change in the price level,** and hence in reproduction cost, in asset valuations on the balance sheet. For ideal planning, depreciation rates should be adjusted to changes in the cost of replacement of capital assets. But balance sheet valuations of capital assets and depreciation rates should be changed only when the change in reproduction costs appears lasting, a factor that may be very difficult to predict.

As a practical matter, asset write-downs are far and away more common than write-ups. The facts that write-ups are frowned upon by accountants and many states prohibit the payment of dividends out of unrealized appreciation of assets discourage upward revaluations of assets.

17·28 CAPITAL ASSET PLANNING

The Accountants' Handbook comments on **price-level write-downs** as follows:

A basic postulate of accounting is the assumption of a stable monetary unit. Any marked fluctuation in the value of the dollar, whether it be upward or downward, reduces the effectiveness of this standard of measurement. Accordingly, the same accounting practices and procedures recommended for an upward price movement should be equally applicable to a movement in the opposite direction. However, many who advocated write-downs in the 1930's as being "sound" and "realistic," now regard proposals to record appraisal values as being "unsound" and "unrealistic."

Departure from a cost basis of accounting for fixed assets is considered by accountants only when the price level change is definite and **relatively stable** in character. Temporary fluctuations are generally ignored due to the long-lived nature of productive facilities. Practical difficulties, however, are encountered in attempting to predicate the stability of prices at a given level. Economic and financial history is replete with instances where anticipated permanent plateaus and valleys in the value of the dollar have quickly passed into oblivion.

Write-downs, like write-ups, must be based on **objective verifiable evidence.** The practice of writing down fixed assets when value has not been impaired for reasons of conservatism or a desire on the part of management to improve the subsequent earnings record of the company deserves severe censure.

APPRECIATION AND DEPRECIATION. The view is sometimes advanced that appreciation of assets may offset depreciation, making the latter unnecessary. This contention has been put forth in connection with **controversies over whether a surplus exists for dividend payments.** Whatever merit this argument may have for some purposes, it is not pertinent to fixed asset administration. All fixed assets, with the exception of land, ultimately decline in value until retirement and replacement. Appreciation in value of plant, equipment, or other fixed assets is an unrealized gain that may vanish at any time, and in any event will ultimately disappear because of wear and tear, obsolescence, etc.

From the viewpoint of financial management, a **primary purpose of depreciation** is to provide for the replacement of fixed assets as it becomes necessary or desirable. This calls for adequate allowance for depreciation. Any appreciation in asset values is pertinent to the problem only because it makes necessary additional provision for replacement. This added provision may take the form of a higher annual rate of depreciation or the application of reinvested earnings for the purpose.

METHODS OF CALCULATING DEPRECIATION. Fixed asset values can be charged off to current cost of operation by various methods. The choice of method for calculating the periodic depreciation allowance has important financial consequences, since the amount deducted **directly affects the size of the profit reported.** Furthermore, if the provision for depreciation exceeds actual current expenditures for capital assets, it results in an addition to working capital. Conversely, if current provision for depreciation is less than the outlay for fixed assets, additional funds must be drawn from working capital, retained profits, or outside sources. Depreciation policies thus affect planning for both fixed and working capital requirements.

Depreciation methods applicable to particular assets should take into account probable replacement requirements. For instance, assets subject to sudden obsolescence should be written off rapidly in the first few years of their productive life. The straight-line method of providing for depreciation under such circumstance might prove inadequate, for the asset may have to be retired long before it has been written off.

Straight-Line Method. The straight-line method is by far the most common. The basic theory behind it is that depreciation is a function of time, and that its amount is uniform with the passage of time. Thus, a fixed asset with an estimated life of 10 years would be depreciated 1/10 yearly or 1/120 each month. This is usually expressed as an annual rate, e.g., 10% per annum. The expression "a 10% rate of depreciation" means that the service life of the asset is assumed to be 10 years.

The straight-line method of depreciation has a number of **advantages** that account for its great popularity. It is simple to apply and easy to calculate. A great volume of data has been assembled regarding straight-line rates applicable to specific types of assets. Because obsolescence and other factors entering into depreciation cannot be measured with any accuracy, the straight-line method is usually considered to give about as accurate a result as any. Some flexibility can be secured, furthermore, since the annual depreciation rate can be changed to reflect a revision of the estimated service life of the asset or obsolescence beyond that originally estimated.

One **criticism** made of the straight-line method is that resale value of an asset often depreciates more rapidly in the early part of its life. But since a primary financial objective of depreciation is to provide resources for eventual replacement of fixed assets, resale value is not a pertinent consideration. A more valid criticism from the financial viewpoint is that maintenance and repair outlays are greater in the later years of the asset's life, so that the total charge against earnings for both depreciation and maintenance actually tends to increase under the straight-line method.

The most effective criticism of the straight-line method, however, is that wear and tear on assets is greatly intensified during periods of **capacity production,** while the large earnings of such periods are not charged proportionately on account of depreciation. At such times, also, repairs may be deferred because of a desire to operate equipment without interruption, or a lack of labor and materials for the purpose. If taxes on income are higher during this period of intensive operation, as occurred during World War II, the result may be quite inequitable to the taxpayer. The attitude of the Treasury Department at that time was, however, that Congress had recognized this and other factors tending to exaggerate taxable income in the carry-back provisions of the revenue law, and therefore it was loath to allow accelerated depreciation due to added wear and tear on assets. In the renegotiation of war contracts, however, additional depreciation on machinery was allowed because of double-shift operation and other special circumstances. Needless to say, there is nothing to prevent corporate managements from deducting additional depreciation, or establishing an appropriation otherwise designated, from earnings after taxes to make additional financial provision for asset replacement.

Declining-Balance Method. The 1954 Internal Revenue Code marked a significant change from previous law in permitting liberalized depreciation methods that increased deductions in the early years of service. Its purpose was to **encourage investment in plant and equipment,** thereby assisting modernization and expansion of the nation's industrial capacity. In addition to the straight-line method, the 1954 Code specifically mentions the declining-balance method, with a rate not exceeding twice the rate that would have been used if the annual allowance had been computed under the straight-line procedure, and the sum-of-the-years-digits method.

In the declining-balance method, the annual depreciation charge represents a fixed percentage of the depreciated book value of an asset or group of assets. This method provides for heavier depreciation deductions in the early years of the life of the asset. **During the initial period** of its life, the usefulness of the asset to the enterprise is most certain, it is likely to be most productive, the obsolescence element is smallest, and maintenance requirements are at a minimum. **In a period of high prices,** this procedure permits a writing down of the book value of the asset at a rapid rate to reflect the expected early decline in replacement cost, so that in later years income will not be burdened by an unduly heavy charge for depreciation.

Objection has been raised chiefly to the **complexity** of this method. The rate of depreciation is applied not to the original cost of the asset, but to the depreciated cost remaining on the books for each year. Furthermore, there will be an undepreciated balance of value at the end of the estimated life of the asset, since the depreciation rate always applies to the remaining valuation after deducting prior depreciation allowances. This is objectionable where the asset does not have substantial final resale value. Grant and Norton (Depreciation) point out that, employing the maximum allowable rate, the declining balance method permits the write-off of about two-fifths of the value of an asset in the first quarter of its estimated average service life and about two-thirds of the value in the first half of its estimated average service life.

Sum-of-the-Years-Digits Method. In this method, like the declining-balance method, a larger amount is written off during the early years and a smaller amount in the later years of an asset's life. It is based on the sum of the digits that correspond to the asset's estimated life. Thus, the numbers representing the periods of life are added and constitute the denominator of a fraction. The numerator is the same numbers in reverse order. For example, $1 + 2 + 3 + 4 + 5 + 6 + 7 + 8 = 36$. For the first year, the fraction would be 8/36; for the second 7/36, and so forth. The total depreciation (cost minus salvage) is multiplied by each of these fractions. Grant and Norton (Depreciation) indicate that this method writes off somewhat more than two-fifths of the value of an asset in the first quarter of its estimated average service life and almost three-quarters in the first half of its estimated average service life. This accelerated write-off, which they point out is more rapid than that possible in any other permissible method, represents the greatest advantage of the sum-of-the-years-digits method.

Interest Method. Funds set aside for depreciation will not be used for a long time to replace assets. In the meantime, they are ordinarily used to acquire other assets, and so contribute to the earnings of the business. If allowance is made for this by adding interest to the depreciation reserve, the total sum accumulated under the straight-line method will exceed the cost of the asset to be replaced.

Under the interest method of calculating depreciation, a **lower annual rate** is set. Interest on the accumulated depreciation reserve is then added to the amount of the annual deduction, which thus increases from year to year.

A practical **objection** that has been advanced against this method is that the total provision for depreciation becomes greater during the later years of the life of the asset, when maintenance and repair costs also are larger, so that earnings are reduced unduly at that time.

Depreciation Based on Production. Depreciation may be based on the number of units produced, machine working hours, or orders received for the products of a particular class of machinery. Where this is done, the object is to correlate depreciation, as a cost of production, with the volume of production. This method ties depreciation very closely to wear and tear, but overlooks such other factors as the action of the elements and obsolescence, so that the aggregate provision may prove inadequate. This will be so particularly if the machinery is idle during considerable periods for lack of orders.

Where depreciation rates are based on production, the effect tends to be to stabilize reported earnings, since deductions will be largest when output is at a high level.

Depreciation Based on Sales or Profits. If management is interested primarily in stabilizing earnings as reported, depreciation in reports to stockholders may be based upon sales or profits. Such a basis will not be acceptable for tax purposes, so that depreciation will have to be calculated on some other basis in the tax return of the business.

One **objection** to this procedure is that, should a succession of years of small sales or profits occur, the provision for depreciation will be inadequate and costs will be understated. Another is that management may arbitrarily manipulate the annual deduction to make a good or bad showing as desired. If a business is relatively stable, as in the public utility field, deduction of depreciation as a uniform percentage of gross revenues may give satisfactory results over a period.

Writing Off Assets on Acquisition. Sometimes the cost of fixed assets has been written off on or shortly after acquisition as a current expense of the business. In such instances, they are carried on the books at a nominal sum, such as $1.

On the surface, this may seem like conservative procedure. Actually, it is the reverse. With the assets written off, there is no charge to earnings on account of depreciation. Therefore, current earnings are overstated and excessive dividends may be paid out. This method is less misleading, though not desirable, if a business must acquire new fixed assets yearly at a fairly regular rate, so that the writing off of assets acquired may give a result similar to more conventional methods of computing depreciation.

FINANCIAL EFFECTS OF DEPRECIATION POLICIES. Within the framework of accepted accounting conventions, management will select a depreciation policy that seems most advantageous, particularly in the light of its effect on tax payments. Although the 1954 Code allows various methods, Grant and Norton believe that generally use will be made of one of the three methods first listed above: the straight-line method, the declining-balance method, and the sum-of-the-years-digits method. They point out that: "It will be noted from the language of the Code that, with the single exception of the sum-of-the-years-digits method, all other new methods are based directly on the declining-balance method in that they must not give greater accumulated deductions at any time during the first two-thirds of life than would be given by the declining-balance method. It is this limitation which causes the authors to question the usefulness of any of these other methods in most situations."

Failure to provide adequate depreciation results in **overstatement of the value of fixed assets** and **overstatement of current profits.** Conversely, too large a provision for depreciation understates current profits and creates secret reserves on the balance sheet in the form of **unduly low fixed asset valuations.** But companies that seek to overstate depreciation in order to create secret reserves may find in time that depreciation has actually been greater than allowed for because of obsolescence, a higher price level, or other unlooked-for developments.

The earnings statement and balance sheet will also be affected by the method used to account for **retirement** of particular assets. Where each fixed asset has its own **individual depreciation allowance,** retirement before the end of its estimated useful life will require a charge to current or retained earnings equal to the undepreciated balance of the asset's value. This may mean heavy charges of this kind from time to time. On the other hand, where the depreciation provision is carried as a **single allowance** against all the fixed assets, this allowance is charged with the original book value of each asset as it is retired and current retained earnings are not affected by retirements. This latter practice, it is found, stimulates replacement of assets. Management is not encouraged to retain obsolete assets that are costly to operate because of an unwillingness to have earnings charged with heavy deductions on account of retirement of assets not fully depreciated on the books.

In all industries, more rapid depreciation of fixed assets tends to encourage replacements because there is then no problem of charging off undepreciated balances of asset values against current or retained earnings.

DEPRECIATION REGULATION. Legislation and its enforcement by government agencies have a profound effect upon depreciation policies. The **Internal Revenue Service,** in passing on depreciation deductions claimed by taxpayers, has the widest influence. Section 167 of the Internal Revenue Code provides that "there shall be allowed as a depreciation deduction a reasonable allowance for the exhaustion, wear and tear (including a reasonable allowance for obsolescence)—(1) of property used in the trade or business, or (2) of property held for the production of income." These amounts are deductible in computing net taxable income. But the burden of proof of the reasonableness of the deduction in each case rests upon the taxpayer. The Internal Revenue Service requires a method of depreciation, once adopted, to be pursued consistently, except where a change receives specific permission.

The 1962 Guidelines. In 1962, the Internal Revenue Service issued new depreciation guidelines and rules that became effective July 12, as Revenue Procedure 62-21. The I.R.S. summarized this procedure as follows (Depreciation Guidelines and Rules):

Revenue Procedure 62-21 provides basic reforms in the guideline lives for depreciation and in the administration of depreciation for tax purposes. It sets forth simpler standards and more objective rules which will facilitate adoption of rapid equipment replacement practices in keeping with current and prospective economic conditions.

It will not, however, supersede existing rules, outstanding arrangements, or established procedures for those who wish to continue to use them.

The Procedure becomes effective immediately and may be used in the preparation of any tax return due after the date of publication. The new guideline lives and new administrative procedures are applicable to all depreciable property, including existing assets as well as new acquisitions.

New guideline lives for machinery and equipment are set forth which, on the whole, average 30 to 40 percent shorter than those previously suggested for use by taxpayers. The new guidelines will automatically permit more rapid depreciation deductions than those presently taken on 70 to 80 percent of the machinery and equipment used by American business. They will not disturb the depreciation taken on the remaining 20 to 30 percent of business assets on which depreciation is now as fast as, or faster than, that provided in the new guidelines.

A central objective of the new Procedure is to facilitate the adoption of depreciable lives even shorter than those set forth in the guidelines, or shorter than those currently in use, provided only that certain standards are met and that subsequent replacement practices are reasonably consistent with the tax lives claimed.

Following the introduction of the new guidelines, the Accounting Principles Board of the American Institute of C.P.A.s issued Interpretive Opinion No. 1, in which it is indicated that with certain stipulated exceptions a company's net income for the period should not be increased by adopting guideline lives for income-tax purposes. "Accordingly, where Guideline lives shorter than the lives used for financial accounting purposes are adopted for income-tax purposes, and there is an excess of tax-return depreciation over book depreciation, provision for deferred income taxes should be made with respect to the part of the excess that is attributable to the adoption of Guideline lives. . . ."

Other Aspects of Depreciation Regulation. Depreciation also enters into the measurement of differences in cost of manufacture, sale, and delivery under the **Robinson-Patman Act.** By this means price differentials may be justified under that law, which forbids price discriminations except where they are based on actual differences in cost (or to meet competition).

The Interstate Commerce Commission, in its regulation of the accounts of **railroads and interstate communications companies,** has had to pass on depreciation policies. The I.C.C. has prescribed rates of depreciation for railroad motive power, cars, and work equipment and requires depreciation accounting for buildings and structures. Track, however, continues to be accounted for on a betterment basis.

In the **public utility** industry depreciation has played a key role in regulation. The Federal Power Commission and the major state regulatory commissions have required regular depreciation of fixed assets over their estimated service life, in place of the replacement and retirement policies common in the past. The regulatory commissions have insisted upon the regular accrual of adequate depreciation so that valuation of property for rate-making purposes will fully reflect accrued depreciation. The amount of the annual depreciation provision is deducted from revenues to measure the rate of return on the rate base. In addition, public utility companies under the jurisdiction of the Federal Power Commission have been required by that body to write down the book value of assets, where they had been written up in the past over original cost, by charges against surplus and earnings.

Management must thus keep in mind tax and regulatory considerations, as well as the requirements of financial policy, in formulating depreciation practices.

Depletion of Wasting Assets

THE DEPLETION PROBLEM. Natural resources that are used up in current operations create a special problem in fixed capital management. A mine or an oil field cannot be replaced, as can a factory or a piece of machinery. When the ore, oil, or other raw material has been extracted, the asset has been depleted and the company must exploit some other mine or field if it is to remain in the business. Hence, part of the earnings from the operation of a wasting asset constitutes a **return of the capital invested.** This portion is designated as depletion.

FINANCIAL SIGNIFICANCE OF DEPLETION. Capital expended to acquire a wasting asset is used, in essence, to acquire by a bulk purchase a large stock of raw material. Through the extraction process, this raw material is then converted into a salable commodity, which may be ore or crude oil or may be a more highly finished product that has been subjected to further processing. Hence, a pro-rata portion of the cost of the natural resource constitutes an **expense** of doing business just as surely as does the cost of raw material in any manufacturing enterprise. But this cost takes the form of a current charge for depletion, rather than the purchase of raw materials from others.

Finney and Miller (Principles of Accounting: Intermediate) state:

Depletion is the exhaustion of the cost or value of a wasting asset, such as a mine, a timber tract, or an oil well, resulting from the conversion of the natural resource into inventories. The **depletion base** is the total cost or value of the wasting asset to be charged to operations during the period of exploitation of the natural resource. If there is a residual land value, it should be recorded in a separate account.

They further point out:

Depreciation must, of course, be provided on buildings and machinery located on a wasting asset. If the life of the wasting asset is estimated to be less than the life of the plant, it is customary to accept the life of the wasting asset as the life of the plant for depreciation purposes. This is done on the theory that the plant will have only a scrap value when it is no longer needed for operations in its present location. As the life of the wasting asset is contingent upon the amount of annual operations, the depreciation of the plant may be computed on the same basis that is used for depletion; that is:

$$\text{Annual depreciation} = (\text{Cost} - \text{Scrap}) \times \frac{\text{Units extracted during year}}{\text{Total estimated units}}$$

Although it is true that depletion is a cost of production of the company exploiting a wasting asset, this does not mean that a natural resource already acquired should not be worked because the sale of the product will not return all costs, including depletion. Since capital has already been invested in the asset, the chief criterion in deciding whether to work it should be whether it yields a margin over actual costs of extraction, refining, and transportation. On the other hand, before a wasting asset is acquired the buyer will want to ascertain **whether it promises to yield a profit over all cost,** including depletion and interest on the capital that will be tied up in the mine, timber land, or other wasting asset.

VALUATION OF WASTING ASSETS. Depletion cannot be computed until the wasting asset has been given a valuation that will provide a basis for calculating the amount to be deducted from earnings. This valuation may be the cost, with or without preliminary development expenses, or it may be some other amount at which the asset will be carried on the books.

Valuation of a wasting asset is often a very difficult matter. The Internal Revenue Code provisions governing valuation acceptable for tax purposes are complex. Broadly, they provide that a natural resource acquired prior to March 1, 1913, can be valued at cost or fair market value at that date, whichever is higher. Most wasting assets acquired after March 1, 1913, are valued at cost, as for computing gains on capital assets sold. In certain instances, notably mines other than coal, metal, and sulphur mines, **discovery value** may be used. This is the fair market value either on the date of discovery or within 30 days thereafter. A complication arises when the mine, oil property, or other wasting asset has been acquired through the issuance of stock, which may be of no par value or with a par or stated value far in excess of the amount that would have been paid for the property had it been purchased for cash. Preliminary development costs of mines should be capitalized, but they may be deducted as expenses when made for oil and gas wells, at the taxpayer's option, for income tax purposes.

Since the wasting asset often has an arbitrary valuation set for tax purposes or to cover stock issued in payment, the annual depletion charge similarly may not reflect in any real sense the loss in value of the asset, or the diminution of the worth of the stockholders' investment. Depletion is a real element of **cost,** but practical valuation difficulties may make its accurate determination impractical.

METHODS OF CALCULATING DEPLETION. Whatever the basis used in setting a valuation for a wasting asset, the charge per unit of product is based in most instances upon the **estimated recoverable content** of the mine, oil field, timber stand, or other wasting asset. This content is fixed in a literal sense, but as a practical matter it may vary greatly through the years with technological changes, improved methods of extraction, and efficiency of operation. Engineers can do little more than hazard a "scientific guess" as to the total amount of the product that can be extracted economically. In the case of mines and other underground resources in particular, quite limited information is usually on hand as extraction starts, but as it proceeds more becomes known about the probable extent of the ultimate recovery. In the light of this additional information, the basis for calculating the depletion charge per unit of product may be changed. For timber lands that are being replanted as trees are cut down, allowance must be made for the resulting prolongation of the life of the asset.

Revision of the unit charge for depletion may radically change the reported earnings of an enterprise. Thus, if the company has invested $1,000,000 in a mine on the assumption that 2,000,000 tons of ore could be extracted from it economically, the depletion charge against earnings would be 50¢ per ton of output. If the company receives $5 per ton and all operating costs aggregate $3 a ton, a profit after depletion of $1.50 a ton is realized. Should it be found shortly after operations begin that the recoverable content of the mine is actually only 1,000,000 tons, the depletion charge should be revised upward to $1 a ton, which would reduce the taxable profit to $1. This is not only necessary for accurate financial reporting, but also to avoid overpayment of income taxes upon earnings after allowable depletion.

For income tax purposes, depletion is allowed only on units **actually sold**, regardless of when they have been extracted.

Percentage Depletion. The Internal Revenue Code permits taxpayers to deduct depletion for certain wasting assets as a **percentage of gross income from the property,** instead of per unit of product. Depletion of oil and gas wells is deductible at the rate of 27½% of the gross income from the property for the taxable year, but it may not exceed 50% of the net income of the taxpayer from the property, without allowing for depletion. Owners of oil and gas wells use percentage depletion, unless depletion per unit of product will give them a larger deduction from taxable income. Percentage depletion is allowed owners of other wasting assets at their option. The rate is 5% of gross income from the property for coal mines, 15% for metal mines, and 23% for sulphur mines, with the same limit of 50% of net income from the property computed without allowance for depletion.

The fact that the taxpayer may over the life of the asset end up deducting more than 100% of its cost under the percentage depletion method has attracted criticism of this procedure. Actually, it reflects the fact that large sums are spent upon the development of natural resources that do not result in finding recoverable products, so that the added tax benefit of percentage depletion from the successful property will offset the other failures that inevitably occur.

Depletion and Financial Reporting. Because of the wide discrepancy between **book** and **actual** values of wasting assets, it has been suggested that managements should compute depletion in statements to stockholders on the basis of engineering data, or that wasting assets be carried at $1 and no pretense at evaluation and depletion for financial reporting purposes be made. A number of companies do not show depletion in their reports to stockholders.

Graham, Dodd, and Cottle (Security Analysis: Principles and Techniques) indicate that investors should restate reported profits by determining an **amortization charge** to write off producing properties at a value based upon the price the investor paid for the stock, rather than upon the cost of the properties to the company. They state:

> The theory of amortization is that it should return over the life of a wasting or depreciating asset enough to repay the cost to the owner. Only after this is provided for can the remaining earnings be considered a true profit on the investment. A company's annual depletion charge is based on its own cost of the ore or oil deposit. But if the investor in the company's stock pays more or less than its net asset value he can usually be considered to be buying his share of the wasting asset at a higher or lower figure than the company's book cost. In calculating the true profits and the return on his investment, he should allow for its amortization over a suitable period of time—presumably the same span as used by the company—but the dollar amount per share may be considerably higher or lower than the company's figure.

Special Problems of Capital Planning

CAPITAL INVESTMENTS AND CASH FLOWS. Capital budgeting may be defined as that area of business activity concerned with choosing the most desirable of proposed investments in capital assets, taking into account the expected life, method of financing, and resultant benefits. The principles of capital budgeting are illustrated in many areas of decision making, such as proposals to expand plant capacity, to replace equipment, to make or buy, to lease or buy, etc. In each instance the investment involves the measurement of the future benefits to determine the worthwhileness of a given proposal. The future benefits are in the form of cash flows and it is the cash flows, their extent and duration, that are the basis for what Bierman and Smidt (The Capital Budgeting Decision) call the measure of investment worth.

MEASURES FOR EVALUATING INVESTMENT PROPOSALS. There are various ways in which investment proposals may be evaluated. The most important are:

1. Payback or payout period
2. Accounting or average rate of return method
3. Discounted cash flow
   a. Time-adjusted rate of return
   b. Excess or net present value method.

Payback or Payout Period. A simple and often employed method for determining the economic desirability of an investment is the payback or payout period. It represents, according to Bierman and Smidt (The Capital Budgeting Decision), "the length of time required for the stream of cash proceeds produced by the investment to equal the original cash outlay," i.e., the time required for the project to pay for itself. The formula is simple:

$$\text{Payback period} = \text{Original investment} \div \text{Annual cash inflow}$$
$$P = I \div E$$

The **annual cash inflow** represents the earnings, that is, the estimated cost savings resulting from the the proposed investment. For example, a machine is offered for $6,000; it has an estimated useful life of 10 years and promises cash savings of $1,200 a year (before depreciation). Hence it will pay for itself in

SPECIAL PROBLEMS OF CAPITAL PLANNING

5 years (i.e., $6,000 ÷ $1,200). If the savings are unevenly distributed in time, then the payback period is determined as in the following illustration:

Investment: $6,000

	Estimated savings	
	Annual	Cumulative
First year	$1,400	$1,400
Second "	1,200	2,600
Third "	1,100	3,700
Fourth "	1,000	4,700
Fifth "	900	5,600
Sixth "	800	6,400
etc.		

It is evident that cost recovery will take place in about 5½ years. In arriving at a decision as to whether this is satisfactory, the payback period must be compared with the **economic life of the asset.** Ordinarily the life of the asset must be substantially longer than the payback period. Thus, if the life span of the asset in the last illustration is 6 years, the project is not worthwhile. If it is 8 or 10 years, it is likely to be worthwhile. The longer the stream of savings continues the greater the margin of safety.

The payback test is little more than a rule-of-thumb, but it has become popular simply because it **measures the time required for investment recovery.** It is not a measure of profitability. If there are a number of proposals to be considered, the available funds for capital acquisitions may be apportioned on the basis of a maximum payback period. Any proposal exceeding such maximum would then be automatically eliminated from consideration. As will be seen below, there are better ways for ranking investment alternatives.

The Accounting or Average Rate of Return Method. The accounting method uses a rate of return to establish the desirability of a given proposal. It is known by various names. The National Association of Accountants refers to it as the "financial statement method" (N.A.A. Research Report No. 35); Anthony (Management Accounting) calls it the "unadjusted return on investment." He further states that when calculated on the initial investment, it will always understate the true rate of return as found under the discounted cash flow methods. Its formula is as follows:

$$\text{Rate of return} = \frac{\text{Annual gross earnings} - \text{Annual depreciation}}{\text{Investment}}$$

$$R = \frac{E - D}{I}$$

Illustration. An asset costs $2,991; it has a 5-year life and estimated savings of $1,000 a year before depreciation. What is the rate of return?

Solution.

$$R = \frac{\$1,000 - \$598}{\$2,991} = \frac{402}{2,991} = 13.44\%$$

This assumes the asset has no salvage value at the expiration of its economic life; the rate of return is based on the **initial** investment. Since the asset shrinks in value from $2,991 to 0, some authorities have suggested calculating a rate of return based on the **average** investment, $\left(\frac{\$2,991 + 0}{2}\right)$ or $1,496. In that case

$$R = \frac{\$402}{\$1,496} = 26.87\%$$

CAPITAL ASSET PLANNING

TIME-ADJUSTED METHODS. The time-adjusted methods make use of the principles of compound interest and present values. Two of the more important are the discounted cash flow, and the excess or net present value methods.

Discounted Cash Flow. The discounted cash flow method attempts to evaluate a proposal in the form of a rate of return that is **applied to the unrecovered capital of each period** instead of to the initial investment. In determining present values of annuities, the annuity payments cover principal and interest. Applied to capital budgeting, this means that each of the periodic cash flows represents a partial recovery of the investment and also yields a return. As stated in N.A.A. Research Bulletin 35: "The rate of return may be defined as the maximum rate of interest that could be paid for the capital employed over the life of an investment without loss on the project."

Figure 7 is a familiar amortization table that shows that if money can be borrowed for anything less than 20% the project can yield a profit. Put another way, the rate of return is ". . . the rate of interest which will discount future net cash inflows from the proposed project down to the amount of the investment in the project" (N.A.A. Research Bulletin 35). In the instant illustration (Fig. 7) the annual cash inflows will do exactly that. The formula is:

$$A_0 = R \, a_{\overline{n}|i}$$
$$= 1{,}000 \times a_{\overline{5}|.20} = 1{,}000 \times 2.991$$
$$= \$2{,}991.$$

(Note: For a discussion of this formula and those underlying the other tables used, see Sec. 27, Mathematics of Finance.)

DATA:

Investment	$2,991
Savings before depreciation	1,000
Economic life of project	5 years
Rate of return	20%

Year	Capital Unrecovered at Beginning of Year	Annual Cash Inflow	Interest at 20%	Capital Recovered
1	$2,991	$1,000	$598	$ 402
2	2,589	1,000	518	482
3	2,107	1,000	421	579
4	1,528	1,000	306	694
5	834*	1,000	167	833*
*Error of $1 due to rounding.				$2,990*

Fig. 7. Amortization table.

The above exhibit assumes that the unrecovered investment at the beginning of each year earns interest for the entire year and that each year's cash inflow is received at the end of the year.

Illustration. A machine with an estimated life of 6 years costs $20,000 and its annual savings from operations are $6,000. What is the discounted cash flow rate of return? Ignore taxes in arriving at a decision.

Solution.

1. Investment $20,000
2. Annual savings 6,000
3. Payback 20,000 ÷ 6,000 .... 3.33 years
4. Rate of return from table (6-year life)................ 19% approx.

The above is the simplest type of situation. Note that the payback of 3.33 years, when expressed in dollars, is really the present value of an annuity of $1 for 6 years. If this factor remains constant but the economic life changes, the rate of return, of course, will also change. Thus, if the life of the machine were expected to be 10 years, the rate of return would be about 27%. If the life expectancy were 4 years, the return would be roughly 8%. These rates of return are obtained from a table (illustrated in Fig. 15 in Sec. 27) that shows the present values of an annuity of $1 per period.

If the periodic cash inflow is not uniform, then the problem becomes more difficult. Such a situation occurs if the cash inflows are unequal in amount, or if some declining balance basis of depreciation is used. (For handling of depreciation, see treatment later in this Section.) In such instances it is necessary to get the **individual present value of each cash inflow.** Here, however, a further difficulty arises: The rate of return can be found only by trial and error.

Illustration. A machine costs $20,000 and produces cash inflows as follows:

Year 1 .... $ 3,000
" 2 5,000
" 3 8,000
" 4 12,000
" 5 6,000
" 6 2,000
$36,000

The total cash inflow for the 6 years is the same as in the previous illustration, but its distribution by years is different. The solution is shown in Fig. 8. The annual present value factors are obtained from a table (such as Fig. 15 in Sec. 27) that is used when it is necessary to get the present value of a lump sum discounted for a definite period.

	Cash Inflows	*P.V. of $1 (18%)	Amt.	*P.V. of $1 (20%)	Amt.
1	*P.V. one year hence of 3,000	.847	$ 2,541	.833	$ 2,499
2	" " two years " " 5,000	.718	3,590	.694	3,470
3	" " three " " " 8,000	.609	4,872	.579	4,632
4	" " four " " " 12,000	.516	6,192	.482	5,784
5	" " five " " " 6,000	.437	2,622	.402	2,412
6	" " six " " " 2,000	.370	740	.335	670
	Total cash inflows		$20,557		$19,467
	Cash outflow (investment)		20,000		20,000
	Excess		+$ 557		−$ 533

* P.V. = Present Value

Fig. 8. Uneven cash flows.

17·40 CAPITAL ASSET PLANNING

By definition the present values of the cash inflows should **exactly balance** the investment; a first trial of 18% shows an excess of $557 cash inflows. This means that the discounting rate used was not high enough. A second trial of 20% produces a deficiency of $533; the discounting rate, therefore, was too high. In the instant case, the true rate of return is about halfway between 18% and 20%, or approximately 19%. In general it is necessary only to obtain a discount rate producing a negative excess and one producing a positive excess. Interpolation to fractions of a per cent is not really necessary, since all figures used in the computations are estimates and hence subject to error.

The Excess Present Value Method. The excess or net present value method is designed to overcome the weakness of the discounted cash flow method. It also uses present values but discounts all cash flows at the minimum desired rate of return, often referred to as **"cost of capital."** (For a detailed presentation of the cost of capital concept see discussion later in this Section.)

With the same illustration as before, the result appears as shown in Fig. 9. (It is assumed that the minimum desired rate of return is 15%.)

The excess of $2,364 means that the investment yields a higher than minimum rate of return and is therefore desirable. If there had been a deficiency, it would mean that the investment would not have been advisable.

Year		Minimum Desired Rate, 15% P.V.	Amt.
1	3,000 at 15%	.870	$ 2,610
2	5,000 " "	.756	3,780
3	8,000 " "	.658	5,264
4	12,000 " "	.572	6,864
5	6,000 " "	.497	2,982
6	2,000 " "	.432	864
	Total cash inflows....................		$22,364
0	Cash outflow (investment)		20,000
	Excess (+) or deficiency (−)		+$ 2,364

Fig. 9. Excess present value calculation.

OTHER FACTORS INVOLVED IN INVESTMENT DECISIONS. Whenever a choice must be made between alternative proposals, certain problems arise whose treatment affects the outcome:

1. Sunk costs and the role of depreciation
2. Disposal value
3. Incremental costs
4. Tax effects
5. Uneven lives
6. Ranking projects

Sunk Costs and Depreciation. The American Accounting Association Committee on Cost Concepts and Standards (Accounting Review, Vol. 27) defines sunk costs as "historical costs which are irrecoverable in a given situation." Kohler (A Dictionary for Accountants) similarly defines sunk cost as "a past cost arising out of a decision which cannot now be revised." For example, in the event of a replacement of an existing machine with a new one before the termination of the useful life of the existing machine, the cost or remaining book value of the existing machine is irrelevant. It is a sunk cost and as such has no bearing on the decision to be reached. What matters is not the past cost, but the **future cost.**

For the same reason, depreciation on the existing machine is irrelevant since it is based on past cost. Likewise, depreciation on the new machine is irrelevant, since the present value formula provides for the recovery of the cost of the new equipment. The only role of sunk costs and depreciation is in connection with taxation, as explained below.

Disposal Value. If the asset to be replaced has a scrap or disposal value, such value acts as a reduction to the capital investment being planned. Frequently the new asset also will have a **residual value** if replaced before the end of its economic life. If the amount is appreciable, it is customary to subtract from the investment figure the present value of the scrap value. Thus the net investment in a machine costing $20,000 with a residual value of $3,000 at the end of 10 years is as follows (assuming a rate of return of 15%):

Gross investment	$20,000
Present value of $3,000 for 10 years at 15%—$3,000 × .247	741
Net investment	$19,259

Incremental Costs and Savings. In all considerations of capital budgeting, only the **additional costs** involved are taken into consideration. This applies both to the original investment as well as to subsequent operations. Thus, as stated above, salvage values are subtracted from the gross investment and only the additional funds being committed to the project are considered. If the new asset promises any operating cost savings, it is necessary to offset additional costs incurred in arriving at the net savings. The costs being considered here are those that would be incurred if the project is carried out but that would be avoided if the project is rejected. Such costs are generally referred to as incremental costs.

CAPITAL BUDGETING AND TAXES. Because of the high income tax rates generally prevailing in this country and elsewhere, it is necessary to take them into account in arriving at a decision concerning a capital asset acquisition. Such taxes affect both the **timing** of the cash flows as well as their **amounts.**

Depreciation, as was noted above, is not a relevant factor in evaluating alternative proposals. Yet it affects the amount of taxes to be paid and hence the cash flows. Moreover, the cash flow may be materially altered by the method of asset amortization adopted, whether straight-line, declining-balance, sum-of-the-years-digits method, etc.

Finally, it is to be noted that where existing assets are disposed of, there may be a question of a **taxable gain or loss on the remaining book value,** even though the book value is basically irrelevant to the question of asset replacement. However, to the extent that taxes are involved, the cash flows are altered.

The application of these principles is illustrated below. Two solutions are presented: the first by the discounted cash flow rate of return, the second by the excess present value method.

Data: Book value of existing machine (original cost less accumulated depreciation)	$12,000
Estimated remaining life	6 years
Disposal value now	7,000

CAPITAL ASSET PLANNING

New fully automatic machine: cost (no residual value) $36,000
Estimated life ..... 6 years
Estimated annual savings
  Labor $10,000
  Material 5,000
Additional annual costs
  Power 1,500
  Maintenance, etc. 3,500
  Minimum desired return 15%

    The **discounted cash flow** solution (see Fig. 10) first develops the net investment and then the annual savings. The total investment is immediately reduced by the realizable disposal value of the old machine. However, since the book value of the old machine is $12,000 and it is being disposed of for $7,000, there is a loss of $5,000 that results in a tax saving of $2,400, based on a tax rate of 48%, so that the net investment is reduced to $26,600.

Cost of new machine	$36,000	
Less disposal value of old machine	7,000	$29,000
Loss on book value of old machine (12,000 − 7,000)	5,000	
Tax saving at 48%		2,400
Net investment		$26,600
Annual Savings		
Labor and material	$15,000	
Less added costs (power, maintenance, etc.)..	5,000	
Before tax savings	$10,000	$10,000
Additional depreciation		
New machine $6,000		
Old machine 2,000	4,000	
Taxable savings	$ 6,000	
Additional tax at 48%		$ 2,880
Post-tax savings		$ 7,120
Payback factor 26,600 ÷ 7,120 =		3.736
Rate of return, approx.		15.48%

Fig. 10. Discounted cash flow return solution.

    The net annual savings before taxes amount to $10,000. For tax purposes, depreciation must now be considered, but only the **additional depreciation**, i.e., the difference in annual depreciation between the old and new machines. The net cost savings of $10,000, less the increased depreciation of $4,000, assuming a straight-line basis, results in total annual savings amounting to $6,000. The net savings after taxes is $3,120 and the cash flow saving is $7,120. These results may also be summarized as follows:

Savings before taxes	$10,000
Additional depreciation	4,000
Balance subject to tax	$ 6,000
Tax at 48%	2,880
Net saving after tax	$ 3,120
Add back depreciation	4,000
Cash flow savings after tax	$ 7,120

    The next step is to obtain the **payback factor,** i.e., the investment divided by the annual savings. The payback period is 3.736 years. This represents the time

SPECIAL PROBLEMS OF CAPITAL PLANNING   **17·43**

required to recover the investment; but this is precisely what the present value of an annuity does. Hence the figure of 3.736 is in effect the present value of an annuity of $1 for a period of six years at an unknown rate of return. The present value table shows the payback, i.e., the present value of $1 per period at various interest rates. The figure of 3.736 lies between 15% and 16%. Interpolation, though not necessary, would yield an adjusted rate of return of 15.48%.

Excess present value solutions:

Net investment as before (cash outflow)........	−$26,600	(Fig. 10)
Present value of annual savings of $7,120 at		
15%: 7,120 × 3.784 = cash inflow	+ 26,942	
Difference	+$ 342	

Since the final result is positive, this means that the proposal will return more than the minimum 15% desired. Unless nonquantitative factors might change the result, the proposal may be accepted. In view, however, of the small excess, this proposal becomes a borderline case. Before a final decision is reached, it would be well to appraise the nonquantitative factors such as customer relations, employee relations, etc. On the basis of the figures alone, the proposal is not attractive.

If a depreciation method other than straight-line is used, such as the **sum-of-the-years-digits method,** it becomes necessary to evaluate each year's savings separately. This is because the stream of savings differs from year to year and cannot, therefore, be solved by the annuity formula. Using the same example as before, the results are as shown in Fig. 11. It is assumed that the old machine is depreciated on a straight-line basis, but that the new machine will use the sum-of-the-years-digits method. The solution uses the net present value method. It shows a more substantial excess of cash inflows over outflows, proving again how important it is, especially in borderline cases, to examine all relevant factors carefully. The reason for the greater excess is the fact that the cash savings of the sum-of-the-years-digits method are larger in the early years when their present values are highest and taper off toward the end when the present value becomes small by comparison.

Unequal Lives. In order to make proper assessments between projects calling for replacement of existing assets, it is desirable to make the comparison for the same number of periods in each case. The difficulty arises from the fact that the present equipment may have a remaining useful life of, say, 4 years while the life expectancy of the proposed new asset is 10 years. Thus, if the new machine is purchased **now** the comparison can be made as of the end of 4 years when the useful life of the old machine is terminated. But at that time the machine that was purchased will have a life expectancy of 6 years and, therefore, its salvage value at that time should be taken into consideration.

Illustration. The Derek Company is considering replacing one of its lathes, Machine A, with a more modern type, Machine B.

Machine A

Cost new, estimated life 10 years	$10,000
Book value now (straight-line depreciation)	4,000
Remaining useful life	4 years
Disposal value now	$ 2,500
" " 4 years hence	1,000
Annual operating costs, exclusive of depreciation............	10,000
Minimum desired return	12%

1.	2.	3.	4.	5.	6.	7.	8.	9.	10.	11.
			Depreciation						P.V. at 15%	
	Pretax	Old	New Machine		Add'l. Depr'n.	Taxable Savings	Tax at	Net Cash Flow		Total
Year	Saving	Machine	Fraction	Amount	5. − 3.	2. − 6.	48%	2. − 8.	from Table	9. × 10.
0	Net Investment (cash outflow) (Fig. 10)								1.0	−$26,600
1	$10,000	$2,000	6/21*	$10,286	$8,286	$1,714	$ 823	$9,177	.870	+$ 7,984
2	10,000	2,000	5/21	8,571	6,571	3,429	1,646	8,354	.756	+ 6,315
3	10,000	2,000	4/21	6,857	4,857	5,143	2,469	7,531	.658	+ 4,955
4	10,000	2,000	3/21	5,143	3,143	6,857	3,292	6,708	.572	+ 3,837
5	10,000	2,000	2/21	3,429	1,429	8,571	4,114	5,886	.497	+ 2,925
6	10,000	2,000	1/21	1,714	−286	10,286	4,937	5,063	.432	+ 2,187
	Total cash inflows									+$28,203
	Excess									$ 1,603

*Sum of digits from 1 through 6 = 21.

Fig. 11. Excess present value applied to sum-of-the-years-digits method.

Derek Company Illustration Solution: 4-year Basis

Incremental Analysis

			Present Value Factor at 12%	Present Value Amount
If Machine B is purchased now:				
Annual operating savings ($10,000 − $3,000) (Note 1)	$7,000			
Additional depreciation ($2,000 − $1,000)	1,000			
Taxable saving	$6,000			
Tax at 48%	2,880			
Post-tax saving (Note 2)	$4,120		3.037	$12,513
At end of 4 years: Disposal value of Machine B (no gain or loss on book value) (Note 3)		$12,000		
Less: Disposal value foregone of Machine A (Note 4)	$1,000			
Capital gain tax at 25%	250	750		
		$11,250	.636	7,155
Proceeds on disposal of Machine A realized now		$ 2,500	1.0	2,500
Loss on book value of Machine A ($4,000 − $2,500)	$1,500			
Tax saved at 48%		$ 720	1.0	720
Total of all cash inflows				$22,888
Investment in Machine B (cash outflow)		$20,000	1.0	20,000
Excess present value (in favor of replacement now)				$ 2,888

Notes on Solution:

Note 1: Only the difference in operating costs is considered. For tax impact, only the additional or incremental depreciation between Machines A and B is taken into account.

Note 2: The same result could be obtained as follows:

Annual operating savings	$7,000
Additional depreciation	1,000
Taxable savings	$6,000
Tax at 48%	2,880
Balance	$3,120
Add back depreciation	1,000
Post-tax saving	$4,120

Note 3: Since the remaining life of Machine A is 4 years, it is necessary, for comparative purposes, to estimate the residual value of Machine B at the end of 4 years.

Note 4: If Machine B is purchased now, the company loses the opportunity to realize $1,000 4 years from now. This is what economists call an **opportunity cost**.

17·45

Machine B

Cost new, estimated life 10 years	$20,000
Disposal value 4 years hence	12,000
" " 10 " "	4,000
Annual operating costs, exclusive of depreciation	3,000

Solution: The comparison is made at the end of 4 years (see table on page 45).

At the end of 4 years, Machine A will have been completely written off. The disposal value is therefore a capital gain.

If the decision is to retain the present equipment it will have to be replaced 4 years from now by machine C, whose life span would then extend another 10 years, i.e., 14 years from now. The problem has been well stated by Horngren (Cost Accounting, a Managerial Approach):

. . . some estimate of residual value is necessary, whether the comparison is made over the remaining life of old equipment or the useful life of the new equipment. If new equipment is to last eight years and old equipment five years, a decision to retain old equipment implies that replacement will be made in five years. Therefore, if a comparison is to be made over eight years, the future replacement cost (five years hence) of the old equipment has to be estimated and also the terminal value of that replacement at the end of the eight-year span under review. This vicious difficulty goes on and on; the practical answer is to make realistic assumptions regarding residual values at a common terminal date. The common date should be as distant as can be considered with confidence.

RANKING PROJECTS. The annual capital budget of a business may include proposals for a great number of projects. Some may have to be adopted because of their urgency, such as an emergency replacement. Some may have to be adopted because of legal requirements (additional fire exits, etc.). The remaining projects must be judged on the basis of the available funds and of the rate of return, i.e., whether they can earn a minimum desired rate of return. Where the excess present value method of evaluating a project is used, it becomes necessary to express each proposal in the form of a **profitability index**. This is the ratio of all cash inflows to the cash outflows. An index over 100 indicates that cash inflows exceed cash outflows and the project is, therefore, desirable, and vice versa.

For the Derek Company illustration above, the profitability index would be computed:

$$\frac{\text{Present value of cash inflows}}{\text{Present value of cash outflows}} = \frac{\$22{,}888}{\$20{,}000} = 114.44$$

There may be alternative proposals relative to the allocation of the available funds. A combination of proposals with the highest rate of return may not always be the best. The optimum combination is made up of investments with the highest **incremental** rate of return or profitability indices. This determines the disposition of the available funds.

Illustration. The following capital items are submitted for consideration (adapted from Horngren, Cost Accounting):

Project	Cost	Profitability Index
1	$ 60M	150
2	50	125
3	70	120
4	20	115
5	50	110
	$250M	

THE COST OF CAPITAL

The total available budget is $200M; since the projects are ranked in order of profitability, project 5 is immediately rejected. Suppose, however, there is the further possibility of substituting project 1a for project 1. The cost of 1a is assumed to be $130M and it has a profitability index of 140.

Solutions:

		Project	Cost I	Profitability Index II	Present Value (I × II)
A.		1	$ 60M	150	$ 90 M
		2	50	125	62.5
		3	70	120	84
		4	20	115	23
			$200M		$259.5M
B.	1a		$130M	140	$182 M
	3		70	120	84
			$200M		$266 M
	2 4 } Rejected				
C.	1a		$130M	140	$182 M
	2		50	125	62.5
	4		20	115	23
			$200M		$267.5M
	3 Rejected				

It is evident that Solution B is preferable to A since its present value is greater than A's. Similarly Solution C is preferable to B. In each case the reason is that the incremental return is greater, even though the profitability index of project 1 is greater than that of project 1a. The incremental approach can be proved as follows:

	Cost	Present Value	Profitability Index
Project 1	$ 60M	$ 90M	
Project 1a	130	182	
Difference	$ 70M	$ 92M	131
Rejections:			
Project 2	$ 50M	$ 62.5M	
4	20	23	
	$ 70M	$ 85.5M	122

What has happened is that the difference or incremental investment of $70M shows a profitability index of 131 as against an index of 122 for the projects that are eliminated.

In Solution C the incremental index is again 131 as between projects 1 and 1a. The rejected project 3 has a profitability index of only 120.

The Cost of Capital

THE GENERAL CONCEPT. Reference to the cost of capital occurs most frequently in connection with discussions of capital allocation decisions. As previously indicated, all capital expenditure projects—except those designated by the management as "strategic" capital outlays—would be considered unacceptable from the stockholder's viewpoint unless the estimated rate of return from a capital proposal exceeded the firm's cost of capital. Thus, cost of capital is visualized as a "hurdle" or **minimum rate of return** that must be earned on a capital investment proposal. The management strives to improve the position of the owners, the common stockholders; this effort involves many decisions in respect to proposed capital expenditures, which in turn must be related to the firm's present and future cost of capital.

The cost of capital to a firm cannot be defined with finality. A slight change in the price of a company's common shares, for example, all other things being equal, will result in a perceptible change in the firm's cost of capital. Moreover, share prices change continually—generally by small percentages but sometimes by substantial amounts. However, though it is difficult to predict a firm's cost of capital with precision, it can be estimated within a reasonable range of accuracy.

Robert W. Johnson (Financial Management) points out:

... It is important that we do not consider the cost of capital to be one single given figure, that is, a cut-off point. Rather it is, a **value in a boundary area.** When we say that a firm's cost of capital for a given amount of financing is 10%, we really mean that as the rate of return after taxes on capital expenditures approaches the neighborhood of 10%, our examination of proposed projects should be increasingly rigorous.

Profit vs. Wealth Maximization. The primary usefulness of the cost of capital concept arises from the fact that, in theory at least, a firm will continue to invest in capital expenditure projects as long as their time discounted rate of return exceeds, or at least is equal to, the cost of capital. The concept of profit maximization may, however, be influenced by a number of other financial considerations. For example, **heavy use of debt financing,** while increasing the stockholders' rate of return, may also tend to reduce the market value of the company's shares because of the lower capitalization rate applied to the income by investors. Yet stockholders are more likely to be interested in the value of their shareholdings than in profits **per se.**

Some writers also point out that the uncertainty attaching to a stream of income from an asset is by itself a sufficient cause for questioning the validity of profits as the variable to be maximized by businessmen. In addition, financial decisions relevant to capital-raising activities are made in the context of circumstances actually existing or expected to exist in the capital and money markets. As a result of these and other considerations, **present value maximization** of owners' wealth is beginning to be increasingly recognized in economic theory as an acceptable expression of a businessman's furthering of his self-interest.

Other Definitions of Cost of Capital. Capital is used by a firm as one of several factors of production. Businessmen compete for it and obtain it subject to restrictions, standards, and demands established in the capital markets, social policy, and the bargaining power possessed by the parties involved. The influence of these factors, in turn, is reflected in the market rates of capitalization. Accordingly, the cost of capital is sometimes defined as a "burden" assumed or as a "sacrifice" suffered by an enterprise in return for the use of capital. It is the "price" paid to capital suppliers for inducing them to entrust their funds to the enterprise. From an internal managerial viewpoint, the cost of capital can be defined alternatively as the cost of **capital inputs.**

Borrowing and Lending Rates. Still another definition of the cost of capital that has been proposed relates to the so-called "borrowing" and "lending" rates.

These concepts were first used by Lutz and Lutz in their analysis of investment decisions of a firm (The Theory of Investment of the Firm). The "borrowing rate" is the rate a firm must pay for funds it acquires. The "lending rate," on the other hand, is the rate a firm can earn by committing its funds to alternative market investments involving the degree of risk comparable to that existing in the firm itself.

Barges has pointed out: ". . . Because of difficulties of determining the 'lending rate' for specific projects and because of the administrative difficulties in applying it, the opportunity cost concept has not received much attention . . ." (The Effect of Capital Structure on the Cost of Capital).

APPLICATIONS OF THE COST OF CAPITAL. Where wealth-maximization is given major emphasis, it is necessary to take into account not only profits but, foremost, **investment values**. The measurement of cost of capital is, therefore, interrelated with the valuation of a business enterprise. As Durand has expressed it, ". . . problems of measuring capital costs are much the same as the problems that arise in trying to appraise the going concern value of a business enterprise . . ." (Conference on Research in Business Finance).

In view of the manifold differences between borrowed and equity capital, a firm's valuation may be affected by mere financing decisions, independent of profits derived from the invested capital. As has been pointed out, a firm's market value will be changed whenever a financing decision causes its capitalization rates to move up or down. A rise in the proportion of debt in the capital structure will tend to increase the volatility and risk of the common stock and vice versa.

These circumstances indicate the need for the **separation of financing decisions from investment decisions**. Each of them may, in turn, affect a firm's cost of capital, and thus its valuation. Moreover, each involves a number of subsidiary issues. For example, a choice between retaining profits or paying them out in higher dividends includes both an investment decision and a financing decision; as such, it is likely to have some repercussions on the cost of capital.

FINANCIAL STRUCTURE VS. CAPITAL STRUCTURE. Typically, measurement of the cost of capital is restricted to items included in the capital structure. Under this definition, **only long-term debt and equity** enter the computations, leaving out all short-term sources of funds. This practice seems to be consistent with other financial analytical techniques, such as the leverage ratio and interest coverage. Although this may be acceptable for some purposes, it is open to the criticism that at least **some short-term credit arrangements are not independent** of the overall financial planning of the firm.

For example, although bank credit may legally take the form of a short-term arrangement subject to renewals, in actuality it may be filling a more permanent need for capital. In addition, the management itself may consciously supplement its long-term financing with short-term arrangements in anticipation of changing conditions in the money and capital markets. It is not difficult to conceive of a number of other situations where a line between a true short-term and a true long-term credit cannot be drawn very easily. It is not the technical classification of items but rather the nature of capital needs that is relevant to cost of capital measurement.

In order to recognize some degree of substitutability among the various types of credit in the debt structure of a firm, some writers explicitly add short-term interest-bearing debt to the value of long-term capital (for example, Weston, Managerial Finance). Others prefer to assume that capital structure and financial structure are identical or interchangeable (Schwartz, The Journal of Finance, Vol. XIV). Whatever a particular executive's preference is with respect to the inclusion of such short-term items in the computation of a firm's overall cost of capital, it appears that their costs should be known at least to the extent that they may influence the choice from among several financing alternatives.

SPECIFIC COSTS OF CAPITAL. As has been mentioned, the measurement of a firm's cost of capital is not an exact procedure. It involves some ambiguities and controversial views and must be based largely on forecasts that, of course, are subject to various margins of error. The computed value for cost of capital should therefore be regarded only as a **reasonable approximation** of the true cost of capital inputs consistent with corporate needs, the conditions under which the company is raising its capital, the state of expectations, and self-imposed policy constraints. Frequently, businesses prefer to employ more than one type of capital, the costs of which may differ widely. Only after the cost of each type of funds has been obtained is it possible to arrive at some idea of the overall, or composite, cost of a firm's capital. Thus, the first step in the measurement of a company's cost of capital is the calculation of each specific cost, which may be defined as ". . . the minimum financial obligation which must be incurred in order to secure the use of capital from a particular source." (Hunt, Williams, and Donaldson, Basic Business Finance.)

Classification of Capital Funds. Capital funds may be classified according to the legal instruments used in their acquisitions—i.e., debt, preferred equity, and common equity. However, such a classification is somewhat inadequate since it fails to recognize the fact that equity capital is frequently "raised" without resort to capital markets. Thus, it may lead to incorrect conclusions with respect to the "cost" of funds that are recouped from operations through nonfunds-flow items, the most important of which is depreciation.

Not only have increased profits presented business firms with opportunities to enlarge their equity base without resorting to the capital markets, but businesses have actually shown a pronounced tendency to rely more heavily on **internal funds,** in satisfying their needs for investment capital, than on external funds. This preference reflects, in large part, the increased cash throw-offs in recent years. And it is reasonable to expect that the role of internal financing will continue to rise. Larger after-tax profits under the 1964 tax law should provide business firms with more investible funds. In addition, more liberal depreciation allowances under the presently allowed accelerated depreciation schedules, investment tax credits, and the increasing capital intensity of our production processes, will give a continued strong impetus to the internal generation of cash.

Consequently, capital funds are additionally classified according to the "locus" of their generation, i.e., whether they are externally or internally generated.

COST OF BORROWED FUNDS. The amount of interest paid periodically to the creditor is the most obvious item in the cost of borrowed funds but it may not be a complete measure of the cost. This is true, for example, of even such a relatively simple arrangement as an unsecured short-term bank credit.

When the full value of the loan is made available to the firm and when there are no other costs of obtaining the loan, its cost is equal to its **nominal or stated rate of interest.** But when a bank discounts the loan by deducting all interest in advance, the **effective rate of interest**—that is, its cost—is somewhat higher than the nominal rate, which is based on the maturity (or "par") value of the loan, whereas the amount actually available is the par value reduced by interest charges. In order to compute the cost of a discounted loan it is necessary to re-

THE COST OF CAPITAL

late interest charges to the amount that the company can actually draw. Thus, in the case of a 90-day, 6% discounted loan of $100,000, the interest is $1,500 and the net proceeds $98,500.

$$\text{Cost of Loan} = \frac{\text{Interest}}{\text{Proceeds}} \;\; \frac{\$1{,}500}{\$98{,}500} = 1.523\% \text{ for 90 days.}$$

Adjusting this to an annual basis—1.523% × 4—the effective rate of interest is 6.092% per annum. The same result is obtained by relating to the net proceeds the imputed annual interest charge based on the face value of the loan:

$$\frac{6\% \times \$100{,}000}{\$98{,}500} = 6.092\%.$$

This is the before-tax cost of the loan. Since interest payments are tax-deductible, the **after-tax cost** is the before-tax cost × (1 − the tax rate). Assuming a 48% corporate tax rate, the after-tax cost of the above loan is:

$$6.092\% \times (1 - .48) = 3.168\%.$$

COSTS INCURRED IN SALE OF SECURITIES. There are four elements of cost incidental to the issue of a security. These are:

1) A **payment of a predetermined amount** to the investment banker who handles the issue. Typically, the banker deducts this amount (the spread) from the selling price of the security (to the public) and remits the balance to the company. (In some instances, of course, the securities may be sold directly to an institution or to the company's own stockholders and the investment banker may not be used at all, or he may be used on a standby basis only.)

2) Frequently the issuing company incurs **other costs,** for example, the cost of designing, engraving, and printing the security certificates, some legal expenses, and the like. The extent to which these costs are absorbed by the underwriters or paid by the issuing company itself depends mainly on the nature of the purchase agreement.

3) **Periodic payments** to security holders in the form of either interest or dividends.

4) Whenever an issue has a definite maturity (or when the company has the right to redeem it, in whole or in part, at its own option), the **final payment** to investors will most likely differ from the amount actually received by the company at the time of the original sale. The extent to which the original net proceeds is less than the retirement payment represents a **"discount"** to the company, whereas a **"premium"** occurs in the opposite case. It must be noted that a discount to the company may reflect a premium to the investor, and vice versa, as shown in the illustrations below.

COST OF BONDS. The specific cost of funds raised by a sale of bonds is customarily computed on a per bond basis. The **net proceeds per bond** are obtained by subtracting the spread and the share of company-paid expenses from the selling price. The financial obligation incurred includes periodic interest payments and the principal, with appropriate adjustments for discounts or premiums.

Assume that a company sells 4½%, 20-year bonds for which investors pay $1,010 per $1,000 par value. Assuming, further, that the spread is $35 and that other expenses paid directly by the company amount to $15, the net proceeds to the company are then $960. Thus, the company is committed to pay $45 interest a year and to repay to the bondholder at the end of 20 years the par value of the bond. What is the cost of these funds?

17·52 CAPITAL ASSET PLANNING

It is usually assumed that the **excess of maturity value** over the net proceeds is accumulated gradually and uniformly over the entire life of the bond. In this example, the accumulation would be at the rate of $2 annually—1/20 of $40 every year. When added to the interest payment of $45, total annual cost (or "sacrifice") becomes $47. The amount of funds available to the company is thus an average of $960 (the amount originally received) and $1,000 (par value), or $980.

The approximate cost of funds is obtained in the following manner:

$$\frac{\text{Sacrifice}}{\text{Proceeds}} = \frac{\$47}{\$980} = 4.796\% \text{ per year.}$$

The steps taken to compute the cost of debt above are summarized in the following formula:

$$\text{Approximate cost} = \frac{I + \dfrac{PV - NP}{n}}{\dfrac{PV + NP}{2}}$$

where I is the dollar amount of annual interest payment, PV is the amount payable at maturity (usually par value), NP is the net proceeds, and n represents the number of years to maturity of the bond.

Similarly, when the company has a "premium," it is assumed that it is being used up gradually and uniformly as a partial offset against interest payments. Again, the same general formula applies, except that the interest cost is reduced by a pro rata fraction of the premium. For example, if the net proceeds were $1,020 (instead of the previously assumed $960), the cost of the issue would be:

$$\frac{\$45 + \dfrac{\$1,000 - \$1,020}{20}}{\dfrac{\$1,000 + \$1,020}{2}} = \frac{\$45 - \$1}{\$1,010} = 4.356\%.$$

Accurate Method. For most purposes the approximate method shown above is quite adequate. A more precise method of computing the effective rate of interest should recognize, however, that the annual accumulations for the discount are kept reinvested and are earning income. It is not necessary to set aside $2 every year in order to have $40 at maturity. The amount that is theoretically set aside each year must be just large enough to give $2 when compounded to the maturity of the bond. That is, the amount to be provided each year should be equal to the present value of $2 at maturity discounted to the year in which it is assumed to be set aside. The rate of discounting is the effective rate of interest on the bond itself.

The problem, therefore, is to find the rate of interest at which the sum of present values of all interest payments of $45 per year plus the present value of $1,000 20 years hence is precisely equal to the net proceeds of $960. The solution may be handled through a discounted cash flow return analysis, as discussed previously. More commonly, however, it is done by means of **bond value "tables"** (see Sec. 27), where the information is conveniently presented. According to the tables, the cost of the issue cited above is 4.814% when net proceeds are $960 and 4.35% when the net proceeds are $1,020.

It should be noted that because of the **flotation costs** and other expenses, the cost of capital to its user is not the same as the yield on investment to its supplier. It was shown, for example, that the bond issue discussed above cost the company 4.814% when the proceeds were $960. The yield to the investor, however, based on the previously assumed selling price of $1,010, comes to 4.424%.

BEFORE AND AFTER-TAX COST OF DEBT. Because of the tax deductibility of interest, it is customary to show the cost of borrowed funds as an after-tax effective rate of interest. Strictly speaking, however, use of a tax-adjusted effective rate of interest is justified only when earnings before interest and taxes are equal to, or exceed the interest charges. When earnings before interest and taxes are negative, the tax shield does not apply and the actual cost of borrowed funds is equal to the before-tax effective rate of interest. With earnings before interest and taxes ranging between zero and the level of interest charges, the cost of credit varies between the before-tax and the after-tax effective rates of interest, the precise rate depending on the extent to which the interest charges are actually earned.

In practice, this refinement can be ignored. The cost of capital should be regarded as a **"continuous"** concept—i.e., extending over the entire life of a contract—rather than an "instantaneous" phenomenon. Moreover, through the carry-forward or carry-backward provisions of the tax laws a firm can take advantage of the tax shield even when earnings in a particular year do not cover all interest charges. Finally, the number of years in which earnings before interest and taxes fall short of interest charges is ordinarily very small, and an occasional failure to earn interest charges is unlikely to have an appreciable effect on the cost of the bond.

COST OF PREFERRED STOCK. From the point of view of the financial manager, preferred equity approaches debt very closely even though its legal status is quite different. Although nonpayment of preferred dividends will not create a condition of default or bring about bankruptcy, it could have a number of other highly undesirable consequences. For this reason the financial manager typically considers the **payment of preferred dividends mandatory** rather than discretionary.

There is an important difference, however, between debt and preferred stock in that debt contracts always specify a maturity date whereas preferred stock is typically considered to be a **"perpetual"** security. "True, some preferred stock issues do carry so-called sinking fund provisions which aim to retire the priority ownership but even so those provisions do not have the force of debt maturities and are not 'requirements' in the unconditional sense." (Waterman, Essays on Business Finance.) Similarly, the preferred is typically made callable at the option of the management. These features tend to put decisions on retirement of the stock in the area of financial "maneuverability."

In general, the method of computing costs is similar to that used for bonds. Assuming that a $5 preferred stock ($100 par) is sold to the public at $105, that the spread is $2, and that other expenses paid by the company amount to $1 per share, the cost of a preferred issue is:

$$\frac{\text{Obligation incurred}}{\text{Proceeds received}} = \frac{5}{105 - (2+1)} = \frac{5}{102} = 4.902\% \text{ per annum.}$$

As the preferred dividend is paid out of the **after-tax** profits, the above method of computation results in an after-tax cost of preferred stock.

The examples used as illustrations of the methods of computing the costs of borrowed funds and preferred stock are oversimplified in the sense that no consideration was given to the fact that the indenture may provide for the **gradual retirement of a bond issue,** either through a sinking fund or through serial redemptions, and that some preferred issues may also include **predetermined retirement schedules.** A sinking fund provision adds to the complexity of the mathematics since the periodic payments will affect the timing and the extent of the flow of funds associated with the issue. The main problem remains the same, however, namely, to find that rate of discount that equates all future flows of funds with the net proceeds received from the issue.

COST OF COMMON STOCK. The cost of common equity is obtained in the same manner as is the cost of senior securities, i.e., by relating "sacrifice" to the "net proceeds." It is not as easily determined, however, since a number of technical and conceptual problems arise.

The fact that all periodic payments for the use of debt and preferred capital are **fixed**, the maturity is definitely known (or nonexistent in the case of preferred stocks), and the amount repayable at retirement (or any other redemption date) is clearly specified, makes it possible to calculate rather precisely the financial obligations associated with these sources of funds.

In contrast, estimates of the cost of common stock are **inexact**. First, common equity may be obtained in a number of ways, e.g., through direct sale of stock to the public, sale of additional shares to present stockholders under pre-emptive rights, and indirect and "delayed" sale by way of convertible securities. The cost of common equity will vary depending on the method by which it is raised.

Second, residual equity differs from senior capital in that it usually gives **unlimited participation in business profits.** Whether or not any dividends are paid, the entire amount of accumulated profits, after tax and provision for the preferred stockholders, belongs to the common shareholders. Since this accumulation will be reflected in the price of the stock, the cost of common stock cannot be construed as a simple ratio of dividends to stock prices.

A stockholder can realize income from his investment either in dividends or in capital gains or both. It is therefore customary to define the **cost of equity** as the ratio of earnings per share to the price per share:

$$\text{Cost of common equity} = \frac{\text{Earnings}}{\text{Proceeds}}.$$

This approach has not been accepted unanimously, some writers preferring to express the cost of common equity as a function of dividends. Some of their views will be presented later in the discussion. In any event, however, the size of the dividend influences the price of the stock.

DIRECT SALE OF COMMON STOCK TO THE PUBLIC. The first step in determining the cost of common stock for a going concern is to find that rate at which the market capitalizes the company's earnings. The second step involves an adjustment in the **capitalization rate** for the difference between the market price of the shares already outstanding and the price per share (net proceeds) from a new issue.

Finding the rate of capitalization for common stock is not an easy matter. When an investor buys a security he buys a stream of anticipated future income. Profits, however, cannot be predicted with certainty and will tend to vary over time. The year to year variations in reported profits may cause the price of the stock to fluctuate, but not necessarily in a direct or proportional manner. To reduce the problem to a manageable level it is usually assumed that **average expected profits** underlie investors' valuations of the security.

The record of past earnings usually reveals a **trend** that is relevant to the future. Consequently, unless there is some acceptable evidence that future profits will differ significantly from past levels, it is customary to use past earnings as a basis for projecting future profits. However, even though management's estimation of the value of the stock may differ from that of the market, the stock can be sold only at a price less than or equal to the price that the investor is willing to pay, which, in turn, is based on information available to him as well as his personal appraisal of the capital markets. Thus, any discrepancy in the valuation of the common equity between the management and the market should be taken into account when the management formulates its overall financial strategy.

Avoidance of Dilution. Management's prime responsibility is to the owners of an enterprise. Accordingly, it is important for the management to take care that, among other things, an investment or a financing decision does not result in a dilution of earnings of the existing residual owners. In terms of capital budgeting, this means that an investment project should be accepted only when it promises to earn at least the equivalent of the earnings per share without the expansion. In terms of financing decisions, earnings will have to increase at least in the same proportion as the number of shares in order to maintain an otherwise expected level of earnings per share.

Dilution occurs when common stock financing reduces earnings per share **(earning power dilution)** or asset value per share **(asset dilution)**. But "because earnings per share are more important than assets per share to the investor, the central problem is not so much whether new financing will dilute book value or asset value, but whether it will dilute earnings per share . . ." (Guthmann and Dougall, Corporate Financial Policy).

Determination of Price per Share. Another major problem that arises in the computation of the capitalization rate for common equity is the selection of the share price to which the expected earnings will be related. First, there are stocks that are not traded at all or that are traded too infrequently to have an "objectively determined market price." Second, prices of stocks that are traded regularly usually fluctuate—sometimes substantially—over a given period of time. Which, then, is the appropriate price to use?

Theoretically the price to use is the price that would exist without the expansion. Since this is highly conjectural, attention is focused on the **existing** market price of the common stock, on the assumption that it very likely reflects the expectations of investors. Thus, considerable value judgment is involved when management attempts to arrive at a **"fair value"** of the stock. This value may be obtained in a number of ways, none of which is completely immune to criticism. Some of the possibilities include: the current market quotations, an average of the past and/or current prices, a market price adjusted for known or expected reactions to similar issues of other companies, or a price that is carefully estimated on the basis of known or expected conditions in the company, in the industry, and in the capital markets.

Computation of Cost. For purposes of illustration the following data are assumed:

1) A company has 1,000,000 shares of common stock outstanding and future average annual earnings are expected to be $5,000,000 after taxes.

2) The company has no senior capital.

3) Its common stock is traded in a narrow range around $50 per share.

4) The contemplated expansion requires $6,000,000 and can be financed, among other possibilities, by the sale of common stock.

5) The investment banker believes that a 10% underpricing will be required to assure a successful distribution and, therefore, the stock will be offered to the public at $45.

6) For underwriting the issue the banker will receive $4 per share; an additional $1 per share will be spent directly by the company. What is the cost of the new common stock issue?

The facts indicate that the market capitalizes common shareholders' profits at 10% ($5/$50). Since all stockholders, new and present, will share alike in the company's profits, the value of the investment of the existing owners will be maintained only when the additional investment earns at least $5 on each new share. It is assumed, additionally, that the incremental earnings are of the same **quality** as previous earnings. (There will usually be a temporary earnings dilution due to the time lag between the raising of funds, the completion of the investment project, and the subsequent generation of new income. However, such a dilution might ensue regardless of the method used to raise the funds and therefore can be conveniently ignored.)

Since net proceeds to the company are $40 per share [$50 − ($5 + $4 + $1)], the cost of this capital is:

$$\frac{\text{Earnings}}{\text{Proceeds}} = \frac{\$5}{\$40} = 12.5\%.$$

The difference between the 10% market rate of capitalization and the 12.5% cost of capital to the company is due entirely to the underpricing and the flotation costs. The same result can be obtained by adjusting the market rate of capitalization for the per share dilution in value. This dilution can be measured, in relation to the market price, in the following manner:

$$\text{Dilution factor} = \frac{\text{Market price} - \text{Net proceeds}}{\text{Market price}} = \frac{\$50 - \$40}{\$50} = .2 \text{ (or 20\%)}$$

and the cost of new equity capital becomes:

$$\frac{\text{Market capitalization rate}}{1 - \text{Dilution factor}} = \frac{10\%}{.8} = 12.5\%.$$

Alternatively, the cost of equity can be obtained as follows:

$$\text{Cost of equity} = \frac{E}{MP \times (1 - DF)} = \frac{\$5}{\$50 \times .8} = 12.5\%$$

where E is expected earnings per share, MP is the market price of the stock, and DF is the dilution factor.

That the cost of the new equity is 12.5% may be proved as follows: When net proceeds are $40 per share it is necessary to sell 150,000 shares of common stock in order to raise $6 million. And:

a. Total number of shares outstanding after the sale of common stock 1,150,000
b. Minimum earnings per share necessary to preserve a market price of $50 .... $5
c. Total earnings needed (a × b) $5,750,000
d. Earnings before expansion $5,000,000
e. Minimum earnings that must be contributed by the new project (d − c) .... $ 750,000
f. Minimum rate of return on new capital ....

$$\frac{\$750{,}000}{\$6{,}000{,}000} \qquad 12.5\%$$

SALE OF COMMON STOCK UNDER PRE-EMPTIVE RIGHTS.

Pre-emptive rights may be granted to stockholders either by common law, by

THE COST OF CAPITAL

state statutes, by the corporate charter, or by the management when it decides to raise the funds through the sale of common stock. Referring to the illustration above, assume that instead of selling the stock to the public, the management has decided to offer it to the existing stockholders at $32 per share. Issuing costs, including fees to an investment banker under a standby arrangement, are $2 per share. Assuming that all shares are promptly subscribed, what is the cost of this offering?

Since net proceeds to the company are $30 per share, it is necessary to sell 200,000 shares in order to raise $6 million. Accordingly, a stockholder is entitled to subscribe to one new share at $32 for each 5 shares he now holds (since there are 1 million shares presently outstanding).

After the offering the common shareholder will have more shares, each worth somewhat less than the previous market price per share, but his proportionate interest (providing, of course, he has exercised his rights) in the company will be unchanged. Such a stockholder will now have six shares instead of the five held previously, with a total value of $282 (five shares at $50 each plus one share at $32). Since the market capitalizes this company's earnings at 10%, it will take $28.20 in earnings to support his total investment of $282. Inasmuch as the earnings on the five shares previously held amounted to $25, the new investment will have to earn at least $3.20 per share ($28.20 − $25.00). Thus, the cost of the issue is:

$$\frac{\text{Required earnings}}{\text{Net proceeds}} = \frac{\$3.20}{\$30} = 10.67\%.$$

It is possible to compute the **cost of a rights offering** by direct reference to the new market value of a share of stock. The theoretical market value of a share ex-rights is:

$$\frac{(50 \times 5) + 32}{6} = \frac{282}{6} = \$47$$

The required earnings on the new investment are:

$$(6 \times \$4.70) - (5 \times \$5) = \$3.20$$

and the cost of the new issue is 10.67% ($3.20/$30).

The difference between 12.5%—the cost of the new common stock sold directly to the public, and 10.67%—the cost of the stock when issued by way of a privileged subscription, is entirely due to the extent of underpricing and the cost of flotation. The effect of these two factors on the cost of capital depends on the method of raising the funds. In a **direct sale to the public**, underpricing tends to increase the cost of capital because it reduces the proceeds to the company while it leaves the level of expected earnings per share unchanged. In a **privileged subscription** the extent of underpricing is irrelevant from the point of view of the cost of capital. It was shown above, for example, that a discount of $18 from the market price of $50 reduced the average value of each share of stock by $3 (to $47 from $50) and that it also reduced the average required earnings per share on the new number of shares by $.30 (to $5 from $4.70). The size of a discount, under the same conditions, is usually higher in a rights offering than in a sale to the public.

As regards flotation costs, assuming identical market conditions, the flotation costs should be lower in a rights offering than in a direct sale. Thus, in most situations there will be a difference in the cost of equity capital between a direct sale and a rights offering.

INDIRECT SALE OF COMMON STOCK THROUGH CONVERTIBLE SECURITIES.

A senior security convertible into common shares is commonly **issued in three types of situations.** First, the convertible security is a financing device by which a corporation may obtain funds through a low-cost bond issue during the early stages of a project, when earnings are low, and have the bond converted to equity capital as earnings rise. Second, it may be sold to attract investors who otherwise would not be willing to commit their funds because of the risks involved. Third, a management may use a convertible security in order to reduce the cost of capital by taking advantage of the anticipated higher future price of the common stock. When converted, the effect of a convertible security on the position of the existing common shareholders will be the same as if the company sold common stock to the public. This means that whenever a convertible security is sold to investors other than existing common shareholders, the latter may face a dilution of control, earnings, and asset values.

The **cost** of a convertible bond can be shown either as the cost of a straight bond or as a cost of equity according to the terms of conversion. The computation of the cost of a convertible bond **as a straight debt instrument** is the same as that of a nonconvertible bond. It is simple and accurate. The calculation of the cost **as an equity-equivalent,** on the other hand, may be beset with difficulties. The time of the conversion can be predicted only in a general way. Also, when the conversion ratio varies over time, as it usually does, the conversion price of the common stock is not known precisely and must be computed with reference to the price that will exist when the expected conversion takes place.

In general, whether the cost of a convertible bond is considered by the management to be equal to the cost of a debt instrument or to the cost of its equity-equivalent depends primarily on the **intentions of the management** and the **reasons for issuing the convertible security.** Should the management intend not to permit its conversion, for example, by calling it before the conditions conducive to conversion set in, a convertible bond would be treated as a straight bond. If, on the other hand, the bond is offered with the hope that it will be converted, its cost should be computed as the cost of a delayed "stock sale."

As before, assume a hypothetical firm that has 1 million shares outstanding and that it expects to earn $5 million without expansion. Its common stock is selling at about $50 per share. It contemplates an expansion project that requires $6 million additional capital. Suppose that the funds can be raised by a sale of 4½%, 20-year debentures, each convertible into 15 shares of common stock. The debenture is priced to net the company $960 per $1,000 face value. The terms of this debenture are identical to the terms of the bond that was used to explain the computation of the cost of a debt instrument, except that, in addition, it is made convertible into common stock. Its cost as a debt instrument would be the same as the cost of the bond, i.e., 4.814% (see page 52). It is further assumed that the management not only expects the debentures to be converted, but, in fact, is issuing them as a method of selling the common stock at a higher price than an outright offering could currently bring.

According to the previous assumptions, net proceeds to the company were $40 per share when the stock was sold directly to the public (see page 56). By means of a convertible debenture, however, the company is able to obtain the equivalent of $64 per common share ($960/15). In addition, before the conversion actually takes place the company has the use of a much cheaper debt issue. The cost of common equity raised in this manner is 9.375%:

$$\frac{\text{Expected earnings per share}}{\text{Net proceeds per share}} = \frac{\$5}{\$64} = 9.375\%.$$

COST OF RETAINED EARNINGS. The increasing tendency of businesses to rely on retention of earnings to satisfy their needs for new capital makes the evaluation of the cost of this source of funds that much more important. The need to estimate the cost of retained earnings stems from the fact that an investment of funds, to be profitable, must also account for the cost of capital inputs. Yet, some businessmen are not fully aware of the importance of imputing cost to retained earnings and may even consider these funds as practically cost-free capital. ". . . This mistaken view seems to rest on the assumption that the corporation is separate from the common stockholders, and that it costs the corporation nothing to withhold the earnings from them . . ." (Johnson, Financial Management).

The generation of profits is a **continuous process,** as is the commitment of funds to assets, at least as far as working capital is concerned. This continuity may tend to divert management's attention from the need to consider the cost of earnings retained in the business. Further, some highly profitable but not too rapidly growing enterprises may be able to obtain most, if not all, of their equity by retaining earnings and thereby virtually eliminate the need to raise equity funds in the capital markets. By foregoing the opportunity to test its investment policies in the capital markets a management may be led to the erroneous conclusion that retained earnings represent a costless type of capital.

In fact, retained earnings are not without cost. This becomes apparent as soon as a decision to retain profits in the business is recognized as ". . . a new act of investment by the existing stockholders, differing from the initial investment only in that the decision to reinvest is made by management rather than by the stockholders." (Robert H. Wessel, Principles of Financial Analysis.) The cost of reinvested profits to stockholders is the **opportunity cost** of such funds to the stockholders, i.e., it is equal to ". . . the earnings that they would otherwise obtain by placing these funds in alternative investments." (R. W. Johnson, Financial Management.)

The cost of retained profits differs from the cost of equity raised by a sale of securities in two respects. First, there is no need for underpricing and no flotation costs are incurred. As a result, net proceeds are equal to the entire amount of profits actually retained. Second, when profits are distributed in the form of cash dividends, the value to the stockholders of the dividends received is less than the value of the distributed profits by the amount of the stockholders' personal tax liability on the dividend income. It follows, therefore, that the cost of retained earnings to the company is less than the market rate of capitalization for equity capital.

The **opportunity cost** of retained earnings to the stockholder is the rate of return that he can obtain by investing the after-tax dividends in alternative opportunities of equal quality. For example, in the illustration used above, a stockholder was willing to pay $50 for a share of stock earning $5 a year because this was the rate that he could have made on other investments with comparable risk. If all earnings were paid out in dividends—$5 per share—and his personal tax rate was, say, 20%, a stockholder could earn, by investing the dividend elsewhere, about 40 cents on each $5 of dividend received ($5 × [1 − t] × 10%). Therefore, based on before-tax dividend—i.e., earnings per share—his return is only 8% ($.40/$5).

The rate of a stockholder's earnings on his dividend income is equal to $i(1-t)$, where i is the market rate of capitalization for this stock and t is the stockholder's personal income tax rate. Consequently, if E is the dollar return from investment of the dividend and P the price of the stock, the cost of retained earnings $= \frac{E(1-t)}{P}$, i.e., the market capitalization rate for equity multiplied by one minus the stockholder's marginal tax rates.

Selecting the Tax Rate. It is apparent that the cost of retained earnings to a firm is a function of the personal income tax rates of its stockholders. However, the multiplicity of the stockholders' tax rates makes application of the formula rather difficult. In a publicly held corporation, where there are a great number of shareholders of various means and incomes, there is no single tax rate that correctly reflects the opportunity cost of retained earnings to every stockholder. (Even in a closely held family business not all of its owners are exactly alike in respect to their objectives, incomes, and tax positions.) The management must therefore exercise its judgment in selecting that tax rate that it thinks most realistically represents the marginal tax of its **"typical"** stockholder. Obviously, this is not an easy task. In some situations a realistic rate can be obtained by a review of the tax status of each stockholder, but this is not practical when there are a large number of stockholders. However, it is not necessary to seek a completely accurate tax rate so long as the rate selected represents a realistic compromise of the tax situations and investment objectives of the stockholders. Such a rate may take into account the approximate number of stockholders falling in each tax bracket and the amounts of capital supplied by large shareholders. Should it be concerned with every stockholder or just those who have held the stock for a minimal—albeit arbitrarily determined—period of time? A "correct" tax rate should also reflect the objectives of the owners—e.g., whether they are interested in a regular dividend income or in capital gains.

An interesting compromise in resolving the **conflict between the regular and the capital gains tax rates** has been advanced by Walter (The Journal of Finance, Vol. 11). In analyzing the effect of taxes on investors' valuation of retained earnings as compared with dividends, he has developed a formula that results in the cost of retained earnings that accounts for the effect of both the regular and the capital gains tax. In symbols,

$$\text{Cost of retained earnings} = \left(\frac{t}{s}\right) R_c$$

where t is one minus the marginal tax rate on personal income, s is one minus the tax rate on capital gains, and R_c is the market capitalization rate for this stock.

Another approach in selecting a rate from among the many marginal tax rates of the stockholders recommends developing an "average marginal tax rate" (Johnson, Financial Management). On the other hand, when conditions are too complex and computations too impractical, management may set an arbitrary rate. For example, Hunt, Williams, and Donaldson (Basic Business Finance), suggest "taking the minimum individual federal tax rate, since all shareholders (except tax-exempt institutions) must pay at least this rate. . . ."

Walter also refers to the marginal tax rate but to him the "marginal" rate is that paid by a marginal **trader** in a security rather than the rate paid by a typical stockholder. (Walter, The Journal of Finance, Vol. 11.)

Disagreement As to Need for Tax Adjustment. There are also writers who do not see the need for adjusting the market capitalization rate for stockholders' tax liability, thus suggesting that the cost of retained earnings is the same as the market rate of capitalization for the common stock. Guthmann and Dougall, for example, state that ". . . to avoid dilution of the rate earned on the total common stock equity, management must earn the same return on retained earnings as on the common stock portion. The cost of capital from both sources is therefore the earnings yield that satisfies the market for the stock itself." (Corporate Financial Policy.)

A similar position is taken by Solomon (The Theory of Financial Management), who concludes that ". . . so long as external opportunities are available, the minimum measure for the cost of internal funds is k_e, regardless of the effect of personal taxes." (k_e is the "yield available on external investments," i.e., the market capitalization rate.) In this context, the cost of retained earnings is the opportunity cost **to the company, not to the stockholder.**

Donaldson and Pfahl (Corporate Finance) agree, in principle, that the cost of retained earnings is equal to the rate of return that ". . . the shareholder himself could earn." This is equivalent to the market capitalization rate for the corporation's stock, adjusted for savings of flotation costs and the tax status of the stockholders. They assume, however, that the cost of retained earnings is ". . . equivalent to the common-stock capital regardless of the tax position of the owners . . ." for, in their view ". . . it does not seem reasonable that management should capitalize on the tax position of its stockholders. . . ."

Weston (Managerial Finance) denies the need for tax adjustment of the market capitalization rate for another reason. In his opinion:

This view implies that there is a direct relation between retained earnings and prices of common stock. Because this relation does not in fact obtain, it is not appropriate to cut down the amount of retained earnings by some percentage factor.

Retained earnings may best be regarded as another form of common-stock investment. Therefore they can appropriately be included in full with common stock in net worth of equity as an element of financing in calculating cost. As a practical matter, the problem does not arise if market values are employed.

COST OF DEPRECIATION FUNDS. All external sources of funds and retained earnings supply a firm with new capital. In contrast, depreciation reflects conversion into cash of funds previously committed to the enterprise. As such, it should not enter the computation of the firm's composite cost of capital. In fact, depreciation is "neutral," inasmuch as it serves only to formally recognize the extent of a gradual consumption of fixed assets; the real source of funds is the income from operations. Therefore, depreciation "provides" funds only to the extent that it is actually earned, i.e., only when consumption of fixed assets attributable to a certain period is "liquefied" by generation of operating revenues.

Productive capacity of fixed assets, on the other hand, does not decline continuously and simultaneously with book adjustments to their unused values, at least not in an exact proportion to the depreciation allowances. Neither does replacement of fixed assets parallel the reduction in their net book values. To this extent funds recovered from income through depreciation charges are available for reinvestment along with other capital obtained from all other sources.

Assignment of cost to depreciation funds has attracted very little attention. There seems to be general agreement, however, that the cost of depreciation funds is its opportunity cost to the common shareholders. Accordingly, a market capitalization rate for common equity in alternative opportunities of like quality is usually accepted as a good measure of the cost of funds recovered through depreciation. Obviously, the underlying thought here is the concern for the preservation of the earning power of the firm, i.e., to its stockholders. It follows that when an internal project cannot earn at least the rate that the stockholder can obtain in an outside investment, the money should be distributed as a partial liquidation dividend and the company should embark upon a gradual dissolution.

Most writers point out, however, that in practice businessmen seldom attempt to assign a cost to depreciation. It is also argued that this omission is usually harmless because the funds required for a firm's profitable investment opportunities, together with its strategic investment projects, usually exceed the amount of funds obtained through depreciation charges.

COMBINED COST OF CAPITAL. A major value of the computation of specific capital costs lies in the fact that it makes possible an evaluation of the overall cost of capital, that is, the combined or composite cost of all capital employed by an enterprise. A firm seldom relies solely on one type of capital funds, most typically employing a combination of creditors' and owners' funds. Further, each of these general sources may include a variety of preferences, priorities, and security provisions. The cost of these various types of funds may differ rather substantially, depending primarily on the nature of the funds raised as well as on the financial strength and the rating of the firm. The combined cost of all capital employed lies somewhere between the least and the most expensive funds. Its computed value represents the measure of the firm's composite cost of capital.

Representing the cost of a "package" of capital funds characteristic of that firm, the overall cost constitutes the "correct" rate in the sense that it allows for a recovery of all capital input costs regardless of the method of raising the funds at a particular moment. Both the magnitude of corporate profits and the wealth of the firm's owners will be enhanced by investing the funds in projects earning in excess of the cost of its capital mix, on the assumption, of course, that marginal investments do not affect materially the quality of the income flows. The opposite would result in converse situations.

The **merit of an investment project** should, therefore, not be judged by comparing the project's expected returns with the cost of the type of capital seemingly raised to finance that particular project. Such a direct association between investment and financing decisions is usually misleading, since when a project is financed through a credit secured by acquired property or some other asset, the creditor tends to rely both on the firm's earning power and the "cushion" provided by the equity. Therefore, it is reasonable to conclude that ". . . there exists on the one hand a group of apparently desirable investment proposals, and on the other, a variety of sources of additional capital funds that, taken together, could supply the financing for the increased investment. In such circumstances, any procedure for assigning the cost of a particular source of capital funds to a specific investment proposal would be arbitrary and capricious." (Bierman and Smidt, The Capital Budgeting Decision.)

Further, costs associated with capital-raising efforts make it impractical to obtain the needed funds simultaneously from a variety of sources, each supplying a small portion of the total capital secured at that time. Thus, economies of scale in the capital-raising activity also suggest the wisdom of uncoupling investment and financing decisions and evaluating capital expenditure decisions in relation to the firm's overall cost of capital. Each financing decision has to be viewed as an integral part of a continuous process of financing the enterprise. Various types of funds are raised on a "package" basis in the sense that they satisfy investors' requirements with regard to a satisfactory mix in the capital structure as well as the corporation's need to preserve—in the long run—a desired balance between borrowed and equity funds.

AVERAGE COST OF CAPITAL. The average cost of capital is an average of specific costs of all types of capital employed by the firm, where each source of funds is assigned a weight corresponding to its relative position in the firm's

THE COST OF CAPITAL   17·63

capital structure. Although conceptually its measurement is simple, in practice a number of problems arise.

Fig. 12 contains essential balance sheet and income statistics for the H(ypothetical) E(xample) Corporation. The data, together with additional information given in Fig. 13, will be used to illustrate the measurement of the average cost of capital for the H. E. Corp. To simplify the computations it is assumed that all

A. Capital Structure

Balance sheet values as of December 31, 1963:	Amount		Per Cent of Total
4½% bank term loan, due Jan. 1, 1969	$ 3,000,000	2.5	
5% 1st mortgage bonds, due Jan. 1, 1980	10,000,000	8.3	
6% subordinated debentures, due Jan. 1, 1975	12,000,000	10.0	
Total long-term debt	$ 25,000,000		20.8
7% cumulative preferred stock, $100 par; 200,000 shares outstanding	20,000,000		16.7
Common stock, $5 par; 2 million shares outstanding	10,000,000	8.3	
Paid-in capital	15,000,000	12.5	
Retained earnings	50,000,000	41.7	62.5
Total capital structure	$120,000,000		100.0
Book value of common per share	$37.50		

B. Income Statistics

From income statement for 12 months ending December 31, 1963:	
Profits before interest and taxes	$26,162,700
Interest charges	1,355,000
Profits before Federal taxes	$24,807,700
Federal income tax (48%)	11,907,700
Profit after taxes	$12,900,000
Preferred dividends	1,400,000
Profits to common equity	$11,500,000
Earnings per share of common stock	$5.75

Fig. 12. Selected balance sheet and income data for H. E. Corp.

Type of Capital	Market Price *	Market Yield **	Capital Structure at Market Values	Per Cent of Total
4½% term loan	At par	4.50%	$ 3,000,000	1.3
5% 1st mortgage bonds	$ 99	5.09	9,900,000	4.1
6% subordinated debentures	106	5.25	12,720,000	5.3
Total long-term debt			$ 25,620,000	10.7
7% preferred stock	118	5.93	23,600,000	9.9
Common stock (P/E ratio of 16.5)	94⅞	6.06	189,750,000	79.4
Total permanent funds			$238,970,000	100.0

* Average price for the year.
** Yields on mortgage bonds and debentures obtained from the bond value tables.

Fig. 13. Computation of the market value of H. E. Corp. capital structure.

fixed income securities were originally sold to investors sufficiently above par to give net proceeds to the corporation exactly equal to the par values. Further, it is assumed in Fig. 13 that the market value of the term loan is equal to its face value. This is equivalent to saying that the market rate of interest for this type and quality of loan is unchanged from what it had been at the time when the loan was granted. (If, however, the rate of interest did actually change, it would be appropriate to adjust the value of this loan to its "market" equivalent.) In addition, it is assumed that there are neither sinking fund nor any other provisions relative to mandatory prepayments or gradual retirements of senior capital. Finally, short-term funds are ignored, mainly on the assumption that they consist primarily of noninterest bearing liabilities or that such liabilities are not significant enough to warrant separate consideration.

Computation of Average Cost. The computation of the average cost of capital requires two steps: (1) the computation of weights to be assigned to each type of funds and (2) the computation of costs of all sources of capital. Once these values are available, the average cost of capital is obtained by adding up the products of the costs of all types of capital multiplied by their appropriate weights. This is done in Fig. 14.

It can be seen that the average cost may be computed in several ways. In the first place, the **weight** of each source can be obtained with reference to their book values or their market values. Secondly, specific capital costs can be either **actual costs** of each issue (sometimes approximated by taking coupon rates) or **market yields**.

Book Values vs. Market Values. Figure 14 reveals that the choice between these two ways of looking at the capital structure will influence a firm's cost of capital. Since cost of capital is used as a cutoff rate for investment projects, a selection of the valuation method of the capital structure will determine the range of acceptable projects and, hence, the firm's profitability as well as its long-term financial position.

The majority of writers prefer to use market values. First, and foremost, it is argued, when an investor considers committing his funds to an enterprise, book values as such are of little importance. What an investor seeks is **adequate compensation** for the risk assumed and a **satisfactory return**. The cost of funds obtained in the past is merely a matter of historical record and may not reflect the company's present ability to raise capital. This is especially true of common stock.

Second, book values do not show the true economic value of an enterprise. They represent the sum total of past financing and investment decisions and, more importantly, reflect a number of arbitrary accounting decisions with respect to capitalization or expensing of certain expenditures, selection of depreciation and amortization schedules, valuation of assets, and the like.

Third, since accounting records are based on historical costs, balance sheet values typically ignore price level changes and therefore do not reflect actual current values.

The use of market values, on the other hand, is also not without difficulties. For example, Barges points out that the use of market values involves the danger of introducing a **bias** into the measurement of the cost of capital. This results from the use of market values in the denominators of both the yield rate to common equity and the debt-equity ratio. Consequently, he prefers the use of the book rather than market values (The Effect of Capital Structure on the Cost of Capital).

THE COST OF CAPITAL

A. Weighted by Book Values

Source of Funds	Weight in Capital Structure,[a] %	Cost of Funds (in %) (at actual rates) Specific[b]	Weighted	Cost of Funds (in %) (at market yields) Specific[c]	Weighted
Term loan	2.5	2.34	.0585	2.34	.0585
1st mortgage bonds	8.3	2.60	.2158	2.65	.2200
Subordinated debentures	10.0	3.12	.3120	2.73	.2730
Preferred stock	16.7	7.00[d]	1.1690	5.93[d]	.9903
Common stock (par) Paid-in capital	20.8	6.06[e]	1.2605	6.06[e]	1.2605
Retained earnings	41.7	4.85[f]	2.0225	4.85[f]	2.0225
	100.0		5.0383		4.8248

B. Weighted by Market Values

Source of Funds	Weight in Capital Structure,[g] %	Cost of Funds (in %) (at actual rates) Specific[b]	Weighted	Cost of Funds (in %) (at market yields) Specific[c]	Weighted
Term loan	1.3	2.34	.0304	2.34	.0304
1st mortgage bonds	4.1	2.60	.1066	2.65	.1087
Subordinated debentures	5.3	3.12	.1654	2.73	.1447
Preferred stock	9.9	7.00[d]	.6930	5.93[d]	.5871
Common equity	79.4	6.06[e]	4.8116	6.06[e]	4.8116
	100.0		5.8070		5.6825

[a] From Fig. 12.
[b] Coupon rate adjusted to after-tax basis.
[c] Cost of debt adjusted to after-tax basis.
[d] Nominal dividend rate or market yield.
[e] Inverse of price/earnings ratio.
[f] Inverse of price/earnings ratio adjusted for an assumed 20% personal income tax liability.
[g] From Fig. 13.

Fig. 14. Computation of average cost of capital for H. E. Corp.

Since the most important purpose of computing cost of capital is its use as a guide in capital investment decisions that will affect the future operations and earning power of the enterprise, the use of book values does not appear to be justified. The **opportunity cost of capital** can best be approximated by reference to the market valuation of corporate securities. Since stock and bond prices change continuously, however, care should be exercised to eliminate the effects of truly short-term supply-demand factors in the capital and money markets as well as short-lived psychological reactions among the investing public. Thus, although market values are preferable, selection of the particular prices is a matter of executive judgment.

On the other hand, conditions may exist where book values may be reasonably representative of market values. This, for example, may occur in low-risk enterprises with high-income stability and rather rapid replacements of fixed assets.

The latter condition, in particular, will tend to minimize inadequacies of accounting and, therefore, tend to bring the book and market values closer together.

Determining the Type of Capital Structure. Another problem that arises in computing average costs is selection of the capital structure from which the weights are obtained. There are several possibilities: (1) current capital structure, either before or after the projected new financing; (2) marginal capital structure, i.e., proportions of various types of capital in the total of funds to be raised at the time; and (3) optimal capital structure.

Using a **current** capital structure can be justified only when it closely resembles or is identical with the optimal capital structure for the firm. Otherwise, this will in practice result in suboptimal investment decisions. In addition, it will tend to perpetuate the existing deficiencies arising from an inappropriate capital structure.

There is even lesser justification for utilizing a **marginal** capital structure, as defined above. Not only is such a capital structure inherently unrelated to the optimal or even the present capital structure, but—more importantly—it assumes that each financing decision is independent of other capital-raising activities, which is an unrealistic view.

Theoretically, the correct capital structure to use for obtaining weights for the various types of funds is the **optimal** capital structure of the firm. An optimal structure, by properly accounting for the effects of risk, leverage, income, control, and other relevant factors, will minimize the overall cost of capital to the firm and provide a "correct" cutoff value for investment decisions.

In practice, however, an optimal capital structure is seldom achieved and, therefore, cannot be precisely determined. Actually, for each company there exists a unique, best mix of debt, preferred stock, and common equity. Too, the cost of capital and the capital structure are interdependent. In view of the above, and also because all computations related to cost of capital and capital structure rely heavily on estimates and forecasts, there probably exists a relatively wide band of capital structures over which the average cost of capital remains relatively constant.

As a result, what is really sought is an acceptable capital structure that, although not determined with the maximum accuracy, permits the computation of the cost of capital that is not far from its optimum value. For this purpose it will be useful to study relevant data of other similar companies employing different proportions of debt and equity. Or, the existing capital structure of the company may be used unless there are compelling reasons to believe that it deviates substantially from the optimal capital structure. This latter approach is often recommended as a reasonable compromise between theory and practice. (For example, by Solomon, The Theory of Financial Management, and by Weston, Managerial Finance.)

Lease Reporting and the Cost of Capital. The leasing of assets is already important in the United States and its importance is growing at an accelerated rate. **Financial leases** are defined as those in which ". . . the lessee agrees to make a series of payments to the lessor which, in total, exceed the purchase price of the asset acquired." (Vancil, Harvard Business Review, Vol. 39.) As such, they are a means of financing acquisition of assets and for that reason are considered by many as, in essence, a form of borrowing. (This view is also presented by Gant in Harvard Business Review, Vol. 37.) In this respect leases are involved in the problem of cost of capital.

In many respects a lease is **similar to a bond**: Both are a source of capital, both require periodic payments, both may contain a clause that allows the lessee or borrower to retire the lease or bond before maturity, and the primary security behind them is often the general credit of the lessee or borrower in addition to the lessor's ownership or lender's claim to the assets involved. (See Nelson, Bureau of Business and Economic Research, Michigan State University, Occasional Paper No. 10.) The decision to lease, acording to Vancil (Harvard Business Review, Vol. 39), ". . . should begin only after a company has previously decided that the purchase of a piece of equipment is desirable. . . ." The decision to obtain the equipment or property is subject to the same criteria as is any other investment decision, whereas the decision to lease is actually a financing decision involving a choice among the available alternatives.

In accounting, lease obligations are usually **reflected in the financial statements** in one of the following two ways. First, they are indicated in balance sheet footnotes or separate schedules to financial statements; this is the more usual method. Second, they are capitalized on the balance sheet on the debit and the credit sides as lease benefits and lease obligations. Among those showing a preference for the capitalization of leases are: Myers (A.I.C.P.A., Accounting Research Study No. 4) and Nelson (Bureau of Business and Economic Research, Michigan State University, Occasional Paper No. 10).

An able argument against the capitalization of lease "benefits and obligations" has been put forward by Cook (Harvard Business Review, Vol. 41). Also in support of this position is the Government Relations Committee of the Financial Analysts Federation, who state: "The Committee does not feel that there should be any adjustment by accountants of the balance sheet, mandatory or otherwise, since if adequate facts are disclosed the analyst can apply his own techniques to suit the particular case." (The Financial Analysts Federation Fourteenth Annual Report, 1960–1961.)

The relevance of this issue to computation of the cost of capital lies in the fact that the choice between capitalization and footnote reporting affects the capital structure of the firm by changing its balance sheet while leaving its income statement unaffected. Under such circumstances, the existence of leases will influence the computation of the cost of capital at least to the extent that the capital markets may not properly reflect lease obligation burdens in securities prices.

ACTUAL VS. MARKET YIELDS. As previously indicated, the computed weights for each type of capital may be applied either to actual (historical) costs of these funds or to yields demanded by the capital market at the time.

In the first approach, fixed-income securities are assigned their actual costs or, sometimes, nominal coupon rates for debt and nominal dividend rates for preferred stock. The cost of common equity is often differentiated between common stock and paid-in capital accounts, on the one hand, and retained earnings, on the other. The cost of par value plus the paid-in capital portion of equity is the market yield on the company's shares; the cost of retained earnings is the market yield adjusted for stockholders' personal tax liability on dividend income (see discussion above on cost of retained earnings). Thus, in essence, this method is a hybrid between the historical specific costs view (for fixed-income securities) and the market yield (common equity) view.

A second variation uses market yields for all types of capital employed. Figure 14 (page 65) illustrates the computation of the average cost of capital with both methods. The difference in the case of the H. E. Corporation is relatively insignificant, but this is due mainly to the relatively low proportion of debt, the closeness between market yields and coupon rates on debt, and the high price-earnings ratio for common stock.

Weston (Managerial Finance) has advanced the following argument in defense of using actual market yields:

Here the economic principle of opportunity costs should obtain. The firm should charge as the cost of its capital what the capital would cost if it were currently to be acquired rather than what it happened to have cost when the capital was acquired.

The difference between current costs and what costs may have been in the past represents a gain (a quasi-rent) because of a favorable purchase price at some time in the past. For current decisions, current facts should be used, not historical information. The cost of debt would not be the coupon rate but the current yields on its bonds at the time of the calculation.

Use of current yields involves the danger, however, of **overemphasizing strictly short-run influences.** In addition, unless a company's securities are actively traded, market yields may be hard to obtain. They may have to be estimated, in which case the results may not be very accurate. Frequently, actual specific costs and current market yields are surprisingly close, as occurs in Fig. 14. The smaller the proportion of fixed-income securities in the capital structure and the closer historical costs are to present market yields, the lesser is the "danger" of using historical costs. Conceptually, though, it is logical to use market yields whenever the capital structure is expressed in market values.

COMMON EQUITY AND AVERAGE COSTS. Another difficulty in the computation of the average cost of capital arises from a certain degree of arbitrariness in measuring the cost of common equity. Since the latter usually comprises the largest single source of funds in the capital structure, its cost will tend to affect the average cost of capital more than any other source of funds. Yet, the computation of the cost of equity capital itself is rather imprecise.

Dividends vs. Earnings. One of the thorniest problems in approaching the valuation of common equity is lack of agreement among financial authorities as to what is more important in determining the price of a share of common stock—dividends or earnings. Some assume that dividends are what the typical stockholder looks for when buying a share of stock. (Williams, The Theory of Investment Value.) Walter accepts "the fundamental premise . . . that, over long periods, stock prices reflect the present values of expected dividends. . . . Granted this premise, retained earnings influence stock prices principally through their effect upon future dividends . . ." (The Journal of Finance, Vol. 11).

A similar assumption is made by Gordon in his book The Investment, Financing and Valuation of the Corporation. His analysis leads to the following conclusions:

. . . There is no choice between earnings and dividends as the variable an investor takes as his expected future income for a share of stock. Only in the special case where earnings are equal to dividends may the former be used. It is nonetheless possible though unlikely that the price of a share is independent of the fraction of earnings the corporation pays in dividends. It is unlikely because the necessary condition is that the corporation's cost of capital be independent of the dividend rate. A corporation's retention rate and rate of growth in its dividend move together, and its cost of capital may rise or fall with the rate of growth in its dividends. The larger the increase in the uncertainty of a dividend with its time in the future and the larger the aversion to risk on the part of investors, the more likely it is that the cost of capital will increase with the growth in the dividend.

A diametrically **opposed view** holds that dividends have little if anything to do with stock prices. For example, Modigliani and Miller state that ". . . the division of the stream of income between cash dividends and retained earnings in any period is a mere detail . . ." (The American Economic Review, Vol. 48). In another discussion of dividends they point out, however, that, ". . . in a world in which the policy of dividend stabilization is widespread, there is no simple way of disentangling the true effect of dividend payments on stock prices from their apparent effect, the latter reflecting only the role of dividends as a proxy measure of long-term earnings anticipations. . . ." The main reason that the "informational content" of dividends has a bearing on the stock prices is that ". . . where a firm has adopted a policy of dividend stabilization with a long established and generally appreciated 'target payout ratio,' investors are likely to (and have good reason to) interpret a change in the dividend rate as a change in management's views of future profit prospects for the firm . . ." (Miller and Modigliani, The Journal of Business, Vol. 34).

Between these two extremes there is the **traditional view** widely held in the financial community that recognizes the importance of **both** dividends and earnings in the valuation of common shares. On the other hand, Solomon (The Theory of Financial Management) states: ". . . The answer to the controversy about whether dividends or earnings determines value is that neither does. When each approach is correctly restated so that it does provide a defensible model, the two models come to exactly the same thing."

Nevertheless, the debate goes on and it will continue as long as there will be some reason to believe that, as Durand put it, ". . . there is a difference between capital gains and income—and especially between unrealized capital gains and realized income . . ." (The American Economic Review, Vol. 49). That is, the argument will persist as long as risks attending investments may cause investors to prefer current dividend income to a delayed capital gain or an enlarged dividend in the future.

Porterfield considers that, in theory, both stock and cash dividends are irrelevant to the stockholder (as ". . . all dividends are liquidating dividends, serving as they do to reduce the assets of the corporation") and that cash dividends like stock dividends have no inherent value, since ". . . cash dividends are merely a means of giving to the stockholder something that he already owns—the heretofore undistributed earnings of the corporation. . . ." But in practice, he admits, ". . . unfortunately, things do not work as ideally as this line of reasoning suggests. Indeed, it is highly probable that for many companies fairly regular and increasing cash dividend payments tend to have a favorable rather than an unfavorable effect on share prices over a period of time." (Harvard Business Review, Vol. 37.)

Harkavy distinguishes between the long-run and the "instantaneous" effect of the retention of earnings on market price. After empirical research, he has concluded that:

1. As of a given time, there is a tendency for stock prices to vary directly with the proportion of earnings distributed.
2. Over a period of years, the stocks of those corporations retaining the greater proportion of earnings tend to exhibit the greater price appreciation. (The Journal of Finance, Vol. 8.)

Therefore, it appears that the traditional view, which holds that both dividends and earnings affect the value of common stock and is in essence a compromise between the two extremes, has much to offer. Financial executives will, no doubt, continue to be mindful of the effects that dividend policies may have on market values of the corporation's stocks. Accordingly, in the event the corporation is contemplating raising new funds, they will tailor their dividend policy in such a way as to facilitate maximization of stock prices in the market and consequently lower the cost of capital to the corporation.

VARIABILITY OF COMPOSITE COST OF CAPITAL. As indicated in the preceding discussion, a firm can influence its cost of capital by varying the proportions of senior and junior capital in the capital structure. Alternatively, given a certain level of earnings on capital employed, a firm's total market value, among other things, also depends on its capital structure.

This can be demonstrated by reference to the following data, assumed to be given. Some $12.5 million is needed to acquire fixed assets and to build up an adequate working capital for a newly organized firm. The firm expects to earn (before profits taxes and financial charges) 12% on these assets, or $1.5 million annually. The required funds can be obtained from a sale of 5% bonds and from a sale of common stock. Net proceeds to the company are assumed to be equal to par value of bonds and to $12.50 per common share. Thereafter, the stock will be traded in the market at about eight times the expected annual earnings per share. Ignoring corporate profits taxes, what is the cost of capital when 10, 30, or 50% of the total amount needed is obtained through the sale of bonds, with the remainder coming from a sale of common stock?

From Figure 15, it is apparent that each increment of debt lowers the average cost of capital and, therefore, brings about a continuous rise in the total market value of the business. The common shareholders are, therefore, the direct beneficiaries of the increasing trading-on-the-equity. With the company's net proceeds from the original sale of stock at $12.50 per share, the following number of shares would be issued under the three financing plans: 900,000 with $1,250,000 (10%) of debt; 700,000 with $3,750,000 (30%) of debt; and 500,000 shares with $6,250,000 (50%) of debt. The corresponding market prices of the common stock on a per share basis (at eight times expected earnings per share) are: $12.77; $15.00; $19.00.

The average cost of capital (weighted by percentages of funds originally obtained—book values) ranges between 11.75% and 8.75%. If, however, market value weights are used—a more realistic approach—the average costs of capital are 11.77%, 10.53%, and 9.52%, respectively. Although Fig. 15 does not show this, it is apparent that under the above assumptions reliance on equity financing alone should be avoided. If all funds were raised by a sale of common stock, 1 million shares would have to be issued. The market price of one share of stock, with $1.50 expected earnings per share, would be $12.00. The total market value of the company would then be $500,000 less than the amount of funds raised ($12 million vs. $12.5 million).

Most authorities agree that the shape of the cost of capital curve is such that it reaches its lowest level at the optimal capital structure and that beyond that point it begins to rise (see Fig. 16).

BUSINESS VALUATION AND COST OF CAPITAL. Business income and cost of capital depend on the business risk and the financial risk. **Business or external risk** is generally defined as the risk affecting the stability of a firm's income as well as the liquidity, safety, and marketability of corporate assets due to factors external to the enterprise. It determines the general level of a firm's capitalization rate (cost of capital) as it ". . . is in large part dictated by the nature of the industry in which a firm is engaged and is not subject to any great extent to the control of the financial decision-maker." (Schwartz, The Journal of Finance, Vol. 14.)

A. Average Cost of Capital

Source of Funds	Specific Before-Tax Cost (%)		Case 1 Weight (%)	Case 1 Cost (%)	Case 2 Weight (%)	Case 2 Cost (%)	Case 3 Weight (%)	Case 3 Cost (%)
			Weighted by Book Values					
5% Bonds	5.0		10	.5	30	1.5	50	2.5
Common stock	12.5		90	11.25	70	8.75	50	6.25
		Total	100	11.75	100	10.25	100	8.75
			Weighted by Market Values					
5% Bonds	5.0		9.8	.490	26.3	1.315	39.7	1.985
Common stock	12.5		90.2	11.275	73.7	9.213	60.3	7.538
		Total	100.0	11.765	100.0	10.528	100.0	9.523

B. Market Value

	Case 1 (bonds = $1,250,000)	Case 2 (bonds = $3,750,000)	Case 3 (bonds = $6,250,000)
Earnings before interest	$ 1,500,000	$ 1,500,000	$ 1,500,000
Interest on debt at 5%	62,500	187,500	312,500
Earnings of common equity [a]	$ 1,437,500	$ 1,312,500	$ 1,187,500
Market value of common equity [b]	$11,500,000	$10,500,000	$ 9,500,000
Market value of debt [c]	1,250,000	3,750,000	6,250,000
Total market value of the firm	$12,750,000	$14,250,000	$15,750,000

[a] Assuming no profit taxes. [b] Capitalized at 12.5%. [c] Selling at par.

Fig. 15. An illustration of the effect of varying financing plans on the cost of capital and the market value of the enterprise.

Fig. 16. Cost of capital to an enterprise.

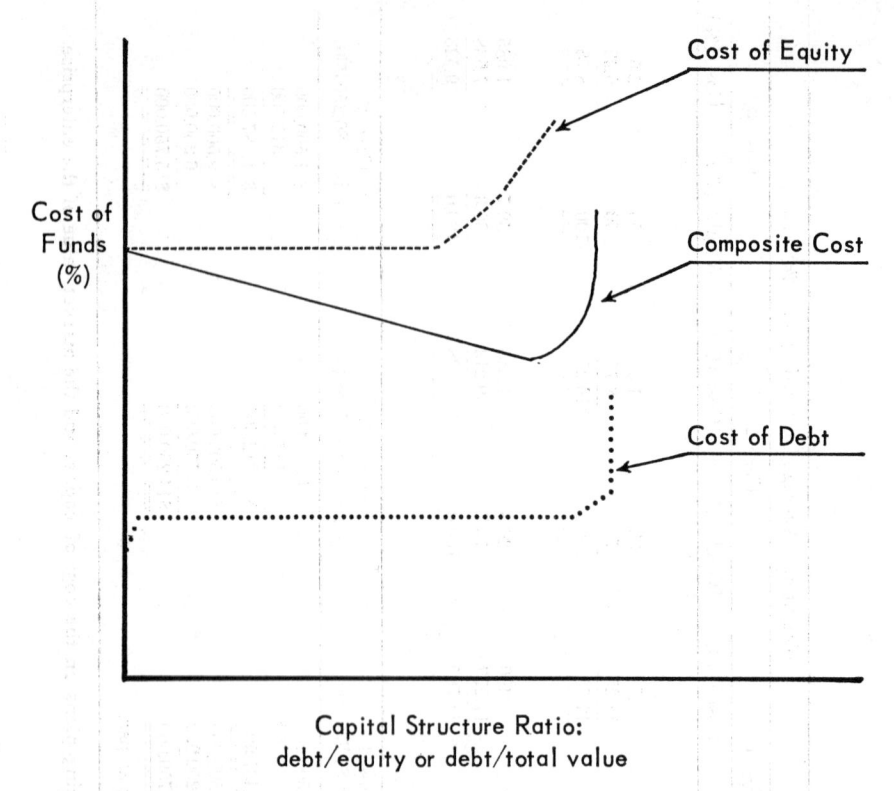

Note: The levels, shapes, and relative positions of all three curves will vary from case to case and with changing circumstances. Also, the curves have been smoothed out, which generally would not be the case in a real world. The diagram is designed merely to show the general behavior of capital costs to a firm.

Financial risk usually refers to uncertainty of the income stream to capital suppliers arising from the firm's capital structure. Since financial risk and financial leverage are interrelated, the two concepts are sometimes used interchangeably.

The concept of financial leverage plays an important part in the theory of the cost of capital. Given the business risk within which a firm operates, the effect on a firm's cost of capital caused by changes in capital structure can be studied by noting sensitivity of market capitalization rates with respect to financial risk.

In 1952, Durand (National Bureau of Economic Research, Conference on Research in Business Finance) indicated that there are essentially two approaches to valuation of a business firm. These are: the **Net Operating Income** (NOI) approach and **Net Income** (NI) approach.

In the NOI approach, which has not received wide acceptance, it is assumed that ". . . the totality of risk incurred by all security holders of a given company cannot be altered by merely changing the capitalization proportions. Such a change could only alter the proportion of the total risk borne by each class of security holder . . . ." Accordingly, a firm's market value and cost of capital remain unaffected and constant regardless of its capital structure. Only the capitalization rates of each security vary. But all changes in these rates are interdependent and interrelated in such a fashion that their influences on the overall capitalization rate for the firm's net operating income cancel out. Thus, nothing can be gained for the cost of capital by varying the capital structure.

In the NI approach, which is today accepted by most financial experts, net income to residual owners is capitalized at an appropriate (market) rate and the capitalized (market) value of equity is then added to the value of debt to give the total market value of the firm. There is not necessarily a direct relationship between the capitalization rates for debt and equity, which permits the value of the firm to change with the introduction of leverage.

The U-Shaped Cost of Capital Curve. In general, it is believed that the composite cost of capital, when plotted against either the debt/equity or the debt/total value ratio, has a U-shaped curve (see Fig. 16). It starts at the same level as the cost of equity curve in an unleveraged firm of its class. From this point of intersection it will decline until it reaches its minimum level at an optimal capital structure, and it will rise again with increasing leverage. The range of capital structures that is operationally meaningful to management is the one extending from pure equity to the optimal capital structure.

It is widely believed that the cost of debt and equity will initially remain constant and then increase, with the cost of equity turning up before the cost of debt. (This will be the case because of the stronger protection that the creditors have in a corporation.) But the increase in specific costs of capital in the area between the pure equity and the optimal capital structure will not be strong enough to offset completely the favorable effect of a gradual replacement of high-cost equity with lower-cost debt. However, **when the proportion of debt becomes excessive,** the marginal cost of borrowing, i.e., the increased cost of debt from raising additional funds plus allowance for an increase in the equity capitalization rate due to the deterioration of the equity's quality, exceeds the average cost of capital, and from that point on each increment of debt will increase the average cost of capital.

Figure 17 illustrates in part the behavior of the cost of capital relative to the financial leverage of the H. E. Corporation. In this example it is assumed that the H. E. Corporation has raised $75 million, or three times as much capital by means of debt as it did previously (see Fig. 12, page 63). Since the total amount of funds is the same as previously, common equity book values are reduced by an appropriate amount.

The **substitution of debt for equity,** as leverage increases, ordinarily will lower the average cost of capital so long as there is no offsetting rise in the equity capitalization rate. Thus when debt constituted 10.7% of the capital structure (weighted by market value), the average cost of capital of the H. E. Corporation was 5.68% (Fig. 14). When an increase in the Corporation's debt brought the ratio to 28.8% of the capital structure, and there was no offsetting change in the capitalization rate, the average cost of capital declined to 5.07%. A further increase in the debt ratio, however, is considered excessive resulting in a rise in the capitalization rate of the common stock from 6.06% to 8%, and an increase in the average cost of capital to 5.97%. (Fig. 17.)

CONCLUDING REMARKS. The cost of capital is a useful concept in formulating a firm's investment policy and its financial strategy. However, the complexity of the problem and the difficulties in the measurement allow the management merely to delineate a range within which the true cost of capital lies. It is the management's job to attempt to narrow this range as much as possible in order to obtain an operationally meaningful measure of the company's

A. Capital Structure

Source of Funds	Book Values $ Amount (000)	Book Values Weight (%)	Market Value I[a] $ Amount (000)	Market Value I[a] Weight (%)	Market Value II[b] $ Amount (000)	Market Value II[b] Weight (%)
Term loan	9,000	7.5	9,000	3.4	9,000	4.0
1st mortgage bonds	30,000	25.0	29,700	11.1	29,700	13.1
Subordinated debentures	36,000	30.0	38,160	14.3	38,160	16.8
Total loans	75,000	62.5	76,860	28.8	76,860	33.9
Preferred stock	20,000	16.7	23,600	8.8	23,600	10.4
Common stock (par)	10,000	8.3	} 166,650	} 62.4	} 126,250	} 55.7
Paid-in capital	15,000	12.5				
Retained earnings						
	$120,000	100.0	$267,110	100.0	$226,710	100.0

B. Average Weighted Cost of Capital

Source of Funds	Weighted at Book Values Using actual specific costs[c]	Weighted at Book Values Using mkt. yields[c]	Weighted at Market Val. I[a] Using actual specific costs[d]	Weighted at Market Val. I[a] Using mkt. yields[d]	Weighted at Market Val. II[b] Using actual specific costs[c]	Weighted at Market Val. II[b] Using mkt. yields[c]
Term loan	.1755%	.1755%	.0796%	.0796%	.0936%	.0936%
First mortgage bonds	.6500	.6625	.2886	.2942	.3406	.3472
Subordinated debentures	.9360	.8190	.4462	.3904	.5242	.4586
Preferred stock	1.1690	.9903	.6160	.5218	.7280	.6167
Common stock and paid-in capital	1.6640[e]	1.6640[e]	3.7814	3.7814	4.4560	4.4560
Retained earnings						
	4.5945%[e]	4.3113%[e]	5.2118%	5.0674%	6.1424%	5.9721%

[a] Common stock selling at 16.5 times earnings per share of $5.05 or at 6.06% capitalization rate.
[b] Common stock selling at 12.5 times earnings per share of $5.05 or at 8% capitalization rate.
[c] Costs from Fig. 14, except for common stock, which is assumed here to sell at P/E ratio of 12.5; weights from above.
[d] Costs from Fig. 14; weights from above.
[e] If, however, common equity continued to sell at 16.5 times earnings per share (6.06% capitalization rate), the cost of equity weighted according to book values would be 1.2605% instead of 1.6640%; the average cost of capital, weighted at book values would change to 4.1910% (if actual specific costs are used) and to 3.9078%, when market yields are used.

Fig. 17. Computation of the cost of capital of the H. E. Corp., with $75,000,000 (at par) of debt securities.

cost of capital. As the cost of capital curve tends to flatten out over a segment of a firm's capital structures (leverages ratios)—within which the cost of capital is almost constant—the computations can be safely based on any capital structure that can be associated with the flat part of the curve. Besides, financial decisions are frequently influenced significantly by factors other than quantitative data.

Since **management's judgment** plays such an important part in the measurement of a firm's cost of capital, false impressions of a nonexistent precision are undesirable. As Biermann and Smidt aptly put it (The Capital Budgeting Decision), ". . . a person who desires neat solutions with one correct answer should avoid the computation of a corporation's cost of capital." But this does not make the concept any less meaningful or useful in making financial decisions. The soundness of the underlying assumptions, the validity of the concept itself, and the operational usefulness of the measured value of the cost of capital are much more important than a high degree of accuracy in the computations.

Risk and Uncertainty

RISK DEFINED. In decision making, management is forced to make choices between alternative courses of action. The quantitative data furnished management are in the form of estimates tending to show what the outcome will be if one or another course of action is chosen. Since these figures relate to the future, they carry with them all the uncertainties associated generally with forecasting. As stated by Dean (Managerial Economics): ". . . these uncertainty characteristics are important when there is much obsolescence of methods or of style, or fickleness and obscurity of forecasting buyers' tastes, particularly in development of new and unknown product lines."

In recent years attempts have been made to apply the laws of **probability** to modify the estimates. Statistically speaking, this involves the measurement of the degree of risk and uncertainty. Spencer and Siegelman (Managerial Economics: Decision Making and Forward Planning) define risk as ". . . the quantitative measurement of an outcome, such as a loss or a gain, in a manner such that the probability of the outcome can be predicted."

Risk, then, is objective. Its probability can be measured with certainty where the outcome characteristics are known in advance, as in coin tossing or throwing of dice. Or the outcome may be predicted on the basis of historical data, where a sufficient number of observations make possible the computation of probability of an outcome. To be valid ". . . the number of cases or observations must be large enough to exhibit stability, they must be repeated in the population or universe, and they must be independent" (i.e., distributed in a random manner) (Spencer and Siegelman). The prediction is made on the basis of a **normal frequency** distribution whose characteristics can then be defined by measuring the central tendency, the dispersion (standard deviation), and skewness.

UNCERTAINTY DEFINED. According to Shubin (Managerial and Industrial Economics):

> Uncertainty arises from developments and fluctuations that cannot be sufficiently foreseen and adequately predicted, such as changes in consumer style tastes and unforeseeable product developments by rival firms . . . . Technological advance also increases uncertainty when it renders obsolete certain productive facilities . . . . Business uncertainty and potential losses derive also from the need to accumulate an inventory of finished goods in advance of sales.

In contrast to risk, uncertainty is **subjective** in nature. The data again pertain to the future, but cannot be objectively verified and predicted as in games of chance. This means that different persons may view a given situation differently, depending upon their varying degrees of optimism or pessimism. Many business decisions, in fact, are the result of combining various estimates into a single figure, and of assigning to each estimate a probability.

APPLICATION TO INVESTMENT DECISIONS. Bierman and Smidt (The Capital Budgeting Decision) suggest a procedure to be followed in the making of investment decisions. Adaptations of this procedure may also be used for other types of decision making such as the following:

1. Determine the present value of the net cash flows for three different assumptions:
   a. Most probable series of events
   b. A reasonably pessimistic series of events
   c. A reasonably optimistic series of events
2. Weight the three present values, using the best information available or using standard weights such as 50 per cent for the most probable and 25 per cent for the most pessimistic and optimistic predictions.
3. The sum of the three weighted present values may be used to represent the present value of the investment, taking uncertainty into consideration . . . .

For example, a sales forecast might be arrived at as follows:

	(1) Probability	(2) Stated Amount	(3) = (1) × (2) Expected Value
Optimistic	.25	$1,000,000	$250,000
Most probable	.50	800,000	400,000
Pessimistic	.25	680,000	170,000
	1.00		$820,000

There are numerous applications of probability theory to decision making. The public accountant makes use of sampling techniques to determine the extent of the audit and the degree of reliance desired in the result. Other uses may be found in budgetary control, both in forecasting sales and the various costs associated with sales; in capital budgeting, as noted above, where it is necessary to determine future cash flows; in problems of maintenance; and in control of inventory.

McKinsey & Company, Inc., have developed a technique for presenting to management "a clear picture of the relative risk and probable odds of coming out ahead or behind in the light of uncertain foreknowledge." Hertz has described the method as follows (Harvard Business Review, Vol. 42):

To carry out the analysis, a company must follow three steps:
1. Estimate the range of values for each of the factors (e.g., range of selling price, sales growth rate, and so on) and within that range the likelihood of occurrence of each value.
2. Select at random from the distribution of values for each factor one particular value. Then combine the value for all the factors and compute the rate of return (or present value) from that combination. For instance, the lowest in the range of prices might be combined with the highest in the range of growth rate and other factors . . . .
3. Do this over and over again to define and evaluate the odds of the occurrence of each possible rate of return. Since there are literally millions of possible combinations of values, we need to test the likelihood that various specific returns on the

RISK AND UNCERTAINTY

investment will occur. This is like finding out by recording the results of a great many throws of what per cent of "7"s or other combinations we may expect in tossing dice. The result will be a listing of the rates of return we might achieve, ranging from a loss (if the factors go against us) to whatever maximum gain is possible with the estimates that have been made.

For each of these rates the chances that it may occur are determined. (Note that a specific return can usually be achieved through more than one combination of events. The more combinations for a given rate, the higher the chances of achieving it—as with "7"s in tossing dice.) The average expectation is the average of the values of all outcomes weighted by the chances of each occurring.

The variability of outcome values from the average is also determined. This is important since, all other factors being equal, management would presumably prefer lower variability for the same return if given the choice.

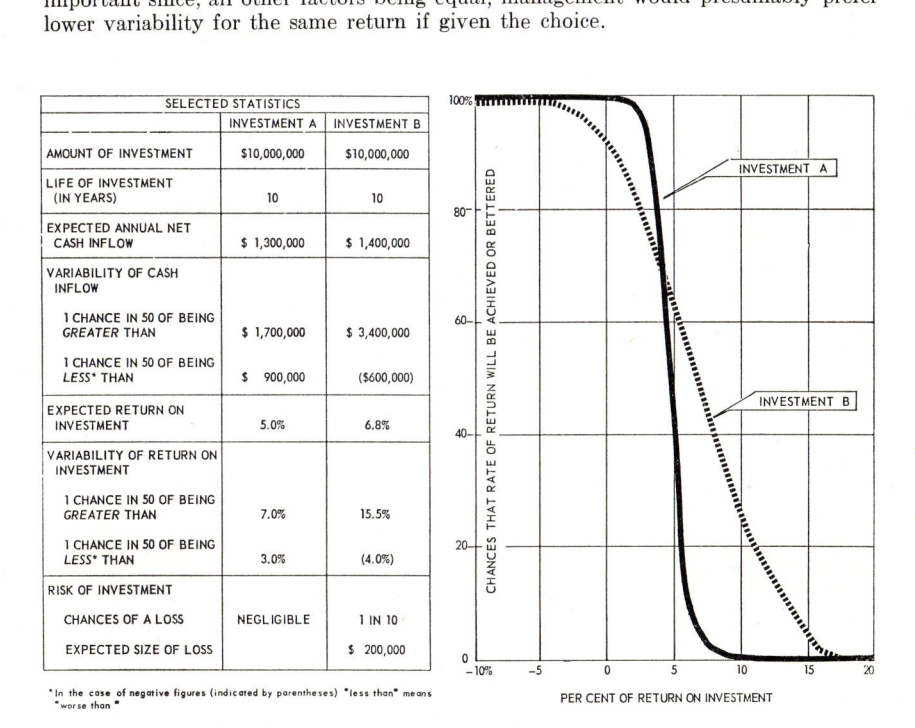

SELECTED STATISTICS	INVESTMENT A	INVESTMENT B
AMOUNT OF INVESTMENT	$10,000,000	$10,000,000
LIFE OF INVESTMENT (IN YEARS)	10	10
EXPECTED ANNUAL NET CASH INFLOW	$ 1,300,000	$ 1,400,000
VARIABILITY OF CASH INFLOW		
1 CHANCE IN 50 OF BEING GREATER THAN	$ 1,700,000	$ 3,400,000
1 CHANCE IN 50 OF BEING LESS* THAN	$ 900,000	($600,000)
EXPECTED RETURN ON INVESTMENT	5.0%	6.8%
VARIABILITY OF RETURN ON INVESTMENT		
1 CHANCE IN 50 OF BEING GREATER THAN	7.0%	15.5%
1 CHANCE IN 50 OF BEING LESS* THAN	3.0%	(4.0%)
RISK OF INVESTMENT		
CHANCES OF A LOSS	NEGLIGIBLE	1 IN 10
EXPECTED SIZE OF LOSS		$ 200,000

*In the case of negative figures (indicated by parentheses) "less than" means "worse than."

Fig. 18. Comparison of two investment opportunities.

According to Hertz, the same technique may be applied to investments by obtaining the expected return and variability of each of a series of investments to determine the effectiveness of various combinations of them in meeting management objectives. Because so many combinations of factors are made, a computer is used to carry out the trial combinations. In this way, management obtains a clear picture of "(1) the expected return based on weighted probabilities of all possible returns, (2) variability of return, and (3) risks." The example (Fig. 18) given by Hertz shows the significance of the method.

The variability of cash inflow and of return on investment and the resulting risk of investment are obtained from computer runs.

SECTION 18

CORPORATE SURPLUSES, RESERVES AND DIVIDENDS

CONTENTS

The Nature of Surplus

	PAGE
Surplus defined	1
Classification of surplus	1
Surplus terminology	2
Decline in use of term "surplus"	2
Improper surplus techniques	2
Understatement of surplus	2
Overstatement of surplus	2

Paid-in Surplus and Revaluation Surplus

Paid-in surplus distinguished from legal capital and undivided profits	3
Sources of paid-in surplus	3
Sale of stock	3
Donations	3
Reacquisition of capital stock	4
Recapitalization	4
Reorganization	4
Business combinations	5
Revaluation surplus	5

Retained Earnings

Sources of retained earnings	6
Charges to retained earnings	6
Administration of retained earnings	6
Deficits	6

"Surplus" or Retained Earnings Reserves

Reserves	7
Valuation reserves	7
Liability reserves	7
Surplus reserves	7
Recent trends in terminology	7
Relationship between funds and reserves	8
Nature of surplus reserves	8
Legal, contractual, and voluntary reserves	8
Accounting for surplus reserves	8
Purposes and types of surplus reserves	9
Reserve for treasury stock	9
Reserve for bonded indebtedness	9
Reserve for contingencies	10
Reserve for plant expansion	10
Reserve for future inventory declines	11
Reserve for insurance	11

Nature and Kinds of Dividends

Dividend defined	11
Cash dividends	12

	PAGE
Stock dividends	12
Stock dividends vs. stock splits	12
Purposes of stock dividends	12
Taxability of stock dividends	13
Valuation of stock dividends	13
Rescission of stock dividends	13
Property dividends	14
Scrip dividends	14
Bond dividends	14

Designation of Dividends

Regular dividend	15
Extra dividends	15
Special dividends	15
Interim and final dividends	15
Liquidating or capital dividends	15
Constructive dividends	16

Types of Dividend Policies

Dividend policy defined	16
Regular dividend policy	16
Regular and extra dividend policy	16
Regular plus stock dividend policy	17
Irregular dividend policy	17
Regular stock dividend policy	17
Property dividend policy	17
Liquidating dividend policy	17
No dividend policy	18
Factors affecting dividend policy	18

Legal Restrictions upon Dividends

Reasons for limitation	18
Common law rules	19
Statutory law	19
The New York statute	19
The capital impairment test	20
The surplus test	20
The profits test	21
The insolvency test	21
Other restrictions	22
Judicial compulsion to declare dividends	22
Effect of dividend declaration	22
Liability for illegal dividends	23

Tax and Financial Aspects of Dividend Policy

Surtax on undistributed earnings	23
Effect on stockholders' taxes	24
Working capital position	25
"Cash flow" analysis	25

CONTENTS (*Continued*)

	Page		Page
Dividend payout ratios	26	Notification of shareholders	28
New capital requirements	26	Preparation of dividend checks	28
Specific objectives	26	Dividend book	29
		Form of record for dividend check delivered at company office (*f*. 1)	29
Mechanics of Declaration and Payment		Form of record for dividend checks sent by mail (*f*. 2)	29
Resolution of the board	27	Special bank account and payment through fiscal agent	30
Stock dividend declarations	27		
Date of record	28		

SECTION 18

CORPORATE SURPLUSES, RESERVES AND DIVIDENDS

The Nature of Surplus

SURPLUS DEFINED. The surplus of a corporation is the excess of the book value of the assets over the sum of the liabilities and the par or stated value of the capital stock. Because legal restrictions applicable to the **impairment of capital** do not apply to surplus, a substantial surplus accords a larger measure of flexibility to corporate management in the formulation of financial policies. For this reason, many managements seek to create a large surplus where one does not exist, or where the surplus has been impaired through operating losses or asset write-downs. The prevailing trend toward the **use of low-par value stock** in corporate capitalization reflects this desire to secure a substantial surplus. In the case of banks and insurance companies, separate surplus and undivided profits accounts are maintained, surplus being considered the more permanent and stable account. Since impairment of the capital of a moneyed institution could lead to its closing and forced liquidation, the surplus of such a corporation is a buffer to protect the capital account from impairment due to losses or asset write-downs.

Surplus, in an accounting sense, is a **stockholders' equity account.** As Donaldson and Pfahl (Corporate Finance) explain, surplus is never anything real or tangible. Consequently, surplus cannot be used in an exchange transaction. Moreover, surplus does not relate to any specific asset or group of assets and it is not owned by any interest.

CLASSIFICATION OF SURPLUS. Surplus is classified by source in order to show the origin of the stockholders' equity. Generally, surplus is divided into **three broad classes:** (1) paid-in (or capital), (2) earned, and (3) revaluation (or reappraisal). The American Institute of Certified Public Accountants (Accounting Research and Terminology Bulletins) distinguishes between the first two classes as follows:

Capital surplus represents (a) capital contributed for shares in excess of their par or stated value, or (b) capital contributed other than for shares.

Earned surplus represents accumulated income or the remainder thereof at the balance sheet date.

Kohler (A Dictionary for Accountants) has defined appraisal surplus as "the excess of estimated depreciated replacement cost, or other basis of measurement, of fixed or other assets over their cost or book value."

The term capital surplus has been used in the past as a generic term to describe any type of surplus other than earned. However, in recent years there has been a tendency to replace this term by more precise designations.

Sometimes the term **donated surplus** is encountered. Donated surplus may result from donations by stockholders or from outsiders, such as donations of land by municipalities and grants-in-aid from governmental agencies. Under the threefold classification cited above, donated surplus is included under paid-in surplus.

Occasionally, the term **discovery surplus** is found, particularly in extractive industries. Discovery surplus is analogous to revaluation surplus and should be similarly classified.

The Securities and Exchange Commission (Regulation S-X) prescribes that separate captions shall be shown for (1) paid-in surplus; (2) surplus arising from revaluation of assets; (3) other capital surplus; and (4) earned surplus.

SURPLUS TERMINOLOGY. The real significance of surplus is frequently misunderstood by investors, creditors and other interested parties. Probably the two **most common misconceptions** are that surplus (1) represents cash funds available for dividends, and (2) denotes "too many," "unneeded," or "excess" liquid assets. Surplus does not represent cash or liquid assets. In fact, there is no necessary correlation between cash and surplus. A newly formed corporation will have substantial cash and no surplus immediately following the sale of capital stock at par value. Conversely, an established corporation may have only a small amount of cash and a substantial surplus upon completion of a major plant expansion program.

Decline in Use of Term "Surplus." The confusion and misunderstanding has prompted both the American Institute of Certified Public Accountants (Accounting Research and Terminology Bulletins) and the American Accounting Association (Accounting and Reporting Standards for Corporate Financial Statements) to recommend discontinuance of the term surplus in favor of the following designations: retained income, retained earnings, or earnings retained in the business for earned surplus; capital received in excess of par or stated value for paid-in surplus; and excess of appraisal or fair value of fixed assets over cost, or appreciation of fixed assets for revaluation surplus.

The A.I.C.P.A.'s annual survey of six hundred corporate reports (Accounting Trends and Techniques) reveals a steady decrease in the use of the term surplus in published reports. For example, only 27% of the companies were still using earned surplus.

IMPROPER SURPLUS TECHNIQUES. The surplus of a corporation may be understated or overstated as a result of changing economic conditions, ignorance of accounting and financial principles, or intent to deceive.

Understatement of Surplus. The principal device for understatement of surplus is the so-called **secret reserve**. Lenhart and Defliese (Montgomery's Auditing) state that the term "secret reserve" denotes the existence of proprietary equities concealed through the understatement or omission of assets, the overstatement of liabilities, or the inclusion of fictitious liabilities. Secret reserves may be deliberate or unintentional. For example, management may willfully write down intangible assets to a nominal amount of $1.00 when the value of such assets has not been impaired; or the estimated income tax liability may be deliberately overstated. In contrast, unintentional secret reserves occur when economic conditions prolong the useful life of a depreciable asset beyond reasonable expectations or when actual warranty costs fall below past averages.

Overstatement of Surplus. The overstatement of surplus would result from practices that are directly the opposite of secret reserves. The capitalizing of revenue expenditures and the omission of accrued liabilities are examples of techniques that will overstate surplus.

Regardless of the specific cause of the misstatement of surplus, **immediate correction is warranted** whenever improper techniques are uncovered.

Paid-in Surplus and Revaluation Surplus

PAID-IN SURPLUS DISTINGUISHED FROM LEGAL CAPITAL AND UNDIVIDED PROFITS. The American Institute of Certified Public Accountants (Accounting Research and Terminology Bulletins) indicates that the stockholders' equity section of a balance sheet should emphasize the distinction between (1) legal capital (the par or stated value of capital stock), (2) capital in excess of legal capital (paid-in surplus), and (3) undivided profits (retained earnings). Paid-in surplus is clearly part of paid-in or contributed capital. For this reason the term "additional paid-in capital" is sometimes used instead of paid-in surplus. In contrast to legal capital, which is not legally available for dividends, paid-in surplus is **legally distributable** in most states.

The distinction between paid-in surplus and retained earnings is of fundamental importance to corporate management, stockholders, and other interested parties. Operating losses and nonrecurring extraneous losses must be charged to retained earnings except in the case of a quasi-reorganization. The S.E.C., for example, stipulates that capital (paid-in) surplus should under no circumstances be used to write off losses that if currently recognized would have been chargeable against income. Thus, such charges as a fire loss, goodwill write-offs, and losses on the sale of investments should be absorbed through retained earnings.

Various purposes may be served through paid-in surplus. In a bank, paid-in surplus provides added protection for depositors and makes possible larger individual loans. In insurance companies paid-in surplus is an added buffer against possible declines in investment values.

SOURCES OF PAID-IN SURPLUS. In published financial statements paid-in surplus is often combined into a single amount. Such disclosure fails to reveal the specific sources of paid-in surplus and is incompatible with sound reporting standards. The principal sources of paid-in surplus are: (1) the sale of capital stock for more than par or stated value, (2) donations and gifts, (3) reacquisition of capital stock, (4) recapitalizations, (5) reorganizations, and (6) business combinations. Each of these sources is discussed below.

Sale of Stock. Paid-in surplus may arise from the sale of par value stock for more than par and no-par value stock for more than the stated value. Paid-in surplus may also be created by the sale of treasury stock at a price that is in excess of the acquisition cost of such shares. The excess results from a **financial rather than an operating transaction.** Accordingly, it is improper to credit such "gains" to retained earnings.

Donations. In some corporations, paid-in capital is created through donations by stockholders or outsiders. Stockholder donations usually involve the return of capital stock to the issuing corporation. Such donations enhance the book value of the shares that remain outstanding but corporate assets are not increased. Eventually the donated shares may be resold, in which case assets and paid-in surplus are increased.

Donations from outsiders may consist of both tangible and intangible properties. The accepted basis of valuation is the **fair market value** of the property at the time of the donation. Donations or gifts may be **conditional** or **uncondi-**

tional. Until the contractual conditions are met it may be desirable to use temporary paid-in surplus accounts in the interest of full disclosure.

Occasionally, donated surplus may also arise from **forgiveness of indebtedness** by stockholders or outsiders.

Reacquisition of Capital Stock. Paid-in surplus may result from the reacquisition of preferred or common stock. **Preferred stock** may be redeemed by call (assuming the terms of issue include a call provision), by purchase in the financial markets, or by negotiation with specific shareholders. When the purchase price is below the net book value of the reacquired shares, paid-in surplus results. Crediting the "gain" to retained earnings is not sanctioned since the redemption of preferred stock is not related to a company's operating activities or its income performance for a given period.

Common shares are sometimes purchased for the treasury with the expectation that they will be re-issued at some time in the future. Either the cost method or the par value method may be used in accounting for treasury stock. Under the cost method, which predominates in practice, the reacquired shares are recorded at their cost. Consequently, the purchase of treasury shares has no effect on paid-in surplus. Under the par value method, which has the greater authoritative support in accounting, paid-in surplus will result if the purchase price is less than the prorata amount paid in on the shares. The paid-in surplus created thereby may be used to absorb "losses" sustained on subsequent acquisition of treasury shares.

Recapitalization. The term recapitalization is used here to describe a modification of paid-in (or contributed) capital without asset revaluation or new financing. The effects of a recapitalization are limited entirely to the stockholders' equity section of a balance sheet. The re-alignments of owners' equity resulting from recapitalizations are relatively minor for insolvency has not occurred and is generally not imminent. Recapitalization may be effected through stock dividends, stock splits, conversion of preferred stock into common stock, and changes from par to no-par stock or vice versa. The paid-in surplus that results from recapitalization should be separately identified to indicate its source. In some cases the designation "Recapitalization Surplus" is used but more specific disclosure is desirable, such as "Surplus From Stock Dividends," "Surplus From Stock Conversion," etc.

Reorganization. Dewing (The Financial Policy of Corporations) defines a reorganization as a **radical adjustment** of the financial structure of a corporation that results from serious financial plight. There are two principal types of reorganizations: (1) an **informal accounting reorganization**, and (2) a **formal legal reorganization**. In the former, generally called a **quasi-reorganization**, the adjustments in the capital structure are made without recourse to the courts; in the latter, the re-alignments are made through the courts in compliance with Federal bankruptcy laws. Typically, a quasi-reorganization involves a downward revaluation of assets, a reduction in the par or stated value of capital stock that produces a paid-in (or capital) surplus, and the absorption of a deficit. As a result of this procedure, assets will be stated in terms of current values that may subsequently permit a company to report increased net income and to resume dividend declarations.

Regardless of the specific form of reorganization, the important feature from an accounting standpoint is the emergence of a **new accounting entity**. The American Institute of Certified Public Accountants (Accounting Research and Terminology Bulletins) has established the following accounting requirements:

When the readjustment has been completed, the company's accounting should be substantially similar to that appropriate for a new company.

After such a readjustment earned surplus previously accumulated cannot properly be carried forward under that title. A new earned surplus account should be established dated to show that it runs from the effective date of the readjustment, and this dating should be disclosed in financial statements until such time as the effective date is no longer deemed to possess any special significance.

Capital surplus originating in such a readjustment is restricted in the same manner as that of a new corporation; charges against it should be only those which may properly be made against the initial surplus of a new corporation.

The S.E.C. (Regulation S-X) indicates that the **dating of retained earnings** should be continued for three years, but in practice it is often continued for longer periods.

Business Combinations. Business combinations may be accomplished through mergers or consolidations. Legally, there is a sharp distinction between these terms. A **merger** occurs when one corporation loses its existence and its assets are combined with those of the surviving entity. A **consolidation** (or amalgamation) results when two or more companies combine to form a new corporation and all of the old companies lose their corporate identities. In business and finance, however, these terms are often used interchangeably.

For accounting purposes, business combinations are classified as being either a purchase or a pooling of interests. The American Institute of Certified Public Accountants (Accounting Research and Terminology Bulletins) indicates that a **purchase** may be described as a business combination of two or more corporations in which an important part of the ownership interests in the acquired corporation or corporations is eliminated. In contrast, a **pooling of interests** occurs when the holders of substantially all of the ownership interests in the constituent corporations become owners of a single corporation that owns the assets and businesses of the constituent companies. Thus, in the typical situation a merger represents a purchase and a consolidation constitutes a pooling of interests.

When a business combination is deemed a purchase the assets of the acquired company should be recorded at their **fair market value** by the purchaser and any retained earnings of the predecessor becomes paid-in surplus to the purchaser. In a pooling of interests, however, the **book value** of assets, if stated in accordance with generally accepted accounting principles, may be continued after making appropriate adjustments to place them on a uniform basis. In addition, the retained earnings of the constituent companies may be carried forward and any increase in stated capital of the new corporation over that of the predecessor companies should be deducted first from the total "capital surplus" and then from the retained earnings of the predecessors.

A **special feature of consolidations** is the recognition of minority interest in the paid-in capital and consolidated surplus of the affiliated companies. Minority interest is generally shown in the consolidated balance sheet as a separate element immediately following the presentation of current and long-term debt.

REVALUATION SURPLUS. The generally accepted basis of accounting for fixed assets is **cost minus depreciation.** Accountants have steadfastly opposed the use of revaluation data and as a result such information normally is not shown in the accounts and statements. The S.E.C. has refused to approve the use of appraised values by new companies, but it has accepted appraisal data for established companies if the appraisal is "based on scientific method." When appraisal data is recorded, the credit is made to revaluation (or appraisal) surplus in order to indicate the specific source of the item.

Legally, revaluation surplus is usually available for both cash and stock dividends. However, accountants have universally rejected this type of surplus as a basis for dividends and corporate managements have seldom found it acceptable.

It is generally agreed that revaluation surplus should not be used to absorb deficits, operating losses, or the write-down of assets that have not been previously subject to an appraisal increase.

Retained Earnings

SOURCES OF RETAINED EARNINGS. Retained earnings represent the undistributed profits of a corporation, from whatever source derived. Retained earnings results from the principal business operations, ancillary activities such as the sale of scrap and income from investments, and extraordinary gains such as the sale of fixed assets for more than book value and income tax refunds. Retained earnings **do not result from** transactions in a company's own stock and transfers from paid-in surplus.

CHARGES TO RETAINED EARNINGS. It is generally agreed that retained earnings are properly charged for (1) the net loss for the period, (2) dividend declarations, and (3) the establishment of retained earnings reserves. Material extraordinary charges are included in the determination of periodic income (or loss) or are charged directly to retained earnings.

Direct charges to retained earnings may also result from **financial transactions** such as stock conversion, stock redemption, and the purchase of treasury shares. If the consideration given exceeds the pro rata amount paid in, the excess is properly chargeable to retained earnings. This treatment is justified on the basis of an implied dividend, a bonus, or a donation to the stockholder who relinquishes his shares.

ADMINISTRATION OF RETAINED EARNINGS. The administration of retained earnings relates to the adoption of retained earnings policies by the board of directors that will afford a **proper balance** among the various interests represented in the enterprise. The basic decision involves a consideration of dividend declarations versus the reinvestment of earnings.

Such purposes as protection of working capital, anticipated plant expansion, compliance with legal and contractual requirements, declaration of regular dividends, and maintenance of a strong market position for a corporation's securities are generally regarded as ethically desirable and administratively proper. Yet, in practice, it is not always easy to accomplish these purposes, taking into account both short- and long-run considerations, from the standpoint of all equities involved.

In recent years, the wide disparity between earnings per share and dividends per share, vague appropriations of retained earnings for equally vague purposes, and the imposition of the accumulated earnings tax have resulted in a more critical appraisal of retained earnings administration. Management clearly has responsibility for disclosing and defending its retained earnings policies.

DEFICITS. A debit balance in retained earnings is called a "deficit." A deficit results when accumulated profits are less than the sum of accumulated losses and dividend declarations. In the absence of other types of surplus, a deficit would cause an impairment of **legal capital.** Generally accepted principles of accounting provide that losses should be charged to retained earnings even if a debit balance is created thereby. Stated in another way, paid-in surplus cannot be used to absorb losses that otherwise would be charged against income.

If a deficit is a temporary situation, no special action is needed because subsequent earnings will fully absorb the deficit. However, if future earnings will be insufficient to cover the deficit, a company may authorize the write-off of the deficit against paid-in surplus via a **quasi-reorganization.** The principal accounting requirement, as explained in the caption "Paid-in Surplus from Reorganizations," is to date the retained earnings of the reorganized company.

While a deficit exists it should be **shown as a deduction** from total paid-in capital in the stockholders' equity section of the balance sheet.

"Surplus" or Retained Earnings Reserves

RESERVES. One of the most overworked and frequently misunderstood terms in business is the word "reserve." The term "reserve" may be used in financial statements in three separate and distinct ways: (1) as an asset valuation account, (2) as an estimated liability, and (3) as a reservation (or appropriation) of retained earnings.

Valuation Reserves. Valuation reserves reflect the **estimated decline** in the value of specific assets that has already occurred. Some valuation reserves, such as reserves for bad debts, marketable securities, and inventories, are deducted within the current asset section in order to show the expected realizable value of the related assets. Other valuation reserves, such as reserves for depreciation and depletion, are offset against related fixed asset accounts to show the unexpired cost (or book value) of the assets.

Liability Reserves. Liability reserves may be used to reveal estimated liabilities at the statement date. Such liabilities represent **known legal obligations** the precise amount of which is indeterminate at the time the balance sheet is prepared. Examples include reserves for income taxes, product warranties, and employee pensions. Liability reserves may be classified as liabilities, as part of stockholders' equity, or in a separate reserve section.

Surplus Reserves. Surplus reserves represent the appropriation or earmarking of retained earnings for some **specific future purpose,** such as plant expansion, retirement of bonds, and contingencies. Generally, surplus reserves are shown in stockholders' equity, but occasionally they are classified in a reserve section.

Recent Trends in Terminology. Both the American Institute of Certified Public Accountants (Accounting Research and Terminology Bulletins) and the American Accounting Association (Accounting and Reporting Standards for Corporate Financial Statements, Supplementary Statement No. 1) have recommended discontinuance of the term "reserves" to identify **asset valuation accounts and estimated liabilities.** Terms such as "estimated uncollectibles," "accumulated depreciation," and "estimated income taxes payable" are suggested as alternative designations. Prevailing practice, as revealed by the American Institute of Certified Public Accountants (Accounting Trends and Techniques), shows a decided trend toward acceptance of these recommendations.

The two accounting organizations differ, however, concerning **surplus reserve** terminology. The A.I.C.P.A. believes the term "reserve" should be used to designate appropriations of retained earnings. The A.A.A., on the other hand, favors the designation "appropriations" of retained earnings. In recommending the complete elimination of the term "reserve," the A.A.A. claims that (1) clarity of financial statement captions would be promoted, (2) nonaccountants would no longer

18·8   CORPORATE SURPLUSES, RESERVES, AND DIVIDENDS

have to deal with a specialized meaning at variance with popular usage, and (3) professional thinking would be freed from a confusing ambiguity.

The American Accounting Association also suggests the elimination of the **reserve section in corporate balance sheets.** Acceptance of this proposal would significantly enhance the understanding of financial statements, for the heterogeneous quasi-liability reserve section would be eliminated.

RELATIONSHIP BETWEEN FUNDS AND RESERVES. Although reserves are frequently considered to be funds by laymen, a clear distinction must be drawn between them. Funds are tangible assets; reserves are segregations of retained earnings. Funds are established by the transfer of cash and/or other assets to the fund; reserves are created by an accounting entry that does not involve a transfer of assets. Funds can be used in exchange transactions; reserves cannot be used as a medium of exchange.

A fund may exist without a related reserve, as is typical with a petty cash fund; a reserve may exist without a related fund, as is typical with a reserve for contingencies. Both a fund and a reserve may exist simultaneously. This situation is described as **funding a reserve.** When a reserve is funded the reservation of retained earnings is accompanied by a transfer of liquid assets from working capital to a special fund. This procedure accomplishes a dual purpose: the reserve assures the retention of earnings in the business, and the fund provides for the accumulation of assets whose use is restricted to the purpose for which the reserve is created. Thus, a "reserve for plant expansion" may be accompanied by a "plant expansion fund."

When either the fund or the reserve, or both, is voluntary, no necessary relationship exists between the amount of the fund and the amount of the reserve. When both are obligatory, the terms of the contract determine the relationship of the amounts.

NATURE OF SURPLUS RESERVES. Surplus reserves represent an informal appropriation of retained earnings. The temporary capitalization removes a portion of retained earnings from the amount available for dividends. The reserves are created by the board of directors, which can increase, decrease, or eliminate them when changing circumstances justify such action. Burtchett and Hicks (Corporation Finance) state that it is often desirable to divert a portion of apparent earnings to surplus reserves in order to meet business contingencies, to act as a buffer for errors in determination of earnings, and to help stabilize dividends.

The reserve does not earmark or restrict any **specific asset** for a specific purpose. It does, however, limit the amount of **total assets** that can be distributed in the form of dividends.

Legal, Contractual, and Voluntary Reserves. There are three basic kinds of surplus reserves: legal, contractual, and voluntary. Legal reserves are required when state laws place a limitation on the combined disbursements for dividends and the purchase of treasury stock. Contractual reserves are set up when bond and/or preferred stock contracts provide for the retention of earnings for the protection of the claims of senior security holders. Voluntary reserves result from the discretionary actions of the board of directors in order to earmark and to disclose the present or potential uses of retained earnings in the business.

Accounting for Surplus Reserves. It is generally recognized in accounting that the determination of **periodic earnings** should not be affected by surplus reserve transactions. Accordingly, establishment of the reserve is effected by a direct transfer from retained earnings, and elimination of the reserve by a direct return to its original source. Under no circumstances should surplus reserves be used to absorb losses ordinarily chargeable against current earnings.

Both the creation and the elimination of the reserve must be **authorized by the board of directors.** Instead of returning the reserve to unrestricted retained earnings the directors may formally capitalize the amount by declaring a stock dividend from the reserve.

Since surplus reserves represent a part of retained earnings they are **classified in the stockholders' equity section of the balance sheet.** The usual presentation is as follows:

Retained Earnings			
Reserves:			
Reserve for Sinking Fund	$500,000		
Reserve for Plant Expansion	400,000		
Reserve for Contingencies	300,000	$1,200,000	
Free		1,000,000	
Total Retained Earnings			$2,200,000

PURPOSES AND TYPES OF SURPLUS RESERVES. Broadly speaking, the purpose of surplus reserves is to show the amount of retained earnings presently unavailable for dividends. However, the reserves may also indicate the specific purposes for which earnings are retained, namely, to maintain legal capital, to provide additional protection for bondholders and preferred stockholders, and to indicate present and potential uses of retained earnings in the business such as to expand plant facilities and to anticipate future contingencies.

The importance of surplus reserves is sometimes exaggerated. Every purpose for which a reserve is established can be accomplished equally well by other means. Moyer and Mautz (Functional Accounting) point out that negative action in the form of no dividend declaration is as effective in retaining earnings in the business as positive action in the form of creation of a reserve. The real protection against future losses and inefficient use of assets lies in the **judicious administration of assets.** A surplus reserve is essentially a disclosure device to indicate the specific nature of future contingencies.

A brief discussion of the principal types of surplus reserves is presented below.

Reserve for Treasury Stock. In the interests of creditors and minority stockholders, some state statutes limit the purchases of shares of a corporation's own stock to the amount of the corporation's surplus account balance. Under such statutes the effect of the expenditure of funds to acquire outstanding stock is to render an amount of surplus corresponding to the cost of the shares unavailable for dividend appropriation. In a study of state corporation laws, Rabel (Journal of Accountancy, Vol. 95) says that surplus restrictions are generally recognized (but not necessarily required) in the thirty-one states that include an "impairment rule" or a "surplus rule" in their statutes. (For explanation of rules, see discussion below under Statutory Law, p. 19.) Under either rule the combined disbursements for dividends and purchases of treasury shares cannot exceed surplus. The **restriction of surplus** may extend only against retained earnings or it may apply against all surplus legally available for dividends. In the states referred to above, only six apply the restriction specifically to retained earnings.

Reserve for Bonded Indebtedness. Many bond contracts require a reserve for bonded indebtedness (often referred to as a **sinking fund reserve**). The

18·10 CORPORATE SURPLUSES, RESERVES, AND DIVIDENDS

purpose of the reserve is to prevent the dissipation of working capital for cash dividends and thereby retain enough cash (or liquid assets) in the business to redeem the bonds periodically or when they mature.

Since the reserve for bonded indebtedness limits the use of cash only for dividends, it may not provide sufficient protection against the impairment of working capital from other uses. Thus, some bond indentures also require the establishment of a bond retirement (sinking) fund. A **bond retirement fund** is created by periodic transfers of cash to a specifically segregated fund that can be used only for the redemption of the bonds. The fund may be under control of the company or it may be administered for the bondholders by a trustee. In either case, the fund is classified as a **noncurrent asset** in the balance sheet. When both a bond sinking fund reserve and a bond sinking fund are required, the relationship between the amount of the two will be determined by the bond contract.

There is some difference of opinion as to whether the fund or the reserve offers greater protection to the bondholder. The prevailing view is that the fund is more important since the bondholder has a specific claim on the fund in the event of forced liquidation. Paton and Paton (Corporation Accounts and Statements) argue, however, that earning power is basically more important than the composition of assets since without earnings default may occur when only a small part of the total requirement has been accumulated.

At maturity the reserve for bonded indebtedness is returned to free retained earnings or it may be used for a stock dividend declaration.

Reserve for Contingencies. Although retained earnings itself is a buffer against uncertainties, many companies use contingency reserves to indicate the specific nature of possible future losses. Examples include losses that may result from pending litigation, strikes, and expropriation of foreign investments by unfriendly governments.

The use of this type of reserve is justified if a specific condition exists or is reasonably imminent, and if the amount of the loss may be estimated with some degree of accuracy. The establishment of **general purpose contingencies** to identify vague and remote circumstances, however, is not recommended, for such reserves may obscure rather than clarify the presentation of stockholders' equity.

Reserve for Plant Expansion. Companies that anticipate a major plant expansion or modernization program may establish a "Reserve for Plant Expansion" or a "Reserve for Additions, Betterments, and Improvements." The purpose of the reserve is to earmark funds and to prevent payment of dividends that could impair the reserve so that the company will be in a better cash position to pay for its expansion program.

Upon completion of the expansion program, the reserve may be returned to free retained earnings. However, since the company's cash position may not permit cash dividends, the directors may decide to formally **capitalize the reserve** through a stock dividend. Such action can be fully justified, for the plant expansion program, in effect, has permanently capitalized a portion of retained earnings.

A closely related reserve is the **"Reserve for Increased Replacement Costs."** As Husband and Dockeray (Modern Corporation Finance) explain, this reserve is intended to recognize situations where depreciation reserves (usually based on original cost) are inadequate for replacement of the physical assets. This procedure has the sanction of the American Institute of Certified Public Accountants (Accounting Research and Terminology Bulletins), who believe it is entirely proper for management to make annual appropriations of net income or surplus in contemplation of replacing facilities at higher price levels.

Reserves for Future Inventory Declines. At the end of an accounting period two types of inventory losses may be recognized in the accounts and statements. Under the lower of cost or market method of inventory costing **known losses** resulting from market declines that have already occurred are recorded by a charge against income and a credit to a valuation reserve. In contrast, **potential losses** expected from future inventory price declines may be recorded in a surplus reserve. The "Reserve for Future Inventory Declines" reveals to all interested parties the possible inventory losses that may occur in the future. If the loss materializes it is charged against income, but the reserve can then be returned to free retained earnings to nullify the effect of the inventory loss on unappropriated retained earnings.

Reserves for Insurance. Any corporation is apt to suffer loss of property values through fire, flood, windstorm, or other natural causes. Protection against a part of such loss may be secured through the purchase of insurance. Not all hazards are known, however, and not all known hazards are insurable. Few, if any, insurance policies afford full protection against possible property loss. Hence, whether a corporation carries its own insurance or buys all the insurance available to it, there will be an **unprotected hazard** that can be covered by a surplus reserve for that purpose. Since these hazards will continue until the enterprise is terminated, the "Reserve for Insurance" is rarely returned to free retained earnings.

Aside from loss to property values, most corporations face other risks requiring insurance, such as **workmen's compensation** and public **liability for accidents** on the premises or **acts of an employee** of the corporation. If a corporation decides to carry self-insurance—in states where this is permitted—or if it cannot buy full coverage by the payment of premiums, provision should be made to meet these hazards. In contrast to fire losses, which are not predictable, these hazards can be determined with reasonable accuracy on the basis of past experience. Moreover, these are bona fide costs of operations and they represent actual liabilities of the company. Accordingly, provision for these events should be made by a charge to expense and a credit to an estimated liability account such as "Estimated Liability for Workmen's Compensation Insurance" or some similar title. In the balance sheet this account is classified as a liability and when workmen's benefits are paid they are charged against the estimated liability.

Nature and Kinds of Dividends

DIVIDEND DEFINED. A dividend involves an appropriation, usually of current or accumulated earnings, that results in a distribution of an equivalent amount of corporate assets to stockholders of a given class on a pro rata basis. The appropriation is made by the board of directors and is usually referred to as declaring a dividend. The **declaration** of a dividend and the **payment** of the dividend represent two separate and distinct steps.

When used alone the term "dividend" usually refers to a declaration from current or accumulated earnings payable in **cash.** However, in many states it is possible to declare dividends from sources other than earnings, and payment may be made in media other than cash. In such instances, full disclosure of the source and medium of payment is generally required, and in any event should be made. Occasionally a dividend represents a return of invested capital but this is not the usual connotation.

CASH DIVIDENDS. The vast majority of dividends are payable in cash. Companies incorporated abroad usually pay dividends in their own currencies, and in some countries there are restrictions on the transfer of dividends to other countries. In others, such as Canada, a **dividend tax** is withheld at the source, so stockholders do not actually receive the full amount declared.

Regular payment of cash dividends generally has a favorable effect on the market value of stock. It should be noted, however, that payment of cash dividends reduces corporate assets, stockholders' equity, and book value per share. Husband and Dockeray (Modern Corporation Finance) indicate that in an abstract sense the increase in shareholder assets may not be genuine. Moreover, Porterfield (Harvard Business Review, Vol. 37) argues that cash dividends theoretically have no value to stockholders and should be a matter of indifference to them.

STOCK DIVIDENDS. In relative importance, stock dividends rank next to cash dividends. Stock dividends may be payable in either preferred or common stock to stockholders of the same or a different class of stock. Ordinarily a stock dividend is payable in common stock to common stockholders. Since this type of dividend does not change either total stockholders' equity or the amount of corporate assets, it has been referred to by some writers as only **nominally** a dividend. Burke (Accounting Review, Vol. 37) therefore suggests the use of the expression **"Stock Distributions in Kind"** to describe the ordinary stock dividend.

Stock Dividends vs. Stock Splits. In a stock dividend additional shares are issued at the par or stated value of shares previously outstanding; in a stock split, the par or stated value is reduced and a proportionate number of additional shares are issued. A distinguishing feature is the **principal intent** of the corporate action: The objective of a stock dividend is the **formal capitalization** of a part of retained earnings, whereas the purpose of a stock split is to increase the **marketability** of the stock. The American Institute of Certified Public Accountants (Accounting Research and Terminology Bulletins Final Edition) recommends that the effect of the event upon market value should be used to validate the avowed purpose of the action. They believe there will be few instances in which the issuance of shares of less than 20% to 25% of the shares previously outstanding will not qualify as a stock dividend.

Purposes of Stock Dividends. Donaldson and Pfahl (Corporate Finance) indicate that the primary reasons for stock dividends are to (1) retain needed cash in the business, (2) pacify stockholders, (3) reduce per share earnings and dividends, and (4) reduce the market price of the stock. The first two reasons are the most important.

The use of stock dividends to conserve cash is considered desirable in a **"growth" company** in order to reduce dependence on capital markets for needed funds. Husband and Dockeray (Modern Corporation Finance) point out that the greatest use of stock dividends is in periods of rapid growth and that growth companies frequently follow a policy of no-cash or low-cash dividends accompanied by stock dividends.

A stock dividend offers several **advantages** to the stockholder. It is not taxable upon receipt and when sold it will receive capital gains treatment. (See discussion of taxability below.) It gives him the opportunity to decide whether to maintain his proportionate interest in the business or to sell the additional shares. If he holds his stock, he will receive increased income whenever the company pays cash dividends.

Stock dividends give corporate directors some control over the earnings, dividends, and market price per share of stock. Ordinarily, of course, the management prefers a good earnings per share ratio and a high market price per share. However, a conspicuously high profit may spur labor union demands for higher wages whereas a high market price may narrow the market for the stock. In order to effect a significant reduction of per share earnings a large stock dividend, say of 50% to 100%, would be necessary, whereas the ordinary stock dividend is often within the range of 2% to 5%. Consequently, if this is the motivating objective the corporate action would be more like a stock split. (See discussion above of Stock Dividends vs. Stock Splits.)

Taxability of Stock Dividends. Under the Internal Revenue Code, the general rule is that stock dividends do not constitute income to the recipient. This rule has been upheld by the Supreme Court, which stated in Eisner v. Macomber, 252 U.S. 189 (1920):

> Far from being a realization of profits to the stockholder it tends rather to postpone such realization, in that the fund represented by the new stock has been transferred from surplus to capital, and is no longer available for actual distribution.

The foregoing applies to all types of stock dividends, including a distribution of stock to a different class of stockholders. When a stock dividend is not taxable, the dividend reduces the **cost price** of the stock for purposes of computing capital gains or losses when the shares are sold.

A stock dividend is **taxable,** however, if (1) the stockholder could elect to receive money or other property, and (2) if the distribution of stock is made in discharge of dividends on preferred shares for the current or preceding taxable year. Stock dividends in discharge of preferred dividend arrearages for years prior to the first year preceding the year of distribution are tax-free within the general rule. For taxable stock dividends, income is measured by the fair market value of the shares received in the distribution.

Valuation of Stock Dividends. Within the requirements of state statutes, the board of directors has the power to determine the amount of surplus to be capitalized when a stock dividend is declared. Normally, the legal requirement is equal to the par or stated value per share.

The American Institute of Certified Public Accountants (Accounting Research and Terminology Bulletins) takes the position that the amount capitalized should bear a reasonable relationship to the **fair value** of the shares distributed. They maintain that the typical dividend (frequently much less than 20%) will not substantially change the market price of the shares previously outstanding and that the recipient accordingly may believe that retained earnings have been capitalized in this amount.

In an effort to prevent abuse of the stock dividend device, the **New York Stock Exchange** has established several **requirements for listed companies.** If the stock dividend represents less than 25% of the shares previously outstanding, the dividend will not be approved unless (1) the company transfers from retained earnings to paid-in capital an amount equal to the **fair value** of the shares and (2) retained earnings for the particular period covered by the dividend is equal to or greater than the aggregate fair value of the dividend.

Rescission of Stock Dividends. Unlike cash dividends, stock dividends do not become a debt of the corporation between the date of declaration and actual payment. The board of directors may rescind a stock dividend any time before it has been distributed, and no liability is thereby incurred.

PROPERTY DIVIDENDS. Dividends payable in noncash assets are "property" dividends. The most common form of property dividends is the distribution of securities held as an investment by the declaring corporation. For this reason a property dividend is sometimes referred to as a **"security" dividend.** Property dividends may be liquidating dividends or they may be distributions of earnings. For example, public utility holding companies have used property dividends to dispose of stock of subsidiaries under the divestment requirements of the Public Utility Holding Company Act. Property dividends may also result from an antitrust action when a corporation is forced to divest itself of stock of other corporations. On occasion, marketable securities held as liquid assets, inventory held for resale, and government bonds have also been distributed as a property dividend.

Property dividends avoid the necessity of selling assets to obtain cash for the payment of dividends. When such assets are not needed in operating the business there can be little objection to this procedure. To the recipient, the fair market value of the property represents **taxable income,** and, as Guthmann and Dougall (Corporate Financial Policy) point out, the corporation saves a tax that might have resulted if it had converted the property into cash.

SCRIP DIVIDENDS. Corporations may sometimes seek to maintain a regular dividend record without paying out cash immediately. This is done by distributing notes payable either at some date in the future or by installments over a period of several years. Such distributions have been called scrip dividends, since notes are issued in small denominations, or for the specific amount payable to each stockholder. The notes usually bear interest and if issued unconditionally they are **negotiable instruments.** Scrip dividends are generally classified as a current liability.

Scrip dividends are actually **deferred or postponed dividends.** They are rarely used and are justified only when a corporation has **actual earnings** that will be converted into cash before the notes become due. Ordinarily it is better to "pass" the dividend until sufficient cash becomes available.

Donaldson and Pfahl (Corporate Finance) point out that scrip dividends to preferred stockholders will not satisfy their prior claims for dividends unless it is so specified in the stock contract or the preferred shareholders agree to such action.

BOND DIVIDENDS. Bond dividends are similar to scrip dividends except the obligation has a longer maturity. The effect of bond dividends is to transform a portion of stockholders' equity, generally retained earnings, into **long-term debt.**

The theory underlying bond dividends is that a corporation, in lieu of selling bonds to other investors, may distribute bonds to stockholders and retain the existing cash for other business purposes. Bond dividends, however, are **not considered sound practice,** on the ground that a corporation should not incur debt except for the actual operating needs of the business. The Interstate Commerce Commission has denied a number of applications by railroads to issue bonds to be distributed as dividends.

To the recipient, a bond dividend is usually considered to represent **income** in the amount of the fair market value of the bond. Paton and Paton (Corporation Accounts and Statements) argue against this interpretation, pointing out that there has been no distribution of corporate assets when the bonds are issued and that payment of the bonds may be postponed indefinitely by exchanges or refundings.

Designation of Dividends

REGULAR DIVIDEND. The term "regular dividend" usually refers to a cash dividend payable on common stock. Such stock normally does not carry a specific dividend rate, nor is any rate expressed in the charter or bylaws. The regularity of the dividend, therefore, results from the actions of the board of directors. When they announce a regular dividend, they imply that they can repeat the dividend periodically, assuming no drastic changes in the circumstances affecting the distribution. Regular dividends generally are declared **quarterly** but occasionally they may be monthly, semi-annually, or annually.

In many companies great effort is exerted to pay a regular dividend over the years, the American Telephone and Telegraph Co. being the classic example. However, in other cases, the dividend has at times been lowered and sometimes passed entirely. On the New York Stock Exchange most of the leading companies have a regular dividend rate on their common stock and approximately eighty corporations have a record of at least fifty consecutive years of cash dividend payments.

EXTRA DIVIDENDS. When a dividend is designated as "extra" it is one declared in addition to the regular dividend and by this designation the board of directors indicates that there is no assurance that the distribution can be repeated. Disclosure of an "extra" is accomplished in some instances by using checks of different color from regular dividend checks and by marking the check "extra dividend." Extra dividends may be paid quarterly or at the end of the year, to reflect better than expected earnings for that year. Some corporations pay regular dividends in cash whereas extras are paid in stock or property. Unusually large extra dividends are often referred to as **"melons."**

SPECIAL DIVIDENDS. A dividend designated as "special" is represented explicitly as being in the nature of a "windfall" to stockholders, and therefore **unlikely to be repeated.** Stockholders are thus placed on notice that they are not justified in assuming that such dividends will recur. Otherwise, there is the possibility that the public will assume that the dividend reflects a regular dividend policy, and the price of the stock might unjustifiably discount the temporarily larger yield. Such dividends often result from an isolated or nonrecurring event, such as a gain on the sale of real estate or a substantial income tax refund.

INTERIM AND FINAL DIVIDENDS. The term "interim dividends" is sometimes used to identify partial distributions of earnings during the year, and the term "final dividend" is employed to indicate the declaration made at the end of the year. Interim dividends may be distributed once or as many as three times **during the year.** The final declaration may not be paid before **the end of the year.** However, it must be paid before the 15th day of the third month following the close of the taxable year to qualify as a distribution under the Section 531 surtax on undistributed earnings.

LIQUIDATING OR CAPITAL DIVIDENDS. When a dividend is designated as "liquidating" or as a return of capital, the stockholder is put on notice that part of the capital is being returned to him, and that the distribution he receives does not come from earnings of the business. Such dividends will not then be looked upon as recurring in nature. Furthermore, stockholders will know that the dividend is not taxable to them, but results rather in a corresponding reduction in the cost of the shares or basis for capital gains tax purposes.

18·16   CORPORATE SURPLUSES, RESERVES, AND DIVIDENDS

Mining companies, investment trusts, and others whose dividends constitute in part or whole a return of capital should make this fact known to the stockholders, regardless of how the dividend is designated in making it public, so they can be guided accordingly in the preparation of their personal income tax returns.

The action of returning a portion of the corporation's permanent capital is not a true dividend. Accordingly, the term **"capital distributions"** is a more appropriate designation.

CONSTRUCTIVE DIVIDENDS. "Constructive" dividends is the term used to describe distributions of corporate assets to stockholders in the ratio of their holdings without formal dividend action. They are sometimes termed **quasi-dividends** and their use is confined generally to closely held corporations. Special problems arise in connection with tax regulations because constructive dividends are sometimes similar to officers' salaries or bonuses. But whereas dividends represent distributions of profits, salaries are **business expenses**. Dividends are not deductible for tax purposes by the corporation, whereas business expenses are. Tax authorities attempt to determine whether the payments bear a closer relationship to services rendered or to stockholdings in distinguishing between the two.

Types of Dividend Policy

DIVIDEND POLICY DEFINED. Wide variety is encountered in dividend policies. As Hunt, Williams, and Donaldson (Basic Business Finance) indicate, the concept of dividend policy implies that businesses, through their boards of directors, evolve a recognizable pattern of cash dividend payments that has a **bearing on future action**. From a study of dividend policies in large industrial corporations, Lintner (American Economic Review, Papers and Proceedings) concludes that in the majority of cases current dividend decisions are intimately related to previous dividend decisions. The principal dividend policies frequently employed by American corporations are described below.

REGULAR DIVIDEND POLICY. Regularity of dividends is an important factor in establishing dividend policy. Present views seem to favor a policy of regular dividend payments.

Graham and Dodd (Security Analysis) claim that the combination of dividend continuity and stability is the most important factor in establishing an investment rating for common stock. Dewing (The Financial Policy of Corporations) asserts that a policy of regular dividends forms a more loyal permanent group of stockholders and helps create a strong credit for borrowing in the open market. Burtchett and Hicks (Corporation Finance) believe that a stable dividend policy indicates conservative operating and financial management as well as a relatively secure and profitable position in the company's industry. Gerstenberg (Financial Organization and Management of Business) also calls attention to possible tax advantages of regular dividends and to the fact that railroad and public utility bonds cannot become legal investments in some states unless the company has a five-year unbroken dividend record.

Companies with relatively **stable earnings** and a **large number of conservative stockholders** are ideally suited for a regular dividend policy. However, companies with fluctuating annual earnings can also maintain a regular dividend policy by paying relatively modest dividends in prosperous years and using accumulated earnings as the basis for dividends in low-income years.

REGULAR AND EXTRA DIVIDEND POLICY. Under a regular and extra dividend policy the stockholder receives a relatively stable regular dividend rate and at times an extra dividend when earnings warrant it. Extra dividends sometimes occur with such frequency that they virtually become a part of regular dividends. If it is believed that the extra dividend can be maintained indefinitely, the directors may decide to raise the regular rate and to drop the extra dividend.

This procedure is illustrated by the following excerpt from a recent annual report of The American Tobacco Co.

For the past several years an extra dividend equivalent to 50 cents per share on the present Common Stock was paid on March 1 of each year. Under the new policy, subject always to business conditions at the time, regular quarterly dividends will be increased 12½ cents per share in place of paying the extra dividend of 50 cents on March 1.

REGULAR PLUS STOCK DIVIDEND POLICY. Gerstenberg (Financial Organization and Management) indicates that this type of dividend policy is used when a corporation (1) wants to continue its record of regular cash payments, (2) has reinvested earnings it wants to capitalize, and (3) wants to distribute to stockholders a part of the additional earnings without using up its cash. As indicated in the discussion of stock dividends, growth companies often adopt a policy of paying small cash dividends plus stock dividends.

IRREGULAR DIVIDEND POLICY. Some corporations prefer to make no attempt to establish a regular dividend rate, but instead vary dividend distributions from year to year and even from quarter to quarter, depending on earnings and other conditions. This may involve dividend declarations every few months but not regularly, or the irregularity may be limited to the rate, with payments declared quarterly, semi-annually, or annually, or on an interim and final basis. This type of dividend policy is particularly suited to companies that have **highly fluctuating earnings**.

REGULAR STOCK DIVIDEND POLICY. A regular stock dividend policy has rarely been used. Continuous stock dividends dilute the capital stock. Both earnings and book value per share may become unsatisfactory, and the market price may fall below a range that will permit later financing. Moreover, not many stockholders are content to defer indefinitely the possibility of receiving cash dividends.

PROPERTY DIVIDEND POLICY. Some enterprises, particularly those that are constantly developing new subsidiaries, distribute securities of other corporations as part or all of their dividend distributions. Holding companies that are required to dissolve also have adopted a property dividend policy to distribute their assets to shareholders.

LIQUIDATING DIVIDEND POLICY. Because of the many uncertainties that surround accurate computation of the depletion charge against earnings, and because it may not be possible to replace an exhausted natural resource by acquiring new property of similar character, dividend policies of **wasting asset enterprises** are affected by special considerations. Policies encountered in such enterprises are:

1. Distribution as dividends of the entire excess of receipts over current disbursements, except for sums required for working capital, without any effort to accumulate a reserve for the replacement of the natural resource. In such cases, it is assumed that when the natural resource has been exhausted, the enterprise will be liquidated. A number of mines and some smaller oil-producing companies have adopted this policy, informing stockholders with each dividend

check of the proportion of the payment that constitutes a return of capital, so that they will not pay income tax thereon.
2. Only a part of the earnings after depletion is paid out in dividends, the balance of net receipts being retained in the business and used to acquire new natural resources or to diversify the enterprise by entering some other type of activity. Thus, an oil-producing company may use funds derived from depletion and undistributed earnings to acquire new oil leases, or to build refining and marketing facilities so as to become less dependent upon wasting assets for future earnings.
3. Depletion reserves and part of the earnings may be retained in the form of cash or government securities, to be utilized in the future as and if occasion arises. The management may decide subsequently to invest these reserves in the same business, to enter some other line of activity, to become a general investment or investment-management company, or to distribute these liquid assets as liquidating dividends. If an efficient organization has been built up to manage a wasting asset that cannot be replaced when exhausted, it is often considered preferable to utilize this organization in some other profitable activity than to dissolve it by liquidation.

NO DIVIDEND POLICY. Some corporations, particularly those in rapidly growing industries, rely entirely upon **re-invested earnings** for new capital rather than on new financing in the capital market. Such companies, therefore, adopt a no-dividend policy and refrain from paying dividends over long periods. Under such a policy, stockholders must look to appreciation of their holdings, stock dividends, and ultimate cash dividends in the remote future rather than to current dividends for a return on their capital. In pursuing this policy, the possible impact of the surtax on unreasonable accumulation of earnings must be weighed. (See discussion of Tax Aspects below, page 23.)

FACTORS AFFECTING DIVIDEND POLICY. The formulation of a dividend policy involves many factors. The first consideration is necessarily the **legal right** of the corporation to distribute net income. Corporation laws of all the states limit dividend payments, and even without statutory restrictions there are common law limitations. In the second place, the distribution of income to stockholders is influenced by the tax consequences, both to the enterprise and to the owners personally. A third factor is the working capital position of a corporation, for it would obviously be shortsighted to pay dividends that could undermine the financial strength of the enterprise and even threaten its future solvency. A fourth basic consideration is the long-term capital requirements of the business and the availability of other sources of funds for expansion. Fifth, a corporation may have specific objectives in view, such as merger with another business. These aims would be furthered by liberal dividend distributions that would make its stock more attractive when offered in exchange for the shares of other concerns. The desire to achieve such a purpose may offset other considerations in shaping dividend policy. A brief discussion of these factors is presented below.

Legal Restrictions upon Dividends

REASONS FOR LIMITATION. The primary reason for restricting dividend declarations by corporations is the **protection of creditors**. The greatest privilege accorded corporations by law is the limitation of the liability of stockholders. In return for this privilege, the courts have sought to protect the capital of the corporation, as originally constituted, from deliberate impairment by dividend distributions or by purchases of its own stock by a corporation. It is one thing for a corporation to amend its charter to reduce the par or stated value of its capital, and to distribute the amount of such capital reduction as a liquidating dividend. But when dividends are paid out of capital without charter amendment, creditors who rely upon the stated capital of the business in granting credit to the enterprise may, in effect, be defrauded.

A second reason for legal limitations upon dividend distributions is the **protection of the stockholders** of the enterprise. The payment of dividends out of capital may mislead stockholders. Dividends that are in fact a return of capital constitute misrepresentation, if not specifically described as such, because they cause persons to pay excessive prices for the shares. Subsequently, when they learn that dividends cannot be maintained because they were actually a return of capital, the market price of the shares will decline and large losses may be incurred.

COMMON LAW RULES. Even apart from state corporation laws that restrict dividend payments, the courts have held that there are basic common law rules limiting the payment of dividends. As long ago as 1824, the United States Supreme Court, in the leading case of Wood v. Dummer, held that dividends could not be paid out of capital until all creditors had been satisfied. The court in this case went so far as to say that the capital of the corporation is "like a trust fund" for the benefit of creditors, but legal writers have since felt that this **trust fund doctrine,** as it is called, goes too far in describing the legal status of corporate capital. Other equity cases have ruled that dividends should be paid only from the profits of a business.

If state laws impose specific legal restrictions upon corporate dividend payments, these take the place of common law precedents. However, because dividend statutes are often brief and general in character, so that they do not provide an adequate guide for the determination of whether dividends can be paid in many cases, courts still refer to equity cases in deciding litigation concerning dividends.

STATUTORY LAW. Dividend laws of the individual states are modified from time to time by statutory amendment and court decisions. There is a great diversity of dividend provisions in state corporation laws although their basic principles are similar. These provisions establish one or more tests to determine the legality of a dividend declaration. The four tests found in state laws, sometimes in various combinations, are:

1. The capital impairment test
2. The surplus test
3. The profits (or earnings) test
4. The insolvency test

The New York Statute. Section 510 of the new Business Corporation Law of New York may be regarded as fairly typical of present-day legislative standards in respect to dividends. This section states:

A corporation may declare and pay dividends or make other distributions in cash or property, including the shares of other corporations, on its outstanding shares, except when currently the corporation is insolvent or would thereby be made insolvent, or when the declaration, payment or distribution would be contrary to any restrictions contained in the certificate of incorporation, subject to the following limitations:

(1) Dividends may be declared or paid and other distributions may be made out of surplus only, so that the net assets of the corporation remaining after such declara-

tion, payment or distribution shall at least equal the amount of its stated capital; except that a corporation engaged in the exploitation of natural resources or other wasting assets, including patents, or formed primarily for the liquidation of specific assets, may declare and pay dividends or make other distribution in excess of its surplus, computed after taking due account of depletion and amortization, to the extent that the cost of the wasting or specific assets has been recovered by depletion reserves, amortization or sale, if the net assets remaining after such dividends or distributions are sufficient to cover the liquidation preferences of shares having such preferences in involuntary liquidation.

(2) When any dividend is paid or any other distribution is made, in whole or in part, from sources other than earned surplus, it shall be accompanied by a written notice (A) disclosing the amounts by which such dividend or distribution affects stated capital, capital surplus and earned surplus, or (B) if such amounts are not determinable at the time of such notice, disclosing the approximate effect of such dividend or distribution upon stated capital, capital surplus and earned surplus and stating that such amounts are not yet determinable.

The Capital Impairment Test. The oldest statutory limitation upon dividend declarations, and one that is found in the common law, is a prohibition of dividend payments that impair capital.

Application of a provision prohibiting capital impairment requires a **definition of "capital."** Court decisions have laid down three such definitions:

1. The par or stated value of capital stock, regardless of whether shares were issued for more or less than such par or stated value.
2. The actual dollar consideration received from the sale of capital stock, which in many cases among older corporations was substantially less than the par or stated value.
3. The capital at the beginning of the accounting period in which dividends are paid. This would mean that the amount of the capital to be kept intact may be reduced by preceding operating losses or write-downs of assets.

Under the first interpretation the capital impairment test is similar to the surplus test, since in many states all types of surplus are available for dividends.

Under the second interpretation **total contributed capital** must be maintained in the business. As a practical matter, this view prevents dividends from paid-in surplus, and in the absence of revaluation surplus, dividends are limited to retained earnings. This interpretation merits both financial and accounting support since dividends are based on current and accumulated earnings.

The third interpretation, namely **capital at the beginning of the period,** does not provide a satisfactory test. Under this view, prior deficits need not be made good out of current earnings before dividends are declared, and capital increases during the period resulting from sources other than earnings are legally available for dividends.

The major deficiencies of the capital impairment test as a basis for dividend declarations are: (1) the lack of agreement concerning the meaning of capital, (2) the fact that a revaluation surplus may be available for cash dividend declarations, and (3) the fact that dividends may be legally declared before eliminating a prior deficit.

The Surplus Test. The majority of state laws now limit dividend declarations to surplus. This means that dividends can legally be declared whenever total assets exceed liabilities and legal capital. In recent years there has been a marked trend in the statutes and in the courts toward an acceptance of sound accounting principles in determining surplus. Pennsylvania, Ohio, Louisiana, and Washington make surplus the sole test in determining the legality of a dividend and Delaware, Georgia, Arkansas, California, and Florida use either a surplus or a net profits test.

Barring any specific statutory prohibition, the surplus test allows **cash dividends to be declared from all types of surplus.** A recent study made by Buttimer (Accounting Review, Vol. 36) reveals the following:

Statutes of thirty-nine states establish paid-in surplus as a legal source for distributions to preferred shareholders, and only twenty-eight of these extend the availability of paid-in surplus for dividend charges to common shareholders. In addition to these twenty-eight, the statutes of California and Minnesota permit common dividend charges to paid-in surplus when there are no preferred shares outstanding.

Graham and Katz (Accounting in Law Practice) indicate that the availability of paid-in surplus for dividends is widely assumed in practice, although there have been few decisions to support this assumption. Guthmann and Dougall (Corporate Financial Policy) point out that "the growing tendency is to limit the use of paid-in surplus to preferred dividends, to restrict the distribution of surplus arising from a reduction of legal capital, and to require that stockholders be given notice when dividends are paid from any source other than earned surplus."

The Profits Test. The profits test is frequently referred to as the net profits or earnings test. There are two legal interpretations of this test: (1) current net profits, and (2) accumulated earnings. Buttimer (Accounting Review, Vol. 36) for example, cites ten states that permit the declaration of dividends from **current profits** despite a deficit in accumulated earnings. The term **"nimble dividends"** is sometimes used to describe this action because the directors have to be quick to declare the dividend before the current earnings are absorbed by the deficit. This interpretation of the profits test is not in accord with sound accounting and financial practice, which holds that prior deficits must be eliminated before a dividend from current earnings is declared.

The **accumulated profits test** provides a sound basis for dividend declarations. The underlying premise is that only profit-derived assets are legally available for dividend distributions. Under this interpretation, dividends are based on accumulated net undistributed earnings from the beginning of a corporation's existence, as determined by generally accepted accounting principles. Bonbright (Valuation of Property) urges the adoption of the accumulated profits test as the **sole criterion** for establishing the legality of a dividend. However, the insistence of the courts upon a liquidation point of view, the difficulty of measuring corporate profits, and the general unfamiliarity of lawyers and judges with accounting principles tend to hinder the wider use of the profits test.

The Insolvency Test. An insolvency test is used in approximately one-third of the states. Often this test is used in conjunction with one of the other statutory restrictions. In essence the insolvency test stipulates that a dividend cannot be declared if such action would make the declaring corporation insolvent. Equity courts would probably apply the insolvency rule if the statute does not do so, on the ground that the payment of a dividend while a corporation is insolvent, or that causes insolvency, is a fraudulent conveyance.

Application of this test involves a definition of the term "insolvency." In California, the term is used either **in the bankruptcy sense,** which means that assets do not suffice to cover liabilities other than capital, or **in the equity sense,** i.e., that the corporation is unable to meet its debts as they mature. In Ohio and Massachusetts, the term is used specifically in the equity sense. If the equity definition of insolvency is used, a corporation whose assets exceed its debts may nevertheless be rendered insolvent by a dividend, if the payment of the dividend absorbs cash that is needed to meet obligations as they mature.

Guthmann and Dougall (Corporate Financial Policy) indicate that this test, when used alone, is less than sound policy requires.

OTHER RESTRICTIONS. A corporation's charter, bylaws, or bond indentures may impose on dividends **restrictions beyond those imposed by statute.** A common restriction limits dividend declarations to retained earnings accumulated after a specified date, to prevent the use of earnings previously accumulated for this purpose. A restriction often inserted to protect preferred stock and bond issues provides that dividends shall not be paid if they will reduce current assets to, say, less than twice current liabilities, or if net working capital will thereby be reduced below a specified amount.

Corporations subject to special regulation may have to conform to additional statutory provisions. Thus, Section 12(c) of the Public Utility Holding Company Act provides that **approval by the S.E.C.** is required for payment of dividends out of capital or unearned surplus by a registered holding company or its subsidiary. Accounting regulations imposed under the Interstate Commerce Act, the Motor Carrier Act, the Federal Water Power Act, and the Federal Communications Act affect dividend declarations by corporations subject to these statutes.

JUDICIAL COMPULSION TO DECLARE DIVIDENDS. Stockholders sometimes seek to compel a corporation to declare dividends on preferred or common stock if the board of directors does not do so even though large earnings are reported. The courts have been loath to interfere, holding that the declaration of a dividend is a matter of business judgment that should be left to the discretion of the board. Also, there is reluctance to overrule a conservative course of action by corporate management.

There have been a few cases, however, where the courts of equity have held that failure to pay dividends imposes an undue sacrifice upon shareholders, or that the purpose of the board in not declaring a dividend is to depress the price of the stock and so induce outside stockholders to sell their holdings.

The most celebrated equity case was Dodge v. Ford Motor Co. (204 Mich. 459, 140 N.W. 668), in which the board of directors of the Ford Motor Co. was ordered to declare a dividend of $19,000,000 out of earnings of more than three times that amount. Referring to Henry Ford's argument that he wanted to put the bulk of the earnings of the corporation back into the business to expand production and employ more men, the court said:

A business corporation is organized and carried on primarily for the profit of the stockholders. The powers of the directors are to be employed for that end. The discretion of the directors is to be exercised in the choice of means to attain that end, and does not extend to a change in the end itself, to the reduction of profits, or to the non-distribution of profits among stockholders in order to devote them to other purposes.

If all stockholders agree to the distribution of a dividend and the directors do not oppose the distribution, such a **"consent dividend"** may be validly distributed in many jurisdictions without specific vote of the board of directors. This will occur only in close corporations.

EFFECT OF DIVIDEND DECLARATION. A dividend that is properly declared creates a debt by the corporation to stockholders. However, if declaration of a dividend violates the statute, or is otherwise illegal, no debt is thereby created. Furthermore, if no announcement has been made of the dividend and stockholders have no knowledge that it has been declared, it may be revoked without stockholders' consent (Hunt v. O'Shea, 69 N.H. 600).

It is realistic to **list cash dividends payable,** if they are legally declared, as a current liability of the corporation. A stock dividend payable, on the other hand, is properly carried along with capital stock outstanding in the stockholders' equity section of the balance sheet.

LIABILITY FOR ILLEGAL DIVIDENDS. Many of the state corporation laws specifically make directors liable for illegal dividend declarations. Creditors of the corporation, a trustee in bankruptcy, or a new management may sue directors to recover sums paid out in dividends that are illegal. A few states make it a misdemeanor for a director to vote for a dividend that impairs capital, and criminal penalties have been imposed in several such cases.

It has been held that a director who attends a meeting at which a dividend is illegally declared becomes liable like a director who votes for it, but that a director who records his vote as opposed to an illegal declaration of dividends thereby escapes personal liability. In Illinois, directors who vote for an illegal dividend are guilty of conspiracy. Delaware and some other jurisdictions make **good faith** a defense if a director is sued because of improper dividend declarations, reliance upon audited financial statements being considered evidence of good faith.

The **right to recover illegal dividends** directly from stockholders is restricted under corporation laws in this country, although it is the prevailing practice under European law. When a dividend payment renders a corporation insolvent, such a distribution is generally recoverable from stockholders. But a number of laws specify that a dividend, even though illegally declared, may not be recovered from the stockholders if they received it in good faith.

Because of civil and sometimes criminal liabilities incurred by directors for improper dividend declarations, it is particularly important that the financial statements used as a basis for dividend actions shall be prepared in accordance with the law of the state in which the corporation is incorporated and pertinent judicial decisions. Otherwise, directors may unwittingly declare a dividend in the belief that a surplus or net profit exists, when under statutory provisions and judicial precedents no surplus would be held available for this purpose. Both creditors and innocent stockholders may bring suit for injuries sustained as a result of illegal dividends.

Tax and Financial Aspects of Dividend Policy

SURTAX ON UNDISTRIBUTED EARNINGS. Section 531 of the Internal Revenue Code provides for a surtax on undistributed earnings. Under the law, earnings are improperly retained when the purpose of the retention is to avoid personal income taxes on shareholders or when the earnings reinvested are in excess of the reasonable needs of the business. The tax is essentially a penalty tax and it is imposed in addition to other corporate income taxes. The tax rates are $27\frac{1}{2}\%$ on unreasonable additions to retained earnings up to \$100,000 in any one year (after excluding \$100,000 of retained earnings) and $38\frac{1}{2}\%$ on annual improper accumulations in excess of \$100,000. These rates apply only to the portion of retained earnings found to be unreasonable.

The 1954 Internal Revenue Code substantially lessened the impact of the tax by transferring the **burden of proof** for unreasonable accumulations from the taxpayer to the **Commissioner of Internal Revenue.** However, the burden of proof will switch to the taxpayer if he fails to submit a statement in response to the Commissioner's tax deficiency notice or if such statement is not supported by facts. The imposition of a penalty is ordinarily not recommended by revenue agents unless:

1. Corporations have not distributed at least 70% of their earnings as taxable dividends.
2. Corporations have invested earnings in securities or other properties unrelated to their normal business activities.
3. Corporations have advanced sums to officers or shareholders in the form of loans out of undistributed profits or surplus from which taxable dividends might have been declared.
4. A majority of the corporation's stock is held by a family group or other small groups of individuals, or by a trust, or trusts, for the benefit of such groups.
5. The corporations' distributions, although exceeding 70% of their earnings, appear to be inadequate when considered in connection with the nature of the business or the financial position of the corporation or corporations, with accumulations of cash or other quick assets that appear to be beyond the reasonable needs of the business.

The reasonable needs of a business depend upon the **specific facts of the situation.** Montgomery's Federal Taxes indicates some of the more important considerations that may be involved:

1. Accumulations to pay off liabilities.
2. Accumulations to finance planned enlargement or modernization of facilities.
3. Accumulations necessary to increase investment to maintain present business.
4. Accumulations necessary to maintain adequate working capital.
5. Accumulations necessary to invest in key man or stockholder life insurance.

The undistributed earnings tax has undoubtedly been a factor in dividend policy, especially in small corporations. The major effects of the tax, however, have been in the actions taken to avoid the liability rather than in the penalties imposed. Unnecessary buildup of plant facilities and premature introduction of new products are a few of the consequences directly or indirectly related to avoid the tax. In reality, as TeKolste (Accounting Review, Vol. 29) explains, most companies need not worry about the tax because their financial positions are not exceedingly fluid and, even when the combination of circumstances indicated above is not present, adequately supported intentions to use the liquid funds will serve to impress the courts favorably. Anderson (Taxation and the American Economy) points out that the Internal Revenue Service has won less than half of such cases, even though only the most flagrant violators have been brought into court.

The surtax on undistributed earnings can be defended if the corporation is used as a vehicle to avoid the imposition of income taxes on stockholders. Such taxation, however, has been opposed on the ground that it tends to discourage corporate savings and to penalize the use of retained earnings for corporate expansion.

EFFECT ON STOCKHOLDERS' TAXES. From the stockholders' viewpoint, liberal dividends are unattractive when received by **persons in the high income brackets.** Wealthy stockholders are generally better off if a smaller proportion of earnings is distributed as dividends, for they can then benefit from appreciation of the market value of their holdings or stock dividends, instead of receiving taxable cash dividend distributions. When this appreciation in value is realized through sale of the stock after the stock has been held for at least six months, the result is a long-term capital gain subject to a maximum tax of 25%, regardless of the surtax bracket of the taxpayer. The larger the extent to which capital stock of a corporation is owned by shareholders in the higher income brackets, therefore, the greater the incentive to limit dividend distributions and to reinvest the larger part of the profits in the business.

Under the Federal tax revisions enacted in 1964, the first $100 of dividends received from domestic corporations is excluded from gross income. The 4% credit on dividends was reduced to 2% in 1964 and eliminated as of January 1, 1965.

WORKING CAPITAL POSITION. Since cash dividends reduce current assets of the corporation, the **effect of dividend distributions** upon the working capital position of the enterprise must be carefully weighed. It is obviously short-sighted and unsound to impair working capital for dividend purposes. Particularly if there is any question about the adequacy of current assets to meet current liabilities and operating expenses, therefore, a **projection of cash requirements** should be made to insure that funds to be used for dividend distributions can be spared.

The fact that current cash holdings are adequate does not alone justify a dividend declaration. If a corporation must borrow some years hence to replenish working capital that has been impaired by dividend distributions, in effect it borrows to pay the dividend. For this reason, a projection of cash income and outgo for a period of 2 years or longer ahead should be weighed in formulating dividend policy where capital resources are scant.

Stock and property dividends, which do not involve a diminution of working capital, are sometimes paid when the need for conserving working capital causes cash dividends to be reduced or eliminated.

"Cash Flow" Analysis. In recent years the concept of "cash flow" has become a major factor in judging the ability of a firm to pay dividends, meet debt requirements, and finance replacement and expansion programs. Mason (A.I.C.P.A., Accounting Research Study No. 2) defines cash flow as follows:

"Cash flow" in financial analysis means net income after adding back expense items which currently do not use funds, such as depreciation. It may also involve deducting revenue items which do not currently provide funds, such as the current amortization of deferred income. It corresponds to the "funds derived from operations" in a statement of source and application of funds.

The term cash flow is not strictly accurate for it is neither cash nor flow. Net income is generally computed on an **accrual basis** rather than a cash basis, and the adding back of depreciation and other items that do not use funds does not indicate the amount of cash provided by operations. Paton (Accounting Review, Vol. 38) vigorously opposes the current usage of cash flow as follows:

The sum of net earnings and the depreciation deduction may often be hopelessly in error as a measure of cash "currently generated" from operations . . . This type of "cash-flow" calculation . . . is intrinsically sloppy and inadequate as a tool in the area of cash administration or fund analysis.

In financial literature such terms as "cash earnings" or "cash income" have been used interchangeably with cash flow. Such terminology not only is inaccurate but it fosters the misconception that cash earnings are either a supplement to or a substitute for net income. Mason (A.I.C.P.A., Accounting Research Study No. 2) specifically denies this connotation of cash flow, pointing out that "in no sense can the amount of cash flow be considered as a substitute for or an improvement upon the net income properly determined, as an indication of the results of operations or the change in financial position."

When cash flow is viewed as the amount of working capital produced by operations, it becomes a valid and useful analytical tool. Consequently, the terms "working capital flow" or "funds flow" might be more appropriate than "cash flow" to describe this item.

DIVIDEND PAYOUT RATIOS. The dividend payout ratio is determined by dividing annual net income into the dividends declared during the same period of time. For all U.S. corporations the average payout ratio of annual earnings has been approximately 50% in recent decades. Stated conversely, this means that 50% of annual net income is reinvested in the business.

Buchanan (The Economics of Corporate Enterprise) states that from an economic point of view earnings should be paid out to the residual owners so long as they can earn a better return elsewhere, considering the relative risks involved. This is referred to as the **marginal principle** of dividend distribution by Johnson (Financial Management). Consequently **alternative investment** opportunities become a major factor in establishing dividend policy.

Under the marginal principle, dividend payout ratios would be relatively high in depression years for there would be limited reinvestment opportunities, and dividend distributions would be relatively low in prosperous times because of an abundance of expansion opportunities. Significantly, in the past three decades, the payment ratio for all U.S. corporations was the highest in 1935–39 (slightly over 100%) and the lowest in 1945–49 (approximately 40%).

Although shareholders generally desire higher payout ratios, Hunt, Williams, and Donaldson (Basic Business Finance) point out that under circumstances of abundant opportunities for profitable expansion it would appear to be in the stockholders' best interests to retain all earnings in the business.

NEW CAPITAL REQUIREMENTS. Even if working capital is adequate to permit a dividend distribution, the need for additional fixed capital may make payments unwise. Fixed, as well as working, capital requirements should be projected, and the available sources for such capital considered before a dividend policy is crystallized.

Even though an expansion program holds out every hope of being profitable, it may not be possible to secure the requisite capital on reasonable terms through new security issues or through loans. Therefore, management may have to look to the reinvestment of earnings as a major or sole source of funds for expansion. In that event, long-term capital needs could well become the chief consideration in the formulation of dividend policy. Hunt, Williams, and Donaldson (Basic Business Finance), in fact, say that given the current level of earnings, dividend policy would be a byproduct of the **capital budget.** If expansion involves substantial risks and may prove unjustified by results, there is added reason to finance it in whole or part from earnings when this is feasible.

SPECIFIC OBJECTIVES. A corporation's dividend policy must normally be based upon legal, tax, working capital, and fixed capital requirements as already indicated. In addition, specific objectives may influence declarations in particular cases. In connection with **new financing** or **mergers,** the board of directors may feel impelled to liberalize dividend distributions to secure more favorable terms. If stockholder dissatisfaction with management or a **proxy battle** has developed, similarly, a larger dividend distribution may be considered expedient to win the favor of shareholders. The desire to **facilitate distribution** of a block of stock held by persons close to management may be a factor also in governing dividend declarations.

Corporations that need to raise large amounts of capital from time to time for **expansion** often adopt a stable dividend policy, since this helps to secure an investment status for capital stock and thus facilitates sale of new shares to investors. A corporation that has an issue of convertible bonds outstanding may raise the dividend rate on its common stock in order to hasten **conversion.** There have been cases where a large cash dividend is declared solely to make conversion attractive, since only bondholders who convert will be entitled to this dividend.

Corporations have shaped their dividend policy at times to further broad corporation objectives. Thus, public utility holding companies have used stocks of subsidiaries for the purpose of distributing property dividends, while cash earnings have been conserved to pay off debt or preferred stock of the holding company. In this way, two objectives are accomplished: **divestment** of subsidiaries and **redemption** of senior securities.

A financial objective that at times assumes major importance is the devotion of most or all of the earnings of a corporation to the **retirement of debt or preferred stock,** if the capital structure has become top-heavy because of loss of earning power or the changed outlook of management. Many railroads have pursued this policy assiduously in recent years, with the result that dividend payments have been small in relation to earnings.

Mechanics of Declaration and Payment

RESOLUTION OF THE BOARD. The authority to declare dividends is vested in the board of directors, ordinarily by **specific statutory authorization.** Only in the case of some closely held corporations are dividends sometimes distributed by consent through **informal agreement** by all the stockholders. A dividend declaration by a board of directors is effected by a resolution approved by a majority or all the directors at a regular or special meeting of the board. This resolution will specify the amount of the dividend, the class of stockholders entitled to receive it, the date of record when the list of shareholders that are to receive the dividend is to be compiled, and the date of payment.

A typical resolution declaring a regular dividend follows:

RESOLVED, That the regular quarterly dividend of .... on the common stock of this Corporation be and it hereby is declared, payable on the ...... day of ...., 19...., to stockholders of record at the close of business on the ...... day of ...., 19.....

STOCK DIVIDEND DECLARATIONS. The procedure of a board of directors in the declaration of a stock dividend follows essentially the following pattern:

First, a resolution is passed that authorizes and justifies the dividend. A common form of such resolution reads as follows:

Whereas, the surplus profits of this Company, amounting to more than $........, have, from time to time, been invested in extensions and betterments to the plant and property of the Company, and in providing additional facilities for its business, and in that manner a large addition has been made to the value of the assets of the Company by withholding from the stockholders moneys which have been fairly earned, and but for the above mentioned expenditures would have been paid to them; and

Whereas, upon a just and fair estimate, the assets of the Company have been in such a manner increased in value over the amount of the capital stock, now issued and outstanding, by at least the said sum of $............; and (If the dividend is to be in no-par value common shares, the foregoing clause may be omitted.)

18·28   CORPORATE SURPLUSES, RESERVES, AND DIVIDENDS

Whereas, the stockholders desire to realize on profits which have been so invested, and to make the same more available, without impairing the property of the Company.

Now, therefore, be it resolved, that from the surplus profits so invested, a dividend of $............ (or, if the dividend is to be in no-par value common shares, of .... shares of common stock without nominal or par value) for each share of the present issued and outstanding common stock of this Company be and is hereby declared, payable on the .... day of ...., 19...., in the capital stock of this Company, to stockholders as shown by the books of the Company at the close of business on the .... day of ...., 19....; and that the president and secretary be directed to issue proper stock certificates representing the same to such stockholders on such date.

As authorized by this resolution, the president and secretary thereupon proceed to issue such stock under the conditions set forth in the resolution. There must be on hand sufficient unissued stock to meet the requirements of the stock dividend. Otherwise, action by the president and secretary must wait upon the **authorization of more stock** by the state and by the stockholders through amendment of the charter in the manner prescribed by the law of the state. Usually such authorization is readily obtained.

DATE OF RECORD. The date of record in dividend declarations will determine when the stock will be quoted **ex-dividend** on the stock exchange, if it is listed, or in over-the-counter trading. Ordinarily, listed shares will be quoted ex-dividend three full business days before the date of record, since settlements are effected on the fourth full business day following the date of the transaction. When the record date falls on a Saturday or holiday, the stock will be quoted ex-dividend on the fourth full business day preceding the date of record.

Only stockholders whose names appear on the corporation's stock books on the date of record will receive the dividend. On stock transferred after the date of record, but before the date of payment, the dividend goes to the seller. If some other arrangement is made, or is required by a stock exchange or the National Association of Securities Dealers, a **due bill** goes to the buyer with the stock, specifying that he or his assignee is entitled to the dividend when paid.

NOTIFICATION OF SHAREHOLDERS. Corporations whose shares are publicly held frequently advertise dividend declarations in the financial columns of newspapers in financial centers, or communities where numerous shareholders reside. Corporations whose shares are closely held may inform stockholders by letter.

The rules of some stock exchanges require listed companies to notify the exchange of all dividend declarations. This is done in order to protect minority stockholders and to prevent shareholders "in the know" from capitalizing on their information before the declaration is made public. As an aid in **identification**, declarations are sometimes numbered in sequence and reference to such numbers is often included in dividend notices.

Many corporations accompany the dividend check with a communication to stockholders containing an interim earnings statement and sometimes other pertinent information. It is in effect an **interim earnings report.** This communication may be printed on a folder within which the dividend check is contained. In other cases, a brief notice only to the effect that it is in payment of specified dividends accompanies the dividend check.

PREPARATION OF DIVIDEND CHECKS. The secretary of the company, if no transfer agent is employed, furnishes the treasurer with a list of stockholders of record. From this list the treasurer will make out the dividend checks.

Larger corporations usually send out special checks in payment of dividends with some identifying words printed thereon, as "Dividend Check" or "Dividend No. ...." If checks are mailed, no formal receipt is required, as the endorsement on the check is sufficient acknowledgment.

DIVIDEND BOOK. Fig. 1 gives a suggested form of the record that the treasurer uses in connection with dividend checks handed to stockholders at the company's office.

X. Y. Z. Manufacturing Company			
Semiannual Dividend No. 24 .... 19.. $3.00			

Name of Stockholder	Address	Number of Shares	Amount of Dividend	We Hereby Acknowledge Receipt of the Accompanying Dividend
....	....	....	....	....
....	....	....	....	....
....	....	....	....	....
....	....	....	....	....

Fig. 1. Form of record for dividend checks delivered at company's office.

Fig. 2 shows a typical record of dividend payments to stockholders as kept by the treasurer upon payments made by **check sent by mail.**

The American Milling Company					
Capital Outstanding $400,000					
Dividend No. 24					Sheet No. 48
List of stockholders of this company as shown by the transfer books at six o'clock P.M., February 15, 19..., and to whom the dividend of five per cent, declared February 12, 19..., is payable on March 1, 19...					
SHARES OUTSTANDING 40,000					RATE OF DIVIDEND 5%

Name of Stockholder	To Whose Order Check Should Be Drawn If Different from That of Stockholder	Mailing Address	Number of Shares	Amount of Dividend Paid	No. of Check Issued in Payment
....	....	....	....	....	....
....	....	....	....	....	....
....	....	....	....	....	....
....	....	....	....	....	....

Fig. 2. Form of record for dividend checks sent by mail.

SPECIAL BANK ACCOUNT AND PAYMENT THROUGH FISCAL AGENT. Payments of cash dividends may be accomplished through a special bank account or through a fiscal agent such as a bank or trust company.

When a special bank account is used, one check can be drawn on the regular bank account for deposit in "X.Y.Z. Co. Dividend Account." The checks to the individual stockholders are then drawn on the special account. With this procedure, it is important to recognize that **distribution of the individual checks** is necessary in order to pay the dividend; the liability is not satisfied by depositing the required funds in the special bank account.

When a fiscal agent is employed, he maintains the stock ledgers and transfer records. Shortly before the date of payment, the declaring corporation transfers the required funds to the fiscal agent. The agent then prepares and mails the checks to stockholders. The **fees** for this work are usually based on the number of checks mailed.

SECTION 19

PENSION AND PROFIT-SHARING PLANS

CONTENTS

Types of Pension Plans

	PAGE
Pension plan defined	1
Necessity for a pension plan	1
Employer's four alternatives on superannuation or disability	1
Dismissal without benefits	1
Continuance on active payroll	2
Unfunded pensions	2
Bookkeeping reserve	2
Funded pension plan	3
Tax aspects of pension plans	3
Taxation of qualified plans	3
Requirements for qualification	4
Deductibility of contributions	4
I.R.S. approval: advance rulings and request for exemption	5

Financing Funded Pension Plans

Method of funding	5
Self-administration (trusteed-securities fund)	5
Deferred group annuities	6
Deposit-administration group annuity	6
Individual retirement income policies	7
Group permanent retirement income	7
Combination plans	7
Advantages and disadvantages of each method of financing	7
Advantages and disadvantages of self-administration	7
Flexibility of contributions	7
No fixed annual contribution commitment	9
Permanence of plan	9
Coverage of pensioners already retired	10
Unusually large accrued liability—older-age employees	10
Disability pensions	10
Change of financing method	10
Comparative cost	11
Advantages and disadvantages of deferred group annuities	11
Third-party guarantees	11
Employee preference	12
Responsibility for employee contributions	12
Registration as a securities issue	12
Administrative cost	12
Advantages and disadvantages of deposit-administration group annuity	12
Advantages and disadvantages of individual retirement income policies	13
Flexibility through borrowing	13
Cost of death benefits	13
Relationship of death benefits to need	14

	PAGE
Costly vesting	14
Revision of retirement income policy plans	14
Cost if coverage is extended	15
Relationship of benefits to earnings	16
Simplicity of administration	16
Cost guarantee	16
Liberal settlement options	16
Advantages and disadvantages of group permanent retirement income	16
Advantages and disadvantages of combination plans	16

Pension Plan Provisions

Eligibility for membership	17
Full coverage	17
Years of service requirement	17
Minimum age requirement	17
Maximum age limitation	18
Effect on eligibility of financing method	18
Salaried employees only	18
Higher-paid employees only	18
Interrelationship of eligibility and financing	19
Normal retirement	19
Age 65 usual	19
Earlier retirement age for women	20
Staggered retirement ages	20
Early retirement	20
Deferred retirement	20
Pension benefit payments	21
Percentage of pay per year of service formula	21
Lower pensions on earnings covered by Social Security	21
Social Security benefits	22
Direct Deduction of Social Security benefits	22
Integration with Federal benefits	22
Earnings increase to covered level	23
Earnings base	23
Past service pensions	24
Maximum pensions	24
Minimum pensions	24
Disability pension benefits	25
Medical benefits for retired employees	25
Benefits for severed employees	25
Vested benefit rights	25
Vesting of retirement income policies	26
Vesting in the form of cash	26
Vesting of past service benefits	26
Return of employee contributions	26
Death benefits	26
Return of employee contributions on death	27

CONTENTS (*Continued*)

	PAGE
Employer contributions	27
Self-administered plans—level percentage of payroll method	27
Group annuity plans—single-premium deferred annuity method	28
Group annuity plans—deposit-administration method	28
Individual policy plans	29
Group permanent retirement income plans.	29
Employee contributions	29
Advisability of providing for employee contributions	29
Trends in use of contributory plans	30
Ratio of employee contributions to benefits	30
Investments	30
Termination of plan	31
Distribution formula	31
Termination of group annuity plans	32
Termination of individual policy plans	32
Early termination—tax penalty	32
Pension committee	32
Trustee	33
Relation of trust to plan	33
Powers and duties	33
Liability	34
Resignation or removal	34
Disclosure and bonding requirements	34

"Money Purchase" vs. "Fixed Benefit" Procedure, and Variable Annuities

Definitions	34
Fixed benefit plan advantages	35
Money purchase plan advantages	35
General considerations	35
Variable annuities	36

Profit-Sharing Plans

Immediate-distribution profit-sharing plans.	36
Objectives	36
Scope and nature	37
Profit-sharing formula	37
Allocations to participants	37
Size of organization	37
Relation to basic compensation	37
Employee reaction	37
Tax status	38
Deferred-distribution profit-sharing plans.	38
Definition	38
Objectives	38
Collective bargaining implications	38
Deferred-distribution profit-sharing plans compared with pension plans	39

Provisions of a Deferred-Distribution Profit-Sharing Plan

	PAGE
Profit-sharing formula	40
15% of compensation limit	40
Method of allocation	41
Actuarially determined pensions not permitted	41
Basis of individual accounts	41
Eligibility for membership	41
Retirement	42
Age pension benefits	42
Use of single-premium annuities	43
Use of ordinary life insurance policies.	43
Disability pension benefits	43
Severance of employment benefits	43
Death benefits	44
Death benefits under ordinary life insurance policies	44
Death benefits under group annuity contract	44
Employee contributions	45
Investments of profit-sharing fund	45
Individual policies	46
Group annuity contract	46
Termination of plan	46
Administrative committee	47
Trustee	47
Compensation	47
Tax rulings	48

Retirement Plans for Self-Employed Individuals

The problem and the solutions	48
Definition of self-employed individuals.	48
Required coverage of plans	48
Vesting requirements	48
Permissible benefits	49
Permissible investments	49
Tax status	49
Treatment of lump sum payments	50
Treatment of death benefits	50
Limitations as to contributions and deductions	50

Government and Union Pension Plans

Federal government pension programs	51
Federal Civil Service system	51
Other Federal programs	51
State and local pension plans	51
Administration of state and local plans	52
Investment restrictions	52
Current investment practice	52
Union plans	53

SECTION 19

PENSION AND PROFIT-SHARING PLANS

Types of Pension Plans

PENSION PLAN DEFINED. The term "pension plan" includes formal or informal procedures by which an income is provided for employees who are retired after attainment of a prearranged age, date, or condition. As herein considered, a pension plan is a formal arrangement made by an employer to anticipate by advance financing, in whole or in part, the responsibility that he considers that he carries to provide retirement benefits for some or all of his employees.

A pension plan is usually part of a broader **employee benefit program** that may include other benefits such as vacations and payments for sickness, hospitalization, death, or termination of employment. Such a program is frequently based upon the broad philosophy of providing protection for employees against the economic hazards not only of old age but also of total and permanent disability, severance of employment, and death. A plan may begin in an abbreviated form and be expanded in time to provide more complete protection against these hazards.

NECESSITY FOR A PENSION PLAN. Any employer who remains in business for any great length of time cannot avoid facing problems and making decisions concerning employees who become superannuated or disabled after years of service. The employer may not recognize these problems, however, until actual cases of superannuation and total and permanent disability appear among his employees after many years of service.

It is a mere question of time until these conditions must be faced. Therefore, the question is not so much whether a pension plan is needed, but rather what kind of a pension plan will best fit into the employer's program.

Employer's Four Alternatives on Superannuation or Disability. The employer has one of four choices concerning the treatment of employees who become superannuated or disabled after long periods of service:

- a. To dismiss aged and disabled employees without benefits; or
- b. To keep them on the active payroll; or
- c. To retire them on pensions financed on a pay-as-you-go basis; or
- d. To establish a funded pension plan under which accruing pension credits are financed as they accumulate during the years of active service.

Each of these procedures has been followed by employers. Before making a choice as to the most satisfactory procedure for a particular employer, the implications of each of the procedures should be considered.

Dismissal Without Benefits. The widespread adoption of pension plans is one of the most striking developments in employee relations. As to **employees**

represented by unions, this trend was given strong impetus by the Inland Steel case, holding that an employer is required, under the National Labor Relations Act, to bargain with its employees' union as to its pension and retirement policies. See Inland Steel Co. v. N.L.R.B., 170 F.2d 247 (7th Cir. 1948). As to **other employees and executives,** the adoption of a plan providing benefits on retirement has, in many cases, become a competitive necessity if the employer wishes to provide compensation comparable to that afforded by others in the same business or industry. But even when this practical necessity does not exist, many employers provide pensions to retired employees because of the widely held view that such payments are part of normal compensation to those who work to retirement age. The **morale of employees,** whether organized or not, would be impaired by a policy of dismissing, without suitable benefits, employees who become superannuated or disabled after many years of service. Such a policy has a detrimental effect not only on the employees as a whole, but on public relations as well. The public relations implications are of particular importance in small communities or localized areas in which the business operates.

Continuance on Active Payroll. Experience has indicated that the employer's second choice, that of keeping superannuated or disabled employees on the active payroll, is sometimes followed as the course of least resistance when an employer finds that the dismissal policy is impracticable. But it is probably the most expensive and unsatisfactory procedure. It involves a **hidden cost progression** that is not recognized at first because it is small. The first to become superannuated usually are few in number because they are generally the survivors of a small group of employees who constituted the original organization. The number of employees who become superannuated then increases steadily over a long period of time. Adverse consequences include not only the high ultimate cost of carrying superannuated employees on the active payroll, but also the detrimental effect on employee morale when promotional channels are blocked and the effect on productive efficiency and production costs of keeping superannuated employees in active service.

Unfunded Pensions. The third choice is the retirement of employees on pensions financed on a **pay-as-you-go basis.** This is an in-between type of procedure that many employers have attempted and abandoned. Among employers who have adopted a policy of paying pensions, the choice of this method has become relatively rare. The chief disadvantage of this procedure is the sharp rise in pension cost as the number of retired employees mounts. Another objection is that employees have no protection against reduction or elimination of pensions financed on a pay-as-you-go basis because of the absence of financial provision to assure payment.

Bookkeeping Reserve. Some employers have endeavored to buttress pay-as-you-go pensions with a supplemental bookkeeping reserve. The reserve accumulated to pay pensions is kept as an asset of the company instead of being segregated in a separate pension trust fund or turned over to an insurance company. This method has a number of disadvantages. One of these is that the employer loses the benefit of tax deductions on any funds that are held in the form of a bookkeeping reserve until the funds are paid to retired employees. Another disadvantage is that the income earned on the bookkeeping reserve is subject to corporate income tax, whereas the income that would be earned on the segregated assets of a qualified pension trust fund, or realized under a plan with insurance company underwriting, is exempt from income taxes.

Funded Pension Plan. The fourth choice, to establish a funded pension plan (with pension financing during the years of active service whether by a trusteed-securities fund or an insured plan), has been found to be the most satisfactory.

1. **Basic advantages of funding.** Employers generally have found that the costs of funded or insured pension plans represent an investment that pays dividends.

A strong indication that funded pension plans are more satisfactory than any other procedure is the fact that although there have been pension systems in this country for over 75 years, there has been a marked expansion in the number of funded plans and a shrinkage in the number of unfunded procedures.

2. **Payroll relief.** A properly funded pension plan helps an employer to retire superannuated and disabled employees, carry out delayed retirements, and effect early retirement of inefficient employees if a business depression makes it necessary to reduce the payroll expense to a minimum in order to meet competition, or even to stay in business. The payroll relief thus gained is financed by contributions made to the funded pension plan in previous more prosperous years. Without a funded pension plan, such employees would entail a current pension or payroll burden; whereas, under a funded plan, such employees are off the payroll, receiving pensions from the pension trust fund or the insurance company.

3. **Other advantages.** Under a funded pension plan, the pension expense is met as a **charge against current production,** instead of being allowed to accumulate as a charge against future operations. Without a funded pension plan, under which the liability to pay future pensions created as a result of current production is financed as it is incurred, present profits are exaggerated at the expense of future profits, and the future competitive position of the business may be jeopardized. Furthermore, the **known cost** of a funded pension plan is at all times a guide indicating whether the benefits and the conditions of payment are feasible from a cost standpoint. Employees appreciate the financing of funded benefits for their future security while they are actively working, whereas active employees tend to discount the value of pay-as-you-go pensions since they usually have little or no assurance that they will ever benefit from such a program. Similarly, retired employees feel less secure if they have to depend on the employer's ability and willingness to continue their pensions on a pay-as-you-go basis instead of receiving pensions under a funded plan.

TAX ASPECTS OF PENSION PLANS. Among the advantages of a funded pension plan are the tax benefits realized under plans that comply with the Internal Revenue Code and are thereby considered qualified plans.

Taxation of Qualified Plans. If the plan meets the requirements of the Code, employer contributions are deductible from taxable corporate income for the years in which contributions are made, within certain limits. The net cost of the plan may thus be reduced considerably. Tax laws of most **states** grant deduction privileges similar to those provided under Federal law.

Moreover, employer contributions for pension and disability benefits under a qualified plan do not constitute taxable income to the employee participants until benefits are actually paid or made available to them. Since the employee is then usually in a lower tax bracket, **considerable savings in taxes** result as compared with the payment of additional compensation to the employee, particularly for executives and higher-paid employees. If all benefits standing to the credit of an employee arising from employer contributions under a qualified plan are distributed to him in one taxable year because of termination of service, the distribution is treated and taxed as a long-term capital gain. Also, income earned under a qualified plan is exempted from tax to the trust or plan. Distributions, to the extent attributable to employer contributions, are not subject to the Federal estate tax, if made to a beneficiary of a deceased employee; in addition, a designation of a beneficiary is similarly exempt from the Federal gift tax. Special rules apply to the taxability of annuity plans of charitable and educational institutions.

If a plan does not meet the requirements of the provisions of the Internal Revenue Code as to qualified plans, employer contributions are deductible from taxable income only if the employee's rights derived from the contributions are nonforfeitable at the time the contribution is paid—i.e., the right to receive the benefits is not forfeited by termination of service for any reason. If the **benefits are nonforfeitable,** the employer's contributions must be included in the employee's current taxable income. If the **benefits are forfeitable,** the employer's contributions will be taxable to the employee only when the benefits are distributed or made available to him, and the employer will never be entitled to a deduction for his contributions. Federal Tax Regulations, Revenue Rulings, "PS" rulings of the Pension Trust Information Service of the Internal Revenue Service, Mimeographs issued by the Commissioner, and "IT" rulings of the Income Tax Unit should be consulted for answers to questions concerning the determination of deductible contributions.

Requirements for Qualification. The Internal Revenue Code requires that a qualified plan must meet the following conditions:

1. Contributions must be for the sole purpose of distributing the corpus and income of the plan or trust to the employees or their beneficiaries.
2. It must be impossible for any part of the fund to be used for purposes other than the exclusive benefit of employees or their beneficiaries prior to the satisfaction of all liabilities under the plan or trust.
3. The plan or trust must benefit either (a) at least 70% of all the employees, or at least 80% of the eligible employees if at least 70% are eligible, excluding in each case those not eligible because of a service requirement of up to 5 years and because of temporary or part-time employment, or (b) employees under an eligibility classification found by the Commissioner of Internal Revenue not to favor officers, shareholders, supervisory employees, or highly compensated employees.
4. The contributions or benefits must not discriminate in favor of employees who are officers, shareholders, supervisory employees, or highly compensated employees; and must not amount to a subterfuge for the distribution of profits to major shareholders.
5. A classification is not considered discriminatory merely because it excludes certain employees such as all employees not paid on a salaried basis or those whose remuneration consists solely of "wages" covered by the Social Security Act, or because contributions or benefits differ for that part of compensation constituting such "wages." But the extent to which such benefits may differ is limited. On the other hand, a classification is not considered discriminatory merely because the contributions or benefits bear a uniform relationship to the total compensation, or the basic or regular compensation, of the employees covered by the plan.
6. The plan or trust meets requirements as to eligibility or employee participation throughout a taxable year if it does so on one day in each quarter thereof.

Deductibility of Contributions. The Internal Revenue Code allows **deductions** from taxable income for **employer contributions** amounting to either (1) sums reasonably necessary to meet the cost of the plan up to 5% of the compensation of the participants, plus (2) any additional amounts that are necessary to meet the cost distributed as a level amount or level percentage of compensation over the future service of each employee, or (3) the normal cost of the plan plus an amount not in excess of 10% of the cost to completely fund or purchase past service or supplementary pension credits as of the date they are included in the plan, determined under regulations prescribed by the Commissioner.

Contributions **in excess** of the amount deductible in any year become deductible in the next succeeding year or years to the extent of the difference between the contributions made and deducted in the succeeding year and the maximum amount that is deductible as described above. Excess contributions may be deductible by the surviving corporation in a corporate reorganization.

I.R.S. Approval: Advance Rulings and Requests for Exemption. Because tax advantages will not be realized unless the plan meets certain requirements, or any subsequent amendments, it is important to secure an advance ruling approving the plan from the Commissioner of Internal Revenue. However, an advance ruling approving the plan does not assure deduction of contributions made under the plan, since the Code provides that contributions to a qualified plan are deductible only if they constitute reasonable compensation for services rendered. These are **subject to review** when a field audit of the tax return is made.

A trust claiming exemption must file information with the Commissioner for **each taxable year** as to the operation of the plan for the particular year. But if the employer has filed the information required to establish the fact that the plan has qualified, the trustee need only file a **request for exemption** stating the names and addresses of the parties to the agreement and the date thereof, the taxable year involved, and copy of a notification from the employer stating that the information has been filed and giving the name of the office where it has been filed.

Financing Funded Pension Plans

METHOD OF FUNDING. A pension plan may be funded by a **trust fund,** commonly called a **self-administered plan,** or by an insurance company, in which case it is called an **insured pension plan,** or by a combination of both. Contributions under a so-called self-administered plan, actuarially determined, are paid to the trustee, normally a trust company, to be directly invested by the trustee in accordance with the provisions of the plan. These plans usually provide for wide discretion and flexibility in the investment of pension funds. Under an insured plan the payments are made directly to an insurance company or contributions are paid to a trustee who merely uses them to pay premiums to an insurance company. The greatest growth in recent years, especially among large enterprises, has been in the use of self-administered pension plans, and the majority of persons covered by private pension plans in the United States are covered under self-administered plans.

SELF-ADMINISTRATION (TRUSTEED-SECURITIES FUND). The term "self-administration" is to some degree a misnomer that has been widely accepted to indicate the trusteed-securities method of financing a plan. Under this type of financing, the employer divests himself of the contributions by irrevocable payment to a trustee. The funds in the hands of the trustee constitute a trust fund that is administered in accordance with the terms of the controlling trust instrument. This type of plan is often called a **self-insured plan,** usually to distinguish it from a plan underwritten by a group annuity contract, or one under which the trustee turns the funds over to an insurance company, usually to pay the premiums under individual or group permanent insurance or annuity policies. In the latter case, the only essential function of the trustee is to apply the contributions to pay premiums and to receive and reapply amounts payable from the insurance company, such as dividends and returns under any policies that are canceled because of the termination of service of employees.

DEFERRED GROUP ANNUITIES. Under the deferred group annuity type of financing, all contributions are paid to an insurance company under a master contract between the employer and the insurance company for the purchase of deferred annuities on a periodic **single premium basis.** Each participant receives a certificate from the insurance company describing his rights. All liability for benefit payments is assumed by the insurance company so long as the required purchase payments are made. A minimum number of employees, such as 50, is usually required for the issuance of a group annuity contract. If the plan is **contributory,** the usual requirement is that at least 75% of the eligible employees must participate. The premium rates and other provisions are generally guaranteed only for the first 5 years, and are subject to change by the insurance company on any anniversary thereafter, although in practice some insurance companies offer additional successive 5-year guaranties. According to the Life Insurance Fact Book for 1963 (Institute of Life Insurance) about 80% of the total number of persons under insured pension plans in the United States are covered by group annuities of either the deferred or deposit-administration type.

DEPOSIT-ADMINISTRATION GROUP ANNUITY. Under the deposit-administration method of financing, employer contributions paid to the insurance company are held and accumulated at compound interest as a **composite, undivided fund** much like a composite self-administered fund. When an employee retires, the single premium required to purchase his retirement income is drawn from this fund. The rate of interest credited on the fund and the single-premium immediate annuity rates applicable at retirement are usually guaranteed for contributions paid during the first 5 years of the contract, on the same basis as is used under deferred group annuity contracts, although some insurance companies guarantee the interest rate only for a limited number of years.

Contributions required under this plan can be estimated within limits, subject to the reserved right of the insurance company to change interest and annuity rate guarantees on contributions made after 5 years from the effective date of the contract. The employer's annual contribution into the deposit-administration fund is determined by the benefits to be provided, the cost of annuities at retirement, the expected mortality and interest rate for the period before retirement, and the age, sex, and earnings of participating employees. Assumed scales of salary increases and expected withdrawal rates may also be taken into account. The cost is usually stated as a **percentage of payroll.** New calculations are made from time to time, to reflect changes in the valuation factors. These require actuarial service.

This type of funding is commonly employed under **noncontributory plans** where the employer pays the entire cost with no contributions from employees, although it is used in some plans involving employee contributions. For example, noncontributory **past service pensions** financed on a deposit-administration basis may be combined with contributory **current service pensions** provided on a typical deferred annuity purchase basis; or the employee contributions may be applied to purchase deferred annuities, the balance of the cost being financed by employer contributions made under the deposit-administration method.

A variant of the deposit-administration contract is a type of contract referred to as an **immediate participation guarantee** contract. Under this type of contract, which is appropriate for large organizations, the interest rate, instead of being fixed, varies each year with the insurance company's earnings on investments; in addition, there is taken into account the actual mortality experience of retired employees and the expenses of the insurance company. Once a retiring employee becomes entitled to benefits, these benefits are fully guaranteed by the insurance company.

INDIVIDUAL RETIREMENT INCOME POLICIES. Generally, under this type of procedure, the employer creates a trust fund and the trustee invests the fund in individual retirement annuity policies, usually combined with an element of life insurance for those who can pass a physical examination. All policies are purchased by the trustee pursuant to the plan and trust agreement. An individual policy is purchased on the life of each participant, generally of the same type that is offered to any person who would purchase a similar policy personally. Such a plan usually calls for the **payment of a level premium under each policy** issued for a participant, based on his age when the policy is issued, the maturity date when the pension is to begin, and the amount of the pension. Annuity policies are purchased for participants who cannot pass a physical examination, with a death benefit usually amounting to the return of premiums or the cash value, whichever is greater.

GROUP PERMANENT RETIREMENT INCOME. This is an outgrowth of the individual retirement income policy concept. It endeavors to overcome some of the obvious disadvantages of individual policies under a plan including sufficient participants to meet the group underwriting requirements of the insurance company, which enables it to issue life insurance protection irrespective of the health of individual participants, and effect economies resulting from group in place of individual procedure. It is sometimes issued without life insurance, but usually with life insurance (as decreasing term) similar to individual retirement income policies.

COMBINATION PLANS. Numerous combinations have been developed to secure as many of the advantages of each method as is possible and to minimize the disadvantages of each, or to accomplish certain specific objectives. For example, instead of using retirement income policies as the sole financing vehicle, ordinary life insurance policies that may be converted into an annuity at or one year before retirement are sometimes used under a combination plan. Contributions are accumulated in a trusteed fund to make an additional payment so that the retirement income will be larger than that available from the cash value of the insurance policy alone.

ADVANTAGES AND DISADVANTAGES OF EACH METHOD OF FINANCING. No method of financing has a monopoly on all advantages, and no method of financing is free of disadvantages. In the following discussions various methods of financing are considered from this point of view.

ADVANTAGES AND DISADVANTAGES OF SELF-ADMINISTRATION. There are a number of considerations in weighing these, in connection with contributions, coverage, contingency of change in financing method, and cost. These aspects of advantage and disadvantage are covered separately in the discussion following.

Flexibility of Contributions. From the employer viewpoint, the outstanding advantage claimed for self-administration is flexibility as to the amount of contributions to be made by the employer from year to year, combined with availability of funds for payment of full benefits to the employees on schedule as they become due. Flexibility with respect to the making of employer contributions varies with each type of funding method.

Maximum flexibility as to contributions is available under the **self-administered type** of plan that uses a **composite fund** that is not earmarked for the benefit of individual participants either before or after retirement. Under this arrangement the effect is that any maximum contributions can be made in good business years and used as a cushion to take the place of contributions in years when the employer may find it necessary or advisable to reduce or suspend the making of contributions. But full pension benefits are payable to the retired participants on schedule as they fall due.

Next in line of flexibility is the combination type, which uses a **self-administered fund** for the period of accumulation before retirement but is **insured when each employee retires.** A single-premium immediate annuity is purchased for him by transferring out of the self-administered fund the single premium necessary to purchase the retirement benefit.

Similar to such a combination plan is the **deposit-administration group annuity** method, under which the insurance company accumulates the contributions in a composite account and does not allocate funds to any particular employee until he is retired, at which time a single-premium immediate annuity is purchased. This method offers contribution flexibility equal to that of a self-administered composite fund with the purchase of annuities at retirement.

Next in line as to flexibility of contributions is the typical **group annuity plan** providing for the purchase of deferred annuities. All employer contributions are allocated to purchase benefits for individual participants. Each participant receives an allocation to his credit for the current year. The **past service pensions** are also purchased for individual participants by allocation of contributions made for this purpose, usually on the oldest-first basis. Under this procedure, the employer may vary the contributions made for past service benefits within fairly broad limits, except that generally such contributions must be made in amounts at least sufficient to purchase the full annuities by the time employees retire. As to contributions for **current service benefits,** there is a grace period of 31 days and a provision under which current service contributions may be suspended for a period of 1 year (in some cases longer, usually with the consent of the insurance company) before the contract, as a whole, will terminate. In the event of a suspension of contributions for current service benefits, it is evident that benefits of all active employee participants will be impaired, unless the employer later pays the suspended contributions on a retroactive basis. If contributions are not resumed at the end of the suspension period, the contract terminates as to further benefits, but the usual provision is that all benefits purchased with employer contributions then become fully vested in employees. If the plan is contributory, terminating employees are then usually allowed to withdraw their own contributions with interest and retain title to the deferred annuity benefits provided with employer contributions.

Contributions under a plan using **retirement income policies** (usually with life insurance) are allocated toward the payment of the current year's premium for each and every participant, commonly funding past and future service benefits in the same policy. This requires fixed level annual premiums with no flexibility, since, if the premiums are not paid or are met by borrowing against the cash value of the policies, benefits are jeopardized. Furthermore, since contributions are allocated to make premium payments for the benefit of particular employees, full benefits will not be available to employees who retire during any period in which full contributions have not been made under the plan. Only if such borrowings are repaid before the employees retire, will their pension benefits be paid on schedule. This disadvantage also applies to a group permanent retirement income contract.

On the other hand, these plans have the advantage of assuring all employees that specific benefits have been financed for them as individuals, whereas under a composite self-administered fund or deposit-administration group annuity the younger employees may receive little or no benefits if the plan should be terminated at a time when benefits are not fully funded, depending on the provisions of the plan or trust agreement.

No Fixed Annual Contribution Commitment. The term "fixed commitment" as used here does not connote a legal obligation committing the employer, since most plans reserve the right to the employer to suspend contributions or terminate the plan. But unless regular annual contributions are made, the plan may fail to provide the employee benefits originally contemplated or may fail to meet requirements for tax qualification. Such a "fixed commitment" of the employer to pay premiums is generally necessary if the plan is insured before and after retirement. Suspension of employer contributions usually results in temporary, and sometimes permanent, impairment of employee benefits. On the other hand, under self-administration (or deposit-administration group annuity) no fixed annual contribution commitment is necessary. This allows flexibility as to the making of employer contributions because, if a composite fund is used, the pensioners can be paid **full pension benefits as they fall due,** the entire composite trust fund being available to pay out benefits on a first-come-first-served basis. For example, if $100,000 is accumulated in a self-administered pension trust fund and the first employees retiring are entitled to pensions aggregating $1,000 per month, they receive their full monthly pension checks from the trust fund (whether or not the full value of their pensions has been accumulated). These, and all subsequent pensioners, receive the payments due them until they die (and sometimes payments are continued thereafter until the death of joint annuitants). No relationship is necessary between the timing of the employer's contributions into the fund for a participant, and the timing of the participant's withdrawal of pension benefits out of the composite fund. So long as contributions are paid in amounts sufficient to pay the cost of benefits for current service and prevent the initial unfunded past service pension liability from increasing for all employees, the pension payments may be made on schedule, the fund will remain actuarially sound, and the plan will meet Treasury requirements. Thus, the employer can diminish or **suspend contributions during recurring depression periods** after making larger payments in prior normal or prosperous periods, but with full pension benefits being paid to retired employees on schedule as required. For example, an employer might make maximum tax-deductible payments for 3 years, thereby funding a considerable amount of the liability for past service pensions and establishing sufficient extra reserves to take the place of normal contributions for current service pension credits that otherwise would be required during the next 2 years if conditions made it desirable to suspend contributions completely during those 2 years. This procedure may be repeated indefinitely. Meanwhile, the plan remains sufficiently funded at all times to pay benefits on schedule and to meet Treasury requirements.

Permanence of Plan. Advocates of self-administration claim that self-administered plans with composite funds are most likely to be permanent. They contend that the inherent flexibility as to the timing of employer contributions under self-administered funding enables the plan to ride out economic storms without the necessity of termination or reduction of employee benefits, whereas a plan entailing more rigidity as to employer contributions may have to be terminated during a period of economic stress.

Advocates of self-administered plans claim that available data showing **why some pension plans have failed** in the past indicate two major causes, both of which favor self-administration or deposit-administration group annuity underwriting. The first reason is that **fixed commitments** to pay insurance premiums became too burdensome in depression years. If plans abandoned for this reason had been self-administered or financed under a deposit-administration group annuity contract, the employers might have been able to suspend or diminish their contributions during depression years, obviating the necessity of terminating the plans. The second cause of plan discontinuance has been **consolidations and reorganizations**. New managements may have been reluctant to assume a "fixed commitment" plan of a predecessor company. Other reasons for abandonment of plans are differences in thinking as to the desirability of formal pension procedures, or the existence of another pension plan of a different type in the company taking over the employer whose plan is abandoned. Advocates claim that a self-administered plan or a deposit-administration group annuity contract is so flexible as to form and financing that either can most readily be adjusted to any other plans that may exist in other companies with which the company may be consolidated or merged.

Coverage of Pensioners Already Retired. If there is a pension roll that is being financed on a current pay-as-you-go basis when the plan is established, it frequently requires less immediate contributions to absorb these pension obligations under a self-administered fund than under an insured plan. Self-administration often gives the employer **more time in which to finance the plan** without interfering with payment of full benefits to all retired employees, past, present and future, directly from a pension trust fund.

Unusually Large Accrued Liability—Older-Age Employees. Similarly, it is contended that if an employer has an unusually large initial accrued liability for past service benefits when a plan is established and he is unable to finance these benefits in full by the time the employees retire and also meet current service benefit costs, such a plan could start with a self-administered or, perhaps, a deposit-administration group annuity plan. This will permit payment of full pension benefits to older employees as they retire and yet give the employer more time to fund his initial past service liability.

Disability Pensions. A major attraction of self-administration is the opportunity to provide total and permanent disability pensions. This is a definite advantage because insurance companies have generally been unwilling to underwrite employee total disability pensions because of adverse experience with individual total disability policies. Total disability pensions can be financed by means of a **supplemental funded procedure.** In fact, supplemental self-administered total and permanent disability benefits may be added to existing self-administered or insured age retirement plans without disturbing their age retirement provisions.

Change of Financing Method. It is generally easier to transfer from self-administration to group annuity underwriting than vice versa, because there is usually no provision for the transfer of reserves from the group annuity contract, and because most group annuity contracts provide for full vesting in employees of title to benefits already purchased on cessation of the group annuity purchase payments. For this reason, it is usually impracticable to change from group annuity to self-administration, or even to transfer from one group annuity insurance carrier to another.

Comparative Cost. Another advantage claimed for self-administration is lower cost to the employer. Differences in initial cost are frequently attributable to differences in benefits and funding procedure. There are often basic **differences in actuarial assumptions and in timing of the contributions** as between self-administered and insured plans. For example, the self-administered plan may assume 3% interest earnings whereas the insured plan may assume that only 2% will be earned, or one plan might assume high rates of mortality whereas another might take lower assumptions for this factor. Also, the self-administered plan may take an advance cost discount for severances, which is not done under typical isured plans.

One of the advantages claimed for trusteed, as against insured, plans is the fact that insurance companies are strictly limited as to their legal power to invest in equities. Trusteed plans, it is contended, are, therefore, a better hedge against **inflation** in that the value of the trust fund will increase with the employer's pension costs. On the other hand, there has been a tendency to relieve insurance companies from these limitations if they are holding the funds of group annuity plans in **separate accounts.**

Each **self-administered pension** case pays its own **true cost,** whereas under **group annuity** contracts there may be an **averaging of costs** for plans of a similar class, thereby leveling the net cost of plans after dividends or rate reductions. Insurance companies claim, however, that in general they strive to have each case reflect its own experience. One method of doing so is by means of the so-called **new money interest rate method.** According to this method, the interest element involved in determining the cost of a group pension plan is computed so that the interest on the increase of the fund for each year of a series of years varies with the average rate of interest earned by the insurance company on new investments during each year, respectively.

In the final analysis, it would appear that an employer would be better served if he gave the question of probable comparative cost less weight in selecting the financing method than other considerations that are important in carrying out the objectives of a pension plan.

ADVANTAGES AND DISADVANTAGES OF DEFERRED GROUP ANNUITIES. Some of the arguments for and against deferred group annuities are as follows:

Third-Party Guarantees. Advocates of group annuities claim that one of the disadvantages of a self-administered plan is that there are no third-party guarantees, leaving the employer in the position of having to meet any shortages in the fund if experience proves less favorable than assumed under the initial actuarial assumptions. Underwriting by an insurance company **assures payment** of the benefits to the employees.

To this argument advocates of **self-administration** reply that if the fund is sufficiently large for **the law of averages** to operate, the history of properly administered funds has demonstrated their soundness and ability to provide benefits on schedule, especially if contributions are made to an independent trustee in amounts comparable to premiums payable to an insurance company, and if investments are similar to those in an insurance company's portfolio.

It is contended by some that plans covering a relatively small number of employees may be safely self-administered because there is no catastrophe hazard in providing age retirement benefits comparable to the hazard in providing death benefits. A large proportion of those covered could die suddenly, but no employees reach retirement age without warning. Furthermore, if there should be a deviation from the assumed mortality experience, it occurs over a period of time sufficient to allow for the financing of fund deficits.

The possibility that deficits may occur under self-administered financing, because of mortality and other experience less favorable to the fund than the original actuarial assumptions, may be offset by the fact that the premium rates under a group annuity contract are subject to change as to annuities purchased after the first 5 years. In the long run, the insurance company's cost will reflect the plan's experience as to mortality, interest, and administrative expenses, so that it will be similar to that under a self-administered fund.

Employee Preference. Group annuity advocates claim that employees prefer the assurance of receiving benefits from an insurance company. Self-administration advocates admit there is merit in this point but feel that there is satisfactory employee acceptance of a fund invested by an independent and competent trustee, and that the other advantages of self-administration are more important factors.

Responsibility for Employee Contributions. Another advantage claimed by group annuity advocates is the avoidance of moral responsibility in the handling of employee contributions under a self-administered trust fund. The counter-argument of self-administration advocates is that employee money can be segregated and invested separately, if desired, in United States government bonds. Furthermore, employee money can be segregated and used to purchase benefits from an insurance company and employer contributions can be self-administered.

Registration as a Securities Issue. If **employee contributions** are made, the self-administered plan may require registration with the Securities and Exchange Commission, whereas no such registration is required for a group annuity plan. But advocates of self-administration point out that, in the first place, no registration is required if the employer pays the entire cost; secondly, that such registration is not necessarily onerous; thirdly, that the requirement of registration applies only to plans in which participation is **voluntary** rather than compulsory; and finally, that the problem can be avoided by placing employee money with an insurance company and investing employer money under self-administration.

Administrative Cost. Advocates of group annuities claim that expenses of self-administration for **trustee fees, actuarial fees,** and so on may exceed corresponding amounts retained by the insurance company. It is countered that the cost of group annuities includes 8% of the gross premium as an initial loading, presumably for expenses. Besides, there are other expenses such as charges when annuities are cancelled on severance of employment. Also, the employer incurs some administration expense under an insured plan, similar to that under a self-administered plan, in connection with record keeping and making reports to the insurance company.

ADVANTAGES AND DISADVANTAGES OF DEPOSIT-ADMINISTRATION GROUP ANNUITY.

Compared to self-administration, advocates of deposit-administration group annuity financing claim, the **investment risk** is eliminated, the rate of interest is guaranteed, and the ultimate cost of the annuities to be purchased is known at least as to contributions during the first 5 years. If the plan is terminated, there is no problem of liquidating securities, possibly in a declining market.

Compared to deferred group annuities, calculation of withdrawal credits and the withholding of surrender charges is avoided, since there is **no direct application of funds** to purchase deferred annuities, and the health of employees upon termination of employment has no significance. Another important advantage of the deposit-administration method is the fact that adjustments in the employer's cost on account of radical changes in any of the factors involved, such as major changes in salary scales, can be more readily spread as a level percentage of payroll over a longer period. A disadvantage as compared to deferred group annuity financing, however, is the fact that a plan financed through a deposit-administration contract, like self-administration, is not automatically and definitely funded as of any given date. The regular contribution of specified amounts or percentages of payroll to the fund does not guarantee that it will be sufficient to meet the cost of all benefits accrued under the plan.

ADVANTAGES AND DISADVANTAGES OF INDIVIDUAL RETIREMENT INCOME POLICIES. Individual policies, it is claimed, are the only practicable method for cases too small in number for group annuity coverage, which usually requires 50 participants, or for self-administration based on the law of averages. Advocates of group annuities admit this, except if insurance companies offer group annuities for groups of less than 50 participants. Advocates of self-administration likewise recognize the hazards of self-administration for small groups after retirement. But many argue that the advantages of self-administration are as important, if not of greater importance, to a **small employer**. Also, under small plans favorable deviations from the assumed experience are just as likely to occur as unfavorable ones. Means can be found to offset the hazard of the lack of risk spread, such as the use of very conservative actuarial assumptions, adjustment of contributions to offset unfavorable experience, or the use of self-administration prior to retirement and insurance company financing thereafter through the purchase of individual single-premium immediate annuities as each employee retires. The latter combination retains flexibility of employer contributions and most of the other advantages inherent in a self-administered plan, avoiding the disadvantages of individual retirement annuity policies.

Flexibility Through Borrowing. Flexibility can be secured with individual policies through the right to borrow on policies to pay premiums in years when contributions may be reduced or suspended. But such borrowing could result in **failure to provide benefits on schedule** as they mature, which may affect employer-employee relations adversely and perhaps create a problem with the Internal Revenue Service in view of its requirement of payment of full employee benefits on schedule and no increase in the current unfunded past service liability as compared to the initial unfunded past service liability, except if the employer has suspended contributions because of demonstrated "business necessity."

Cost of Death Benefits. A major criticism of retirement income with insurance policies is that the provision of vested death benefits generally increases employer costs from 60% to 100% as compared with the cost of a pure pension system that provides no death benefits from employer contributions. Although death benefits are desirable, their cost may result in inadequate age and disability pensions.

Relationship of Death Benefits to Need. An anomaly in the individual retirement income (with insurance) policy procedure is that death benefits tend to change in inverse ratio to the need for them. Under typical plans of this type, no death benefits are provided during a waiting period after employees are hired, usually 3 to 5 years, after which death benefits of employees who are insurable usually amount to about 3 years' salary. This is the case if a pension of 36% of salary is provided with the typical provision for insurance equal to 100 times the monthly pension. For typical employees, the coverage increases to a peak of about 4½ years' salary immediately before retirement, through substituting the cash value of the policy as the death benefit when it exceeds the face amount of insurance. Thus, coverage increases at a time when the employee's children have usually become self-supporting. The coverage drops to about 3.6 years' salary at retirement, and, under the usual 120 months' certain and for life annuity provision, subsequently decreases by 10% each year, until no death benefit coverage is provided 10 years after retirement.

The **uninsurable participants** in the same plan would receive death benefits dependent on their age as well as their years of premium-paying membership in the plan. For example, the uninsurable young man aged 30 at entry would accumulate about one-tenth of a year's salary each year. Thus it would require about 10 years of membership to build up 1 year's salary as his death benefit. An uninsurable older man, aged 55, would accumulate close to one-half year's salary as a death benefit per year, so that it would require but 2 years of membership to build up 1 year's salary as his death benefit.

Advocates of both group annuities and self-administration argue that individual policies carrying an insurance element should never be used if the group is large enough for some form of **group underwriting** (25 or 50 employees according to the state insurance law and insurance company rules), because of the effect on employee relations of denying insurance to those who, for reasons of health, cannot be insured under a plan using individual policies. The usual group life insurance plan on a 1-year renewable-term basis offers protection to all employees after 3, 6, or 12 months' service, giving insurance to the younger short-service employees who generally have the most acute dependency problems.

Costly Vesting. There is a tendency toward more complete vesting of benefits under individual policy plans. This tendency increases the cost. The usual practice of turning over the policy to an **employee who resigns or is discharged**, to permit him to continue the insurance, creates the anomaly of giving departing employees cash values instead of deferred benefits, defeating the fundamental purpose of a pension plan. This situation is not encountered under typical self-administered or group annuity plans. Although liberal vesting provisions upon severance of employment are desirable, they may give protection at a cost that the employer is not able or willing to assume. Under group annuity and self-administered plans, the vesting provisions are designed to provide retirement benefits for employees with long service who leave the company. In retirement income policies, life insurance protection favors earlier and more liberal vesting, to enable the departing employee to continue the life insurance.

Revision of Retirement Income Policy Plans. Disadvantages of retirement income policies in pension plans can be partially or wholly eliminated. One way is to **halt the use of retirement income policies**, keeping in force only those already purchased. Only part of subsequent employer contributions need then be used to pay premiums on the old policies, the remainder of the contributions (usually up to the maximum deductible for tax purposes) being placed in a self-administered securities account in the pension trust fund to provide pensions either through self-administration, group annuities, or the purchase of annuities at retirement, or to pay premiums in years when other funds are not available.

Another way is to **convert existing retirement income policies** for insurable employees into ordinary life insurance policies in the same insurance company, dated back to the original age and date of issue. Suppose, for example, a pension plan is 4 years old, and a $10,000 retirement income policy was issued for an employee at age 40 on which four premiums have been paid. This policy would require an annual premium of, say, $556, and would have a current cash surrender value of $1,496. If this policy were converted into an ordinary life insurance policy as of age 40, the annual ordinary life premium would be $309, a reduction of $247 in annual premium, and the cash value of the converted ordinary life policy would be $539. The insurance company would be asked to refund to the trustee the difference between the current cash surrender values of the two policies, or $957. This $957 would be deposited in a supplemental self-administered pension trust fund invested in securities such as United States government bonds. Thereafter, ordinary life insurance policies would be used for any death benefits for new participants and to cover salary increases for old participants, and the balance of employer contributions would be held in the self-administered account. At retirement, the pension provided for the employee would be obtained in part by applying the cash value of the ordinary life insurance policy under its annuity settlement option, the balance coming from the self-administered account. If desired, the balance of the pension could be purchased from the insurance company instead of being paid out of a self-administered fund, so that the **entire pension would come from one source.** Many insurance companies will accept the supplemental self-administered payment and issue the balance of the annuity at rates guaranteed when the ordinary life insurance is purchased.

Under this combination of ordinary life insurance and self-administration, every employee is not only assured his **full pension at retirement** if contributions are made as contemplated, but it will be possible for the employer to keep his costs lower or to provide larger pensions by savings anticipated from **less liberal severance benefits,** since severing employees will receive ordinary life insurance policies instead of higher cost retirement income policies. These savings can be increased by reducing the face amount of the ordinary life insurance. Usually, retirement income policies have a face amount 100 times the monthly retirement benefit, which would be equivalent to 3 years' salary on a 36% pension plan. The ordinary life insurance may be reduced to 2 years' salary or 1 year's salary, there being no need to relate the face amount of ordinary life insurance to the pension.

Cost If Coverage Is Extended. Another objection to individual retirement income policies with insurance is that in many cases such policies are originally issued under plans with limited coverage, and the cost may become prohibitive when **more participants** are included. For example, a plan confined to employees having at least 5 years of service may have included only 10% of the total number of employees originally, but such employees may constitute 40% of the staff later. Expansion of coverage may also result from **union requests** for extension to hourly workers of a plan previously confined to salaried employees or those earning more than the amount covered by Social Security. **Consolidations or mergers** may bring an influx of new participants. The increase in cost due to expansion of coverage is much greater if the plan utilizes individual policies, not only because of the tendency to provide costly death benefits, but also because of the further tendency to vest these policies in participants upon severance.

Relationship of Benefits to Earnings. Another objection to the use of individual policies is that salary increases and decreases can only be made operative within the available minimum units of, say, $500 or $1,000 face amount of insurance, or $5 or $10 a month of pension benefits. Under self-administration or group annuities, benefits can be made to follow earnings to a penny. This objection is most serious for low-paid groups.

Simplicity of Administration. An advantage of individual policies is that a policy is issued on the life of each participant, and a descriptive certificate describing benefits is given him. Upon severance, retirement, or death, the policy is usually delivered to the participant or his beneficiary.

Cost Guarantee. The annual premium cost is guaranteed for the life of each individual policy, whereas there is no guarantee as to annuity costs after the first 5 years under a group annuity contract and the cost of self-administration will vary with actual experience. On the other hand, overall higher costs of these plans offset the value of the rate guarantee. Furthermore, there is no assurance that individual contracts of a particular type will be available in future years with the same provisions and rates, which may lead to differences in severance benefits, settlement options, and so on, between participants entering the plan in different years.

Liberal Settlement Options. Under individual policies there are usually more liberal settlement options than with group annuity financing. For example, the joint annuitant option may be elected at any time before retirement, whereas a group annuity contract usually bars election of this option within 5 years before the retirement date, unless the employee is in good health.

ADVANTAGES AND DISADVANTAGES OF GROUP PERMANENT RETIREMENT INCOME. Advocates of group permanent retirement income policy plans claim that they retain the advantages of the **lifetime rate guarantee** offered by individual policies and, at the same time, overcome the disadvantages of individual selection on the basis of health and of extra loading charges for expenses. But critics argue that group permanent retirement income plans are subject to most of the objections applicable to individual retirement income policies, particularly the **level premium method of financing**, which does not allow as much flexibility in making contributions as do self-administration and group annuity financing. They also point out that the use of employer contributions to provide death benefits and more liberal severance benefits generally results in a cost increase of some 60% to 100%, as in the case of individual retirement income policies.

Group permanent retirement income contracts generally offer more liberal terms concerning the election of optional benefit forms than group annuity underwriting.

ADVANTAGES AND DISADVANTAGES OF COMBINATION PLANS. To minimize the disadvantages of the several types of pension financing, and to accomplish special objectives, employers sometimes use a **combination of funding methods.**

An example of a combination plan to keep the initial cost as low as possible under plans involving employee contributions for future service benefits is to **self-administer pensions** for past service and to employ **group annuity** financing for future service benefits provided in part out of employee contributions.

Some of the disadvantages of using individual level premium policies may be obviated by accumulating the contributions in a self-administered trust fund

until retirement, when individual single-premium immediate annuity contracts are purchased.

Another procedure that is gaining in popularity and bids fair to be used in place of retirement income policies is the combination of **self-administration with ordinary life insurance.** Either individual ordinary life policies or group permanent ordinary life may be used. Such policies provide part of the pension benefits purchased at retirement with the cash values. The balance of the pension benefits, in accordance with the plan formula, may be provided by making contributions into a self-administered fund. Sometimes, however, the ordinary life insurance policy contains a **conversion privilege** whereby it may be converted into a policy providing the full annuity specified by the plan, the sum needed for conversion being drawn out of the self-administered fund. This plan has the contribution flexibility of self-administration before retirement and is fully insured after retirement, avoiding the problem of erratic mortality among annuitants.

A combination similar to the foregoing is that of **deposit-administration group annuity** combined with **group permanent ordinary life insurance.**

Pension Plan Provisions

ELIGIBILITY FOR MEMBERSHIP. Important provisions bearing on this are as follows:

Full Coverage. The inclusion of all regular employees is highly desirable in order completely to solve the retirement problem. Unionized employees will generally have a separate pension plan based upon the applicable collective bargaining agreement.

Years of Service Requirement. A common eligibility provision restricts participation to employees who have completed a specified period of service. Aside from reducing the benefits and the cost, this restriction also eliminates employees whose employment is most likely to terminate, thereby reducing record keeping and administrative expenses. A usual requirement limits eligibility to employees with not less than 1 year of service. The least liberal requirements do not often exceed 5 years of employment before an employee becomes eligible for membership in the plan. If a plan is designed to satisfy the percentage requirement of the Internal Revenue Code as to **nondiscrimination in coverage,** the required period of employment as a condition of eligibility may not exceed 5 years.

Minimum Age Requirement. Participation is sometimes restricted by excluding employees who have not reached a specified age. Exclusion of younger employees reduces record keeping, and requires contributions over a smaller number of years. However, it may defer part of the true cost of the plan until employees become eligible and reduce benefits drastically, since retroactive credits are not given as a rule. Another reason for a minimum age requirement under contributory plans is that young employees may not wish to participate, with retirement many years in the future. If they become eligible at an older age, they are more likely to join the plan, since they will then know that they will remain with the employer and retirement security will have assumed greater importance. A fairly **long service requirement** for eligibility gives the same effect. Minimum age requirements are more general in insured plans. In self-administered plans, there is less purpose in a minimum age requirement unless the objective is to reduce the cost by limiting the number of years for which pension credit is given.

Maximum Age Limitation. Employees who have reached a stated maximum age are sometimes excluded to **avoid high initial past service costs** and the need for contributions that exceed amounts deductible for tax purposes. An example is the exclusion of employees over age 65. Such employees are usually carried on the payroll as active or retired employees. Another example is the use of age 55 as the limit, with age 65 as the normal retirement age. The latter rule results in a gap in the plan for 10 years, and in failure to provide for retirement of older employees who have usually contributed most to the success of the business. Provisions of this type are more frequently found in plans using retirement income policies of insurance companies that require at least ten annual premiums under such policies. Advocates of insured financing contend that in the long run exclusion of overage employees is not a material point because such employees can be pensioned on a current **pay-as-you-go basis**. But the employer is placed at a disadvantage because he is carrying the double load of funding his pension plan and paying pensions to overage employees in bad years as well as in good, whereas under the self-administered plan he merely has the one fund to support on a flexible contributions basis. Also, overage employees are obviously better off because managements, stockholders, consolidations, reorganizations, or depression cycles cannot deprive them of the protection of the self-administered fund.

Effect on Eligibility of Financing Method. Flexibility of employer contributions without interference with the provision of pensions on schedule is also sought through eligibility for membership provisions. Self-administration facilitates the inclusion of employees over the normal retirement age and retired employees who are on the pension roll at the time the plan begins. If self-administered financing is not used, the likelihood of excluding aged employees increases in the following order: deposit-administration group annuity, typical deferred group annuity (with past service benefits financed on the oldest-first principle), level premium retirement income policy (individual policies or group permanent contract).

Salaried Employees Only. Where management decides not to provide coverage for all employees, it is usual to confine the plan to the salaried group. Some reasons for this are:

  a. In some situations management considers that the union organization of the wage earners has or will obtain all that can be allocated to them in the form of compensation and other benefits, and hence only the salaried (nonunion) employees need be included. Frequently, wage-earners represented by a union have a separate pension plan established under the collective bargaining agreement.
  b. The executive and higher-ranking members of the personnel upon whom rest decisions of policy, and upon whom depends the success of the company, are in the salaried group.

Higher-Paid Employees Only. It has been decided in many cases to limit eligibility to employees earning over a specified amount, usually **the amount of earnings covered by Social Security,** because of the lack of Social Security benefits on earnings in excess of this limit.

A factor influencing a decision to exclude lower-paid employees, such as those earning less than the amount covered by Social Security benefits, is a requirement of the Internal Revenue Service that the plan provide no more benefit per dollar of earnings in excess of the minimum specified than the highest paid of those excluded receive under the Social Security Act, the criterion used being 150% of the primary insurance benefits. For this reason, pensions provided for eligible employees (e.g., those earning more than the amount covered by Social Security) may be too low to provide adequate retirement incomes, causing difficulty in effecting retirements in actual practice.

Thus, the employer finds that the Social Security Act usually does not solve his problem of superannuated or disabled employees covered solely by the Act, while his own plan for employees earning more than amounts covered by the Act is likewise inadequate. The employer may be asked to keep employees on the payroll or to provide them with suitable pensions.

Interrelationship of Eligibility and Financing. The question of eligibility is related to the method of financing and the **vested rights** to benefits granted employees. If an employer wishes to provide benefits only for long-service, higher salaried employees, a **provision for vested rights** may be preferred under which title to benefits provided by employer contributions will be vested in those employees in the event of severance of employment, contingent only on completion of a short period of service or membership in the plan. Or there may be complete vesting from the outset. Having arrived at this decision, the employer could use either a group annuity contract or individual retirement annuities (with or without insurance), or the latter's equivalent under a group permanent retirement annuity plan, for each of these insured types of financing allocates the employer's contributions to the **specific benefit of each named participant.** However, if the employer desires a plan for all regular employees so that survivors may be entitled to an age or disability pension, and a high future turnover is expected, he will generally find that a group annuity contract, self-administration, or a combination of these is better. The individual retirement income or the group permanent retirement income policy methods of financing do not lend themselves to full-coverage, high-turnover types of plans, not only because of inflexible contribution and benefit provisions, but because of the high cost of the death benefits, vested rights, and surrender charges involved.

Employers frequently confine their investigations to one type of funding method, such as individual retirement income contracts or the practical equivalent of a group permanent retirement income plan, and as a result have unwittingly adopted a plan confined to the higher-paid, low-turnover group, such as employees earning salaries in excess of the amount covered by Social Security who have at least 5 years of service. This "puts the cart before the horse" by allowing limitations of the financing method to control eligibility provisions.

NORMAL RETIREMENT. Certain age provisions are important, as follows:

Age 65 Usual. Most pension plans specify age 65 as the normal retirement age. Although the age at which employee efficiency declines to a point making retirement desirable varies greatly with individuals, and sometimes depends upon the character of employment, there is general agreement that age 65 is typical for most employees and that retention in service beyond that age is undesirable under ordinary circumstances. The Social Security Act, however, permits both men and women to retire with reduced benefits at the age of 62.

A retirement date commonly used is the first of the month following attainment of age 65. The anniversary date of the plan nearest age 65 is also frequently employed, particularly if retirement income policies are used as the financing vehicle.

Earlier Retirement Age for Women. Some plans specify a lower retirement age for women than for men, such as 60 or 55. The number of female employees and the nature of the business are determining factors. If adequate benefits are provided, this practice may increase the cost of the plan substantially. Women will collect pensions over a longer period of time, not only because of their earlier retirement but because they commonly live longer. The **lack of Federal benefits** until age 62 is reached is also an influencing factor. This problem is sometimes partially met by adjusting the pension paid before and after age 62 to provide a constant income including Federal benefits. A smaller pension will be paid women employees because they will have fewer years of service for which benefits are credited, unless they are accorded special treatment in the benefit formula. Some employers do not believe that this is a serious consideration, however, because women generally have smaller family obligations than men.

Staggered Retirement Ages. Instead of excluding older employees from coverage, some plans require a **minimum number of years of membership** under the plan before retirement, such as 10, so that employees aged 56 at commencement of the plan retire at age 66, those aged 57 retire at age 67, etc. Such a provision frequently is coupled with provision for **immediate retirement** of those who have reached a specified age, such as 70. The treatment of the older employees is closely related to the type of funding. This requirement postpones the time when the superannuation problem will be solved and the full advantages of the plan realized.

EARLY RETIREMENT. Many plans allow employees to retire at early ages, such as within 10 years before the normal retirement date, on reduced actuarially equivalent annuities, subject to approval of the employer or the pension committee. This enables an employer to retire employees who may be disabled or who, for any of a variety of reasons, should be retired before the normal retirement date. Pensions provided in case of early retirement are, however, usually so low as to be unsatisfactory. For example, a male employee who would have been entitled to $100 a month pension if he had worked to age 65 and retired after 35 years of service might find that his actuarially reduced early retirement benefit would be only $33.94 per month at age 55, or $57.45 at age 60. These figures apply under a plan providing benefits, expressed as a percentage of pay for each year of service, financed entirely by the employer, with annuity costs based on the 1937 Standard Annuity Table with 2½% interest. A constant salary is assumed. The sharp **reduction in income** if retirement occurs many years before the normal retirement date is one reason for the common provision restricting early retirement to the 10-year period before the normal retirement date. Some plans allow employees who retire before age 65 to select an **adjusted annuity** so that their total income, including Federal primary insurance benefits, will be constant both before and after age 65, when the Federal benefit begins.

DEFERRED RETIREMENT. It is usual to provide that, with the consent of the employer, an employee may remain in active service after the normal retirement date. Unless properly administered, however, such a provision may lead to many late retirements, thereby defeating the basic objectives of the plan. To avoid pressure on supervisors and executives by individuals who wish to remain in service, which is particularly apt to occur if the pensions are low in relation to final salary at normal retirement age, it is sometimes specified that retention after the normal retirement date is permissible only with the **year-to-year consent** of the pension committee or the board of directors. As a rule,

no credit for service after the normal retirement date is given in computing retirement benefits. To allow such credit would encourage late retirement, thereby tending to defeat the purposes of the plan.

Under insured plans, contributions generally cease and the annuity payments begin on the normal retirement date, although some group annuity plans provide that any employee who remains in active service after the normal retirement date may leave his pension payments with the insurance company at interest to be used to purchase additional retirement income when he actually retires. Under self-administered plans, the usual practice is to make no pension payments until actual retirement.

PENSION BENEFIT PAYMENTS. Determination of the formula for computing pensions payable to employees reaching the normal retirement date involves a number of considerations varying with the circumstances and desires of each employer. Cost considerations have frequently resulted in pensions so low as to cause employees to resist retirement, making the plan ineffective. It is obvious that if pensions are too low, so that retirements do not occur, the purposes of the plan have not been fulfilled. On the other hand, pensions should not be too large because the expense of the plan will then be unduly burdensome.

Percentage of Pay per Year of Service Formula. Before the Social Security Act came into operation, pensions provided under formal plans were generally expressed as a **uniform percentage of employee earnings** for each year of credited service. Rates ranged from 1% to 2%. For example, 1% was generally used in railroad retirement plans, so that an employee retiring after, say, 35 years of service received a pension of 35% of earnings, the earnings basis generally being the average received during the last 10 years of service. Plans in other industries tended to be more generous, particularly if labor costs were a relatively lower percentage of total costs. Typical oil company plans, for example, based pensions on 2% of earnings for each year of credited service.

Lower Pensions on Earnings Covered by Social Security. Following enactment of the Social Security Act, many plans were revised to reduce pensions credited on the amount of annual earnings that were subject to the Act. Plans formerly using a 2% factor were generally changed to provide 1% of the amount of annual earnings covered by the Act plus 2% of the excess. Plans that had uniformly provided 1½% of pay per year of service were generally changed to provide ¾ of 1% of the covered earnings and 1½% of the excess for each year of credited service. Plans having a **breaking point** based on a **fixed dollar amount,** which in turn is determined by the amount of annual earnings covered by the Social Security Act, must be changed each time the amount covered by Social Security is changed if it is the employer's intention to make the breaking point coincide with the Social Security Act.

It is still fairly common, however, to use a **uniform percentage of all earnings** per year of service, with the thought that higher-paid employees are better able to take care of their needs after retirement. For example, a number of plans financed entirely at employer expense specify pensions amounting to 1% of earnings per year of service for all participants as a supplement to Social Security benefits.

To provide more uniform total retirement incomes, including Federal benefits, some plans grant a **rising percentage of pay per year** of service up to the amount of annual earnings covered by Social Security benefits; for example, using $4,800 as the amount of annual earnings covered by Social Security, ¾ of 1% of the first $2,400, plus 1% of the next $2,400, plus 1½% of the excess above $4,800. A few plans exclude credit on the first $100 of monthly earnings for the same reason. These procedures sometimes result in inadequate total retirement incomes for lower-paid employees, because they are close to the subsistence level and consequently require a higher retirement income relative to earnings. If the plan is of the money-purchase type with employer contributions fixed as a percentage of employee earnings, the contributions frequently vary with employee earnings brackets to make the pensions approximate the desired result when added to the Federal benefits. Money-purchase plans are discussed below.

Social Security Benefits. The Federal old age benefits vary considerably on a percentage of pay per year of coverage basis, so that private plans providing a uniform percentage of pay on the amount of annual earnings covered by Social Security result in total private and government benefits that favor lower-paid employees, in whose favor the Federal benefits are weighted. The **Federal primary insurance benefit** payable to a qualified individual is based upon a table forming part of the Social Security Act.

If a retired employee has a wife who is aged 62 or over, a wife's insurance benefit equal to 50% of the employee's primary insurance benefit (or any larger benefit to which the wife may be entitled on account of her own coverage) becomes payable. Since wives of employees retiring at 65 generally average 5 or 6 years younger, Social Security benefits payable to wives are usually disregarded in considering the adequacy of pensions provided under a private plan, as are benefits payable for dependent children and parents of retired employees.

Direct Deduction of Social Security Benefits. A number of plans, particularly those under which employees make no contributions, provide for direct deduction of Social Security primary insurance benefits from pensions otherwise provided under the plan. Because the tax for such benefits is **levied equally on employees and employers,** however, some plans deduct only one-half of the primary insurance benefits.

The practice of making a direct deduction for government benefits has a number of disadvantages. Employees are likely to criticize a procedure under which the employer appears to take credit for benefits the employees know are provided in part by their contributions and in part perhaps by government subsidy. Difficulty will also arise in the event of changes in the government benefit formula. Since government benefits depend entirely on the employee's employment and wage history, they cannot be accurately determined until he retires, leading to difficulty in accurately computing the cost of the pension credits accumulating under the plan. For these reasons, a majority of funded pension plans contain a pension formula that does not directly include government benefits as a factor, but provides pensions that are payable separate from and in addition to Social Security benefits.

Integration with Federal Benefits. Under some pension plans, lower-paid employees are excluded on the premise that the government has taken over the problem of providing for retirement of such employees. Sometimes a plan excluding employees earning less than the amount covered by Social Security has been adopted and announced as constituting merely a first step in the development of a comprehensive pension program. If, however, the plan provides no pension for these employees, it cannot solve the retirement problem realistically (1) because the Federal benefits alone are inadequate for most employees and (2) because of the Internal Revenue Service's position that if pensions are provided only for the higher-paid employees the pensions must **integrate** with the Federal benefits, i.e., pensions based on earnings in excess of the amount specified in the plan must be relatively no greater than 150% of the Federal primary insurance benefits payable to the highest-paid excluded employees. The basis of this requirement is that the Social Security Act provides not only a primary insurance benefit payable to the employee but other benefits; the total Social Security benefits are calculated to be worth 150% of the primary insurance benefit. Rulings issued by the Commissioner of Internal Revenue prescribe detailed tests to be used in determining whether the required integration exists with respect to Social Security benefits provided by the Social Security Act as amended.

Earnings Increase to Covered Level. One of the difficulties encountered in the operation of plans granting pensions only on the excess of earnings above the amount covered by Social Security has been the very low pensions provided for long-service employees who enter the plan late in life when their earnings rise above that amount. If this occurs after the plan has been established, there is generally no provision for the employee's past service, and his future service pension may be quite small.

Earnings Base. The earnings base to which the pension percentage is to be applied is an important consideration. Most of the early, unfunded pension plans used the **final rate of employee earnings** as the basis for computing pensions, or an **average of the earnings** during the final or the highest-paid 5 or 10 years of service, to avoid impairment of pensions that might be caused by earnings decreases that may occur late in life as a result of declining employee efficiency. The use of final or final average earnings is desirable to make the pensions bear as close a relationship as possible to living standards at retirement. However, if final or final average earnings are used, the cost of benefits cannot be computed as accurately as if pensions are based on the **actual amount earned** during each year of service (average earnings basis), because any assumed rate of final earnings may not be realized in actual practice. For this reason, insurance companies generally will not underwrite the cost of pensions based on final or final average employee earnings under group annuity contracts, but there are many instances of self-administered plans in which pensions are based on final earnings or an average of final earnings during the last years of service, the cost sometimes being estimated in accordance with an assumed scale of salary increases.

For purposes of integration with Social Security, it is permissible to use the 5 consecutive years that will produce the highest average for the employee. Under plans that credit pensions on the basis of **actual earnings for future service,** it is common practice to compute past service pensions on the rate of earnings as of the date of the plan's establishment, rather than on past average earnings, because past earnings records are not available in suitable form or because of a desire to provide pensions related as closely as is feasible to the standard of living before retirement.

If there are employees covered by the plan who are compensated on a fluctuating basis, such as **salesmen on commission,** provision is frequently made for the use of an average of past actual earnings over a designated number of years, such as 5, 7, or even 10, as a basis for computing past service pensions. If some employees are paid on a piecework or other incentive basis of compensation, it is common to use an average of their actual earnings over a period of weeks or months prior to the establishment of the plan to determine past service pensions.

Overtime earnings are generally excluded from the earnings base because such earnings are irregular and are not usually considered a proper gauge for determining the employee's standard of living. **Bonus payments,** although not generally included in earnings used for pension computation purposes, have in some cases been included if they are fixed in accordance with a predetermined formula. Inclusion of discretionary bonus payments may be considered by the Internal Revenue Service as introducing the possibility of prohibited discrimination in favor of highly compensated employees.

Past Service Pensions. Past service pensions are frequently credited at a lower rate than future service pensions to hold down past service cost, and because past service pensions are generally based on employee earnings as of the date of establishing the plan rather than on the lower average of past earnings. The cost may be further reduced by eliminating credit for past service before a stated age, such as 25, 30, or 35, or credit may be eliminated for an initial period of service. These restrictions frequently correspond to eligibility requirements for coverage by the plan. A pension plan that provides past service credits for all prior service of original, but not subsequent, participants will be considered discriminatory for tax purposes if it contains a minimum age requirement or a waiting period of more than one year for subsequent participants. A **minimum age restriction** for eligibility and past service pension computation purposes sometimes tends to engender dissatisfaction on the part of younger employees who may feel discriminated against by reason of the fact that their first years of service are not credited, whereas the first years of service of employees hired at older ages are recognized for the purposes of the plan, particularly because it often cuts off an important portion of the total benefits that would otherwise be payable to long service employees.

Maximum Pensions. Employers may establish **pension ceilings,** either by limiting the dollar amount of pensions or limiting the compensation on which pensions are credited. The wisdom of maximum pensions is being questioned for a number of reasons. The first is that the cost of superannuation strikes heaviest if pensions are so small as to discourage retirement by executives. If they do not retire, promotions are blocked and younger employees become dissatisfied. Very high personal income taxes have made it difficult for higher-paid employees to accumulate retirement reserves from savings. The need for **adequate pensions relative to compensation** is, therefore, as vital for top management as for rank-and-file employees. A low pension ceiling forces many employers to pay costly discretionary supplemental pensions financed on a pay-as-you-go basis. Removal of a maximum on pensions usually increases the total cost of the plan by only a comparatively small amount. There is a trend away from pension ceilings.

Minimum Pensions. These have assumed importance as a result of **union negotiations** on pensions. Prior to the pressure imposed by the unions for minimum pensions, some employers placed a floor under pension benefits so that no employee would be expected to retire on a pension of less than $10 or $20 per month in addition to Social Security benefits, but many felt that all employees should be treated uniformly on the basis of earnings and length of service. Minimum pensions were quite common in plans using individual policies because of the minimum unit requirements of the insurance company. Minimum pensions established recently have generally been of the flat-benefit type, ranging from $100 per month to $125 per month after 25 or 30 years of service, including primary Social Security benefits, with benefits reduced for less years of service at retirement than specified.

DISABILITY PENSION BENEFITS. Under many plans the only benefits available for disabled employees are the reduced **actuarially equivalent age retirement pensions.** These benefits are generally too small for an effective total and permanent disability pension. The Social Security Act provides disability benefits equal to the amount a disabled employee would have received as an old age pension. But because of the relatively small amount of such Social Security pension, some form of supplemental disability benefit is necessary.

Since insurance companies will not generally underwrite additional pensions for disabled employees except on the basis of annuity costs applicable to employees retiring in ordinary health, practically all insured plans provide no supplemental pensions for totally and permanently disabled employees other than the actuarially reduced age pensions. However, it is becoming more frequent under self-administered plans to provide pensions for employees who become totally and permanently disabled. Usually there is a minimum eligibility period, such as 10 or 15 years of service. The benefit is based on a percentage of pay for each year of service from the date of employment to the date of disability. In addition, some plans provide minimum pensions for disability, such as 25% of pay but not more than the pension that would have been accumulated if the employee had remained in service to the normal retirement date. As a result of union negotiations, minimum disability benefits have been included in many plans. This type of minimum is usually included in a plan that provides an **age retirement minimum benefit,** including Social Security, and the applicable minimum disability benefit after age 65 is based upon a recomputation at age 65, using the age retirement minimum benefit formula. Amounts payable under **workmen's compensation laws** may be deducted from the benefits otherwise payable. Disability pensions may be financed out of the general fund established under the plan or a separate fund or account may be established for this purpose. It is usual to include a specific definition of total and permanent disability. A **medical certificate** stating that the disability is total and likely to be permanent is generally required, and **periodic physical examinations** are called for. If desired, it is provided that adverse disability pension benefit experience will not impair the age retirement fund.

MEDICAL BENEFITS FOR RETIRED EMPLOYEES. Under an amendment to the Internal Revenue Code made in 1962, a pension plan may provide for the payment of benefits for sickness, accident, hospitalization, and medical expenses of retired employees, their spouses, and dependents. Such medical benefits are permissible only if they are subordinate to the retirement benefits under the plan, the employer's contributions for such benefits are reasonable and ascertainable, and a separate account is maintained for such benefits. The plan must provide that on the satisfaction of all liabilities under the plan to provide such benefits, any **excess** shall be returned to the employer. Payment of medical benefits under pension plans for retired employees is not taxable.

BENEFITS FOR SEVERED EMPLOYEES. These provisions involve certain questions of vesting and return of contributions such as:

Vested Benefit Rights. The vesting of title to benefits for employees whose service terminates before the qualifications for retirement have been met creates problems. For economy or other reasons, some employers provide no vesting of benefits financed with employer contributions except upon retirement, including approved early retirement and retirement because of total and permanent disability. Employees, on the other hand, prefer full vesting of benefits provided by employer contributions on termination of service at any time and for any reason. The extent to which vesting is to be provided under the plan is one of the major decisions an employer must make. There has been a trend toward providing vested pension benefits after some **specified period of service.**

The cost of such severance benefits must be considered in the light of the **basic purpose** of the plan and the **amount** the employer is able and willing to contribute. The ultimate cost of a liberal vesting provision may result in inadequate pensions, since most of the employer's contributions may be used up to finance benefits for employees who leave before they become superannuated or disabled. The proportion of the participants who leave before retirement is generally much greater than the proportion who remain. The granting of title to employer-financed benefits after many years of service is less expensive, since there are likely to be fewer terminations after as much as, say, 20 years of service, or after 20 years of service and attainment of age 50 or 55, although the cost per employee is greater than for a short-service employee.

Vesting of Retirement Income Policies. If retirement income policies are used (either individual or group permanent) and vested rights are granted, the policies are usually delivered to departing employees who then have all ownership rights, including the privilege of surrendering them for their cash value.

Vesting in the Form of Cash. It is undesirable to allow departing employees who have vested rights to receive cash representing the employer contributions made for them, in lieu of the retirement benefits to which they would otherwise be entitled, except in settlement of very small pension amounts. Such a practice defeats the basic purpose of the plan, which is to provide security following retirement. It may also encourage employees to leave, possibly to enter the service of a competitor. Under plans that are self-administered or underwritten by a group annuity contract, employees leaving the company before retirement qualifications have been met obtain vested rights only to **deferred annuities,** beginning when they reach the normal retirement date, although the right is sometimes given the terminating employee to have his vested annuity begin earlier in an actuarially reduced amount.

Vesting of Past Service Benefits. Vesting of annuities frequently differs as regards annuities for service before and after the date of establishment of the plan. A number of years of membership in the plan are sometimes required for the vesting of past service annuities, especially under contributory plans, to preclude employees from joining the plan and leaving shortly thereafter, taking with them title to full benefits, financed entirely at employer expense, for their past service.

Return of Employee Contributions. If employee contributions are made under the plan, the amount the employee has contributed is returned, usually with interest, on termination of employment. In group annuity or self-administered plans, any vested right to benefits financed with employer contributions is usually contingent upon the employee not withdrawing his own contributions. But most group annuity contracts provide that if the contract is discontinued as to further benefit purchases, employees leaving the service thereafter may withdraw their own contributions while retaining title to the deferred annuities provided by contributions of the employer.

DEATH BENEFITS. Most self-administered and group annuity plans provide little or no death benefits out of employer contributions to a pension plan.

Death benefits provided under an employee benefit program are usually in the form of supplemental life insurance, such as **group term life** insurance, **group permanent ordinary life**, or **group permanent paid-up life**, the latter two types providing permanent paid-up insurance protection on termination of employment or after retirement; of these kinds of insurance, the most frequent is group term life insurance.

The typical individual retirement income policy with insurance pension plan (or the practically equivalent group permanent retirement income with insurance plan) provides employees with death benefits financed by employer contributions. Such a program usually increases employer costs 60 to 100% as compared to a pension plan without death benefits financed with employer contributions. Treasury tax regulations require that death benefits under qualified pension plans, whether provided by insurance or otherwise, must be incidental to pension benefits.

Return of Employee Contributions on Death. If employee contributions that are not applied specifically to purchase life insurance are made under a pension plan, they are usually returned to the employee's beneficiary with interest if the employee dies before retirement. On death after retirement, the employee's beneficiary normally receives the difference between the amount that would have been payable had the employee died immediately before retirement and the pension payments he has received after retirement.

Most plans allow employees to elect **optional annuity forms**, such as a reduced actuarially equivalent joint and survivor annuity providing for continuance of all or a fraction of the employee's reduced annuity during the lifetime of a surviving joint annuitant, or sometimes a larger life annuity with no benefit on death following retirement.

EMPLOYER CONTRIBUTIONS. Employer contributions may be determined under any one of several deferred annuity accounting methods.

Self-Administered Plans—Level Percentage of Payroll Method. Under self-administered plans, any of several actuarially acceptable methods of cost computation may be used. One frequently employed is the so-called "level percentage of payroll" method, under which the actuary computes the percentage of pay that should be contributed according to sex for each age at entry to provide the specified benefits, taking account of future mortality and interest, and sometimes also of assumed future increases in employee earnings and rates of separation from service. The level percentages of pay determined for each age at entry are applied to the payroll distribution of participating employees to arrive at an **overall percentage** of the payroll of participants, which is contributed by the employer each year until a revaluation or change in underlying actuarial assumptions necessitates revision. This method has at times been employed only for **future service benefits** after the date of establishment of the plan, with financing of **previous service benefits** under the **single premium method** of accounting.

Another procedure is to compute payroll percentages on the basis of the ages at which employees would have entered the plan if it had always been in effect. The present value of the future expected payments of the level percentages (normal cost) is then subtracted from the present value of all benefits to be provided under the plan, to arrive at past service cost. This method often has the effect of reducing the normal cost of the plan and increasing the past service cost, thereby allowing the employer greater flexibility in meeting the costs.

Group Annuity Plans—Single-Premium Deferred Annuity Method. Under a typical group annuity plan, the exact amount of annuity commencing at the normal retirement date that is credited for each period of service is purchased currently. The cost varies according to the sex of the employees and their age when the benefits are purchased, under the so-called single-premium method of accounting for the cost of deferred annuities. The cost also depends, of course, on earnings of the employee.

If **employee contributions** are made, the employer contributions cover the balance of the periodic single-premium cost of the benefits provided under the plan, if the benefit is a percentage of earnings for each year of service. Under this method, employer cost per dollar of annuity is much greater for older than for younger employees. Advocates of money purchase plans or level payment methods of accounting contend that in the event of a period of poor business, when few young employees are hired, the cost to the employer of a fixed benefit plan based on single-premium accounting will increase as a percentage of payroll at a time when it will be most burdensome. On the other hand, it is pointed out by advocates of fixed benefit plans and the single-premium method of accounting that during such times there are usually substantial withdrawal credits resulting from employee terminations that are usually applied to reduce the cost to the employer of purchasing benefits for current service, tending to offset any increase in employer cost relative to payroll. The **level premium method** of accounting has been used under a few group annuity contracts, but it has not been favored by the insurance companies for administrative reasons and a desire to avoid long-term cost guarantees.

Under the usual group annuity contract, past service annuities are also purchased on a single-premium basis, so that the cost for each employee depends on his sex and his age at the time the benefits are purchased. To avoid the possibility of receiving large amounts of employer contributions in times when investment conditions may be unfavorable to the insurance company, group annuity contracts commonly fix the annual past service contribution amount on the basis of the number of years over which the employer desires to amortize it, but there is frequently a provision allowing variation, such as a minimum of ½ and a maximum of 1½ or 2 times the stated annual payment.

Group Annuity Plans—Deposit-Administration Method. An alternative to the purchase of deferred annuities under a group annuity contract is the so-called group annuity "deposit-administration" method. Available only for larger organizations, a deposit fund is maintained under this method with the insurance company to provide the sums required to purchase immediate annuities for employees when they retire. The amount of the fund and contributions for current and past service benefits may be determined by methods similar to those used under self-administration. They are usually based upon a level percentage of the compensation of all participating employees, estimated as sufficient to purchase the benefits when employees retire, with a discount for anticipated mortality and interest, and usually with an assumed scale of salary increase and a discount for anticipated future terminations from service. The insurance company guarantees the rate of interest to be paid on funds deposited during the first 5 years of the contract and the cost of the annuities to be purchased with such funds when employees retire. There may be a limitation on the number of years for which the interest rate will be guaranteed.

The principal advantage of the deposit-administration method is that the employer has greater latitude as to the amount of the contributions that may be made under the plan from year to year. A **surrender charge** by the insurance company when employee benefits are canceled because of termination of service under the usual contract for the purchase of deferred group annuities is also avoided. Another possible advantage is that the employer cost depends on actual mortality experience among active employees. If mortality is greater than expected by the table used by the insurance company in computing deferred annuity premium rates, the cost of the plan is correspondingly lower. On the other hand, there is a risk that the opposite may occur. Because there is no guarantee by the insurance company that the deposit-administration fund will be sufficient to meet the cost of benefits, especially since the insurance company does not guarantee the rates applicable to funds deposited after the first 5 contract years, most group annuity plans have used the deferred annuity purchase method rather than deposit-administration. Because deposit-administration offers greater flexibility in making employer contributions, it may be used to a greater extent in the future.

A type of deposit-administration contract is the **immediate-participation guarantee contract.** Under this method of funding, the interest rate credited on funds deposited varies with the earnings of the insurance company; the employer's contribution also takes into account the actual mortality experience of retired employees and actual insurance company expenses.

Individual Policy Plans. If level-premium individual policies are used to provide all of the benefits, the contributions are those required to meet the premiums as they fall due, reduced by dividends and recoveries such as the cash value of policies surrendered on severance of employment. The **gross premium cost** remains constant for each employee once the policy has been issued, except that it may rise for employees whose earnings increase by the amount of the premium required for new policies taken out to provide benefits with respect to earnings increases. In such cases, the cost will rise not only because of the additional coverage, but also because of the higher premium payable under policies issued at older ages.

Group Permanent Retirement Income Plans. These plans are financed in a manner similar to individual policy plans, except that the insurance company reserves the right to increase premium rates or change provisions as to new coverage after the first 5 years of the plan.

EMPLOYEE CONTRIBUTIONS. Certain questions in connection with these are as follows:

Advisability of Providing for Employee Contributions. There are two schools of thought regarding the advisability of requiring employees to contribute to the cost of their pensions. Advocates of a **contributory plan** point out that employee contributions make it possible to provide more adequate pensions than can be financed if the employer pays the entire cost. Also, if employees contribute they have a sense of proprietorship in the plan that is not otherwise obtainable. Advocates of **noncontributory plans,** on the other hand, point out that (1) the contributions of employees frequently do not finance more than one-fourth of the benefits provided under the plan; (2) the net gain to the employer resulting from employee contributions is not the full amount of the contributions, but is the amount of those contributions less the tax deduction that would be available to the employer if he made the contributions; (3) employee contributions are less effective in providing pensions than employer contributions because of the usual provision for the return of employee contributions on death; (4) if employees contribute they are more likely to demand a voice in the administration of the plan; (5) since it is generally inadvisable to require compulsory participation of all eligible employees in a contributory plan, especially for employees in service when the plan begins, there is the possibility that some eligible employees will not join, thereby creating a retirement problem on their account; (6) there is a much greater tendency under contributory plans to provide liberal vested rights to the benefits financed with employer contributions upon termination of service before retirement, which may absorb a considerable proportion of employer contributions that might otherwise be used to provide more adequate pensions under a noncontributory plan for those who survive in service to old age or disability; and (7) the Securities and Exchange Commission has taken the position that **registration of contributory, self-administered plans** is required for disclosure purposes when participation in the plan is voluntary. (Registration can be avoided by investing employee contributions with an insurance company and employer contributions in a self-administered fund. Registration is not required for contributory group annuity plans.)

Trends in Use of Contributory Plans. Although most earlier pension plans in the United States did not require employee contributions, a large proportion of those established in the depression of the 30's were contributory. There has, however, in recent years been a noticeable tendency to make pension plans noncontributory.

Ratio of Employee Contributions to Benefits. Under fixed benefit plans of the contributory type, there are a great variety of employee contribution formulas. Under plans providing benefits that vary according to the employee earnings brackets to take account of Federal benefits, it is common to use the **same ratio of employee contributions to benefits** throughout. For example, employees may contribute 2% of pay for each 1% of benefit, so that under a plan providing pensions amounting to ¾ of 1% of the first $3,600 of annual earnings plus 1½% of the excess for each year of service, employees contribute 1½% of the first $3,600 plus 3% of the excess. There is frequently a greater ratio of employee contributions to benefits in the **higher earnings brackets,** however, which may be justified in part because higher-paid employees are generally older than the others, making their benefits more costly. Many other ratios of contributions to benefits are used.

With the increasing cost of annuities in recent years there has been a tendency to use a **higher ratio of employee contributions to benefits,** and many plans specify employee contributions that are equal to as much as three or more times the benefits provided as a percentage of pay per year of service. Under money-purchase plans, employee contributions are set as a percentage of earnings, sometimes varying with the earnings brackets which with employer contributions in a specified ratio are designed to produce the desired total retirement incomes, including Social Security benefits, if insurance company annuity rates (or annuity values used under a self-administered plan) are not changed.

It is also possible to provide for **voluntary, unmatched employee contributions** but these, according to a Treasury ruling, may not exceed 10% of compensation.

INVESTMENTS. Since a pension plan is designed to provide economic security to employees against the major economic hazards of old age or disability and sometimes death, some companies consider it advisable to confine investments under self-administered plans to securities specified as **legal investments** for insurance companies, savings banks, or trust funds. Since 1950, however, the investment in common stock of a substantial portion of the assets of a self-administered pension plan has become much more frequent. In the decade of the 1950's the assets of all private pension funds, as measured by book value, more than quadrupled. The most rapid growth was shown by the **noninsured corporate pension funds.** At the end of 1961, according to S.E.C. data, the market value of the assets of these funds was $39 billion. Of this total, common stock made up 50% (as against only 32% in 1956), corporate bonds 36% (as against 45% in 1956), U.S. government securities 5% (as against 12.5% in 1956), and preferred stock and miscellaneous assets the remainder. Reserves of the insured pension funds were estimated at over $20 billion, at book value.

Under insured plans, the contributions are automatically invested in accordance with the laws of the states in which the insurance company operates. In a self-administered plan, the investment powers are laid down in the trust instrument. If it is desired to invest in **employer securities,** it is generally advisable to restrict investments to senior obligations such as bonds or preferred stock. If such investments are made, a full disclosure to the Commissioner of Internal Revenue is required to make certain that the plan continues to qualify under the Internal Revenue Code, and that, in particular, it continues to operate for the exclusive benefit of the employees. Provisions of the Code relating to so-called **"prohibited transactions"** between a tax-exempt employee trust and the employer, such as those prohibiting the lending of money to an employee without adequate security and a reasonable rate of interest, may prevent the acquisition by the trust of unsecured debentures of the employer.

TERMINATION OF PLAN. If the plan is completely **self-administered** it need not necessarily be liquidated and distributed immediately after contributions cease. It may go on providing **full benefits** until the fund is exhausted. Or, to assure continued fund solvency, provision may be made to **change the benefits** from time to time as indicated by periodic valuations of the benefit liabilities and the fund assets, the change being made pro rata on the basis provided by the plan. It is usual to provide for the **liquidation** of the fund at a time to be determined by the administrative committee or the board of directors of the employer. Some plans and trust agreements merely provide that the assets shall be liquidated and distributed in a nondiscriminatory manner, as determined by the committee. To avoid the possibility of dissatisfaction when the assets are distributed, however, detailed provisions concerning distributions among employees and pensioners are often included in the trust instrument. In any event, upon termination of a pension plan or discontinuance of contributions, the plan must provide, for tax purposes, that the **rights of all employees to accrued benefits shall be nonforfeitable.**

Distribution Formula. If a **self-administered plan** is terminated and the fund liquidated, it is sometimes provided that the assets will be distributed in the following order:

1. For the purchase from an insurance company of full retirement benefits for retired participants.
2. For the purchase of full retirement benefits for participants who have reached normal retirement age but have not retired.
3. For the purchase of retirement benefits for participants who have reached an age within a specified number of years of the normal retirement date, upon the basis of reserve liabilities at the date of liquidation, using the actuarial principles underlying the plan.
4. For the purchase of retirement benefits for all other participants upon the basis of their respective reserve liabilities, similarly determined.

In the event that assets do not suffice to purchase all of the foregoing, they are applied to the purchase of benefits in full for each group **in sequence,** and to purchase **reduced benefits in a uniform ratio** for the participants included in the group for which the remaining assets are insufficient to purchase benefits in full. There are many other distribution formulas, some of which give precedence only to retired employees or to those eligible for retirement.

In other cases, no provision is made for payment of pensions following liquidation of the fund, provision being made for payments in cash based on the reserve liabilities for benefits that had been credited under the plan, proportionately adjusted if necessary to the proceeds of liquidated fund assets.

Any **surplus** remaining after satisfaction of all pension liabilities, contingent and fixed, is the result of an overestimate of such liability and may be refunded to the employer.

Termination of Group Annuity Plans. Group annuity contracts usually provide that after the contract is discontinued as to further benefit purchases, none of the benefits provided by employer contributions can be canceled. There is thus **complete vesting** of all benefits provided with contributions of the employer. If employee contributions have been made under the plan, the usual provision is to allow those who leave the company's employ after the termination to withdraw their own contributions with interest, without forfeiting the benefits provided with employer contributions.

Termination of Individual Policy Plans. If individual policies are held at the time the plan is terminated, the usual provision is to deliver to each participant the policies that have been taken out for him, subject to the right of the committee or trustee to have the policies endorsed in a manner restricting surrender for cash. He may then decide whether to continue the premium payments in whole or in part, convert the policy to another type, surrender the policy for its available cash value, or take paid-up benefits.

Early Termination—Tax Penalty. The tax regulations state that if a plan is discontinued for reasons other than business necessity within a few years after its establishment, **tax deductions may be disallowed** with respect to the employer contributions that have been made under the plan. This is based on the view that one of the fundamental requirements for qualification is the permanency of the plan. This generally applies only to the **"open" tax years,** usually the last three. There should, therefore, be substantial certainty before a plan is established that, on the basis of past earnings and future prospects of the business, it will be possible to continue the plan indefinitely. The Internal Revenue Service has stated that a reduction of profits or the occurrence of business losses will not necessarily be considered a valid reason for the discontinuance of a plan. Under Treasury rulings special limitations are applicable to pensions payable to higher paid employees if a plan is terminated within the first 10 years of its operation.

It is important to note that **suspension of employer contributions** may be equivalent to termination of a plan with respect to the possibility of retroactive tax penalties. It is possible to suspend contributions without penalty if benefits under the plan are not affected at any time, and if the unfunded cost at any time does not exceed the unfunded past service cost as of the date of establishment of the plan.

PENSION COMMITTEE. Under plans of the completely or partially **self-administered** type, including plans using individual policies, it is desirable that there be a committee to supervise and be responsible for administrative detail. The committee is usually appointed by the board of directors. The committee usually comprises not less than three nor more than five members who may or may not be plan participants or company officials, and is empowered to act by a majority vote. Committee members usually serve without compensation but are reimbursed for actual expenses, usually by the trust fund but sometimes by the employer. The committee lays down regulations for the administration of the plan and interprets, construes, corrects, and supplies any omissions in the provisions of the plan in a manner that does not discriminate in favor of officers, shareholders, supervisory or highly paid employees. The committee also adopts the actuarial assumptions underlying the plan, determines the contributions to be made, directs the trustee to make payments out of the trust fund, and, if the plan or trust so provides, passes on trust investments and actions of the trustee. It is common to include a provision exempting the committee from **liability** for their acts, individually and severally, except when due to wilful misconduct or gross negligence. It is usual to bar a committee member from acting on decisions affecting his individual rights under the plan. The committee supplies information and assistance to participants, pensioners, and beneficiaries.

A committee is not required as a rule for a plan underwritten by means of a group annuity contract, since conditions governing the payment of contributions and benefits are stated in the contract. Problems that may arise are usually settled by discussion between the insurance company and the employer.

TRUSTEE. All types of pension plans, except those underwritten by a group annuity contract, usually require the setting up of a trust. A bank or trust company commonly acts as trustee, although an individual or individuals, often executives or employees serving without pay, may act in this capacity. The following discussion deals with certain provisions regarding the trustee. (See also Sec. 6, Corporate Fiduciaries, Trusts, and Agencies.)

Relation of Trust to Plan. There are two schools of thought concerning the **relation of the plan and trust agreement.** Some trustees require that the trust agreement be separate and distinct from the plan. In these cases, the trust agreement is made a part of the plan by reference, but the plan is not made a part of the agreement. This is done primarily to protect the trustee from responsibility for official notice of plan details. The other school of thought holds that the plan and trust agreement should be in one document, thereby providing for all matters to be brought officially to the trustee's attention. Since the trust is irrevocable as to contributions made to it, the trustee must be empowered to carry out the terms of the plan and the trust even if the employer is no longer in existence or associated with the trust.

Powers and Duties. The powers and duties of the trustee are described at length in the **trust agreement.** The trustee is given the power to hold, invest, and reinvest the fund and fund income, and to perform routine duties connected with investments. The power to select investments may be given entirely to the trustee, the trustee may make investments subject to the approval of the pension committee, or the committee may be given full power to instruct the trustee concerning investments. Cash is retained in amounts necessary to meet obligations under the plan as determined by the trustee or the pension committee.

If the plan is completely **self-administered,** the trustee may make benefit payments directly to beneficiaries, or the amounts required may be paid to the committee for disbursement as benefit payments.

If **insurance or annuity policies are purchased,** the trust instrument specifies that the trustee shall be the absolute owner of the policies, and that all of the incidents of ownership shall be exercised by the trustee alone, as directed by the committee or as requested by the participants in accordance with the terms of the plan.

Liability. The trustee is generally protected from liability for any fund losses not caused by its own gross negligence.

Resignation or Removal. The trust instrument specifies the manner in which the trustee may be removed and replaced, generally after 30 or 60 days following notice of action by the board of directors. The trustee is permitted to resign after similar notice to the board of directors.

DISCLOSURE AND BONDING REQUIREMENTS. The Federal **Welfare and Pension Plans Disclosure Act,** which became effective in 1959, requires the filing of a **description of employee welfare and pension plans** covering more than 25 employees if interstate commerce is involved. The types of welfare benefits as to which a report is required are medical, surgical, or hospital care or benefits in the case of sickness, accident, disability, death, or unemployment. Pension benefits include benefits under insured and uninsured pension plans and profit-sharing plans providing retirement benefits. In addition, **annual financial reports** are required to be filed as to welfare and pension plans covering 100 or more employees. These descriptions and annual reports are filed with the United States Department of Labor; the Secretary of Labor prescribes the contents of the required reports and has enforcement powers. The responsibility for the reports is placed upon the **"administrator of the plan,"** which is either the company providing the benefits or the employee organization that provides benefits for its members or the joint board established by a collective bargaining agreement.

In 1962, the Federal statute was amended to require the **bonding** of administrators, officers, and employees who handle plan funds. The bond must be at least 10% of the funds handled with a maximum amount of $500,000, subject to increase by the Secretary of Labor.

In addition to Federal statute, a number of **states** including New York, Massachusetts, Connecticut, Washington, and Wisconsin have statutes regulating and requiring disclosure of employee welfare plans. Some state statutes have provisions designed to avoid duplication of reporting.

"Money Purchase" vs. "Fixed Benefit" Procedure, and Variable Annuities

DEFINITIONS. Benefits are determined under a pension plan by one of two methods:

1. The **"fixed benefit"** or **"definite benefit"** method, under which pensions are determined as a fixed percentage of employee earnings for each year of credited service, or more infrequently as a flat percentage of the earnings of participants or a flat amount. The flat percentage basis is associated usually with plans employing retirement income policies.

This fixed benefit method is by far the most popular. If the plan involves employee contributions, each employee contributes a stated percentage of earnings and the employer pays the balance of the cost of the benefits for current service, which varies according to the sex and age of the employees.

2. The **"money purchase"** method, under which contributions instead of benefits are fixed as a percentage of employee earnings, and current service pensions

are those that can be purchased with the contributions made at each age. Consequently, the benefits vary not only with the amounts contributed, but also in accordance with the annuity rates applicable at each age.

Pensions for past service are usually on a fixed benefit basis, being a percentage of pay times the years of credited service under either type of plan.

FIXED BENEFIT PLAN ADVANTAGES. Fixed benefit plans have the following advantages: The amount of pension may be readily estimated on the basis of assumed employee earnings without reference to annuity costs; lower employer contributions are made at the younger ages, which permit larger contributions for employees nearing retirement; the cost of vesting annuities in employees who are most apt to sever employment is lower; the benefit objective is not changed because of future changes in basic annuity costs; and pensions are more closely related to the final rate of employee earnings.

MONEY PURCHASE PLAN ADVANTAGES. Money purchase plans have the following advantages: Each employee is always aware of the amount the employer is contributing for him; employer cost may be a more constant percentage of payroll; larger benefits are available for employees retired before the normal retirement age because of disability or other reasons than under a fixed benefit plan financed on the single-premium basis; and no benefit precedent is established that might be difficult to maintain if annuity costs increase.

GENERAL CONSIDERATIONS. Advocates of fixed benefit plans contend that money purchase plans have been outmoded by increasing annuity costs due to lower interest rates and the greater longevity of employees and pensioners. **Increased annuity costs** reduce pensions below the original objective of a money purchase plan, unless contributions are correspondingly increased. Because it has usually not been advisable to increase employee contributions under money purchase plans, employers in such cases have met higher costs by **increasing the matching ratio,** the employer contributing $1.50, $2, or more, for each $1 of employee contributions. It is contended that, if this is to be the experience under a money purchase plan, a **fixed benefit plan** with the employer automatically paying the full amount of any cost increase is preferable, since the advantage cited in favor of the money purchase procedure that annuity cost increases could be shared between employee and employer is more theoretical than practical.

The ease with which the amount of the pension may be estimated under a fixed benefit plan is its chief advantage. Money purchase plan advocates contend, however, that pensions under such plans can be readily estimated by multiplying the amount the employee contributes by a factor taken from a table usually included in such plans. The pension thus estimated, however, does not take account of future increases in annuity costs.

Fixed benefit advocates point out that relatively small pensions are provided for the future service of older employees under money purchase plans, and that if earnings increase rapidly the pension will not rise proportionately. Furthermore, lower future service benefits for older employees make larger past service pensions necessary. Money purchase advocates counter that all employees should be treated alike from a cost standpoint, and that the higher cost for older employees under a fixed benefit plan will cause an employer to hesitate in hiring new employees in the middle and older age groups, which is socially undesirable.

Money purchase plan advocates feel it encourages **participation by younger employees** for whom comparatively small employer contributions are made under fixed benefit procedure. Fixed benefit advocates counter that the money purchase arrangement places too much of the employer contributions on the younger, high turnover employees, and that vested rights given these younger employees are costly, resulting in smaller pensions for the older employees who are most likely to constitute a retirement problem.

Fixed benefit plans have always greatly outnumbered money purchase plans. Money purchase procedure is confined almost exclusively to plans toward the cost of which employees contribute, and they are mostly of the group annuity type.

VARIABLE ANNUITIES. An increasingly important kind of pension plan that may be either of the money purchase type or the fixed benefit type is that providing for payment of a variable annuity. Arrangements providing for variable benefits have received increasing recognition as a means of keeping pension benefits in line with increases in the cost of living.

An example of a money purchase type of plan involving variable benefits is that of the College Retirement Equities Fund. Under this system, the employer and employee each contributes a stated percentage of the employee's salary. These contributions are accumulated for the individual employee in either a **fixed dollar fund** or an **equity fund** and are represented by a number of units in the respective funds. The employee may choose to have up to one-half of the contributions on his behalf placed in the equity fund. The amount of the pension on retirement attributable to the employee's units in the equity fund varies with the **market value** of the units.

Alternatively, a pension fund that is not a money purchase type may provide for payment of variable benefits in the form of a life annuity. Such a plan is that providing for the payment of **equity annuities** to employees of the Long Island Lighting Company, of New York. The amount in the annuity depends upon changes in the value of the portion of the trust fund invested in equities.

Another type of variable benefit plan is that which pays a pension that is keyed to a **cost-of-living index,** such as that of the United States Labor Department. A plan of this type is the pension plan of National Airlines. In case of such a plan, the investments of the trust include both fixed income investments and common stocks on the theory that the value of the trust investments will tend to vary with the cost of living (Washington and Rothschild, Compensating the Corporate Executive).

Profit-Sharing Plans

IMMEDIATE-DISTRIBUTION PROFIT-SHARING PLANS. An immediate-distribution profit-sharing plan provides compensation **additional to take-home pay** as a reward for better-than-average performance as measured by the profits of the enterprise. None of the shared profits are stored for future delivery. The plan is thus essentially a **bonus plan** dependent upon profits, the distributions usually being made annually.

Objectives. Among reasons for establishing immediate-distribution profit-sharing plans has been a desire to **unify the interests of the business and employees** and instill a "feeling of partnership"; to give employees a stake in the private enterprise system; to increase employee initiative and efficiency; to eliminate wasteful practices; and to improve employee goodwill and loyalty generally. Another reason may be a desire to avoid increases in wage and salary rates that would be difficult to remove in times of poor business.

Scope and Nature. Immediate-distribution profit-sharing plans may be confined to one or more employees. The employer may decide who are to receive the bonuses and the division of the shared profits. The procedure may be formal or entirely discretionary with the employer. In contrast, **deferred-distribution profit-sharing plans** that qualify under the Internal Revenue Code must include a nondiscriminatory method of allocation of employer contributions among the participants, who must then include a broad class of employees as under pension plans, such as all salaried employees or all earning above a stated sum. Most deferred-distribution profit-sharing plans include all regular salaried employees who have completed a specified period of service.

Profit-Sharing Formula. The formula to determine the portion of profits to be shared under an immediate-distribution profit-sharing plan may be based on profits **before or after taxes.** The percentage used will naturally be lower if it is applied to profits before taxes. To assure a fair return to stockholders, many plans provide that dividends or earnings on invested capital at a specified rate will be deducted before determining the amount of profits to be divided among employees.

Allocations to Participants. Under an immediate-distribution profit-sharing plan it is possible to weight allocations to participants according to length of service as well as compensation, although distributions are frequently based entirely on compensation only. In many cases, no formal method of allocation is specified, distributions being based on individual merit, in the discretion of the employer.

Size of Organization. Many surveys have concluded that profit-sharing plans are more effective in promoting employee efficiency in **small** organizations where individual effort has a more direct bearing on profits than in larger enterprises, particularly those engaged in mass production where the individual employee can do comparatively little to control the volume of production, and where his efforts have but a small effect on the amount he receives under the plan.

Relation to Basic Compensation. Profit-sharing plans of the immediate-distribution type are sometimes established to give compensation increases in prosperous times that will automatically lapse during periods of poor business. Employees will not usually accept such a basis of compensation unless it is clearly a supplement to a competitive wage scale. If good employee relations are to be maintained, basic rates of compensation must be paid that are in line with those paid by the industry and the community. High personal income taxes have minimized the attractiveness of profit-sharing cash bonuses to executives. On the other hand, it has become a frequent practice for corporations to adopt **deferred compensation** arrangements for executives, providing for payment of a portion of each executive's compensation after retirement. Such arrangements may base the amount of deferred compensation upon profits of the corporation during employment; the participating executive does not acquire an interest in a fund, but instead must look to the contractual obligation of the employer to pay the deferred compensation at the times specified in the plan or agreement (Washington and Rothschild, Compensating the Corporate Executive).

Employee Reaction. A profit-sharing plan must provide reasonably large returns to individual participants if it is to promote employee goodwill and efficiency. Organized labor favors inclusion of all employees, as against provision of larger shares for a relatively small group of long service employees. Profit-sharing is likely to be most effective, therefore, in industries where labor cost is a low percentage of gross sales, making it possible to make substantial payments to individual employees.

A **leading cause of discontinuance** of immediate-distribution profit-sharing plans has been employee dissatisfaction. The employees become accustomed to receiving extra compensation when profits are substantial and gear their living standards accordingly; when the extra compensation is reduced or eliminated because business is poor, they tend to look upon the reduction as a pay cut. Also, dissatisfaction results from delay in making distributions, which may occur as much as a year after the profits resulting from employee effort have actually been earned. The distribution is commonly made by a single annual payment. Although employees are likely to be enthusiastic at that time, interest may be lacking during the remainder of the year.

It is essential that a continuous educational effort be made to impress employees with the principles of the plan so that there will be a minimum of dissatisfaction when the profit-sharing distribution is reduced or eliminated.

The history of immediate-distribution profit-sharing plans reveals no steady growth in the movement. More plans are established during periods of prosperity, but there is a high rate of discontinuance in ensuing depressions. Profit-sharing plans may be compared to common stocks in that they both appear attractive to the majority in boom times and unattractive during depressions.

Tax Status. Under the immediate-distribution type of profit-sharing plan, the amounts received by employees are subject to personal income tax. The employer's profit-sharing contributions are deductible from his taxable income if the test of the income tax regulations as to reasonableness of total employee compensation is met.

DEFERRED-DISTRIBUTION PROFIT-SHARING PLANS. Such plans have a number of objectives and collective bargaining implications.

Definition. A deferred-distribution profit-sharing plan is one of the kinds of qualified plans under the Internal Revenue Code, so that the employer may deduct his contributions from taxable income and no income tax need be paid by employee participants until the year when benefits are actually received, and the trust itself is exempt from tax.

Such a deferred-distribution profit-sharing plan may be defined as an arrangement to share profits with employees under a **fixed formula** as to allocation of employer contributions, the profits shared being accumulated in a **trust fund** and paid out to employees on the happening of specified contingencies, such as the completion of a specified number of years of membership in the plan, the attainment of a certain age, occurrence of disability, severance of employment, or death.

Objectives. Employers may use profit-sharing to finance **retirement benefits**, instead of contributions based on actuarially computed costs or premiums paid to an insurance company for pensions credited in relation to employee earnings and length of service. Another objective has been the provision of **death benefits** out of credits in the profit-sharing trust fund, sometimes supplemented by the purchase of life insurance policies out of each participant's share. **Severance benefits** also have been a consideration, especially for long service employees.

Collective Bargaining Implications. A number of large corporations have profit-sharing plans covering unionized workers. A notable example is the plan of American Motors Corporation. If a plan is made applicable to workers represented by a union, the terms of the plan are subject to collective bargaining (N.L.R.B. vs. Black-Clawson Co., 210 F. 2d 523 [6th Cir. 1954]).

Deferred-Distribution Profit-Sharing Plans Compared with Pension Plans. If an employer can afford both an adequate pension plan and a deferred-distribution profit-sharing plan, it may be desirable to adopt both.

But some employers are unable or unwilling to undertake both types of plans. It then becomes a question of which plan should be established. If the employer has employees who constitute a present problem of superannuation or disability, a pension plan is needed to provide for them and other employees who will have to be retired because of age or disability in the next 15 or 20 years. If the employer establishes a deferred-distribution profit-sharing plan, he will still be faced with the expense and problem of providing for superannuated and disabled employees for many years before profit-sharing can provide adequate benefits for them. One reason for this is that the Internal Revenue Service usually does not permit a deferred-distribution profit-sharing plan to make **adequate provision for past service** except, perhaps, for the lowest-paid participants, for allocations must not discriminate in favor of highly paid employees. This means that allocations generally cannot be made in accordance with length of service or age, since the oldest employees who have served for the longest periods are usually paid more than others. Another reason why profit-sharing provides less adequate pensions in the early years of a plan is that sums allocated to individual participants who remain in service to retirement are distributed in cash or applied to buy retirement benefits under a money-purchase procedure, so that the amount of the benefit of the participants depends upon their years of membership in the plan. As a result, the retirement benefits are relatively small for employees who are of advanced age when the plan is established, and who constitute the most pressing retirement or disability problem. Under a **self-administered** pension plan, contributions need not be allocated to individual accounts, but the whole fund may be used for the sole purpose of providing pensions on a first-come-first-served basis for those who actually retire. Assuming the same employer contributions as under a pension plan, a deferred-distribution profit-sharing plan usually disburses more money for death and severance benefits, leaving less for pensions.

If a substantial part of the amounts allocated to participants are paid out to them while they are in active service, little will be left to provide benefits on retirement because of old age or disability, or in the event of death or severance.

To illustrate the operation of a profit-sharing plan as compared with a pension plan, let us assume a **deferred-distribution profit-sharing plan** under which approximately one-third of the contributions are used for death benefits, since provision is usually made for payment to a participant's beneficiary of his full account when he dies. Payments to employees leaving the company's employ depend on turnover before retirement and forfeiture provisions, but might absorb another one-third of the contributions. Thus, only about one-third of the total would be left to provide pensions.

Even assuming that the amounts allocated to participants are not diminished by distributions during their active service but are held intact until retirement, the most that can be used to provide retirement benefits are the **maximum tax deductible contributions of 15%** of the compensation of participants for the years during which they are members of the plan, together with fund earnings and any severance forfeitures that have been apportioned to individual accounts, reduced by amounts that may have been paid for life insurance. The amount credited to the individual's account is applied to provide retirement benefits on a money-purchase basis, which means that much more will be provided for young than for older entrants, and more will be provided for males than females.

A **pension plan,** on the other hand, may utilize all available funds for pensions. None of the employer contributions need be used for death or severance benefits, and the entire fund can be used to pay pensions. In addition, under a pension plan the employer may contribute and deduct from his taxable income more than 15% of the aggregate compensation of participants if actuarially required under the plan.

On the other hand, there are many instances in which a fixed obligation to pay pensions under a pension plan may be considered unwise in spite of permissible flexibility as to funding. Moreover, a qualified profit-sharing plan, unlike a pension plan, may provide for the **re-allocation of forfeitures** among the remaining participants, and for distributions to participants in case of hardship or other events. Profit-sharing plans and pension plans may both provide incidental life insurance; there is no tax requirement in the case of profit-sharing plans that death benefits (other than life insurance) be merely incidental and, in fact, profit-sharing plans usually provide for the payment to a deceased employee's beneficiary of the total amount credited to his account at the time of death.

Provisions of a Deferred-Distribution Profit-Sharing Plan

PROFIT-SHARING FORMULA. The Treasury Department formerly required, as a condition of qualification, a **fixed formula** to determine the amount of the employer's contribution. At present, the regulations require only **regular and substantial contributions.** But a fixed formula may still be desirable, both to avoid a Treasury contention that a failure to make contributions is a termination of the plan and as a matter of employee relations.

A formula, if used, may simply commit the employer to contribute a specified percentage of the profits each year, but it is much more common to provide for contributions based on a **specified percentage of the profits** in excess of (1) a flat dollar figure, (2) a percentage of invested capital, or (3) dividend payments to stockholders. Special provision may be made for contingency reserves, adjustments in taxes for previous years, and other items. Under some plans, the profits are shared with employees on a **progressive scale,** so that the larger the profits the larger will be the proportion contributed under the profit-sharing plan.

15% of Compensation Limit. A maximum on annual contributions of 15% of the compensation of participating employees is also usually included, because of the provision of the tax law limiting **deductible contributions** under profit-sharing plans to that amount. But it is not necessary to restrict contributions to 15% of the aggregate compensation of participants in any particular year, since the law allows larger contributions if less than 15% of the compensation of participants was contributed in previous years. It is provided, however, that the additional deduction because of lower contributions in previous years cannot exceed 15% of the compensation of covered employees in the later year. It is possible, therefore, to contribute and deduct in one year as much as 30% of the compensation of participants. Similarly, if a contribution in excess of the 15% limit is made in a particular year, the excess may be carried forward for tax purposes and used in years in which less than the maximum is contributed.

Profit-sharing trust **carryovers** may be used by the surviving corporation in a corporate reorganization.

If an employer has both a qualified pension plan and a qualified profit-sharing plan, the Code provides an **overall limitation** to the effect that not more than 25% of compensation of participating employees may be deducted in any one year.

METHOD OF ALLOCATION. For tax approval, a profit-sharing plan must contain **a specific formula** describing the method of allocating the profits shared among participating employees. This formula **must not discriminate** in favor of officers, shareholders, supervisory, or highly compensated employees.

As a practical matter, shares of individual employees often cannot vary with **length of service,** since those with the longest service are generally compensated at higher rates than other employees. Even if such a procedure were nondiscriminatory at the outset, it might prove unsafe in later years, since the distribution method must be nondiscriminatory for each year of the plan. The simplest and safest allocation method, therefore, is to distribute the profits shared in direct proportion to the compensation of employees. This makes it impossible to provide adequate retirement benefits under a profit-sharing plan except for those retiring many years after the plan begins. Although it is sometimes possible for an employer to secure approval for an allocation formula that takes into account the years of past service of lower-paid employees, arranged so that it would not favor the higher-paid employees in any year, such a procedure would not provide adequate pensions for higher-paid employees or lower-paid employees retiring after a short period of membership.

Actuarially Determined Pensions Not Permitted. It is not possible for a tax-qualified profit-sharing plan to provide specific pensions upon an actuarial basis, regardless of profits, because the Internal Revenue Code provides that a profit-sharing trust does not include "any trust designed to provide benefits upon retirement and covering a period of years, if under the plan the amounts to be contributed by the employer can be determined actuarially. . . ." [§ 404 (a) (3) (A)].

Basis of Individual Accounts. The plan may establish individual accounts in dollars for participating employees with annual apportionment of contributions, generally in proportion to employee compensation, and with apportionment of fund increments or losses pro rata. Individual accounts are sometimes established in terms of **units** having an initial stated value, such as $1, which are revalued thereafter by dividing total assets held under the plan by the number of outstanding units. Annual contributions are then allocated to individual accounts in terms of units. The unit method simplifies accounting computations.

Under a unit formula, the interests of new and old participants should be protected from dilution by dividing the amount in the fund, before a new contribution is made, by the number of units outstanding before the addition of new units, to determine the unit value used in apportioning current contributions.

The **Treasury Department** requires allocation to the accounts of participants under a profit-sharing plan of all of the assets of the trust, at least once a year, on the basis of market value. Such allocation includes all realized income and forfeitures (if the plan provides for the re-allocation of forfeited accounts).

ELIGIBILITY FOR MEMBERSHIP. Under the Internal Revenue Code, the eligibility provisions of a deferred-distribution profit-sharing plan may not discriminate in favor of stockholders or supervisory or highly compensated employees. For this reason, it is common to include all regular employees who have completed a specified period of service, usually not more than 5 years. **Eligibility under profit-sharing** is subject to the same considerations as **eligibility under pension plans,** with the exception that employees are not generally excluded because of age. Also, to secure tax approval of a profit-sharing plan confined to employees earning more than the amount covered by Social Security, it must be integrated with Social Security benefits, as with a pension plan.

RETIREMENT. It is usual under deferred-distribution profit-sharing plans to provide for normal retirement of employees, generally when they reach age 65. If a portion of the fund has been allocated to purchase annuity benefits, these generally commence under provisions similar to those of pension plans. Because of the **absence of any fixed retirement annuity concept** such as is usually applicable under a pension plan, profit-sharing plans generally do not include provisions for actuarially equivalent annuities for employees who retire before the normal retirement date, as is common under pension plans. If the profit-sharing plan uses a group annuity contract, such a provision may be included, however, and reduced incomes beginning at earlier ages are available if individual policies are employed.

A profit-sharing plan geared to retirement should contain detailed provisions for retirement of employees after the normal retirement date and a provision preventing employees who continue to work after the normal retirement age from receiving an allocation from the subsequent annual profit-sharing contribution of the employer. As has been noted, **benefits** under a profit-sharing plan are not necessarily payable only on retirement but may be payable after a fixed number of years or the happening of some event, such as illness, disability, financial hardship, termination of employment, or death. The minimum number of years during which funds must be accumulated is two.

AGE PENSION BENEFITS. Retirement benefits payable for life, either through the purchase of annuities or a self-administered funded procedure, are sometimes absent under profit-sharing plans. Instead, provision is made for a **lump-sum distribution** to retiring employees or a **distribution in installments** over a specified period of years. The absence of provision for benefits payable for life may be caused by a desire to have the accumulation paid out in one sum so that it will constitute a **"capital gain"** subject to income tax at a reduced rate. Another reason may be the small amounts credited to individual employees who retire during the early years of the plan because it is usually impossible to allocate contributions on the basis of length of service, which would introduce discrimination in favor of the highly compensated older group. After a plan has operated successfully for a number of years, however, and amounts credited to participants have become substantial, it may be amended to provide for life benefits through the purchase of annuities or a self-administered fund. Because adequate account cannot usually be taken of past service under a profit-sharing plan, it cannot fulfill the functions of a pension plan for many years after it is established.

If a plan provides for the distribution of all or a substantial portion of the employee's share in the profit-sharing fund while he is in active service, under a provision that allocations will be held for, say, 10 years in the employee's account and then paid out to him over the ensuing 10 years, it is obvious that only relatively small sums will be left for retirement benefits.

If a profit-sharing plan is operated in conjunction with a pension plan, the Internal Revenue Service will not permit contributions made under profit-sharing to be used as a **"feeder"** to the pension plan, except that employee contributions to the pension plan may be paid from amounts allocated to their accounts under profit-sharing. Amounts so applied then constitute currently taxable income to employees.

Use of Single-Premium Annuities. If **retirement benefits** are a primary objective of profit-sharing, a part or all of the annual contributions may be made to purchase single-premium deferred annuities, using either individual or group annuity contracts. Although level annual premium annuity policies are sometimes used, this is seldom desirable because of the possibility of losses due to possible lapse of the policies if future profit-sharing distributions prove insufficient to pay premiums due. It is possible, however, to provide that if the amount in an employee's account is insufficient to pay an annual premium, he shall have the **option to contribute** a sufficient amount to make up the deficiency.

Use of Ordinary Life Insurance Policies. To avoid the inflexibility of level premium annuity contracts, the plan may provide for the purchase of level premium ordinary life insurance policies. A portion of each year's contribution is used to pay the **annual premium,** starting with ¼ or ⅓ of the first year's allocation, the remainder being held in the employee's individual account and invested in securities in the profit-sharing trust fund, which may be applied to meet premium payments in years when profits are low, to convert the life insurance policy to an annuity contract at retirement, or to purchase a supplemental annuity at retirement.

DISABILITY PENSION BENEFITS. Under the usual type of **self-administered profit-sharing plan,** with distributions on severance of employment, death, or retirement, benefits provided in the event of severance because of disability are usually the same as those for severance of employment or retirement, except that any provision for forfeiture on severance is not applicable. The disabled participant then receives his full share, either in a lump sum or in stipulated installments over a period of time. With a **group annuity contract,** the same provisions for actuarially reduced annuities on early retirement may apply as are found in group annuity pension plans. If **individual retirement income policies** are employed, the disabled employee is given the privilege of electing one of the options included in the policy, either a cash settlement, a reduced annuity, or continuance of premium payments for the life insurance protection offered by the policy. Because of the limitation on the tax deductibility of employer contributions and requirements as to allocation among participating employees, the problem of taking care of employees who become disabled in the early years of operation cannot be adequately solved under a profit-sharing plan, regardless of how allocations are applied.

SEVERANCE OF EMPLOYMENT BENEFITS. In contradistinction to pension plans, profit-sharing plans frequently provide **cash benefits** on termination of service. Amounts paid to employees in a lump sum in one year, representing allocations then credited under profit-sharing plans, are taxable to the employee at the favorable long-term capital gain rate.

It is advisable to provide that a **participant shall not have an absolute right** to receive his share in the fund upon severance of employment or termination of the plan, but rather that such right be subject to discretion of the trustee or committee as to the time of payment. If the participant is given the choice, he may be taxable on the basis of constructive receipt upon the entire amount ultimately distributable to him, whether or not actually paid in a lump sum.

Forfeiture of all or a portion of an employee's credit is common if his service terminates before completion of a specified number of years of service or participation in the plan. A **graduated scale** is often used to determine the amount to be paid or forfeited. For example, employees who leave the employ of the company may be entitled to 10% of their credit for each year of participation in the plan, up to 100% after 10 years. Although a forfeiture provision for employees who leave in the early years is justified because it permits the accumulation of larger benefits for those who stay, it is disadvantageous because it detracts from the employer's effort to secure increased employee cooperation in view of the possible forfeit of benefits.

DEATH BENEFITS. Although death benefits are not absolutely necessary under profit-sharing plans, they are logical if one objective of the plan is to stimulate employee cooperation and carry out the profit-sharing concept. Under the usual deferred-distribution profit-sharing plan with assets held in a trust fund, the accumulated share of an employee who dies is normally paid to a **beneficiary** designated by the employee. If no beneficiary has been designated, or if the beneficiary does not survive the employee, provision is usually made for payment to the **employee's estate,** although some plans, particularly those using group annuity financing, specify that in this event payment may be made to the employee's relatives in a listed order of preference. The employee has the right to change the beneficiary at any time.

Death Benefits Under Ordinary Life Insurance Policies. Under a plan using ordinary life policies, the administrative committee procures an individual or group permanent ordinary life insurance policy for each insurable employee in an amount that can be purchased with ¼ or ⅓ of the share of the profits allocated to the employee in the year the policy is purchased. As a protective measure, the annual life insurance premium is usually not greater than an amount equal to 5% of the employee's basic compensation, so that in no event will the annual cost exceed ⅓ of the 15% of compensation allowed as the maximum employer tax deductible contributions to the plan. With ordinary life insurance, **ownership of the policies is vested in the trustee,** except that participants may designate beneficiaries and modes of settlement. Upon the death of employees under a plan that provides death benefits through life insurance, beneficiaries designated by the employees and named in the policies receive the benefits directly from the insurance company in accordance with the terms of the policy

If this procedure is followed and life insurance benefits are paid for with a portion of the employee's accumulated share of the profits, the cost of the pure life insurance element and the loading charges of the policies will reduce amounts available for other contingencies such as severance, disability, or age retirement, leaving the **cash surrender value** of the policies available for these purposes.

Some ordinary life insurance policies may be **converted** into an annuity by application of amounts in the employee's individual account, as well as the cash value of the ordinary life insurance policy, to this purpose.

Death Benefits Under Group Annuity Contract. If group annuities carrying full death benefits are purchased with the employer contributions, they will be about 60% of those provided with employer contributions on a no-return-at-death basis under a pension plan. This reduction results not only from payments made to beneficiaries of those who die before retirement, but also from the purchase of **full cash refund annuities** instead of life annuities providing no return on death after retirement.

EMPLOYEE CONTRIBUTIONS. If employees are asked to contribute, there **must be an incentive** for them to do so in the form of a minimum annual employer payment. Otherwise, there will be little incentive for employees to contribute in years when there are no profits to be shared, and they may lose interest and withdraw from the plan. In an increasing number of plans, employees are asked to contribute under a **subsidized savings arrangement**, the company guaranteeing interest at a fairly high rate and offering the further inducement of participation in profits. A provision for **voluntary employee contributions** (permissible up to 10% of compensation according to Treasury ruling) may have an attraction to highly compensated employees, since the income and capital gains attributable to such contributions will accumulate tax-free and may eventually be received as part of a lump sum payment, taxable as a long-term capital gain.

INVESTMENTS OF PROFIT-SHARING FUND. If the objective of a deferred-distribution profit-sharing plan is to provide basic economic security against the hazards of old age, disability, unemployment, or death, it has sometimes been considered advisable to confine investments to securities legal for insurance companies or trust funds. Some employers, however, have felt that **investment in securities of the employer** may be desirable in profit-sharing plans (1) to secure a greater return on the fund, or (2) to promote the "partnership principle" through greater participation in the success of the business. Since 1950 there has been a marked increase in the use of the employer's common stock as an investment by qualified profit-sharing plans of large corporations listed on stock exchanges. Such plans usually involve employee contributions matched to a varying extent by employer contributions. Some permit additional voluntary contributions by employees. This practice has proved successful for enterprises that have been **consistently profitable.** But since this can only be determined "by hindsight," it may not be advisable to invest a profit-sharing fund in securities of a company having cyclical earnings unless a separate and adequate pension plan assures economic security. A drastic decline in the value of the employer's stock may prove unfortunate, especially if it should occur at a time when profits as well as employment opportunities are reduced. In this event, not only is there insecurity as to the employee's job, but the employee's future security is also placed in jeopardy. **Stock of closely held companies** may not be a suitable investment because of the Treasury's requirement of a fair rate of return and unrestricted transferability.

Full disclosure of investments that are made in employer securities must be made to the Commissioner of Internal Revenue to make certain that the plan continues to qualify under the Internal Revenue Code. Obviously, participating employees also should be informed concerning such investments. The purchase by the trust of bonds or other obligations of the employer may involve a **"prohibited transaction"** entailing the loss of the tax-exempt status of the trust. Such transactions include, in general, lending money to the employer without adequate security and without a reasonable rate of interest. Exceptions apply to unsecured debt acquired upon the open market or from an underwriter or the issuer itself at prices not less favorable than those paid by persons independent of the issuer.

If employee contributions are made under the plan, it is even more desirable that a **conservative investment policy** be followed, at least for amounts they contribute. The common practice is to use obligations of the United States government or life insurance or annuity policies.

Some plans give employees at least a partial voice in investment policy. Treasury rulings require that if any employees are given the right to have their interests in the profit-sharing trust invested in earmarked accounts, this right must be given to all the participants.

Advocates of self-administration contend that a profit-sharing plan, by its very nature, should be invested only in securities, and no commitment should be made for annual premium payments on insurance policies because of uncertainty as to profits.

Individual Policies. An advantage claimed for the use of individual policies in a profit-sharing plan is that **larger death benefits** may thereby be provided in the early years of the plan than would be available by merely paying the amount accumulated to the credit of employees who die. Because of the fluctuating nature of the contributions made under a profit-sharing plan, however, it is generally inadvisable to take out insurance policies for employees when the plan is first established, unless the business is quite stable and there is assurance of steady contributions in future years. It is possible that if insurance policies are taken out at the outset, the original participants may receive insurance protection whereas later participants may not because of a lack of profits after they become eligible.

Annual premium policies should not be used as the sole investment vehicle under a profit-sharing plan because of the fixed yearly premium required. They should be used only as a **partial investment** in conjunction with a fund invested in securities. The supplemental investment fund must ordinarily be quite substantial because, if little or no profit should be available for the purposes of the plan over a period of years, it would become necessary to borrow on policies to meet the premium cost, to reduce the amount of the policies, or to allow them to lapse. This is almost certain to occur if policies are issued for employees who enter the plan a year or two before curtailment or elimination of profit-sharing contributions. Combination procedures have been developed, such as investing ⅓ or ¼ of the first year's allocation for each employee in an annual premium ordinary life insurance or retirement income (with insurance) policy, the remainder being held in reserve as a cushion to pay premiums in subsequent years. Additional policies are then added from time to time when financially feasible.

Group Annuity Contract. A group annuity contract may be used as an investment vehicle for a profit-sharing plan. Each employee's share of the profits is used to purchase a typical **single-premium deferred annuity** under a master group annuity contract. From the viewpoint of the insurance company, it is advantageous to underwrite only plans of more **stable employers** if there is reasonable expectation of substantial and continuous profit-sharing contributions. One of the larger insurance companies requires that at least 100 employees be covered but may write a contract covering as few as 50 if the initial premium is substantial and the prospect for continued payments of premiums is favorable. Premiums are payable entirely by the employer up to a maximum of 20% of an individual's salary. A premium of at least $50 for each employee covered must be paid in a period of 3 years, a requirement that could not be met if there should be a prolonged period of low profits. Special approval of the insurance company is required if premiums in any one year exceed $500,000. Annuity premium rates are guaranteed only for the usual first 5 years of the contract.

TERMINATION OF PLAN. A profit-sharing plan usually reserves the right to the employer to terminate profit-sharing contributions, whereupon the fund continues to operate and distributions are made to employees until it is liquidated. Upon termination of a profit-sharing plan or discontinuance of contributions, the rights of all employee participants must become fully vested. Because of the **tax requirements** as to allocation of employer contributions among all participants, there is no problem of discrimination in favor of highly compensated employees, such as exists in the case of a pension plan. A termination of a profit-sharing plan or discontinuance of employer contributions without a business reason may cause the Internal Revenue Service to question whether the plan satisfied the requirements of the Code as to permanency of qualified employee plans.

ADMINISTRATIVE COMMITTEE. An administrative committee is needed to operate a profit-sharing plan. This committee, usually of 3 or 5 members, may be **appointed by the board of directors**, but employee participants are sometimes permitted to select one or more of the committee members. In some cases members are elected by each of several classes of employees, such as salaried employees and wage earners. The fact that a member of the committee is also an officer, director, or stockholder of the employer, or a participant, does not disqualify him from serving as a committee member, except for decisions affecting his own rights under the plan.

Members of the committee **usually act without compensation**, but are reimbursed for actual expenses. Reimbursement is usually from the trust fund, but in some cases it is made by the employer. The plan usually provides that no member of a committee is liable for any act or decision, except his own when performed in bad faith.

The **committee decides administrative questions** arising under the plan. It construes the plan for all parties. Action taken or instructions given by the committee must not discriminate in favor of officers, shareholders, or supervisory or highly compensated employees. Depending upon arrangements with the trustee, the committee may supervise the keeping of employee accounts, including the apportionment of employer contributions. The committee may also pass on benefit payments out of the fund by the trustee or make these payments itself. The committee maintains contact with employees, supplying information and assistance to participants, annuitants, and their beneficiaries.

If individual policies are used under the plan, the committee arranges for issuance of policies and their delivery to the trustee with instructions as to premium payments. If a group annuity contract is used, the committee has few functions, but it is usually necessary, especially if all amounts contributed under the plan are not applied to the purchase of benefits under the group annuity contract.

TRUSTEE. An **irrevocable trust** must be created for a deferred-distribution profit-sharing plan, and a trustee appointed to hold title to and invest the trust fund. A bank or trust company may be appointed trustee, or an individual or individuals may act in this capacity.

The **powers of a trustee** under a deferred-distribution profit-sharing plan are generally as broad as those granted trustees of pension plans. As under a self-administered pension plan and trust, the trustee is empowered to hold, invest, and reinvest the fund and income thereon, and to perform all duties incident to investment. Under some plans and trust instruments, the trustee keeps records of individual accounts and apportions profit-sharing contributions, fund earnings, and amounts released by forfeitures. The trustee is generally required to make periodic statements concerning the condition of the fund.

Compensation. The trustee is usually compensated for services, as set forth in a separate agreement, except if the trustee is an individual associated with the employer willing to act without pay. Expenses of the trustee are paid either from the fund or by the employer.

Tax Rulings. The trustee should keep itself protected from year to year by requesting rulings from the Commissioner of Internal Revenue as to the tax-exempt position of the trust. The regulations require an **annual information return,** but the trustee is not required to duplicate the information filed by the employer as to the plan.

Retirement Plans for Self-Employed Individuals

THE PROBLEM AND THE SOLUTIONS. The Internal Revenue Code, prior to its amendment in 1962, provided favorable tax treatment to pension and profit-sharing plans only for individuals who had the status of employees. An individual engaged in business as a sole proprietor or a partnership might have such plans for his or its employees but the employer or the members of the partnership could not be covered since they were not employees. Incorporation enabled the proprietors, as corporate employees, to receive pension and profit-sharing plan benefits as well as other tax-favored employee benefits. Many self-employed, however, namely **those engaged in professions,** such as lawyers, accountants, doctors, dentists, engineers, and architects, could not incorporate because of state law requirements that such professions be conducted in unincorporated form. This led to a large number of state statutes permitting some or all of the professions to be carried on by professional associations or corporations and these statutes opened the way for professional persons to become employees for tax purposes. Then, Congress passed H. R. 10, the **Self-Employed Individuals Tax Retirement Act of 1962,** which permits self-employed individuals to be treated as employees for pension and profit-sharing plan purposes, but only within rather narrow limitations and subject to various specific requirements.

DEFINITION OF SELF-EMPLOYED INDIVIDUALS. The term "owner-employee" in this law includes an owner of an unincorporated business or one who owns more than 10% of either the capital interest or the profits interest of a partnership. To be eligible, the person must perform personal services. A member of a partnership whose interest falls below 10% is treated as an employee rather than an owner-employee. The tax treatment of an owner-employee is less favorable than that of his employees in various respects.

REQUIRED COVERAGE OF PLANS. The requirements as to coverage of employees are more stringent than those applicable to other qualified plans. In the case of plans that cover owner-employees, **all employees must be included** if they have been employed for three years or more, excluding only part-time and seasonal employees. If a self-employed individual controls another unincorporated business (by means of more than 50% ownership of either the capital interest or the profits interest), the plan must also cover the employees of that business.

Vesting Requirements. The plan of a self-employed individual that covers his employees must provide for **immediate vesting** of all contributions made for the employees. In this respect, the law is also more stringent than that applicable to other qualified plans. This does not mean that if an employee's employment is terminated, he must receive his benefits immediately, but only that his benefits may not be forfeited. His share of the fund may be held until his retirement date.

PERMISSIBLE BENEFITS. A plan covering an owner-employee may be either a pension or profit-sharing plan. In the case of a profit-sharing plan, there must be a formula for determining the amount of the contributions to be made for employees other than owner-employees. This tax requirement, although formerly made, no longer exists as to other profit-sharing plans.

In respect of any owner-employees no benefits may be paid prior to age 59½, except in case of prior permanent disability or death. In addition, the plan must provide for the distribution of the entire interest of an owner-employee in the year in which he reaches an age of 70½, except that the plan may provide for payment beginning with such age over the joint life expectancy of the owner-employee and his wife. In the case of employees and self-employed individuals who are not owner-employees the year in which distributions must begin is that in which the individual reaches the age of 70½ or retires, whichever is later.

In the case of the **death of an owner-employee** before receiving distribution of his entire interest, the law requires either (1) distribution of his interest to his beneficiary within five years or within five years of the death of his wife, if that is later; or (2) the purchase of an annuity for his beneficiary within that period. If payments have begun at the time of his death, they may continue over the joint life expectancy of the owner-employee and his wife.

PERMISSIBLE INVESTMENTS. Funds of plans covering owner-employees may be invested only in the following ways:

1. By making contributions to a trust of which a bank or trust company is the trustee. The owner-employee or some other person may direct the investment of the trust fund.

2. By making contributions to a trust that uses annuity, endowment, or life insurance contracts of a life insurance company to fund the benefits under the trust, if the life insurance company supplies information annually to the Treasury Department about trust transactions affecting owner-employees. In case of such a trust, the trustee need not be a bank or trust company.

3. By investing contributions under a custodial arrangement with a bank, but only if the contributions are to be invested in "open-end" mutual funds or in annuity, endowment, or insurance contracts.

4. By purchasing nontransferable "face-amount certificates," issued by companies registered under the Investment Company Act of 1940. Under these certificates, the holder receives at maturity the face amount, in cash or in periodic installments.

5. By purchasing in the name of the employee a special series of United States government bonds that are not transferable and not redeemable until the holder attains the age of 59½ years, becomes disabled, or dies, whichever occurs first.

TAX STATUS. The chief tax advantage that an owner-employee may derive as a participant in a qualified plan is the fact that the earnings on his contributions accumulate **tax-free** until his retirement. Eventually, he will be subject to tax as ordinary income on the previously deductible portion of his contributions, plus any increment on his share of the trust subject to the limitation of the tax mentioned below to lump sum payments. Presumably, however, the plan benefits will be paid to him at a time when his other income has been reduced, so that the applicable tax rate on the distributions will be less than if the tax is paid currently. He can estimate the tax saving from making deductible contributions and having them increase tax-free at an assumed rate prior to retirement, as against paying a normal income tax on these contributions, accumulating the balance after taxes of the amounts that would have been contributed and receiving taxable income at the same assumed rate on the balance. **If he has employees,** he must take into account as part of the calculation the cost of making comparable contributions on their behalf. In addition, he must consider that the funds that go into the retirement plan are tied up and cannot be withdrawn for other purposes without incurring the penalties applicable to premature distributions.

Treatment of Lump Sum Payments. The treatment of lump sum payments to employees as long-term capital gains, subject to tax at a reduced rate, is denied to owner-employees themselves. Instead, in case of a lump sum distribution, the tax of an owner-employee is limited by an averaging device to **five times the increase in tax** that would result from including one-fifth of the taxable portion of the distribution in his gross income in the year of receipt. This provision does not apply to the special retirement plan government bonds previously mentioned; the beneficiary is taxable upon their redemption.

Treatment of Death Benefits. A death benefit paid under a plan that includes an owner-employee will generally be subject to tax to the beneficiary to the same extent as it would have been to the plan participant. In the case of an employee, a $5,000 **death benefit exclusion** is allowed to the beneficiary for income tax purposes; this exclusion is not allowed to the beneficiary of an owner-employee. The estate and gift tax exclusions applicable to benefits under qualified plans attributable to employer contributions also do not apply to owner-employees.

Limitations As to Contributions and Deductions. If the plan covers employees of an owner-employee, the contributions on their behalf must be made on the same basis as those made for the owner-employee. The maximum amount that may be contributed under a qualified plan for an owner-employee is limited to $2,500 or 10% of earned income, whichever is less. This limitation does not apply to other employees. Contributions for the self-employed are deductible only to the extent of one-half thereof, so that the maximum contribution for an owner-employee is $1,250.

No portion of any **contributions for life insurance protection or accident or health insurance,** whether or not incidental to the plan, may be deducted.

An **exception to the limitation** to 10% of earned income is that in which the owner-employee purchases an annuity, life insurance, or endowment contract providing for the payment of premiums of not more than 10% of his average income for the three years prior to the purchase of the contract. In this case, payment of the premium does not constitute an excess contribution when his earned income in subsequent years falls below this average amount. His deduction is, however, limited to 10% of earned income. In no case may the total annual premium on all such contracts exceed $2,500. Purchases of bonds under United States government bond purchase plans also are not subject to the rules as to excess contributions.

A plan that covers an owner-employee may also permit additional **voluntary contributions** by an owner-employee (as an employee) of another 10% of earned income or $2,500, whichever is less, if the plan also covers employees and they are given the same right; no deduction is, however, allowable as to such additional voluntary contributions.

Government and Union Pension Plans

FEDERAL GOVERNMENT PENSION PROGRAMS. Federal Civil Service System. A formal retirement program for Federal Civil Service employees was inaugurated in 1920 with contributions by the covered members of 3½% of their pay. Since then the members' contribution has been increased to 6½% with the Federal government making up the balance necessary to pay benefits related to highest five-year salary and length of service. As of mid-1963 the Federal Civil Service retirement program covered 2,400,000 actively contributing employee members plus over 150,000 inactive members (not yet eligible to draw benefits) plus 425,000 retirees and 175,000 surviving beneficiaries. Present member and Federal contributions have not been sufficient to avoid the accumulation of a **substantial deficit** ($20 billion) in the required reserves according to government actuaries.

Other Federal Programs. The retirement role of the Federal government was greatly expanded as a result of the economic depression of the 1930's and the ensuing unemployment. In 1935 the Social Security program—**Old Age and Survivors and Disability Insurance (O.A.S.D.I.)**—was enacted and has been greatly extended in scope since. At the present time O.A.S.D.I. has seventy-seven million members and fourteen million people are receiving some type of benefit, according to the Department of Health, Education and Welfare.

The Social Security program was immediately followed by special legislation on behalf of the depressed railroad industry in the form of the **Railroad Retirement Act of 1935.** Although these programs are also contributory, they are not fully funded but proceed on a partial pay-as-you-go basis backed by the substantial taxing power of the national government.

Military pensions have always been noncontributory on a pay-as-you-go basis, disbursed directly from general tax revenues by the Veterans Administration.

Asset Reserves of Federal Programs. As of 1963 asset reserves had been accumulated by the three major Federal retirement systems, as follows:

Federal O.A.S.D.I.	$18.3 billion
U. S. Civil Service Commission	12.6 billion
Railroad Retirement Administration	3.7 billion

These reserves are all invested in special issues of U. S. Treasury bonds.

STATE AND LOCAL PENSION PLANS. State and local pension systems, as reported by the U. S. Bureau of the Census, now cover over 5,367,000 employees plus 740,000 retirees or their beneficiaries. More than half the state and local employees are also covered by the **Federal social security (O.A.S.D.I.) program.** These systems, in contrast to collectively bargained industrial pension benefits, are created by complex statutes setting forth, in detail, administrative, benefit, and investment provisions. Being agencies of the government, they do not have to conform to the complex regulations (Section 401) of the Internal Revenue Service to secure tax-exemption.

The investment portfolio of state and local pension systems now aggregates $23.3 billion. New York City systems, covering employees, teachers, police, and firemen, have now accumulated assets exceeding $3.5 billion that are under the direct control and management of the City Comptroller.

Administration of State and Local Plans. In general, they are administered by a **board of trustees,** some appointed by the governor or mayor and others elected by employee groups and administered by an executive secretary and his staff. The board of trustees determine, within the ambit of the governing statute, administrative policy, whereas the detail work is carried out by the executive secretary and his staff. Sometimes the administration or investment of the pension assets is under the direct control of the chief fiscal officer of the state or municipality.

Although these pension funds are the fiduciary responsibility of the trustees or other statutorily designated officers, many trustees and officers seek **professional guidance** from the financial community in the form of advice from investment counselors, banks, trust companies, or others.

Municipal funds are **never trusteed with banks** in the sense that industrial plan pension assets may be and seldom are carried with insurance companies.

Contributions are usually joint with a recent tendency for the municipality to contribute a larger proportion to ease the immediate tax burden of the employee.

Investment Restrictions. Accumulated pension assets must be invested strictly in accordance with **statutory standards.** In times past these investment provisions have been quite restrictive and limited to the same type of securities as were deemed appropriate for the investment of surplus tax receipts or sinking funds. With their growing size an awareness arose that these pension funds, although a public trust carrying the highest degree of fiduciary obligation, did not have the same investment characteristics as short-term state or city treasury monies. Because of the long-term nature of these funds, investment yield, as well as safety, becomes a major concern. The **importance of earnings** on these accumulations is forcefully illustrated by the fact that an increase in the effective yield of pension assets of 1%, will, because of the working of compound interest, reduce pension costs by about 20%. Investment to secure high earnings, consistent with prudence, then becomes important.

Current Investment Practice. Many enabling acts have been amended during the past decade to provide more investment freedom, greater diversification, and higher yields. Many statutes now permit investment in corporate bonds and real estate mortgages with a lesser number authorizing investment in common stock. Overall changes in portfolio composition, however, take time to accomplish.

As reported by the U. S. Bureau of the Census, pension fund assets were invested as follows as of the close of 1962:

Assets	Amount (in millions)	Per cent
I. Government Securities		
Federal	$ 6,112	26.3%
Own government	2,503	10.8
Other state and local	1,545	6.7
II. Nongovernmental Securities		
Corporate bonds	9,523	41.0
Corporate stocks	694	3.0
Real estate and mortgages	2,053	8.3
Loans to members	8	.1
Miscellaneous	569	2.5
Cash and deposits	287	1.3
III. Total	$23,294	100.0%

GOVERNMENT AND UNION PENSION PLANS

This portfolio distribution is, of course, heavily weighted by past restrictive investment statutes and policies and does not give a correct picture of **present investment policies.** During 1962 state and municipal pension funds had a net increase in assets of $2.4 billion that was invested by the trustees as follows:

Assets	Amount (in millions)	Per Cent
I. Government Securities		
Federal	$ 122	5.0%
Own government	(184)	(7.6)
Other state and local	(171)	(7.1)
II. Nongovernmental Securities		
Corporate bonds	2,055	85.0
Corporate stocks	211	8.7
Real estate and mortgages	334	13.8
Miscellaneous	34	1.4
Cash and deposits (net changes)	18	.8
III. Total	$2,419	100.0%

UNION PLANS. True union pension funds are few in number and aggregate less than a billion dollars of assets in contrast to the $40 billion of corporate trusteed funds plus an additional $18 billion of assets in the form of reserves with insurance companies.

In general, **union funds are most conservatively managed** with a high concentration in Federal securities and Federal guaranteed or insured mortgages.

Many industrial funds have joint employer and employee boards of trustees and are governed by Section 302 of the Labor Management Act of 1947 (Taft-Hartley) and the Federal Welfare and Pension Plans Disclosure Act (see p. 34).

Union plans have the limitation that **contributions** by members are made after the payment of income taxes on wages received. Increased benefits must come directly from increased contributions by the union member. In contrast with industrial plans benefits can be bargained for and charged against the general corporate earning power.

SECTION 20

CORPORATE EXPANSION, COMBINATION AND COOPERATION

CONTENTS

Business Expansion

	PAGE
Pattern of expansion	1
Motives for expansion	1
Summary of key motives	1
Development of a sound expansion policy	2
Direction of expansion	2
Factors determining need of financing	3
Expansion and working capital needs	3
Internal expansion	3

Expansion by Combination

Definitions	4
Advantages of combinations	4
Increase of profits	5
Potential difficulties	5
Federal antitrust legislation	6
Planning for future combinations	6
Considerations in selecting the form of business combination	7
Ease of effecting the combination	7
Ease of financing	7
Degree of management control	7
Flexibility and permanence	7
Taxation	7
The trend of mergers	7

The Purchase of Assets

When purchase of assets is used	8
Tax advantages	9
Necessity for stockholder consent	9
Procedure	9
Preliminary negotiations	10
Tentative agreement of sale	10
Approval of directors	10
Approval of stockholders	10
Transfer of assets and consideration	11
Paying off dissenting stockholders	11
Dissolution of selling company	11
Position of purchasing company	11
Authorization of stock for expansion purposes	11
Position of selling company	12
Legal aspects	12
Stockholders' consent	12
Right of appraisal	13
Rights of creditors in sale of assets	13
Mortgage liens of the selling company	14
Obligations of seller	14
Subjects of sale	14
Provisions regarding consideration	15

	PAGE
Preferred stock of selling company	15
Advantages and disadvantages of purchase of assets	16
Advantages	16
Disadvantages	16

Consolidations and Mergers

Definition of consolidation	17
Charter rights of consolidated companies	17
Legal factors	17
Statutory and administrative provisions	17
State laws governing consolidations	18
Effect of consolidation	19
Procedure in effecting consolidation	19
Rights of dissenting stockholders	20
Rights of creditors in consolidations and mergers	20
Treatment of mortgage liens	21
Definition of merger	21
Power of corporations to merge	22
Merger procedure	22
Advantages and disadvantages of consolidations and mergers	22
Advantages	22
Disadvantages	22
Terms of consolidations and mergers	23

Financial and Accounting Factors in Combinations

Valuation problems	24
Accounting analysis	24
Engineering analysis	24
Economic analysis	24
Nonbalance sheet factors	24
Nature of consideration	24
Methods of valuation	25
Valuation based on capitalized earning power	25
Goodwill or going concern value	26
Market value	26
Investment value	26
Book value	26
Cost less depreciation	27
Reproduction cost	27
Substitution cost	27
Accounting problems in asset transfers	27
Valuation of plant and equipment	27
Effect of plant valuation on production costs	28
Valuation of intangible assets	28

CONTENTS (*Continued*)

	Page
Valuation of current assets	28
Effect of merger or consolidation on surplus	29
Distinction between purchase and pooling of interests	29
Financial steps in promoting a combination	29
Determining basis of share exchange	30
Relative earnings per share	30
Relative book value per share	30
Relative net working capital per share	30
Relative market value per share	30
Hidden assets	30
Strategic elements	31
Relative strength of management	31
Bargaining factors	31

Combination by Lease

Leases as a means of expansion	31
Lease agreements	31
Status of lessor corporation	32
Corporate existence and acts of lessor	32
Power of corporations to lease assets	32
Statutes governing lease of assets	33
Industrial leases	33
Railroad leases	33
Form of rental	34
Guaranty of rental	34
Difficulties in drafting equitable lease agreements	34
Mergers to end leases	34

Holding Companies

Use of holding company method of combination	34
Definition and types of holding companies	35
Holding company with one subsidiary	35
Holding-operating companies	35
Laws respecting formation of holding companies	35
Trusts as combination device	36
Control through voting trusts	36
Acquisition of stock control	36
Purchase for cash	36
Acquisition of control through exchange of stock	36
Dealings between parent and subsidiary	37
Financing subsidiary's capital requirements	37
Advantages and disadvantages of the holding company device	37

	Page
Advantages	37
Disadvantages	38
Maintaining corporate existence after transfer of assets	39
Creation of subsidiaries by parent company	39
Subsidiaries organized for legal reasons	39
Subsidiaries to facilitate management and operations	40
Subsidiaries to secure goodwill	40
Subsidiaries to limit parent company's liability	40
Intercorporate readjustments	40
Foreign subsidiaries	40
Abuse of parent-subsidiary relation	41
Protection afforded minority stockholders by courts	41
Instrumentality rule	41
The deep rock doctrine	42
Public utility holding companies	42
Unsound financial practices	43
Regulation of public utility holding companies	43
Registration of utility holding companies	43
Regulation of new security issues of utility holding companies	43
Acquisition of securities and properties	44
Simplification and integration of holding-company systems	44
Supervision of intercompany loans, dividends, security transactions, etc.	44
Periodic reports and accounts and records	45
Regulation of interstate electric utility companies under the Federal Power Act	45
Use of Massachusetts trust	45
Regulation of other holding companies	45

Other Types of Business Combination or Cooperation

Cartels	46
Types	46
Restrictions on use in the United States	46
Webb-Pomerene Act associations	46
Trade associations	46
Long-term sales contracts	47
Community of interest	47
Mutual stock ownership	47
Jointly owned subsidiaries and facilities	48
Voluntary chains	48

SECTION 20

CORPORATE EXPANSION, COMBINATION AND COOPERATION

Business Expansion

PATTERN OF EXPANSION. Business organization in the United States has been characterized by the development of large corporations that control a substantial proportion of business wealth. Large corporations and corporate groups have come into existence as a consequence of two basic patterns of expansion: (1) internal growth, and (2) combination. This section is concerned with a discussion of the various methods utilized in effecting business combinations.

MOTIVES FOR EXPANSION. Whether a business expands or not will depend on the **policies of its management** as well as the **opportunities** it may have for extending its operations. From deliberate choice the management may prefer to keep within its present scale of operations. Many small concerns have elected to remain small and are not interested in expansion or combination.

However, numerous business concerns have found it difficult to stand still and yet hold their own with competitors. They have been forced either to expand or to sell out to larger concerns. In order to secure a larger sales volume so as to improve utilization of plant facilities and reduce costs, **expansion of marketing territory** becomes necessary. Similarly, a business may find it necessary to integrate more fully its operations or **add to its line of products** so as to reduce unit costs to the level of competitors' costs. Rising costs tend to force expansion to secure the offsetting economies of large-scale operation. A high level of business activity places a premium on the enlargement of capacity. Personnel considerations may stimulate expansion, for a capable management of a smaller concern may want to improve opportunities of key employees to secure larger incomes through expansion of the business, and if such a policy is not adopted those individuals may leave for jobs in a larger and more aggressive business. Every business, to remain successful, may have to formulate an expansion policy and be ready to seize opportunities to grow when presented.

Management may make poor decisions in day-to-day operations, but **proper decisions** as to the wisdom of expanding may readily offset these mistakes. On the other hand, efficiency in routine operations cannot compensate for one erroneous major decision as to increasing the size of the business when economic conditions do not justify expansion, or the failure to expand when changing economic or competitive conditions make this necessary.

Summary of Key Motives. Some of the more important motives for expansion are:

1. To maintain the concern's relative position in an industry.
2. To reduce production costs through larger-scale operations.
3. To reduce costs of distribution.

20·2 CORPORATE EXPANSION, COMBINATION, AND COOPERATION

4. To take advantage of greater technical skill, research facilities, and better credit of larger companies.
5. To reduce or eliminate destructive competition and price-cutting.
6. To obtain tax savings through absorption of other companies.
7. To broaden markets or to stabilize the business by adding offsetting products.
8. To extend management, engineering, and financial advantages through diversification.
9. To facilitate a "sell-out" of close corporations through combination and public financing.
10. To enable embarrassed companies to carry on through combination with stronger and better managed companies.
11. To provide opportunities for public sales of securities.
12. To satisfy the desire of executives to expand.

In general, these motives reflect the desire to increase the profits of the business, or at least to conserve or stabilize profits. From an **economic viewpoint**, expansion can be on a sound basis only if the rate of return on the additional capital investment is at least equal to that obtainable from investment in comparable business enterprises.

DEVELOPMENT OF A SOUND EXPANSION POLICY. Whether expansion will be carried on by internal growth or combination will be determined largely by the financial position of the company, transportation costs, the most economic size of producing unit, location of markets, the extent to which the territory is already well served by existing units, and opportunities for acquisition of desired facilities. To some degree the **pattern** that business expansion takes may be simply a matter of accident or sudden opportunity rather than the result of carefully balanced judgment. Regardless of the pattern, every well-managed corporation must develop a sound expansion policy. Such a policy should embrace the following objectives:

1. Improve existing products.
2. Improve and expand distribution facilities.
3. Increase service to consumers.
4. Widen uses for products.
5. Develop new products.
6. Conduct research on possible future demands.
7. Discover and study combination opportunities.
8. Conduct research and make evaluations of new inventions, processes, etc.
9. Promote development of new markets.
10. Effect a full utilization of manufacturing capacity.

Direction of Expansion. Irrespective of whether expansion is primarily "external" or "internal," there are five main approaches to expansion: (1) horizontal, (2) vertical, (3) circular, (4) research, and (5) diversification.

Horizontal expansion takes place at the same stage of the economic process. Thus, a combination of manufacturers of the same line of products, or of jobbers, constitutes horizontal expansion.

Vertical expansion involves integration of two or more successive stages in the economic process from raw material production to sale of the finished product. The United States Steel Corp. is an example of vertical expansion. Through its subsidiaries, it is engaged in mining, processing, transportation, manufacturing, and distribution.

Circular expansion involves the addition of units that produce different products that can be distributed through the same channels. An outstanding example is General Foods, which combines manufacturers of various products sold through grocers.

A leading example of expansion built around **research** is E. I. du Pont de Nemours & Co., Inc., which expands in almost any direction its research laboratories' findings point to.

Corporations that expand through **diversification,** such as Textron or General Dynamics, act on the principle that even totally unrelated businesses may be operated more successfully through centralized management and control.

FACTORS DETERMINING NEED OF FINANCING. The need of financing in expansion depends upon the amount of cash derived from depreciation, retained earnings, and surplus working capital in relation to the new capital required. If **public financing** is practical, or combinations can be effected by **exchange of stock,** there is added incentive to expand aggressively as opportunity offers.

In the railroad, public utility, and other heavy industries, if a heavy plant investment is required and the rate of earnings on capital investment is relatively low, expansion almost always results in financing. In the manufacture of aluminum a large supply of cheap electrical power is needed, so that a heavy investment in hydroelectric properties has been necessary.

EXPANSION AND WORKING CAPITAL NEEDS. If expansion is the result of **growing demand for a company's products,** working capital needs usually expand at the same or a declining ratio to sales. Distributing facilities and warehouse inventories may be used to handle a larger volume up to a point. Horizontal expansion through combining with other companies operating in the same field and in overlapping territories may result in a decline in working capital needs in relation to sales. On the other hand, in vertical integration working capital requirements expand at an increasing ratio to sales. This is most clearly demonstrated when a distributing company takes over a manufacturing concern supplying it with goods, or when a plant is built to supply goods formerly bought in the open market. Under such conditions, sales may not expand at all, although working capital may have to be increased not only to provide inventories of raw material and goods in process, but also to provide a reserve against the risk of loss through the necessity of carrying these larger inventories over a longer period of time. **Risks** are substantial in industries if raw material cost is large in proportion to total costs and if prices of materials are subject to wide changes, as in cotton goods manufacture, sugar refining, and meat packing.

INTERNAL EXPANSION. The more important **advantages** of expanding internally rather than by acquisition of other enterprises are that it tends to:

1. Avoid liability to minority stockholders or creditors of acquired companies.
2. Avoid need for obtaining stockholders' consent to combinations.
3. Avoid valuation problems.
4. Avoid alterations to make new facilities suitable.
5. Embody latest advances in newly built facilities.
6. Forestall construction of like plant by competitor.
7. Take advantage of low-cost sources of raw material, power, and labor supply.
8. Entrench the company as a low-cost producer in its industry.

On the other hand, there may be certain **disadvantages.** If new plant construction is not paid for out of internally generated working capital, new financing will be necessary. Moreover, construction is a comparatively prolonged process, and meanwhile there is not only a loss of return on capital tied up but also the possibility of rival concerns obtaining certain competitive advantages. Furthermore, time and money are required to place a new plant in operation.

20·4 CORPORATE EXPANSION, COMBINATION, AND COOPERATION

Personnel must be engaged and trained, and other expenses incurred before actual commencement of operations. If a new line of business is being entered, advertising and other expenditures must be made to develop the market and establish goodwill in the trade. Lastly, additional working capital must be obtained to support additional inventories and receivables.

Expansion by Combination

DEFINITIONS. Expansion by combination takes a variety of forms. Instead of constructing a new plant, a concern may acquire one by purchase or merger. It may lease quarters, thus dispensing with the necessity of building for itself.

The generic term "combination" covers all the methods whereby two or more existing businesses may gain some of the advantages of **joint ownership** through various forms of intercorporate relations.

The **chief types** of intercorporate relations, each of which is discussed elsewhere in this section, are:

1. **Purchase** of all or part of the assets of another concern.
2. **Consolidation,** or the fusion of two or more existing corporations into a newly organized corporation.
3. **Merger,** or the absorption of one or more existing businesses by an existing corporation.
4. The **lease** of the assets and business of another concern.
5. **Holding company,** or the purchase by one corporation of a controlling stock interest in one or more other corporations.
6. **Community of interest,** or the joint control of separate corporations by means of common ownership of stock by a small number of persons. Similarly, two or more corporations may own one another's stock, and the resulting harmony of interest may be made even more effective by interlocking directorates.
7. **Cartels,** consisting of contractual agreements among concerns in the same field of business to divide the market and limit competition among themselves. These are generally illegal except in the export field.
8. **Trade associations,** in so far as they cooperate to study accounting problems, labor relations, government relations, price policies, and other matters of common interest.
9. **Voluntary chains,** consisting of a large number of retail units that contract with a central organization to provide the benefits of pooled purchasing and unified management.
10. **Use of jointly owned facilities** or jointly owned subsidiaries by two or more concerns.
11. **Long-term contracts** whereby one concern buys all or most of the output of another.

It should be observed that types 6 through 11 above are types of intercorporate relations that involve **no formal combination** of the enterprises involved. But they have been utilized for many of the same reasons that combinations have been employed. Moreover, they may be forerunners of combination at a later date.

ADVANTAGES OF COMBINATIONS. Expansion by combination has certain advantages as well as disadvantages, compared with internal expansion. Combination requires no cash if it can be effected through exchange of securities. No time is lost in having additional plant capacity in operation. There is less risk because past operating results are known. If an entire business is acquired, the buying corporation comes into possession of goodwill also. Combinations do not increase the productive capacity of an industry, and therefore do not lead to excessive capacity and disturbed markets. Moreover, combinations offer an opportunity of acquiring valuable managerial skill, new customers, new processes, and additional working capital, as well as additional plant facilities.

In recent years, new factors have stimulated business combinations. The desire to achieve **capital gains** and other tax advantages through the purchase and sale of whole businesses is one of these.

Increase of Profits. The **ultimate economic motive** for business combination is to increase or stabilize profits. This may be achieved by:

1. An increase in sales volume.
2. Higher or more stable prices.
3. A reduction in expenses.

Economies sought by combination include the following:

Buying
Assured and steady supply of materials.
Unification of buying departments and staffs.
Bulk purchases.
Greater opportunity for comparison and selection.
Cheaper credit and better discounts.
Standardization of materials.

Manufacture
Standardization and improvement of product.
Specialization of plants and labor.
Improvements in plant.
Use of by-products.
Equalized distribution of work.

Selling and Distribution
Transportation economies.
Unification of selling departments and staffs.
Extension of export trade.
Collective advertising and promotion.
Lower costs of distribution through direct selling.

Research
Interchange of data and experience.
Standardization and interchange of costings.
Collection and dissemination of trade statistics.
Promotion of scientific and technical research.
Tax research and study.

General
Lower management costs.
Lower financing costs.
Better labor relations with qualified personnel men.
Possible tax savings through deductible loss carryovers.

Potential Difficulties. Economies are not always realized from combinations as expected. Even when realized, a considerable expenditure of additional funds may be required. Plants may have to be altered at considerable expense before **full coordination of operations** is achieved. It is not always possible to reduce the personnel immediately. If the sales force is reduced, a loss of business may result. In any event it can hardly be expected that the entire trade of the acquired business can be retained, except when the acquisition is consummated in such a manner that the public does not become aware of the change.

Unless the businesses combined naturally complement each other, the time and money expended in coordination and physical consolidation of production and marketing facilities may result in a permanent increase in the unit cost of production. Another factor of potential weakness is that many business combinations are put together at the top of the business cycle when earnings are high and values inflated with the consequence that the combination may result in an overcapitalized and weak financial strucure. Finally, properties may be added too quickly to allow for proper coordination and control. Hence, it is easy to understand why expected savings or higher earnings may not materialize.

FEDERAL ANTITRUST LEGISLATION. Aside from state laws and possible opposition from dissenting stockholders, the principal **legal obstacles** that may be involved in business combinations are the Federal antitrust laws, notably the Sherman Act and the Clayton Act. The former, enacted in 1890, declared illegal monopolies and combinations in restraint of trade. The Clayton Act, as originally passed in 1914, prohibited, among other things, the acquisition by one corporation of the stock of another where the effect "may be substantially to lessen competition." The law was broadened by an amendment in 1950 that also included acquisition of **assets,** as distinguished from **stock,** among the prohibited actions. Most of the antitrust cases in recent years arising out of business combinations have been instituted under the Clayton Act, either by the Department of Justice or the Federal Trade Commission.

Since the 1950 amendment, enforcement of the law has been considerably intensified and broadened (see Arthur H. Dean, Some Significant Aspects of the Law Concerning Mergers, in American Management Association, Corporate Mergers and Acquisitions). Moreover, uncertainty as to the attitude that may be taken by the Department of Justice, the F.T.C. and the courts and the fear of being involved in protracted antitrust proceedings have at times **tended to deter mergers.**

PLANNING FOR FUTURE COMBINATIONS. If a corporation is contemplating expansion through combination, the following **preparatory measures** are desirable:

1. The management should assure its **control,** for opposition may develop that could use the combination proposal as a reason for changing the management. Also, the management will want to protect its control from undue dilution as a result of the exchanges of securities in the combination.

2. The stronger its **current financial position,** the better the bargaining position of a corporation negotiating a combination. Cash may be required in substantial amounts to pay off dissenters. Dependence on borrowing to provide the cash needs of the combination may prove a boomerang should the enlarged concern enter a period of declining sales and earnings that would give rise to difficulty in meeting interest and principal on the indebtedness.

3. The **investment status of the common stock** should be built up, as this will inevitably assure a superior bargaining position in formulating the terms of exchange of shares.

4. An **investment banking connection** is helpful in assuring strong financial sponsorship of the combination and any underwriting that may be required.

5. A **strong competitive position** in the industry gives a company a better bargaining position in the negotiation. If a company has established an outstanding name for itself in the eyes of the public, its customers, and the trade, the goodwill element should weigh heavily in its favor in the terms reached for the exchange of securities.

6. If possible, a combination should be put through in the earlier part of an **upswing of the business cycle,** so as to get the benefits of improving business

conditions. However, many combinations are put through near the top of the cycle, so that often the result is overcapitalization. Adequate preparations for a combination program will enable management to time its actions properly.

CONSIDERATIONS IN SELECTING THE FORM OF BUSINESS COMBINATION. In choosing among the various methods of combination, management should weigh certain factors with relation to the goals. Primary considerations in the selection of the form of business combination are:

Ease of Effecting the Combination. Certain types of business combinations are easier to effect than others. Thus, in many states it is easier to effect the combination through purchase of assets than by means of merger. For example, the Delaware law specifies that a majority vote of the stockholders of the selling corporation is all that is necessary to effect such a combination, whereas if the merger or consolidation device is used a two-thirds vote of the stockholders of each of the constituent corporations is required. Similarly, the extent to which dissenters may cause trouble will influence the type of combination selected.

Ease of Financing. The **size of the capital outlay** necessary to effect combination by means of the various methods will often greatly influence the particular method chosen. Thus, at times the holding company device may be most feasible because of the possibility of buying a controlling stock interest mainly with the proceeds of a loan secured by the stock.

Degree of Management Control. In selecting a particular type of business combination, corporate management must necessarily consider the extent to which it will retain control over the expanding enterprise. For example, if the properties are to be operated by means of a partly owned holding company, the **control may be lost** in the future. The issuance of additional stock to effect mergers or purchases of assets of other enterprises may dilute stockholdings of management, and so shift control to others.

Flexibility and Permanence. These factors are most important both at the time of expansion and at a later date when adjustments and changes may be desirable. Obviously the merger and consolidation are the least flexible and the most permanent, since the absorbed corporations go out of existence. Purchase of assets may involve only part of the assets of the selling corporation, or, if the entire assets are involved, the purchase terms may not involve an assumption of the selling corporation's liabilities. Similarly, if expansion is effected through the holding company device, **separation of the controlled properties** may be effected in the future through sale of the stock of the subsidiary.

Taxation. Consideration must be given to the tax burden that the particular combination imposes on each of the corporations and on their security holders. Thus, the tax on intercorporate dividends and the stringent requirements for filing consolidated tax returns have encouraged the use of **mergers and consolidations in preference to the holding company device.** A sale of assets may involve a heavy capital gains tax. The Revenue Act distinguishes between taxable and tax-free exchanges.

THE TREND OF MERGERS. As McCarthy (Acquisitions and Mergers) points out, the period since World War II has marked the third of the major waves of industrial combinations in the U.S. The first took place around the turn of the century and the second from 1925 to 1931. Each of the intervening periods, however, witnessed a large number of mergers. As a general rule, corporate combinations tend to increase in number and magnitude along with rises in general business activity and stock prices.

According to Federal Trade Commission data, the number of mergers and acquisitions totaled 5,625 in the 11½ years from 1951 to mid-1962, or an average of 489 a year. Whereas earlier mergers were largely of the horizontal type, later periods saw **increasing emphasis on vertical combinations** leading to the creation of numerous integrated companies embracing raw materials production, manufacturing, and distribution. Since the 1950's there has also been a sharp **increase in diversified systems** and of acquisitions made for the purpose of offsetting tax-loss carryovers against large taxable profits.

The Purchase of Assets

WHEN PURCHASE OF ASSETS IS USED. The purchase of assets is a legal device frequently employed to effect a **combination of two or more concerns.** Thus, if companies A and B desire to combine, the directors negotiate a sales contract whereby B, with the consent of its stockholders, agrees to transfer to A all or a substantial part of its assets for a consideration consisting of stock or other securities, and less often of cash. Company A may assume the debts of company B or a certain stipulated portion of them. The **transfer of title** is effected by ordinary instruments of conveyance. Company B, upon receiving A's stock, most frequently distributes these shares to its shareholders and dissolves if the sale involves all of its assets, although it may continue purely as a holding company owning securities in A.

The purchase of assets device has been used under various conditions. An existing company may simultaneously purchase assets of two or more other going concerns. A new company may be organized by promoters to purchase the assets and business of several existing concerns.

A sale of assets may be used also in **breaking up an enterprise** into several parts to segregate risks or for other reasons. A corporation engaged in several lines of business may decide to organize a separate company for each line and sell to it the property and business belonging to that line. Receiving the stocks of the newly formed companies, it may distribute these holdings among its stockholders and dissolve, or it may continue as a holding company.

Failing companies are sometimes taken over through purchase of their assets by more successful concerns to extricate them from their difficulties. A sale of assets is also used as a device in effecting **voluntary reorganizations.** A new corporation is formed that purchases the assets and business of the old. Transfer of assets by sale is also often resorted to in internal corporate readjustments, as between parent and subsidiary companies or between subsidiaries.

A business may purchase the tangible assets of another, such as plants, equipment, and inventories, leaving out other assets not wanted or whose valuation cannot be agreed upon, as well as the goodwill.

In the purchase of **branch plants** of other companies, without acquisition of their business as a whole, contracts of the vendor corporation with respect to the operation of the plant must be examined carefully. As an inducement to bring new plants into a city, power companies often give very favorable rates under contracts that may not be extended on the same basis to a subsequent purchaser of these plants. The same may be true of favorable agreements sometimes executed with city officials on tax assessments, water rates, etc., when a new plant was built.

Tax Advantages. Frequently, the tax advantages may be the principal factor in the choice of purchase of assets as the form used to effect combination. For example, if a **closely held corporation** sold out its net assets at a profit, the maximum tax rate on this capital gain would be 25%, in contrast to the 48% rate on corporation income (as of January 1, 1965) and rates ranging up to 70% on dividend income. If payment for the net assets or the stock were received in the form of an equivalent amount of stock of the acquiring company, the selling stockholders would not realize any taxable gain or loss when the transaction took place.

There might also be important tax advantages for the acquiring company. If the purchaser bought the net assets of a company or bought its capital stock with the intention of liquidating the acquired company within two years, it would be entitled to **increase the original tax basis** of the seller to the fair market value of the assets acquired. Consequently, if the former tax basis for the tangible assets were considerably below the current market value, it might be possible to recover a substantial part of the purchase price through subsequent tax savings as the inventories were disposed of and fixed assets depreciated. (McCarthy, Acquisitions and Mergers.)

The **1954 Internal Revenue Code** clarified and in some ways broadened the tax advantages that may be derived through purchase of assets and mergers. For example, it provided that **some cash may be used** in an acquisition of assets mainly in exchange for voting stock without sacrificing the tax-free exchange provisions. The revised Code also permitted the distribution to shareholders, under a one-year plan of liquidation, of the proceeds of a sale of assets without subjecting the corporation to tax on any gains realized. The tax status of acquisitions and mergers is a highly complicated subject requiring expert advice.

Necessity for Stockholder Consent. Whether or not **consent of the vendor company's stockholders** is required hinges on the importance of the property being sold, except if statutory or charter provisions specifically call for such approval by a vote of stockholders. (Also, see below, "Approval of Stockholders" and "Stockholders' Consent.") If the property sold is an integral part of the vendor's business and the character of the business will be substantially changed through the sale, then consent of the stockholders is needed. In some instances it is only when the **goodwill** is sold along with the tangible property that the consent of the stockholders of the selling corporation is required. A selling corporation's business may be of such a nature that its profits are made by the sale of its tangible assets in one transaction. In such an event, the company continues in business with the proceeds of the sale and prepares for another such transaction. Real estate development companies are an example of such a business. Stockholders' consent to sales in such instances is not required.

PROCEDURE. The initiative in the purchase of the assets and business of another concern is generally taken by the management of the expanding company. However, the original idea of the purchase may be conceived by other persons such as promoters, bankers, or large stockholders.

If it is thought that the management of the concern to be bought is likely to be hostile to the transaction, it may be advisable to carry on preliminary negotiations with large stockholders with a view to obtaining their cooperation or of purchasing their stock to obtain working control before purchase negotiations are begun. An **option** may be sought on the assets, pending further investigation and negotiations. In some instances, purchase in the open market of the stock of the company to be taken over may be the first step in the absorption of another concern by purchase of assets. However, it may be difficult to accumulate large amounts of stock in the open market without forcing the price up to a point where the purchase price of the assets will be raised. It is highly desirable to obtain the cooperation of the directors of the concern to be absorbed at the outset, for in so doing the danger of trouble later on with a large group of dissenting minority stockholders is usually lessened.

Ordinarily, the steps taken to effect a combination by the purchase of the property, goodwill, and business of one corporation by another are as follows:

Preliminary Negotiations. Negotiations are usually initiated at the instance of the boards of directors between representatives of the two companies, who may be members of the boards, officers, or lawyers. Other persons may participate in the negotiations including promoters, bankers, and disinterested intermediaries who may be called in to arbitrate disputed points.

It may be agreed at the very outset that pending negotiations and the consummation of the sale, neither company will declare dividends at a rate greater than usual and that neither will issue stock rights during the period, since the terms of sale may have to be changed if this is done.

Tentative Agreement of Sale. If the negotiations are successful, a plan and agreement of sale setting forth terms and conditions is drawn. This agreement requires approval by the board of directors, stockholders, and state or Federal regulatory commissions that may have jurisdiction.

Approval of Directors. The plan and agreement of sale is submitted to the respective boards of directors for their approval, or for such changes as they may see fit to propose. In the latter event, the agreement is returned for further negotiations between the representatives of the corporations concerned.

Approval of Stockholders. Following approval by the board of directors, the board of the selling company recommends the plan to its voting stockholders as required by the statute or its certificate of incorporation. A special meeting of stockholders is called, and a committee of directors may be appointed to solicit proxies. Notice of the meeting sent to the stockholders will be accompanied by a statement from the president of the corporation explaining the terms and advantages of the proposed sale and urging favorable action. If permitted by the statute, instead of calling a meeting of the stockholders the board may seek their **written consent.** Forms will be prepared in that event and mailed to the stockholders who, by signing and returning the forms, give approval to the sale; or consent may be secured by means of a **deposit agreement** under which assenting shares are deposited with a trust company.

Transfer of Assets and Consideration. When approval of the desired proportion of stockholders has been obtained, a bill of sale, deed of transfer, or other instruments of conveyance are prepared by the attorneys, as in ordinary sales of personal or real property. The business, assets, and goodwill of the company, as specified in the agreement, are thereby formally transferred to the purchasing company, which undertakes to pay the stipulated consideration, including the assumption of all or some of the selling company's **liabilities.** Instead of the property being conveyed to the purchasing company, the contract of sale may provide that it be turned over to its nominees or subsidiaries. At the time of the execution of the bill of sale, certain of the purchased assets may be resold immediately to other parties.

The consideration received by the selling company, including securities, may be distributed among its stockholders according to a plan that may be voted upon at the meeting that sanctioned the sale of assets.

Paying Off Dissenting Stockholders. One of the last steps in the proceeding is paying off dissenting stockholders in accordance with the procedure laid down by the statute. Although the law or charter prescribes the minimum majority of stockholders whose assent is necessary for a sale of assets, efforts should be made to secure **as many assents as possible** to keep the dissenting minority, whose holdings must be appraised and paid off in cash, to small proportions. (See also, "Right of Appraisal," below.) Otherwise, a considerable sum of money may have to be paid out, which may necessitate **new financing** to effect the combination. One advantage of the purchase of assets with stock or other securities is that new financing is thereby avoided. This advantage is lost to the extent that cash settlements must be made with objecting minority stockholders.

Dissolution of Selling Company. If the selling company has sold all its assets, it may be desired to dissolve the corporation upon consummation of the transaction. The directors will then order the appropriate legal steps to terminate the life of the corporation. Dissolution need not necessarily follow, however. In some instances the selling corporation remains in existence to hold the securities received for its assets, to go into some other business, or to settle tax or other liabilities. Thus, the Adams Express Co. sold its properties in 1918 to the American Railway Express Co. for stock of the latter company. This stock was gradually sold and the proceeds reinvested, and Adams Express Co. became an investment trust.

Under the New York Business Corporation Law (§ 909 b):

. . . whenever a transaction involves a sale, lease, exchange or other disposition of all or substantially all the assets of the corporation, including its name, to a new corporation formed under the **same name as the existing corporation,** upon the expiration of thirty days from the filing of the certificate of incorporation of the new corporation, with the consent of the state tax commission attached, the existing corporation shall be dissolved, unless, before the end of such thirty-day period, such corporation has changed its name.

POSITION OF PURCHASING COMPANY. So far as the purchasing company is concerned, the transaction is **no different from ordinary purchases of large amounts.** Action by the board of directors is all that is required, unless charter or statutory provisions require assent of stockholders. Usually there are no such provisions, and the only restraint exercised by the stockholders of the purchasing company is in authorizing additional stock if used as consideration in the purchase. Such authorization may be required for this purpose. On the other hand, if a considerable amount of stock is already authorized, to be issued at the discretion of the directors, the latter can proceed unhampered with the purchase of the assets of other concerns. The fact that consent of the purchasing company's stockholders is not generally required is one advantage of this method of combination over consolidation or merger.

Authorization of Stock for Expansion Purposes. A concern that has adopted a policy of expansion by acquisition of assets of other concerns will usually place at the disposal of the directors ample amounts of authorized but unissued stock for their use in taking immediate advantage of opportunities to acquire desirable properties. Otherwise, the directors have to apply to the stockholders for authorization of an increase in capital stock as a necessary preliminary to the consummation of a purchase of assets of another concern. By granting such authorization only as negotiations for new acquisitions are entered into, stockholders of the purchasing company can exercise **full control over the activities of the directors** in this respect, even though directors of purchasing companies are not by law required to obtain specific permission of stockholders before entering into contracts for the purchase of other businesses.

POSITION OF SELLING COMPANY. The selling corporation must be solvent and in full control of its assets. A sale of its business when **knowingly insolvent** would constitute a fraud upon its creditors. Assets of an insolvent company, whether or not under control of trustees in liquidation or bankruptcy, are in the nature of a trust fund held for the benefit of creditors. If management has custody of the assets, it must act for creditors rather than stockholders, and under such conditions it cannot dispose of the business. However, assets of a bankrupt enterprise may be sold by a trustee in bankruptcy, with court approval, or as part of a plan of reorganization.

LEGAL ASPECTS. In all of these proceedings, the requirements of the law and the charter provisions must be scrupulously observed. Any failure in this respect affords dissenting stockholders of the selling company an opportunity to appeal to a court to enjoin the entire transaction. Provided the legal formalities are observed and the transaction is carried out in fairness to the minority stockholders, the latter have no grounds for attacking the sale and are obliged to accept the appraised value of their shares as prescribed by the statute.

There are usually no statutory or charter limitations on the power to transfer business assets, except the requirement of **stockholders' consent** (see below). Under common law, a corporation has the power to dispose of its business as an entirety with the unanimous consent of stockholders. However, if a clause is inserted in the charter forbidding sale of the business, such a provision is controlling inasmuch as it is a part of the contract that the stockholders have entered into with each other and with the state.

General statutory provisions relating to sale of assets do not apply to **railroads or public utilities.** Such enterprises are usually required to secure approval of regulatory agencies before they can sell part or all of their assets, particularly their franchises.

In a sale of assets, as well as in a merger or consolidation, care must be taken to observe the registration and filing provisions of the **Securities Act of 1933** applying to newly issued securities and those of the **Securities Exchange Act of 1934** applying to listed securities. The necessary information must also be supplied to the stock exchanges **for listed securities.**

Stockholders' Consent. Statutes generally permit the sale of assets if a specified majority of the stockholders consent or vote in the affirmative at a meeting duly called to consider the proposed sale. (See also, above, "Necessity for Stockholders' Consent" and "Approval of Stockholders.")

A sale of the assets and business of a corporation is an extraordinary corporate transaction that is not contemplated by the charter, unless there is a special provision to that effect. Under the laws of the forty states permitting the sale of all the assets of a business, the approval required ranges from a majority to four-fifths of the stockholders. A two-thirds vote is stipulated in the statutes of New York, New Jersey, Maryland, and Ohio. In some states, a distinction is made between a sale for cash and a sale for other consideration. When **cash** is the consideration, the statute may require approval of only a bare majority of the stockholders, whereas when the consideration is **stock** or other securities, a two-thirds vote may be required. In a number of states, if a corporation cannot meet its matured liabilities the directors may authorize a sale of assets by majority or a two-thirds vote.

Right of Appraisal. The laws of most states provide for the appraisal and purchase for cash of **dissenting stockholders'** shares. From the standpoint of nonassenting stockholders, the transfer of all the corporate assets is treated as a practical dissolution. Stockholders who do not wish to assume new risks are thus allowed by the statute to insist on receiving the fair cash value of their holdings. Apart from the protective provisions of the statutes, courts of equity afford dissenting stockholders protection against fraud or oppression.

A stockholder who votes against the sale of assets has a stated period of time, usually at least 20 days, within which to make demand upon the corporation for payment for his stock at its **fair value** as of the date of dissent. Unless the demand is made within the specified period, the stockholder must accept the amount tendered by the corporation, which must, however, be reasonable. If the dissenting stockholder and the corporation fail to agree upon a fair value for the stock, provision is made for the appointment of **disinterested appraisers,** usually three, who appraise the value of the stock without regard to any appreciation or depreciation in value that may result from the sale of assets. The appraisers may be appointed by a court, or one may be appointed by the dissenting stockholders, another by the corporation, and the third by the two already selected. The award of the appraisers may be **final and conclusive** or it may have to be **confirmed by the court** that appointed the appraisers. As finally settled, the award becomes the liability of the corporation and is collectible like any other debt.

From the time of the stockholder's dissent from the action of the majority in the sale of assets, his **status as a stockholder virtually ceases.** Not only does he lose his voting power, but he is no longer entitled to dividends. Although this is the common law, it is expressly provided for in some statutes. A stockholder may withdraw his dissent only with the consent of the corporation. His right to cash payment ceases if the corporation abandons its plan to sell its assets.

The New York Business Corporation Law (§ 910 a) does not make available to a stockholder "the right to receive payment of the fair value of his shares" in a sale of assets wholly for cash and "where the shareholders' authorization thereof is conditioned upon the distribution of all of the net proceeds of such transaction to the shareholders in accordance with their respective interests within one year after the date of such transaction and upon the dissolution of the corporation."

RIGHTS OF CREDITORS IN SALE OF ASSETS. Creditors of a corporation selling its assets as an entirety have no power to object to the sale, unless it defrauds them. They have extended credit to the corporation with full knowledge of its power to dispose of its property. If the corporation exercises that power, creditors can object only if they are deprived of their rights.

The question of creditor rights arises only when assets are sold for securities of the purchasing company, and not when sold for fair cash value. It is usually held that transfer of corporate property for shares of another corporation makes the purchasing corporation liable for the debts of the seller to the extent of the value of property received from the seller. Creditors of the seller **can follow assets** when transferred to the purchasing corporation and satisfy their claims from them by judicial process. They are not required to look alone to the securities received as consideration in the sale of the assets. However, when the vendor corporation receives money sufficient to pay its debts, or property that can be used for this purpose, the purchasing corporation will not, in the absence of a specific contract or fraud of a substantial character, be held liable for debts of the selling corporation.

In a sale of assets full provision is ordinarily made in the agreement for the selling company's indebtedness. This usually involves the **assumption by the purchasing company of all debts** and obligations, the stock or money consideration being paid for the net assets after deducting such debt. Creditors of the selling company thus obtain the same status as creditors of the buying company. Debts are not thus assumed, however, unless expressly so agreed. Creditors of the selling company also have a prior claim to the assets transferred to the purchasing company.

Mortgage Liens of the Selling Company. A mortgage or other lien placed on the assets while in the possession of the selling corporation usually remains undisturbed by the transfer of such assets. A purchasing company that assumes a mortgage on assets cannot sell or pledge bonds not previously issued by the selling company so as to give them an equal lien with the bonds previously issued by the selling company. An **after-acquired clause** in the indenture under which the assumed bonds were issued becomes of no effect, according to the weight of authority, and such a clause cannot be made to apply to property acquired by the purchasing company after the date of acquisition of the assets of the selling company.

OBLIGATIONS OF SELLER. The purchasing company may undertake to assume all or only certain specified liabilities of the seller. It may, for example, not take over the current liabilities, and in that event certain assets, including cash, receivables, and possibly also certain inventories, may be left with the selling company for the liquidation of this indebtedness. Or the contract may stipulate that the selling company shall retain its cash and receive an additional amount from the purchasing company to pay off the unassumed liabilities.

Assumption of bonds by the purchasing company may be by **supplemental indenture.** On the other hand, the selling company may be obliged by the terms of the sales contract to retire its outstanding bonds, if they are redeemable, with funds indirectly furnished by the purchasing company. **Bondholders** may also be offered stock or other securities of the purchasing company in exchange, which is done when the selling company is in an embarrassed condition. Occasionally, to facilitate the distribution of the proceeds of sale, retirement of the selling company's redeemable **preferred stock** occurs prior to the transfer of assets. If the sales contract provides for payment entirely in cash, the selling company may prefer to pay off its own liabilities. Then the consideration paid by the purchasing company covers gross assets exclusive of cash. If any of the liabilities are liens against specific assets, arrangements may be made for a portion of the purchase money to be paid to the indenture trustee who will pay off these obligations.

The purchasing company may have to provide for **stock purchase warrants** that the selling company has outstanding. This is usually done by giving holders of the warrants the right to purchase at the stated price an amount of the buying company's stock equivalent to the shares of the selling company to which they are entitled to subscribe. The purchasing company may have to enter into a similar undertaking with respect to convertible bonds the selling company may have outstanding.

SUBJECTS OF SALE. In the purchase of a business, the contract of sale should stipulate whether it is merely the **tangible assets** of the selling company that are being bought, or whether intangibles are to be transferred as well, including the selling company's **goodwill,** trade names, and contracts. In the latter instance, the selling company's business is being purchased as a going concern.

Dissolution of the selling company may be stipulated in the sales contract. If immediate dissolution is impossible, it may be provided that immediately upon the execution of the sale, the selling company will change its name so that the purchasing company may have full benefit of the goodwill attaching to the old name. A new company may be formed as a subsidiary of the buying company with the old name to act as a selling company only, in order to preserve the name as a good-will asset. It has been held that a corporation that purchases all the property and goodwill of another at a dissolution sale has the **exclusive right to use the corporate name** of the selling company, at least to the extent of showing that the purchaser corporation is the successor of the selling corporation.

PROVISIONS REGARDING CONSIDERATION. The nature and amount of the consideration and the manner of payment should be set forth in the **sales contract.** The consideration paid by the purchasing company for the net assets involved in the sale (the total assets to be taken over less liabilities to be assumed) usually consists of its stock, either common alone or common and preferred. It may also be exclusively or partially cash, which is usually paid to enable the selling company to retire indebtedness not assumed by the purchasing company or to redeem the selling company's preferred stock. Sale for stock may have an advantage over sale for cash in that a precise dollar valuation of the assets may not be necessary. Selling company stockholders may be offered an option of stock or cash. Part or all of the consideration may also consist of bonds. Tax savings may be the paramount consideration since a sale of assets for stock may be deemed a **tax-free exchange** whereas in a cash sale a profit or loss may be realized.

Purchases of assets entirely or mainly for cash are comparatively rare when the concerns acquired are relatively large. The new financing that such transactions require is something that purchasing companies usually avoid. Purchase of assets with bonds creates fixed charges just like the sale of bonds to raise funds for payment in cash.

Serial notes are often issued in payment for assets when the purchase is not large and the earnings of the purchaser are ample to retire the notes over a few years. The notes may be secured by a **vendor's lien.** This device is most used among smaller enterprises whose credit is not such as to permit financing through a public offering of its securities.

Payment in stock is less usual when part of the physical assets, but not the whole business of the company, is sold. In a partial sale of assets, cash or its equivalent in the form of bonds and notes is usually demanded. Payment in stock is occasionally made for tangible assets transferred between companies having a community of interest.

What securities of the purchasing company will be offered and accepted in payment will depend in a large measure on the relative strength of each company's bargaining position and the shrewdness with which its representatives conduct their negotiations. The classes of securities of the selling company outstanding and their rights and priorities are factors that must be reckoned with, as well as the wishes of large stockholders. Demand for **payment in cash** or **fixed income-bearing securities** is usual when the ownership of the selling company is largely identical with its management, and a change of management is contemplated following the sale. Losing control over their investment, these persons usually want security of income.

PREFERRED STOCK OF SELLING COMPANY. If the selling company has preferred stock outstanding it is usually necessary to offer in exchange a comparable class of stock. Purchasers of preferred stocks are primarily interested in stability of income, and, unless their company is in an embarrassed position and has suspended dividends on the preferred, it is difficult to induce holders of preferred to accept a junior security in exchange. It may be necessary also to offer an inducement in the shape of slightly higher income, a convertible feature, or a small bonus in common stock to bring the preferred holders into line. This is especially true when the selling company is an old, well-established company with a long record of regular dividend payments, and the preferred is non-callable or is entitled to a high price in liquidation.

ADVANTAGES AND DISADVANTAGES OF PURCHASE OF ASSETS. Advantages and disadvantages of the purchase-of-assets method of combination may be summarized as follows:

Advantages.

1. It is easier to effect than a merger or consolidation in that in most states only stockholders of the selling corporation have to approve. No action on the part of the stockholders of the buying corporation is required unless the buying corporation finds it necessary to increase its authorized capital stock in order to effect whole or part payment for the assets to be acquired.
2. It is a more flexible method of combination as compared to certain others in that only part of the assets may be desired and partial purchase may be made, whereas a merger involves the acquisition of all the assets of the absorbed concern. Similarly, the purchasing company may undertake to assume all or only some liabilities of the selling corporation. Agreement on terms is more likely when some assets and liabilities can be left out of the deal.
3. It may be the only practical method of combining corporations organized under state laws that prohibit merger or consolidation of a domestic corporation with a foreign corporation.
4. The purchase-of-assets method does not involve the legal details attendant upon the formation of a new corporation.
5. There may be a tax advantage, if the sale permits realization of a capital loss on a taxable exchange.

Disadvantages.

1. The statutes of some states regard the distribution of stock received in exchange for assets as a transaction distinct from the sale of the assets, and separate consent of the stockholders must be received. Even if the stockholder has voted for the sale of the assets and business of his company, he may still object to the distribution in liquidation of the securities of the purchasing company received and may insist upon receipt of cash, although some courts have ruled that when stock taken in exchange in a sale of assets has an established market value it may be considered an equivalent of money.
2. As under other statutory methods of business combination, dissenting stockholders of the selling corporation may avail themselves of their statutory appraisal rights. This may require such large cash payments as to make combination by this method impractical. Moreover, if dissenting stockholders are held entitled to a high price, the additional money must come out of the proceeds of the sale, unless the liability is specifically assumed by the buying company, since the court's decision cannot alter the terms of the sale. This fact explains why the board of a selling corporation usually reserves the right to cancel the sale until after the period has elapsed during which dissent may be registered.
3. Legal objections have sometimes been raised if it is the intention to have the selling corporation remain as a holding company or investment trust. In such cases it has been argued that a corporation has no power to sell its assets and remain in existence as a holding company except by express statutory consent.

4. The sale of assets may result in a heavy Federal tax liability to the selling corporation if a gain is thereby realized, unless the transaction is held by the Internal Revenue Service to constitute a tax-free exchange under the Revenue Act, upon which no gain or loss has been registered.

The purchase of assets, regardless of whether all or only part of the assets of the selling corporation are to be acquired, necessarily involves the problem of **valuation.** Since this problem is also of great importance in effecting mergers and consolidations, discussion of valuation technique is reserved for a later part of this Section.

Consolidations and Mergers

DEFINITION OF CONSOLIDATION. In a consolidation, two or more companies by agreement and under legislative authority become united into a new corporation, organized for the purpose, which takes over their property, rights, privileges, contracts, and franchises, whether of a public or private nature, and assumes their liabilities and other obligations. Generally, stockholders of the consolidating companies exchange their shares for stock of the consolidated company and thus become stockholders of the latter, though they may be partly paid off in cash or receive in exchange for part of their holdings bonds or other obligations of the consolidated company.

Charter Rights of Consolidated Companies. The new or consolidated corporation succeeds to the charter rights of the original or constituent companies, and in this respect differs from a corporation organized merely to purchase the property and business of a number of going concerns. The charter rights of the selling company do not pass to the purchasing company, but are canceled and cease to exist with the dissolution of the selling company. In a corporation newly formed to purchase the assets and business of others, such a corporation has a charter of its own quite independent of the charters of the selling companies.

LEGAL FACTORS. A corporation has no inherent or common-law right to consolidate with other corporations. The **power cannot be implied,** and corporations cannot consolidate unless the state has expressly authorized them to do so, either by a provision in their charters or the charter of one of them, or by a special act passed after their creation and before consolidation, provided such special act is constitutional, or by a general law. As expressed in effect by Fletcher (Law of Private Corporations), legislative authority is just as vital to a valid consolidation of existing corporations as it is to the creation of a corporation in the first instance.

If at the time a corporation is created there is no constitutional or charter provision or statute authorizing a consolidation, and the state has not reserved the right by constitutional or statutory provision to amend or repeal the charter, a consolidation cannot be effected without the **consent of all the stockholders** of the constituent companies. To allow a subsequent consolidation statute to have this effect would impair the obligation of the contracts between the corporations and the dissenting stockholders. If, however, there is a reservation of the right to amend or repeal corporation charters, all corporations are subject to any consolidation statute that may be enacted after their incorporation.

Statutory and Administrative Provisions. The general statutory provisions for consolidation usually relate to private business corporations. There are special provisions to cover consolidation of railroads, public utilities, banks, insurance companies, savings banks, and other enterprises that are subject to public regulation in one form or another, although in some states there is but one statute for all corporations. Railroads and public utilities may have to observe conditions laid down by the public service commissions, which may include obtaining the commission's permission and approval of the terms. The Interstate Commerce Commission must approve consolidation (or merger) of interstate railroad corporations. Similarly, the Securities and Exchange Commission under the Public Utility Holding Company Act of 1935 must approve mergers of registered public utility holding companies and their subsidiaries. Consolidations and mergers among state banks are usually effected with the consent and under the supervision of the State Superintendent of Banking, and also the Federal Reserve Board in the instance of state member banks. In national banks supervision is the responsibility of the Comptroller of the Currency. Similar supervision may be exercised over consolidations of insurance companies by the State Superintendent of Insurance.

State Laws Governing Consolidations. Many, if not all, states have provisions for consolidations on their statute books. These are the **sole authority** for consummating a consolidation and they must be carefully observed. The statutes governing consolidations prescribe what corporations may be consolidated, the manner and the procedure of effecting the consolidation, the rights of the stockholders and creditors of the old constituent companies, the rights and privileges of the new consolidated company, and the status of the consolidating companies for a period after the act of consolidation.

Restrictions laid down in the different state statutes affecting consolidations differ widely. Consolidation of parallel railroads or competing companies or domestic with foreign corporations (those organized in other states) may be prohibited. Consolidations may be restricted to corporations organized to carry on business of the same or similar nature. Under some statutes, the new corporations resulting from consolidation must be organized under the laws of the state.

§ 901 of the new **Business Corporation Law of New York State**, which applies to all corporations other than specially regulated companies (banks, railroads, insurance companies, etc.), states:

"Power of merger or consolidation.—(a) Two or more domestic corporations may, as provided in this chapter:

(1) Merge into a single corporation which shall be one of the constituent corporations; or

(2) Consolidate into a single corporation which shall be a new corporation to be formed pursuant to the consolidation."

§ 902 requires **approval by the board** of each corporation of the plan of merger or consolidation and specifies the information that must be included in the plan. Authorization of the plan by holders of at least **two-thirds of all outstanding shares** entitled to vote on it (each class voting separately) is provided for in § 903. A **certificate of merger or consolidation** must be filed with the New York State Department of State.

With regard to the **merger of a subsidiary** corporation, § 905a states: "Any domestic corporation owning at least ninety-five percent of the outstanding shares of each class of another domestic corporation or corporations may merge such other corporation or corporations into itself without the authorization of the shareholders of either corporation."

The merger or consolidation of **domestic and foreign** corporations is authorized under § 907 as follows: "One or more foreign corporations and one or more domestic corporations may be merged or consolidated into a corporation of this state or of another jurisdiction, if such merger or consolidation is permitted by the laws of the jurisdiction under which each such foreign corporation is incorporated."

EFFECT OF CONSOLIDATION. The effect of the consolidation is to fuse the constituent companies into a single corporate unit. However, some statutes authorizing consolidation provide for the continuance of the consolidating companies as corporate entities for a certain period, such as 2 or 3 years, for maintaining or defending suits pending at the time of consolidation, adjusting liabilities or transferring property, or for the protection of creditors' claims. As the new consolidated corporation assumes the entire liabilities of the constituent corporations, only damage suits can arise. As a general rule, recent court decisions lean toward the realistic conception of dissolution by consolidation (or merger), unless the statutes of the states in which the corporations are chartered definitely indicate a contrary contention.

By the act of consolidation the new corporation **succeeds to the title of all properties** of the constituent companies as provided in the agreement of consolidation. No instrument of conveyance, assignment, or other act of transfer is necessary under the provisions of most state laws. Similarly, no formal assignment of contracts or claims of consolidating companies is necessary to pass title to them, though there may be a provision to that effect in the statute or the consolidation agreement. Debtors of the constituent companies become **debtors of the consolidated company,** which may therefore sue on a note formerly held by one of the constituent companies. But to enforce claims the consolidated corporation must show compliance with all the requirements of the law authorizing the consolidation.

PROCEDURE IN EFFECTING CONSOLIDATION. Although the laws vary from to state, the procedure is generally as follows:

1. **Agreement on terms between negotiators.** It is only after a period of negotiation between the officials of the companies concerned, and often interested outside promoters, that a formal agreement is drawn up embodying the terms of the consolidation.

2. **Approval of the terms of consolidation by the board of directors of each constituent corporation.** This approval is effected by the passage of resolutions containing the terms of the consolidation and the method and basis of exchange of the securities. The resolutions also direct that the consolidation plan be submitted to the shareholders for their vote.

3. **Obtaining stockholders' consent.** After the agreement of consolidation has been approved by the directors of the several consolidating companies, it is submitted to their stockholders for final ratification. For this purpose a special meeting of the stockholders is called. The statute frequently sets forth the precise manner of calling such a meeting. The stockholders may vote in person, or by proxy, and if the required majority of the voting shares as provided in the statute adopt the plan of consolidation, it becomes effective as soon as certain other legal formalities are completed. The statute prescribes the majority of the voting stock that must approve a consolidation, usually two-thirds. However, this does not preclude the stipulation by corporations of a higher proportion in their certificates of incorporation, or a lower one but not less than a stated minimum.

4. **Execution of consolidation agreement.** The next step is to obtain the signatures of the president and secretary of each of the consolidating corporations and, with the filing of the signed agreement in the office of the Secretary of State or some other state official, the agreement becomes the act of or articles of con-

solidation, and the consolidated company comes into existence. Certified copies of the agreement may also have to be recorded in the counties in which each of the consolidating companies has recorded its original certificate of incorporation. Election of the board of directors ordinarily takes place immediately after the filing of the articles of consolidation.

5. **Exchange of securities.** In accordance with the terms of the plan of consolidation the securities of the new corporation and any other consideration will be distributed among the stockholders of the constitutent corporations.

6. **Settlement with dissenting stockholders.** One of the last steps in the procedure is the cash settlement with dissenting stockholders in accordance with the procedure laid down by state law.

RIGHTS OF DISSENTING STOCKHOLDERS. Dissenting stockholders who have voted against the consolidation proposal at the special meeting of stockholders, or who refrained from voting there, may file objection to the consolidation and obtain the relief specified in the state law. Most statutes on consolidation provide for **appraisal rights** for dissenting stockholders.

The **New York Business Corporation Law** (§ 910) provides that any shareholder of a domestic corporation who does not assent to a merger or consolidation shall have the right, by complying with § 623 (which sets forth the procedure to enforce a shareholder's right to receive payment for shares), to "receive payment of the fair value of his shares and the other rights and benefits provided by such action."

This right is not available to a **shareholder of the surviving corporation** in a merger unless the merger effects one or more of the following changes in the shareholder's rights, as specified in § 806 (b6):

(A) alters or abolishes any preferential right of any outstanding shares having preferences; or (B) creates, alters or abolishes any provision or right in respect of the redemption of any outstanding shares; or (C) alters or abolishes any preemptive right of such holders to acquire shares or other securities; or (D) excludes or limits the right of such holder to vote on any matter, except as such right may be limited by the voting rights given to new shares then being authorized of any existing or new class.

Stockholders who object to a proposed consolidation may attempt to block the consummation thereof by bringing an action to enjoin the consolidation on the ground that the terms of exchange of securities are **fraudulent**. Stockholders of one of the constituent corporations may claim that they are getting unfair treatment as compared to that accorded the stockholders in the other constituent corporations. Similarly, one class of stockholders of a constituent corporation may argue that other classes of stock of the same corporation are unjustifiably receiving preferential treatment. In either case it is claimed that improper dilution of equity and control results. Other grounds of action have included the claim that proper legal procedure to effect a consolidation was not followed, or that the consolidation would constitute an ultra vires act or a violation of antitrust laws.

RIGHTS OF CREDITORS IN CONSOLIDATIONS AND MERGERS. Creditors of the constituent corporations are allowed no voice in the decision to consolidate. They can bring suits to halt consolidation only on the basis of fraud, unfairness, or because of the illegality of the mode of consolidation. If the legislative authority to consolidate existed when they became creditors of the consolidating corporations, the legal presumption is that they acted with full knowledge of the power of the corporations to consolidate and they are thereby estopped from refusing to become creditors of the consolidated corporation. If the legislative authority was granted only after they became creditors, they are not restricted to a remedy against the consolidated company, but they may **follow the assets** of the consolidating corporations into the hands of the consolidated corporation.

There is a conflict of authority as to whether **unsecured creditors** of a constituent corporation acquire a lien on its property as it passes into the hands of the consolidated corporation. Usually statutes provide for the assumption of debts by the new company, but some statutes do not relieve the constitutent companies of their respective liabilities. Nor are stockholders of the constituent companies released from their liabilities, if any exist, by reason of the consolidation.

The **New York statute** regarding the position of creditors of the constituent companies is as follows [§ 906 (30)]:

The surviving or consolidated corporation shall assume and be liable for all the liabilities, obligations and penalties of each of the constituent corporations. No liability or obligation due or to become due, claim or demand for any cause existing against any such corporation, or any shareholder, officer or director thereof, shall be released or impaired by such merger or consolidation. No action or proceeding, whether civil or criminal, then pending by or against any such constituent corporation, or any shareholder, officer or director thereof, shall abate or be discontinued by such merger or consolidation, but may be enforced, prosecuted, settled or compromised as if such merger or consolidation had not occurred, or such surviving or consolidated corporation may be substituted in such action or special proceeding in place of any constituent corporation.

TREATMENT OF MORTGAGE LIENS. Liens on the property of the constituent concerns are not affected by any sale of property, consolidation, or merger, unless the holder of the obligation agrees otherwise. Mortgages of the constituent companies remain liens on the mortgaged property after that property has been transferred to the consolidated corporation. Issuance of bonds by the consolidated corporation in connection with the consolidation will depend upon the statute and the agreement of consolidation. If one of the constituent corporations executed a mortgage to secure bonds that were to be issued in the future acquisition of property by it, the consolidated company may not issue its own bonds under such mortgage unless the mortgage indenture permits such an issue.

After-acquired property clauses in the mortgage indentures of a constituent corporation are usually rendered of no effect by the consolidation, so that property acquired by the consolidated corporation from the other constituent companies or after the consolidation does not become subject to such mortgages. Liens on property taken over by the consolidated corporations have priority over liens subsequently executed.

DEFINITION OF MERGER. A merger is the absorption of one or more existing corporations by another existing corporation. Mergers differ from consolidations, therefore, in that the absorbing corporation is not a newly formed corporation. When corporation A is absorbed or merged into corporation B, a going concern, the latter succeeds to all A's property, rights, privileges, immunities, and franchises, whether of a public or private nature, and at the same time assumes all of A's liabilities and other claims against A. As a result of the merger, corporation B becomes the successor of corporation A in the eyes of the law.

POWER OF CORPORATIONS TO MERGE. Like the power to consolidate, the power to merge is derived strictly **from legislative enactment**. Without the existence of a statute conferring such power, no corporation of that state can participate in a merger. The power to consolidate does not necessarily imply the power to merge.

What corporation may take part in a merger, the manner of effecting mergers, the precise rights, liabilities, and obligations of the absorbing corporation, and the rights of stockholders and creditors of the absorbed corporations are regulated in varying detail by the statutes. Usually, under the statutes corporations that may consolidate may also form a merger.

In many states, including Delaware, Ohio, and New Jersey, the same statutory provisions apply to both mergers and consolidations.

MERGER PROCEDURE. Merger procedure is similar to that of consolidation. An **agreement** of merger is drawn up and signed by the officers and directors of the absorbing concern and of those to be merged, and is then submitted for the **approval** of a prescribed majority of voting stockholders at a special meeting called for the purpose. The merger becomes effective with the filing of this agreement in the office of the Secretary of State, or in the manner required by statute.

The terms of the merger, including the basis for the exchange of stock between the absorbing corporation and stockholders of the merged corporations, must be stated in the agreement. Dissenting stockholders have the same rights as in the case of a sale of assets or consolidation. The rights of creditors of the merged companies are similar to those of the constituent companies in consolidations.

ADVANTAGES AND DISADVANTAGES OF CONSOLIDATIONS AND MERGERS. As methods of business combination, the advantages and disadvantages of the consolidation or merger device are:

Advantages.
1. Consolidations and mergers are generally treated by the Internal Revenue Service as tax-free exchanges that lead to no gain or loss.
2. Consolidations and mergers constitute permanent forms of combination that result in the management obtaining complete control. In this respect they differ from looser forms of combination such as a holding company and a partly owned subsidiary.
3. Consolidations and mergers result in centralized administration as compared to the holding company structure where there is often divided authority and the expense of keeping a number of corporate organizations in existence.

Disadvantages.
1. Consolidations and mergers have an element of inflexibility in that it is necessary to take in all the assets and liabilities of the corporations being consolidated or merged. The purchase of assets is usually a more desirable method of combination if only part of a corporation's assets may need to be purchased, and only some of the liabilities assumed.
2. It is necessary to get approval of the stockholders of each corporation involved in a consolidation or merger, whereas in the purchase of assets only stockholders of the selling corporation have to approve, and in a holding company arrangement approval of stockholders is not required at all.
3. Consolidations and mergers often create personnel problems, particularly with respect to executives of the various companies.
4. Determination of terms of exchange often proves a stumbling block, since each corporation and class of stockholders will endeavor to receive favorable treatment. The valuation problem is reduced to a minimum if the holding company device is employed.

Since mergers and consolidations have much in common, no attempt has been made to discuss the advantages and disadvantages of each separately. However, certain differences between the two devices do exist, and under given conditions **one device may be preferable to the other** provided the statutes permit a choice. Thus, if a small corporation is being fused with a large corporation (with a variety of outstanding stock issues) it will usually be simpler to merge the smaller into the larger corporation. Similarly, dissolution of the larger corporation might be inadvisable because of the goodwill established or inability to pass a valuable franchise privilege to the consolidated corporation. Conversely, consolidation might be preferable in other situations. For example, by eliminating the corporate entities of the constituent companies, consolidation makes possible greater freedom in setting up the new organization.

TERMS OF CONSOLIDATIONS AND MERGERS. Inasmuch as consolidations and mergers are subject to statutory regulation, the terms will have to conform to the **statutory provisions.** In some states it would appear that the identity of the stockholders of the several corporations must remain unchanged just before and after consolidation. Therefore stock may be issued only to the shareholders of the consolidating or merging concerns, though the stock so issued need not be in the same class as that surrendered. Other states, however, have more liberal provisions that permit the consolidated or absorbing concern to exchange cash and their obligations, in addition to stock, for the shares of the several companies entering into the consolidation or merger.

In view of the many and complicated factors involved—legal, financial, tax, accounting, personnel, etc.—the terms of each combination necessarily have to be worked out to suit each individual situation. Generally, the **surviving company,** both in the case of mergers and purchases of assets, turns over its common stock in exchange for the capital stock or net assets of the company acquired. In such a transaction the selling stockholders are usually not required to report either a gain or a loss on the securities received. There are many variations, however. The acquiring company may, for example, at least in some states, be permitted to issue preferred voting stock, or nonvoting stock, or even debt securities as part or full consideration (McCarthy, Acquisitions and Mergers). In these situations the tax or accounting treatment may be different in each case.

At times the deal may include arrangements for the selling stockholders to **dispose of part of the securities** received in an exchange in order to obtain some cash while at the same time preserving their tax-free status. The same aim can be realized by having the surviving company redeem part of the stock of the company to be absorbed prior to effecting the exchange of stock. In some instances the combination may be made in two stages: The absorbing company first acquires a sizable block of stock of the other company on the open market. Then it endeavors to obtain a controlling interest either through negotiations with the management and leading stockholders or through proxy solicitation. Sometimes different classes of stock may be issued to different holders of common stock of the merged company. For example, the largest stockholders may be offered convertible preferred and the others ordinary common, with the terms of conversion and voting power adjusted to suit the parties involved.

At times the acquiring company may agree to repurchase part or all of the capital stock issued to the seller at a **stipulated price and time.** Part of the purchase price, whether the deal involves payment of cash or capital stock, may be made contingent on future operating results. Sometimes the acquisition may be financed on an installment basis involving a down-payment and interest-bearing notes for the remainder. Many other possibilities might be cited.

Financial and Accounting Factors in Combinations

VALUATION PROBLEMS. Consolidations and mergers, like the purchase of assets, give rise to complex valuation problems. Not only must tangible and intangible assets of diverse character be valued, but securities issued in exchange similarly must be fairly appraised.

As a prelude to the formulation of terms, the following types of analyses are generally made by the negotiating parties:

Accounting Analysis. An independent accounting firm is often engaged to audit each company's books with the purpose of making the balance sheet and income statements of each corporation as comparable and uniform as possible. This analysis should extend to accounting policies as well as the accuracy of the figures, and attempt to iron out differences in depreciation policies, provision for bad debts and contingencies, officer and employee compensation, etc.

Engineering Analysis. This analysis is designed to establish the technological position and operating characteristics of each company. It will include an analysis of the physical layout of the building, the modernity of the processes employed, raw material resources, and the flexibility and efficiency of each company's operations.

Economic Analysis. This survey will deal with the elements **external** to corporate operations, such as respective market areas, competitive conditions, the industry outlook, and probable public reaction to the combination.

If the above analyses do not introduce stumbling blocks, the next step is the establishment of values for the merger, consolidation, or purchase of assets.

Nonbalance Sheet Factors. The facts that must be taken into consideration in valuation other than those in balance sheets and income accounts are so many and diverse that it is rare that a price is set except after long-drawn-out negotiations in which the human equation plays an important part and that may be affected by such factors as:

1. Distribution of the stock.
2. Requirements of large stockholders.
3. Management.
4. State of business.
5. Condition of the securities market.
6. Nature of the consideration.
7. Whether merely assets or both assets and business are being acquired.

Nature of Consideration. Of the factors listed above, the nature of the consideration usually affects the valuation problem most. If the purchase of assets method is used and cash alone is given in payment, valuation of the assets and business of the selling company alone is needed. On the other hand, if an exchange of securities is involved then it becomes necessary to value the securities given in payment as well. Moreover, the nature of the consideration is important in determining whether or not the combination is tax-free.

Further, as McCarthy (Acquisitions and Mergers) states, it is quite possible for the same company to have a different value or "price" depending upon the nature of the consideration involved, for example:

1. **A cash offer** could be higher than that proposed in an exchange of securities because the purchaser would recover part of the price paid through reductions in federal income taxes resulting from a stepped-up tax basis of assets ac-

FINANCIAL AND ACCOUNTING FACTORS IN COMBINATIONS

quired. Also, a seller generally would require a higher price in a cash deal than in an exchange of securities because of the immediate income tax consequences.

2. **An exchange of securities offer** of a company in a "glamour" industry whose stock was selling at a very high price-earnings ratio could be much more generous than one whose stock was selling on a conservative basis relative to earnings and dividend yield.

METHODS OF VALUATION. Although many attempts have been made to evolve formulas for the valuation of business enterprises by engineers, accountants, courts of law, and others, they are of limited use to practical business men in attempting to set a price on a company to be acquired as a part of an expansion program. The valuation of the assets and business of a concern usually involves consideration of **several bases** of value. Which bases of value will be given most weight may depend upon such factors as the characteristics of the industry and how eager the parties are to effect a combination. The bases of value that may be given consideration are:

1. Capitalized earning power.
2. Goodwill or going concern value.
3. Market value.
4. Investment value.
5. Book value.
6. Cost less depreciation.
7. Reproduction cost.
8. Substitution cost.

Valuation Based on Capitalized Earning Power. The most common method of valuation applied to intercorporate transfers of assets, favored by legal precedent as well as sound financial principles, is the capitalization of the earning power of the corporation whose assets and business are being valued. This method involves agreement upon two factors: (1) the amount of earning power and (2) the rate at which this amount should be capitalized.

1. **Determination of earning power.** The usual manner of arriving at a figure that will fairly represent earning power is to average annual net income for a period of, say, 3 or 5 years, on the theory that the best indication of future possibilities is the achievements of the past. A weighted average giving more weight to recent earnings may be used. Adjustments should be made for abnormal operating results, and every effort should be made to reach a figure that would reasonably reflect earning power under normal operating conditions in the future. Account must be taken of whether the business is well seasoned and well established, or only recently organized, and one whose initial success may prove to be only a "flash in the pan." Due consideration must be given to depreciation policies, treatment of research and development expenditures, and pension policies.

As indicated previously, none of the constituent corporations will necessarily accept the earnings figures of the others as reported in their financial statements. Independent firms of accountants and engineers may be engaged to examine the books and the assets and give an impartial report on the record of earnings.

2. **Determination of capitalization rate.** The rate at which earning power is to be capitalized represents the rate of return that the business in question should earn on its value. This rate has been expressed also as the number of years' earnings required to amortize the purchase price. The rate will depend upon stability of earnings, the rate of increase in earnings, and the many factors affecting the long-term and short-term outlook for the company. The more speculative the

business, the higher the capitalization rate will be, and vice versa. The extent to which earnings may be affected by the leverage factor in the capital structure must also be taken into account.

If the acquisition involves the entire assets and business of another concern, the purchasing company will arrive at a rate for capitalizing the earning power of the selling company by determining first its own rate of earnings on invested capital. If a company regularly earns 15% on its own invested capital, it will want to acquire new properties on a comparable basis if possible.

Goodwill or Going Concern Value. Another method of determining the value of a going concern is as follows: From the average annual earnings for the years taken, a certain rate of return on tangible assets is deducted. The remainder represents the company's **excess earning power,** which, capitalized on the basis of a certain number of years' purchase, gives the value of the goodwill. The value of the goodwill, added to the value of the tangible assets, constitutes the value of the company as a going concern.

Market Value. In determining the value of an enterprise, market values of its securities are often given a great deal of consideration. Market quotations usually discount the future, giving weight to such **intangible** yet important factors as the rate of growth in earnings, abilities of the management, prospects of the industry in which the company operates, and strategic values possessed by the company because of patents, location, good banking sponsorship, etc. More important, security holders are largely influenced in deciding whether to accept terms offered them by the relation of these terms to prevailing market values.

This method can best be applied when there is a **broad market** for the company's securities. To arrive at a fair figure there must be assurance that there are no temporary abnormal factors at play in the market to cause quotations that might be regarded as fictitious. To reduce the chances of error because of such abnormalities, quotations may be averaged over a period of time, provided there have been no wide variations in quotations during the period that might produce an average figure of questionable usefulness in determining values.

The **total value** of all classes of stock outstanding based on the market quotations agreed upon will represent the value of net assets, that is, total assets less the amount of liabilities. Should this basis of value be accepted this would be the consideration paid if the acquiring company assumes all the liabilities of the selling concern. Otherwise there should be added to the value of the net assets the amount of the liabilities not assumed by the purchasing company.

Investment Value. If the concern being sold has been recently organized and represents largely a promotion to develop a new process or invention, investment value is often given weight in determining the sale price. Investment value represents the amount of cash actually paid in to develop the enterprise and bring it up to its present state of productivity. To the amount of cash paid in is added compound interest at an agreed rate from the time of payment to the time when the properties began to pay a return on the investment.

Book Value. If the accounting policies of the selling company have been conservative and ample charge-offs for depreciation, obsolescence, and inventory losses have been made, book value may represent a fair and equitable basis of value in the determination of purchase price. However, the book value might represent, in part, a write-up of assets through revaluation by appraisal that may or may not be justified. The use of book value has the advantage of convenience and speed, often important considerations in effecting combinations. Then too, the use of book values does not necessitate a field investigation of the properties. If the management of the selling company is hostile to the purchase, it may be impossible to place engineers in the plants and auditors on the books to secure a valuation by more elaborate methods.

Cost Less Depreciation. This basis of value has the advantage over book value in that a write-up of assets would not be included. Fairness of this basis, however, depends to a great extent upon the company's depreciation policies. This basis of value has the disadvantage of not giving weight to changes in **price levels**, and it is not possible to value intangibles by this method.

Reproduction Cost. A definition of reproduction cost would be the cost of duplicating the properties to be acquired at prices prevailing as of the date of valuation. Real estate would be valued on the basis of market values of adjacent property. Plant would be valued on the basis of use of the same materials and specifications, and equipment at cost of replacement. However, reproduction would provide a new plant, whereas the plant to be acquired may be many years old. Therefore, proper allowance must be made for the **condition of the properties** and the cost of bringing them up to the state of **efficiency desired**. Like cost less depreciation, this basis of value does not provide a practical method of valuing intangibles and, therefore, supplementary methods must be used.

Substitution Cost. Whereas reproduction cost assumes the construction of an exactly similar plant, substitution cost is based on the cost of constructing a plant that would possess the same utility to the purchaser and would have the same capacity, but that might not necessarily be similar in design and materials or located in the same place. Here again, allowance must be made for the age of the plant considered for acquisition.

Substitution cost, reproduction cost, and actual cost less depreciation are useful as bases of valuation when the **plant and other physical properties** are most important and the business or goodwill are secondary considerations. These bases of value are most commonly used among concerns producing bulk commodities and other unbranded goods, where price rather than brand name is the determining factor in marketing the product.

ACCOUNTING PROBLEMS IN ASSET TRANSFERS. For accounting purposes, the acquiring company must distribute the total consideration paid among the various assets taken over, as it would otherwise be impossible to compute depreciation and to account for individual assets. In recording the acquired assets on the books of the buying, consolidated, or merging company, book values, market values, or replacement values may be used. However, care must be taken not to ignore the essential legal elements in the transaction. Courts construe combinations not by what they are called but by their **inherent nature**, and the precise steps used in carrying out the combinations determine in their eyes the nature of the combinations.

Valuation of Plant and Equipment. As the transfer of assets is in the nature of a sale from one corporation to another, current market values are ordinarily the logical basis for valuation, unless, as with public utilities, regulatory authorities prescribe otherwise. If they are not available, then the nearest approach to market values should be adopted. Land may be taken at **appraised value**. If the plant is small and particularly if it is suited to a variety of uses, market value can usually be readily determined. Large plants are rarely the subject of individual sale, and therefore have no determinable market value.

Accordingly, the method of valuation employed is usually **reproduction cost**, that is, the current cost of construction, with proper allowance for the present physical state of the property. The plant and equipment are appraised on the basis of replacement cost less depreciation for wear and tear as well as for obsolescence, which is frequently referred to as the "sound value" of the plant. However, proper regard must be had to the productive efficiency of the plant.

If the plant is to be carried on the books of the acquiring company at a **higher value** than it has been on the books of the selling or constituent company, care should be exercised in determining that such an increase is justified, for it may be questioned later by disgruntled stockholders or by creditors. This is particularly true if the acquisition is financed by exchange of stock.

Effect of Plant Valuation on Production Costs. Consideration must also be given to the effect that new values assigned to plant and equipment will have on the cost of production and consequently on the net operating results. If the transfer of assets is made in a **period of rising prices,** so that the plant will be carried at a higher value than it has been on the books of the selling company, heavier depreciation charges will add to the production cost and reduce the margin of profit on sales, although, if selling prices of the products are rising at the same time, the effect of increased depreciation charges may be completely offset. Under reverse conditions, **when the general level of prices is declining** and replacement cost of the plant, less depreciation, is below the book value given it by the selling company, depreciation charges based on a lower plant value will reduce production costs and increase the profit margin. Here also, the resulting reduction in cost may be entirely balanced by the lower price the company may be getting for its product.

Valuation of Intangible Assets. If the company whose business is acquired has been **successful,** the probabilities are that the total value of the tangible assets determined in the manner described above will be substantially less than the consideration paid for the business as determined by capitalization of earnings. The difference will be the value of the intangible elements of the going concern, generally known as **"Goodwill,"** "Goodwill, trade-marks, and trade names," "Goodwill and patents," etc. Inasmuch as this excess of consideration over tangible asset values taken over represents an actual investment, such items may be carried on the balance sheet as an asset by the purchasing company.

If the concern taken over is a **failing** one, the value fixed for its business is likely to be less than the replacement or market value of the tangible assets. If the acquiring company follows conservative practice, it will carry the assets taken over at the **consideration paid.**

From a managerial viewpoint there is an advantage in placing assets purchased on the books at **market or replacement value,** when this is below cost. Because of such purchase, the management may achieve good operating results merely because depreciation allowances will be smaller on the lower asset values.

Valuation of Current Assets. The transfer of current assets of one business to another does not usually involve accounting problems comparable to the valuation of plant and equipment on the acquiring company's books. Current assets will generally be transferred to the books of the acquiring company at the same amount as shown on the seller's or constituent corporation's books. The only exceptions would be receivables of doubtful liquidity and inventory that has declined in value. In such an instance, restatement of book values would be proper practice.

Effect of Merger or Consolidation on Surplus. Whether any addition to the surplus of the absorbing concern results from the merger or consolidation will depend, first, on the **securities issued** by it, and, secondly, on the **values assigned** to the assets of the absorbed concerns. Whether the transfer changes the character of the surplus and renders it paid-in surplus, or whether earned surplus of the absorbed corporations continues as such on the books of the absorbing corporation, are questions that depend for their answers on the **nature of the consolidation** or merger and **provisions of the statute** authorizing the combination.

Distinction Between Purchase and Pooling of Interests. A relatively recent development is the distinction between the accounting treatment of a purchase and that of a pooling of interests. For this purpose, a purchase is regarded as a business combination "in which an important part of the ownership interests in the acquired corporation is eliminated," whereas a pooling of interests is described as a combination "in which the holders of substantially all of the ownership interests in the constituent corporation become the owners of a single corporation." (See American Institute of Certified Public Accountants, Business Combinations, Bulletin No. 48.) Thus, cash deals or those involving other than voting securities are "purchases," whereas an exchange of voting stock usually, although not always, results in a "pooling of interests."

In a **purchase,** the net assets of the acquired company are recorded at cost and are measured in cash or the fair value of securities or other property turned over, or at the fair value of the property acquired, whichever appears more reasonable. To the extent that the purchase cost is not allocable to tangible assets and intangible assets amortizable for tax purposes, there is goodwill that is generally dealt with by periodic charges to future income.

In a **pooling of interests,** the combined financial position of the constituent companies is, in effect, the same as though they had been previously affiliated. Therefore, no "goodwill" is created. The "fair market value" of the capital stock of the surviving company is disregarded and the net book assets of the absorbed or purchased companies are carried forward in the combined enterprise. Appropriate adjustments are made in the asset and capital and surplus accounts to take care of **differences in balance sheet treatment.** The great majority of combinations involving large companies are effected by exchanges of voting capital stock and are therefore considered pooling transactions. (See American Institute of Certified Public Accountants, Accounting Trends and Techniques.)

FINANCIAL STEPS IN PROMOTING A COMBINATION. The financial steps involved in a business combination are similar to those involved in the promotion of a new enterprise. The initiative may be taken by the management or representatives of one of the constituent corporations, in which event it is commonly termed an **inside combination**; or it may be taken by outside interests—usually a professional promoter or investment bankers. The advantage of an **outside promotion** of a combination lies in the fact that the professional promoter can maintain a neutral position in the negotiations and the interested parties tend to regard his opinions with more confidence.

A promoter usually employs one or the other of two approaches in effecting a combination. In what is termed the **bargaining method** the promoter estimates what the earnings will be after the combination has been completed through taking actual combined earnings of the constituent companies and adding savings expected from the combination. These pro forma earnings are then capitalized at a rate that is assumed to be a fair rate of capitalization at the time. The promoter then proceeds to negotiate the acceptance of securities, representing their capitalized value by the constituent corporations, on terms that will usually leave him an amount sufficient to compensate him for his services.

In the **option method,** the promoter procures options on the assets or business of the several corporations, dealing with each separately on the best terms that can be obtained. Ordinarily, the option is based on a cash consideration, but when the time comes to take up the option, securities of the new or surviving corporation are offered as alternative consideration to the security holders of the constituent corporations. The promoter usually protects himself against possible refusal of the stockholders of the constituent companies to accept the new securities by arranging with an investment banking syndicate to buy the securities not taken up by owners of constituent concerns who demand cash for their holdings.

DETERMINING BASIS OF SHARE EXCHANGE. The terms on which the purchasing, merging, or consolidated corporation will distribute its shares to shareholders of the acquired corporations are usually based on the following factors:

Relative Earnings per Share. Most enterprises are valued by capitalizing their earnings. What period of earnings should be used and what rate of capitalization employed? The **nature and record of the enterprise** and its industry and **prospective economic conditions** will largely determine the answers to these questions. Furthermore, stability of net income available for dividends will be affected by the capital structure of the corporation—large senior security issues will impart a leverage character to the common stock of a company. Similarly, the trend of earnings must be given proper weight as indicative of a growing or declining enterprise.

Relative Book Value per Share. A comparison of the book value per share of each corporation's stock indicates the respective net worth and the relative capital investment represented. As a practical matter it should be recognized that stockholders who have made large investments in their holdings are going to insist that some weight be given to this fact even though current earnings on such capital investment may be relatively small. The **shortcomings** of book value as a basis of share exchange are that it is not indicative of current value and that it is a poor basis for comparative values due to the nonuniformity of accounting methods employed by different concerns. A precombination accounting analysis could make financial statements of different businesses comparable, however.

Relative Net Working Capital per Share. This factor will indicate the relative contribution by each company to the liquid assets of the combination. Since a strong net working capital position is an important prerequisite to a successful combination, and since owners can normally withdraw liquid assets for their own use, this factor must be given considerable weight.

Relative Market Value per Share. If stocks are traded in on the securities market, it is possible to compare relative values placed on the shares by the public. Often, however, security holders feel the market price does not adequately reflect the value of their holdings, and insist that the more fundamental factors already mentioned receive greatest weight in setting the terms of exchange.

The above factors provide a basis for negotiation. Less tangible factors that may affect the terms finally agreed upon are:

Hidden Assets. A corporation may own assets that are not producing earnings currently, but that are worth substantially more than their book value, such as timber, oil, or natural gas properties that may eventually produce large earnings, but are not being exploited currently.

Strategic Elements. In some combinations the share exchange may be affected by the fact that one corporation controls certain valuable processes or has an excellent research department that at the time of the combination is not fully reflected in its earnings. Security owners will want these advantages recognized in the terms of exchange.

Relative Strength of Management. One corporation may possess a management of outstanding skill and reputation, and weight may have to be given to this factor. In some instances, however, it can be argued that superior management has already been reflected in that company's earnings and the market value of its stock.

Bargaining Factors. The terms of the share exchange may reflect to a considerable degree the relative skill of the participants in bargaining.

Combination by Lease

LEASES AS A MEANS OF EXPANSION. In industries where the investment in fixed assets is heavy and the return is relatively stable, a lease of assets may be the most suitable method of combination. This device has been used most in the **railroad and street railway industries.** Although industrial concerns lease property and equipment extensively in order to expand operations without making large investments, the lease method is seldom used to effect industrial combinations.

The **chief advantage** of this method of combination is that no cash payment or issue of securities is required to obtain use of additional facilities. Negotiation and effectuation of leases are relatively simple. The consent of only the shareholders of the lessor corporation is required.

Disadvantages of the lease become apparent in times of depression when fixed rentals payable by companies that have resorted to this method of expansion may become burdensome. Higher fixed charges may affect adversely the credit of the lessee, especially since leased property cannot be placed under the lessee's mortgage bonds. Also, economic changes may cut into the earning power of the leased properties, so that, unless the lease has contingent clauses to guard against such eventualities, the lessee corporation may find itself with outmoded facilities the earning power of which will not be sufficient to cover even a part of the fixed rental.

Double taxation results from leases, furthermore, since the courts have held that lessor corporations are subject to the corporate income tax even if the rental is paid directly to the lessor's stockholders.

LEASE AGREEMENTS. Essentially, a lease of all or substantially all the assets of one corporation to another resembles an ordinary real estate lease. The lessor concern turns over its property to the lessee for a stated term of years, under specified conditions. In return, the lessee pays the lessor a rental and covenants to pay taxes and other expenses, and at the termination of the lease to return the property in as good a condition as that in which it was received.

Intercorporate leases go far beyond the ordinary lease of real estate in that they provide for the transfer not only of the lessor's real property, but also of the personalty, including stocks or bonds that the lessor may hold in subsidiary companies. Stocks may be assigned to the lessee to enable it to vote them and exercise control over the subsidiaries in place of the lessor.

If a lessor corporation happens to be a lessee in relation to the property of other corporations, these leases are assigned to its lessee so that the latter will have complete control over all properties operated by the lessor. Furthermore, the lessor assigns to the lessee its rights, franchises, privileges, and interest in outstanding contracts, in order that it may enjoy the full use of the leased property precisely as though the property were its own.

A **lessee is entitled to all income** derived from the operation of leased property. So that it may operate and finance the properties and enter into all necessary contracts, the lessee is appointed the lessor's agent. Moreover, the lessee may be given the right to sell land and other leased property, provided it replaces assets sold with others of equal value. To give the lessee capacity to enter into such transactions, it may be made the lessor's lawful attorney. On the other hand, the **lessee takes the property subject to all existing debts,** liens, and other incumbrances, and assumes the lessor's other obligations under outstanding leases and other contracts. The lessee undertakes to protect the property by bringing suit in the name of the lessor at its own expense, to defend all suits brought against the lessor, and to hold it harmless against all costs, losses, damages, and claims.

STATUS OF LESSOR CORPORATION. As a result of the lease, the lessor or **proprietory company** may become little more than a shell. The only property that may remain in its possession may be its corporate seal, the stockholders' and directors' books, and the stock and transfer books. Even the nominal expense of keeping these records is usually paid by the lessee. The lessor company's only source of income may be the rental, which may be paid as dividends directly to its stockholders. On the other hand, it has no expenses to meet. All **operating expenses** of the property, as well as interest on its obligations, and some or all taxes are defrayed by the lessee, which also undertakes to satisfy other claims that might arise against the lessor as the result of lawsuits.

Corporate Existence and Acts of Lessor. The lessor continues to function as a corporation. Its stockholders will hold annual meetings to elect directors, who will meet occasionally to take such action at the request of the lessee as may be necessary so that all legal formalities may be observed in connection with the issue of additional stock or bonds or other corporate transactions.

The **terms of the lease** may bind the lessor to act or refrain from acting in practically all corporate matters at the will of the lessee, which thus takes over for the period of the lease all its corporate powers. On the other hand, the lessee corporation must pay promptly the rental and interest on the lessor's obligations, and fulfill other covenants of the lease. Any default in this respect will, by the conditions of the lease, operate to terminate the agreement and permit the lessor to take possession of the property and file suit for damages for breach of the lease contract.

Power of Corporations to Lease Assets. A corporation's power to lease its assets is similar to its power to sell its assets as an entirety. Like the sale of assets, leasing all its property is not a part of the ordinary business of a corporation, and hence it is not within the power of its directors to execute such an agreement. Such a lease requires action by the stockholders, which must be unanimous unless the statute permits action by a stated majority, as is generally the case.

Regulated corporations, such as railroads and public utilities, require approval of a lease of their property by regulatory commissions having jurisdiction over them.

The Interstate Commerce Act empowers the **Interstate Commerce Commission** to authorize acquisition of control of one carrier by another "under a lease or by the purchase of stock or in any other manner not involving the consolidation of such carriers into a single system for ownership and operation," when such control is found to be in the public interest. The Commission's approval must also be obtained when a railroad assumes the liabilities of another corporation, including a lessor.

STATUTES GOVERNING LEASE OF ASSETS. In practically all states, statutes have been enacted permitting corporations, both private and quasi-public, to lease their property if approval of a certain majority of the stockholders has been secured. Frequently the same provisions apply to leases and sales of assets, authorizing such transactions if a stated majority of the voting stockholders approve at a special meeting called for the purpose. This majority may be a bare majority, two-thirds, or three-quarters, according to the particular statute.

The provisions apply to lessor companies that surrender possession of their property, and not to the lessees. A corporation may lease another by action of its board of directors, unless the charter requires the approval of stockholders for such contracts.

Dissenting stockholders under a number of statutes may demand the fair value of their shares in cash, if necessary, after an appraisal conducted as prescribed in the statute. **Creditors of the lessor** corporation cannot prevent the execution of a lease except on the ground of fraud.

Special statutes in a number of states apply to railroads and public utilities, the lease of which requires approval of the Public Service Commission. The **right to make a lease** may be restricted by statute to corporations domiciled within the state, or to cases where the lessor and lessee corporations are engaged in similar lines of business.

INDUSTRIAL LEASES. Leases are seldom resorted to by industrial companies to effect **combinations**, except among mining, oil, and gas companies, department stores, and motion picture chains, and the property leased in these cases may consist of little more than real estate. The earning power of a manufacturing or trading company rests in large measure on its goodwill, and it is not practicable as a rule to transfer this intangible asset without selling all the assets and allowing the vendee to use the vendor's name. If a business is based on a well-protected patent or trade-mark, the earning power could be transferred to a certain extent by the lease of this intangible asset along with the tangible assets. However, there are serious obstacles in the way of such agreements. The successful exploitation of a patent, for example, depends greatly upon the ability of the management, and this may not be acquired by the lessee corporation. Moreover, the obligation assumed by the lessee corporation to pay a rental is a fixed charge, equivalent to the payment of interest on a bonded indebtedness. Manufacturing and trading concerns ordinarily do not want to burden themselves with heavy fixed charges.

RAILROAD LEASES. A number of large railroad systems have been built up through the amalgamation of small connecting lines, to a considerable extent by leases. In many instances, the lease was favored to accomplish this end because no financing was needed. Although the lessee railroad might have little or no stock interest in the lessor road at the time of the execution of the lease, it has been customary to acquire stock ownership by later purchases, with many leased lines finally being absorbed through merger.

FORM OF RENTAL. Practically all important leases involve a **fixed rental**. Commonly these rentals take the form of a fixed rate of dividend payable on the stock of the lessor corporation. The amount of stock on which the dividend is payable may be increased during the term of the lease, if it is provided that additional shares may be issued for capital improvements.

Contingent rentals may be based on (1) gross earnings of the leased properties from all sources or (2) net earnings of the leased lines. These contingent rentals are features of the older leases executed when the earning power of leased lines was not predictable.

Guaranty of Rental. In addition to obligating itself to the lessor corporation to pay the rental, a lessee may guarantee payment to the lessor's stockholders by specific endorsement on each stock certificate. By virtue of this guaranty, stockholders can sue the lessee corporation directly in their own right in the event of default. Under the **Bankruptcy Act**, however, such endorsement does not make a material difference in the position of guaranteed stock issues.

DIFFICULTIES IN DRAFTING EQUITABLE LEASE AGREEMENTS. Leases of corporate property usually run for extended periods of time. Railroad leases for the most part cover from 50 to 999 years, and may be for perpetuity. There are instances where a lease runs for the life of the lessor, and if that is limited the lease may be renewable with the renewal of the lessor's charter. In Pennsylvania, perpetual leases are considered sales.

Because of changes that may take place during the long periods covered by leases, disputes are likely to arise over the **interpretation of lease provisions**. It is not always possible for those drafting the agreement to foresee and provide for all of the contingencies that may arise during the lease's life. For example, many leases were written before the 16th Amendment to the Constitution legalized income taxes, and many leases did not specify whether the lessee or the lessor would be liable for the payment of income tax on the lessor's income. In a number of cases, the Treasury attached the lease rental to secure income taxes due it by the lessor corporation, and the amount of dividend received by the lessor's stockholders was reduced by the income tax paid on such income.

MERGERS TO END LEASES. Because the Treasury levies an income tax upon the net income of a lessor corporation, the lease device is distinctly unfavorable from a tax standpoint. Hence, a number of leases have been terminated through merger of the lessor into lessee corporations.

Holding Companies

USE OF HOLDING COMPANY METHOD OF COMBINATION. Acquisition of control by a corporation of one or more other corporations through stock ownership has been a common method of effecting business combinations in practically all fields of enterprise. The use of this method of combination has extended even to commercial banking, particularly in areas where legal restrictions limit the establishment of branches.

Effective control over one corporation by another may be exercised with varying degrees of stock ownership. Usually a **majority interest** is necessary to insure the election of the subsidiary's directors by the holding company, particularly in a moderate-sized company at whose meetings a large proportion of the stockholders are likely to vote either in person or by proxy. In larger corporations, effective control of a subsidiary can often be exercised with minority stockholdings, for most small stockholders have no interest in use of the voting power in such cases.

DEFINITION AND TYPES OF HOLDING COMPANIES. A holding company is one that holds stock in other companies for purposes of **control** rather than for mere investment. If a corporation owns a majority of stock in another with no idea of exercising control, but simply for the return that the investment will bring, it is not an actual holding company, although it may be regarded potentially as such. For example, an investment trust may happen to own a majority of the stock in a business corporation, but instead of voting the stock directly and controlling the company, it may be satisfied to send in its proxy for its stockholdings to the management in the same manner as other stockholders.

A corporation that has acquired a controlling stock interest in a number of other corporations may be a **pure holding** company or a **holding and operating** company. In the former instance, its assets will consist solely of its holdings of stocks and bonds, cash, and advances it may have made on short- or long-term account to subsidiary companies. Its chief sources of income are the dividends, interest, and perhaps fees received from these companies. The subsidiaries in turn may be subholding or operating companies.

If a law defines a holding company, such **statutory definition** takes the place of the above definition, which is based on common usage, in the application of the statute. Thus, the Public Utility Holding Company Act defines a holding company, for its purposes, as "any company which directly or indirectly owns, controls, or holds with power to vote, 10 percentum or more of the outstanding voting securities of a public-utility company . . ."

Holding Company with One Subsidiary. Practically all pure holding companies own the stock of at least two companies, since the purpose of their organization is to unify control of two or more companies. However, it is sometimes advantageous to form a holding company to hold the stock of a single operating company. The object then is not combination but to achieve some other end. It may be desirable, for example, to leave intact an operating company organized under the laws of one state and yet take advantage of the incorporation laws of another state. In that event, a holding company is formed that will exchange its stock for that of the operating company and thus become a pure holding company for that single subsidiary. Later it may acquire stock control of other companies as opportunity offers.

Holding-Operating Companies. The other form of holding company is a corporation that is at once an operating and a holding company. A manufacturing company, for example, may hold stock interests in one or more subsidiaries. Whether it is generally considered a holding company will depend upon the proportion of its assets represented by stockholdings.

Many parent corporations are primarily operating companies, with stockholdings in subsidiaries constituting a comparatively small portion of their total assets. Frequently the subsidiaries are not acquired but are incorporated to conduct some part of the business than can better be carried on by a separate corporation.

LAWS RESPECTING FORMATION OF HOLDING COMPANIES. Prior to 1888, all holding companies that came into prominence derived their power from special legislative acts giving them charter privileges denied other corporations. In a few states, the power to hold stock of another is expressly limited by law, but the **limitation** applies to only certain types of companies. Most statutes now permit corporations to hold stock in another corporation for whatever purpose, and the holding company has become a major instrument of combination through stock control.

TRUSTS AS COMBINATION DEVICE. In the period before holding company statutes existed, the trust was used to effect large business combinations. Shareholders of the companies involved assigned their stock to trustees who took title to and voted the shares. In exchange they received **certificates of beneficial interest** in the trust that entitled them to dividends declared by the trustees out of the trust's funds and, in the event of dissolution, a ratable portion of the net assets. The trustees thus became stockholders of the several companies, and by electing their directors exercised common control over them.

The original Standard Oil Trust was the most famous example of this form of business combination. It was attacked in the Ohio courts, and a decision was rendered dissolving the trust as an illegal grant of authority by the Standard Oil Co. of Ohio to the Standard Oil trustees. Courts of other states also frowned on the use of the trust device to control corporations. These court decisions resulted in the holding company replacing the trust as a device for intercorporate combination.

Control Through Voting Trusts. A number of statutes expressly authorize voting trusts upon compliance with certain conditions. The trust is used occasionally to effect combinations, but its use is restricted to smaller concerns. Smaller companies at times find it convenient to combine by having their stockholders place their shareholdings in the hands of one or two trustees, receiving certificates of beneficial interest in return.

ACQUISITION OF STOCK CONTROL. If ownership of the stock of a company in which a controlling stock interest is sought is concentrated in a few hands, the owners may be sought out and dealings carried on with them directly. This is not practicable in the instance of companies of any size whose stockholders may be numerous and widely scattered. Under such conditions other methods must be resorted to, particularly if a majority of the stock is sought.

Purchase for Cash. If it is decided to pay cash for the stock, purchasing may be done in the open market, by private negotiations, or both. It is often impracticable to acquire any sizable quantity of the stock by market purchases. Such buying, and the rumors to which it may give rise, will raise the price of the stock before the desired number of shares has been secured. Usually the buying will be spread over a considerable period of time and done as quietly as possible to avoid such a **run-up in the price.** By concealing its accumulation of the stock through having it transferred to dummy holders or carrying it with brokers, the purchasing company may succeed in keeping the management of the company being acquired in the dark as to changing ownership until it has accumulated the desired block of stock and is ready, just before the annual meeting or earlier, to announce its control of the company. However, the requirement, under the Securities Exchange Act of 1934, of **public disclosure of stock dealings** of a holder of more than 10% of the stock of a registered company makes this procedure more difficult.

Acquisition of Control Through Exchange of Stock. When it is planned to acquire control by an exchange of stock or other securities, an offer must be made to the stockholders of the company sought. Usually it is advisable first to approach its directors and large shareholders to enlist their cooperation in the plan. These discussions will determine the terms. If, with the announcement of the terms, the directors issue a statement recommending the exchange of stock as in the best interest of the stockholders, organized opposition may be forestalled and stockholders will be so much more likely to agree to the exchange.

The offer frequently stipulates that the offer of exchange will become operative only if holders of a stated majority of the stock agree to turn in their stocks. In that event, stockholders desiring to exchange their shares will be asked to deposit their stock by a certain date with a named depositary under a deposit agreement.

The **consideration** paid in the acquisition of stock in other companies may consist of cash or securities. If a large number of shares is involved, cash settlement will usually be avoided as it would require new financing on the part of the purchasing company. Stock is the most common consideration, but the purchasing company may issue bonds in full or part payment. Sometimes, collateral trust bonds are issued, with the stock acquired pledged as security. The bonds can be issued directly in exchange for the stock or sold to raise cash if the desired stock is to be acquired for cash.

DEALINGS BETWEEN PARENT AND SUBSIDIARY. Parent-subsidiary relations largely depend upon whether the subsidiary is **wholly** or only **partly owned.** When there is a minority interest outstanding, the subsidiary must be treated as a separate and independent entity, if the parent is to avoid possible liability. The parent may require the payment of interest on advances it makes to the subsidiary, and even demand the deposit of collateral security provided the advance is really required for the subsidiary's business. Whether a subsidiary is wholly or partly owned, the parent company is legally entitled only to the share of a subsidiary's profit that is distributed by **formal dividend declaration.**

Financing Subsidiary's Capital Requirements. A subsidiary may be financially self-contained and not require financial assistance. If, however, it is compelled to seek **additional funds,** these may be obtained from the parent company if the latter has the money or can raise it on better terms than can the subsidiary. Advances may be made on open book account, represented by interest-bearing demand notes given the parent company, or funded by the issuance of bonds or stock that the parent company may retain as permanent investments. On the other hand, if the subsidiary enjoys a **good credit rating** with investors, the parent may resell the subsidiary's securities it holds, with or without a guaranty of dividends or interest, and principal at maturity of bonds.

Sometimes a subsidiary's credit is so well established that it can do its own public financing with stocks or bonds, and enjoy a regular line of credit with banks. If it issues stock to the public, this may be preferred or a special class not possessing voting power in order that the parent company's control may not be disturbed.

ADVANTAGES AND DISADVANTAGES OF THE HOLDING COMPANY DEVICE. Combination by acquisition of a stock interest in one or more companies has distinct advantages and certain disadvantages.

Advantages. The major advantages obtained are as follows:

1. It is not necessary to secure formal consent of stockholders, or to pay off a dissenting minority in cash, as in the case of the purchase of assets, consolidations, or mergers.

2. A going concern is taken over intact and continued as such, so that there is no loss of goodwill with either the public or employees. This is particularly true if the stock acquisition is effected quietly by private purchase from a comparatively few large stockholders.
3. If cash is paid, a sum far less than the net value of the assets of the acquired subsidiary need be invested to acquire control. The holding company device makes it possible to acquire control of large properties with a minimum of investment, for only that part of the voting stock of the subsidiary sufficient to exercise control need be purchased. If the subsidiaries, and perhaps the holding company as well, are financed in part by senior nonvoting securities, control can be secured with a relatively small investment. A holding company can pledge stock of subsidiaries owned as security for a collateral trust bond issue, to reduce its investment further.
4. No assumption or guaranty of a subsidiary's liabilities is necessary. Thus, the parent company is insulated against the liabilities of subsidiaries, if the **"instrumentality rule"** (see below) is not applied. This insulation from liabilities of a subsidiary may be of considerable importance when (1) expansion occurs into a field subject to unusual risks, or (2) future regulation by the government may compel separation of subsidiaries from parent control.
5. The holding company has an advantage over the merger or consolidation in that it is easier to divorce an unprofitable unit from the whole.
6. The holding company device may make possible combination of enterprises that could not legally be fused under direct ownership of one corporation.
7. The holding company is advantageous if it is desirable from an administrative viewpoint to decentralize operations by products, territories, or otherwise. The holding company structure has been effectively used to segregate unlike businesses or different operating functions; to obtain local capital; to preserve goodwill; and to meet regional regulation and taxation situations.

Disadvantages. The ownership of subsidiary companies has certain drawbacks, the seriousness of which will depend on circumstances. The more important disadvantages are:

1. Minority interests may prove troublesome. If subsidiaries are only partly owned, the minority stockholders may be a source of annoyance to the holding company. They may charge the holding company with diverting earnings from the subsidiary by improper accounting methods. They may also restrict the management's ability to adjust operations to changing conditions and new opportunities. Even though a holding company may have the statutory power to effect the desired change, a recalcitrant minority interest may seek the intervention of a court of equity on the ground of fraud, and the parent may find it necessary to buy out the minority interest. Partly because of this possibility, many industrial companies seek to eliminate minority interests in subsidiaries as soon as this can be done.
2. The **expense** of creating and maintaining separate corporate organizations. Franchise taxes must be paid by each corporation, and each corporation must submit reports to the state and regulatory agencies. The costs of records of directors' and stockholders' meetings must be considered. Particularly in times of slack business when expenditures are being curtailed in every direction, the number of subsidiaries may be reduced through absorption of subsidiaries by the parent or other subsidiaries.
3. A holding company structure may prove unstable. **"Pyramiding"** was carried to an extreme in the public utility field, and was a main reason for the collapse of several large utility holding company systems. Further, if subsidiary earnings fall off, income may cease to flow to the parent. If a subsidiary is unable to pay dividends on a cumulative preferred stock issue with contingent voting power held by the public, control may be lost by the parent. If a subsidiary defaults on its obligations and is reorganized, the parent company's stockholdings may be wiped out altogether.

4. Present **income tax laws** work to the disadvantage of a holding company. A parent company must own 95% or more of its subsidiaries' voting stock (and 95% of each class of nonvoting stock, other than preferred, of at least one subsidiary) to file a consolidated return. This requirement serves to offset the advantage of controlling a subsidiary by holding a majority or less of the voting stock. Furthermore, a penalty of 2% is imposed on the filing of a consolidated tax return. In addition, the holding company has to pay an intercorporate dividend tax of 15% of the corporate normal and surtax rate on dividends received. Tax considerations have been a major reason for the simplification of many holding company structures during the past decade. However, there are still many instances where a holding company structure gives net tax advantages, as when a motion picture chain incorporates each theatre separately so that it is taxed as a small business.
5. Unfavorable legislation affecting holding companies, especially in the public utility field.

MAINTAINING CORPORATE EXISTENCE AFTER TRANSFER OF ASSETS. A company may acquire the stock of another corporation and have the latter's assets transferred to itself or some other subsidiary. Instead of dissolving the newly acquired subsidiary, however, it may maintain its corporate existence by the payment of the **annual franchise tax** in order to prevent others from appropriating its name, which may have a trade value.

CREATION OF SUBSIDIARIES BY PARENT COMPANY. Subsidiary companies are not only purchased and acquired to effect combinations, but are also created by the parent company. For various reasons, the parent company may segregate certain assets by turning them over to a newly formed subsidiary, all of whose stock it will own with the exception possibly of directors' qualifying shares. The amount of assets turned over and the size of the capital stock with which the subsidiary is organized will depend on the function it is to perform and the financial relationship it will maintain with the parent organization. The purpose of its creation may be such that it will not require any considerable amount of capital. On the other hand, it may need a great deal of capital for expansion. If it is to conduct business on the parent company's credit, having its notes endorsed and its accounts guaranteed by the latter, its **capital stock may be of a nominal amount.** In that event, the parent company is actually liable for the subsidiary company's liabilities.

Subsidiaries Organized for Legal Reasons. Frequent recourse is had to the organization of subsidiary companies to circumvent legal obstacles, to avoid burdens otherwise imposed by the law, or to take advantage of a particular law. Under our Federal system, which makes **every corporation created in one state foreign in every other state,** subsidiaries are organized to do business in other states, if restrictions are imposed on foreign corporations or they are required to pay special taxes and fees.

State laws of a restrictive or regulatory character may make it advisable to form a subsidiary to conduct some of the activities of the business. A timber company may encounter difficulties in acquiring the right of way for a private logging railway to a tract of timber land it owns. It can organize a railroad company that, as a common carrier, enjoys the right of eminent domain and is able to condemn land necessary for its road. A general business corporation, among its other activities, may be engaged in a business that makes it subject to regulation by the State Public Service Commission. It will free itself of considerable annoyance by incorporating the public utility business in a separate subsidiary that will be so regulated.

Subsidiaries To Facilitate Management and Operations. If the parent is engaged in two or more independent lines of business, segregation of the activities by organizing subsidiaries may promote more effective management and more economical and efficient operation. The internal corporate organization may follow the lines of the functional divisions of a business. One subsidiary may be formed to take over the sales division. Other departments may be similarly incorporated.

Scientific and research activities of the organization may be grouped in one separate corporation. Subsidiaries are also organized to hold and develop real estate. After combinations of large corporations, the rearrangement of operations necessary to realize anticipated economies is often effected through the organization of subsidiary companies.

Subsidiaries To Secure Goodwill. When branch plants or selling organizations are established, it may be desirable to incorporate them separately and place prominent local men on the board. By this means, this particular division of the company's business becomes more intimately identified with the community it is intended to serve and local goodwill is obtained.

The **segregation** in a subsidiary of some new line of business taken on by a corporation may be desirable to protect the established goodwill of the parent in connection with its old line. Thus, a publishing house of many years' standing may have developed a nationwide reputation for handling books appealing to more intellectual tastes. If it desires to handle in addition publications with a wide popular appeal, it may organize a new subsidiary for this new business, so that the public interested in more serious works may not get the impression that the company is changing the character of its publications.

On the other hand, an acquired subsidiary may be stripped of all assets and become an **inactive corporation** whose existence will be maintained merely to prevent appropriation of its name, with its trade value, by others who desire to enter the same field.

Subsidiaries To Limit Parent Company's Liability. When a corporation is launching some hazardous business, one that is highly **speculative** or that may possibly give rise to heavy claims for damages, it may be able to limit the possible loss by organizing a subsidiary to engage in that particular activity. Similarly, a corporation may make certain undertakings that later handicap its financial and other arrangements. At times these obligations may be legally avoided by the formation of subsidiary companies. An example of such practice is the organization of subsidiaries to evade the **after-acquired property clause** in trust indentures securing mortgage bond issues.

Intercorporate Readjustments. A holding company organization with a number of subsidiary companies may from time to time effect intercorporate readjustments to fit changing economic conditions, tax laws, regulatory statutes, or financing requirements. Assets and functions may be reparceled among existing subsidiaries for more advantageous grouping. New subsidiaries may be formed to take over certain activities of the old, or subsidiaries may be combined with others or with the parent company. The legal devices used will be the same as between independent corporations. **Transfer of assets** will occur through sales, consolidation, or merger, and stockholdings may be sold by one subsidiary to another or to the parent corporation. (See also in Sec. 21, beginning p. 22.)

Foreign Subsidiaries. Manufacturers having factories, warehouses, or sales offices in foreign countries quite frequently find it advantageous or necessary to have them separately incorporated under the laws of those countries. Often, the parent would labor under legal handicaps if it owned the factories or other facilities directly. National prejudices may hamper the business of a foreign enterprise in that country. A minority interest in the subsidiary may be offered to the public in the foreign country in order to establish its character as locally owned.

Foreign subsidiaries have become of increasing importance since the Second World War. The most rapid expansion has taken place in Western Europe as U.S. firms, desirous of availing themselves of the tariff preferences accorded to companies organized in the European Common Market and European Free Trade Association countries, have established thousands of new enterprises in those areas. The profitability of some of these concerns was affected by a change in the **Revenue Act of 1962**. Under the new rules, 90% of the earnings of foreign **sales** subsidiaries are subject to U.S. corporate income taxes in the year earned. Profits of **manufacturing** subsidiaries, however, continue to be taxed only when they are transferred to the U.S.

ABUSE OF PARENT-SUBSIDIARY RELATION. A holding or parent corporation owning a controlling interest in a subsidiary is considered by the courts to assume a **fiduciary relationship** to the minority stockholders and to be charged with the duty of exercising a high degree of good faith, care, and diligence for the protection of such minority interests. This doctrine has been extended and clarified by more recent Supreme Court decisions. (See Deep Rock doctrine below.)

Protection Afforded Minority Stockholders by Courts. Minority stockholders have secured relief from the courts when a parent company has **exploited the subsidiary in its own interest** and adversely to the interest of the latter's minority shareholders. Such cases have involved diversion of business and income from a partly owned subsidiary to the parent company or a wholly owned subsidiary, particularly when the parent and the partly owned subsidiary were competitors. In flagrant cases, the parent has attempted to bankrupt the subsidiary by depriving it of lucrative business so as to come into full control. When a parent has, through the controlled board of directors, attempted to foist on the subsidiary unfavorable contracts, including sale or lease of assets and intercorporate loans, or has failed to observe contracts with the subsidiary, minority stockholders have likewise received the protection of the courts.

The courts have also intervened at the instance of minority shareholders to enjoin consolidation of the subsidiary with the parent or other subsidiaries, or the dissolution of the subsidiary, even though the procedure was in strict conformity with the statutory provisions, when the palpable reason for the consolidation, merger, or dissolution was to get rid of some contract between parent and subsidiary, unfavorable to the former, such as a lease of assets (Boyd v. New York & Harlem R. R. Co., 220 Fed. 174 [D. C. N. Y., 1915]), or when the terms of a proposed consolidation or merger were unfair to minority stockholders of the subsidiary.

INSTRUMENTALITY RULE. One important reason for the use of the holding company device has been to insulate the parent and each subsidiary from liabilities incurred by another subsidiary. As a result, creditors have found on occasion that they cannot collect debts due them because insufficient assets are held by the debtor subsidiary, although such debts may have been incurred for the benefit of the parent or the holding company system as a whole. The courts have attempted to meet this situation through the application of what has been termed the "instrumentality rule." The "instrumentality rule" holds that a parent company will be **liable for debts** of a subsidiary if it can be shown that the parent uses the subsidiary as a mere "instrumentality," "agency," or "adjunct," so that one is the "alter ego" of the other. This is particularly the case if the subsidiary is formed with a nominal capital stock and has no independent organization through which to function, the main purpose of its existence being apparently the evasion of liability or some law.

The Deep Rock Doctrine. Parent-subsidiary relationships have been clarified to a large extent by a series of United States Supreme Court decisions of which the first and most important was the "Deep Rock" case, Taylor v. Standard Gas Electric Co., 306 U. S. 307 (1939). This case involved the attempt of the parent company, Standard Gas, to assert a **prior claim**, as creditor on account of advances, to the assets of its subsidiary, the Deep Rock Oil Corporation, which was being reorganized. The court subordinated the claim of Standard Gas to publicly held preferred stock of Deep Rock. The basis of the decision was (1) the history of spoliation, mismanagement, and faithless stewardship of the affairs of the subsidiary by the parent to the detriment of public investors, and (2) the failure of Standard Gas to capitalize the subsidiary adequately by providing it with sufficient equity capital when it was formed. As expanded in subsequent decisions, the "Deep Rock Doctrine" holds that a **holding company is a fiduciary.** Its powers are powers in trust and must be exercised for the protection of the entire community of interests in the corporation—creditors as well as stockholders. The application of this doctrine has been of increasing importance in the field of intercorporate relations.

PUBLIC UTILITY HOLDING COMPANIES. The holding company reached its highest development in the public utility field, particularly among electric light and power and gas companies. Less than ten holding-company systems formerly conducted the major portion of the electric light and power business of the country. These systems comprised a holding company at the top of the structure, with one or more intermediate subholding companies between it and the operating companies. The major holding companies did not in every instance own a majority of the stock of the subholding or operating companies, but a sufficient minority interest was held to insure effective control in view of the widely scattered stockholdings.

A number of factors brought about the **dominance of holding companies** in the utility industry. Early control of basic patents by the Bell System and the advantages of a unified system of countrywide communication explain the great success of the American Telephone & Telegraph Co. Earlier combinations of local operating units in contiguous territories were formed to avoid destructive rate reductions and increase efficiency. Later giant combinations of scattered, diverse utilities were attributed by Bonbright and Means (The Holding Company) chiefly to the greater financial strength of a large utility system as compared with a local property, and the efficiency and economy of centralized management or supervision by organizations of experts. Other reasons were the desire of engineering and manufacturing groups to secure control of a maximum number of utility properties in order to sell them commodities and services, and the desire of bankers to control utility managements in order to underwrite their security issues. The Electric Bond & Share Co. was originally organized by the General Electric Co. to give financial assistance to utility companies purchasing its products. The Stone & Webster system was formed in 1924 in order to prevent companies for which the firm of Stone & Webster furnished engineering and management service from falling into other hands. The United Corp. was organized by the banking firms of J. P. Morgan & Co., Drexel & Co., and Bonbright & Co. to retain control over a large group of utilities in the East.

Unsound Financial Practices. In the years of depression following 1929, unsound practices developed in the financing of some public utility holding companies. Several holding companies were forced to lean heavily upon their operating subsidiaries for financial support. **"Upstream" loans** from subsidiary to parent were made, and the operating companies' credit was even used to provide funds for unrelated ventures of the controlling financial interests. Dividend policies of operating companies at times were guided by stockholders' demands rather than by the need for funds on the part of the holding companies, even if such distributions were unwise.

Such abuses, although by no means typical of public utility holding companies generally, caused the enactment of the Public Utility Holding Company Act of 1935.

REGULATION OF PUBLIC UTILITY HOLDING COMPANIES. Under the Public Utility Holding Company Act of 1935, the Federal government has obtained drastic regulatory powers over holding companies controlling electric and gas operating companies. These holding companies are not subject to the jurisdiction of the state public service commissions, which have supervision only over utility **operating** companies. The Act aims to eliminate abuses that have characterized the formation and operation of holding companies.

The **Public Utility Holding Company Act,** which provides for the dissolution as well as the regulation of utility holding companies, is administered by the Securities and Exchange Commission. The S.E.C. supervises security transactions by holding companies and their subsidiaries, the acquisition of securities and properties by holding companies and proxies, intercompany loans, and service, sales, and construction contracts that holding companies or nonoperating subsidiaries may have with operating utility subsidiaries.

Registration of Utility Holding Companies. Companies subject to the Act are holding companies having electric and gas subsidiaries in more than one state, and their subsidiaries. Such holding companies are required to register with the Securities and Exchange Commission. The **registration statement** includes complete corporate information, and balance sheets and income statements for several years. Unless a holding company is registered with the Commission it is barred from the use of the mails or from engaging in any form of interstate activity, including the sale and distribution of its securities or those of its subsidiaries. The Commission may upon application exempt, from the obligation to register, holding companies whose operations are predominantly intrastate in character, or that are only incidentally or temporarily holding companies, or whose chief source of income is public utility companies operating abroad.

Regulation of New Security Issues of Utility Holding Companies. Before a registered holding company or any of its subsidiaries may issue securities, it must file with the S.E.C. a **declaration** including information and documents required to register a security under the Securities Act of 1933, and any additional information that the Commission may require. Issue of securities is not permitted until the declaration has been approved by the Commission and becomes effective. This provision does not apply to certain short-term note issues. Before approving issuance, the S.E.C. must be satisfied that the character of the security is justified by the financial set-up of the issuing company and that the terms of sale are reasonable and not detrimental to the interests of the public, investors, and consumers. In May 1941 Rule U-50 was adopted by the Commission which requires **competitive bidding** in the sale of securities (other than short-term notes) by a registered holding company or any of its subsidiaries.

Acquisition of Securities and Properties. A holding company or any of its subsidiaries may not purchase securities of other companies or properties without the Commission's approval. Whether securities or properties are purchased, the Commission, before granting permission, must satisfy itself that the new acquisition will not tend to **undue concentration** of control of public utility companies or unduly complicate the capital structure of the holding company system making the acquisition, and that the consideration paid for the securities or properties is reasonable.

Simplification and Integration of Holding-Company Systems. The provisions of the Act relating to simplification and integration of holding company systems constitute its most drastic and significant part. The simplification standards [§ 11b(2)] are twofold: (1) the capital structure of a holding company and each subsidiary must not be unduly complicated, and a fair and equitable distribution of voting power must exist among the stockholders, and (2) the intercorporate structure is limited to **three layers** of corporate entities, i.e., a holding company cannot have a subsidiary whose subsidiary is itself a holding company (**"grandfather" clause**).

The integration provisions [see § 11b(1)] limit holding companies to a single integrated system. The Act defines an integrated system for electric power and light public utilities as "one or more units of generating plants and/or transmission lines and/or distributing facilities whose utility assets, whether owned by one or more electric utility companies, are physically interconnected or capable of physical interconnection and which under normal conditions may be economically operated as a single interconnected and coordinated system confined in its operations to a single area or region, in one or more states, not so large as to impair (considering the state of the act and the area or region affected) the advantages of localized management, efficient operation, and the effectiveness of regulation." The S.E.C. has interpreted the integration provisions of the Act to limit a holding company to one compact operating system that must be in one or more adjoining states. (See also Sec. 21, p. 24.)

Supervision of Intercompany Loans, Dividends, Security Transactions, Etc. Regulation and supervision by the S.E.C. of other activities of holding company systems are provided for by the Act. The law prohibits:

1. "Upstream" financing, or borrowing by holding companies from their subsidiaries.
2. Contributions in support of any political candidate or party by a holding company or any subsidiary.

The following activities may be carried on by the holding company or its subsidiaries only in accordance with regulations prescribed by the Commission:

1. Intercompany loans within the holding-company system other than loans by subsidiaries to the holding company.
2. Payment of dividends and acquisition, retirement or redemption of securities.
3. Sale of any assets, including securities of other companies.
4. Intercompany transactions within the holding-company system.

HOLDING COMPANIES

5. Solicitation of proxies.
6. Lobbying before Congress, the Securities and Exchange Commission, or the Federal Power Commission.

The Act also aims to prevent abuses in connection with **contracts** that holding companies, or companies especially organized for the purpose, have with subsidiary companies.

Periodic Reports and Accounts and Records. The Commission may require annual, quarterly, and other periodic reports from registered holding companies and mutual service companies. Officers and directors of holding companies are required to file a statement of the securities they own in the holding company or any subsidiary, and to report monthly any change in their holdings. Officers and directors may be required to **refund** to the corporation any profit from the purchase and sale, or short sale and covering purchase of any securities of an affiliated company, made within a period of less than 6 months. No officer or director of a bank or trust company, and no partner or representative of an investment banking firm or of any corporation controlled by a bank, trust company, or investment banking firm, may serve as an officer or director of a holding company or any of its subsidiaries, except as the Commission may permit.

Regulation of Interstate Electric Utility Companies Under the Federal Power Act. An amendment to the Federal Water Power Act, known as the Federal Power Act, subjects to regulation by the Federal Power Commission electric utility companies transmitting and selling electric energy across state lines. Rates that electric companies may charge for current are under the control of the Commission, with whom schedules must be filed. The Commission also passes on the issuance of new securities by companies under its jurisdiction, as well as the purchase, sale, or lease of properties of a value in excess of $50,000 and mergers or consolidations.

Without the Commission's sanction there may be no **interlocking directorates** between the companies and no officer of one company may serve as an officer of another company. Likewise, subject to the Commission's approval, a director or officer of an electric utility company may not serve in a similar capacity with any organization doing a security underwriting business, or with any company supplying electrical equipment to electric utility companies. If provisions relating to the regulation of electric companies by the Federal Power Commission are in conflict with provisions of the Public Utility Holding Company Act, the latter prevail.

Use of Massachusetts Trust. In Massachusetts, no foreign corporation (incorporated in another state) owning a majority of the capital stock of a public utility in that state may issue stocks or bonds based upon the property of that utility unless such issue has been specifically authorized by Massachusetts. As none has been so authorized, this law has prevented foreign holding companies from obtaining direct control of local utilities in that state. They have instead resorted to indirect means of acquiring control through the organization of voluntary associations or Massachusetts trusts (see Section 12 on Forms of Business Organization).

REGULATION OF OTHER HOLDING COMPANIES. There is little regulation of holding companies in the industrial field with the exception of the air transport industry, which is regulated by the Civil Aeronautics Board. The Clayton Anti-Trust Act prohibits the acquisition of stock of one corporation by another if the effect is "to substantially lessen competition."

In the **railroad** field, the Emergency Transportation Act of 1933 gave the Interstate Commerce Commission jurisdiction over the acquisition of stocks of railroad companies for control purposes by any person after June 16, 1933. Railroad holding companies formed prior to 1933 are not affected, for this statute, unlike the Public Utility Holding Company Act, is not retroactive in character.

There are few pure holding companies among railroads. In most instances, the large railroad systems consist of parent operating companies that own stock of subsidiaries or lease them, for they were developed before the organization of pure holding companies was possible under state statutes.

Bank holding companies are subject to special regulation under the jurisdiction of the Board of Governors of the Federal Reserve System.

Other Types of Business Combination or Cooperation

CARTELS. A cartel may be described as an agreement among business enterprises to limit competition among themselves. The agreement may take the form of a written contract or an oral gentlemen's agreement.

Types. Cartels may be divided into five basic types. Some belong to one type, whereas others are a combination of several.

1. **Price cartel.** This type sets either uniform or minimum prices. It represents an attempt to eliminate price cutting within an industry through contractual agreement, rather than by combination.

2. **Division of output.** In this type, limitation of production and division of output by quotas for each member are jointly agreed upon, to fit supply to demand.

3. **Division of territory.** The territorial cartel assigns market areas on an exclusive basis to its members.

4. **Single selling agency.** A more advanced type of cartel involves the use of one selling agency that sells for all the members, distributing orders among them under a prearranged schedule of quotas.

5. **Patent pools.** In this type of cartel the associated companies agree to interchange patents. The companies owning the patents may retain title to the patents and license other members to use them. Another method involves transfer of title to the patents to a trustee, who licenses members of the cartel to use them. A third method calls for formation of a new corporation for the purpose of holding title to the patents.

Restrictions on Use in the United States. Although permitted in some foreign countries, cartels are, for the most part, prohibited in the United States by the antitrust laws. In the United States, exemptions from the legal prohibition of activities in "restraint of trade" are provided in a number of industries, including agricultural cooperative marketing associations (under the Capper-Volstead Act of 1922) and railroads with the approval of the Interstate Commerce Commission (under the Transportation Act of 1920).

Webb-Pomerene Act Associations. The Webb-Pomerene Act was enacted by Congress in 1918 to exempt from the provisions of the Sherman and Clayton Acts associations engaging solely in **export trade**. These export associations enabled United States exporters to form united fronts on prices, market quotas, and sales policies as do foreign cartels. However, when export associations join in agreements that restrain trade in the United States, they are held illegal.

TRADE ASSOCIATIONS. A type of business cooperation not involving formal combination is the trade association, which has been defined as "a voluntary organization formed to promote the mutual interests of enterprises engaged in the same kind of business." Such associations exist in virtually every industry, both on a regional and national scale. Among the **functions** they perform for their members are collection and dissemination of statistical data relating to production, prices and sales, political representation, industry self-regulation, arbitration of commercial disputes, collective bargaining, setting up of uniform accounting systems, industrial research, market research, advertising and promotional activities, credit services, cooperative buying, and transportation problems. In some instances these activities were used to limit production, fix prices, or otherwise restrict competition and were declared illegal.

LONG-TERM SALES CONTRACTS. A contract under which one company has the exclusive right to use or sell the products or services of another may result in substantial economies in production and distribution without loss of corporate identity by either party. Frequently, such an arrangement may be the **forerunner of a formal combination** through acquisition of stock or purchase of assets.

COMMUNITY OF INTEREST. The community of interest consists of corporations brought within the same sphere of influence by means of common ownership of stock by one person or a small group of persons who are held together by common interest, family relationship, or long acquaintance. This influence is often made more effective by the use of **interlocking directorates,** the same individuals sitting on the several boards of directors. So long as the stockholders remain in agreement, such an affiliation may be as effective in coordinating the policies of two companies as the ownership of the one by the other, or of both by a holding company.

Since such companies will tend to work in harmony with one another, some of the advantages of combination may be achieved. The community of interest has played an important part in the railroad, public utility, and industrial fields. The Standard Oil companies constitute an informal community of interest, the holdings of the Rockefeller family in the several Standard Oil corporations constituting a unifying influence.

Interlocking directorates are **prohibited by law** in several fields at the present time. Thus, the Clayton Act of 1914 made it illegal for an individual to be a director of more than one national bank with deposits and net worth of over $5,000,000, or of more than one industrial corporation with net worth of over $1,000,000 if the companies are, or have been, competitors. Similarly, the Banking Act of 1933, in connection with the divorce of investment from commercial banking activities, prohibited an officer or director of a Federal Reserve member bank from serving as an officer or director of a securities company. The Transportation Act of 1920 made interlocking directorates in the railroad industry subject to approval by the Interstate Commerce Commission.

A community of interest may be effected **without formal steps.** Its use, however, is subject to several **disadvantages.** First, there is no centralized control and its success depends on the influence of the common stockholding interest in separate corporations. Secondly, the advantages of unified large-scale operation are not usually realized. In the third place, a community of interest lacks permanence in that sale of stock by some holders ends the arrangement.

Mutual Stock Ownership. A community of interest may be effected by mutual stock ownership. The petroleum industry affords outstanding examples, the best known being the Royal Dutch-Shell combination, which was achieved between two previously quite competitive enterprises when each bought a large block of stock in the other. If such a relationship exists it is easier to effect uniformity in production, pricing, and marketing policies. In many instances mutual stock ownership has served as a **prelude to fuller combination** through merger or consolidation.

JOINTLY OWNED SUBSIDIARIES AND FACILITIES. Another variation of the community of interest of increasing importance is the formation of a subsidiary that is controlled jointly by two or more independent corporations that desire to combine their efforts along certain lines. For example, the Brunswick Pulp and Paper Co. is controlled jointly by Scott Paper Co. and Mead Corporation, each owning 50% of Brunswick's capital stock. Carthage Hydrocol, Inc., was formed in 1946 by eight corporations, including The Texas Co., The Chicago Corp., United Gas Corp., and Gulf States Oil Co., for the purpose of manufacturing gasoline and by-products from natural gas. Electric Energy, Inc., was organized by five electric utility companies to generate power for the Paducah project of the U.S. Atomic Energy Commission.

In some instances two companies have found it more advantageous, from a tax standpoint, to operate a jointly owned plant without organizing it as a separate corporation.

VOLUNTARY CHAINS. A method utilized by small businesses to obtain some of the benefits of large scale operation without losing their identities is the voluntary chain. This device involves assumption of specified managerial functions over a large number of retail stores by a **central organization** through contract. These functions may include purchasing, advertising, store design, and assistance in administration and merchandising activities.

An outstanding example of the voluntary chain is the Independent Grocers Alliance, a national organization of independent retailers grouped around their local wholesale grocery houses, which hold exclusive I.G.A. franchises for a defined geographical area.

Other examples of voluntary chains are the independent Rexall chain, with the United Rexall Drug Co. as the central organization, and the Howard Johnson restaurant chain.

SECTION 21

RECAPITALIZATIONS AND READJUSTMENTS

CONTENTS

Nature and Causes of Changes in Capital Structure
Changing economic conditions and capital structures 1
Recapitalizations, readjustments, and reorganizations 1

Common Stock Recapitalizations
Legal requirements 2
Changes in number of shares 3
  Stock split-ups and stock dividends 3
  Reverse splits or share consolidation 3
Changes in par or stated value 4
  Changes from par to no-par stock 4
  Changes from no-par to par stock 4
  Increase or decrease in par or stated value.. 4
Capital account reductions 4
  Methods of effecting capital stock reductions 5
  Purposes accomplished by capital stock reductions 5
  Arguments for and against asset writedowns 6
  Creditors' and preferred shareholders' interest in capital stock reductions 6
  Capital distributions 7
Reclassification of stock 7
  Reasons for reclassifying stock capitalization 8

Preferred Stock Recapitalizations and Readjustments
General principles and legal restrictions 9
Purposes of preferred stock recapitalizations. 9
  Elimination of burdensome charter provisions 10
  Exchange for a lower dividend issue 10
  Exchange for other securities 10
  Clear-up arrearages on cumulative preferred stock 10
Meeting the special problems of arrearages .. 11
  Legal factors 11
  Methods of clearing up arrearages 12
  Meeting the problem of dissent 12
  Examples of arrearage settlements 13

Debt Readjustments
Circumstances necessitating debt readjustment 14

Main types of readjustments 14
  Extension of maturities 14
  Reduction of interest rate 15
  Reduction of principal 15
  Other indenture changes 15
Inducements to bondholders 15
Legal aspects of debt readjustments 15
  Dissenters' rights 15
  Mechanics of debt readjustment 16
How bond readjustments are effected 16
  Negotiation with large holders 16
  Presenting the plan 17
  Securing assents 17
  Establishing effective date 17
  A bank loan 17
Debt readjustments under special legislation.. 17
Small business readjustments 17
Compositions 17
  Number of creditors necessary to a composition settlement 18
  Acceptance considerations 18
  When to agree to compositions 18
Assignments 19
  Advantages of assignments 19
  Common law and statutory assignments 19
  Assignment an act of bankruptcy 19
  Rights of creditors 20
  Assignees 20
  Duties of assignees 20
Creditors' committees 20
  How committees operate 21
  Creditor voting trustees 21
  Advantages of creditors' committees 21
  Disadvantages of creditors' committees ... 22
Credit adjustment bureaus 22

Intercorporate Readjustments
Changes in corporate structure of a holding company system 22
Reasons for intercorporate changes 22
Intercorporate readjustment methods 23
Simplification and integration under the Public Utility Holding Company Act 24
Simplification and integration methods ... 24

Voluntary Liquidations
Liquidation defined 25
Wasting asset industries 25
Liquidation to avoid insolvency 25
Procedure in voluntary liquidation 25
Liquidating agency 26

CONTENTS (Continued)

Corporate Dissolution

	Page
Meaning of dissolution	26
Methods of dissolution	27
Legislative revocation of charter	27
Dissolution by expiration of charter	27
Dissolution effected by happening of some contingency	27
Dissolution from misuse and nonuse of powers	28
Voluntary dissolution	28

SECTION 21

RECAPITALIZATIONS AND READJUSTMENTS

Nature and Causes of Changes in Capital Structure

CHANGING ECONOMIC CONDITIONS AND CAPITAL STRUCTURES. The capital structure of a business reflects management decisions over a long period of time and the condition of the security markets at the time of successive security sales. The capital structure may consist of a single class of stock, or it may be complicated by several issues of bonds and preferred stock, the characteristics of which may vary considerably. The **rights of each class** of security holders are determined by contract. Contract rights of bondholders are set forth in the bond indenture, whereas rights of stockholders are set forth in the certificate of incorporation and, in some instances, the bylaws. Rights of security holders are relatively fixed in nature, and can be modified only by proper legal steps.

On the other hand, economic conditions are in a constant state of flux. Fortunes of corporations change. One enterprise may suffer a long series of operating deficits, whereas another may encounter a sustained period of success. In either event, a remolding of the capital structure may become desirable or necessary to facilitate new financing or for other purposes. For example, when a corporation experiences **large operating deficits** or a sharp decline in the value of its assets, it may be desirable to increase the surplus so that the needed charge-offs may be made without impairing capital and preventing payment of dividends from future earnings. Conversely, when a corporation develops very **large earning power** so that its stock is selling at a high price, it may be sound policy to bring down the price by increasing the number of shares outstanding through a stock split or a stock dividend. These and other changes in the capital structure may provide opportunities for strengthening a company's financial position by improving the investment status and broadening the market for its securities.

RECAPITALIZATIONS, READJUSTMENTS, AND REORGANIZATIONS. A distinction may be drawn between corporate recapitalizations, readjustments, and reorganizations. Recapitalizations involve a **rearrangement** of the capital accounts only. Readjustments, as the term is used here, involve **changes in the rights and preferences** of preferred stock provisions, and bonds, or the intercorporate structure of a parent company and its subsidiaries. Reorganization is ordinarily used to describe **revision** of capital structures under the jurisdiction of a court (see Sec. 22). Reorganization through the courts permits dealing with **potential dissenters** in a manner that may be difficult or impossible in voluntary recapitalizations and readjustments.

These distinctions are not observed strictly by either businessmen or lawyers. The revenue laws, in fact, refer to changes of all three types as "reorganizations." Recapitalizations and readjustments take place **outside the courts** and constitute a change in the form, provisions, or amount of the outstanding securities through voluntary action on the part of the security holders, as distinguished from the **involuntary judicial procedure** involved in corporate reorganization. Readjustments of a more serious nature are commonly proposed by management when a business is an economic or financial failure. But even a prosperous corporation may find it advantageous to effect a recapitalization under certain conditions.

Broadly speaking, recapitalizations and readjustments may involve: (a) a change in the size of one or more security issues; (b) a modification of contractual rights of one or more classes of securities; (c) a revaluation of capital accounts; and (d) a revaluation of asset values. Although such rearrangements are normally voluntary, legislation such as the Public Utility Holding Company Act of 1935 or action required under antitrust decisions may compel managements to undertake them. Recapitalizations and readjustments cannot be classified easily, since nomenclature is not standardized. Any classification is to a considerable extent arbitrary, and in practice the terms are often used to describe identical situations. It must also be kept in mind that a recapitalization is one of the transactions that the Internal Revenue Code terms a "reorganization" for **tax purposes.** (Ordinarily a recapitalization is regarded as a "tax-free reorganization." However, when securities received in an exchange are subsequently disposed of, the gain or loss must be computed for tax purposes.)

Common Stock Recapitalizations

LEGAL REQUIREMENTS. Changes in the number of authorized shares or the par or stated value of common stock require **charter amendment,** and therefore the **consent of stockholders** as a class. They are usually effected by a vote of stockholders after the directors have passed a resolution recommending the change in the authorized capital stock and the basis on which the newly authorized shares are to be exchanged for the old, which are to be canceled. What vote of the stockholders is required to sanction the readjustment will depend upon the nature of the adjustment and the provisions of the statute and certificate of incorporation.

The **New York Business Corporation Law,** for example, states (§ 801) that "a corporation may amend its certificate of incorporation, from time to time, in any and as many respects as may be desired, if such amendment contains only such provisions as might be lawfully contained in an original certificate of incorporation filed at the time of making such amendment." This section also sets forth some of the specific matters in respect to which the certificate may be amended. These include the right to change the aggregate number of authorized shares or the number of shares of any class; to change the par value of any class of stock; to change shares with par value into those without par value, and vice versa; to reduce stated capital under certain conditions; and to fix, change, or abolish the designations and the rights, preferences, and limitations of any class or series, including provisions in respect to undeclared dividends, redemption of shares, and pre-emptive rights.

These amendments may be **authorized by vote of holders of a majority** of all outstanding shares entitled to vote (§ 803). In addition, holders of a majority of any class of stock must approve any proposed amendment that would exclude or limit their voting rights or otherwise adversely affect or subordinate their rights (§ 804). Similar provisions are contained in the statutes of many other states. In a number of states, however, a two-thirds vote, instead of a simple majority, is required.

COMMON STOCK RECAPITALIZATIONS

CHANGES IN NUMBER OF SHARES. This type of recapitalization involves a split-up (or stock split), a split-down (reverse split), or a stock dividend; with or without a change in the par value or stated value of the shares.

Stock Split-Ups and Stock Dividends. A stock split-up occurs when a class of stock is **divided** into a greater number of shares without change in the capital account. It involves a reduction in the par or stated value of shares. Such changes are of rather frequent occurrence, with the 2 for 1 ratio the most common. In this instance the par or stated value per share of stock must be cut in half since the dollar amount of capital stock remains unchanged. The 3 for 1 ratio is also widely used, an outstanding example being the 3 for 1 split in the common stock of the American Telephone and Telegraph Co. in 1959. Many other variations above or below these ratios have also been employed.

A corresponding **increase** in the number of shares may also be accomplished by a large stock dividend, of 100% or 200%, for example. But this would involve debiting surplus and crediting capital by the amount of the dividend, whereas a stock split does not affect the surplus account. A split-up requires approval of stockholders for requisite charter amendments, whereas a stock dividend is paid at the discretion of the board of directors if authorized but unissued stock is available.

The more common **reasons for split-ups** are:

1. To reduce the market price of outstanding stock to what is believed a more popular price range, thus broadening the market for a company's stock. In particular, a lower selling price may be sought as a prelude to new financing.

2. To facilitate a public offering of stock by shareholders of close corporations, sometimes because of high estate and inheritance taxes. A conspicuous example was the 10 for 1 split, in December 1958, of the common stock of the Great Atlantic & Pacific Tea Co. prior to the disposal of some of the stock owned by members of the Hartford family.

3. To pave the way for mergers, consolidations, or holding company acquisitions. (See Kent, Corporate Financial Management.)

4. To widen the distribution of a corporation's stock so as to make less likely concentration of ownership by outsiders who may seek to displace the management.

5. To avoid an appearance of excessive per-share earnings.

6. To stimulate consumer interest and identification through wider distribution of stock ownership.

Reverse Splits or Share Consolidation. In years of prosperity, when corporation earnings are large and stock market prices are high, the subdivision of shares by means of stock split-ups and stock dividends and the issuance of stock subscription rights at a low price are frequent. The reverse practice is encountered when earnings and stock prices are low. Some corporations that split their stock in boom years, and others, may find their shares selling at such low prices as to render them unsatisfactory as collateral for loans. Moreover, the corporation's credit and ability to sell new stock may be affected adversely when its shares are quoted at too low a price. **Consolidation of shares** may be effected by increasing the par value of each share, or the stated value of no-par shares, and exchanging one new share for so many outstanding. In the case of no-par stock without stated value, the consolidation of shares is brought about by simply reducing the number of shares represented by the capital account. New stock certificates are then issued representing the smaller number of shares, and exchanged for those outstanding. Reverse splits or consolidations are much less common than split-ups.

CHANGES IN PAR OR STATED VALUE. This type of common stock recapitalization involves only the par or stated value of the shares, without change in the number outstanding.

Changes from Par to No-Par Stock. Numerous corporations that originally issued par value shares have subsequently changed to no-par. In some instances, the reason for the change has been to facilitate **new financing** when the outstanding stock was selling below par and it was desired to float a new issue of common stock. Another reason has been to pave the way for certain **corporate transactions**, such as new acquisitions, consolidations, and reorganizations, in which exchanges of securities are involved.

The value at which no-par shares are carried on the balance sheet after the change from par value stock will depend upon the circumstances in each case. The **capital stock account** may be left undisturbed so that the no-par shares, if equal in number to the previous par value shares, will have a stated or capital value equal to the par shares. Or the capital stock account may be reduced through transfer to capital surplus of part of the old par value. This is sometimes done if it is desired to write down the book value of assets without creating a deficit.

Changes from No-Par to Par Stock. The change from no-par to low par value has become common, since the use of low par values has to a large extent deprived no-par value stock of its former advantages. To effect stock split-ups, no-par shares offer no particular advantage over par value shares, since the par value can be reduced virtually to any amount. Legal uncertainties connected with the use of no-par shares and lower franchise and transfer taxes have also caused numerous shifts from no-par to low par value.

Increase or Decrease in Par or Stated Value. When the par or stated value of common stock is increased or decreased, **adjustments** are made between the capital stock and capital surplus accounts. A decrease in the capital stock account is more common than an increase, since a larger surplus is usually desired.

An increase or decrease in the par value of capital stock requires an amendment of the charter in accordance with the procedure previously outlined. Under the laws of many states, a change in the stated value of no-par stock can be made by the directors, unless the charter provides otherwise.

CAPITAL ACCOUNT REDUCTIONS. A decrease in the capital stock account on the balance sheet, and a corresponding increase in "capital surplus," results from a lowering of par or stated value or a reduction in the number of shares outstanding. The **disposition of the surplus** resulting from stock reduction is regulated by some statutes.

The **New York statute** (§ 517 of the Business Corporation Law) states that any surplus resulting from reduction of stated capital shall be capital surplus. A corporation may apply any part of its capital surplus to elimination of any deficit in the earned surplus upon approval by vote of the shareholders. Such action must be disclosed to shareholders "in the next financial statement furnished by the corporation to its shareholders or in the first notice of dividend or share distribution that is furnished to shareholders between the date of such elimination of a deficit in the earned surplus account and the next financial statement, and in any event within six months of the date of such action."

Methods of Effecting Capital Stock Reductions. Methods of effecting a reduction of the capital stock account with an accompanying increase in surplus are:

1. By **retiring shares:**
   a. Purchased in the open market at a price that is less than the balance sheet value per share.
   b. Purchased under an offer to stockholders to buy shares from them at a given price (less than the balance sheet value) in proportion to their holdings.
   c. Purchased from stockholders who offer to sell to the company at specified prices in response to a request for tenders. (The tender prices accepted will be less than the balance sheet value.)
   d. Donated to the corporation.

2. By **reducing the par value** of shares having par value, **or the stated value** of no-par shares having stated value, or by diminishing the declared capital in the case of no-par shares without stated value.

3. By **changing stock of par value to no-par stock** of lower stated value; **or vice versa,** by changing no-par stock with stated value to stock with a lower par value; or by changing par or stated value stock to no-par stock without stated value having a smaller capital value; or by changing no-par stock without stated value into stock with a lower par or stated value than the previous capitalized value per share.

4. By **reducing the number of shares** without changing the par or stated value, or the capitalized value of shares in the case of no-par shares without stated value, through a reverse split-up.

Two or more of these methods may be combined in effecting a capital stock reduction.

Purposes Accomplished by Capital Stock Reductions. The following are the most common purposes achieved by reductions in capital stock:

1. **Elimination of an earned surplus deficit.** The capital surplus created by the reduction in capital stock is employed to write off the deficit in the "earned surplus" account. Deficit elimination serves to improve the appearance of the balance sheet and allows the corporation to pay dividends from current or subsequent earnings. This device was used frequently in the depression of the 1930's. The New York Stock Exchange forbids the use of capital surplus to absorb earned surplus deficits without obtaining the approval of stockholders and notifying the Exchange.

2. **Writing off goodwill and other intangibles.** Even in normal times, when values are stable or rising, corporations resort at times to capital stock reduction for the purpose of writing down a questionable goodwill or other intangible item on the balance sheet. If a company already has an ample surplus or is accumulating one very rapidly from current earnings, the goodwill account may be written off against it at once or in installments, and there is no necessity to resort to the expedient of reinforcing surplus from the capital stock account. A conspicuous instance of this kind was the elimination, some years ago, of a $50,000,000 goodwill item from the accounts of the Woolworth Co. by a series of charges to its surplus account extending over a period of several years. If, however, the surplus account is inadequate, a capital surplus can be created through reduction of capital. Such write-downs should, of course, conform to accepted accounting principles.

3. **Writing down tangible asset values.** Writing down of values against the capital stock account was extended to all types of the assets during the depression

of the '30's. Investment trusts found that their security holdings declined in market value to a point where surpluses were extinguished and capital stock impaired. They were generally unable to pay dividends on their preferred stock until this impairment was corrected, although current earnings sufficed for such disbursements. By revaluing security holdings on their books at current market quotations, securing a surplus for the corresponding charge-offs by reducing their capital stock, future earnings were made available for dividend payments.

Industrial companies wrote down fixed assets, inventories, and other assets to lower replacement values and obtained surplus to effect these charge-offs by reducing their stock capitalizations. Many also set up larger reserves against doubtful receivables and other claims through charges against such newly created surplus.

4. **Creating general reserves.** The transfer from the capital stock account to capital surplus may also be used to set up general reserves for such purposes as (a) future revaluation of assets or (b) general contingencies.

Arguments For and Against Asset Write-Downs. Most capital stock reductions are effected for the purpose of writing down asset values. The principal value of such a procedure is that it enables a corporation to present a **better financial picture** by writing down overvalued assets—usually fixed assets, both tangible and intangible—without incurring a deficit. Suppose, for example, a company with total assets of $20,000,000 and capital and surplus of $12,000,000 (consisting of common stock $11,000,000 and surplus $1,000,000) has earnings of $500,000 a year. This is equivalent to 2½% on total assets and 4.2% on the book value of the owners' equity, both ratios being considerably under par for the industry. It is recognized, however, that fixed assets are substantially overvalued, as measured by reasonable present-day valuations. A decision is therefore made to reduce the book value of plant and equipment and to write off patents and goodwill, resulting in a total decline in assets of $6,000,000. At the same time, the surplus is increased to $6,500,000 by reducing the par value per share by 50%. As a result of these transactions, the revised balance sheet now shows total assets of $14,000,000 and capital accounts of $6,000,000 ($5,500,000 capital and $500,000 surplus).

On this basis the annual profits of $500,000 amount to 3.6% of assets and 8.3% of owners' equity. Moreover, future earnings should be increased because of the smaller **depreciation** charges. This, in turn, will make possible larger dividends and strengthen the corporation's credit and its ability to arrange new financing. Care should be exercised, however, to avoid overstatement of earnings and payment of excessive dividends through overlarge write-downs resulting in inadequate depreciation charges.

Asset write-downs should not be made because of declines in the price level that may prove temporary. It is always justifiable to reduce capital so as to write off obsolete assets. Similarly, if there is good reason to believe that replacement values will remain lower than book values, write-downs are justifiable to bring a corporation's asset valuations and depreciation allowances into line with those of its competitors.

Creditors' and Preferred Shareholders' Interest in Capital Stock Reductions. Capital stock reductions are effected by stockholder action. Creditors normally have no voice in the matter, even though their interests may be affected because the capital stock affords a margin of protection to them. But if they can prove that their **interests will be adversely affected,** the courts may intervene. The law presumes that creditors and others enter into dealings with the corporation with full knowledge of its power to reduce its capital stock. But many state statutes provide that capital stock may not be reduced unless the assets remaining after the reduction are sufficient to pay the debts. The **New York Business Corporation Law** [§ 513(a)] states: "A corporation may purchase its own shares, or redeem its redeemable shares, out of surplus except when currently the corporation is insolvent or would thereby be made insolvent."

Any attempt by a corporation with heavy liabilities to effect a drastic cut in its capital stock by purchasing and retiring shares, or by making capital distributions to its stockholders, would probably be enjoined as a **fraud upon creditors.** Many of the statutes also require a corporation to **publish the facts of a reduction in capital** to protect the public in future dealings with the corporation. A certificate reporting such reduction must be filed with the Secretary of State or otherwise, in the same manner as the certificate of incorporation.

The **New York law** also contains the following provision [§ 806(b)(3)] to protect owners of **preferred stock:** "No reduction of stated capital shall be made by amendment unless after such reduction the stated capital exceeds the aggregate preferential amount payable upon all issued shares having preferential rights in assets upon involuntary liquidation plus the par value of all other issued shares with par value."

Capital Distributions. Distributions of part or all of the capital of a corporation may be made with the consent of the stockholders. If they are paid as **liquidating dividends,** they are made with a view to winding up the corporation. Capital distributions may take the form of cash or securities of other corporations. Preliminary to a capital distribution, stockholders vote to reduce the capital and authorize the directors to distribute the capital thus released to stockholders. Mining companies usually do not require specific authority of stockholders to make such distributions. If complete liquidation is contemplated, appropriate action must be taken under the statute and charter. Capital distributions are not considered income subject to taxation.

RECLASSIFICATION OF STOCK. Reclassification is a type of recapitalization involving a change in the capital stock structure of the corporation, through exchanging one or more classes of shares for classes of stock previously outstanding. Commonly it involves exchange of preferred for common or common for preferred.

A reclassification **may be restricted** to a portion of a corporation's capital stock. Thus, several outstanding preferred issues may be consolidated into one, or into one new preferred issue and additional common stock. Or a single preferred issue may, by exchange, be divided into two new preferred issues, one having priority over the other, or into a new preferred and additional common stock.

Stock reclassifications require **amendment of the charter** with the requisite **consent of stockholders.** The statutes may provide that major characteristics of a stock issue may be altered only with the consent of the holders of a specified majority of the stock. Thus, the Delaware law provides that capital stock may be reclassified and the "preferences, or relative, participating, optional, or other special rights of shares, or the qualifications, limitations or restrictions of such rights" may be changed by amendment of the certificate of incorporation upon the affirmative vote of a majority of the shares entitled to vote. But it further provides that

... if any such proposed amendment would alter or change the preferences, special rights or powers given to any one or more classes of stock by the certificate of incorporation, so as to affect such class or classes of stock adversely, or would increase or decrease the amount of the authorized stock of such class or classes of stock, or would increase or decrease the par value thereof, then the holders of the stock of each class of stock so affected by the amendment shall be entitled to vote as a class upon such amendment, whether by the terms of the certificate of incorporation such class would be entitled to vote or not; and the affirmative vote of a majority in interest of each such class so affected by the amendment shall be necessary to the adoption thereof, in addition to the affirmative vote of a majority of every other class of stock entitled to vote thereon.

Some statutes accord appraisal rights to dissenting stockholders in reclassifications.

Reasons for Reclassifying Stock Capitalization. Among common reasons for reclassifying stock capitalization are:

1. To bring the capital structure into line with earnings, as where preferred dividends are not earned year after year.
2. To create a better medium or media for financing or for making new acquisitions by exchange of stock.
3. To readjust the capital structure of a closely held corporation so as to facilitate public distribution of its securities.
4. To reduce voting stock outstanding.
5. To simplify the capital structure.
6. To conform to regulatory requirements, as in public utilities.
7. To enable large stockholders to recover their investment by giving them non-voting preferred that they can sell.
8. To fund arrearages on preferred dividends.
9. To eliminate noncallable, high dividend preferred issues.

Reclassification of capital stock to facilitate new financing or to acquire properties or stock of other corporations by payment in shares is frequent. Of its own accord or upon the advice of issuing bankers, a company may decide that its capital structure is not adapted to its needs. A particular type of stock may be in vogue among investors, and reclassification of the existing capital structure may be needed to provide such stock. Even apart from the tastes of investors, a corporation may have to remold its capital structure from time to time to bring it into line with prevailing conditions.

Owners of a **closely held corporation**—members of a family or a small group of friends—may decide to seek public participation in ownership. They may be actuated in this decision by a desire to diversify their own investments, or they may wish to relinquish control and retire from active management. Whatever the reason, it may be necessary to rearrange the capital structure so as to give stockholders shares that can be sold more readily. Numerous corporations have combined several preferred stock issues into one through an exchange of shares.

Reclassification of the capital structure **may be equivalent to payment of an extra cash dividend,** as is illustrated by the following case. A corporation had capital stock of $30,000,000, consisting of 300,000 common shares of a par value of $100, and a surplus of $20,000,000. It exchanged for these common shares $15,000,000 of redeemable preferred stock and 600,000 shares of new no-par common shares that were assigned a stated value of $25, or $15,000,000 for the total new common stock. A few years later the company redeemed the preferred stock at par, thus reducing its capital stock to $15,000,000. The original capital of $30,000,000 was thus restored, while stockholders had received $15,000,000 in cash through redemption of the preferred.

Similarly, if each share of common is exchanged for one share of new common and one of preferred, the shareholders can sell part or all of their preferred without reducing their proportionate share of the common. In one instance a group that had obtained control of a holding company by acquiring a **large block of common**, put through this type of recapitalization and subsequently sold in a public offering their preferred stock at a price that enabled them to **recoup most of their original investment**.

A stock reclassification may involve **adjustments between the capital stock and surplus accounts** if the par or stated value of the new stock issued is different from that of the stock for which it is exchanged.

Preferred Stock Recapitalizations and Readjustments

GENERAL PRINCIPLES AND LEGAL RESTRICTIONS. Like the common stockholder, the preferred stockholder is a part-owner of the business. Preferred and common shareholders alike have a position that contrasts with that of creditors. Recapitalizations of the nature described above may involve preferred as well as common stockholders. However, as the name indicates, preferred holders are given certain preferences over common holders, and in time these rights may conflict with a corporation's needs and welfare. **Readjustment of the terms and rights** of preferred stock is then desirable. This may usually be effected by amendment of the charter, although some courts have held that the right to accumulated back dividends on cumulative preferred stock is a vested right that each individual stockholder may insist upon, regardless of charter amendments.

Corporation laws of many states authorize changes in preferred stock provisions by a **specified vote of stockholders.** Thus, the **New York Business Corporation Law** includes specifically among the matters in respect to which a corporation may **amend its certificate of incorporation,** from time to time, the right: "To fix, change or abolish the designations of any authorized class or any series thereof and the relative rights, preferences and limitations of any shares of any authorized class or any series thereof, whether issued or unissued, including any provisions in respect of any undeclared dividends, whether or not cumulative or accrued, or the redemption of any shares, or any preemptive right to acquire shares or other securities" [§ 801(b)(12)]. It is further provided [§ 801(b)(13)] that the certificate may be amended: "As to the shares of any preferred class, then or theretofore authorized, which may be issued **in series,** to grant authority to the board or to change or revoke the authority of the board to establish and designate series and to fix the variations in the relative rights, preferences and limitations as between series."

As previously indicated, in New York authorized amendments may be approved by a majority of all outstanding shares entitled to vote thereon (§ 803) and, in addition, by a majority of all outstanding shares of any **class,** voting as a class, on any amendments limiting, excluding, or adversely affecting their rights (§ 804). Many statutory or charter provisions specify that a two-thirds vote of the preferred stock is necessary to change preference rights. The New York statute also provides, as do some other state statutes, that a **dissenting stockholder** who does not consent to a change in his preferential rights effected by an amendment of the certificate is entitled to surrender his stock and to have its appraised value paid to him by the corporation [§ 806(b)(6)].

PURPOSES OF PREFERRED STOCK RECAPITALIZATIONS. Although preferred stock does not burden a corporation with fixed interest charges or the problem of maturities, it may nevertheless prove troublesome to management and common stockholders. Among the more common purposes of effecting a preferred stock readjustment are the following:

Elimination of Burdensome Charter Provisions. Corporations on occasion find themselves hampered in their financial transactions by reason of some restrictive charter provision relating to preferred stock. Such a provision may deprive the corporation of the power to issue funded debt or additional preferred stock without permission of a specified percentage of the preferred shares. Other typical provisions include working capital covenants and restrictions on common stock dividend payments. To give the management greater freedom in financing, consent of the preferred stockholders can be sought to modify such charter provisions. For this concession preferred **stockholders are usually compensated** in some manner, for example, through retirement of part of the issue.

Exchange for a Lower Dividend Issue. If preferred stock is noncallable, an exchange for a lower dividend issue may be difficult unless it is effected by charter amendment. To obtain the required approval, the stockholders may be offered a **conversion privilege** or some common stock. If the preferred shares are callable, unexchanged shares can be called for redemption. There have been instances, however, where even when the stock was callable, the management preferred to effect an exchange through amendment of the certificate in order to avoid the expense of redemption. Among the advantages that might induce stockholders to vote for the plan would be that an exchange would be tax-free whereas the redemption premium received over the stockholders' cost would constitute either regular taxable income or capital gain.

Exchange for Other Securities. A corporation may desire to exchange preferred stock for other securities for simplification or income tax savings. For example, in 1958 Corn Products Refining Co., as an incident to a merger with its subsidiary, Corn Products Co., exchanged its 7% noncallable preferred (par value $100) into $175 of 4⅝% subordinated debentures. The shareholders' yield was thus increased from 7 to 8.1%. In the same year Deere & Co. offered $500 of 4½% subordinated debentures in exchange for fourteen shares of 7% noncallable, cumulative preferred (par value $20), increasing the shareholders' income from 7 to nearly 7.9%. The advantage to the company in these instances arises because **interest paid bondholders is deductible** for income tax purposes whereas preferred stock dividends are not deductible.

Clear-Up Arrearages on Cumulative Preferred Stock. By far the most common type of preferred stock readjustment is the **compromise settlement** of arrearages of unpaid dividends on cumulative preferred stock. Few corporations with heavy accruals of unpaid dividends on preferred stocks pay them off in cash, in accordance with the terms of the contract. A notable exception was the Alleghany Corporation, which in 1958 cleared up a 27-year accumulation on its 5½% preferred by paying $149.87½ a share.

Heavy accumulations of unpaid preferred dividends adversely affect a corporation's credit, prevent new financing with either preferred or common stock, and bar dividends on common stock even though earnings are large. Sale of common stock in particular is not practicable when dividend payments are made remote by the existence of large arrearages on the preferred. Also, failure to pay preferred dividends may, under charter provisions, **shift voting control** to preferred stockholders, and common stockholders may be eager to regain control through a plan of readjustment to clear up arrearages.

The problem of arrearages is now not nearly as serious as in earlier periods, particularly the years following the depression of the 1930's. In 1941, of the 401 domestic preferred stocks listed on the New York Stock Exchange, 116, or 29%, were in arrears. Twenty years later, only ten of the 402 listed stocks were in arrears. (See discussion in Hunt, Williams, and Donaldson, Basic Business Finance.)

MEETING THE SPECIAL PROBLEMS OF ARREARAGES. As the claims of the preferred stockholder for back dividends constitute claims against the corporation's surplus in preference to those of the common stockholder, any compromise involving cancellation of these claims is, in fact, a compromise between **conflicting interests** of preferred and common stockholders. The compromise proposal generally comes from the management, which usually represents common stockholders. In making a proposal for adjustment of the arrearages on the preferred stock, the following reasons are commonly advanced for carrying out such a plan:

1. The adjustment plan would eliminate arrearages without the need for heavy cash distributions that would impair the working capital position of the corporation.
2. Improvement of the credit of the corporation.
3. Resumption of current dividend payments to the corporation's stockholders.
4. Improvement of the market position and salability of the corporation's securities.
5. Simplification of the corporation's capital structure, with the clearing up of preferred dividend accumulations as one phase of the operation.

A readjustment plan of this kind **usually benefits common stockholders** directly, since elimination of the preferred dividend arrearages brings the common stock closer to dividend payments. The problem is one of making sufficient concessions to the preferred to obtain their consent to releasing their claim to back dividends in cash.

Legal Factors. The courts have held that changes in dividend rates, sinking fund provisions, and voting rights of preferred stock are **changes in preference rights** that may be effected by amending the certificate of incorporation. However, claims of preferred stockholders to accumulated unpaid dividends or past due sinking fund payments have been held by some jurisdictions to constitute **contract** or **vested property** rights that cannot be eliminated by amending the certificate of incorporation. In such jurisdictions, dissenting preferred stockholders can insist on receiving back dividends in cash before any dividends are paid on a junior class of stock, provided the readjustment plan involves eliminating the accrued dividends through charter amendment. Other jurisdictions such as New York permit elimination of accrued preferred dividends by charter amendment if this is authorized by statute, with the right of appraisal given dissenting stockholders.

A preferred **stockholder who objects** to a proposed readjustment plan designed to reduce or eliminate his back dividends can:

1. Vote against the proposed plan.
2. Attempt to have its execution enjoined in the courts if fraud is involved.
3. Insist on his contract rights, which involve receipt of back dividends in full before any dividend is paid on the common. The effectiveness of this action depends on the particular jurisdiction and the device employed to eliminate the accruals.
4. Ask for an appraisal of his preferred stock and payment of the appraisal price in cash, if the statute so provides.

If the right of appraisal exists and dissenters are substantial in number, the cash requirements to pay them off may prove a stumbling block to the readjustment plan, because too much cash would be drained out of the corporation in this way. Hence, some corporations provide that a plan to readjust preferred dividend arrearages shall become effective only if a specified percentage, say 90%, of the preferred is deposited or voted in favor of the plan, although the directors may retain the right to declare it effective if a smaller percentage approves.

The **Public Utility Holding Co. Act** of 1935 grants the Securities and Exchange Commission powers under §§ 11(e), 6(a), and 7(e) to force capital stock readjustments. When a plan of integration and simplification, which may involve clearing up preferred dividend arrearages, has been approved by the S.E.C., the latter may apply to a court of equity for an order enforcing the terms of the recapitalization plan upon all stockholders, who are enjoined from interfering with its execution. [United Light & Power Co., S.E.C. Holding Co. Act Release No. 4215; 51 F. Supp. 217 (D. Del.; 1943), affirmed in 323 U. S. 624 (1945).] In that case, the United States Supreme Court ruled that "where pre-existing contract provisions exist which produce results at variance with a legislative policy which was not foreseeable at the time the contract was made, they cannot be permitted to operate."

Methods of Clearing Up Arrearages. In clearing up dividend arrearages on cumulative preferred stock, terms have varied widely. Broadly speaking, a corporation may employ one of **two main approaches.** The first approach is to leave the outstanding preferred stock undisturbed and simply **provide for the settlement** of the dividend arrearages. Thus, a corporation might ask preferred stockholders to agree to the cancellation of dividend accumulations in return for raising the dividend rate or adding a conversion or dividend participation feature to the preferred stock. Similarly, the corporation might propose to satisfy the arrears by means of (a) the issuance of dividend arrears certificates, (b) the issuance of additional preferred stock of the same class, (c) the issuance of a new senior or junior preferred stock (a conversion or participation feature might be included as a provision of the new preferred stock), (d) the issuance of bonds, or (e) the issuance of additional common stock.

This approach is unsuitable for a corporation that does not expect its operations to be more profitable in the future, for it will only be a matter of time before new arrearages accumulate. In fact, the issuance of bonds or additional preferred stock in settlement of arrears only increases prior claims to the corporation's earnings. In such instances, preferred dividend requirements should be reduced or perhaps eliminated entirely.

The second approach involves an **exchange of other securities** for preferred stock. Holders may be asked to exchange their preferred stock and the arrearages thereon for (a) a preferred stock with a lower dividend rate, (b) new preferred stock that is noncumulative, (c) common stock, (d) bonds with a low interest rate, or (e) a combination of the foregoing, such as a reduced amount of preferred stock and common. Very often, a cash payment or a conversion privilege is added to induce acceptance of the offer.

Meeting the Problem of Dissent. The problem of a dissenting minority has caused corporations to utilize various devices to overcome this difficulty in clearing up dividend arrearages on the preferred stock. The particular device employed will depend to a considerable extent on the **law of the state** of incorporation and other pertinent circumstances. The following are some of the devices used:

Preferred stockholders who assent may be given **added compensation** such as (a) making the new preferred stock convertible into common, (b) placing a sinking fund on the new preferred stock, (c) the payment of a cash bonus, (d) issuing a new higher dividend-paying preferred stock, and (e) funding the old preferred stock with its arrears into bonds.

Assenters may be given **prior preferred stock in exchange,** which will place them ahead of nonassenting preferred stockholders in future dividend distributions. Since the right to future dividends is a preference, a prior preferred issue can be put out under most statutes by amendment of the charter. By placing dissenters in a junior position as regards payment of back dividends as well as future dividend distributions, this device acts as an indirect method of coercing dissenters.

The **merger** device has been utilized frequently by corporations desiring to clear arrearages on an outstanding preferred stock issue. The corporation enters into a merger with a subsidiary and, as part of the merger plan, exchanges its preferred stock with unpaid back dividends for new preferred and common stock. The merger provisions of many corporation laws provide for appraisal and cash payment of dissenting stockholders. Although the merger device provides a method of coercing dissenting preferred stockholders in readjustment plans, it has certain disadvantages Stockholders may seek to enjoin the merger on the ground that it is not bona fide, but the courts have been disinclined to intervene in such cases. A second disadvantage lies in the right of appraisal.

Examples of Arrearage Settlements. Sometimes a **combination** of some of the above-mentioned methods is used in effecting an adjustment plan. For example, in a plan offered to the stockholders of the Missouri, Kansas & Texas Railway and approved by them in 1958, the stockholders received in exchange for each share of 7% preferred stock of $100 par value plus $167.75 of unpaid back dividends the following: one $100 5½% 75-year subordinated income debenture; a $110 dividend arrears certificate (in effect a noninterest-bearing promissory note) that represented a prior claim on future income; and one share of $10 par common stock. Since the old preferred as well as the new common had voting rights, no change of control could take place. At the time the plan was approved, the par value of the preferred totaled $67 million and the arrearages $112 million, and in only 9 of the previous 27 years had there been any earnings on the common stock. (See discussion in Wessel, Principles of Financial Analysis.)

Another plan involving the use of **bonds** was that effected by the Maine Central Railroad Co. in 1959, whereby each share of $100 par value preferred with arrearages of $55 was exchanged for $150 of 5½% income debenture bonds and $5 in cash.

In a thorough recapitalization of the Ward Baking Co. in 1945, involving both common and preferred stock, each share of $7 preferred (with arrears of over $57) received in exchange $25 of 5½% 25-year subordinated debentures, ¼ share of new 5½% cumulative preferred stock (par value $100), and 2½ shares of common.

In 1951 holders of 5½% cumulative preferred ($100 par) of Hotel Corp. of America, with $11 in dividend arrears, received in exchange for each share 4.4 shares of new 5% cumulative **convertible** ($25 par), making a total of $110. Three years later, however, holders of the new preferred were offered 5 shares of common in exchange for each share.

In 1945 the Guantanamo Sugar Co. completed a readjustment plan that provided for the exchange of one share of $8 preferred stock ($100 par) with arrears of $120 per share for 2⅓ shares of $5 cumulative convertible preferred stock (no par). The convertible preferred could be converted at any time before July 1, 1950, into 8 shares of common stock. At the time of the voting on the plan the common stock was selling at a price high enough to make the **conversion feature** an effective sweetening device to induce acceptance of the plan by the $8 preferred shareholders.

In instances where the old preferred stock is exchanged for **common stock only**, the plan may accord quite drastic treatment to the old common. Thus, Puget Sound Power & Light Co. in 1943 effected a reclassification whereby each share of $6 preferred stock with dividend arrears of $60.50 a share received 8 shares of new $10 par common stock. The old common stockholders received 1/20 of a share of new common stock for each old share held, so that the old common stockholders received only 3.03% of the new common stock.

Debt Readjustments

CIRCUMSTANCES NECESSITATING DEBT READJUSTMENT. Debt adjustments illustrate even more than do capital stock modifications a conflict between law and economics. Corporations that borrow incur **rigid legal obligations** that changing economic conditions may make it impossible for them to fulfill. This is particularly true in industries that have passed their growth stage and those quite sensitive to the business cycle.

Situations often arise in which it is to the interest of the creditors and the debtor corporation to **avoid legal proceedings,** with accompanying heavy expense, undesirable publicity, and shrinkage in asset values, and to effect a voluntary readjustment of outstanding debt. Circumstances that determine whether or not readjustment should be considered include the following:

1. **Managerial ability.** If management has the capacity and qualifications to run the business successfully, a reorganization that may force it out of office becomes undesirable.
2. **Degree of financial embarrassment.** When financial embarrassment is temporary and future prospects are reasonably good, debt readjustments are logical.
3. **Nature of embarrassment.** If the difficulty is only inability to meet a heavy debt maturity, readjustment rather than reorganization is the indicated remedy.
4. **Debt ownership.** If holders of debt can readily be made to agree to a readjustment, a costly, drawn-out legal reorganization becomes unnecessary.

MAIN TYPES OF READJUSTMENTS. The main types of readjustments are:

Extension of Maturities. One of the most frequent occasions when corporations are forced to **appeal to bond or noteholders for relief** is at the maturity of such obligations. Present and prospective earnings may be quite sufficient to provide for fixed charges, and working capital may be adequate for ordinary needs. Nevertheless, cash resources may not suffice to pay off the principal of maturing obligations, and refinancing or refunding of such obligations may not be practical because of unsatisfactory securities market conditions. Similarly, the unfavorable position of the industry at the time may render the flotation of a new issue on reasonable terms impracticable or very burdensome.

We are not concerned here with extensions of maturing obligations of corporations with a strong credit standing, with or without underwriting by investment bankers. Unassenting bondholders in such instances receive their principal promptly on maturity.

Reduction of Interest Rate. Where **fixed charges** prove burdensome, a corporation may seek to reduce the interest rate on its debt. Thus, International Railway Co. (Buffalo, N. Y.) proposed in 1938 a reduction of the interest rate on its $18,208,000 refunding and improvement 5% bonds due 1962. Approximately 98% of the bondholders consented to a reduction in the fixed interest rate to 3% and the placing of the remaining 2% on a contingent basis, payment depending on earnings.

Reduction of Principal. Although unable to pay off or refund its debt in full, a corporation may have sufficient cash to handle a smaller debt. For example, in 1958 the Studebaker-Packard Corp. effected a plan whereby a group of twenty large banks and three life insurance companies reduced the debt of $55 million owed to them by the company by $22 million and accepted in return $16.5 million of preferred stock convertible into common after January 1, 1961. Because of the **subsequent rapid rise in the price** of the stock, most of the creditors were able to recover all or a large part of their original claims.

Other Indenture Changes. Corporations may find it desirable to get security holders' consent to other changes in a bond indenture or note agreement, such as postponement of interest or sinking fund payments or termination of a sinking fund requirement. Bondholders may be asked to accept **interest-bearing scrip** or **preferred stock** in lieu of cash for matured coupons. Not infrequently, a corporation may have urgent need of additional capital and may ask bondholders to **release certain assets** from their lien so that they can be pledged for new loans or sold. Bondholders may also be asked to subordinate their liens to new creditors. Some corporations have obtained the consent of their bondholders to **relax indenture requirements** for the maintenance of certain minimum ratios between current assets and current liabilities, current assets and funded debt, and stockholders' equity and funded debt.

INDUCEMENTS TO BONDHOLDERS. A corporation will usually find it desirable to offer incentives to induce bondholders to agree to an extension of maturity or other concessions. The interest rate may be raised or the principal amount increased indirectly through a higher call price or maturity value. Additional security may be offered in the shape of increased collateral or an additional mortgage lien. A sinking fund may be provided where none had been stipulated before, the sale of senior securities may be barred, or payment of dividends on the common stock may be restricted during the extended life of the obligations. A stock bonus or cash premium has been offered in a number of cases. A convertible feature may be added to the securities to enhance the attractiveness of the readjustment offer.

LEGAL ASPECTS OF DEBT READJUSTMENTS. Voluntary debt readjustments are more difficult to effect than in the past. The reasons are (a) growing realization by creditors that Chapter X and Chapter XI of the Federal Bankruptcy Act accord them **fuller protection** than older reorganizations and readjustment procedures (see Sec. 22 on Reorganizations and Bankruptcy), and (b) the many instances in which **dissenters have secured full payment** when due.

Dissenters' Rights. As regards interest and principal payments, the individual bondholder possesses a contract right under his bond. He cannot be coerced ordinarily to reduce or postpone interest or principal due him. In a few instances, however, bond indentures have provided that, by vote of a specified proportion of bondholders, interest or principal may be postponed for a period after the due date. It is customary to provide for 30 to 60 days' **grace period** with respect to interest payments. Existence of a right to postpone principal payments has been held to impair negotiability of a bond issue.

As regards provisions other than those relating to payment of interest and principal, it is common practice to include an **indenture provision that it may be amended** by vote of bondholders, usually a 66⅔% or 75% vote. Sinking fund provisions, maintenance and replacement fund provisions, dividend restrictions, working capital covenants, and so on can often be modified or eliminated by amendment of the indenture. In the event of **default** of interest or principal, the typical indenture provides that if the trustee fails to act an individual bondholder can sue to collect his obligation. The chief problem in a debt readjustment proposal is thus to keep the number of dissenters within a number that the corporation is able to pay off in cash.

Mechanics of Debt Readjustment. In soliciting consent of bondholders to a debt readjustment plan, the corporation usually resorts to (a) exchange of certificates of deposit, (b) stamping of bonds as assented, or (c) deposit of bonds with a trust company without issuing certificates in exchange.

The use of **certificates of deposit** customarily involves the deposit by the bondholder of his bond with a named depositary under an agreement empowering the corporation to execute the plan, provided deposits are made by holders of a sufficient proportion of the securities. Upon deposit of his bond, the bondholder receives a transferable certificate of deposit evidencing his approval of the debt readjustment plan. In exchange for this certificate, he will receive new securities if the plan is declared operative. There are several **disadvantages** to the corporation in the use of certificates of deposit. These are: (a) the certificate of deposit may sell lower than nondeposited bonds, which discourages further deposits; (b) the procedure is relatively costly; and (c) certificates of deposit require registration with the S.E.C. under the Securities Act of 1933 unless the original security was exempt, as in the case of railroad securities. Stamping of bonds may be less costly, but it has the same disadvantage with respect to sales at lower prices in the market and registration. [Associated Gas & Electric Co., 99 F. (2d) 795, where stamping of bonds was held to in effect create a new security.] Deposit of securities with the right to withdraw at any time up to the effective date avoids the need for certificates of deposit or stamping, but involves risk of heavy withdrawals of deposited securities.

In effecting debt readjustment plans, **registration of the new securities** issued in exchange for the old is required under the Securities Act of 1933, unless it can be shown that commissions are not paid to secure assents. Similarly, any material change in the indenture will require its qualification by the S.E.C. under the Trust Indenture Act of 1939. This qualification requirement applies even though the original bonds were issued prior to 1939.

HOW BOND READJUSTMENTS ARE EFFECTED. A corporation will frequently seek the advice and assistance of the **investment bankers** who marketed the bonds in carrying out a readjustment of debt. In general, the following points should be kept in mind in proceeding with a plan to effect a debt readjustment:

Negotiation with Large Holders. It is wise to discuss the proposed readjustment with large bondholders before announcing a plan publicly, so as to assure substantial support in advance. It is a great advantage to announce agreement by large institutional bondholders in formally presenting a plan for approval.

Presenting the Plan. The management should draw up a letter to bondholders, signed by the senior officer of the company, to explain the financial problems confronting the corporation and the proposed solution. This letter should stress the advantages to bondholders in approving the debt readjustment plan.

Securing Assents. It generally is desirable to place the operation under the **jurisdiction of one executive** who will set up a staff consisting of employees of the company, or others specially retained, to solicit assents. A **security dealer** may be retained for a fee to aid in this task, and a commission may be allowed brokers for securing assents. A **list of bondholders** is a prerequisite. The indenture trustee will help in compiling such a list, since the Trust Indenture Act requires him to maintain a list of names and addresses of known bondholders.

Once active solicitation of assents starts, the officer in charge should attempt to secure **favorable publicity** for the plan. Frequent follow-up letters to bondholders will hasten deposits. It is common to emphasize the heavy expense and uncertainty of bankruptcy proceedings in advertisements and letters.

Establishing Effective Date. Usually the plan will not be declared operative by the corporation unless holders of the bulk of the issue have assented. The percentage required will depend usually upon the cash position of the corporation, since dissenters will have to be paid off in cash. It usually varies from 75% to 90%. Once a plan has been declared operative, the corporation will fix an early date for exchanging new securities for the old.

A Bank Loan. Consummation of a debt readjustment plan has been assured in some instances through willingness of bankers to advance funds to pay off dissenters. A loan for this purpose is usually contingent upon (a) the corporation's obtaining a **prescribed percentage of assents** and/or (b) the corporation's ability to put up **satisfactory collateral** to secure the funds advanced by the banks.

DEBT READJUSTMENTS UNDER SPECIAL LEGISLATION. §§ 11(c), 6(a), and 7(e) of the **Public Utility Holding Company Act of 1935** authorize the S.E.C. to force debt readjustment plans on dissenting bondholders. The contractual right of a bondholder to insist upon payment in cash may be modified under this law, and he may be compelled to accept securities of approximately equivalent value instead. [S.E.C.'s decision in the Standard Gas & Electric Co. case, Holding Co. Act Release No. 5430; affirmed 151 Fed. (2d) 326.]

Similarly, the **Mahaffie Act** [§ 20(b) of the Interstate Commerce Act] provides a means whereby debts of a railroad may be readjusted under a plan approved by the holders of at least three-fourths of each class of debt affected. Such a plan, which is solely under the jurisdiction of the Interstate Commerce Commission, is binding on all creditors.

SMALL BUSINESS READJUSTMENTS. If a business is small and the creditors few, financial difficulties may be solved through **friendly debt adjustments.** Types of voluntary debt readjustment are discussed below.

COMPOSITIONS. "Composition with creditors is an arrangement between a debtor and his creditors, the latter agreeing with the debtor, and mutually among themselves, to receive and the debtor to pay, a certain part or portion of the demands in full payment and discharge of the debt." (Anderman v. Meier, 91 Minn. 413.)

"A composition agreement is an agreement as well between the creditors themselves as between the creditors and their debtor. Each creditor agrees to receive the sum fixed by the agreement in full of his debt." (Reynolds v. Pennsylvania Oil Co., 150 Cal. 629.)

"In all compositions the creditors are moved by some advantage to be obtained in a distribution of property or money by the debtor, or by fixed payments to be made by him securing to each a certain proportion of his assets." (Henry v. Patterson, 57 Pa. 346.)

Such a settlement is usually brought about on the initiative of the debtor, who submits the terms of a proposed compromise. The proposal may be made to creditors individually, or at a **creditors' meeting** called for the express purpose of considering it. The latter method is more conducive to success, for when creditors are relatively numerous some may not be amicably disposed toward the debtor, but the other creditors may induce them to go along.

Number of Creditors Necessary to a Composition Settlement. One creditor alone cannot make a composition. (An arrangement with a single creditor is sometimes called an "accord.") If two or more creditors agree to a composition, it will be valid and binding on them and on the debtor if there is no requirement that the agreement to become effective must be entered into by a greater number of creditors. (Van Bokkelen v. Taylor, 62 N. Y. 105.) If the composition agreement provides that it shall not become effective until a certain number of creditors, all, or a majority, shall have agreed to it, the composition does not become operative until the required number agree. (Day v. Jones, 150 Mass. 231.)

The debtor may enter into a composition with **only one class** of creditors, such as his unsecured creditors. (Zoebisch v. Van Minden, 120 N. Y. 406.)

"An agreement for composition may be entered into by a part of the creditors of an insolvent debtor, and in such a case it will be binding only upon those who enter into it. In such a case, the creditors who do not enter into the agreement may proceed to collect or to settle their claims in their own way. If such a creditor makes a better settlement than those who agree to the composition, or obtains any other advantage, he will be permitted to retain it." (Atlas Engine Works v. Seymour First National Bank, 50 Ind. A. 549.)

Acceptance Considerations. Offers in composition should never be considered by creditors when there is well-founded **suspicion of fraud** on the part of the debtors. Creditors are entitled to know the facts and figures about the debtor's business, and where the funds are coming from to pay the creditors agreeing to the compositions. Creditors should insist that the money, or satisfactory security for it, is actually put up before consenting and signing composition agreements.

When To Agree to Compositions. Composition settlements under certain circumstances are the most effective and economical means of dealing with embarrassed debtors. Creditors must join at times with debtors in absorbing losses. Such arrangements have often enabled debtors to recover from financial adversity, with subsequent **benefit to the creditors** with whom they continue to transact business, as well as to themselves.

Creditors are interested in obtaining as large settlements as possible on their claims. Compositions are at times preferable for two reasons: (1) the amounts of settlement are definite, (2) the amounts realized are likely to be greater than can be expected from forced liquidations accompanied by heavy court and legal expenses. Thus, let us assume that the balance sheet of a business shows that the total assets amount to 75% of the liabilities. As a going concern, the assets may be worth that much, but if forced liquidation is resorted to the assets may, and very likely will, realize a great deal less than the book value. Hence, if the business is forced into bankruptcy, with the expenses and losses incident to such a procedure, the creditors might receive liquidating dividends aggregating only about 25% of their claims. A composition settlement of 50% of the claims would obviously be better for all concerned. Although the creditors would receive 50% of their claims instead of 25% the debtor could remain in business with some assets and without the stigma of bankruptcy.

ASSIGNMENTS. Specific assignments for the benefit of creditors and general assignments (assignments in trust for the benefit of creditors) involve the **transfer of assets of debtors to trustees,** to be managed by them pending the settlement of creditors' claims. "An assignment is substantially a transfer, actual or constructive, with the clear intent at the time to part with all interest in the thing transferred and with a full knowledge of the rights so transferred." (Ormond v. Connecticut Mut. L. Ins. Co., 145 N. C. 140.)

Assignments of **property in trust** for the benefit of creditors have been approved by both state and Federal courts. The only restriction is the general one providing for the setting aside of assignments on the ground of fraud.

Advantages of Assignments. Assignments for the benefit of creditors provide a means whereby embarrassed debtors may adjust their affairs with creditors. They combine the advantages of amicable adjustments with some aspects of bankruptcy. The advantages are:

1. Expenses of administration are less than in bankruptcy proceedings.
2. Under assignments a time limit is not set for settling the affairs of debtors, and trustees may hold the assets until they can be sold under favorable conditions or returned to the debtor, whereas in bankruptcy they are often sold at forced sale.
3. There is less undesirable publicity attached to assignments than to bankruptcy proceedings.
4. The administration of debtors' estates under assignments is a private matter between trustees and creditors, whereas in bankruptcy it is a matter of public record.

COMMON LAW AND STATUTORY ASSIGNMENTS. Assignments may be effected either under the common law or state statutes.

The common law assignment differs from the statutory assignment principally in the fact that it is not recorded and administration of the assets is conducted under the supervision of a committee of creditors rather than a court. It rests generally on the **consent of the creditors,** and serves as a legal basis for a friendly adjustment in accordance with the terms of the instrument of assignment. In a statutory assignment, the powers of the assignee as defined in the assignment instrument are subject to the **provisions of the statute.** At common law an insolvent debtor may make an assignment giving preference to certain creditors or classes of creditors, but only some statutes permit this.

All states have **insolvency laws** under which debtors may assign their property to trustees for the purpose of liquidation and distribution of proceeds among creditors. Statutory assignments have been largely displaced by bankruptcy proceedings, although common law assignments are still in use.

Assignment an Act of Bankruptcy. Under the Federal bankruptcy laws, an assignment for the benefit of creditors is an act of bankruptcy. As the Federal law supersedes state laws as regards bankruptcies, dissatisfied creditors may have assignments set aside simply by filing petitions in bankruptcy.

Although creditors have this privilege, it may be unwise to exercise it, particularly if they are satisfied as to the good faith of the debtor, and the honesty and ability of the assignee.

Rights of Creditors. If creditors have consented to assignments they are estopped from filing petitions in bankruptcy. For this reason creditors should not consent to assignments until they know the facts and have faith in the assignees. Creditors have a **right to an accounting** from assignees, and if this is not furnished pressure may be brought by proper application to the courts. The consent of all creditors to an assignment makes it proof against attack by bankruptcy petition.

Assignees. Assignees may be named by debtors when making assignments. If none is designated, the court will select them. Debtors have the right to select their own assignees, and are under **no obligation** to consult the wishes of creditors provided the persons selected are capable of performing the duties involved. Although selected by debtors, the assignees are supposed to act in the interest of the creditors. Assignees may or may not be creditors of the assignors.

Duties of Assignees. When assignees receive assignments from debtors, they are formally recognized as assignees. Their duties are:

1. To give public notice of assignment and their appointment as assignees.
2. To execute bonds for the faithful performance of trust.
3. To take possession of the property listed in the schedules accompanying the assignments.
4. To collect the debts due the assignors.
5. To sell the property transferred under the assignments.
6. Out of the proceeds of sale and debts collected, to pay the expenses of realization and distribute to creditors dividends on their claims. Dividends are usually paid from time to time as funds accumulate in the hands of assignees.
7. To turn over to the assignors funds left in the hands of assignees after paying the claims of the creditors in full.
8. To file an accounting that generally closes the estate.

Assignees hold a **fiduciary relation** to their assignors and to the creditors. Good faith is essential. They may be held personally liable for misconduct or breach of trust. They are expected to make an accounting of their transactions and may be removed from office for violation of trust. They are liable for property or money lost by negligence.

CREDITORS' COMMITTEES. Operation of businesses by creditors' committees resembles an assignment in that the management of an embarrassed enterprise is taken over by creditors. The **chief requirements** usually are:

1. That existing creditors subordinate and extend their claims.
2. That banks or creditors advance sufficient new money to operate the businesses, the new advances to be entitled to a priority in repayment.
3. That the management of the businesses pass into the hands of committees chosen by the creditors.
4. That the businesses be returned to the proprietors when the debts are paid in full.

The foregoing requisites **may be incorporated into a single contract** between the business in financial difficulties, the creditors who subordinate their claims and extend aid, and bankers who may advance new money. The same result may be accomplished by a series of agreements as each situation is met, one being made conditional upon the others.

Creditors, in **appointing committees,** generally give the larger creditors representation and attempt to select the men best qualified to manage the debtors' affairs. The size of a committee is governed by several factors, such as the magnitude of the concern, the number of creditors, and the variety of interests involved. For efficiency, committees should be as small as conditions permit. Committees of three can handle business problems more easily than larger ones, but sometimes it is necessary to have larger committees to obtain the support and cooperation of all creditor groups. If this is necessary, it is desirable to appoint a small but active executive committee with considerable authority. In practice, banks that subscribe additional money are the most influential members.

How Committees Operate. Generally the committees formulate and supervise policies to be followed in handling the debtors' affairs. Actual management is often delegated to a member best qualified. Frequently the creditors employ a qualified executive to act as their representative and pass on all matters relating to the routine management of the business. He may be appointed treasurer or controller. This **appointee** should be able, within a short time, to advise creditors whether the business can recover or should be liquidated. If the business cannot be continued as constituted, reorganization may be necessary. If reorganization also is not feasible and it becomes necessary to liquidate, the creditors' committees may supervise the liquidation.

Creditor Voting Trustees. In a corporation, a **voting trust** may be set up under the creditors' agreement, and broad powers given the voting trustees, including the power to elect new directors and officers and to liquidate the business if they see fit. The trustees may have to elect "dummy" directors, as men of standing are not disposed to appear as directors of a failing business. Although entirely new officers may be installed, it is better to avoid this for the sake of outward appearances if an attempt is to be made to save the business. The old president may be allowed to continue, but he may be deprived of his former powers, and the active administration of the business taken over by a general manager selected by the voting trustees designated by creditors. A clerk in the office of the counsel of the creditors' committee may serve as secretary for the corporation, and the treasurer may be an employee of the firm of accountants engaged to make an audit of the company's affairs and keep the accounts for the trustees.

Advantages of Creditors' Committees. Creditors' committees provide:

1. **Greater freedom of action.** Creditors' committees have greater freedom of action and adaptability to changing business conditions, without the hampering influence of statutes or legal precedents and the necessity for obtaining judicial approval for every important business move.

2. **Efficiency and economy.** Expenses and costs of creditors' committees are less than in bankruptcy organizations. The members of creditors' committees, by reason of their desire to safeguard their interests, give much time to working out solutions of the debtors' problems and sometimes act without compensation.

In many instances, members of creditors' committees and their counsel are substantially compensated for their services. But usually this follows successful administration.

3. **Expeditiousness.** Administration of a business under a court's jurisdiction is often a long-drawn-out affair, whereas creditors' committees are chiefly interested in settling the claims of the creditors quickly and being relieved from their work as soon as possible.

4. **Absence of unfavorable publicity.** Unfavorable financial publicity has a detrimental influence on any business. Under creditors' committees concerns are not subject to the widespread publicity incident to court proceedings. The only publicity under creditors' committees is that of credit reporting agencies and credit departments of banks and creditors.

5. **Retention of organization.** Under creditors' committees the personnel of business organizations are generally kept intact, with the exception of unnecessary and inefficient employees and possibly the treasurer or controller, who may be temporarily superseded by the representatives of the creditors' committees.

Disadvantages of Creditors' Committees. Creditors' committees do not possess certain powers of bankruptcy trustees. Disadvantages are:

1. **Inability to set aside unprofitable contracts.** Trustees in a bankruptcy reorganization may move to set aside contracts that are burdensome or unprofitable. Committees of creditors could do away with such contracts only by consent of the parties to the burdensome contracts.

2. **Inability to set aside questionable claims.** Courts may exclude questionable claims of creditors. Committees of creditors may find it far more difficult to resist questionable claims.

3. **Inability to stop creditors' actions.** The greatest benefit in reorganization under the Bankruptcy Act is the court's power to enjoin actions by creditors. Creditors' committees do not possess such powers. They are limited to persuasion and negotiation, and if they fail their other solution is to pay off insistent creditors.

CREDIT ADJUSTMENT BUREAUS. Creditor committee management, as an alternative for proceedings under the Federal Bankruptcy Act, has been strongly supported by the **National Association of Credit Management**, which has implemented the procedure. Settlement of the affairs of a corporation in an embarrassed financial condition can be handled by a creditors' committee working through its own liquidating agent, or an adjustment bureau on the approved list of the Association. Throughout the country, member associations of the National Assn. of Credit Management have created and fostered approved adjustment bureaus that specialize in liquidating insolvent businesses and rehabilitating embarrassed debtors without resort to the Bankruptcy Act.

Intercorporate Readjustments

CHANGES IN CORPORATE STRUCTURE OF A HOLDING COMPANY SYSTEM. Intercorporate readjustments involve change in the corporate structure of a holding company system. Corporate structures of **expanding** enterprises may assume a complicated form. The process of expansion often results in the acquisition of control of a number of other corporations. Subsequently, **simplification** of intercorporate structure may be desirable for greater economy and efficiency of operation, to facilitate financing, for tax reasons or because of regulatory requirements. The trend among large industrial, railroad, and public utility enterprises has been to reduce the number of corporate entities constituting a holding company system. In some instances, however, tax considerations have encouraged the formation of new subsidiaries.

REASONS FOR INTERCORPORATE CHANGES. There are several reasons why it may become desirable or necessary to make intercorporate changes (see also Sec. 20):

1. **To reduce taxes.** Reduction in the number of corporate entities composing a holding company system will result in a saving in both corporate franchise taxes

and income taxes. A holding company must pay a tax on dividends received from a subsidiary equal to 15% of the corporate income and surtax rate. If the corporate normal and surtax is 48%, the effective intercorporate dividend tax rate is thus 7.2% (or 15% × 48%). Furthermore, present tax laws place a penalty of 2% on the filing of consolidated returns by two or more corporations, and a parent must own 95% or more of the subsidiaries' voting stock (and 95% of each class of nonvoting stock other than preferred stock of at least one subsidiary) to be qualified to file a consolidated income tax return.

The tax factor has also been of considerable influence in stimulating intercorporate readjustments involving **leases**. The Federal government taxes lessor corporations as the recipient of income. In many cases the courts have decided that the provisions of the lease agreement make the lessee liable for the lessor's taxes. The additional tax burden imposed on lessee railroads under such decisions caused several of them to merge with leased lines. (See Delaware, Lackawanna & Western R. R. mergers with a number of leased lines.)

Special tax treatment is accorded distributions of stock in one or more subsidiaries formed to take over assets of which a corporation is divesting itself. Under certain circumstances, such distributions are designated as tax-free exchanges, so that no tax need be paid on their receipt by stockholders. A distribution of stock of a newly formed subsidiary is termed a **spin-off** when it is distributed without affecting the outstanding stock of the distributing company; it is a **split-off** when the new shares are exchanged for part of the stock of the parent; and it is a **split-up** when shares in subsidiaries are exchanged for all the stock of the parent, which is then in effect dissolved. Corporations that have developed products or activities not directly related to their main business may find such tax-free distributions very desirable for their shareholders, who otherwise may be subject to full taxation of a property dividend at regular rates.

2. **To facilitate financing.** Simplification of corporate structure may permit a stronger mortgage to be created and more stable earning power to be achieved (Consolidated Edison Co. of N. Y. 1946 refinancing).

3. **Management reasons.** The underlying motive for intercorporate simplification may be a desire by management to reduce overhead expense and to reorganize production and distribution facilities. This has been a most important reason for the simplification of the Standard Oil parent groups during the past two decades.

4. **Legal compulsion.** The Public Utility Holding Company Act of 1935, chief example of this factor, requires the simplification and dissolution of intercorporate structures of registered public utility holding company systems to meet two tests, namely, (a) the corporate simplification test and (b) the integration test. § 11(b)(2) of this law provides that a holding company may not have a subsidiary whose subsidiary is in turn a holding company (simplification). Similarly, § 11(b)(1) provides that the operating subsidiaries of a holding company must be limited to an integrated area in one or adjoining states.

INTERCORPORATE READJUSTMENT METHODS. Such readjustments can be effected by the following procedures:

1. **Formation or liquidation of subsidiaries.** Intercorporate readjustment may involve forming new or dissolving existing subsidiaries.

2. **Merger of subsidiaries.** Numerous large enterprises have reduced the number of their subsidiaries by merging them into other subsidiary corporations, or by absorbing some of the subsidiaries into the parent company.

3. Merger with lessor corporations. Railroad and traction companies have simplified their intercorporate structures by mergers with corporations whose properties they have previously operated under leases.

4. Liquidation of holding company. The holding company may be liquidated entirely for financial reasons or because of legal compulsion. In either event, securities of operating subsidiaries are distributed in exchange for those of the holding company.

5. Exchange of securities. Some utility holding companies, to meet the integration requirement, turned over their interest in certain subsidiaries to other holding companies having adjoining properties in exchange for stocks of operating utilities they desired or cash.

SIMPLIFICATION AND INTEGRATION UNDER THE PUBLIC UTILITY HOLDING COMPANY ACT. Simplification and integration under the Public Utility Holding Company Act of 1935 created a number of problems in intercorporate adjustments. The chief of these were:

1. **The need of paying off senior securities** of the top and intermediate holding companies, either in cash or through an exchange for portfolio securities.

2. **Disposal of small, isolated properties.** This could be done by competitive or private sale, or through an exchange of properties with other holding companies.

3. **Elimination of intermediate holding companies.** This often involved claims and counterclaims for mismanagement, etc., requiring settlements or extended litigation. Until such problems could be ironed out, simplification and integration was necessarily delayed.

4. **Relative participation of bondholders, preferred stockholders, and common stockholders** in the assets of a holding company, where these do not suffice to cover prior securities. The S.E.C. gave **junior stock** a participation of about 5% in such cases where it had no present book value, in recognition of the fact that a going concern was being liquidated because of statutory compulsion. (Otis & Co. v. S.E.C., 323 U.S. 624.)

SIMPLIFICATION AND INTEGRATION METHODS. Among the measures taken to effect simplification and integration of holding company systems are:

1. **Sales of operating subsidiary securities to the public,** proceeds being used to pay off prior securities of holding company. (See sale of Empire District Electric Co. common stock by Cities Service Power & Light Co.)

2. **Use of current earnings to retire prior securities,** after which the balance of the portfolio is distributed to common stockholders. (The North American Co. utilized this method, paying dividends on its common stock in shares of some of its subsidiaries, while cash earnings went to retire bonds of the parent company.)

3. **Direct exchanges of portfolio securities** for prior securities of the holding company. (The United Corp. used this method with particular success.)

4. **Sale through the issuance of rights** to holding company stockholders entitling them to subscribe to portfolio securities, the proceeds going to retire prior securities. (Sale of Pennsylvania Power & Light Co. common stock by National Power & Light Co. to its own stockholders.)

5. **Reclassification of the holding company capital structure** into a single class of common stock, followed by distribution of stock of subsidiaries in an agreed-upon reclassification ratio. (United Light & Power plan.)

Voluntary Liquidations

LIQUIDATION DEFINED. Liquidation involves conversion of assets into cash to discharge liabilities, distribution of the balance of assets among the stockholders, and legal steps to effect dissolution of the corporation. The **distribution of assets** must be in accordance with the respective rights and preferences of the several classes of creditors and stockholders. Ordinarily, assets are turned into cash prior to making the distributions, but a corporation owning stocks or bonds of other companies may distribute these among its stockholders pro rata.

WASTING ASSET INDUSTRIES. Liquidation may follow from a number of causes. Concerns engaged in wasting asset industries such as mining, oil extraction, lumbering, and stone-quarrying will in time be forced to liquidate unless new reserves of the wasting assets are acquired or they shift to some other business. The shrinkage in the business is reflected in the allowance for depletion, and the distribution of depletion reserves as distributions to stockholders is tantamount to gradual liquidation of the enterprise.

The **amount credited to depletion** is usually based on the original cost of the property (less any residual value it may have), estimated recoverable reserves, and the rate at which the reserves of ore, lumber, or other assets are being used up. For example, a coal mine purchased for $1,000,000 is estimated to have a value as land after the exhaustion of the coal deposits of $10,000. The net cost of the coal deposit is thus $990,000. If estimates place the amount of recoverable coal at 4,000,000 tons, then for each ton mined $.2475 should be credited to the depletion reserve out of the sales price of each ton extracted. The purchase price of the mine is thus gradually recovered in cash as the mined coal is marketed. Unless this accumulating cash is used to purchase new mining properties or other assets, the only alternative is to declare capital distributions or liquidating dividends from time to time, thereby gradually returning to the stockholders their original investment. For tax purposes the Internal Revenue Code sets **specific depletion allowances** that may be deducted in some extractive industries, expressed as a percentage of gross value of the product.

Reinvestment in other assets may not be wise if a management is specialized. If a company has decided not to extend its operations beyond the exhaustion of its present reserves, a wiser course may be to declare dividends in partial liquidation from time to time. Such distributions are not taxable as ordinary income to the stockholders. Simultaneously, ordinary taxable dividends may be paid out of current profits. Stockholders should be informed of the amount that is a capital distribution, and so not subject to tax as ordinary income.

LIQUIDATION TO AVOID INSOLVENCY. A concern may be solvent, but its operations may be showing persistent losses, working capital may be depleted, and the prospects for improvement uncertain. To avoid further impairment of assets through operating losses, the directors may decide to liquidate and return to stockholders whatever of their investment remains. Even a prosperous concern may vote to liquidate if it foresees a decided change for the worse in general conditions or in its own fortunes, or if the management wishes to retire and does not want to turn over direction of the affairs of the business to others.

PROCEDURE IN VOLUNTARY LIQUIDATION. Statutes provide for the manner of voluntary liquidation. The following procedure is typical.

1. **A vote by the required proportion of stockholders,** either of those having voting power only, or of all classes regardless of whether they have voting power. The proportion may be a bare majority, two-thirds, or higher. The charter may prescribe some other proportion that, however, may not be less than the minimum set by statute.

2. **Appointment of liquidating trustees or agents.** Under the statutes, the directors may be constituted liquidating trustees, or trustees may be appointed by the stockholders from their own number. As the company has voted to dissolve, title to the assets is no longer in the corporation but passes to the liquidating trustees, who hold them in trust for the benefit, first, of creditors and other claimants, and after them for the benefit of the stockholders. Assets may be followed, in the interest of creditors, into the hands of stockholders after final distribution. The liquidating trustees may engage one or more liquidating agents to act under their supervision. On the application of a creditor or stockholder, a court of competent jurisdiction may appoint a receiver to take charge of the assets for liquidation under the court's supervision.

3. The **assets are sold** by the liquidating trustees, the liquidating agent or the receiver.

4. **Extinguishment of all claims and liabilities** from proceeds of liquidation.

5. **Declaration of a liquidation dividend** or dividends by liquidating trustees, agents, or receiver. Such declaration may not be permitted until after a certain period has elapsed from the date of the corporation's dissolution, to assure that claims have been asserted and paid. In January 1959, the Cuban-Atlantic Sugar Co. distributed a third and final liquidating dividend consisting of cash and stock of two subsidiaries. It turned over, however, about $1 per share to a subsidiary, which accepted responsibility for the remaining liabilities. If some stockholders have not paid the subscription price in full, they are entitled to share the dividends only in proportion to the amount of their payments.

6. **Surrender for cancellation of stock certificates** by shareholders on the receipt of the final liquidating dividend. Liquidation is generally a protracted process because of the nonliquid character of certain assets and the time required to settle claims and liabilities. **Dividends in partial liquidation** may be paid in the meantime as the required cash is accumulated. In some instances, the amount of each liquidation is stamped or endorsed on the stock certificate. This is done while the stock transfer books remain open and shares change hands, to inform buyers that part of the capital has been returned.

LIQUIDATING AGENCY. If liquidation is protracted, assets may be turned over to a new liquidating corporation or trust to hold them pending their sale. The original corporation can then be dissolved forthwith.

Corporate Dissolution

MEANING OF DISSOLUTION. As stated by Fletcher (Law of Private Corporations), a corporation is dissolved when the **franchise to be a corporation,** conferred upon it by the state in which it is incorporated, is extinguished and the corporate existence is terminated. Dissolution involves observance of certain legal formalities. Without these a corporation may continue to exist, even as an empty shell, after it has ceased doing business and no meetings of stockholders or directors are being held. However, discontinuance of business, as well as insolvency, although not technically dissolution, practically confers upon creditors the rights that they have under technical dissolution—to recover unpaid stock subscriptions from stockholders if the assets are insufficient to meet the liabilities.

METHODS OF DISSOLUTION. A corporation may be dissolved in one of the following ways:

1. By act of the legislature.
2. By expiration of the period fixed in the charter for the life of the corporation.
3. By the happening of some contingency prescribed in the charter.
4. By failure or by loss of some essential part of the corporation.
5. By forfeiture of the charter by judicial proceedings.
6. By voluntary surrender of the charter, as previously discussed.

LEGISLATIVE REVOCATION OF CHARTER. The legislature may revoke the charter of a corporation only if it has reserved that right **by constitutional or statutory provision**, as is generally the procedure, or by a clause in a charter granted by special act. Such a provision then becomes a part of the contract between the state and the corporation. Without such provision repeal of the charter without the corporation's consent would be in violation of the obligation of a contract, which is prohibited by the Constitution of the United States. However, absence of such provision does not prevent the legislature from repealing a charter if the corporation has violated its contract with the state by some act of omission or commission. This right is rarely invoked.

DISSOLUTION BY EXPIRATION OF CHARTER. Statutes generally require that the charter state the period of corporate existence, and when that period has elapsed the life of the corporation automatically ceases. However, a corporation whose term of life is about to elapse may in most states **extend its existence** by complying with certain statutory provisions. A charter may limit the exercise of a certain power for a specified number of years without otherwise limiting the length of corporate life. In some states, **corporate life can be shortened by amendment of the charter**, and advantage is taken of this provision to dissolve the corporation.

DISSOLUTION EFFECTED BY HAPPENING OF SOME CONTINGENCY. Statutes may prescribe certain acts or omissions to act on the part of the corporation that automatically effect dissolution without any court proceedings instituted by the state. For example, failure to commence business within a certain time after incorporation may end the corporate existence. Such conditions, however, must be so plain that the legislation is unmistakable, according to Fletcher (Law of Private Corporations), as courts are ordinarily inclined to be liberal in this respect and view failure to fulfill a condition imposed by statute or charter as merely a cause for the forfeiture of the charter in an action brought by the state specifically for that purpose, and not as working forfeiture automatically.

There is no **legal dissolution, without specific statutory provision** to that effect, even if the corporation has not only ceased exercising its powers but has disposed of all of its property and distributed the proceeds to the stockholders, until the charter has been surrendered and its surrender has been accepted by the state. Likewise, insolvency, assignment for benefit of creditors, bankruptcy proceedings, failure to pay taxes, etc., are causes of dissolution but do not work automatic dissolution unless so provided by statute. On the other hand, in consolidations and mergers, the consolidating or merged companies are dissolved by the act of consolidation or merger.

DISSOLUTION FROM MISUSE AND NONUSE OF POWERS. If a corporation has either misused or failed to use its franchises and powers, court action may be brought against it to bring about the forfeiture of its charter by the state, represented by the attorney general or otherwise. For example, the **New York Business Corporation Law** [§ 1101(a)] provides that: "The attorney-general may bring an action for the dissolution of a corporation upon one or more of the following grounds:

1) That the corporation procured its formation through fraudulent misrepresentation or concealment of a material fact.

2) That the corporation has exceeded the authority conferred upon it by law, or has violated any provision of law whereby it has forfeited its charter, or carried on, conducted or transacted its business in a persistently fraudulent or illegal manner, or by the abuse of its powers contrary to the public policy of the state has become liable to be dissolved."

Minority stockholders or creditors are permitted to institute such proceedings only by express statutory provisions. Courts generally, however, show reluctance to deprive corporations of their charters except in flagrant cases, in which the ultra vires acts involve essential provisions of the law or charter and are matters of interest to the public. As a general rule, the dissolution will be granted only if the attorney general is able to show that some serious **injury to the public** has resulted because of the misuse or nonuse of the corporate form and the corporation's charter (Bergh-Conyngton, Business Law). In New York (Business Corporation Law, § 1104) proceedings for judicial dissolution may also be initiated by a petition presented by holders of half of all outstanding shares (unless otherwise provided in the certificate of incorporation) setting forth that the directors or shareholders are so divided respecting the corporation's affairs that the votes required for action cannot be obtained; or that because of internal dissension, dissolution would be beneficial to the shareholders.

VOLUNTARY DISSOLUTION. Such dissolution, in the absence of a statute making special provision for it, can only be brought about by the unanimous consent of all the stockholders. A majority of the stockholders can under those conditions effect dissolution only if the corporation is unable to fulfill the purposes of its incorporation and it is not a quasi-public corporation (railroad or public utility). In most states, however, statutes have been enacted that permit the dissolution of corporations by a **vote of a specified majority** of the stock outstanding. If there are two or more classes of stock, the permission of each class may be required. Under the New York Business Corporation Law (§ 1001), **nonjudicial dissolution** may be effected by the vote of holders of two-thirds of all outstanding shares entitled to vote thereon. Special statutes authorize the dissolution of such corporations as **banks, trust companies, insurance companies, and savings and loan associations.** In some states, all claims against the corporation must be settled before a corporation can dissolve itself.

The **corporate existence** may be continued for a stated period after formal dissolution but only to wind the company up. Thus, in Delaware all corporations, whether they expire by limitation or are otherwise dissolved, continue as bodies corporate for three years thereafter for the purpose of prosecuting or defending suits and enabling them to liquidate their affairs—to dispose of and convey their property and to divide their capital, but not to continue the business for which they were established.

SECTION 22

REORGANIZATIONS AND BANKRUPTCY

CONTENTS

Definitions and History
	PAGE
Reorganization defined	1
Tax vs. financial definition	1
Arrangements	1
Equity reorganizations	1
Insolvency defined	2
History of reorganization procedure	2
The Bankruptcy Act of 1938	3

Reorganizations Under Chapter X
Steps in reorganization under Chapter X	3
Filing of the petition	3
Contents of petition	4
Appraisal of petition	4
Appointment of trustees	5
Trustee's investigation	5
Trustee's statement and notice to creditors and stockholders	5
Formulation and approval of a plan of reorganization	6
Statutory requirements	6
Hearing on the reorganization plan	6
Advisory report by the S.E.C.	6
Approval of plan by the court	7
Submission of plan to security holders	7
Acceptance by creditors	7
Confirmation of the plan by the court	7
Effect of confirmation	8
Final decree	8
Compensation and allowances	8
Representation of security holders	8

Railroad Reorganization
Special factors	9
Judge may confirm plan without acceptance	9
Holders of equipment trust issues exempt from stay against creditors	10
Railroad readjustments	10

The Reorganization Plan
Legal limitations	10
Plan must be "fair and equitable"	10
Valuation of property	11
Prospective earning power	11
Preparation for reorganization	11
Objectives of the plan	11
Reduction of fixed charges	12
Elimination of burdensome maturities	12
Provision of adequate working capital	12
Facilitating future financing	13
Assuring sound financial policy	13

	PAGE
Presentation of a reorganization plan	13
Hypothetical plan in table form	14

Protective Committees in Reorganizations
Formation of committees	14
Authorization	14
Authorization form used in a Chapter X reorganization (f. 1)	15
Deposit agreement	16
Expenses of the committee	16
Pledge of deposited securities	16
Statutory control of protective committees	16

Arrangements Under Chapter XI
Definition	17
Filing a petition	17
Proceedings	18
Confirmation	18
Statutory criteria	18
Effect of confirmation	18

Bankruptcy
Bankruptcy laws of the United States	18
Purpose of bankruptcy	18
Federal bankruptcy law and state insolvency and other laws	19
Courts of bankruptcy	19
Geographical jurisdiction	20
Commencement of bankruptcy proceedings	20
Voluntary bankruptcy	20
The voluntary petition	20
Filing of schedules	20
Power of corporate directors to petition bankruptcy	21
Involuntary bankruptcy	21
Acts of bankruptcy	21
Adjudication of bankrupt	23
Provisional remedies for safeguard of debtor's property	24
Receiver in bankruptcy	24
Function of receiver	25
Referee in bankruptcy	25
Referee's powers	25
Referee's duties	25
Compensation of referee	26
Creditor meetings	26
Creditors' committees	26
Voting at creditors' meetings	26
Proving of claims	26
What debts may be proved	27

CONTENTS (*Continued*)

	PAGE
Allowed claims	28
Duties of bankrupt	29
Examination of the bankrupt	29
Concealment of property and records	29
Trustee in bankruptcy	30
Trustee's duties	30
Trustee's accounts	30
Compensation of trustee	31
Trustee's title to property	31
Transfer of powers and documents to trustee	31
Bankrupt's exemptions	32
Voidable preferences	32
Fraudulent transfers	32
Continuance of business	33
Partnerships in bankruptcy	33
Summary jurisdiction of the bankruptcy court	34
Adverse claimants	34
Jurisdiction of state and other courts over bankrupt's property	34
Sale of property	35
Payment of debts with priorities	36
Order of priority	36
Declaration and payment of dividends to creditors	36
Closing of the bankrupt estate	37
Reopening of bankrupt estate	37
Discharge of bankrupt	37
When discharge not allowed	37
Revocation of discharge	38
Debts not affected by discharge	38

Wage Earners' Plans

Instituting the proceeding	38
Petition and presentation of plan	39
Acceptance of plan	39
Confirmation by the court and discharge of the debtor	39

Agricultural Compositions and Extensions

Special treatment for farmers	39
Definition of farmer	39
Procedure	40
Adjudication of bankruptcy	40

SECTION 22

REORGANIZATIONS AND BANKRUPTCY

Definitions and History

REORGANIZATION DEFINED. The term "reorganization" is sometimes used to describe a voluntary readjustment of corporate debt and capital stock, as well as one effected by order of a court. But in financial usage it is generally limited to plans that change the terms of corporate indebtedness, and incidentally of capital stock, which are effected under Chapter X or Section 77 of the Bankruptcy Act.

Tax vs. Financial Definition. In tax, as distinct from financial, usage, the term is defined much more broadly to distinguish tax-free from taxable exchanges of securities or other property. Section 368 of the Internal Revenue Code of 1954 defines reorganization for tax purposes as follows:

(1) The term "reorganization" means (A) a statutory merger or consolidation, or (B) the acquisition by one corporation, in exchange solely for all or a part of its voting stock, of stock of another corporation if immediately after the acquisition the acquiring corporation has control of such other corporation (whether or not the acquiring corporation had control immediately before the acquisition); (C) the acquisition by one corporation, in exchange solely for all or a part of its voting stock (or in exchange solely for all or a part of the voting stock of another corporation which is in control of the acquiring corporation), of substantially all of the properties of another corporation, but in determining whether the exchange is solely for stock the assumption by the acquiring corporation of a liability of the other, or the fact that property acquired is subject to a liability, shall be disregarded; (D) a transfer by a corporation of all or a part of its assets to another corporation if immediately after the transfer the transferor, or one or more of its shareholders (including persons who were shareholders immediately before the transfer), or any combination thereof, is in control of the corporation to which the assets are transferred; but only if, in pursuance of the plan, stock or securities of the corporation to which the assets are transferred are distributed in a transaction which qualifies under sections 354–6 [dealing with tax-free exchanges]; (E) a recapitalization; or (F) a mere change in identity, form, or place of organization, however effected.

Arrangements. The National Bankruptcy Act as amended in 1938 authorized, under Chapter XI, a distinct procedure, arrangements, to simplify statutory reorganization for smaller corporations. By accelerating reorganizations of smaller enterprises Congress sought to clear Federal court calendars of such cases more quickly and to reduce the expense and time consumed.

Equity Reorganizations. Equity reorganizations have become virtually a thing of the past as the result of the enactment of the reorganization sections of the National Bankruptcy Act in 1933 and subsequent years. Since equity remedies become unavailable when statutes are enacted covering the same subjects, equity proceedings for reorganization are now initiated only in the very rare instances a corporation cannot reorganize under the Bankruptcy Act because it does not meet the statutory requirements. Equity receivers are still appointed on occasion if a conflict among stockholders over the election of the board of directors or charges of fraud may cause a court to appoint its representative to take over a business enterprise pending the conclusion of litigation. Also, the thousands of precedents handed down by the courts in past equity reorganizations still govern many aspects of bankruptcy reorganizations, for Chapter X of the Bankruptcy Act specifies in Section 115:

> The Court shall have and may exercise all the powers, not inconsistent with the provisions of this chapter, which a court of the United States would have if it had appointed a receiver in equity of the property of the debtor on the ground of insolvency or inability to meet its debts as they mature.

INSOLVENCY DEFINED. Insolvency has been defined differently in the Bankruptcy Act and by courts of equity. A debtor may be said to be insolvent either in the **bankruptcy** or in the **equity** sense, depending upon which of these two definitions is used. Section I of the **Bankruptcy Act** gives the following definition:

> A person shall be deemed insolvent within the provision of this Act whenever the aggregate of his property, exclusive of any property which he may have conveyed, transferred, concealed, removed, or permitted to be concealed or removed, with intent to defraud, hinder, or delay his creditors, shall not at a fair valuation be sufficient in amount to pay his debts.

Equity courts, on the other hand, have defined insolvency as inability to meet debts as they mature. Therefore, a corporation whose assets largely exceed its liabilities may nevertheless be found insolvent in an equity sense because it cannot meet currently maturing debts. The reorganization provisions of the Bankruptcy Act may be used by corporations that are insolvent in either sense.

HISTORY OF REORGANIZATION PROCEDURE. The Constitution of the United States provides that "Congress shall have power to establish . . . uniform laws on the subject of bankruptcies throughout the United States."

This clause is the basis for Federal regulation of bankruptcy and reorganization. Until 1898, however, Congress had not enacted a permanent bankruptcy statute, so that state laws applied in each jurisdiction. With the enactment of the Bankruptcy Act of 1898, Congress asserted its Constitutional authority over bankruptcies and the state laws lapsed.

For many years, however, the Bankruptcy Act contemplated exclusively the **liquidation** of the assets of the debtor for the benefit of creditors, rather than reorganization and continued operation. With statutory authority for reorganization lacking, embarrassed debtors resorted to equity proceedings, and numerous precedents established by the Federal courts in these cases provided a standardized procedure for the reorganization of business enterprises through the device of a **foreclosure sale** of the property for the benefit of creditors. Because of the absence of adequate supervision over such proceedings and the desire to reduce the cost and time required to effect reorganizations, Congress in 1933 and 1934 provided for the first time corporate reorganization procedures under the Bankruptcy Act. Section 77 of the Bankruptcy Act was enacted for railroad reorganizations, and Section 77B for reorganization of other corporations. In practice, Section 77B was found to favor debtors unduly at the expense of creditors, and in the drastically revised Bankruptcy Act enacted in 1938 Section 77B was replaced by Chapter X

THE BANKRUPTCY ACT OF 1938. The Bankruptcy Act of 1938 codified bankruptcy legislation passed by Congress up to that time. Chapters I through VII are concerned with bankruptcy proper, which contemplates a liquidation of the debtor's assets for the benefit of creditors. Chapter VIII includes Section 77, which was carried over from the old law intact, applicable to railroad reorganizations. Chapter IX, applicable to counties, municipalities, taxing, and special assessment districts, was made permanent in 1946.

The most comprehensive reorganization procedure is Chapter X, entitled Corporate Reorganizations. Chapter XI provides the simplified procedure known as Arrangements. Chapter XII outlines a procedure for Real Property Arrangements by Persons Other Than Corporations. Chapter XIII covers Wage Earners' Plans. Chapter XIV applies to reorganizations arising out of Maritime Commission Liens. A simplified procedure for readjustment of **railroad** capital structures, Section 20b of the Interstate Commerce Act, is conducted under the interstate commerce, rather than the bankruptcy, power of Congress.

Reorganizations Under Chapter X

Chapter X and Section 77 have strengthened the protection given creditors as against stockholders, and senior as against junior creditors, in corporate reorganizations. The investment status of corporate bonds has been enhanced to the extent that legal priorities can do so.

STEPS IN REORGANIZATION UNDER CHAPTER X. The Bankruptcy Act provides for the following steps in effecting reorganizations under Chapter X:

1. Filing of the petition.
2. Appointment of trustees.
3. Formulation of a plan of reorganization.
4. Hearing on the reorganization plan.
5. Preparation of an advisory report by the S.E.C.
6. Approval of plan by the court.
7. Submission of plan to security holders.
8. Confirmation of the plan by the court, and its consummation.

Under the final decree of confirmation by the court, the reorganization plan becomes binding upon **dissenters.** This final decree takes the place of the foreclosure sale that was used to consummate reorganizations in equity proceedings, as a result of which dissenters were either wiped out or became entitled to their pro-rata share of the proceeds of foreclosure, after deduction of expenses.

Filing of the Petition. A petition to reorganize a corporation under Chapter X of the Bankruptcy Act may be brought by the corporation itself, by three or more creditors whose claims aggregate $5,000 or more, or by an indenture trustee. Virtually all such petitions are filed, as a practical matter, by the debtor corporation. The petition should be filed with the court in whose territory the corporation has had its principal place of business or its principal assets for the preceding 6 months. In the case of a subsidiary corporation, the petition may be filed either in the court in whose territory it has its principal place of business or in a court that has already approved a petition to reorganize by or against its parent corporation.

Contents of Petition. Each petition filed under Chapter X must state, as required by Section 130:

(1) that the corporation is insolvent or unable to pay its debts as they mature;
(2) the applicable jurisdictional facts requisite under this chapter;
(3) the nature of the business of the corporation;
(4) the assets, liabilities, capital stock, and financial condition of the corporation;
(5) the nature of all pending proceedings affecting the property of the corporation known to the petitioner or petitioners and the courts in which they are pending;
(6) the status of any plan of reorganization, readjustment, or liquidation affecting the property of the corporation, pending either in connection with or without any judicial proceeding;
(7) the specific facts showing the need for relief under this chapter and why adequate relief cannot be obtained under chapter XI of this Act; and
(8) the desire of the petitioner or petitioners that a plan be effected.

Every petition under Chapter X must specify why adequate relief cannot be obtained under the shorter and simpler Chapter XI procedure. Chapter XI is not applicable to secured debts, and has been held inapplicable to corporations requiring a thorough financial reorganization or whose securities are held publicly. A statement of the pertinent facts would automatically meet this statutory requirement.

An **involuntary petition** to reorganize under Chapter X, brought by creditors or an indenture trustee, must add the following, as required by Section 131:

(1) that the corporation was adjudged a bankrupt in a pending proceeding in bankruptcy; or
(2) that a receiver or trustee has been appointed for or has taken charge of all or the greater portion of the property of the corporation in a pending equity proceeding; or
(3) that an indenture trustee or a mortgagee under a mortgage is, by reason of a default, in possession of all or the greater portion of the property of the corporation; or
(4) that a proceeding to foreclose a mortgage or to enforce a lien against all or the greater portion of the property of the corporation is pending; or
(5) that the corporation has committed an act of bankruptcy within four months prior to the filing of the petition.

Appraisal of Petition. The judge will enter an order approving a petition by a debtor to reorganize under Chapter X if satisfied that it complies with the requirements of Chapter X and has been filed in **good faith**. If not so satisfied, he is required to dismiss the petition. In the case of an involuntary petition brought by creditors or an indenture trustee, the debtor must file an answer controverting the facts alleged before 10 days, or a longer period if allowed by the court. If a satisfactory answer is not filed, the judge will enter an order approving the petition if it complies with the requirements of Chapter X and has been filed in good faith.

The statute specifies in Section 146 that a petition shall be deemed **not to be filed in good faith** if:

(1) the petitioning creditors have acquired their claims for the purpose of filing the petition; or
(2) adequate relief would be obtainable by a debtor's petition under the provisions of Chapter XI of this Act; or
(3) it is unreasonable to expect that a plan of reorganization can be effected; or
(4) a prior proceeding is pending in any court and it appears that the interests of creditors and stockholders would be best subserved in such prior proceeding.

An order of the court approving a petition to reorganize will automatically **stay mortgage foreclosure,** equity receivership or bankruptcy proceedings, and any other action to enforce a lien against a debtor's property, unless the court should order otherwise.

Appointment of Trustees. The judge will appoint one or more trustees to conduct the business of the debtor, pending reorganization, if liabilities aggregate $250,000 or more. If the liabilities are less than $250,000, the judge retains discretion whether to appoint a trustee or continue the corporation in possession. Trustees and their attorneys must be **"disinterested,"** which under the provisions of Section 158 bars any person if:

(1) he is a creditor or stockholder of the debtor; or
(2) he is or was an underwriter of any of the outstanding securities of the debtor or within five years prior to the date of the filing of the petition was the underwriter of any securities of the debtor; or
(3) he is, or was within two years prior to the date of the filing of the petition, a director, officer, or employee of the debtor or any such underwriter, or an attorney for the debtor or such underwriter; or
(4) it appears that he has, by reason of any other direct or indirect relationship to, connection with, or interest in the debtor or such underwriter, or for any reason an interest materially adverse to the interests of any class of creditors or stockholders.

To facilitate management of the business pending reorganization, the judge may appoint a director, officer, or employee of the debtor as an **additional trustee.** Furthermore, a trustee may employ an attorney who is not disinterested to represent him for any specified purpose other than the reorganization proceeding, with the approval of the judge.

Trustee's Investigation. If the judge so directs, the trustee is required by Section 167 to:

(1) investigate the acts, conduct, property, liabilities, and financial condition of the debtor, the operation of its business and the desirability of the continuance thereof, and any other matter relevant to the proceeding or to the formulation of a plan, and report thereon to the judge;
(2) examine the directors and officers of the debtor and any other witnesses concerning the foregoing matters or any of them;
(3) report to the judge any facts ascertained by him pertaining to fraud, misconduct, mismanagement and irregularities, and to any causes of action available to the estate.

The purpose of this provision is to assure that claims against the management of the debtor corporation arising out of past acts shall be prosecuted if the judge believes a basis for such action exists. The decision whether or not such an investigation shall be prosecuted rests with the court.

Trustee's Statement and Notice to Creditors and Stockholders. The trustee is required to submit a brief statement to the court at an early date summarizing his investigation of the property, the liabilities and financial condition of the debtor, and his conclusion whether continuance of the business is desirable. He must also give notice to creditors and stockholders that they may submit proposals for a reorganization plan to him within a specified time. This gives the key role in formulating a plan to the trustee, rather than to the old corporate management as was usually the case in the past.

FORMULATION AND APPROVAL OF A PLAN OF REORGANIZATION.
The judge is required to fix a time within which the trustee shall prepare and file a plan of reorganization, or a report stating his reasons why a plan cannot be carried out. For corporations with liabilities of less than $250,000, if the debtor is continued in possession, a disinterested person may be appointed as **"examiner"** by the judge to prepare and file a plan and perform other duties of a trustee.

Statutory Requirements. A plan of reorganization under Chapter X must conform to the following statutory requirements outlined in Section 216:

(1) shall include in respect to creditors generally or some class of them, secured or unsecured, and may include in respect to stockholders generally or some class of them, provisions altering or modifying their rights, either through the issuance of new securities of any character or otherwise;
(2) may deal with all or any part of the property of the debtor;
(3) shall provide for the payment of all costs and expenses of administration and other allowances which may be approved or made by the judge;
(4) may provide for the rejection of any executory contract except contracts in the public authority;
(5) shall specify what claims, if any, are to be paid in cash in full;
(6) shall specify the creditors or stockholders or any class of them not to be affected by the plan and the provisions, if any, with respect to them.

A **plan may provide,** to assure its execution, for the sale of corporate property; a merger of the debtor with one or more other corporations; the sale of property subject to or free of lien, or the issuance for cash of new securities, property, or other securities.

If a lease or other executory contract is rejected during reorganization, or in the reorganization plan, any person injured thereby may file a claim as a creditor. The law limits the claim of a landlord, if an unexpired lease of real estate is rejected, to 3 years' rent following the date of surrender of the premises, plus unpaid accrued rent.

Hearing on the Reorganization Plan. The judge is required to hold a hearing on the reorganization plan following the expiration of the time allowed the trustee to file his plan. At this hearing, objections to the plan, amendments thereto, or other plans may be presented by the debtor corporation or by any creditor or stockholder.

Following this hearing, the judge must submit the plan or plans presented to the **Securities and Exchange Commission** if the indebtedness exceeds $3,000,000 and may do so at his discretion if the indebtedness is less than this sum.

Advisory Report by the S.E.C. The Securities and Exchange Commission is authorized under Chapter X to appear as a party to a reorganization proceeding, either upon its own motion if approved by the judge or if requested by him. It is customary for the Commission to become a party if **substantial amounts** of securities of the debtor corporation are **held by the public.**

The **judge may fix a date** by which the Commission's report shall be filed. Until this report is filed, the S.E.C. notifies the judge that it will not file a report, or the date fixed has expired, whichever first occurs, the judge may not enter an order approving the plan.

The **S.E.C. report discusses** whether the plan or plans submitted are (1) feasible and (2) fair and equitable. A plan is **feasible** if it will place the corporation in a position where it is unlikely to suffer renewed financial embarrassment.

A plan is **fair and equitable** if it treats each class of securities or creditors in accordance with its legal priority.

Approval of Plan by the Court. The judge, in entering an order approving one or more plans of reorganization submitted by the trustee or others, must find that it (1) complies with the requirements of the law covering the reorganization plan, as contained in Section 216 of Chapter X of the Bankruptcy Act; (2) is fair and equitable; (3) is feasible. The requirements of Section 216 are outlined above under Formulation of a Plan of Reorganization.

Submission of Plan to Security Holders. The judge, in approving the plan, is required to **set a time** within which the creditors and stockholders affected may accept the plan. For this purpose, the judge must fix the division of creditors and stockholders into classes according to the nature of their claims and stock. It is important to each class of securities to know whether it is placed in a separate class, for this may determine whether the requisite approval will be forthcoming. Security holders are **not considered affected** by a plan if they are either **undisturbed** or **wiped out entirely**.

The **trustee is required to transmit** to creditors and stockholders affected by a plan, to aid them in voting, the following:

(1) the plan or plans approved, together with a summary thereof;
(2) the opinion of the judge, if any, approving the plan, or plans, or a summary thereof approved;
(3) the report, if any, filed in the proceeding by the Securities and Exchange Commission, or a summary thereof prepared by the Securities and Exchange Commission; and
(4) such other matters as the judge may deem necessary or desirable for the information of creditors and stockholders.

It is forbidden, without the court's consent, to solicit acceptance of a plan, conditional or unconditional, until the court has entered an order approving the plan and its transmittal to creditors and stockholders.

Acceptance by Creditors. A plan is considered accepted by any class of creditors if acceptances in writing are filed in the court on behalf of **creditors holding two-thirds in amount** of the claims filed and allowed of that class. If the debtor has not been found insolvent, acceptances must also be filed by or on behalf of holders of the **majority of stock,** of which proofs have been filed and allowed. To prevent persons with conflicting interests from pushing through or preventing the adoption of a plan, the statute provides:

If the acceptance or failure to accept a plan by the holder of any claim or stock is not in good faith, in the light of or irrespective of the time of acquisition thereof, the judge may, after hearing upon notice, direct that such claim or stock be disqualified for the purpose of determining the requisite majority for the acceptance of a plan.

Confirmation of the Plan by the Court. Following acceptance of the plan by creditors and stockholders affected, the judge must call a hearing, notice of which must be given the debtor corporation, creditors, stockholders, indenture trustees, the Secretary of the Treasury, the Securities and Exchange Commission, and any other persons designated by the judge, to consider confirmation of the plan. The judge is to confirm the plan if he is satisfied that the following requirements of Section 221 have been met:

(1) the statutory standards applicable to a plan of reorganization, and satisfaction of claims of the United States Treasury against the debtor have been complied with;

(2) the plan is fair and equitable, and feasible;
(3) the proposal of the plan and its acceptance are in good faith and have not been made or procured by means or promises forbidden by this Act;
(4) all payments made or promised by the debtor or by a corporation issuing securities or acquiring property under the plan or by any other person, for services and for costs and expenses in, or in connection with, the proceeding or in connection with the plan and incident to the reorganization, have been fully disclosed to the judge and are reasonable or, if to be fixed after confirmation of the plan, will be subject to the approval of the judge; and
(5) the identity, qualifications, and affiliations of the persons who are to be directors or officers, or voting trustees, if any, upon the consummation of the plan, have been fully disclosed, and that the appointment of such persons to such offices, or their continuance therein, is equitable, compatible with the interests of the creditors and stockholders and consistent with public policy.

Effect of Confirmation. Once confirmed, a plan becomes **binding** upon the debtor, upon every other corporation issuing securities or acquiring property under the plan, and upon all creditors and stockholders whether or not they are affected by the plan, have accepted it, or have filed proofs of their claims or interests.

Final Decree. Upon consummation of the plan, Section 228 provides that the judge shall enter a final decree:

(1) discharging the debtor from all its debts and liabilities and terminating all rights and interests of stockholders of the debtor, except as provided in the plan or in the order confirming the plan or in the order directing or authorizing the transfer or retention of property;
(2) discharging the trustee, if any;
(3) making such provisions by way of injunction or otherwise as may be equitable; and
(4) closing the estate.

The judge may also specify that, not sooner than 5 years after the final decree, holders of securities who have not presented or surrendered them shall not participate in distributions under the plan. Securities or cash remaining unclaimed at the **expiration** of such time becomes the property of the debtor, or of the new corporation if one is set up to acquire the assets of the debtor under the plan.

COMPENSATION AND ALLOWANCES. The judge must pass on costs and expenses incurred by creditors, trustees and their attorneys, attorneys for petitioning creditors, a referee, or a special master in Chapter X proceedings. The judge may also allow reasonable compensation for services rendered by indenture trustees, depositaries, reorganization managers, committees or representatives of creditors or stockholders, or attorneys or agents of the foregoing. A **separate hearing** is held to consider applications for these allowances. Each person claiming compensation for services rendered or reimbursement for costs and expenses incurred in a Chapter X proceeding must file with the court a statement under oath showing acquisition or transfers of claims or stock interests after the commencement of the proceeding. No compensation or reimbursement will be allowed to any committee or attorney, or other person acting in the proceedings in a representative or fiduciary capacity, who at any time after undertaking to act in this capacity has purchased or sold such claims or stock without the prior consent or subsequent approval of the judge.

REPRESENTATION OF SECURITY HOLDERS. Chapter X regulates persons or committees representing more than twelve creditors or stockholders in a reorganization proceeding, as well as indenture trustees. Under Section 111, each such person, committee, or trustee must file a statement with the court under oath containing:

(1) a copy of the instrument, if any, whereby such person, committee, or indenture trustee is empowered to act on behalf of creditors or stockholders;
(2) a recital of the pertinent facts and circumstances in connection with the employment of such person or indenture trustee, and, in the case of a committee, the name or names of the person or persons at whose instance, directly or indirectly, such employment was arranged or the committee was organized or formed or agreed to act;
(3) with reference to the time of the employment of such person, or the organization or formation of such committee, or the appearance in the proceeding of any indenture trustee, a showing of the amounts of claims or stock owned by such person, the members of such committee or such indenture trustee, the times when acquired, the amounts paid therefor, and any sales or other disposition thereof; and
(4) a showing of the claims or stock represented by such person or committee and the respective amounts thereof, with an averment that each holder of such claims or stock acquired them at least one year before the filing of the petition or with a showing of the times of acquisition thereof.

The judge may **disregard any provision of a depositary agreement,** proxy, power of attorney, or indenture that he finds to be unfair or not consistent with public policy. A claim or stock acquired by members of a protective committee, indenture trustee, an agent, or an attorney representing creditors or stockholders may be limited, in its treatment in reorganization, to the actual consideration paid.

A fuller discussion of protective committee operation is given below.

Railroad Reorganization

SPECIAL FACTORS. Section 77 of the Bankruptcy Act differs from Chapter X in one fundamental respect—the **Interstate Commerce Commission is given the key role** in the procedure, rather than the mere advisory part assigned to the Securities and Exchange Commission in Chapter X cases. Plans of reorganization are filed in the first instance with the Commission, which issues an examiner's report on a **plan of reorganization** and subsequently its own final plan. Until a plan has been issued by the Commission, either one filed with it or one of its own, the court cannot proceed. Furthermore, the Interstate Commerce Commission ballots security holders following approval of its plan by the court. The role of the court in railroad reorganization was severely curtailed by the United States Supreme Court in the Chicago, Milwaukee, St. Paul & Pacific, and Western Pacific cases, decided in 1943. In those cases, the highest court ruled that findings as to valuation and other facts by the Commission shall be final, and not subject to review by the courts, whose jurisdiction is limited to seeing that the procedure followed has conformed to the requirements of the law.

Judge May Confirm Plan Without Acceptance. One provision of Section 77 states that the judge may confirm a plan of reorganization that has not been accepted by two-thirds in amount of each class of creditors or stockholders affected, if he finds "that it makes adequate provision for fair and equitable treatment of the claims or interests of those rejecting it, that the rejection is not reasonably justified, that the plan otherwise conforms to all of the applicable requirements of the section."

Holders of Equipment Trust Issues Exempt from Stay Against Creditors. Section 77 exempts holders of railroad equipment issues from the general stay against creditors enforcing their claims. The theory is that such obligations will become impaired in value if the holders are not permitted to act promptly to protect their interests in the event of reorganization.

RAILROAD READJUSTMENTS. A greatly simplified procedure for the readjustment of railroad capital structures was provided by the **Mahaffie Act** of 1948 under Section 20b of the Interstate Commerce Act. Amended in 1957, the law specifies that the provisions of **any class** of railroad securities may be altered or modified with the approval of the Interstate Commerce Commission, **without further submission to a court.** This avoids the need for a drastic recasting of capital structure to modify the terms of a maturing bond issue or to effect other changes, since the rigid "fair and equitable" test of the Bankruptcy Act is not applicable (see below). Section 20b does not apply to equipment trust certificates or to any evidences of debt of a carrier secured solely by equipment.

The **authority of the Commission** under this law is **"exclusive and plenary."** Approval by the I.C.C. relieves the railroads "from the operations of all restraints, limitations, and prohibitions of law, Federal, state, or municipal, insofar as they may be necessary to enable them to make and carry into effect" the approved changes. A plan of modification under Section 20b is submitted to the Commission by the railroad corporation with evidence of approval by a substantial number of holders of the issues affected. After approval by the Commission and of at least 75% of each class of securities affected, the modification then becomes **compulsory for all holders** of such securities.

The Reorganization Plan

LEGAL LIMITATIONS. The statutes and court decisions interpreting them have circumscribed in essential respects the nature of corporate reorganization plans.

Plan Must Be "Fair and Equitable." The statutes require that a plan of reorganization must be "fair and equitable." The United States Supreme Court has interpreted this term to give it a very concrete significance. A plan will not be considered fair and equitable unless it is consistent with standards laid down by the United States Supreme Court in a long line of cases, of which the best known is Northern Pacific Railway Co. v. Boyd [228 U.S. 482 (1913)]. The Boyd case principle was confirmed anew for statutory reorganization in Case v. Los Angeles Lumber Products Co. [308 U.S. 106 (1939)]. In this latter case, the leading decision governing present-day corporate reorganization, the Supreme Court required that senior creditors or stockholders shall be covered in full with new securities issued in reorganization before junior issues may participate in the plan. Even if senior and junior security holders have agreed to a compromise plan, the court is required to ignore this and to make an independent finding that priorities have been recognized. This ruling is known as the **doctrine of absolute priority,** which rejects the theory that a plan of reorganization is designed "for the relief of debtors" and requires that priority of claim be recognized literally.

To make a plan of reorganization feasible, the same class of securities of the reorganized company may have to be issued to two or more classes of claims of the corporation undergoing reorganization. In that event, senior securities may be given a larger amount of the new securities per dollar of claim, as **"equitable compensation"** for the loss of their prior position.

VALUATION OF PROPERTY. The doctrine of absolute priority makes it necessary to secure a valuation of the property of the corporation undergoing reorganization, to determine which securities are to be recognized and which must be wiped out because of a lack of equity. In the eyes of the law, such securities are not wiped out by the reorganization plan; rather the court is held merely to recognize a loss in value that has already taken place.

Prospective Earning Power. The United States Supreme Court in Consolidated Rock Products Co. v. Du Bois (312 U.S. 510), as well as in railroad cases, has held that a valuation of property for reorganization purposes shall be based upon prospective earning power, rather than the original cost of assets. Similarly, in determining the treatment of individual security issues, the earning power of the property upon which they have a lien will determine relative treatment. The court in the Consolidated Rock Products Co. case said that "the criterion of earning power is the essential one if the enterprise is to be freed from the heavy hand of past errors, miscalculations or disaster and if the allocation of securities among the various claimants is to be fair and equitable."

PREPARATION FOR REORGANIZATION. During operation of the property of the debtor by the trustee, important preparations can be made for reorganization. Since interest does not have to be paid, earnings can be devoted to making up deferred maintenance and effecting necessary property improvements. Burdensome leases and other contracts can be rejected, accrued taxes paid, and activities that reduce earning power curtailed or eliminated. The trustee can also build up cash so that the enterprise will have a stronger working capital position at the time of reorganization.

Trustees may with the court's approval pay off prior obligations, with a view to simplifying the capital structure of the reorganized enterprise. On the other hand, trustees may borrow for needed expenditures through the issuance of **trustee certificates,** which may be exchanged for prior lien obligations at the time of reorganization if they are not paid off before or at that time. Trustees may apply to the court to make interest payments on outstanding obligations from time to time, if earnings and cash position justify and if they want to prevent accumulation of unpaid interest that adds to the debts of the corporation. Since the claim to unpaid interest normally ranks *pari passu* with claims to principal, delay in reorganization may largely increase prior obligations coming ahead of the stock. Accumulation of dividends on cumulative preferred stock has the same effect as far as the common is concerned.

OBJECTIVES OF THE PLAN. A sound plan of reorganization will achieve the following five objectives:

1. Reduce fixed charges.
2. Eliminate burdensome debt maturities.
3. Assure adequate working capital.
4. Facilitate the raising of new capital in the future.
5. Pave the way for a sound financial policy after reorganization.

In addition, a plan of reorganization may provide for a sounder business basis for the enterprise through:

1. Dropping departments or activities that reduce earning power.
2. Adding departments or activities, through merger or otherwise, that increase earning power.
3. Providing competent management.

Reduction of Fixed Charges. No reorganization plan is "feasible," and will be approved by regulatory commissions and courts as such, unless fixed charges are reduced to a level that can be earned with a margin even in less favorable years. If earnings of a corporation are sensitive to the business cycle, fixed charges should be limited to an amount that can be covered in all but the very worst depression years. There are several ways by which fixed charges can be reduced in reorganization plans. These are:

1. A lowering of the rate of interest on outstanding bonds, particularly if it is higher than the prevailing level.
2. Substitution of income bonds in part or whole for fixed interest obligations.
3. Fixed interest bonds may be exchanged in part for preferred or common stock. In more drastic reorganizations, if severe loss of earning power makes even the payment of contingent interest questionable, this is preferable.
4. Part or all of the funded debt may be retired, during trusteeship or at the time of reorganization, by the use of cash derived from the sale of unnecessary assets or from earnings.
5. Through sinking fund provisions; through arrangements for liquidation of assets after reorganization, the proceeds to be applied to additional debt reduction; by making bonds convertible and by issuing stock purchase warrants, funds from the exercise of which must be applied to debt retirement.

If the earning power of a business tends to disappear entirely in depressions, serious consideration should be given to the substitution of contingent interest bonds or stock for all outstanding fixed interest debt.

Elimination of Burdensome Maturities. A reorganization cannot be successful, and therefore the plan will not be considered feasible by regulatory agencies or the courts, if the debtor is left with burdensome debts that will mature within a few years after the reorganization. Hence, the plan should leave no substantial debt maturities during a period of 5 or 10 years, and preferably longer, after the plan becomes effective. Burdensome debt maturities may be eliminated by:

1. Extension of the maturity of obligations.
2. Provision of adequate sinking funds.
3. Provision of sufficient cash under the terms of the reorganization plan to meet maturities over a period of years.
4. Underwriting arrangements with bankers to assure funds for early maturities from the sale of new issues.
5. Negotiation of sale of assets pledged to secure debts coming due within the near future, perhaps with the purchaser assuming the obligations.
6. Granting of conversion privileges to bonds coming due within a limited period of years.

Provision of Adequate Working Capital. A plan of reorganization must seek to assure that the company will not encounter financial embarrassment again following its emergence from the jurisdiction of the courts. This objective requires that working capital not only shall be adequate for immediate needs, but shall provide a margin for contingencies, visible and possible. Unless adequate working capital is provided, a plan of reorganization is not "feasible"

THE REORGANIZATION PLAN

as that term has been defined by the Securities and Exchange Commission and the courts.

In many instances, additional cash must be raised as part of the plan of reorganization. Among the **methods commonly used to raise cash** are:

1. Assessment of stockholders, who either receive new securities for the assessment or merely retain their old equity. Assessments have become unusual, although they were quite common in equity reorganizations.
2. Sale of new bonds, preferred stock, or common stock to underwriters, to security holders of the company, or to other buyers.
3. Issuance of stock-purchase warrants to security holders or others, exercisable within a short period.
4. A term loan may be secured from a bank or an insurance company.
5. A corporation may dispose of unnecessary assets, including securities of subsidiaries no longer needed by the business.
6. Sometimes reorganization is postponed for a period so that cash can be accumulated out of earnings during the trusteeship.

Facilitating Future Financing. A sound reorganization should provide not only adequate working capital immediately but also reasonable assurance that new capital can be raised for expansion and other needs in the future. This can be done by:

1. Authorizing a prior lien mortgage, under which bonds would be sold in the future to provide new capital as needed.
2. Having valuable assets on hand free of lien, that can be pledged for loans if necessary.
3. Establishing a capital fund out of earnings before interest need be paid upon income bonds.
4. Authorizing a prior preferred stock issue to raise new capital.
5. Providing adequate sinking funds on outstanding bond issues, so that they can be retired over a period of years to strengthen the company's credit and thus facilitate new financing on attractive terms.
6. Limiting the common stock issue, so that these shares can achieve an investment status in time and become a suitable vehicle for new financing.
7. Simplification of the reorganized corporation's capital structure through the elimination of divisional, collateral trust, and other obligations, and through absorption of publicly held securities of subsidiaries.

Assuring Sound Financial Policy. The plan of reorganization can include safeguards to help prevent a recurrence of financial strain in the future. These may take the form of:

1. Sinking funds on outstanding bonds and other debts.
2. Dividend limitations for the initial period following reorganization.
3. Low call prices on bonds and preferred stock issued, to facilitate future refunding at lower interest and dividend rates.
4. Election to the board of directors of representatives of creditors, who would favor conservative financial policies.
5. Accounting adjustments, to eliminate any overstatement of asset values.

PRESENTATION OF A REORGANIZATION PLAN. The more complex the capitalization of a corporation undergoing reorganization, the more difficult it is to present the salient facts about the plan in understandable form to the security holders affected. This is often done in tabular form, to make clear at a glance the status of the enterprise before and after reorganization, and the treatment to be accorded each security issue. **Two tables** are customarily included in presenting a more complex reorganization plan. One shows the effect of the plan upon total capitalization and annual charges, and the other the treatment of each security issue. In industrial reorganizations, if only a few classes of securities and creditors are involved, shorter tables or a mere description of the treatment of each class of security may suffice for a clear presentation of the plan to security holders and others interested.

Hypothetical Plan in Table Form. The effect of a simplified, hypothetical Chapter X reorganization on the debt and fixed charges of an industrial corporation is illustrated in the following tabulation:

Before Reorganization			After Reorganization		
	Debt	Annual Interest Charges		Debt	Annual Interest Charges (contingent)
1st mortgage 5% bonds	$5,000,000	$250,000	4% income bonds	$5,000,000	$200,000
Secured bank loans (5%)	3,000,000	150,000	4% income bonds	3,000,000	120,000
6% debentures	4,500,000	270,000	Receive, pro rata, $2,000,000 of 4% noncumulative preferred stock and $6,000,000 of common stock		
Trade creditors	3,500,000	—			
	$16,000,000	$670,000		$8,000,000	$320,000

In the above example it is assumed that the secured creditors receive 4% income bonds in exchange for their claims and the unsecured creditors all of the preferred and common stock of the reorganized corporation. The equity of the old stockholders is wiped out, since creditor claims exceed the valuation of assets on the date of reorganization.

Protective Committees in Reorganizations

FORMATION OF COMMITTEES. When a corporation encounters financial difficulties and a reorganization of its financial structure is imminent, committees may be appointed to look after the interests of the various classes of bondholders, other creditors, and stockholders. It is generally advisable to have a **committee for each class** of security holders having a distinct interest in the company to protect. For a single committee to represent two or more classes may lead to charges that the committee is favoring one class as against another.

A protective committee is a more or less **self-appointed body.** Stockholders' committees may be organized at the instance of the management of the corporation. But unless members of the committee are well known or are connected with substantial enterprises or institutions, or are large security holders themselves, other security holders may be skeptical about permitting them to represent their interests. The committee may be composed mainly of representatives of the bankers, large holders, and others who will lend it prestige and standing.

Each committee elects one of its members as chairman, appoints counsel to advise it on the legal problems that are likely to arise, and appoints a secretary who will attend to administrative details.

AUTHORIZATION. In earlier reorganization proceedings, security holders signified their desire to have the protective committee represent them by depositing their securities with a trust company in exchange for **certificates of deposit**. Under the Securities Act of 1933, the certificates of deposit might, however, be subject to registration with the S.E.C. To avoid this complication, as well as the prospect that certificates of deposit could be less marketable or sell at a lower price, a much less cumbersome procedure was evolved that does not require the actual deposit of securities. This takes the form of a simple authorization to the protective committee to represent the security holder in the reorganization proceedings. The authorization, which may be revoked at any time, does not prevent the owner from disposing of his securities at will. This simpler procedure is now ordinarily used in Chapter X reorganizations. A typical form used for such an authorization is shown below (Fig. 1).

PROTECTIVE COMMITTEE FOR FIRST AND REFUNDING 5% BONDS OF HUDSON & MANHATTAN RAILROAD COMPANY

299 Madison Avenue
New York 17, N. Y.

AUTHORIZATION

The undersigned, being the owner of $ principal amount of First and Refunding 5% Bonds of Hudson & Manhattan Railroad Company, hereby authorizes George J. Wise, Ralph H. Haas and Lloyd E. Dewey, and their successors and additions, a Committee:

To represent the undersigned in connection with the reorganization proceedings of Hudson & Manhattan Railroad Company under the United States Bankruptcy Act, and to appear before any court, commission or other body in connection with the affairs of said corporation or its subsidiaries, and to negotiate and take such action as the Committee may deem necessary or proper for the protection of the interests of the holders of said First and Refunding 5% Bonds.

This authorization (a) does not affect the right of the undersigned to dispose of the bonds at any time; (b) does not authorize the Committee to accept or reject, on behalf of the undersigned, any plan of reorganization; (c) does not impose any lien or charge on the bonds or any financial obligation on the undersigned for the expenses or compensation of the Committee; application for same will be made to the Court at the conclusion of the reorganization proceedings.

This authorization may be revoked by the undersigned at any time without cost or expense.

WITNESS the signature of the undersigned this   day of   , 1956.

SIGNATURE ....

Please typewrite or print the following:

Name of Holder ....

Street Address ....

City and State ....

Principal amount of Bonds owned $..............................

If bonds were acquired after August 10, 1953, please state date when acquired
....

Fig. 1. Authorization form used in a Chapter X reorganization.

If a committee solicits authorizations for a security listed on a national exchange, it must comply with the proxy regulations of the S.E.C.

DEPOSIT AGREEMENT. One of the first duties of a protective committee's counsel may be to draft the agreement under which holders will be asked to deposit their securities or claims with the committee. In return depositing bondholders or stockholders receive from the depositary its certificates of deposit issued to represent the deposited securities. These may be admitted to dealings on the stock exchange in place of the securities they displace.

The purpose of the agreement is often to place the committee practically in the position of the owners of the securities deposited, with power to pursue all the remedies open to them. In addition to the **general grant of power** to take necessary steps to protect the interests of the depositors, the agreement usually contains a long enumeration of **specific powers** as well as disclaimers of liability. Although making the document bulky, the enumeration of specific powers is considered necessary because of the attitude of the courts in construing provisions strictly against the committee and in favor of the depositors.

The agreement commonly provides that the **depositors may withdraw** at any time upon payment of their proportion of the committee's expenses.

EXPENSES OF THE COMMITTEE. These expenses include the cost of publicity, etc., compensation received by the committee's counsel, its secretary, the depositary, and its own members, unless these latter contribute their service gratis, as they not infrequently do. When the reorganization plan has been confirmed, the court may allow payment of part or all of the expenses by the debtor corporation. Depositing security holders are assessed their pro-rata share of the expenses if the court does not allow the debtor to pay them, or if they withdraw before reorganization.

Pledge of Deposited Securities. To defray expenses a protective committee may contract loans and for this purpose it may pledge deposited securities under the authority granted it by the deposit agreement. The committee may also use the deposited securities as a pledge to indemnify the bondholders' trustee for any expense, loss, or liability it may incur in taking action under the indenture at the request of the committee, which has the authority to make such request by reason of its being holder of the proportion of the bonds stipulated in the indenture.

STATUTORY CONTROL OF PROTECTIVE COMMITTEES. The Bankruptcy Act bars a protective committee from soliciting acceptances, conditional or unconditional, of a plan of reorganization until after entry of an order approving the plan and the transmittal of this order to creditors and stockholders, unless the court gives specific authority for such solicitation. Section 211 of the Bankruptcy Act, as stated above, requires a committee representing more than twelve creditors or stockholders to file with the court a copy of the instrument under which it functions, and other pertinent data. Section 213 further provides that a protective committee can be heard or allowed to intervene in a proceeding under Chapter X only if it shall have satisfied the court that it has "complied with all applicable laws regulating the activities and personnel of such persons."

Section 77 of the Bankruptcy Act provides that no committee or person may solicit deposit of securities of railroads during reorganization, or proxies to act for security owners, until such solicitation has been authorized by the Interstate Commerce Commission after a hearing. However, the law makes an **exception** for persons acting in their own interest, groups of not more than 25 bona fide holders of securities, or mutual institutions acting together for their own interests. The Interstate Commerce Commission requires that applicants for authority to act for other security holders, as a protective committee or otherwise, must file a sworn statement providing information required by the Commission's rules and regulations.

Arrangements Under Chapter XI

DEFINITION. An arrangement is defined in the statute as a "plan of a debtor for the settlement, satisfaction, or extension of the time of payment of his unsecured debts." It may include:

(1) provisions for treatment of unsecured debts on a parity one with the other, or for the division of such debts into classes and the treatment thereof in different ways or upon different terms;
(2) provisions for the rejection of any executory contract;
(3) provisions for specific undertakings of the debtor during any period of extension provided for by the arrangement, including provisions for payments on account;
(4) provisions for the termination, under specified conditions, of any period of extension provided by the arrangement;
(5) provisions for continuation of the debtor's business with or without supervision or control by a receiver or by a committee of creditors or otherwise;
(6) provisions for payment of debts incurred after the filing of the petition and during the pendency of the arrangement, in priority over the debts affected by such arrangement; and
(7) provisions for retention of jurisdiction by the court until provisions of the arrangement, after its confirmation, have been performed.

When proceedings are brought under Chapter XI that should have been brought under Chapter X, Section 328, of the Bankruptcy Act authorizes the Securities and Exchange Commission to make application to the court to dismiss the proceeding unless the petition that initiated it is amended to comply with the protective requirements of Chapter X. The courts have held that Chapter XI is not available to a debtor both when there are **publicly held securities** and when the corporation has need of a **thorough-going reorganization** and recasting of its capital structure. It cannot be used to effect reorganization of companies with **complex capital structures.**

FILING A PETITION. A petition to effect an arrangement must always be filed by the debtor corporation. This may be done either before or after adjudication in bankruptcy. A petition must state "that the debtor is insolvent or unable to pay his debts as they mature," and set forth the provisions of the arrangement proposed or include a statement that the debtor intends to propose an arrangement. It must be accompanied by a statement of the executory contracts of the debtor, and a statement and schedules of his affairs, if one was not previously filed.

The court may, upon application of the debtor, grant a **stay** of adjudication or of the administration of the estate in bankruptcy, following filing of the petition to effect an arrangement. The mere act of filing does not act as such a stay automatically. The court may direct the debtor to file a **bond** with approved sureties indemnifying the estate against subsequent loss, pending confirmation of an arrangement.

PROCEEDINGS. The court may appoint a **receiver** for the property of the debtor corporation, and one or more appraisers to prepare an inventory of its property. Also, the judge may refer the proceeding to a **referee**.

The statute requires the court to call a **meeting of creditors** within ten days after the petition is filed giving written notice of 15 to 30 days. The **notice** must be accompanied by a summary of liabilities and appraisal of the assets, if one had been made. At this meeting, the judge or referee presides, passing upon proofs of claims and receiving written acceptances of creditors on the proposed arrangement. In an arrangement, unlike a statutory reorganization, acceptances may be sought before the filing of a petition, as well as afterward.

If no receiver or trustee is appointed, the management of the debtor remains in possession of the property.

CONFIRMATION. If all creditors affected have accepted an arrangement in writing, the court may confirm it forthwith. Otherwise, an application for confirmation is to be filed with the court after the arrangement has been **accepted in writing by a majority** in number and amount of all creditors, or if the creditors are divided into classes, by a majority in number and amount of the creditors of each class affected by the arrangement.

Money or securities to be distributed to creditors affected by the arrangement must be deposited with the court before confirmation.

Statutory Criteria. Before a court may confirm an arrangement, it must under Section 366 see that it conforms to the following five tests:

(1) the provisions of Chapter XI have been complied with;
(2) it is for the best interests of the creditors;
(3) it is fair and equitable and feasible;
(4) the debtor has not been guilty of any of the acts or failed to perform any of the duties which would be a bar to the discharge of a bankrupt; and
(5) the proposal and its acceptance are in good faith and have not been made or procured by any means, promises, or acts forbidden in the Act.

Effect of Confirmation. Following confirmation, an arrangement is binding not only upon the creditors affected, but upon all creditors of the debtor corporation. An amendment added in 1958 provides a procedure whereby, if the court has retained jurisdiction, the arrangement may be modified after confirmation.

Bankruptcy

BANKRUPTCY LAWS OF THE UNITED STATES. The Constitution of the United States, in Article I, Section 8, Clause 4, provides that: "Congress shall have power to establish . . . uniform laws on the subject of bankruptcies throughout the United States." Under this power, Congress has enacted four successive bankruptcy laws: the Act of 1800, repealed in 1803; the Act of 1841, repealed in 1843; the Act of 1867, repealed in 1878; and the Act of 1898, amended principally by the Bankruptcy Act of 1938, known popularly as the **Chandler Act.** Since then there have been frequent amendments but they are of lesser importance. The **bankruptcy laws in force** at present consist of (1) the Act of 1898, (2) its several amendments, (3) certain **General Orders** adopted by the Supreme Court of the United States, and (4) the equity rules prescribed by that court for the lower Federal courts.

PURPOSE OF BANKRUPTCY. The primary purpose of bankruptcy proper is to **take over the assets** of the insolvent debtor, reduce them to money, and distribute the proceeds, after the satisfaction of secured and priority claims, among the general creditors in proportion to their respective claims as filed with and allowed by the bankruptcy court. Before the enactment of the bankruptcy law, except in states that had their own bankruptcy or insolvency laws, the common law rule prevailed that "the law favors the diligent creditor." Hence, creditors who first appeared on the scene with sheriffs armed with writs of attachment or executions had their claims satisfied in full, whereas subsequently appearing creditors found little if any of the debtor's assets left for the payment of their claims. Bankruptcy laws, including the Federal, **substitute equity for the common law,** and their rule is equality, not diligence. The debtor's estate is seized by the bankruptcy court and creditors share in the assets pro rata.

A second purpose of the present bankruptcy law is to place an insolvent business under the control of the court for **reorganization,** so that liquidation may be avoided. In 1933 and 1934 the Act was amended to provide relief for insolvent debtors through reorganization.

Another purpose of the present bankruptcy law is to **relieve unfortunate but honest debtors** of the unsatisfied portion of their debts, with certain exceptions, after they have surrendered all their assets, in order to afford them an opportunity to reinstate themselves in business if they can. They are also allowed certain exemptions, being permitted to retain property of a certain kind and value that is not subject to seizure by the bankruptcy courts. The discharge of the bankrupt, however, is viewed by courts as a distinctly secondary purpose of the Bankruptcy Law and not an essential characteristic.

FEDERAL BANKRUPTCY LAW AND STATE INSOLVENCY AND OTHER LAWS. States are permitted to have bankruptcy or insolvency laws so long as there is no Federal bankruptcy law. Prior to the enactment of the present Federal law, many states had insolvency laws in force, some of which in their essential features were similar to the subsequently enacted Federal statute. However, with the passage of the Federal law the state statutes became suspended, being now valid and continuing in operation only to the extent that they are not in conflict with the Federal law. No state court has power to interfere with the operation of the Bankruptcy Act and restrain a debtor from taking advantage of its provisions.

However, **assignments made by debtors** for the benefit of creditors and receiverships in state courts are nullified only when the debtors are adjudicated bankrupts in the Federal courts. In the meantime, state courts are not disturbed in their custody of debtors' property without their consent. Moreover, the Federal law takes cognizance of state laws relating to certain rights of the parties to the bankrupt proceedings, such as exemptions, priority of payment, dower rights, mortgages, etc. The Federal bankruptcy courts also follow state courts in dealing with property rights regulated by state law, unless the provisions of the Bankruptcy Act require a different construction from the state court decisions.

COURTS OF BANKRUPTCY. The judicial administration of the Bankruptcy Act is placed in the **Federal district courts "sitting in bankruptcy."** When so sitting, they are **courts of equity** and not of law. However, they must administer the bankruptcy proceedings pending before them in accordance with the provisions of the Act and the General Orders of the U.S. Supreme Court, and not allow themselves the latitude of any broad and unlimited equity power. Being equitable in nature they can punish for contempt of court. Thus, if a bankrupt conceals property belonging to his estate, the court can punish him summarily for contempt to force obedience to its orders. This is not held to be any violation of the constitutional prohibition against imprisonment for debt. In general, any intentional interference with the law on the part of the bankrupt or the creditors is punishable for contempt. In the exercise of its equitable powers, the bankruptcy court can also issue injunctions restraining the commission of any acts that would hamper the proper administration of the bankruptcy proceedings.

Geographical Jurisdiction. A particular district court, sitting in bankruptcy, has the power to adjudicate the bankruptcy only of persons (including corporations) who have had their principal place of business or their domicile within the confines of the court's district for the preceding 6 months or the greater portion of this period. The **principal place of business** of a corporation is where its principal business is transacted, or where its assets are mainly located, and not necessarily where it is incorporated. If the debtor has neither place of business nor residence but has property in the United States, the court in whose district the property is located has jurisdiction.

The jurisdiction of a bankruptcy court is **confined to its district**. If it is desired, for example, to recover property belonging to the bankrupt's estate but located in another judicial district, or to examine persons in another district concerning the acts, conduct, and property of the bankrupt, **ancillary proceedings** must be instituted in the court of that district by petitioning it for the issuance of the proper order or subpoena.

COMMENCEMENT OF BANKRUPTCY PROCEEDINGS. These proceedings are begun when a petition is filed with the court praying that the debtor be adjudged a bankrupt. The petition may be filed by the debtor himself, in which case it is known as a **voluntary** petition. Or it may be filed by one or more creditors against the debtor, in which case it is known as an **involuntary** petition. The petitions are made on the official forms prescribed by the U.S. Supreme Court.

VOLUNTARY BANKRUPTCY. All persons, partnerships, and corporations, capable of contracting and who owe debts, except municipal, railroad, insurance, or banking corporations or building and loan associations, may make an application to the court for voluntary bankruptcy. The term "corporation" as used in the Bankruptcy Act includes "limited or other partnership associations organized under laws making the subscribed capital alone responsible for the debts of the association; joint stock companies, unincorporated companies, and associations and any business conducted by a trustee or trustees wherein the beneficial interest or ownership is evidenced by a certificate or other written instrument."

THE VOLUNTARY PETITION. Separate official forms are prescribed for the voluntary petition of an individual, a partnership, and a corporation. In each the petitioner, after stating that his principal place of business or his residence has been in the judicial district for the greater part of 6 months immediately preceding the filing of the petition, and that he owes debts that he is unable to pay in full, expresses his willingness to surrender all his property except such as is exempt by state law, and his desire to obtain the benefit of the Bankruptcy Act.

Although the official form of voluntary petition provides for an **allegation of insolvency** (debts exceeding the assets), there is nothing in the law requiring the applicant to be insolvent.

Filing of Schedules. With the filing of a voluntary petition, the debtor must submit schedules, on official forms, showing in detail the **amount and kind of**

property, and its location, a list of the creditors with the addresses of their residences if known (if unknown, that fact must be stated), the amounts due each of them, the consideration thereof, and the special security held by creditors, if any. The schedules should also set forth the **exempt property** that the petitioner claims by right of state law. The statements of assets and liabilities should set forth the major items specifically and with such detail as to be capable of identification. **Damage suits** and creditors' claims of whatever nature, although apparently groundless, should also be stated at the maximum amount alleged to be due. **Contingent liabilities** should be included. Provision is also made for the listing of the books, papers, deeds, and writings relating to the bankrupt's business and estate, as the court takes possession of these in taking over the petitioner's assets. A **knowing omission or misstatement** in the schedules may not only bar the petitioner from a discharge of his debts but may make him liable to criminal prosecution for false swearing.

Power of Corporate Directors To Petition Bankruptcy. Corporations, both business and nonprofit, with the exceptions noted above, may be adjudged voluntary bankrupts. Whether **directors of a corporation, without authority** from the stockholders, have the power to file a petition in voluntary bankruptcy depends upon the laws of the state in which the corporation is organized and its charter provisions. According to the trend of authority, in the absence of charter restrictions, the directors may on their own responsibility petition for voluntary bankruptcy. On the other hand, an **officer of a corporation** has no authority to file such a petition unless it has been conferred upon him by the directors. It has been held that state statutes that prohibit the sale, assignment, or transfer of the property and franchise of a corporation without the consent of a certain proportion of the stockholders do not prohibit the filing of a voluntary petition by directors. [Bell v. Blessing (C.C.A. 9th Cir.), 35 Am. B.R. 672, 225 Fed. 750.]

INVOLUNTARY BANKRUPTCY. Creditors may file a petition in bankruptcy against any person, partnership, or corporation owing debts of $1,000 or over, except the following:

1. Wage earners.
2. Farmers, defined as individuals whose wages do not exceed $1,500 per year.
3. Municipal, railroad, insurance, or banking corporations, or building and loan associations.

When the **number of creditors totals 12 or more,** the petition may be filed by three or more creditors having provable claims or claims aggregating $500 or more above any specific security they may hold. When the **total number of creditors is less than 12,** one such creditor may file the petition.

No schedules of the bankrupt's assets and liabilities accompany the petition as these will have to be filed by the debtor himself should he be adjudged a bankrupt.

ACTS OF BANKRUPTCY. The Bankruptcy Act is not intended to cover all cases of insolvency to the exclusion of judicial proceedings in state courts. The statute gives bankruptcy courts jurisdiction only in certain instances—those in which within 4 months before the filing of the bankruptcy petition one of the six specified "acts of bankruptcy" has been committed. These acts, however, **apply only to involuntary bankruptcies.** A voluntary petition in bankruptcy may be filed by anyone regardless of whether or not he has committed an act of bankruptcy. The filing of the voluntary petition is in itself regarded as an act of bankruptcy.

The "six" acts of bankruptcy actually consist of any one of the following four actions:

a. Fraud on the part of the alleged bankrupt.
b. Giving an unfair advantage to one creditor over another either by way of preferential transfer or by permitting the seizure of assets through legal proceedings.
c. Attempting to keep the administration of the insolvent estate out of the bankruptcy court, as in the case of receivership and the general assignment for the benefit of creditors.
d. The business admits its insolvency and is willing to be liquidated.

The six acts of bankruptcy are as follows:

1. **The debtor, within the stipulated four months, has conveyed, transferred, concealed, removed, or permitted to be concealed or removed, any part of his property with intent to hinder, delay, or defraud his creditors.**

The intent to defraud creditors by disposing of property is the essence of this act of bankruptcy. Moreover, the intent need not always be actual but may be constructive, or intent attributed to the bankrupt by virtue of the circumstances. The statute does not prevent an insolvent person from disposing of his property provided there is no intent on his part to hinder, delay, or defraud the creditors. The insolvency of the debtor is not necessary to be shown in connection with this act, and it is a **complete defense** to a petition alleging the first act of bankruptcy to show that the alleged bankrupt was not insolvent at the time of the filing of the petition. The term "transfer" as used here and elsewhere in the statute is defined as the "sale and every other and different mode of disposing of or parting with property absolutely or conditionally, as payment, pledge, mortgage, gift or security."

2. **The debtor has transferred, while insolvent, any portion of his property to one or more of his creditors with intent to prefer such creditor or creditors over his other creditors.**

Preference is the essence of this act. The preference must be intentional on the part of the debtor, but the interest of the preferred creditor is immaterial, as it is not necessary to show that he knew that the payment was preferential. In view of the definition of "transfer" in the statute the preference may consist in giving a mortgage or a pledge of property, for example, to a pre-existing creditor. However, if the mortgage is given in the ordinary course of business, in order to obtain a new loan, no preference is intended, and no act of bankruptcy is committed.

3. **The debtor has, while insolvent, suffered or permitted any creditor to obtain a lien upon any of his property through legal proceedings and has not vacated or discharged such lien within 30 days or at least 5 days before the date set for any sale or other disposition of such property.**

This is known as the **passive act of bankruptcy**, since the debtor commits no overt act but merely fails, while insolvent, to prevent a creditor from obtaining an advantage over others through legal process. The intention of the bankrupt is not material. If the element of intent is also present he has also extended a preference under the second act of bankruptcy. This third act of bankruptcy is mainly committed by those who permit judgments and liens to be obtained against them. An attachment in itself is not enough to constitute this act of bankruptcy unless it is followed by a judgment permitting the sale of the property; if a lien is procured by a creditor in legal proceedings but no steps are taken to bring about a "sale or other disposition" of property, the lien later might become a preference.

4. Debtor has made a general assignment for the benefit of creditors.

Under this act of bankruptcy, an assignment for the benefit of creditors, even though without preferences, is an act of bankruptcy regardless of the debtor's intent or his solvency or insolvency. Assignments may be made under state laws, but they permit creditors to throw debtors into bankruptcy if the petitions are filed in the following 4 months.

5. While insolvent or unable to pay his debts as they mature, the debtor has procured, permitted, or suffered voluntarily or involuntarily the appointment of a receiver or trustee to take charge of his property.

Insolvency is a requisite element of this act of bankruptcy if a receiver, statutory or in equity, is appointed to take over the debtor's property. It must be the actual cause of the appointment. To avoid bankruptcy, corporations, when seeking friendly or consent receivership, make it a practice to claim solvency in the application. In the hearing on a bankruptcy petition the records of the court appointing the receiver may be used to prove solvency or insolvency.

An agreement to wind up the affairs of a corporation when insolvent by assigning all its property to its directors as trustees in liquidation is an act of bankruptcy.

6. Debtor has admitted in writing his inability to pay his indebtedness and his willingness to be adjudged a bankrupt on that ground.

This act of bankruptcy is tantamount to voluntary bankruptcy, and natural persons will usually prefer the more direct method of the latter. It is used primarily in cases where the debtor has no objection to being adjudicated a bankrupt but does not wish to undertake the proceeding himself and advance the necessary fees. The act was of greater importance in relation to business corporations when they did not enjoy their present unrestricted right to apply for voluntary bankruptcy. The power of directors to declare the corporation's inability to pay its debts and willingness to be adjudged a bankrupt is the same as in applications for voluntary bankruptcy.

ADJUDICATON OF BANKRUPT. A voluntary petition for bankruptcy is adjudicated immediately. No one is permitted to contest such adjudication except in partnership proceedings that partake of the nature of both voluntary and involuntary bankruptcy. If the petition is drawn up in accordance with the statutory requirements and makes out a prima facie case, the judge must make the adjudication.

In involuntary proceedings, the defendant is served with a subpoena and a copy of the petition and if personal service cannot be made, notice is given by publication once a week for two consecutive weeks. The hearing on the petition is held before the judge, but, since the proceedings are in equity, there is no jury unless the judge decides to call one to act purely in an advisory capacity, or unless the debtor takes advantage of his right under the law of filing an application for a jury trial to decide whether or not he was insolvent at the time of the petition and whether or not he committed an act of bankruptcy in the 4 months immediately preceding the date of the petition. If no jury is demanded, the judge may refer the hearings to a master in chancery, who may be a referee, to take and hear the evidence and report the findings to the judge.

After the judge has heard the evidence as submitted by the bankrupt and other parties in interest, including creditors, for or against the debtor, he either dismisses the case for want of sufficient evidence that the debtor is insolvent and has committed an act of bankruptcy within the stipulated time, or he adjudicates him a bankrupt. With this latter decision the court takes immediate charge of the debtor's property and the machinery is started to wind up his estate. The case is referred to a referee who supervises the administration of the estate with a view to its liquidation and the distribution of the proceeds among the creditors.

If the alleged bankrupt fails to respond to the subpoena he is adjudicated a bankrupt by **default,** if the evidence furnished by the petition is sufficient and objections on the part of other creditors, if any, are overruled.

PROVISIONAL REMEDIES FOR SAFEGUARD OF DEBTOR'S PROPERTY. After a petition is filed in involuntary bankruptcy, or after the adjudication of the bankrupt and before the selection of a trustee to take active charge of the bankrupt's estate, several remedies are available to creditors to prevent the depletion of the estate or to prevent any action on the part of the bankrupt that would tend to defeat the proceedings. These are as follows:

1. **Provisional seizure of the property by a species of attachment.** Upon proof by affidavit that a debtor against whom an involuntary petition is pending has committed an act of bankruptcy and that he is neglecting his property, so that it is deteriorating in value, the judge may issue a warrant to a marshal to seize and hold the property subject to further orders. The property may, however, be released if the debtor gives bond that he will turn it over or pay its value to the trustee, should he be adjudged a bankrupt.

2. **Issuance of injunction.** An injunction may be issued to restrain the debtor, or a third party in possession of property alleged to belong to the debtor's estate, from disposing of the property until proper action can be taken.

3. **Arrest, detention, and extradition of bankrupt.** Upon satisfactory proof by the affidavits of two persons that the alleged bankrupt is about to leave the judicial district in order to avoid examination, the court may issue a warrant to a marshal directing him to bring the debtor forthwith before the court for examination. If, upon hearing of the evidence, the allegations are found to be true, the court may order the marshal to keep the debtor in custody for not over 10 days, but not, however, to imprison him, until he has been examined, or given bail to appear for examination. If the debtor happens to be in another district when the warrant for his apprehension is issued, he may be extradited in the same manner as a person under indictment.

4. **Suits by creditors.** Creditors may file suits for the recovery of property fraudently transferred or concealed by the alleged bankrupt. They will be reimbursed for the costs if he is adjudicated a bankrupt and the property is recovered.

5. **Appointment of a receiver.**

RECEIVER IN BANKRUPTCY. Prior to the adjudication of the bankrupt and the subsequent selection of a trustee, the bankrupt remains in undisturbed possession of his property. In a proper case, however, at any time between the filing of the bankruptcy petition and the selection of a trustee and his assumption of his duties, upon the petition of any creditors having provable claims or the debtor himself, **the court may take over actual possession of the debtor's estate** through the appointment of a receiver or by a direction to a marshal. The only ground for the appointment of a receiver in bankruptcy is that it is absolutely necessary for the preservation of the estate. Title to the property, however, remains in the bankrupt until the adjudication and selection of a trustee. In ordinary practice the receiver is frequently continued as trustee.

Function of Receiver. The receiver's function is to preserve and not to administer the debtor's estate, as the latter function is subsequently performed by the trustee in case of adjudication. The receiver, therefore, merely takes custody of the property and not title to it. He may, however, sell perishable assets and may, when authorized by the court, continue operating the business for a limited period if that will tend to preserve the value of the property. He may be sued in state courts for acts done while conducting the business. The weight of authority is against his right to sue to recover property, which duty is later performed by the trustee.

The exact **powers of the receiver** are defined in the order of the court (judge or referee) appointing him. Upon his assumption of office, his first duty is to make an **inventory of the assets** and when authorized by the court he may borrow money, issuing receiver's certificates therefor. As the court's jurisdiction over the debtor's estate does not extend beyond the limits of its district, ancillary receivers must be appointed in other districts to enter upon the custody of any property found there. At the first meeting of the creditors after the adjudication of the bankrupt, the receiver submits a report and turns over the property to the trustee.

In the **absence of the appointment of a receiver,** it is the duty of the bankrupt to see that his property is preserved until the appointment of a trustee.

REFEREE IN BANKRUPTCY. The referee is a judicial officer of the bankruptcy court, to whom bankruptcy cases are usually referred after adjudication, and who sits in them practically as a judge, with certain limitations. He is appointed for a term of 6 years, and as his appointment may be renewed after the expiration of each term, his tenure in office may in that manner be prolonged indefinitely.

Referee's Powers. Referees are invested with wide jurisdiction, subject always to a review by the judge. They may perform such of the duties as are conferred on the courts by the Act, except as specifically restricted. Among their more important powers are to make adjudications or dismiss petitions; administer oaths and examine persons as witnesses and require the production of documents in proceedings before them; in the absence of the judge or his inability to act, exercise his powers for the taking possession and releasing of the property of the bankrupt; grant, revoke, or deny discharges; confirm, or refuse to confirm, arrangements or wage earners' plans; or set aside the confirmations and reinstate the cases.

Referee's Duties. The referee's first act is to see that the bankrupt files his schedule of assets and list of creditors and that they are drawn up properly. If the **bankrupt has absconded,** subpoenas may be issued by the referee to all persons who are likely to have some knowledge of the bankrupt's business affairs, and schedules may be prepared from the evidence produced by these witnesses and from the bankrupt's books.

Other duties that the law specifically prescribes for the referee include the following:

1. Give notices to creditors of meetings or of other actions for which they are entitled to previous notice.
2. Furnish any information regarding the bankrupt estate requested by parties in interest.
3. Transmit to the clerks papers needed in any proceedings in courts and secure the return of such papers after they have been used.

4. Declare dividends and cause to be prepared dividend sheets showing the dividends declared and to whom payable.
5. Keep a record of the case and the filed documents, and at the conclusion of the case transmit it to the clerk of the court, where it remains open to inspection.

Compensation of Referee. Referees are paid out of the referees' salary fund that is raised by fees collected from bankruptcy cases and paid into the United States Treasury.

CREDITOR MEETINGS. Not less than 10 and not more than 30 days after adjudication the referee calls the **first meeting** of the creditors. The referee presides at the meeting, and the first business to be transacted is the proving of claims of creditors and their allowance by the referee. When the status of the creditors is thus established, they proceed to the examination of the bankrupt and the election of one or three trustees to take title and enter upon the active administration of the bankrupt estate.

Trustees are elected by a majority vote in number and amount of claims of all creditors whose claims have been allowed and who are present. Certain creditors such as relatives, directors, or stockholders of a corporation that is bankrupt, and the bankrupt's spouse are not allowed to vote for a trustee.

Creditors' Committees. Creditors may, at their first meeting, appoint a committee of not less than three creditors, which committee may consult and advise with and make recommendations to the trustee in the performance of his duties. Such committee is **chosen by a majority** computed as in the case of the election of a trustee. It has no power to control the administration of the estate, but has the right to be heard by the court.

Other **meetings of creditors after the first** may be held at any time or place as may be agreed upon in writing by all the creditors whose claims have been allowed by the referee. The referee is also compelled to call a meeting of creditors whenever one-fourth or more in number of those who have proved their claims file a written request for it. It is customary, however, for the referee to keep adjourning the first meeting in order to avoid calling special meetings.

Voting at Creditors' Meetings. Bankruptcy proceedings are conducted to a considerable extent by a vote of creditors. In actual practice, however, creditors vote only in the election of the trustee and the fixing of the amount of his bond as a matter of right. The referee rules on other questions though he will consult with creditors and ask for their vote.

The creditors pass on all matters submitted to them by a **majority vote in both number and the amount** of the claims of all those present. However, only claims that have been allowed by the referee are entitled to vote. Those who have several assigned claims have only one vote. As bankruptcy proceedings are conducted solely in the interest of the general creditors, those having **secured or priority claims** cannot vote except for the amount by which their claims exceed the probable value of the security or priority as determined by the referee upon application. They may vote, however, if they surrender their security or priority. As to any other matter than participation in voting, any creditor having a provable claim, whether he has proved it or not, is entitled to be heard, as for example, in the examination of the bankrupt. Creditors need not be present at meetings in person, but may be represented by proxy or attorney.

No given quorum is required at creditors' meetings.

PROVING OF CLAIMS. Proof of claim is a technical term used in bankruptcy with reference to the formal filing with the referee, by each creditor, of a sworn statement setting forth his claim. The proof must set forth the consideration given for the debt and what security, if any, is held against the debt. Secured and priority claims must be proved on separate forms. If a **claim was assigned** before the adjudication of the bankrupt, the assignee files the proof of claim in his own name. If the assignment is made after adjudication but before the claim was proved, the claimant's proof must be supported by the affidavit of the owner of the claim at the time of adjudication. When a proved claim is assigned, the referee should be given notice, and he will then notify the one who filed the proof, giving him 10 days in which to deny the assignment to the claim. An agent may prove a debt for a sufficient reason, such as the illness of the principal.

Many of the claims will be proved at the **first meeting of creditors**, in order that they may be allowed by the referee and entitle their owners to participate in the voting. However, creditors have until 6 months from the date first fixed for the first meeting of creditors in which to file their claims.

It is a crime punishable by imprisonment for a period not exceeding 5 years to present a **false proof of claim** against the estate of a bankrupt.

Whenever a **claim is based upon an instrument in writing**, as a note or a bond, it must be filed with the proof of claim until the claim is formally allowed by the referee, whereupon it may be withdrawn and a copy substituted in its place. It is customary to attach the original and a copy to the proof of claim and request the referee to return the original. If an instrument draws interest, the interest is to be computed to the date of the filing of the bankruptcy petition. In case of **lost or destroyed instruments**, the facts concerning their loss and destruction should also be set forth in the proof of the debt.

Indorsers, guarantors, and sureties may prove, in the name of creditors, any claim on which they are secondarily liable and that the creditors have failed to prove. If they discharge such claims, they succeed to the rights of the creditors.

The **trustee for bonds** issued by a corporation in bankruptcy may file a proof of claim for the entire issue, but in view of conflicting legal decisions, this is not regarded sufficient, and the individual bondholders must also file their separate claims, accompanied by the bond certificates. If there is a protective committee to represent the bondholders, its secretary sends forms of proofs of claims to those who have deposited their bonds with the committee and attends to the details of filing the proofs in their behalf. The referee may issue informal receipts for the bonds thus filed.

WHAT DEBTS MAY BE PROVED. The question of whether or not a debt is provable, as the term is used in bankruptcy, turns upon its status at the time of the filing of the bankruptcy petition. Claims not owing at that time are not provable. But in order that the debt may be owing at the time of the bankruptcy petition it is not necessary that it should be due then nor that damages be liquidated.

Debts that may be proved against the bankrupt estate are:

1. Fixed liabilities, as evidenced by a judgment or an instrument in writing, absolutely owing at the time of the filing of the bankruptcy petition, whether then payable or not, with any interest thereon that would have been recoverable at that date or with a rebate of interest upon such as were not then payable and did not bear interest.
2. Debts due as costs taxable against an involuntary bankrupt who was at the time of the filing of the petition against him plaintiff in a cause of action that would pass to the trustee and that the trustee declines to prosecute after notice.

3. Debts founded upon a claim for taxable costs incurred in good faith by a creditor before the filing of the petition in bankruptcy in an action to recover a provable debt.
4. Debts founded on open accounts, or on contracts expressed or implied.
5. Provable debts reduced to judgments after filing of the petition and before the consideration of the bankrupt's application for a discharge, less costs incurred and interest accrued after the filing of the petition and up to the time of the entry of such judgment.
6. Debts founded upon an award of an industrial accident commission.
7. Amount of any damages, as evidenced by a judgment in an action for negligence instituted against bankrupt before filing of the petition.
8. Contingent debts and contingent contractual liabilities.
9. Claims for damages respecting executory contracts, including future rents. The claim of a landlord for damages is limited to not more than one year's rent without acceleration for the year next succeeding the date of the surrender of the premises or the date of re-entry of the landlord, whichever first occurs, plus an amount equal to the unpaid rent accrued, without acceleration, up to such date.

Unliquidated claims against the bankrupt may, pursuant to application to the court, be liquidated in such manner as it shall direct, and may thereafter be proved and allowed against his estate.

The **provability of claims is not dependent upon their validity**, as that is a matter that the referee passes on in allowing claims after they are proved. It is necessary to distinguish proved claims as the term is applied in bankruptcy from claims subsequently allowed, as the owners of these two classes of claims have a different status. Any creditor with a provable claim may participate in the examination of the bankrupt, but only a creditor with an allowed claim may vote in creditors' meetings. The allowance or disallowance of a claim for voting purposes at the first meeting is not necessarily binding for dividend purposes.

ALLOWED CLAIMS. After claims are proved, that is, filed in proper form as explained above, they are either allowed or rejected. The **difference between proving and allowing** is that between evidence and judgment. All proved debts must be allowed by the court, usually the referee, unless objection is made to their allowance by some party in interest. The referee may, however, upon his own motion postpone allowance of any proved claim for good cause and not immediately enter an order allowing it. Before the election of the trustee, either the bankrupt or any creditor may object to a claim, or if already allowed, petition for its re-examination, provided the estate has not been wound up. After the election of the trustee, all objections and petitions for re-examination are made by the trustee or in his name, and he may use his own judgment in the matter. Upon his refusal when urged to take action, however, a creditor or the bankrupt may file his objections or petitions for examinations; or the court may compel the trustee to take action.

It is only the owners of allowed claims who may participate in all the proceedings of creditors' meetings and share in the dividends declared from the bankrupt estate. **Secured and priority claims,** although they must be proved, are not allowable debts except for such sums as the referee decides are owing on them over and above the value of the security or the priority. Secured claims in this connection only include debts secured by property belonging to the bankrupt estate. Hence, a note bearing an accommodation endorsement, or a debt secured by property other than that of the bankrupt, is an allowable claim.

DUTIES OF BANKRUPT. In addition to submitting schedules of his assets and liabilities, the law imposes certain other duties upon the bankrupt:
1. To attend the first meeting of his creditors if directed by the court to do so, and also the hearing upon his application for a discharge from his debts and at such other times as the court shall order.
2. To comply with all lawful orders of the court, which is usually the referee.
3. To examine the correctness of all proofs of claims filed against his estate. As a rule, the bankrupt sits by as the claims are called off at the first meeting of creditors and informs the referee whether they are correct or not.
4. To execute to the trustee, when appointed, transfers of all his property in foreign countries.
5. To execute and deliver such papers as shall be ordered by the court. If, for example, he owns a seat on a stock exchange, he must execute the necessary papers to enable the trustee to sell it.
6. To inform the trustee immediately of any attempt on the part of his creditors, or other persons, to evade the provisions of the Bankruptcy Law, should any such attempt come to his knowledge.
7. In case of any person having to his knowledge proved a false claim against his estate, to disclose that fact immediately to the trustee.
8. To prepare, make oath to, and file in court within 5 days after adjudication, if an involuntary bankrupt, and with his petition, if a voluntary bankrupt, a schedule of his property and a list of his creditors. The schedule must show both in detail.
9. To file in triplicate with the court, at least 5 days prior to the first meeting of creditors, a statement of his affairs in such form as may be prescribed by the Supreme Court.
10. When present at the first meeting of creditors and at such other times as the court may order, to submit to an examination concerning the conduct of his business, the cause of his bankruptcy, his dealings with his creditors and other persons, the amount, kind, and whereabouts of his property, and, in addition, all matters that may affect the administration and settlement of his estate. No testimony given by the bankrupt may be offered in evidence against him in any criminal proceedings. Such proceedings, however, may be instituted against him as a result of what is disclosed by the examination into his conduct of the business, but other evidence must be produced in the prosecution of the trial. Evidence taken in the bankrupt's examination may, however, be used against him in the hearing upon his application for a discharge or in other hearings connected with the bankruptcy proceedings.

EXAMINATION OF THE BANKRUPT. The bankrupt may be required to appear before the court, or before the judge of any state court, to be examined concerning the bankrupt's acts, conduct, or property. Any designated person, including the bankrupt's spouse, despite any state law to the contrary, may also be examined. It is mandatory upon the trustee to examine the bankrupt unless he already has been fully examined by the referee, receiver, or creditors. It is mandatory, too, for the judge or referee, whichever presides at the first meeting of creditors, to examine the bankrupt, and he may permit the creditors to examine him.

Ample opportunity is given for the examination of a dishonest bankrupt and these examinations should result in the disclosure of his past illegal actions, if any have occurred.

CONCEALMENT OF PROPERTY AND RECORDS. It is a crime punishable by imprisonment for a period not exceeding 5 years, or fine of not to exceed $5,000, or both, knowingly and fraudulently to conceal from trustee, receiver, marshal, or other court officer charged with the control and custody of the bankrupt's property, any property belonging to the estate; or to receive any material amount of property from the bankrupt after the filing of the bankruptcy petition with the intent to defeat the Act; or to conceal, falsify, mutilate, or destroy any books, documents, or records relating to the affairs of the bankrupt.

Whenever any trustee, referee, or receiver has grounds for believing that any offense under the Bankruptcy Act has been committed, it is his duty under the law to report the facts to the United States attorney of the district for such action as he may deem necessary.

TRUSTEE IN BANKRUPTCY. The trustee is the **officer of the court** who upon election takes charge of the administration and settlement of the bankrupt estate. He is elected, subject to the judge's or referee's approval, at the first meeting of creditors. Before assuming office he must enter into a **bond** for the faithful performance of his duties, the amount of which is also fixed by a vote of the owners of allowed debts.

The **number of trustees** may be either one or three, as determined by the creditors. If three are appointed, the concurrence of two of them is requisite for action.

Trustee's Duties. The law contemplates that the bankrupt estate will be settled with all possible speed in order to **conserve the assets for the benefit of the general creditors.** It is, therefore, the duty of the trustee to promptly take possession of all assets, bringing suit against so-called "adverse claimants," or third parties in possession of assets that in the judgment of the trustee belong to the bankrupt, recovering property from those who were given unlawful preferences or to whom unlawful transfers were made by the bankrupt, defending the estate generally against void or voidable liens and priorities of payments. The trustee represents the interests of the general or unsecured creditors and the bankrupt, for whose benefit primarily the Bankruptcy Law has been enacted. With the approval of the referee he may compromise any controversy arising out of the administration of the estate on such terms as he may deem for the best interests of the estate.

Property in the hands of the trustee should be liquidated at the earliest possible moment under the supervision of the court. The trustee himself may act as **salesman or auctioneer,** and for that reason it is best to appoint as trustee a business man with selling ability, preferably one who has had experience in the same line of business as the bankrupt and one residing or having his business office in the same district. The services of **special masters or auctioneers** may be used in the liquidation of the estate, though they add greatly to the expense of administration. In prosecuting his work, the trustee is expected to use his best judgment, though he will find it profitable to consult with creditors and enlist their interest in securing bids for property he is trying to sell. He must **deposit all money** coming into his possession in one of the designated depositaries for the receipt of bankruptcy court funds. To prosecute or defend suits he may engage attorneys, and he may incur other expenses that he pays by check on the depositary countersigned by the referee.

Trustee's Accounts. The trustee must keep **regular accounts** showing the amounts received and the amounts disbursed, and must file with the referee periodically a **written report of the condition of the estate**—the first within the first month after his appointment and one every 2 months thereafter. Within 10 days after his qualification, he must file a certified copy of the court decree in the office where conveyances of real estate are recorded, in every county where the bankrupt owns real estate not exempt from execution.

The trustee's accounts and papers are **open to inspection** by officers and all proper parties, including the creditors, who are entitled to receive from him other pertinent information. He must pay **dividends to the creditors** within 10 days after they are declared by the referee. Fifteen days before the date fixed for the final meeting of the creditors, after the bankrupt estate has been wound up and settled, he is required to file with the referee a **final report and account**, and at the final meeting of the creditors, he must submit a detailed statement of the estate. When his final report is approved by the referee, he is discharged.

Compensation Of Trustee. The trustee's compensation consists of minor fees and such commissions as the referee may allow on all monies he disburses or turns over to any persons or corporations, subject to maximum percentages. The maximum amounts apply to trustees who do not conduct the normal business operations of the bankrupt; if trustees actually conduct the business the allowance is doubled. **If there are three trustees,** the referee apportions the fees and commissions among them according to the services they have actually rendered, all three receiving in the aggregate only what one would have received if he had been the sole appointee.

Trustee's Title to Property. Immediately upon qualifying, the trustee takes title by operation of law to all the bankrupt's property, including his books, documents, papers, etc., in this country. He takes title to the bankrupt's property for the benefit of the creditors as of the date of the filing of the petition in bankrupcy. However, the property he takes over is only that which the bankrupt was possessed of at the time of the filing of bankruptcy petition, including the subsequent profits and earnings of such property, and including later substitutions through sale, purchase, or exchange. The exception is the property for which the bankrupt claims exemption under state law. Title to all property acquired independently after the filing of the petition, as that obtained on credit or for the bankrupt's labor or services, or by gift or bequest, does not vest in the trustee. Such property belongs to the bankrupt, clear of the claims of all creditors save those who become such after the commencement of the bankruptcy proceedings or those who for statutory reasons are not affected by the bankrupt's discharge. However, if subsequently any composition arranged with the creditors is set aside or the bankrupt's discharge is revoked, the trustee is vested with title to all property of the bankrupt as of the date of the setting aside of the composition or the revoking of the discharge.

The **trustee takes the bankrupt's property subject to all valid claims,** liens, and equities. He has no better title than the bankrupt had at the time of the filing of the petition, except as the status of the title was modified by any fraud of the bankrupt. Legal liens and preferences obtained within 4 months preceding the bankruptcy petition are void.

Transfer of Powers and Documents to Trustee. The trustee, in addition to taking title to property that the bankrupt is capable of transferring or that can be seized by judicial process, also takes over certain powers, rights, and documents that are not always regarded as strictly transferable or leviable:

1. Documents relating to bankrupt's property.
2. Powers that he might have exercised for his own benefit, but not those that he might have exercised for some other person.
3. Rights of action arising upon contracts or from the unlawful taking or detention of, or injury to, his property.

If the bankrupt is carrying an **insurance policy,** payable to himself, his estate, or personal representatives, that has a cash surrender value, he is permitted to hold the policy free of all claims of creditors if he pays the trustee a sum equal to this value, or gives security for its payment.

BANKRUPT'S EXEMPTIONS. In every state there are statutes freeing certain property of debtors from seizure, by judicial process, for the benefit of creditors. These exemption provisions specify the type of property, their value, and who may claim the exemptions. The **personal property exemption** may include household articles, tools, and clothing of a certain value. The **homestead** may also be exempt up to a certain amount, as well as the wages of laborers, mechanics, and employees.

The bankrupt, when preparing his schedules, may make claim to exemption under the law of the state in which he has resided for the 6 months or the greater portion of the 6 months immediately preceding the bankruptcy petition. If he files his claim, the trustee does not take title to the exempt property, and one of the latter's first duties on entering upon office is to set aside the property—both the kind and amount claimed by the bankrupt as exempt—and make a report to the referee. A hearing is held on this report and both bankrupt and creditors may take exception to it. By agreement with the bankrupt, **exempt property may be sold** along with other property as an entirety, and the bankrupt be allowed his exemptions out of the proceeds. Liens obtained by legal proceedings within 4 months preceding the bankruptcy petition upon property later claimed by the bankrupt as exempt are not annulled by the bankruptcy proceedings.

A debtor may **waive his right to exemptions** by specific surrender of them or by failure to claim them when filing his schedules. In the former case, the usual method is a **waiver-note** running to a particular creditor. In a number of states, a waiver of exemption is void as against public policy.

VOIDABLE PREFERENCES. A bankrupt gives a voidable preference if, being insolvent, he has within the 4 months immediately preceding the filing of the bankruptcy petition, or between the filing of the petition and adjudication, procured or permitted a judgment to be entered against himself or made a transfer of any of his property, and the effect of such judgment or transfer is to enable any of the creditors to obtain a greater percentage of the debt due him than any other creditor of the same class. Such preferences are voidable and the trustee may bring action to recover such property, provided the creditor receiving such preference had reasonable cause to believe that such judgment or transfer would effect a preference. The preference can be extended only to one having a provable claim.

Likewise **any lien** obtained against bankrupt's property by legal process, which was begun not more than 4 months before the filing of a bankruptcy petition, such as attachment, garnishment, or equity receivership, is dissolved by the adjudication of the bankrupt if it appears that the lien was obtained and permitted while the defendant was insolvent, or the party benefited had reasonable cause to believe that the defendant was insolvent, or if such lien was sought and permitted in fraud of the provisions of the Bankruptcy Act. Liens, however, given and accepted in good faith are not affected by this provision. Similarly, statutory liens, such as mechanics' liens, are also excepted from the provision.

FRAUDULENT TRANSFERS. Transfers of property made by the bankrupt when insolvent within the 4 months immediately preceding adjudication, for the purpose of hindering, delaying, or defrauding creditors, are void and the trustee may bring action to recover the property or its value. The burden of proof is on the transferee, who must prove his own good faith and that he has given a fair consideration for the property. An example of a **fraudulent transfer** is the sale of the entire stock of goods for less than cost.

CONTINUANCE OF BUSINESS. A receiver, marshal, or trustee when appointed may be authorized by the court to continue the business of the bankrupt for a limited period, which may be extended and re-extended a number of times. The purpose of this is to preserve a going business and thus sell it as such. A trustee under this authority may have implied **power to borrow money;** or power may be expressly conferred upon him by the court. Orders of the court with respect to the powers of receiver or trustee are regarded as notice to all persons, and it is the duty of those dealing with a receiver or trustee to inquire concerning the extent of his authority.

Courts authorize referees, after consultation with creditors, to permit trustees in bankruptcy to **reject property of bankrupt that is onerous and unprofitable** and that will prove burdensome rather than beneficial to the estate. Thus, if property is mortgaged for more than its value, the court may direct the surrender of the property to the mortgagee upon such conditions as may be considered best. Trustees, like receivers in equity, may either **assume or renounce executory contracts** of the bankrupt. A trustee may assume or reject the lease of a bankrupt tenant within a reasonable time after adjudication.

PARTNERSHIPS IN BANKRUPTCY. A partnership is considered a **legal entity** in bankruptcy proceedings separate and distinct from its members. It owns its property and owes its debts apart from the individual property and debts of its members. It may, therefore, be adjudged a bankrupt without the individual partners being adjudged, or it may be adjudged jointly with one or more or all its general partners. If a petition is filed in behalf of a partnership by less than all the general partners it must allege that the partnership is insolvent. The creditors of the partnership appoint the trustee, who usually is also trustee of the bankrupt partner or partners. The court that has jurisdiction of one of the general partners has jurisdiction over all, including partnership, property. In the case of **involuntary bankruptcy,** the firm or member acting within the scope of the partnership must have committed the act of bankruptcy. The commission of an act of bankruptcy as to partnership property by one of the partners amounts to an act of bankruptcy. The law directs that **partnership property** be appropriated to the payment of partnership debts and the property of the individual partners to the payment of their respective individual debts. If any surplus remains of the property of any partner after paying his debts, it is to be added to the partnership assets and to be applied to the payment of the partnership debts. Any surplus of the partnership property remaining after paying the partnership debts is to be added to the assets of the individual partners in proportion to their respective interests in the partnership.

The court (referee) may permit the proof of the claims of the partnership estate against the individual estates, and vice versa, and may **marshal the assets** of the partnership estate and the individual estates so as to prevent preferences and secure the equitable distribution of property of the several estates. In the event that one or more but not all the partners are adjudged bankrupts, the partnership property cannot be administered in bankruptcy except by consent of the partners not adjudged bankrupts; but the general partners not adjudged bankrupt must settle the partnership business as expeditiously as possible and account for the interest of the bankrupt partner or partners. If all the general partners are adjudged bankrupt the partnership is also adjudged bankrupt.

A **partnership may be adjudged a bankrupt after its dissolution** if there has as yet been no final settlement. Since an estate of a deceased debtor cannot be adjudged a bankrupt, it follows, according to some authorities, that a partnership, one member of which is dead, cannot be adjudged a bankrupt. Surviving members can be so adjudged as individuals.

SUMMARY JURISDICTION OF THE BANKRUPTCY COURT. The trustee may seize, if he can do so peaceably, property belonging to the bankrupt estate that is being withheld by a bankrupt or by some one who claims no beneficial interest in it. If peaceable seizure is impossible, he obtains an order from the referee requiring the party in possession to surrender the property under penalty of contempt. The order is obtained in what is known as a summary proceeding, which is ordinarily begun without summons or subpoena and is usually tried upon affidavits and at short notice, or is determined in an ex parte manner. Power of the referee thus to proceed summarily depends upon whether the subject matter of the proceeding is in the possession of the court, actually or constructively.

The same summary jurisdiction is exercised by the bankruptcy court in determining the **rights of third parties claiming property** in the custody of the trustee, no regular or plenary suit being required. There are likely to be many articles in the bankrupt's possession, when he is adjudicated, that do not belong to him, such as goods left in storage, for repairs, on consignment, or approval. These may be **reclaimed by their owners** from the trustee by summary proceedings. Liens upon and interests in property in the custody of the bankruptcy court (receiver, marshal, or trustee) may be passed upon by the court by summary proceedings and the validity and priority of the liens determined.

Although the trustee is vested with title to bankrupt's property wherever it is located in the United States, he cannot assert his rights by proceedings, summary or plenary, in the court of which he is an officer with regard to property located in other judicial districts. He must institute **ancillary proceedings** in the courts of those districts.

ADVERSE CLAIMANTS. These are third parties having no interest in the bankruptcy suit, either as bankrupt or creditors, who are in possession of and claim title to certain property that the trustee claims as belonging to the bankrupt estate. They are outside the jurisdiction of the bankruptcy court and the trustee can only assert his rights by bringing a **formal, plenary suit** against them in the proper court. The law provides that in all controversies at law and equity, as distinguished from proceedings in bankruptcy, between trustee and adverse claimants concerning property acquired or claimed by the trustee, the United States district courts have jurisdiction in the same manner and to the same extent as if the bankruptcy proceedings had not been instituted and such controversies had been between the bankrupt and the adverse claimant.

JURISDICTION OF STATE AND OTHER COURTS OVER BANKRUPT'S PROPERTY. The following is adapted from A Business Man's Manual of Bankruptcy Law by Remington:

If property afterward claimed by the bankruptcy trustee is taken into custody by a state court (or any court other than the bankruptcy court in question) before the bankruptcy petition is filed, the state court, or such other court, continues to retain jurisdiction over the entire matter involving the property, except in three instances, and all the trustee can do is to get himself admitted as a party to the case in the state court and litigate his rights there. The three exceptions are as follows:

1. When possession by the state court has created a **lien by legal proceedings within four months of the filing of the bankruptcy petition** and while the debtor is insolvent, the state court does not retain jurisdiction, but the property affected must be surrendered to the bankruptcy court.

2. When the property at the time of bankruptcy is **in the possession of an assignee for the benefit of creditors or of a receiver or trustee appointed outside of bankruptcy,** and when the assignment, receivership, or trusteeship is created within 4 months preceding the filing of the bankruptcy petition, the bankruptcy court, upon adjudication of the bankrupt, supersedes the court appointing the assignee, receiver, or trustee, and takes over the property involved for administration in bankruptcy.

3. When property at the time of bankruptcy is in the custody of the state court under **state insolvency or state bankruptcy proceedings,** or proceedings amounting to such, such proceedings are superseded by the Federal bankruptcy proceedings. This, however, does not apply to general assignments for benefit of creditors. It is, therefore, important to distinguish between a true state insolvency law, which is absolutely suspended by the Bankruptcy Act, and the general assignment law, which is only voidable by the institution of bankruptcy proceedings within the prescribed 4 months' period. To be a bankruptcy law a statute must provide the machinery for throwing a debtor into insolvency involuntarily and for completely administering his assets. General assignment laws simply provide a system for administering voluntary assignments in trust. It has always been possible for a debtor to deed his property in trust, and to pay all or some class of creditors, and equity has always had jurisdiction to compel the proper carrying out of such trusts.

Some states have bankruptcy laws even providing for the **discharge of the bankrupt.** This does not contravene the article of the United States Constitution prohibiting a state to pass any laws impairing the obligation of a contract, first, because of the rule of law that an existing statute is to be read into every contract as a part of its terms, and second, because the law applies to the creditors of the state, and creditors of other states must consent to the proceedings before they are allowed to share in dividends.

SALE OF PROPERTY. When the trustee is prepared to sell a portion of the bankrupt's property, he files a petition with the referee and secures a permitting order. Ten days' notice must thereupon be given of the forthcoming sale to all creditors who have proved their claims, whether their claims have been allowed or not. No such notice is necessary, however, if the property is of a perishable nature. The sale must be conducted at public auction unless the referee authorizes a private sale. Each parcel of the bankrupt property must be **appraised by three disinterested appraisers** appointed by and reporting to the court or referee, and no sale may be made for less than 75% of the appraised value, except by approval of the court. The bankrupt or any of the creditors may bid at the sale, but not the trustee, referee, appraisers, or any of their agents. A **reorganization committee** or a reorganized corporation may also bid.

The trustee's sale is a **judicial sale** so that the rule of caveat emptor applies, the sale passing only such interest as the trustee has title to. In a judicial sale property in the custody of the court is sold while the proceedings concerning it are still pending, the court being the actual seller, and the sale is not consummated and the purchaser does not take title until the sale is confirmed by the court. Nothing but fraud, accident, a mistake, or some other cause for which equity would void a like sale warrants a court in avoiding a confirmation of sale.

Property may be sold by the trustee subject to any **existing liens,** or it may be sold, without the lienholder's consent, free of these liens, which in that case pass to the proceeds. However, ordinarily a **sale free of liens** should not be ordered unless the lienholders request it and there is reasonable prospect that a surplus will remain for the general creditors. When the purchaser is one of the lienholders, he may apply the value of the lien upon the purchase price.

The **costs and expenses of the preservation and sale of each piece of property** are paid out of the proceeds of its sale, even though they are not enough to satisfy in full any existing liens on the property.

PAYMENT OF DEBTS WITH PRIORITIES. The Bankruptcy Act prescribes a certain order of priority in the payment of the several classes of creditors out of the net amount of property left after the segregation of property belonging to adverse claimants, secured creditors, and the exemptions, and after the payment of the expenses of the individual sales.

Order of Priority. The order of priority is as follows:

1. **Administrative expenses,** the actual and necessary expenses of preserving the bankrupt estate. Filing fees paid by creditors in involuntary cases, and reasonable expenses in recovering to the estate property transferred or concealed by the bankrupt. Cost of administration and one attorney's fee as the court may allow, for services actually rendered to creditors in involuntary cases and to the bankrupt in voluntary and involuntary cases.
2. **Wages** due to wage-earners and salesmen on salary or commission basis, earned within 3 months before the commencement of bankruptcy proceedings, not to exceed $600 for each such claimant.
3. The **reasonable costs of creditors** resulting in the refusal, revocation, or setting aside of an arrangement, a wage earner's plan, a bankrupt's discharge, or the conviction of any person of an offense under the Act.
4. **Taxes** to United States, state, county, district, or municipality.
5. **Debts** owing to any person who by the laws of the states or the United States is **entitled to priority.** (Term "person" includes corporations, the United States, the several states and territories of the United States.) **Rent** owing to a landlord who is entitled to occupancy of the premises, and that accrued within 3 months prior to bankruptcy.

When a creditor has **security for his debt** the security must be surrendered or sold to entitle him to any payment along with the general creditors.

DECLARATION AND PAYMENT OF DIVIDENDS TO CREDITORS. The residue of the bankrupt estate, after the payment of the priorities, belongs to the general creditors, in whose interest it has been primarily administered. Dividends of an equal per cent are declared on all allowed claims. The **first distribution** must be declared within 30 days after the first date set for the first meeting of creditors if by then there is cash enough in the estate to pay 5% on the claims already allowed. The first dividend must not exceed one half of what is likely to remain for the general creditors after the payment of all prior claims, and all costs of administration that will probably be incurred. **Dividends after the first** are to be declared upon the same terms as the first and as often as the amount equals 10% or more, and upon the closing of the estate. After the expiration of 6 months following the first date set for the first meeting only one dividend need be declared. Creditors having claims allowed after one or more dividend declarations are entitled to receive the previous dividends before another dividend is declared to all the creditors. The final dividend is not to be declared until 3 months after the declaration of the first dividend in order to permit the belated creditors to share in the estate.

Although the law provides for distribution to creditors in equal proportions, it will not disturb creditors in the possession of the earlier dividends if the balance of the estate is not sufficient to pay the same proportion to creditors appearing later with allowed claims. If the bankrupt is also such in a foreign court, creditors residing in the United States are first to be paid a dividend equal to that distributed by the foreign court to creditors abroad before any payments are made out of the proceeds of the estate located in this country to the foreign creditors. Ten days' notice of dividend declarations and payments must be given by mail to creditors. The dividends cannot be attached and the trustee cannot be garnisheed for dividends in his hands. **Dividends that remain unclaimed** for 60 days after the final dividend has been declared must be paid into the court by the trustee.

CLOSING OF THE BANKRUPT ESTATE. Final accounts of the **trustee** must be filed with the referee 15 days before the date fixed for the final meeting of creditors, who are thereby given an opportunity to examine accounts and thus place themselves in a position to ask pertinent questions of the trustee at the meeting. The creditors receive 10 days' notice of the meeting.

If the trustee's accounts show proper administration of the estate and distribution of the assets, they are **approved by the referee,** who **discharges the trustee and closes the estate,** an order to that effect being entered. The referee thereupon certifies to the report and transmits it to the court clerk, along with the records, which thereafter constitute the record and files of the bankruptcy court in the case.

REOPENING OF BANKRUPT ESTATE. The judge of the bankruptcy court may reopen the estate upon the application of a creditor made within a reasonable time, if evidence is submitted that the estate was not completely administered. The common ground for reopening is the discovery of additional assets that existed when the bankruptcy petition was filed and therefore belonged to the estate. Upon reopening, a new trustee is appointed, the old trustee not being reinstated. When the administration of the reopened estate is completed, it is again closed in the manner described above.

DISCHARGE OF BANKRUPT. This is a release granted by the court from all debts that remain unsatisfied from the bankrupt estate, with certain exceptions. **Bankrupts, other than corporations** and those classified as corporations, do not have to apply for a discharge. Adjudication operates as an application for discharge. A **corporation** may, within 6 months after its adjudication, file an application for its discharge, though there is no particular purpose in a corporation filing an application, since bankruptcy usually means the demise of the corporation even if its business is continued by a reorganized corporation. After the bankrupt has been examined the court fixes a time for **filing objections to his discharge.** Creditors have 30 days' notice in which to file objections to the bankrupt's discharge and, if objections are filed, 10 days' notice of the hearing on the objections. Discharge may be opposed for cause by the trustee, creditors, the United States attorney, or such other attorney as the Attorney General may designate. The court grants the discharge if it is not opposed.

When Discharge Not Allowed. The bankrupt must be accorded the relief he seeks unless he is guilty of one of the following acts:

1. Has committed any offense punishable by imprisonment under the provisions of the Act.

2. Has destroyed, mutilated, falsified, concealed, or failed to keep books of account or records from which his financial condition and business transactions might be ascertained.
3. Has obtained money or property on credit, or obtained an extension or renewal of credit, by issuing a false financial statement.
4. At any time within the 12 months immediately preceding the filing of the application, has transferred, removed, destroyed, or concealed any of his property with intent to hinder, delay, or defraud his creditors.
5. Has been granted a discharge in bankruptcy within previous 6 years, or had a composition, arrangement, or wage earners' plan.
6. Has refused to obey any lawful order of, or to answer any material question approved by, the court in the course of the bankruptcy proceedings.
7. Has failed to explain satisfactorily any losses of assets or deficiency of assets.

Revocation of Discharge. Upon application of any party in interest made within one year after the discharge, if the applicant has not been guilty of any lack of proper diligence in the matter, the judge may **revoke the discharge** if it is shown upon trial that it was obtained through the fraud of the bankrupt and the petitioner had no knowledge of the fraud before the granting of the discharge. In the event of such revocation the property acquired by the bankrupt after adjudication is applied in payment of the claims of creditors who sold such property to the bankrupt, and the residue, if any, to debts owing at the time of adjudication.

Debts Not Affected by Discharge. A discharge only affects debts incurred before bankruptcy and only those that are provable, except the following:

1. Taxes of the United States, the state, county, district, and municipality in which the bankrupt resides.
2. Liabilities for obtaining property by false pretenses or false representations, or for obtaining money by a false financial statement, or for wilful and malicious injuries to the person or property of another or for alimony due or to become due, or for maintenance or support of wife or child, or for seduction of an unmarried woman, or for breach of promise of marriage accompanied by seduction, or for criminal conversation.
3. Debts that have not been duly scheduled in time for proof and allowance, with the names of the creditors, if known to the bankrupt, unless such creditors had notice or actual knowledge of the proceedings in bankruptcy.
4. Those created by bankrupt's fraud, embezzlement, misappropriation, or defalcation while acting as an officer or in any fiduciary capacity.
5. Those for wages due to wage-earners and salesmen on salary or commission basis, which have been earned within 3 months of the commencement of bankruptcy proceedings.
6. Those due for money received from an employee and retained to secure the faithful performance by the employee of the terms of the contract of employment.

The liability of any person who is a **co-debtor** with the bankrupt, or is a **guarantor**, or in any manner a **surety** for him, is not altered by the bankrupt's discharge.

Wage Earners' Plans

INSTITUTING THE PROCEEDING. The Bankruptcy Act provides (Chapter XIII) that a wage earner whose principal income is derived from wages, salaries, or commissions may institute a voluntary proceeding to effect a settlement of his debts out of future earnings. Wage earners' plans may provide for settlements with secured and unsecured creditors upon any terms. The plan deals with the **unsecured creditors as a class** but must deal with **secured creditors individually.** The court in which the proceeding is commenced has exclusive jurisdiction of the debtor and his property wherever located and of his earnings and wages during the period of the consummation of the plan. The court may permit the rejection of executory contracts of the debtor; extend, for cause, the time for taking any steps in the proceeding; and enjoin, or stay until final decree, the commencement or continuation of suits including any proceeding to enforce any lien upon the debtor's property.

Petition and Presentation of Plan. The debtor must set forth in his petition that he is insolvent or unable to pay his debts as they mature, and that he desires to effect an extension or composition, or both, with his creditors. A **first meeting of creditors** is called promptly at which the debtor must present his plan. The **plan must include** provisions dealing with unsecured debts generally, upon any terms; provisions for submission of future earnings of the debtor to the supervision and control of the court; that the court may, during the period of the plan, increase or decrease the amount of any of the installment payments, or extend or shorten the time for any such payments if the debtor's circumstances so warrant or require; and may include a plan for dealing with secured debts severally upon any terms; may provide for priority of payment as between secured and unsecured debts affected by the plan, and for the rejection of executory contracts.

Acceptance of Plan. The debtor may procure the acceptances, which must be in writing, of the creditors before or after the filing of his petition. The plan must be accepted by **all the secured creditors** affected by the plan, and by **a majority** in number and amount of **unsecured creditors** whose claims have been approved and allowed before the conclusion of the first meeting of creditors. If a plan cannot be agreed upon, the alternatives are to dismiss the proceedings or adjudge the debtor a bankrupt.

Confirmation by the Court and Discharge of the Debtor. Upon confirmation by the court, the plan becomes binding on the debtor and all creditors. Upon completion of all payments to be made under the plan, the court enters an order discharging the debtor from all his debts provided for in the plan, except debts that are not dischargeable in a regular bankruptcy proceeding, unless such creditors have accepted the plan. The debtor may be discharged by the court three years after the confirmation of the plan even though all payments under the plan have not been completed.

Agricultural Compositions and Extensions

SPECIAL TREATMENT FOR FARMERS. Special provision is made for the relief of distressed farmers in **Section 75 of the Bankruptcy Act of 1938.** Any farmer who is insolvent or unable to meet his debts as they become due may make application to the court to effect a composition or an extension of time to pay his debts. The Act also enables a farmer who has been unable to effect a settlement with his creditors to retain possession of his property under the supervision of the court, have its value fixed by independent appraisers, and repurchase it over an extended period of time.

Definition of Farmer. For the purpose of these provisions of the Bankruptcy Act, the term "farmer" means any individual who personally is engaged primarily in farming operations, and includes the personal representative of a deceased farmer. A farmer is deemed a resident of the county in which he conducts his farming operations.

Procedure. In general, the procedure followed by the farmer under Section 75 is similar to that prescribed for insolvent debtors in other sections of the Act. There are a **number of exceptions** of which the following are the more important:

1. The Act provides for the appointment of a **"conciliation commissioner."** The conciliation commissioners have vested in them many of the functions of the referees in regular bankruptcy proceedings. Among their qualifications, they must be familiar with agricultural methods and conditions and not engaged in any business that would prejudice fair action in proceedings under this section. After the filing of the petition and prior to the confirmation of the plan the court exercises such control over the farmer's property as it deems to the best interests of the farmer and his creditors. When requested, a conciliation commissioner is required to assist a farmer in preparing and filing a petition for composition proceedings and in handling all subsequent matters concerned with the proceedings. **Farmers are not obliged to be represented by attorneys** in such proceedings.

2. Except upon petition made to and granted by the judge after hearing and report by the conciliation commissioner, **the following proceedings may not be maintained** in any court or otherwise against the farmer or his property after he has filed his petition for composition or extension and prior to the confirmation or other disposition by the court of the composition or extension proposal:

    a. Proceedings for any demand, debt, or account, including any money demand.
    b. For foreclosure of a mortgage on land, or for cancellation, or specific performance of an agreement for sale of land or for recovery of possession of land.
    c. To acquire title to land by any tax sale.
    d. Issuance of any execution, attachment, or garnishment.
    e. Sale of land under or in satisfaction of any judgment or mechanic's lien.
    f. Seizure, distress sale, or other proceedings under an execution or under any lease, lien, chattel mortgage, conditional sale agreement, crop payment agreement, or mortgage.

The foregoing prohibitions do not apply to proceedings maintained against a farmer for the collection of **taxes**, or interest or penalties in connection with such taxes; nor to proceedings affecting solely property **other than that used in farming** operations or comprising the **home or household effects** of the farmer or his family.

ADJUDICATION OF BANKRUPTCY. If a farmer fails to obtain the acceptance by creditors of his composition or extension proposal, or if he feels aggrieved by the composition and extension, he may petition to be **adjudged a bankrupt.** At the time of the first hearing he may petition the court that all his property be appraised and that he be allowed to retain possession of all or a portion of his property by paying for it under terms and conditions set forth in the Act.

SECTION 23

COMMODITY TRADING

CONTENTS

Evolution and Nature of Futures Trading

	Page
Trading methods	1
Distinction between cash and futures markets	1
Origin and scope of futures exchanges	2
Selling on samples	2
Growth of futures trading	2
Types of commodities traded	2
Commodities adapted to futures trading	3
Volume of trading	3
Commodity exchanges abroad	3
The futures contract	3
Legal nature of contract	3
Main features of contract	4
Deliverable grades of commodities	4
Basis grade of a commodity	4
Examples of basis grades	5
Determination of differentials	5
Delivery rules	6
Delivery points	6

Organization and Functions of Commodity Exchanges

	Page
Form of organization	6
Purpose of exchanges	6
Memberships	7
Management	7
Standing committees	7
Rules and regulations	8
Chief functions of futures exchanges	8
The market function	8
The price risk insurance function	8
Diffusion of risks	9
Free versus controlled markets	9

Regulation of Commodity Exchanges

	Page
Early legislative moves	9
The Cotton Futures Act	9
The Grain Futures Act	10
The Commodity Exchange Act of 1936	10
Administration	10
Commodities covered	11
Contract markets	11
Prevention of manipulation	11
Curbs on speculative trading	11
Prevention of squeezes	11
Handling of customer's funds	12

	Page
Enforcement of the Commodity Exchange Act	12
Reports on holdings	13
Special calls	13
Penalties	13
Self-regulation of exchanges	13
Margin rules	14

Mechanism of Futures Trading

	Page
Trading facilities	14
Handling of orders	14
Market and limit orders	15
Short selling	15
Stop-loss orders	15
Execution of commodity orders	15
Contract units	16
Job lot trading	16
Price fluctuations	16
Minimum fluctuations	16
Daily fluctuation limits	16
Trading and position limits	17
Margin practices	17
Extension of credit	18
Commission rates	18
Liquidation of futures contracts	18
Liquidation by deliveries on contract	18
Seller's options	18
First notice day	18
Delivery notices	19
Notice procedure	19
Liquidation through offset	19
Switching	20
Liquidation through settlement	20

Clearing House Functions

	Page
Need for central clearing	20
Evolution of clearing methods	21
The modern clearing house	21
Basic theory of the clearing house	21
Purposes of the clearing house	22
Financial safeguards	22
Daily reports on transactions	22
Original margins	22
Margin variation	22
Handling of deliveries	23

Hedging

	Page
Theory and practice of hedging	23
Definition of hedging	23
Major types of hedges	23
Processor's hedge	23

CONTENTS (*Continued*)

	Page
Importer's hedge	24
Dealer's hedge	24
Producer's hedge	24
Manufacturer's hedge	24
Hedging inventories	25
Hedging versus speculation	25
Tax status	25
Limitations of hedging	25
Deviations in price spreads	25
Basis gains and losses	25
Expected and unexpected basis changes	26
Hedging and insurance	26
Problems in hedging	26
Placing a hedge	26
Shifting a hedge	26
Hedging balances	27
Anticipating hedge requirements	27
Buying cotton on call	27
Mechanics of "call cotton" transaction	28

Interpreting Futures Markets

Importance of market information	29
Price spreads	29
Trading volume	29
Open interest figures	29
Open interest reports	30
Open interest formula	30
Delivery cycles	30
Danger signals	30
Deliverable stocks	31

Speculation in Commodity Futures

Role of speculation	31
Sources of information	31

Spot Commodity Markets

Cash dealings in commodities	32
Determination of spot prices	32
Price reporting	32
Trade terms used in cash commodity transactions	33
"F.A.S. (named port)"	33
"F.O.B. (named point)"	33
"Freight equalized"	34
"C.A.F. (named destination)"	34
"Delivered (named destination)"	34
"In store"	35

SECTION 23

COMMODITY TRADING

Evolution and Nature of Futures Trading

TRADING METHODS. Trading in commodities is the lifeblood of the economy. Evolution of trading methods has characterized the development of the modern economy, particularly during the past 100 years.

With the development of modern transportation and communications, commodity trading methods had to be adjusted to longer distances between the place of origin and that of consumption of many commodities, as well as to the long periods of time that often elapse between production and final consumption. It became impossible to buy many commodities on sight or even "on sample."

Trading of commodities against cash in hand ceased to be sufficient to satisfy the needs of a rapidly expanding economy. Contract forms had to be developed that would permit bridging the gap in distances and in time involved in the flow of commodities from producer to consumer. The ultimate result of this trend was the development of markets on which commodities are traded on the basis of strict specifications rather than on sample, and where they may be bought or sold well in advance of actual possession. The markets developed for these purposes are called **commodity futures exchanges.** Because trading on them is based on carefully developed contract forms and is conducted according to strict trading rules, these markets are also known as "organized" commodity markets. Only a few "spot" markets are conducted as organized markets.

Commodities today are bought and sold either on "cash" markets or on these "futures" markets. Cash markets are called **spot markets**, to indicate when immediate fulfillment of a contract is intended.

Distinction Between Cash and Futures Markets. Despite the origin of these two types of commodity markets, the chief difference between them today is not the time element involved in the delivery of a commodity. In this respect, the commonly used terms are distinctly misleading.

Dealings in cash markets are mostly for immediate delivery, but they may also be for "forward" or "to arrive" delivery, in which case a specific delivery date is set in the contract. Usually this is a specified month. Actually a huge volume of business today is conducted on this basis.

On the other hand, trading in futures markets may be for delivery in the current month. Consequently, such contracts may be terminated within a very brief period.

The chief difference between cash and futures markets lies in the **form of contract** used, rather than in the delivery periods involved.

In spot (or cash) markets, commodities are bought and sold in specific lots and grades with a definite delivery date specified.

On futures markets, commodities are bought and sold on the basis of standard contracts established by organized commodity exchanges. These contracts may not be altered in individual transactions, and differ from each other only as far as prices and delivery months are concerned, which are left to the determination of the contracting parties. This forms the basis for the legal definition of a futures contract.

ORIGIN AND SCOPE OF FUTURES EXCHANGES. The development of modern futures exchanges was a process of gradual evolution. Trading in contracts for commodities for future delivery started on an informal basis, before the adoption of formal rules, around the middle of the 19th century.

The principle of definite time contracts grew out of dealings in "to-arrive" contracts. The practice of selling on a "to-arrive" basis developed around the middle of the last century, both in the cotton trade in this country and in England and in the American grain trade following the opening of the West and the necessity of linking the new western producing areas with Chicago as the established grain trading center.

The desirability of quoting **regular prices** for such forward contracts and for the development of **uniform trading practices** led to the organization of the Chicago Board of Trade in 1848. By 1859 trading in contracts for future delivery was well developed, and in 1869 the Chicago Board of Trade adopted its first rules for the regulation of trading in "futures" contracts.

Selling on Samples. In the cotton trade the development of modern formalized trading practices goes back to the **advent of the steamship.** Shipping cotton by sailing vessels became extremely hazardous as soon as news between the two continents began to travel by faster steamboats. Since this created considerable price risks, the practice developed of taking samples from bales that were being shipped to Liverpool and offering them for sale in New York "to arrive" at Liverpool. If not sold in New York, these samples were sent by steamer to Liverpool and offered for sale there. In 1863 the Liverpool Cotton Association adopted written rules for dealing in such "to-arrive" contracts.

The next important step forward was the completion of the **transatlantic cable** in 1866. Because of the greater speed of communication between the continents, trading by samples became antiquated and was replaced by selling on the basis of an established specified grade, usually "middling—nothing below low middling." Active dealing in these cotton contracts developed in New York and in 1870 the **New York Cotton Exchange** was organized. At Liverpool, trading in cotton futures contracts began in 1875.

GROWTH OF FUTURES TRADING. Although futures trading in grains and cotton emerged gradually from older trade practices, futures trading in other commodities was organized by taking over, with minor modifications, practices developed in grains and cotton. **Up to World War I,** diversification in futures markets developed only gradually; **after World War I** the number of commodities traded on organized futures exchanges expanded more rapidly. During World War II, trading in most futures markets was suspended or came to a standstill, because of establishment of price ceilings and allocation controls. The grain and cotton markets remained open. Futures markets resumed active trading, with minor exceptions, in 1947.

Types of Commodities Traded. Since the establishment of futures trading in grains in or about 1859 and in cotton in or about 1869, trading in a large number of "new" commodities has been established. These include lard, coffee, flaxseed, cottonseed oil, butter and eggs, cocoa, rubber, silk, tin, copper, hides, burlap, millfeeds, cottonseed, cottonseed meal, wool tops, potatoes, molasses, silver, lead, zinc, wool, tallow, soybeans, tobacco, black pepper, soybean oil, soybean meal, onions, platinum, grain sorghums, turkeys, pork bellies, and chicken broilers.

This is only the approximate order, and the list may not be complete. Some of these "died on the vine" because of the lack of trade interest. Some are inactive but may come to life again. In the various futures markets studies are often made to determine the feasibility of establishing trading in additional commodities. In all probability more commodities will be added to the trading list from time to time.

Commodities Adapted to Futures Trading. Not all commodities are adapted to futures trading, as was amply demonstrated by the failure of experiments with futures markets for tobacco, fuel oil, and gasoline. To provide a suitable trading medium for a futures market, a commodity must meet certain **qualifications**. It must be sold in bulk; it must be interchangeable, susceptible to grading, and relatively imperishable. In addition, demand and supply must be uncertain, so that it is subject to wide price fluctuations from time to time, and the futures market must enjoy substantial trade acceptance.

Volume of Trading. In 1939, futures trading aggregated 2,423,623 contracts (in units of each exchange). Grains accounted for 60% of this total and cotton 18%. All other futures markets accounted for 22%, with sugar, cocoa, hides, rubber, eggs, and cottonseed oil trading the more active.

In 1962, the volume of futures trading on all exchanges in the United States totaled 5,179,975 contracts, according to the Association of Commodity Exchange Firms, Inc., of New York. Trading in grains (wheat, corn, oats, and rye) accounted for 48.5% of this total, whereas trading in cotton was only $6/10$ of 1%. The volume of wool trading, from the standpoint of number of contracts, was larger than cotton. The sharp contraction in cotton trading reflected the artificially high level of **government price supports** to growers and consequent freezing of prices within narrow limits. Commodities such as soybeans, soybean oil and meal, eggs, potatoes, sugar, and cocoa were actively traded.

Commodity Exchanges Abroad. Commodity futures trading is conducted on a worldwide basis. Up to the outbreak of World War II, trading was featured by a keen rivalry between American and British commodity markets for the leading world role. The war set back futures trading in England even more than in the United States. Major commodity exchanges were also located in Canada, Brazil, Argentina, France, Germany, The Netherlands, Japan, and other countries. Many of these were revived after the war but because of **foreign exchange restrictions** and **government controls** have not assumed their former importance.

THE FUTURES CONTRACT. A futures contract is a legal agreement to deliver or accept a definite quantity of a particular commodity during a specified calendar month at an agreed price. It is enforceable by law and under the rules of the exchange concerned.

Legal Nature of Contract. The seller of a futures contract has the right to deliver, on due notice, the actual commodity at any time during the **delivery month** specified in the contract. The buyer is under obligation to accept such delivery against full payment according to the rules and regulations of the exchanges, unless he terminates his contract through an **offsetting transaction** by selling a futures contract.

The fact that very few futures contracts are actually fulfilled by delivery does not change the basic legal nature of the contract. Consequently, it is incorrect to describe the futures contract as an option, as is frequently done. Futures exchanges, although not dealing in actual commodities, deal in **rights to the commodity**. These rights can be legally enforced.

The United States Supreme Court has held that **trading in commodity futures does not constitute gambling**. (Justice Holmes of the United States Supreme Court in an appeal of the case of Christie Grain & Stock Co., et al. v. Chicago Board of Trade, 1905, 798 U. S. 236.)

So long as an exchange makes ample provision for sellers or buyers to make or take delivery if they so choose, the presumption is that actual delivery is intended or contemplated. If this right is withdrawn, as in bucketing trades or by private agreement, it may be inferred that delivery is neither intended nor contemplated, and that the parties to such agreements were merely betting on price differences. Such practices are prohibited by law and under the regulations of the exchanges.

The only optional element involved in a futures contract is the fact that the seller may decide, within the specified delivery month of the contract, on what day of the month and—again within the exchange rules—which grade of the commodity he wants to deliver. This is usually called the **"seller's" option**. (For details see discussion of the liquidation of futures contracts below.)

Main Features of Contract. The modern futures contract embodies the following special features:

1. It covers the sale of a stipulated amount of the commodity.
2. It refers to a specified grade of this commodity.
3. The seller is given the choice of making delivery at any date between specified limits.
4. Enforcement of the contract is insured by cash margins that are deposited by each of the contracting parties.

Deliverable Grades of Commodities. The price at which a futures contract is quoted refers to a particular grade of the commodity that is described in the contract and is known as the **"basis"** or **"contract"** grade. However, the commodities delivered on such contract may be either of the contract grade or of some other grade, which may be delivered at the seller's choice at a price above or below the contract price. The number of deliverable grades varies on different exchanges, as does the method of determining the price differentials.

The need for a basis contract arises from the fact that commodities traded on organized exchanges have many grades that are well recognized in the trade. Determination of the number of grades that shall be tenderable against exchange contracts and what shall be the basis grade poses one of the most important and far-reaching problems of the exchange, since the usability of the exchanges depends largely on this factor.

Basis Grade of a Commodity. The basis or contract grade—that named in the contract—is usually the one in widest commercial use. Other deliverable grades may be superior or inferior in quality to the basis grade. Hence they may command either premiums over or discounts under the price for the basis grade.

Experience has shown that **price manipulation** may occur if tenderable grades represent too small a proportion of the total supply of the commodity. If tenderable grades are too numerous, the less desirable grades tend to be delivered on exchange contracts. As the buyer must allow for the fact that he may be tendered the least desirable grade if he accepts delivery, the whole futures price structure may be depressed. In both instances, the value of an exchange for hedging purposes will be diminished.

Grading may be done solely in accordance with the bylaws and regulations of an exchange; or grading standards may be prescribed by law.

Examples of Basis Grades. Practices of the exchanges vary greatly. One extreme is in the **rubber futures contract** that is based on a single deliverable grade—No. 1 standard ribbed smoked sheets. A commodity with one of the most complex systems of deliverable grades is cotton.

The **New York Cotton Futures Contract** is based on 1-in. cotton. Originally based on ⅞ in. and later on $^{15}/_{16}$ in. cotton, the present contract reflects the steady improvement in the quality of the American cotton crop. Nonrain grown (irrigated) cotton now may be tendered on contract, but must be designated as such. Cotton with a Micronaire reading of less than 3.5 (the weight in micrograms per inch of fiber) cannot be delivered on contract. Cotton of less than this reading tends to cause spinning and dyeing difficulties. Staples of $^{29}/_{32}$ in. and over are tenderable on contract. Those under 1 in. are tenderable at **full commercial discounts**, whereas staples of 1$^{1}/_{32}$ in. and 1$^{1}/_{16}$ in. are tenderable at **full commercial premiums** over 1 in. Cotton over 1$^{1}/_{16}$ in. may be tendered but seldom is, since the premium therefor is calculated as the full commercial premium for 1$^{1}/_{16}$ in. plus 75% of the difference in premium between 1$^{1}/_{16}$ in. and the longer staple.

The following grades may be tendered on contracts: White cotton—Good Middling, Strict Middling, Middling, Strict Low Middling, and Low Middling; Spotted cotton—Good Middling, and Strict Middling. Cotton reduced in grade for preparation, or in staple for character, or in value for any reason is not tenderable.

Exemplifying practice in the grain futures market, deliverable grades on the **Chicago Board of Trade Wheat contract** are as follows:

No. 1 Dark Hard Winter Wheat	1½¢ Premium
No. 1 Dark Northern Spring Wheat, Heavy	1½¢ Premium
No. 1 Hard Winter Wheat	1¢ Premium
No. 1 Red Winter Wheat	1¢ Premium
No. 1 Yellow Hard Winter Wheat	1¢ Premium
No. 1 Northern Spring Wheat, Heavy	1¢ Premium
No. 2 Dark Hard Winter Wheat	½¢ Premium
No. 1 Dark Northern Spring Wheat	½¢ Premium
No. 2 Hard Winter Wheat	Contract Price
No. 2 Red Winter Wheat	Contract Price
No. 2 Yellow Hard Winter Wheat	Contract Price
No. 1 Northern Spring Wheat	Contract Price
No. 3 Hard Winter Wheat	1¢ Discount
No. 3 Yellow Hard Winter Wheat	1¢ Discount
No. 3 Red Winter Wheat	1¢ Discount

Determination of Differentials. Methods used in the determination of differentials for deliverable grades vary among individual exchanges, but in each instance the procedure is specifically covered by the rules of the exchange. There are two major types of differentials: **fixed** or **variable**.

A typical case of fixed differentials was the hides futures contract formerly used on Commodity Exchange, Inc., New York. The basis grade of this contract was light native cow hides. In addition, four other grades were deliverable at the basis price. Four grades commanded premiums ranging from 1¼ cents to

½ cent per pound while nine were discount grades deliverable at specified discounts ranging from ½ cent down to 1¼ cents per pound.

Variable differentials are used in the cotton futures market. The grade differentials for deliveries on cotton futures contracts are determined on the basis of average commercial differentials prevailing from day to day in **bona fide spot markets,** officially designated by the Secretary of Agriculture under the U.S. Cotton Futures Act. The spot market differentials are established at each market by a committee consisting of spot cotton trade members who must be approved by the Department of Agriculture. These committees meet daily and establish prices for grades and staples. Those for deliverable grades are wired to the Department of Agriculture, which then calculates the average of the grade and staple differentials above and below Middling inch and sends them to the markets.

Delivery Rules. The futures contract usually specifies delivery during one of the next 12 to 18 calendar months. This means that the commodities can be bought or sold on futures contracts as far as 1 to 1½ years ahead. In some instances trading is permissible only 6 to 8 months ahead.

It must be borne in mind, however, that each futures transaction is for **one specific delivery month** only. Contracts are generally designated according to their delivery months. Trading is conducted in May wheat, July cotton, September corn, or January hides.

Trading is normally concentrated in 4 to 6 active delivery months, while the other positions are inactive. Thus, the active trading months in grains are March, May, July, September, and December futures, while trading in cotton futures is active in the March, May, July, October, and December deliveries.

The seller has the entire delivery month during which to make delivery on his contract. This protects him against delays in transportation.

Delivery Points. Actual deliveries on futures contracts are effected by transfer of **warehouse receipts.** In some cases exchange rules permit delivery of commodities in cars on track within the switching limits of specified cities. However, the contracts used by the various exchanges specify where the commodities to be delivered on contract shall be located. These locations—they range in number on various contracts from one to a substantial number—are called delivery points.

Organization and Functions of Commodity Exchanges

FORM OF ORGANIZATION. Organized commodity exchanges in the United States are a direct outgrowth of the boards of trade and chambers of commerce that were formed to regulate trading in grain at large terminal points. The older ones were chartered by special acts of the legislature, such as the **Chicago Board of Trade** Incorporation Act of 1859. Newer ones are membership corporations, not operated for profit.

Purpose of Exchanges. The preamble to the Rules and Regulations of The Board of Trade of the City of Chicago spells out the objects of the Board of Trade as follows:

  To maintain a Commercial Exchange;
  To promote uniformity in the customs and usages of merchants;
  To inculcate principles of justice and equity in trade;
  To facilitate the speedy adjustment of business disputes;
  To acquire and to disseminate valuable commercial and economic information;

And, generally, to secure to its members the benefits of cooperation in the furtherance of their legitimate pursuits.

MEMBERSHIPS. Membership in commodity exchanges is through qualifications by election and purchase of an exchange seat. The value of these seats has fluctuated sharply. It is determined by the **outlook for trading volume,** which largely determines how profitable membership in an exchange will be, and the value of exchange assets.

Exchange seats are limited in number, so that they can be acquired only through transfer from another member. Thus New York Cotton Exchange memberships total 450.

MANAGEMENT. The central government of commodity exchanges is vested in a president, one or several vice-presidents, a treasurer, and a governing body usually known as Board of Governors or Board of Managers. Officers and governors are elected annually. The administrative work is largely done by a salaried secretary of the exchange.

STANDING COMMITTEES. A number of standing committees, though subject to final authority of the Board of Governors, exert great powers. The names and the work of some of these committees are as follows:

The Arbitration Committee adjusts differences among exchange members. Voluntary or compulsory arbitration of disputes between members plays an important role in commodity exchange practices. Prototype for voluntary arbitration is the Chicago Board of Trade, whose rules state that, "The policy of the Association is to encourage, but not to compel the arbitration of disputes." Arbitrators possess wide judicial power including the right to subpoena members. Decisions of the arbitration committee are binding upon the parties and enforceable under the bylaws of the exchange by disciplinary action. **Appeals** against such decisions are allowed, in which case special committees appointed by the Board of Governors usually have the right to issue final decisions.

The Business Conduct Committee investigates alleged misconduct on the part of a member, on its own initiative or by direction of the Board of Governors. Strong business conduct committees are responsible for the fact that few abuses occur in commodity exchange practice. Membership discipline on these exchanges is very strict. When formal complaints are issued against a member, the **Supervisory Committee** assumes jurisdiction. If the Supervisory Committee finds against a defendant, the **Board of Governors** fixes penalties.

The Floor Committee has jurisdiction over business conduct on the floor of the exchange and trading rules. It has the authority to decide disputes arising from bids offered or acceptances in regular trading on the spot.

The Quotations Committee is charged with the enforcement of quotation rules and the settlement on the floor of disputes over price quotations. It meets daily to establish official "bid and asked" quotations and nominal quotes for inactive trading months.

The Committee on Commissions prescribes and enforces rigidly minimum commission rate schedules. Splitting of commissions and discrimination between large or small customers are prohibited.

The Committee on Information and Statistics collects all data and news of significance to the operation of the exchange. Complete, correct, and fast assimilation of all news bearing on the **supply and demand** position of a commodity is of paramount importance in commodity trading.

The Grading and Warehousing Committee has the important duty of supervising the Inspection Bureau of the exchange, which is in charge of grading and weighing commodities for certification. It approves and supervises warehouses licensed by the exchange for the storage of commodities that may be delivered on futures contracts.

RULES AND REGULATIONS. All commodity exchanges have tightly drawn bylaws and rules that govern business procedures and the conduct of their members. These rules and regulations are strictly enforced. Upon their soundness depends the value of the services rendered by these exchanges.

CHIEF FUNCTIONS OF FUTURES EXCHANGES. Futures or commodity exchanges provide a market place where members trade under established rules and regulations and where orders from buyers and sellers from every quarter of the globe are executed by member brokers. Some commodity exchanges maintain facilities for spot trading, but their primary purpose is to provide a market for future delivery contracts.

The chief functions of the commodity exchanges are twofold:

1. They provide a continuous market for the commodities traded.
2. They make possible protection of commodity positions, incurred in the regular course of business, against price fluctuations through offsetting positions in the futures markets. This price protection is called **hedging**.

These two functions of the futures markets are best described as their market function and their price risk insurance function.

The Market Function. Futures exchanges provide a market place and machinery where sales and purchases of a commodity can be made at any time.

It often is asserted that, without the exchanges, there would be no **continuous market** in these commodities. Consequently, potential sellers or buyers would not, at all times, know exactly the price at which they can purchase or sell. This argument goes on to say that though farmers or producers may never use the mechanism of the exchange to dispose of their output—although they can easily do so—the existence of the exchange assures their ability to sell when they want to, at prices that can be checked readily against prevailing exchange quotations. However, this really is true only when the exchanges are an integral part of the marketing system of the particular commodities, and when trading is in large volume and active. In numerous instances, the exchanges are an **adjunct** to the marketing system and not an integral part. In the case of some of the "minor" commodities, there may be no futures trading for days on end and quotations may be purely nominal, i.e., bid and asked prices at the opening, the several "calls" during the day, and the close.

Futures exchanges not only provide buyers and sellers with a continuous market—where orders from all parts of the country can be executed within a few minutes—but make for more **orderly markets** in which price changes between transactions—with rare exceptions—are only fractional. There are no off-the-record dealings on these exchanges; all trades are made in full view at a trading ring by public outcry.

The Price Risk Insurance Function. The fact that usually a considerable period elapses between the production and consumption of a commodity involves serious price risks. During this period the commodity is owned by someone—this may be either the producer, a processor or handler, or the ultimate consumer. Whoever he is, the owner is confronted with the possibility of unforeseen **price fluctuations** that could cause severe losses.

If futures exchanges did not provide a mechanism for protection against such price risks, distribution costs would be materially higher. Through the exchanges, positions in a cash commodity—either in the form of a commitment to deliver at a later date at a specified price or in the form of inventory—may be offset by positions in the futures market. Thus, somebody "long" in the cash market may offset this position by going "short" in the futures market, and vice versa.

The practice of buying or selling futures to counterbalance an existing position in the cash market, and thus avoid the risk of unforeseen price fluctuations, is called "hedging," which is discussed at length below.

Diffusion of Risks. By far the most important role of futures exchanges is their diffusion of economic risks, which otherwise would have to be carried by relatively few people—producers, processors, or dealers. But futures markets can function only if buyers and sellers are standing by at all times to take over these risks. Since trade buyers and sellers may not be on hand at any given time, "outside participation" or speculation is also required.

Hedging alone—despite the fact that it may be done on both sides of the market—does not assure a functioning futures market. A **two-way market** requires also speculative participation. This need is clearly recognized by the exchanges and administrative agencies. Commodity exchange regulation is aimed at the prevention only of excessive speculation.

Free versus Controlled Markets. Since the major function of commodity exchanges is protection against price risks, they are a feature of free trading in commodities. If prices of commodities are fixed by law or by international agreement, the price insurance function of the futures market loses its importance.

Domestic or international price support measures do not necessarily doom trading in commodity futures, so long as rigid price fixing is avoided. If such controls permit fluctuations between upper and lower price limits, future markets still serve a useful purpose.

Regulation of Commodity Exchanges

EARLY LEGISLATIVE MOVES. Attempts to regulate commodity exchanges are almost as old as futures trading itself. Their main purpose has been the protection of the affected trades and the public against abuses. During the late 90's several attempts were made to outlaw futures trading altogether as mere "gambling." Charges of price-manipulation led to numerous investigations of the exchanges and their practices. In 1892 prohibition of **short selling** in commodity markets came within an inch of becoming the law of the land through the so-called Hatch Bill. Germany, in 1896, actually outlawed short selling with the result that completely one-sided markets were created that could not function properly.

Following the turn of the century, attempts to prohibit futures trading were replaced by a trend toward government supervision.

The three basic commodity exchange laws in this country are:

1. The Cotton Futures Act of 1915.
2. The Grain Futures Act of 1922.
3. The Commodity Exchange Act of 1936.

The Cotton Futures Act. The Cotton Futures Act grew out of the refusal of the New York Cotton Exchange to change its system of fixing differentials for various grades of cotton deliverable against futures contracts. The shortcomings of the **"fixed difference" system** used in earlier years had become apparent in

1906 when, due to extremely poor weather conditions, a scarcity of high quality cotton developed and, as a result, the spread between high and lower grades in the spot markets widened sharply.

The exchange's Revision Committee, which under exchange rules determined fixed differentials twice a year, failed to recognize these conditions, so that it became advantageous to deliver low grade cotton on futures contracts. Futures prices were thereby depressed, and the market lost its value as a medium for hedging. The Commissioner of Corporations suggested switching to a **system of commercial differences**, and when the exchange failed to do so the Cotton Futures Act made use of commercial differences mandatory. The Act also provides for the use of standards set by the Department of Agriculture, and establishes a system of inspection, grading, and labeling of bales under the supervision of officials of the Department.

The Grain Futures Act. Principal objectives of the Grain Futures Act, passed in 1922, were:

1. To prevent misuse of grain futures exchanges that might result in "sudden and unreasonable fluctuations in prices" and in the cornering of grain.
2. To prevent dissemination of false or misleading reports concerning crop or market conditions.
3. To open the contract markets for producers by preventing the arbitrary exclusion of properly formed and conducted cooperative associations of producers engaged in the cash grain business.

To keep the market under observance, the Grain Futures Administration required daily reports on open commitments in wheat, corn, or oats futures of 200,000 bushels or more.

The Commodity Exchange Act of 1936 is an amendment to the Grain Futures Act.

THE COMMODITY EXCHANGE ACT OF 1936. This Act is based upon the findings of Congress that commodity futures markets are affected with a national public interest, that the commodity exchanges are an integral part of the agricultural marketing system, and that, since futures trading and prices are susceptible to speculation, manipulation, and control and to sudden and unreasonable price fluctuations, regulation of trading in the commodities specified in the law is essential in the public interest. Regulation under the Act is directed not to the restriction of legitimate competition but to the improvement of the markets as price-registering mechanisms.

The Act **prohibits undesirable practices**—such as price manipulation and cornering of a commodity; cheating, defrauding, or making false reports to customers by brokerage houses; disseminating false crop or market information; and entering into fictitious transactions. It requires that futures **commission merchants** and **floor brokers** be **registered** and that a futures commission merchant provide protection of customers' funds.

Administration. There are three levels of authority under the Act. The highest level is the **Commodity Exchange Commission**, which consists of the Secretary of Agriculture (Chairman), the Secretary of Commerce, and the Attorney General. The next highest level is the Secretary of Agriculture, acting alone, and below him is the **Commodity Exchange Authority** headed by the **Act Administrator**. The Authority is a part of the United States Department of Agriculture. Administration and enforcement of the Act is carried out for the most part by the Authority and the Act Administrator.

Commodities Covered. The term "commodity" as used in the Commodity Exchange Act applies to agricultural products and to products processed therefrom (such as cottonseed oil and cottonseed meal from cottonseed). The Act has been amended several times to include commodities not listed in the original Act and presumably may be amended further to include some of the commodities in which futures trading has been instituted during the past few years. As of February 1, 1963, the commodities subject to the Act included: wheat, corn, oats, rye, barley, flaxseed, rice, grain sorghums, millfeeds, butter, eggs, potatoes, onions, cotton, wool, wool tops, fats and oils (lard, tallow, cottonseed oil, peanut oil, soybean oil, and all other fats and oils), soybeans, cottonseed, peanuts, cottonseed meal, and soybean meal.

Contract Markets. The Act requires that all futures transactions in the commodities covered by the Act be made on an exchange that has applied to and has been designated by the Secretary of Agriculture as a contract market. A number of commodity exchanges do not fall under the purview of the Act. Among these are such leading exchanges as the New York Coffee and Sugar Exchange, the New York Cocoa Exchange, and the New York Commodity Exchange.

Prevention of Manipulation. To prevent manipulation and corners, the Commodity Exchange Act makes it unlawful to execute transactions in regulated commodities:

1. If such transaction is commonly known to the trade as a **wash sale, cross trade,** or **accommodation trade,** or if it is a **fictitious** sale;
2. If such transaction is commonly known to the trade as **privilege indemnity, bid, offer, put, call, advance guaranty,** or **decline guaranty,** or
3. If such transaction is used to cause any price to be reported, registered, or recorded that is not a true or bona fide price.

What constitutes "manipulation" has been more precisely defined by court decisions interpreting the Act. This is treated in considerable length by Campbell (Trading in Futures Under the Commodity Exchange Act, booklet reprinted from The George Washington Law Review, Vol. 26).

Curbs on Speculative Trading. The Act authorizes the fixing of limits by the Commodity Exchange Commission on the amount of trading that may be done by any person each day, as well as on the amount of speculative open commitments that may be held by any one interest.

Different limits may be fixed for different commodities, markets, futures, or delivery months. Also, limits do not have to be the same for buying and selling operations. Spreading or straddling operations may be exempted from the trading limits. Bona fide hedging transactions are exempted from any limitation on sales and open commitments. Limits apply to futures commission merchants or floor brokers only to the extent that they are not made on behalf of or for the account of customers. **Trading limits** may be imposed only by the Commodity Exchange Commission after due notice and opportunity for hearing. A number of orders have been issued under this provision of the Act, covering grains, generally, rye specifically, cotton, soybeans, eggs, and fats and oils.

Prevention of Squeezes. The prevention of "squeezes" or congestion in current delivery months is one of the most difficult problems of commodity exchange procedure and supervision.

There are two major types of squeezes:

1. If a discrepancy develops between the amount of outstanding futures contracts and available supplies that can be delivered against such contracts, it is called a

"natural squeeze." This is most apt to happen toward the end of the season when crops are short.

2. If a discrepancy between the volume of outstanding futures contracts and deliverable supplies results because supplies are tightly held by a small number of trade interests or speculators, the squeeze is an **artificial** one, commonly called a **"corner."**

The Commodity Exchange Act contains a special provision [section 5a(4)] designed to prevent excessive price fluctuations due to squeezes by enabling the Secretary of Agriculture to require the establishment of a **cease-trading period.** Under this provision the Secretary of Agriculture may direct a contract market to "provide for a period, after trading and contracts of sale of any commodity for future delivery in a delivery month has ceased, during which contracts of sale of such commodity for future delivery in such month may be satisfied by the delivery of the actual cash commodity."

The purpose of this provision is to enable persons who sold futures contracts to ship the actual commodity for delivery on the contract from considerable distances to the delivery point after trading in the contract for that month has stopped. This will tend to make holders of long contracts considerably more willing to even up their positions before trading in a delivery month stops, unless they want to take delivery on the contract.

The Secretary of Agriculture has ordered contract markets to maintain a period of not less than 3 business days and not more than 10 business days during which contracts for future delivery in the current delivery month may be settled by delivery of the actual cash commodity after trading in such contracts has ceased.

Handling of Customers' Funds. The Commodity Exchange Act requires strict segregation of customers' **margin moneys.** Futures commission merchants must treat such amounts as belonging to the customers, and may not use them in their own business or for extending credit to others.

On October 10, 1936, upon advice of the Solicitor of the United States Department of Agriculture, it was ruled that full compliance with these provisions of the Act requires segregation not only of customers' funds received to margin or guarantee trades but also of funds and equities accruing to customers as a result of payments received from the **Clearing House Association** of a contract market covering settlements to the market each day. On August 11, 1937, it was officially announced that the Commodity Exchange Authority would "view with disfavor all contracts between futures commission merchants and customers which purport to give a commission firm blanket authority to use customers' funds as it sees fit." There is no objection, however, to bona fide agreements whereby customers, trading in commodities not covered by the Act, authorize the transfer of funds from one account to another as needed to avoid margin calls.

ENFORCEMENT OF THE COMMODITY EXCHANGE ACT. Enforcement of the Act is based on:

1. Designation of Commodity Exchanges as "contract markets" by the Secretary of Agriculture upon application.
2. Registration of futures commission merchants and floor brokers by the Secretary of Agriculture.

No futures commission merchant may solicit or accept orders for the purchase or sale of any commodity for future delivery unless he is registered with the Secretary of Agriculture and his **registration** has not expired. These registrations have to be renewed every year.

Registrations may be suspended or revoked (after due notice and hearing) for violation of any provision of the Act or regulation issued by the Secretary of Agriculture. These require the keeping of proper books and records, which must be held open to inspection by representatives of the Department of Agriculture or the Department of Justice.

On July 14, 1937, the Secretary of Agriculture published an extensive set of **Rules and Regulations** to facilitate application of the Commodity Exchange Act. These rules and regulations have been amended repeatedly, and are available in booklet form at the United States Department of Agriculture, Washington, D.C.

Reports on Holdings. Supervision of regulated futures markets is facilitated by an elaborate system of daily reports to the Commodity Exchange Authority.

Each clearing member of a contract market must report daily the total of all **open accounts** "long" and "short" carried at the beginning and end of the business day, as well as the net position of all accounts open on his books and the daily volume and quantity of cash commodities delivered on or received on futures contracts. Such reports must be filed at the local office of the Commodity Exchange Authority not later than 30 minutes before the official opening of the market on the following business day.

In addition to these reports, daily reports are required of all persons holding or controlling **open contracts** of specified size. Every person who holds or controls open contracts in any one future of any regulated commodity on any one contract market that equal or exceed the amounts fixed by the Secretary of Agriculture for reporting purposes shall report these on the specified forms. Such reports are due daily, except that if on any day such person has no trades or transactions in any future previously reported and there has been no change in the open contracts, the last report shall be considered as his report on open contracts in all intervening days.

Special Calls. Whenever in the judgment of the Act Administrator a **danger of congestion** exists in any delivery month, each member of a contract market and each futures commission merchant may be called upon to report all accounts carried by him that show open contracts in any designated delivery month equal to or in excess of the amount specified in the call. The above limits do not apply in such cases.

Penalties. The Commodity Exchange Act has real "teeth" in its penalty provisions. Fines of up to $10,000, or imprisonment up to one year (or both) is provided for violation of the following provisions of the Act: failure of commission merchants or floor brokers to register; wilful errors in reporting contracts to the Secretary of Agriculture; attempts to operate outside contract markets or false representation as members of a contract market; violations of trading and position limits set by the Commodity Exchange Commission; attempts to manipulate exchange prices or to corner a commodity; or careless transmission of misleading or false market information in interstate commerce.

Failure or refusal of an exchange to comply with provisions of the Act is punishable with (1) suspension for a period up to 6 months, (2) revocation of its designation as a contract market, and (3) issuance of a "cease and desist" order. These actions on the part of the Commodity Exchange Commission require notice and hearing. Failure to comply with a cease and desist order is punishable by fine of $500 to $10,000, imprisonment of 6 months to a year, or both. Each day during which such order is ignored constitutes a separate offense.

SELF-REGULATION OF EXCHANGES. The Commodity Exchange Act has set the pattern for futures trading that is followed also by exchanges that are not subject to the Act because they deal in **"unregulated"** commodities. Most provisions of the Act reflected practices enforced by exchange bylaws even before the Act was passed as desirable measures of self-regulation. Self-regulation seeks to prevent "any conduct detrimental to the best interest of the exchange or the welfare of the United States."

Under the bylaws of Commodity Exchange, Inc., for instance, exchange members may be suspended or expelled by the Board of Governors on any one of nine different counts, including refusal to submit to and abide by arbitration decisions, misstatement of facts in advertisements, disreputable or fraudulent transactions, and insolvency.

Margin Rules. One important matter left entirely to self-regulation by commodity exchanges is the margining of futures transactions.

The Commodity Exchange Act, although requiring segregation and separate handling of customers' margin moneys, does not now give the government the authority to fix margin requirements. In circumvention of the Commodity Exchange Act the Administration in March 1946 used the Emergency Price Control Act of 1942 to force the cotton futures exchanges in New York, New Orleans, and Chicago to raise their margin requirements sharply. The Administration's argument was that stricter control of speculation in cotton futures was essential to carry out the mandate of the Price Control Act. Use of this device to fix margin requirements ended automatically when price controls were discontinued.

The basic margin rule, adopted voluntarily by all futures exchanges, is that initial margins on speculative accounts required from customers shall not be smaller than those fixed for clearing members of the exchanges. This rule was adopted by the Chicago Board of Trade in 1934 and by the New York Cotton Exchange in 1937, following an informal request of the Commodity Exchange Administration.

If commodity exchanges permit the opening of trade accounts—as distinguished from speculative transactions—on credit without deposit of margins—the bylaws usually set **maximum limits** for the extension of such credit.

Mechanism of Futures Trading

TRADING FACILITIES. Trading in commodity futures is carried out at trading **rings** at the various commodity exchanges. On the grain exchanges these are called **pits**. Usually there is a separate pit or ring for each commodity traded.

Blackboards, in full view of the trading ring, serve to register all transactions. Quotations are also distributed by ticker, similar to the stock ticker.

The trading floor is connected with commission house and dealers' offices by direct wires. This enables execution of buying or selling orders in a matter of minutes from all parts of the country covered by the net of commission house branch offices. Private wire systems connect virtually every sizable city in the United States with Chicago, New York, and other futures trading centers.

HANDLING OF ORDERS. Buying or selling orders for futures contracts—regardless of whether they are for trade accounts or speculators—are routed through **commission houses.** Most commission houses handling securities are equipped to handle commodity orders also. The larger commission houses are members of virtually all or at least the major commodity exchanges.

The actual execution of orders at the trading rings is handled by **floor brokers.** Their chief function is to act as brokers for other exchange members. They are brokers' brokers. Both commission brokers and floor brokers frequently trade for their own account, but exchanges prohibit members from acting as agent and principal in the same transaction.

Traders on commodity exchanges fall into two categories: **hedgers,** who use the futures markets to avoid speculative risks in their business resulting from price fluctuations, and **speculators,** who go into these markets to profit by price fluctuations.

Floor traders who seek to profit from daily price fluctuations by brief commitments are called **scalpers.** This activity is not restricted to exchange members, but nonmembers are hampered in such in-and-out trading by commission and clearing costs, as well as the fact that they are not in contant touch with ring activity.

One type of speculator in commodity trading is the **straddler** or **spreader.** Straddlers seek to capitalize on changes in the spread between quotations for different delivery months in a futures market, or between different futures markets in the same commodity. They buy in one market or one specific delivery month, while at the same time selling short an equal amount in another market or another specific delivery month. Sometimes spreads are tried between two commodities; such as wheat and corn; or cottonseed oil and lard. Such operations are based either on known seasonal developments or on the fact that "normal" price relationships in futures markets sometimes become temporarily distorted. (The term "straddler" is used in cotton trading; "spreader" in the grain trade.)

MARKET AND LIMIT ORDERS. Orders to buy or sell commodity futures can be either "at the market" or at a price limit. Practice corresponds exactly with that used in securities trading.

SHORT SELLING. There are no restrictions on short selling of commodity futures contracts other than the trading limits established for grains and cotton by the Commodity Exchange Authority, which apply to transactions on the long side of the market as well as on short sales. The Commodity Exchange Commission may establish different limits for longs and shorts. These limits are for speculative accounts only.

No limits whatsoever apply to trade accounts. Without unrestricted short selling in commodity futures, these markets could not be used for hedging purchases.

STOP–LOSS ORDERS. Widely used in futures markets for purposes of price protection is the "stop-loss" order. It reads something like this: "Sell 10 December wheat contracts at $1.50, stop." This type of order is used when a trader wants to protect book profits on long positions against sudden market breaks, or if he wants to limit his loss when he enters a futures market. As long as the market is above the "stop," such an order remains a limited order. However, as soon as the stop price is reached or passed, the order becomes a market order, to be executed at the best price obtainable. There is thus no guaranty that the order will be executed at the stop point. Particularly in **thin markets,** fluctuations between transactions may be so wide that the market goes right through the stop point. Furthermore, it occurs frequently that in a **declining market** a large number of stop-loss orders become effective at the same point, which will aggravate a declining price trend.

EXECUTION OF COMMODITY ORDERS. Quotations on futures exchanges are determined by **open outcry.** On most exchanges trading is opened by a special "call." This is a means of establishing opening prices for all delivery months in an orderly manner, instead of plunging at once into general trading.

Each trading month is called out in succession and offers to buy and sell are made for that month only. Sales may or may not occur at the opening call. When the call is finished, regular trading begins. The call procedure usually is repeated at least twice, and in some instances three times, during each trading session.

Futures markets **quotations** are reported daily in the financial press and in other large newspapers. Daily price reports show opening and closing prices, as well as the daily high and low for each delivery month.

In addition to price quotations, daily information is given on the volume of trading and on open commitments. The latter figures are published a day late.

All trades at the ring must be made at the market. An offer to sell at the ring is open to the first buyer who meets the price. A bid must be closed with the first broker who offers a lot at the same price.

The lowest offer and the highest bid constitute the **price limit** for the market. A seller cannot offer his lot "all or none"; but if there are simultaneous acceptances, one for all and the other for part of the lot, the former gets preference.

Trading hours are rigidly regulated, but vary somewhat among exchanges. No trades may be made before or after trading hours. All orders unexecuted at the closing gong must await the opening of the exchange on the following business day.

Trading hours are relatively short—usually from 3 hours and 40 minutes to 5 hours, depending on the exchange—for concentration of trading within a relatively brief but active period better reflects demand and supply than dispersion of orders over a longer part of the day. It is also felt that shorter trading periods discourage manipulation.

CONTRACT UNITS. Trading in futures is done on the basis of specified contract units or multiples thereof. Thus the standard grain contract is for 5,000 bushels and the standard (New York) cotton contract for 100 bales.

JOB LOT TRADING. A few futures markets have facilities for trading in job lots, similar to trading in odd lots of securities. Job lot **sizes** also are fixed by exchange rules. Thus, the Chicago Board of Trade permits job lot sales in lots of 1,000 bushels in all grains, with the exception of oats, which may be traded in lots of 2,000 bushels.

Prices for job lots are quoted ⅛ cent per bushel above and below the market for purchases and sales, respectively.

Trading in cotton futures at the New Orleans Cotton Exchange is in 50-bale lots, but this is the basic contract unit at that exchange rather than a special job lot.

PRICE FLUCTUATIONS. In market operations price fluctuations are governed in part by regulations to prevent excesses of a manipulative nature.

Minimum Fluctuations. To fulfill their function as sensitive market barometers, quotations on futures markets are permitted to fluctuate by a very small fractions under exchange bylaws. These are known as "minimum fluctuations." Grains fluctuate by ⅛ cent per bushel, or only $6.25 on a full 5,000-bushel contract. Rubber, cotton, coffee, sugar, cocoa, and cottonseed oil futures move up and down in fractions of 1/100 cent per pound.

Daily Fluctuation Limits. To curb excessive speculation nearly all futures exchanges limit price changes permitted to occur during a single trading session. The Chicago Board of Trade limits the daily advance or decline in wheat futures to 10 cents per bushel. Once the price hits the permissible limit, prices are quoted bid or offered at the limit, and orders can be executed only if the price falls within the daily limit.

Most exchanges figure the daily fluctuation limit up and down from the previous closing price. The possible daily **maximum range** is thus double the limit, or 20 cents in the case of wheat. In some instances, however, the maximum range is the amount of fluctuation either above or below the previous close.

Daily fluctuation limits are not uniformly approved in the trades. Critics say that

1. Such limits immobilize futures markets at times; and therefore
2. Jeopardize the hedging function because it may become impossible at times to place or lift hedges.

This is aggravated if a succession of limit advances or declines occurs.

TRADING AND POSITION LIMITS. The most far-reaching restrictions on futures trading are the limits on the volume of daily trading permitted each person and the amount of open commitments that may be held by nontrade members. Several commodity exchanges in the past have from time to time imposed such limitations if they were believed necessary in the interest of the exchange and the public. The best-known example of this type of voluntary restriction was the so-called "gentlemen's agreement" between the Chicago Board of Trade and the Administration in the late 30's under which speculative holdings were restricted to an amount of 5,000,000 bushels.

Such voluntary restrictions were not believed sufficient by the Commodity Exchange Administration, however. The Commodity Exchange Act gives the Commodity Exchange Commission authority to fix daily trading and position limits, and the Commission has issued a number of orders fixing such limits.

MARGIN PRACTICES. The role of margins in commodity futures trading differs from that in the security markets. Although buying and selling of securities on organized stock exchanges may be for cash or on margin, trading in commodity futures on organized exchanges is **never on a cash basis.** Margins in security accounts constitute part payment for securities purchased. But margins in futures trading only bind seller and buyer to a contract that actually will not be consummated until a later date. For this reason, commodity margins always have been lower than security margins.

There are two classes of commodity margins:

1. The margins that clearing house members must pay into their clearing house accounts to safeguard fulfillment of their potential financial obligations.
2. The margins that commission house merchants require from their customers.

Customers' margins usually are moderately higher than **clearing house margins,** averaging about 10% of the purchase value of a futures contract, although they are not formally based on percentages of contract value. They frequently are increased in times of erratic price movements in a futures market. A call for **additional margin** is usually issued when the actual margin has been reduced by a change in price to 75% of the original requirement. When price movements are erratic margin requirements usually are raised by the Clearing House Associations. The cotton exchanges now have margins directly tied to fluctuations in the price. In the case of grains, changes are ordered from time to time as conditions warrant.

Minimum margin requirements usually are higher for speculative accounts than for hedging or spreading operations. On grain hedging transactions the initial margin is the clearing house requirement as a minimum. No Chicago Board of

Trade member may carry for a customer hedging or spreading transactions in grain when the customer's account, figured to the market, would result in a deficit.

EXTENSION OF CREDIT. Some exchanges permit the extension of credit—instead of initial margins—in the case of hedge positions for trade accounts, as contrasted with speculative transactions. But the trend has been away from this practice.

COMMISSION RATES. All commodity exchanges have rules fixing minimum commission rates to prevent unfair competition between commission houses in the solicitation of business. Splitting of commissions is prohibited.

Commodity futures commissions usually are expressed in terms of the full commission for a "round-turn" transaction, consisting of a purchase and subsequent sale of a contract, or vice versa.

Commission rates are much lower for **exchange members** than for **nonmembers**. Commission rates on commodity futures are considerably lower than comparative costs in security trading.

LIQUIDATION OF FUTURES CONTRACTS. Futures contracts can be liquidated in three ways: through delivery of the actual commodity; through offset—sale or purchase—in the futures market; or, in cases of emergency, through settlement by order of the affected commodity exchange.

LIQUIDATION BY DELIVERIES ON CONTRACT. Although only a small proportion of futures contracts are settled by actual delivery of commodities, it is important to remember that legally every **buyer** of a futures contract obligates himself to accept and pay in full for the commodity specified in the contract if he holds his contract until maturity.

Similarly, the **seller** is under obligation to deliver and receive payment for a stipulated amount of the commodity. Through orders given through their respective brokers, the traders on both sides of the transaction are under contract to make or take delivery of the physical commodity unless sometime prior to the maturity of that contract their obligations are cancelled out.

Intimate knowledge of **grades** that may be delivered against a futures contract, and of the **differentials** applicable in case of delivery, is of paramount importance for trade or industrial firms intending to make use of a futures market. (See **deliverable grades** and **determination of differentials** under the discussion above of "The Futures Contract.")

Rules and regulations on deliveries of actual commodities against futures contracts are very rigid.

Seller's Options. Although futures contracts restrict deliveries to the delivery month specified in the contract, the seller has two important options:

1. He can choose the day during the delivery months on which he wants to make delivery on his contract.
2. It is his privilege to determine which of the deliverable grades he wants to deliver.

The exchange rules require that a seller declare his intention to deliver one or several days ahead of time. Of particular importance in commodity trading is the day on which intentions to deliver on a contract may first be declared. The day is called the "first notice day."

First Notice Day. This day marks the period for the final liquidation of a maturing futures contract. Usually it is preceded by a considerable amount of contract liquidation on the part of longs or shorts who do not intend to make or take delivery on their contracts. The intention to deliver on a futures contract is signified by the issuance of a **"delivery notice"** or **"transferable notice."**

Trading in a futures contract stops a specified number of days before the end of the delivery month, to give sellers some additional time to make deliveries before the end of the month.

The last day of trading in a maturing contract is called the **expiration day** of the contract, or simply the "last trading day." The period during which deliveries may still be made while trading in the maturing future has stopped is called the **cease-trading period.** In grains, this is 7 business days by special order of the Commodity Exchange Authority. Intentions to deliver must be declared 1 day in advance of actual delivery.

Cotton exchanges require the issuance of delivery notices 5 days ahead of intended delivery, and set the last date for delivery at 7 days before the end of the delivery month. The practical effect of this is to stop trading in a delivery month at least 12 business days before the end of the month.

Most other futures markets permit trading in the maturing contract up to a day or two previous to the end of the delivery month, and require issuance of delivery notices only a day ahead of the date of intended delivery.

Delivery Notices. The delivery notice informs the buyer actual delivery is planned and specifies the grade of the commodity that the seller—in accordance with the exchange regulations on deliverable grades—intends to deliver.

Deliveries on futures contracts must be made at **specified delivery points** out of stocks in warehouses officially licensed by the exchange. Furthermore, the contract requires that the **grade and weight** of the commodity be officially determined by a licensed inspector. In some instances inspections are made under direction of federal or state governments; in others the exchanges themselves provide the facilities. Deliveries are facilitated through transfer of warehouse receipts from seller to buyer.

Notice Procedure. Delivery notices are handled through the clearing house of each commodity exchange. The seller delivers his notice to the clearing house; then it is up to the clearing house to deliver it to someone who is long a contract.

Methods used by various clearing houses to determine the buyer to whom a notice should be sent vary, but a notice is deemed accepted by a buyer unless it is passed on to a different buyer within a certain time limit. This limit is sometimes as little as 20 minutes after receipt of the notice. If notices are passed on in such a way it is said that they are **"circulating,"** until **"stopped"** by someone. The readiness with which delivery notices are stopped by traders indicates the technical condition of a futures market.

LIQUIDATION THROUGH OFFSET. Normally 98% to 99% of all outstanding contracts are liquidated through an offsetting transaction on the futures market rather than through delivery.

If a trader in January buys one hide futures contract calling for the delivery of 40,000 pounds of hides during the month of June and if some time between January and June he gives an order to sell one hide futures contract, the later sale will offset his original purchase. As a result, his contractual obligation to accept delivery and pay for 40,000 pounds of hides is nullified.

The possibility of liquidating futures contracts through offset is one prerequisite for the use of futures markets for hedging purposes.

A futures market fulfills its function best if the percentage of deliveries on contract is virtually nil. A sharp increase in deliveries—preceded by an increase in certificated stocks in licensed warehouses that may be used for such deliveries—usually indicates that the futures contract is not functioning smoothly. The suspicion in such instances is that the exchange differentials for deliverable grades are no longer in line with commercial differences, so that sellers are better off to make deliveries.

Switching. Liquidation of futures contracts through offset can be effected either through outright liquidation of a position or through switching from one delivery month into a later one. A switching operation consists of two separate transactions: the sale of a nearby delivery and the simultaneous purchase of a deferred delivery; or vice versa. Switching plays an important role in commodity trading. It is used to maintain a position in the futures market either for trade purposes (hedging) or for speculative reasons.

Commission rates for switches are the same as for a regular **round-turn operation**, consisting of a purchase and subsequent sale or vice versa.

LIQUIDATION THROUGH SETTLEMENT. The bylaws of all futures exchanges authorize the exchange to order settlement of futures contracts at a **specified price**, if such action is held necessary in the best interests of the trade. Use of this authority is restricted to emergencies, particularly an extreme price squeeze on shorts due to an acute shortage of spot supplies. Exchanges are reluctant to make use of this authority, for it contradicts the principle of free and open markets.

If a severe shortage of deliverable spot supplies is threatened, commodity exchanges occasionally order trading in a delivery month restricted to the liquidation of outstanding contracts several weeks or even months ahead of the formal expiration date of the contract. If liquidation at a settlement price becomes necessary, great care must be exercised by the exchanges to set a **fair price** that does not favor unduly longs or shorts.

Clearing House Functions

NEED FOR CENTRAL CLEARING. Modern commodity exchanges could not function properly without a streamlined mechanism for clearing futures transactions. Clearing organizations play an even more important role in **commodity trading** than they do in securities trading, because not only money differences but also the contracts themselves are cleared centrally.

As has been shown in the preceding discussion, the bulk of all transactions in futures contracts is liquidated through offsetting transactions rather than through actual delivery of the commodity. This, as the Supreme Court held in the famous Christie case (1905), accords with the legal nature of the futures contract. It would not be feasible to carry all futures contracts bought or sold on the books of exchange members until maturity, and then to settle them through circulation of transferable notices. Such a system would be extremely burdensome, and would unnecessarily strain the financial reserves of commission merchants and traders alike, as all open commitments then would have to remain fully margined.

Transactions in commodity futures are made between members of the exchanges. Since the number of commission houses is relatively small, they trade back and forth among themselves. Market positions that offset each other are thereby built up each day. Instead of carrying such offsetting positions on their books until maturity, commission houses turn to the clearing house to match up trades of the same character and clear them from the records of the brokers who have handled them.

EVOLUTION OF CLEARING METHODS. The search for appropriate methods for clearing commodity futures transactions is as old as trading in futures contracts itself. Early forms were the **direct settlement** or **"ring settlement."** Under this system brokers, involved in either buying and selling transactions, formed a "ring" to close out their respective positions. This system was slow at best, as it involved considerable scurrying around from office to office to establish a complete ring that could function to close up a series of trades. If rings could not be formed, contracts were frequently settled by transfer through substitution of one principal for another. If this, too, could not be accomplished, contracts had to be carried along until maturity and then settled by actual delivery, or at least through circulation of transferable notices.

Attempts to streamline these settlement procedures led step by step to the evolution of the modern clearing house system. Members of the Chicago Board of Trade formed, in 1884, a clearing system for the purpose of handling money balances growing out of futures trades. This was facilitated through the use of a daily "settlement price."

The **settlement price** in commodity clearing house procedure is a price set by a commodity exchange official to which all trades are adjusted at the conclusion of each day's trading. Usually it is the closing price or the nearest even price when the market closes. The settlement price has nothing to do with the actual trading on the exchange; it is merely an internal mechanism used in determining credit and debit balances in interbroker relations.

The first complete clearing system was set up by the Minneapolis Chamber of Commerce in 1891. The Minneapolis clearing system became the pattern for all future exchanges although, in the course of time, a number of important improvements were developed.

THE MODERN CLEARING HOUSE. Every commodity exchange now works through a clearing association. This is usually a corporation separate from the exchange and independent of it. A typical example is the **New York Commodity Clearing Corporation.**

Membership in clearing associations or corporations is restricted to members of the respective commodity exchanges, but not all exchange members are clearing house members. Actually only larger exchange members usually acquire membership in the clearing house; other exchange members "clear" their transactions through clearing house members. Although the New York Cotton Exchange has 450 members, the Clearing Corporation is capitalized with only 150 shares and limits each clearing member to 1 share. In Chicago, with a Board of Trade membership of over 1,600, clearing house members in the past have averaged not more than about 150.

Operating expenses of the clearing association are defrayed from a special clearing fee levied on all members of the association (and through them on nonmembers). If fees are larger than needed, dividends are paid to the clearing house members at the end of a year.

Basic Theory of the Clearing House. The basic conception of the clearing house is that it takes the place of the buying or selling exchange member. It is substituted as seller to all buyers, and as buyer to all sellers. In this way a maximum number of direct settlements are automatically made possible at the close of every trading session.

Purposes of the Clearing House. The certificate of incorporation of the New York Commodity Clearing Corporation states its purposes as follows:

1. The purchase and sale of cotton, wool, and wool tops for future delivery and the acquisition of contracts made in accordance with the rules of the New York Cotton Exchange and of the Wool Associates of the New York Cotton Exchange and the **assumption of the obligations arising under such contracts.**
2. The settling, adjusting, and clearing for compensation of such contracts.
3. The buying, selling, receiving, carrying, storing, and delivering of cotton, wool, and wool tops in connection with the first two objectives.
4. The protection of the association against loss in its business by establishing a Guaranty Fund to be raised by contributions and/or assessments.

FINANCIAL SAFEGUARDS. In view of the central role of clearing associations in futures trading, an elaborate system of protection for clearing house members exists. The clearing house has to make good in case of a member's default on his obligation. Financial protection is provided through:

1. The permanent guaranty fund carried by all clearing associations.
2. Margining of all outstanding member obligations.

The New York Commodity Clearing Corporation maintains a guaranty fund of $7,500 for each clearing member. Guaranty funds in other exchange clearing associations vary from $5,000 to $15,000 per member.

DAILY REPORTS ON TRANSACTIONS. All clearing house members submit daily reports on their transactions to the clearing association, as well as their net commitments.

Every transaction on a commodity exchange is first registered on a **confirmation slip.** From these confirmation slips—checked as to accuracy at the end of each trading session—each clearing member prepares daily **purchase and sales sheets** and a **recapitulation sheet** showing his previous positions and daily sales. These sheets must be submitted to the clearing associations within a specified number of hours after the close of trading, and serve for the determination of the member's margin obligations with the clearing associations.

ORIGINAL MARGINS. Since the clearing association assumes the financial risk under each outstanding contract, an adequate margin must be kept by each clearing member at all times. The regulations are very specific as to original margins to be paid into the clearing association by members. In most instances they are scaled according to the **size of the net commitments held by a member.**

Thus, the New York Coffee and Sugar Clearing Association, Inc., scales its original margin coffee requirements as follows:

For "B" and "W" contracts,
 $1,000 for the first 200 contracts
 $1,500 for the next 200 contracts (up to 400)
 $2,000 for the next 100 (up to 500)
 $3,000 for the next 300 (up to 800)
 $4,000 for those over 800
For "M" contracts, the margin requirements are 20% higher.

Original margin requirements for straddle positions usually are considerably smaller. Some clearing associations do not demand any clearing house margins on such positions.

MARGIN VARIATION. All outstanding futures contracts are adjusted to the daily closing price each day through the clearing association. This prevents margin impairment and enables members to withdraw profits on outstanding commitments from clearing house margin accounts.

In case of wide price fluctuations during one trading session, the clearing association may call for **additional margins** during the day. Such calls must be met within one hour after delivery.

Losses paid to the clearing association or profits received from it by a clearing member reflect the customer-client position of the clearing member or exchange members for whom the clearing member did the clearing. Additional margin calls are passed on to the client, whereas profits received are credited to the client.

HANDLING OF DELIVERIES. An important function of the clearing associations is the handling of deliveries of actual commodities against future contracts at maturity through the issuance of delivery or transferable notices, as described under Deliveries on Contract.

Hedging

THEORY AND PRACTICE OF HEDGING. The modern futures contract was evolved to minimize price risks inherent in shipping commodities over long distances or in the time lag between production of a commodity and its consumption. The futures markets enable producers, processors, dealers, or manufacturers to pass on the risk of price changes between purchase and sale or purchase and consumption of a commodity to the broad group of buyers of futures contracts, and thereby minimize this price risk for themselves. This function of the futures market is called **hedging**.

Definition of Hedging. The **purpose** of hedging is to avoid or minimize price risks in connection with obligations to receive or deliver commodities, or positions in cash commodity markets. A hedge has been defined as "a sale or purchase of a contract for future delivery against a previous purchase or sale of an equal quantity of the same commodity or an equivalent quantity of another commodity that has a parallel price movement, and where it is expected that the transaction in the contract market will be cancelled by an offset transaction at the time the contemplated spot transaction is completed and before the futures contract matures." (Cox, N. Y. Jour. Commerce.)

Expressed even more broadly, hedging is the practice of buying or selling futures to counterbalance an existing position in the trade market, and thus avoid the risk of unforeseen major movements in price. (Hoffman, Futures Trading Upon Organized Commodity Markets in the United States.)

MAJOR TYPES OF HEDGES. Producers, manufacturers, importers, or dealers depend for their livelihood on an expected reasonable merchandising profit, manufacturing profit, or a commission. Unexpected price fluctuations can completely wipe out their anticipated normal income and cause heavy losses unless they protect themselves through proper use of futures markets. It is no exaggeration to say that futures markets exist primarily for the purpose of providing hedging facilities for the trades and industries whose commodities are traded on such markets.

The folowing examples show how this form of price protection can be utilized by various trade interests.

Processor's Hedge. A flour miller has made a contract in July to deliver 5,000 barrels of flour in December. He will not need the wheat to fill this contract until November; yet there is no way of telling what the price of wheat will be at that time. To protect himself against a rise in the price of wheat between July and November that might wipe out his expected profit, he immediately buys five December futures contracts on the Chicago Board of Trade (since it will take 25,000 bushels of wheat to mill 5,000 barrels of flour). Assuming that wheat prices, between the time of the flour sale and the actual wheat purchase in November, rise 2 cents a bushel, the miller will lose 2 cents a bushel on his flour contract, but at the same time he will make a profit of about the same amount on his purchase of December wheat futures. He has thus successfully "protected" his merchandising profit.

Importer's Hedge. An importer of crude rubber has contracted with a producer in British Malaya to import 100 long tons of crude rubber into New York at a price of, say, 30 cents per pound without having an immediate buyer for this rubber. Should the price or rubber decline 3 cents per pound while it is in transit, a loss of $6,720 would result for the importer unless he protected himself against just such a possibility. This he can do by selling ten futures contracts on the rubber exchange at the time he buys the actual rubber in Malaya. If he has done this and the price of rubber declines 3 cents per pound before he can resell it, his account will show a profit of 3 cents a pound on the ten contracts he has sold on the exchange, to offset the loss on the sale of actual rubber.

Dealer's Hedge. A cotton merchant in a southern port receives an order from a spinner abroad for cotton of a specified grade and staple that usually commands a premium over the basis grade. He agrees to sell such cotton for delivery in December, although the contract is made at a time when the crop has not yet been harvested and possibly has not even been planted. The risk to which this merchant has exposed himself by entering into an unqualified contract can easily result in heavy loss. Normally he expects to earn a commission of 1% on such sale. But if the price of cotton were to advance 5 cents a pound between the time when the contract is made with the foreign spinner and the time when the merchant enters the market to buy the cotton for shipment, this would not only wipe out his anticipated profit but cause a ruinous loss. The only way he can protect himself against such possibility is to buy immediately an equivalent amount of December cotton contracts.

Producer's Hedge. A mining company expects to produce 5,000 tons of copper during the next 6 months. Its executives feel that, although present copper prices are high enough to realize a satisfactory profit, the trend is toward lower copper prices. If the company is unable to find buyers in the cash market who are willing to purchase the expected 5,000-ton output at a satisfactory price, it can turn to the copper futures market in order to sell copper futures to the extent of 5,000 tons. As the copper then is mined and sold to consumers, futures will be purchased back on the exchange. Assuming that copper prices actually do go down during this period, the company will offset losses from cash sales of the copper with profits on the futures transaction.

Manufacturer's Hedge. If a manufacturer is compelled to set prices on his products a considerable time ahead of actual manufacture and he does not want to increase the products' prices later on, unexpected price advances in his major raw materials may severely cut his profit margins. If raw materials he needs are traded on a futures exchange, he can minimize this risk by purchasing futures contracts equivalent to his manufacturing requirements, unless he has already purchased the commodity at a satisfactory price on the cash market. Although this is not a perfect hedge, it is a procedure that may prove extremely beneficial to the manufacturer. A case in point is the purchase of hide futures as a protection against rising leather prices, once a manufacturer has committed himself to specific selling prices over a considerable period.

Hedging Inventories. Declines in the value of inventories constitute one of the greatest business risks. The danger is aggravated in declining markets because buyers may withdraw entirely. Futures exchanges offer the opportunity to hedge inventories by selling futures. The futures contracts are sold as inventories are liquidated in regular channels of trade.

Besides protecting the value of commodities in store, such hedging of inventories greatly facilitates financing because banks extend more liberal credit lines if inventories are hedged.

HEDGING VERSUS SPECULATION. The aim of hedging is to segregate the elements of merchandising and speculation in business. A hedger, in protecting himself against undue price risks, foregoes the possibility of speculative price gains if prices should move in his favor. Many concerns do not follow a policy of **constant hedging,** but use this device only if they are in particular doubt regarding prospective market trends. Such "stop-gap" hedging involves a combination of speculation and hedging.

Although hedges theoretically may be in the buying or selling side of the market, hedging operations are preponderantly on the short side of the futures markets. Buying hedges are encountered most in the cotton market. In no case, therefore, does hedging alone provide a balanced futures market; it must be complemented by speculative activity.

TAX STATUS. Profits and losses resulting from hedge transactions are considered ordinary business income or expense for income tax purposes. The Internal Revenue Service takes a rather narrow view in defining a "hedge" for tax purposes, however.

LIMITATIONS OF HEDGING. Hedging relies on a basic assumption that in cash and futures markets **price movements** are **parallel.** This is generally true because:

1. Futures contracts can be converted into the cash commodity if either buyer or seller desires. Thus, the "price relationship between the two is very much the same as that of a convertible bond to the stock into which it may be exchanged." (Hoffman, Futures Trading Upon Organized Commodity Markets in the United States.)
2. Experienced exchange traders constantly watch the price relation of cash and futures markets for spreading operation opportunities, which help maintain parallel price movements between cash and futures prices.
3. Both cash and futures prices are determined by the same basic demand and supply factors.

Yet, at times, cash and futures prices may drift apart.

Deviations in Price Spreads. Price discrepancies between futures and cash markets may occur near the end of a crop year when short supplies strengthen the cash price. Also, the basis grade on which the futures contract is based may be out of line with the grade of the commodity needed by the hedger. Such risks are known as **"basis risks."** Because of them, hedging operations are far from a simple matter, and qualified persons should be consulted by those without experience in such transactions.

Basis Gains and Losses. The hedger is more concerned with the **spread** between prices in the spot and futures markets than with the price **trend.**

Transactions in the spot market frequently are not in the basis or contract grade, particularly in the cotton trade. Numerous varieties of cotton either command a premium over the basis grade or are quoted at a discount under that grade. In trade terminology, if a grade commands a premium it is quoted so many points "on" the price of a specific futures delivery. If a discount exists, it is quoted so many points "off" the delivery month. Thus, a sale of cotton may be of strict low middling grade at "60 points off December," or it may be of good middling at "50 points on December."

For the hedger this spread between the December contract and the specific grade involved in his cash transaction is all-important. The difference between the two is known as "basis." Consequently, hedging is often called **"trading in basis."** In other words, the spread between spot and futures prices is the **base** on which the hedge is built. Shifts in this base or foundation may upset the whole hedge. Changes in the basis yield a profit in case the spread between the two prices changes in the hedger's favor, a loss if the opposite is true. These changes are called "basis gains" or "basis losses."

Expected and Unexpected Basis Changes. Basis gains or losses fall into two groups: those that can be **reasonably expected** and others that are **entirely unexpected.** Most important among expected basis gains or losses are those due to carrying the commodity forward in point of time within a given season, changes in the condition or quality of the commodity, and changes in location.

Most important among unexpected factors is the weather. The dividing line between changes that are expected and those that are not is largely a matter of experience and ability to appraise present and future market conditions.

HEDGING AND INSURANCE. Because "basis" losses may occur, hedging does not provide a foolproof guaranty against loss. It would be misleading to say that hedging is insurance. This is not to minimize the economic importance of hedging, but to emphasize its complexity. It is an involved procedure that must be mastered for good results. Wholesale handlers of grains and cotton, dealers, merchants, elevator interests, or shippers are most likely to profit by skillful handling of hedges, or to lose because foreseeable basis changes were not considered. This fact applies both to the placement of hedges and shifting from one delivery into another.

PROBLEMS IN HEDGING. Many perplexing problems arise in connection with hedging and these problems necessitate making definite decisions as to the action to take.

Placing a Hedge. The initial decision facing a hedger is where to place the hedge. This involves selection of the futures market if several are available (such as Chicago and Minneapolis), and selection of the **specific delivery month** in which the hedge is to be placed.

One should then determine whether the normal price relation between different markets or delivery months has been temporarily disturbed. If this is the case, good reason exists to select one market over another, or one delivery month over another. If one market is abnormally high in relation to another when the hedge is placed, it should be used for a hedge **sale** but not for purchasing a futures contract as a hedge.

It is important to avoid **inactive delivery months** in placing hedges, since this may give rise to grave difficulties when the hedge is to be closed out or "lifted."

Shifting a Hedge. Normally a delivery month will be selected that closely approximates the time when the corresponding position in the cash commodity will be terminated. Where hedges will run for a longer period, this may involve a shift from a nearby delivery month into a more distant delivery. If this becomes necessary, hedgers are well advised not to delay switching too long. To avoid **erratic price movements** in the maturing month—which are common and can destroy a large part of the price protection for the hedger—hedges should be shifted into forward positions before a delivery month matures. Squeezes are most likely to occur when a delivery enters into its final liquidation phase.

Hedging Balances. Hedging enters into the operations of a dealer, merchant, or processor only to the extent that an uncovered **net commitment** exists in the cash commodity. If a company or person is long and short equal amounts in the cash market, this in itself constitutes a hedge. When a terminal operator has 2,000,000 bushels of wheat in store but forward sales of 200,000 bushels on his books, his net cash market position amounts to 1,800,000 bushels. This is the amount to be covered through sales of 1,800,000 bushels in the futures market. If he later sells another 100,000 bushels of cash wheat, a similar amount of futures is bought back and his short position in the futures market reduced to 1,700,000 bushels.

Anticipating Hedge Requirements. If a dealer or merchant expects heavy hedge selling at the time a crop begins to move in volume, and he has a fair idea of the amount of hedges he will place, he may decide to start selling futures in small quantities before the start of the heavy crop movement. He thus anticipates his hedge requirements. This constitutes an open speculation until the cash commodity is actually acquired.

Buying Cotton on Call. Cotton mills requiring special grades of cotton that are scarce and expensive like to cover their spinning needs far in advance, preferably before a crop has been harvested. But uncertainties over sales and price prospects frequently make them hesitant to purchase such cotton far in advance at fixed prices—regardless of what the price trend may be between the time of purchase and when they actually need the cotton. Although hedging could be used, a different system of handling such mill purchases from merchants has been developed in the cotton market. Under this system the purchase price for such spot cotton is not fixed outright; instead mill and cotton merchants merely agree on a **premium** over or a discount under a designated futures delivery at which the mill is to get such cotton later on. The buyer then has the privilege of selecting the exact time of delivery. When he finally calls for delivery, he pays the actual price of the specified delivery month plus the agreed upon premium or discount of so and so many points "on or off this contract." This practice is known as buying cotton on call. When the mill calls for the cotton it **"fixes the price."**

This system works in practice as follows: A mill estimates its cotton needs for the next year at 5,000 bales of strict middling white 1-in. Texas cotton. It wants to secure this cotton by buying it on call. The mill contacts a cotton merchant and finds that he is willing to sell such cotton at a price of 100 points "on May." This price includes the merchant's profit as well as shipping costs to the mill. In calculating the differential, all likely basis changes are taken into account by the merchant. Whenever the mill wants the cotton or part of it, it notifies the merchant and pays the May futures price on the day the cotton is called plus the "on" difference of 100 points.

If the cotton is not called previous to the termination of the contract with the merchant, it is automatically called on the last day unless an arrangement is made for extension of the contract.

Under this call arrangement the mill is not protected against price changes in cotton, but it has the assurance that it will get the desired grade when it wants it. The **price risk** is transferred to the merchant, who is under obligation to deliver on call the particular grade of cotton at whatever the price may then be, plus the agreed upon premium covering his costs and profit. He has to go out and buy the desired grade immediately, but he obtains hedge protection by selling futures from the time he buys the cotton until the date it is called by the mill.

The Commodity Exchange Authority published, until 1962, weekly figures on unfixed call cotton which helped evaluate the futures market. This was discontinued because of a sharp decline in the number of reporting traders.

To carry this type of transaction one step further, the merchant may buy the desired type of cotton from a farmer on a similar **open price basis.** He may agree with the farmer that the sale shall be consummated at a price of, say, 20 points on May, or allow the farmer to fix the price whenever he wishes, as long as it is within an agreed period.

Mechanics of "Call Cotton" Transaction. The mechanics of the complete transaction when cotton is both bought and sold "on call"—so that both the farmer and the mill have the right to fix the price when they choose—are as follows:

	Debit	Credit
Jan. 2—Merchant bought from a farmer 100 bales Middling 1 in. at Houston at 20 points on May futures, allowing the farmer to fix the price when he chose, but before April 16. (May was then 34¢.)		
Jan. 29—The merchant sold the cotton to a mill in Greensboro, on buyer's call, at 135 points on May, of which 90 points were for freight, futures commission, and other expenses. He gave the mill the right to fix the price when it pleased but before April 16. (The market then was 34.80¢ for May.)		
Feb. 10—The farmer notified the merchant he wanted to fix the price for his sale on the basis of 34.90¢, then ruling for May. This made the sale price 34.90¢ plus .20 or 35.10¢ and the amount paid the farmer was ...	$17,550.00	
(The farmer probably received $12,000 on account when he delivered cotton immediately and it was agreed final adjustment would be made when the price was fixed.) At the same time the merchant sold a May futures contract at 34.90¢		$17,450.00
Apr. 15—The mill notified the merchant to fix the price on its purchase from the merchant at the then current level of 32.80¢ per pound for May, making the sale price to the mill 32.80¢ plus 1.35, or 34.15¢. The merchant received from the mill		17,075.00
The merchant, at the time of shipping to the mill, would have to pay freight, and all other charges, equal to 90 points, or	450.00	
On the same date that the price to the mill was fixed, the merchant bought one May contract. The price level then was 32.80¢ making the value	16,400.00	
The total result of the completed spot transaction and the liquidated futures hedge was therefore	$34,400.00	$34,525.00
Making a gross profit of	125.00	

Interpreting Futures Markets

IMPORTANCE OF MARKET INFORMATION. The two basic prerequisites for successful utilization of futures markets by trade interests or speculators are:

1. Proper use of all available market information.
2. Correct interpretation of technical market factors.

A great wealth of statistical and general information is available on all commodities that are traded on futures exchanges.

Each exchange provides a complete service on news and statistical data on its own commodities that is available to its members and, through the medium of the trade press and the commission brokers, to the public at large. This information includes government reports on the progress of agricultural crops, statistical information gathered by the exchanges themselves, private crop reports, and market reports issued by individual exchange members. Weather reports also must be closely followed.

PRICE SPREADS. Changes in the price relationship between different delivery months in a futures market offer valuable clues to changes in market conditions. Normally the distant delivery months are quoted at **premiums** over nearby months. These premiums reflect carrying charges for the commodity, chiefly storage in warehouses, insurance, and credit costs.

Taking the hide futures market as an example, it costs about 10 points per month (or .1 cent per pound) to carry hides in warehouses. Therefore, the hide futures market normally shows a spread of 10 points per month; or 30 points between each of the active positions that are 3 months apart.

Deviations in quotations from such carrying charge schedules seldom go far, since the trade constantly watches differences for arbitrage or spreading possibilities. It is significant, therefore, when the normal relation between delivery months is upset and nearby positions go to premiums over distant months. This points to the development of spot supply shortages, or at least considerable nervousness over the possibility that congestion or even a squeeze may develop in a maturing delivery month.

TRADING VOLUME. All futures exchanges publish daily volume figures that indicate the breadth of a futures market. If trading volume is low, the value of the market for hedging purposes is diminished, as the placing or lifting of even moderate hedges may be possible only at considerable price concessions.

The combined trading volume of all futures markets gives the **overall picture.** In periods of active commodity trading before World War II, the combined daily trading volume in all futures markets frequently averaged as high as 15,000 to 20,000 contracts per day. Technical factors may distort volume figures, as when heavy switching takes place from one delivery month into another.

OPEN INTEREST FIGURES. One of the most important differences between security and commodity markets lies in the fact that, although in the stock market the number of shares of each issue is fixed, the number of futures contracts is a constantly changing market factor without any limitation. The number of contracts outstanding in each commodity and in each delivery month, as well as changes from day to day and over extended periods of time, is a factor of great importance in evaluating trends in futures markets.

The total number of futures contracts that remain undelivered at any one time is called the "open interest." Other terms used are "open commitments" or "open contracts." Short and long commitments in a futures market—or in each delivery month—must always be the same, since no futures contract can be sold without a buyer, and vice versa. Hence long and short commitments are not added up in calculating the open interest, but each contract is counted only once. If the open interest in a futures market is reported at 1,000 contracts, this means that there are 1,000 long and 1,000 short positions open.

Open Interest Reports. Up to a few years ago the size of open commitments was an unknown market factor in all futures markets but grain. The Grain Futures Administration started publication of these data in 1923. Nearly all exchanges now supply **daily figures** on the size of, and changes in, open futures commitments. It is generally recognized that proper use of these figures is very helpful in an appraisal of changes in the technical position of futures markets.

Open Interest Formula. Changes in the open interest frequently explain price changes. A rising market may be due either to new buying or short covering. Conversely, a declining market may reflect liquidation or short selling. Changes in the open interest on days when these price movements occur permit a determination of the real factors behind the price change. Short covering causes a decline in the open interest, as does liquidation of futures contracts during a declining market. Conversely, short selling and new buying add to the open interest.

The following formula shows these various possibilities in graphic form:

Price up	Open interest up	New buying
	Open interest down	Short covering
Price down	Open interest down	Liquidation
	Open interest up	Short selling

DELIVERY CYCLES. Open interest figures are of particular value because they are given for each delivery month separately. This permits their use in evaluating the technical condition of individual delivery months.

The "life" of each futures delivery is limited. Trading starts on a specified day from scratch, meaning that on that particular day no open interest exists in this position. At the other end of its life span, trading in each delivery month ends at a fixed date—the last trading date. Similarly, deliveries on a futures contract never can be made before the "first notice" day.

These dates, particularly the first notice day and the last trading day, are of great importance in determining the technical state of the market at any particular time. The **rate of liquidation** just prior to the first notice day can be measured by changes in the open interest.

DANGER SIGNALS. Since open interest figures permit traders to follow the development of each delivery month, and particularly switching operations from one into another delivery, they function as danger signals for the quick detection of maladjustments in a delivery month. If, with the approach of the maturity of a futures contract, the open interest in that month fails to show a normal contraction, something is likely to be wrong. Deviations from the normal rate of liquidation may be due to stubbornness on the part of longs or shorts. In either case prices during the delivery month are likely to be extremely sensitive, and erratic price swings may occur.

DELIVERABLE STOCKS. The key to the situation usually is found in the size of the stocks of the commodity available for delivery on contract. Therefore, open interest changes must be considered in conjunction with the size of these stocks as reported daily by the exchanges. If stocks are low in relationship to the open interest in the maturing month, longs may feel encouraged to hold on to their commitments, thus pushing the price up. Conversely, if stocks are large in relationship in the open interest in the maturing month, the shorts would appear to have the better of the argument, with prices likely to come down under pressure.

Since only **specified grades** of a commodity may be delivered on a futures contract, it is important to know the exact size of these stocks at all times. First-hand indicators of their size are stocks in licensed warehouses. However, consideration must also be given to available supplies that have not yet been, but could be, certificated in time for delivery against a contract. Usually, only 24 to 48 hours are required to rush additional certifications through. Usually, changes in deliverable stocks in licensed warehouses during the last month of trading in an active delivery are at least equally as important as the absolute size of the stocks, since they hint trade intentions with regard to deliveries on the contract.

Speculation in Commodity Futures

ROLE OF SPECULATION. In the commodity futures markets, speculative activity on both sides of the market helps to provide a broad base and to minimize price fluctuations when sizable buy or sell orders are placed. The speculator, whether on the long side or the short side, is welcomed in the futures markets. By trying to make a profit through the purchase or sale of futures contracts he assumes much of the price risks in these markets. Without speculative activity, futures trading lags.

For the speculator the futures markets offer big **leverage** and usually quick action. Margin requirements are small relative to the value of the commodities traded and if the speculator's judgment proves to be correct he sometimes can profit by many times his original "investment", i.e., the margin requirement.

SOURCES OF INFORMATION. Some speculators rely heavily upon **vertical price charts,** showing the high, low, and closing price for each day, in their trading operations. Details of the methods used, as well as much detailed information important to speculators, may be found in Modern Futures Trading by Gerald Gold, published by Commodity Research Bureau, Inc. Also much used by speculators are other publications of this company, including a weekly futures market service, a weekly commodity chart service, and an annual yearbook of commodity charts and statistics.

As in securities, there are a number of **"tipster" services** that furnish buying and selling recommendations on commodity futures to subscribers. Usually, although not always, these recommendations are based on "chart readings."

The **Association of Commodity Exchange Firms, Inc.,** with headquarters in New York, informs its members of any proposed legislation that may affect futures trading and advises them on new and revised governmental regulations. The Association also compiles and publishes the monthly volume of trading on all U.S. commodity exchanges and is the only source that reports the volume on all individual contracts.

Along with the increased trading volume has arisen a demand for **specialized training facilities** in the field of commodity futures. To meet this demand the Association inaugurated some years ago the "Commodity Futures Correspondence Course." This is used by leading commission houses to train their account representatives both in classes in New York and in branch offices throughout the country.

Spot Commodity Markets

CASH DEALINGS IN COMMODITIES. Cash dealings in commodities are not normally conducted on organized exchanges. There are only a few exceptions from this rule, such as the spot markets maintained by most grain and cotton exchanges, the Savannah naval stores market, and the tobacco auction markets in the South. Even in these instances procedure is far less standardized and controlled than in the case of futures exchanges. Grain exchanges with spot cash market facilities generally provide a reporting service for recording cash grain transactions and have definite rules relating to confirmation of trades, surrender of documents, arbitration of disputes, defaults on contracts, commission rates, etc.

Cash dealings—whether for immediate or forward delivery—are not conducted on the basis of highly developed, uniform contracts. Buyers and sellers in cash commodity markets may modify a contract in whatever detail they desire. The most common terms in cash markets are for immediate and for 3 months' delivery. However, forward delivery terms vary greatly, and can be fixed to suit every possible situation as regards buyers' needs. A popular practice is to purchase **"on contract."** This is an arrangement under which a buyer contracts with a supplier for his needs for a whole season or an otherwise determined period, and deliveries are made according to a carefully determined schedule on the buyer's call. The buyer does not usually pay the price that prevails when the contract is made, but that prevailing at the time of each delivery. This method is widely used in supplying fuel needs for industrial and private users.

DETERMINATION OF SPOT PRICES. A major difference between futures and spot markets is the form of price reporting. Although every price, in a free market, in the final analysis must reflect the relationship between supply and demand forces, most spot markets lack the price continuity and the open pricing through outcry in full public view that is one of the chief advantages of the futures markets. Price changes in spot markets between successive transactions are frequently wider than in futures trading.

The lack of concentration of spot dealings in most commodities under one roof—such as an exchange provides—frequently results in difficulties in determining the exact spot price for most commodities from day to day. Here again, such spot markets as cotton, grains, and naval stores are the exception rather than the rule. In cotton, especially, a highly developed system of determining and reporting spot prices exists. In most fields, spot price reporting is done by **trade publications** rather than by the trades themselves. Accuracy depends largely on the experience and skill of the reporters used by the trade press for this purpose.

Price Reporting. Trade publications usually attempt in their spot price reporting to show the price at the close of trading each day that most nearly reflects the prevailing market. Instances where small lots of a commodity, such as distress lots, are offered at a lower price are usually ignored, although they may be mentioned. In some instances, all prices are reported at which **actual**

dealings have occurred during the day, even if only small transactions took place at the outside points of the range. This is usually a less satisfactory form of reporting, for it fails to indicate what the prevailing market in a commodity really is.

In most publications where price ranges for spot prices are shown, this range does not indicate **bid and asked prices,** but rather the range in **asked** prices, since it is the exception rather than the rule in these markets that a uniform asked price is quoted by all sellers.

If no transaction has occurred at the price range shown, prices usually are given as "nominal." Prices shown in the trade press are either at the manufacturers' or wholesale level. Because of the great number of variations existing in the quotation of spot prices, care must be taken to ascertain the exact significance of any given quotation before it is used.

TRADE TERMS USED IN CASH COMMODITY TRANSACTIONS.

Although buyers and sellers of cash commodities have complete freedom in determining contract terms for individual transactions, such business is greatly facilitated by the use of well-established trade terms. Obligations of sellers and buyers under these various contract forms are as follows:

"F.A.S. (Named Port)." Under this quotation, in which F.A.S. is the abreviation for free alongside ship:

Seller must:

1. Transport goods to seaboard.
2. Store goods in warehouse or on wharf, if necessary, but in any case at risk and expense of buyer.
3. Place goods alongside vessel, either in a lighter or on the wharf, or, in the event buyer fails or refuses to furnish vessel upon arrival of goods at seaboard, store in warehouse or hold in cars at buyer's expense.
4. Be responsible for loss and/or damage to goods until they have been delivered alongside ship or on wharf or stored in warehouse.

Buyer must:

1. Be responsible for loss and/or damage thereafter, and for insurance and/or demurrage and car service.
2. Handle all subsequent movement of the goods.
3. Furnish vessel ready and able to receive goods on their arrival at seaboard.
4. Pay cost of hoisting goods into vessel if weight of goods is too great for ship's tackle.

"F.O.B. (Named Point)." Under this quotation, in which F.O.B. means free on board:

Seller must:

1. Furnish a railroad or privately owned car that shall be suitable for transportation of the product sold; properly cleaned and equipped to receive the produce; in apparent good order and condition to protect the goods under reasonable and normal handling by the carrier.
2. Place goods on or in cars.
3. Secure railroad bill of lading.
4. Be responsible for loss and/or damage to goods until they have been placed on or in cars and a bill of lading secured from carrier.

Buyer must:

1. Furnish seller with shipping permit if any required.
2. Furnish the seller with full and complete instructions for shipping, routing, inspecting, weighing, icing, and re-icing, or specifically authorize the seller to

act for him in these matters, in which case the seller assumes no responsibility other than to use his (the seller's) best judgment.
3. Assume all shrinkage, expense, loss, and/or damage to goods after seller has complied with his obligations as set forth above.

"Freight Equalized." Under this quotation:

Seller must:
1. Furnish cars the same as under F.O.B. rules.
2. Place goods on or in cars.
3. Secure railroad bill of lading.
4. Pay or allow any costs of freight or transportation by cheapest suitable all-rail route from shipping point to destination beyond the named city in excess of such costs had shipment been made from the named city to same destination. If such costs to destination are less than on shipment from the named city, seller shall be entitled to add such difference to the invoice.
5. Make any necessary freight contract in accordance with buyer's shipping and routing instructions.

Buyer must:
1. Furnish seller with shipping permit if any required.
2. Furnish the seller with full and complete instructions for shipping, inspecting, weighing, routing, icing, and re-icing, or specifically authorize the seller to act for him in these matters, in which case the seller assumes no responsibility other than to use his (the seller's) best judgment.
3. Assume all expense, loss of, and/or damage to goods after seller has fulfilled his obligations as above.

"C.A.F. (Named Destination)." Under this quotation, in which C.A.F. stands for cost and freight:

Seller must:
1. Furnish cars the same as under F.O.B.
2. Place goods on or in cars.
3. Secure any necessary freight contract or shipping permit.
4. Secure railroad bill of lading, same to be endorsed "Lighterage Free" if so requested by buyer, provided this can be done without additional expense to seller.
5. Pay (or allow) freight between one point of shipment and destination.
6. Be responsible for any loss of or damage to goods until they have been placed on or in cars and the bill of lading secured from carrier—seller not being responsible for delivery of goods at destination.

Buyer must:
1. Assume any expense, shrinkage, loss of, and/or damage to goods after seller has fulfilled his obligations as above.

"Delivered (Named Destination)." Under this quotation:

Seller must:
1. Furnish cars as specified under F.O.B. rule.
2. Place goods on or in cars.
3. Secure any necessary freight contract or shipping permit.
4. Secure railroad bill of lading.
5. Pay (or allow) freight between point of shipment and destination.
6. Assume all responsibility for expense, shrinkage, loss of, and/or damage to goods until they are delivered by carrier at destination named.

Buyer must:
1. Assume any expense, shrinkage, loss of, and/or damage to goods after arrival of goods at destination named.

"In Store." Under this quotation:

Seller must:
1. Furnish buyer with a warehouse receipt or delivery order showing where stored and with suitable endorsement or instructions to warehouseman to surrender goods to buyer.
2. Pay (or allow) all storage, insurance, or other charges up to date of sale to buyer.
3. Be responsible for any loss of, and/or damage to, the goods up to time of delivery of warehouse receipt or delivery order, but not thereafter.
4. Refund to buyer any shortage shown by the official certificate of inspection.

Buyer must:
1. Accept such warehouse receipts or delivery order as actual transfer of title to property from seller to buyer, and assume any expense, shrinkage, loss of, and/or damage to goods thereafter.
2. Notify the seller within 2 days after receipt of such warehouse receipt, delivery order, or document transferring title, of his desire to have such goods officially inspected and/or officially weighed. His failure to notify the seller of such desire within the time specified above shall constitute an acceptance of the goods and a termination of seller's liability for their condition and/or weight.

SECTION 24

NEGOTIABLE INSTRUMENTS

CONTENTS

Origin, Governing Law, and Classification of Instruments

	Page
Origin of negotiable instruments and governing law	1
Codification movement	1
Characteristics of negotiable instruments	1
Classification of instruments	2
Promissory notes	2
Promissory note made by individual (f. 1)	2
Bill of exchange or draft	2
A typical draft or bill of exchange (f. 2)	2
Check	3
Certificate of deposit	3

Negotiability

General requirements for negotiability	3
Definitions and explanations	3
"Writing" and signature	3
Unconditional promise to pay	3
"Sum certain"	4
Money	4
"Payable on demand"	4
"Determinable future time"	5
Installment note specifying fixed times of payment (f. 3)	5
"Payment to order"	5
Non-negotiable note, payable to a specified person only (f. 4)	5
"Payable to bearer"	6
Last indorsement in blank	6
Additional provisions not affecting negotiability	6
Collateral security	6
Omissions not affecting negotiability	6
Signature by agent	7
Agent's authority	7
Forged signatures	7
Presumption as to date of instrument	7
Ante-dated and post-dated	7
When date may be inserted	7
Blanks in the instrument	7
Amount	8
"With interest" added	8
Construction where instrument is ambiguous	8
Interest	8
Alteration of instrument	8
Where negligence contributed to alteration	9
Material alteration	9
Consideration	9
What constitutes consideration	9
Effect of want of consideration	9
Illegal consideration	9
Instruments issued in violation of law	10

Negotiation: Delivery and Indorsement

	Page
What constitutes negotiation	10
"Delivery"	10
Stolen instrument	10
Conditional delivery	10
Incomplete instrument not delivered	11
"Indorsement"	11
Kinds of indorsement	11
Kinds of indorsement (f. 5)	11
Special indorsement	11
Indorsement in blank	11
Blank indorsement; how changed to special indorsement	11
Restrictive indorsement	11
Effect of restrictive indorsement; rights of indorsee	12
Qualified indorsement	12
Conditional indorsement	12
Method of indorsement	13
Indorsement must be of entire instrument	13
When person deemed indorser	13
Indorsement where payable to two or more persons	13
Indorsement where name is wrong	13
Effect of indorsement by infant or corporation	13
Forged indorsement	13
Bearer instruments	13
Certification of check with forged indorsement	13
Bank's liability for payment	14
Striking out indorsement	14
Transfer without indorsement	14
When prior party may negotiate instrument	14

Rights, Liabilities, and Warranties

What constitutes holder in due course	14
What constitutes holder for value	15
All holders presumed holders in due course but status may be challenged	15
Person not deemed holder in due course	15
Notice before full amount is paid	15
When title is defective	15
Notice of defect	16
Rights of holder in due course	17
When a negotiable instrument is subject to original defenses	17
Liability of parties in connection with negotiable instruments	18
Liability of maker	18
Liability of drawer	18
Liability of acceptor	18
Liability of guarantor	18
Liability of indorser	19

NEGOTIABLE INSTRUMENTS

CONTENTS (*Continued*)

	PAGE
Liability of indorser where paper is negotiable by delivery	19
Order in which indorsers are liable	19
Liability of irregular indorser	19
Liability of accommodation party	20
Liability of person signing as agent	20
Signature by corporate officers	21
Liability of person signing in trade or assumed name	21
Warranties	21
Warranties on presentment and transfer	22

Presentment, Payment, Notice of Dishonor, Protest, and Discharge

"Presentment"	22
When presentment for payment is necessary	22
Presentment for acceptance	23
When presentment for payment may be dispensed with	23
What constitutes sufficient presentment for payment	23
Time of presentment	24
Delay in presentment	24
Rights of party to whom presentment is made	24
What constitutes payment in due course	25
When instrument is dishonored	25
Notice of dishonor	25
Where notice must be sent	26
Notice to subsequent party; time of notice	26
Waiver of notice	26
Waiver of demand and notice by indorser (*f.* 6)	26
Who is affected by waiver	27
Waiver of protest	27
When notice is dispensed with	27
When notice need not be given drawer	27
Notice of non-payment where acceptance is refused	27
Protest	27
Notice of protest (*f.* 7)	27
Certificate of service of notice of protest (*f.* 8)	28
Discharge	28
When persons secondarily liable are discharged	29
Right of party who discharges instrument	29
Renunciation of rights by holder	29

Bills of Exchange

Nature of bills of exchange	30
Bill not an assignment of funds in the hands of drawee	30
Bill addressed to more than one drawee	30
When bill may be treated as promissory note	30
Referee in case of need	30
Bills of exchange in a set	30
Rights of holders where different parts are negotiated	30
Liability of holder who indorses two or more parts of a set to different persons	30
Acceptance of bills drawn in sets	31
Payment by acceptor of bills drawn in sets	31
Effect of discharging one of a set	31
Inland and foreign bills of exchange	31
Presentment for acceptance	31
Requirements covering presentment	31
Where presentment is excused	31
Acceptance of bill of exchange	32

	PAGE
Accepted bill of exchange (*f.* 9)	32
Holder entitled to acceptance on face of bill	32
Acceptance by separate instrument	32
Time allowed drawee to accept	32
Liability of drawee retaining or destroying bill	33
Acceptance of incomplete, overdue, or dishonored bill	33
General and qualified acceptances	33
Qualified acceptance	33
Rights of parties as to qualified acceptance	33
When dishonored by non-acceptance	34
Notice of dishonor	34
Protest for non-acceptance and non-payment	34
Contents of protest	34
When and where protest must be made	34
Protest before maturity where acceptor is insolvent	35
Protest where bill is lost, destroyed, or detained	35
When protest is dispensed with	35
Acceptance for honor	35

Trade and Banker's Acceptances

Trade acceptances	35
Trade acceptance (*f.* 10)	35
Banker's acceptance	36

Checks

Checks	36
Within what time a check must be presented	36
Certification of check	36
Certified check (*f.* 11)	37
When check operates as an assignment	37
New York State provisions	37
No stopping payment after certification	37
Recovery of a forged check	38
Legal effect of indorsements	38
Duty and responsibility of bank collecting agents	39

Interest

Definition	40
Lawful interest	40
Contractual and implied interest	40
Rate of interest after maturity	41
When interest starts	41
Stopping of interest	41
"United States Rule"	42
Mercantile rule	42

Usury

Definition	42
Three necessary elements	42
Main test	42
Which state's law governs	43
Exceptions to the general usury rule	43
Transactions not classified as usurious	43
Discounting	43
Capital contribution of a partner	43
Loans to corporations	43
Sale of negotiable instrument	43
Sale of property	43
When contract is void	44
When interest is forfeited	44
New York State Rule	44
Criminal liability	44

SECTION 24

NEGOTIABLE INSTRUMENTS

Origin, Governing Law, and Classification of Instruments

ORIGIN OF NEGOTIABLE INSTRUMENTS AND GOVERNING LAW. Negotiable instruments include checks, drafts, promissory notes, bills of exchange, and other credit instruments that serve as **substitutes for money**. These instruments were developed by merchants to meet requirements of trade. The law of negotiable instruments grew out of the ethical rules and customs of merchants, generally referred to as the **law merchant**, much of which gradually became a part of the **common law**.

Codification Movement. In the late nineteenth century a movement toward codification of the common law of negotiable instruments started in England and spread to this country where it led to the preparation of the **Uniform Negotiable Instruments Act (U.N.I. Act)**. This Act was eventually adopted by all of the states, with minor modifications in some instances due to local needs. The next step in this country was the drive, still in process, for one uniform code that would make some changes in the law and would cover not only negotiable instruments but other commercial transactions as well, such as the law of sales and the law governing secured transactions. The result has been the **Uniform Commercial Code** (U.C. Code), first adopted by Pennsylvania in 1953 and now adopted by a large number of states, including New York, California, Illinois, Massachusetts, Michigan, New Jersey and Ohio, with several additional states presently considering its adoption. When adopted, the Code replaces the Uniform Negotiable Instruments Act and expressly repeals those provisions of the Act that are inconsistent with the Code. In a broad sense, however, the inconsistencies and differences are not too numerous.

In sum then, the **present law** governing negotiable instruments in the majority of states is the Uniform Negotiable Instruments Act, with a large number of states having replaced or considering replacement of the Act with the Uniform Commercial Code. On occasion the **common law** and even the **law merchant** must also be considered for though both the Act and Code are attempted codifications of the common law, it is still often necessary to go to the original source for an interpretation of a particular rule in the light of its history.

Throughout the discussion below, the Act alone is referred to if the Act and Code are consistent, but if they differ, the differences are presented.

CHARACTERISTICS OF NEGOTIABLE INSTRUMENTS. The main characteristics of a negotiable instrument are simplicity of form, the ease with which it is transferred, and the advantageous legal position that a holder in due course possesses. It is intended that negotiable instruments be transferred freely from hand to hand and as nearly as is possible **like money**—free of any defenses that an earlier holder may have asserted, and additionally free from claims of other parties. Generally speaking, **negotiable instruments** and **commercial paper** are similar terms and may be used interchangeably.

CLASSIFICATION OF INSTRUMENTS. Although there are many types of negotiable instruments, they may be broadly classified as: promissory notes, drafts or bills of exchange, checks, and certificates of deposit.

Promissory Notes. A promissory note is an unconditional promise in writing made by one person to another, signed by the maker, engaging to pay on demand or at a fixed or determinable future time a sum certain in money to order or to bearer. (See U.N.I. Act, § 184.) An ordinary form of promissory note made by an individual is shown in Fig. 1.

Fig. 1. Promissory note made by individual.

Bill of Exchange or Draft. "A bill of exchange is an unconditional order in writing addressed by one person to another, signed by the person giving it, requiring the person to whom it is addressed to pay on demand or at a fixed or determinable future time, a sum certain in money to order or to bearer." (U. N. I. Act, § 126.) Fig. 2 illustrates a typical bill of exchange. (See discussion under Bills of Exchange p. 30, below.)

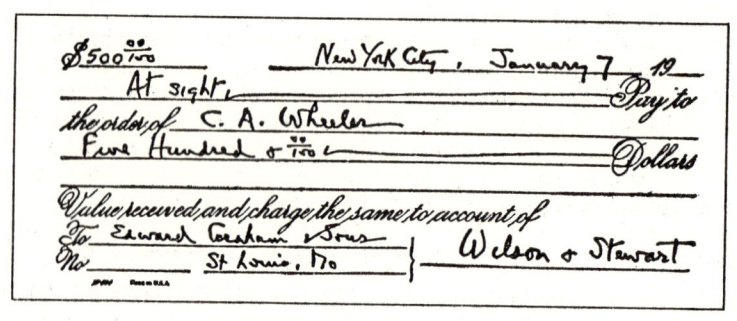

Fig. 2. A typical draft or bill of exchange.

"An **inland bill of exchange** is a bill which is, or on its face purports to be, both drawn and payable within the State. Any other bill is a foreign bill." (U. N. I. Act, § 129.)

Check. "A check is a bill of exchange drawn on a bank payable on demand." (U. N. I. Act, § 185). The Uniform Commercial Code [Art. 3-104(2)(b)] describes a "check" as a draft drawn on a bank and payable on demand. (For a more detailed discussion of checks, see the separate heading below, page 36.)

Certificate of Deposit. A certificate of deposit is an acknowledgment by a bank of the receipt of money with an engagement to repay it. [U. C. Code § 3-104(2)(c).]

Negotiability

GENERAL REQUIREMENTS FOR NEGOTIABILITY. "An instrument to be negotiable must conform to the following requirements:

1. It must be in writing and signed by the maker or drawer;
2. Must contain an unconditional promise or order to pay a sum certain in money;
3. Must be payable on demand, or at a fixed or determinable future time;
4. Must be payable to order or to bearer; and
5. Where the instrument is addressed to a drawee, he must be named or otherwise indicated therein with reasonable certainty." (U.N.I. Act, § 1.)

DEFINITIONS AND EXPLANATIONS. The principal terms used in the five "general requirements" for negotiability are explained below:

"Writing" and Signature. May be with pencil, ink, crayon, or any means to record a signature (25 Minn. 160), or figures or a mark may be used in lieu of the proper name, and a party thereby intending to may bind himself just as effectively by using such (1 Denio. 471). Under the Uniform Commercial Code, "signature" includes **symbol, trade name, or any word or mark.**

Unconditional Promise To Pay. Under the Uniform Commercial Code, a promise is an **undertaking** and must be more than the acknowledgment of a debt.

"An unqualified order or promise to pay is **unconditional . . . though coupled with:**

1. An indication of a particular fund out of which reimbursement is to be made or a particular account to be debited with the amount; or
2. A statement of the transaction which gives rise to the instrument. But an order or promise to pay out of a particular fund is not unconditional." (U.N.I Act, § 3.)

The Uniform Commercial Code enlarges this section as follows:

"(1) A promise or order otherwise unconditional is **not made conditional** by the fact that the instrument

(a) is subject to implied or constructive conditions; or
(b) states its consideration, whether performed or promised, or the transaction which gave rise to the instrument, or that the promise or order is made or the instrument matures in accordance with or "as per" such transaction; or
(c) refers to or states that it arises out of a separate agreement or refers to a separate agreement for rights as to prepayment or acceleration; or
(d) states that it is drawn under a letter of credit; or
(e) states that it is secured, whether by mortgage, reservation of title or otherwise; or
(f) indicates a particular account to be debited or any other fund or source from which reimbursement is expected; or

(g) is limited to payment out of a particular fund or the proceeds of a particular source, if the instrument is issued by a government or governmental agency or unit; or

(h) is limited to payment out of the entire assets of a partnership, unincorporated association, trust or estate by or on behalf of which the instrument is issued.

"(2) A promise or order is **not unconditional** if the instrument

(a) states that it is subject to or governed by any other agreement; or

(b) states that it is to be paid only out of a particular fund or source except as provided in this section." (§ 3–105.)

"**Sum Certain.**" The sum payable is a sum certain although it is to be paid:

1. With interest; or
2. By stated installments; or
3. By stated installments with a provision that upon default in payment of any installment or of interest, the whole shall become due; or
4. With exchange, whether at a fixed rate or at the current rate; or
5. With costs of collection or an attorney's fee, in case payment shall not be made at maturity. (U.N.I. Act, § 2.)

The Uniform Commercial Code expands this by covering **discounts and foreign money** as follows:

6. With a stated discount or addition if paid before or after the date fixed for payment; or
7. With exchange or less exchange, whether at a fixed rate or at the current rate.

In general, the requirement as to a "sum certain" is met if **sufficient information** is given so that by computation a fixed sum can be arrived at.

Money. The Uniform Commercial Code contains the following provisions with regard to the kind of money **valid** for payment:

(1) An instrument is payable in money if the medium of exchange in which it is payable is money at the time the instrument is made. An instrument payable in "currency" or "current funds" is payable in money.

(2) A promise or order to pay a sum stated in foreign currency is for a sum certain in money and may be satisfied by payment of that number of dollars which the stated foreign currency will purchase at the buying sight rate for that currency on the day on which the instrument is payable, or, if payable on demand, on the day of demand. (§ 3–107.)

A written promise to pay a **sum of money in goods** is not a valid negotiable note but is a mere contract.

"**Payable on Demand.**" "An instrument is payable on demand:

1. where it is expressed to be payable on demand, or at sight, or on presentation; or
2. in which no time for payment is expressed.

"Where an instrument is issued, accepted or indorsed when overdue, it is, as regards the person so issuing, accepting or indorsing it, payable on demand." (U. N. I. Act, § 7.)

If a note is payable on demand with no qualifying provisions, it is due as of the date of execution and delivery. (32 N.Y.S. 2d 239; 237 Ala. 658; 202 N.Y. App. Div. 499.)

"**Determinable Future Time.**" "An instrument is payable at a determinable future time, which is expressed to be payable:

1. At a fixed period after date or sight; or
2. On or before a fixed determinable future time specified therein [see installment note specifying the fixed times of payment, Fig. 3]; or
3. On or at a fixed period after the occurrence of a specified event, which is certain to happen, although the time of happening be uncertain." (U.N.I. Act, § 4.)

The Code eliminates 3. above, but, like the Act, contains the following sentence: "An instrument payable upon a contingency is not negotiable, and the happening of the event does not cure the defect." (U.N.I. Act, § 4.)

$250.00   New York, June 1st, 19—.

For value received, I promise to pay to the order of Richard Roe, at the Safe Trust Company, No. 1 Fifth Avenue, New York City, the sum of Two hundred fifty and no/100 dollars, in installments as follows:

On the 1st day of July, 19—, Fifty dollars,
On the 1st day of August, 19—, Fifty dollars,
On the 1st day of September, 19—, Fifty dollars,
On the 1st day of October, 19—, Fifty dollars,
On the 1st day of November, 19—, Fifty dollars,

all with interest from date, at the rate of six per centum per annum.

                                                John Doe.

Fig. 3. Installment note specifying fixed times of payment.

"**Payable to Order.**" "The instrument is payable to order where it is drawn payable to the order of a specified person or to him or his order. It may be drawn payable to the order of:

1. A payee who is not maker, drawer or drawee; or
2. A drawer or maker; or
3. A drawee; or
4. Two or more payees generally; or
5. One or some of several payees; or
6. The holder of an office for the time being.

"Where the instrument is payable to order, the payee must be named or otherwise indicated therein with reasonable certainty." (U. N. I. Act, § 8.)

An instrument payable to a **specified person without the word "order"** is not negotiable. (209 Ky. 230.) Such a note is shown in Fig. 4.

$100.00   New York, June 1st, 19—.

Thirty days after date, I promise to pay to John Doe,
One Hundred Dollars, for value received with interest.
                                                Richard Roe

Fig. 4. Nonnegotiable note, payable to a specified person only.

24·6   NEGOTIABLE INSTRUMENTS

A **check drawn in the "alternative"** is negotiable. (257 N.Y. 441; 114 Neb. 230.)

A check **payable to the holder of an office,** such as Commissioner of Internal Revenue, is negotiable. (6 N.Y. 124.)

Negotiability is not affected by an instrument drawn to the order of **several payees** jointly. (257 N.Y. 441.)

"Payable to Bearer." The instrument is payable to bearer:

1. When it is expressed to be so payable; or
2. When it is payable to a person therein or bearer, or
3. When it is payable to the order of a fictitious or non-existing person. and such fact was known to the person making it so payable, or
4. When the name of the payee does not purport to be the name of any person; or
5. When the only or last indorsement is an indorsement in blank." (U.N.I. Act, § 9.)

The Uniform Commercial Code § 3–111 omits 3. and 4. above and states: "An instrument is payable to bearer when by its terms it is payable to

(a) bearer or the order of bearer; or
(b) a specified person or bearer; or
(c) "cash" or the order of "cash," or any other indication which does not purport to designate a specific payee."

A check **payable to a particular bearer,** such as "to the order of bearer B. Cohen," is not payable to a bearer generally and cannot be negotiated without the indorsement of the payee named. (68 N.Y.S. 35; 162 S.W. 314.)

Last Indorsement in Blank. An indorsement in blank will not make a non-negotiable instrument negotiable. (25 N.Y.S. 2nd 157; 155 N.C. 47.)

ADDITIONAL PROVISIONS NOT AFFECTING NEGOTIABILITY. "An instrument which contains an order or promise to do any act in addition to the payment of money is not negotiable. But the negotiable character of an instrument otherwise negotiable is not affected by a provision which:

1. Authorizes the sale of collateral securities in case the instrument be not paid at maturity; or
2. Authorizes a confession of judgment if the instrument be not paid at maturity; or
3. Waives the benefit of any law intended for the advantage or protection of the obligor; or
4. Gives the holder an election to require something to be done in lieu of payment of money." (U.N.I. Act, § 5.)

Collateral Security. A promise to furnish additional collateral if the original collateral decreases in value, further to secure an instrument for the payment of money, does not render the instrument nonnegotiable. (164 N.E. 113; 128 Mass. 129.)

OMISSIONS NOT AFFECTING NEGOTIABILITY. "The validity and negotiable character of an instrument are not affected by the fact that:

1. It is not dated; or
2. Does not specify the value given, or that any value has been given therefor; or
3. Does not specify the place where it is drawn or the place where it is payable; or
4. Bears a seal; or

5. Designates a particular kind of current money in which payment is to be made." (U.N.I. Act, § 6.)

SIGNATURE BY AGENT. "The signature of any party may be made by a duly appointed agent. No particular form of appointment is necessary for this purpose; and the authority of the agent may be established as in other cases of agency." (U.N.I. Act, § 19.)

Agent's Authority. An authority to make or indorse negotiable paper is subject to strict interpretation. The power will be construed as extending only to paper executed or indorsed in the business of the principal. **Third parties** cannot rely upon the agent's mere assumption of authority. They are bound to inquire as to the power of the agent. (52 N.Y.S. 681.)

FORGED SIGNATURES. "Where a signature is forged or made without authority of the person whose signature it purports to be, it is wholly inoperative, and no right to retain the instrument, or to give a discharge therefor, or to enforce payment thereof against any party thereto, can be acquired through or under such signature, unless the party, against whom it is sought to enforce such right, is precluded from setting up the forgery or want of authority." (U.N.I. Act, § 23.)

"Though a person may be deceived as to the name of a man with whom he is dealing, if he dealt with and intended to deal with the visible person before him, a check may be properly endorsed by the impostor." (10 N.E. 2d 457.) (See also Forged Indorsement, page 13, below.)

PRESUMPTION AS TO DATE OF INSTRUMENT. "Where the instrument or an acceptance or any indorsement thereon is dated, such date is deemed prima facie to be the true date of the making, drawing, acceptance or indorsement as the case may be." (U.N.I. Act, § 11.)

Ante-Dated and Post-Dated. "The instrument is not invalid for the reason only that it is ante-dated or post-dated, provided this is not done for an illegal or fraudulent purpose. The person to whom an instrument so dated is delivered, acquires title thereto as of the date of delivery." (U. N. I. Act, § 12.)

An instrument post-dated or ante-dated for an **illegal purpose** is void to all persons having knowledge of it. Otherwise it is good. [8 Wend. (N.Y.) 478; 282 N.Y.S. 202.]

When Date May Be Inserted. "Where an instrument expressed to be payable at a fixed period after date is issued undated, or where the acceptance of an instrument payable at a fixed period after sight is undated, any holder may insert therein the true date of issue or acceptance, and the instrument shall be payable accordingly. The insertion of a wrong date does not void the instrument in the hands of a subsequent holder in due course; but as to him, the date so inserted is to be recorded as the true date." (U.N.I. Act, § 13, 54 N.Y. 234; 122 S.W. 756.)

BLANKS IN THE INSTRUMENT. "Where the instrument is wanting in any material particular, the person in possession thereof has a prima facie authority to complete it by filling up the blanks therein. And a signature on a blank paper delivered by the person making the signature in order that the paper may be converted into a negotiable instrument, operates as **prima facie authority** to fill it up as such for any amount. In order, however, that any such instrument, when completed, may be enforced against any person who became a party thereto prior to its completion, it must be filled up strictly in accordance with the authority given and within a reasonable time. But if any such instrument, after completion, is negotiated to a holder in due course, it is valid and effectual for all purposes in his hands, and he may enforce it as if it had been filled up strictly in accordance with the authority given and within a reasonable time." (U.N.I. Act, § 14.)

Amount. One who accepts a draft with the amount in blank is **liable to a bona fide holder thereof** for the amount filled in, although such amount is larger than was contemplated by the acceptor. (21 N.Y. 531.)

"With Interest" Added. The holder is not permitted to add words that change the obligation from a noninterest-bearing to an interest-bearing one. (100 N.Y. 150, 2 N.E. 247.)

CONSTRUCTION WHERE INSTRUMENT IS AMBIGUOUS. "Where the language of the instrument is ambiguous, or there are omissions therein, the following rules of construction apply:

1. Where the sum payable is expressed in words and also in figures and there is a discrepancy between the two, **the sum denoted by the words is the sum payable;** but if the words are ambiguous or uncertain, reference may be had to the figures to fix the amount;
2. Where the instrument provides for the payment of interest, without specifying the date from which interest is to run, the **interest runs from the date of the instrument,** and if the instrument is undated, from the issue thereof;
3. Where the instrument is not dated, it will be considered to be **dated as of the time it was issued;**
4. Where there is a conflict between the written and printed provisions of the instrument, the **written provisions prevail;**
5. Where the instrument is so ambiguous that there is doubt whether it is a bill or note, the holder may treat it as either at his election;
6. Where the signature is so placed upon the instrument that it is not clear in what capacity the person making the same intended to sign, he is to be deemed an endorser;
7. Where an instrument containing the words "I promise to pay" is signed by two or more persons, they are deemed to be jointly and severally liable thereon." (U.N.I. Act, § 17.)

Interest. Subdivision 2 of this Section of the Uniform Negotiable Instruments Act refers to the computation of interest only when there is an agreement to pay interest. It does not apply if the instrument does not provide for interest. (139 N.Y. App. Div. 603.) When an instrument is payable with interest and rate is not specified, the **legal rate** of the place of issue is presumed. (86 Neb. 103.)

ALTERATION OF INSTRUMENT. "Where a negotiable instrument is materially altered without the assent of all parties liable thereon, it is voided, except as against a party who has himself made, authorized or assented to the alteration and subsequent indorsers. But when an instrument has been materially altered and is in the hands of a holder in due course, not a party to the alteration, he may enforce payment thereof according to its original tenor." (U.N.I. Act, § 124.)

If the maker of an instrument leaves a blank space that enables a forger to raise the amount thereof, the liability of the maker or an indorser is not affected by alleged negligence in signing or indorsing the carelessly drawn instrument, but a holder in due course can only enforce it according to its original tenor. (87 N.E. 779.) If the mere inspection of a check discloses that there has been an alteration, a transferee thereof cannot be a holder in due course. (131 Tenn. 42;

98 N.Y.S. 667.) Adding the words "with interest" is a material alteration. (220 Mass. 247.) Changing an order instrument to a bearer instrument is a material alteration. (151 N.W. 100.) An alteration of the place of payment is a material alteration. (235 N.Y. App. Div. 704.)

Where Negligence Contributed to Alteration. The Uniform Commercial Code would seem to affirm these provisions on alterations but raises the question of negligence as a cause of the alteration:

Any person who by his negligence substantially contributes to a material alteration of the instrument or to the making of an unauthorized signature is precluded from asserting the alteration or lack of authority against a holder in due course or against a drawee or other payor who pays the instrument in good faith and in accordance with the reasonable commercial standards of the drawee's or payor's business. (§ 3-406.)

Material Alteration. "Any alteration which changes:

1. The date;
2. The sum payable, either for principal or interest;
3. The time or place of payment;
4. The principal or relations of the parties;
5. The medium or currency in which payment is to be made; or which adds a place of payment where no place of payment is specified, or any other change or addition which alters the effect of the instrument in any respect is a material alteration." (U.N.I. Act, § 125.)

CONSIDERATION. "Every negotiable instrument is deemed prima facie to have been issued for a valuable consideration; and every person whose signature appears thereon to have become a party thereto for value." (U.N.I. Act, § 24.)

This is so even though the words "Value Received" are not present. These words are now regarded merely as surplusage.

If an action is brought on a negotiable instrument, in order to raise the question of lack of consideration, the defendant must allege affirmatively that the instrument was without consideration. (185 N.Y.S. 66; 215 Iowa 215.)

What Constitutes Consideration. "**Value** is any consideration sufficient to support a **simple contract.** An antecedent or pre-existing debt constitutes value; and is deemed such whether the instrument is payable on demand or at a future time." (U.N.I. Act, § 25.)

"A valuable consideration may consist of some right, interest, profit or benefit accruing to one party, or some forbearance, detriment, loss or responsibility given, suffered, or undertaken by the other." (108 N.E. 558; 145 S.E. 619.)

EFFECT OF WANT OF CONSIDERATION. "Absence or failure of consideration is a matter of defense as against any person not a holder in due course; and partial failure of consideration is a defense pro tanto whether the failure is of ascertained and liquidated amount or otherwise." (U.N.I. Act, § 28.)

As between the original parties, the consideration of an instrument is a subject of inquiry. The maker may show that it was not given for a sufficient consideration, and it is immaterial whether the note is negotiable or nonnegotiable. (60 N.Y. 146; 291 N.Y.S. 302.) A holder in due course may enforce a negotiable instrument though there was an absence or failure of the consideration as between the original parties. (89 N.E. 1106; 109 N.Y.S. 818.)

Illegal Consideration. Instruments based on an illegal consideration are void. (173 N.E. 895.)

INSTRUMENTS ISSUED IN VIOLATION OF LAW. An instrument given for an **illegal consideration** can nevertheless be enforced by a bona fide purchaser, unless the statute expressly declares the instrument to be void. A check or note given for **a gambling debt** in some states is absolutely void. Usury makes an ordinary instrument unenforceable even by a bona fide purchaser (91 S.E. 7; 223 N.Y. 401), except as in the case of New York where a bank forfeits the usurious interest but may recover the principal amount of the obligation. (New York Banking Law, Section 108.)

However, there is a **tendency on the part of the courts** to uphold negotiable instruments in the hands of a bona fide holder since "the business of the country is done so largely by means of commercial paper that the interests of commerce require that a promissory note, fair on its face, should be as negotiable as a government bond. Every restriction upon the circulation of negotiable paper is an injury to the State, for it tends to derange trade and hinders the transaction of business." (Chemical National Bank v. Kellogg, 183 N.Y. 92.)

Negotiation: Delivery and Indorsement

WHAT CONSTITUTES NEGOTIATION. "An instrument is negotiated when it is transferred from one person to another in such manner as to constitute the transferee the holder thereof. If **payable to bearer,** it is negotiated by delivery; if **payable to order,** it is negotiated by the indorsement of the holder completed by delivery." (U.N.I. Act, § 30.)

"DELIVERY." To complete a negotiation, there must be a voluntary delivery of the instrument to the payee. There is a **presumption,** however, that if an instrument is in the hands of a holder in due course, there was a valid delivery of the instrument at the time of its inception.

The Uniform Negotiable Instruments Act, § 16, states

> Every contract on a negotiable instrument is **incomplete and revocable until delivery** of the instrument for the purpose of giving effect thereto. As between immediate parties, and as regards a remote party, other than a holder in due course, the delivery, in order to be effectual, must be made either by or under the authority of the party making, drawing, accepting or indorsing as the case may be; and in such case the delivery may be shown to have been conditional, or for a special purpose only, and not for the purpose of transferring the property in the instrument. But where the instrument is in the hands of a holder in due course, a valid delivery thereof by all parties prior to him so as to make them liable to him is conclusively presumed. And where the instrument is no longer in the possession of a party whose signature appears thereon, a valid and intentional delivery by him is presumed until the contrary is proved.

Act and intention are the essential constituents of a delivery that makes an instrument operative according to its terms. Whenever there has been a delivery of the instrument for the purpose of giving it such effect, it becomes a present and completed contract. (111 N.E. 263.)

Stolen Instrument. When a negotiable instrument, complete on its face, is stolen from the maker or other party before delivery, a subsequent holder in due course will acquire a good title as against the person from whom it was stolen. (190 N.Y. 167; 82 N.E. 1108.)

Conditional Delivery. A **certificate of deposit** issued by a bank is one of the class of instruments where the section declares that delivery "may be shown to have been conditional or for a special purpose only." (140 N.Y.S. 231; 110 N.Y. 654.)

Incomplete Instrument Not Delivered. "Where an incomplete instrument has not been delivered, it will not, if completed and negotiated, without authority, be a valid contract in the hands of any holder, as against any person whose signature was placed thereon before delivery." (U.N.I. Act, § 15.) The Uniform Commercial Code abolishes the foregoing (§ 3–305), with the result that it is no longer a real defense against a holder in due course.

"**INDORSEMENT.**" Indorsement is the technical act of signing one's name, with or without words of qualification, to an instrument for purpose of transfer.

KINDS OF INDORSEMENT. "An indorsement may be either special or in blank; and it may also be either restrictive or qualified, or conditional" (U.N.I. Act, § 33). Fig. 5 shows how indorsements of various kinds are worded.

Pay to the order of John Richards. Richard Roe	*Special Indorsement*
Richard Roe	*Blank Indorsement*
Pay to John Doe only Richard Roe	*Restrictive Indorsement*
Pay without recourse to order of Ben Boe Richard Roe	*Qualified Indorsement*
On the next arrival of the Queen Mary in New York, Pay to the order of Jim Smith. Richard Roe	*Conditional Indorsement*

Fig. 5. Kinds of indorsement.

Special Indorsement. "A special indorsement specifies the person to whom, or to whose order the instrument is to be payable; and the indorsement of such indorsee is necessary to the further negotiation of the instrument." (U.N.I. Act, § 34.)

Indorsement in Blank. "An indorsement in blank specifies no indorsee, and an instrument so indorsed is payable to bearer, and may be negotiated by delivery." (U.N.I. Act, § 34.)

Possession of a negotiable instrument indorsed in blank by the payee is presumptive evidence of the possessor's title to it. (211 N.Y.S. 486; 203 Ala. 446.)

Blank Indorsement; How Changed to Special Indorsement. "The holder may convert a blank indorsement into a special indorsement by writing over the signature of the indorser in blank any contract consistent with the character of the indorsement." (U.N.I. Act, § 35.)

Restrictive Indorsement. "An indorsement is restrictive, which either:

1. Prohibits the further negotiation of the instrument; or
2. Constitutes the indorsee the agent of the indorser; or
3. Vests the title in the indorsee in trust for or to the use of some other person

"But the mere absence of words implying power to negotiate does not make an indorsement restrictive." (U.N.I. Act, § 36.)

An indorsement **"For Deposit"** was held restrictive and prohibited further negotiation for any purpose except for collection for deposit to indorser's account. (277 N.Y. 223; 14 N.E. 2d 46.)

The U. C. Code states that an indorsement is restrictive if conditional or if it purports to prohibit further negotiation or uses the terms "for deposit" or "for collection" or "pay any bank."

Effect of Restrictive Indorsement; Rights of Indorsee. "A restrictive indorsement confers upon the indorsee the right:

1. To receive payment of the instrument;
2. To bring any action that the indorser could bring;
3. To transfer his rights as such indorsee, where the form of the indorsement authorizes him to do so.

"But all **subsequent indorsees** acquire only the title of the first indorsee under the restrictive indorsement." (U.N.I. Act, § 37.)

An indorsement of a check **"For collection"** passes title to the check by reason of the fact that the indorsee in such case can sue in his own name or indorse the instrument to another for collection. (8 F. Supp. 72; 277 N.Y. 223.)

The Uniform Commercial Code further regulates the effect of a restrictive indorsement by stating:

(1) No restrictive indorsement prevents further transfer or negotiation of the instrument.

(2) An intermediary bank, or a payor bank which is not the depositary bank, is neither given notice nor otherwise affected by a restrictive indorsement of any person except the bank's immediate transferor or the person presenting for payment.

(3) Except for an intermediary bank, any transferee under an indorsement which is conditional or includes the words "for collection," "for deposit," "pay any bank," or like terms (sub. paragraphs (a) and (c) of Section 3–205) must pay or apply any value given by him for or on the security of the instrument consistently with the indorsement and to the extent that he does so he becomes a holder for value.

(4) The first taker under an indorsement for the benefit of the indorser or another person (sub. paragraph (d) of Section 3–205) must pay or apply any value given by him for or on the security of the instrument consistently with the indorsement and to the extent that he does so he becomes a holder for value. A later holder for value is neither given notice nor otherwise affected by such restrictive indorsement unless he has knowledge that a fiduciary or other person has negotiated the instrument in any transaction for his own benefit or otherwise in breach of duty (subsection (2) of § 3–304).

Qualified Indorsement. "A qualified indorsement constitutes the indorser a mere assignor of the title to the instrument. It may be made by adding to the indorser's signature the words **'Without recourse'** or any words of similar import. Such an indorsement does not impair the negotiable character of the instrument." (U.N.I. Act, § 38. See 172 Mich. 159; 262 N.Y. 215; 65 Ore. 450.)

Conditional Indorsement. "Where an indorsement is conditional, a party required to pay the instrument may disregard the condition, and make payment to the indorsee or his transferee, whether the condition has been fulfilled or not. But any person to whom an instrument so indorsed is negotiated, will hold the same, or the proceeds thereof, subject to the rights of the person indorsing it conditionally." (U.N.I. Act, § 39.)

METHOD OF INDORSEMENT. "The indorsement must be written on the instrument itself or upon a paper attached thereto. The signature of the indorser without additional words is a sufficient indorsement." (U.N.I. Act, § 31.)

An indorsement written in pencil is sufficient. And it may be by a mark or with the figures 1-2-8 with no name, if the indorser intends to bind himself thereby. [6 Hill (N.Y.) 443.]

Indorsement Must Be of Entire Instrument. "The indorsement must be an indorsement of the entire instrument. An indorsement which purports to transfer to the indorsee a part only of the amount payable, or which purports to transfer the instrument to two or more indorsees severally, does not operate as a negotiation of the instrument. But where the instrument has been **paid in part**, it may be indorsed as to the residue." (U.N.I. Act, § 32.)

The U. C. Code provides that if the endorsement purports to be of less than the entire amount, it operates only as a partial assignment.

When Person Deemed Indorser. "A person placing his signature upon an instrument, otherwise than as maker, drawer, or acceptor, is deemed to be an indorser, unless he clearly indicates by appropriate words his **intention to be bound in some other capacity.**" (U.N.I. Act, § 63.)

This intention must be made clear and distinct by appropriate language. (170 Fed. 434.) The **president of a corporation** by writing his mere name upon the back of a note, without addition of any qualifying language, becomes an indorser within the meaning of this section. (163 N.Y.S. 97.)

Indorsement Where Payable to Two or More Persons. "Where an instrument is payable to the order of two or more payees or indorsees who are not partners, all must indorse, unless the one indorsing has authority to indorse for the others." (U.N.I. Act, § 41.)

Indorsement Where Name Is Wrong. "Where the name of a payee or indorsee is wrongly designated or misspelled, he may indorse the instrument as therein described, adding, if he thinks fit, his proper signature." (U.N.I. Act, § 43.)

The Uniform Commercial Code provides that a transferee may require both signatures when paying value for the instrument.

EFFECT OF INDORSEMENT BY INFANT OR CORPORATION. "The indorsement or assignment of the instrument by a corporation or by an infant passes the property therein, notwithstanding that from want of capacity, the corporation or infant may incur no liability thereon." (U.N.I. Act, § 22.)

FORGED INDORSEMENT. If an instrument is not payable to bearer, so that the indorsement of the payee is required, title thereto cannot be transferred if the indorsement of the payee is forged and any bank or person making payment on the forged indorsement does so at his own peril. (85 N.E. 829; 112 F. 2d 409.)

Bearer Instruments. If an instrument is payable to bearer, since it may be negotiated without indorsement, the forgery of an indorsement on such an instrument does not preclude a transferee from acquiring good title thereto. (85 N.E. 829.)

Certification of Check with Forged Indorsement. If a wrong-doing forger procures certification of a check, funds represented thereby do not pass from the drawer and he can recover the same from the bank that has charged such debit to his account. (112 N.E. 1053).

Bank's Liability for Payment. A bank paying on a forged check indorsement to a person other than the payee gives the depositor an action against the bank. (33 N.Y.S. 2d 885; 246 N.W. 178.) A bank depositor is under a duty to detect forgeries of his **own signature,** but ordinarily he is in no position to know the **signatures of payees** and he therefore is under no duty to detect forged indorsements. (39 N.E. 2d 897.)

STRIKING OUT INDORSEMENT. "The holder may at any time strike out any indorsement which is not necessary to his title. The indorser whose indorsement is struck out, and all indorsers subsequent to him, are thereby **relieved from liability** on the instrument." (U.N.I. Act, § 48.)

TRANSFER WITHOUT INDORSEMENT. "Where the holder of an instrument payable to his order transfers it for value without indorsing it, the transfer vests in the transferee such title as the transferor had therein, and the transferee acquires, in addition, the right to have the indorsement of the transferor. But for the purpose of determining whether the transferee is a holder in due course, the negotiation takes effect as of the time when the indorsement is actually made." (U.N.I. Act, § 49.) As to depositary banks, the Code provides the bank may supply the missing indorsement of its depositor.

WHEN PRIOR PARTY MAY NEGOTIATE INSTRUMENT. "Where an instrument is negotiated back to a prior party, such party may, subject to the provisions of this Act, reissue and further negotiate the same. But he is not entitled to enforce payment thereof against any **intervening party** to whom he was personally liable." (U.N.I. Act, § 50.)

Rights, Liabilities, and Warranties

WHAT CONSTITUTES HOLDER IN DUE COURSE. "A holder in due course is a holder who has taken the instrument under the following conditions:

1. That it is complete and regular upon its face;
2. That he became the holder of it before it was overdue, and without notice that it had been previously dishonored, if such was the fact;
3. That he took it in good faith and for value;
4. That at the time it was negotiated to him, he had no notice of any infirmity in the instrument or defect in the title of the person negotiating it." (U.N.I. Act, § 52.)

A holder **for value** of an instrument is to be distinguished from a holder in due course. A holder in due course is one who has no notice of any defect in the title of the person negotiating the instrument. (143 N.Y.S. 762; 173 Va. 168.) A purchaser who takes a negotiable instrument with unfilled blanks is put on inquiry and may not become a holder in due course. (25 N.Y.S. 2nd 157; 220 Mass. 445.) Ordinarily a payee of a negotiable instrument will not be in the position of a holder in due course under the Uniform Negotiable Instruments Act. (173 N.Y. App. Div. 821; 192 N.C. 330.)

A **bank discounting paper** and merely placing the amount to the credit of the customer does not become a holder in due course. (180 N.Y. 346.) But if the sum so credited is drawn on, the bank becomes a holder in due course to that extent.

The requirements of a holder in due course are changed to some extent by the Uniform Commercial Code:

(1) A holder in due course is a holder who takes the instrument
   (a) for value; and
   (b) in good faith; and
   (c) without notice that it is overdue or has been dishonored or of any defense against or claim to it on the part of any person.
(2) A payee may be a holder in due course.
(3) A holder does not become a holder in due course of an instrument:
   (a) by purchase of it at judicial sale or by taking it under legal process; or
   (b) by acquiring it in taking over an estate; or
   (c) by purchasing it as a part of a bulk transaction not in regular course of business of the transferor.
(4) A purchaser of a limited interest can be a holder in due course only to the extent of the interest purchased (§ 3–302.)

What Constitutes Holder for Value. "Where value has at any time been given for the instrument, the holder is deemed a holder for value in respect to all parties who became such prior to that time." (U.N.I. Act, § 26.)

"Where the **holder has a lien** on the instrument, arising either from contract or by implication of law, he is deemed a holder for value to the extent of his lien." (U.N.I. Act, § 27.)

The above is enlarged by the Uniform Commercial Code as follows:

"A holder takes the instrument for value

   (a) to the extent that the agreed consideration has been performed or that he acquires a security interest in or a lien on the instrument otherwise than by legal process; or
   (b) when he takes the instrument in payment of or as security for an antecedent claim against any person whether or not the claim is due; or
   (c) when he gives a negotiable instrument for it or makes an irrevocable commitment to a third person." (§ 3–303.)

ALL HOLDERS PRESUMED HOLDERS IN DUE COURSE BUT STATUS MAY BE CHALLENGED. "Every holder is deemed prima facie to be a holder in due course; but when it is shown that the title of any person who has negotiated the instrument was defective, the burden is on the holder to prove that he or some person under whom he claims, acquired the title as holder in due course. But the last mentioned rule does not apply in favor of a party who became bound on the instrument **prior to the acquisition** of such defective title." (U.N.I. Act, § 59.)

Person Not Deemed Holder in Due Course. "Where an instrument payable on demand is negotiated an **unreasonable length of time** after its issue, the holder is not deemed a holder in due course." (U.N.I. Act, § 53.)

The Uniform Commercial Code says a reasonable time is thirty days.

Notice Before Full Amount Is Paid. "Where the transferee receives notice of any infirmity in the instrument or defect in the title of the person negotiating the same, before he has paid the full amount agreed to be paid therefor, he will be deemed a holder in due course only to the extent of the amount theretofore paid by him." (U.N.I. Act, § 54.)

WHEN TITLE IS DEFECTIVE. "The title of a person who negotiates an instrument is defective within the meaning of this Act when he obtained the instrument, or any signature thereto, by fraud, duress, or force and fear, or other unlawful means, or for an illegal consideration, or when he negotiates it in breach of faith, or under such circumstances as amounts to a fraud." (U.N.I. Act, § 55.)

A Federal Reserve bank that accepted for collection a check that had been indorsed "For Deposit" by the payee, and subsequently by another in blank, was liable to the true owner for loss for "bad faith" in failing to inquire into the significance of the indorsement. (14 N.E. 2d 46.)

Notice of Defect. "To constitute notice of an infirmity in the instrument or defect in the title of the person negotiating the same, the person to whom it is negotiated must have had **actual knowledge** of the infirmity or defect, or knowledge of such facts that his action in taking the instrument amounted to bad faith." (U.N.I. Act, § 56. See Section 95, N.Y. Negotiable Instruments Law, for a stricter section.) For actual notice see 102 U.S. 442; 148 N.Y. 652.

The transferee is not required to make an inquiry. (175 Minn. 287; 150 N.Y. 59.) A **purchase at a discount,** even though it is large, is not sufficient to deprive the holder of the rights of a holder in due course. If, however, the discount is very large and there are other factors, they may be considered together to determine if he became a holder in good faith. (156 N.Y. App. Div. 9.)

The Uniform Commercial Code is much more specific wherein it provides:

(1) The purchaser has notice of a claim or defense if
    (a) the instrument is so incomplete, bears such visible evidence of forgery or alteration, or is otherwise so irregular as to call into question its validity, terms or ownership or to create an ambiguity as to the party to pay; or
    (b) the purchaser has notice that the obligation of any party is voidable in whole or in part, or that all parties have been discharged.

(2) The purchaser has notice of a claim against the instrument when he has knowledge that a fiduciary has negotiated the instrument in payment of or as security for his own debt or in any transaction for his own benefit or otherwise in breach of duty.

(3) The purchaser has notice that an instrument is **overdue** if he has reason to know
    (a) that any part of the principal amount is overdue or that there is an uncured default in payment of another instrument of the same series; or
    (b) that acceleration of the instrument has been made; or
    (c) that he is taking a demand instrument after demand has been made or more than a reasonable length of time after the issue. A reasonable time for a check drawn and payable within the states and territories of the United States and the District of Columbia is presumed to be thirty days.

(4) Knowledge of the following facts does not of itself give the purchaser notice of a defense or claim
    (a) that the instrument is antedated or postdated;
    (b) that it was issued or negotiated in return for an executory promise or accompanied by a separate agreement, unless the purchaser has notice that a defense or claim has arisen from the terms thereof;
    (c) that any party has assigned for accommodation;
    (d) that an incomplete instrument has been completed, unless the purchaser has notice of any improper completion;
    (e) that any person negotiating the instrument is or was a fiduciary;
    (f) that there has been default in payment of interest on the instrument or in payment of any other instrument, except one of the same series.

(5) The filing or recording of a document does not of itself constitute notice within the provisions of this Article to a person who would otherwise be a holder in due course.

RIGHTS, LIABILITIES, AND WARRANTIES

(6) To be effective notice must be received at such time and in such manner as to give a reasonable opportunity to act on it.

(7) In any event, to constitute notice of a claim or defense, the purchaser must have knowledge of the claim or defense or knowledge of such facts that his action in taking the instrument amounts to bad faith. If the **purchaser is an organization** and maintains within the organization reasonable routines for communicating significant information to the appropriate part of the organization apparently concerned, the individual conducting the transaction on behalf of the purchaser must have the knowledge. (§ 3–304.)

RIGHTS OF HOLDER IN DUE COURSE. "A holder in due course holds the instrument free from any defect of title of prior parties, and free from defenses available to prior parties among themselves, and may enforce payment of the instrument for the full amount thereof against all parties liable thereon." (U.N.I. Act, § 57.) The holder of a note is presumed to be the owner thereof (49 N.E. 1101), and he may sue thereon in his own name. (U.N.I. Act, § 51.)

The Uniform Commercial Code § 3–304 (supra page 16) would seem to qualify this to some extent. The code also specifies:

"To the extent that a holder is a holder in due course he takes the instrument free from

(1) all claims to it on the part of any person; and
(2) all defenses of any party to the instrument with whom the holder has not dealt except
  (a) infancy, to the extent that it is a defense to a simple contract; and
  (b) such other incapacity, or duress, or illegality of the transaction, as renders the obligation of the party a nullity; and
  (c) such misrepresentation as has induced the party to sign the instrument with neither knowledge nor reasonable opportunity to obtain knowledge of its character or its essential terms; and
  (d) discharge in insolvency proceedings; and
  (e) any other discharge of which the holder has notice when he takes the instrument." (§ 3–305.)

WHEN A NEGOTIABLE INSTRUMENT IS SUBJECT TO ORIGINAL DEFENSES. "In the hands of any holder other than a holder in due course, a negotiable instrument is subject to the same defenses as if it were nonnegotiable. But a holder who derives his title through a holder in due course and who is not himself a party to any fraud or illegality affecting the instrument, has all the rights of such former holder in respect of all parties prior to the latter." (U.N.I. Act, § 58.)

The Uniform Commercial Code provides:

"Unless he has the right of a holder in due course any person takes the instrument subject to

(a) all valid claims to it on the part of any person; and. . . .
(d) the defense that he or a person through whom he holds the instrument acquired it by theft, or that payment or satisfaction to such holder would be inconsistent with the terms of a restrictive indorsement. The claim of any **third person** to the instrument is not otherwise available as a defense to any party liable thereon unless the third person himself defends the action for such party." (§ 3–306.)

A **transferee** of a negotiable instrument who is not a holder in due course and who did not acquire the instrument from one who is takes a title that is subject to the equities between the original parties. (182 La. 649; 2 N.Y. App. Div. 240.) Because a past due note has passed through innocent hands before maturity and is thus free from equitable defenses, it is of no consequence that one who acquires it after its maturity may have had notice of an original infirmity. (150 Pac. 571.)

LIABILITY OF PARTIES IN CONNECTION WITH NEGOTIABLE INSTRUMENTS. Liability attaches to persons concerned as makers, drawers, acceptors, indorsers, or otherwise handling negotiable instruments.

Liability of Maker. "The maker of a negotiable instrument by making it, engages that he will pay it according to its tenor; and admits the existence of the payee and his then capacity to indorse." (U.N.I. Act, § 60.)

The maker of a note is **jointly liable** on the note with the **co-maker.** (19 N.Y.S. 2d 457.) The maker is **primarily liable** even though he signs only for accommodation. (81 Ohio State 348.)

Liability of Drawer. "The drawer by drawing the instrument, admits the existence of the payee and his then capacity to indorse and engages that on due presentment the instrument will be accepted or paid, or both, according to its tenor, and that if it be dishonored and the necessary proceedings on dishonor be duly taken, he will pay the amount thereof to the holder, or to any subsequent indorser who may be compelled to pay it. But the drawer may insert in the instrument an **express stipulation negativing or limiting** his own liability to the holder." (U.N.I. Act, § 61.)

The distinction between checks and bills of exchange, as respects drawer's obligations, is founded upon mercantile custom and is destroyed by this Section. (280 N.Y. 135.)

Liability of Acceptor. "The acceptor by accepting the instrument, engages that he will pay it according to the tenor of his acceptance; and admits:

1. The existence of the drawer, the genuineness of his signature, and his capacity and authority to draw the instrument; and
2. The existence of the payee and his then capacity to indorse." (U.N.I. Act, § 62.)

Although the drawee of a bill is bound to know the signature of the drawer, he is not required to have any knowledge of the signature of the payee. If the drawee pays a draft on a forged indorsement and thereby is unable to charge the payment against the drawer, he is entitled to recover the money from the one to whom it was paid. (91 N.Y. 74.)

The acceptor is estopped from asserting the incapacity of the drawer if the instrument is drawn by an infant, married woman, or a corporation without such power. (54 Penn. State 302.) The drawee cannot hold the drawer if the acceptance was for accommodation until the drawee has paid the instrument. (80 Virginia 369.) The Uniform Commercial Code makes more definite the liability of the various parties:

(1) The **maker** or **acceptor** engages that he will pay the instrument according to its tenor at the time of his engagement or as completed pursuant to Section 3–115 on incomplete instruments.

(3) By making, drawing or accepting the party admits as against all subsequent parties including the drawee the existence of the payee and his then capacity to indorse. (§ 3–413.)

Liability of Guarantor. The Uniform Commercial Code seems to add a new statutory form of liability for a guarantor:

(1) **Payment guaranteed** or equivalent words added to a signature mean that the signer engages that if the instrument is not paid when due he will pay it according to its tenor without resort by the holder to any other party.

(2) **Collection guaranteed** or equivalent words added to a signature mean that the signer engages that if the instrument is not paid when due he will pay it according to its tenor, but only after the holder has reduced his claim against the maker or acceptor to judgment and execution has been returned unsatisfied, or after the maker or acceptor has become insolvent or it is otherwise apparent that it is useless to proceed against him.

(3) Words of guaranty which do not otherwise specify guarantee payment.

(4) No words of guaranty added to the signature of a sole maker or acceptor affect his liability on the instrument. Such words added to the signature of one of two or more makers or acceptors create a presumption that the signature is for the accommodation of the others.

(5) When words of guaranty are used presentment, notice of dishonor and protest are not necessary to charge the user.

(6) Any guaranty written on the instrument is enforceable notwithstanding any statute of frauds. (§ 3–416.)

LIABILITY OF INDORSER. Every indorser who indorses without qualification warrants to all subsequent holders in due course:

1. The matters and things mentioned in Subdivisions 1, 2 and 3 of the section below on Warranties; and
2. That the instrument is at the time of his indorsement valid and subsisting. And in addition, he engages that on due presentment, it shall be accepted or paid, or both, as the case may be, according to its tenor, and that if it be dishonored, and the necessary proceedings on dishonor be duly taken, he will pay the amount thereof to the holder, or to any subsequent indorser who may be compelled to pay it. (U.N.I. Act, § 66.)

Thus the obligation of the indorser is that, if the maker fails to pay, he, the indorser, is obligated if the proper steps are taken. (109 N.E. 481; 163 Cal. 485.)

An indorser guarantees the genuineness of all prior indorsements. (223 N.W. 780; 281 N.Y. 162.) Likewise the indorser of a check under forged indorsements of payees warrants the genuineness of the indorsements of the payees. (286 N.Y.S. 859.) The fact is that each indorsement of a promissory note is a **separate contract**, standing apart from that of the maker or any other indorser. (75 N.E. 1103.)

Liability of Indorser Where Paper Is Negotiable by Delivery. "Where a person places his indorsement on an instrument negotiable by delivery, he incurs all the liabilities of an indorser." (U.N.I. Act, § 67.)

Order in Which Indorsers Are Liable. "As respects one another, indorsers are liable prima facie in the order in which they indorse; but evidence is admissible to show that as between or among themselves, they have agreed otherwise. **Joint payees** or **joint indorsees** who indorse are deemed to indorse jointly and severally." (U.N.I. Act, § 68.)

In the absence of an agreement between two accommodation indorsers that they shall be liable between themselves as co-sureties, they are liable in the order that their names appear. (9 N.E. 109.)

Liability of Irregular Indorser. "Where a person not otherwise a party to an instrument, places thereon his signature in blank before delivery, he is liable as indorser in accordance with the following rules:

1. If the instrument is payable to the order of a third person, he is liable to the payee and to all subsequent parties.
2. If the instrument is payable to the order of the maker or drawer, or is payable to bearer, he is liable to all parties subsequent to the maker or drawer.

3. If he signs for the accommodation of the payee, he is liable to all parties subsequent to the payee." (U.N.I. Act, § 64.)

By this section a prior rule that an irregular indorser was presumed to be a second indorser was changed. Such an indorser is now presumed to be liable in several different situations according to the language of this section. (192 N.Y. 499; 85 N.E. 682.)

LIABILITY OF ACCOMMODATION PARTY. "An accommodation party is one who has signed the instrument as maker, drawer, acceptor, or indorser, without receiving value therefor, and for the purpose of lending his name to some other person. Such a person is liable on the instrument to a holder for value, notwithstanding such holder at the time of taking the instrument knew him to be only an accommodation party." (U.N.I. Act, § 29.)

The Uniform Commercial Code enlarges and clarifies the liability of an accommodation party as follows:

(1) An accommodation party is one who signs the instrument in any capacity for the purpose of lending his name to another party to it.

(2) When the instrument has been taken for value before it is due the accommodation party is liable in the capacity in which he has signed even though the taker knows of the accommodation.

(3) As against a holder in due course and without notice of the accommodation **oral proof** of the accommodation is not admissible to give the accommodation party the benefit of discharges dependent on his character as such. In other cases the accomodation character may be shown by oral proof.

(4) An indorsement which shows that it is not in the chain of title is notice of its accommodation character.

(5) An accommodation party is not liable to the party accommodated, and if he pays the instrument has a right of recourse on the instrument against such party.

(6) An accommodation party warrants to any subsequent holder who is not the party accommodated and who takes the instrument in good faith that
   (a) all signatures are genuine or authorized; and
   (b) the instrument has not been materially altered; and
   (c) all prior parties had capacity to contract; and
   (d) he has no knowledge of any insolvency proceeding instituted with respect to the maker or acceptor or the drawer of an unaccepted instrument.
   (§ 3–415.)

An **accommodation maker is liable primarily** to **the payee** or his assignee, and is not liable merely as a surety. (245 N.Y.S. 372; 159 N.W. 737.)

If one **indorses** a note for the accommodation of the maker, he becomes a mere surety. (131 N.Y.S. 157; 28 R.I. 338.)

Corporations are without power to become accommodation parties. (55 Fed. 465; 211 N.Y. 154.)

A **partner** has no power to indorse the firm name for the accommodation of a third party. (44 N.Y. 680.)

A holder for value of a negotiable instrument is entitled to recover the amount thereof from an accommodation indorser, although he knew at the time of taking the instrument that it was accommodation paper. (73 N.E. 1129.)

LIABILITY OF PERSON SIGNING AS AGENT. "Where the instrument contains or a person adds to his signature words indicating that he signs for or on behalf of a principal, or in a **representative capacity,** he is not liable on the instrument if he was **duly authorized;** but the mere addition of words describing him as an agent, or as filling a representative character, without disclosing his principal, does not exempt him from personal liability." (U.N.I. Act, § 20.)

If an agent signs an instrument with the addition of words that are merely descriptive and the payee knows that such person is merely acting as agent for another and that he does not intend to bind himself individually, the agent is not personally liable to the payee. (107 N.Y. App. Div. 491.)

Signature by Corporate Officers. If a note is signed not in the name of the corporation, but in the name of an officer with an addition of the office he holds, the name of the office is deemed merely descriptive, and the officer is, as against a holder in due course of the instrument, liable individually and the corporation is not liable. (44 N.E. 1038.)

If, however, the instrument is subscribed with the name of a corporation and the name of an individual with the designation "Treas.," it is an obligation of the corporation, not of the Treasurer individually. (66 N.Y. 145.)

LIABILITY OF PERSON SIGNING IN TRADE OR ASSUMED NAME.
One who signs in a trade or assumed name will be liable to the same extent as if he had signed in his own name. (U.N.I. Act, § 18.)

WARRANTIES. "Every person negotiating an instrument by **delivery** or by a **qualified indorsement** warrants:

1. That the instrument is genuine and in all respects what it purports to be;
2. That he has good title to it;
3. That all prior parties had capacity to contract;
4. That he has no knowledge of any fact which would impair the validity of the instrument or render it valueless. But when the negotiation is by delivery only, the warranty extends in favor of no holder other than the immediate transferee. The provisions of subdivision 3 of this section do not apply to persons negotiating public or corporate securities, other than bills and notes." (U.N.I. Act, § 65.)

A transferor of negotiable paper by assigning without indorsement warrants under this section only against his own knowledge of invalidity and not against the fact of invalidity. This is true whether the instrument be bearer paper or unindorsed order paper. (48 Fed. 2d 574.)

The Uniform Commercial Code enlarges this section to read:

(2) Any person who transfers an instrument and receives consideration warrants to his transferee and if the transfer is by indorsement to any subsequent holder who takes the instrument in good faith that
    (a) he has a good title to the instrument or is authorized to obtain payment or acceptance on behalf of one who has a good title and the transfer is otherwise rightful; and
    (b) all signatures are genuine or authorized; and
    (c) the instrument has not been materially altered; and
    (d) no defense of any party is good against him; and
    (e) he has no knowledge of any insolvency proceeding instituted with respect to the maker or acceptor or the drawer of an unaccepted instrument.
(3) By transferring "without recourse" the transferor limits the obligation stated in subsection (2) (d) to a warranty that he has no knowledge of such a defense.
(4) A selling agent or broker who does not disclose the fact that he is acting only as such gives the warranties provided in this section, but if he makes such disclosure warrants only his good faith and authority. (§ 3–417 (2), (3), 4).)

Although it is a rule that, upon the sale of a note, there is an implied warranty by the vendor of the **genuineness** of the instrument, no warranty will be implied if the contract of sale was made in such form as to exclude the warranty of genuineness, as when the vendor expressly declines to warrant the genuineness of the note. (60 N.Y. 528.)

The seller of a **forged instrument** is liable to the purchaser even though he acted in good faith. (232 S.W. 456.)

WARRANTIES ON PRESENTMENT AND TRANSFER. The Uniform Commercial Code provides the following:

(1) Any person who obtains payment or acceptance and any prior transferor warrants to a person who in good faith pays or accepts that
    (a) he has a good title to the instrument or is authorized to obtain payment or acceptance on behalf of one who has a good title; and
    (b) he has no knowledge that the signature of the maker or drawer is unauthorized, except that this warranty is not given by a holder in due course acting in good faith
        (i) to a maker with respect to the maker's own signature; or
        (ii) to a drawer with respect to the drawer's own signature, whether or or not the drawer is also the drawee; or
        (iii) to an acceptor of a draft if the holder in due course took the draft after the acceptance or obtained the acceptance without knowledge that the drawer's signature was unauthorized; and
    (c) the instrument has not been materially altered, except that this warranty is not given by a holder in due course acting in good faith
        (i) to the maker of a note; or
        (ii) to the drawer of a draft whether or not the drawer is also the drawee; or
        (iii) to the acceptor of a draft with respect to an alteration made prior to the acceptance if the holder in due course took the draft after the acceptance, even though the acceptance provided "payable as originally drawn" or equivalent terms; or
        (iv) to the acceptor of a draft with respect to an alteration made after the acceptance. (§ 3–417 (1).)

Presentment, Payment, Notice of Dishonor, Protest, and Discharge

"PRESENTMENT." Presentment is a demand for acceptance or payment made upon the maker, acceptor, drawee, or other payor by or on behalf of the holder (U. C. Code, § 3–504 (1)).

WHEN PRESENTMENT FOR PAYMENT IS NECESSARY. "Presentment for payment is not necessary in order to charge the person primarily liable on the instrument; . . . But except as herein otherwise provided, presentment for payment is necessary in order to charge the drawer and indorsers." (U.N.I. Act, § 70.)

In essence, this means that presentment is necessary only to fix the liability of the parties who are **secondarily liable.** The maker or acceptor, being a primary obligor, remains liable even though the instrument is not presented for payment. The only effect that nonpresentment has on the primary parties is to stop the running of interest as against them. Indorsers and secondary parties may waive the necessity of presentment. (22 N.E. 371.)

The Uniform Commercial Code modifies this provision as follows:

(1) Presentment is necessary to charge secondary parties as follows . . . .
    (b) presentment for payment is necessary to charge any indorser;
    (c) in the case of any drawer, the acceptor of a draft payable at a bank or the maker of a note payable at a bank, presentment for payment is neces-

sary, but failure to make presentment discharges such drawer, acceptor or maker only in very special circumstances and then only to a limited degree as stated in 3–502 (1) (b)

(4) Notwithstanding any provision of this section, neither presentment nor notice of dishonor nor protest is necessary to charge an indorser who has indorsed an instrument **after maturity.** (§ 3–501.)

PRESENTMENT FOR ACCEPTANCE. See discussion below under Bills of Exchange, p. 31.

WHEN PRESENTMENT FOR PAYMENT MAY BE DISPENSED WITH. "Presentment for payment is dispensed with:

1. Where, after the exercise of reasonable diligence, presentment as required by this Act cannot be made;
2. Where the drawee is a fictitious person;
3. By waiver of presentment expressed or implied." (U.N.I. Act. § 82.)

The insolvency of a maker or acceptor does not dispense with the necessity for presentment. (68 N.W. 677; 27 N.E. 251.)

"Presentment for payment is not required in order to charge the indorser where the instrument was made or accepted for his **accommodation,** and he has no reason to expect that the instrument will be paid if presented." (U.N.I. Act, § 80.)

Under the U. C. Code, presentment may be entirely excused in the following circumstances:

(2) Presentment or notice or protest as the case may be is entirely **excused** when
  (a) the party to be charged has waived it expressly or by implication either before or after it is due; or
  (b) such party has himself dishonored the instrument or has countermanded payment or otherwise has no reason to expect or right to require that the instrument be accepted or paid; or
  (c) by reasonable diligence the presentment or protest cannot be made or the notice given.

(3) Presentment is also entirely excused when
  (a) the maker, acceptor or drawee of any instrument except a documentary draft is dead or in insolvency proceedings instituted after the issue of the instrument; or
  (b) acceptance or payment is refused but not for want of proper presentment. (§ 3–511.)

WHAT CONSTITUTES SUFFICIENT PRESENTMENT FOR PAYMENT. "Presentment for payment to be sufficient, must be made:

1. By the holder, or by some person authorized to receive payment on his behalf;
2. At a reasonable hour on a business day;
3. At a proper place as herein defined;
4. To the person primarily liable on the instrument, or if he is absent or inaccessible, to any person found at the place where the presentment is made." (U.N.I. Act, § 72.)

Under the U.C. Code presentment may be made:
  (a) by mail, in which event the time of presentment is determined by the time of receipt of the mail; or
  (b) through a clearing house; or
  (c) at the place of acceptance or payment specified in the instrument or if there be none at the place of business or residence of the party to accept or pay. If neither the party to accept or pay nor anyone authorized to act for him is present or accessible at such place presentment is excused.

(3) It may be made:
    (a) to any one of two or more makers, acceptors, drawees or other payers; or
    (b) to any person who has authority to make or refuse the acceptance or payment.

(4) It may be made as provided in Section 4–204; except as provided in that section, a draft accepted or a note made payable at a bank in the United States must be presented at such bank. (U.C. Code § 3–504.)

Time of Presentment. "Where the instrument is not payable on demand, presentation must be made on the day it falls due. Where it is **payable on demand**, presentment must be made within a reasonable time after its issue, except that in case of a bill of exchange, presentment for payment will be sufficient if made within a reasonable time after the last negotiation thereof." (U.N.I. Act, § 71.)

The Uniform Commercial Code enlarges this section as follows:

(1) Unless a different time is expressed in the instrument, the time for any presentment is determined as follows:
    (a) where an instrument is payable at or a fixed period after a stated date any presentment for acceptance must be made on or before the date it is payable;
    (b) where an instrument is payable after sight it must either be presented for acceptance or negotiated within a reasonable time after date or issue whichever is later;
    (c) where an instrument shows the date on which it is payable presentment for payment is due on that date;
    (d) where an instrument is accelerated presentment for payment is due within a reasonable time after the acceleration;
    (e) with respect to the liability of any secondary party presentment for acceptance or payment of any other instrument is due within a reasonable time after such party becomes liable thereon.

(2) A reasonable time for presentment is determined by the nature of the instrument, any usage of banking or trade and the facts of the particular case. In the case of an **uncertified check** which is drawn and payable within the United States and which is not a draft drawn by a bank the following are presumed to be reasonable periods within which to present for payment or to initiate bank collection:
    (a) with respect to the liability of the drawer, thirty days after date or issue whichever is later; and
    (b) with respect to the liability of an indorser, seven days after his indorsement.

(3) Where any presentment is due on a day which is not a full business day for either the person making presentment or the party to pay or accept, presentment is due on the next following day which is a full business day for both parties.

(4) Presentment to be sufficient must be made at a reasonable hour, and if at a bank during the banking day. (§ 3–503.)

Delay in Presentment. "Delay in making presentment for payment is excused when the delay is caused by circumstances beyond the control of the holder and not imputable to his default, misconduct or negligence. When the cause of delay ceases to operate, presentment must be made with reasonable diligence." (U.N.I. Act, § 81.)

RIGHTS OF PARTY TO WHOM PRESENTMENT IS MADE. Under the Uniform Commercial Code,

    (1) The party to whom presentment is made may without dishonor require
        (a) **exhibition** of the instrument [this is also true under the U.N.I. Act]; and
        (b) reasonable **identification** of the person making presentment and evidence of his authority to make it if made for another; and

(c) that the instrument be produced for acceptance or payment at a **place specified** in it, or if there be none at any place reasonable in the circumstances; and

(d) a signed **receipt** on the instrument for any partial or full payment and its surrender upon full payment.

(2) Failure to comply with any such requirement invalidates the presentment but the person presenting has a reasonable time in which to comply and the time for acceptance or payment runs from the time of compliance. (§ 3–505.)

WHAT CONSTITUTES PAYMENT IN DUE COURSE. "Payment is made in due course when it is made at or after the maturity of the instrument to the holder thereof in good faith and without notice that his title is defective." (U.N.I. Act, § 88.)

WHEN INSTRUMENT IS DISHONORED. "The instrument is dishonored by **non-payment** when:

1. It is duly presented for payment and payment is refused or cannot be obtained; or
2. Presentment is excused and the instrument is overdue and unpaid," (U.N.I. Act, § 83.)

The U. C. Code provides: "An instrument is dishonored when (a) a necessary or optional presentment is duly made and due acceptance or payment is refused or cannot be obtained within the prescribed time or in case of bank collections the instrument is seasonably returned by the midnight deadline" (§ 4–301).

Return of an instrument for lack of proper indorsement is not dishonor. (§ 3–507.)

NOTICE OF DISHONOR. "Except as is herein otherwise provided, when a negotiable instrument has been dishonored by non-acceptance or non-payment, notice of dishonor must be given to the drawer and to each indorser, and any drawer or indorser to whom such notice is not given is discharged." (U.N.I. Act, § 89.)

Such notice of dishonor is shown in the notice of protest, Fig. 7, page 27.

The object of the requirement of this notice of dishonor is to put the indorser in possession of the material facts on which his own liability is founded, so that he may take necessary measures for his own security against those who are liable to him. (22 N.E. 371.) Except when waived or excused, notice of dishonor is an essential element to hold the indorser of a negotiable instrument. (22 N.E. 371.) An **accommodation indorser,** to be held, most be given notice of dishonor like any other indorser. (279 N.Y. 775.) If a **note** is given to a bank for collection and it is dishonored, it is the duty of the bank to give notice of dishonor to its customer. (148 N.C. 362.)

The foregoing applies only to parties secondarily liable. A pure guarantor does not come under the rule requiring such notice. (2 N.Y. 225.)

"The notice may be given by or on behalf of the holder, or by or on behalf of any party to the instrument who might be compelled to pay it to the holder, and who, upon taking it up, would have a right to reimbursement from the party to whom the notice is given." (U.N.I. Act, § 90.)

Although a maker cannot on his behalf give a notice of dishonor, he may do it as an agent on behalf of the holder. (105 N.Y. App. Div. 433.) The notice must be given by either the holder or a duly constituted agent. (16 N.Y. 235.)

The Uniform Commercial Code enlarges this section by stating:

(1) Notice of dishonor may be given to any person who may be liable **on the instrument by or** on behalf of the holder or any party who has himself received

notice, or any other party who can be compelled to pay the instrument. In addition an agent or bank in whose hands the instrument is dishonored may give notice to his principal or customer or to another agent or bank from which the instrument was received.

(2) Any necessary notice must be given by a bank before its midnight deadline and by any other person before midnight of the third business day after dishonor or receipt of notice of dishonor.

(3) Notice may be given in any reasonable manner. It **may be oral or written** and in any terms which identify the instrument and state that it has been dishonored. A misdescription which does not mislead the party notified does not vitiate the notice. Sending the instrument bearing a stamp, ticket or writing stating that acceptance or payment has been refused or sending a notice of debit with respect to the instrument is sufficient.

(4) Written notice is given when sent although it is not received. . . .

(8) Notice operates for the benefit of all parties who have rights on the instrument against the party notified. (§ 3–508.)

Mere knowledge of dishonor is not equivalent to notice thereof. The notice must come from one entitled to look to the party for payment and must inform him that the note has been duly presented for payment, that it has been dishonored, and that the holder looks to him for payment. (279 N.Y. 775; 18 N.E. 2d 862.)

Where Notice Must Be Sent. "Where a party has added an address to his signature, notice of dishonor must be sent to that address; but if he has not given such address, then the notice must be sent as follows:

1. Either to the Post Office nearest to his place of residence, or to the Post Office where he is accustomed to receive his letters; or
2. If he live in one place, and have his place of business in another, notice may be sent to either place; or
3. If he is sojourning in another place, notice may be sent to the place where he is sojourning."

But if the notice is actually received by the party within the time specified in this act, it will be sufficient, though not sent in accordance with the requirements of this section. (U.N.I. Act, § 108.)

Notice to Subsequent Party; Time of Notice. "Where a party receives notice of dishonor, he has, after the receipt of such notice, the same time for giving notice to antecedent parties that the holder has after the dishonor." (U.N.I. Act, § 107.)

WAIVER OF NOTICE. "Notice of dishonor may be waived, either before the time of giving notice has arrived or after the omission to give due notice, and waiver may be expressed or implied." (U.N.I. § 109.) (See Fig. 6.)

I, John Doe, do hereby, for value received, waive demand, notice of demand, and nonpayment, protest, and notice of protest of the within note. Dated, June 1st, 19—.

John Doe

Fig. 6. Waiver of demand and notice by indorser.

The liability of an indorser generally depends upon the **implied conditions** that the instrument shall be duly presented at its maturity and that notice of dishonor shall be transmitted to the indorser. But these conditions are for the benefit of the indorser and may be waived by him, either verbally, in writing **or** as a result of implication and usage, or from any understanding between the parties that is sufficient to prove the waiver. (22 N.E. 371.)

Who Is Affected by Waiver. "Where the waiver is embodied in the instrument itself, it is binding upon all parties; but where it is written above the signature of an indorser, it binds him only." (U.N.I. Act, § 110.)

Waiver of Protest. "A waiver of protest, whether in the case of a foreign bill of exchange or other negotiable instrument, is deemed to be a waiver not only of a formal protest, but also of presentment and notice of dishonor." (U.N.I. Act, § 111.)

WHEN NOTICE IS DISPENSED WITH. "Notice of dishonor is dispensed with when, after the exercise of **reasonable diligence,** it cannot be given to or does not reach the parties sought to be charged." (U.N.I. Act, § 112.)

It has been held that if the indorser had no place of residence that the reasonable diligence of the holder could enable him to discover, the law would dispense with giving regular notice. (7 N.Y. 266.) If a holder does not know or cannot find the address of the maker, he is under a duty to inquire for it of the other parties to the instrument. (48 N.Y. App. Div. 188.)

When Notice Need Not Be Given Drawer. "Notice of dishonor is not required to be given to the drawer in either of the following cases:

1. Where the drawer and drawee are the same person;
2. Where the drawee is a fictitious person or a person not having capacity to contract;
3. Where the drawer is the person to whom the instrument is presented for payment;
4. Where the drawer has no right to expect or require that the drawee or acceptor will honor the instrument;
5. Where the drawer has countermanded payment." (U.N.I. Act, § 114.)

Notice of Non-payment Where Acceptance Is Refused. "Where due notice of dishonor by non-acceptance has been given, notice of a subsequent dishonor by non-payment is not necessary, unless in the meantime the instrument has been accepted." (U.N.I. Act, § 116.)

PROTEST. "Where any negotiable instrument has been dishonored, it may be protested for non-acceptance or non-payment, as the case may be; but protest

---

To John Doe:

Please take notice that a note made by Richard Roe for the sum of One hundred dollars, dated June 1st, 1946, payable thirty days after date to Ben Boe or his order and indorsed by you, has been presented by me, at the request of the holders thereof, to Richard Roe at No. 1 Fifth Avenue, Borough of Manhattan, City of New York, and that payment being duly demanded, was refused, whereupon, by direction of such holders, the same has been protested by me, and payment thereof is hereby requested of you.

July 1st, 19—.
  (Seal)

                              Henry Hoe
                    Notary Public New York County No. 1
                    Register No. 1-H-1
                    Commission expires March 30, 19—.

Fig. 7. Notice of protest.

is not required except in the case of **foreign bills of exchange**." (U.N.I. Act, § 118.) A notice of protest is shown in Fig. 7.

Formal protest by a notary public is not essential to hold the indorser of a promissory note. (138 N.Y. App. Div. 339.) Although protest is not legally required in the case of nonpayment of inland bills of exchange, it is desirable to have a **certificate of a notary** setting forth presentation and demand for payment where it may become necessary to bring legal action. Without such certificate, it is sometimes difficult to prove these facts in court. (240 Pa. State 328.) A certificate of service of notice of protest is shown in Fig. 8.

United States of America, ⎫
State of New York, ⎬ ss:
County of New York, ⎭

I, John Doe, a notary public of the State of New York, duly commissioned and sworn, do hereby certify, that on the 1st day of June, 19—, due notice of the protest of the before mentioned bill was served on Richard Roe personally, and upon Ben Boe, by putting the same into the post-office directed to him at No. 1 Fifth Avenue, New York City, which place was the reputed residence of the person to whom the notice was directed, and the post-office address nearest thereto, and that said notice was mailed at Hudson River Station Post-office, New York City, in a sealed envelope with postage prepaid.

(Seal)

John Doe
Notary Public, New York County No. 1
Register No. 1–D–1
Commission expires March 30, 19—.

Fig. 8. Certificate of service of notice of protest.

DISCHARGE. "A negotiable instrument is discharged:

1. By payment in due course by or on behalf of the principal debtor;
2. By payment in due course by the party accommodated, where the instrument is made or accepted for accommodation;
3. By the intentional cancellation thereof by the holder;
4. By any other act which will discharge a simple contract for the payment of money;
5. When the principal debtor becomes the holder of the instrument at or after maturity in his own right." (U.N.I. Act, § 119.)

The words in subdivision 5 "in his own right" merely exclude such a case as that of a maker acquiring the instrument in a representative capacity. (94 N.Y. App. Div. 474.)

The Uniform Commercial Code states:

(1) The liability of any party is discharged to the extent of his payment or satisfaction to the holder even though it is made with knowledge of a claim of another person to the instrument unless prior to such payment or satisfaction the person making the claim either supplies indemnity deemed adequate by the party seeking the discharge or enjoins payment or satisfaction by order of a court of competent jurisdiction in an action in which the adverse claimant and the holder are parties. This subsection does not, however, result in the discharge of the liability
    (a) of a party who in bad faith pays or satisfies a holder who acquired the instrument by theft or who (unless having the rights of a holder in due course) holds through one who so acquired it; or

(b) of a party (other than an intermediary bank or a payor bank which is not a depositary bank) who pays or satisfies the holder of an instrument which has been restrictively indorsed in a manner not consistent with the terms of such restrictive indorsement.

(2) Payment or satisfaction may be made with the consent of the holder by any person including a stranger to the instrument. Surrender of the instrument to such a person gives him the rights of a transferee (Section 3–201). (Code Art. 3–603.)

The payment of an **accommodation note** by the party accommodated discharges the instrument. (101 N.Y.S. 101.) One of two co-makers, who signed for the accommodation of the other, can pay the instrument and recover on it against his co-maker who received the consideration. (281 Fed. 715.)

When Persons Secondarily Liable Are Discharged. "A person secondarily liable on the instrument is discharged:

1. By any act which discharges the instrument;
2. By the intentional cancellation of his signature by the holder;
3. By the discharge of a prior party;
4. By a valid tender of payment made by a prior party;
5. By a release of the principal debtor, unless the holder's right of recourse against the parties secondarily liable is expressly reserved;
6. By any agreement binding upon the holder to extend the time of payment or to postpone the holder's right to enforce the instrument, unless made with the assent of the party secondarily liable, or unless the right of recourse against such party is expressly reserved." (U.N.I. Act, § 120.)

The Uniform Commercial Code enlarges on the question of cancellation and renunciation:

"(1) The holder of an instrument may even without consideration discharge any party

(a) in any manner apparent on the face of the instrument or the indorsement, as by intentionally cancelling the instrument or the party's signature by destruction or mutilation, or by striking out the party's signature; or
(b) by renouncing his rights by a writing signed and delivered or by surrender of the instrument to the party to be discharged."

Any act that discharges a prior indorser discharges all subsequent indorsers for the reason, that on making payment, each indorser is entitled to have recourse to all indorsers preceding him. (174 N.Y. 222.) The giving of any security by the maker or prior indorser for the payment is not payment, nor does it discharge subsequent indorsers. (176 Pa. State 513.) An **extension of time** made after the maturity of a note will discharge the indorser. (143 N.Y.S. 1017.)

Right of Party Who Discharges Instrument. "Where the instrument is paid by a party secondarily liable thereon, it is not discharged; but the party so paying it is remitted to his former rights as regards all prior parties, and he may strike out his own and all subsequent indorsements, and again negotiate the instrument, except:

1. Where it is payable to the order of a third person, and has been paid by the drawer; and
2. Where it was made or accepted for accommodation and has been paid by the party accommodated." (U.N.I. Act, § 121.)

Renunciation of Rights by Holder. "The holder may expressly renounce his rights against any party to the instrument, before, at or after its maturity. An absolute and unconditional renunciation of his rights against the principal debtor, made at or after the maturity of the instrument, discharges the instrument. But a renunciation does not affect the rights of a holder in due course without notice. A renunciation must be **in writing**, unless the instrument is delivered up to the person primarily liable thereon." (U.N.I. Act, § 122.)

Bills of Exchange

NATURE OF BILLS OF EXCHANGE. "A bill of exchange is an unconditional order in writing addressed by one person to another, signed by the person giving it, requiring the person to whom it is addressed to pay on demand or at a fixed or determinable future time a sum certain in money to order or to bearer." (U.N.I. Act, § 126.) Fig. 2, p. 2 above, illustrates a typical bill of exchange.

Bill Not an Assignment of Funds in the Hands of Drawee. "A bill of itself does not operate as an assignment of the funds in the hands of the drawee available for the payment thereof, and the drawee is not liable on the bill unless and until he accepts the same." (U.N.I. Act, § 127.)

The Uniform Commercial Code enlarges this section by stating:

(2) Nothing in this section shall affect any liability in contract, tort or otherwise arising from any letter of credit or other obligation or representation which is not an acceptance. (§ 3–409.)

Bill Addressed to More Than One Drawee. "A bill may be addressed to two or more drawees jointly, whether they are partners or not; but not to two or more drawees in the alternative or in succession." (U.N.I. Act, § 128.)

When Bill May Be Treated As Promissory Note. "Where in a bill, the drawer and drawee are the **same person**, or where the drawee is a **fictitious person**, or a **person not having capacity** to contract, the holder may treat the instrument at his option, either as a bill of exchange or a promissory note." (U.N.I. Act, § 130.)

Referee in Case of Need. "The drawer of a bill and any indorser may insert thereon the name of a person to whom the holder may resort in case of need, that is to say, in case the bill is dishonored by non-acceptance or non-payment. Such person is called the Referee in case of need. It is in the option of the holder to resort to the Referee in case of need or not, as he may see fit." (U.N.I. Act, § 131.)

BILLS OF EXCHANGE IN A SET. "Where a bill is drawn in a set, each part of the set being numbered and containing a reference to the other parts, the whole of the parts constitute one bill." (U.N.I. Act, § 178.)

Rights of Holders Where Different Parts Are Negotiated. "Where two or more parts of a set are negotiated to different holders in due course, the holder whose title first accrues is as between such holders the true owner of the bill. But nothing in this section affects the rights of a person who in due course accepts or pays the first part presented to him." (U.N.I. Act, § 179.)

Liability of Holder Who Indorses Two or More Parts of a Set to Different Persons. "Where the holder of a set indorses two or more parts to different persons, he is liable on every such part, and every indorser subsequent to him is liable on the part he has himself indorsed, as if such parts were separate bills." (U.N.I. Act, § 180.)

Acceptance of Bills Drawn in Sets. "The acceptance may be written on any part and it must be written on one part only. (See discussion of Acceptance, below, p. 32.) If the drawee accepts more than one part, and such accepted parts are negotiated to different holders in due course, he is liable on every such part as if it were a separate bill." (U.N.I. Act, § 181.)

Payment by Acceptor of Bills Drawn in Sets. "When the acceptor of a bill drawn in a set pays it, without requiring the part bearing his acceptance to be delivered to him, and that part at maturity is outstanding in the hands of a holder in due course, he is liable to the holder thereon." (U.N.I. Act, § 182.)

Effect of Discharging One of a Set. "Except as herein otherwise provided, where any one part of a bill drawn in a set is discharged by payment or otherwise, the whole bill is discharged." (U.N.I. Act, § 183.)

INLAND AND FOREIGN BILLS OF EXCHANGE. "An inland bill of exchange is a bill which is, or on its face purports to be, both **drawn and payable within the State.** Any other bill is a foreign bill. Unless the contrary appears on the face of the bill, the holder may treat it as an inland bill." (U.N.I. Act, § 129.)

A bill of exchange drawn in a foreign state upon a party in this state has long been considered a foreign bill. (49 N.Y. 269.)

A foreign check is a foreign bill of exchange, not an inland bill. (159 N.Y. App. Div. 389.)

PRESENTMENT FOR ACCEPTANCE. "Presentment for acceptance must be made:

1. Where the bill is payable after sight or in any other case where presentment for acceptance is necessary in order to fix the maturity of the instrument; or
2. Where the bill expressly stipulates that it shall be presented for acceptance; or
3. Where a bill is drawn payable elsewhere than at the residence or place of business of the drawee." (U.N.I. Act, § 143.)

"In no other case is presentment for acceptance necessary in order to render any party to the bill liable."

It is the duty of a bank or individual receiving a bill for collection to **use due diligence** in presenting it. Failure to do so or failure to give notice makes him liable for any loss that the holder may sustain. (9 N.Y. 582.)

Requirements Covering Presentment. "Presentment for acceptance must be made by or on behalf of the holder at a reasonable hour, on a business day, and before the bill is overdue, to the drawee or some person authorized to accept or refuse acceptance on his behalf; and

1. Where a bill is addressed to **two or more drawees** who are not partners, presentment must be made to them all, unless one has authority to accept or refuse acceptance for all, in which case presentment may be made to him only;
2. Where the **drawee is dead,** presentment may be made to his personal representative;
3. Where the drawee has been adjudged a **bankrupt or an insolvent,** or has made an assignment for the benefit of creditors, presentment may be made to him or to his trustee or assignee." (U.N.I. Act, § 145.)

Where Presentment Is Excused. "Presentment for acceptance is excused and a **bill may be treated as dishonored** by non-acceptance in the following cases:

1. Where the drawee is dead or has absconded, or is a fictitious person or a person not having capacity to contract by bill;
2. Where after the exercise of reasonable diligence, presentment cannot be made;
3. Where, although presentment has been irregular, acceptance has been refused on some other ground." (U.N.I. Act, § 148.)

ACCEPTANCE OF BILL OF EXCHANGE. "The acceptance of a bill is the signification by the drawee of his assent to the order of the drawer. The acceptance must be in writing and signed by the drawee. It must not express that the drawee will perform his promise by any other means than the payment of money." (U.N.I. Act, § 132.)

Upon acceptance, a bill of exchange **becomes in effect a promissory note,** the acceptor standing in the place of the maker and becoming primarily liable, and the maker standing in the place of a first indorser. (237 N.Y. App. Div. 723.)

The Uniform Commercial Code states:

(1) The maker or acceptor engages that he will pay the instrument according to its tenor at the time of his engagement or as completed pursuant to Section 3–115 on incomplete instruments.

(2) By making, drawing or accepting the party admits as against all subsequent parties including the drawee the existence of the payee and his then capacity to indorse. (§ 3–413.)

The usual method of accepting a bill of exchange is to write across the face of the bill "Accepted," subscribed by the drawee's signature. (See Fig. 9.)

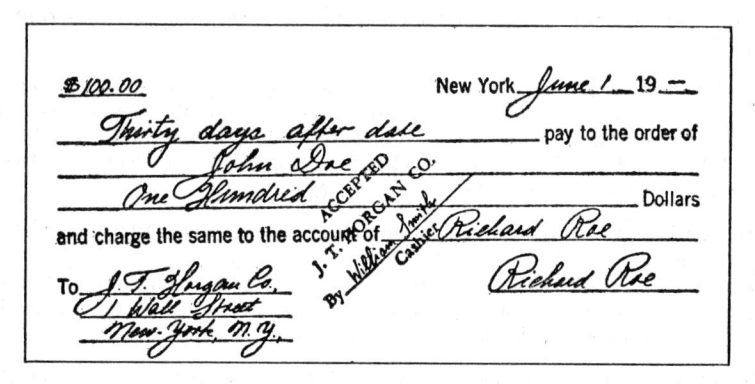

Fig. 9. Accepted bill of exchange.

Holder Entitled to Acceptance on Face of Bill. "The holder of a bill presenting the same for acceptance may require that the acceptance be written on the bill, and if such request is refused, may treat the bill as dishonored." (U.N.I. Act, § 133.)

Acceptance by Separate Instrument. "Where an acceptance is written on a paper other than the bill itself, it does not bind the acceptor, except in favor of a person to whom it is shown and who, on the faith thereof receives the bill for value." (U.N.I. Act, § 134.) The Uniform Commercial Code would seem to override this section in that it provides the acceptance must be written on the draft (§ 3–410 (1)) and completed by delivery.

Time Allowed Drawee To Accept. "The drawee is allowed twenty-four hours after presentment in which to decide whether or not he will accept the bill; but the acceptance, if given, dates as of the day of presentation." (U.N.I. Act, § 136.)

The Uniform Commercial Code extends this time to the end of the next business day:

(1) Acceptance may be deferred without dishonor until the close of the next business day following presentment. The holder may also in a good faith effort to obtain acceptance and without either dishonor of the instrument or discharge of secondary parties allow **postponement** of acceptance for an additional business day. (§ 3–506.)

Liability of Drawee Retaining or Destroying Bill. "Where a drawee to whom a bill is delivered for acceptance destroys the same, or refuses within twenty-four hours after such delivery, or within such other period as the holder may allow, to return the bill accepted or non-accepted to the holder, he will be deemed to have accepted the same." (U.N.I. Act, § 137.)

The Uniform Commercial Code makes a drawer **guilty of conversion** if he refuses to return the bill or if it is paid on a forged indorsement. (§ 3–419.)

A check is regarded as a bill of exchange payable on demand and is within the doctrine that the drawee will be deemed to have accepted when he refuses to return it within 24 hours after its delivery for acceptance. (91 N.Y.S. 276.)

Acceptance of Incomplete, Overdue, or Dishonored Bill. "A bill may be accepted before it has been signed by the drawer, or while otherwise incomplete, or when it is overdue, or after it has been dishonored by a previous refusal to accept, or by the non-payment. But when a bill payable after sight is dishonored by non-acceptance and the drawee subsequently accepts it, the holder, in the absence of any different agreement, is entitled to have the bill accepted as of the date of first presentment." (U.N.I. Act, § 138.)

GENERAL AND QUALIFIED ACCEPTANCES. "An acceptance is either general or qualified. A general acceptance assents without qualification to the order of the drawer. A qualified acceptance in express terms varies the effect of the bill as drawn." (U.N.I. Act, § 139.)

Qualified Acceptance. "An acceptance is qualified which is:

1. **Conditional,** that is to say, which makes payment by the acceptor dependent on the fulfillment of a condition therein stated;
2. **Partial,** that is to say, an acceptance to pay part only of the amount for which the bill is drawn;
3. **Local,** that is to say, an acceptance to pay only at a particular place;
4. Qualified as to **time;**
5. The acceptance of some **one or more of the drawees but not of all.**" (U.N.I. Act, § 141.)

Rights of Parties as to Qualified Acceptance. "The holder may refuse to take a qualified acceptance, and if he does not obtain an unqualified acceptance, he may treat the bill as dishonored by non-acceptance. Where a qualified acceptance is taken, the drawer and indorsers are discharged from liability on the bill, unless they have expressly or impliedly authorized the holder to take a qualified acceptance, or subsequently assented thereto. When the drawer or an indorser receives notice of a qualified acceptance, he must within a reasonable time express his dissent to the holder, or he will be deemed to have assented thereto." (U.N.I. Act, § 142.)

A bank acting as collecting agent has no authority to receive anything else than an unqualified acceptance. (9 N.Y. 582.)

When Dishonored by Non-Acceptance. "A bill is dishonored by non-acceptance:

1. When it is duly presented for acceptance, and such an acceptance as is prescribed by this Act is refused or cannot be obtained; or
2. When presentment for acceptance is excused and the bill is not accepted." (U.N.I. Act, § 149.)

"Where a bill is duly presented for acceptance and is not accepted within the prescribed time, the person presenting it **must treat the bill as dishonored** by non-acceptance or he loses the right of recourse against the drawer and indorsers." (U.N.I. Act, § 150.)

"When a bill is dishonored by non-acceptance, an immediate **right of recourse** against the drawers and indorsers accrues to the holder, and no presentment for payment is necessary." (U.N.I. Act, § 151.)

NOTICE OF DISHONOR. See discussion on page 25 above.

PROTEST FOR NON-ACCEPTANCE AND NON-PAYMENT. "Where a foreign bill appearing on its face to be such is dishonored by non-acceptance, it must be duly protested for non-acceptance, and where such a bill which has not previously been dishonored by non-acceptance is dishonored by non-payment, it must be duly protested for non-payment. If it is not so protested, the drawer and indorsers are discharged. Where a bill does not appear on its face to be a foreign bill, protest thereof in case of dishonor is unnecessary." (U.N.I. Act, § 152.) (See also Protest, page 27 above.)

Protest has long been required to hold the indorser on a foreign bill of exchange (49 N.Y. 269); but protest on a promissory note is not required to be made by a notary public. All that is required is a demand for payment and due notice of dishonor. (7 N.Y. 266.)

"A bill which has been protested for non-acceptance may be subsequently protested for non-payment." (U.N.I. Act, § 157.)

Protest may be made by:

1. A notary public; or
2. By any respectable resident of the place where the bill is dishonored, in the presence of two or more credible witnesses. (U.N.I. Act, § 154.)

Contents of Protest. "The protest must be annexed to the bill, or must contain a copy thereof, and must be under the hand and seal of the Notary making it, and must specify:

1. The time and place of presentment;
2. The fact that presentment was made and the manner thereof;
3. The cause or reason for protesting the bill;
4. The demand made and the answer given, if any, or the fact that the drawee or acceptor could not be found." (U.N.I. Act, § 153.)

"In many states, statutes have made the certificate of the notary prima facie evidence of the facts of presentment, demand, non-payment and notice of dishonor. Therefore, while protest is not required in cases of promissory notes and inland bills, it is usual to protest these instruments also, when dishonored, since the notary's certificate of protest is the most convenient and certain mode of proving the facts." (Brannan's Negotiable Instruments Law.)

When and Where Protest Must Be Made. "When a bill is protested, such protest must be made on the **day of its dishonor**, unless delay is excused." (U.N.I. Act, § 155.)

"A bill must be protested at the **place** where it is dishonored, except that when a bill drawn payable at the place of business or residence of some person other than the drawee has been dishonored by non-acceptance, it must be protested for non-payment at the place where it is expressed to be payable and no further presentment for payment to, or demand on, the drawee is necessary." (U.N.I. Act, § 156.)

Protest Before Maturity Where Acceptor Is Insolvent. "Where an acceptor has been adjudged a bankrupt or an insolvent, or has made an assignment for the benefit of creditors, before the bill matures, the holder may cause the bill to be protested for better security against the drawer and indorsers." (U.N.I. Act, § 158.)

Protest Where Bill Is Lost, Destroyed, or Detained. "Where a bill is lost or destroyed, or is wrongfully detained from the person entitled to hold it, protest may be made on a **copy** or **written particulars** thereof." (U.N.I. Act, § 160.)

WHEN PROTEST IS DISPENSED WITH. "Protest is dispensed with by any circumstances which would dispense with notice of dishonor. Delay in noting or protesting is excused when delay is caused by circumstances beyond the control of the holder and not imputable to his default, misconduct or negligence. When the cause of delay ceases to operate, the bill must be noted or protested with reasonable diligence." (U.N.I. Act, § 159.)

ACCEPTANCE FOR HONOR. "Where a bill of exchange has been protested for dishonor by non-acceptance or protested for better security and is not overdue, any person not being a party already liable thereon may, with the consent of the holder, intervene and accept the bill **supra protest** for the honor of any party liable thereon or for the honor of the person for whose account the bill is drawn. The acceptance for honor may be for part only of the sum for which the bill is drawn; and where there has been an acceptance for honor for one party, there may be a further acceptance by a different person for the honor of another party." (U.N.I. Act, § 161.)

Trade and Banker's Acceptances

TRADE ACCEPTANCES. "A trade acceptance is a 'draft or bill of exchange drawn by the seller on the purchaser of goods sold, and accepted by such purchaser' (Regulations Fed. Reserve Board relating to Acceptance, Section A, Paragraph V, Subd. a).'' (241 N.Y. 239.) (See Fig. 10.)

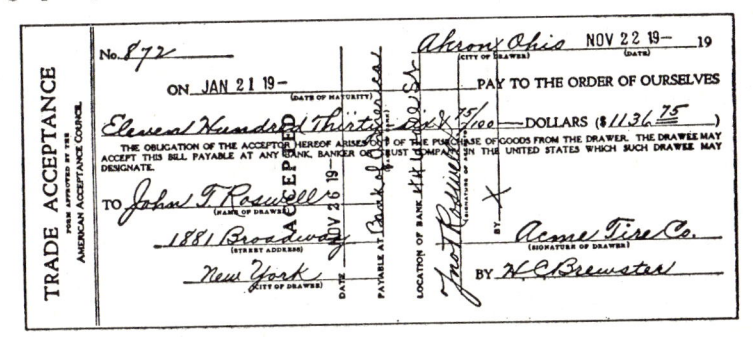

Fig. 10. Trade acceptance.

It might thus be stated that a trade acceptance is a **special form of a bill of exchange** drawn by the seller of goods to his purchaser and then accepted by the purchaser. If drawn and executed in conformity with the Uniform Negotiable Instruments Act or the Uniform Commercial Code it is a negotiable instrument and is governed by such law. A trade acceptance is different from a promissory note in that it is drawn by one person on another, whereas the promissory note is drawn by one person to the order of another.

The Uniform Negotiable Instruments Act and the Uniform Commercial Code specifically provide that the negotiability of an instrument is not to be affected by the fact that it contains on its face "a statement of the transaction which gives rise to the instrument." The courts have literally interpreted the wording used. For safety's sake, the language should be limited to the statement "The transaction which gives rise to this instrument is the purchase of goods by the acceptor from the drawer." Any provision giving a **title retention clause** in the trade acceptance has been held to render it nonnegotiable. (159 N.E. 625.) The Code would allow title retention and not make it nonnegotiable. (§ 3–105 (1) (e).)

BANKER'S ACCEPTANCE. "A banker's acceptance is a draft or bill of exchange of which the acceptor is a bank or banker engaged generally in the business of granting banker's acceptance credits." (241 N.Y. 239.)

Checks

CHECKS. "A check is a bill of exchange drawn on a bank payable on demand." (U.N.I. Act, § 185.) The Uniform Commercial Code describes a check as a draft drawn on a bank and payable on demand. (§ 3–104(2)(b).)

"Checks are but inland bills of exchange, and subject to all the rules applicable to instruments of that character, and impose no obligation upon the drawee until accepted; and until presented and paid, are revocable by the drawer, who has the legal control of the moneys to his credit until acceptance of payment of the checks." (46 N.Y. 82; 107 N.Y. 179.)

A **bank cashier's check**, whether certified or not, is construed under the statute as a bill of exchange payable on demand. (143 N.C. 102.) The only essential difference between a check and a bill of exchange is that a check is drawn upon a bank or banker. (8 N.Y. 190.)

Within What Time a Check Must Be Presented. "A check must be presented for payment within a reasonable time after its issue or the drawer will be discharged from liability thereon to the extent of the loss caused by the delay." (U.N.I. Act, § 186.)

The courts have construed that reasonable time ends with the end of the next business day after delivery of the check. (128 N.Y. App. Div. 131: 98 S.W. 2d 320.)

The Uniform Commercial Code treats as follows the question of **"stale" checks**:

A bank is under no obligation to a customer having a checking account to pay a check, other than a certified check, which is presented more than six months after its date, but it may charge its customer's account for a payment made thereafter in good faith. (§ 4–404.)

Certification of Check. "Where a check is certified by the bank on which it is drawn, the certification is equivalent to an acceptance." (U.N.I. Act, § 187.) (See Fig. 11.)

The effect of certification by a bank before delivery to the payee is that the bank guarantees the genuineness of the signature of the drawer, that it has in its custody sufficient funds to meet the check, and that it agrees that the money shall not be withdrawn to the prejudice of the holder of the check. (79 N.Y. App. Div. 409.) The payee of a check, by procuring certification, accepts the bank as his debtor and releases the drawer of the check. (99 Fla. 745; 196 N.Y.S. 629.) But if the drawer obtains certification before delivery, he is not discharged from liability. (217 N.Y. 726.)

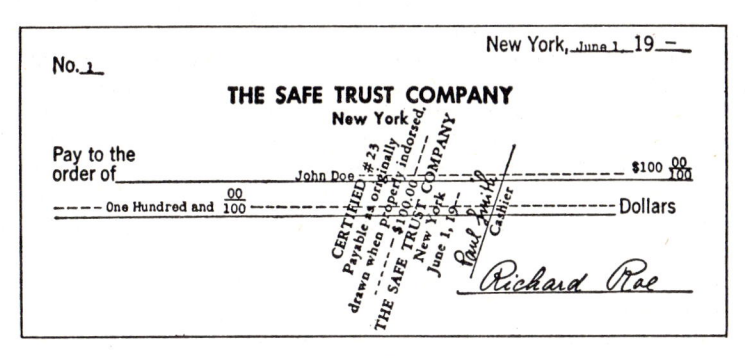

Fig. 11. Certified check.

"Where the holder of a check procures it to be accepted or certified, **the drawer and all indorsers are discharged** from liability thereon." (U.N.I. Act, § 188.)

When Check Operates As an Assignment. "A check of itself does not operate as an assignment of any part of the funds to the credit of the drawer with the bank, and the bank is not liable to the holder, unless and until it accepts or certifies the check." (U.N.I. Act, § 189.)

Prior to the enactment of this section, it was a well-established rule that a check in the usual form, unless accepted or certified by the bank, did not operate as an assignment of the depositor's funds. (32 N.E. 38.) The holder of an uncertified check has **no cause of action against the drawee bank for refusal to pay** the check, even though the maker had sufficient funds on deposit. (186 S.W. 471.) The depositor, however, being a party to a contract of deposit with the bank, may sue the bank for injury to his credit. (134 N.Y. 368.)

Under the Uniform Commercial Code the **liability of the bank for a wrongful dishonor** is fixed:

A payor bank is liable to its customer for damages proximately caused by the wrongful dishonor of an item. When the dishonor occurs through mistake liability is limited to actual damages proved. If so proximately caused and proved damages may include damages for an arrest or prosecution of the customer or other consequential damages. Whether any consequential damages are proximately caused by the wrongful dishonor is a question of fact to be determined in each case. (§ 4–402.)

NEW YORK STATE PROVISIONS. The following provisions in force in the State of New York are **not** a part of the Uniform Negotiable Instruments Act. The section numbers as given refer to the **Negotiable Instruments Law of New York.**

NO STOPPING PAYMENT AFTER CERTIFICATION. § 325–a. "A bank, banker or trust company which has certified a check, note or other instrument for the payment of money at the request of the drawee, payee or holder thereof, shall not thereafter be required to stop or refuse payment thereof upon the order, demand or request of the drawee or of any other party thereto."

However, the new Code states that before certification a customer may order his bank to stop payment, provided the bank has a reasonable time to do so. An oral stop order is only valid for 14 days, but if confirmed in writing for 6 months. (§ 4–403.)

RECOVERY OF A FORGED CHECK. § 326. "No bank shall be liable to a depositor for the payment by it of a forged or raised check, unless within one year after the return to the depositor of the voucher of such payment, such depositor shall notify the bank that the check so paid was forged or raised."

Although the drawer of a check may be liable if he draws the instrument in an incomplete form so as to facilitate or invite fraudulent alterations, the law does not require him to prepare the check so that nobody can successfully tamper with it. (63 N.E. 969.)

LEGAL EFFECT OF INDORSEMENTS. § 350-C. "An indorsement of an item by the payee or other depositor, 'for deposit' shall be deemed a restrictive indorsement and indicate that the indorsee bank is an agent for collection and not owner of the item.

"An indorsement 'pay any bank or banker' or having equivalent words shall be deemed a **restrictive** indorsement and shall indicate the creation of an agency relation in any subsequent bank to whom the paper is forwarded unless coupled with words indicating the creation of a trustee relationship; and such indorsement or other restrictive indorsement whether creating an agency or trustee relationship shall constitute a guaranty by the indorser to all subsequent holders and to the drawee or payor of the genuineness of and the authority to make prior indorsements and also to save the drawee or payor harmless in the event any prior indorsement appearing thereon is defective or irregular in any respect unless such indorsement is coupled with appropriate words disclaiming such liability as guarantor.

"Where a deposited item is payable to bearer or indorsed by the depositor in blank or by special indorsement, the fact that such item is so payable or indorsed shall not change the relation of agent of the bank of deposit to the depositor, but subsequent holders shall have the right to rely on the presumption that the bank of deposit is the owner of the item. The indorsement of an item by the bank of deposit or any subsequent holder in blank or by special indorsement or its delivery when payable to bearer, shall carry the presumption that the indorsee or transferee is owner provided there is nothing upon the face of the paper or in any prior indorsement to indicate an agency or trustee relation of any prior party. But where an item is deposited or is received for collection indorsed specially or in blank, the bank may convert such an indorsement into a restrictive indorsement by writing over the signature of the indorser the words 'for deposit' or 'for collection,' or other restrictive words to negative the presumption that such bank of deposit or indorsee bank is owner; and in the case of an item deposited or received for collection payable to bearer, may negative such presumption by indorsing thereon the words 'Received for deposit' or 'Received for collection' or words of like import."

The Code, however, does not limit negotiability so stringently under such an indorsement. (§ 3–206.) (See Restrictive Indorsements supra page 11.)

RESPONSIBILITY FOR COLLECTION: WHEN ACTION SEASONABLE.
  (1) A collecting bank must use ordinary care in
    (a) presenting an item or sending it for presentment; and

(b) sending notice of dishonor or non-payment or returning an item other than a documentary draft to the bank's transferor or directly to the depositary bank under subsection (2) of Section 4–212 after learning that the item has not been paid or accepted, as the case may be; and
(c) settling for an item when the bank receives final settlement; and
(d) making or providing for any necessary protest; and
(e) notifying its transferor of any loss or delay in transit within a reasonable time after discovery thereof.

(3) Subject to subsection (1) (a), a bank is not liable for the insolvency, neglect, misconduct, mistake or default of **another** bank or person or for loss or destruction of an item in transit, or in the possession of others. (§ 4–202.)

PRESUMPTION AND DURATION OF AGENCY STATUS OF COLLECTING BANKS AND PROVISIONAL STATUS OF CREDITS; APPLICABILITY OF ARTICLE; ITEM ENDORSED "PAY ANY BANK."

(1) Unless a contrary intent clearly appears and prior to the time that a settlement given by a collecting bank for an item is, or becomes final (subsection (3) of Section 4–211 and Sections 4–212 and 4–213) the bank is an agent or sub-agent of the owner of the item and any settlement given for the item is provisional. This provision applies regardless of the form of indorsement or lack of indorsement and even though credit given for the item is subject to immediate withdrawal as of right or is in fact withdrawn; but the continuance of ownership of an item by its owner and any rights of the owner to proceeds of the item are subject to rights of a collecting bank such as those resulting from outstanding advances on the item and valid rights of set-off. When an item is handled by banks for purposes of presentment, payment and collection, the relevant provisions of this Article apply even though action of parties clearly establishes that a particular bank has purchased the item and is the owner of it.

(2) After an item has been indorsed with the words "pay any bank" or the like, only a bank may acquire the rights of a holder
(a) until the item has been returned to the customer initiating the collection; or
(b) until the item has been specially indorsed by a bank to a person who is not a bank. (§ 4–201.)

METHODS OF SENDING AND PRESENTING: SENDING DIRECT TO PAYOR BANK.

(1) A collecting bank must send items by reasonably prompt method taking into consideration any relevant instructions, the nature of the item, the number of such items on hand, and the cost of collection involved and the method generally used by it or others to present such items.
(2) A collecting bank may send
(a) any item direct to the payor bank;
(b) any item to any non-bank payor if authorized by its transferor; and
(c) any item other than documentary drafts to any non-bank payor, if authorized by Federal Reserve regulation or operating letter, clearing house rule or the like.
(3) Presentment may be made by a presenting bank at a place where the payor bank has requested that presentment be made. (§ 4–204.)

DUTY AND RESPONSIBILITY OF BANK COLLECTING AGENTS. Section 350-D. "It shall be the duty of the initial or any subsequent agent collecting bank to exercise **ordinary care** in the collection of an item and when such duty is performed such bank shall not be responsible if for any cause payment is not received in money or an unconditional credit given on the books of another bank, when such agent bank has requested or accepted. An initial or subsequent agent collecting bank shall be liable for its own lack of exercise of ordinary care but shall not be liable for the neglect, misconduct, mistakes or defaults of any other agent bank or of the drawee or payor bank."

A bank receiving a check for collection acts as agent and may be liable upon proof of its failure to exercise ordinary care. (244 N.Y. App. Div. 68.)

Interest

DEFINITION. Interest is "money to be paid for the use of capital, on a loan of money, or forbearance of a debt and becomes part of and incident to a debt; or it is damages for the detention of a debt due, and fixed by law, at a given rate, in proportion to the amount of money lent, or detained, and the time for which it is thus lent or detained." (8 Gray Mass. 267, 278.)

Compound interest is "interest added to the principal as the former becomes due, and thereafter made to bear interest." (3 Dak. 449.) Compound interest is not favored by the courts and will not be allowed unless authorized by statute or by contract, expressed or implied. (43 Fed. 231.) The legal rate of interest is the rate prescribed by law which is to prevail in the absence of any special agreement between the parties.

LAWFUL INTEREST. This is any rate of interest agreed upon by the parties, but not in excess of the maximum rate fixed by statute. The rate of interest permitted by statute is fixed by state law and varies among the states. The only safe course is to determine the rate set by statute in the jurisdiction in question. In general, in the absence of agreement, if interest is to be paid the rate is governed by the law of the place where the contract was made. (149 U.S. 122.) If, however, a contract involving interest is made in one state and the contract is to be performed in another state, the law of the **place of performance** will govern. (142 U.S. 101.) It has also been held that the parties may agree to be bound by the interest laws of the **place where the contract was entered into**, instead of the place of performance. (13 Fed. 198.)

Interest laws, since they are statutes and are in derogation of common law, must be strictly construed.

Under some statutes a usurious instrument is void, and the holder of such an instrument cannot recover either interest or principal. Exceptions to this rule are mentioned below.

CONTRACTUAL AND IMPLIED INTEREST. A promissory note ordinarily does not bear interest prior to its maturity, unless it is an interest bearing obligation and actually contains the words "with interest." In that event, interest is to be computed from the date of the instrument. (147 N.E. 641.) But all written instruments referring to the payment of money, whether interest-bearing or noninterest-bearing, carry with them an implied promise to pay interest if the debt is not paid when due. (129 U.S. 601.)

If **invoices** accompanying goods contain the terms of sale, together with words to the effect that bills are to bear interest after maturity, and the consignee accepts them without objection, they constitute a contract for the payment of such interest. (187 Ill. 283.) Under certain circumstances, also, well-known and long-established customs generally followed within the trade that interest is to be payable under certain conditions result in an implied contract to pay interest. (161 N.Y. 530.) "This knowledge may be established by presumptive as well as direct evidence. It may be inferred from the uniformity and long continuance of the usage, from the fact that a party has for some time been in the particular

INTEREST **24·41**

trade to which it relates, from the previous dealings between the parties, or from any other facts tending to show its general notoriety." (64 Mass. 250.)

As a general rule, **interest is not allowed on an open and running account.** It may be agreed by the parties, however, that interest is to be paid on the amount actually due when it has been ascertained. If this is the case, there is no law prohibiting such a contract. In the case of settled accounts interest will be allowed if the balance due has been agreed upon by the parties. (88 U.S. 105.)

With **unliquidated claims** if the amount due cannot be determined by any method of computation, it is implied that no interest is to run prior to the entry of a verdict or decision in the case in question. (232 Pac. 1002.)

RATE OF INTEREST AFTER MATURITY. The Federal courts follow the rule that interest on an obligation after maturity is computed at the legal rate. (51 Fed. 2d 46.) In many states, however, the rate of interest agreed upon by the parties in their agreement continues after maturity as well as before maturity. (112 Mass. 63.)

When Interest Starts. Interest runs on an interest-bearing obligation from the date of the instrument or from the time agreed upon by the parties. If no agreement is made, the interest runs from the date the principal becomes due. (233 U.S. 261.) In some obligations such as debts, due bills, and obligations payable on demand, interest does not begin to accrue until demand for payment is made. (119 N.Y. 62.) "Interest does not begin to run from the date of such note, unless expressly reserved, because interest, unless stipulated for, is only allowed as damages in default of payment, and the maker is not considered in default until payment is demanded or suit is brought, which is a judicial demand." (119 Atlantic 420.)

In the case of an instrument payable at a **fixed time,** interest will begin to run although no demand for payment is made.

STOPPING OF INTEREST. The accruing of interest will stop under the following circumstances:

1. On payment of the principal of the debt.
2. Improper acts of the creditor making it impossible for the debtor to pay the debt. (58 Fed. 653.)
3. Laches. If the creditor delays unreasonably in pressing his claim against the debtor, he forfeits interest which cannot be collected. (110 U.S. 174.)
4. Absence of the creditor. If the creditor cannot be found or is absent from the country and has left no agent to collect the debt, interest will cease if the debtor has made diligent effort to find his creditor.
5. Valid tender. "The reason for such a rule rests in the fact that the person to whom the tender was made, if the same tender is sufficient to satisfy him for his debt and for his costs, is bound to take it, and if he does not, while the debt is not paid, the liability of the debtor for interest is suspended." (179 N. Y. App. Div. 57.) It should be noted, however, that a tender of payment before maturity is not valid and does not stop the running of interest. The tender must indicate that the debtor is ready, willing, and able to pay the debt according to the terms thereof and his tender must be unconditional and in the proper amount. The circumstances of the offer must be such that it leaves the creditor free to accept the amount offered without prejudice, and the amount tendered is all that is due. A check, even though certified, is not a good tender. (100 S.E. 37.) In the case of a promissory note payable at a bank, sufficient tender is made if there is money to pay the note on deposit to the maker's credit in the bank on the date payment is due.

6. Payment suspended by court order. If the payment of a debt is suspended by an order of a court of proper jurisdiction, interest ceases to accumulate. (149 U.S. 95.)

7. Deposit in court. A deposit made in a court of proper jurisdiction at the direction of the court suspends the accumulation of interest.

"UNITED STATES RULE." What is generally known as the United States Rule for computing interest on **partial payments** is set forth in 1 Johns. (N.Y.) 136:

The rule for casting interest, where partial payments have been made, is to apply the payment, in the first place, to the discharge of the interest then due. If the payment exceeds the interest, the surplus goes toward discharging the principal, and the subsequent interest is to be computed on the balance of principal remaining due. If the payment be less than the interest, the surplus of the interest must not be taken to augment the principal; the interest continues on the former principal until the period when the payments, taken together, exceed the interest due, and then the surplus is to be applied toward discharging the principal; and interest is to be computed on that balance as aforesaid.

In general, the foregoing rule in computing interest is followed by the courts if the contracts of the parties or the usages of trade do not indicate the use of some other theory or method of computing interest. In the **administration of estates and relations with the government,** this method is also followed.

MERCANTILE RULE. As against the United States Rule, there is the Mercantile Rule that provides that if it is the agreement of the parties or the custom of trade, the balance of the debt due is computed by calculating the interest on each item of the debt on one side, and allowing interest for each payment on the other.

Usury

DEFINITION. "Usury consists of extorting or taking a rate of interest for money beyond what is allowed by law. It is not necessary that money should be actually advanced, in order to constitute the offense of usury, but any pretense or contrivance whatever, to gain more than legal interest, where it is the intent of the parties to contract for a loan, will make the contract usurious." [3 Johns. (N.Y.) 206.]

Three Necessary Elements. "Three things must unite to render any contract usurious.

"First, there must be a loan, express or implied. Second, there must be an agreement that the money lent or, which is the same thing, that which is lent for the purpose of raising money shall be repaid without conditions or contingency. And, third, there must be an agreement to pay a higher rate of interest than that allowed by statute." (4 N.Y. 363.)

Main Test. The main test of any usurious contract is that, if it is performed, it will result in producing to the lender a **higher rate of interest than is allowed by law.** Under the usury laws, it would appear that the **lender alone** is the violator of the law and it is against him that penalties are to be enforced.

It is a requirement of procedural law that if a defense of usury is to be used, it **must be affirmatively pleaded** and proved by the borrower inasmuch as there is a presumption that all contracts are intended to be lawful. (120 N.E. 694.)

Which State's Law Governs. The place where a contract is executed determines the rights and liabilities of the parties involved, and the usury laws of that particular state apply. The **intent** of the parties must be in good faith and not for the purpose of evading the usury laws of another state. Provided the arrangement is not a mere device to evade the usury laws of a sister state, a note made in one state, payable in another, may lawfully bear a rate of interest permitted in either state. (43 Fed. 2d 730.)

EXCEPTIONS TO THE GENERAL USURY RULE. In most states by special statute certain types of corporations, associations, and banking organizations are permitted to charge higher rates of interest than is allowed the ordinary lender. Personal loan companies and industrial banking companies in some instances can charge up to 3% per month. Since these institutions function under special statute, reference must be had to the law in question to determine the maximum rates they may charge.

To obviate **unfair competition** between them, state and national banks are permitted to charge the same rate of interest in the jurisdiction in which they are located. If there is no rate fixed by law, a national bank may charge 7%. Another exception not to be classed with the above is the duly licensed pawn broker whose loans are secured by the pledge of personal property. By special statute in most states, he is allowed to charge a higher rate of interest.

There are other exceptions, such as "call money" in New York. The General Business Law of that state, Section 379, provides that on any loan not less than $5,000 secured by warehouse receipts, bills of lading, certificates of stock, certificates of deposit, bills of exchange, bonds, or other negotiable instruments pledged as collateral, it shall be lawful to receive or to contract to receive and collect, as compensation for making such loan, any sum to be agreed upon in writing by the parties to the transaction.

TRANSACTIONS NOT CLASSIFIED AS USURIOUS. Certain transactions are not considered usurious. These are as follows:

Discounting. The mercantile custom of deducting interest in advance on short-term paper does not make the transaction usurious. (12 N.Y. 223.) Compound interest is not usury. (37 N.E. 840.)

Capital Contribution of a Partner. This is not a loan, and therefore any interest paid on such an investment, even though in excess of the lawful rate, does not constitute usury. (91 N.Y. 43.)

Loans to Corporations. In New York and many other states, under most circumstances most corporate debtors cannot plead usury as a defense. The net result is that interest can be charged a corporation at any rate the traffic will bear, which in effect repeals the usury laws for most corporate obligations. (15 N.Y. 9.) The underlying reason for this is that usury laws were passed to protect helpless needy borrowers from the lender. But corporations can secure capital from a large number of persons to satisfy their needs, and so they are not considered to require protection of usury statutes.

Sale of Negotiable Instrument. To make a transaction usurious, the usury must arise at the inception of the contract or the instrument. The mere sale of a negotiable instrument by a holder at a substantial discount will not constitute usury.

Sale of Property. No sale or exchange of property can become usurious under any conditions. But such a sale cannot be used merely for a cloak to hide what is on its face a usurious transaction. If a borrower, as a condition to his obtaining a loan, is compelled to purchase property at an exorbitant price, even though the money loaned bears lawful interest, it is considered to be a usurious transaction. (101 N.Y. 643.) As a general proposition the courts will look with disfavor on any device, no matter how skillfully devised, resorted to as a cover for usurious loans. The form of the transaction may be set aside to discover the **real intent** of the parties, and if the transaction is basically usurious, the courts will treat it as unlawful.

WHEN CONTRACT IS VOID. When a usurious contract is void under the statutes, the lender cannot enforce it.

WHEN INTEREST IS FORFEITED. When the statutes declare that all interest is forfeited in a usurious contract, the lender may nevertheless recover the principal. (N.Y. Banking Law, Section 108.)

In those states where the statute declares the excess over the legal rate of interest to be forfeited, the lender can recover the principal and legal interest. (39 Ind. 305.)

NEW YORK STATE RULE. In New York, the maximum rate of interest permitted by law is 6% per annum. Usurious contracts are void and the lender forfeits both principal and interest, except in the case of banks and other exempt lenders. A mortgage or other security given for a usurious loan is also void, and the bond and mortgage can be canceled without paying back what has been received. (N.Y. General Business Law, §§ 370–382.)

If the interest payments have been made in excess of the legal rate, they can be recovered by the borrower.

CRIMINAL LIABILITY. In some states the taking of usurious interest is specifically made a misdemeanor and subjects the lender to criminal prosecution.

SECTION 25

RISK MANAGEMENT AND INSURANCE

CONTENTS

Nature of Business Risks
	PAGE
Risk management and control	1
The risk manager	1
Role of economists	2
"Risk" defined	2
Static risks	2
Risk survey and analysis	2
Probability and the law of large numbers	2
Financial exposure	3

Areas of Risk
Losses of property values	3
Direct and indirect property losses	3
Additional expenses associated with property damage	4
Losses directly affecting income	4
Business interruption	4
Risks assumed through rental or other agreements	5
Losses due to destruction of records	5
Losses from death or disability of key personnel	5
Liability to public and employees	5
Workmen's Compensation laws	5
Losses due to dishonesty or other criminal acts	5

Dealing with Risk
Available alternatives	6
Control of risk and loss	6
Cost of risk	6
Benefits from loss control	6
Methods of loss reduction	7
Assumption of risk and loss	7
Self-insurance	7
Conditions necessary for self-insurance	8
Purchasing commercial insurance	8
Availability of insurance	8
Cost of commercial vs. self-insurance	9
Other risk transfer devices	10
Use of leased property	10
Construction contracts	10
Bailments	10
Sales contracts	10
Suretyship	11

Commercial Insurance Coverage
Regulation of the insurance business	11
The insurance policy	11
Standardization of policies	11
Types of policies	12

	PAGE
Schedule and package policies	12
Floater and general cover or multiple location policies	12
Comprehensive and "all-risk" policies	12
Important policy clauses	13
Co-insurance clause	13
Pro rata liability clause	13
Pro rata distribution clause	13
Replacement cost clause	13
Mortgagee clause	14
Subrogation clause	14
Apportionment clause	14

Insurance Against Physical Damage to Property
Fire and allied lines	14
Extended coverage endorsement (EC)	14
Additional extended coverage (AEC)	15
Business coverages—multiple line	15
Jewelers' block policy	15
Mercantile block policy—commercial property coverage	15
Manufacturers' output policy	15
Other business multiple-line coverages	16
Ocean marine policies	16
Ocean marine losses	17
Features of ocean marine policies	17
Inland marine policies	17
Transportation policies	18
Floater contracts	19
Instrumentalities of transportation	19
Automobile physical damage policy	20
Types of automobile coverage	20
Steam boiler and machinery insurance	20
Other policies	20

Policies Insuring Against Consequential Losses
Loss of income	21
Business interruption insurance	21
Contingent business interruption insurance	21
Extra expense insurance	21
Rents and rental value insurance	21
Leasehold interest insurance	22
Profits insurance	22
Temperature damage insurance	22
Other consequential loss coverage	22

Crime Insurance
Definitions	22
Theft and larceny	22

RISK MANAGEMENT AND INSURANCE

CONTENTS (Continued)

	PAGE
Burglary	23
Robbery	23
Characteristics of crime coverages	23
Business coverages	23
Mercantile open stock burglary policy	23
Mercantile open stock theft policy	23
Mercantile safe burglary policy	23
Mercantile interior robbery, messenger robbery, paymaster robbery policies	23
Money and securities broad-form policy	23
Blanket crime policy; comprehensive dishonesty, disappearance, and destruction (3-D) policy; broad-form storekeepers' policy	24
Financial institution coverages	24

Fidelity and Surety Bonding

Bonds compared with insurance	24
Fidelity bonds	25
Individual bond	25
Name schedule bond	25
Position schedule bond	25
Blanket bonds	25
Surety bonds	25

Liability Insurance

Liability and negligence	26
Negligence a form of tort	26
Culpable negligence and defenses	26
Employer liability	27
Liability of landlords and tenants	27
Liability of a tenant	28
Product liability	28
Professional liability	28
Liability for acts of agents	28
Liability of automobile owners and operators	29
Liability of the owner	29
Liability of the operator	29
Liability of a nonowner employer	29
Bailment liability	29
Liability imposed by a contract	29
Miscellaneous liability	30

	PAGE
Insurance coverage available	30
Protection provided by insurance	30

Business Uses of Life Insurance

Provision for loss of key men and business continuation	31
Key man insurance	31
Business continuation—individual proprietorships	32
Business continuation—partnerships	32
Business continuation—close corporations	33
Programs for employees	34
Split dollar plan	34
Salary continuation or deferred compensation plans	35
Employee death benefit of $5,000	35
Group insurance and pension plans	35
Example of a split dollar insurance plan	36

Considerations in Selecting Insurers

Importance of proper selection	37
Types of private insurers	37
Intercompany organizations	37
Admitted insurers	37
Scope of underwriting authority	38
Monoline or single-line companies	38
Multiple-line companies	38
"All-lines" companies	38
Distribution channels	38
Direct distribution	38
Indirect distribution (the American Agency System)	38
Insurance brokers	39
Distribution systems not mutually exclusive	39
Claims services	39
Loss prevention services	40
Financial soundness of insurers	40
The role of regulation	40
Sources of information	40
Measuring financial soundness	40
Financial safety of fire and casualty insurance companies	41
Financial safety of life insurance companies	41

SECTION 25

RISK MANAGEMENT AND INSURANCE

Nature of Business Risks

RISK MANAGEMENT AND CONTROL. Management is constantly faced with a multitude of risks, those inherent in the dynamic or speculative nature of business that produce a profit or loss and those involving perils to people or property that can result only in damage and loss. Business risk management or risk control is concerned with these latter **static** risks. Control of static risks can be vital to the survival of an enterprise. "Many businesses fail each year because of losses resulting from risks that were unknown or from risks which, although known to exist, were not the subject of adequate insurance protection or effective loss preventing measures." (Johnson, American Management Association Report No. 38.)

The **objective** of risk management is to minimize the cost to and impact on the business of static risks. To accomplish this, risk management, as MacDonald (Business Risk Management) points out, engages in two basic areas of activity: (1) prevention and reduction of the likelihood and extent of destructive occurrences such as fires, thefts, and other casualties, and (2) provision for economic survival when mishaps do occur.

The Risk Manager. Responsibility for risk management is most frequently placed in the hands of a top-ranking member of management, a financial vice-president, treasurer, assistant treasurer, or controller. However, MacDonald (Business Risk Management) argues that a financial officer may not have a sufficiently broad range of interest. He advocates that the executive who is made responsible for risk control should be linked directly to the office of the company's chief executive, since the proper performance of the function necessitates a continuing interest in and accessibility to many dissimilar areas of activity, and such an overall perspective is usually possible only through that office. In MacDonald's view, an **adequate risk control program** requires, "(a) intensive analysis of plans and methods in such diverse areas as production, research, marketing, advertising, plant construction, procurement, job training, contracting for services and maintenance of facilities; (b) breadth and depth of understanding of insurance principles, contracts, and markets; and (c) continuously expanding knowledge of techniques for prevention of accidents, fires, thefts and other destructive or damaging occurrences."

The **specific role and responsibilities** of the risk manager or director of risk control have been summarized as follows (Rogers, The Journal of Insurance, Vol. XXX):

First, he must have an accurate knowledge of the properties and operations of his employer.

Second, he needs to analyze the hazards that confront those properties and arise out of the operations.

Third, it is important that he carry out a program aimed at eliminating or reducing hazards to the extent possible.

Finally, he must be able to arrange and administer a program of insurance or self-insurance to prevent heavy financial inroads due to risks he cannot eliminate.

Role of Economists. There is an increasing awareness and concern on the part of economists of the influence of risk and uncertainty on economic activity. Because insurance is the major institutional device for handling the problem of static risk and, further, because the insurance industry is an important segment of the total domestic economy, economists are delving further into the science of risk and insurance.

The growing field of insurance economics is concerned with (Athearn, The Journal of Insurance, Vol. XXIX):

(1) The analysis of conditions giving rise to the need for the insurance device, (2) the analysis of the problems of those providing insurance service, (3) analysis of the place of the institution—and industry—of insurance in the economy, (4) efforts to integrate the analysis of risk and insurance with economic theory, and (5) efforts to develop separate principles of risk and insurance to supplement the present body of economic theory where the latter provides an incomplete framework for insurance economics. The insurance economist is concerned with risk, uncertainty and insurance because risk causes uncertainty, which has undesirable economic effects, and insurance is a major institutional arrangement for coping with risk.

"RISK" DEFINED. Viewed as an economic entity, risk is defined as uncertainty regarding the occurrence of an economic loss. When it is very likely or almost certain that a loss will occur, the **degree** of risk is quite low. At the same time, if it were nearly impossible for a loss to occur, we would again say that the risk is low. Risk is at a maximum when uncertainty is greatest.

Static Risks. Speculative or **dynamic** risks are those in which, as a result of the risk, the business may suffer a loss or enjoy a profit. Static, or pure, risks are defined as those that can result only in loss to the exposed party. They stem from: perils of nature, fraud and criminal violations, adverse legal decisions, damage to the property of others, and the death of key employees or owners. A **peril** may be defined as a contingency that may cause loss, and a **hazard** as a condition that makes occurrence of the peril more likely. Greene states (Risk and Insurance) that the definition of a hazard might be expanded ". . . to include conditions that make the loss more severe, once the peril has occurred and has caused a loss." To a large extent the efforts of the risk manager are directed toward the reduction or elimination of the contributing perils and hazards.

RISK SURVEY AND ANALYSIS. Modern risk management begins with the **identification** of all exposures to possible loss. This requires, among other things, careful analysis of potential loss to physical property of all kinds, possible losses due to unexpected interruption of business, losses due to commission of crimes, exposure to liability claims of individuals arising from any type of operation and ownership or agency relationship in which the business may be involved, and losses resulting from death or disability of key personnel. Insurance companies, brokers, and independent risk managers have developed a variety of **schedules, forms, and charts** to assist in this type of analysis. The study should be exhaustive since any exposure overlooked may create a loss that could be crippling to a business.

Probability and the Law of Large Numbers. Probability, which is based on the law of large numbers, relates to the long-run chance of the occurrence of some event. The law of large numbers asserts that in respect to random events, the projected experience of an event (e.g., a loss) will approach as a limit the actual experience, provided the forecast is based on a large enough number of exposure units and that the occurrence of the event is completely fortuitous, or random, in nature. The larger the number of units involved, the more closely will the projected events approximate the actual events.

Insurers base their operations on probability and they are interested in determining the average loss that will occur to the exposed units in a like class. The **insured**, on the other hand, is concerned with risk and the uncertainty as to whether the loss will happen to him as an individual person or business.

Financial Exposure. The maximum dollar amount of a potential loss should be estimated in respect to each loss exposure, and in the measurement of this potential dollar loss the aggregate of all losses that can result from a single event should be included. It is imperative that this measurement be made in order that adequate provision be made for loss possibility. Moreover, **maximum** loss exposure is the important element—not modal or **average** (mean) loss. "The greater the potential loss, the more important is the risk." (Angell, Insurance— Principles and Practices.) Average loss exposure is a useful concept, but it must be combined with some measure of the deviation from the average to be an adequate guide for planning.

In the measurement of the total dollar damage that can result from a single event, consideration must be given to the entire area to which damage could occur. The term **catastrophe area** is sometimes used to describe this entire area. It includes all losses that may result to property, real and personal, to persons, to income, and those that may result from any additional expenses incurred. For example, damage to explosive inventory could cause damage to the building, personnel, other inventory, leased or rented property, property of others, and a loss of profits.

Areas of Risk

LOSSES OF PROPERTY VALUES. Property already accumulated and committed to a business undertaking is exposed to risk and consequent damage. Damage to property may also cause the reduction or even total loss of profits for one or more periods. The business properties subject to damage are included within the following subgroups (Magee, Property Insurance):

1. **Real property,** including buildings owned, rented or leased, and other real property or fixtures attached to real property which would embrace such things as alterations in progress, escalators, power machinery, signs, and pressure vessels.
2. **Personal property,** including inventory, cash and checks, furniture and fixtures, and cars, trucks, boats, and airplanes, among other things.

Direct and Indirect Property Losses. In estimating the loss potential, the risk manager must evaluate both the direct and indirect losses that may occur, as well as additional expenses that may be involved. If the cause of the loss is the immediate and direct precipitant of the loss, the loss is called a direct loss. Direct losses may be of two types: **on-premise** and **extended.** "When the peril that causes the loss is actuated on the same premises where the damaged or destroyed property is located, the loss is an on-premise property loss. If the peril that causes the loss is actuated away from the premises where the damaged or destroyed property is located, the loss is an extended direct property loss."

(Mehr and Hedges, Risk Management in the Business Enterprise.) For example, direct damage to one of the retaining dams in a farm's irrigation system would be considered an on-premise loss, whereas the loss of crops served by the irrigation system due to flooding or scorching of the unwatered property might be considered an extended property loss. Other examples of extended loss are damage caused by smoke and damage caused by water or chemicals used to extinguish a fire, if these occur on other premises.

The two major sources of indirect property loss are **damage caused by a change in environmental conditions** and **damage to an integral part of a set.** For example, in the irrigation system cited above, it is possible that the flooding might reach and temporarily disrupt an on-premise power system. The damage to the power system might, in turn, turn off all refrigeration units or shut down a production line, which might result not only in loss of production and related profits but also in partially or completely destroying the inventory. The damage to the power system is a direct loss—loss due to the flood, whereas the loss of the inventory would be an indirect loss, stemming, however, from a common initial peril.

Additional Expenses Associated with Property Damage. Further sources of property losses are those expenses that may have to be incurred in **clearing the premises for rebuilding.** Local laws or regulations may require that when the damage exceeds a stipulated amount the entire building must be torn down or completely modified to bring it up to present building standards. A firm that sustains property damage may further find that even though the salvage value of the plant does not equal the cost of tearing it down, the expense will have to be incurred.

LOSSES DIRECTLY AFFECTING INCOME. The measure of direct property loss is the cost of replacing the damaged property less any salvage value. However, if there is a **loss to inventory,** the direct loss is probably greater than the cost of replacing the inventory. Even though the new inventory is sold at a profit, the delay in replacement could be extensive, and the time value of money is such that a dollar of profits today is more valuable than a dollar of profits tomorrow.

Business Interruption. Property losses may interfere with or completely stop the operation of the business, as well as operations in other businesses. Since these losses generally cannot be promptly restored, they may result in a lengthy interruption of the business process. While the enterprise is shut down or crippled it may well lose not only current business but also the future business of valuable customers who may also have suffered losses due, for example, to lack of product to sell or lack of a part essential to the assembly of a finished product. The customer firm may be forced to purchase the goods elsewhere, possibly at a higher price, thus decreasing its net income through increased operation costs. (Schultz and Bardwell, Property Insurance.)

A company could reduce this type of risk by using **several suppliers** or by using a **supplier who has provided internally** for such a contingency. For example, a supplying firm may spread its productive capacity geographically so that the probability of loss of its entire capacity is virtually eliminated.

Some types of businesses **cannot close down,** and if this is the case the business may have to incur exceptional costs to continue in operation. The added costs of carrying on such a business (e.g., a private hospital) in substitute facilities may be extraordinarily high, and the facilities may not be nearly as satisfactory to the customer.

Risks Assumed Through Rental or Other Agreements. The terms of a contract may cause a firm to risk loss due to delay or other default of the party with whom the firm contracts, or a happening caused by events beyond the control of either party. These would be losses in addition to those strictly defined as business interruption losses. For example, the particular terms of a rental or lease agreement may obligate the tenant to make rental payments even if a building is temporarily rendered uninhabitable.

Losses Due to Destruction of Records. The loss of many types of records can be costly to a business. Such a loss may result in duplication of expenses (proof of payment lost), in loss of income (destruction of accounts receivable), and even in the loss of particular customers (destruction of technical data, etc.).

LOSSES FROM DEATH OR DISABILITY OF KEY PERSONNEL.

Inasmuch as the most valuable ingredient of many businesses is the ability of their management teams, the loss from death or disability of key personnel in some companies may be disastrous or extremely expensive. For example, **loss of key accounts** may result from the death of a particular salesman or sales executive (Huebner and Black, Life Insurance).

LIABILITY TO PUBLIC AND EMPLOYEES.

In the conduct of its affairs, a business constantly faces the possibility of being held liable to outsiders and its employees for personal injuries and property damages that are alleged to be the result of some failure or negligence on the part of the business. An injured party is afforded the legal remedy of bringing a suit or claim for damages. Since the **number and variety of claims and suits** seem to be limited only by the imagination of man, the cost of defending against them may be substantial. And when the injured are successful, the cost to the business may be much larger than most losses to physical property.

The business may also be held liable for the **misconduct of any employee or agent** while acting within the scope of his employment. Risk managers find this type of exposure to be one of the most difficult to control (Magee, General Insurance).

Workmen's Compensation Laws. In many states claims by employees for physical injury sustained during the course of their employment are administered through procedures established by Workmen's Compensation laws. These statutes provide an administrative proceeding for recovery of damages, such proceeding replacing and barring resort by the injured claimant to a legal suit. Usually, schedules determining the amounts to be paid as compensation for different types of injuries are established. The laws also provide that insurance coverage be maintained by all firms subject to the law to satisfy any awards of damages to employees. The insurance coverage is available through private commercial insurance companies. Though the procedure is heavily regulated, the area of risk covered cannot be ignored by the risk manager as the cost of the required insurance is usually directly related to the firm's claims experience.

LOSSES DUE TO DISHONESTY OR OTHER CRIMINAL ACTS.

The commission of a crime may result in the loss of property and income. Even if the criminal is apprehended there is no assurance that there will be a full, or even partial, restitution of the loss. **Criminal perils that a business is subject to** include the following: burglary, robbery, embezzlement, forgery, conversion (theft), and vandalism. The risk manager views these perils with the same concern as other perils and acts to see that they are reduced to the extent possible and economical. He then decides what steps should be taken to handle the remaining risk.

Dealing with Risk

AVAILABLE ALTERNATIVES. Unless an individual firm has a large enough number of "exposed" units for the law of large numbers to apply and make the happening of certain occurrences definitely predictable, the firm cannot very well reduce its own exposure to risk. Therefore, only a very few firms can reduce their exposure and virtually every firm must deal with one or more risks that could cause major losses. Every firm inevitably does confront each of the risks it is exposed to—though the confrontation may be the end result of anything from a well-thought-out program to haphazard or involuntary choice due to ignorance or inaction.

The skillful risk manager, as suggested above, first familiarizes himself with all the risks to which his firm may be exposed. He then proceeds to decide which of the following **four alternatives** to pursue in dealing with each type of risk:

1. Control the risk and/or loss
2. Assume the risk
3. Self-insure
4. Transfer the risk through the purchase of commercial insurance or through other devices.

CONTROL OF RISK AND LOSS. The control of risk and loss involves measures directed toward their reduction or elimination. If all possibility of loss is eliminated, the risk is also eliminated. Decisions regarding control of risk and loss must first of all take into account the costs involved.

Cost of Risk. According to Mehr and Hedges (Risk Management in the Business Enterprise):

Cost of risk has been defined as cost which would not be incurred if future losses were known. If losses are higher because of their uncertainty, then by definition these losses will include some cost of risk. The cost of risk, however, is not the entire amount by which the cost of uncertain losses will exceed cost of losses that are certain. If the onset of the losses could be foreseen, usually something would be done about them, and that "something" would itself cost something. Therefore, the difference between cost under certainty and cost under uncertainty would be the net difference between the cost of "doing something" about the loss before it occurs and the extra cost suffered because nothing was done. Because it is not always feasible to do something effective, it may turn out that the cost of risk is zero. Even if losses were fully known in advance, the only practicable treatment might still be simply to suffer them. Then, and only then, is the cost of risk zero.

Thus, a distinction may be made between the **cost of the loss itself** and the **costs incurred because of the uncertainty that a loss may occur.** The latter costs would be the dollar amount of the insurance premiums if the risk is transferred to an insurer, or the cost of keeping funds available to provide for a loss if the risk is assumed.

Benefits from Loss Control. Whether a firm bears or transfers the risk of a loss, successful loss prevention activities will be financially advantageous to the firm, provided, of course, the cost of such activities does not exceed the benefits derived therefrom. Loss prevention may benefit the firm in several ways. **If the risk of loss is transferred to an insurer,** the latter may reduce the insurance costs to the extent it deems the firm's loss-prevention activities successful.

Further, the amount of losses is rarely covered in its entirety by insurance, and the value of the losses avoided is saved to the firm. **If the firm assumes its own risks,** it is financially better off to the extent of the dollar reduction in loss less the costs of the loss-reduction activities.

Methods of Loss Reduction. Loss prevention and control may to some extent be carried on by everyone, but if the amounts involved are large, **trained specialists** should be used, whether as permanent staff members or on a consulting basis.

Many insurers provide loss-prevention counsel of high quality to the insured party. From their own experience with prior losses they are often able to point out steps that can be taken to reduce the probability of a loss. They may have on their staffs professionally trained and experienced people who devote themselves to a study of ways of reducing losses.

ASSUMPTION OF RISK AND LOSS. Risk assumption, the equivalent of noninsurance, takes place when a firm, consciously or unconsciously, assumes a given risk or risks. A firm's risk assumption may be either planned or unplanned.

Unplanned risk assumption occurs when the party concerned is not cognizant of a given risk or, although cognizant of it, feels that the probability of loss is so remote that no allowance need be made for it. When such a loss occurs, the firm must bear the cost, the consequences depending, of course, upon the magnitude of the loss and the firm's ability to absorb it.

Planned assumption of risk and the connected loss occurs when a firm is cognizant of a particular loss exposure but believes that the dollar amount is relatively inconsequential and, therefore, decides to absorb it if it should occur. A fund or reserve may be established for such losses, or they may be assumed on a current basis. In the latter instance the company is, in effect, gambling on the occurrence of a loss. Sometimes this decision is dictated by a critical need for funds. In any event, the maximum loss that could occur in a given period should be estimated as closely as possible, so that the management can act with open eyes.

Lenders and other suppliers of funds, including trade creditors, should be cognizant of any risk to their commitment resulting from the user's inadequate plans for assuming, avoiding, or transferring the risks to which it is exposed.

SELF-INSURANCE. Self-insurance is defined as a deliberate program of the exposed party to provide for his own insurance. It occurs when a firm recognizes a loss potential and decides that its financial consequences could be more than the firm should try to absorb without making some allowance in advance. Thus, self-insurance is distinguished from risk assumption.

The insurance buyer is becoming increasingly aware of the fact that mere trading of dollars with an insurance company does not constitute effective risk management. In their attempts to popularize the use of a **deductible,** insurance companies themselves recognize that the insured is frequently better off if he bears part of the risk himself. When a business achieves a size where constant exposure to some peril produces losses that are regular and predictable in nature, the accountant will write these losses off as business expenses. Although the firm has absorbed these costs, it has avoided paying for insurance that would, in these circumstances, exceed the cost of the losses themselves. Commercial insurance exists primarily to provide a means for meeting unusual and crippling losses.

Firms self-insure in order to save money since, generally speaking, when commercial insurance is purchased, 40 to 50% of the premium dollar may go for the insurer's expenses. In addition, a firm may self-insure when commercial insurance is not available at all or only at a prohibitive cost. For a discussion of comparative costs of self-insurance as against commercial insurance see "Cost of Commercial vs. Self-Insurance," page 9.

A genuine self-insurance plan, involving scientific methods of measuring risk and of setting aside reserves, may cost more when managed by the business firm than by the specialized insurance company, but there may be situations where it can be done to advantage.

The use of larger and larger deductibles as a type of self-insurance seems to be reasonable. A loss that would have been considered large thirty years ago has shrunk in significance because of inflation, the increase in scale of business, and higher taxes, so that many firms realize they can **absorb much larger losses** without embarrassment.

The risk manager, conscious of the high cost of risk-bearing, whoever does the job, should never consider resorting to insurance until all of the methods for reducing or eliminating risks have been exhausted.

Conditions Necessary for Self-Insurance. Basically, for self-insurance to be advisable the same general conditions must exist as are required for any insurer to operate. That is, the party should have a **large number of nearly homogeneous units** subject to the loss, these exposed units should **not be subject to catastrophic hazard,** and the firm should have some **historical experience** upon which to determine the probability of loss (Angell, Insurance). By a "large" number of units is meant a number sufficient to make operable the law of large numbers.

In spite of the possible saving, many firms **prefer not to self-insure.** For one thing, it takes time to build up a fund for complete self-insurance. While this fund is being built up, the firm may carry some commercial insurance or may seek to transfer the risk in some other way. As the fund grows, the amount of externally purchased insurance may drop, and eventually the firm may completely self-insure in respect to a particular loss exposure. The company may find, however, that the alternative uses of the money committed to the fund offer a rate of return so attractive that the purchase of commercial insurance, although expensive in some respects, actually represents the optimum use of funds. (See "Cost of Commercial vs. Self-Insurance," below.)

Companies must also take into account the fact that the static risks are random not only in respect to **place of occurrence** but also in respect to **time.** To be fully covered in the event of a loss occurring in the near future may mean that commercial insurance is a must, at least initially.

PURCHASING COMMERCIAL INSURANCE. Normally the firm obtains insurance when it has been decided that this is the least costly manner of providing for the risk or the only practical method available for dealing with it (Angell, Insurance). The decision to buy insurance should be continually re-examined in the light of changed conditions, and the risk manager should continually ask the questions: Should the firm insure? Is the coverage adequate? Is the coverage excessive?

Availability of Insurance. Not all the risks can be transferred, and commercial insurance, which is one form of risk transfer, is not always available nor always economically feasible. For insurance to be available for purchase the following conditions must exist:

1. The loss must be determinable and measurable.
2. The chance of loss must be small enough so that the sale of insurance is economically feasible.
3. There must be a sufficiently large number of independent exposures.
4. The objects to be insured must be sufficiently homogeneous so that reliable statistics can be formulated.
5. There must be randomness of loss.
6. It must be possible to predict the losses with reasonable accuracy.
7. The insurer's cost of operation must be reasonably low.
8. There must be a large enough number of exposed firms seeking this coverage.

Insurance will be made commercially available only if the risk is insurable as indicated above. It must be available at a **reasonable cost,** or for all practical purposes it is considered unavailable.

Cost of Commercial vs. Self-Insurance. The basic criterion in deciding on the method of dealing with risk is **comparative cost.** Care must be taken, however, to be sure that the comparative costs are correctly evaluated, and this analysis must be carried on continually—or at least periodically.

Most firms have more profitable uses for money than they have funds available. Thus, costly as commercial insurance may be, the cost of opportunities lost by building up and holding a fund for self-insurance purposes may exceed the cost of the insurance. The following example, comparing the relative cost of funded risk assumption and that of the purchase of commercial insurance, demonstrates a method used to evaluate the alternative means of providing for a risk.

Assume that a firm has a maximum loss exposure in respect to a particular asset of $100,000 and is studying the advisability of carrying commercial insurance to the full extent of the loss or of establishing a fund to cover potential loss. In evaluating the costs, the following assumptions will be made:

Federal income tax rate applicable, 48%
Municipal income tax rate applicable, 8%
Total income taxes, 56%
Internal, pretax, rate of return on invested assets, 22%
Rate of return on short-term investments, 3½%
Average loss exposure for this type of asset is such that losses paid for by the insurer have been running at 60% of premiums.
The loss costs are related to the average loss rate.
Average losses are $5,000 per year.

Risk Assumption Funded

Average loss		$ 5,000
Income on $100,000 fund at 3½%	$ 3,500	
Potential income derived from internal investment of $100,000 at 22%	22,000	
Opportunity cost		18,500
Gross cost of risk and loss before taxes...........		$23,500
Net cost if average loss materializes, after allowance of 56% tax rate (net dollar amount of loss, and potential income on the fund)		$10,340

Commercial Insurance

Average losses of $5,000 assumed to be 60% of the premium. Premium covers both cost of losses and risks	$8,333
Net cost of carrying insurance after allowance of 56% tax rate applicable	$3,667

Under the above assumed conditions, it is apparent that the cost of commercial insurance is considerably less than that of risk assumption through setting up of a fund.

In comparing one alternative with another, all costs, both direct and indirect, should be taken into consideration. These costs may include those of defense in law suits arising out of the loss, costs of loss adjustment, and cost of records that must be maintained.

OTHER RISK TRANSFER DEVICES. Risks can also be transferred to parties other than an insurer. As Mehr and Hedges (Risk Management in the Business Enterprise) state: "The variety of ways in which risks may be transferred by contract is limited only by the ingenuity of the contracting parties. . . ." Some of the other devices of risk transfer are indicated below.

Use of Leased Property. When a firm leases either real or personal property the risks of ownership continue to be borne by the lessor unless they are transferred by contract to the lessee. However, the reason for leasing property is rarely for the sole purpose of transferring the risks of ownership, and the lessee does not escape the related costs since the lessor must provide for these risks, and the lease payments will undoubtedly reflect the cost of assuming them.

Construction Contracts. A firm contracting for the erection of a building or other real property may thereby transfer some, but probably not all, risks to the contractor. The agreement may provide, for example, that any physical damage, thefts, or vandalism occurring during the construction period are the **responsibility of the contractor.** However, the engagement of an outside contractor does not automatically and completely absolve the party who contracted for the work from all the risks involved. The law may hold the **contracting party liable** for a variety of risks—for example, injuries that result from the nature of the work being performed. A firm using an independent contractor to perform specific work would be well advised to obtain expert help in providing for these possible liabilities, as the law of liability is very complex, and the financial consequences could be critical.

Bailments. A bailment exists when one party (the bailor) voluntarily places goods with another (the bailee) for sale, processing, safekeeping, servicing, or for some other purpose. This generally excludes common carriers, although even here, in some jurisdictions, a bailment is deemed to exist. **State laws** distributing risk between a bailor and a bailee vary widely and in order for a bailor to adequately protect himself he should determine in advance what risks, if any, the law transfers to the bailee. Then, if existing laws do not make clear which party bears the risks, or if the law permits the parties to distribute the risk in whatever manner they choose, the responsibility for each different risk and/or loss should be **plainly stipulated in the contract** of bailment.

Sales Contracts. In purchasing property a firm may, through contract, have the **seller assume all risk** of loss until the goods are deposited with the buyer. The **seller may carry the risk himself,** as he would do if the goods were delivered by his own carrier, or he may transfer the risk to a public carrier.

Again, as with bailments, the extent to which the risks can be transferred depends upon the particular state's laws and upon the contract between the shipper and the carrier.

In **selling any tangible goods** for use or consumption, situations arise in which there may be losses due to negligent manufacture or other defect. In many instances the manufacturer, processor, bottler, or canner may agree to protect its distributors or retailers from any damage or injury suits that may result.

Suretyship. Risk may also be transferred to a surety. A surety is one who promises a second party that a third party will perform (the job contracted for). Should the third party fail, the surety then must perform or indemnify the second party for the lack of performance. Any legal party can act as a surety, but contracts of suretyship are most commonly issued by corporations that make it a business. (Angell, Insurance—Principles and Practices.)

Commercial Insurance Coverage

REGULATION OF THE INSURANCE BUSINESS. It has been held (South Eastern Underwriters Association *et al.*, 322 U. S. 533 1944) that insurance is in interstate commerce and is therefore subject to Federal regulation. Federal statutes apply in various situations, particularly those involving the Federal antitrust acts. In practice, however, insurance is regulated for the most part by the **individual states.** (Rohrer, State Regulation of Insurance.) Companies are regulated by the states in which they are incorporated and, in addition, are subject to extraterritorial regulation by the states in which they do business. As an example, the State of New York subjects "foreign" companies doing business in the state to "reasonable" compliance with the New York Code under the "Appleton Rule" (New York Insurance Law, Article 4, § 42, paragraph 5).

Each state is free to enact insurance legislation as it pleases, although there are a number of cases in which **uniform legislation** has been adopted by a majority of the states. One of the major achievements of the **National Association of Insurance Commissioners,** composed of representatives of all the states, "has been the promulgating of uniform state laws with regard to insurance and the recommending of such laws to the various state legislatures." (Angell, Insurance.)

The state controls the insurance business through the courts, the legislature, and an administrative agency under an official known as **Insurance Commissioner,** Superintendent of Insurance, or similar title. This official is the most important of the state's control media, according to Kulp (Casualty Insurance), because of his difficult and essential role of executing the continuing mass of complex legislation. Among the Commissioner's **principal powers** are the granting of licenses to transact business, the examination in detail of the condition of insurers, and the investigation of complaints.

THE INSURANCE POLICY. The insurance policy is a complex legal document, and a thorough understanding of its component parts is mandatory for the insured party. The basic policy is made up of declarations, the insuring agreements, exclusions, and conditions. In addition there may be endorsements and/or riders.

Standardization of Policies. Insurance policies have to some extent become standardized by law, by competition among insurers, by company agreement, and by custom. According to Angell (Insurance):

Standardization is generally of benefit to the insured since it permits him to know that policies will read the same regardless of which company they are purchased from. This also simplifies adjustment problems in the event a loss occurs and contracts are in force in more than one company. An advantage both to the policyholder and the company is that under a standard policy a body of court decisions gradually accumulates which has interpreted the various words of the policy.

There is no **standard policy** in universal use throughout the United States. However, such basic forms as the standard fire policy, the standard workmen's compensation and employers' liability policy, and the standard automobile liability policy are used by most if not all insurers and approved by a majority of the states. Also, every state has statutes requiring the inclusion of certain **standard provisions** in certain kinds of policies.

TYPES OF POLICIES. A **specific policy** is one that insures specifically designated property for a stipulated amount. A **blanket policy** covers more than one class of property at a given location (such as "Dwelling and Contents") or property located at more than one location.

Schedule and Package Policies. A schedule policy provides specific protection for more than one type of property or interest (personal property floaters); against several enumerated perils and hazards (owner's, landlord's, and tenant's liability); or against several exposures to loss as listed or indicated in the schedule (schedule bond).

A package policy is one that combines different coverages, such as fire and extended coverage, theft, personal liability, and often a medical payments coverage (as in the homeowners policy) in **one contract**. It requires the purchase of fixed or minimum amounts of insurance under each coverage.

Floater and General Cover or Multiple Location Policies. A floater policy covers property wherever it may be located, including **goods in transit** but usually excluding property on the premises of the insured's principal place of business. Because it covers goods in transit it is usually written as an inland marine floater.

A general cover or multiple location policy provides automatic **coverage for fluctuating inventories at several locations.** Periodic reporting of the amounts of stock located at the various places is usually required. This policy was designed to meet the requirements of firms having many stores or warehouses, often in different states. Since it does not cover goods in transit, it is not a floater type of policy.

Comprehensive and "All-Risk" Policies. The term comprehensive may be used to describe a broad class of property, as in the "contents form" of the fire policy; to describe a broad group of perils or hazards insured against, as in the comprehensive auto policy; or to describe a broad package of coverages, such as are found in the comprehensive dwelling form and other broad-form coverages.

An "all-risk" type of policy insures against any loss of property from any peril to which it might be exposed. Since the coverage is so general and inclusive it is necessary for the insurance company to state specific **exceptions** where there are good reasons for making them. Hence, in an "all-risk" type of policy it is more important to know what is in the exceptions than to know what is in the insuring agreement.

The more specialized the business of risk management becomes, the less certain it is that all insurance needs should be met in one package. Package and "all-risk" policies offer many advantages for the average insurance buyer, but to the extent that they offer coverage of risks that the insured may rather bear in some other manner, they may prevent rather than aid in the specialized treatment of risk.

IMPORTANT POLICY CLAUSES. The following clauses are often found in property insurance policies.

Co-insurance Clause. This clause is designed to encourage the insured to take insurance amounting to a certain per cent of the actual value of the property covered. Otherwise, he will be paid for only a fraction of any loss sustained, even if the loss is small. The operation of an 80% co-insurance clause may be illustrated as follows:

Property value	$50,000
Insured for	$30,000
Insurance required under 80% clause	$40,000
Loss	$ 5,000

When property is covered by a policy that contains a co-insurance clause, the insurance company pays that proportion of the loss that the insurance taken bears to the amount of insurance required by the clause. In the above case, therefore, the insurer would pay ¾ of $5,000, or $3,750, and the insured as "co-insurer" would pay $1,250.

At first glance it might appear that this clause is introduced to force the policy holder to carry large amounts of insurance, but in fact its use is necessary for the **setting of equitable rates.** Since the majority of losses to property are only partial, the necessary rate per $100 of exposure drops off rapidly as the per cent of value insured increases. If all insurance buyers wished to insure to only 20% of value, for example, the premium rate per $100 would be much higher than if most of them took insurance to 80% of value.

Use of a system of **graded rates** would offer an alternative to the use of the co-insurance clause. Premium rates under this plan would vary from policy to policy with the ratio of the amount of insurance purchased to the actual value of the property. It is believed, however, that the use of a graded system of rates would add substantially to insurance costs.

Pro Rata Liability Clause. This is a clause that limits a particular insurance company's liability in respect to a given loss to that proportion of the loss that the insurance issued by that company bears to the total insurance. If all insurance policies are alike, the clause causes little difficulty; if they might differ in endorsements or clauses attached, making them **"nonconcurrent,"** problems may arise in securing an adjustment of losses that is fair to both the insured and the insurance company. (Magee, General Insurance.)

Pro Rata Distribution Clause. If a blanket policy covers several locations, this clause has the effect of distributing the coverage among the different locations in the proportion that the values of the individual locations bear to the total value of all locations at the time of a loss. Without this clause a small blanket policy might be adequate to give complete indemnity for losses to large property values at separate locations. (Magee, General Insurance.)

Replacement Cost Clause. Under most property insurance policies the insurance company agrees to indemnify the insured for an amount equal to the "actual cash value." This takes into consideration appreciation, depreciation, and obsolescence. Under replacement-cost coverage it is possible for the insured to recover "the replacement cost of the building structure or any part thereof identical with such building structure on the same premises and intended for the same occupancy and use." This is subject to the **limitation** of the face value of the policy and other limitations that may be stated in the clause. (Mehr and Cammack, Principles of Insurance.)

Mortgagee Clause. When this clause is included in a mortgagor's policy for the benefit of a mortgagee, the effect is to provide a separate contract between the company and the mortgagee. The latter's right to payment in event of a loss will not be invalidated by any action that the insurance company may take against the mortgagor because of any act or neglect on his part. The mortgagee assumes responsibility, however, for notifying the company of "any change of ownership or occupancy or increase of hazard which shall come to the knowledge of said mortgagee (or trustee) and, unless permitted by this policy, it shall be noted thereon and the mortgagee (or trustee) shall, on demand, pay the premium for such increased hazard for the term of use thereof." (Rodda, Fire and Property Insurance.)

Subrogation Clause. This clause is included to make clear in various situations the intention and right of the insurance company, upon the payment of a claim, to **take over the right of action** that the insured may possess against any party responsible or liable, in any manner, for the loss. (Greene, Risk and Insurance.)

Apportionment Clause. This clause appears in connection with the extended coverage endorsement of the standard fire policy (see below). It is similar in its effect to the pro rata liability clause with the difference that it prorates the liability of the company to pay for losses from perils other than fire to the proportion that the fire insurance under the given policy bears to the total amount of fire insurance covering the property.

Insurance Against Physical Damage to Property

FIRE AND ALLIED LINES. The basic standard fire policy is the form originally adopted by New York State in 1943 and now **mandatory** in practically all states. It protects against the perils of direct loss by fire, by lightning, and by removal from the premises of property endangered by the perils insured against. It covers only at specific locations, and only the specific interests of the insured party described in the contract. It may cover both building and contents, or either separately, depending upon the interest of the insured. The policy is subject to numerous stipulations, conditions, and exclusions, each of which should be clearly understood by the insured.

Inasmuch as the standard fire policy specifies the perils covered, it differs from the all-risk or all-perils type of policy; in specifying the exact location of the property covered, it differs from a floating type policy; and in specifying the maximum amount of insurance provided, it differs from automatic or reporting forms of coverage.

Extended Coverage Endorsement (EC). Since the standard policy itself provides that insurance against additional perils may be provided by written endorsements added to the policy, it has long been the practice to cover several additional perils. These are the perils of: windstorm, hail, explosion, riot and civil

INSURANCE AGAINST PHYSICAL DAMAGE TO PROPERTY   25·15

commotion, aircraft, vehicles, and smoke. These added perils are subject to the same exact definition and to the same kind of conditions, exclusions, and limitations as the standard policy, but they are also subject to **special limitations** included on the endorsement itself. This endorsement has long made the fire policy a multiple-peril coverage, constituting the basic protection ordinarily acquired in the purchase of "fire" insurance.

Additional Extended Coverage (AEC). Ten additional perils may be covered in a fire policy by the use of this additional endorsement. They are (a) water damage from plumbing and heating systems, (b) rupture or bursting of steam or hot water heating systems, (c) vandalism and malicious mischief, (d) vehicles owned or operated by the insured or a tenant, (e) fall of trees, (f) objects falling from the weight of ice, snow, or sleet, (g) freezing of plumbing, heating, and the like, (h) collapse, (i) landslide, and (j) glass breakage. None of these perils overlaps those covered by the extended coverage endorsement. The vehicle coverage of the EC endorsement, for instance, does not cover vehicles owned or operated by the insured or a tenant. Fall of trees may cause damage when not a direct result of a peril covered in the EC endorsement, and glass breakage, though covered as a loss when caused directly by an insured peril, may be caused by perils not otherwise listed. (Angell, Insurance.)

BUSINESS COVERAGES—MULTIPLE LINE. Business policies, now written under the sanction of multiple line laws (see page 38), allow fire and casualty coverages to be written in the same contract. (Michelbacher, Multiple-line Insurance.) These policies are even more inclusive than those available with the EC and AEC endorsements added to the standard fire policy. They are formed by extending the standard fire policy to cover "all risks" to the described property, subject, however, to specific exclusions. In this type of policy the **exclusions** are as important to the insured as the perils actually covered. Examples of these broad coverages follow.

Jewelers' Block Policy. The first business multiple line coverage to be sold, this floater may be used by jewelry retailers, wholesalers, or manufacturers. It is written as inland marine coverage (see page 17) and covers all risks of loss or damage to a jeweler's stock anywhere in the United States. It also covers property entrusted to the jeweler by others, and the coverage may be extended to include the theft of money. With the endorsements that are permitted, it may be said to cover every possible business loss to which a jeweler may be exposed.

Mercantile Block Policy—Commercial Property Coverage. This policy, made up by attaching the proper form to the standard fire policy, insures against all risks of direct physical loss of or to property covered while anywhere within the continental United States or in transit in Canada. Property covered consists of (1) stocks of merchandise, (2) fixtures, furniture, and equipment, and (3) the insured's interest in improvements and betterment of the premises.

It is written with a deductible and provides for the monthly reporting of values located at different places as in the multiple location fire insurance policy. As in all "all-risk" types of policies, the specific exclusions as to property, perils, and situations must be carefully analyzed by the insured.

Manufacturers' Output Policy. This policy provides manufacturers with all-risk coverage of **personal property located off the insured's premises.** It is a new multiple line policy and not merely an extension of the standard fire policy. It is written on a reporting form basis and specifies three limits of liability: at each location, on any one conveyance, and while property is located at conventions or fairs. It does not cover real estate except for improvements and betterments.

Other Business Multiple-Line Coverages. The industrial property form, public institutions form, and office contents special form are available on an all-risk basis, and new forms are being constantly developed in this highly fluid and competitive industry.

OCEAN MARINE POLICIES. The field of marine insurance is divided into two major divisions: ocean marine and inland marine. The feature common to both of them is that they cover property in movement from place to place or property used in some manner to assist in the movement of goods.

Ocean marine insurance is the oldest branch of the insurance business, and many of its features show the influence of the practices and customs developed among the individual underwriters in London. There is no standard policy in use today, but a considerable amount of **standardization** in the important clauses has been achieved through the activities of the American Institute of Marine Underwriters. (Mowbray and Blanchard, Insurance: Its Theory and Practice in the United States.)

Marine policies continue in many instances to use **phraseology** from the 17th century or earlier. The reason for this, according to Angell (Insurance), is not to confuse the insured, but to continue the use of language that has been interpreted many times and that is therefore definite in nature. The following example from an early insuring agreement is still typical of statements used in policies issued by American companies, although the wording has now been somewhat modernized; the perils covered remain essentially the same.

Touching the Adventures and Perils which we the Assurers are contented to bear and to take upon us in this Voyage, they are of the Seas, Men-of-War, Fires, Enemies, Pirates, Rovers, Thieves, Jettisons, Letters of Mart and Countermart, Surprisals, Takings at Sea, Arrests, Restraints and Detainments of all Kings, Princes and People, of what Nation, Condition, or quality soever, Barratry of the Master and Mariners . . . and it is agreed by us, the Insurers that this Writing or Policy of Assurance shall be of as much Force and Effect as the surest Writing or Policy of Assurance heretofore made in Lombard Street, or in the Royal Exchange, or elsewhere in London.

The typical policy covers:

1. **Perils of the Sea,** which are those associated with the natural hazards of a voyage such as sinking, stranding, overturning, collision, lightning, and action of the wind and waves.
2. **Perils on the Sea,** which include fire; jettisons, the throwing overboard of all or a part of the cargo; barratry of the masters and mariners, the equivalent of embezzlement; and "all other perils." "All other perils" would seem to make this policy an all-risk coverage, but what is meant by the phrase is that the policy will cover perils which are related to those already enumerated. The policy is definitely **not an "all-risk" policy.**
3. **Additional Perils,** which may be added by agreement. The policy may be extended to cover theft, leakage, spoilage of refrigerated foods and pilferage. A clause extending coverage to losses attributable to latent defects in machinery, hull, and appurtenances, and known as the **Inchmaree clause,** is frequently added. Liability for damage to another ship, its cargo and other interests may be provided by the added endorsement of a **running-down clause.** Additional liability for damage caused upon or by the insured's own ship may be covered by a **protection and indemnity policy.** A **warehouse to warehouse clause** may extend coverage to perils upon the land, including fire, earthquake, flood and collision. In the case of cargo insurance, it is possible to

INSURANCE AGAINST PHYSICAL DAMAGE TO PROPERTY 25·17

add an endorsement making the policy cover "all risks" of certain types. (Huebner and Black, Property Insurance.)

Ocean Marine Losses. Marine losses may be **partial** or **total,** falling upon one interest alone, such as the owner of cargo, or shared by all interests involved in a voyage, including the owner of the ship and the owner of the cargo as well as one who owns only the freight interest.

The word **"average"** is used in ocean marine insurance to refer to a loss that is less than a total loss. Hence, partial losses may be either a **"particular** average loss," involving only one interest, or a **"general** average loss," which is borne proportionally by all interests when it results from the fact that some or all cargo must be voluntarily sacrificed to save an entire ship. The settlement of general average losses is a highly technical matter usually entrusted to specialized **"general average adjusters."** Policies frequently specify the rules to be followed (e.g., York-Antwerp Rules) in settling such losses. (Magee, General Insurance.)

Features of Ocean Marine Policies. Policies in ocean marine insurance may be used to protect any one of three different interests: (1) that of owners or charterers and of mortgagees in the hull, machinery, and equipment; (2) that of owners, consignees, commission merchants, and others in the cargo; and (3) that of owners or charterers of ships in freight charges that may be collectible only if the voyage is successfully completed. The latter interest is rarely insured in a separate policy, but is generally included in valuing the hull and cargo interests.

The **builder's-risk policy** is essentially a shore cover and relates to the construction and initial trial period of the vessel. Policies may be issued to insure against **"total loss only"** or **"port risk only,"** the latter covering the vessel only while in port or dry-dock.

Policies may be issued to cover a particular voyage, on an annual or term basis, or as an **open policy** in which there is no expiration date stated. The great majority of marine policies are written on an "open" basis. Cargo policies may cover one particular type of goods or general cargo, and they may cover "on deck" or "underdeck." Because many types of cargo are particularly susceptible to damage during an ocean trip, a clause known as the **memorandum clause** is used to provide that any loss less than a specified percentage of the total value will not be paid. This is not a true deductible clause, because if the loss exceeds the stated percentage it will be paid in full.

A straight deductible is also used in marine insurance and may read: "Free of particular average under 5 per cent, which is deductible." Thus, in the case of a 15% loss, the insurance company would pay 10%. Any type of loss may also be covered by another type of deductible known as a **franchise clause.** As in the case of the memorandum clause, nothing will be paid if the loss is less than a stated per cent; but if it exceeds this percentage, it will be paid in full.

Cargo insurance in both the ocean marine and inland marine divisions is all the more essential for the sending or receiving firm that bears the risk because of the relatively low degree of liability for which the carriers may be held responsible. This is true whether goods are sent by ship, railroad, truck, or airplane.

INLAND MARINE POLICIES. Inland marine lines of insurance have assumed growing importance in recent years. This has been due, in part, to the great increase in the need for transportation coverage on land and in the air and the widespread nature of modern business operations. In competition with fire and casualty carriers, who long operated under the restraint of monoline laws (see page 38), inland marine carriers found opportunities to exploit their relative freedom to combine coverages in a multiple line type of policy. For this reason they have been a powerful force in the development of the all-risk type of coverage. (Schultz and Schultz, The Journal of Insurance, Vol. XXVIII.)

The expansion of inland marine insurance writing was partially checked in 1933 when the National Convention of Insurance Commissioners drew up a "**Nationwide Definition** and Interpretation of the Insuring Powers of Marine and Transportation Underwriters." This was revised in 1953 and has since become law in nearly all of the states. Although this brought about some semblance of order to the competitive practices of the various companies, it did not prevent the continued demand for the "multiple perils" type of coverage from affecting the fire and casualty lines as well.

Inland marine coverages fall into three major groups: (1) transportation policies, (2) floater policies, and (3) policies covering instrumentalities of transportation. There are a large number of policies in each category, but within each group they share the same general character. (Rodda, Inland Marine and Transportation Insurance.)

Transportation Policies. The basic transportation policy is the **inland transit floater policy,** which is completed for each special class of transportation insurance by the attachment of special forms to fit the particular needs of the insured. (Angell, Insurance.) The coverage may be procured by either the carrier or by the owner of the goods. The carrier is interested primarily in protecting itself against its legal liability for loss and will usually not purchase insurance covering direct physical loss.

The land carrier has a higher degree of responsibility for the care of goods entrusted to him than does the ocean carrier, but he is not responsible for losses due to: (1) a so-called act of God, which is generally defined as an unusual natural disturbance such as flood, earthquake, storm, or lightning; (2) the war hazard; (3) damage or destruction of property by a public authority; (4) any fault or neglect on the part of the shipper, such as goods being carelessly packed, with a loss resulting from this cause; and (5) inherent vice, referring to any quality of an article that makes it tend to destroy itself. Even if a carrier may be held to be legally liable, there may be long delays before an equitable adjustment may be obtained, and a shipper may find it advantageous to rely upon relatively prompt settlement by the insurance company, leaving it to the insurer, whose rights arise out of subrogation, to collect, if possible, from the carrier. A further need for insurance stems from the fact that the owner will often accept a "**released bill of lading**" from the carrier, limiting the amount of loss for which the carrier may be responsible.

The principal types of policies covering direct losses are: (1) **trip transit policies,** covering single shipments, and (2) **annual transit policies,** which may be written to cover incoming shipments of businessmen as well as outgoing shipments and which may be written on both an annual and an open form. The **annual-readjustment form** provides for the advance payment of an annual premium, with an adjustment at the end of the year. The open policy requires a monthly reporting of shipments covered, with premiums being due and payable when the report is made. The coverage provided is the same in both forms. Other policies include railway express policies, motor truck transportation owners policy, parcel post policies, department store floaters, first class mail and registered mail, and others covering a wide variety of special situations.

The most widely used policy covering the liability of the carrier is the **motor carriers' cargo liability policy.** The growing importance of this coverage is due both to the great increase in truck hauling and to pressure from state legislatures that have become increasingly concerned with the ability of truckers to assume liability for goods entrusted to their care. These policies may be written on a blanket form covering up to a fixed limit of liability on each truck, with an annual premium charged for the total liability assumed for all trucks; or they may be written on a form fixing a limit of liability on each truck but also subject to a limit of liability for any casualty that may involve more than one truck. The premium is calculated on gross earnings reported monthly by the insured.

Floater Contracts. A floater policy is one that follows the property, i.e., "floats along" wherever it may go. Coverage under such contracts may be worldwide, although some of them are limited to the continental United States, and includes all risks, subject, however, to listed exclusions. As in the case of the transportation policy, a scheduled "property floater" or "inland floater" is used as the basic policy, and many different forms may be attached to fit it to the particular needs of the insured. Many forms are issued subject to a deductible.

Floaters used to cover business property, wherever it may be located, may be issued to protect the interests of owners or bailees. In fact, it was out of this line that the first "all-risk" (or block) policy, the **jewelers' block policy**, developed (see page 15). In this type of policy, the extensions of fire and allied lines merge with those of inland marine lines in a new class known as multiple line coverages.

Some of the better known **commercial floaters** covering an owner's interest are:

1. Contractors' equipment floater.
2. Installation risks floater.
3. Installment sales floater.
4. Mobile agricultural equipment floater.
5. Physicians' and surgeons' floater.
6. Radium floater.

Floaters are also issued to cover the liability of the bailee for goods entrusted to his care. Such liability may be either legally imposed or voluntarily assumed. Aside from his liability, a bailee may have an interest in the goods of others because of the possible loss of payment for his services. Among the floaters used for these purposes are:

1. Floor plan insurance.
2. Laundries' and dry cleaners' insurance.
3. Furriers' customers' insurance.
4. Cold storage locker insurance.

Instrumentalities of Transportation. The "Nationwide Definition" (see page 18) authorizes inland marine companies to cover a wide variety of property not movable in itself but generally characterized by some feature relating it to a transportation risk. (Snider, ed., Readings in Property and Casualty Insurance.) Such property includes:

1. Bridges and tunnels.
2. Pipelines.
3. Wharves and piers.
4. Power transmission lines, telephone and telegraph lines, neon signs.

Builders'-risk contracts may be written to cover such property during the construction process. (Angell, Insurance.)

AUTOMOBILE PHYSICAL DAMAGE POLICY. Insurance against physical damage to automobiles is usually written today in conjunction with bodily injury and property damage liability insurance to provide a broad coverage for car owners. The automobile physical damage policy is usually written on a standard form agreed upon by the **American Mutual Alliance** (an organization representing mutual companies) and the **National Automobile Underwriters Association** (representing stock insurance companies). The form is used by most companies represented in these two groups, but it is not required by law. (Brainard, Automobile Insurance.)

Types of Automobile Coverage. The first page of the auto policy contains a schedule of coverage under which the company may be bound and indicating the specific premium charge to be paid for each coverage, together with the limits of liability to be assumed. Three of these coverages relate to the liability portion of the contract, the others being comprehensive (excluding collision); collision; fire, lightning, and transportation; theft; combined additional coverage; towing and labor costs; and uninsured motorists.

The **comprehensive coverage** is an all-risk coverage and covers against losses from fire, theft, transportation, windstorm, hail, earthquake, and explosion. Essentially it provides coverage against every physical loss except those arising from collision. Many policies combine the comprehensive coverage with the collision liability coverages to provide nearly complete protection for the car owner. Towing and labor cost is not included in the comprehensive, however, nor is protection available against failure to collect a judgment against an uninsured motorist.

The **combined additional coverage** protects against the perils of windstorm, hail, earthquake, explosion, riot or civil commotion, forced landing or falling of any aircraft, flood or rising waters, malicious mischief or vandalism, external discharge or leakage of water except loss resulting from rain, snow, or sleet whether or not wind driven. When combined with the fire and theft coverages it provides much the same protection as the comprehensive but on a specified perils basis. The comprehensive is broader and more inclusive.

STEAM BOILER AND MACHINERY INSURANCE. Boiler and machinery insurance is primarily a physical damage cover although it is sold as a casualty coverage. Companies undertaking to provide insurance covering losses to steam boilers and machinery have discovered that periodic and extensive inspection can reduce losses arising from this source to a minimum. Much of the premium collected by these companies, accordingly, is in the nature of a **service charge** instead of a true insurance premium. The business is highly specialized and is concentrated in a relatively few companies. Because of its specialized nature, liability for losses of this type is usually excluded from practically all other property insurance contracts. (Angell, Insurance.)

The basic policy is incomplete without the attachment of a number of schedules that define the "object" to be insured and the "accident" with respect to that object. The policy covers the insured against loss to the object, as defined, caused by the accident described in the schedules. The objects covered by the policy may be boilers and pressure vessels or machinery. Losses covered may be for damage to the property itself, for bodily injury liability to others, and for property damage liability to others.

OTHER POLICIES. A great variety of additional policies are written to cover losses to material property from a number of other exposures. Some of these are necessary because of particular exclusions written into more comprehensive policies. Among these coverages may be mentioned those against flood water damage, sprinkler leakage, glass damage, and hail. (Magee, General Insurance.)

Policies Insuring Against Consequential Losses

LOSS OF INCOME. The fire insurance policy, even in its broadened and "all-risk" forms, provides indemnity only for direct physical loss to property resulting from the perils insured against. There are other losses, however, that occur as a consequence of an interruption to business, and these must be insured under separate policies. The losses suffered may be related to the time period during which the business is not able to operate at full capacity, or they may be unrelated to the time taken to resume operations. So-called **time-element losses** would include: (1) loss of the income impossible to earn during the period of interruption; (2) inability to recover fixed expenses or any continuing expenses from operations during the period of interruption; and (3) extra expenses incurred if it is necessary to carry on operations in spite of the loss to physical equipment. Among the consequential **losses that are unrelated to the time element** are: (1) losses to perishables on account of temperature changes; (2) loss of profit on goods manufactured; (3) loss of leasehold interests when a lease is cancelable following a fire; (4) and losses growing out of errors and omissions in placing insurance. (Magee, General Insurance.)

BUSINESS INTERRUPTION INSURANCE. This policy promises to indemnify the insured for the loss of income that would have been realized had the business continued to operate. Had the business continued to operate it might have had a profit, it might have been barely breaking even, or it might have been operating at a loss. Even in the latter instance, however, coverage may be helpful if it can be shown that a greater loss is suffered when operations are interrupted. One of the problems connected with the underwriting of consequential loss insurance is the determination of the amount of insurable value tied up in the continuation of the business. This insurance is available in several different forms adaptable to the special requirements of the type of business interrupted.

Contingent Business Interruption Insurance. This form is available to cover losses from business interruption that are caused not by a loss to the insured's physical property but by a loss to the property of either suppliers of materials, parts, or services, or purchasers of the finished product of the insured business.

EXTRA EXPENSE INSURANCE. In some types of business it might be considered necessary to incur sizable additional expenses, even those required to carry on business at another location, in order to be able to continue the supply of a product or a service to the public. Such extra expense would not ordinarily be covered by business interruption insurance, although under that policy extra expenses are covered to the extent that loss under the policy is reduced. This is insurance that indemnifies only for necessary additional expenses incurred, and does not cover the loss of profits and income suffered as a consequence of a loss.

RENTS AND RENTAL VALUE INSURANCE. If **property becomes untenantable** because of damages sustained, there may be loss of use if it is being occupied by an owner; a loss of rental income to the owner if occupied by a tenant; or loss of rent to the tenant if he is still obligated to pay it under his lease contract. Time-element losses of this nature are insurable under rents and rental value insurance policies.

LEASEHOLD INTEREST INSURANCE. A tenant may hold a long-term lease calling for payment of rent considerably below current market prices. If terms of the lease allow the landlord to cancel because of property damage, the tenant could suffer an immediate loss that would not be related to the time taken to restore the property to tenantable condition. This value can be estimated by determining the discounted value of the series of rent increases the tenant could have expected during the period of the lease. On the other hand, if the lease were not canceled, the tenant could suffer a loss of rental value that would depend upon the time element. Both of these sources of loss are insurable under the leasehold interest form.

PROFITS INSURANCE. Loss of profits that could have been expected from the continuation of the business in the future are insurable, of course, under business interruption forms. These do not, however, cover the loss of profits that a business would suffer from the **destruction of goods ready for sale** at the time of the loss. Fire insurance covers the actual cash value of goods lost but without allowance for profit. Business interruption insurance covers loss of future profits only. If the insured wishes to cover the loss of profits already earned on goods ready for delivery, he needs profits insurance as well.

TEMPERATURE DAMAGE INSURANCE. Indemnity is sometimes collectible under a fire insurance policy for losses resulting from a change in temperature brought about by damage to refrigerating equipment. As a general rule, however, such losses are considered to be consequential, not direct, and hence are not covered by the standard policy. In cases where losses of this type are likely to occur, such as in creameries, breweries, greenhouses, packing plants, or cold storage warehouses, insurance companies often seek to clarify the situation by using a clause **exempting the company from liability** due to temperature changes. On the other hand, the dwelling, buildings, and contents form contains a consequential loss assumption clause **affirming the intention of the company to cover such losses.** In cases where there is doubt or where there is a clause denying liability, this type of consequential loss may be specifically covered.

OTHER CONSEQUENTIAL LOSS COVERAGE. Consequential loss coverages are also available in the following forms: delayed profits insurance, contingent profits insurance, excess rental value, accounts receivable insurance, contract of supply, match parts or sets, replacement cost and depreciation, and unearned premium insurance.

Crime Insurance

DEFINITIONS. Crime insurance is written by casualty companies to protect the insured against losses by burglary, robbery, theft, forgery, embezzlement, and other dishonest acts. Definitions of these crimes appear in the statutes of most states, but to avoid any possibility of uncertainty, insurers define them exactly for the purpose of the contract. The following are fairly typical of some of these definitions.

Theft and Larceny. Both of these terms are used to describe, in broad terms, the taking of property with intent to defraud. They cover all kinds of theft, whether it be with or without violence, by forcible entry or not.

Burglary. Burglary means the felonious abstraction of insured property and always involves breaking and entering for the purpose. It is required that entry be made by actual force and that there shall be visible marks made by tools, explosives, or other means.

Robbery. Robbery means the taking of insured property by violence or intimidation. It includes taking the property by violence, or the threat of violence, from the custodian of the property or when such a person has been killed or rendered unconscious by either malicious or accidental means.

CHARACTERISTICS OF CRIME COVERAGES. Some of the general characteristics of crime coverages distinguishing them from other types of policies are given by Angell (Insurance—Principles and Practices), as follows:

1. The act insured against is a violation of the law. The act covered by a crime policy may either be a felony or a misdemeanor but it is always an illegal act.
2. There is a considerable amount of adverse selection, and crime coverages tend to be purchased only by persons who feel they are exposed to a high degree of risk.
3. The crimes insured against are defined in the policy, and the policy definition governs regardless of any statutory definition.
4. Policies are generally specified-risk contracts. However, a few coverages are written on an all-risk basis.
5. The property insured is often of high value, since it is natural for criminals to be attracted to especially valuable property.
6. Co-insurance is often required as a means of combating the tendency toward underinsurance.

Crime coverages fall naturally into three categories: personal coverages providing for residence protection, business coverages primarily for mercantile establishments, and financial institution coverages. Only a few of the many policies available are listed below.

BUSINESS COVERAGES. These include the following important forms of protection against crime.

Mercantile Open Stock Burglary Policy. This is a policy protecting the insured against loss of merchandise that is not kept in a safe and that is taken by a burglar or robber while the premises are not open for business. It covers, in addition, damages to the premises or property resulting from the attempt to commit the theft.

Mercantile Open Stock Theft Policy. This policy adds the broader coverage, loss by theft, to the mercantile open stock burglary policy. Since the inclusion of theft broadens the policy considerably, it is subject to some strict underwriting considerations, among which is the use of a $50 deductible.

Mercantile Safe Burglary Policy. This contract is written for a wide variety of businesses to provide protection for money, securities, and other property usually kept in safes or vaults. The policy, however, covers losses only where the safe is forced open. In addition, it provides coverage for damages to the premises, including furniture and equipment.

Mercantile Interior Robbery, Messenger Robbery, Paymaster Robbery Policies. These are all policies protecting against losses resulting from robbery occurring under various conditions.

Money and Securities Broad-form Policy. Since this policy covers a type of property that is both easier to steal than merchandise and generally of higher value in small bulk, it has become one of the most important crime coverages sold. The policy gives **very broad protection** against dishonesty and for losses arising from both inside and outside the premises. It also covers losses resulting from destruction, disappearance, and wrongful abstraction.

Blanket Crime Policy; Comprehensive Dishonesty, Disappearance, and Destruction (3-D) Policy; Broad-form Storekeepers' Policy. Each of these policies is a **package policy** providing the most comprehensive crime protection that mercantile, industrial, and commercial organizations can buy. The broadform storekeepers' policy does for the small businessman what the 3-D policy does for the large organization. It does not provide, however, for the flexibility in coverages and amounts taken that the 3-D permits.

FINANCIAL INSTITUTION COVERAGES. Crime protection for financial institutions is provided through the use of several classes of forgery bonds, bankers' blanket bonds, the bank burglary and robbery policy, and the combination safe depository policy. (Angell, Insurance.)

Fidelity and Surety Bonding

BONDS COMPARED WITH INSURANCE. A bond that protects against losses resulting from a principal's dishonesty or his inability to perform as expected serves much the same purpose as an insurance policy. There are, however, some significant **differences between bonding and insuring.**

1. A bond always involves three parties: the **principal**, whose actions, lack of ability, or dishonesty may be the cause of the loss; the **obligee**, who is protected and indemnified in case of loss; and the **surety**, who stands in the same position as the insurance company. In an insurance contract there are usually only two parties: the insured and the insurer.
2. A principal purchases a bond to protect someone else, not himself, as is the case in the purchase of an insurance policy.
3. When a bond is secured, the bonding company has satisfied itself that there is little likelihood of a default or a loss. Losses are expected and anticipated by insurance companies.
4. Some person is always responsible for bonded losses. Someone can be held liable, and salvage or the right to use subrogation is always available. The principal is always liable to the surety for the repayment of any losses paid on his account. Insurance losses are accidental, and, although the right of subrogation exists in many cases where legal responsibility can be proved, it is used only in the unusual situation.
5. It is sometimes said that premiums on a bond are in the nature of service fees and that giving a bond constitutes the extension of credit. In insurance, premiums are paid to build up a reserve out of which losses are expected to be paid.
6. There are a number of other differences, such as: the indefinite period of the bond, the absence of cancellation privileges, the ability of a surety to demand collateral deposits, the use of joint accounts, and the use of suretyship.

The amount of the bond is referred to as the **penalty** rather than the face, and bonds may be written either for a fixed amount or without any specific limitation on the indemnity.

There are also important **differences between fidelity bonds and surety bonds.**

1. Fidelity bonds involve dishonesty and guilt, whereas surety bonds are more likely to involve the question of ability, capacity, or mistakes.

2. Fidelity bonds come closer to insurance inasmuch as there is recognition that some losses are certain to appear. Crime coverages written by casualty insurance companies are so similar to fidelity coverages as to make the line separating them virtually indistinguishable. (Angell, Insurance.)

FIDELITY BONDS. Most fidelity bonds are written to cover the possible dishonesty of employees. They protect the employer against the loss of any kind of property and, within the scope of the contract, they cover against all losses. Hence, they may be regarded as an "all-risk" type of coverage. The bond applies only if there is a **dishonest intent** on the employee's part; it does not cover mistakes innocently made. It will cover, however, against losses to an employer if the employee has assisted others in dishonest acts by deliberate carelessness or passive acceptance of the situation—even if he does not hope to gain for himself. Bonds may be written in several different ways.

Individual Bond. This is used where an employer wishes to cover a single employee. It covers only during the period of his employment and will not cover another employee who takes his place. An individual bond protects the employer against any dishonest act of that employee committed during the term of his employment and discovered within a stated period, often one year. The period within which losses must be discovered if the bond is to indemnify is called the **discovery period** and is usually specifically defined in fidelity bonds.

Name Schedule Bond. This bond covers several different employees named in the bond. The individual penalty applying need not be the same but must be stated for each employee. The bond usually designates an employee's position, but it will cover for any loss for which he is responsible. Employees may be deleted from the bond or new ones added, but they are not included automatically when they take the position of a former employee listed in the bond.

Position Schedule Bond. This is a schedule bond covering several different employees but identifying them by position held rather than by name. The number of occupants of each position must be stated in the bond. A penalty is stated for each separate position. Some bonds provide temporary automatic coverage for certain newly created positions and for increases in the number of persons occupying a given position.

Blanket Bonds. These bonds are issued to cover a group of employees under one master contract. They generally cover everyone in the insured's employ, and new employees as they are hired. Under a blanket bond it is not necessary to identify a particular employee, as is required under a name or position bond. There are two major blanket bonds sold to commercial establishments: the **primary commercial blanket bond** and the **blanket position bond.** They offer essentially the same protection and differ chiefly in the manner in which they apply to losses involving more than one employee. In the blanket position bond the penalty applies for each employee involved in a loss, whereas for the primary commercial blanket bond the penalty represents the maximum that the employer may collect for any single loss. If under both bonds the penalty was set at $10,000 and five employees were involved in a loss, the blanket position bond might pay $50,000, whereas the maximum indemnity on the primary bond would still be $10,000.

SURETY BONDS. In most cases surety bonds are contracts of indemnity, paying to the extent that an obligee has suffered a loss. Some bonds, however, known as **forfeiture bonds,** provide that the amount of the penalty will be paid under the conditions of the policy without the need of proving a loss. Compared with insurance policies, the bond stipulations are usually short and to the point. The name of the bond generally is sufficient to indicate the nature of the protection it affords and the purpose for which it was written. Some of the more important surety bonds are listed below:

1. Court or Judicial Bonds
    a. Fiduciary Bonds: Probate Bonds and Bankruptcy Trust Bonds
    b. Litigation Bonds: Bonds required in Civil Proceedings (Attachment, Repletion, Injunction); Release of Attachment Bonds (Appeal, Stay of Execution); Bonds Required for Admiralty Proceedings (General Coverage Bond)
2. Contract Bonds
    a. Bid Bonds
    b. Performance Bonds
3. Public Official Bonds
4. United States Government Bonds

Liability Insurance

LIABILITY AND NEGLIGENCE. Liability insurance is available to cover the costs to the insured if he has been held legally responsible for bodily injuries or property damage to employees or members of the public. A proper appraisal of this complex type of exposure requires, first of all, a basic understanding of the legal background.

Negligence is defined as failure to exercise the **degree of care** required by law, or "as a failure to exercise all due care." (Angell, Insurance.) Negligence often gives rise to liability claims, and the liability may result not only from one's own acts but from the acts of agents or employees. The law interprets "the degree of care" required to be that conduct expected of a reasonably prudent individual acting in the same circumstances.

Liability suits can be both frequent and costly, and the risk manager must appraise these contingencies and determine how the firm will provide for the possible financial consequences. If the company operates without a plan, the end result may be financial disaster or a cost far in excess of that required to assume or transfer the risk.

Individuals can incur liability in various ways. There is personal liability, employer liability, landlord and tenant liability, professional liability, product liability, liability in connection with the ownership and operation of an automobile, liability for agents, and miscellaneous liability.

Negligence a Form of Tort. An injury to another arising other than out of breach of contract is a tort. An injury, in the eyes of the law, results when a person's rights are wrongfully invaded.

Negligence is an example of a tort, as are libel, assault, and slander. The concern of the risk manager is not exclusively directed to negligence, but risk transfer devices are available for this tort, whereas for other torts insurance is not generally available. For an event to be insurable it must be fortuitous, and as assault, slander, and libel are not accidental occurrences they are not insurable events. Management, of course, must also be made fully cognizant of the possible financial consequences of these noninsurable torts. (Mehr and Hedges, Risk Management in the Business Enterprise.)

Culpable Negligence and Defenses. For an act to be deemed negligent, it must be a **voluntary act.** The voluntary act may be intentional or unintentional, but even if unintentional the act is not excused under the law, and liability claims are not negated on this basis. Intentional negligence may give rise to both criminal and civil action, whereas unintentional negligence will give rise to civil action only.

In order for damages to be awarded as a result of a negligent act, the act must be the proximate (contributing) cause of the loss, and it must be possible to connect the injury with the act. Even when a party is guilty of a negligent act, however, there are **legal defenses** that may be raised. These defenses include contributory negligence and assumed risk. (Mehr and Hedges, Risk Management in the Business Enterprise.)

In the event that there was negligence on behalf of all parties involved, it may be that none of the parties can collect for damages, even if the bulk of the negligence is attributed to one of the parties. The defendant can raise the defense of the claimant's **contributory negligence.**

Under many circumstances a party assumes certain risks when he enters the property of another. If under these circumstances there is an injury in connection with one of these assumed risks, the damage sustained is considered to be the result of his own actions and not those of the property owner. Should the injured party bring legal action against the party owning (or operating) the property, the defendant can raise the defense of **assumed risk.**

At one time an employer could avoid liability by showing that the negligence was that of the injured party's fellow worker. However, with the passage of workmen's compensation and employer's liability statutes, this defense has been nearly eliminated.

EMPLOYER LIABILITY. Employers have been held responsible for certain standards of care owed to their employees. Breach of these standards may give rise to damage suits, and the defenses of the employer are quite limited. The **standards of care** typically required are as follows: The employer must provide a safe place to work, and when danger exists the employee must be warned. The employer must employ reasonably competent individuals, and they must be provided with adequate tools. The employer must have and enforce proper rules of conduct in order to minimize the possible hazards. (Magee, General Insurance.)

LIABILITY OF LANDLORDS AND TENANTS. The owner of real property and/or his tenants owe a certain degree of care to those who enter the premises. Three **classes of individuals who may be affected** are: invitees, licensees, and trespassers. The degree of care that is owed to these various classes of persons varies widely.

The greatest degree of care is owed to an **invitee,** an individual who is on the premises for his own benefit as well as for that of the occupant or owner. For example, a customer in a retail store is an invitee and if he should suffer injuries due to negligence other than his own while on the premises, liability could result.

Licensees, such as delivery men and messengers, might also suffer injuries (due to negligence) while on someone else's property, but the courts tend to hold the owner or occupant innocent of negligence provided he has taken reasonable steps to warn a licensee of a particular danger.

Trespassers, who are legally defined as all persons other than invitees or licensees, may also be injured while on the premises, but no positive standard of care is usually owed to such a person. In most cases, if the trespasser is injured by or through some hazard, even though hidden, the owner or occupant will probably not be held liable. An exception may arise in respect to that described by the law as an **attractive nuisance.**

If a party, business or individual, maintains, for example, a swimming pool, it may be held in some jurisdictions to be an "attractive nuisance." If the pool is used by a certain type of trespasser, usually a child, he may be considered to be an invitee, thus exposing the owner to liability should death or injury ensue. This doctrine varies from state to state, and it would be the duty of the risk manager to ascertain the liability that might result from the maintenance of such a hazard and to properly provide for the exposure.

Liability of a Tenant. It is generally accepted under the law that the operators, or tenants, of real property take on whatever legal duties the landlord normally owes to members of the public. In some cases, however, the courts have held that the landlord does not completely succeed in transferring his liability to the operator or tenant because, for example, the landlord may not have abandoned all of the premises to the occupant.

To some extent, legal responsibility may be shifted between owner and operator, or tenant, but there are certain **exceptions**. Examples of situations where responsibilities generally cannot be shifted are where losses were due to violations of pertinent ordinances or to failure to exercise reasonable care in making excavations.

PRODUCT LIABILITY. A firm may incur liability in connection with a product that it manufactures, processes, or distributes. If injury to person or property results from the use or consumption of a faulty product, there may be grounds for legal action in the courts. Such actions are generally based on one of two conditions: breach of warranty or negligence.

Negligence, which is the main concern of the risk manager, may arise in respect to particular products where, for example, some impurities or foreign objects are found in the products. It is difficult for the injured party to prove negligence, but the courts have generally held that he may infer negligence from the facts and a judgment may be rendered in his favor. The injured party may recover not only for out-of-pocket expenses incurred but may also be granted an award for such things as mental distress. (Mehr and Hedges, Risk Management in the Business Enterprise.)

PROFESSIONAL LIABILITY. Professional liability involves physicians, pharmacists, dentists, lawyers, accountants, and other professional people, as well as contractors under what have come to be known as **malpractice suits.** The seller of professional services, as well as a contractor, is required to exercise reasonable care in the performance of his services, and if negligence can be shown these parties may be held liable. The financial liability may extend beyond that of the direct losses or costs to include **remuneration for psychic damages.**

In the case of the contractor, he may be held liable for all of the damages that result from the voluntary installation or erection of property. The injuries may be to both persons and property. Further, if the negligence of the contractor causes injury while he is still in actual control of the property, his liability is similar to that of the owner or occupant of real property. (Mehr and Hedges, Risk Management in the Business Enterprise.)

LIABILITY FOR ACTS OF AGENTS. If the agent of a party is acting within the scope of his authority or employment, the employer may be held liable for the agent's negligence. If, however, through his voluntary act an agent brings injury to a third party, the agent may be held personally liable.

It is important to distinguish between the actions of an agent and the actions of an **independent contractor.** Even though the independent contractor may be performing work for another, the latter is not usually held liable for the negligence of the contractor. If, however, the employer controls or closely supervises the work of the contractor, he may be held liable for the contractor's work.

An individual who may not in fact be an agent of another party may be held to be an **agent by estoppel.** Estoppel arises, for example, when an employer by his words or actions leads others to believe that an individual is his agent. In this case, the law may estop him from denying that the party was in fact his agent, and he may therefore be held liable for the negligent acts of the party.

LIABILITY OF AUTOMOBILE OWNERS AND OPERATORS. In the event of an automobile accident caused by **negligence** or **misconduct** the following parties may be legally liable: the operator, whether owner or nonowner; the automobile owner for the negligence of those operating his car; an employer, even though he may not be the owner, for the negligence of agents or employees using automobiles in the employer's business.

Liability of the Owner. The owner of an automobile is generally held liable for the negligent operation (or maintenance) of his car by a minor or for the negligence of an operator driving with the owner's permission.

Liability of the Operator. If the operator of an automobile is adjudged negligent he is generally held legally liable, although, as cited above, his employer may be the one held liable. The risk manager must determine the limits of the loss exposure in the various jurisdictions in which his company operates, and he must make adequate provisions for the maximum loss exposure.

Liability of a Nonowner Employer. An employer, even though he is not the owner of the car (the salesman may provide his own car or cars may be leased), may be held liable for the negligent acts of his agents or employees committed in connection with the operation of an automobile. This does not mean that the employer may be held liable for all the negligent acts of his employees. The employee operator may, as stated above, be held personally liable for the damages resulting from his negligent operation if it can be shown that he was guilty of intentional or voluntary negligence.

BAILMENT LIABILITY. In the handling of property for another, a bailee-bailor relationship arises. The bailee, who has physical possession of the property, is required to exercise the care that a reasonably prudent man would exercise over his own property. Typical of the liability that is created by bailments is that which arises in respect to such businesses as automobile garages, dry cleaners and laundries, and various storage operations. It must be noted that the degree of care that may reasonably be expected is greater when the bailee accepts property for profit.

The liability of a bailee can be **altered by contract.** For such a contract to be binding, however, it must be consummated in accordance with the prescribed requirements of the particular jurisdiction. Some attempts to shift or avoid liability by conditions stated on a parking lot ticket or bank deposit stub, for example, may not be recognized by the court as establishing an enforceable agreement.

LIABILITY IMPOSED BY A CONTRACT. A business may agree to assume, in whole or in part, the common law or other (i.e., contractual) liability of another party, provided the agreement is not in contravention of public policy or statute. It is imperative that the risk manager provide for the liability exposure that has thus been created. A typical liability of this kind is found in permits from municipal authorities, certain types of railroad agreements, and in contracts to supply goods or services.

MISCELLANEOUS LIABILITY. In addition to the specific liabilities cited above, there has evolved from both cases and statutes a body of decisions establishing the liability of an owner of an animal; of a trustee for beneficiaries; of an employer sponsoring an athletic team; of an employer who serves liquor to employees and to the public; among others. The risk manager must be cognizant of these potential loss exposures and take steps to provide for those risks that he feels the firm should not assume.

INSURANCE COVERAGE AVAILABLE. Coverages fall into three classes: **personal liability**, business liability, and professional liability. Within each of these classes liability may be incurred in a variety of situations, as the following partial listing for the business and professional categories illustrates.

Business liability: ownership or operation of factories, stores, warehouses, or any site under the control and responsibility of the insured; ownership and operation of any vehicle, including automobiles, airplanes, and boats, construction machinery, and equipment of all sorts; responsibility for a product the use of which may result in an injury; liability to employees or agents for injuries or losses sustained during the course of their employment; liability assumed by contract and contingent liability growing out of the existence of subcontracts, tenants, and agents of all sorts; and special types of liability, such as those arising from the use of elevators, published information giving rise to libel suits, etc.

Professional liability: malpractice suits arising from errors and mistakes made by a wide range of professional persons, as well as trustees, directors, etc.

PROTECTION PROVIDED BY INSURANCE. Each type of liability coverage has important provisions relating to that coverage alone. It is possible, however, to indicate in a general way the nature of the protection afforded by all liability contracts. The insurance company generally obligates itself to pay:

1. The amount of judgments awarded by a court, subject to the limits stated in the policy. Such limits are stated separately with respect to bodily injury and to property damage. The bodily injury limits usually specify the maximum payable on behalf of any one person, with a larger maximum stated as the amount that will be paid on behalf of all persons injured in one accident. Thus, limits might be stated: $50,000/$100,000.
2. All costs incurred in defense of the suit, including cases where the insured is not liable because the suit is groundless, false, or fraudulent. This includes costs assessed by the court; premiums on bonds needed, such as appeal bonds and release of attachment bonds; and interest accruing after entry of judgment and up to the time when the company pays.
3. Expenses incurred in giving emergency medical and surgical aid at the time of an accident.
4. Expenses incurred in assisting in the defense against a suit at the request of the insurance company, not including, however, the loss of earnings.

The amounts payable by the company to cover the expenses incurred in a suit and for immediate medical relief are in addition to any sum that might have to be paid pursuant to a judgment.

Some liability policies are written to cover all exposure to liability on a comprehensive basis, whereas others cover only a single, specifically defined liability hazard. The **comprehensive general liability policy** as a business cover and the comprehensive personal liability policy are the most important examples of the former, while the elevator, sports, and dog policies are examples of the latter.

There are a number of **exclusions** generally found in liability policies, including intentional injury, damage to property in the care, custody, or control of the insured, war risk, and liability assumed under contract. Other exclusions listed are usually designed to prevent duplication of coverage where the risk is expected to be covered by other insurance, such as automobile or workmen's compensation.

Business Uses of Life Insurance

PROVISION FOR LOSS OF KEY MEN AND BUSINESS CONTINUATION. Business uses of life insurance grow out of the need to provide indemnity for losses arising from the uncertainties of human lives. Death, disability, and sickness may disrupt a business as seriously as they do a family, and insurance offers the only practical and effective means of dealing with them. The special consideration given by states and the Federal government to the protection of funds set aside for these purposes gives special inducements for using life insurance in several business situations. Important tax savings may be effected in a number of ways, but competent professional assistance and advice from attorneys and accountants as well as insurance men are essential.

The **large corporation** with widely held and actively traded stock outstanding is not normally plagued with problems of business continuation. The division between ownership and management in corporations is usually clear; frequent and continual change in both management and ownership is to be expected. The death of a key man in an important managerial position may pose important problems for the corporation, but rarely would his death or that of an important stockholder jeopardize the continuation of the business. (Monroe, in Gregg, ed., Life and Health Insurance Handbook.)

Smaller businesses—whether organized as individual proprietorships, partnerships, or close corporations—are often promoted, owned, and managed by one or a few individuals to such a degree that the death of a top man may be expected to bring the business to an end. This is especially true in the case of the individual proprietorship, for the proprietor and the business are one and the same. This is true also in the case of a partnership, for although there may be surviving partners, the partnership as such is automatically dissolved. A close corporation may survive the death of the principal stockholder, and the interests of such a stockholder may more easily be transferred, sold, or otherwise disposed of; but it, too, may be so dependent upon the life of the key man that his death may make it difficult for the business to survive. Life insurance is not the answer to all of the problems connected with the continuation of such businesses, but it can be used to provide funds for the purchase of the interests of the deceased according to a previously arranged plan. If forced liquidation can be avoided, and problems of valuation, transfer of interest, and tax liability anticipated ahead of time, the business may at least have a sporting chance to survive. (Zeigen, and Mintz, in Gregg, ed., Life and Health Insurance Handbook.)

KEY MAN INSURANCE. The continued success of a business may depend upon the life of a single man or the lives of a small group of men. Their importance may be due to special talents or knowledge, to special skills in organization and management, or to special creative drives and inspirations. The loss of such men may be as crippling to the business as the loss of a major part of its capital equipment. Life insurance policies payable to the firm may serve to indemnify it for the loss of such a key man.

Business Continuation—Individual Proprietorships. An individual proprietorship ceases upon the death of the owner. Although its assets may be taken over by a member of the family, or by employees or other persons who may then continue to operate the business in any form they may elect, there are serious **difficulties in the way of making the transfer.** The heirs of the estate, the creditors of both the estate and of the business, and that ever-present representative from the Internal Revenue Service must all be satisfied before those who take over the business are free to worry alone about their business problems. The executor or administrator of the estate of the deceased has a responsibility to each of these claimants, and for his own protection he must usually liquidate and distribute the estate as quickly as he can. Unfortunately, forced liquidation may result in substantial losses to the value of the estate. A substantial amount of life insurance payable immediately upon the death of the proprietor can simplify the problems of the executor considerably. Money will be available for the care of the family, creditors may be satisfied without pressing upon the estate, and the estate tax may be paid before the estate has to be liquidated. Orderly liquidation may be carried out to preserve the value of the properties.

Another means of providing for the transfer of the individual proprietorship intact and at a good price to the estate is through a **"buy-and-sell agreement."** The individual proprietor, during his lifetime, can enter into a buy-and-sell agreement that provides for the transfer of the business upon his death to the contracting party at a fixed price or according to a specified valuation formula. This has the advantage of the estate's receiving the valuation that the proprietor himself places upon the business. If the valuation is reasonable, it is also likely to be accepted by the government for tax purposes. Buy-and-sell agreements usually involve key employees as the purchasing parties. They are likely to have a real interest in the continuation of the business and may wish to guarantee or improve their existing status. The proprietor on the other hand may seek through such an agreement their continued loyalty and the orderly transfer of his business after his death. The agreement can usually be funded through life insurance taken out upon the life of the proprietor that would amount to all or a substantial part of the agreed to price for the business. The use of insurance can be combined with a program of payments out of the earnings of the business or other forms of compensation to make up the total price to be paid for the proprietor's interest.

Regardless of the means used, it is to the advantage of all parties concerned to have sufficient funds available immediately upon the death of an individual proprietor to avoid a forced liquidation of the business. Life insurance still offers one of the most practical means of supplying these funds.

Business Continuation—Partnerships. According to common law and most state statutes, the death of a partner automatically dissolves a partnership unless the partnership agreement specifically provides for its continuation. The possibility of **automatic dissolution** creates problems for the partnership similar to those faced by a sole proprietorship upon the death of the proprietor. Funds will be needed immediately for the support of the dependents of the deceased partner, for the creditors of the business who might have depended upon his credit worthiness and who may not wish to extend their credit further—especially at this time, and for the payment of any estate taxes that may be due.

There are **additional problems** growing out of the death of a partner. A difference in opinion can easily develop between the heirs of the deceased and the remaining partners as to the proper valuation to be placed upon the share of the deceased. The former are likely to capitalize the earnings of the deceased at an even higher ratio than the tax collector, and may fail to take into consideration how much of his income represented personal earnings not reflected in tangible assets of the business. The partners, on the other hand, would like to acquire his share of the business at a figure that might enable them to carry on in spite of the loss of his services. If forced liquidation is the only means of deciding the issue, it may result in considerable loss to all.

Since it is usually impossible to anticipate when the partnership is likely to be dissolved by death, or which partner is to be taken first, life insurance offers an effective and economical means for accumulating the funds needed immediately for the continued operation of the business or the purchase of the deceased partner's share.

The solution usually offered for these problems is to include a buy-and-sell provision in the partnership agreement or to draw up a separate agreement under which the surviving partners agree to buy and the deceased partner's estate is obligated to sell his interest. Such an agreement needs to be very carefully drawn and may require considerable ingenuity on the part of attorneys, accountants, trust officers, and insurance advisors. The actual valuation of each partner's share must be agreed upon in advance. It may be established as a fixed amount, which may need to be revised periodically as the partners' interests in the business change; or it may be valued through the use of a formula. Such a buy-and-sell agreement is the heart of a partnership continuation plan and should be effective in solving questions of valuation to the satisfaction of heirs, surviving partners, and, if certain conditions are met, the government.

The insurance needed to fund the obligation of the living partners to buy can be arranged by an **exchange of policies** wherein each partner purchases insurance upon the lives of each of the others in such an amount as will provide for the purchase of each partner's share. As the value of the partner's share in the business increases, additional insurance may be provided, or the partners may assume an obligation to pay the balance due the estate of the deceased partner out of the earnings of the business. Premiums may be paid by each partner, or they may be treated as an expense of the partnership and taken indirectly from each partner's share of the earnings. The deceased partner's estate will own insurance on the lives of the living partners. Such insurance can then be allowed to lapse, the cash value, if any, being taken by his estate, or it may be provided that the remaining partners may purchase the insurance upon their own lives. (Mintz, Insurance for Business Continuation—Partnerships.)

Business Continuation—Close Corporations. It might at first appear that there should be few difficulties connected with the transfer of a deceased stockholder's interest in a close corporation. The stock in such a business may be sold, given, or bequeathed by the owner without affecting the status or the assets of the corporation. A new officer should be able to step into the position of the deceased, and the business would continue as before. Unfortunately, it often is not this simple. The business may legally be in the form of a corporation, but in effect the principal stockholder may have been in the position of sole proprietor or a partner in the business. The death of such a stockholder may prove to be as disruptive to the business as the death of a sole proprietor or a partner.

The corporation may have to be terminated because no one else has the knowledge or the skill required to carry on the business. It is true that the heirs and the executor of the estate may be in a better position with respect to the creditors of the business than in the case of the proprietorship or partnership, but the creditors are likely to be just as concerned about their ability to collect what is due them from the corporation. If stock is transferred to members of the deceased's family, they may not be able to obtain dividends upon their shares, for the greater part of the earnings may be needed, as in the past, to pay the salaries of the officers. **If the heirs wish to sell their shares** and to divorce themselves from the business, they are likely to discover that the shares have no established market values. If a buy-and-sell or stock purchase agreement has not been worked out, it may be difficult to arrive at a proper valuation of the shares. On the other hand, **if the shares in the deceased's estate are not sold** and are held as an investment, there is danger that the stockholders are in for a lifetime of dispute as to what should be the proper distribution of the earnings. Fortunately, it is possible, as in the case of the proprietorship and the partnership, for skilled attorneys, accountants, trust officers, and insurance men to work out suitable stock retirement or stock purchase agreements that may protect the interests of the heirs and surviving stockholders, and insure the orderly continuation of the business. Not all of the stockholders need to be included in a buy-and-sell agreement, but if the plan provides for the retirement of the stock, all must participate. The corporation might be able to accumulate a surplus sufficient for the purpose, but in most cases it will be advantageous to fund the agreements by the purchase of life insurance.

Under a **stock retirement plan** where all stockholders benefit proportionately from a reduction in the number of shares outstanding, the corporation should own the insurance as well as being designated beneficiary, and, of course, should pay premiums out of the earnings of the corporation. The corporation receives the proceeds of the policy upon the death of a stockholder and uses these to retire the stock. It will still own policies upon the remaining stockholders, and these may still continue to serve their original purpose. In **stock purchase plans** the stockholders take out insurance on each other's lives and pay the premiums. Proceeds of the policies are used to purchase deceased stockholders' shares according to the terms of the buy-and-sell agreement. The insurance owned by the deceased must be transferred to the survivors if the cross-purchase agreement is to remain in effect.

PROGRAMS FOR EMPLOYEES. Insurance may also be used effectively in instances where additional direct financial inducements may lose their charm because of high income tax rates. The company may provide for salary continuation after death or retirement, or for attractive pensions and group insurance of various kinds. It may also provide for life insurance payable to the key man's family with premiums payable wholly or in large part by the company, as in the split dollar plan. In special situations these plans may not only serve to protect the company's interest in the key man but may also produce some tax advantages for it as well. (Mehr and Osler, Modern Life Insurance.)

Split Dollar Plan. This is an ingenious plan serving to assist individual executives in the purchase of "personal" life insurance at nominal cost. It offers particular **advantages to younger executives** by providing large amounts of insurance during the early years when most needed. It is also designed to tie their loyalties more firmly to the assisting concern. Under this plan the business firm pays that part of the premium that represents the cash value of the policy in the first year and the increases in cash value in each subsequent year. In return, the business firm retains ownership of the cash value of the policy. Therefore, if the cash value of the policy is $41.00 upon payment of the first premium, the firm would pay only $41.00 of the first premium and would be entitled upon the death of the insured to receive $41.00 of the face amount of the policy. In the second year, if the cash value rises to $1,041.00, the firm will pay that part of the premium which represents the increase in value, $1,000.00, and will then become entitled to $1,041.00 of the face amount of the policy. The insured pays only that part of the annual premium that exceeds the increase in the cash value on the policy. Thus, the firm can provide an important benefit to the executive at a cost to it of only the interest lost on the amounts tied up in the policy. After a few years no further payment is required from the executive as the cash value of the policy reaches the cost of the annual premium. The amount of insurance available to him under such an arrangement is equal to the difference between the face value of the policy and the cash surrender value, which is owned by the firm. This is usually sufficient to provide him with substantial amounts of life insurance at very low cost, as shown by the example on page 36.

Salary Continuation or Deferred Compensation Plans. Current high income tax rates naturally make attractive any legal and effective method of deferring compensation until a later age, when reduced income will usually place the individual in a lower income tax bracket. Profit-sharing and stock option plans have been quite popular for this purpose. (See Section 19, Pensions and Profit-Sharing Plans.) Insurance may also be used advantageously for the same purpose, taking the form either of a formal pension plan or one in which specific insurance policies upon the life of the employee provide the funds for the purpose. If the employee is to receive a **tax benefit,** the plan has to be carefully drawn. Should it be held that he currently has vested rights to such compensation, he would be liable for taxes. The employer is not likely to obtain an immediate tax advantage in providing for such a plan, but a later advantage may accrue to him because of his ability to pay the compensation out of untaxed insurance dollars obtained from the insurance policy. Plans of this nature have to be drawn up with great care and are often of doubtful effectiveness because of the uncertainty surrounding future decisions of the Internal Revenue Service.

Employee Death Benefit of $5,000. The Internal Revenue Code provides that the employee's beneficiaries may exclude from gross income amounts up to $5,000 received from a company as an employee death benefit. It is possible, therefore, for an employer to arrange to pay this amount as a death benefit, with tax advantages to the family of the employee and to the employer as well. If insurance is used to fund the program, the employer is not allowed to treat premiums paid as a business expense, but he is allowed to receive the $5,000 from an insurance policy as tax-free income. When he pays the $5,000 out to the family of the employee, that amount may be treated as a business expense. Since 48% of this would otherwise have been payable as corporate income tax, he is in effect making this payment with 52-cent dollars.

Group Insurance and Pension Plans. The services of life insurance companies are also used to provide important employee **fringe benefits** in the form of group life insurance and group accident and health protection. In addition, many employers use the insurance company to provide an insured or guaranteed type of pension or retirement program (see Section 19, Pension and Profit-Sharing Plans). Life insurance companies maintain large departments with highly trained personnel to assist in such programs.

Age of Key Man for Whom the Plan Is Arranged: 35
Plan of Insurance: $50,000 of Ordinary Life
Gross Annual Premium: $1,382.00

Year	Payments by the Employer: (Premiums, up to Cash Value, less Dividends)	Employer Receives This Cash Value on Death of the Insured	Employee's Family Receives on Death of the Insured	Payments by the Insured
1	$ 41.00	$ 41.00	$49,959.00	$1,341.00
2	1,000.00	1,041.00	48,959.00	120.56
3	1,008.50	2,049.50	47,950.50	95.00
4	1,017.50	3,067.00	46,933.00	68.00
5	1,025.50	4,092.50	45,907.50	22.00
6	1,032.50	5,125.00	44,875.00	15.50
.	Employer pays full premium from the 7th year on	Cash value in policy equal to total payments $19,036.00	30,964.00	Employee pays nothing more

Note: Gross Annual Premium is reduced after first year by dividends (amounts not shown) and therefore amount paid by employer, plus amount paid by insured after first year, does not add up to gross annual premium.

Example of a Split Dollar Insurance Plan

25·36

Considerations in Selecting Insurers

IMPORTANCE OF PROPER SELECTION. Not all insurance companies have the same costs or the same financial strength and stability, and the quality and quantity of the services they offer may differ markedly. The risk manager of a firm must be familiar with the type of companies offering insurance, how the market is organized, the kinds and extent of services offered, and the financial soundness of the insurers. All are important factors to consider in obtaining for the firm the desired coverage at the lowest cost commensurate with financial safety. "Cost," as used here, means the measure of both direct and indirect costs, adjusted for offsetting benefits.

TYPES OF PRIVATE INSURERS. An insurance carrier may be a **stock company** organized for profit, with capital and surplus subscribed by the investing stockholders. It may be a **nonstock, nonprofit entity**, such as a mutual company or a reciprocal exchange. In these latter companies the policy-holders contribute all of the funds, and they may be liable for special assessments in case additional funds are needed. Once a surplus or guarantee fund of sufficient size is built up, however, the policy-holders may be freed from responsibility for additional assessments. In a reciprocal exchange, the policy-holder is also the insurer, and his individual account is credited for his premium deposits and debited for his share of the losses.

A considerable amount of insurance is placed in this country with Lloyds of London. A **Lloyds association** is an association of individual underwriters who individually accept liability for a stipulated fraction of the loss in each policy. Although Lloyds of London enjoys an international reputation, attempts to establish similar associations in this country have not been particularly successful.

Intercompany Organizations. Insurance is by nature a cooperative undertaking, so that it is not surprising that commercial insurers should find it advantageous to form a number of intercompany associations. These are designed to fill a variety of needs, including those of rate making, loss prevention, re-insurance, adjustment of losses, handling of claims, mutual exchange of information of all kinds, education, regulation of business practices—in fact, every aspect of insurance company activities. They exist on national, state, and local levels, and there are usually separate organizations representing the mutual and the stock companies.

ADMITTED INSURERS. Commercial insurance companies acquire the right to sell insurance in a particular state by complying with the specific statutes regulating, limiting, and controlling the issuance of charters. (See "Regulation of the Insurance Business," page 11.) **Insurers must be licensed** in each state in which they do business and for each line of insurance that they write. When a state grants a license to an insurer to write a particular line or lines of insurance, the insurer is said to be an admitted insurer.

Admission to additional states is, of course, of great value to the insurance company since its sales potential is thereby enlarged. In order to be licensed in a given state, **additional qualifications** may have to be met by the insurer. For example, New York imposes very high requirements on those companies domiciled in the state. For foreign companies to be licensed to transact business within New York, they must reasonably comply with the New York requirements.

SCOPE OF UNDERWRITING AUTHORITY. State laws also regulate the extent of the coverage that insurance companies are permitted to offer.

Monoline or Single-Line Companies. Before the 1940's the insurance laws of most of the states permitted an insurance company to secure a charter to write only one line of insurance, e.g. life, fire, marine, or casualty. Such restrictions were imposed in the belief that specialization was desirable, that there were substantial differences in the various lines, and that public regulation might be easier if such differences were recognized. Even though fleets or groups of related companies were chartered to overcome these restrictions, casualty and property coverages could not usually be combined in one policy. (Snider, ed., Readings in Property and Casualty Insurance.)

The risk manager may find that, for his company's purposes, a firm specializing in one line or a few lines only offers the best service and more coverage than is available from a multiple-line company.

Multiple-Line Companies. Because of the growing demand for all-risk policies and the severe competition offered to fire and casualty carriers by foreign companies and marine insurance companies (see "Inland Marine Policies," page 18), the states have modified their laws to some extent to permit multiple-line policies to be issued. New York authorized companies operating in that state to issue multiple-line insurance policies in 1949, and because of the importance and influence of the New York Insurance Code the change from monoline to multiple-line coverage was considered an accomplished fact.

The insured company may find that the multiple-line writer offers the most advantageous coverage, since in writing many lines, costs may be reduced. He also may accommodate the insured by writing a **line not normally economically available** or, in fact, not available at all.

"All-Lines" Companies. An "all-lines" contract as a single policy cannot provide coverage against all losses arising from the ownership of property and from the loss of life, even though the name seems to imply that it can. (McGill, ed., All Lines Insurance.) It is possible, however, for casualty and fire companies to be combined with life companies in various types of ownership groups, permitting agents for such companies to offer insurance covering all known needs. This is what is now known as "All-Lines Insurance."

DISTRIBUTION CHANNELS. Basically, insurance is marketed either on a direct basis, where the agent or underwriter reports directly to the insurer, or on an indirect basis, where one or more middlemen are involved. This latter system is called the American Agency System and dominates the distribution of **property lines;** the direct method of distribution dominates the **life insurance field.**

Direct Distribution. This method of distribution is one where the insurance salesman, usually called an agent or an underwriter, is directly responsible to and is supervised by the insurer himself or by his authorized representative, a general agent. Neither the salesman nor the general agent can bind the company he represents; that is, he cannot consummate the contract and he exercises no control over the premium.

Indirect Distribution (The American Agency System). In the indirect system of distribution **at least three parties** are involved: the insurer, the general agent, and the local agent. The **general agent** is a middleman, and his role is similar in some respects to that of the wholesaler who stands between the manufacturer, or processor, and the retailer. (Snider, ed., Readings in Property and Casualty Insurance.)

The general agent, under this arrangement, has far-reaching powers. He can bind the insurer; he has some leeway within which to negotiate the price of the contract (if allowed under state regulations); and he has some authority for regulating the work of the local agent. The business he produces within the limits of the agreed terms is paid for by the insurer at an established rate.

The **local agent,** or retailer, is also an independent middleman who deals directly with the insured. He may represent one or more companies, and in most instances he has the power to bind the insurer. The agent normally collects the premiums and remits them, less his commission, to the insurer. Greene (Risk and Insurance) states: "The local agent 'owns' the business he writes. That is, he has the legal rights of access to customer files and to solicit the renewal of policies."

Insurance Brokers. An insurance broker, like the general and local agents in the indirect distribution method, is a middleman between the insurer and the insured. Unlike the agent, however, brokers are not technically considered to be representatives of the insurers; they are actually agents of the insurance buyer. Nevertheless, it is the insurer who directly pays a commission to the broker in return for the business he has generated.

Distribution Systems Not Mutually Exclusive. A given insurance company may use a combination of distribution methods or may change at any time from one distribution system to another. For example, Fortune National Life Insurance Company's 1963 report stated:

During 1962, the Agency Department initiated the organization of a full-time General Agency plan. Seven such agencies are now operating; our goal is to have at least one in each state of operation. Brokerage business is still encouraged, and this should develop even more rapidly under our general agency plan.

CLAIMS SERVICES. The insurer's management of his **claims department** is of vital concern to both the insurer and the insured. In many cases the entire picture that the insured has of a particular insurer is that which he has obtained directly when involved in settling a claim with his insurer, or that which he has obtained indirectly through the most effective of all advertising, **word of mouth** from someone who has settled a claim.

The function of the claims department is to establish the **dollar amount of the payment to be made** (which, of course, is often subject to disagreement between insured and insurer) and to determine the time **when such payment is to be made.** Niggardly claims settlement or long delays in making the payment, or both, can cause much ill will and add to the insured's expenses. Since fire and property contracts are of short duration the insured may readily seek out a new insurer if dissatisfied.

In the process of establishing the amount of a claim, the insurer may use both his own personnel and **independent adjusters.** The use of independent adjusters may help to reduce the insurer's costs (by reducing the number of personnel needed) and may well speed up the settlement of claims. The insurer's own claims department will, nevertheless, retain the responsibility for setting the dollar amount of the loss, apply the terms of the policy to the particular loss, and approve the payment of the claim.

The claims function is most important in the property insurance field because of the complex problems that may arise in determining the true value and exact cause of the partial losses that occur so often.

LOSS PREVENTION SERVICES. Insurers are directly concerned with loss prevention because the insurer endeavors to spread the losses that occur among those who carry the insurance. Further, insurers realize that an insured party may, consciously or unconsciously, exercise less than the maximum care in acting to reduce hazards. If the insurer, through his actions or those of interindustry loss prevention groups, can reduce the probability of loss, the cost of the insurance will fall and, hopefully, more of the firms exposed to this risk will find commercial insurance economical and advisable. Also, of course, if actual losses in any period are greater than the forecast losses on which the prepaid premiums are based, the insurer's profits are reduced and his **loss ratio** (losses incurred as a percentage of premiums earned) increased. The latter ratio is often used as a criterion in selecting an insurer as it is generally reasoned that the lower the loss and expense ratios, the more efficient, and hence the more desirable, the insurer. This criterion, however, is not an adequate or full test of an insurer's efficiency, since the ratio is made up of components that can be manipulated and are at times not strictly comparable as between companies.

The insurers have sponsored some groups and activities that have been effective in reducing losses. Among these are the **Underwriters Laboratories,** which test new products, generally of an electrical type but including any apparatus that could start a fire, and the **National Safety Council,** which has been instrumental in promoting traffic safety.

FINANCIAL SOUNDNESS OF INSURERS. The financial safety of an insurance company is of primary importance to the insured, and if doubt as to the insurer's financial safety exists, no cost concessions should induce the prospective policy holder to place his business with that company.

The Role of Regulation. Regulation of insurance companies (see discussion on page 11) is concerned with the financial soundness of the insurer in order to protect the people who rely on the insurer to fulfill the "future" contract. Regulation, however, does not assure the financial soundness of the carrier. For example, it has been reported that between 1930 and 1962 nearly 7% (384 companies) of the property and liability insurers failed to meet their obligations ("Surety and Stability," Journal of American Insurance, Vol. XXVIII).

The **minimum financial qualifications** imposed upon insurers by the various states differ in a number of respects, and these differences may be critical. Further, even those companies domiciled within a single state may vary widely in financial soundness.

Sources of Information. Since every insurance company operating within a state must file a **detailed annual statement** with the state insurance department, the risk manager has a vast amount of data at his disposal. In addition, the pertinent figures on most insurers are available in such publications as Best's Digest of Insurance Stocks, Best's Fire and Casualty Aggregates and Averages, and The Spectator Insurance Yearbooks.

Measuring Financial Soundness. To analyze the financial strength of an insurer, the analyst follows the same basic principles that are used in the analysis of any company (see Sec. 7, Security Analysis, and Sec. 8, Financial Reports). There are, however, some special items to consider, just as there are in nearly every industry.

The **reserves** or liabilities of insurers are of special importance, according to Greene (Risk and Insurance), who adds that "an understanding of how the reserves are developed is necessary before an intelligent judgment can be made as to the 'net worth' of the insurer."

The reserves of an insurer are of **several types**: reserves for current claims, reserves for future claims, and securities valuation reserves. The first two are set by regulatory authorities at levels felt to be adequate to assure payment of claims as they come due. Securities valuation reserves are required only of life and fraternal benefit societies to provide for possible fluctuations in security holdings.

Other important items in the analysis of an insurance company include: the ratio of policy holders' surplus (which includes reinvested earnings and funds contributed by the owners) to debt, the earnings record on underwriting activities, the loss ratio, the investment experience and the composition of the insurer's portfolio, and the liquidating value.

Financial Safety of Fire and Casualty Insurance Companies. Fire and casualty companies have considerable freedom of choice in their investments for amounts over and above those that the regulatory authorities require to be held in the form of cash and high-grade bonds. According to Jordan and Dougall, (Investments):

. . . Although the existing regulations vary from state to state, in general, funds equal to minimum capital required must be invested in Government bonds and/or approved mortgages; funds equal to a portion of the unearned premium and the loss reserves must be invested in approved Government and/or corporate bond issues. The remaining funds may be invested in both bonds and stocks, as long as the issuers are solvent and have maintained adequate interest and dividend records.

Opinions regarding the investments of insurance companies vary. In respect to multiple-line companies, in which are included most fire and casualty companies, Schultz and Schultz write as follows (The Journal of Insurance, Vol. XXVIII):

. . . Of all the state statutes considered . . . the Illinois approach appears to be the most sound. In effect, this state suggests that a multiple-line insurer owes its primary obligation to the insureds, not to stockholders . . . and requires that companies domiciled under its laws invest their funds accordingly.

Jordan and Dougall (Investments) state that:

. . . the first measure of safety is the composition of the assets. The higher the proportion of cash and high grade bonds to liabilities, and to liabilities plus capital, the less the hazard from variations in the market value of the portfolio. It also follows that a very conservative portfolio brings in lower investment income, but this may be offset, through careful selection of risks, by a favorable loss record.

Financial Safety of Life Insurance Companies. In spite of the fact that insurance companies are closely regulated and that the business is conducted on a very scientific basis, **failure** of life insurance companies is not uncommon, even though in recent years failures have been due primarily to misuse of assets. The risk manager would be well advised to plan with care the placement of his insurance business.

The main points to be checked, according to Jordan and Dougall (Investments) include:

. . . (1) mortality experience, actual versus actuarial (obtained from Best's Life Reports); (2) percentage distribution of assets; (3) net investment income as a per cent of admitted assets (this stems from the distribution of assets among various types of high or low-yielding investments); (4) expense ratio (per cent of premium income spent for expenses); (5) gain from operations (this reflects rate of growth, mortality experience, and cost control); (6) percentage of insurance in force represented by each main type of policy; (7) growth of insurance in force (since the entire cost of placing new business on the books is met in the first year, and this cost will subsequently be recovered, the new business has an earnings potential that is worth from $2 to $20 per $1,000 of new insurance written, depending on the type of policy).

Since the average life contract is written for a long time period and since the primary problem of life companies is in making investments, state regulatory authorities are concerned with these investments, how they are valued, and whether there is an adequate reserve established to meet value fluctuations.

SECTION 26

REAL ESTATE FINANCE

CONTENTS

Sources of Real Estate Financing
	PAGE
Financial institutions	1
Mortgage debt outstanding (in millions of dollars) (f. 1)	2
Mortgage debt by type of lender—one- to four-family nonfarm homes (f. 2)	3
Savings and loan associations	1
Mortgage activity of savings and loan associations, 1957–1963 (in millions of dollars) (f. 3)	4
Commercial banks	4
Mortgage loans held by commercial banks, 1957–1963 (in millions of dollars) (f. 4)	5
Mutual savings banks	6
Mortgage loans held by mutual savings banks, 1957–1963 (in millions of dollars) (f. 5)	6
Life insurance companies	6
Mortgage holdings of life insurance companies, 1957–1963 (in millions of dollars) (f. 6)	7
Nonfarm mortgage loans of life insurance companies held by type of property, 1957–1962 (in millions of dollars) (f. 7)	7
Nonfiduciary organizations	7
The mortgage company	8
Nonfarm mortgage recordings, by type of lender, 1950–1962 (percentage distribution based on dollar volume) (f. 8)	9
The Federal National Mortgage Association	8
The real estate investment corporation	9
Savings and loan holding companies	10
Real estate investment trusts	10
Pension and endowment funds	10
Individuals and miscellaneous sources	11
State and community development commissions	11
Syndicates	11

Real Estate Financing Instruments
The note and mortgage	12
Mortgage loan repayment plans	12
Straight-term loans	12
Amortized loans	12
Partial amortization loans	12
Mortgage liens	13
Mortgage insurance and conventional loans	13

	PAGE
The trust deed	14
Special features of mortgage financing	14
Construction loans	14
Land development financing	15
Leasehold mortgages	15
Open-end mortgages	15
Package mortgages	16
Share collateral mortgages	16

Options, Escrows, and Land Trusts
Options	16
Escrows	17
The land trust	17

Long-Term Leases
Purposes and types	17
Net leases	17
Gross leases	18
Typical provision of leases	19
Variable rent leases	19

Real Estate Valuation and Investment Analysis
Investment features of real estate	20
Risk characteristics	20
Rating of realty investment (f. 9)	21
Environmental and physical characteristics	20
Type of property	22
Market trends	22
Nature of property rights	22
Financing arrangements	23
Influence of leverage	23
Depreciation and tax factors	24
Real estate valuation	25
Market comparison approach	26
Income capitalization analysis	26
Cost of replacement approach	26

Financing Selected Real Estate Projects
Sales and leasebacks	26
Illustration of a sale and leaseback	27
Office buildings	28
The competitive office building	28
Professional buildings	29
Shopping centers	29
A shopping center case analysis	31

SECTION 26

REAL ESTATE FINANCE

Sources of Real Estate Financing

FINANCIAL INSTITUTIONS. The greater part of real estate financing by financial institutions is effected through **mortgage loans**. Only life insurance companies are prominent investors in **equity interests** in real estate, and even in their case equity investments account for only 3% of total assets, as against 36% for mortgages.

Figure 1 shows the total mortgage debt outstanding in the United States, 1957–1963, classified according to type of investor and type of property. At the end of 1963, 65% of the mortgage debt outstanding was on one- to four-family houses, 29% on multifamily and commercial properties, and 6% on farm properties. Of the total debt, financial institutions (commercial and savings banks, savings and loan associations, and life insurance companies) held 77% and of the one- to four-family mortgages, 86%. Figure 2 shows the percentage distribution of mortgage debt held by principal nonfarm home mortgage lenders. (See also discussion in Sec. 2, pp. 36–38.)

Savings and Loan Associations. Savings and loan associations, also called building and loan associations and cooperative banks, held at the end of 1962 43% of the home mortgage loans outstanding on one- to four-family dwellings. The savings and loan associations are primarily **home mortgage lenders**. Ordinarily, from 80% to 90% of an association's assets are in the form of mortgage loans, and most of these are on one- to four-family dwellings. (See Federal Home Loan Bank Board, Savings and Home Financing Chart Book.)

Savings associations may be chartered by the Federal Home Loan Bank Board under §5 of the Homeowners Loan Act of 1933. Associations may also be chartered by the various states. Although the Federal associations comprise less than a third of the total number, they accounted for about 53% of the approximately $1 billion in assets held by all savings associations in 1963. (See Ewalt, A Business Reborn, and the United States Savings and Loan League, Savings and Loan Fact Book.)

The lending authority of associations chartered by the states varies from state to state, whereas the lending authority of the federally chartered associations is set by the provisions of the Homeowners Loan Act of 1933, as amended, and regulations of the Home Loan Bank Board. (See Rules and Regulations for the Federal Savings and Loan System, Federal Home Loan Bank Board.) The lending powers of the state associations vary somewhat from those of the Federal associations.

A summary of the **lending authority of federally chartered** savings and loan associations follows:

a. Federal associations may lend on the security of their own shares in amounts up to 100% of the value of the shares pledged; on the security of first liens on

	All properties					Nonfarm						Farm	
End of period	All holders	Financial institutions[1]	Other holders[2]		All holders	1- to 4-family houses			Multifamily and commercial properties[3]				Financial institutions[1]	Other holders[4]
			U.S. agencies	Individuals and others		Total	Finan. institutions[1]	Other holders	Total	Finan. institutions[1]	Other holders	All holders		
1957	156.5	119.7	7.4	29.3	146.1	107.6	89.9	17.7	38.5	25.8	12.7	10.4	4.0	6.4
1958	171.8	131.5	7.8	32.5	160.7	117.7	98.5	19.2	43.0	28.8	14.2	11.1	4.2	6.9
1959	190.8	145.5	10.0	35.3	178.7	130.9	109.2	21.6	47.9	31.9	16.0	12.1	4.5	7.6
1960	206.8	157.6	11.2	38.0	194.0	141.3	117.9	23.4	52.7	35.0	17.7	12.8	4.7	8.2
1961	226.3	172.6	11.8	41.9	212.4	153.1	128.2	24.9	59.3	39.4	19.9	13.9	5.0	8.9
1962 p	251.6	192.5	12.2	47.0	236.4	166.5	140.4	26.0	69.9	46.6	23.4	15.2	5.5	9.7
1963 p	280.9	216.9	11.2	52.9	264.2	182.2	156.0	26.2	82.0	54.8	27.2	16.8	6.2	10.6

p—preliminary.

[1] Commercial banks (including nondeposit trust cos. but not trust depts.), mutual savings banks, life insurance cos., and savings and loan assns.
[2] U.S. agencies are F.N.M.A., F.H.A., V.A., P.H.A., Farmers Home Admin., and Federal land banks, and in earlier years, R.F.C., H.O.L.C., and F.F.M.C. Other U.S. agencies (amounts small or current separate data are not readily available) included with "individuals and others."
[3] Derived figures; includes small amounts of farm loans held by savings and loan assns.
[4] Derived figures; includes debt held by Federal land banks and Farmers Home Admin.

Fig. 1. Mortgage debt outstanding (in millions of dollars). (Source: Federal Reserve Bulletin, May 1964.)

homes or combinations of homes and business real estate, if the property is located within one hundred miles of the home office of the association and provided that the loan principal does not exceed $35,000; associations may invest additional sums up to 20% of assets in improved nonresidential real estate and without regard to the $35,000 and one-hundred-mile limits; associations may lend up to 5% of assets on real estate located in any one of the standard metropolitan areas of the United States; associations may invest sums not to exceed 20% of assets without regard to the one-hundred-mile limitation by purchasing participating interests of not more than 50% in loans made by other associations insured by the Federal Savings and Loan Insurance Corporation; the total of the loans made under the exceptions may not exceed 30% of the assets of the association.

Percentage Distribution

December 31	Savings and Loan Associations	Life Insurance Companies	Commercial Banks	Individuals and Others	Mutual Savings Banks	F.N.M.A.	Total
1950	29.0	18.8	21.0	18.7	9.6	2.9	100.0
1951	28.7	20.5	19.9	17.1	10.3	3.5	100.0
1952	30.2	20.1	19.2	16.1	10.6	3.8	100.0
1953	31.8	20.0	18.2	15.3	11.1	3.6	100.0
1954	33.0	20.0	17.6	14.4	11.9	3.1	100.0
1955	34.0	20.0	17.1	13.5	12.6	2.8	100.0
1956	34.4	20.3	16.4	12.9	13.1	2.9	100.0
1957	35.3	19.9	15.2	13.0	13.1	3.5	100.0
1958	36.5	19.0	15.0	13.2	13.3	3.0	100.0
1959	37.8	18.0	14.7	12.8	12.9	3.8	100.0
1960	39.2	17.6	13.6	12.7	13.0	3.9	100.0
1961	41.1	16.8	13.1	12.4	13.1	3.5	100.0
1962 p	42.5	16.0	13.1	12.1	13.2	3.1	100.0

p—preliminary

Fig. 2. Mortgage debt by type of lender—one- to four-family nonfarm homes. (Source: Federal Home Loan Bank Board.)

b. Federal associations may grant loans insured by the Federal Housing Administration and loans insured or guaranteed by the Veterans Administration on the terms approved by the agencies.

c. Property improvement loans not in excess of $3,500 and 5-year terms, F.H.A. Title I loans, and unsecured loans guaranteed by the Veterans Administration may be made, but the total of all such loans may not exceed 15% of assets.

d. Associations with reserves and undivided profits in excess of 5% of withdrawable accounts may invest up to 5% of such accounts in land acquisition and development loans within the one-hundred-mile primary lending area. The loans may be for up to 70% of the value of the land plus 70% of development costs and may extend for up to 3 years.

e. An association's amortized real estate loans on one- to four-family properties may extend for periods of not longer than 25 years and may be for 75% of the appraised value; this limit may be increased to 80% of appraised value if the membership of the association approves.

f. An association may also grant a 30-year loan, provided the loan is made upon the security of a first lien upon real estate upon which there is located a completed structure designed for residential use for one family. The principal obligation of the loan must not exceed $26,500, and the loan may be for 90% of the value of the real estate up to $25,000 plus 80% of the value in excess of $25,000. The loan contract must provide for monthly installments equivalent to one-twelfth of estimated annual taxes, assessments, and insurance premiums, as well as interest and principal on the loan.

The **state-chartered** associations typically can make the same kinds of loans on terms generally comparable to those of the Federal associations. In addition, some state-chartered associations are allowed to make equity investments in real estate. Federally chartered associations acquire equity interests in real estate ordinarily only through foreclosure proceedings.

Of the loans made by savings and loan associations in 1963, 40% were for homes purchased, 28.5% were to finance construction of one- to four-family dwellings, and the remainder were divided among share-account loans, home improvement loans, loan participations, land acquisition and development loans, and loans on nonresidential real estate (see Fig. 3). Further details on savings and loan associations are given in Sec. 4 (Savings Institutions).

	Loans made			Loans outstanding (end of period)			
Period	Total [1]	New construction	Home purchase	Total [2]	F.H.A.-insured	V.A.-guaranteed	Conventional [2]
1957	10,160	3,484	4,591	40,007	1,643	7,011	31,353
1958	12,182	4,050	5,172	45,627	2,206	7,077	36,344
1959	15,151	5,201	6,613	53,141	2,995	7,186	42,960
1960	14,304	4,678	6,132	60,070	3,524	7,222	49,324
1961	17,364	5,081	7,207	68,834	4,167	7,152	57,515
1962	20,754	5,979	8,524	78,770	4,476	7,010	67,284
1963	24,734	7,038	9,920	90,849	4,685	6,960	79,204

[1] Includes loans for repairs, additions and alterations, refinancing, etc. not shown separately.
[2] Beginning with 1958 includes shares pledged against mortgage loans.

Fig. 3. Mortgage activity of savings and loan associations, 1957–1963 (in millions of dollars). (Source: Federal Reserve Bulletin, May 1964.)

Commercial Banks. Commercial banks participate in real estate financing by making real estate mortgage loans, construction loans, and working capital loans to construction companies; providing lines of credit to mortgage companies; and warehousing mortgages for financial institutions seeking mortgage investments but having temporarily inadequate investable funds.

The real estate lending authority of **national banks** is established in Title 12 of the United States Code (the Federal Reserve Act, §24), which gives national banks the authority to make mortgage loans secured by first liens on improved real estate. A loan may be for up to 75% of appraised value if the term does not exceed 20 years and the principal is to be fully amortized during the term of the loan. A loan may be for 66⅔% of the value if at least 40% of the loan is to be amortized within 10 years. A loan contract that does not provide for principal reduction may not exceed 50% of value and a term of 5 years.

National banks may grant F.H.A. and V.A. loans according to the terms approved by the agencies. These loans are not subject to the limitations cited above.

The real estate loans of a national bank may not at any time be greater than the amount of the capital stock of the bank plus its unimpaired surplus, or 60% of the amount of its time and savings deposits, whichever is the greater.

National banks may lend **to finance construction** of industrial or commercial buildings. Such loans may have maturities not to exceed 18 months, provided there are arrangements for a regular mortgage loan to refinance the construction loan upon the completion of the building. Similar loans for the construction of residential or farm buildings may have maturities not to exceed 9 months. The construction loans need not be secured by the pledge of real estate but ordinarily they are also mortgage loans. The aggregate amount of construction loans may not exceed 100% of a bank's paid-in and unimpaired capital and surplus.

The lending powers of **state-chartered banks** vary from state to state, but on the whole they tend to be similar to those of national banks.

In banking statistics only mortgage loans of banks are classified as **real estate loans.** All other loans to finance real estate activity, directly or indirectly, including construction loans, are classified as **commercial and industrial loans.** Real estate loans have comprised about 25% of the total loans of all commercial banks in recent years. Sixty-seven per cent of the bank-held mortgage loans at the end of 1963 were on residential real estate, and 62% of the home loans were of the conventional type (see Fig. 4).

		Residential					
End of period	Total	Total	F.H.A.-insured	V.A.-guaranteed	Conventional	Other non-farm	Farm
1957	23,337	17,147	4,823	3,589	8,735	4,823	1,367
1958	25,523	18,591	5,476	3,335	9,780	5,461	1,471
1959	28,145	20,320	6,122	3,161	11,037	6,237	1,588
1960	28,806	20,362	5,851	2,859	11,652	6,796	1,648
1961	30,442	21,225	5,975	2,627	12,623	7,470	1,747
1962	34,476	23,482	6,520	2,654	14,308	8,972	2,022
1963	39,414	26,476	7,105	2,862	16,509	10,611	2,327

Fig. 4. Mortgage loans held by commercial banks, 1957–1963 (in millions of dollars). (Source: Federal Reserve Bulletin, May 1964.)

In April 1964, the beginning of the construction season, construction loans of weekly reporting member banks constituted about 5% of their total commercial and industrial loans.

Commercial banks are not only an important direct source of real estate and mortgage credit, but their role as a facilitator of real estate activity through loans to other financial institutions and construction companies and through construction loans is also significant. Banks were an especially important source of **indirect real estate credit** during the mid-1950's when the demand for mortgage loans was very heavy relative to the available funds of savings institutions. Life insurance companies in particular resorted to **"warehousing"** arrangements with commercial banks under which the company would make a block of loans, perhaps F.H.A. or V.A. loans, acceptable to the commercial bank. The loans in turn would be sold to the bank on a repurchase basis, with the insurance company reacquiring the loans on a prearranged schedule.

Mutual Savings Banks. At the end of 1962 mutual savings banks held 13% of the outstanding home mortgage loans on one- to four-family dwellings, and 70% of their assets consisted of real estate mortgages. The lending authority of savings banks varies from state to state but the banks typically may grant loans ranging from 66⅔% to 80% of value and extending from 20 to 25 years.

Savings banks lend mostly on **residential real estate**. The savings banks held $36 billion in real estate loans at the end of 1963. Of these, 90% were residential loans divided fairly equally among conventional loans, V.A. loans, and F.H.A. loans (see Fig. 5).

End of period	Total	Residential Total	F.H.A.-insured	V.A.-guaranteed	Conventional	Other nonfarm	Farm
1957	21,169	19,010	4,669	7,790	6,551	2,102	57
1958	23,263	20,935	5,501	8,360	7,073	2,275	53
1959	24,992	22,486	6,276	8,589	7,622	2,451	55
1960	26,935	24,306	7,074	8,986	8,246	2,575	54
1961	29,145	26,341	8,045	9,267	9,028	2,753	51
1962	32,320	29,181	9,238	9,787	10,156	3,088	51
1963	36,224	32,718	10,684	10,490	11,544	3,454	52

Fig. 5. Mortgage loans held by mutual savings banks, 1957–1963 (in millions of dollars). (Source: Federal Reserve Bulletin, May 1964.)

Mutual savings banks have been active investors in the post-World War II **housing booms**. F.H.A.-insured and V.A.-guaranteed loans have been particularly attractive investments for the savings banks because they permit the banks to participate in the financing of housing activity outside their own primary lending areas. (See further discussion in Sec. 4 on Savings Institutions.)

Life Insurance Companies. Life insurance companies are both lenders and equity investors in real estate. Moreover, they hold mortgages on commercial, industrial, and institutional real estate, and multifamily units as well as on one- to four-family houses (see Figs. 6 and 7).

At the end of 1962, insurance companies held 16% of the home mortgage loans outstanding on one- to four-family dwellings. (For details on life insurance company investments, see Sec. 4, pp. 37–39.) Of their **total mortgage holdings** (including farm mortgages), nearly 43% were on properties other than one- to four-family units.

In addition to mortgage holdings, life insurance companies held $4.3 billion in equity investments in real estate at the end of 1963. Mortgages constituted 36% and equity investments 3% of their total assets at that time. Life insurance companies are chartered by the various states; their **lending and investing powers** vary from state to state. Life insurance companies typically are permitted to make residential loans ranging from 66⅔ to 75–80% of value. The terms on residential real estate are ordinarily limited either by custom or prac-

SOURCES OF REAL ESTATE FINANCING 26·7

tice to 25 to 30 years. On multifamily and commercial real estate, mortgage terms more commonly fall between 60 and 70% of value and run for terms of 15 to 20 and sometimes 25 years.

		Nonfarm				
Period	Total	Total	F.H.A.- insured	V.A.- guar- anteed	Other	Farm
1957	35,236	32,652	6,751	7,721	18,180	2,584
1958	37,062	34,395	7,443	7,433	19,519	2,667
1959	39,197	36,370	8,273	7,086	21,011	2,827
1960	41,771	38,789	9,032	6,901	22,856	2,982
1961	44,203	41,033	9,665	6,553	24,815	3,170
1962	46,902	43,502	10,176	6,395	26,931	3,400
1963	50,543	46,753	10,790	6,411	29,552	3,790

Fig. 6. Mortgage holdings of life insurance companies, 1957–1963 (in millions of dollars). (Source: Federal Reserve Bulletin, May 1964.)

December 31	1 to 4 Family	Multifamily	Commercial	Total
1957	21,441	3,551	7,660	32,652
1958	22,374	3,547	8,474	34,395
1959	23,583	3,666	9,121	36,370
1960	24,879	3,865	10,045	38,789
1961	25,776	4,250	11,007	41,033
1962 p	26,984	4,670	11,928	43,582

p—preliminary.

Fig. 7. Nonfarm mortgage loans of life insurance companies held by type of property, 1957–1962 (in millions of dollars). (Source: Federal Home Loan Bank Board.)

Of the real estate owned by life companies, about one-third represents **company-used property**. The companies were particularly active in the real estate field in the late 'fifties and early 'sixties through their office building projects in both downtown and suburban areas.

Life insurance companies also pioneered in large-scale apartment house developments in the 1950's. Only a tenth of life company equity investments was in residential properties at the end of 1962. Nearly three-fifths represented investments in **commercial properties** such as office buildings, department stores, factories, and shopping centers. Many of these holdings were acquired on a purchase and leaseback arrangement.

NONFIDUCIARY ORGANIZATIONS. Of the nonfiduciary organizations engaged in real estate financing, mortgage companies are by far the most important. Real estate investment corporations also played a prominent part in the post-World War II construction boom, particularly in commercial buildings.

The Mortgage Company. The mortgage company is typically a corporation whose **principal activity** is originating and servicing mortgage loans for institutional investors. It is chartered the same way as any other corporation, and since it is nonfiduciary in nature there is a minimum of Federal or state supervision. The mortgage company typically has a small equity investment relative to its volume of business and relies largely on commercial bank credit.

Most mortgage companies engage in a number of activities related to the origination and servicing of mortgages, including real estate brokerage and management, insurance, construction, and land development. Many operate primarily as correspondents of life insurance companies, mutual savings banks, savings and loan associations, pension funds, and other financial institutions, acting as intermediaries between borrowers and investors. (See Bryant, Mortgage Lending.)

Mortgage companies typically originate loans on the basis of commitments from institutional investors to purchase completed mortgages of given characteristics. Ordinarily they hold the loans in their own portfolios for a very short time before selling them to the ultimate investor. A significant and profitable part of their operations is **loan servicing**—that is, the collection of monthly payments on mortgage loans for the mortgagee. The standard fee for residential mortgage loans is $\frac{1}{2}$ of 1% of the outstanding balance of the loan. The fees for servicing loans on commercial and multifamily property are not standard, but usually range from $\frac{1}{8}$% to $\frac{3}{8}$% of the outstanding balance. (See Klaman, Occasional Paper 60, National Bureau of Economic Research.)

Although mortgage companies originate conventional loans, the greater part of their business in the post-World War II years has been in the origination and servicing of **F.H.A. and V.A. loans** for institutional investors seeking to develop nationally diversified residential mortgage portfolios. Regulations concerning F.H.A. and V.A.-approved mortgagees represent the **principal type of public regulation** of the companies. In order to qualify as a F.H.A.-approved mortgagee, the mortgage company must have a minimum capital of $100,000, and $250,000 if the company is to operate in noncontiguous states.

The mortgage company relies heavily on **bank borrowings** to finance its operations. It is not unusual for a company to have total liabilities outstanding, largely bank credit, of six to eight times the size of the equity funds in the company. Since it operates mainly on borrowed funds, it typically sells the mortgages it makes as quickly as possible. The role of the mortgage companies (which account for the bulk of "other mortgagees") in originating mortgage loans is illustrated in Fig. 8.

In 1962, mortgage companies originated a larger percentage of nonfarm mortgages than any other lender except savings and loan associations. Savings banks and insurance companies, which were relatively small-scale originators, acquired their loans mainly from the mortgage companies. Serving as intermediaries between the geographically concentrated savings banks and life insurance companies and would-be home purchasers all over the country, the mortgage companies played a major role in developing the national market in F.H.A. and V.A. loans after World War II. Lending terms offered by the companies are essentially the same as those of the financial institutions to which the completed mortgage loans are sold. There were between 800 and 1,000 full-time private mortgage companies operating in the United States in 1963.

The Federal National Mortgage Association. The F.N.M.A. (usually called Fanny Mae), a constituent of the Housing and Home Finance Agency, is a federally chartered mortgage company dealing only in F.H.A. and V.A. loans

SOURCES OF REAL ESTATE FINANCING

made by **private lenders**. The principal activity of the F.N.M.A. is to provide a **secondary market** through the purchase and resale of government underwritten mortgages. At the end of 1963 its mortgage holdings totaled $4.7 billion. Most of its funds are supplied by the Federal government and the remainder is obtained through the sale of debentures to private investors.

Year	Savings and Loan Associations	Mutual Savings Banks	Commercial Banks	Insurance Companies	Individuals	Other Mortgagees	Total
1950	31.3	6.6	20.8	10.0	14.2	17.1	100.0
1951	32.3	6.2	20.5	9.8	16.1	15.1	100.0
1952	35.8	6.3	20.0	7.9	15.3	14.7	100.0
1953	37.4	6.7	18.6	7.5	14.4	15.4	100.0
1954	36.2	6.5	18.5	7.7	12.5	18.6	100.0
1955	36.7	6.5	19.7	6.8	11.8	18.5	100.0
1956	35.2	6.7	20.2	6.6	13.1	18.2	100.0
1957	38.0	5.9	17.6	6.1	14.7	17.7	100.0
1958	38.4	6.0	19.0	5.3	12.5	18.8	100.0
1959	40.6	5.5	18.1	4.7	12.2	18.9	100.0
1960	41.4	5.3	15.4	4.5	13.6	19.8	100.0
1961	43.8	5.6	16.0	3.7	11.7	19.2	100.0
1962	44.3	5.7	17.1	3.6	10.4	18.9	100.0

Fig. 8. Nonfarm mortgage recordings, by type of lender, 1950–1962 (percentage distribution based on dollar volume). (Source: Savings and Loan Fact Book, 1963.)

The Real Estate Investment Corporation. The real estate investment corporation is typically a closely held company developed for the purpose of acquiring and holding a single property. Real estate corporations are frequently used in the development of shopping centers, office buildings, hotels, industrial districts, and large apartment buildings. The holding company system is sometimes used to develop a multicorporate real estate complex and occasionally to amplify the leverage opportunities in real estate investments.

During the **building boom of the 1920's,** the real estate investment corporation, financed by the public flotation of real estate bonds, was very popular. (See Hoagland and Stone, Real Estate Finance.) The corporations and their bonds fell sharply from favor during the **depression of the 1930's,** however, and did not return to popularity until the late 1950's. The privately held corporations were a major influence in the nationwide post-World War II boom in shopping centers and office buildings.

In contrast to the situation in the 1920's, real estate investment corporations during the **postwar period** have for the most part sought equity capital from the security markets and relied on loans from financial institutions for real estate credit.

Most real estate investment corporations are privately held. The stocks of almost all the public corporations are traded in the over-the-counter markets. Perhaps a dozen of these corporations achieved prominence in the financial world between 1955 and 1964. Their reputations were built largely on spectacular leverage situations or untaxed returns to equity holders made possible through the use of rapid depreciation plans authorized by the Internal Revenue Act of 1954. Many of the publicly held companies participating in the New York office building boom of the late 1950's, which combined high leverage with nontaxable capital returns, experienced serious financial problems and incurred public disfavor between 1961 and 1963.

Savings and Loan Holding Companies. A special type of real estate financial corporation developed after World War II is the savings and loan holding company. During the latter half of the 1950's many mutual savings and loan associations were converted to stock companies in which **stockholders have equity interests,** in contrast to the semicreditor interest of the savings shareholders. An owner of capital stock can benefit from capital appreciation, whereas a holder of a savings account can accumulate only interest on his savings.

Savings and loan holding stock companies have been established throughout the United States, but notably in California. Cash dividends to stockholders in the individual associations or in the holding companies have been infrequent, interest in the stocks being based chiefly on hope of capital appreciation. A few of the holding companies are listed on organized exchanges, but for the most part the stocks of both the companies and the associations are traded **over the counter** or held **privately.**

Real Estate Investment Trusts. The trust, long used in Massachusetts and Illinois as a form of organization allowing multiple ownership of real estate, acquired preferential tax status in 1960, effective 1961, through the Real Estate Investment Trust Act, an amendment to the Internal Revenue Code of 1954. The Act limits the tax liability of qualifying trusts that distribute 90% or more of their ordinary income. Qualifying requirements of the investment trusts are extensive, but a qualified trust has to pay the Federal corporate income tax only on its retained earnings.

To qualify for this favorable tax treatment, a real estate investment trust must be (1) a legally unincorporated trust, (2) managed by trustees, (3) the type of organization that would be taxed as a corporation except for the provisions of the Real Estate Investment Trust Act, and (4) held by one hundred or more persons holding transferable shares or certificates of beneficial interest. It must be an investment organization and not an operating company holding property primarily for sale to customers. It must not be a personal holding company (that is, five or fewer individuals may not, directly or indirectly, own more than 50% of the trust).

A qualifying trust must have at least 75% of its assets in real estate, cash, and government securities. Ninety per cent or more of its gross income must be obtained from rents from real property, dividends, interest on mortgages, gains from the sale of securities and real property, and abatements and refunds of taxes on real property. At least three-fourths of the trust income must be derived from real estate alone. Fewer than ten real estate investment trusts had attained prominence in the financial markets by 1964 (see also Sec. 12).

Pension and Endowment Funds. The annual net acquisition of financial assets of noninsured pension funds increased from $3.2 billion in 1959 to $4 billion in 1963. In 1947 the portfolios were mostly in government securities but since then they have been shifted heavily into bonds and stocks. Mortgage and real estate holdings of the pension funds are relatively small. (See Ricks, Research Report 23, and Sec. 19 on Pensions and Profit-Sharing Plans.)

SOURCES OF REAL ESTATE FINANCING

Pension funds have traditionally been disinterested in real estate mortgages because of the origination and servicing problems. Only the managers of very large funds are inclined to include real estate in their investment portfolios in order to increase yield and diversification. These investments are largely in the form of **sale and leaseback contracts.** The greater part of the investments of **college and university endowment funds** is in corporate securities. Relatively few endowment funds participate extensively in real estate investments. These funds deal almost exclusively in mortgages on commercial and industrial property, sales and leasebacks, and occasionally equity investments in commercial and office building properties.

A few universities actively search for real estate investments. Stanford University is one of the most aggressive investors. This school undertook a land development program in 1951 and has created an industrial park of about 400 acres and a shopping center of 65 acres, and is developing an office building complex of another 65 acres. Columbia University owns Rockefeller Center in New York City, the University of Washington owns several blocks in the heart of downtown Seattle, and a number of other universities own large commercial and office properties. On the whole, however, the endowment funds are a relatively small source of real estate finance. Ricks (Research Report No. 23) found in a study of ten large university endowment funds that their total endowments amounted to approximately $21 billion in 1961 and that mortgages represented 2.8% of their assets; long-term real estate, 3.9%; and operated real estate, 0.6%.

INDIVIDUALS AND MISCELLANEOUS SOURCES. Although institutional investors have taken an increasing share of the mortgage investments in the postwar years, individual investors have long been an important source of mortgage financing. At the end of 1963, the Home Loan Bank Board estimated that 11% of the one- to four-family nonfarm mortgage debt was held by "individuals and others," as against 28% in 1946. This category includes trust funds, mortgage companies, and individual investors, but the greater part of the debt is held by private individuals. The individual investor most often makes loans directly on the basis of private solicitation but sometimes buys loans through mortgage companies. The terms offered by individuals are not standardized and are adapted to meet particular borrowing situations.

State and Community Development Commissions. The efforts of states and communities to develop the economies of their areas have resulted in the creation of organizations to **promote business and industry** through such incentives as low-interest real estate loans, capital grants, long-term leases, gifts of buildings and sites, tax abatement, guarantees on loans obtained from financial institutions, and development of facilities available for purchase or lease. Manufacturing firms seeking new locations can often find appropriate sites and an opportunity of minimizing real estate development expenses through programs of state or community development commissions.

Syndicates. Syndicates are commonly used in the development of real estate subdivisions, housing projects, and the acquisition of single units of high-value property. A syndicate may be brought together through a corporation, a trust, a partnership, or simply through the holding of real estate in joint tenancy or tenancy in common. The designation of a group as a syndicate does not refer to the form of organization but is merely applied to **investors brought together for one particular purpose.** Whereas syndicates generally undertake projects that are to be completed in a relatively short span of time, real estate syndicates are not necessarily of the short-term variety.

Real Estate Financing Instruments

THE NOTE AND MORTGAGE. The basic instruments of real estate finance are the note and the real estate mortgage. The note is evidence of a debt, and the mortgage pledges real property as security for the obligation. The note and the mortgage may be two **separate** instruments, or they may be **merged** into one.

The note and the mortgage do not have to be in any particular physical form. **Standard arrangements** typically contain the following: the mortgagor's (borrower's) promise to pay a specific sum and the terms of repayment; what constitutes default and the consequences of default; a description of the pledged property; and details of covenants and contractual agreements between the borrower and the lender (mortgagee). The note and the mortgage must be signed by the borrower.

Ordinarily the real estate mortgage pledges property to secure a debt of one person to another person or single institution. In the case of the corporate mortgage bond, in contrast, a single borrower pledges specific property for the protection of multiple creditors (see discussion in Sec. 14).

MORTGAGE LOAN REPAYMENT PLANS. Nearly all mortgage loans are now of the fully amortized variety, with straight-term and partial amortization loans being used in special situations.

Straight-Term Loans. The oldest form of mortgage loan is the straight-term loan, written typically for 1 to 5 years. The contract ordinarily requires the payment of interest on the total debt outstanding—monthly, quarterly, or annually—with the entire debt coming due at the end of the loan term. Straight-term loans seldom run for more than 5 years and usually do not exceed 50 to 60% of the appraised value of the pledged property. The straight-term loan was used extensively in real estate finance before World War I and in the 1920's, but gave way to partially and fully amortized loans in the 1930's and in the post-World War II period. The straight-term loan is now used principally for **interim financing situations** and represents only a small part of real estate mortgages.

Amortized Loans. The fully amortized loan was pioneered by savings and loan associations and achieved national prominence through its use by the Home Owners Loan Corporation during its lending period 1933 to 1936. In this plan **periodic payments**—usually monthly—cover interest on the unrepaid portion of the debt and full repayment of the debt within the contract term. The typical residential amortized mortgage loan is a level-payment monthly annuity. As the unpaid portion of the loan declines, the share of the monthly payment going to principal increases and that going to interest decreases.

Partial Amortization Loans. In 1935 national banks received authority to make partial amortization loans, typically called **"balloon payment"** loans. Such loans are usually employed in situations in which **refinancing** of the unamortized portion of the loan is contemplated. For example, if a loan were to extend for 10 years with amortization of 40% of the original principal, the unpaid 60% represents the balloon payment falling due at the end of the original term. The 60% might then be refinanced through a new loan. The balloon payment loan is used in special circumstances and in situations when a fully amortized long-term loan acceptable to borrowers is not available.

MORTGAGE LIENS. Institutional mortgages invariably carry a **first** claim against the real estate pledged as security. There are many situations in real estate finance in which second and third mortgages are also used.

Under a **second mortgage** the mortgagee's claim to the property is subordinated to a previously existing pledge. The second mortgage is common in commercial financing, but appears most often in the sale of houses by individuals when the price exceeds the combined amount of an available first mortgage loan and the buyer's cash resources. In such instances, if the seller is willing to extend credit to the buyer, he frequently takes a second mortgage. Maturities of the notes are usually shorter than those of the first mortgage loan, commonly running from 3 to 5 or 10 years.

Second and even **third** mortgages were prominent in real estate finance in the 1920's, but during the depression of the 1930's the junior mortgage holders suffered severely. With the increased availability of low down-payment, fully amortized loans, the demand for second mortgages in residential financing has fallen sharply.

The **purchase money** mortgage is used in a situation in which a purchaser buying property partly on credit from the seller pledges as security the property being purchased. The purchaser takes the property subject to the claim of the seller, which has priority over any other mortgage loan the buyer may subsequently obtain. The purchase money mortgage is used most often in land acquisition and subdivision development projects. It is common for the seller to agree that his lien will be subordinated to a claim of an institutional lender supplying either land development or construction funds.

MORTGAGE INSURANCE AND CONVENTIONAL LOANS. Loans made by lending institutions in which the risk of loss is borne by the institution without regard to insurance are called conventional loans. These comprise the bulk of all mortgages.

Mortgage insurance was first developed in the 1920's, but the depression of the 1930's brought with it losses too great for private mortgage companies to absorb. In 1934 the Federal Housing Administration was created to develop a **government-insured loan program.** In 1944, with the passage of the Servicemen's Readjustment Act, there was created the Veterans Administration guaranteed and insured loan program, originally only **for veterans** of World War II and subsequently extended to veterans of the Korean conflict. The F.H.A. and V.A. programs provide standards for loan terms and for properties eligible for security. Institutions making loans according to these standards are insured or guaranteed against lossses.

The F.H.A. program calls for 100% insurance on each eligible loan, whereas the V.A. guarantee is for 60% of the loan, but not in excess of $7,500. In practice, the Veterans Administration has been able to acquire properties from distressed veteran borrowers and to reimburse lenders in full. The F.H.A. reimburses lenders holding defaulted mortgages with 3-year debentures.

Government-underwritten mortgages took their largest share of the market in 1950, when F.H.A. home loans accounted for 11% of nonfarm mortgage recordings and V.A. loans, 16%. Since 1960, conventional loans have accounted for over four-fifths of annual nonfarm mortgage recordings.

With the development of a few small privately owned mortgage insurance companies, **private mortgage insurance** again became available in the latter part of the 1950's. In 1957 the Mortgage Guaranty Insurance Company of Milwaukee offered a program of mortgage insurance for qualified savings and loan associations. The company insures against loss the top 20% of a conventional eligible loan. As of June 30, 1963, the company had insurance in force of nearly $1.2 billion.

THE TRUST DEED. The trust deed has virtually supplanted the mortgage in a few states, particularly California, and is commonly used throughout the United States in transactions involving substantial amounts of funds. (See Weimer and Hoyt, Principles of Real Estate.) The trust deed provides for the conveyance of the title of pledged property to a **third party** (the trustee) who holds it in trust as security for the payment of an obligation by a borrower to a lender (or beneficiary). Thus, in a trust deed situation there are three parties as compared to the two parties in an ordinary real estate mortgage transaction. In the event of a **default**, the trustee must protect the rights of the beneficiary either by selling the property or undertaking foreclosure proceedings. If the debt is repaid without default, the trustee is instructed to reconvey title to the debtor.

SPECIAL FEATURES OF MORTGAGE FINANCING. The great majority of all real estate mortgages are written to secure a debt by the pledge of one specific piece of real property. Modifications in the standard mortgage arrangements are common in the financing of different phases of real estate activity. The most important ones are described below.

Construction Loans. The most common type of construction financing is the construction loan, the proceeds of which are disbursed to the borrower as the building progresses. (Weimer and Hoyt, Principles of Real Estate.) The loan is evidenced by a note or a series of short-term notes drawn at intervals during the construction period. This **interim financing** is repaid from the proceeds of the regular mortgage loan once the project is completed and may be an integral part of the long-term financing arrangements.

Construction loan **disbursement schedules** are adapted to the particular situations. Some loans permit payouts as specific phases of a project are completed. For example, 25% may be paid out when the foundation is completed, 25% when the structure is under roof and rough plumbing and wiring are installed, 35% when the structure is completed and ready for occupancy, and 15% after the period for filing mechanics' liens has elapsed. Other payout systems permit the borrower to draw loan funds in amounts equal to a certain percentage of the cost of the work completed for which payment has not already been made. The balance is disbursed after the project is completed and accepted. Some payout systems simply require the builder to submit bills to the lender for payment as work on the project progresses. The borrower typically pays interest during the construction period and begins periodic repayments at the completion of construction or after some time span, such as 6 months, whichever first occurs.

Construction loans are made by all types of real estate lenders, but primarily by commercial banks and savings and loan associations. Bank loans ordinarily are evidenced by short-term notes that require refinancing. Loans of the savings and loan associations tend to be longer term, with disbursements spaced during the construction period.

The **principal risks** to the lenders in real estate financing are failure of project completion within a reasonable time and at a cost commensurate with the value of the completed property, and subservience of the mortgage lien to mechanics' liens. The amount of analysis and supervision required for construction loans is greater than for the ordinary mortgage loan. Accordingly, it is customary for lenders to charge a special fee, which may range from 1% to 2½% of the principal amount. In addition, interest rates on construction loans tend to run from ¼% to ½% higher than for a loan on a completed unit.

Land Development Financing. Subdivision developers typically are responsible for the installation of the necessary capital facilities, which are generally very costly and consequently require credit arrangements. The cost of converting a farm into a residential subdivision, for example, usually runs from three to six times the investment in the raw land. Most of the institutional lenders are permitted to grant loans for land development, federally chartered savings and loan associations and some state associations having specific authority to make such loans.

The form of mortgage note most often used in land development financing of subdivisions is the **blanket mortgage,** which attaches to each lot in the subdivision. As the project is completed and the lots are ready for sale, an individual lot may be removed as security for the loan upon the payment of a stipulated sum. The release payments typically are set at such levels that the entire loan will be repaid before all of the pledged lots have been presented for release.

Leasehold Mortgages. Leasehold mortgages are common in the financing of large-scale properties such as office buildings, shopping centers, and even some industrial properties. The leasehold mortgage figures in the following kind of transaction: A leases a tract of land to B on which B builds an office building. B, in turn, executes space leases with building tenants. As security for his mortgage loan B pledges his rights as a lessee in the land and the rents due under the lease contracts with the tenants.

Leasehold financing is very common in financing investment real estate. In effect, the real security for the mortgage is the credit standing of the tenants.

The leasehold mortgage is often used **in combination** with other financing in the subdividing of property interests in a single unit of real estate. An outstanding example, described by McDonald in Fortune, is one in which William Zeckendorf first acquired full interest in No. 2 Park Avenue, a Manhattan office building, in which the rentals netted $1 million annually and which had prospects for substantial rental increases. He then leased the entire property to an investor for (1) an initial payment of $1.5 million cash, (2) a note for $3.5 million secured by a pledge of the leases to the building's tenants, and (3) an annual rental of $600,000. Zeckendorf, in turn, borrowed $6,750,000 secured by a pledge of his interest in the leased fee and reversion, and another $2,250,000 secured by a second mortgage on the leased fee. Subdivision of the interest in the property thus resulted in a cash flow to Zeckendorf of $10.5 million from the two mortgages and the sale of the lease, a note for $3.5 million, and an equity valued at $1.2 million, for a total of $15.2 million. The property had a market value of $10 million before the interests were divided, the increased worth resulting from the fractionalization of the interests that began with the creation of the top leasehold estate.

Open-End Mortgages. The open-end mortgage is an ordinary mortgage that includes provisions for securing future advances to the borrower (Weimer and Hoyt, Principles of Real Estate). If an **additional advance** is made, the lender need acquire only a note, since the advance is secured by the original mortgage, which stipulates that the mortgage is to secure the original debt plus additional advances that may be made.

The open-end mortgage is used most often in residential financing. Although open-end advances could be used for any purpose, most lenders restrict them to the financing of improvement, expansion, or remodeling of the property covered by the original mortgage. The advance is evidenced by a note ordinarily repayable over the unexpired term of the original note.

The lender must be certain that the additional advances are **covered by the original mortgage.** In a majority of states the mere inclusion of the open-end provision in the mortgage instrument protects future advances, but in some states the lender must determine that no intervening liens have been created that would rank ahead of his claim.

Package Mortgages. A package mortgage is created when chattels (personal property) are converted to real property and are included along with the real estate as part of the security in a mortgage transaction. The package mortgage is frequently used in residential financing and commonly includes such items of equipment as plumbing accessories, air conditioning systems, awnings, blinds, cabinets and bookcases, dishwashers, fireplace accessories, floor coverings, garbage disposal units, laundry equipment, radiator covers, ranges, refrigerators, screens, and storm doors. The items to be covered are listed in the mortgage, which ordinarily also includes a **covenant attaching a claim to replacements.** Some lenders require on such equipment as washers, dryers, and stoves a certificate reading, "This appliance or equipment has been installed here by the owner as a part of this real estate and is included in any mortgage or conveyance."

Share Collateral Mortgages. The share collateral mortgage is a specialty of savings and loan associations that can lend not only upon the security of real estate but also on their own share accounts. Such loans are used only when a qualified borrower requires a loan **in excess of 80% of appraised value.** Associations unwilling to grant 90% loans or F.H.A. and V.A. loans are frequently willing to make share collateral loans because of the extra protection made available to the lending institution. The plan has been used in financing both single homes and tract houses.

In an example described by Theobald (The Magazine of Prefabrication) the seller of a home had an offer for $10,500 with a down payment of $1,500. The First Federal Savings and Loan Association of Peoria appraised the property for $10,000 and was willing to make an $8,000 conventional loan to the buyer. The real estate broker involved suggested to the seller that he consummate the transaction by agreeing to put up as collateral a $1,000 First Federal savings account. The First Federal thus made a loan for $9,000, based upon 80% of the appraised value and 100% of the seller's share account. The agreement provided that the $1,000 would be released to the seller when the loan was paid down to $7,500. Until such time he would collect dividends, or could sell the account to another investor who, of course, would be bound by the original collateral agreement. In such a sale, any appreciation over the face value would be taxable as a capital gain.

Options, Escrows, and Land Trusts

OPTIONS. An option is a contract in which a seller gives a buyer a **specified period of time** during which he has the right to call for the execution of a transaction on some predetermined basis. The option is particularly useful in the acquisition of land for building or subdividing. Once the buyer has an option securing his right to complete the transaction, he is then free to undertake such actions as financing, obtaining zoning amendments, or processing a subdivision plot.

According to Kratovil (Real Estate Law), "If, within the time specified in the option, the optionee gives the owner notice that he elects to exercise the option, the option then ripens into a contract of sale. If the optionee lets the specified time go by without taking any action, he has no further rights in the land nor can he recover from the landowner the money paid for the option."

ESCROWS. An escrow is an arrangement in which a third party serves to protect the interests of two or more contracting parties while conditions upon which the contract is contingent are being fulfilled or after a default. It is not unusual in real estate transactions for the seller to be unable to satisfy his mortgage until he receives the proceeds from the buyer. The buyer, in turn, or his mortgagee, will be unwilling to pay the full purchase price to the seller until the mortgage claim against the seller's property has been satisfied. The escrow arrangement allows this impasse to be overcome. The escrow holder, a **disinterested third party** who is free to act only upon the instructions contained in the escrow agreement, may collect all the papers, releases, and monies necessary to the transaction and effect the exchanges with full protection to all parties.

The escrow period may be a relatively short time, to allow for the completion of a title search or the arrangement of financing. It may, however, extend for months or years, during which a long-term contract for the purchase of land is fulfilled. (See Kratovil, Real Estate Law.)

THE LAND TRUST. A land trust is created by a deed in trust under which the grantor conveys to a trustee, usually a corporate trustee, a title to property to be held for a **specified beneficiary.** The warranty deed conveying the title of property must be recorded in the public records, but the trust agreement need not be recorded and, accordingly, the identity of the beneficiary need not become public information. The beneficiary may be the creator of the trust.

The land trust is used both for the holding of single properties and for the assembling of parcels of land. It permits privacy of ownership, limited liability for beneficiaries, and multiple ownership without the legal complexities of joint tenancies or tenancies in common. Interests in trusts may be conveyed simply by assignment of the beneficial interest. (See Garrett, Legal Aspects of Land Trusts.)

Long-Term Leases

PURPOSES AND TYPES. A long-term lease is often used instead of mortgage financing by firms wishing to conserve working capital or even to free working capital invested in real estate. In some instances the **deductibility of interest** as an expense for income tax purposes makes leasing more economical for business firms than buying real property on a mortgage since interest is deductible as a business expense whereas principal repayments are not. Long-term real estate leases are of two types: net leases under which the tenant pays all charges of every description; and gross leases, under which the tenant pays a given rental to the owner, who assumes the entire burden of management. (See Kahn, Case, and Schimmel, Real Estate Appraisal and Investment.)

NET LEASES. There are three standard forms of the net lease: (1) the ninety-nine-year lease, (2) the twenty-one-year lease, and (3) the long-term net lease. The **ninety-nine-year** lease is likely to appear to the owner of the real estate as a sale on an annuity basis. This type of lease is usually made on large pieces of valuable land and is typically regarded as a well-secured, long-term investment on a net basis. Frequently it results from the inability to sell the property because of complications with an estate, or a desire to avoid reinvestment of proceeds of the sale or to defer payment of a capital gains tax.

Ninety-nine-year leases are often used on prime commercial or office building sites. The lessee may agree to purchase for cash any buildings on the site and then replace them with a new building. The lessor receives a net rental—that is, the tenant pays in addition to the rent the taxes, water rates, insurance, and operating expenses of the building. Typically, ninety-nine-year leases made subsequent to 1945 include provisions for rental adjustments to combat inflation.

The **twenty-one-year** lease, characteristic of New York real estate, is basically a ground lease. It differs from the ninety-nine-year lease mainly in that under the ground lease, if there are improvements the tenant purchases the improvements, but is not obliged to erect a new building. If there are no improvements, or if the improvements are obsolete, the tenant may, at his option, erect a new structure. Additional characteristics follow:

. . . The twenty-one-year lease usually gives the tenant one to three options to renew for additional terms of twenty-one years each. The rent paid is also net, the tenant paying all other charges. There may or may not be step-up provisions for the rentals. The renewal options provide that one or two years prior to the expiration of the original term the tenant must signify his intention to exercise his renewal privilege. The renewal options may specify that the rent be set at a percentage of the market value at the time of renewal or at a predetermined figure, but, in any event, the rental in the renewal period is hardly ever set at a figure below the amount paid in the preceding term.

An exception to this general rule will occur where sales-leaseback transactions have been entered into. In these cases, particularly where insurance companies are involved, the initial rental is set at a figure sufficient to completely amortize the initial investment by the company with interest on the outstanding balances during the first term lease. The renewal options then call for sharply reduced rentals for the succeeding term. But sales-leaseback transactions are more in the nature of financial arrangements between insurance companies and substantial tenants than they are real estate transactions. In these cases, the credit rating of the tenants, the former owners, is at least as important as the value of the property as security for the lease. (See further discussion later in this Section.) (Kahn, Case, and Schimmel, Real Estate Appraisal and Investment.)

In the **long-term net lease,** the lessee is typically the property user, who will occupy all or the greater portion of the building. The term of the lease is usually for 20 years or longer and is written on a net rental basis. Ordinarily it is on improved property, and the lessee is not expected to erect a structure or provide improvements to it.

Long-term net leases usually have the following provisions: (1) The landlord has no problem of management, the tenant relieving him of this burden and paying all operating charges. The landlord receives his monthly or quarterly rental and pays interest and amortization on the mortgage, if there is one. (2) The landlord is not obligated to make any repairs. In the event of fire or other casualty causing damage or destruction of the building, the tenant is obligated to repair or rebuild; and if the insurance proceeds are insufficient, the tenant makes up the deficiency. Rent does not cease for any reason.

GROSS LEASES. Gross leases are the most common types of lease contracts and are typical of rental situations involving ordinary properties. Normally they contain no provision for periodic rent adjustments, and there are no standard arrangements regarding renewals.

The tenant pays a given rental to the owner, who has the burden of management. The leases sometimes require the lessee to pay the real estate taxes in excess of a certain stipulated amount. Tenants may also be assessed for operating expenses of certain types, such as snow removal, and institutional advertising and grounds care in the case of shopping centers.

On commercial properties the rent is frequently based upon gross revenues of the tenant, with a stipulated minimum below which rents may not fall. A summary of percentage lease rates on selected types of properties is given in Percentage Leases (The National Institute of Real Estate Brokers).

TYPICAL PROVISION OF LEASES. The essential parts of the real estate lease are the names of the parties, the extent and boundaries of the properties, the term of the lease, the amount of the rent, and the time of payment and execution by the parties. (Levinson, The University of Illinois Law Forum.)

In addition, there are many topics that typically are covered in **detailed leases.** According to Levinson (The University of Illinois Law Forum), these include the following: (1) description of the premises, including detailed description of the building; (2) the rental term, including form, timing, and place of payment; (3) details on the payment of taxes, including provision for lessee to contest taxes; (4) maintenance and care of buildings, including indemnity to owner for loss and damages, repairs to be made by lessee, and prohibition against using the premises for unlawful purposes; (5) repairs and insurance—the lessee's obligation to keep buildings in good repair and to insure the property up to a certain percentage of value, with directions on the loss payable; (6) covenants regarding liens; (7) covenants regarding waste (changing the premises, deliberate destruction, or failing to repair damage); (8) construction of a new building, including a specified time limit, character of construction, architectural and engineering details, evidence of availability of financing and financial feasibility of construction, protection of lessor with respect to expense and mechanics' liens, and limitation on the removal of buildings; (9) deposits and application of security; (10) rebuilding in the event of injury or destruction; (11) alterations and improvements, including conditions under which improvements and rebuilding should take place; (12) vesting in the lessor of buildings built by the lessee; (13) limitation on right of lessor to mortgage; (14) lessee's rights for the assignment of the lease; (15) lessee's rights for mortgaging the leasehold; (16) limitations on subleases; (17) purchase options on behalf of the lessee; (18) provision for adjustment of rights of lessee and lessor in the event of condemnation of premises; and (19) controls on party-wall agreements.

VARIABLE RENT LEASES. The longer the term of the lease, the greater the possibility that the real flow of rent to the lessor will be diminished by inflation, rising taxes, or changes in the productive capacity of the property. Several devices have been used to alter lease payments to meet changed conditions. Among such variable leases are the expense-participating lease, the step-up or step-down lease, the reappraisal lease, the percentage lease, and leases based upon a cost-of-living index. (See Denz, The University of Illinois Law Forum.)

Step-up or step-down leases and **reappraisal** leases are likely to be burdensome to one or the other of the parties and difficult to administer. The generally accepted minimum period between reappraisals is 2 years, and the generally accepted maximum is 5 years. With regard to the reappraisal lease, Denz states:

> As a practical matter, it is not infallible and there are several significant disadvantages. The parties do not have a firm lease the entire term because the rent to be paid during certain periods of the term of the lease will be determined by strangers to the contract. The uncertainty attendant upon this situation is a mental

hazard to both the landlord and the tenant and a hindrance to the sale of the building, as well as to the sale of the business . . .

In addition to objecting to the uncertainty attending appraisals, the parties often object to the inconvenience and expense incident to the process. It appears that if the appraisal accomplishes its purpose, the inconvenience and expense are amply justified by the result.

Leases adjusted according to changes in some **price index,** such as the Consumers' Price Index, may frustrate as well as protect the parties to a lease. To guard against too frequent readjustment, the leases usually prohibit an adjustment more frequently than once a year, and then only if the index has changed by not less than a stipulated percentage.

The **percentage** lease is the most common of all the variable leases. Inasmuch as the rent payment is expressed as a percentage of gross sales, such a lease automatically takes into account inflation, changes in the productivity of the site, and variable performances by the tenant. Current operating data provide the basis for rent determination without the necessity for special calculations or reviews.

Real Estate Valuation and Investment Analysis

INVESTMENT FEATURES OF REAL ESTATE. The features of real estate of major interest to both lenders and equity investors are value stability and investment safety; investment yield, in terms of both certainty and stability; marketability or investment liquidity; capital appreciation; protection from inflation; and tax minimization opportunities. Real estate, however, cannot be rated as a homogeneous investment area. Different types of real estate have different investment attributes. In Fig. 9 Kahn, Case, and Schimmel classify the principal types of real estate according to their investment qualities.

RISK CHARACTERISTICS. The risks inherent in any particular real estate investment may arise from the following factors: (1) environmental and physical characteristics of the real estate, (2) the type of property, (3) market trends, (4) the nature of the property rights involved, and (5) the financing arrangements of the investor.

Environmental and Physical Characteristics. The physical characteristics of real estate obviously determine its capacity to produce useful services.

One of the most significant criteria is the **functional character of the design,** which may influence the profitability of operations of a business using the structure, maintenance costs, and, of course, the rents that can be obtained from the property. Other important physical attributes are quality of construction, convertibility, architectural style, and adaptation of the structure to the site.

The **quality of construction** should be measured in terms of whether or not the building will be capable of performing its functions satisfactorily during the entire economic life of the structure. Another test is whether or not the physical qualities will require unusually heavy maintenance expense.

The **architectural style** and the **adaptation of the structure to the site** are largely esthetic considerations. But each may influence the uses to which the building may be put as well as the efficiency with which the property can be used.

Very few individual pieces of real estate are important enough to alter the character of a neighborhood or district. To a great extent, the value characteristics of real estate are determined by the attributes of the neighborhood, district, or the immediate environment of the property.

REAL ESTATE VALUATION AND INVESTMENT ANALYSIS 26·21

Type of Investment	Safety of Initial Investment	Safety of Annual Earnings	Capital Appreciation	Liquidity	Income Tax Shelter	Inflationary Protection
Apartment houses (middle income)	E	E	E	E	G	E†
Apartment houses (luxury)	F	F	F	F	G	E†
Office buildings (multitenant, in city)	G	G	G	E	F	E†
Office buildings (one national tenant, suburb)	F	G*	P*	E*	E	N
Office buildings (multitenant, suburb)	P	F	P	P	E	G
Retail property (average tenant, in city)	F	P	N	F	P	F
Retail property (one national tenant, in city)	F	G*	P	E*	P	N‡
Retail property (shopping centers)	F	G	G	G	E	P‡
Retail property (one national tenant, suburb)	G	G*	P*	E*	E	N‡
Loft buildings (multitenant)	G	G	F	F	G	G†
Industrial buildings (one national tenant)	G	G*	P*	E*	E	N
Gas stations (one national tenant, highway)	F	F*	P*	E*	E	P
Gas stations (one national tenant, in city)	E	G*	G	E*	F	P

Code: E—excellent; G—good; F—fair; P—poor; N—negative.

* Assume rental is at market, lease has many years to run, and purchase price is fair.
† Under free market conditions, otherwise poor.
‡ Unless percentage lease, then excellent.

Fig. 9. Rating of realty investment. (Source: Kahn, Case, and Schimmel, Real Estate Appraisal and Investment.)

Type of Property. The investment characteristics of real estate are influenced by the type of property involved. All other things being equal, certain types of realty have more safety than others. While drawing attention to the dangers of generalizations, Kahn, Case, and Schimmel point out:

... Usually, safe realty investments include middle-income apartment houses, well-rented office buildings, retail property with choice occupancy, and industrial buildings and gas stations with national tenants under long-term leases. Motels, hotels, bowling alleys, theaters, nursing homes, and similar properties are considered risky because they are not actually realty investments. They involve the operation of a business on realty premises. It is true that the business may be thought of as the renting of bed space, alley space, motel unit space, or theater seat space, any of which can be compared with store, office, or apartment space; nevertheless, it is a highly specialized form of operation. The returns should include a realty return, a business management return, and an entrepreneurial risk return. (Kahn, Case, and Schimmel, Real Estate Appraisal and Investments.)

The degree to which a structure is a **special purpose** building influences its investment attributes. Obviously, the greater number of uses to which a building may be put, the lower the investment risk.

Market Trends. The investment quality of real estate is, of course, influenced by national business trends, regional economic developments, and especially the strength of the economic base of the area in which the property is located.

Rights in some kinds of properties, such as office buildings, shopping centers, supermarkets, and industrial parks, are traded **nationally,** whereas other parcels of real estate are traded strictly within the **immediate vicinity** of the property. Whether the investment market is large or small, the fundamental strength of the property lies in the economic conditions in the area in which the property offers its services.

Nature of Property Rights. The totality of rights in real property is represented by **fee ownership.** However, the fee may be fractionalized, with many different strata of rights being involved in the accounting for the full ownership. The character of the rights held by a particular investor influences the risk characteristics of the investment.

The **safest** realty investment, according to Kahn, Case, and Schimmel (Real Estate Appraisal and Investment), is the ownership of land under a large modern building that is well designed and a proper improvement for the land. If the rent is not paid on the ground lease, the land owner typically has the right to acquire the building placed upon the land. Consequently, the builder and any mortgagees of the building will do everything possible to see that rent payments are made according to the lease.

The **most hazardous** period for the owner of the leased land fee will be the period of construction until the building is rented. Usually the ground owner will require a security deposit and/or a completion bond to protect himself until the building is actually completed and rented.

Prudently created **first mortgages** are another low-risk realty investment. Mortgage risks are generally related to the amount of equity of the borrower, the anticipated relationship of property net income to debt service, and the amount of the debt relative to the anticipated income and value stability of the property. In residential real estate, the ratio of the loan to the appraised value of the property is considered very important. In investment real estate, greater emphasis is put on the relationship between net property income and mortgage interest and amortization charges. Depending upon the expected stability of income of the property, mortgage lenders may require a net earnings stream anticipated to be from 1½ to 2½ times the annual debt charges. In the financing of shopping centers and office buildings, lenders sometimes limit a loan to a magnitude that will permit the debt service to be covered from the rents paid by the principal tenants (those with the highest credit ratings) less operating expenses for the entire project.

Although **loan-to-value** ratios are also given consideration on loans to investment property, the loan-to-value test is not nearly as significant as the **income-to-debt service** test. In fact, the two relationships are interrelated since the value of investment property is usually determined from anticipated property net income.

FINANCING ARRANGEMENTS. The investment character of a fee interest in improved property is directly related to the financial obligations involved. A leaseholder's interest may have risk characteristics comparable to those of a fee holder, depending upon the position of the leasehold and whether or not the leaseholder is an investor in improvements. The greater the number of mortgage commitments and subleases a leaseholder has, the greater the risks of the leasehold position tend to be.

Influence of Leverage. The amount of leverage involved in either a fee or a leasehold situation may be a factor that determines whether a particular program represents an investment or a speculation. An example taken from Kahn, Case, and Schimmel (Real Estate Appraisal and Investment), illustrates the hazards and advantages of leverage.

A property was purchased, free and clear, for $80,000, and there is a net return, before depreciation, of $10,000, or 12½ per cent.

A $50,000 first mortgage is placed against the realty, with annual payments of $3,750 including interest charges of 5½ per cent. The net cash flow is reduced to $6,250, but now the owner's cash investment is reduced to $30,000. The return is now 20.8 per cent.

If he now obtains $15,000 against a second mortgage and pays $1,650 per annum, including 8 per cent interest, the net cash flow is reduced to $4,600 but he will only have an investment of $15,000 and the return will be over 30 per cent.

These mortgages are not obtained without cost, and this will reduce the return to the investor, for his investment will be somewhat higher than that stated in this example. However, the results will be nearly as effective as shown.

The investor who has $80,000 cash can repeat this same process in the purchase of about five properties, and, instead of being satisfied with a cash flow of $10,000, he will actually have about $23,000. In addition, amortization is the repayment of the mortgage indebtedness, and he will be increasing his portion of the property ownership with each payment. He will also be able to reduce his income-tax liability because the mortgage interest is an expense against his earnings.

Obviously, such a fine situation must also have some negative factors. First of all, it must be understood that the mortgage interest rate on the first mortgage was stated to be 5½ per cent and that on the second mortgage, 8 per cent. Why are these mortgage investors willing to take a lower return than the over-all rate of 12½ per cent available to the realty? The reason is obvious. They are taking the safer portion of the investment.

Property values would have to decline more than 33⅓ per cent before it would be possible for the first mortgage holder to lose any of its money. (Since its mortgage is being decreased by the regular amortization payments, the actual decrease in value would have to be greater.) Even then, only a portion of its investment would be lost. However, a loss in value of 20 per cent would wipe out the property owner completely, and the second mortgagee would lose a little, unless the amortization had reduced the mortgage sufficiently.

Another way of showing this is to indicate that, before mortgage financing, $10,000 a year was available to the owner but that, after the two mortgages were placed against it, debt charges totaled $5,400, leaving only $4,600 to the owner. Now let us suppose that a combination of a rent loss and an operating increase occurred. A total income loss of $5,000 would leave the property owner with a deficit of $400. He would, therefore, have to pay to own this realty. He would have a negative return on his investment. If he had not mortgaged the realty, his return would still be $5,000 on an $80,000 investment, or over 6 per cent.

The speculative investor can also show that a $5,000 increase in rental return would give the free and clear investor $15,000 net income on an $80,000 investment, or a return of a bit under 19 per cent, while, with the mortgages stated above, the thin equity holder would have a return of $9,600 on an investment of $15,000, or 64 per cent.

The figures given in this example are not indicative of market conditions affecting any particular investment but are offered to indicate clearly potentialities of leverage. Typically, the most skilled professional investors utilize this system. They have even devised additional methods of investing and applying leverage by separating the fee from the leasehold and also trading in leasehold positions.

Depreciation and Tax Factors. The investment characteristics of the equity position in a high leverage situation are strongly influenced by the relationship of principal repayments on a mortgage and depreciation allowances deductible from income subject to the Federal income tax. Real estate is sometimes thought of as a tax shelter because of the depreciation allowances, but the tax allowances are not without **disadvantages.**

Suppose that an investor acquired a property at a market price of $250,000, with a first mortgage for $170,000, having annual mortgage payments of $12,000. The investor chose to depreciate his property for Federal income tax purposes over a period of 33⅓ years on the **declining-balance method,** which allows depreciation to be 200% of that which would be allowed under the straight-line method of depreciation. Suppose in this instance that the depreciable part of the investment—the building—represented $200,000. Further assume that the annual net income from the property remains stable at $15,000 and that the first year's mortgage payment of $12,000 consists of $8,400 interest and $3,600 principal. On the basis of a 33⅓-year life, the depreciation allowance would be 6% of $200,000, or $12,000; the second year, 6% of $188,000, or $11,280; the third year, 6% of $176,720, or about $10,603; and so on. Exhibit 1 shows the cash flow and the income tax liability at the end of the first year.

Exhibit 1

Net Income from Property		$15,000
Mortgage Payment		
Interest	$8,400	
Principal	3,600	
		12,000
Cash in Hand		$ 3,000
Income Tax Liability		
Income		$15,000
Less Depreciation	$12.000	
Interest on Mortgage	8.400	20,400
TAXABLE INCOME		$−5,400

Thus, at the end of the first year the investor has cash in hand of $3,000 that is not subject to an income tax liability, and a tax **offset** against other income of $5,400.

The investor's position will be reversed in some future year. Assume that the $15,000 net income continues and that at some point the division between principal and interest in the mortgage payment is reversed, with interest amounting to $3,600 and principal, $8,400. Inasmuch as the depreciation allowance continues at 6% of a declining amount, it declines each year. Assume that in the year under consideration it has fallen to $2,400. Exhibit 2 shows the cash flow and the taxable income in the assumed year.

Exhibit 2

Net Income from Property		$15,000
Mortgage Payment		
Interest	$3,600	
Principal	8,400	
		12,000
Cash Flow		$ 3,000
Income Tax Liability		
Income		$15,000
Less Depreciation	$2,400	
Interest	3,600	
		6,000
Taxable Income		$ 9,000
Cash Available from Investment		$ 3,000

The taxable income to the investor is $9,000, whereas cash available is only $3,000. If the investor is in a 30% or higher tax bracket, his cash flow from the project will no more than equal and possibly be less than the tax due.

In addition to the declining balance method of depreciation, the Internal Revenue Service permits the **sum-of-the-digits approach**. By assuming that the anticipated life of the property is 10 years, an investor would determine the sum of the integers from 1 through 10 (total: 55). The depreciation for the first year would be 10/55 of the depreciable investment, in the second year 9/55, and so on.

The rapid depreciation plans, if used wisely, can give a high-leverage investor an unusually large return on his equity. It is not uncommon for an investor using a rapid write-off plan to dispose of the property when the depreciation allowance approximately equals the principal repayment portion of the mortgage loan. The differential between the sales price and the undepreciated balance of the investment in the property would be treated as a capital gain or loss.

REAL ESTATE VALUATION. Appraisals made for mortgage lenders differ little from analyses made for equity investors. The mortgage lender seeks to determine the probability that the debt will be satisfied according to schedule and that, in the event of default, the property value will be large enough to cover the outstanding loan balance. The equity investor seeks essentially the same information since the probable rate of return on his equity is closely related to the value of the property and the mortgage terms. He is also interested in depreciation allowances, in the property's value stability, and especially in the prospects for capital gains.

Three standard approaches to **value analysis** are in use: (1) market comparison, (2) income capitalization, and (3) cost of replacement. Each of the methods seeks to determine the present worth of the future benefits to be derived from the property. It is rare that data are available that permit the satisfactory use of all three methods in a single value analysis.

Market Comparison Approach. Whenever a property is of a type actually traded in the real estate markets, the appraiser or analyst will endeavor to ascertain what the consensus of the market would be as to the present worth of the future benefits of the subject property, as determined by what has been paid for similar properties. The basic technique of the market comparison method is to find evidence of sales of properties that took place under market conditions comparable to those at the given time. The **comparison units** should be properties with physical, legal, environmental, and financing characteristics similar to those of the property being evaluated. To find truly comparable situations is the most difficult part of market comparison appraising. This method is used in the valuation of all kinds of property and is employed whenever possible, even though other appraisal methods may also be used in the analysis.

Income Capitalization Analysis. The capitalization of income approach is used whenever it is possible to estimate the net income stream of the property. The value analysis of investment property almost always involves income capitalization appraising. The basic objective is to estimate a **reasonable net income stream** for the economic life of the property and to translate this into a present worth estimate, frequently through the use of annuity factors. This requires estimating the remaining economic life of the property, gross income potentials, and probable operating expenses.

Market comparison techniques also come into play in the income capitalization analysis, since the process involves the application of appropriate capitalization rates to the projected net income. The rates selected must be close to those being earned by investors in properties of comparable risks.

Cost of Replacement Approach. Certain kinds of real property are not readily traded in the market and produce no measurable money income. Ordinarily, special purpose amenity producing properties are valued or analyzed on a cost of replacement basis. In an effort to determine the value of a nonmarket, non-income-producing property, the question is posed: What would it cost to replace the present property with a newly created unit of real estate that would offer a totality of future services similar to those of the property under consideration?

Since a new structure would embody technological advances in the given field, the analysis technique is divided essentially into two parts: (1) estimation of the cost to replace the subject structure with new facilities that would render comparable services, and (2) measurement of the differences in productivity between the subject property and the hypothetical replacement. In other words, the estimated cost must reflect the productivity differences between the real subject and the compared replacement. The differential is called depreciation or penalty, so that the method of valuation is called either the **"replacement cost less depreciation"** method or the **"penalized cost of replacement"** approach.

The replacement cost method is extremely difficult to employ and is used infrequently. Cost estimates made without regard to depreciation or penalties are commonly used in investment program analysis. (See Kahn, Case, and Schimmel, Real Estate Appraisal and Investment.)

Financing Selected Real Estate Projects

SALES AND LEASEBACKS. A sale and leaseback arrangement is one in which the owner of real estate sells it to an investor under an agreement in which the seller leases the property for a stipulated period. Properties most often involved in sales and leasebacks are office buildings, retail outlets, shopping centers, and industrial properties.

Occasionally, an apartment building is involved in a sale and leaseback transaction. The investor is frequently a life insurance company or a university endowment fund. The transaction usually involves either fully developed property, or vacant land sold to an investor who agrees to build a structure according to the specifications of the leaseback tenant.

Sales and leasebacks became popular during the late 1940's and have been used extensively in the post-World War II plant expansion and real estate investment booms. They have been favored by industrial companies that desire to improve their working capital position by recapturing their investment in real estate. Inasmuch as rent is deductible for income tax purposes when a lease involves property used for business or investment, some companies sell their property and lease it back in order to improve their current operating position.

Financial institutions and endowment funds investing in leasebacks have considerable leeway with respect to the terms and have been able to effect advantageous deals. The transactions usually involve large sums of money and therefore relatively low investment management costs. The leaseback tenants are typically highly rated corporations with great financial strength. The purchaser is also in a position to realize gains from capital appreciation, should such occur. Most institutional investors acquiring leasebacks recover their investment in the property during the first term of the lease unless the term is unusually short so that the residual value of the property will be unusually high.

Sale and leaseback transactions, although conceptually simple, may be very complicated in detail, especially if they involve the construction of a building to meet the needs of a particular user. The leases are typically written for terms of 21 to 25 years, with renewal periods that will give the selling corporation the right to use the property for varying periods, but frequently as long as 100 years.

The **price** at which the property is sold to an institutional investor is not necessarily the same as the current market price. The purchaser might be willing to pay a premium price that would be reflected in the higher rents received under the lease. The selling corporation, in turn, would have a gain taxable at capital gains rates while the higher rents would be tax-deductible as operating expenses.

There is **no standard relationship** between interest rates charged on mortgages and yields required on sale and leaseback transactions. According to Ricks (Research Report 23), the yields required on leaseback versus mortgages differ among insurance companies depending on the standards they set up for leasebacks and their investment objectives. In instances where the company looks upon the deal as a partial inflation hedge, the leaseback yield may be lower than mortgage rates.

Illustration of a Sale and Leaseback. Kahn, Case, and Schimmel (Real Estate Appraisal and Investment) describe the essentials of a sale and leaseback transaction, involving a well-known multitenant office building sold to and leased back from a life insurance company:

A group of investors purchased the property at an all-cash price of $8,750,000 and simultaneously sold it to the insurance company for $7,000,000. The investors also had to invest approximately $250,000 additional cash for working capital and organizational cost. They also had to borrow funds from a bank for building modernization.

The lease rental was $525,000 for ten years and $456,000 for about fourteen years. It can be seen that the insurance company's return, on the $7,000,000, was 7½ per cent for the initial period and then was reduced to about 6½ per cent. This income is completely net to the insurance company, with the operating group paying all charges against the realty. However, the insurance company did not consider the rental to be all income. As is usually done, it credited part to interest income and the balance to working off the investment.

The lease called for three twenty-one-year renewal terms at a rental of $210,000 each. At the end of the three renewal terms, the realty became the unencumbered property of the insurance company.

The insurance company received a very advantageous deal that has worked out very well. The tenant-investors have also done very well. Their financing was in a larger amount than is available in normal mortgage financing. In addition, the entire rental payment was tax-deductible. They were also able to use the difference between the original cost and the sales price (about $2,000,000) as a tax base for the leasehold investment. Naturally, they were not entitled to normal building depreciation, as the building was insurance-company property. However, all leasehold improvements could be written off during the term of the original twenty-four-year lease.

OFFICE BUILDINGS. The corporate symbol office building has become prominent in recent years with the construction of the New York office buildings of Seagram's, Lever Brothers, and Union Carbide; the Inland Steel Building in Chicago; and the Humble Oil Building in Houston. Insurance companies have also built notable office buildings carrying the company names. Although the prestige buildings attract the most public attention, the greater part of office space, however, is in the competitive rental buildings in which the principal tenant may occupy 30% or less of the building space. It is not unusual for a multi-tenant building to carry the name of the chief tenant if that company occupies as much as 25 to 30% of the space. Quite often it is the completion of a lease with an A.A.A. tenant for 25 to 30% of the building space that allows the project developer to proceed with the program.

The value of an office building is, of course, dependent upon the net earnings available to cover debt service and returns on the equity. The greater the share of the building space under quality leases, the easier the financing is.

The Competitive Office Building. The competitive office building can be found both in central business districts and in outlying shopping centers and commercial clusters. The smaller the community, the more likely the building is part of a structure in which the principal occupant is a bank, a department store, or a specialized retail outlet.

Kahn, Case, and Schimmel describe commercial office buildings as follows (Real Estate Appraisal and Investment):

The commercial rental buildings will be created for main, regional, or local offices of commercial firms; service organizations such as insurance companies, realtors, and accountants; legal, medical, and dental offices; and some sales and showrooms.

In larger communities, buildings will be created to serve specific groups. In a city like Chicago or New York, separate office and showroom buildings tend to be centers for such specialized tenants as lawyers; realtors; toy showrooms; shippers; boys' or men's clothiers; buyers' offices; manufacturers of cotton, woolen, or silk textiles; securities dealers; insurance agents or companies; produce dealers (with different buildings for different types of products); advertisers; furniture companies; fine-arts dealers; dealers in gifts; and numerous other categories. Furthermore, certain buildings will cater to one type of merchandise within a specific price range.

Buildings which become highly specialized can often retain their economic strength for a longer period than either the age of the structure or the suitability of the neighborhood might indicate. This is due to the benefits of the business being concentrated under one roof. In this way, the firm's customers find it easier to deal with it.

Commercial office buildings in the United States are sometimes divided into **two classes**: those built and occupied before 1932, and those constructed since 1947. The post-World War II office boom started in New York in 1947 with the conversion of apartments to office buildings. By the mid-1950's, office developments were going on in all major United States cities.

The older class of office buildings were often financed with mortgage bonds and multiple traditional mortgages, frequently with a very small equity base, narrowly held. The postwar speculative buildings have been financed for the most part with mortgage loans from insurance companies that run for 20 to 25 years and are based upon the credit strength of tenants who have signed long-term leases. Construction money is usually dependent on a mortgage loan commitment, but in some instances builders have been able to finance construction on the basis of a lease commitment from a principal high-credit tenant.

The **speculative office building** is one in which there is likely to be not only high capital but also high operating leverage. The operating expenses of an office building, including management and administration but excluding financial charges, may range from 40 to 60% of the total rent collections. The expenses for a given building tend to be relatively stable so that a rise in gross collections, either from rent increases or a reduction in vacancies, tends to exceed the rate of increase in operating expenses. Accordingly, net income available to equity holders will expand more than proportionately with the increases in gross revenue.

The **breakdown of expenses** varies widely from building to building. The summary on page 30 of a recent financial statement for a 21-story office building built in the 1920's in a choice location in New York, with about 330,000 square feet of rentable space, manually operated elevators, and almost complete air conditioning composed of several systems, is representative of office building accounts.

Professional Buildings. Since the end of World War II, the relatively small professional office building has become prominent. Medical-dental buildings in particular have been developed outside of central business districts in many cities.

The medical-dental buildings are often owned by the building's tenants. Such buildings are expensive to construct and operating costs are typically high. Accordingly, investment in them may be advantageous to a tenant-owner but not necessarily attractive to an outside investor.

The professional building is typically financed by an amortized mortgage loan. The mortgages usually require that leases be arranged in advance, and they generally favor situations where owner-investors are also tenants.

Shopping Centers. A few shopping centers were developed in outlying areas prior to World War II, but the real boom occurred between 1947 and 1960. So many centers were developed in the latter part of the 1950's that in metropolitan areas the keenest competition was not so much between the shopping centers and downtown areas as among the new shopping centers themselves.

Insurance companies have been the principal investors in shopping centers, although all types of institutional lenders and endowment funds have supplied mortgage loans to developers. The demise of a few centers and the poor financial performance of many others have led mortgage lenders to be increasingly severe in providing financing.

A **long-term mortgage commitment** is the key to the development. Mortgage lenders typically require center developers to have signed leases with major tenants with suitable credit ratings and to have a sufficient number of these

INCOME
(Per Square Foot per Annum)

Basic rent collections =	$5.05	
Store overage =	.22	
Total collections =	$5.27	= 100%
Expenses		
Operating =	$ .92	
Repairs and maintenance =	.14	
Taxes and insurance =	1.01	
Management and administration =	.24	
	$2.31	= 44%
Tenant and building alterations =	$ .14	
	$2.45	= 46%
Net income free and clear =	$2.82	= 54%

EXPENSE BREAKDOWN
(Per Square Foot per Annum)

Fixed Charges	
Real estate taxes =	$.96
General insurance =	.048
(net including employees)	
Operating Expenses	
Payroll =	.72
Payroll surcharges =	.07
Heat =	.08
Miscellaneous =	.06
Repair and Maintenance	
Supplies =	.03
Painting =	.05
Repairs =	.06
Management and Administration	
Management commissions =	.08
Leasing commissions, averaged =	.09
Legal, accounting, advertising, administration, etc. =	.07

leases so that the income from the principal tenants alone could cover operating expenses and debt service. The principal tenants are usually a department store, a variety store, or a supermarket, depending upon the size of the center.

Loan terms are ordinarily for 15 to 20 and sometimes 25 years. Although the relationship between projected earnings and debt service is the key factor, the loan-to-value ratio test is also important. The shopping center loan is rarely for more than 65 to 70% of the appraised value of the property.

Several factors present **difficulties for shopping center development and financing.** It is now almost impossible to find a site that is not already within the trading area of an existing center or will probably not be encroached upon by another newly developed center. Since the financing is so dependent upon anticipation of good tenants with high credit standings, the first-rate tenants are actively sought and are ordinarily in a position to bargain to their advantage. Many center developers have given break-even arrangements or even subsidized positions to attract name tenants, only to discover that other tenants could not be attracted on less favorable terms—or, even worse, that the small tenants could not generate sufficient sales to produce enough rent to cover operating expenses, debt service, and a return on the equity.

The following are the principal **investment criteria** used in evaluating a shopping center. (See Kahn, Case, and Schimmel, Real Estate Appraisal and Investment.)

1. Mortgage lenders will expect about 70% of the rental income of the center to be derived from tenants having a net worth of over $1,000,000. The income from the prime tenants alone must be sufficient to meet operating expenses, real estate taxes, and debt charges. Only minimum guaranteed rents are included in the calculation. Lenders typically will not include in a mortgage analysis projected rents over and above the minimum guarantee of a percentage lease.
2. The mortgage should have a maturity of not less than 10 years and preferably an amortization schedule of 15 to 20 years.
3. While secondary financing with junior mortgages is common in shopping center projects, junior financing should be avoided whenever possible.
4. A complete analysis of the shopping center market and its growth potential are prerequisites to investment. The long-run potential for gross sales increases and, therefore, rent increases from percentage leases should be determined.
5. Equity investors in shopping centers ordinarily expect a return on equity of from 10–12% to 18–20%.

A Shopping Center Case Analysis. The following review of a shopping center investment is adapted from Kahn, Case, and Schimmel (Real Estate Appraisal and Investment). This midwestern shopping center is well located, with access on two roads. It covers 35 acres on the fringe of a large city and in a residential growth area.

The center was built with 175,000 square feet of ground floor stores and another 70,000 square feet of basement and mezzanine. The development costs included land and improvements, $105,000; parking lot, $275,000; buildings, $2,662,000; leasehold improvements for tenants, $187,000; total, $3,229,000.

The development costs represent about $16 per square foot of ground floor area for buildings (including tenant improvements) and about $1.60 per square foot for parking lot improvements. Land costs were 60 cents per square foot. The total project thus cost about $18.20 per square foot of ground floor area.

Income and expense data for 1961 are presented in Exhibit 3.

The total income for the center in 1961 amounted to less than $2 per square foot of ground floor area. Rental income at the rate of $2.50 or more per square foot would be necessary to produce a minimum satisfactory return on the total investment in the center. The net operating income of about $228,000 is only about 7% return on the total capital investment of $3,229,000, well below the desired minimum, which is usually 12%. It must be noted that this return includes depreciation and is before debt service. Moreover, $90,000 of the net operating income is based on tenant sales and is not a firm obligation. Finally, no allowance is made for possible vacancies.

The developer obtained unusually favorable mortgage financing. In this instance the loan totaled $2,600,000, which represented about 80% of the total cost and over 90% of the estimated value of the center. (A mortgage loan on a center ordinarily would not exceed two-thirds of value. The favorable loan was apparently available because 70% of the space was to be occupied by highly rated

Exhibit 3

Income		
Guaranteed rental:		
Fixed minimum		$249,060
Straight percentage (no minimum)		34,953
Percentage excess		55,189
Utilities and maintenance		4,156
Taxes and insurance		1,844
Other		1,629
Total income:		$346,800 *
Expenses—Operating		
Advertising		$ 3,600
Leasing commission		959
Insurance		10,223
Janitors' salaries		3,930
Janitors' supplies		27
Management fee paid local representative		8,596
Repairs and maintenance:		
Buildings		2,248
Parking lot		642
Utilities		5,179
Taxes:		
Property	$76,863	
State income tax	5,118	81,981
Legal and audit		1,778
Total cash operating expenses:		$119,100 *
Net operating income (before capital charges and depreciation).		$227,700
Capital Charges		
Interest on mortgage	$123,888	
Amortization of mortgages	66,752	
	$190,640	
Net income to equity (before depreciation):		$ 37,000

* Note: Last two figures have been dropped in income and expense totals.

tenants.) The operating costs for the center are about 68 cents per square foot of ground floor space, of which 44 cents are for real estate taxes and 24 cents for general operation. The $3,600 spent for advertising is abnormally low for a center of this size. It would not be unusual to see an annual expenditure for advertising for this type of center of at least $20,000 per year. The low promotional budget was probably a factor in the relatively small rental income.

At this time the mortgage had been paid down to about $2,230,000. If an investor were interested in buying this shopping center to earn at a rate of about 12% on his investment, he would pay no more than about $300,000 above the mortgage $\left(\dfrac{\$37,000}{0.12}\right)$. This would bring the total price to about $2,500,000, which is approximately $700,000 less than the original investment in the center. On this basis the developer would suffer a substantial loss.

SECTION 27

MATHEMATICS OF FINANCE

CONTENTS

Types of Interest

	PAGE
Definitions	1
Principal	1
Rate	1
Time	1
Basic types of interest	1
Computing elapsed time in days	2
Use of tables	2
The number of each day of the year counting from January 1 (f. 1)	2
Exact number of days in loan period (f. 2)	3
Accruing interest on bonds	3

Ordinary Interest

Basic formula	4
Short-cut methods for computing ordinary interest	4
Breaking up the time element	5
Odd interest rates	5
One-day rule	6

Exact Interest

Nature of exact interest	7
Finding the value of 1/73	7
Illustrative page of interest tables; exact interest on $100 of principal (f. 3)	8
Use of exact interest tables	8
Interest on United States government securities	9
Exact number of days in 6-month interest period (f. 4)	9
Interest for 1 day on $1,000 at different rates and periods (f. 5)	9
Anticipation	10
Exact interest per $100 of principal (basis 365-day year) at indicated time and rates (f. 6)	11

Bank Discount

Loans and discounts defined	12
Types of notes	13
Interest-bearing promissory note (f. 7)	13
Noninterest-bearing promissory note (f. 8)	13
Basis for calculating proceeds	13
Due date of notes	13
Computing proceeds and discount on noninterest-bearing paper	14
Discounting interest-bearing paper	14
Finding principal to yield given proceeds	15

	PAGE
Computation of interest under partial payment plans	15
The Merchant's Rule	15
The United States Rule	16
Bank discount vs. true discount	16
Relation of bank discount rate to true discount rate	17

Chain Discounts

Definition of chain discount	18
Finding equivalent single discount	18
Net cost factor tables	20
Typical page of a net cost factor table (f. 9)	19

Compound Interest

Compound interest definitions	20
Finding the compound amount	21
Arithmetical solution	21
Solution by formula	21
Compound interest table giving accumulated amounts (f. 10)	22–23
Value of $(1+i)^n$ from prepared tables	24
Value of $(1+i)^n$ by logarithms	24
Definition of present value	25
Finding present value from tables	25
Compound interest table giving present value (f. 11)	26–27
Finding present values by logs	28
Other converse cases	28
Finding value of n	28
Finding value of i	29

Annuities

Definitions	30
Ordinary annuity	30
Annuity due	30
Deferred annuity	30
Amount or final value of annuity	30
Perpetuity	30
Life annuity	30
Annuity certain	30
Final value of ordinary annuity	30
Final value formula	31
Computation of final value by logarithms	31
Annuity valuation table giving amount of annuity (f. 12)	32–33
Sinking fund calculations	34
Finding amount of sinking fund installments	34
Finding the number of payments to sinking fund	35

CONTENTS (*Continued*)

	PAGE
Annuity that $1 will buy (*f*. 13)	36–37
Schedule of sinking fund installments (*f*. 14)	38
Final value of annuity due	38
Present value of ordinary annuity	39
Present value of $1 per annum (*f*. 15)	40–41
Proof of amortization of loan (*f*. 16)	42
Annuity that $1 will buy	42
Finding the number of payments to amortize a loan	43
Schedule of interest payments and bond retirements for serial bond issue (*f*. 17)	44
Present value of annuity due	45

Bond Valuation

Definitions	45
Bond	45
Premium and discount on bonds	45
Nominal and effective interest rates	45
Determining basis price of bonds	46
Short method for finding basis price	46
Amortization schedule	47
Schedule of amortization (*f*. 18)	47
Short-cut method for discount bonds	47
Schedule of accumulation	48
Accumulation table for $10,000 bond (*f*. 19)	48
Bond valuation tables	48
Finding price of a bond when the yield is known	49

	PAGE
Finding yield when basis price is known	49
Basis price for bonds bought between interest dates	49
Bond table page (*f*. 20)	50
Accruing bond interest between interest dates	52
Determining profit or loss on sale of bonds	52
Finding yield between interest dates	53

Logarithms

Definition and uses	54
Characteristics of logs	55
Log tables	55
Finding the log of a number	55
Sample page from table of logarithms to seven decimal places (*f*. 21)	56
Interpolation	57
Finding the anti-log	58
Using logs to solve problems	58
Case I	58
Case II	58
Typical page from a 6-place log table (*f*. 22)	59
Typical page from a 6-place log table (*f*. 23)	60
Typical page from a 6-place log table (*f*. 24)	61
Typical page from a 6-place log table (*f*. 25)	62
Case III	63
Case IV	64
Case V	65

SECTION 27

MATHEMATICS OF FINANCE

Types of Interest

DEFINITIONS. Interest is ordinarily defined as consideration paid for the use of money. To the borrower it represents the cost of the loan, to the lender it is a source of income. The amount of interest depends on three factors:

1. Principal.
2. Rate.
3. Time.

Principal. The principal is any sum of money upon which interest is to be computed. It may represent invested capital, as in the instance of partnership equities, or a loan in the form of notes or the more formal bond indentures.

Rate. The interest rate is usually expressed as a percentage of the principal per unit of time; for example, 4% per annum, 3% semi-annually, etc.

Time. The time refers to the period for which interest is to be calculated. Unless otherwise stated, interest formulas use the year as a unit.

BASIC TYPES OF INTEREST. There are two basic types of interest, simple and compound. These may be represented as follows:

1. Simple interest.
    a. Ordinary.
    b. Exact—commercial practice.
    c. Exact—government securities.
2. Compound.

Simple interest refers to interest that is always computed on the original principal. If the interest is not paid when due, it is not added to the principal. Thus the amount of interest is always **proportional** to the time.

Ordinary interest represents a type of simple interest computed on a 360-day year, commonly referred to as the **commercial year.** Under this method the year is divided into 12 months of 30 days each. Although the method is used in many commercial transactions, modifications are often introduced. For example, in discounting commercial paper, ordinary interest is calculated, but it is based upon the exact number of days in the discount period.

Exact interest is interest based on a 365-day year, or 366 days in leap years. It is generally employed by banks in allowing interest on daily balances, also in governmental calculations other than interest on government securities. In the latter instance special tables are available from which the accrued interest may be read.

Compound Interest. See presentation later in this Section (pages 20–29).

MATHEMATICS OF FINANCE

COMPUTING ELAPSED TIME IN DAYS. The most common method in computing the number of days between two dates is either to include the first day and exclude the last or vice versa. Thus, to find the number of days between July 12 and October 23, proceed as follows:

Excluding July 12, there are in

July	19 days
August	31 days
September	30 days
October	23 days
Total	103 days

Use of Tables. Figure 1 shows a convenient table for use in computing the elapsed number of days. The days in the calendar, beginning with January 1, are numbered consecutively from 1 to 365. Hence, to find the number of days

NUMBER OF EACH DAY OF YEAR FROM JANUARY 1

Days	Jan.	Feb.	Mar.	Apr.	May	June	July	Aug.	Sep.	Oct.	Nov.	Dec.
1	1	32	60	91	121	152	182	213	244	274	305	335
2	2	33	61	92	122	153	183	214	245	275	306	336
3	3	34	62	93	123	154	184	215	246	276	307	337
4	4	35	63	94	124	155	185	216	247	277	308	338
5	5	36	64	95	125	156	186	217	248	278	309	339
6	6	37	65	96	126	157	187	218	249	279	310	340
7	7	38	66	97	127	158	188	219	250	280	311	341
8	8	39	67	98	128	159	189	220	251	281	312	342
9	9	40	68	99	129	160	190	221	252	282	313	343
10	10	41	69	100	130	161	191	222	253	283	314	344
11	11	42	70	101	131	162	192	223	254	284	315	345
12	12	43	71	102	132	163	193	224	255	285	316	346
13	13	44	72	103	133	164	194	225	256	286	317	347
14	14	45	73	104	134	165	195	226	257	287	318	348
15	15	46	74	105	135	166	196	227	258	288	319	349
16	16	47	75	106	136	167	197	228	259	289	320	350
17	17	48	76	107	137	168	198	229	260	290	321	351
18	18	49	77	108	138	169	199	230	261	291	322	352
19	19	50	78	109	139	170	200	231	262	292	323	353
20	20	51	79	110	140	171	201	232	263	293	324	354
21	21	52	80	111	141	172	202	233	264	294	325	355
22	22	53	81	112	142	173	203	234	265	295	326	356
23	23	54	82	113	143	174	204	235	266	296	327	357
24	24	55	83	114	144	175	205	236	267	297	328	358
25	25	56	84	115	145	176	206	237	268	298	329	359
26	26	57	85	116	146	177	207	238	269	299	330	360
27	27	58	86	117	147	178	208	239	270	300	331	361
28	28	59	87	118	148	179	209	240	271	301	332	362
29	29	..	88	119	149	180	210	241	272	302	333	363
30	30	..	89	120	150	181	211	242	273	303	334	364
31	31	..	90	...	151	...	212	243	...	304	...	365

* For leap years the number of the day is one greater than the tabulated number after February 28.

Fig. 1. The number of each day of the year counting from January 1.

between any two calendar dates, simply look up in the table the numbers corresponding to these dates and subtract the lower from the higher. The illustrations below are taken from Lang and Schlauch (Tables for Mathematics of Business and Finance).

TYPES OF INTEREST 27·3

Example 1. Find the elapsed time from May 14 to September 22. From Fig. 1,

> September 22 .... 265 days
> May 14 .... 134 days
> Elapsed time .... 131 days

Example 2. Find the elapsed time from October 28, 1963, to March 10, 1964. From October 28 to the end of the year, there are

$$365 - 301 = 64 \text{ days}$$

> From December 31 to March 10 (adding an extra
> day, because 1964 is a leap year) .... = 70 days
> Elapsed time .... = 134 days

The table shown in Fig. 2 represents another method for figuring elapsed time that is sometimes more convenient. The table shows the number of days

From Any Day of	To the Same Day of the Next											
	Jan.	Feb.	Mar.	Apr.	May	June	July	Aug.	Sept.	Oct.	Nov.	Dec.
Jan..	365	31	59	90	120	151	181	212	243	273	304	334
Feb..	334	365	28	59	89	120	150	181	212	242	273	303
Mar.	306	337	365	31	61	92	122	153	184	214	245	275
Apr..	275	306	334	365	30	61	91	122	153	183	214	244
May.	245	276	304	335	365	30	61	92	123	153	184	214
June	214	245	273	304	334	365	30	61	92	122	153	183
July.	184	215	243	274	304	335	365	31	62	92	123	153
Aug.	153	184	212	243	273	304	334	365	31	61	92	122
Sept.	122	153	181	212	242	273	303	334	365	30	61	91
Oct..	92	123	151	182	212	243	273	304	335	365	31	61
Nov.	61	92	120	151	181	212	242	273	304	334	365	30
Dec.	31	62	90	121	151	182	212	243	274	304	335	365

Fig. 2. Exact number of days in loan period.

between any day of one month to the same day in another month. Using the same illustrations as above, the following calculations show how the method works.

Example 1. Using Fig. 2, find May in the left-hand column and follow it across the page to the column headed September; the number is 123. This means that

> From May 14 to September 14 represents .... 123 days
> From September 14 to 22 equals .... 8 days
> Elapsed time .... 131 days

Example 2. In Fig. 2 follow the October line across the page to the March column. The table reads 151, meaning that from October 28, 1963, to March 28 of the next year equals 151 days. Since 1964 is a leap year and the time interval contains February 29,

> One day is added, resulting in .... 152 days
> Next, count back from March 28 to March 10 .... 18 days
> Elapsed time .... 134 days

Accruing Interest on Bonds. See discussion later in this Section under "Bond Valuation."

Ordinary Interest

BASIC FORMULA. Ordinary interest is the product of the principal, the rate, and the time:

$$i = prt$$

where i = Amount of interest
p = Principal
r = Rate
t = Time expressed in years

For example, to find the ordinary interest on $12,148.72 for 153 days at 4% (per year), the formula yields:

$$12,148.72 \times \frac{4}{100} \times \frac{153}{360} = \$206.53$$

This is the basic method, but for computation purposes it is somewhat awkward. Fortunately, a number of short-cuts are available.

SHORT-CUT METHODS FOR COMPUTING ORDINARY INTEREST. Interest rates of 4%, 4½%, and 6% lend themselves to short-cut methods of computation. These consist of finding the number of days required to produce decimal equivalents of the principal. The decimals most commonly used are 1% and .1%, thus making computation possible through a mere shifting of the decimal point. The first step required is to divide the 360-day year by the given interest rate to determine the number of days required to produce 1%. Thus, 6% a year is equivalent to 1% in 60 days (i.e., 360 divided by 6), etc. The short-cut formulas may then be tabulated as follows:

6%:
For 60 days, point off **two** decimals in principal.
For 6 days, point off **three** decimals in principal.
For 1 day, point off **three** decimals and divide by 6.

4½%:
For 80 days, point off **two** decimals in principal.
For 8 days, point off **three** decimals in principal.
For 1 day, point off **three** decimals and divide by 8.

4%:
For 90 days, point off **two** decimals in principal.
For 9 days, point off **three** decimals in principal.
For 1 day, point off **three** decimals and divide by 9.

Examples. Find the interest on the following: Answer:
1. $1,513.82   9 days   4% per annum $ 1.51
2. $6,818.71   80 days   4½% per annum $68.19
3. $4,253.64   1 day   6% per annum $ .71

BREAKING UP THE TIME ELEMENT. To find the interest for periods other than the key days mentioned above, the best procedure is to break up the time element so as to yield the key days or aliquot parts thereof. By an **aliquot part** is meant a fraction containing the number 1 in the numerator (e.g., one-third, one-fifth, etc.). The examples below serve to illustrate the method.

Examples. Find the interest for the following:
1. $1,628.39 at 6%   for 72 days.
2. $2,839.27 at 4½%   for 88 days.
3. $3,102.15 at 4%   for 140 days.
4. $2,825.17 at 4½%   for 23 days.
5. $4,031.73 at 6%   for 53 days.

ORDINARY INTEREST   27·5

Solutions: 1. 60 days............ $16.284
               12 "   ....   3.257 (⅕ of 60 days)
               72 " $19.54
            2. 80 days............ $28.393
                8 "   ....   2.839 (⅒ of 80 days)
               88 " $31.23
            3. 90 days............ $31.022
               45 "   ....   15.511 (½ of 90 days)
                5 "   ....   1.723 (⅑ of 45 days)
              140 " $48.26
            4. 20 days............ $ 7.063 (¼ of 80 days)
                2 "   ....   .706 (⅒ of 20 days)
                1 "   ....   .353 (½ of 2 days)
               23 "   .... $ 8.12
            5. 30 days............ $20.159 (½ of 60 days)
               20 "   ....   13.439 (⅓ of 60 days)
                3 "   ....   2.016 (⅒ of 30 days)
               53 " $35.61

In those instances where the interest rates represent aliquot parts or multiples of the basic rates, calculation is most easily effected by using the base rate and dividing or multiplying by the appropriate factor.

Examples. Find ordinary interest on the following:
   1. $7,385.29 at 2% for 161 days.
   2. $6,428.17 at 3% for 117 days.
   3. $5,047.82 at 9% for 57 days.

Solutions: 1. **4% Base:**
               90 days .... $ 73.853
               30 "   ....   24.618 (⅓ of 90 days)
               30 "   ....   24.618 (⅓ of 90 days)
               10 "   ....   8.206 (⅓ of 30 days)
                1 day   ....   .821 (⅒ of 10 days)
              161 days at 4% $132.116
               2%   .... $ 66.06 (½ of 4%)
            2. **6% Base:**
              120 days .... $128.563 (Twice 60 days)
              − 3 "   ....   3.214 (½ of 6 days)
              117 days at 6%.......... $125.35
               3%   .... $ 62.68
            3. **4½% Base:**
               40 days .... $ 25.239
                8 " 5.048
                8 " 5.048
                1 day 631
               57 days at 4½% ...... $ 35.966
               9%   .... $ 71.93 (Twice 4½%)

ODD INTEREST RATES. Interest calculations other than those mentioned above are best handled by assuming a convenient base and adding or subtracting the necessary fraction to yield the desired interest rate. Thus, if interest is to be calculated at 5½%, proceed with a base of 6% and subtract 1/12 of the total (½% equals 1/12 of 6%).

Examples. Find ordinary interest on the following:
1. $1,648.97 at 6½% for 157 days.
2. $1,642.83 at 4¼% for 13 days.
3. $3,807.28 at 2½% for 73 days.

Solutions: 1. Base 6%

120 days	....	$32.979	(Twice 60 days)
30 "	....	8.245	(½ of 60 days)
6 "	....	1.649	
1 "	....	.275	
157 "	at 6%........	$43.148	
Add 1/12 of 6%		3.596	
6½%		$46.74	

2. Base 4%

9 days	....	$ 1.643	
3 "	....	.548	(⅓ of 9 days)
1 "	....	.183	(⅓ of 3 days)
13 "	at 4%	$ 2.374	
Add 1/16 of 4%		.148	
4¼%		$ 2.52	

3. Base 6%

60 days	....	$38.073	
12 "	....	7.615	(⅕ of 60 days)
1 "	....	.635	
73 "	at 6%	$46.323	
3%		$23.162	(½ of 6%)
Less ⅙ of 3%		3.860	
2½%		$19.30	

ONE–DAY RULE. Another short-cut method for calculating simple interest consists of multiplying the principal by the number of days and calculating interest for one day on the product. The basis for this method lies in the interchange of principal and days. Thus the interest on $2,500 for 10 days is the same as the interest on $25,000 for 1 day. The latter principal is obtained by multiplying $2,500 by 10. This method is particularly apt where the number of days represents an aliquot part of 100 or 1,000.

Examples. Find ordinary interest on the following:
1. $2,439.55 at 3½% for 125 days.
2. $3,347.24 at 5½% for 25 days.

Solutions: 1. 8) 2439550   (125 = ⅛ of 1000)
          304943.75   Principal for 1 day
          $33.883   Interest for 1 day at 4%
                      (Point off 3 places and divide by 9)
          −4.235   Less ⅛ of 4%
          $29.65   Interest at 3½%

2. 4) 334724   (25 = ¼ of 100)
       83681   Principal for 1 day
       $13.947   Interest for 1 day at 6%
       −1.162   Less 1/12 of 6%
       $12.79   Interest at 5½%

Exact Interest

NATURE OF EXACT INTEREST. A given amount of principal earns in 365 days as much exact interest as the same principal earns in 360 days at ordinary interest. For 360 days therefore the exact interest is only 360/365 of the amount of ordinary interest. For practical purposes it is easier to compute ordinary interest first and then to adjust the result to get exact interest.

Since
$$360/365 = 72/73$$
it is evident that exact interest is 72/73 of ordinary interest; therefore to calculate exact interest, figure ordinary interest and subtract 1/73.

Finding the Value of 1/73. After calculating ordinary interest, the quickest way to figure 1/73, according to Schlauch and Lang (Mathematics of Business and Finance) is by use of an empirical formula as follows:

1. Take 1% of the figure representing ordinary interest.
2. Add one-third of the above.
3. Add one-tenth of Step 2.
4. Add one-tenth of Step 3.
5. The total of steps 1, 2, 3, 4 is an excellent approximation of 1/73.

Example 1. Find the exact interest on $27,345.69 for 114 days at 3½%.

Ordinary interest, 4% Base:

```
      90 days  ..........  $273.457
      18   "   ..........    54.691   (Twice 9, or ⅕ of 90)
       6   "   ..........    18.230   (⅓ of 18)
4% — 114   "   ..........  $346.378
Less ⅛ of 4%                 43.297
3½%, ordinary               $303.081
Less 1/73:
      1%        $3.030
      1/3        1.010
                  .101
                  .010       − 4.151
Exact interest              $298.93
```

Example 2. Municipal taxes in the town of X are due November 1 and may be paid without penalty up to and including November 30. Thereafter an interest penalty is charged at 7% per annum from the first due date (November 1). For a tax bill of $4,850, find the total paid to the town, if payment is made on December 11 of the same year.

Solution:

a. Elapsed time November 1 to December 11 (Fig. 1), 40 days
b. Ordinary interest, 6% base

```
    30 days ..................  $ 24.25    (½ of 60)
    10    "  ..................    8.083   (⅓ of 30)
    40    "  at 6% ............  $ 32.333
    Add ⅙ of 6% ...............    5.389
    7%, ordinary ..............  $ 37.722
    Less 1/73 .................    − .517
    Exact interest, 7% ........  $ 37.21
    Amount of bill ............   4,850.00
    Total paid ................  $4,887.21
```

27·8 MATHEMATICS OF FINANCE

No.of Days	¼%	½%	1%	1½%	2%	No.of Days
1	.000 685	.001 370	.002 740	.004 110	.005 479	1
2	.001 370	.002 740	.005 479	.008 219	.010 959	2
3	.002 055	.004 110	.008 219	.012 329	.016 438	3
4	.002 740	.005 479	.010 959	.016 438	.021 918	4
5	.003 425	.006 849	.013 699	.020 548	.027 397	5
6	.004 110	.008 219	.016 438	.024 658	.032 877	6
7	.004 795	.009 589	.019 178	.028 767	.038 356	7
8	.005 479	.010 959	.021 918	.032 877	.043 836	8
9	.006 164	.012 329	.024 658	.036 986	.049 315	9
10	.006 849	.013 699	.027 397	.041 096	.054 795	10
20	.013 699	.027 397	.054 795	.082 192	.109 589	20
30	.020 548	.041 096	.082 192	.123 288	.164 384	30
40	.027 397	.054 795	.109 589	.164 384	.219 178	40
50	.034 247	.068 493	.136 986	.205 479	.273 973	50
60	.041 096	.082 192	.164 384	.246 575	.328 767	60
70	.047 945	.095 890	.191 781	.287 671	.383 562	70
80	.054 795	.109 589	.219 178	.328 767	.438 356	80
90	.061 644	.123 288	.246 575	.369 863	.493 151	90
100	.068 493	.136 986	.273 973	.410 959	.547 945	100
110	.075 342	.150 685	.301 370	.452 055	.602 740	110
120	.082 192	.164 384	.328 767	.493 151	.657 534	120
130	.089 041	.178 082	.356 164	.534 247	.712 329	130
140	.095 890	.191 781	.383 562	.575 342	.767 123	140
150	.102 740	.205 479	.410 959	.616 438	.821 918	150
160	.109 589	.219 178	.438 356	.657 534	.876 712	160
170	.116 438	.232 877	.465 753	.698 630	.931 507	170
180	.123 288	.246 575	.493 151	.739 726	.986 301	180
190	.130 137	.260 274	.520 548	.780 822	1.041 096	190
200	.136 986	.273 973	.547 945	.821 918	1.095 890	200
210	.143 836	.287 671	.575 342	.863 014	1.150 685	210
220	.150 685	.301 370	.602 740	.904 110	1.205 479	220
230	.157 534	.315 068	.630 137	.945 205	1.260 274	230
240	.164 384	.328 767	.657 534	.986 301	1.315 068	240
250	.171 233	.342 466	.684 932	1.027 397	1.369 863	250
260	.178 082	.356 164	.712 329	1.068 493	1.424 658	260
270	.184 932	.369 863	.739 726	1.109 589	1.479 452	270
280	.191 781	.383 562	.767 123	1.150 685	1.534 247	280
290	.198 630	.397 260	.794 521	1.191 781	1.589 041	290
300	.205 479	.410 959	.821 918	1.232 877	1.643 836	300
310	.212 329	.424 658	.849 315	1.273 973	1.698 630	310
320	.219 178	.438 356	.876 712	1.315 068	1.753 425	320
330	.226 027	.452 055	.904 110	1.356 164	1.808 219	330
340	.232 877	.465 753	.931 507	1.397 260	1.863 014	340
350	.239 726	.479 452	.958 904	1.438 356	1.917 808	350
360	.246 575	.493 151	.986 301	1.479 452	1.972 603	360

Fig. 3. Illustrative page of interest tables; exact interest on $100 of principal.

Use of Exact Interest Tables. Figure 3 shows a page from a specially prepared exact interest table, taken from Schlauch and Lang (Mathematics of Business and Finance). The interest shown is for $100 of principal. By combining the number of days and interest rates, and adjusting for the principal, the interest on any amount for any number of days can be figured.

Example. Find the exact interest on $5,732.48 for 163 days at 2¾%.

EXACT INTEREST 27·9

Solution (Fig. 3):

	¼%	½%	2%	Total per Hundred Dollars
1o0 days	.109589	.219178	.876712	
3 days	.002055	.004110	.016438	
163 days	.111644	.223288	.893150	$1.228082

Interest on $5,732.48 is therefore

$$57.3248 \times 1.228082 = \underline{\$70.40}$$

To shorten the work involved, expanded tables may be constructed showing exact interest computations for a larger number of interest rates and a variety of principal amounts.

INTEREST ON UNITED STATES GOVERNMENT SECURITIES.

Interest on bonds or notes issued by the United States government is computed on the basis of exact interest for the exact number of days falling within the interest period. Figure 4 shows that the length of an interest period may vary

Ending Dates	Ordinary Year	Leap Year
January 1 or 15	184	184
February 1 or 15	184	184
March 1 or 15	181	182
April 1 or 15	182	183
May 1 or 15	181	182
June 1 or 15	182	183
July 1 or 15	181	182
August 1 or 15	181	182
September 1 or 15	184	184
October 1 or 15	183	183
November 1 or 15	184	184
December 1 or 15	183	183

Fig. 4. Exact number of days in 6-month interest period.

from 181 days to 184 days. Consequently a table may be constructed showing the **daily accrual of interest** based upon the varying lengths of the interest periods. Part of such a table is shown in Fig. 5. This table has been constructed to conform with rules of the Treasury Department in computing interest on securities issued by the United States government.

To compute the interest accrual on a government security, Figs. 4 and 5 must be used together. First determine the number of days in the interest period by reference to Fig. 4. Then select the appropriate column in Fig. 5 to obtain the

Rate per Annum %	Length of Period in Days			
	184	183	182	181
2	$.05434783	$.05464481	$.05494505	$.05524862
2½	.06793478	.06830601	.06868132	.06906077
2¾	.07472826	.07513661	.07554945	.07596685

Fig. 5. Interest for 1 day on $1,000 at different rates and periods.

daily accrual per $1,000. Finally adjust the latter figure for the number of days to be accrued and for the principal amount. To illustrate:

Example 1. Find the accrued interest on November 12, 1967, on $10,000 of United States Treasury 2½s, interest dates March 15 and September 15.

Solution: November 12 falls in the 6-month period between September 15 and the following March 15. Reference to Fig. 4 shows that the period ending March 15 has 182 days (since 1968 is a leap year). Figure 5 shows a daily accrual per $1,000 of $.06868132 for a 2½% bond during a 182-day period.

From September 15 to November 12 represents 58 days (see Fig. 1).

Hence the final calculation is:

$$10 \times \$.06868132 \times 58 = \underline{\underline{\$39.84}}$$

Example 2. Find the accrued interest on May 12, 1966, on $10,000 of United States Treasury 2½% bonds, interest dates March 15 and September 15.

Solution:

1. Period ending September 15 (Fig. 4) .... 184 days
2. Daily accrual per $1,000 (Fig. 5) .... $.06793478
3. Number of days to be accrued, March 15 to May 12 (Fig. 1) .... 58 days
4. 10 × $.06793478 × 58 = ... $39.40

Note that in both illustrations, the principal, interest rate, and accrual period are the same, but the amounts accrued are different because the interest periods differ in length.

ANTICIPATION. This is a customary term used in connection with purchase invoices that have extra dating where interest is allowed if payment is made before the expiration of the final due date of the invoice. The effect of the extra dating is to extend the time within which a proffered cash discount may be taken. Thus, if merchandise is purchased at 2%, 10 days, 90 days extra, with anticipation at 6%, a discount of 2% is allowed for payment any time within 100 days. In addition, the purchaser may deduct interest for the number of days before the final due date. The exact procedure is first to find the amount payable on the last day of the discount period. From this amount is deducted **exact interest** at the stipulated anticipation rate for the number of days anticipated.

Example. An invoice is dated April 12, 1966, for $5,653.75, terms 2%, 10 days, 60 days extra, f.o.b. destination, anticipation at 6%. The purchaser paid $45.60 freight. What was the amount due if payment was made on May 22, 1966?

The number of days from April 12 to May 22 is 40. Hence payment is anticipated 30 days. The calculation appears as follows:

Invoice	$5,653.75
Less freight paid	45.60
Net invoice	$5,608.15
Less 2% discount	112.16
Balance subject to anticipation	$5,495.99
Anticipation for 30 days at 6% per annum (exact)..	27.10
Amount payable on May 22, 1966	$5,468.89

It is the custom with some stores to compute the discount on the face of the invoice and the anticipation on the net amount after deducting the discount,

EXACT INTEREST

Anticipation Rates and Percentages

$$100 \times \text{Per Annum Rate} \times \frac{\text{Days effective}}{365}$$

Days	\multicolumn{9}{c}{PER ANNUM RATES}
	1%	2%	3%	4%	5%	6%	7%	8%	9%	10%
1	.00274	.00548	.00822	.01096	.01370	.01644	.01918	.02192	.02466	.02740
2	.00548	.01096	.01644	.02192	.02740	.03288	.03836	.04384	.04932	.05479
3	.00822	.01644	.02466	.03288	.04110	.04932	.05753	.06575	.07397	.08219
4	.01096	.02192	.03288	.04384	.05479	.06575	.07671	.08767	.09863	.10959
5	.01370	.02740	.04110	.05479	.06849	.08219	.09589	.10959	.12329	.13699
6	.01644	.03288	.04932	.06575	.08219	.09863	.11507	.13151	.14795	.16438
7	.01918	.03836	.05753	.07671	.09589	.11507	.13425	.15342	.17260	.19178
8	.02192	.04384	.06575	.08767	.10959	.13151	.15342	.17534	.19726	.21918
9	.02466	.04932	.07397	.09863	.12329	.14795	.17260	.19726	.22192	.24658
10	.02740	.05479	.08219	.10959	.13699	.16438	.19178	.21918	.24658	.27397
11	.03014	.06027	.09041	.12055	.15068	.18082	.21096	.24110	.27123	.30137
12	.03288	.06575	.09863	.13151	.16438	.19726	.23014	.26301	.29589	.32877
13	.03562	.07123	.10685	.14247	.17808	.21370	.24932	.28493	.32055	.35616
14	.03836	.07671	.11507	.15342	.19178	.23014	.26849	.30685	.34521	.38356
15	.04110	.08219	.12329	.16438	.20548	.24658	.28767	.32877	.36986	.41096
16	.04384	.08767	.13151	.17534	.21918	.26301	.30685	.35068	.39452	.43836
17	.04658	.09315	.13973	.18630	.23288	.27945	.32603	.37260	.41918	.46575
18	.04932	.09863	.14795	.19726	.24658	.29589	.34521	.39452	.44384	.49315
19	.05205	.10411	.15616	.20822	.26027	.31233	.36438	.41644	.46849	.52055
20	.05479	.10959	.16438	.21918	.27397	.32877	.38356	.43836	.49315	.54795
21	.05753	.11507	.17260	.23014	.28767	.34521	.40274	.46027	.51781	.57534
22	.06027	.12055	.18082	.24110	.30137	.36164	.42192	.48219	.54247	.60274
23	.06301	.12603	.18904	.25205	.31507	.37808	.44110	.50411	.56712	.63014
24	.06575	.13151	.19726	.26301	.32877	.39452	.46027	.52603	.59178	.65753
25	.06849	.13699	.20548	.27397	.34247	.41096	.47945	.54795	.61644	.68493
26	.07123	.14247	.21370	.28493	.35616	.42740	.49863	.56986	.64110	.71233
27	.07397	.14795	.22192	.29589	.36986	.44384	.51781	.59178	.66575	.73973
28	.07671	.15342	.23014	.30685	.38356	.46027	.53699	.61370	.69041	.76712
29	.07945	.15890	.23836	.31781	.39726	.47671	.55616	.63562	.71507	.79452
30	.08219	.16438	.24658	.32877	.41096	.49315	.57534	.65753	.73973	.82192
31	.08493	.16986	.25479	.33973	.42466	.50959	.59452	.67945	.76438	.84932
32	.08767	.17534	.26301	.35068	.43836	.52603	.61370	.70137	.78904	.87671
33	.09041	.18082	.27123	.36164	.45205	.54247	.63288	.72329	.81370	.90411
34	.09315	.18630	.27945	.37260	.46575	.55890	.65205	.74521	.83836	.93151
35	.09589	.19178	.28767	.38356	.47945	.57534	.67123	.76712	.86301	.95890
36	.09863	.19726	.29589	.39452	.49315	.59178	.69041	.78904	.88767	.98630
37	.10137	.20274	.30411	.40548	.50685	.60822	.70959	.81096	.91233	1.01370
38	.10411	.20822	.31233	.41644	.52055	.62466	.72877	.83288	.93699	1.04110
39	.10685	.21370	.32055	.42740	.53425	.64110	.74795	.85479	.96164	1.06849
40	.10959	.21918	.32877	.43836	.54795	.65753	.76712	.87671	.98630	1.09589
41	.11233	.22466	.33699	.44932	.56164	.67397	.78630	.89863	1.01096	1.12329
42	.11507	.23014	.34521	.46027	.57534	.69041	.80548	.92055	1.03562	1.15068
43	.11781	.23562	.35342	.47123	.58904	.70685	.82466	.94247	1.06027	1.17808
44	.12055	.24110	.36164	.48219	.60274	.72329	.84384	.96438	1.08493	1.20548
45	.12329	.24658	.36986	.49315	.61644	.73973	.86301	.98630	1.10959	1.23288
46	.12603	.25205	.37808	.50411	.63014	.75616	.88219	1.00822	1.13425	1.26027
47	.12877	.25753	.38630	.51507	.64384	.77260	.90137	1.03014	1.15890	1.28767
48	.13151	.26301	.39452	.52603	.65753	.78904	.92055	1.05205	1.18356	1.31507
49	.13425	.26849	.40274	.53699	.67123	.80548	.93973	1.07397	1.20822	1.34247
50	.13699	.27397	.41096	.54795	.68493	.82192	.95890	1.09589	1.23288	1.36986

Fig. 6. Exact interest per $100 of principal (basis 365-day year) at indicated time and rates.

finally deducting the freight charges. This plan, which favors the purchaser, is illustrated below:

Invoice	$5,653.75
Less 2% discount	113.08
Balance	$5,540.67
Anticipation for 30 days at 6% per annum	27.33
Balance	$5,513.34
Less freight paid	45.60
Amount of check	$5,467.74

In **computing anticipation on invoices,** Fig. 6, adapted from publications of the Controllers' Congress of the National Retail Dry Goods Association (now called the National Retail Merchants Association), may be used. This table shows the **exact interest** (based on a 365-day year) on $100 of principal for the indicated time and rates. Thus, the interest for 30 days per $100 at 6% is $.49315. Using the first illustration above,

$$54.9599 \times \$.49315 = \$27.11$$

In the second illustration the calculation is as follows:

$$55.4067 \times \$4.9315 = \$27.32$$

Extra dating is sometimes secured by stores as a result of certain trade customs. Invoices are frequently dated, say, 2%, 10 days, e.o.m. (end of month). This means that if an invoice is dated June 17, it is due 10 days after the end of June, i.e., July 10. Both discount and anticipation would then be allowed if payment is made before July 10.

Again, purchase orders sometimes contain conditional clauses in which "the seller agrees that merchandise shipped on or after the twenty-fifth of a month, will be billed as of the first of the following month." Thus, merchandise shipped on April 26, terms 2%, 10 days, is billed as of May 1, with discount and anticipation available until May 10. Ordinarily the anticipation may not amount to much because of the short time. However, if the above quoted clause is coupled with e.o.m. dating, the effect is to secure an extra month's dating. In short, if goods are shipped on April 26, terms 2%, 10 days, e.o.m., and the purchase order contains the above billing clause, the invoice becomes due on June 10, that is, 10 days after the first of the month in which the invoice would otherwise fall due.

Bank Discount

LOANS AND DISCOUNTS DEFINED. One of the important functions of a commercial bank is the making of loans. These loans produce a source of income for the bank and fulfill a necessary function in the economic life of the community served by the bank. Technically loans are distinguished from discounts chiefly by the fact that, in the case of loans, interest is paid periodically, during the existence of the loan or at its maturity, whereas in the case of discounts the interest or "discount" is deducted at the time the advance is made. Thus, in the case of a $1,000 loan at 6% for 6 months, the borrower receives $1,000 and pays back $1,030 at the end of 6 months. On the other hand, if he discounts a $1,000 note at 6%, he receives $970 and pays back $1,000 at the end of the 6-month term. In short, bank discount is the consideration deducted by the bank from the face of a note or draft prior to its maturity date.

In recent years finance companies and banks have been making **long-term loans,** especially in the field of home financing. These loans are usually amortized, principal and interest, through equal monthly payments. They are dealt with later in this Section in connection with annuities.

TYPES OF NOTES. Notes may be variously classified, but for computation purposes it is necessary only to know whether a note is **interest-bearing** or **noninterest-bearing** (Figs. 7 and 8).

```
$ 3400 00/100                        New York   April 2 19 —
      Two (2) months      AFTER DATE    I    PROMISE TO PAY TO
THE ORDER OF              Barrow & Co.
      Thirty-four hundred and 00/100  ~~~~~~~~~  DOLLARS
AT              Irving Trust Co. with interest @ 5%
VALUE RECEIVED
No.  1    DUE June 2 19—                     J. Doe
```

Fig. 7. Interest-bearing promissory note.

In discounting a note, the bank pays only what the note is worth at the time of discount. Thus, a noninterest-bearing note is worth its face value at maturity and not before. Hence, any time before maturity the note is valued at less than face value by the amount of interest the bank charges. An interest-bearing note, however, provided the interest and discount rates are the same, is worth approximately its face value on the date of issue and thereafter increases in value each day by the amount of interest earned until maturity.

```
$ 500 00/100                         New York   May 15 19 —
      Twenty (20) days     AFTER DATE    I    PROMISE TO PAY TO
THE ORDER OF                 J. Doe
      Five hundred and 00/100 ~~~~~~~~~~~~  DOLLARS
AT                   Irving Trust Co.
VALUE RECEIVED
No.  273                                     R. Roe
```

Fig. 8. Noninterest-bearing promissory note.

The amount that a bank pays for a note or that it credits to a borrower's account is called the **proceeds** of the note.

BASIS FOR CALCULATING PROCEEDS. Ordinarily, banks use the actual number of days in figuring the discount period on short-term notes, but interest or discount is computed on the basis of a 360-day year (ordinary interest). In the case of the Federal Reserve system, **exact** interest is used.

DUE DATE OF NOTES. Promissory notes are payable at a stated number of either days or months after date. In the case of **drafts**, a draft may be payable so many days **after date** or **after sight**. If days are specified, the exact number of days is counted. Thus, if the note states "sixty days after date ..." and is dated May 14, it is due July 13 (see Fig. 1). However, when months are specified, the note falls due in the month of maturity on the same date as is specified in the date of the note. For example, a note dated May 14 due in 2 months is due on July 14.

If a note is dated on the last day of a 31-day month, and falls due in a 30-day month, the due date would be the last day of the 30-day month. To illustrate, a note dated May 31, due in four months, matures on September 30. But a note dated May 31, due in 120 days, is payable September 28.

COMPUTING PROCEEDS AND DISCOUNT ON NONINTEREST-BEARING PAPER. Three steps are necessary to calculate the proceeds or deposit credit:

1. Calculate the time from the discount date to maturity.
2. Compute the interest to maturity for the time computed in Step 1. This is the discount.
3. Deduct the discount from the face value.

Example 1. Find the proceeds or deposit credit on a note for $1,875, dated July 5, for 30 days, discounted at 4% per annum on the date of issue.

The note is due August 4, that is, 30 days from July 5.

Face value of note	$1,875.00
Discount, 30 days, 4% on $1,875	−6.25
Proceeds	$1,868.75

Example 2. Find the proceeds on a note for $2,863.79 dated February 8, 1966, due in 60 days, discounted on March 2 at 4½% per annum.

Maturity date	April 9, 1966
Time to maturity (March 2 to April 9)	38 days
Face value	$2,863.79
Discount on above for 38 days at 4½%:	
40 days	$14.319
2 days (¼ of 8 days)	−.716
38 days	
	−13.60
Proceeds	$2,850.19

DISCOUNTING INTEREST-BEARING PAPER. The general rule in discounting interest-bearing paper is to compute the maturity value and then to discount the maturity value. In calculating the maturity value, the interest from the date of the note to maturity is added to the face value. Next the discount is computed for the discount period and deducted from the maturity value.

Example. Find the proceeds on a 5% note for $5,350, dated August 12, 1966, due in 3 months, and discounted on September 27, 1966, at 4%.

Maturity date	November 12, 1966
Maturity value:	
1. Face value	$5,350.00
2. Interest August 12 to November 12	−68.36
(92 days on $5,350 at 5%)	
Maturity value	$5,418.36
Discount from September 27 to November 12 (46 days, 4%)	−27.69
Proceeds	$5,390.67

FINDING PRINCIPAL TO YIELD GIVEN PROCEEDS. Occasionally it becomes necessary to reverse the above process; that is, a debtor wishes to borrow enough so that the proceeds will exactly cover the net amount of an invoice that is to be paid. Thus the face value of the note is unknown. If the note is **noninterest-bearing,** the face value to yield the given proceeds is found by dividing the given proceeds by the proceeds of $1. The expression "proceeds of one dollar" means one dollar minus the interest or discount on $1.

Example. A merchant arranges to pay for a shipment by borrowing the exact amount required to pay the invoice. The net amount of the invoice is $5,960.34 and the bank agrees to discount the merchant's note at 4% for 120 days.

 I. Proceeds of $1 for 120 days at 4% = $1 − $.01⅓ = $.98⅔

 II. $\dfrac{\text{Given proceeds}}{\text{Proceeds of \$1}} = \dfrac{\$5,960.34}{.98\frac{2}{3}} = \dfrac{\$17,881.02}{2.96} = \underline{\$6,040.89}$

 Proof:

Face value		$6,040.89
Interest 120 days at 4%:		
90 days	$60.409	
30 days	20.136	80.55
Proceeds		$5,960.34

COMPUTATION OF INTEREST UNDER PARTIAL PAYMENT PLANS. When a short-term indebtedness is reduced through periodic payments, the interest is computed upon either one of two bases. The basis used commonly among business men is known as the "Merchant's Rule." This method gives the results more quickly but not as accurately as the computation under the other, the "United States Rule."

The Merchant's Rule. In following the Merchant's Rule, the interest is computed upon the total indebtedness from the date of inception to the date of maturity, and from this total is deducted the interest earned from the date that each partial payment is made to the date of maturity of the debt.

Example. The following payments were made on a $16,500, 6% note, dated June 22, 1966, due in 6 months:

    October 20, 1966 .... $ 300
    November 15, 1966 3,500

What is the amount due at maturity?

Solution:

June 22	Face value		$16,500.00
December 22	Interest at 6% on above, June 22 to December 22 = 183 days		503.25
	Maturity value of note		$17,003.25
October 20	First payment	$ 300.00	
	Interest on above October 20 to December 22 = 63 days	3.15	
November 15	Second payment	3,500.00	
	Interest on above November 15 to December 22 = 37 days	21.58	
	Total credits		3,824.73
December 22	Maturity: Balance due		$13,178.52

27·16 MATHEMATICS OF FINANCE

The United States Rule. Under the United States Rule, each installment is first applied against the interest due at the date the partial payment is made, and the balance of the installment is then applied to reduce the principal. Interest is always computed upon the reduced principal. In the event that a partial payment is insufficient to cover the accrued interest, it is held in suspense. There is no reduction of principal until the suspended payment together with subsequent payments exceeds the accrued interest. Using the same figures as in the example for the Merchant's Rule, the solution appears as follows:

June 22	Face value		$16,500.00
October 20	First payment	$ 300.00	
	Interest on $16,500 for 120 days (June 22 to October 20)	330.00	
	Reduction of principal		—0—
November 15	Second payment	$3,500.00	
	Add first payment	300.00	
	Total	$3,800.00	
	Interest on $16,500 for 146 days (June 22 to November 15)	401.50	
	Reduction of principal		3,398.50
	Balance due		$13,101.50
December 22	Maturity		
	Interest on $13,101.50 for 37 days (November 15 to December 22)		80.79
	Balance due		$13,182.29

BANK DISCOUNT VS. TRUE DISCOUNT. In a discounting operation, the interest charge, as in the case of noninterest-bearing notes, is taken out in advance. Thus the borrower receives the maturity value minus the discount. He is paying interest calculated on the maturity value for the use of a smaller sum, the proceeds. A 60-day note for $1,000, discounted at 6%, yields $990 proceeds. The borrower pays $10 for the use of $990, which is therefore more than 6%. The discount calculated as above is called bank discount. So-called true discount is an interest charge based on the **present value** of the note, that is, on a sum that at the discount rate would produce the face value of the note. To find the present value of a note, it is necessary merely to divide the maturity value by the amount of $1 (at the given rate and for the given time). The "amount of $1" means one dollar plus the interest on $1.

Example. Find the proceeds and present value of a note for $5,632.50, dated June 22, 1966, due in 90 days, and discounted at 4½% per annum on July 27, 1966.

I. Proceeds

The note is due September 20, 1966 (Fig. 1)
Maturity value (since this is a noninterest-bearing note) $5,632.50
Discount at 4½% for 55 days; i.e., from July 27 to September 20 (Fig. 2):

40 days	$28.163	(½ of 80 days)	
10 days	7.041	(¼ of 40 days)	
5 days	3.520	(½ of 10 days)	
55 days	$38.72		

	38.72
Proceeds	$5,593.78

BANK DISCOUNT 27·17

II. Present Value

1. Maturity value $5,632.50
2. Amount of $1 at 4½% per annum for 55 days:
    (Using one-day rule, find the interest on $55 for 1 day at 4½%)
    .055 ÷ 8 = ... .006⅞
    Add $1.000
    Amount of $1 .... 1.006⅞
3. Present value $5,632.50 ÷ 1.006⅞ = 45,060 ÷ 8.055 .... $5,594.04

In the above problem the bank discount is $38.72; the true discount is $38.46 (i.e., $5,632.50 − $5,594.04). This means that if $5,594.04 is invested for 55 days at 4½% per annum it should produce $5,632.50.

PROOF:
Present value $5,594.04
Interest on above at 4½% for 55 days:
    40 .... $27.970
    10 .... 6.993
    5 .... 3.497
    55 .... 38.46
Maturity value $5,632.50

Relation of Bank Discount Rate to True Discount Rate. Since the bank discount is based on a larger sum than the borrower receives, he evidently pays more than the indicated rate of interest. To discover the true interest rate, it is necessary to express the bank discount as a percentage of the proceeds, assuming the loan ran for one year. Actually, the time a loan runs and the amount are immaterial, since the calculation can be put on a unit dollar basis. The illustration below is taken from Schlauch and Lang (Mathematics of Business and Finance).

Example. A note for $10,000, due in 4 months, is discounted at 6% per annum. What is the equivalent annual interest charge?

Solution: (a) Here it is necessary to compute the **annual** discount, that is, treat the note as if it had one year to run; thus:

    Maturity value $10,000.00
    Discount 6%, one year 600.00
    Proceeds .... $ 9,400.00

The borrower, in effect, pays $600 for the use of $9,400 for a year. Hence the interest rate is

$$\frac{600}{9,400} = .0683 = \underline{6.383\%}$$

Solution: (b) By putting the calculation on a unit dollar basis a general formula may be derived as follows:

    Maturity value $1.00
    Discount .... .06
    Proceeds .... $ .94

$$\text{Interest rate} = \frac{.06}{.94} = .06383 = 6.383\%$$

Let d = Discount rate; this will also equal the
        amount of discount in one year

27·18   MATHEMATICS OF FINANCE

Then $1 - d$ = Proceeds of $1 due in one year
r = Interest rate

Hence $r = \dfrac{d}{1-d}$

In the above problem, substitution in the formula yields

$$\frac{.06}{.94} = 6.383\%$$

Thus a discount rate of 6% per annum is equal to an annual interest charge of 6.383% approximately. To convert one into the other, it is not necessary to know anything about a particular loan transaction except the discount rate.

Chain Discounts

DEFINITION OF CHAIN DISCOUNT. Chain discounts are two or more discounts that are applied in succession to a quoted price. The latter is usually referred to as the **list price**, that is, the price at which the item is listed in the manufacturer's or jobber's catalog. Each discount is applied to the net amount remaining after the previous discount has been taken. For example, an article quoted at $25 less 30 and 10 means $25 less 30%, and then less 10% on the diminished amount.

List price	$25.00
Less first discount—30%	7.50
Balance	$17.50
Less second discount—10%	1.75
Net price	$15.75

If many chain discounts are involved in connection with a given list price, the above method may be cumbersome. An alternative method is to multiply the list price by the net cost factors, that is, the percentage remaining after deducting the chain discount from 100%. Thus, in the above example, the purchaser pays

$$\$25 \times 70\% \times 90\% = 25 \times .63 = \$15.75.$$

FINDING EQUIVALENT SINGLE DISCOUNT. It is often convenient to convert chain discounts into equivalent single discounts. According to Schlauch and Lang (Mathematics of Business and Finance), to find an equivalent single discount rate equal to two chain discounts, add the discounts and subtract their product.

Examples. Find single discounts equal to chain discounts of:

1. 40 and 30
2. 20 and 20
3. 15 and 10
4. 20 and 5
5. 10 and 5

Solutions:

1.	.40	2.	.20	3.	.15	4.	.20	5.	.10
	+.30		+.20		+.10		+.05		+.05
	.70		.40		.25		.25		.15
	−.12		−.04		−.015		−.01		−.005
	.58		.36		.235		.24		.145
	58%		36%		23.5%		24%		14.5%

CHAIN DISCOUNTS

	10%	12½%	15%	16⅔%
Net	.900 000	.875 000	.850 000	.833 333
And 2½	.877 500	.853 125	.828 750	.812 500
And 5	.855 000	.831 250	.807 500	.791 667
5 and 2½	.833 625	.810 469	.787 312	.771 875
5 and 5	.812 250	.789 687	.767 125	.752 083
5, 5, and 2½	.791 944	.769 945	.747 947	.733 281
And 7½	.832 500	.809 375	.786 250	.770 833
7½ and 2½	.811 687	.789 141	.766 594	.751 562
7½ and 5	.790 875	.768 906	.746 937	.732 292
And 10	.810 000	.787 500	.765 000	.750 000
10 and 2½	.789 750	.767 812	.745 875	.731 250
10 and 5	.769 500	.748 125	.726 750	.712 500
10, 5, and 2½	.750 262	.729 422	.708 581	.694 687
10 and 10	.729 000	.708 750	.688 500	.675 000
10, 10, and 2½	.710 775	.691 031	.671 287	.658 125
10, 10, and 5	.692 550	.673 312	.654 075	.641 250
10, 10, 5, and 2½	.675 236	.656 480	.637 723	.625 219
10, 10, and 10	.656 100	.637 875	.619 650	.607 500

	20%	22½%	25%	27½%
Net	.800 000	.775 000	.750 000	.725 000
And 2½	.780 000	.755 625	.731 250	.706 875
And 5	.760 000	.736 250	.712 500	.688 750
5 and 2½	.741 000	.717 844	.694 687	.671 531
5 and 5	.722 000	.699 437	.676 875	.654 312
5, 5, and 2½	.703 950	.681 952	.659 953	.637 955
And 7½	.740 000	.716 875	.693 750	.670 625
7½ and 2½	.721 500	.698 953	.676 406	.653 859
7½ and 5	.703 000	.681 031	.659 062	.637 094
And 10	.720 000	.697 500	.675 000	.652 500
10 and 2½	.702 000	.680 062	.658 125	.636 187
10 and 5	.684 000	.662 625	.641 250	.619 875
10, 5, and 2½	.666 900	.646 059	.625 219	.604 378
10 and 10	.648 000	.627 750	.607 500	.587 250
10, 10, and 2½	.631 800	.612 056	.592 312	.572 569
10, 10, and 5	.615 600	.596 362	.577 125	.557 887
10, 10, 5, and 2½	.600 210	.581 453	.562 697	.543 940
10, 10, and 10	.583 200	.564 975	.546 750	.528 525

Fig. 9. Typical page of a net cost factor table.

In practice, the decimal points are not put in, in order to speed up the work. Thus problem 5 above would be solved: $10 + 5 = 15$, minus $.5 = 14.5\%$. In fact, these problems can and should be done mentally.

The same rule may be applied to three or more chain discounts, provided only two discounts are taken at a time. The order in which the discounts are taken is immaterial.

Examples. Find equivalent single discounts for the following:

    6. 40, 20, and 10   8. 20, 5, and 5
    7. 30, 10, and 5   9. 15, 5, and 2

Solutions:

6.		7.		8.		9.	
	40		30		20		15
	+20		+10		+ 5		+ 5
	60		40		25		20
	− 8		− 3		− 1		− .75
	52		37		24		19.25
	+10		+ 5		+ 5		+ 2
	62		42		29		21.25
	− 5.2		− 1.85		− 1.2		− .385
	56.8%		40.15%		27.8%		20.865%

NET COST FACTOR TABLES. Tables showing net cost factors resulting from the application of chain discounts are sometimes available. No such table can be complete, since the variety and combinations of discounts are infinite. As a matter of fact, each concern may construct its own tables based upon the most common combinations of discounts encountered by it. Figure 9, taken from Lang and Schlauch (Tables for Mathematics of Business and Finance), represents a sample page of such a table. Its application is illustrated below.

Example 1. Find the net cost of an article listed at $64.50 subject to discounts of 15, 10, and 5%.

In Fig. 9, run down the 15% column to a point opposite 10 and 5. The net cost factor is .726750. Hence the net cost of the article is

$$\$64.50 \times .726750 = \$46.88$$

Example 2. Find the net cost of an article listed at $83.25 less 20, 15, and 10%.

Fig. 9 does not show this particular combination of discounts. From the 15% column, the 15 and 10 combination may be used as a first step, or the 20 and 10 combination may be used from the 20% column. Using the latter the net cost for 20 and 10 is .720. Hence,

$$\$83.25 \times .72 = \$59.94$$

This amount is subject to a further discount of 15% or a net cost factor of 85%.

$$\$59.94 \times .85 = \$50.95$$

Note that the order in which the discounts are taken is immaterial.

Compound Interest

COMPOUND INTEREST DEFINITIONS. In compound interest calculations, the interest is computed at the end of each fiscal period and added to the principal at the beginning, the total representing the new principal on the basis of which a new interest calculation is made. Compound interest may therefore be defined as that form of interest in which the interest for each period is added to the principal. Because of the fact that interest is added to the principal, and interest for the next period is calculated on the new total, interest is said to be **converted** into principal.

The time for which interest is calculated and converted is known as the **conversion period**. It represents the elapsed time between two successive interest dates. The time—that is, the conversion period—may be a month, or a quarterly, semi-annual, or annual period, or any other convenient time period.

COMPOUND INTEREST

The conversion period is sometimes referred to as an **accumulation period** because the principal accumulates—that is, it increases by the amount of interest added to the principal. No such term was necessary in the instance of simple interest, because the interest was not converted but always computed on the original principal. But in compound interest, the interest is computed on an ever-increasing amount, because of the repeated addition to the existing principal.

FINDING THE COMPOUND AMOUNT. Several methods are available for finding the compound amount.

1. By arithmetic.
2. By formula.

Arithmetical Solution. Find the compound amount on $1,500 for 3 years at 6% per annum, compounded semi-annually (or at 3% per 6 months).

Investment	$1,500.00
Interest 6 months, $1,500 at 3%	45.00
Amount at end of first 6 months	$1,545.00
Interest 6 months, $1,545 at 3%	46.35
Amount at end of second 6 months	$1,591.35
Interest 6 months, $1,591.35 at 3%	47.74
Amount at end of third 6 months	$1,639.09
Interest 6 months, $1,639.09 at 3%	49.17
Amount at end of fourth 6 months	$1,688.26
Interest 6 months, $1,688.26 at 3%	50.65
Amount at end of fifth 6 months	$1,738.91
Interest 6 months, $1,738.91 at 3%	52.17
Compound amount at end of 3 years	$1,791.08

Solution by Formula. If the principal amount is reduced to unity, say $1, the above can be restated as follows:

Investment	$1.00
Interest 6 months, $1 at 3% or	.03
Amount at end of first 6 months	$1.03
Interest 6 months, $1.03 at 3%	.0309
Amount at end of second 6 months	$1.0609
Interest 6 months, $1.0609 at 3%	.031827
Amount at end of third 6 months	$1.092727
Interest 6 months, $1.092727 at 3%	.032782
Amount at end of fourth 6 months	$1.125509
Interest 6 months, $1.125509 at 3%	.033765
Amount at end of fifth 6 months	$1.159274
Interest 6 months, $1.159274 at 3%	.034778
Compound amount at end of 3 years	$1.194052

It is obvious therefore that if the rate of interest per period is represented by i, the statement immediately above may be recast as follows:

Compound amount at end of first 6 months	$1.03	$= (1 + i)$
" " " " " second 6 "	1.0609	$= (1 + i)^2$
" " " " " third 6 "	1.092727	$= (1 + i)^3$
" " " " " fourth 6 "	1.125509	$= (1 + i)^4$
" " " " " fifth 6 "	1.159274	$= (1 + i)^5$
" " " " " sixth 6 "	1.194052	$= (1 + i)^6$

$s = (1 + i)^n$

AMOUNT OF 1 AT

Periods	1%	1 1/4%	1 1/2%	1 3/4%	2%	2 1/4%	2 1/2%
0	1.	1.	1.	1.	1.	1.	1.
1	1.01	1.0125	1.015	1.0175	1.02	1.0225	1.025
2	1.0201	1.02515625	1.030225	1.03530625	1.0404	1.04550625	1.050625
3	1.030301	1.03797070	1.04567838	1.05342411	1.061208	1.06903014	1.07689063
4	1.04060401	1.05094534	1.06136355	1.07185903	1.08243216	1.09308332	1.10381289
5	1.05101005	1.06408215	1.07728400	1.09061656	1.10408080	1.11767769	1.13140821
6	1.06152015	1.07738318	1.09344326	1.10970235	1.12616242	1.14282544	1.15969342
7	1.07213535	1.09085047	1.10984491	1.12912215	1.14868567	1.16853901	1.18868575
8	1.08285671	1.10448610	1.12649259	1.14888178	1.17165938	1.19483114	1.21840290
9	1.09368527	1.11829218	1.14338998	1.16898721	1.19509257	1.22171484	1.24886297
10	1.10462213	1.13227083	1.16054083	1.18944449	1.21899442	1.24920343	1.28008454
11	1.11566835	1.14642422	1.17794894	1.21025977	1.24337431	1.27731050	1.31208666
12	1.12682503	1.16075452	1.19561817	1.23143931	1.26824179	1.30604999	1.34488882
13	1.13809328	1.17526395	1.21355244	1.25298950	1.29360663	1.33543611	1.37851104
14	1.14947421	1.18995475	1.23175573	1.27491682	1.31947876	1.36548343	1.41297382
15	1.16096896	1.20482918	1.25023207	1.29722786	1.34586834	1.39620680	1.44829817
16	1.17257864	1.21988955	1.26898555	1.31992935	1.37278571	1.42762146	1.48450562
17	1.18430443	1.23513817	1.28802033	1.34302811	1.40024142	1.45974294	1.52161826
18	1.19614748	1.25057739	1.30734064	1.36653111	1.42824625	1.49258716	1.55965872
19	1.20810895	1.26620961	1.32695075	1.39044540	1.45681117	1.52617037	1.59865019
20	1.22019004	1.28203723	1.34685501	1.41477820	1.48594740	1.56050920	1.63861644
21	1.23239194	1.29806270	1.36705783	1.43953681	1.51566634	1.59562066	1.67958185
22	1.24471586	1.31428848	1.38756370	1.46472871	1.54597967	1.63152212	1.72157140
23	1.25716302	1.33071709	1.40837715	1.49036146	1.57689926	1.66823137	1.76461068
24	1.26973465	1.34735105	1.42950281	1.51644279	1.60843725	1.70576658	1.80872595
25	1.28243200	1.36419294	1.45094535	1.54298054	1.64060599	1.74414632	1.85394410
26	1.29525631	1.38124535	1.47270953	1.56998269	1.67341811	1.78338962	1.90029270
27	1.30820888	1.39851092	1.49480018	1.59745739	1.70688648	1.82351588	1.94780002
28	1.32129097	1.41599230	1.51722218	1.62541290	1.74102421	1.86454499	1.99649502
29	1.33450388	1.43369221	1.53998051	1.65385762	1.77584469	1.90649725	2.04640739
30	1.34784892	1.45161336	1.56308022	1.68280013	1.81136158	1.94939344	2.09756758
31	1.36132740	1.46975853	1.58652642	1.71224913	1.84758882	1.99325479	2.15000677
32	1.37494068	1.48813051	1.61032432	1.74221349	1.88454059	2.03810303	2.20375694
33	1.38869009	1.50673214	1.63447918	1.77270223	1.92223140	2.08396034	2.25885086
34	1.40257699	1.52556629	1.65899637	1.80372452	1.96067603	2.13084945	2.31532213
35	1.41660276	1.54463587	1.68388132	1.83528970	1.99988955	2.17879356	2.37320519
36	1.43076878	1.56394382	1.70913954	1.86740727	2.03988734	2.22781642	2.43253532
37	1.44507647	1.58349312	1.73477663	1.90008689	2.08068509	2.27794229	2.49334870
38	1.45952724	1.60328678	1.76079828	1.93333841	2.12229879	2.32919599	2.55568242
39	1.47412251	1.62332787	1.78721025	1.96717184	2.16474477	2.38160290	2.61957448
40	1.48886373	1.64361946	1.81401841	2.00159734	2.20803966	2.43518897	2.68506384
41	1.50375237	1.66416471	1.84122868	2.03662530	2.25220046	2.48998072	2.75219043
42	1.51878989	1.68496677	1.86884712	2.07226624	2.29724447	2.54600528	2.82099520
43	1.53397779	1.70602885	1.89687982	2.10853090	2.34318936	2.60329040	2.89152008
44	1.54931757	1.72735421	1.92533302	2.14543019	2.39005314	2.66186444	2.96380808
45	1.56481075	1.74894614	1.95421301	2.18297522	2.43785421	2.72175639	3.03790328
46	1.58045685	1.77080797	1.98352621	2.22117728	2.48661129	2.78299590	3.11385086
47	1.59626344	1.79294306	2.01327910	2.26004789	2.53634351	2.84561331	3.19169713
48	1.61222608	1.81535485	2.04347829	2.29959872	2.58707039	2.90963961	3.27148956
49	1.62834834	1.83804679	2.07413046	2.33984770	2.63881179	2.97510650	3.35327680
50	1.64463182	1.86102237	2.10524242	2.38078893	2.69158803	3.04204640	3.43710872
55	1.72852457	1.98028070	2.26794398	2.59652785	2.97173067	3.40002740	3.88877303
60	1.81669670	2.10718135	2.44321978	2.83181628	3.28103079	3.80013479	4.39978975
65	1.90936649	2.24221407	2.63204158	3.08842574	3.62252311	4.24732588	4.97795826
70	2.00676337	2.38589997	2.83545629	3.36828827	3.99955822	4.74714140	5.63210286
75	2.10912847	2.53879358	3.05459171	3.67351098	4.41583546	5.30577405	6.37220743
80	2.21671522	2.70148494	3.29066279	4.00639192	4.87543916	5.93014530	7.20956782
85	2.32978997	2.87460191	3.54497838	4.36943740	5.38287878	6.62799112	8.15696424
90	2.44863267	3.05881260	3.81894851	4.76538080	5.94313313	7.40795782	9.22885633
95	2.57353755	3.25482789	4.11409214	5.19720324	6.56169920	8.27970921	10.44160385
100	2.70481383	3.46340427	4.43204565	5.66815594	7.24464612	9.25404630	11.81371635

Fig. 10. Compound interest table

COMPOUND INTEREST

$s = (1 + i)^n$

Periods	2 3/4%	3%	3 1/2%	4%	4 1/2%	5%	6%
0	1.	1.	1.	1.	1.	1.	1.
1	1.0275	1.03	1.035	1.04	1.045	1.05	1.06
2	1.05575625	1.0609	1.071225	1.0816	1.092025	1.1025	1.1236
3	1.08478955	1.092727	1.10871788	1.124864	1.14116613	1.157625	1.191016
4	1.11462126	1.12550881	1.14752300	1.16985856	1.19251860	1.21550625	1.26247696
5	1.14527334	1.15927407	1.18768631	1.21665290	1.24618194	1.27628156	1.33822558
6	1.17676836	1.19405230	1.22925533	1.26531902	1.30226012	1.34009564	1.41851911
7	1.20912949	1.22987387	1.27227926	1.31593178	1.36086183	1.40710042	1.50363026
8	1.24238055	1.26677008	1.31680904	1.36856905	1.42210061	1.47745544	1.59384807
9	1.27654602	1.30477318	1.36289735	1.42331181	1.48609514	1.55132822	1.68947896
10	1.31165103	1.34391638	1.41059876	1.48024428	1.55296942	1.62889463	1.79084770
11	1.34772144	1.38423387	1.45996972	1.53945406	1.62285305	1.71033936	1.89829856
12	1.38478378	1.42576089	1.51106866	1.60103222	1.69588143	1.79585633	2.01219647
13	1.42286533	1.46853371	1.56395606	1.66507351	1.77219610	1.88564914	2.13292826
14	1.46199413	1.51258972	1.61869452	1.73167645	1.85194492	1.97993160	2.26090396
15	1.50219896	1.55796742	1.67534883	1.80094351	1.93528244	2.07892818	2.39655819
16	1.54350944	1.60470644	1.73398604	1.87298125	2.02237015	2.18287459	2.54035168
17	1.58595595	1.65284763	1.79467555	1.94790050	2.11337681	2.29201832	2.69277279
18	1.62956973	1.70243306	1.85748920	2.02581652	2.20847877	2.40661923	2.85433915
19	1.67438290	1.75350605	1.92250132	2.10684918	2.30786031	2.52695020	3.02559950
20	1.72042843	1.80611123	1.98978886	2.19112314	2.41171402	2.65329771	3.20713547
21	1.76774021	1.86029457	2.05943147	2.27876807	2.52024116	2.78596259	3.39956360
22	1.81635307	1.91610341	2.13151158	2.36991879	2.63365201	2.92526072	3.60353742
23	1.86630278	1.97358651	2.20611448	2.46471554	2.75216635	3.07152376	3.81974966
24	1.91762610	2.03279411	2.28332849	2.56330416	2.87601383	3.22509994	4.04893464
25	1.97036082	2.09377793	2.36324498	2.66583633	3.00543446	3.38635494	4.29187072
26	2.02454575	2.15659127	2.44595856	2.77246978	3.14067901	3.55567269	4.54938296
27	2.08022075	2.22128901	2.53156711	2.88336858	3.28200956	3.73345632	4.82234594
28	2.13742682	2.28792768	2.62017196	2.99870332	3.42969999	3.92012914	5.11168670
29	2.19620606	2.35656551	2.71187798	3.11865145	3.58403649	4.11613560	5.41838790
30	2.25660173	2.42726247	2.80679370	3.24339751	3.74531813	4.32194238	5.74349117
31	2.31865828	2.50008035	2.90503148	3.37313341	3.91385745	4.53803949	6.08810064
32	2.38242138	2.57508276	3.00670759	3.50805875	4.08998104	4.76494147	6.45338668
33	2.44793797	2.65233524	3.11194235	3.64838110	4.27403018	5.00318854	6.84058988
34	2.51525626	2.73190530	3.22086033	3.79431634	4.46636154	5.25334797	7.25102528
35	2.58442581	2.81386245	3.33359045	3.94608899	4.66734781	5.51601537	7.68608679
36	2.65549752	2.89827833	3.45026611	4.10393255	4.87737846	5.79181614	8.14725200
37	2.72852370	2.98522668	3.57102543	4.26808986	5.09686049	6.08140694	8.63608712
38	2.80355810	3.07478348	3.69601132	4.43881345	5.32621921	6.38547729	9.15425235
39	2.88065595	3.16702698	3.82537171	4.61636599	5.56589908	6.70475115	9.70350749
40	2.95987399	3.26203779	3.95925972	4.80102063	5.81636454	7.03998871	10.28571794
41	3.04127052	3.35989893	4.09783381	4.99306145	6.07810094	7.39198815	10.90286101
42	3.12490546	3.46069589	4.24125799	5.19278391	6.35161548	7.76158756	11.55703267
43	3.21084036	3.56451677	4.38970202	5.40049527	6.63743818	8.14966693	12.25045463
44	3.29913847	3.67145227	4.54334160	5.61651508	6.93612290	8.55715028	12.98548191
45	3.38986478	3.78159584	4.70235855	5.84117568	7.24824843	8.98500779	13.76461083
46	3.43808606	3.89504372	4.86694110	6.07482271	7.57441961	9.43425818	14.59048748
47	3.57887003	4.01189503	5.03728404	6.31781562	7.91526849	9.90597109	15.46591673
48	3.67728988	4.13225188	5.21358898	6.57052824	8.27145557	10.40126965	16.39387173
49	3.77841535	4.25621944	5.39606459	6.83334937	8.64367107	10.92133313	17.37750403
50	3.88232177	4.38390602	5.58492686	7.10668335	9.03263627	11.46739979	18.42015427
55	4.44631964	5.08214859	6.63314114	8.64636692	11.25630817	14.63563092	24.65032159
60	5.09225136	5.89160310	7.87809090	10.51962741	14.02740793	18.67918589	32.98769085
65	5.83201974	6.82998273	9.35670068	12.79873522	17.48070239	23.83990056	44.14497165
70	6.67925676	7.91782191	11.11282526	15.57161835	21.78413558	30.42642554	59.07593018
75	7.64957472	9.17892567	13.19855038	18.94525466	27.14699629	38.83268592	79.05692079
80	8.76085402	10.64089056	15.67573754	23.04979907	33.83009643	49.56144107	105.79599348
85	10.03357261	12.33570855	18.61785881	28.04360494	42.15845513	63.25435344	141.57890449
90	11.49118322	14.30046711	22.11217595	34.11933334	52.53710530	80.73036505	189.46451123
95	13.16054584	16.57816077	26.26232856	41.51138594	65.47079168	103.03467645	253.54625498
100	15.07242234	19.21863198	31.19140798	50.50494818	81.58851803	131.50125785	339.30208351

giving accumulated amounts.

Thus the compound amount of $1,500 for 3 years at 6%, converted semi-annually, is

$$\$1{,}500 \times 1.194052 = \$1{,}791.08$$

The difference between the compound amount and the original principal is the compound interest.

Compound amount, end of 3 years	$1,791.08
Principal at beginning	1,500.00
Compound interest	$ 291.08

Similarly for n periods the compound amount for $1 is $s = (1+i)^n$. In this formula

$s =$ Compound amount of $1
$i =$ Interest rate
$n =$ Number of periods

The compound amount of any given number of dollars can then be found easily by multiplying the principal by the value of $(1+i)^n$. In general terms,

$$A = P(1+i)^n$$

where $A =$ Compound amount of any number of dollars
$P =$ Any principal, i.e., initial investment

Value of $(1+i)^n$ from Prepared Tables. The arithmetical method for finding the compound amount is obviously too cumbersome. The formula may be solved either through the use of prepared tables or by logarithms. Fig. 10 gives the compound amount of $1 for periods from one to 100, for various interest rates. The use of the table is illustrated below.

Example. Find the compound amount of $2,634.56 for 12 years at 3½% annually.

$$A = P \times (1+i)^n$$
$$= \$2{,}634.56 \times 1.035^{12}$$

Locate the 3½% column in Fig. 10; run down the column to the twelfth period. The figure on that line represents the compound amount of $1 for 12 years at 3½%; in short, 1.035^{12}. Hence,

$$A = \$2{,}634.56 \times 1.51106866$$
$$= \$3{,}981$$

Value of $(1+i)^n$ by Logarithms. There are many occasions when prepared tables cannot be used. This condition occurs when the time for which the compound amount is to be found is beyond the table limits, in this case, 50 interest periods. Again the given interest rate may be one not found in the tables. In both instances, the best solution is through the use of logarithms.

Example. Find the compound amount of $4,950 for 5 years at 6% per annum, converted monthly.

This is equivalent to compounding at ½% for 60 interest periods. Hence,

$$A = 4{,}950 \times (1.005)^{60}$$
$$\log A = \log 4950 + 60 \log 1.005.$$

COMPOUND INTEREST

This may be solved through the use of any standard logarithm table. The following solution is based on Lang and Schlauch (Tables for Mathematics of Business and Finance).

$$\begin{array}{rl} \log 4950 = & 3.694605 \\ \log 1.005 = & .00216606 \\ \times\ 60 & .129964 \\ \hline \log A = & 3.824569 \\ A = & \$6{,}676.80 \end{array}$$

(For an explanation of logarithms, see the latter part of this Section.)

DEFINITION OF PRESENT VALUE. The general formula $A = P(1 + i)^n$ may be used to find any of the variables contained in it. The most common converse case is finding the present value (P). This is the value at the present moment of money due at a future time. It is the reciprocal of the compound amount, and may also be defined as that sum of money that, when placed at compound interest for the full number of periods involved, will amount to the given sum.

Example. $1,500 at compound interest for 6 periods at 3% per period will amount to $1,791.08. Hence the present worth of $1,791.08 due 6 periods hence at 3% per period compounded is $1,500.

The formula for the present value of $1 is:

$$v^n = \frac{1}{(1+i)^n}, \text{ in which}$$

v^n = Present value of $1
i = Interest rate
n = Number of periods

The formula for the present value of any number of dollars is:

$$P = A \times \frac{1}{(1+i)^n}, \text{ i.e., } Av^n$$

This formula is used whenever prepared present value tables are available. When, because of table limitations, logarithms must be used, the formula is more convenient for computation when written in the form

$$P = \frac{A}{(1+i)^n}$$

In these formulas

A = Given sum; i.e., the compound amount, the end value after n conversion periods
P = Present value, the initial investment

FINDING PRESENT VALUE FROM TABLES. Figure 11 shows the present value of $1 for a number of interest rates for every period from 1 to 50 and at greater intervals thereafter. The use of the table is illustrated below.

Example. Find the present value of $6,975 for 6 years at 2% per annum.

Fig. 11 shows the present value of $1 for 6 periods ($v^6$) at 2% is $.88797138.

$$P = A \times v^6 \text{ at } 2\%$$
$$P = 6{,}975 \times .88797138 = \$6{,}193.60$$

The difference between the present value and the given compound amount is called the **compound discount.** In the above illustration, the compound discount is

$$\$6{,}975 - \$6{,}193.60 = \$781.40$$

The compound discount represents the amount of interest that $6,913.60 would earn in 6 years at 2% per annum.

27·26 MATHEMATICS OF FINANCE

$$v^n = \frac{1}{(1+i)^n} = (1+i)^{-n}$$

PRESENT VALUE OF

Periods	1%	1 1/4%	1 1/2%	1 3/4%	2%	2 1/4%	2 1/2%
0	1.	1.	1.	1.	1.	1.	1.
1	0.99009901	0.98765432	0.98522167	0.98280098	0.98039216	0.97799511	0.97560976
2	0.98029605	0.97546106	0.97066175	0.96589777	0.96116878	0.95647444	0.95181440
3	0.97059015	0.96341833	0.95631699	0.94928528	0.94232233	0.93542732	0.92859941
4	0.96098034	0.95152428	0.94218423	0.93295851	0.92384543	0.91484335	0.90595064
5	0.95146569	0.93977706	0.92826033	0.91691254	0.90573081	0.89471232	0.88385429
6	0.94204524	0.92817488	0.91454219	0.90114254	0.88797138	0.87502427	0.86229687
7	0.93271805	0.91671593	0.90102679	0.88564378	0.87056018	0.85576946	0.84126524
8	0.92348322	0.90539845	0.88771112	0.87041157	0.85349037	0.83693835	0.82074657
9	0.91433982	0.89422069	0.87459224	0.85544135	0.83675527	0.81852161	0.80072836
10	0.90528695	0.88318093	0.86166723	0.84072860	0.82034830	0.80051013	0.78119840
11	0.89632372	0.87227746	0.84893323	0.82626889	0.80426304	0.78289499	0.76214478
12	0.88744923	0.86150860	0.83638742	0.81205788	0.78849318	0.76566748	0.74355589
13	0.87866260	0.85087269	0.82402702	0.79809128	0.77303253	0.74881905	0.72542038
14	0.86996297	0.84036809	0.81184928	0.78436490	0.75787502	0.73234137	0.70772720
15	0.86134947	0.82999318	0.79985150	0.77087459	0.74301473	0.71622628	0.69046556
16	0.85282126	0.81974635	0.78803104	0.75761631	0.72844581	0.70046580	0.67362493
17	0.84437749	0.80962602	0.77638526	0.74458605	0.71416256	0.68505212	0.65719506
18	0.83601731	0.79963064	0.76491159	0.73177990	0.70015937	0.66997763	0.64116591
19	0.82773992	0.78975866	0.75360747	0.71919401	0.68643076	0.65523484	0.62552772
20	0.81954447	0.78000855	0.74247042	0.70682458	0.67297133	0.64081647	0.61027094
21	0.81143017	0.77037881	0.73149795	0.69466789	0.65977582	0.62671538	0.59538629
22	0.80339621	0.76086796	0.72068763	0.68272028	0.64683904	0.61292457	0.58086467
23	0.79544179	0.75147453	0.71003708	0.67097817	0.63415592	0.59943724	0.56669724
24	0.78756613	0.74219707	0.69954392	0.65943800	0.62172149	0.58624668	0.55287535
25	0.77976844	0.73303414	0.68920583	0.64809632	0.60953087	0.57334639	0.53939059
26	0.77204796	0.72398434	0.67902052	0.63694970	0.59757928	0.56072997	0.52623472
27	0.76440392	0.71504626	0.66898574	0.62599479	0.58586204	0.54839117	0.51339973
28	0.75683557	0.70621853	0.65909925	0.61522829	0.57437455	0.53632388	0.50087778
29	0.74934215	0.69749978	0.64935887	0.60464697	0.56311231	0.52452213	0.48866125
30	0.74192292	0.68888867	0.63976243	0.59424764	0.55207089	0.51298008	0.47674269
31	0.73457715	0.68038387	0.63030781	0.58402716	0.54124597	0.50169201	0.46511481
32	0.72730411	0.67198407	0.62099292	0.57398247	0.53063330	0.49065233	0.45377055
33	0.72010307	0.66368797	0.61181568	0.56411053	0.52022873	0.47985558	0.44270298
34	0.71297334	0.65549429	0.60277407	0.55440839	0.51002817	0.46929641	0.43190534
35	0.70591420	0.64740177	0.59386608	0.54487311	0.50002761	0.45896960	0.42137107
36	0.69892495	0.63940916	0.58508974	0.53550183	0.49022315	0.44887002	0.41109372
37	0.69200490	0.63151522	0.57644309	0.52629172	0.48061093	0.43899268	0.40106705
38	0.68515337	0.62371873	0.56792423	0.51724002	0.47118719	0.42933270	0.39128492
39	0.67836967	0.61601850	0.55953126	0.50834400	0.46194822	0.41988528	0.38174139
40	0.67165314	0.60841334	0.55126232	0.49960098	0.45289042	0.41064575	0.37243062
41	0.66500311	0.60090206	0.54311559	0.49100834	0.44401021	0.40160954	0.36334695
42	0.65841892	0.59348352	0.53508925	0.48256348	0.43530413	0.39277216	0.35448483
43	0.65189992	0.58615656	0.52718153	0.47426386	0.42676875	0.38412925	0.34583886
44	0.64544546	0.57892006	0.51939067	0.46610699	0.41840074	0.37567653	0.33740376
45	0.63905492	0.57177290	0.51171494	0.45809040	0.41019680	0.36740981	0.32917440
46	0.63272764	0.56471397	0.50415265	0.45021170	0.40215373	0.35932500	0.32114576
47	0.62646301	0.55774219	0.49670212	0.44246850	0.39426836	0.35141809	0.31331294
48	0.62026041	0.55085649	0.48936170	0.43485848	0.38653761	0.34368518	0.30567116
49	0.61411921	0.54405579	0.48212975	0.42737934	0.37895844	0.33612242	0.29821576
50	0.60803882	0.53733905	0.47500468	0.42002883	0.37152788	0.32872608	0.29094221
55	0.57852808	0.50497892	0.44092800	0.38512970	0.33650425	0.29411528	0.25715052
60	0.55044962	0.47456760	0.40929597	0.35313025	0.30478227	0.26314856	0.22728359
65	0.52373392	0.44598775	0.37993321	0.32378956	0.27605069	0.23544226	0.20088557
70	0.49831486	0.41912905	0.35267692	0.29688670	0.25002761	0.21065309	0.17755358
75	0.47412949	0.39388787	0.32737599	0.27221914	0.22645771	0.18847391	0.15693149
80	0.45111794	0.37016679	0.30389015	0.24960114	0.20510973	0.16862993	0.13870457
85	0.42922324	0.34787426	0.28208917	0.22886242	0.18577420	0.15087528	0.12259463
90	0.40839119	0.32692425	0.26185218	0.20984682	0.16826142	0.13498997	0.10835579
95	0.38857020	0.30723591	0.24306699	0.19241118	0.15239955	0.12077719	0.09477073
100	0.36971121	0.28873326	0.22562944	0.17642422	0.13803297	0.10806084	0.08464737

Fig. 11. Compound interest table

COMPOUND INTEREST

1 AT COMPOUND INTEREST

$$v^n = \frac{1}{(1+i)^n} = (1+i)^{-n}$$

Periods	2 3/4%	3%	3 1/2%	4%	4 1/2%	5%	6%
0	1.	1.	1.	1.	1.	1.	1.
1	0.97323601	0.97087379	0.96618357	0.96153846	0.95693780	0.95238095	0.94339623
2	0.94718833	0.94259591	0.93351070	0.92455621	0.91572995	0.90702948	0.88999644
3	0.92183779	0.91514166	0.90194271	0.88899636	0.87629660	0.86383760	0.83961928
4	0.89716573	0.88848705	0.87144223	0.85480419	0.83856134	0.82270247	0.79209366
5	0.87315400	0.86260878	0.84197317	0.82192711	0.80245105	0.78352617	0.74725817
6	0.84978491	0.83748426	0.81350064	0.79031453	0.76789574	0.74621540	0.70496054
7	0.82704128	0.81309151	0.78599096	0.75991781	0.73482846	0.71068133	0.66505711
8	0.80490635	0.78940923	0.75941156	0.73069021	0.70318513	0.67683936	0.62741237
9	0.78336385	0.76641673	0.73373097	0.70258674	0.67290443	0.64460892	0.59189846
10	0.76239791	0.74409391	0.70891881	0.67556417	0.64392768	0.61391325	0.55839478
11	0.74199310	0.72242128	0.68494571	0.64958093	0.61619874	0.58467929	0.52678753
12	0.72213440	0.70137988	0.66178330	0.62459705	0.58966386	0.55683742	0.49696936
13	0.70280720	0.68095134	0.63940415	0.60057409	0.56427164	0.53032135	0.46883902
14	0.68399728	0.66111781	0.61778179	0.57747508	0.53997286	0.50506795	0.44230096
15	0.66569078	0.64186195	0.59689062	0.55526450	0.51672044	0.48101710	0.41726506
16	0.64787424	0.62316694	0.57670591	0.53390818	0.49446932	0.45811152	0.39364628
17	0.63053454	0.60501645	0.55720378	0.51337325	0.47317639	0.43629669	0.37136442
18	0.61365892	0.58739461	0.53836114	0.49362812	0.45280037	0.41552065	0.35034379
19	0.59723496	0.57028603	0.52015569	0.47464242	0.43330179	0.39573396	0.33051301
20	0.58125057	0.55367575	0.50256588	0.45638695	0.41464286	0.37688948	0.31180473
21	0.56569398	0.53754928	0.48557090	0.43883360	0.39678743	0.35894236	0.29415540
22	0.55055375	0.52189250	0.46915063	0.42195539	0.37970089	0.34184987	0.27750540
23	0.53581874	0.50669175	0.45328563	0.40572633	0.36335013	0.32557131	0.26179726
24	0.52147809	0.49193374	0.43795713	0.39012147	0.34770347	0.31006791	0.24697855
25	0.50752126	0.47760557	0.42314699	0.37511680	0.33273060	0.29530277	0.23299863
26	0.49393796	0.46369473	0.40883767	0.36068923	0.31840248	0.28124073	0.21981003
27	0.48071821	0.45018906	0.39501224	0.34681657	0.30469137	0.26784832	0.20736795
28	0.46785227	0.43707675	0.38165434	0.33347747	0.29157069	0.25509364	0.19563014
29	0.45533068	0.42434636	0.36874815	0.32065141	0.27901502	0.24294632	0.18455674
30	0.44314421	0.41198676	0.35627841	0.30831867	0.26700002	0.23137745	0.17411013
31	0.43128391	0.39998715	0.34423035	0.29646026	0.25550241	0.22035947	0.16425484
32	0.41974103	0.38833703	0.33258971	0.28505794	0.24449991	0.20986617	0.15495740
33	0.40850708	0.37702625	0.32134271	0.27409417	0.23397121	0.19987254	0.14618622
34	0.39757380	0.36604490	0.31047605	0.26355209	0.22389589	0.19035480	0.13791153
35	0.38693314	0.35538340	0.29997686	0.25341547	0.21425444	0.18129029	0.13010052
36	0.37657727	0.34503243	0.28983272	0.24366872	0.20502817	0.17265741	0.12274077
37	0.36649856	0.33498294	0.28003161	0.23429685	0.19619921	0.16443563	0.11579318
38	0.35668959	0.32522615	0.27056194	0.22528543	0.18775044	0.15660536	0.10923885
39	0.34714316	0.31575355	0.26141250	0.21662061	0.17966549	0.14914797	0.10305552
40	0.33785222	0.30655684	0.25257247	0.20828904	0.17192870	0.14204568	0.09722219
41	0.32880995	0.29762800	0.24403137	0.20027793	0.16452507	0.13528160	0.09171905
42	0.32000968	0.28895922	0.23577910	0.19257493	0.15744026	0.12883962	0.08652740
43	0.31144495	0.28054294	0.22780590	0.18516820	0.15066054	0.12270440	0.08162962
44	0.30310944	0.27237178	0.22010231	0.17804635	0.14417276	0.11686133	0.07700908
45	0.29499792	0.26443862	0.21265924	0.17119841	0.13796437	0.11129651	0.07265007
46	0.28710172	0.25673653	0.20546787	0.16461386	0.13202332	0.10599668	0.06853781
47	0.27941773	0.24925876	0.19851968	0.15828256	0.12633810	0.10094921	0.06465831
48	0.27193940	0.24199880	0.19180645	0.15219476	0.12089771	0.09614211	0.06099840
49	0.26466122	0.23495029	0.18532024	0.14634112	0.11569158	0.09156391	0.05754566
50	0.25757783	0.22810708	0.17905337	0.14071262	0.11070965	0.08720373	0.05428836
55	0.22490511	0.19676717	0.15075814	0.11565551	0.08883907	0.06832640	0.04056742
60	0.19637679	0.16973309	0.12693431	0.09506040	0.07128901	0.05353552	0.03031434
65	0.17146718	0.14641325	0.10687528	0.07813272	0.05720594	0.04194648	0.02265264
70	0.14971726	0.12629736	0.08998612	0.06421940	0.04590497	0.03286617	0.01692737
75	0.13072622	0.10894521	0.07576590	0.05278367	0.03683649	0.02575150	0.01264911
80	0.11414412	0.09397710	0.06379285	0.04338433	0.02955948	0.02017698	0.00945215
85	0.09966540	0.08106547	0.05371187	0.03565875	0.02372003	0.01580919	0.00706320
90	0.08702324	0.06992779	0.04522395	0.02930890	0.01903417	0.01238691	0.00527803
95	0.07598469	0.06032032	0.03807735	0.02408978	0.01527399	0.00970547	0.00394405
100	0.06634634	0.05203284	0.03206011	0.01980004	0.01225663	0.00760449	0.00294723

giving present value.

FINDING PRESENT VALUES BY LOGS. If the number of periods or the interest rate is not given by the table, logarithms may be used to find the present value, as in the example below.

Example. Find the present value of $7,418 at ¼% quarterly for 10 years. Ten years are equivalent to 40 interest periods.

$$P = \frac{7418}{(1.0025)^{40}}$$

$\log P = \log 7418 - 40 \log 1.0025$

$\log 7418 = 3.870287$

$\log 1.0025 = .00108438$

$ \times 40 .043375$

$\log P = 3.826912$

$P = \$6{,}712.90$

OTHER CONVERSE CASES. Occasionally it becomes necessary to find how long it will take for a given sum to amount to another sum at some future time; or what interest rate is being realized on a given principal. In short, the problem is to find n or i in the general formula. These may be found either by interpolation in a table or by logarithms.

Finding Value of n. The example below illustrates two methods for finding n.

Example. How long will it take for $765 to amount to $1,350 if money is worth 3½% per annum.

By logarithms:

$A = P \times (1 + i)^n$

$1350 = 765 \times 1.035^n$

$\log 1350 = \log 765 + n \log 1.035$

$n \log 1.035 = \log 1350 - \log 765$

$n = \dfrac{\log 1350 - \log 765}{\log 1.035}$

$n = \dfrac{3.130334 - 2.883661}{.014940}$

$n = \dfrac{.246673}{.014940} = \underline{\underline{16.5}}$ years

A general formula based on the above demonstration can be worked out as follows:

$$n = \frac{\log A - \log P}{\log (1 + i)}$$

By interpolation:

$A = P \times (1 + i)^n$

$1350 = 765 \times 1.035^n$

$1.035^n = \dfrac{1350}{765} = 1.7647$

COMPOUND INTEREST 27·29

Now consult Fig. 10, and locate in the 3½% column a value just above and one just below the value given above. The procedure is as follows:

(1) Years	(2) Tabular Difference	(3) Given Difference
16	1.7340	1.7340
?		1.7647
17	1.7947	
	.0607	.0307

$$\frac{307}{607} = .5$$

Hence $n = 16 + .5 = \underline{\underline{16.5}}$ years

Finding Value of i. The logarithmic method and also the solution by interpolation are illustrated below.

Example. Find the yield on United States government bonds sold at $18.75 redeemable in 10 years for $25.

By logarithms: These are not coupon bonds, but bonds sold on a discount basis.

$$A = P(1+i)^n$$
$$25 = 18.75(1+i)^{10}$$
$$(1+i)^{10} = \frac{25}{18.75} = \frac{4}{3}$$
$$10 \log(1+i) = \log 4 - \log 3$$
$$\log(1+i) = \frac{\log 4 - \log 3}{10}$$
$$= \frac{.602060 - .477121}{10}$$
$$= \frac{.124939}{10} = .012494$$
$$1 + i = 1.0292$$
$$i = .0292 = \underline{\underline{2.92\%}}$$

By interpolation: Proceed as in the previous solution.

$$(1+i)^{10} = 4/3 = 1.3333$$

Now look in Fig. 10 on the tenth line and find values on that line just above and below 1.3333. The value is evidently between 2¾% and 3%. The computation is as follows:

Rate	Tabular Difference	Given Difference
2¾%	1.3117	1.3117
?		1.3333
3%	1.3439	
.25%	.0322	.0216

A jump in the table of ¼% increases the compound amount by roughly $.03. Hence the change in rate for the difference in column (3) is:

$$\frac{.0216}{.0322} \times .25\%$$
$$= \frac{216}{322} \times .0025 = .0017 = .17\%$$

Hence $i = 2.75\% + .17\% = \underline{\underline{2.92\%}}$

Annuities

DEFINITIONS. An annuity is the payment of a fixed sum of money at uniform intervals of time. An **example** of an annuity is rent on the use of property. Payments of annuities are commonly called **rents**.

Ordinary Annuity. An ordinary annuity is a series of equal payments each of which is made at the end of a period of time.

Annuity Due. An annuity due is one in which the payments are due at the beginning of each payment period.

A life insurance premium is an example of an annuity due since such premiums are always payable in advance.

Deferred Annuity. A deferred annuity is one in which payments are due after a number of periods have elapsed.

Amount or Final Value of Annuity. The total of all annuity payments made, together with the interest earned by these payments, is the amount of an annuity. It is technically referred to as the **final value** of an annuity.

Perpetuity. An annuity in which the payments continue without end is a perpetuity. An example of this type is to be found in the payments made from endowment funds.

Life Annuity. An annuity whose duration depends on the life expectancy of one or more persons is called a **contingent** or life annuity.

Annuity Certain. This is an annuity that has a definite number of periods to run.

Example. A mortgage on a piece of property is to be paid off through 20 equal periodic payments beginning 4 years from the present time. This is an ordinary annuity certain deferred 4 years; it is certain, because it runs for 5 years, once it becomes effective.

FINAL VALUE OF ORDINARY ANNUITY. The total accumulation of an annuity may be found by two methods. In the first or arithmetical method, the interest is computed on the accumulations to date and added to the principal together with the new payment. The second method compounds each payment from the date of the payment to the end of the annuity series. The arithmetical method is illustrated below:

Example.

Payment end of first year	$ 200.00
Interest second year (4%)	8.00
Payment end of second year	200.00
Total end of second year	$ 408.00
Interest third year	16.32
Payment end of third year	200.00
Total end of third year	$ 624.32
Interest fourth year	24.97
Payment end of fourth year	200.00
Total end of fourth year	$ 849.29
Interest fifth year	33.97
Payment end of fifth year	200.00
Total accumulation (final value)	$1,083.26

ANNUITIES

In effect, the final value of an annuity is the sum of the compound amounts of the individual payments. Thus in the diagram below, the first payment made at the end of the first year bears interest for 4 years, the second for 3 years.

	1967	1968	1969	1970	1971
Payments (end of each year).	$1	$1	$1	$1	$1
Compound Amount (end of 1971)	1.04^4	1.04^3	1.04^2	1.04	1
Total Value	1.16985856 +	1.124864 +	1.0816 +	1.04 +	1 = $5.41632256

Assuming money is worth 4%, the compound amount of each $1 payment is shown underneath the payments in the diagram. When the values are totaled, it is found that an ordinary annuity of $1 per year annually for 5 years at 4% amounts to $5.41632256. For an annuity of $200 under these conditions, the final amount is

$$200 \times 5.41632256 = \underline{\$1{,}083.26}.$$

Instead of laboriously calculating the compound amount of each payment, recourse may be had to prepared annuity tables, Fig. 12. Thus in the illustration above, the answer may be found directly in the 4% column on line 5 in Fig. 12.

Final Value Formula. The symbol for the final value of an ordinary annuity of $1 per annum is $s_{\overline{n}|i}$ (read italic s sub n at i%). The formula is

$$s_{\overline{n}|i} = \frac{(1+i)^n - 1}{i}$$

in which i = Interest rate
n = Number of periods

The numerator of the fraction is evidently the compound interest.

$$\text{Hence, } s_{\overline{n}|i} = \frac{\text{Compound interest}}{\text{Interest rate}}$$

The final value for any number of dollars is expressed by the following formula:

$$A_n = R\, s_{\overline{n}|i}$$

in which A = The final value of the annuity
R = Amount of each payment (rent)

Example. Find the amount of an annuity of $2,000 received semi-annually for 10 years when invested at 4% per annum.

$$A_n = R \times s_{\overline{n}|i}$$
$$A_{20} = 2{,}000 \times s_{\overline{20}|.02}$$
$$= 2{,}000 \times 24.2973698 \text{ (Fig. 12)}$$
$$A_{20} = \underline{\$48{,}594.74}$$

Note that interest is at 2% per period for 20 periods; hence look for the value in the 2% column, line 20 of Fig. 12.

Computation of Final Value by Logarithms. If the interest rate or the number of conversion periods is not found in the table, recourse must be had to solution by logarithms. The example below illustrates the method.

$$s_{\overline{n}|i} = \frac{(1+i)^n - 1}{i}$$

AMOUNT OF ANNUITY

Periods	1%	1 1/4%	1 1/2%	1 3/4%	2%	2 1/4%	2 1/2%
1	1.	1.	1.	1.	1.	1.	1.
2	2.01	2.0125	2.015	2.0175	2.02	2.0225	2.025
3	3.0301	3.03765625	3.045225	3.05280625	3.0604	3.06800625	3.075625
4	4.060401	4.07562695	4.09090338	4.10623036	4.121608	4.13703639	4.15251563
5	5.10100501	5.12657229	5.15226693	5.17808939	5.20404016	5.23011971	5.25632852
6	6.15201506	6.19065444	6.22955093	6.26870596	6.30812096	6.34779740	6.38773673
7	7.21353521	7.26803762	7.32299419	7.37840831	7.43428338	7.49062284	7.54743015
8	8.28567056	8.35888809	8.43283911	8.50753045	8.58296905	8.65916186	8.73611590
9	9.36852727	9.46337420	9.55933169	9.65641224	9.75462843	9.85399300	9.95451880
10	10.46221254	10.58166637	10.70272167	10.82539945	10.94972100	11.07570784	11.20338177
11	11.56683467	11.71393720	11.86326249	12.01484394	12.16871542	12.32491127	12.48346631
12	12.68250301	12.86036142	13.04121143	13.22510371	13.41208973	13.60222177	13.79555297
13	13.80932804	14.02111594	14.23682960	14.45654303	14.68033152	14.90827176	15.14044179
14	14.94742132	15.19637988	15.45038205	15.70953253	15.97393815	16.24370788	16.51895284
15	16.09689554	16.38633463	16.68213778	16.98444935	17.29341692	17.60919130	17.93192666
16	17.25786449	17.59116382	17.93236984	18.28167721	18.63928525	19.00539811	19.38022483
17	18.43044314	18.81105336	19.20135539	19.60160656	20.01207096	20.43301957	20.86473045
18	19.61474757	20.04619153	20.48937572	20.94463468	21.41231238	21.89276251	22.38634871
19	20.81089504	21.29676893	21.79671636	22.31116578	22.84055863	23.38534966	23.94600743
20	22.01900399	22.56297854	23.12366710	23.70161119	24.29736980	24.91152003	25.54465761
21	23.23919403	23.84501577	24.47052211	25.11638938	25.78331719	26.47202923	27.18327405
22	24.47158598	25.14307847	25.83757994	26.55592620	27.29898354	28.06764989	28.86285590
23	25.71630183	26.45736695	27.22514364	28.02065490	28.84496321	29.69917201	30.58442730
24	26.97346485	27.78808403	28.63352080	29.51101637	30.42186247	31.36740338	32.34903798
25	28.24319950	29.13543508	30.06302361	31.02745915	32.03029972	33.07316996	34.15776393
26	29.52563150	30.49962802	31.51396896	32.57043969	33.67090572	34.81731628	36.01170803
27	30.82088781	31.88087337	32.98667850	34.14042238	35.34432383	36.60070590	37.91200073
28	32.12909669	33.27938429	34.48147867	35.73787977	37.05121031	38.42422178	39.85980075
29	33.45038766	34.69537659	35.99870085	37.36329267	38.79223451	40.28876677	41.85629577
30	34.78489153	36.12906880	37.53868137	39.01715029	40.56807921	42.19526402	43.90270316
31	36.13274045	37.58068216	39.10176159	40.69995042	42.37944079	44.14465746	46.00027074
32	37.49406785	39.05044069	40.68828801	42.41219955	44.22702961	46.13791226	48.15027751
33	38.86900853	40.53857120	42.29861233	44.15441305	46.11157020	48.17601528	50.35403445
34	40.25769862	42.04530334	43.93309152	45.92711527	48.03380160	50.25997563	52.61288531
35	41.66027560	43.57086963	45.59208789	47.73083979	49.99447763	52.39082508	54.92820744
36	43.07687836	45.11550550	47.27596921	49.56612949	51.99436719	54.56961864	57.30141263
37	44.50764714	46.67944932	48.98510874	51.43353675	54.03425453	56.79743506	59.73394794
38	45.95272361	48.26294243	50.71988538	53.33362365	56.11493962	59.07537735	62.22729664
39	47.41225085	49.86622921	52.48068366	55.26696206	58.23723841	61.40457334	64.78297906
40	48.88637336	51.48955708	54.26789391	57.23413390	60.40198318	63.78617624	67.40255354
41	50.37523709	53.13317654	56.08191232	59.23573124	62.61002284	66.22136521	70.08761737
42	51.87898946	54.79734125	57.92314100	61.27235654	64.86222330	68.71134592	72.83980781
43	53.39777936	56.48230801	59.79198812	63.34462278	67.15946777	71.25735121	75.66080300
44	54.93175715	58.18833687	61.68886794	65.45315367	69.50265712	73.86064161	78.55232308
45	56.48107472	59.91569108	63.61420096	67.59858386	71.89271027	76.52250605	81.51613110
46	58.04588547	61.66463721	65.56841398	69.78155908	74.33056447	79.24426243	84.55403443
47	59.62634432	63.43544518	67.55194018	72.00273637	76.81717576	82.02725834	87.66788530
48	61.22260777	65.22838824	69.56521929	74.26278425	79.35351927	84.87287165	90.85958243
49	62.83483385	67.04374310	71.60869758	76.56238298	81.94058966	87.78251126	94.13107199
50	64.46318218	68.88178989	73.68282804	78.90222468	84.57940145	90.75761776	97.48434879
55	72.85245735	78.42245562	84.52959893	91.23016259	98.58653365	106.66788460	115.55092136
60	81.66966986	88.57450776	96.21465171	104.67521588	114.05153942	124.45043493	135.99158995
65	90.93664882	99.37712526	108.80277215	119.33861370	131.12615541	144.32559477	159.11833027
70	100.67633684	110.87199776	122.36375295	135.33075826	149.97791114	166.53961758	185.28411421

Fig. 12. Annuity valuation

ANNUITIES

OF 1 AT END OF EACH PERIOD

$$s_{\overline{n}|i} = \frac{(1+i)^n - 1}{i}$$

Periods	2 3/4%	3%	3 1/2%	4%	4 1/2%	5%	6%
1	1.	1.	1.	1.	1.	1.	1.
2	2.0275	2.03	2.035	2.04	2.045	2.05	2.06
3	3.08325625	3.0909	3.106225	3.1216	3.137025	3.1525	3.1836
4	4.16804580	4.183627	4.21494288	4.246464	4.27819113	4.310125	4.374616
5	5.28266706	5.30913581	5.36246588	5.41632256	5.47070973	5.52563125	5.63709296
6	6.42794040	6.46840988	6.55015218	6.63297546	6.71689166	6.80191281	6.97531854
7	7.60470876	7.66246218	7.77940751	7.89829448	8.01915179	8.14200845	8.39383765
8	8.81383825	8.89233605	9.05168677	9.21422626	9.38001362	9.54910888	9.89746791
9	10.05621880	10.15910613	10.36849581	10.58279531	10.80211423	11.02656432	11.49131598
10	11.33276482	11.46387931	11.73139316	12.00610712	12.28820937	12.57789254	13.18079494
11	12.64441585	12.80779569	13.14199192	13.48635141	13.84117879	14.20678716	14.97164264
12	13.99213729	14.19202956	14.60196164	15.02580546	15.46403184	15.91712652	16.86994120
13	15.37692107	15.61779045	16.11303030	16.62683768	17.15991327	17.71298285	18.88213767
14	16.79978639	17.08632416	17.67698636	18.29191119	18.93210937	19.59863199	21.01506593
15	18.26178052	18.59891389	19.29568088	20.02358764	20.78405429	21.57856359	23.27596988
16	19.76397948	20.15688130	20.97102971	21.82453114	22.71933673	23.65749177	25.67252808
17	21.30748892	21.76158774	22.70501575	23.69751239	24.74170689	25.84036636	28.21287976
18	22.89344487	23.41443537	24.49969130	25.64541288	26.85508370	28.13238467	30.90565255
19	24.52301460	25.11686844	26.35718050	27.67122940	29.06356246	30.53900391	33.75999170
20	26.19739750	26.87037449	28.27968181	29.77807858	31.37142277	33.06595410	36.78559120
21	27.91782593	28.67648572	30.26947068	31.96920172	33.78313680	35.71925181	39.99272668
22	29.68556615	30.53678030	32.32890215	34.24796979	36.30337795	38.50521440	43.39229028
23	31.50191921	32.45288370	34.46041373	36.61788858	38.93702996	41.43047512	46.99582769
24	33.36822199	34.42647022	36.66652821	39.08260412	41.68919631	44.50199887	50.81557735
25	35.28584810	36.45926432	38.94985669	41.64590829	44.56521015	47.72709882	54.86451200
26	37.25620892	38.55304225	41.31310168	44.31174462	47.57064460	51.11345376	59.15638272
27	39.28075467	40.70963352	43.75906024	47.08421440	50.71132361	54.66912645	63.70576568
28	41.36097542	42.93092252	46.29062734	49.96758298	53.99333317	58.40258277	68.52811162
29	43.49840224	45.21885020	48.91079930	52.96628630	57.42303316	62.32271191	73.63979832
30	45.69460830	47.57541571	51.62267728	56.08493775	61.00706966	66.43884750	79.05818622
31	47.95121003	50.00267818	54.42947098	59.32833526	64.75238779	70.76078988	84.80167739
32	50.26986831	52.50275852	57.33450247	62.70146867	68.66624524	75.29882937	90.88977803
33	52.65228969	55.07784128	60.34121005	66.20952742	72.75622628	80.06377084	97.34316471
34	55.10022765	57.73017652	63.45315240	69.85790851	77.03025646	85.06695938	104.18375460
35	57.61548391	60.46208181	66.67401274	73.65222486	81.49661800	90.32030735	111.43477987
36	60.19990972	63.27594427	70.00760318	77.59831385	86.16396581	95.83632272	119.12086666
37	62.85540724	66.17422259	73.45786930	81.70224640	91.04134427	101.62813886	127.26811866
38	65.58393094	69.15944927	77.02889472	85.97033626	96.13820476	107.70954580	135.90420578
39	68.38748904	72.23423275	80.72490604	90.40914971	101.46442398	114.09502309	145.05845813
40	71.26814499	75.40125973	84.55027775	95.02551570	107.03032306	120.79977424	154.76196562
41	74.22801898	78.66329753	88.50953747	99.82653633	112.84668760	127.83976295	165.04768356
42	77.26928950	82.02319645	92.60737128	104.81959778	118.92478854	135.23175110	175.95054457
43	80.39419496	85.48389234	96.84862928	110.01238169	125.27640402	142.99333866	187.50757724
44	83.60503532	89.04840911	101.23833130	115.41287696	131.91384220	151.14300559	199.75803188
45	86.90417379	92.71986139	105.78167290	121.02939204	138.84996510	159.70015587	212.74351379
46	90.29403857	96.50145723	110.48403145	126.87056772	146.09821353	168.68516366	226.50812462
47	93.77712463	100.39650095	115.35097255	132.94539043	153.67263314	178.11942185	241.09861210
48	97.35599556	104.40839598	120.38825659	139.26320604	161.58790163	188.02539294	256.56452882
49	101.03328544	108.54064785	125.60184557	145.83373429	169.85935720	198.42666259	272.95840055
50	104.81170079	112.79686729	130.99791016	152.66708366	178.50302828	209.34799572	290.33590458
55	125.32071411	136.07161972	160.94688984	191.15917299	227.91795938	272.71261833	394.17202657
60	148.80914038	163.05343680	196.51688288	237.99068520	289.49795398	353.58371788	533.12818089
65	175.70980889	194.33275782	238.76287650	294.96838045	366.23783096	456.79801118	719.08286076
70	206.51842746	230.59406374	288.93786459	364.29045876	461.86967955	588.52851071	967.93216965

table giving amount of annuity.

Example. Find the final value of an ordinary annuity of $1,365 a year for 12 years at 3.2%.

$$A_{12} = 1{,}365 \times s_{\overline{12}|.032}$$

$$= 1{,}365 \times \frac{1.032^{12} - 1}{.032}$$

The first step is to find the value by logs of 1.032^{12} and then substitute it in the above fraction.

$$12 \log 1.032 = 12 \times .013680 = .164160$$
$$1.032^{12} = 1.4594$$

$$A_{12} = 1{,}365 \times \frac{1.4594 - 1}{.032}$$

$$= \frac{1{,}365 \times .4594}{.032}$$

$$= \$19{,}596.25$$

SINKING FUND CALCULATIONS. Sinking funds are commonly used to accumulate, by periodic contributions, sufficient amounts for the extinction of a debt or the replacement of an asset. In the latter event, the fund is more generally referred to as a replacement fund. In either instance the periodic payments are annuity rentals. Many bond issues of both private and municipal corporations are of the sinking fund type. The payments are usually turned over to a trustee or municipal sinking fund commission that invests these amounts and accumulates them to maturity or uses them to retire some of the bonds each year. In some issues, no part of the debt is extinguished until maturity even if the trustee invests his receipts in the bonds to be redeemed. In the latter case, he merely collects the coupons and adds the interest to the sinking fund just as in the case of investment in any other bonds.

There are two mathematical problems involved in the **flotation** of sinking fund bond issues. The first is one of determining what sum shall be set aside periodically to provide the required amount at maturity. The other problem is concerned with determining the life span of the bond issues once the size of the periodic sinking fund payment the corporation can afford to make is known. These are presented below.

Finding Amount of Sinking Fund Installments. Determination of the installment or rent necessary to be set aside periodically is equivalent to finding R in the annuity formula.

$$A_n = R\, s_{\overline{n}|i}$$

$$R = \frac{A_n}{s_{\overline{n}|i}} = A_n \times \frac{1}{s_{\overline{n}|i}}$$

The second form of the formula is used when tables giving value of $\dfrac{1}{s_{\overline{n}|i}}$ are available. The first is used when logarithms are necessary.

The value of $\dfrac{1}{s_{\overline{n}|i}}$ is obtained from a special table (Fig. 13) that makes computation of the rent extremely simple. It represents the periodic payment of an annuity that will amount to $1 in n periods. However, Fig. 13 does not give the values of $\dfrac{1}{s_{\overline{n}|i}}$ directly. It shows instead the values of $\dfrac{1}{a_{\overline{n}|i}}$ usually referred to as the annuity that $1 will buy, that is, the annuity whose present value is $1. The same table may, however, be used to find both values because of the following relationship existing between them:

$$\frac{1}{a_{\overline{n}|i}} = \frac{1}{s_{\overline{n}|i}} + i.$$

Fig. 13 actually shows the values of $\dfrac{1}{a_{\overline{n}|i}}$. To find $\dfrac{1}{s_{\overline{n}|i}}$ use the following derived from the above equation:

$$\frac{1}{s_{\overline{n}|i}} = \frac{1}{a_{\overline{n}|i}} - i \qquad (I)$$

Hence to find $\dfrac{1}{s_{\overline{n}|i}}$, look in Fig. 13 and subtract the interest rate.

Example. A corporation on June 1, 1967, issued bonds due June 1, 1973, to the amount of $200,000. Provision was made to set up a sinking fund to retire the entire issue by means of semi-annual payments. If the fund earns 3% semi-annually, what is the size of each installment?

There are 12 payments compounded at 3% every 6 months.

$$R = A_{12} \times \frac{1}{s_{\overline{12}|.03}}$$

$R = 200{,}000 \times .0704621$ (Fig. 13   .1004621 − .03)
    = **$14,092.42**

The schedule in Fig. 14 shows the periodic amounts set up and the interest earned on the accumulated balances in the sinking fund. The total semi-annual installments plus the accumulated interest earned by the sinking fund equal $200,000, the accumulated amount in the sinking fund June 1, 1973, the date of maturity of the bonds. If logarithms are necessary, see solution later in this Section, page 65.

Finding the Number of Payments to Sinking Fund. A corporation floating a sinking fund bond issue needs to prepare a long-range budget to determine what it can spare for sinking fund payments. Once that is known, the time to build up the proper size sinking fund can easily be calculated. This involves finding the number of payments (n in the formula) from which the maturity of the bonds may be determined. The simplest solution is through interpolation in Fig. 12. For logarithmic solution, see presentation later in this Section, page 64.

Example. A corporation wishes to raise $300,000 through the issuance of 5% sinking fund bonds. It can spare $50,000 a year for sinking fund purposes and interest on the bonds. If the fund earns 4½%, when should the bonds be made to mature?

Total annual payment	$50,000.00
Annual interest charge (300,000 × .05)	15,000.00
Sinking fund contribution	$35,000.00

$$s_{\overline{n}|.045} = 300{,}000 \div 35{,}000$$
$$= 8.5714286.$$

$$\frac{1}{a_{\overline{n}|i}} = \frac{i}{1-\frac{1}{(1+i)^n}}; \quad \frac{1}{s_{\overline{n}|i}} = \frac{1}{a_{\overline{n}|i}} - i$$

PERIODIC PAYMENT REQUIRED

n	1%	1 1/4%	1 1/2%	1 3/4%	2%	2 1/4%	2 1/2%
1	1.0100 000	1.0125 000	1.0150 000	1.0175 000	1.0200 000	1.0225 000	1.0250 000
2	0.5075 124	0.5093 944	0.5112 779	0.5131 630	0.5150 495	0.5169 376	0.5188 272
3	0.3400 221	0.3417 012	0.3433 830	0.3450 675	0.3467 547	0.3484 446	0.3051 372
4	0.2562 811	0.2578 610	0.2594 448	0.2610 324	0.2626 238	0.2642 189	0.2658 179
5	0.2060 398	0.2075 621	0.2090 893	0.2106 214	0.2121 584	0.2137 002	0.2152 469
6	0.1725 484	0.1740 338	0.1755 252	0.1770 226	0.1785 258	0.1800 350	0.1815 500
7	0.1486 283	0.1500 887	0.1515 562	0.1530 306	0.1545 120	0.1560 003	0.1574 954
8	0.1306 903	0.1321 331	0.1335 840	0.1350 429	0.1365 098	0.1379 846	0.1394 674
9	0.1167 404	0.1181 706	0.1196 098	0.1210 561	0.1225 154	0.1239 817	0.1254 569
10	0.1055 821	0.1070 031	0.1084 342	0.1098 753	0.1113 265	0.1127 877	0.1142 588
11	0.0964 541	0.0978 684	0.0992 938	0.1007 304	0.1021 779	0.1036 365	0.1051 060
12	0.0888 488	0.0902 583	0.0916 800	0.0931 138	0.0945 596	0.0960 174	0.0974 871
13	0.0824 148	0.0838 210	0.0852 404	0.0866 728	0.0881 184	0.0895 769	0.0910 483
14	0.0769 012	0.0783 052	0.0797 233	0.0811 556	0.0826 020	0.0840 623	0.0855 365
15	0.0721 238	0.0735 265	0.0749 444	0.0763 774	0.0778 255	0.0792 885	0.0807 665
16	0.0679 446	0.0693 467	0.0707 651	0.0721 996	0.0736 501	0.0751 166	0.0765 990
17	0.0642 581	0.0656 602	0.0670 797	0.0685 162	0.0699 698	0.0714 404	0.0729 278
18	0.0609 821	0.0623 848	0.0638 058	0.0652 449	0.0667 021	0.0681 772	0.0696 701
19	0.0580 518	0.0594 555	0.0608 785	0.0623 206	0.0637 818	0.0652 618	0.0667 606
20	0.0554 153	0.0568 204	0.0582 457	0.0596 912	0.0611 567	0.0626 421	0.0641 471
21	0.0530 308	0.0544 375	0.0558 655	0.0573 146	0.0587 848	0.0602 757	0.0617 873
22	0.0508 637	0.0522 724	0.0537 033	0.0551 564	0.0566 314	0.0581 282	0.0596 466
23	0.0488 858	0.0502 967	0.0517 308	0.0531 880	0.0546 681	0.0561 710	0.0576 964
24	0.0470 735	0.0484 867	0.0499 241	0.0513 857	0.0528 711	0.0543 802	0.0559 128
25	0.0454 068	0.0468 225	0.0482 635	0.0497 295	0.0512 204	0.0527 360	0.0542 759
26	0.0438 689	0.0452 873	0.0467 320	0.0482 027	0.0496 992	0.0512 213	0.0527 688
27	0.0424 455	0.0438 668	0.0453 153	0.0467 908	0.0482 931	0.0498 219	0.0513 769
28	0.0411 244	0.0425 486	0.0440 011	0.0454 815	0.0469 897	0.0485 253	0.0500 879
29	0.0398 950	0.0413 223	0.0427 788	0.0442 642	0.0457 784	0.0473 208	0.0488 913
30	0.0387 481	0.0401 785	0.0416 392	0.0431 298	0.0446 499	0.0461 993	0.0477 776
31	0.0376 757	0.0391 094	0.0405 743	0.0420 701	0.0435 964	0.0451 528	0.0467 390
32	0.0366 709	0.0381 079	0.0395 771	0.0410 781	0.0426 106	0.0441 742	0.0457 683
33	0.0357 274	0.0371 679	0.0386 414	0.0401 478	0.0416 865	0.0432 572	0.0448 594
34	0.0348 400	0.0362 839	0.0377 619	0.0392 736	0.0408 187	0.0423 966	0.0440 068
35	0.0340 037	0.0354 511	0.0369 336	0.0384 508	0.0400 022	0.0415 873	0.0432 056
36	0.0332 143	0.0346 653	0.0361 524	0.0376 751	0.0392 329	0.0408 252	0.0424 516
37	0.0324 681	0.0339 227	0.0354 144	0.0369 426	0.0385 068	0.0401 064	0.0417 409
38	0.0317 615	0.0332 198	0.0347 161	0.0362 499	0.0378 206	0.0394 275	0.0410 701
39	0.0310 916	0.0325 537	0.0340 546	0.0355 940	0.0371 711	0.0387 854	0.0404 362
40	0.0304 556	0.0319 214	0.0334 271	0.0349 721	0.0365 558	0.0381 774	0.0398 362
41	0.0298 510	0.0313 206	0.0328 311	0.0343 817	0.0359 719	0.0376 009	0.0392 679
42	0.0292 756	0.0307 491	0.0322 643	0.0338 206	0.0354 173	0.0370 536	0.0387 288
43	0.0287 274	0.0302 047	0.0317 247	0.0332 867	0.0348 899	0.0365 336	0.0382 169
44	0.0282 044	0.0296 856	0.0312 104	0.0327 781	0.0343 879	0.0360 390	0.0377 304
45	0.0277 051	0.0291 901	0.0307 198	0.0322 932	0.0339 096	0.0355 681	0.0372 675
46	0.0272 278	0.0287 168	0.0302 513	0.0318 304	0.0334 534	0.0351 192	0.0368 268
47	0.0267 711	0.0282 641	0.0298 034	0.0313 884	0.0330 179	0.0346 911	0.0364 067
48	0.0263 338	0.0278 308	0.0293 750	0.0309 657	0.0326 018	0.0342 823	0.0360 060
49	0.0259 147	0.0274 156	0.0289 648	0.0305 612	0.0322 040	0.0338 918	0.0356 235
50	0.0255 127	0.0270 176	0.0285 717	0.0301 739	0.0318 232	0.0335 184	0.0352 581
60	0.0222 445	0.0237 899	0.0253 934	0.0270 534	0.0287 680	0.0305 353	0.0323 534
70	0.0199 328	0.0215 194	0.0231 724	0.0248 893	0.0266 677	0.0285 046	0.0303 971
80	0.0182 189	0.0198 465	0.0215 483	0.0233 209	0.0251 607	0.0270 638	0.0290 260
90	0.0169 031	0.0185 715	0.0203 211	0.0221 476	0.0240 460	0.0260 113	0.0280 381
100	0.0158 657	0.0175 743	0.0193 706	0.0212 488	0.0232 027	0.0252 259	0.0273 119

Fig. 13. Annuity

ANNUITIES

TO AMORTIZE $1 AND INTEREST

$$\frac{1}{a_{\overline{n}|i}} = \frac{i}{1 - \frac{1}{(1+i)^n}}$$

n	3%	3 1/2%	4%	4 1/2%	5%	6%	7%
1	1.0300 000	1.0350 000	1.0400 000	1.0450 000	1.0500 000	1.0600 000	1.0700 000
2	0.5226 108	0.5264 005	0.5301 961	0.5339 976	0.5378 049	0.5454 369	0.5530 918
3	0.3535 304	0.3569 342	0.3603 485	0.3637 734	0.3672 086	0.3741 098	0.3810 517
4	0.2690 271	0.2722 511	0.2754 901	0.2787 437	0.2820 118	0.2885 915	0.2952 281
5	0.2183 546	0.2214 814	0.2246 271	0.2277 916	0.2309 748	0.2373 964	0.2438 907
6	0.1845 975	0.1876 682	0.1907 619	0.1938 784	0.1970 175	0.2033 626	0.2097 958
7	0.1605 064	0.1635 445	0.1666 096	0.1697 015	0.1728 198	0.1791 350	0.1855 532
8	0.1424 564	0.1454 767	0.1485 278	0.1516 097	0.1547 218	0.1610 359	0.1674 678
9	0.1284 339	0.1314 460	0.1344 930	0.1375 745	0.1406 901	0.1470 222	0.1534 865
10	0.1172 305	0.1202 414	0.1232 909	0.1263 788	0.1295 046	0.1358 680	0.1423 775
11	0.1080 775	0.1110 920	0.1141 490	0.1172 482	0.1203 889	0.1267 929	0.1333 569
12	0.1004 621	0.1034 840	0.1065 522	0.1096 662	0.1128 254	0.1192 770	0.1259 020
13	0.0940 295	0.0970 616	0.1001 437	0.1032 754	0.1064 558	0.1129 601	0.1196 509
14	0.0885 263	0.0915 707	0.0946 690	0.0978 203	0.1010 240	0.1075 849	0.1143 449
15	0.0837 666	0.0868 251	0.0899 411	0.0931 138	0.0963 423	0.1029 628	0.1097 946
16	0.0796 109	0.0826 848	0.0858 200	0.0890 154	0.0922 699	0.0989 521	0.1058 577
17	0.0759 525	0.0790 431	0.0821 985	0.0854 176	0.0886 991	0.0954 448	0.1024 252
18	0.0727 087	0.0758 168	0.0789 933	0.0822 369	0.0855 462	0.0923 565	0.0994 126
19	0.0698 139	0.0729 403	0.0761 386	0.0794 073	0.0827 450	0.0896 209	0.0967 530
20	0.0672 157	0.0703 611	0.0735 818	0.0768 761	0.0802 426	0.0871 846	0.0943 929
21	0.0648 718	0.0680 366	0.0712 801	0.0746 006	0.0779 961	0.0850 046	0.0922 890
22	0.0627 474	0.0659 321	0.0691 988	0.0725 457	0.0759 705	0.0830 456	0.0904 058
23	0.0608 139	0.0640 188	0.0673 091	0.0706 825	0.0741 368	0.0812 785	0.0887 139
24	0.0590 474	0.0622 728	0.0655 868	0.0689 870	0.0724 709	0.0796 790	0.0871 890
25	0.0574 279	0.0606 740	0.0640 120	0.0674 390	0.0709 525	0.0782 267	0.0858 105
26	0.0559 383	0.0592 054	0.0625 674	0.0660 214	0.0695 643	0.0769 044	0.0845 610
27	0.0545 624	0.0578 524	0.0612 385	0.0647 195	0.0682 919	0.0756 972	0.0834 257
28	0.0532 932	0.0566 026	0.0600 130	0.0635 208	0.0671 225	0.0745 926	0.0823 919
29	0.0521 147	0.0554 454	0.0588 799	0.0624 146	0.0660 455	0.0735 796	0.0814 487
30	0.0510 193	0.0543 713	0.0578 301	0.0613 915	0.0650 514	0.0726 489	0.0805 864
31	0.0499 989	0.0533 724	0.0568 554	0.0604 435	0.0641 321	0.0717 922	0.0797 969
32	0.0490 466	0.0524 415	0.0559 486	0.0595 632	0.0632 804	0.0710 023	0.0790 729
33	0.0481 567	0.0515 724	0.0551 036	0.0587 445	0.0624 900	0.0702 729	0.0784 081
34	0.0473 220	0.0507 597	0.0543 148	0.0579 819	0.0617 555	0.0695 984	0.0777 967
35	0.0465 393	0.0499 984	0.0535 773	0.0572 705	0.0610 717	0.0689 739	0.0772 340
36	0.0458 038	0.0492 842	0.0528 869	0.0566 058	0.0604 345	0.0683 948	0.0767 153
37	0.0451 116	0.0486 133	0.0522 396	0.0559 840	0.0598 398	0.0678 574	0.0762 369
38	0.0444 593	0.0479 821	0.0516 319	0.0554 017	0.0592 842	0.0673 581	0.0757 951
39	0.0438 439	0.0473 878	0.0510 608	0.0548 557	0.0587 646	0.0668 938	0.0753 868
40	0.0432 624	0.0468 273	0.0505 235	0.0543 432	0.0582 782	0.0664 615	0.0750 091
41	0.0427 124	0.0462 982	0.0500 174	0.0538 616	0.0578 223	0.0660 589	0.0746 596
42	0.0421 917	0.0457 983	0.0495 402	0.0534 087	0.0573 947	0.0656 834	0.0743 359
43	0.0416 981	0.0453 254	0.0490 899	0.0529 824	0.0569 933	0.0653 331	0.0740 359
44	0.0412 299	0.0448 777	0.0486 645	0.0525 807	0.0566 163	0.0650 061	0.0737 577
45	0.0407 852	0.0444 534	0.0482 625	0.0522 020	0.0562 617	0.0647 005	0.0734 996
46	0.0403 625	0.0440 511	0.0478 821	0.0518 447	0.0559 282	0.0644 149	0.0732 600
47	0.0399 605	0.0436 692	0.0475 219	0.0515 073	0.0556 142	0.0641 477	0.0730 374
48	0.0395 778	0.0433 065	0.0471 807	0.0511 886	0.0553 184	0.0638 977	0.0728 307
49	0.0392 131	0.0429 617	0.0468 571	0.0508 872	0.0550 397	0.0636 636	0.0726 385
50	0.0388 655	0.0426 337	0.0465 502	0.0506 022	0.0547 767	0.0634 443	0.0724 599
60	0.0361 330	0.0400 886	0.0442 018	0.0484 543	0.0528 282	0.0618 757	0.0712 292
70	0.0343 366	0.0384 610	0.0427 451	0.0471 651	0.0516 992	0.0610 331	0.0706 195
80	0.0331 118	0.0373 849	0.0418 141	0.0463 707	0.0510 296	0.0605 725	0.0703 136
90	0.0322 556	0.0366 578	0.0412 078	0.0458 732	0.0506 271	0.0603 184	0.0701 590
100	0.0316 467	0.0361 593	0.0408 080	0.0455 584	0.0503 831	0.0601 774	0.0700 808

that $1 will buy.

Date	Semiannual Installment	Interest at 3% on Accumulated Sinking Fund	Total Additions to Sinking Fund	Accumulated Amounts in Sinking Fund
June 1, 1967	....	....	....	....
December 1, 1967	$ 14,092.42	....	$ 14,092.42	$ 14,092.42
June 1, 1968	14,092.42	$ 422.77	14,515.19	28,607.61
December 1, 1968	14,092.42	858.23	14,950.65	43,558.26
June 1, 1969	14,092.42	1,306.75	15,399.17	58,957.43
December 1, 1969	14,092.42	1,768.71	15,861.13	74,818.56
June 1, 1970	14,092.42	2,244.55	16,336.97	91,155.53
December 1, 1970	14,092.42	2,734.66	16,827.08	107,982.61
June 1, 1971	14,092.42	3,239.48	17,331.90	125,314.51
December 1, 1971	14,092.42	3,759.43	17,851.85	143,166.36
June 1, 1972	14,092.42	4,294.99	18,387.41	161,553.77
December 1, 1972	14,092.42	4,846.61	18,939.03	180,492.80
June 1, 1973	14,092.42	5,414.78	19,507.20	200,000.00
	$169,109.04	$ 30,890.96	$200,000.00	

Fig. 14. Schedule of sinking fund installments.

Now look in Fig. 12 in the 4½% column for an amount directly above and below the given figure. The time is evidently between 7 and 8 years. Since the results are approximations in any event, only four decimals are used.

	Tabular Difference	Given Difference
7 years	8.0192	8.0192
?		8.5714
8 years	9.3800	
	1.3608	.5522

$$n = 7 + \frac{.5522}{1.3608} = \underline{\underline{7.41}} \text{ years approximately}$$

Since bond maturities such as this are practically unknown, the borrower must decide whether the bonds are to mature in 8 or 7 years. If $50,000 represents the limit of what the borrower can spare, the maturity must be extended to 8 years, and the exact amount of R (sinking fund contribution) recalculated. If a maturity of 7 years is more desirable, the total annual burden will be greater than $50,000 and can easily be found by the formula for R.

FINAL VALUE OF ANNUITY DUE. In the case of an annuity due, the payments are made at the beginning rather than at the close of the period. Hence the last payment earns interest for the period. The symbol for the final value of an annuity due of $1 is $s_{\overline{n}|i}$ (read Roman s sub n at $i\%$). The simplest formula for it is:

$$s_{\overline{n}|i} = s_{\overline{n+1}|} - 1.$$

This formula makes possible the use of the regular annuity tables as shown in the examples below.

Example. Find the final value of an annuity due of $6,500 for 10 years at 3%

$$A_{10} \text{ Due} = R\, s_{\overline{10}|.03}$$
$$= \$6{,}500 \times (s_{\overline{11}|.03} - 1)$$
$$= \$6{,}500 \times 11.80779569$$
$$= \underline{\underline{\$76{,}750.67}}$$

In looking up $s_{\overline{10}|.03}$, start in the 3% column in Fig. 12, read the figure on the eleventh line, and subtract $1; that is, look up $s_{\overline{11}|.03}$ and decrease this value by $1.

PRESENT VALUE OF ORDINARY ANNUITY. The present value of an annuity is an amount that represents the sum of the discounted or present values of a series of equal payments made at uniform time intervals. Note that the future payments are equal, but are discounted. Hence, each payment represents in part principal and in part interest on the remaining debt. This is in contrast to final value problems where payments are accumulated to wipe out a future debt at maturity. Hence, wherever the annuity payments represent principal and interest, the problem is one of present value.

The symbol to represent the present value of a single dollar per annum payable at the end of each year, i.e., an ordinary annuity of $1, is $a_{\overline{n}|i}$ (read italic *a* sub *n* at *i*%). The formula is as follows:

$$a_{\overline{n}|i} = \frac{1 - \frac{1}{(1+i)^n}}{i}$$

$$= \frac{\text{Compound discount}}{\text{Interest rate}}$$

Fig. 15 shows the present values represented by the above formula and may therefore be used to solve present value problems. The present value of any number of dollars is represented by the following formula:

$$A_0 = R\, a_{\overline{n}|i}$$

in which A_0 = The present value of R dollars
R = Amount of each annuity payment

Example. A corporation owning a patent with an 8-year life receives a quarterly royalty in the amount of $5,500. At what value shall it set up this asset upon its balance sheet, assuming that money is worth 5% per annum?

Fig. 15 shows the present value of an annuity of $1 at 1¼% for 32 periods as 26.2412742.

$$\$5{,}500 \times 26.24127418 = \$144{,}327.01$$

This is the required value of the asset.

Example 2. A lumber company signs a contract with a syndicate that owns in fee a large tract of timber land. The company agrees to cut 120,000,000 feet of timber a year for 6 years and to pay $360,000 a year for the cut timber. The syndicate, desiring to anticipate the payments under its contract, applies to its bankers for the cash value

$$a_{\overline{n}|i} = \frac{1 - \dfrac{1}{(1+i)^n}}{i} = \frac{1 - v^n}{i}$$

PRESENT VALUE OF ANNUITY

Periods	1%	1 1/4%	1 1/2%	1 3/4%	2%	2 1/4%	2 1/2%
1	0.99009901	0.98765432	0.98522167	0.98280098	0.98039216	0.97799511	0.97560976
2	1.97039506	1.96311538	1.95588342	1.94869875	1.94156094	1.93446955	1.92742415
3	2.94098521	2.92653371	2.91220042	2.89798403	2.88388327	2.86989687	2.85602356
4	3.90196555	3.87805798	3.85438465	3.83094254	3.80772870	3.78474021	3.76197421
5	4.85343124	4.81783504	4.78264497	4.74785508	4.71345951	4.67945253	4.64582850
6	5.79547647	5.74600992	5.69718717	5.64899762	5.60143089	5.55447680	5.50812536
7	6.72819453	6.66272585	6.59821396	6.53464139	6.47199107	6.41024626	6.34939060
8	7.65167775	7.56812429	7.48592508	7.40505297	7.32548144	7.24718461	7.17013717
9	8.56601758	8.46234498	8.36051732	8.26049432	8.16223671	8.06570622	7.97086553
10	9.47130453	9.34552591	9.22218455	9.10122291	8.98258501	8.86621635	8.75206393
11	10.36762825	10.21780337	10.07111779	9.92749181	9.78684805	9.64911134	9.51420871
12	11.25507747	11.07931197	10.90750521	10.73954969	10.57534122	10.41477882	10.25776460
13	12.13374007	11.93018466	11.73153222	11.53764097	11.34837375	11.16359787	10.98318497
14	13.00370304	12.77055275	12.54338150	12.32200587	12.10624877	11.89593924	11.69091217
15	13.86505252	13.60054592	13.34323301	13.09288046	12.84926350	12.61216551	12.38137773
16	14.71787378	14.42029227	14.13126405	13.85049677	13.57770931	13.31263131	13.05500266
17	15.56225127	15.22991829	14.90764931	14.59508282	14.29187188	13.99768343	13.71219772
18	16.39826858	16.02954893	15.67256089	15.32686272	14.99203125	14.66766106	14.35336363
19	17.22600850	16.81930759	16.42616837	16.04605673	15.67846201	15.32289590	14.97889134
20	18.04555297	17.59931613	17.16863879	16.75288130	16.35143334	15.96371237	15.58916229
21	18.85698313	18.36969495	17.90013673	17.44754919	17.01120916	16.59042775	16.18454857
22	19.66037934	19.13056291	18.62082437	18.13026948	17.65804820	17.20335232	16.76541324
23	20.45582113	19.88203744	19.33086145	18.80124764	18.29220412	17.80278955	17.33211048
24	21.24338726	20.62423451	20.03040537	19.46068565	18.91392560	18.38903624	17.88498583
25	22.02315570	21.35726865	20.71961120	20.10878196	19.52345647	18.96238263	18.42437642
26	22.79520366	22.08125299	21.39863172	20.74573166	20.12103576	19.52311260	18.95061114
27	23.55960759	22.79629925	22.06761746	21.37172644	20.70689780	20.07150376	19.46401087
28	24.31644316	23.50251778	22.72671671	21.98695474	21.28127236	20.60782764	19.96488866
29	25.06578530	24.20001756	23.37607558	22.59160171	21.84438466	21.13234977	20.45354991
30	25.80770822	24.88890623	24.01583801	23.18584934	22.39645555	21.64532985	20.93029259
31	26.54228537	25.56929010	24.64614582	23.76987650	22.93770152	22.14702186	21.39540741
32	27.26958947	26.24127418	25.26713874	24.34385897	23.46833482	22.63767419	21.84917796
33	27.98969255	26.90496215	25.87895442	24.90796951	23.98856355	23.11752977	22.29188094
34	28.70266589	27.56045644	26.48172849	25.46237789	24.49859172	23.58682618	22.72378628
35	29.40858009	28.20785822	27.07559458	26.00725100	24.99861933	24.04579577	23.14515734
36	30.10750504	28.84726737	27.66068431	26.54275283	25.48884248	24.49466579	23.55625107
37	30.79950994	29.47878259	28.23712740	27.06904455	25.96945341	24.93365848	23.95731812
38	31.48466330	30.10250133	28.80505163	27.58628457	26.44064060	25.36299118	24.34860304
39	32.16303298	30.71851983	29.36458288	28.09462857	26.90258883	25.78287646	24.73034443
40	32.83468611	31.32693316	29.91584520	28.59422955	27.35547924	26.19352221	25.10277505
41	33.49968922	31.92783522	30.45896079	29.08523789	27.79948945	26.59513174	25.46612200
42	34.15810814	32.52131874	30.99405004	29.56780136	28.23479358	26.98790390	25.82060683
43	34.81000806	33.10747530	31.52123157	30.04206522	28.66156233	27.37203316	26.16644569
44	35.45545352	33.68639536	32.04062223	30.50817221	29.07996307	27.74770969	26.50384945
45	36.09450844	34.25816825	32.55233718	30.96626261	29.49015987	28.11511950	26.83302386
46	36.72723608	34.82288222	33.05648983	31.41647431	29.89231360	28.47444450	27.15416962
47	37.35369909	35.38062442	33.55319195	31.85894281	30.28658196	28.82586259	27.46748255
48	37.97395949	35.93148091	34.04255365	32.29380129	30.67311957	29.16954777	27.77315371
49	38.58807871	36.47553670	34.52468339	32.72118063	31.05207801	29.50567019	28.07136947
50	39.19611753	37.01287574	34.99968807	33.14120946	31.42360589	29.83439627	28.36231168
55	42.14719216	39.60168667	37.27146681	35.13544550	33.17478752	31.37265438	29.71397928
60	44.95503841	42.03459179	39.38026889	36.96398552	34.76088668	32.74895285	30.90865649
65	47.62660777	44.32098022	41.33778618	38.64059678	36.19746555	33.98034405	31.96457705
70	50.16851435	46.46967562	43.15487183	40.17790267	37.49861929	35.08208492	32.89785698
75	52.58705124	48.48897027	44.84160034	41.58747771	38.67711433	36.06782605	33.72274044
80	54.88820611	50.38665706	46.40732349	42.87993474	39.74451359	36.94978079	34.45181722
85	57.07767600	52.17005958	47.86072218	44.06500479	40.71128909	37.73887655	35.09621486
90	59.16088148	53.84606035	49.20985422	45.15161037	41.58692916	38.44489025	35.66576848
95	61.14298002	55.42112744	50.46220054	46.14793265	42.38002254	39.07656940	36.16917089
100	63.02887877	56.90133936	51.62470367	47.06147304	43.09835164	39.64174052	36.61410526

Fig. 15. Present value

ANNUITIES 27·41

OF $1 AT END OF EACH PERIOD

$$a_{\overline{n}|i} = \frac{1 - \frac{1}{(1+i)^n}}{i} = \frac{1 - v^n}{i}$$

Periods	2 3/4%	3%	3 1/2%	4%	4 1/2%	5%	6%
1	0.97323601	0.97087379	0.96618357	0.96153846	0.95693780	0.95238095	0.94339623
2	1.92042434	1.91346970	1.89969428	1.88609467	1.87266775	1.85941043	1.83339267
3	2.84226213	2.82861135	2.80163698	2.77509103	2.74896435	2.72324803	2.67301195
4	3.73942787	3.71709840	3.67307921	3.62989522	3.58752570	3.54595050	3.46510561
5	4.61258186	4.57970719	4.51505238	4.45182233	4.38997674	4.32947667	4.21236379
6	5.46236678	5.41719144	5.32855302	5.24213686	5.15787248	5.07569206	4.91732433
7	6.28940806	6.23028296	6.11454398	6.00205467	5.89270094	5.78637340	5.58238144
8	7.09431441	7.01969219	6.87395554	6.73274487	6.59588607	6.46321276	6.20979381
9	7.87767826	7.78610892	7.60768651	7.43533161	7.26879050	7.10782168	6.80169227
10	8.64007616	8.53020284	8.31660532	8.11089578	7.91271818	7.72173493	7.36008705
11	9.38206926	9.25262411	9.00155104	8.76047671	8.52891692	8.30641422	7.88687458
12	10.10420366	9.95400399	9.66333433	9.38507376	9.11858076	8.86325164	8.38384394
13	10.80701086	10.63495533	10.30273849	9.98564785	9.68285242	9.39357299	8.85268296
14	11.49100814	11.29607314	10.92052028	10.56312293	10.22282528	9.89864094	9.29498393
15	12.15669892	11.93793509	11.51741090	11.11838743	10.73954573	10.37965804	9.71224899
16	12.80457315	12.56110203	12.09411681	11.65229561	11.23401505	10.83776956	10.10589527
17	13.43510769	13.16611847	12.65132059	12.16566885	11.70719143	11.27406625	10.47725969
18	14.04876661	13.75351308	13.18968173	12.65929697	12.15999180	11.68958690	10.82760348
19	14.64600157	14.32379911	13.70983742	13.13393940	12.59329359	12.08532086	11.15811649
20	15.22725213	14.87747486	14.21240330	13.59032634	13.00793645	12.46221034	11.46992122
21	15.79294612	15.41502414	14.69797420	14.02915995	13.40472388	12.82115271	11.76407662
22	16.34349987	15.93691664	15.16712484	14.45111533	13.78442476	13.16300258	12.04158172
23	16.87931861	16.44360839	15.62041047	14.85684167	14.14777489	13.48857388	12.30337898
24	17.40079670	16.93554212	16.05836760	15.24696314	14.49547837	13.79864179	12.55035753
25	17.90831795	17.41314769	16.48151459	15.62207994	14.82820896	14.09394457	12.78335616
26	18.40225592	17.87684242	16.89035226	15.98276918	15.14661145	14.37518530	13.00316619
27	18.88297413	18.32703147	17.28536451	16.32958575	15.45130282	14.64303362	13.21053414
28	19.35082640	18.76410823	17.66701885	16.66306322	15.74287351	14.89812726	13.40616428
29	19.80615708	19.18845459	18.03576700	16.98371463	16.02188853	15.14107358	13.59072102
30	20.24930130	19.60044135	18.39204541	17.29203330	16.28888854	15.37245103	13.76483115
31	20.68058520	20.00042849	18.73627576	17.58849356	16.54439095	15.59281050	13.92908599
32	21.10032623	20.38876553	19.06886547	17.87355150	16.78889086	15.80267667	14.08404339
33	21.50883332	20.76579178	19.39020818	18.14764567	17.02286207	16.00254921	14.23022961
34	21.90640712	21.13183668	19.70068423	18.41119776	17.24675796	16.19290401	14.36814114
35	22.29334026	21.48722007	20.00066110	18.66461323	17.46101240	16.37419429	14.49824636
36	22.66991753	21.83225250	20.29049381	18.90828195	17.66604058	16.54685171	14.62098713
37	23.03641620	22.16723544	20.57052542	19.14257880	17.86223979	16.71128734	14.73678031
38	23.39310568	22.49246159	20.84108736	19.36786423	18.04999023	16.86789271	14.84601916
39	23.74024884	22.80821513	21.10249987	19.58448484	18.22965572	17.01704067	14.94907468
40	24.07810106	23.11477197	21.35507234	19.79277388	18.40158442	17.15908635	15.04629687
41	24.40691101	23.41239997	21.59910371	19.99305181	18.56610949	17.29436796	15.13801592
42	24.72692069	23.70135920	21.83488281	20.18562674	18.72354975	17.42320758	15.22454332
43	25.03836563	23.98190213	22.06268870	20.37079494	18.87421029	17.54591198	15.30617294
44	25.34147507	24.25427392	22.28279102	20.54884129	19.01838305	17.66277331	15.38318202
45	25.63647209	24.51871254	22.49545026	20.72003970	19.15634742	17.77406982	15.45583209
46	25.92357381	24.77544907	22.70091813	20.88465356	19.28837074	17.88006650	15.52436990
47	26.20299154	25.02470783	22.89943780	21.04293612	19.41470884	17.98101571	15.58902821
48	26.47493094	25.26670664	23.09124425	21.19513088	19.53560654	18.07715782	15.65002661
49	26.73959215	25.50165693	23.27656450	21.34147200	19.65129813	18.16872173	15.70757227
50	26.99716998	25.72976401	23.45561787	21.48218462	19.76200778	18.25592546	15.76186064
55	28.18526879	26.77442764	24.26405323	22.10861218	20.24802057	18.63347796	15.99054297
60	29.22266201	27.67556367	24.94473412	22.62348997	20.63802204	18.92928952	16.16142771
65	30.12846605	28.45289152	25.51784916	23.04668199	20.95097913	19.16107033	16.28912272
70	30.91937247	29.12342135	26.00039664	23.39451498	21.20211187	19.34267665	16.38454387
75	31.60995558	29.70182628	26.40668868	23.68040834	21.40363360	19.48496995	16.45584810
80	32.21294098	30.20076345	26.74877567	23.91539185	21.56534493	19.59646048	16.50913077
85	32.73944009	30.63115103	27.03680373	24.10853116	21.69511035	19.68381623	16.54894668
90	33.19915489	31.00240714	27.27931564	24.26727759	21.79924075	19.75226174	16.57869944
95	33.60055671	31.32265592	27.48350415	24.39775559	21.88280030	19.80589059	16.60093244
100	33.95104232	31.59890534	27.65542540	24.50499900	21.94985274	19.84791020	16.61754623

of $1 per annum.

of the contract, offering as security the contract itself and a mortgage on the timber land. What is the present worth of the contract calculated on a 4% basis?

$$A_0 = 360{,}000 \times a_{\overline{6}|.04}$$
$$= \$360{,}000 \times 5.24213686$$
$$= \underline{\$1{,}887{,}169.28}$$

This answer represents the amount the syndicate can borrow on its contract. This means that six annual payments of $360,000 will pay off the loan and the interest on the outstanding balances. The proof is submitted in Fig. 16, which shows the amortization of the loan.

Year	Amount Outstanding at Beginning of Period	Interest at 4% on Outstanding Balance	Annuity Payment	Principal Repaid
1	$1,887,169.28	$ 75,486.77	$ 360,000.00	$ 284,513.23
2	1,602,656.05	64,106.24	360,000.00	295,893.76
3	1,306,762.29	52,270.49	360,000.00	307,729.51
4	999,032.78	39,961.31	360,000.00	320,038.69
5	678,994.09	27,159.76	360,000.00	332,840.24
6	346,153.85	13,846.15	360,000.00	346,153.85
		$272,830.72	$2,160,000.00	$1,887,169.28

Fig. 16. Proof of amortization of loan.

ANNUITY THAT $1 WILL BUY. The annuity that $1 will buy is equivalent to a series of annuity payments the sum of whose present values is $1. This type of problem is found where the size of the annuity rent (R) is to be determined. The formula is as follows:

$$R = A_0 \times \frac{1}{a_{\overline{n}|i}}$$

The fraction is the reciprocal of the present value of $1 and represents the annuity that $1 will purchase. Special tables are available and these make the computation quite easy. Fig. 13 shows the values of the above fraction whose use is illustrated below.

Example 1. Mr. X buys a property for $25,000, agreeing to pay $2,500 down and the balance in 15 equal annual installments that include interest at 5%. What is the size of each installment?

The debt amounts to $22,500 after deduction of the down payment.

$$R = A_0 \times \frac{1}{a_{\overline{n}|i}}$$
$$= \$22{,}500 \times \frac{1}{a_{\overline{15}|.05}}$$
$$= \$22{,}500 \times .0963423$$
$$= \underline{\$2{,}167.70}$$

ANNUITIES

Example 2. The Steel Wire Co. floated a $300,000, 6% bond issue on May 1, 1966, due May 1, 1974. Interest is payable semi-annually; the bonds are in denominations of $1,000, and callable at par and accrued interest. What is the standard rent that will wipe out the debt and interest?

$$R = A_0 \times \frac{1}{a_{\overline{16}|.03}}$$
$$= 300,000 \times .0796109$$
$$= \$23,883.27$$

In Fig. 17 is shown a table of bond retirements. Since the bonds are issued in fixed denominations, the total semi-annual charge cannot be exactly as stated above, but should be kept as near that figure as possible. Thus on November 1, 1966, $9,000 of the $23,883.27 is due as interest and the balance of $14,883.27 can be applied against principal outstanding. But the bonds must be retired in even amounts; in this case fifteen bonds are retired. As a result, the first year involves an expenditure of $24,000 instead of $23,883. The excess payment is reflected in the column showing the excess or deficiency of any one period. A cumulative column is also provided; the purpose is to keep the cumulative error as low as possible. In the case of a $1,000 bond the maximum deviation from the standard charge should not exceed ±$500, that is, half the value of the bond. In case the cumulative error threatens to become more than $500, it is best to redeem one bond more or less, so as to keep the error within the stated limits.

FINDING THE NUMBER OF PAYMENTS TO AMORTIZE A LOAN.

If the amount that can be spared for principal and interest is known, the borrower must also know how long it will take to amortize the debt. This involves finding n, that is, the number of payments to be made.

Example. The Brass Fixture Co. on July 1, 1965, issued $300,000, 6% bonds, interest payable semi-annually. The bonds are in denominations of $1,000 and are to be redeemed at par and accrued interest. How long will it take to pay them off if the corporation has budgeted $25,000 each period for interest and bond redemption?

$$R = \frac{A_0}{a_{\overline{n}|i}}$$

$$25,000 = \frac{300,000}{a_{\overline{n}|.03}}$$

$$a_{\overline{n}|.03} = \frac{300,000}{25,000} = 12$$

Now look for the nearest values in the 3% column of Fig. 15 and interpolate. Evidently n lies between 15 and 16 periods.

15 years	11.9379	11.9379
n years		12.0000
16 years	12.5611	
Tabular difference	.6232	
Given difference		.0621

$$n = 15 + \frac{621}{6,232} = \underline{\underline{15.1}} \text{ semi-annual periods.}$$

The value of n may also be found by logs. See presentation later.

Date	Outstanding	Interest at 3%	Amount Retired	Amount To Pay Interest and Retire Bonds	Number of Bonds Retired	Over (+) and Short (−) Current	Over (+) and Short (−) Cumulative
May 1, 1966	$300,000	....	....	....	..	....	....
November 1, 1966	300,000	$ 9,000	$ 15,000	$ 24,000	15	+117	+117
May 1, 1967	285,000	8,550	15,000	23,550	15	−333	−216
November 1, 1967	270,000	8,100	16,000	24,100	16	+217	+ 1
May 1, 1968	254,000	7,620	16,000	23,620	16	−263	−262
November 1, 1968	238,000	7,140	17,000	24,140	17	+257	− 5
May 1, 1969	221,000	6,630	17,000	23,630	17	−253	−258
November 1, 1969	204,000	6,120	18,000	24,120	18	+237	− 21
May 1, 1970	186,000	5,580	18,000	23,580	18	−303	−324
November 1, 1970	168,000	5,040	19,000	24,040	19	+157	−167
May 1, 1971	149,000	4,470	20,000	24,470	20	+587	+420
November 1, 1971	129,000	3,870	20,000	23,870	20	− 13	+407
May 1, 1972	109,000	3,270	20,000	23,270	20	−613	−206
November 1, 1972	89,000	2,670	21,000	23,670	21	−213	−419
May 1, 1973	68,000	2,040	22,000	24,040	22	+157	−262
November 1, 1973	46,000	1,380	23,000	24,380	23	+497	+235
May 1, 1974	23,000	690	23,000	23,690	23	−193	+ 42
		$82,170	$300,000	$382,170	300		

Fig. 17. Schedule of interest payments and bond retirements for serial bond issue.

PRESENT VALUE OF ANNUITY DUE. The symbol for the present value of an annuity due of $1 per period is $a_{\overline{n}|i}$ (read Roman a sub n at $i\%$). The formula is as follows:

$$a_{\overline{n}|i} = a_{\overline{n-1}|i} + 1$$

This means that the present value tables for ordinary annuities (Fig. 15) may be used in computing the present value of an annuity due. For instance, if $a_{\overline{12}|.03}$ is wanted, it can be found by looking in the 3% column of Fig. 15 on line 11 and adding $1. In this case the answer is 10.25262411.

Example. What is the cash value of a lease that has 7 years to run and that calls for rentals of $1,365 quarterly, payable in advance? Assume money is worth 4% per annum, compounded quarterly.

The lease has 28 periods to run and is discounted at 1% per period. Since payments are made in advance it is an annuity due.

$$A_0 \text{ Due} = R\, a_{\overline{28}|.01}$$
$$= 1{,}365\, (a_{\overline{27}|.01} + 1)$$
$$= 1{,}365 \times 24.55960759$$
$$= \underline{\underline{\$33{,}523.86}}$$

Bond Valuation

DEFINITIONS. The following definitions are in order:

Bond. A bond may be defined as a long-time promissory note under seal. It promises to pay to the owner of the bond a specified principal sum called the face value on a definite date in the future, called the maturity date. It also promises to pay the interest based on the face value on the interest dates as called for in the bond indenture.

The **par value** of a bond is the amount stated on its face. The **redemption value** is the price at which the bond will be redeemed. In many issues this is the same as the par value; in others, premiums are paid when bonds are redeemed before or at maturity.

Premium and Discount on Bonds. When bonds sell at a price greater than par, they are said to sell at a **premium**, and when at a price less than par they are said to sell at a **discount**.

Nominal and Effective Interest Rates. The nominal rate, also known as the **coupon rate** or the **cash rate**, is the rate, based on the par value, stipulated in the bond.

The **effective rate**, also called the **yield** or **market rate**, is the return that the bonds earn on the price at which they are purchased if they are held to maturity. Note that the yield is based on the price paid for the bond, not on its par value. When the nominal rate is in excess of the yield rate, that is, in excess of what in the opinion of the market is considered a fair rate of return for that type of security, the bond sells at a **premium**. When the bond rate is less than the yield rate, the bond sells at a **discount**. The amount of the premium or discount can be mathematically determined and is based on principles of compound interest and annuities.

DETERMINING BASIS PRICE OF BONDS.

The price at which a bond will sell on the open market depends on a number of factors:

1. The security for the payment of the principal and interest.
2. The bond rate.
3. The rate realized by like investments, or to be realized by the investor.
4. The time to the maturity of the bond.
5. The price at which the bond will be redeemed.

From a purely mathematical point of view, once the desired yield is known, the basis price, that is, the purchase price, of a bond depends on two factors:

1. The present value of the principal.
2. The present value of the interest payments.

The sum of these two present values represents the basis price of the bond. The first factor represents the present value of a lump sum, the second the present value of an annuity.

Example. What is the price paid by Mr. X on November 1, 1965, for 100 bonds, par value $100,000, paying 5% nominal to yield 4½%? The bonds pay interest May and November 1, through coupons, and mature November 1, 1968.

The nominal rate per period is 2½%, the effective rate 2¼%.

I. The present value of the principal six periods from now is

$$P = A \times v^n$$
$$P = 100{,}000 \times v^6 \text{ at } 2\tfrac{1}{4}\%$$
$$= \$100{,}000 \times .87502427 \text{ (Fig. 11)}$$
$$= \$87{,}502.43$$

II. The present value of the coupons is calculated by means of the annuity formula. The size of each coupon is determined from the nominal rate. In this example, the semi-annual coupons have a face value of $2,500 (i.e., $100,000 × 2½%). Their present value is then found:

$$A_0 = R\, a_{\overline{n}|i}$$
$$= 2{,}500 \times a_{\overline{6}|.02\tfrac{1}{4}}$$
$$= 2{,}500 \times 5.55447680 \text{ (Fig. 15)}$$
$$= \$13{,}886.19$$

Basis price of bonds:

$$\$87{,}502.43 + 13{,}886.19 = \$101{,}388.62$$

Note that the yield rate is always used except for calculating the amount of each coupon.

Short Method for Finding Basis Price. Since the difference between the coupon and yield rates gives rise to premium or discount on bonds, it is possible to compute the premium, and hence the basis price, directly from such difference. This method is illustrated below, using the same example as above.

	Rate	Amount
Nominal interest	= 2.50%	$2,500
Effective interest	= 2.25%	2,250
Excess interest	=	$ 250

BOND VALUATION

The bond pays $2,500 interest per period. It should pay $2,250 in order to sell at par. There is, therefore, $250 excess interest per period.

The excess interest constitutes an annuity for the life of the bond. The present value of this annuity represents the premium to be paid.

$$A_0 = R\, a_{\overline{n}|i}$$
$$= 250 \times a_{\overline{6}|.0225}$$
$$= 250 \times 5.55447680 = \$\ 1{,}388.62 \text{ premium}$$

Par value	100,000.00
Basis price	$101,388.62

AMORTIZATION SCHEDULE. Although an investor may have paid a premium for the bond, generally speaking, he collects only the par value at maturity. This shrinkage in value takes place gradually during the life of the bond. It means that each coupon collection represents two things:

1. Return on the investment at the yield rate.
2. Partial return of the premium paid.

That this is the case can be shown by a so-called amortization table. The table in Fig. 18 is based on the premium bond illustrated in the last example.

Date	Coupon Income 2½%	Effective Income 2¼%	Amortization	Remaining Book Value
November 1, 1965	....	....	....	$101,388.62
May 1, 1966	$ 2,500	$ 2,281.25	$ 218.75	101,169.87
November 1, 1966	2,500	2,276.32	223.68	100,946.19
May 1, 1967	2,500	2,271.29	228.71	100,717.48
November 1, 1967	2,500	2,266.14	233.86	100,483.62
May 1, 1968	2,500	2,260.88	239.12	100,244.50
November 1, 1968	2,500	2,255.50	244.50	100,000.00
	$15,000	$13,611.38	$1,388.62	

Fig. 18. Schedule of amortization.

The coupon income is 2½% a period based on the par value of the bonds. The effective income or yield is 2¼% based on the remaining investment. Thus, on May 1, 1966, 2¼% is earned on $101,388.62, or $2,281.25. This is the true income for the period. The balance of the $2,500 coupon interest collected on that day represents a partial liquidation of the investment. Hence, the book value is reduced on May 1, 1966, by $218.75. Six months later, the effective income is 2¼% of the new book value of $101,169.87, etc.

SHORT-CUT METHOD FOR DISCOUNT BONDS. The short-cut method illustrated above works equally well for bonds selling at a discount, as shown in the example below.

Example. Find the basis price of a $10,000 bond paying 3% nominal February and August 1, to yield 3½%. The bond was purchased February 1, 1966, and matures August 1, 1969.

	Rate	Amount
Nominal interest	1.50%	$150
Effective interest	1.75%	175
Deficiency of interest		$ 25

$$A_0 = 25 \times a_{\overline{7}|.0175}$$
$$= 25 \times 6.53464139 \text{ (Fig. 15)}$$

Discount	= $ 163.37
Par value	10,000.00
Basis price	$ 9,836.63

SCHEDULE OF ACCUMULATION. A bond purchased at a discount approaches par or other redemption value gradually. The increase in value is spread over the life of the bond. Hence, the **true income** each period consists of:

1. Coupon interest.
2. Increase in book value, known as the accumulation.

The table in Fig. 19 shows an accumulation table for the last illustration, under the short-cut method for discount bonds.

Date	Coupon Interest 1½%	Effective Interest 1¾%	Accumulation	New Book Value
February 1, 1966	....	......	......	$9,836.63
August 1, 1966	150	$172.14	$22.14	9,858.77
February 1, 1967	150	172.53	22.53	9,881.30
August 1, 1967	150	172.92	22.92	9,904.22
February 1, 1968	150	173.33	23.33	9,927.55
August 1, 1968	150	173.73	23.73	9,951.28
February 1, 1969	150	174.15	24.15	9,975.43
August 1, 1969	150	174.57	24.57	10,000.00
	$1,050	$1,213.37	$163.37	

Fig. 19. Accumulation table for $10,000 bond.

The figures in the effective interest column are obtained by taking 1¾% of the last book value. Thus on August 1, 1966, 1¾% of $9,836.63 yields $172.14, etc. Six months later 1¾% of $9,858.77 amounts to $172.53, etc. In each instance, the difference between coupon and yield interest is **added** to the previous book value.

BOND VALUATION TABLES. Bond tables have been devised to simplify the labor involved in determining:

1. The price to be paid when the yield is known.
2. The yield when the cost is known.

BOND VALUATION 27·49

Thus it is possible to read the basis price of a bond directly from the table. The **standard bond tables** usually give the value of a million dollar bond correct to the nearest cent for a great variety of nominal and effective interest rates and for periods ranging from 6 months to 50 years at 6-month intervals, and at longer intervals thereafter. **Sprague's Extended Bond Tables** cover coupon rates from 3% to 7% and yields from 2½% to 5%. Special formulas and tables are provided for other rates and for bonds with quarterly or annual coupons. Fig. 20 shows one page from these tables. The following problems illustrate the uses of the tables.

Finding Price of a Bond When the Yield Is Known.

Example. An advertisement contains in part the following information, "These 3½% bonds maturing in 9 years will yield the purchaser 4.23% per annum on his investment." What price shall be paid for the bonds? This is similar to the problem above except that the yield rate is not found in the table but will have to be obtained by interpolation.

Proceed as follows: In the 3½% table (Fig. 20) in the column headed 9 years, set down the price of a $1,000 bond at 4.20 and 4.25%.

	Yields	
Prices	Tabular Diff.	Given Diff.
$947.99	4.20%	4.20%
?		4.23%
944.39	4.25%	
$ 3.60	.05%	.03%

Thus an increase of .05% in yield corresponds to a decrease of $3.60 in the basis price of the bond. The difference between 4.20% and the given yield of 4.23% amounts to .03%. Hence the change in basis price is

$$\frac{.03}{.05} \times \$3.60 = \frac{3}{5} \times 3.60 = \underline{\underline{\$2.16}}$$

Since the basis price decreases as the yield increases, the price to be paid in this case is $947.99 − $2.16 = $945.83.

Finding Yield When Basis Price Is Known. A frequent problem is that of determining the yield when the basis price, i.e., the quoted price, is known. The problem is not easily solved by ordinary mathematical devices, but the yield can easily be approximated by the use of bond tables.

Example. What yield is realized on a 3½% bond maturing in 10 years and quoted at 95?

At 95 the price is $950.00 for a $1,000 bond. Turn to the 3½% table (Fig. 20) in the column headed 10 years. The price is found to be between the values corresponding to the yields of 4.10 and 4.15% in the left-hand column. By interpolation the yield of the given bond is found to be 4.115%.

BASIS PRICE FOR BONDS BOUGHT BETWEEN INTEREST DATES. The basis price of a bond changes from day to day. Hence, if a bond is bought between interest dates, its basis price must be computed by interpolation between the basis prices of the last preceding and next succeeding interest dates. In addition, the purchaser will have to pay **accrued interest** on the bonds to the seller for the time since the last interest date.

Bonds may be quoted either "and interest" or "flat." The **"and-interest" price** is the quoted price plus the accrued interest. The **"flat" price** includes

VALUES TO THE NEAREST CENT, OF A 3½% BOND FOR $1,000,000, INTEREST PAYABLE SEMI-ANNUALLY

Net Inc.	8 Years	8 1/2 Years	9 Years	9 1/2 Years	10 Years
2 50	1 072 101 46	1 076 149 59	1 080 147 74	1 084 096 54	1 087 996 58
2 55	1 068 357 29	1 072 186 91	1 075 968 32	1 079 702 11	1 083 388 91
2 60	1 064 628 15	1 068 241 02	1 071 807 52	1 075 328 26	1 078 803 81
2 65	1 060 913 97	1 064 311 84	1 067 665 27	1 070 974 86	1 074 241 16
2 70	1 057 214 68	1 060 399 29	1 063 541 48	1 066 641 82	1 069 700 86
2 75	1 053 530 23	1 056 503 31	1 059 436 06	1 062 329 04	1 065 182 77
2 80	1 049 860 54	1 052 623 80	1 055 348 92	1 058 036 41	1 060 686 79
2 85	1 046 205 55	1 048 760 71	1 051 279 97	1 053 763 83	1 056 212 80
2 90	1 042 565 20	1 044 913 95	1 047 229 12	1 049 511 21	1 051 760 68
2 95	1 038 939 42	1 041 083 44	1 043 196 30	1 045 278 44	1 047 330 32
3 00	1 035 328 16	1 037 269 12	1 039 181 40	1 041 065 42	1 042 921 60
3 05	1 031 731 35	1 033 470 91	1 035 184 35	1 036 872 05	1 038 534 40
3 10	1 028 148 92	1 029 688 74	1 031 205 06	1 032 698 24	1 034 168 63
3 15	1 024 580 81	1 025 922 53	1 027 243 45	1 028 543 88	1 029 824 15
3 20	1 021 026 97	1 022 172 22	1 023 299 43	1 024 408 88	1 025 500 87
3 25	1 017 487 33	1 018 437 72	1 019 372 91	1 020 293 15	1 021 198 67
3 30	1 013 961 83	1 014 718 97	1 015 463 81	1 016 196 57	1 016 917 43
3 35	1 010 450 41	1 011 015 89	1 011 572 06	1 012 119 06	1 012 657 06
3 40	1 006 953 00	1 007 328 42	1 007 697 56	1 008 060 53	1 008 417 43
3 45	1 003 469 55	1 003 656 48	1 003 840 23	1 004 020 87	1 004 198 45
3 50	1 000 000 00	1 000 000 00	1 000 000 00	1 000 000 00	1 000 000 00
3 55	996 544 28	996 358 91	996 176 78	995 997 81	995 821 97
3 60	993 102 35	992 733 15	992 370 48	992 014 22	991 664 27
3 65	989 674 12	989 122 64	988 581 03	988 049 13	987 526 77
3 70	986 259 56	985 527 31	984 808 35	984 102 46	983 409 38
3 75	982 858 60	981 947 09	981 052 36	980 174 09	979 311 99
3 80	979 471 17	978 381 92	977 312 97	976 263 96	975 234 50
3 85	976 097 23	974 831 72	973 590 11	972 371 95	971 176 80
3 90	972 736 72	971 296 44	969 883 70	968 497 99	967 138 79
3 95	969 389 57	967 775 99	966 193 67	964 641 99	963 120 36
4 00	966 055 73	964 270 32	962 519 92	960 803 84	959 121 42
4 05	962 735 14	960 779 36	958 862 39	956 983 48	955 141 85
4 10	959 427 74	957 303 03	955 221 00	953 180 79	951 181 57
4 15	956 133 49	953 841 28	951 595 67	949 395 71	947 240 47
4 20	952 852 31	950 394 04	947 986 33	945 628 13	943 318 45
4 25	949 584 16	946 961 24	944 392 89	941 877 98	939 415 40
4 30	946 328 98	943 542 81	940 815 28	938 145 16	935 531 24
4 35	943 086 72	940 138 70	937 253 44	934 429 59	931 665 86
4 40	939 857 31	936 748 83	933 707 27	930 731 19	927 819 17
4 45	936 640 70	933 373 15	930 176 72	927 049 86	923 991 06
4 50	933 436 84	930 011 58	926 661 69	923 385 52	920 181 44
4 55	930 245 68	926 664 07	923 162 13	919 738 09	916 390 21
4 60	927 067 15	923 330 55	919 677 96	916 107 48	912 617 29
4 65	923 901 21	920 010 96	916 209 09	912 493 62	908 862 56
4 70	920 747 80	916 705 23	912 755 47	908 896 41	905 125 95
4 75	917 606 86	913 413 30	909 317 02	905 315 77	901 407 35
4 80	914 478 35	910 135 11	905 893 66	901 751 62	897 706 66
4 85	911 362 21	906 870 60	902 485 33	898 203 89	894 023.81
4 90	908 258 39	903 619 71	899 091 95	894 672 48	890 358 69
4 95	905 166 83	900 382 36	895 713 46	891 157 31	886 711 21
5 00	902 087 48	897 158 52	892 349 77	887 658 31	883 081 28

Fig. 20. Bond table page.

BOND VALUATION 27·51

the accrued interest in the quotation. To find the value of a bond between interest dates, proceed as follows:

1. Find the basis price on the preceding interest day and on the succeeding interest day, and thus determine the decrease or increase in book value for the entire period.
2. Find the fractional part of the period that has elapsed to the day of purchase. Find this fractional part of the period's change in book value.
3. Add to the book value of the preceding interest day the increase found in (2) or subtract from it the decrease found in (2) for the part of the period that has elapsed. The result is the "and-interest" price or "ex-interest" price.
4. Add to the ex-interest price in either instance the accrued interest, or seller's share of the current period's bond interest. The result is the **total price** or flat price.

Example. Find the "and-interest" and "flat" prices for a $1,000 bond, due February 1, 1976, bearing interest at 3½% per annum, payable February 1 and August 1, if purchased April 1, 1966, to yield 2.9%.

The life of the bond on the last interest date (February 1, 1966) was 10 years; at the next interest date it has 9½ years to run. The basis prices on these two dates can be found by the methods presented earlier (determining the basis prices of bonds) or by reference to bond tables (Fig. 20). From the latter the values of the bond to yield 2.9% are as follows:

1. 10 years (Feb. 1, 1966) $1,051.76
   9½ years (Aug. 1, 1966) 1,049.51
   Amortization for 6 months .... $ 2.25
2. From February 1 to April 1 is ⅓ of a period. Therefore the basis price decreased ⅓ × $2.25 .... $ .75
3. "And-interest" price April 1, 1966 = $1,051.76 − $.75 = $1,051.01
4. Accrued interest:
   3½% per annum on $1,000 for 2 months 5.83
   Flat price $1,056.84

It is possible also to determine the flat price directly. The seller is entitled to the book value on the preceding interest day, plus interest on this value at the yield rate, for the time elapsed since that day. The procedure is stated by Schlauch and Lang (Mathematics of Business and Finance) as follows:

1. Find the basis price on the preceding interest day.
2. Find the time elapsed since the last interest day, and add to the basis price on the preceding interest day interest on it at the yield rate for the elapsed time on a 360-day year basis. The result is the **total price**.
3. From the total price **subtract** the accrued interest. The result is the and-interest price or the ex-interest price.

Using the same illustration as above the method works out as follows:

1. February 1, 1966, basis price $1,051.76
2. Interest at 2.9% per annum for 2 months on above 5.08
3. April 1, 1966, flat price $1,056.84

If only the total price to be paid by the purchaser or to be received by the seller is wanted, this method offers a short-cut. For the purpose of setting up a schedule of amortization or accumulation, the and-interest price must be used.

The first four lines of the amortization table for the above bond appear as follows:

Date	3½% Bond Interest	2.9% Effective Interest	Amortization	Book Value
April 1, 1966				$1,051.01
August 1, 1966	$11.67	$10.17	$1.50	1,049.51
February 1, 1967	17.50	15.22	2.28	1,047.23
August 1, 1967	17.50	15.18	2.32	1,044.91

The figures for August 1, 1966, are obtained as follows:

1. Bond interest. The total coupon interest for a period is $17.50, one-third of which ($5.83) was paid over to the vendor on April 1. Hence, the net interest collected on August 1 is $11.67.
2. Effective interest. This must be calculated on the basis price as of the last interest date (February 1, 1966) for 4 months. In this case $1,051.76 at 2.9% for 4 months $10.17.
3. Amortization. Difference between the two preceding columns. $11.67 − $10.17 = $1.50. It could also be found by taking the amortization for the full 6-month period ($2.25) and subtracting the amortization from February 1 to April 1 ($.75).
4. Book value. Book value April 1, 1966, less current amortization. $1,051.01 − $1.50 = $1,049.51.

ACCRUING BOND INTEREST BETWEEN INTEREST DATES. The interest accrued at time of purchase or sale depends on whether the bond is a corporate or a government bond. For **corporate bonds** delivery must be made on the fourth working day after the sale and interest is accrued on the basis of a 360-day year up to and including the day before delivery. In the case of **government bonds,** delivery is on the next working day, and the seller receives interest up to and including the day of the sale.

The rules are further clarified by the Committee on Securities of the New York Stock Exchange as follows:

Interest at the rate specified on a bond dealt in "and-interest" shall be computed on a basis of a 360-day year, i.e., each calendar month shall be considered to be 1/12 of 360 days, and each period from a date in one month to the same date in the following month shall be considered to be 30 days.

Note: The number of elapsed days shall be computed in accordance with the examples given in the following table:

From	To
30th or 31st	1st of the following month to be figured as 1 day.
30th or 31st	30th of the following month to be figured as 30 days.
30th or 31st	31st of the following month to be figured as 30 days.
30th or 31st	1st of the second following month to be figured as one month, one day.

Thus if a January and July 15 bond were bought on March 15, 2 months are said to have elapsed since January 15. If a June and December 1 bond were bought on January 16, following the above rule there are:

From December 1 to January 1	30 days
From January 1 to January 16	15 days
Elapsed time	45 days

DETERMINING PROFIT OR LOSS ON SALE OF BONDS. When bonds that have been purchased as an investment are subsequently sold, the

BOND VALUATION   **27·53**

profit or loss on the transaction is determined by comparison of the book value (i.e., the and-interest price) on the date of sale with the selling price. The example below illustrates the procedure.

Example. On January 1, 1966, Mr. A bought a $1,000 bond bearing 3½%, January and July 1, due July 1, 1974, at a price to yield 3% if kept to maturity. On March 1, 1966, he sold the bond for $1070.90 and interest. Find the profit realized on the sale.

March 1 falls between interest dates. Hence, find the basis prices on January 1, 1966, and July 1, 1966, and interpolate.

January 1, 1966, basis price	$1,037.27
July 1, 1966, basis price	1,035.33
Difference for 6-month period	$ 1.94
January 1 to March 1 (2 months or ⅓ of $1.94)	$ .65
March 1, 1966, basis price ($1,037.27 − $.65)	$1,036.62
Selling price	1,070.90
Profit on sale	$ 34.28

The profit figure represents the capital gain for tax purposes and is of course exclusive of the coupon interest less amortization regularly reported as income.

FINDING YIELD BETWEEN INTEREST DATES. In this type of problem a double interpolation is required. First it is necessary to find basis prices above and below the quoted price on the date of purchase or sale. Next an interpolation is made for the yield.

Example 1. Find the yield on a $1,000 3½% bond, January and July 1, due July 1, 1975, if purchased March 1, 1966, at 104¼ and interest.

On March 1, 1966, the bond had 9 years and 4 months to run. The first step is to read from Fig. 20 the values for 9½ years and 9 years that bracket the given price of $1,042.50 and to write down the yields corresponding to them, as in columns (2) and (4) below:

(1)	(2)	(3)	(4)	(5)
		9 Years,		(2) − (4)
Yield	9½ Years	4 Months	9 Years	Difference
2.95%	$1,045.28	$1,044.59	$1,043.20	$2.08
3.00%	1,041.07	1,040.44	1,039.18	1.89

The differences in the last column represent the change in book value for a 6-month period. A change in the time interval of 2 months (i.e., from 9½ years to 9 years and 4 months) would change the book value by one-third of the difference.

Book value, January 1, 1966	$1,045.28
⅓ of $2.08	.69
Book value, March 1, 1966	$1,044.59

In the same way the book value corresponding to a 3% yield is determined to be $1,040.44. These interpolated values are inserted in column (3) above. There is thus one value above the given quotation corresponding to a yield of 2.95% and one below, corresponding to a yield of 3%. To find the yield at the quoted price, interpolate in column (3) as follows:

2.95%	$1,044.59	$1,044.59
?		1,042.50
3.00%	1,040.44	
.05%	$ 4.15	$ 2.09

$$\frac{209}{415} \times .05\% = .025\%$$

Hence the required yield is

$$2.95\% + .025\% = \underline{\underline{2.975\%}}$$

Example 2. Find the yield on a $1,000 bond, 3½% February and August 15, due August 15, 1975, purchased March 15, 1967, at 94⅞ and accrued interest.

The interest date preceding the date of purchase was February 15, 1967, at which time the bond had 8½ years to run.

(1)	(2)	(3)	(4)	(5)
		8 Years		
Yield	8½ Years	5 Months	8 Years	Difference
4.20%	$950.39	$950.80	$952.85	$2.46
4.25%	946.96	947.40	949.58	2.62
4.30%	943.54	944.00	946.33	2.79

For 8½ years the yield is between 4.20% and 4.25%. But for 8 years the yield is between 4.25% and 4.30%. Hence three sets of figures are copied from Fig. 20, and horizontal interpolation is made for 8 years and 5 months. It then becomes evident from column (3) that the next higher and the next lower prices occur on lines 1 and 2 of the above table. Line 3 is therefore discarded and interpolation for the yield made as follows:

4.20%	$950.80	$950.80
?		948.75
4.25%	947.40	
.05%	$ 3.40	$ 2.05

$$\frac{205}{340} \times .05\% = .030\%$$

Yield rate = 4.20% + .030% = 4.230%

Logarithms

DEFINITION AND USES. The use of logarithms reduces multiplication and division to simple addition and subtraction, respectively. The task of extracting roots and raising numbers to powers is also enormously simplified. The logarithm (or log) of a number is generally defined as the power to which 10 must be raised to produce that number. Thus the log of 100 is 2, because $10^2 = 100$; the log of 10,000 is 4, because $10^4 = 10,000$. As a background for further discussion the following tabulation will be useful:

$10^{-4} =$	.0001	that is, the log of	.0001	$= -4$
$10^{-3} =$	.001	" " " " "	.001	$= -3$
$10^{-2} =$	.01	" " " " "	.01	$= -2$
$10^{-1} =$	.1	" " " " "	.1	$= -1$
$10^0 =$	1.	" " " " "	1.	$= 0$
$10^1 =$	10.	" " " " "	10.	$= 1$
$10^2 =$	100.	" " " " "	100.	$= 2$
$10^3 =$	1,000.	" " " " "	1,000.	$= 3$
$10^4 =$	10,000.	" " " " "	10,000.	$= 4$

This table can of course be extended up or down indefinitely.

The next step is to consider the significance of fractional or decimal powers of 10 such as $10^{1.25}$ or $10^{3.451\,172}$. It is obvious that the value of $10^{1.25}$ lies between 10^1 and 10^2 and therefore between 10 and 100. (It is 17.783.) Likewise $10^{3.451\,172}$ lies between 10^3 and 10^4 and therefore between 1,000 and 10,000. (It is 2,826.)

LOGARITHMS   **27·55**

These relationships may be restated as follows: The log of 17.783 is 1.25; the log of 2,826 is 3.451 172.

From the foregoing it should be clear that the logs of all numbers other than the even powers of 10 will consist of a whole number and a decimal. The whole number part of each log can be determined by inspection. The decimal part of the log can be determined practicably only by reference to a log table.

The whole number part of a log is called the **characteristic**; the decimal part is referred to as the **mantissa**. In looking up the log of a number only the mantissa is given by the table.

CHARACTERISTICS OF LOGS. For even powers of 10, the log does not have a fractional part, as is evident from the tabulation above. For numbers from 1 to 10, the characteristic is 0; from 10 to 100, the characteristic is 1; from 100 to 1,000 it is 2, etc. In short, from 1 up, the characteristic is always positive and is one less than the number of digits to the left of the decimal point.

For numbers between 0 and 1, that is, for pure decimals, the characteristic is always negative and one greater than the number of zeros immediately following the decimal point.

Example 1. Numbers greater than 1:

$$\begin{array}{ll} 769 & \text{— characteristic is } 2 \\ 164.34\ — & \text{``}\qquad\text{`` } 2 \\ 16.043\ — & \text{``}\qquad\text{`` } 1 \\ 14{,}701.2\ — & \text{``}\qquad\text{`` } 4 \end{array}$$

Example 2. Pure decimals:

$$\begin{array}{ll} .6 & \text{— characteristic is } \bar{1} \\ .4302\ — & \text{``}\qquad\text{`` } \bar{1} \\ .0714\ — & \text{``}\qquad\text{`` } \bar{2} \\ .000615\ — & \text{``}\qquad\text{`` } \bar{4} \end{array}$$

LOG TABLES. Log tables are published as appendices in many mathematics books, and as separate volumes. Commonly available tables are carried out to six or seven decimals and provide sufficient accuracy for ordinary purposes. Tables up to twenty or more decimals are used for certain purposes. The logs of certain especially important numbers such as typical interest rates are often given in special tables to a considerable number of places. Kent's tables (Compound Interest and Annuity Tables) give 10-place logs of 168 fractional interest rates (in the form $1 + i$) for the most commonly useful rates from 1/20 of 1% to 10%.

The usual form of 7-place log tables (see Fig. 21 for sample page) lists the first four digits of the number down the left margin of the page, the last digit of the number across the top of the page, and the decimal part of the corresponding logs (i.e., the mantissa) in ten columns on the body of the page. Since the first two or three digits of the mantissa repeat for considerable ranges, they are often placed in a special column at the left and shown only when they change.

FINDING THE LOG OF A NUMBER. By reference to the sample page shown (Fig. 21), the technique of finding the log of a number may be illustrated. To find the log of 10,326, look down the number column at the left to number 1032 and along its line to the column headed 6. The number 9321 together with the first three nonrepeated digits at left gives the complete mantissa, .013 9321. The whole number part of the log (its **characteristic**) is 4, since the number 10,326 lies between 10,000 and 100,000. Thus the complete log is 4.013 9321. If the number had been 1,032.6, the process of finding its log would have been the

Sample Page from Table of Logarithms to Seven Decimal Places

No.		0	1	2	3	4	5	6	7	8	9
1000	000	0000	0434	0869	1303	1737	2171	2605	3039	3473	3907
01		4341	4775	5208	5642	6076	6510	6943	7377	7810	8244
02		8677	9111	9544	9977	0411	0844	1277	1710	2143	2576
03	001	3009	3442	3875	4308	4741	5174	5607	6039	6472	6905
04		7337	7770	8202	8635	9067	9499	9932	0364	0796	1228
05	002	1661	2093	2525	2957	3389	3821	4253	4685	5116	5548
06		5980	6411	6843	7275	7706	8138	8569	9001	9432	9863
07	003	0295	0726	1157	1588	2019	2451	2882	3313	3744	4174
08		4605	5036	5467	5898	6328	6759	7190	7620	8051	8481
09		8912	9342	9772	0203	0633	1063	1493	1924	2354	2784
10	004	3214	3644	4074	4504	4933	5363	5793	6223	6652	7082
1011		7512	7941	8371	8800	9229	9659	0088	0517	0947	1376
12	005	1805	2234	2663	3092	3521	3950	4379	4808	5237	5666
13		6094	6523	6952	7380	7809	8238	8666	9094	9523	9951
14	006	0380	0808	1236	1664	2092	2521	2949	3377	3805	4233
15		4660	5088	5516	5944	6372	6799	7227	7655	8082	8510
16		8937	9365	9792	0219	0647	1074	1501	1928	2355	2782
17	007	3210	3637	4064	4490	4917	5344	5771	6198	6624	7051
18		7478	7904	8331	8757	9184	9610	0037	0463	0889	1316
19	008	1742	2168	2594	3020	3446	3872	4298	4724	5150	5576
20		6002	6427	6853	7279	7704	8130	8556	8981	9407	9832
1021	009	0257	0683	1108	1533	1959	2384	2809	3234	3659	4084
22		4509	4934	5359	5784	6208	6633	7058	7483	7907	8332
23		8756	9181	9605	0030	0454	0878	1303	1727	2151	2575
24	010	3000	3424	3848	4272	4696	5120	5544	5967	6391	6815
25		7239	7662	8086	8510	8933	9357	9780	0204	0627	1050
26	011	1474	1897	2320	2743	3166	3590	4013	4436	4859	5282
27		5704	6127	6550	6973	7396	7818	8241	8664	9086	9509
28		9931	0354	0776	1198	1621	2043	2465	2887	3310	3732
29	012	4154	4576	4998	5420	5842	6264	6685	7107	7529	7951
30		8372	8794	9215	9637	0059	0480	0901	1323	1744	2165
1031	013	2587	3008	3429	3850	4271	4692	5113	5534	5955	6376
32		6797	7218	7639	8059	8480	8901	9321	9742	0162	0583
33	014	1003	1424	1844	2264	2685	3105	3525	3945	4365	4785
34		5205	5625	6045	6465	6885	7305	7725	8144	8564	8984
35		9403	9823	0243	0662	1082	1501	1920	2340	2759	3178
36	015	3598	4017	4436	4855	5274	5693	6112	6531	6950	7369
37		7788	8206	8625	9044	9462	9881	0300	0718	1137	1555
38	016	1974	2392	2810	3229	3647	4065	4483	4901	5319	5737
39		6155	6573	6991	7409	7827	8245	8663	9080	9498	9916
40	017	0333	0751	1168	1586	2003	2421	2838	3256	3673	4090
1041		4507	4924	5342	5759	6176	6593	7010	7427	7844	8260
42		8677	9094	9511	9927	0344	0761	1177	1594	2010	2427
43	018	2843	3259	3676	4092	4508	4925	5341	5757	6173	6589
44		7005	7421	7837	8253	8669	9084	9500	9916	0332	0747
45	019	1163	1578	1994	2410	2825	3240	3656	4071	4486	4902
46		5317	5732	6147	6562	6977	7392	7807	8222	8637	9052
47		9467	9882	0296	0711	1126	1540	1955	2369	2784	3198
48	020	3613	4027	4442	4856	5270	5684	6099	6513	6927	7341
49		7755	8160	8583	8997	9411	9824	0238	0652	1066	1479
1050	021	1893	2307	2720	3134	3547	3961	4374	4787	5201	5614

Fig. 21. Sample page from table of logarithms to seven decimal places.

LOGARITHMS

same, since it is composed of the same sequence of digits, except that its characteristic would have been 3 and the resulting log 3.013 9321.

In the table, the light ruling above the last four digits of some of the mantissas indicates that those four digits are to be used with the nonrepeated digits on the next lower line. For instance, the log of 10,352 is 4.015 0243; the log of 104.26 is 2.018 1177. Some tables employ an asterisk as a reminder to the user that he should go to the lower line for the first digits.

Finding the characteristic for numbers less than 10 and for decimals is simply an extension of this process as is seen by an inspection of the following:

log	10,326	=	4.013 9321	
log	1,032.6	=	3.013 9321	
log	103.26	=	2.013 9321	
log	10.326	=	1.013 9321	
log	1.0326	=	.013 9321	
log	.10326	=	−1 + .013 9321	(or 9.013 9321 − 10)
log	.010326	=	−2 + .013 9321	(or 8.013 9321 − 10)
log	.0010326	=	−3 + .013 9321	(or 7.013 9321 − 10)
log	.00010326	=	−4 + .013 9321	(or 6.013 9321 − 10)

Log .010326 can be written in the two methods shown or as $\bar{2}.0139321$, the mantissa remaining positive. All three methods are mathematically identical. The method of showing it as 8.013 9321 − 10 is preferred by some in actual calculations.

INTERPOLATION. When it is necessary to find the log of a number that is not given directly in the table, recourse may be had to interpolation. Find, for example, the log of 103,265 in the sample log table given. The table gives directly the mantissa for 103,260, which is .013 9321, and for 103,270, which is .013 9742. Since the selected number lies half-way between 103,260 and 103,270 by the general rules of interpolation its mantissa will lie half-way between the mantissas of those numbers and may be calculated as follows:

$$.013\,9321 + \tfrac{1}{2}(.013\,9742 - .013\,9321) = .013\,9532$$

Having found the mantissa, the characteristic is determined and the complete log is 5.013 9532. Similarly, it may be assumed that the log of 103,263 lies 3/10 of the way from log of 103,260 to log of 103,270. The calculation is as follows:

$$.013\,9321 + 3/10(.013\,9742 - .013\,9321) = .013\,9447$$

and the complete log is 5.013 9447.

The differences between successive mantissas on the sample page vary from 435 to 413. Most log tables include on the margins of the pages small tables of proportional parts to facilitate the calculation of the interpolation. The excerpt given is illustrative. For the number 103,263 the mantissa (using the table of proportional parts) is calculated as follows:

	P. P. 421
.1	42.1
.2	84.2
.3	126.3
.4	168.4
.5	210.5
.6	252.6
.7	294.7
.8	336.8
.9	378.9

.013 9321 + .0000126 = .013 9447

FINDING THE ANTI-LOG. Finding the number whose log is known (i.e., the anti-log) is the reverse of the process of finding the log when the number is known.

Example. Find the anti-log of 2.018 0135. Referring to Fig. 21, the given mantissa of .018 0135 is found to lie between the tabulated mantissas of .017 9927 and .018 0344, corresponding to the number 10423 and 10424, respectively. The computation is then arranged as follows:

$$2.0180135$$
$$2.0179927 \text{ corresponds to } 10423$$
$$\frac{208}{417} = .5 \text{ interpolation}$$
$$\text{Anti-log } 2.0180135 = \underline{\underline{104.235}}$$

The procedure is thus to find the next lower mantissa in the log table and to write down the number corresponding to it in the left-hand margin as well as the one at the top of the column. The difference between the given log and the next lower one (.0000208, but written simply as 208) is divided by the tabular difference (between the next lower and next higher log or 417). The quotient, .5, is added to the previously found figure. The final step is placing the decimal point. Since the given characteristic is 2, the number is 104.235.

With a characteristic of zero and the given mantissa of .018 0135 the anti-log is 1.04235. Given the logarithm 7.018 0135 − 10 the anti-log is .00104235.

USING LOGS TO SOLVE PROBLEMS. The use of logs in solving problems depends entirely on knowledge of the laws of exponents or powers. These laws may be demonstrated by setting up a series of parallel illustrations simple enough to be checked by actual arithmetic calculation.

Case I. To multiply numbers:

    a. $x^2 \times x^5 = x^7$ (by the laws of algebra)
    b. $2^2 \times 2^4 = 2^6$ (i.e., $4 \times 16 = 64$)
    c. $10^3 \times 10^4 = 10^7$ (i.e., $1{,}000 \times 10{,}000 = 10{,}000{,}000$)
    d. $10^{4.006\ 8510} \times 10^{2.012\ 1198} = 10^{6.018\ 9708} = 1{,}044{,}650$*
        (i.e., $10{,}159 \times 102.83 = 1{,}044{,}649.97$ *)

*There is a slight error if 7-place logs are used for figures as large as these. The answer is 1,044,650.

The rule illustrated by this demonstration is as follows: To multiply two or more numbers, add their logs and find the anti-log.

Example. Multiply $578.3 \times .0016122$.

    log 578.3   = 2.762153   (Table Fig. 24)
    log .0016122 = $\overline{3}$.207419   (Table Fig. 22, interpolated)
                  $\overline{1}$.969572
                  $\overline{1}$.969556   corresponds to 9323
                      $\frac{16}{46} = .3$ interpolation
    Answer   .93233

Case II. To divide numbers:

    a. $x^9 \div x^4 = x^5$ (by the laws of algebra)
    b. $2^5 \div 2^2 = 2^3$ (i.e., $32 \div 4 = 8$)
    c. $10^6 \div 10^4 = 10^2$ (i.e., $1{,}000{,}000 \div 10{,}000 = 100$)
    d. $10^{3.019\ 3240} \div 10^{1.016\ 0300} = 10^{2.003\ 2940} = 100.761$
        (i.e., $1{,}045.5 \div 10.376 = 100.761$, to 3 decimal places)
    e. $10^{1.016\ 0300} \div 10^{3.019\ 3240} = 10^{7.996\ 7060-10} = .0099244$
        (i.e., $10.376 \div 1{,}045.5 = .0099244$, to 3 decimal places)

LOGARITHMS 27·59

N.	0	1	2	3	4	5	6	7	8	9	Diff.
150	17 6091	6381	6670	6959	7248	7536	7825	8113	8401	8689	289
1	8977	9264	9552	9839	18 0126	0413	0699	0986	1272	1558	287
2	18 1844	2129	2415	2700	2985	3270	3555	3839	4123	4407	285
3	4691	4975	5259	5542	5825	6108	6391	6674	6956	7239	283
4	7521	7803	8084	8366	8647	8928	9209	9490	9771	19 0051	281
155	19 0332	0612	0892	1171	1451	1730	2010	2289	2567	2846	279
6	3125	3403	3681	3959	4237	4514	4792	5069	5346	5623	278
7	5900	6176	6453	6729	7005	7281	7556	7832	8107	8382	276
8	8657	8932	9206	9481	9755	20 0029	0303	0577	0850	1124	274
9	20 1397	1670	1943	2216	2488	2761	3033	3305	3577	3848	272
160	4120	4391	4663	4934	5204	5475	5746	6016	6286	6556	271
1	6826	7096	7365	7634	7904	8173	8441	8710	8979	9247	269
2	9515	9783	21 0051	0319	0586	0853	1121	1388	1654	1921	267
3	21 2188	2454	2720	2986	3252	3518	3783	4049	4314	4579	266
4	4844	5109	5373	5638	5902	6166	6430	6694	6957	7221	264
165	7484	7747	8010	8273	8536	8798	9060	9323	9585	9846	262
6	22 0108	0370	0631	0892	1153	1414	1675	1936	2196	2456	261
7	2716	2976	3236	3496	3755	4015	4274	4533	4792	5051	259
8	5309	5568	5826	6084	6342	6600	6858	7115	7372	7630	258
9	7887	8144	8400	8657	8913	9170	9426	9682	9938	23 0193	256

PROPORTIONAL PARTS

Diff.	1	2	3	4	5	6	7	8	9
290	29.0	58.0	87.0	116.0	145.0	174.0	203.0	232.0	261.0
289	28.9	57.8	86.7	115.6	144.5	173.4	202.3	231.2	260.1
288	28.8	57.6	86.4	115.2	144.0	172.8	201.6	230.4	259.2
287	28.7	57.4	86.1	114.8	143.5	172.2	200.9	229.6	258.3
286	28.6	57.2	85.8	114.4	143.0	171.6	200.2	228.8	257.4
285	28.5	57.0	85.5	114.0	142.5	171.0	199.5	228.0	256.5
284	28.4	56.8	85.2	113.6	142.0	170.4	198.8	227.2	255.6
283	28.3	56.6	84.9	113.2	141.5	169.8	198.1	226.4	254.7
282	28.2	56.4	84.6	112.8	141.0	169.2	197.4	225.6	253.8
281	28.1	56.2	84.3	112.4	140.5	168.6	196.7	224.8	252.9
280	28.0	56.0	84.0	112.0	140.0	168.0	196.0	224.0	252.0
279	27.9	55.8	83.7	111.6	139.5	167.4	195.3	223.2	251.1
278	27.8	55.6	83.4	111.2	139.0	166.8	194.6	222.4	250.2
277	27.7	55.4	83.1	110.8	138.5	166.2	193.9	221.6	249.3
276	27.6	55.2	82.8	110.4	138.0	165.6	193.2	220.8	248.4
275	27.5	55.0	82.5	110.0	137.5	165.0	192.5	220.0	247.5
274	27.4	54.8	82.2	109.6	137.0	164.4	191.8	219.2	246.6
273	27.3	54.6	81.9	109.2	136.5	163.8	191.1	218.4	245.7
272	27.2	54.4	81.6	108.8	136.0	163.2	190.4	217.6	244.8
271	27.1	54.2	81.3	108.4	135.5	162.6	189.7	216.8	243.9
270	27.0	54.0	81.0	108.0	135.0	162.0	189.0	216.0	243.0
269	26.9	53.8	80.7	107.6	134.5	161.4	188.3	215.2	242.1
268	26.8	53.6	80.4	107.2	134.0	160.8	187.6	214.4	241.2
267	26.7	53.4	80.1	106.8	133.5	160.2	186.9	213.6	240.3
266	26.6	53.2	79.8	106.4	133.0	159.6	186.2	212.8	239.4
265	26.5	53.0	79.5	106.0	132.5	159.0	185.5	212.0	238.5
264	26.4	52.8	79.2	105.6	132.0	158.4	184.8	211.2	237.6
263	26.3	52.6	78.9	105.2	131.5	157.8	184.1	210.4	236.7
262	26.2	52.4	78.6	104.8	131.0	157.2	183.4	209.6	235.8
261	26.1	52.2	78.3	104.4	130.5	156.6	182.7	208.8	234.9
260	26.0	52.0	78.0	104.0	130.0	156.0	182.0	208.0	234.0
259	25.9	51.8	77.7	103.6	129.5	155.4	181.3	207.2	233.1

Fig. 22. Typical page from a 6-place log table.

27·60 MATHEMATICS OF FINANCE

N.	0	1	2	3	4	5	6	7	8	9	Diff.
340	53 1479	1607	1734	1862	1990	2117	2245	2372	2500	2627	128
1	2754	2882	3009	3136	3264	3391	3518	3645	3772	3899	127
2	4026	4153	4280	4407	4534	4661	4787	4914	5041	5167	127
3	5294	5421	5547	5674	5800	5927	6053	6180	6306	6432	126
4	6558	6685	6811	6937	7063	7189	7315	7441	7567	7693	126
345	7819	7945	8071	8197	8322	8448	8574	8699	8825	8951	126
6	9076	9202	9327	9452	9578	9703	9829	9954	54 0079	0204	125
7	54 0329	0455	0580	0705	0830	0955	1080	1205	1330	1454	125
8	1579	1704	1829	1953	2078	2203	2327	2452	2576	2701	125
9	2825	2950	3074	3199	3323	3447	3571	3696	3820	3944	124
350	4068	4192	4316	4440	4564	4688	4812	4936	5060	5183	124
1	5307	5431	5555	5678	5802	5925	6049	6172	6296	6419	124
2	6543	6666	6789	6913	7036	7159	7282	7405	7529	7652	123
3	7775	7898	8021	8144	8267	8389	8512	8635	8758	8881	123
4	9003	9126	9249	9371	9494	9616	9739	9861	9984	55 0106	123
355	55 0228	0351	0473	0595	0717	0840	0962	1084	1206	1328	122
6	1450	1572	1694	1816	1938	2060	2181	2303	2425	2547	122
7	2668	2790	2911	3033	3155	3276	3398	3519	3640	3762	121
8	3883	4004	4126	4247	4368	4489	4610	4731	4852	4973	121
9	5094	5215	5336	5457	5578	5699	5820	5940	6061	6182	121
360	6303	6423	6544	6664	6785	6905	7026	7146	7267	7387	120
1	7507	7627	7748	7868	7988	8108	8228	8349	8469	8589	120
2	8709	8829	8948	9068	9188	9308	9428	9548	9667	9787	120
3	9907	56 0026	0146	0265	0385	0504	0624	0743	0863	0982	119
4	56 1101	1221	1340	1459	1578	1698	1817	1936	2055	2174	119
365	2293	2412	2531	2650	2769	2887	3006	3125	3244	3362	119
6	3481	3600	3718	3837	3955	4074	4192	4311	4429	4548	119
7	4666	4784	4903	5021	5139	5257	5376	5494	5612	5730	118
8	5848	5966	6084	6202	6320	6437	6555	6673	6791	6909	118
9	7026	7144	7262	7379	7497	7614	7732	7849	7967	8084	118
370	8202	8319	8436	8554	8671	8788	8905	9023	9140	9257	117
1	9374	9491	9608	9725	9842	9959	57 0076	0193	0309	0426	117
2	57 0543	0660	0776	0893	1010	1126	1243	1359	1476	1592	117
3	1709	1825	1942	2058	2174	2291	2407	2523	2639	2755	116
4	2872	2988	3104	3220	3336	3452	3568	3684	3800	3915	116
375	4031	4147	4263	4379	4494	4610	4726	4841	4957	5072	116
6	5188	5303	5419	5534	5650	5765	5880	5996	6111	6226	115
7	6341	6457	6572	6687	6802	6917	7032	7147	7262	7377	115
8	7492	7607	7722	7836	7951	8066	8181	8295	8410	8525	115
9	8639	8754	8868	8983	9097	9212	9326	9441	9555	9669	114

PROPORTIONAL PARTS

Diff.	1	2	3	4	5	6	7	8	9
127	12.7	25.4	38.1	50.8	63.5	76.2	88.9	101.6	114.3
126	12.6	25.2	37.8	50.4	63.0	75.6	88.2	100.8	113.4
125	12.5	25.0	37.5	50.0	62.5	75.0	87.5	100.0	112.5
124	12.4	24.8	37.2	49.6	62.0	74.4	86.8	99.2	111.6
123	12.3	24.6	36.9	49.2	61.5	73.8	86.1	98.4	110.7
122	12.2	24.4	36.6	48.8	61.0	73.2	85.4	97.6	109.8
121	12.1	24.2	36.3	48.4	60.5	72.6	84.7	96.8	108.9
120	12.0	24.0	36.0	48.0	60.0	72.0	84.0	96.0	108.0
119	11.9	23.8	35.7	47.6	59.5	71.4	83.3	95.2	107.1
118	11.8	23.6	35.4	47.2	59.0	70.8	82.6	94.4	106.2
117	11.7	23.4	35.1	46.8	58.5	70.2	81.9	93.6	105.3
116	11.6	23.2	34.8	46.4	58.0	69.6	81.2	92.8	104.4
115	11.5	23.0	34.5	46.0	57.5	69.0	80.5	92.0	103.5
114	11.4	22.8	34.2	45.6	57.0	68.4	79.8	91.2	102.6

Fig. 23. Typical page from a 6-place log table.

LOGARITHMS 27·61

N.	0	1	2	3	4	5	6	7	8	9	Diff.
545	73 6397	6476	6556	6635	6715	6795	6874	6954	7034	7113	
6	7193	7272	7352	7431	7511	7590	7670	7749	7829	7908	
7	7987	8067	8146	8225	8305	8384	8463	8543	8622	8701	
8	8781	8860	8939	9018	9097	9177	9256	9335	9414	9493	
9	9572	9651	9731	9810	9889	9968	74 0047	0126	0205	0284	79
550	74 0363	0442	0521	0600	0678	0757	0836	0915	0994	1073	
1	1152	1230	1309	1388	1467	1546	1624	1703	1782	1860	
2	1939	2018	2096	2175	2254	2332	2411	2489	2568	2647	
3	2725	2804	2882	2961	3039	3118	3196	3275	3353	3431	
4	3510	3588	3667	3745	3823	3902	3980	4058	4136	4215	
555	4293	4371	4449	4528	4606	4684	4762	4840	4919	4997	
6	5075	5153	5231	5309	5387	5465	5543	5621	5699	5777	78
7	5855	5933	6011	6089	6167	6245	6323	6401	6479	6556	
8	6634	6712	6790	6868	6945	7023	7101	7179	7256	7334	
9	7412	7489	7567	7645	7722	7800	7878	7955	8033	8110	
560	8188	8266	8343	8421	8498	8576	8653	8731	8808	8885	
1	8963	9040	9118	9195	9272	9350	9427	9504	9582	9659	
2	9736	9814	9891	9968	75 0045	0123	0200	0277	0354	0431	
3	75 0508	0586	0663	0740	0817	0894	0971	1048	1125	1202	
4	1279	1356	1433	1510	1587	1664	1741	1818	1895	1972	77
565	2048	2125	2202	2279	2356	2433	2509	2586	2663	2740	
6	2816	2893	2970	3047	3123	3200	3277	3353	3430	3506	
7	3583	3660	3736	3813	3889	3966	4042	4119	4195	4272	
8	4348	4425	4501	4578	4654	4730	4807	4883	4960	5036	
9	5112	5189	5265	5341	5417	5494	5570	5646	5722	5799	
570	5875	5951	6027	6103	6180	6256	6332	6408	6484	6560	
1	6636	6712	6788	6864	6940	7016	7092	7168	7244	7320	76
2	7396	7472	7548	7624	7700	7775	7851	7927	8003	8079	
3	8155	8230	8306	8382	8458	8533	8609	8685	8761	8836	
4	8912	8988	9063	9139	9214	9290	9366	9441	9517	9592	
575	9668	9743	9819	9894	9970	76 0045	0121	0196	0272	0347	
6	76 0422	0498	0573	0649	0724	0799	0875	0950	1025	1101	
7	1176	1251	1326	1402	1477	1552	1627	1702	1778	1853	
8	1928	2003	2078	2153	2228	2303	2378	2453	2529	2604	75
9	2679	2754	2829	2904	2978	3053	3128	3203	3278	3353	
580	3428	3503	3578	3653	3727	3802	3877	3952	4027	4101	
1	4176	4251	4326	4400	4475	4550	4624	4699	4774	4848	
2	4923	4998	5072	5147	5221	5296	5370	5445	5520	5594	
3	5669	5743	5818	5892	5966	6041	6115	6190	6264	6338	
4	6413	6487	6562	6636	6710	6785	6859	6933	7007	7082	
585	7156	7230	7304	7379	7453	7527	7601	7675	7749	7823	
6	7898	7972	8046	8120	8194	8268	8342	8416	8490	8564	74
7	8638	8712	8786	8860	8934	9008	9082	9156	9230	9303	
8	9377	9451	9525	9599	9673	9746	9820	9894	9968	77 0042	
9	77 0115	0189	0263	0336	0410	0484	0557	0631	0705	0778	

PROPORTIONAL PARTS

Diff.	1	2	3	4	5	6	7	8	9
79	7.9	15.8	23.7	31.6	39.5	47.4	55.3	63.2	71.1
78	7.8	15.6	23.4	31.2	39.0	46.8	54.6	62.4	70.2
77	7.7	15.4	23.1	30.8	38.5	46.2	53.9	61.6	69.3
76	7.6	15.2	22.8	30.4	38.0	45.6	53.2	60.8	68.4
75	7.5	15.0	22.5	30.0	37.5	45.0	52.5	60.0	67.5

Fig. 24. Typical page from a 6-place log table.

MATHEMATICS OF FINANCE

N.	0	1	2	3	4	5	6	7	8	9	Diff.
900	95 4243	4291	4339	4387	4435	4484	4532	4580	4628	4677	
1	4725	4773	4821	4869	4918	4966	5014	5062	5110	5158	
2	5207	5255	5303	5351	5399	5447	5495	5543	5592	5640	
3	5688	5736	5784	5832	5880	5928	5976	6024	6072	6120	
4	6168	6216	6265	6313	6361	6409	6457	6505	6553	6601	48
905	6649	6697	6745	6793	6840	6888	6936	6984	7032	7080	
6	7128	7176	7224	7272	7320	7368	7416	7464	7512	7559	
7	7607	7655	7703	7751	7799	7847	7894	7942	7990	8038	
8	8086	8134	8181	8229	8277	8325	8373	8421	8468	8516	
9	8564	8612	8659	8707	8755	8803	8850	8898	8946	8994	
910	9041	9089	9137	9185	9232	9280	9328	9375	9423	9471	
1	9518	9566	9614	9661	9709	9757	9804	9852	9900	9947	
2	9995	96 0042	0090	0138	0185	0233	0280	0328	0376	0423	
3	96 0471	0518	0566	0613	0661	0709	0756	0804	0851	0899	
4	0946	0994	1041	1089	1136	1184	1231	1279	1326	1374	
915	1421	1469	1516	1563	1611	1658	1706	1753	1801	1848	
6	1895	1943	1990	2038	2085	2132	2180	2227	2275	2322	
7	2369	2417	2464	2511	2559	2606	2653	2701	2748	2795	
8	2843	2890	2937	2985	3032	3079	3126	3174	3221	3268	
9	3316	3363	3410	3457	3504	3552	3599	3646	3693	3741	
920	3788	3835	3882	3929	3977	4024	4071	4118	4165	4212	
1	4260	4307	4354	4401	4448	4495	4542	4590	4637	4684	
2	4731	4778	4825	4872	4919	4966	5013	5061	5108	5155	
3	5202	5249	5296	5343	5390	5437	5484	5531	5578	5625	
4	5672	5719	5766	5813	5860	5907	5954	6001	6048	6095	47
925	6142	6189	6236	6283	6329	6376	8423	6470	6517	6564	
6	6611	6658	6705	6752	6799	6845	6892	5939	6986	7033	
7	7080	7127	7173	7220	7267	7314	7361	7408	7454	7501	
8	7548	7595	7642	7688	7735	7782	7829	7875	7922	7969	
9	8016	8062	8109	8156	8203	8249	8296	8343	8390	8436	
930	8483	8530	8576	8623	8670	8716	8763	8810	8856	8903	
1	8950	8996	9043	9090	9136	9183	9229	9276	9323	9369	
2	9416	9463	9509	9556	9602	9649	9695	9742	9789	9835	
3	9882	9928	9975	97 0021	0068	0114	0161	0207	0254	0300	
4	97 0347	0393	0440	0486	0533	0579	0626	0672	0719	0765	
935	0812	0858	0904	0951	0997	1044	1090	1137	1183	1299	
6	1276	1322	1369	1415	1461	1508	1554	1601	1647	1693	
7	1740	1786	1832	1879	1925	1971	2018	2064	2110	2157	
8	2203	2249	2295	2342	2388	2434	2481	2527	2573	2619	
9	2666	2712	2758	2804	2851	2897	2943	2989	3035	3082	
940	3128	3174	3220	3266	3313	3359	3405	3451	3497	3543	
1	3590	3636	3682	3728	3774	3820	3866	3913	3959	4005	
2	4051	4097	4143	4189	4235	4281	4327	4374	4420	4466	
3	4512	4558	4604	4650	4696	4742	4788	4834	4880	4926	
4	4972	5018	5064	5110	5156	5202	5248	5294	5340	5386	46
945	5432	5478	5524	5570	5616	5662	5707	5753	5799	5845	
6	5891	5937	5983	6029	6075	6121	6167	6212	6258	6304	
7	6350	6396	6442	6488	6533	6579	6625	6671	6717	6763	
8	6808	6854	6900	6946	6992	7037	7083	7129	7175	7220	
9	7266	7312	7358	7403	7449	7495	7541	7586	7632	7678	

PROPORTIONAL PARTS

Diff.	1	2	3	4	5	6	7	8	9
47	4.7	9.4	14.1	18.8	23.5	28.2	32.9	37.6	42.3
46	4.6	9.2	13.8	18.4	23.0	27.6	32.2	36.8	41.4
45	4.5	9.0	13.5	18.0	22.5	27.0	31.5	36.0	40.5
44	4.4	8.8	13.2	17.6	22.0	26.4	30.8	35.2	39.6
43	4.3	8.6	12.9	17.2	21.5	25.8	30.1	34.4	38.7

Fig. 25. Typical page from a 6-place log table.

LOGARITHMS 27·63

The rule illustrated by this demonstration is as follows: To divide one number into another, subtract the log of the divisor from the log of the dividend and find the anti-log.

Example 1. Divide 563.41 by 15.532.

$$\begin{aligned}
\log 563.41 &= 2.750825 \\
\log 15.532 &= 1.191227 \\
\hline
&1.559598 \\
&1.559548 \quad \text{corresponds to 3627} \\
\hline
&\frac{50}{119} = .4 \text{ interpolation}
\end{aligned}$$

Answer 36.274

Example 2. Divide 54.83 by .09464

$$\begin{aligned}
\log 54.83 &= 1.739018 \\
\log .09464 &= \overline{2}.976075 \\
\hline
&2.762943 \\
&2.762904 \quad \text{corresponds to 5793} \\
\hline
&\frac{39}{74} = .5 \text{ interpolation}
\end{aligned}$$

Answer 579.35

Note that in subtracting the negative from the positive characteristic, it is necessary to change the sign of the former, then add.

Case III. To raise to a power:

    a. $(x^2)^4 = x^{2 \times 4} = x^8$ (by the laws of algebra)
    b. $(2^3)^4 = 2^{3 \times 4} = 2^{12}$ [i.e., $(8)^4 = 2^{12} = 4,096$]
    c. $(10^4)^2 = 10^{4 \times 2} = 10^8$ [i.e., $(10,000)^2 = 10^8 = 100,000,000$]
    d. $(10^{3.017\ 8677})^3 = 10^{9.053\ 6031} = 1,131,400,000$ *
    [i.e., $(1,042)^3 = 1,131,366,088$ by actual multiplication]

* A six-place table yields this answer; a seven-place table yields 1,131,370,000.

The rule illustrated by this demonstration is as follows: To raise any number to a power, multiply its log by the exponent of the power and find the anti-log.

Example. Case III is applicable to compound interest problems where annuity or interest tables are not available or fail to give the desired information.

Find the compound amount of $905.40 for 10 years at 3.32%.
The formula for the compound amount developed earlier in this Section is:

$$\begin{aligned}
A &= P \times (1 + i)^n \\
A &= 905.40 \times 1.0332^{10} \\
\log A &= \log 905.40 + 10 \log 1.0332 \\
\log 905.40 &= 2.956840 \text{ (Fig. 25)} \\
\log 1.0332 &= .0141844 \\
&\underline{\times 10} \underline{.141844} \\
&3.098684 \\
&3.098644 \text{ corresponds to 1255 *} \\
&\frac{40}{346} = .1 \text{ interpolation}
\end{aligned}$$

Answer $1255.10

* Figure not given in sample table.

27·64　MATHEMATICS OF FINANCE

Case IV. To find a root:

a. $\sqrt[3]{x^{12}} = x^{12 \div 3} = x^4$ (by the laws of algebra)
b. $\sqrt[3]{2^6} = 2^{6 \div 3} = 2^2 = 4$ (i.e., $\sqrt[3]{64} = 4$)
c. $\sqrt[4]{10^8} = 10^{8 \div 4} = 10^2 = 100$ (i.e., $\sqrt[4]{100{,}000{,}000} = 100$)
d. $\sqrt[5]{10^{5.456\ 5760}} = 10^{5.456\ 5760 \div 5} = 10^{1.091\ 3152} = 12.34$
    (i.e., $\sqrt[5]{286{,}138} = 12.34$)

The rule illustrated by this demonstration is as follows: To find the root of any number, divide the log of the number by the index of the root and find the anti-log.

In the following illustrations, finding the value of n is equivalent to extracting the nth root.

Example 1. How long will it take for 1,675 to accumulate to 2,000 at 3% per annum?

$$A = P \times (1+i)^n$$
$$2000 = 1675 \times (1.03)^n$$
$$\log 2000 = \log 1675 + n \log (1.03)$$
$$n \log 1.03 = \log 2000 - \log 1675$$
$$n = \frac{\log 2000 - \log 1675}{\log 1.03}$$
$$= \frac{3.301030 - 3.224015}{.012837}$$
$$= \frac{.077015}{.012837} = 6$$
$$n = 6 \text{ years}$$

Example 2. Company A on July 1, 1965, issued $300,000 bonds, 6%, interest payable semi-annually. The bonds are in denominations of $1,000 and are to be redeemed at par and accrued interest. How long will it take to pay them off if the corporation has budgeted $25,000 each period for interest and bond redemption?

$$A_0 = R \times a_{\overline{n}|i}$$

$$300{,}000 = 25{,}000 \times \frac{1 - \frac{1}{1.03^n}}{.03}$$

$$\frac{300{,}000 \times .03}{25{,}000} = 1 - \frac{1}{1.03^n}$$

$$.36 = 1 - \frac{1}{1.03^n}$$

$$\frac{1}{1.03^n} = 1 - .36 = .64$$

$$1.03^n = \frac{1}{.64}$$

$$n \log 1.03 = \log 1 - \log .64$$
$$n = \frac{\log 1 - \log .64}{\log 1.03}$$
$$n = \frac{0 - \overline{1}.806180}{.012837} = \frac{-(-1 + .806180)}{.012837}$$
$$= \frac{-(-.193820)}{.012837} = \frac{.193820}{.012837}$$
$$n = \underline{15.1} \text{ semi-annual periods.}$$

LOGARITHMS 27·65

Case V. Successive calculations: When the solution of a practical problem requires several successive calculations, the final result may often be determined by a careful manipulation of the logs without the necessity of finding the antilogs for partial solutions.

Example 1. A corporation on January 1, 1967, issued bonds due January 1, 1975, in the amount of \$250,000. The bonds are to be retired by a sinking fund to which semi-annual payments are to be made. If the fund earns 1.7% per period on an average, what is the size of each payment?

The formula developed earlier in this section is

$$R = A_n \times \frac{1}{s_{\overline{n}|i}}$$

There are 16 payments. Hence

$$R = 250{,}000 \times \frac{1}{s_{\overline{16}|.017}}$$

Since 1.7% is not in the table (Fig. 13), logs must be used.

$$R = 250{,}000 \times \frac{.017}{1.017^{16} - 1}$$

$$= 250{,}000 \times \frac{.017}{1.3096 - 1}$$

$$= 250{,}000 \times \frac{.017}{.3096}$$

$$\log 1.017 = .007321$$
$$\times 16$$
$$\overline{.117136}$$
$$.116940 \text{ corresponds to } 1309$$
$$\frac{196}{331} = .6 \text{ interpolation}$$

$$1.017^{16} = 1.3096$$

The calculation of 1.017^{16} is shown above to the right. Its value is then substituted in the formula. The problem can now be finished by logs.

$$\begin{aligned}
\log 250{,}000 &= 5.397940 \\
+ \log .017 &= \overline{2}.230449 \\
- \log .3096 &= \overline{(1.490801)}^* \\
\log R &= \overline{4.137588}
\end{aligned}$$

$$4.137354 \text{ corresponds to } 1372$$
$$\frac{234}{317} = .7 \text{ interpolation}$$

$$R = \$13{,}727$$

*Figure not given in sample table.

Example 2. The calculation of the geometric average of ten numbers requires the finding of the product of the ten numbers, and then the extraction of the 10th root of the product. Using logs, this is accomplished as follows:

$$\begin{aligned}
\log 16 &= 1.204\ 1200 \\
\log 18 &= 1.255\ 2725 \\
\log 19 &= 1.278\ 7536 \\
\log 19.2 &= 1.283\ 3012 \\
\log 19.6 &= 1.292\ 2561 \\
\log 19.9 &= 1.298\ 8531 \\
\log 20 &= 1.301\ 0300 \\
\log 20.5 &- 1.311\ 7539 \\
\log 21 &= 1.322\ 2193 \\
\log 23 &- 1.361\ 7278 \\
\log \text{ of the product} &= 12.909\ 2875 \\
\log \text{ of the 10}^{\text{th}} \text{ root} &= 12.909\ 2875 \div 10 = 1.290\ 9288
\end{aligned}$$

10th root = geometric average = 19.5402

SOURCES

In the preparation of the FINANCIAL HANDBOOK, reference has been made to virtually the entire literature of finance and related areas. With full appreciation for the value and significance of the contributions to the field made by the authors and publishers of all of these works, the editor of the HANDBOOK wishes to give special acknowledgment to the publications cited in the Fourth Edition.

Special acknowledgment is also made to organizations and government agencies for materials from their journals, bulletins, reports, transactions, and research.

Books, Periodicals, and Reports

Accounting and Reporting Standards for Corporate Financial Statements and Preceding Statements and Supplements. Columbus, Ohio: American Accounting Asso.

Accounting Research and Terminology Bulletins, Final Edition. New York: American Institute of Certified Public Accountants, 1961.

Accounting Review

Accounting Series Release No. 4, Administrative Policy on Financial Statements. Washington, D.C.: Securities and Exchange Commission.

Accounting Series Release No. 27. Washington, D.C.: Securities and Exchange Commission.

Accounting Trends and Techniques. 16th ed. New York: American Institute of Certified Public Accountants, 1962.

ALLEN, WILLIAM R., and ALLEN, CLARK LEE (eds.). *Foreign Trade and Finance—Essays in International Economic Equilibrium and Adjustment.* New York: The Macmillan Co., 1959.

The American Economic Review

AMLING, FREDERICK. *Some Determinants of Capital Expenditure Decision in the Largest Industrial, Public Utility, Transportation and Merchandising Corporations in the United States.* Oxford, Ohio: School of Bus. Adm., Miami U., 1963.

ANDERSON, WILLIAM H. *Taxation and the American Economy: An Economic, Legal, and Administrative Analysis.* Englewood Cliffs, N.J.: Prentice-Hall, Inc., 1951.

ANGELL, FRANK J. *Insurance—Principles and Practices.* New York: The Ronald Press Co., 1959.

Annual Rate Turnover of Demand Deposits. New York: Federal Reserve Bank.

Annual Report of the Board of Governors of the Federal Reserve System. Washington, D.C.: Board of Governors, Federal Reserve System.

Annual Reports of the Federal Deposit Insurance Corporation. Washington, D.C.: Federal Deposit Insurance Corporation.

Annual Reports of the S.E.C. Washington, D.C.: Securities and Exchange Commission.

Annual Statistics of Electric Utilities in the United States, Privately Owned. Washington, D.C.: Federal Power Commission.

Annual Statistics of Electric Utilities in the United States, Publicly Owned. Washington, D.C.: Federal Power Commission.

Annual Statistics of Railways in the United States. Washington, D.C.: Interstate Commerce Commission.

ANTHONY, ROBERT N. *Management Accounting—Text and Cases.* Rev. ed. Homewood, Ill.: Richard D. Irwin, Inc., 1960.

ASCHHEIM, JOSEPH. *Techniques of Monetary Control.* Baltimore: Johns Hopkins Press, 1961.

Bank of England Weekly Returns

BARDES, PHILIP; BARNES, WILLIAM T.; FISH, JAMES B., JR.; STUETZER, HERMAN, JR.; and YAGER, PAUL D. (eds.). *Montgomery's Federal Taxes*. 39th ed. New York: The Ronald Press Co. 1964.

BARGES, ALEXANDER. *The Effect of Capital Structure on the Cost of Capital*. Englewood Cliffs, N.J.: Prentice-Hall, Inc., 1963.

BEAMAN, WALTER H. *Paying Taxes to Other States—State and Local Taxation of Non-Resident Businesses*. New York: The Ronald Press Co., 1963.

BELLEMORE, DOUGLAS H. *Investments: Principles, Practices and Analysis*. 2d ed. New York: Simmons-Boardman, 1960.

BERGH, LOUIS O., CONYNGTON, THOMAS, and KASSOFF, EDWIN. *Business Law*. 6th ed. New York: The Ronald Press Co., 1964.

Best's Digest of Insurance Stocks

Best's Fire and Casualty Aggregates

BEUTEL, FREDERICK K. (ed.). *Brannan's Negotiable Instruments Law*. 7th ed. Cincinnati, Ohio: W. H. Anderson Co.

BIERMAN, HAROLD, JR., and SMIDT, SEYMOUR. *The Capital Budgeting Decision*. New York: The Macmillan Co., 1960.

Blue List Daily. New York: Blue List Publishing Co.

BOGEN, J. I., and KROOS, H. *Security Credit: Its Economic Role and Regulation*. Englewood Cliffs, N.J.: Prentice-Hall, Inc., 1960.

BONBRIGHT, JAMES C. *The Valuation of Property; A Treatise on the Appraisal of Property for Different Legal Purposes*. 2 vols. Published under the auspices of the Columbia University Council for Research in the Social Sciences. New York: McGraw-Hill Book Co., Inc., 1937.

BONBRIGHT, JAMES C., and MEANS, G. C. *The Holding Company; Its Public Significance and Its Regulation*. New York: McGraw-Hill Book Co., Inc., 1932.

BRAINARD, CALVIN H. *Automobile Insurance*. Homewood, Ill.: Richard D. Irwin, Inc., 1961.

BRYANT, W. R. *Mortgage Lending*. 2d ed. New York: McGraw-Hill Book Co., Inc., 1962.

BUCHANAN, N. S. *The Economics of Corporate Enterprise*. New York: Holt, Rinehart & Winston, Inc., 1940.

BURTCHETT, F. F., and HICKS, C. M. *Corporation Finance*. 3d ed. Lincoln, Neb.: Johnsen Publishing Co., 1959.

Business Combinations, Bulletin No. 48. Committee on Accounting Procedure. New York: American Institute of Certified Public Accountants.

The Cash Budget. Policyholders Service Bureau. New York: Metropolitan Life Insurance Co.

Cash Flow Analysis for Managerial Control, N.A.A. Research Report No. 38. New York: National Association of Accountants.

CLENDENIN, JOHN C. *Introduction to Investments*. 3d ed. New York: McGraw-Hill Book Co., Inc., 1960.

Columbia Law Review

The Commercial Banking Industry, a monograph prepared for the Commission on Money and Credit by the American Bankers Association. Englewood Cliffs, N.J.: Prentice-Hall, Inc., 1962.

Commodity Chart Service Weekly. New York: Commodity Research Bureau, Inc.

Commodity Futures Correspondence Course. New York: Association of Commodity Exchange Firms, Inc.

Commodity Yearbooks. New York: Commodity Research Bureau, Inc.

Company Organization of the Finance Function, Research Study 55. New York: American Management Association.

COMRIE, L. J. (ed.). *Chambers' Six Figure Mathematical Tables*. 2 vols., 2d ed. Princeton, N.J.: D. Van Nostrand Co., Inc., 1949.

Condition of Weekly Reporting Member Banks in New York and Chicago, H43. New York: Federal Reserve Bank.

Conference on Research in Business Finance. Universities–National Bureau Committee for Economic Research. Princeton, N.J.: Princeton University Press, 1952.

Consolidated Financial Statements, Accounting Research Bulletin No. 51. New York: American Institute of Certified Public Accountants.
Consumers Monthly Price Index. Wash., D.C.: U.S. Dept. of Labor and Statistics.
Controlling Capital Expenditures, Studies in Business Policy, No. 62. New York: National Industrial Conference Board, Inc.
Corporate Mergers and Acquisitions; Basic Financial, Legal and Policy Aspects. New York: American Management Association, 1958.
Credit Union Year Books. Madison, Wis.: Credit Union National Association.
CROSSE, HOWARD D. *Management Policies for Commercial Banks.* Englewood Cliffs, N.J.: Prentice-Hall, Inc., 1962.
CRUMP, N. E. *ABC of the Foreign Exchanges.* 13 ed. London: Macmillan, 1963.
Current Application of Direct Costing, Research Report No. 37. New York: National Association of Accountants.
CURTIS, EDWARD T. *Company Organization of the Finance Function, Research Study No. 55.* New York: American Management Association.
The Daily Bond Buyer. New York: The Bond Buyer.
Daily Statement of the U.S. Treasury
DEAN, JOEL. *Capital Budgeting.* New York: Columbia University Press, 1951.
DEAN, JOEL. *Managerial Economics.* Englewood Cliffs, N.J.: Prentice-Hall, Inc. 1951.
DENZ, R. E. *Lease Provisions Designed To Meet Changing Economic Conditions.* The University of Illinois Law Forum, Fall, 1952.
Depreciation Guidelines and Rules, Internal Revenue Service Publication No. 456 (7–62). U.S. Treasury Dept. Wash., D.C.: Government Printing Office, 1962.
DEWING, ARTHUR J. *The Financial Policy of Corporations.* 2 vols., 5th ed. New York: The Ronald Press Co., 1953.
DICKEY, ROBERT I. (ed.). *Accountants' Cost Handbook.* 2d ed. New York: The Ronald Press Co., 1960.
DONALDSON, E. F., and PFAHL, J. K. *Corporate Finance—Policy and Management.* 2d ed. New York: The Ronald Press Co., 1963.
DONALDSON, GORDON. *Corporate Debt Capacity: A Study of Corporate Debt Policy and the Determination of Corporate Debt Capacity.* Boston: Harvard University, Graduate School of Business Administration, 1961.
Dun and Bradstreet, Inc., Analytical Report
Dun and Bradstreet, Inc., Reference Book
Economic Monthly Indicators. Joint Economic Committee of Congress. Washington, D.C.: U.S. Government, Superintendent of Documents.
EINZIG, P. *A Dynamic Theory of Forward Exchange.* N.Y.: Macmillan, 1961.
EINZIG, P. *Foreign Dollar Loans in Europe.* London: Macmillan, 1965.
Employee Retirement Systems of State and Local Governments. United States Bureau of the Census. Washington, D.C.: Government Printing Office, 1962.
Executive Committee Control Charts. Wilmington, Del.: E. I. DuPont de Nemours & Co., 1959.
EWALT, J. E. *A Business Reborn.* Chicago: American Savings and Loan Institute Press, 1952.
Factors Affecting Bank Reserve and Condition. Weekly Statement of Federal Reserve Banks, H41. Consolidated Statement of Condition of 12 Federal Reserve Banks. New York: Board of Governors, Federal Reserve System.
Factory (formerly *Factory Management and Maintenance*)
Facts and Figures—Mutual Savings Banking Annual. New York: National Association of Mutual Savings Banks.
Federal Reserve Monthly Bulletin
The Federal Reserve System, Purposes and Functions. 4th ed. Washington, D.C.: Board of Governors, Federal Reserve System, 1961.
The Federal Reserve and the Treasury, a study prepared by the Commission on Money and Credit. Englewood Cliffs, N.J.: Prentice-Hall, Inc., 1963.
Federal Reserve Weekly Statement
Federal Securities Weekly Law Reports. New York: Commerce Clearing House.
FILER, HERBERT, SR. *Understanding Put and Call Options.* N.Y.: Crown, 1959.

Financial Executive
FINNEY, H. A., and MILLER, H. E. *Principles of Accounting: Intermediate.* 5th ed. Englewood Cliffs, N.J.: Prentice-Hall, Inc., 1958.
FLETCHER, WILLIAM M. *Cyclopedia of the Law of Private Corporations.* 20 vols. Permanent ed., supplemented. Chicago, Ill.: Callaghan & Co.
Forecasting Financial Requirements, Financial Management Series No. 87. New York: American Management Association.
Fortune
FOULKE, ROY A. *Practical Financial Statement Analysis.* 5th ed. New York: McGraw-Hill Book Co., Inc., 1961.
FOULKE, ROY A. *Twenty-Five Years of the Fourteen Important Ratios.* New York: Dun and Bradstreet, Inc., 1957.
14 Important Ratios in 72 Lines of Business. N.Y.: Dun and Bradstreet, Inc., 1962.
FOUSEK, PETER G. *Foreign Central Banking: The Instruments of Monetary Policy.* New York: The Federal Reserve Bank, 1957.
FRIEDMAN, M. *A Program for Monetary Stability.* N.Y.: Fordham U. Pr., 1960.
Fundamentals of Investment Banking. 7th print. Investment Bankers Association of America. Englewood Cliffs, N.J.: Prentice-Hall, Inc., 1962.
Futures Market Service Weekly. New York: Commodity Research Bureau, Inc.
GAINES, T. C. *Techniques of Treasury Debt Management.* New York: Free Press of Glencoe, Inc., 1962.
GARDNER, FRED V. *Variable Budget Control Through Management by Exception and Dynamic Costs.* New York: McGraw-Hill Book Co., Inc., 1940.
GARRETT, WILLIAM B. *Legal Aspects of Land Trusts.* Chicago, Ill.
The George Washington Law Review
GERSTENBERG, CHARLES W. *Financial Organization and Management of Business.* 4th ed., rev. Englewood Cliffs, N.J.: Prentice-Hall, Inc., 1959.
Getting the Most Out of Your Computer. New York: McKinsey and Company, Inc., 1963.
GOLD, GERALD. *Modern Futures Trading.* New York: Commodity Research Bureau, Inc., 1959 (rev. 1961).
GORDON, MYRON J. *The Investment, Financing and Valuation of the Corporation.* Homewood, Ill.: Richard D. Irwin, Inc., 1962.
GORDON, ROBERT A. *Business Leadership in the Large Corporation.* Washington, D.C.: Brookings Institution, 1945.
GRAHAM, BENJAMIN, DODD, DAVID L., and COTTLE, SIDNEY. *Security Analysis—Principles and Techniques.* 4th ed. New York: McGraw-Hill Book Co., Inc., 1962.
GRAHAM, W. J., and KATZ, W. G. *Accounting in Law Practice.* Chicago: Callaghan & Co.
GRANGE, WILLIAM J., and WOODBURY, THOMAS C. *Corporation Law for Officers and Directors—Operating Procedures.* 2d ed. New York: The Ronald Press Co., 1964.
GRANT, EUGENE L., and NORTON, PAUL T., JR. *Depreciation.* Rev. printing. New York: The Ronald Press Co., 1955.
GREENE, MARK R. *Risk and Insurance.* Cincinnati, Ohio: South-Western Publishing Co., Inc., 1962.
GUTHMANN, H. G., and DOUGALL, H. E. *Corporate Financial Policy.* 4th ed. Englewood Cliffs, N.J.: Prentice-Hall, Inc., 1962.
Harvard Business Review
HAYES, DOUGLAS A. *Investments: Analysis and Management.* New York: The Macmillan Co., 1961.
HECKERT, J. BROOKS, and WILLSON, JAMES D. *Business Budgeting and Control.* 2d ed. New York: The Ronald Press Co., 1955.
HEISER, HERMAN C. *Budgeting—Principles and Practice.* New York: The Ronald Press Co., 1959.
HICKMAN, WALTER B. *Corporate Bond Quality and Investor Experience,* National Bureau of Economic Research. Princeton, N.J.: Princeton University Press, 1958.
HOAGLAND, H. E., and STONE, L. D. *Real Estate Finance.* Rev. ed. Homewood, Ill.: Richard D. Irwin, Inc., 1961.

SOURCES A·5

HOFFMAN, GEORGE W. *Futures Trading Upon Organized Commodity Markets in the United States.* Philadelphia: University of Pennsylvania Press, 1932.

HOFFMAN, RAYMOND A. *Inventories—A Guide to Their Control, Costing, and Effect Upon Income and Taxes.* New York: The Ronald Press Co., 1962.

HOLDEN, P. E., FISH, L. S., and SMITH, U. L. *Top-Management Organization and Control.* New ed. New York: McGraw-Hill Book Co., Inc., 1951.

HOLMES, A. R. *The New York Foreign Exchange Market.* New York: The Federal Reserve Bank, 1959.

HOMER, SIDNEY. *A History of Interest Rates.* New Brunswick, N.J.: Rutgers University Press, 1963.

HORNGREN, CHARLES T. *Cost Accounting—A Managerial Approach.* Englewood Cliffs, N.J.: Prentice-Hall, Inc., 1962.

HUEBNER, S. S., and BLACK, KENNETH, JR. *Life Insurance.* 5th ed. New York: Appleton-Century-Crofts, Inc., 1958.

HUEBNER, S. S. and BLACK, KENNETH, JR. *Property Insurance.* New York: Appleton-Century-Cofts, Inc., 1957.

HUNT, PEARSON, WILLIAMS, CHARLES M., and DONALDSON, GORDON. *Basic Business Finance.* Rev. ed. Homewood, Ill.: Richard D. Irwin, Inc., 1961.

HUSBAND, W. H., and DOCKERAY, J. C. *Modern Corporation Finance.* 5th ed. Homewood, Ill.: Richard D. Irwin, Inc., 1962.

Instructions of the Comptroller of the Currency Relative to the Organization and Powers of National Banks. Washington, D.C.: Government Printing Office.

Interpretive Opinion Bulletin No. 1. Accounting Principles Board. New York: American Institute of Certified Public Accountants.

Interpretive Opinion Bulletin No. 3. Accounting Principles Board. New York: American Institute of Certified Public Accountants.

Investment Companies, 1962. New York: Arthur Wiesenberger and Co.

Investment Outlook Annual. New York: Bankers Trust Co.

JOHNSON, ELLIOT A. *Corporate Insurance: Management and Markets, Report No. 38.* New York: American Management Association.

JOHNSON, ROBERT W. *Financial Management.* Boston, Mass.: Allyn & Bacon, Inc., 1959.

JORDAN, DAVID, and DOUGALL, HERBERT E. *Investments.* 7th ed. Englewood Cliffs, N.J.: Prentice-Hall, Inc., 1960.

The Journal of Accountancy
Journal of American Insurance
The Journal of Business
The Journal of Commerce
The Journal of Finance
Journal of Risk and Insurance

KAHN, S. A., CASE, F. E., and SCHIMMEL, A. *Real Estate Appraisal and Investment.* New York: The Ronald Press Co., 1963.

KELLEY, RICHARD E. (ed.). *S.B.I.C.'s—Suppliers of Venture Capital.* Annual. Los Angeles, Calif.: Keyfax Publications, Inc.

KENEN, P. B. *International Economics.* Englewood Cliffs, Prentice–Hall, 1964.

KENT, FREDERICK C., and KENT, MAUDE E. *Compound Interest and Annuity Tables.* New York: McGraw-Hill Book Co., Inc.

KENT, RAYMOND P. *Corporate Financial Management.* Homewood, Ill.: Richard D. Irwin, Inc., 1960.

KETCHUM, MARSHALL D., and KENDALL, LEON T. *Readings in Financial Institutions.* Boston: Houghton Mifflin Co., 1965.

KINLEY, JOHN R. *Corporate Directorship Practices; Studies in Business Policy, No. 103.* Rev. ed. New York: National Industrial Conference Board.

KLAMAN, S. B. *The Post-War Rise of Mortgage Companies.* Occasional Paper 60, National Bureau of Economic Research, 1959.

KOHLER, ERIC L. *A Dictionary for Accountants.* 3d ed. Englewood Cliffs, N.J.: Prentice-Hall Inc., 1963.

KRATOVIL, R. *Real Estate Law.* 3d ed. Englewood Cliffs, N.J.: Prentice Hall, 1958.

KREPS, CLIFTON H., JR. *Money, Banking, and Monetary Policy.* New York: The Ronald Press Company, 1962.
KREPS, C. H., JR., and LAPKIN, D. T. *Improving the Competition for Funds Between Commercial Banks and Thrift Institutions,* Research Paper 11. Chapel Hill, N.C.: School of Business Administration, University of North Carolina.
KREPS, CLIFTON H., JR., and LAPKIN, DAVID T. *Public Regulation and Operating Conventions Affecting Sources of Funds of Commercial Banks and Thrift Institutions,* a research study prepared for the Commission on Money and Credit. New York: Commission on Money and Credit, 1960.
KULP, C. A. *Casualty Insurance.* 3d ed. New York: The Ronald Press Co., 1956.
LEFFLER, GEORGE L., and FARWELL, LORING C. *The Stock Market.* 3d ed. New York: The Ronald Press Co., 1963.
LENHART, N. J., and DEFLIESE, P. L. *Montgomery's Auditing.* 8th ed. New York: The Ronald Press Co., 1957.
LEVINSON, D. *Basic Principles of Real Estate Leases.* The University of Illinois Law Forum, Fall, 1952.
Life and Health Insurance Handbook. GREGG, D. W. (ed.). Homewood, Ill.: Richard D. Irwin, Inc., 1955.
Life Insurance Fact Book, 1964. New York: Institute of Life Insurance.
Life Insurance Review of 1963. New York: Institute of Life Insurance.
LOSS, LOUIS. *Securities Regulation.* 3 vols. 2d ed. Boston, Mass.: Little, Brown & Co., 1961.
LOSS, LOUIS, and COWETT, E. M. *Blue Sky Law.* Boston, Mass.: Little, Brown & Co., 1958.
LUDTKE, JAMES B. *The American Financial System.* Boston, Mass.: Allyn & Bacon, Inc., 1961.
LUTZ, FRIEDRICH, and LUTZ, VERA. *The Theory of Investment of the Firm.* Princeton, N.J.: Princeton University Press, 1951.
LYON, ROGER A. *Investment Portfolio Management in the Commercial Bank.* New Brunswick, N.J.: Rutgers University Press, 1960.
MCCARTHY, GEORGE D. *Acquisitions and Mergers.* New York: The Ronald Press Co., 1963.
MACDONALD, D. L. *Business Risk Management.* New York: The Ronald Press Co.
MCGILL, DAN M. (ed.). *All Lines Insurance.* Homewood, Ill.: Richard D. Irwin, Inc., 1960.
The Magazine of Prefabrication
MAGEE, JOHN H. *General Insurance.* 6th ed. Homewood, Ill.: Richard D. Irwin, Inc., 1961.
MAGEE, JOHN H. *Property Insurance.* 3d ed. Homewood, Ill.: Richard D. Irwin, Inc., 1955.
Managing Company Cash, Studies in Business Policy, No. 99. New York: National Industrial Conference Board, Inc.
MASON, PERRY. *"Cash Flow" Analysis and the Funds Statement, Accounting Research Study No. 2.* New York: American Institute of Certified Public Accountants.
MEHR, ROBERT I., and CAMMACK, EMERSON. *Principles of Insurance.* 3d ed. Homewood, Ill.: Richard D. Irwin, Inc., 1961.
MEHR, ROBERT I., and HEDGES, R. A. *Risk Management in the Business Enterprise.* Homewood, Ill.: Richard D. Irwin, Inc., 1963.
MEHR, ROBERT I., and OSLER, R. W. *Modern Life Insurance.* 3d ed. New York: The Macmillan Co., 1961.
Member Bank Call Reports. Federal Reserve Board. Washington, D.C.: Board of Governors, Federal Reserve System.
MICHELBACHER, G. F. *Multiple-line Insurance.* New York: McGraw-Hill Book Co., Inc., 1957.
MILL, JOHN STUART. *Principles of Political Economy—With Some of Their Applications to Social Philosophy.* ASHLEY, W. J. (ed.). New York: Augustus M. Kelley.

SOURCES

Money Borrowed Monthly Report, M.F. 4. New York: New York Stock Exchange.
Monthly Investment Plan Quarterly. New York: New York Stock Exchange.
Monthly Statistical Bulletin of the S.E.C.
Moody's Banks and Finance
Moody's Bond Survey
Moody's Dividend Record
Moody's Industrials
Moody's Municipals and Governments
Moody's Public Utilities
Moody's Transportation
MOWBRAY, A. H., and BLANCHARD, R. H. *Insurance: Its Theory and Practice in the United States.* 5th ed. New York: McGraw-Hill Book Co., Inc., 1961.
MOYER, C. A., and MAUTZ, R. K. *Functional Accounting.* 2d ed. New York: John Wiley & Sons, Inc., 1951.
MYERS, JOHN H. *Reporting of Leases in Financial Statements, Accounting Research Study No. 4.* New York: American Institute of Certified Public Accountants.
N.A.A. Bulletin
N.A.S.D. Manual D-5, ff. Washington, D.C.: National Association of Securities Dealers, Inc.
National Daily Quotation Service. New York: National Quotation Bureau, Inc.
National Monthly Bond Summary. New York: National Quotation Bureau, Inc.
National Monthly Stock Summary. New York: National Quotation Bureau, Inc.
NELSON, A. TOM. *The Impact of Leases on Financial Analysis,* Occasional Paper No. 10. East Lansing, Mich.: Bureau of Business and Economic Research, Michigan State University.
New York Stock Exchange Guide. New York: Commerce Clearing House, Inc.
1962 Annual Report to the President and Congress. Washington, D.C.: Small Business Administration.
Odd-Lot and Round-Lot Transactions Weekly. Washington, D.C.: Securities and Exchange Commission.
O'NEAL, FOREST H. *Close Corporations; Law and Practice.* 2 vols. Chicago, Ill.: Callaghan & Co., 1958.
O'NEAL, FOREST H., and DERWIN, JORDAN. *Expulsion or Oppression of Business Associates: "Squeeze-Outs" in Small Enterprises.* Prepared under the Small Business Administration Management Research Grant Program. Durham, N.C.: Duke University Press, 1961.
PACKEL, ISRAEL. *Law of Corporations.* 3d ed. New York: Matthew Bender & Co., Inc., 1956.
Par and Rate List for Collecting Checks, Drafts, Notes, Etc. Winston-Salem, N.C.: Wachovia Bank and Trust Co.
PATON, W. A., with the assistance of PATON, W. A., JR. *Corporation Accounts and Statements: An Advanced Course.* New York: The Macmillan Co., 1955.
PATON, WILLIAM A., with the assistance of PATON, WILLIAM A., JR. *Asset Accounting—An Intermediate Course.* New York: The Macmillan Co., 1952.
Percentage Leases. 9th ed. Chicago: The National Institute of Real Estate Brokers, 1957.
PFLOMM, NORMAN E. *Financial Committees, Studies in Business Policy, No. 105.* New York: National Industrial Conference Board, Inc.
Quarterly Report on Corporations, U.S. Department of Commerce. Washington, D.C.: Department of Commerce.
RAPPAPORT, LOUIS H. *S.E.C. Accounting Practice and Procedure.* 2d ed. New York: The Ronald Press Co., 1963.
Regulations of the Secretary of Agriculture Under The Commodity Exchange Act as Amended. Washington, D.C.: United States Department of Agriculture.
REIERSON, ROY L. *The Investment Outlook for 1964.* New York: Bankers Trust Company.
REMINGTON, HAROLD. *On Bankruptcy.* Rev. ed. by HUGG, JABEZ. Rochester, N.Y.: Lawyers Co-operative Publishing Co., 1963.

Report of the Special Study of Securities Markets, House Document No. 95. Washington, D.C.: Securities and Exchange Commission.

Restatement and Revision of Accounting Research Bulletins Nos. 1 through 42, Accounting Research Bulletin No. 43. New York: American Institute of Certified Public Accountants.

Restatement of Trusts (Second). 3 vols. Philadelphia, Pa.: American Law Institute, 1959.

Return on Capital as a Guide to Managerial Decisions, Research Report No. 35. New York: National Association of Accountants.

Review and Résumé, Accounting Terminology Bulletin No. 1. New York: American Institute of Certified Public Accountants.

RICKS, R. B. *Recent Trends in Institutional Real Estate Investment, Research Report 23.* Center for Real Estate and Urban Economics. University of California, Berkeley, 1964.

RIPLEY, WILLIAM Z. *Main Street and Wall Street.* Boston, Mass.: Little, Brown & Co., 1926.

ROBINSON, ROLAND I. (ed.). *Financial Institutions.* 3d ed. Homewood, Ill.: Richard D. Irwin, Inc., 1960.

ROBINSON, ROLAND I. *The Management of Bank Funds.* 2d ed. New York: McGraw-Hill Book Co., Inc., 1962.

ROBINSON, ROLAND S. *Post-War Market for State and Local Government Securities.* National Bureau of Economic Research. Princeton, N.J.: Princeton University Press, 1960.

RODDA, WILLIAM H. *Fire and Property Insurance.* Englewood Cliffs, N.J.: Prentice-Hall, Inc., 1956.

RODDA, WILLIAM H. *Inland Marine and Transportation Insurance.* 2d ed. Englewood Cliffs, N.J.: Prentice-Hall, Inc., 1958.

ROHRER, M. *State Regulation of Insurance.* Berkeley, Calif.: University of California Bureau of Public Administration, 1951.

S.E.C. Official Monthly Summary of Security Transactions and Holdings. Washington, D.C.: Government Printing Office, Superintendent of Documents.

SAMUELSON, PAUL A. *Economics—An Introductory Analysis.* New York: McGraw-Hill Book Co., Inc., 1961.

Savings and Home Financing Chart Book, Federal Home Loan Bank Board, 1963.

Savings and Loan Fact Books. Chicago, Ill.: United States Savings and Loan League.

SCHIFF, MICHAEL, and BENNINGER, LAWRENCE J. *Cost Accounting.* 2d ed. New York: The Ronald Press Co., 1963.

SCHLAUCH, WILLIAM S., and LANG, THEODORE. *Mathematics of Business and Finance.* New York: The Ronald Press Co., 1937.

SCHLAUCH, WILLIAM S., and LANG, THEODORE. *Tables for Mathematics of Business and Finance.* New York: The Ronald Press Co., 1937.

SCHULTZ, R. E., and BARDWELL, E. C. *Property Insurance.* New York: Rinehart & Co., Inc., 1959.

SCOTT, AUSTIN W. *Law of Trusts*, 5 vols., 2d ed. Boston, Mass.: Little, Brown & Co., 1956.

SCOTT, WILLIAM R. *Constitution and Finance of English, Scottish, and Irish Joint Stock Companies in 1720.* 3 vols. Gloucester, Mass.: Peter Smith, 1910–1912.

Securities Act Release No. 4552. Washington, D.C.: Securities and Exchange Commission.

SEGHERS, PAUL D., REINHART, WILLIAM J., and NIMAROFF, SELWYN. *Essentially Equivalent to a Dividend.* New York: The Ronald Press Co., 1960.

SHUBIN, JOHN A. *Managerial and Industrial Economics.* New York: The Ronald Press Co., 1961.

SNIDER, H. WAYNE (ed.). *Readings in Property and Casualty Insurance.* Homewood, Ill.: Richard D. Irwin, Inc., 1959.

SOLOMON, EZRA. *The Theory of Financial Management.* New York: Columbia University Press, 1963.

Southern Economic Journal

The Spectator Annual Insurance Yearbook. Philadelphia: Chilton Co.

SPENCER, MILTON H., and SIEGELMAN, LOUIS. *Managerial Economics—Decision Making and Forward Planning.* Homewood, Ill.: Richard D. Irwin, Inc., 1959.

Standard and Poor's Bond Guide

Standard and Poor's Dividend Record

Standard and Poor's Standard Corporation Record

Standard and Poor's Trade and Securities Statistics

Study of Check Collection System. Report of the Joint Committee on Check Collection System to the American Bankers Association, Association of Reserve City Bankers, and Conference of Presidents of the Federal Reserve Banks. New York: 1954.

Techniques in Inventory Management, Res. Rep. No. 40. N.Y.: Nat'l Asso. of Acc'ts.

THORN RICHARD S. *Monetary Theory and Policy—Major Contributions to Contemporary thought.* New York: Random House, Inc., 1966.

Time Schedules, Operating Circular No. 8. Richmond, Va.: Federal Reserve Bank

TRESCOTT, PAUL B. *Financing American Enterprise.* New York: Harper & Row, 1963.

TRIFFIN, ROBERT. *The World Money Maze.* New Haven: Yale University Press, 1966.

The Unique Manual and National Underwriter Life Reports, 1963. Cincinnati, Ohio: The National Underwriter Company.

The Variation of Costs with Volume, Research Report No. 16. New York: National Association of Accountants.

VEGA, GEORG. *Seven Place Logarithmic Tables of Numbers and Trigonometrical Functions.* Reprint. New York: Hafner Publishing Co., 1957.

VEGA, GEORG. *Ten Place Logarithms, Including Wolfram's Tables of Natural Logarithms.* Reprint from ed. of 1794. N.Y.: Hafner Publ. Co., 1958.

VORIS, WILLIAM. *The Management of Production.* New York: The Ronald Press Co., 1960.

WASHINGTON, GEORGE T., and BISHOP, JOSEPH W. *Indemnifying the Corporate Executive—Business, Legal, and Tax Aspects of Reimbursement for Personal Liability.* New York: The Ronald Press Co., 1963.

WASHINGTON, GEORGE T., and ROTHSCHILD, V. HENRY, 2D. *Compensating the Corporate Executive.* 2 vols., 3d ed. New York: The Ronald Press Co., 1962.

WATERMAN, MERWIN H. *Essays on Business Finance.* Ann Arbor, Mich.: Masterco Press, 1962.

The Weekly Bond Buyer. New York: The Bond Buyer.

WEIMER, A. M., and HOYT, H. *Principles of Real Estate.* 4th ed. New York: The Ronald Press Co., 1960.

WELFLING, WELDON. *Bank Investments.* New York: American Institute of Banking, 1963.

WESSEL, ROBERT H. *Principles of Financial Analysis; A Study of Financial Management.* New York: The Macmillan Co., 1961.

WESTON, J. FRED. *Managerial Finance.* New York: Holt, Rinehart & Winston, Inc., 1962.

WILLIAMS, JOHN B. *Theory of Investment Value.* New York: Augustus M. Kelley, 1938.

WIXON, RUFUS (ed.). *Accountants' Handbook.* 4th ed. New York: The Ronald Press Co., 1956.

Yale Law Journal

YOUNG, JOHN PARKE. *The International Economy.* 4th ed. New York: The Ronald Press Co., 1963.

Organizations and Government Agencies

AMERICAN ACCOUNTING ASSOCIATION (A.A.A.)

AMERICAN BANKERS ASSOCIATION (A.B.A.)

AMERICAN INSTITUTE OF CERTIFIED PUBLIC ACCOUNTANTS (A.I.C.P.A.)

AMERICAN INSTITUTE OF MARINE UNDERWRITERS (A.I.M.U.)

AMERICAN MUTUAL INSURANCE ALLIANCE (A.M.I.A.)

AMERICAN STOCK EXCHANGE
ASSOCIATION OF COMMODITY EXCHANGE FIRMS, INC.
BANK OF ENGLAND
BANK FOR INTERNATIONAL SETTLEMENTS
BOARD OF TRADE OF THE CITY OF CHICAGO
BUREAU OF FEDERAL CREDIT UNIONS OF THE U.S. DEPARTMENT OF HEALTH, EDUCATION, AND WELFARE
COMMODITY CLEARING CORPORATION
COMMODITY EXCHANGE COMMISSION
FEDERAL DEPOSIT INSURANCE CORPORATION (F.D.I.C.)
FEDERAL HOME LOAN BANK SYSTEM
FEDERAL HOUSING ADMINISTRATION (F.H.A.)
FEDERAL NATIONAL MORTGAGE ASSOCIATION (F.N.M.A.)
FEDERAL POWER COMMISSION (F.P.C.)
FEDERAL RESERVE BOARD
FEDERAL SAVINGS AND LOAN INSURANCE CORPORATION
FEDERAL TRADE COMMISSION (F.T.C.)
FINANCIAL ANALYSTS FEDERATION
HOUSING AND HOME FINANCE AGENCY (H.H.F.A.)
INSTITUTE OF LIFE INSURANCE
INSTITUTIONAL SECURITIES CORPORATION
INTER-AMERICAN DEVELOPMENT BANK
INTERNAL REVENUE SERVICE (I.R.S.)
INTERNATIONAL BANK FOR RECONSTRUCTION AND DEVELOPMENT (WORLD BANK)
INTERNATIONAL FINANCE CORPORATION (I.F.C.)
INTERNATIONAL MONETARY FUND (I.M.F)
INTERSTATE COMMERCE COMMISSION (I.C.C.)
INVESTMENT BANKERS ASSOCIATION OF AMERICA
INVESTMENT COMPANY INSTITUTE
LIFE INSURANCE ASSOCIATION OF AMERICA
NATIONAL ASSOCIATION OF ACCOUNTANTS (N.A.A.)
NATIONAL ASSOCIATION OF CREDIT MANAGEMENT
NATIONAL ASSOCIATION OF INSURANCE COMMISSIONERS
NATIONAL ASSOCIATION OF MUTUAL SAVINGS BANKS
NATIONAL ASSOCIATION OF SECURITIES DEALERS, INC. (N.A.S.D.)
NATIONAL AUTOMOBILE UNDERWRITERS ASSOCIATION
NATIONAL INDUSTRIAL CONFERENCE BOARD (N.I.C.B.)
NATIONAL QUOTATION BUREAU, INC.
NATIONAL RETAIL MERCHANTS ASSOCIATION
NATIONAL SAFETY COUNCIL
NEW YORK CLEARING HOUSE ASSOCIATION
NEW YORK STOCK EXCHANGE
NORTH AMERICAN SECURITIES ADMINISTRATORS (formerly, THE NATIONAL ASSOCIATION OF SECURITIES COMMISSIONERS)
PUT AND CALL BROKERS AND DEALERS ASSOCIATION, INC.
SECURITIES AND EXCHANGE COMMISSION (S.E.C.)
SMALL BUSINESS ADMINISTRATION (S.B.A.)
UNITED STATES DEPARTMENT OF AGRICULTURE
UNITED STATES DEPARTMENT OF COMMERCE
UNITED STATES DEPARTMENT OF LABOR
UNITED STATES DEPARTMENT OF THE TREASURY
VETERANS ADMINISTRATION (V.A.)

GENERAL INDEX

Bold face numbers, followed by a dot, refer to sections;
light face numbers following are the pages of the section.

Acceptance Market, 1·11–12
  Federal Reserve Banks and, 1·12
Acceptances
  Banker's, 5·31, 16·5, 24·36
  Bills of exchange, 24·32–33
  Domestic trade, 5·31
  General and qualified, 24·33
  Of time drafts, 3·9
  Trade, 3·26, 24·35–36
    Domestic, 5·31
Accommodation Paper, 5·31
Accommodation Party, Negotiable instruments, 24·20
Accountant's Certificates, 8·27–28
  Registration statements, 9·38
Accounting
  Analysis, 20·24
  Asset transfer, 20·27–29
  Cash or accrual, 8·29
  Certification of reports, 8·27–28
  Combinations, 20·24–31
  Distinction between purchase and pooling of interests, 20·29
  Effect of changes in method, 7·13
  Effect of merger or consolidation on surplus, 20·29
  For surplus reserves, 18·8–9
  Industrial concerns, 7·12–13
  Interstate Commerce Commission regulations, 8·3
  Investment banking houses, 9·26–27
  Investment companies, 4·27–30
  Securities Exchange Act requirements, 8·2–3, 10·49–50
  Standards, 10·9, 10·49–50
  Valuation of current assets, 20·28
  Valuation of intangible assets, 20·28
  Valuation of plant and equipment, 20·27–28
Accounting or Average Return Method, For evaluating investments, 17·22, 17·37
Accounts
  Chart of, 15·19
  Classification of, 8·14–16
  Receivable, 15·34, 16·6–7
    As collateral, 5·30
    As security, 5·30
    Balance sheet treatment, 8·16–17
    Credit policies and, 15·34
    Financing, 16·14–15
    Turnover, 16·10
  Trustees in bankruptcy, 22·30–31
Accrual Basis, In income statements, 8·29
Acid-Test, Statement analysis ratio, 8·32–33
Administrators, Estate, 6·6–7
  Ancillary, 6·6
  Fees and commission, 6·20

Administrators (*Continued*)
  Ordinary, 6·6
  Temporary, 6·6–7
  Trusts, 6·6–7
Advance Refundings, 11·11
  Treasury policies, 11·21
After-Acquired Property Clause, 20·14, 20·40
  Mortgage bonds, 14·19–20
Agencies
  Consumer credit, 5·34
  Corporate fiduciaries as, 6·1–24
  Fiscal agents, 6·23
  Function for corporations, 6·23–24
  Liquidating, 21·26
  Transfer agents, 6·23
Agency for International Development (A.I.D.), 3·30–31
Agents
  By estoppel, 25·29
  Coupon-paying, 6·23
  Independent contractor differs from, 25·28
  Liability for acts of, 25·28–29
  Signature on negotiable instruments, 24·7
    Authority, 24·7
  Stock subscription, 6·24
  Transfer, 6·23, 13·3
Agreements
  Creating a trust by, 6·8
  Hypothecation, 10·38
  Leases, 20·31–32
  Partnership, 12·5
  Selling group, 9·21–22
  Syndicates, 12·6–7
Alteration, Of negotiable instruments, 24·8–9
Alternative Projects
  Evaluating, 17·22
  Financial planning, 15·3
  Risk and uncertainty, 17·75–77
American Bankers Association, 2·23
American Depositary Receipts, 3·28–29, 10·10, 10·57
American Institute of Banking, 2·23
"American Shares," 10·57
American Telephone and Telegraph Co., 7·21
Amortization
  Bonded debt, 14·36
  Debt financing and, 14·4
  Finding number of payments, 27·43–44
  Of bonds, 14·36
  Of deferred charges, 8·19
Annual Meetings, 8·5
Annual Reports, 8·4–5
Annuities
  Mathematical methods, 27·30–45
    Annuity that $1 will buy, 27·42–43
    Definitions, 27·30

G·1

GENERAL INDEX

Annuities (*Continued*)
  Mathematical methods (*Continued*)
    Final value of annuity due, **27**·38–39
    Final value of ordinary annuity, **27**·30–34
      Computation by logarithms, **27**·31–34
      Formula, **27**·31
    Finding the number of payments to amortize a loan, **27**·43–44
    Present value of annuity due, **27**·45
    Present value of ordinary annuity, **27**·39–42
    Sinking fund calculations, **27**·34–38
      Finding the amount of installments, **27**·34–35
      Finding the number of payments, **27**·35–38
      Schedule of installments, **27**·38
    Tables
      Amound of annuity of $1 at end of each period, **27**·32–33
      Annuity that $1 will buy, **27**·36–37
      Present value of annuity of $1 at end of each period, **27**·40–41
  Pension plans, **19**·36
    Deferred group, **19**·11–12
Anti-Fraud Laws, **9**·45
Antitrust Legislation, **20**·6
Appraisals
  Purchase of assets, **20**·13
  Real estate, **26**·25–26
Appreciation, **17**·28
Appropriation Requests, **17**·16–18
  Approval of, **17**·18
  Blanket, **17**·18
  Forms, **17**·17
Appropriations Committees, **17**·14–16
Arbitrage, **10**·58
  Foreign exchange, **3**·11
  In securities, **3**·11, **10**·58
  Types of, **10**·58
Arrangements
  Confirmation, **22**·18
  Definition, **22**·17
  Deposit, **22**·16
  Filing a petition, **22**·17
  Proceedings, **22**·18
  Under Chapter XI, **22**·17–18
Arrearages, Preferred stock, **21**·10–14
Assets
  Accounting problems in transfer of, **20**·27–29
  Book value, **18**·5
  Capital (See also "Capital, Assets")
    Fixed, **17**·1–4
    Planning, **17**·1–77
    Surplus, **17**·7
  Classification of, **8**·13
  Collection of trust assets, **6**·11–12
  Current, **8**·16–17, **16**·1
    Administration of, **16**·4–9
    Net, **16**·1
    Planning, **16**·1–3
  Definition, **8**·13
  Distribution of, **21**·25
  Fair market value, **18**·5
  Fixed, **16**·4
    In relation to total assets, **17**·2–3
    Leasing of, **14**·42–44
    Ratio of owners' equity to, **8**·33
    Ratio to funded debt, **8**·35
    Turnover, **17**·10–11
  Intangible, **8**·18–19, **17**·1
    Fixed, **17**·2
    Valuation of, **20**·28
  Preference of preferred stock, **13**·20–21

Assets (*Continued*)
  Purchase of, **20**·8–17 (See also "Purchase of Assets")
  Ratios, in statement analysis, **8**·32–34
  Tangible fixed, **17**·2
  Wasting, **17**·33–36
  Write-downs, **21**·5–6
Assignees, Corporate fiduciary as, **6**·7
Assignments, **21**·19–22
  Act of bankruptcy, **21**·19–20
  Advantages of, **21**·19
  Assignees, **6**·7, **21**·20
    Duties of, **21**·20
  Checks used as, **24**·37
  Creditors' committees, **21**·20–22
  Legal aspects, **21**·19–20
  Rights of creditors, **21**·20
Association of Commodity Exchange Firms, Inc., **23**·31
Assumed Bonds, **14**·29–30
Auction Basis, Securities market, **10**·1–3
Auditors, Independent, **8**·28
Authority To Purchase, **3**·25–26
Authorizations, Chapter X reorganizations, **22**·15
Automobiles, Analysis of securities, **7**·14
  Insurance policies
    Liability, **25**·29
    Physical damage, **25**·20
    Type of coverage, **25**·20

Bailment Liabilities, **25**·29
Balance of Payments, **3**·1–2
  British problem, **1**·28–29
  Deficit, **1**·27
  Payments transactions, **3**·2
  Role of gold, **3**·3–4
Balance Sheets
  Analysis of, **8**·13–22
    Comparative, **8**·40–42
  Assets, **8**·13
  Brokerage houses, **10**·37
  Classification of accounts, **8**·14–16
  Comparative, **8**·40–42, **16**·17
  Condensed, **15**·2
  Contingent liabilities, **8**·20–21
  Contributed capital, **8**·21
  Credit analysis, use in, **8**·30–31
  Current assets, **8**·16–17
    Cash and cash items, **8**·16
    Determination of cost, **8**·17
    Inventories, **8**·17
    Marketable securities, **8**·16
    Notes and accounts receivable, **8**·16–17
  Current liabilities, **8**·19–20
  Deferred charges, **8**·19
  Definition, **8**·13–14
  Form, **8**·14–15
  Intangibles, **8**·18–19
  Investments, **8**·17–18
  Liabilities and equity, **8**·13–14
  Long-term (fixed) liabilities, **8**·20
  No-par stock in, **13**·8–9
    Objectionable methods of, **13**·9
  Preferred stock, **8**·21
  Projections, **15**·26–29
    Period of, **15**·26
    Review of, **15**·29
  Property, plant and equipment, **8**·18
  Ratios, **8**·32–34
    Acid-test, **8**·32–33
    Current, **8**·32
    Current liabilities to owners' equity, **8**·33
    Fixed assets to funded debt, **8**·35

GENERAL INDEX G·3

Balance Sheets (*Continued*)
 Ratios (*Continued*)
  Fixed assets to owners' equity, 8·33
  Funded debt to net working capital, 8·33
  Funded debt to total capitalization, 8·34–35
  Inventory to net working capital, 8·33–34
  Owners' equity to total assets, 8·34
 Reserve section, 18·8
 Retained earnings, 8·22
 Uniform reporting, 8·15
Balanced Funds, 4·25
Bank Credit, 2·4
 Monetary aspects, 2·9
Bank for Cooperatives, Obligations of, 11·7
"Bank Holiday," 2·24
Bank Merger Act of 1960, 2·20
Bank of Amsterdam, 2·10
Bank of England, 2·10
 Weekly statement, 1·29–30
Bank of the United States, 2·6, 2·12
Banker's Acceptances, 1·11, 2·35, 5·31, 16·5, 24·36
Banker's Bill, 1·11
Banking Acts
 Of 1864, 5·6
 Of 1933, 2·20, 5·5–6
 Of 1935, 2·20
Bankruptcy, 22·18–38
 Acts of, 22·21–23
 Adjudication of, 22·23–24, 22·40
 Adverse claimants, 22·34
 Agricultural compositions and extensions, 22·39–40
 Assignment, 21·19–22
 Bankrupts
  Concealment of property and records, 22·29–30
  Duties of, 22·29
  Examination of, 22·29
  Exemptions, 22·32
  Fraudulent transfers, 22·32–33
  Jurisdiction of courts over property of, 22·34–35
  Voidable preferences, 22·32
 Claims, 22·26–27
  Allowed, 22·28
  Unliquidated, 22·28
 Closing of bankrupt estate, 22·37
 Commencement of proceedings, 22·20
 Continuance of business, 22·33
 Courts of, 22·19–20
  Summary jurisdiction of, 22·34
 Creditor meetings, 22·26
  Voting at, 22·26
 Debts that may be proved, 22·27–28
 Declaration and payment of dividends to creditors, 22·36–37
 Discharge of, 22·37–38
  Debts not affected by, 22·38
  Revocation of, 22·38
 Federal and state laws, 22·18–19
 Indorsers, guarantors, and sureties, 22·27
 Involuntary, 22·31
 Laws, 22·18
 Partnerships, 22·33–34
 Payment of debts with priorities, 22·36
  Order of priority, 22·36
 Provisional remedies for safeguard of debtor's property, 22·24
 Purpose of, 22·18–19
 Receivers, 22·24–25
  Function of, 22·25
  Powers of, 22·25

Bankruptcy (*Continued*)
 Referees, 22·25–26
  Compensation, 22·26
  Powers and duties, 22·25–26
 Reopening of bankrupt estate, 22·31
 Sale of property, 22·35–36
 Trustees, 22·30–32
  Accounts, 22·30–31
  Compensation of, 22·31
  Duties, 22·30
  Number of, 22·30
  Title to property, 22·31
  Transfer of power and documents to, 22·31–32
 Voluntary, 22·20–21
  Petition, 22·20–21
 Wage earners' plans, 22·38–39
Bankruptcy Act of 1938, 22·3, 22·18
 Agricultural compositions and extensions, 22·39–40
 Arrangements under Chapter XI, 22·17–18
 Reorganizations under Chapter X, 22·3–9
 Wage earners' plans, 22·38–39
Banks and Banking, 2·10–24
 American Bankers Association, 2·23
 As fiduciaries, 6·1, 6·21–22
 Bank stocks, 7·15
 Branch and group banking, 2·21–23
  Controversy, 2·22–23
 Capital requirements, 5·2
 Cashier's checks, 24·36
 Central banks, 2·11
 Chain banking, 2·22
 Charter, 5·1–2
 Checking accounts (See "Checks and Checking Accounts")
 Collection services, 5·20–21
 Commercial (See "Commercial Banks")
 Competition, 2·27, 5·5
 Credit department, 5·33
 Deposits, 5·3–9, 5·14–15, 16·4–5
  Account analysis, 5·17–19
  Competition for, 5·5
  Creation of, 2·11
  Demand, 2·2, 5·3
  Federal Deposit Insurance Corporation, 2·19, 5·6–9
  In credit management, 2·11
  Liabilities of bank, 5·9
  Payment of interest, 5·5–6
  Right of set-off, 5·9
  Savings, 5·4
  Surplus cash and, 16·4–5
  Time, 5·4
  Trends in, 2·25–26
  Turnover, 1·24
 Directors, 5·2–3, 12·29
 Discount, computing, 27·12–18
 Dual system, 2·13
 Earnings, 2·27
 Evolution of banking, 2·10
 Examinations, 5·3
 Failures, 2·24
 Federal Deposit Insurance Corporation, 2·19, 5·6–9
 Federal Reserve System, 2·13–18 (See also "Federal Reserve System")
 Foreign, agencies of, 3·16–17
 Foreign branches of American, 3·15
 Foreign departments, 3·13–15
 Government regulation of, 2·19–20, 5·2–3
 Group, 2·21–23
 Historical background, 2·12–13
 Holding companies, 2·21–22, 20·46

Banks and Banking (*Continued*)
  Industrial, 2·41
  Interbank deposits, 2·11
  Interbank relations, 2·23
  International (See "International Banking")
  International Bank for Reconstruction and Development, 3·31
  International departments of, 3·13–15
  International Monetary Fund, 3·31
  Interpretation of statistics, 1·14–25
  Investment, 2·10–24, 9·8–27 (See also "Investment Banking")
  Investment department, 5·26
  Investments of, 2·26, 5·21–27, 9·6
    Department, 5·26
    Portfolio policy, 5·24–25
    Preference for government obligations, 5·22–23
    Profits from sale of, 5·25–26
    Ratio of capital funds to "risk assets," 5·25
    Real estate mortgages, 5·26–27, 26·4–6
    Securities eligible for purchase, 5·21–22
    Tax switching, 5·26
    Valuation of, 5·23–24
      Government classifications, 5·24
  Legislation, 2·12–13, 2·19–21
  Liquidity, 5·22
  Loans, 5·27–34
    Consumer, 5·34
    Credit analysis, 5·32–33
    Importance of, 5·27–28
    Line of credit, 5·33–34
    Secured, 5·29–30
    Security loans, 5·30–31
    Source of working capital, 16·14
    Types of, 5·28–29
    Uses of, 5·28
  Mergers and branches, 2·20
  Mutual savings, 26·6
  National, 2·12–13, 5·2, 6·2–3, 26·5
  Organization procedures, 5·1–3
  Paying on forged indorsements, 24·14
  Personal trust business, 6·4–7
  Portfolio policy, 5·24–25
  Privately managed, 2·10
  Proposals for banking unification, 2·23–24
  "Real bills" doctrine, 2·26
  Real estate financing, 5·26–27, 26·4–6
  Regulatory legislation, 2·12–13, 2·19–21, 5·2–9
    Availability and cost of credit, 2·20–21
    Bank supervision and examination, 2·21
    Loans and investments, 2·21
    Mergers and branches, 2·20
  Reviewing departments, 6·16
  Savings, 4·3–12 (See also "Savings Banks")
  Securities analysis departments, 6·16–17
  Services offered depositors, 5·4–5
    Checks, 5·4
    Collection services, 5·4–5, 5·19–20
    Payroll services, 5·5
  State-chartered, 2·13, 5·2, 6·2, 26·5
  Statistics, interpretation of, 1·14–25
  Stocks, 7·15
  Systems, 2·10–24
    Federal Reserve, 2·13–18 (See also "Federal Reserve System")
    Foreign, 1·27–30
    Monetary Policy, 2·28–33
    United States, 2·12–24
  Time deposits, 16·4–5
  Trends, 2·24–27
    Bank earnings, 2·27
    From 1920's to Postwar, 2·24

Banks and Banking (*Continued*)
  Trends (*Continued*)
    Growth of bank investments, 2·26
    In bank loans, 2·25–26
    Negotiable certificates of time deposit, 2·26–27
  Trust companies (See "Trust Companies")
  Trust department management, 6·4
    Services provided by, 6·18–19
  Trusts, 6·2–3 (See also "Trusts")
  "Warehousing" arrangements with life insurance companies, 26·5
Beneficiaries, of Trusts, 6·12
Benefit Payments, Pension plans, 19·21–29
Bid and Asked Quotations, 10·2–3
Bidding, Competitive, securities, 9·13
Bills of Exchange, 3·2, 24·2, 24·30–35
  Acceptance for honor, 24·35
  Acceptance of, 24·32–33
  Foreign, 24·31
  General and qualified acceptances, 24·33
  In a set, 24·30–31
  Inland, 24·2, 24·31
  Nature of, 24·30
  Presentment for acceptance, 24·31–32
  Protest for nonacceptance and nonpayment, 24·34–35
  When dishonored by nonacceptance, 24·34
  When protest is dispensed with, 24·35
  When treated as promissory note, 24·30
Bills of Lading, 5·29, 16·15
  As collateral, 5·29, 16·15
"Bills Only," Federal Reserve policy, 11·15
Bimetallic Standard, 2·3, 2·6
Blue Sky Laws, 9·43–52
  Common provision and the Uniform Securities Act, 9·45–50
  Exemptions under, 9·50–52
  Federal statutes and, 9·44
  Historical background, 9·43–44
  Promoters, 12·15
  Real estate syndicates, 12·7
  Types of, 9·44–45
Board of Directors, 12·27–33
  Authorized to declare dividends, 18·27
  Committees, 12·31–32
    Executive and finance, 12·31
    Limitations on powers, 12·31–32
  Conflict of interest, 12·33
  Consolidations approved by, 20·19
  Election, 12·28
  Financial executives, 15·37–38
  Financial planning functions, 15·36–39
    Committees, 15·38–39
    Reports to, 15·38
  Legal status, 12·27
  Liability, 12·29–30
    Imposed by statute, 12·29–30
    Indemnification, 12·30
  Meetings, 12·32–33
    Quorums, 12·32–33
    Special, 12·32
  Power to petition bankruptcy, 22·21
  Purchase of assets approved by, 20·10
  Qualifications, 12·27–28
  Resignation and removal, 12·28–39
  Statutory provisions, 12·27–29
  Stock subscription rights approved by, 13·25–26
Bond Market, Treasury policies and, 11·19–20
Bondholders
  Individual action of, 14·14–15
  Remedies of, 14·13–14
  Trustees for, under indenture, 6·22

GENERAL INDEX

G·5

Bonding Requirements, 25·24–26
  Compared with insurance, 25·24–25
  Fidelity bonds, 25·25
  Pension plans, 19·34
  Surety bonds, 25·25–26
Bonds, 14·5–42 (See also "Securities," "Stocks")
  Adjustment, 14·28
  Advantages of debt financing, 14·1–2
  Amortization schedule, 27·47
  Analysis, 7·4–8
    Convertible, 7·6
    Credit of the obligor, 7·4–5
    Earnings coverage of interest charges, 7·4
    Earnings coverage of junior bond interest, 7·5
    Objective of, 7·4
    Protective provisions of bond issue, 7·5
  "And-interest" price, 27·49
  Assumed, 14·29–30
  Basis price for bonds brought between interest dates, 27·49–52
  Bearer, 14·6
  Blue List, 10·44
  Bond room, 10·39–40
  Brokers and dealers, 10·9
  Callable, 14·35–37
    Serial bonds, 14·38
  Certification of, 14·8–9
  Characteristics, 14·5–7
  Collateral trust, 14·21–23
    Consolidations, merger, or sale of assets of subsidiary, 14·23
    Nature of security, 14·21–22
    Pledged securities, 14·22–23
    Types of, 14·21–22
  Commissions and transfer taxes, 10·41
  Convertible, 9·7, 14·30–35, 17·58
    Advantages and disadvantages, 14·31
    Conversion rights, 14·30–31
    Factors influencing conversion, 14·34
    Fixing conversion rate, 14·32
    Interest and dividend adjustments, 14·32
    Protective features against dilution or destruction, 14·33–34
    Ratio or price, 14·31–32
    Subscription privileges, 14·32–33
    Time of conversion, 14·32
    With warrants, 14·34–35
  Corporate trustees, 14·8–9, 14·10
  Costs incurred in sale of, 17·51–52
  Coupon, 10·40, 14·5–6
  Debentures, 14·25–26
    Characteristics, 14·25
    Common provisions, 14·25
    Conversion privileges, 14·26
    Subordinated, 14·26
    Use of, 14·25–26
  Deed of trust, 14·5
  Definition, 14·5, 27·45
  Denominations, 14·5
  Depositary, 11·10
  Discount, 27·47–48
  Dividends, 18·14
  Dollar, 10·44
  Equipment, 14·23
  Equipment obligations
    Character of, 14·23–24
    Conditional sale plan, 14·24
    Covenants, 14·24–25
    Equipment mortgage plan, 14·24
    Philadelphia plan, 14·24
  Fidelity, 25·25
  "Flat" price, 27·49–50
  Forfeiture, 25·25–26

Bonds (*Continued*)
  Government, 5·23 (See also "Government Securities")
  Guaranteed, 14·26–28
    Form of guaranty, 14·27
    Legal position, 14·27–28
    Purpose, 14·26
    Value of guaranty, 14·27
  Held in the treasury, 14·30
  Income, 14·28–29
    Cumulative and noncumulative, 14·28–29
    Determining income and basis of payments, 14·28
    Nature of, 14·28
    Payment of interest, 14·28
    Reasons for use of, 14·29
  Indentures, 14·7–17
    Acceleration of maturity in cases of default, 14·14
    Certification of bonds, 14·8–9
    Changes in, 14·16–17
    Conditions governing issue of, 14·12
    Consolidations and mergers, 14·16
    Corporate trustees, 14·8–9
    Grant of assignment of trust, 14·12
    Individual action of bondholders, 14·14–15
    Names of parties, 14·11
    Need for, 14·7–8
    "No recourse" clause, 14.16
    Particular covenants, 14·12–13
    Period of grace, 14·14
    Preamble, 14·11
    Provisions, 14·11–17
    Required by the Act, 14·10–11
    Releases of mortgaged property, 14·15–16
    Remedies of trustees and bondholders, 14·13–14
    Supplemental, 14·17
    Trust Indenture Act of 1939, 14·9–11
  Interest dates
    Accruing bond interest between, 27·52
    Basis price for bonds bought between, 27·49–52
    Yield between, 27·53–54
  Interest payments, 14·7
  Interest rates, 1·1–3
    Mathematical computations, 27·45–54
  Joint, 14·29
  "Large" and "small," 10·40
  Liberty, 11·21–22
  Listed, 10·14
  Loans of, 10·41
  Lost or destroyed, 14·6
  Market for, 7·6
  Market indicators, 10·31
  Miscellaneous classes, 14·29–30
  Mortgage, 14·17–21
    Closed mortgage, 14·18
    Issuance of bonds against deposit of cash with trustee, 14·19
    Issued in series, 14·19
    On after-acquired property, 14·19–20
    Open-end and limited open-end, 14·18–19
    Restrictions on, 14·18–19
    Purpose of, 14·17–18
    Scope of lien and mortgage bond titles, 14·20–21
  Municipal, 9·13, 11·26–29
  Net proceeds per bond, 17·51
  Option warrants, 9·7
  Par value, 27·45
  Participating, 14·30
  Premium and discount, 27·45

Bonds (*Continued*)
Pricing of issues, 9·18
 Determining basis, 27·46
  Short method for, 27·46–47
 Influence of money market on, 11·19
Protective provisions, 7·5
Public regulation, 14·4–5
Ratings, 7·5–6
Readjustments, 21·16–17
Redemption of, 14·35–36, 27·45
Refunding, 14·39–40
 At maturity, 14·40
 Before maturity, 14·39–40
 Extensions, 14·40
Registered, 10·40, 14·6
 Only as to principal, 14·6
Reserve for bonded indebtedness, 18·9–10
Retirement of bonded debt, 14·35–37
 Amortization through sinking fund, 14·36
 Call feature, 14·35–36
 Method of redemption, 14·35–36
Revenue, 11·27
Sale of, determining profit or loss, 27·52–53
Schedule of accumulation, 27·48
Serial, 14·37–38
 Callable, 14·38
 Characteristics, 14·37–38
 Comparison of sinking fund and, 14·38
 Size of maturities, 14·4, 14·38
Sinking fund for, 14·13, 14·36–37
Source of working capital, 16·12
Special assessment, 11·27
State and municipal, 10·44, 11·24–29
 Purpose of borrowing, 11·24–25
 Tax status, 11·25
Surety, 9·47, 25·25–26
Tax-exempt, 7·6
Terminal, 14·21
Terms of payment, 14·7
 Payable in gold, 14·7
Trading on the Exchange, 10·39–41
 Commissions and taxes, 10·41
 Good delivery, 10·40–41
 "Nine Bond Rule," 10·39
 Quotation, 10·39–40
Treasury, 11·7, 11·13
 Investment Series A, 11·9
 Investment Series B-1975–80, 11·9–10
Trust indenture, 14·5
Trustees, 6·22
 For bondholders under indenture, 6·22
 Individual co-trustee for corporate, 6·22–23
Trustees' or receivers' certificates, 14·30
Types of, 9·7
United States Savings Bonds, 11·8–9
 Redemption values and investment yields, 11·9
 Series E and H bonds, 11·8
Unlisted bond market, 10·44
Valuation, 27·45–54
 Accruing interest between interest dates, 27·52
 Finding price when yield is known, 27·49
 Finding yield when basis price is known, 27·49
 Nominal and effective interest rates, 27·45
 Tables, 27·48–49, 27·50
Voting, 14·30
With warrants, 14·34–35
Yield between interest dates, 27·53–54
Bonus Stock, 9·7, 13·28
Book Value of Assets, 18·5
Average cost of capital, 17·64–66
Method of valuation, 20·26–27

Borrowing
Bonds, 14·2–3 (See also "Bonds")
Cash forecasts and, 16·32
Cost of borrowed funds, 17·50–51
Equipment obligations, 14·23–25
Leasing of fixed assets, 14·42–44
Long-term and intermediate-term, 14·1–44
Measuring capacity, 14·3–4
 Margin of safety, 14·4
Notes, 14·2–3 (See also "Notes")
Power to incur debt, 14·4
Principles and forms of, 14·1–5
 Debt financing, 14·1–4
 Debt vs. equity capital, 14·1
 Power to incur debt, 14·4
 Public regulation of bond issues, 14·4–5
Private placements, 14·41–42
Rates, 17·48–49
Short-term vs. long-term, 14·2, 16·17
Term loans, 14·40–41
Types of, 14·2–3
Unsecured vs. secured, 14·2
Branch Banking, 2·21–23
Branch Plants, 20·8
Breach of Trust, 6·17, 6·18
Break-Even Analysis, 15·20–22
Charts, 15·20–21
For profitability of product lines, 15·22
Brokerage Houses, 10·35–39
Balance sheet, 10·37
Customer's statement, 10·35–37
Examination of member firms, 10·39
Financing, 10·37–38
Loaning rates, 10·23
Organization of, 10·35
Registered representatives, 10·35
Restrictions on broker borrowing, 10·38–39
Sources of funds for, 10·38
 Hypothecation agreement, 10·38
 Lending customer's stocks to short sellers, 10·38
Brokers and Dealers, 10·4–5
Associate, 10·8
Bond, 10·9
Borrowing, restrictions on, 10·38–39
Commissions on stocks, 10·16–17, 10·21
Commodity trading, 23·14
Distinction between roles, 10·4–5
Federal regulation, 10·54–56
Floor, 10·7
Foreign Exchange, 3·6
Hypothecation agreement, 10·38
Inspection by S.E.C., 10·55
Interest charges, 10·34–35
Licensing, 9·44
Loans, 1·10–11
 Margin requirements, 1·11
Put and call, 10·25–27
Registration of, 10·54
Relations with customers, 10·34
Security, 10·4–5
Self-regulation, 10·54–55
"Street" holders, 10·14
Transactions, 9·41–42, 10·55
Uniform Securities Act, 9·46–47
"Two-dollar," 10·7
Budget Policy, 11·4–5
Budget message of the President, 11·5
Budgets and Budgeting
Appropriation, 15·7
Capital, 16·30, 17·12–21
 Advantages, 17·12–13
 And cash planning, 17·20–21
 Appropriations committee, 17·14–16

GENERAL INDEX

Budgets and Budgeting (*Continued*)
Capital (*Continued*)
Appropriation requests, **17**·16–18
Approval of, **17**·18
Form, **17**·17
Authorization of cash distributions, **17**·21
Controlling expenditures, **17**·18–20
Company organization, **17**·19–20
Coverage, **17**·12
Facilities committee, **17**·15
Preparation, **17**·13–14
Ranking projects, **17**·46–47
Selection of projects, **17**·14
Taxes and, **17**·41–46
Cash, **16**·24–33
Definition, **15**·5–6
Departmental, **15**·6
Directors, **17**·13
Estimated statements, **8**·27
Financial planning and, **15**·1, **15**·5–8
Use of computers, **15**·4
Fixed or forecast, **15**·7
Flexible, **15**·7, **15**·22–23
Installing, **15**·23
Interpreting, **15**·22–23
Use in profit planning, **15**·22–23
Period, **15**·7–8
Plant and equipment, **17**·13
Procedures, **15**·6
Purchase, **16**·31
Standards, **8**·39
Types of, **15**·7
Use of budgets in financial planning, **15**·6–7
Use of computers, **15**·4
Working capital, **16**·18
Builders'-Risk Contracts, 25·19
Bulls and Bears, 10·22
Business Combinations (See "Combinations, Corporate")
Business Conditions
Adjusting business to economic conditions, **15**·34–35
And financial planning, **15**·33–35
Forecasting, **15**·33
Influence of external factors, **15**·33
Business Cycle
Debt financing and, **14**·3
Effect on money market, **1**·26–27
Effect on working capital, **16**·11–12
Business Expansion (See "Expansion, Business")
Business Interruption
Insurance, **25**·21
Losses due to, **25**·4
Business Organizations, 12·1–36
Business trusts, **12**·8–9
Corporations, **12**·12–36
Board of directors, **12**·27–33
Officers, **12**·33–36
Stockholders' meetings, **12**·23–27
Factors in selecting proper form, **12**·1–3
Changing the form, **12**·3
Continuity, **12**·2
Financing, **12**·1
Liability, **12**·2
Management, **12**·2–3
Taxation, **12**·1–2
Individual proprietorships, **12**·3
Joint stock companies, **12**·10
Mutuals and cooperatives, **12**·10–12
Partnerships, **12**·3–6
Professional corporations, **12**·12
Real estate investment trusts, **12**·9
Selecting form of, **12**·1–3
Syndicates, **12**·6–7

Business Trusts, 12·8–9
Advantages and disadvantages, **12**·9
Length of life, **12**·8–9
Liabilities, **12**·8
Method of formation, **12**·8
Tax status, **12**·9
Buy-and-sell agreements, 25·32
Bylaws, Corporate, 12·22–23
Power to make, **12**·22
Provisions, **12**·22–23, **15**·37

"C.A.F. (Named destination)" Quotation, 23·34
Obligations of sellers and buyers, **23**·34
Cables
International department of banks, **3**·15
Transfers, **3**·7
Call Feature, Bonds, **14**·35–37
Callable Preferred Stock, 13·21–22
Calls and Puts, 10·26
Canadian Securities, 10·57
Capital
Assets
Depreciation, **17**·23–33
Insurance on, **17**·7–8
Nature of, **17**·1–2
Obsolescence, **17**·9–10
Planning (See "Capital Asset Planning")
Surplus, **17**·7
Bank, requirements, **5**·2
Budget, **17**·12–21
Circulating, **16**·1
Contributed, **8**·21
Cost of, **17**·47–75
Actual vs. market yields, **17**·67–68
Applications of, **17**·49
Average, **17**·62–67
Book values vs. market values, **17**·64–66
Computation of, **17**·64
Avoidance of dilution, **17**·55
Before- and after-tax cost of debt, **17**·53
Borrowing and lending rates, **17**·48–49
Business valuation and, **17**·70–73
Combined, **17**·62
Common equity and average costs, **17**·68–70
Cost of common stock, **17**·54
Depreciation funds, **17**·61–62
Direct sale of common stock to public, **17**·54–56
Dividends vs. earnings, **17**·68–70
Effect of financing plans on, **17**·71
General concept, **17**·47–48
Lease reporting and, **17**·66–67
Management's judgment, **17**·75
Preferred stock, **17**·53–54
Profit vs. wealth maximization, **17**·48
Retained earnings, **17**·59–61
Sale of bonds, **17**·51–52
Sale of common stock, **17**·54–58
Sale of securities, **17**·51
Specific costs, **17**·50
U-shaped curve, **17**·73
Variability of composite, **17**·70
Debt vs. equity capital, **14**·1
Demand for, **9**·1–2
Factors influencing, **9**·1–2
Distributions, **18**·16, **21**·7
Dividends, **18**·15–16
Expenditures
Balanced capital investments, **17**·5–7
Controlling, **17**·4, **17**·18–20
Effect on future operating costs, **17**·5
Financial planning and, **17**·9
Fixed asset turnover, **17**·10–11
Handling surplus capital assets, **17**·7

Capital *(Continued)*
  Expenditures *(Continued)*
    Investment tax credit, **17**·11–12
    Long-range, **17**·8–9
    Planning, **17**·4–12
    Purchase of additional equipment, **17**·6–7
    Timing, **17**·9
  Financial planning, **15**·1
    Special problems, **17**·36–47
  Fixed, management of, **15**·1
  Funds, **17**·50
    Railroad reorganizations, **14**·29
  Impairment of, **18**·1, **18**·6
    Dividend declarations, **18**·20
    Tests of, **18**·20
  Investments
    And cash flows, **17**·36
    Balanced, **17**·5–7
    Measures for evaluating, **17**·36–40
  Net working
    Ratio of inventory to, **8**·33
    Ratio to funded debt, **8**·33
    Turnovers of, **8**·38
  New, requirements, **18**·26
  New corporations, **12**·16
  Operating, **16**·1
  Opportunity cost of, **17**·59, **17**·65
  Rate of return, **17**·48
  Ratio of funded debt to total capitalization, **8**·34–35
  Small business investment companies, **9**·5
  Stock (See "Capital Stock")
  Structure, **17**·49–50
    Current, **17**·66
    Determining type of, **17**·66
    Economic condition changes and, **21**·1
    Industrial securities, **7**·13
    Nature and causes of changes in, **21**·1–2
  Supply of, **9**·2–6
    For the small enterprises, **9**·2–4
    Investment of savings, **9**·2
  Surplus, **18**·1
  Working (See "Working Capital")
Capital Asset Planning, 17·1–77
  Capital budget, **17**·12–21
  Capital expenditures, **17**·4–12
  Cost of capital, **17**·47–75
  Depletion of wasting assets, **17**·33–36
  Depreciation, **17**·23–33
  Estimating profitability of investments, **17**·22–23
  Nature of fixed capital, **17**·1–4
  Risk and uncertainty, **17**·75–77
  Special problems, **17**·36–47
Capital Budget, 17·12–21
Capital Gains
  Tax rates, **17**·60
  Through combinations, **20**·5
Capital Market, 1·8
Capital Stock, 8·21
  Bylaw provisions, **12**·22
  Creating general reserves, **21**·6
  Elimination of earned surplus deficit, **21**·5
  Reacquisition of, **18**·4
  Recapitalization
    Reclassification of stock, **21**·7–9
  Reductions, **21**·4–7
    Capital distributions, **21**·7
    Creditors' interest in, **21**·6–7
    Methods of, **21**·5–7
    Purpose of, **21**·5–7
    Stockholders' interest in, **21**·6–7
  Writing down tangible asset values, **21**·5–6
  Writing off goodwill and other intangibles, **21**·5

Capitalization
  Definition, **8**·34
  Public utility companies, **7**·19–20
  Rate, determination of, **20**·25–26
  Ratios, in statement analysis, **8**·34–35
  Recapitalizations, **18**·4, **21**·1–14 (See also "Recapitalizations")
Capitalized Earning Power, 20·25–26
Cartels, 20·46
  Restrictions on use, **20**·46
  Types of, **20**·46
  Webb-Pomerene Act Associations, **20**·46
Cash, 16·4
  Administration as working capital, **16**·4
  Balance sheet treatment, **8**·16
  Budget or forecast, **15**·1, **16**·24–33
    Cash receipts and disbursements method, **16**·27–28
    Forecasting collections from sales, **16**·28–30
    Forecasting disbursements, **16**·30–32
    Forecasts by adjusted earnings method, **16**·31
    Integrating cash forecasts and the business program, **16**·25
    Predetermined balance sheet method, **16**·31
    Preparation of, **16**·27–32
    Progressive, **16**·26
    Significance of, **16**·24
    Uses of, **16**·27
    Working capital differentials method, **16**·31–32
  Capital budget and cash planning, **17**·20–21
  Commodity transactions, **23**·32–34
  Corporations operating abroad, **16**·4
  Dealings in commodities, **23**·32
  Discounts, **16**·6, **16**·13
  Dividends, **18**·12
  Earnings, **18**·25
  Fixed capital expenditures and, **17**·20–21
  Forecasts, **16**·25
    And borrowing, **16**·32
    Long-term, **16**·25–26
    Shorter-term, **16**·26
  Income, **18**·25
    Versus profit, **16**·24
  Investment of surplus, **16**·4–6
  "Iron reserve," **16**·5
  Planning and control program, **16**·33
  Reserves, **16**·2
  Surplus, investment of, **16**·4–6
  Tax considerations, **16**·6
  Utilizing more efficiently, **16**·32–33
    Controlling rate of cash outflow, **16**·33
    Reduction of bank balances, **16**·33
"Cash Flow" Analysis, 18·25–26
  Capital investments and, **17**·36
  Controlling rate of outflow, **16**·33
  Discounted method, **17**·23, **17**·38–40, **17**·42
  Industrial securities, **7**·12
Central Banks, 2·11
Certificates
  No-par value stock, **13**·10
  Of beneficial interest, **12**·8, **20**·36
  Of deposit, **21**·16, **22**·15, **24**·3
  Of incorporation, **12**·19, **13**·7
  Of indebtedness, **5**·23, **11**·7, **16**·5
  Scrip, **13**·31
  Stock, **13**·1–3
  Trustees' or receivers', **14**·30, **22**·11
  Voting trust, **13**·17–18
Certification
  Financial statements, **8**·27–28
  Of checks, **5**·15, **24**·36–37
Chain Discounts, 27·18–20
  Definition, **27**·18

Chain Discounts (*Continued*)
Finding equivalent single discount, 28·18–20
Net cost factor tables, 27·19–20
Chains, Voluntary, 20·48
Chandler Act, 22·18
Charitable Trusts, 6·11
Charters, Corporate
Bank, 5·1–2
Dissolution by expiration of, 21·27
Elimination of burdensome provisions, 21·10
Legislative revocation of, 21·27
Charts and Charting
Break-even, 15·20
Of accounts, 15·19
Stock price movements, 10·31
Checks and Checking Accounts, 5·9–21
Advantages of a personal account, 5·10
As an assignment, 24·37
Bank cashier's checks, 24·36
Bank services, 5·4
Certification of checks, 5·15, 24·36–37
Stopping payment not permitted, 24·37–38
Clearing work, 5·10
Definition, 24·3
Deposit account analysis, 5·17–19
Exchange and collection charges, 5·19–20, 24·39–40
Handled by Federal Reserve, 2·16
Nonpar banks, 5·20
Par clearance system, 5·19–20
Increased use of demand deposits as money, 5·9–10
Indorsements, 24·38–39
Joint accounts, 5·11–12
Local clearing house, 2·23
Making a deposit, 5·14
Negotiable instrument, 24·36
New York State provisions, 24·37–40
Opening accounts, 5·10–11
Corporate deposit account, 5·11–13
Partnership accounts, 5·11
Presentment for payment, time for, 24·36
Reconciliation of accounts, 5·15–17
Recovery of forged, 24·38
Selecting a bank, 5·10
Service charges, 5·19
Stop-payment orders, 5·15, 24·37–38
Travelers', 3·28
Types of, 5·10
When deposited items are available for withdrawal, 5·14–15
Chemical and Drug Stocks, Industry analysis, 7·14
Chicago Board of Trade, 23·6–7
Claims, Bankruptcy, 22·26–27
Clearance, Par, bank, 2·16, 5·19–20
Clearing Transactions, 5·4–5
Commodity trading, 23·20–23
Over-the-counter market, 10·43–44
Security transactions, 10·28–29
Clinics, Unincorporated, 12·12
Closed-End Companies, 4·24
Coinage, 2·8
Collateral Security, Negotiable instruments, 24·6
Collateral Trust Bonds, 14·21–23
Collections
Estimating, from sales, 16·28–30
Foreign trade, 3·12–13, 3·16–19
From customers, estimating, 15·34
Par, banks, 2·16, 5·19–20
Service, of banks, 5·4–5, 5·19–20
Combinations, Corporate, 20·4–8 (See also "Mergers")

Combinations, Corporate (*Continued*)
Advantages, 20·4–6
Economies, 20·5
Increases of profits, 20·5
Antitrust legislation, 20·6
By lease, 20·31–34
Cartels, 20·46
Community of interest, 20·47–48
Definitions, 20·4
Determining bases of share exchange, 20·30–31
Financial and accounting factors, 20·24–31
Jointly owned subsidiaries and facilities, 20·48
Planning for future, 20·6–7
Potential difficulties, 20·5–6
Selecting form of, 20·7
Tax advantages, 20·7
Trade associations, 20·46–47
Trend of mergers, 20·7–8
Types of, 20·4
Valuation factors, 20·24–27
Voluntary chains, 20·48
Commercial Banks, 2·10–11
Consumer credit, 2·38
Examinations, 5·3
Foreign exchange business, 3·5
How deposits are created, 2·11
Interbank deposits, 2·11
Investments of, 9·6
In government securities, 11·11–12
In state and local issues, 11·28–29
Loanable funds, 1·23–25
Mortgage loans, 2·36
New financing, 9·12
Number of, 2·19
Organization, 5·1–3
Procedures, 5·1–34
Real estate financing, 26·4–6
Role in banking system, 2·10–11
Savings departments, 4·4, 4·5, 4·11–12
Source of financing prospects, 9·12
Taxes, 4·18–19
Commercial Credit
Credit reports, 8·6–7
Foreign, 3·14
Commercial Finance Companies, 2·35
Commercial Paper, 2·34, 16·5
Market, 1·12–13
Promissory notes, 1·12–13
Volume outstanding, 1·12–13
Commission Houses, 10·7
Commission on Money and Credit, 2·23–24
Commissions (See also "Fees")
Bond transactions, 10·41
Brokerage, 10·16–17, 10·21
Commitments, Underwriting, 9·15
Committee on Financial Institutions, 2·24
Committees
Appropriation, 17·15–16
Board of directors, 15·38–39
Finance, 15·38–39
Reorganizations, 22·15–17
Commodities, Loans on, 16·15–16
Commodity Exchange Act of 1936, 23·10–12
Administration, 23·10
Commodities covered, 23·11
Curbs on speculative trading, 23·11
Enforcement, 23·12–13
Handling of customers' funds, 23·12
Margin rules, 23·14
Prevention of manipulation, 23·11
Prevention of squeezes, 23·11–12
Reports on holdings, 23·13
Self-regulation of exchanges, 23·13–14

GENERAL INDEX

Commodity Exchange Act of 1936 (*Continued*)
  Special calls, **23·**13
  Penalties, **23·**13
Commodity Exchange Authority, 23·10
Commodity Exchange Commission, 23·10
Commodity Trading, 23·1-35
  Basis grade, **23·**4-5
  Cash markets, **23·**1-2
  Cash transactions, **23·**32-34
    Determination of spot prices, **23·**32-33
    Trade terms used, **23·**33-35
  Clearing house functions, **23·**20-23
    Daily reports on transactions, **23·**22
    Evolution of methods, **23·**21
    Financial safeguards, **23·**22
    Handling of deliveries, **23·**23
    Margin variation, **23·**22-23
    Need for central clearing, **23·**20-21
    New York Commodity Clearing Corp., **23·**21-22
    Original margins, **23·**22
  Commission rates, **23·**18
  Contract units, **23·**16
  "Corner," **23·**12
  Cotton Futures Act, **23·**9-10
  Credit, extension of, **23·**18
  Daily reports on transactions, **23·**22
  Danger signals, **23·**30
  Deliverable grades, **23·**4-5
  Deliverable stocks, **23·**31
  Delivery cycles, **23·**30
  Exchanges, **10·**2, **23·**1, **23·**6-9
    Diffusion of risks, **23·**9
    Form of organizations, **23·**6-7
    Free versus controlled markets, **23·**9
    Functions, **23·**8-9
    In foreign countries, **23·**3
    Management, **23·**7
    Market function, **23·**8
    Memberships, **23·**7
    Regulation of, **23·**9-14
      Commodity Exchange Act of 1936, **23·**10-12
      Early moves, **23·**9-10
      Grain Futures Act, **23·**10
    Rules and regulations, **23·**8
    Self-regulation of, **23·**13-14
    Standing committees, **23·**7-8
  Facilities, **23·**14
  Floor brokers, **23·**14
  Futures contract, **23·**3-6
    Basis grade of a commodity, **23·**4-5
    Chicago Board of Trade Wheat Contract, **23·**5
    Deliverable grades, **23·**4
    Delivery rules, **23·**6
    Determination of differentials, **23·**5-6
    Legal nature of, **23·**3-4
    Liquidation, **23·**18-20
    Main features, **23·**4-6
    New York Cotton Futures Contract, **23·**5
  Futures markets, **23·**1-2
  Futures trading, **23·**14-30
    Commodities adapted to, **23·**3
    Evolution and nature of, **23·**1-6
    Growth of, **23·**2-4
    Interpreting futures markets, **23·**29-31
      Price spreads, **23·**29
    Mechanism of, **23·**14-30
    Origin and scope of, **23·**2
    Selling on samples, **23·**2
    Types of commodities traded, **23·**2-3
    Volume of, **23·**3
  Hedging, **23·**23-28 (See also "Hedging")
  Job lot, **23·**16

Commodity Trading (*Continued*)
  Liquidation of futures contracts, **23·**18-20
    By deliveries on contract, **23·**18-19
    Delivery notices, **23·**19
    First notice day, **23·**18-19
    Seller's options, **23·**18
    Switching, **23·**20
    Through offset, **23·**19-20
    Through settlement, **23·**20
  Margins, **23·**14, **23·**17-18, **23·**22-23
  Market information, **23·**29
  Methods, **23·**1-2
  Open interest figures, **23·**29-30
    Formula, **23·**30
    Reports, **23·**30
  Orders, **23·**14-15
    Market and limit, **23·**15
    Short selling, **23·**15
    Stop-loss, **23·**15
  Position limits, **23·**17
  Price fluctuations, **23·**16-17
  Price reporting, **23·**32-33
    Bid and asked prices, **23·**33
  Price spreads, **23·**29
  Quotations, **23·**15-16
  Regulation of exchanges, **23·**9-14
  Short selling, **23·**9-10, **23·**15
  Speculation in futures, **23·**31-32
    Role of, **23·**31
    Sources of information, **23·**31-32
  Spot markets, **23·**32-34
    Bona fide, **23·**6
    Cash dealings in commodities, **23·**32
    Determination of price, **23·**32-33
    Trade terms used, **23·**33-35
  Squeezes, **23·**11-12
  Traders, hedgers, and speculators, **23·**15
  Volume, **23·**29
Common Stock (See "Stocks, Common")
Community Development Commissions, Real estate financing by, **26·**11
Community of Interest, 20·47-48
  Jointly owned subsidiaries and facilities, **20·**48
  Mutual stock ownership, **20·**47-48
Compensation
  Corporate officers, **12·**36
  Directors, **12·**30-31
  Executives, **12·**36
  Promoters, **12·**13-14
  Trustees in bankruptcy, **22·**31
  Underwriters, **9·**18-19
Competitive Bidding, For purchase of new issues, **9·**13
Composition Settlements, 21·17-19
  Acceptance considerations, **21·**18
  Number of creditors, **21·**18
  When to agree to, **21·**18-19
Compound Interest, 27·20-29
Comptrollers, 12·35
Computers, For financial planning, **15·**3-5
Conditional Sale Plans, 14·24
Confirmation, Of stock purchase, **10·**16
Conflict of Interest, Directors, **12·**33
Considerations
  Consolidations and mergers, **20·**24-25
  Negotiable instruments, **24·**9
  Purchase of assets, **20·**15
Consignments, 3·17
Consolidated Statements, 8·22-25
  Advantages and limitations, **8·**22-23
  Inclusion and exclusion of subsidiaries, **8·**23
  Intercompany items and transactions, **8·**25
  Investment in consolidated subsidiaries, **8·**24
  Purpose, **8·**22

Consolidated Statements (*Continued*)
 Reconciliation of dividends received from and earnings of unconsolidated subsidiaries, 8·24
Consolidations, 18·5 (See also "Mergers")
 Accounting problems in asset transfers, 20·27–29
 Advantages and disadvantages, 20·22–23
 Agreement on terms, 20·19
  Execution of, 20·19–20
 Approval of board of directors, 20·19
 Charter rights, 20·17
 Collateral trust bonds, 14·23
 Consideration, 20·24
 Definition, 20·17
 Effect of, 20·19
  On surplus, 20·29
 Financial and accounting factors, 20·24–31
 Legal factors, 20·17–19
  Consent of all stockholders, 20·17
  State laws, 20·18–19
  Statutory and administrative provisions, 20·17–18
 Nonbalance sheet factors, 20·24
 Procedures in effecting, 20·19–20
 Rights of creditors, 20·20–21
 Rights of dissenting stockholders, 20·20
 Stockholders' consent, 20·19
 Terms of, 20·23
 Treatment of mortgage liens, 20·21
 Valuation problems, 20·24
  Methods of, 20·25–27
Construction
 Contracts, 25·10
 Loans, 26·14
Consumer Credit, 2·38–41, 5·34
 Effective rates of interest, 2·41
 Noninstallment credit, 2·38
 Sources of, 2·39–41, 5·34
Consumer Finance Companies, 2·40–41
Contingencies
 Funds for meeting, 16·2–3
 Need for additional working capital, 16·11
 Provisions for, 15·34
 Reserve for, 18·10
Contingent Liabilities, Balance sheet treatment, 8·20–21
Contingent Voting, 13·15
Contracts
 Builders'-risk, 25·19
 Construction, 25·10
 Futures, 23·3–6
 Pre-incorporation, 12·15–16
 Purchase group, 9·18
 Sales, 20·15, 25·10–11
  Long-term, 20·47
 Underwriting, 9·14–16
 When-issued, 10·19
Controllers, 12·35
 Duties of, 15·35–36
Controls and Controlling
 Capital expenditures, 17·18–20
 Of foreign exchange, 3·10–11
 Of risk and loss, 25·6–7
Convertible Bonds, 14·30–35
Convertible Preferred Stock, 13·22
Convertible Securities, 17·58
Cooperatives, 12·10–12
 Advantages and disadvantages, 12·11
 Forms of, 12·11
 Tax treatment, 12·11
Corners
 Commodity trading, 23·12
 Security trading, 10·24
  Control of, 10·24
  Technical, 10·24

Corporate Fiduciaries, 6·1–4
Corporations, 12·12–23
 Agency functions of fiduciaries, 6·23–24
 Alien, 12·20
 Annual meetings, 8·5
 Annual reports, 8·4–5
 Bank deposit account, 5·11–12
 Banks and trust companies as fiduciaries, 6·21–22
 Board of directors, 12·27–33 (See also "Board of Directors")
 Business expansion, 20·1–4
  Development of policy, 20·2–3
  Motives for, 20·1–2
  Pattern of, 20·1
 Bylaws, 12·22–23
 Capital structure, 7·13
 Cartels, 20·46
 Certificate of incorporation, 12·19
 Charter, 12·20–21
  Amendments to, 12·21–22
  Legislative revocation of, 21·27
 Choice of state of incorporation, 12·16–17
  State laws, 12·18
  State taxes, 12·17
 Closely held, 20·9, 21·8
  Business continuation and key man insurance, 25·33–34
 Combinations, 18·5, 20·4–8
  Accounting problems in asset transfers, 20·27–29
  Advantages, 20·4–6
  Antitrust legislation, 20·6
  By means of leases, 20·31–34
  Cartels, 20·46
  Community of interest, 20·47–48
  Definitions, 20·4
  Determining bases of share exchange, 20·30–31
  Financial and accounting factors, 20·24–31
  Financial steps in promoting, 20·29–30
  Holding companies, 20·34–46
  Mutual stock ownership, 20·47–48
  Types of, 20·4
 Community of interest
  Jointly owned subsidiaries and facilities, 20·48
  Mutual stock ownership, 20·47–48
  Voluntary chains, 20·48
 Consolidations and mergers, 6·24, 18·5, 20·17–23 (See also "Consolidations," "Mergers")
 Debt vs. equity capital, 14·1
 Delaware incorporation, 12·17–18
 Dissolution, 21·26–28
  By expiration of charter, 21·27
  Effected by happening of some contingency, 21·27
  From misuse and nonuse of powers, 21·28
  Meaning of, 21·26–27
  Methods of, 21·27
  Voluntary, 21·28
 Dividends (See "Dividends")
 Domestic, 12·20
 Edge Act, 3·15–16
 Evaluation of divisions, 15·16–17
 Expansion, 20·1–4
  Circular, 20·2–3
  Combinations, 20·4–8
  Development of sound policy, 20·2–3
  Factors determining need of financing, 20·3
  Horizontal, 20·2
  Internal, 20·3–4
  Vertical, 20·2
  Working capital needs, 20·3
 Fiduciary functions for, 6·1–4, 6·21–23

Corporations (*Continued*)
 Financial and accounting factors in combinations, 20·24-31
 Financial statements (See "Financial Statements")
 Financial steps in promoting, 20·29-30
 Foreign, 12·17, 12·20, 20·39
  Consolidations and mergers, 20·18-19
  Restriction on, 12·20
 Franchise tax, 20·30
 Holding companies, 20, 34-46 (See also "Holding Companies")
 Incorporation process, 12·19
 Intercorporate readjustments, 21·22-24
  Holding companies, 21·22
  Methods, 21·23-24
  Reasons for, 21·22-23
  To reduce taxes, 21·22-23
 Investments
  In Government securities, 11·12
  In state and local issues, 11·28-29
 Loans to, 24·43-44
 Long-term sales contracts, 20·47
 Maintaining corporate existence after transfer of assets, 20·30
 Mergers, 18·5 (See also "Mergers")
 Mutual, 12·10-12
 Name of, 12·18-19
 Officers, 12·33-36
  Compensation, 12·36
  Controller, 12·35
  Powers and duties, 12·34-36
  Qualifications, 12·33-34
  Secretary, 12·35-36
  Titles and functions, 12·33
  Treasurer, 12·34-35
 Opening a corporate deposit account, 5·11-13
 Operating abroad, 16·4
 Organization, 12·12-13
  Advantages and disadvantages, 12·13
 Parent-subsidiary relations, 20·39-41 (See also "Subsidiaries, Corporate")
 Pooling of interests, 18·5
 Power to incur debt, 14·4
 Pre-incorporation contracts, 12·15-16
 Promotions, 12·13-15
  Compensation of promoters, 12·13-14
  Function of promoters, 12·13
  Legal status, 12·14
 Provision for loss of key men and business continuation, 25·31
 Purchase of assets, 20·8-17 (See also "Purchase of Assets")
 Raising capital, 12·16
 Readjustments, 21·14-28
 Recapitalizations, 6·24, 21·1-14
 Reorganizations, 21·1-18 (See also "Reorganizations")
 Retained earnings, 18·6-7
 Signature of officers, 24·21
 Statements by executives or spokesmen, 8·5
 Stockholders' meetings, 12·23-27
 Stockholder's relationship to, 13·1
 Subchapter S, 12·3
 Subsidiaries (See "Subsidiaries, Corporate")
 Surpluses, 18·1-3
  Retained earnings reserves, 18·7-11
 Trade associations, 20·46-47
 Valuation problems, 20·24-27
  Plant and equipment, 20·27-28
 Voluntary liquidations, 21·25-26
Cost Less Depreciation, Method of valuation, 20·27
Cost of Goods Sold, In income statement, 8·9-10

Costs
 Advertising, 15·32
 Computers for estimating, 15·4
 Cost-volume-profit relationship, 15·17-19
  Decomposing costs, 15·18-19
   Methods employed, 15·19
 Decomposing, 15·18-19
 Depreciation, 17·27
 Direct costing, 15·23-25
  Benefits of, 15·25
  In practice, 15·24-25
  Use by management, 15·24
 Incremental, 17·41
 Incurred in sale of securities, 17·51
 Less depreciation, 20·27
 Marginal, 15·17
 Of bonds, 17·51-52
 Of borrowed funds, 17·50-51
 Of capital, 17·47-75 (See also "Capital, Cost of")
 Of retained earnings, 17·59-61
 Operating, 17·27
  Expansion and, 15·30-31
 Opportunity, 17·59
 Product, and working capital, 16·10
 Production, 15·31-32
 Replacement, valuation method, 26·26
 Reproduction, 20·27
 Selling, 15·32
 Substitution, 20·27
 Sunk, 17·40-41
 Variable, 15·18
Cotton, Buying on call, 23·27-28
Cotton Futures Act, 23·9-10
Council of Economic Advisors, 1·2
Counsel, Investment, 4·33-34
Coupons
 Bonds, 10·40, 14·5-6
 Obligations, 11·10-11
Courts
 Of bankruptcy, 22·19-20
 Of equity, 22·2, 22·19
 Reorganizations plans approved by, 22·7-8
Credit
 Analysis, 5·32-33, 8·30-31
 Bank, 2·4
 Classes of, 2·4
 Consumer, 2·4, 2·38-41, 5·34
 Customer credit limits, 16·6
 Department in banks, 5·33
 Files, 5·2-3
 Financial statement analysis, 8·30-31
 Installment, 2·4
 Instruments, 5·20-21
  Foreign exchange transactions, 3·7-10
 Investment or commercial, 2·4
 Maximum ledger balances, 16·6
  And receivables, 16·6-7
 Policies, 2·4
  Effect of economic conditions, 15·34
 Role of, 2·4
 Security, 10·33-34
  Regulation of, 10·33-34
 Sources of information, 8·6-7
  Dun & Bradstreet, Inc., 8·6-7
  National Credit Office, 8·7
  Robert Morris Associates, 8·7
Credit Control Policies
 Federal Reserve System, 1·3, 1·5, 1·20-21
 Government debt management policies, 11·5-6
 Limitations of, 2·33
 Monetary and credit management, 2·28-33
 Open-market operations, 2·31
 Reserve credit and, 2·30

GENERAL INDEX

G·13

Credit Control Policies (*Continued*)
  Techniques, **2**·30–31
  Through member bank reserves, **2**·17–18
Credit Unions, **2**·40, **4**·16–17
  Functions and operations, **4**·16
  Loans and charges, **4**·17
  Membership, **4**·16–17
  Organization, **4**·16–17
  Taxes, **4**·17
Creditors
  Committees, **21**·20–22
    Advantages of, **21**·21–22
    Meetings, **22**·26
    Operations of, **21**·21
    Requirements, **21**·20–21
    Voting trustees, **21**·21
  Composition settlements, **21**·17–18
    Acceptance considerations, **21**·18
    Number of creditors necessary, **21**·18
    When to agree to, **21**·18–19
  Corporate dissolutions, **21**·28
  Interest in capital stock reductions, **21**·6–7
  Reorganizations
    Plan accepted by, **22**·7
    Trustee's statement and notice to, **22**·5
  Rights of
    Assignments, **21**·20
    In consolidations and mergers, **20**·20–21
    In sale of assets, **20**·13–14
  Selective uses of ratios, **8**·39–40
Crime Insurance, **25**·22–24
Cumulative Preferred Stock, **13**·19–20
Cumulative Voting, **13**·14–15
Currencies, **2**·1–2
  Convertible, **3**·11
  Devaluation of U. S., **2**·7
  Federal Reserve, **2**·6–7
  Free vs. controlled, **3**·11–12
  In circulation, **2**·8–9
Current Assets, **8**·16–17 (See also "Assets")
  Administration as working capital, **16**·4–9
    Cash, **16**·4
    Investment of surplus cash, **16**·4–6
    Receivables, **16**·6–7
  Planning, **16**·1–33
    Cash budget, **16**·24–33
  Valuation of, **20**·28
Current Liabilities
  Balance sheet treatment, **8**·19–20
  Deferred revenue or income, **8**·20
  Definition, **8**·19
Current Ratio, In statement analysis, **8**·32
Custodian Accounts, **6**·19
  Fees and commissions, **6**·21
Customers
  As buyers of securities, **9**·8
  Relations with brokers, **10**·34
  Sale of stock to, **13**·25
  Statements from brokerage houses, **10**·35–36

Dealers (See also "Brokers and Dealers")
  Bond, **10**·9
  In government securities, **11**·12–13
  Odd-lot, **10**·8
  Specialists, **10**·8
Death Benefits
  Employee insurance plans, **25**·35
  Profit-sharing plans, **19**·44
  Retirement plans for self-employed, **19**·50
Debenture Bonds, **14**·25–26
Debt Financing, **14**·1–2
  Advantages, **14**·1
  Amortization and, **14**·4
  Business cycle and, **14**·3

Debt Financing (*Continued*)
  Disadvantages, **14**·1–2
  Leasing of fixed assets, **14**·42–44
  Long-term industry trend and, **14**·3
  Measuring borrowing capacity, **14**·3–4
  Power to incur debt, **14**·4
    Corporate authorization, **14**·4
  Principles of, **14**·3–4
  Private placements, **14**·41–42
  Term loans, **14**·40–41
Debts
  Before- and after-tax cost of, **17**·53
  Equity capital vs., **14**·1
  Funded
    Ratio of fixed assets to, **8**·35
    Ratio to net working capital, **8**·33
    Ratio to total capitalization, **8**·34–35
  Long-term and intermediate-term, **14**·1–44
  National (See "National Debt")
  Payment of
    Bankruptcies, **22**·36
  Provable, against bankrupt estate, **22**·27–28
  Readjustments, **21**·14–22
    Assignments, **21**·19–22
    Bonds, **21**·16–17
    Circumstances necessitating, **21**·14
    Composition settlements, **21**·17–19
    Credit adjustment bureaus, **21**·22
    Creditors' committees, **21**·20–22
    Legal aspects, **21**·15–16
    Small business, **21**·17
    Types of, **21**·14–15
    Under special legislation, **21**·17
  Substitution for equity, **17**·73
Decision Making, **17**·75–77 (See also "Alternative Projects")
Declining-Balance Methods, For computing depreciation, **17**·29–30
Deeds of Trust, **6**·8, **12**·8, **26**·14
Deferred Charges
  Amortization of, **8**·19
  Balance sheet treatment, **8**·19
  Writing off, **8**·19
Deferred Income, As liability, **8**·20
Deficit Financing, **11**·21
Delaware Incorporation, **12**·17–18
  No-par value stock, **13**·7
"Delivered (named Destination)," **23**·34
  Obligations of sellers and buyers, **23**·34
Delivery Notices, Commodity trading, **23**·19
Delivery of Securities, **10**·28–29
  Government obligations, **11**·15
Demand Deposits, **5**·3–4
  Definition, **2**·1–2
  Increased use as money, **5**·9–10
  Turnover of, **1**·23
Depletion, **17**·33–36
  Financial reporting and, **17**·35–36
  Financial significance of, **17**·33–34
  In income statement, **8**·11–12
  Income tax treatment, **8**·12
  Methods of calculating, **17**·35–36
  Of wasting assets, **17**·33–36
  Percentage, **17**·35
  Valuation of wasting assets, **17**·34–35
Depositary Bonds, **11**·10
Deposits, Bank, **5**·3–9
Depreciation, **8**·10–11, **17**·23–33
  Allocating the cost of fixed assets, **8**·10, **17**·23–24
  Appreciation and, **17**·28
  As source of working capital, **16**·16
  Cost of funds, **17**·61–62
    Assignment of cost to, **17**·61–62

GENERAL INDEX

Depreciation (*Continued*)
  Cost of operation, **17**·27
  Effect of inadequate, **17**·26–27
  Effect on working capital, **17**·26
  Financial effects of policies, **17**·31–32
  Government regulation, **17**·32–33
  Impact of changing price levels, **17**·27–28
  In financial analysis, **8**·10–11
  In income statement, **8**·10–11
  Inadequate, effect of, **17**·26–27
  Industrial securities, **7**·12
  Maintenance vs., **17**·25–26
  Methods of calculating, **8**·11, **17**·28–31
    Based on production, **17**·30–31
    Based on sales or profits, **17**·31
    Declining-balance method, **17**·29–30
    Interest method, **17**·30
    Straight-line method, **17**·28–29
    Sum-of-the-years-digits method, **17**·30
    Writing off assets on acquisition, **17**·31
  Objectives, **17**·23
  Obsolescence of capital assets, **17**·25
  Price-level write-downs, **17**·28
  Property, **8**·18
  Real estate investments, **26**·24–25
  S.E.C. policy, **8**·10–11
  Sunk costs and, **17**·40–41
Depression, Effect on banking system, **2**·24
Devaluation, Of U. S. currency, **2**·7
  Chief effect of, **2**·7
  Gold standard and, **2**·7
Direct Costing, **15**·23–25
  In profit planning, **15**·23–25
  Tool of management, **15**·24
Directors
  Banks, **5**·2–3
  Board of, **12**·27–33 (See also "Board of Directors")
  Committees, **15**·38–39
  Compensation, **12**·30–31
  Conflict of interest, **12**·33
  Election, **12**·28
  Financial planning, responsiblity for, **15**·36–39
  Interlocking directorates, **20**·45, **20**·47
  Liabilities, **12**·29–30
  Qualifications, **12**·27–28
  Resignation and removal, **12**·28–29
  Term of office, **12**·28
Disability Benefits
  Pension plans, **19**·10, **19**·25
  Profit-sharing plans, **19**·43
Discharge, Of negotiable instruments, **24**·28–30
Disclosure Requirements
  Listing securities on stock exchange, **10**·9
  Pension plans, **19**·34
  Profit-sharing plans, **19**·45–46
  Securities Act of 1933, **9**·27–28
Discount Rate, **2**·31
  Federal Reserve System, **1**·20
Discounted Cash-Flow Method, For evaluating investments, **17**·23, **17**·38–40, **17**·42
Discounts, **24**·43
  Bank, **27**·12–18
    Basis for calculating proceeds, **27**·13
    Computation of interest under partial payment plans, **27**·15
    Definition, **27**·12–13
    Due date of notes, **27**·13–14
    Finding principal to yield given proceeds, **27**·15
    Interest-bearing paper, **27**·14
    On noninterest-bearing paper, **27**·14
    Types of notes, **27**·13
    Versus true, **27**·16–18

Discounts (*Continued*)
  Bonds, **27**·45
  Cash, **16**·6, **16**·13
  Chain, **27**·18–20
    Definition, **27**·18
    Finding equivalent single discount, **27**·18–20
    Net cost factor tables, **27**·19–20
  Definition, **27**·12–13
  Loans differ from, **5**·28–29
  Negotiable instruments, **24**·4
  Sale of securities, **17**·51
Disposal Value of Assets, **17**·41
Dissenters' Rights
  Debt readjustments, **21**·15–16
  Preferred stock recapitalizations, **21**·9, **21**·12-13
  Reorganizations, **22**·3
Dissolution, Corporate, **21**·26–28
  By expiration of charter, **21**·27
  Effected by happening of some contingency, **21**·27
  From misuse and nonuse of powers, **21**·28
  Meaning, **21**·26–27
  Methods of, **21**·27
  Voluntary, **21**·28
Distribution Statement, **10**·9
Distributions of Securities, **9**·8
  Exchange, **10**·22
  Foreign issues, **10**·57–58
  Primary, **9**·8
  Secondary, **9**·8, **10**·21
Diversification, And working capital needs, **16**·11
Dividends
  Arrearages on preferred stock, **21**·11–14
  Bonds, **18**·14
    Convertible, **14**·32
  Bylaws provisions, **12**·22–23
  Cash, **18**·12
  Consent, **18**·22
  Construction, **18**·16
  Declaration, **18**·11, **18**·27–30
    Date of record, **18**·28
    Effect of, **18**·22–23
    Notification of shareholders, **18**·28
    Resolution of the board, **18**·27
    Stock dividends, **18**·27–28
  Definition, **18**·11
  Designation of, **18**·15–16
  Earnings versus, **17**·68–70
  Effect on working capital, **18**·25–26
  Ex-dividend, **10**·18, **18**·28
  Extra and special, **18**·15, **18**·16–17
  Industrial securities, **7**·13
  Insured banks, restrictions, **5**·8-9
  Interim and final, **18**·15
  Legal restrictions, **18**·18–23
    Approval by S.E.C., **18**·22
    Capital impairment test, **18**·20
    Common law rules, **18**·19
    Effect of declaration, **18**·22–23
    Insolvency test, **18**·21–22
    Judicial compulsion to declare dividends, **18**·22
    Liability for illegal, **18**·23
    New York Statute, **18**·19–20
    Profits test, **18**·21
    Reasons for limitation, **18**·18–19
    Statutory law, **18**·19–22
    Surplus test, **18**·20–21
  Liquidating or capital, **18**·15–16, **18**·17–18
  Nature and kinds of, **18**·11–14
  On common stock, **13**·23
  On pledged securities, **14**·22

GENERAL INDEX

Dividends (*Continued*)
Payment of, **18**·11, **18**·27–30
  Dividend book, **18**·29
  Fiscal agent for, **18**·30
  Preparation of dividend checks, **18**·28–29
  Special bank account, **18**·30
  To creditors, **22**·36–37
Payout ratios, **18**·26
Policy, **18**·16–18
  Definition, **18**·16
  Factors affecting, **18**·18
  Irregular, **18**·17
  Liquidating dividends, **18**·17–18
  New capital requirements, **18**·26
  No dividend, **18**·18
  Property, **18**·17
  Regular, **18**·16
  Regular and extra, **18**·16–17
  Regular plus stock dividends, **18**·17
  Regular stock dividend, **18**·17
  Specific objectives, **18**·26–27
  Tax and financial aspects, **18**·23–27
Preferred stock, **13**·19–20
Price-earnings ratio and, **7**·9
Property, **18**·14, **18**·17
Quasi-dividends, **18**·16
Regular, **18**·15, **18**·16–17
Scrip, **18**·14
"Security," **18**·14
Stock, **18**·12–14
  Purposes of, **18**·12–13
  Rescission, **18**·13
  Taxability of, **18**·13
  Valuation, **18**·13
  Versus stock splits, **18**·12
Subsidiaries, **8**·24
Tax treatment, **18**·12–13, **18**·23–25
  Effect on stockholders' taxes, **18**·24–25
  Surtax on undistributed earnings, **18**·23–24
Dollar Cost Averaging, **7**·2
Dollar Drain, **2**·29
Dollar Exchange, Acceptances drawn to create, **1**·12
Domestic Trade Acceptances, **5**·31
Donated Stock, **13**·4, **18**·3
Dow Theory of Stock Price Movements, **10**·31
Drafts, **3**·8–9, **24**·2
Advance on, **3**·21
Clean, **3**·17–18
Collection, **3**·17–18, **3**·19–20
Discount of, **3**·21
Documentary, **3**·18, **3**·26
Documents attached to, **3**·26
Due date, **27**·13–14
Sight, **3**·8–9, **3**·17
Time, **3**·9
Due Bills, **10**·18
Dun & Bradstreet, Inc., **8**·6–7
Working capital ratios, **16**·18–23

Earned Surplus, **18**·1 (See also "Retained Earnings")
Earnings
Capitalized, **20**·25–26
Determination of, **20**·25
Determining, **15**·14
Dilution of, **17**·55
Dividends versus, **17**·68–70
Investment analysis factor, **8**·30
Per share of common stock, **7**·8
Prospective industrial securities, **7**·11–12
Reinvestment of, **16**·12
Retained (See "Retained Earnings")
Subsidiaries, **8**·24

Earnings (*Continued*)
Surtax on undistributed, **18**·23–24
Economic Conditions
Adjusting business to, **15**·34–35
Inventories, **15**·34
Effect on investment funds, **9**·1–2, **20**·24
Economic Indicators, **1**·2
Economists, Role of, **25**·2
Edge Act Corporations, **3**·15–16
Electric Light and Power Industry, **7**·21
Emergencies, Trusts for, **6**·11
Emergency Banking Act, 1933, **2**·24
Employees
Contributions
  Pension plans, **19**·29–30
  Profit-sharing plans, **19**·45
Insurance plans for, **25**·34–36
  Employee death benefits, **25**·35
  Group, **25**·35
  Salary continuation or deferred compensation plans, **25**·35
  Split dollar plan, **25**·34–35
Loans to, **16**·6
Sale of stock to, **9**·8, **13**·25
Savings plans, **13**·25
Stock purchases, **9**·8
Employers
Contributions to pension plans, **19**·27–29
Liability insurance, **25**·27
Endowment Funds, Mortgage financing, **26**·10–11
Engineering, Analysis, **20**·24
Equipment
Balance sheet treatment, **8**·18
Leasing, **14**·44
Obsolescence, **17**·6–7
Purchases of, **15**·35, **17**·6–7
Replacement investments, **17**·6
Unequal lives, **17**·43
Valuation of, **20**·27–28
Equipment Mortgage Plan, **14**·24
Equipment Obligations, **14**·23–25
Conditional sale plan, **14**·24
Covenants in agreements, **14**·24–25
Philadelphia plan, **14**·24
Equipment Trusts, **14**·23
Equity
Balance sheet treatment, **8**·13–14
Courts, **22**·2, **22**·19
Investments, **7**·1
Reorganizations, **22**·1–2
Substitution of debt for, **17**·73
Escrow Accounts, **6**·19, **26**·17
Evaluating
Alternative projects, **17**·22
Investment proposals, **17**·22–23, **17**·36–37
Examinations
Auditing, **9**·14
Engineering, **9**·14
Legal, **9**·14
Examiners, Reorganization proceedings, **22**·6
Excess Present Value Method, Evaluating investments, **17**·40, **17**·43
Exchange Act of 1934 (See "Securities Exchange Act of 1934")
Exchange Distributions, **10**·22
Exchange Offerings, **11**·11
Exchange Stabilization, **2**·28
Period following World War II, **2**·29
Upward revaluation, **2**·28–29
Exchanges
Commodity (See "Commodity Trading, Exchanges")
Futures trading, **23**·2

GENERAL INDEX

Exchanges (*Continued*)
Security, **10**·1, **10**·2 (See also "Securities Trading")
Stock, **10**·2-3
Ex-Dividend, Stocks, **10**·18
Executives
Compensation, **12**·36
Indemnification of, **12**·30
Pension and profit-sharing plans, **12**·36
Executors
Administrative duties, **6**·5
Fees and commissions, **6**·20
Final settlement, **6**·6
Functions of, **6**·5-6
Preparation of inventory, **6**·5
Probating will, **6**·5
Expansion, Business, 20·1-4
Anticipated, capital expenditures for, **17**·9
Circular, **20**·2-3
Combinations, **20**·4-8
Development of a sound policy, **20**·2-3
Estimating additional capacity, **15**·31
Factors to be considered, **15**·30-32
Financial planning, **15**·30-33
Financing, **20**·3
Forecast of demand and selling prices, **15**·31
Forecast of economic conditions, **15**·30-31
Horizontal, **20**·2
Increased working capital requirements, **15**·32
Internal, **20**·3-4
Leases as a means of, **20**·31
Long-term goals, **15**·30
Motives for, **20**·1-2
Pattern of, **20**·1
Profitability of, **15**·33
Reserves for, **18**·10
Selling and advertising costs, **15**·32
Vertical, **20**·2
Working capital needs, **16**·11, **20**·3
Expenses
Fixed, **15**·18
In financial reports, **8**·29
Variable, **15**·18
Export-Import Bank, 3·30
Exporters, Foreign trade financing, **3**·17-18
Ex-rights, Stock, **10**·18

"F.A.S. (Named Port)," **23**·33
Obligations of sellers and buyers, **23**·33
"F.O.B. (Named Point)," **23**·33
Obligations of sellers and buyers, **23**·33-34
Factors, 2·35, **16**·14
Fair Market Value, 18·5
Farmers
Adjudication of bankruptcy, **22**·40
Bankruptcy proceedings, **22**·39-40
Federal Advisory Council, 2·13
Federal Agencies
Credit control policies, **1**·3, **1**·5
Mortgage financing, **2**·37
Obligations, **16**·5
Federal Communication Commission (F.C.C.), **7**·18
Federal Deposit Insurance Corporation (F.D.I.C.), 2·19, **5**·6-9
Bank examinations by, **5**·3
Insured banks, **5**·6-7
Payment of insured deposits, **5**·8
Prevention of unsound practices, **5**·7-8
Federal Funds
Market, **1**·13
Market rate, **1**·13
Reserve balances, **1**·13
Types of, **1**·13

Federal Home Loan Bank System, 4·15
Obligations of, **11**·7
Federal Housing Administration (F.H.A.), **2**·37, **5**·27
Mortgages, **7**·7, **26**·8, **26**·13
Federal Intermediate Credit Banks, Obligations of, **11**·7
Federal Land Banks, Obligations of, **11**·7
Federal National Mortgage Association, 1·5, **2**·37, **26**·8-9
Obligations of, **11**·7
Federal Power Act, 20·45
Federal Power Commission, 7·18
Competitive bidding required, **9**·13
Depreciation regulation, **17**·33
Public utility regulations, **7**·18, **8**·6
Federal Regulation (See "Government Regulations")
Federal Reserve Act, 2·13
On foreign branches of banks, **3**·15
Federal Reserve Banks, 2·15-17
Acceptance market and, **1**·12
Assets and liabilities, 1963, **1**·14-17, **2**·16
Capital accounts, **1**·18-19
Credit, **1**·18-19
Control of, **1**·20
Excess reserves, **1**·18
Foreign branches and affiliates, **3**·16-17
Free reserves, **1**·19
Government securities, **11**·12
Government securities market, role in, **11**·5
Liabilities of, **1**·17
Loans and advances to member banks, **1**·23-25, **2**·16
Rediscount rates, **11**·18
Reserve balances, **1**·13
Statement, consolidated, **1**·14-19
Assets of Federal Reserve banks, **1**·14-17
Acceptances—bought outright, **1**·16
Cash, **1**·16
Discounts and advances, **1**·16
Gold Certificate account, **1**·14
Gold Certificate Reserves, **1**·14-15
Redemption Fund for Federal Reserve Notes, **1**·14
Capital accounts, **1**·18-19
Liabilities, **1**·17
Statement of reporting member banks, **1**·21-25
Federal Reserve Board, 1·20, **2**·13, **2**·15
Federal Reserve Bulletin, 2·15
Flow of Funds/Saving statistics, **1**·8
Sources of consumer credit, **2**·38
Federal Reserve Notes, 2·7
Federal Reserve System, 2·13-18
Abandonment of "Bills Only" policy, **11**·15
Annual rate of turnover of demand deposits, **2**·5
Banks, **2**·15-16 (See also "Federal Reserve Banks")
Boundaries of Federal Reserve districts, **2**·14
Collection of checks and other services, **2**·16
Credit control policies, **1**·3, **1**·5, **1**·20, **2**·28-33
"Accord" with Treasury, **2**·32
Discount rate, **1**·20
Effect on prices of government securities, **11**·19
Instruments of, **1**·20
Member bank reserves, **2**·17-18
Open market purchases, **1**·20
Postwar, **2**·31-32
Power to vary legal reserve requirements, **1**·20
Regulation of loans on securities, **1**·20

GENERAL INDEX

Federal Reserve System (*Continued*)
  Credit control policies (*Continued*)
    Bank reserves, **2**·30
      Subject to constant change, **1**·5
    Techniques of, **2**·30–31
  Credit outstanding, **2**·9
  Currency, **2**·6–7
  Discount rate, **2**·16
  Easy money policy, **2**·31
  Excess reserves, **2**·17–18, **2**·32
  Legal reserve requirements, **2**·17
  Member bank reserves, **2**·17–19
  Member banks, **2**·13, **2**·17–19
  Membership, **2**·17
  Monetary controls
    Federal Reserve powers, **2**·34
    Over nonbank financial institutions, **2**·34–35
  Monetary policy, **2**·28–33
    Control and bank reserves, **2**·30
    Definitions and objectives, **2**·28
    Exchange stabilization, **2**·28–29
    Money supply and the price level, **2**·29
  Open Market Committee, **2**·13, **2**·15, **11**·15
  Operations, in money market, **11**·15–16, **11**·19–20
  Par clearance system, **5**·19–20
  Repurchase agreements, **2**·16
  Role in government securities market, **11**·15–16
Federal Savings and Loan Insurance Corp., **4**·15
Fees
  Custodian accounts, **6**·21
  Executors, administrators, and guardians, **6**·20
  Finders, **9**·12
  For filing registration statement, **9**·35
  Investment Supervisory Services, **6**·21
  Personal trust, **6**·20–21
    Registration of broker-dealers, agents, and investment advisers, **9**·46–47
  Security registration, **10**·16–17
  Trust accounts, **6**·29–31
  Trustees, **6**·20–21
  Underwriters' "spread," **9**·18–19
Fiat Money, **2**·4
Fidelity Bonds, **25**·25
Fiduciaries, **6**·1–4 (See also "Trusts")
  Corporate, **6**·1–4
    Advantages, **6**·3–4
    Evolution of, **6**·2–3
    Definition, **6**·1
    Establishment and growth of, **6**·1
    Liabilities of, **6**·17–18
    Trust companies and banks as, **6**·1, **6**·21–22
Field Warehouse Loans, **5**·30, **16**·15
FIFO (First-in first-out method of inventory valuation), **8**·10, **16**·9
Finance Companies, **15**·38–39
  Analysis of stock, **7**·16
Financial Data
  Short-term credit information, **8**·6–7
  Sources of, **8**·4–7
Financial Enterprises
  Security analysis, **7**·14–16
    Bank stocks, **7**·15
    Insurance stocks, **7**·15–16
Financial Institutions, **2**·33–41 (See also "Banks and Banking")
  Monetary controls over nonbank, **2**·34–35
  Real estate financing, **26**·1–7
Financial Planning, **15**·1–39
  Alternative plans, **15**·3
  Budgeting and, **15**·5–8

G·17

Financial Planning (*Continued*)
  Capital expenditures and, **17**·9
  Comprehensive character, **15**·2–3
  Computers used for, **15**·3–5
  Concepts, **15**·1
  Continuous, **15**·3
  Current asset planning, **16**·1–33
  Definition and scope, **15**·1–5
  Financial statement projections, **15**·25–30
  For expansions, **15**·30–33
    Estimating additional capacity, **15**·31
    Forecast of demand and selling prices, **15**·31
    Forecast of economic conditions, **15**·30–31
    Increased working capital requirements, **15**·32
    Long-term goal, **15**·30
    Production costs at increased volume, **15**·31–32
    Profitability of, **15**·33
    Selling and advertising costs, **15**·32
  Organization for, **15**·35–39
    Board of directors, **15**·36–39
    Responsibility for, **15**·35–36
  Profit planning, **15**·8–25
Financial Reporting Services, **8**·6
Financial Reports, **8**·1–44 (See also "Financial Statements")
  Analysis of, **8**·28–31
  Annual reports, **8**·4–5
  Balance sheets, **8**·13–22 (See also "Balance Sheets")
  Certification of, **8**·27–28
  Consolidated statements, **8**·22–23
  Evolution of, **8**·1–4
    Early corporate reports, **8**·1
    I.C.C. regulation, **8**·3
  Income statements, **8**·7–13 (See also "Income Statement")
  Interim, **8**·5
  New York Stock Exchange requirements, **8**·1–2
  S.E.C. requirements, **8**·2–3, **8**·5–6
  Sources of financial data, **8**·4–7
    Financial reporting services, **8**·6
    Information from the company, **8**·4–5
    S.E.C. information, **8**·5–6
    Short-term credit information, **8**·6–7
  To board of directors, **15**·38
  Trend toward "humanizing," **8**·3–4
Financial Statements
  Analysis, **7**·13, **8**·28–31
    Cash or accrual accounting, **8**·29
    Comparative, **8**·31, **8**·40–43
    Credit analysis, **8**·30–31
    Expenses subject to managerial discretion, **8**·29
    For financial management, **8**·31
    Investment analysis, **8**·30
    Need for, **8**·28
    Purposes of, **8**·29–30
    Ratios, **8**·31–39
  Application of funds, **8**·40–42
  Auditor's examinations and reports, **10**·50
  Balance sheets, **8**·13–22 (See also "Balance Sheets")
    Certification of, **8**·27–28
    Form of report, **8**·28
    Standards for, **8**·27–28
  Consolidated, **7**·13, **8**·22–23
  Estimated statements, **8**·27
  Funds statement, **8**·25–27
  Income statements, **8**·7–13 (See also "Income Statement")
  Pro-forma statements, **15**·25–26
  Projections of, **8**·44, **15**·25–30

Financial Statements (*Continued*)
  Railroads, **7**·24
  Ratio analysis, **8**·31–39
    Income statements, **8**·35–36
    Interstatement, **8**·36–38
    Significant ratios, **8**·31–32
  S.E.C. regulations, **10**·49–50
  Securities Act of 1933, **9**·38
  Statement of retained earnings, **8**·25
  Statement of variation of working capital, **16**·17
Financial Vice-President, **15**·35–36
Financing
  Accounts receivable, **16**·14–15
  Debt, **14**·1–44
  Expansions, **15**·30–33
  Foreign trade, **3**·15–27
  Inventories, **16**·15–16
  Proposals for, **9**·11–13
  Public, **12**·1
  Small businesses, **16**·13
Finders, Of financial proposals, **9**·11–12
  Fee, **9**·12
Finished Goods, Inventories of, **16**·7
Fire Insurance, **25**·14–15
Fiscal Agents
  For payment of dividends, **18**·30
  Trust companies as, **6**·23
Fiscal Policy, **11**·4–5
Fixed Assets, **16**·4
  Ratios, in statement analysis, **8**·33, **8**·35
Fixed Capital Assets, **17**·1–4
  Components, **17**·2
  Economic nature of, **17**·2
  In relation to total assets, **17**·2–3
  Insurance on, **17**·7–8
  Nature of, **17**·1–4
  Recovery of tangible assets, **17**·3–4
  Turnover, **17**·10–11
  Valuation of fixed tangible assets, **17**·4
Fixed Tangible Assets
  Recovery of, **17**·3–4
  Valuation of, **17**·4
Flexible Budgets, **15**·7
"Floating Debt," Government, **11**·2–3
Floor Traders, New York Stock Exchange, **10**·7–8
Forecasts and Forecasting
  Balance sheet projections, **15**·26–29
  Budgets, **15**·7 (See also "Budgets and Budgeting")
  Business conditions, **15**·33
  Capital expenditures, **17**·8–9
  Cash, **16**·25
    Long-term, **16**·25–26
    Receipts from sales, **16**·28–30
    Shorter-term, **16**·26
  Economic conditions, **15**·30–31
  Financial statements, **15**·25–30
  Operating, **15**·27
  Profit and loss statements, **15**·26–27
  Retained earnings, **15**·29–30
Foreclosure Sales, **22**·2
Foreign Aid Programs, **2**·29
  Financing, **3**·30–32
Foreign Corporations, **12**·17
  Trust company as, **6**·23
Foreign Countries, Government securities held by, **11**·12
Foreign Exchange, **3**·4–13
  Brokers, **3**·6
  Cable transfers, **3**·7
  Control of, **3**·11–12
  Free vs. controlled currencies, **3**·11–12

Foreign Exchange (*Continued*)
  Future transactions, **3**·9–10
  Market, **3**·10
  Hedging, **3**·9–10
  Mail transfers, **3**·7–8
  Markets, **3**·5–13
    Nature and functions of, **3**·5
    New York, **3**·5
  Quotation of rates of exchange, **3**·6–7
    Open market and commercial rates, **3**·6–7
    Types of exchange quoted, **3**·7
  Sight drafts, **3**·8–9
  Speculation in exchange, **3**·10–11
  Spot transactions, **3**·9–10
  Time drafts, **3**·9
  Types of credit instruments, **3**·7–9
Foreign Money Markets, **1**·27–30
Foreign Securities
  Arbitrage, **10**·58
  Distribution of blocks of foreign issues, **10**·57–58
  Interest equalization tax, **10**·56–57
  Investment in, **10**·56–57
  Markets for, **10**·58
  Organization dealing in, **10**·57
Foreign Subsidiaries, **20**·40–41
Foreign Trade Financing, **3**·17–29
  American Depositary receipts, **3**·28–29
  By exporters, **3**·17–18
  By exporter's bank, **3**·21
  By importers, **3**·18–21
  By importer's bank, **3**·21–26
  Risks in, **3**·17
  Travelers' checks, **3**·28
  U. S. government and international agencies, **3**·30–32
Forfeiture Bonds, **25**·25–26
Forgeries
  Checks, **24**·38
  Indorsements, **24**·13–14
  Negotiable instruments, **24**·7
Forms
  Authorizations, reorganizations, **22**·15
  Balance sheets, **8**·14–15
  Certification of independent public auditors, **8**·28
  Income statements, **8**·8
  Operating reports, **15**·12
  Par value stock certificate, **13**·6
  Proxies, **13**·16
  Statement of retained earnings, **8**·25
  Stock subscription, **13**·18
  Subscription warrant, **13**·27
Founders' Shares, **13**·23–24
Fractional Shares, **13**·30–31
Franchises
  Public utilities, **7**·16–17
  Taxes, **20**·30
Fraud
  Antifraud provisions, Uniform Securities Act, **9**·45
  In the sale of securities, **9**·28
  Transactions of brokers and dealers, **10**·55–56
". . . Freight Equalized," Quotation, **23**·34
  Obligations of sellers and buyers, **23**·34
Full Disclosure Requirements (See "Disclosure Requirements")
"Full-Paid and Nonassessable" Stock, **13**·5
Funded Debt
  Ratios, in statement analysis, **8**·34–35
  Valuation of, **8**·20
Funds
  Contingency, **16**·2–3
  Flow, **18**·26

Funds (*Continued*)
   Measuring supply and demand of, **1·**6–8
   Relationship between reserves and, **18·**8
   Sources of, **1·**6
   Sources of information, **1·**7–8
   Statement, **8·**25–27
   Users of, **1·**7
Futures Trading (See also "Commodity Trading")
   Evolution and nature of, **23·**1–6
   Futures contract, **23·**3–6
   Growth of, **23·**2–3
   Interpreting, **23·**29–31
   Origin and scope of futures exchanges, **23·**2
   Types of commodities traded, **23·**2–3
   Volume of trading, **23·**3

Gas Industry, **7·**21
Going Concern Value, **20·**26
Gold
   As Reserve Asset, **3·**3–4
   Balance of Payments, **3·**3
   Bonds payable in, **14·**7
   Changes in stocks, **2·**11
   For settling international accounts, **3·**1–2
Gold Certificate Reserve, **2·**9
Gold Certificates, **2·**7
Gold Reserve Act, **2·**7
Gold Standard, **2·**2
   Devaluation and, **2·**7
Goods-In-Process, Inventories, **16·**7
Goodwill
   Subsidiaries to secure, **20·**40
   Valuation of, **20·**26, **20·**28
   Writing off, **21·**5
Government Obligations, **10·**1, **11·**1–29
   Certificates of indebtedness, **11·**7
   Characteristics of, **11·**6–11
      Prompt payment, **11·**6
   Dealers in, **11·**12–13
   Depositary bonds, **11·**10
   Factors affecting prices and yields, **11·**17–24
      Effects of Treasury policies, **11·**20–21
      Influence of Federal Reserve policies, **11·**19
      Major market movements, **11·**21–24
      Money market conditions and bond prices, **11·**17–19
      Supply and demand, **11·**18
      Nonmanaged factors, **11·**21
      Volume of short-term investments, **11·**18
   Federal agency issues, **11·**7–8, **16·**5
      Attractive features, **11·**8
   For bank investments, **5·**21–22
   Foreign Series and Foreign Currency series, **11·**10
   Interest on, **27·**9–10
   Investment risks, **11·**6
   Market for, **11·**11–17
      Classes of investors, **11·**11–12
      Dealers, **11·**12–13
      Delivery of securities, **11·**15
      Long-range picture, **11·**23–24
      Major movements, **11·**21–24
         Trends since World War II, **11·**22–24
      Operation and size of, **11·**13–15
      Quotations, **11·**14
      Role of Federal Reserve System, **11·**15–16
         Abandonment of "Bills Only" policy, **11·**15
   Marketable issues, **11·**7
   Municipal bonds, **11·**26–29
   National debt, **11·**1–6
   Nonmarketable obligations, **11·**9–10
   Public housing authorities' obligations, **11·**27
   Purchases by banks, **2·**10, **5·**22–23

Government Obligations (*Continued*)
   Repurchase agreements, **2·**16, **16·**5
   Selection of, **11·**6–7
   Short-term, **1·**10, **1·**16–17
   State and municipal bonds, **11·**24–29
      Purpose of borrowing, **11·**24–25
   Tax status, **11·**10, **11·**25
   Trading, **11·**12–15
   Treasury bills, **11·**7
   Treasury bonds
      Investment Series A, **11·**9
      Investment Series B-1975-80, **11·**9–10
      R.E.A. Series, **11·**10
   Treasury financing techniques, **11·**10–11
      Advance refundings, **11·**11
      Coupon obligations, **11·**10
      Exchange offerings, **11·**11
      Tax-anticipation issues, **11·**10
      Treasury bill auctions, **11·**10
   Treasury notes, **11·**7
   Treasury obligations, **16·**5
      Long-term, **16·**5
      Short-term, **16·**5
   Types of, **5·**23
   United States savings bonds, **11·**8–9
      Redemption values and investment yields, **11·**9
      Series E bonds, **11·**8
      Series H bonds, **11·**8–9
   Yield patterns, **11·**16–17
      Factors affecting prices and, **11·**17–24
Government Regulations
   Banking, **2·**19–20, **5·**2–3
   Business combinations, **20·**6
   Depreciation, **17·**32–33
   Insurance companies, **25·**11, **25·**40
   Investment companies, **4·**31–33
   Public utility industries, **7·**18, **20·**43–45
   Railroads, **7·**21–22, **8·**3
   Securities trading, **10·**46–56, **14·**4–5
Government Securities (See "Government Obligations")
Government Trust Accounts, **11·**12
Grades, Commodities, **23·**4–5
Grain Futures Act, **23·**10
Greenbacks, **2·**6
Group Annuity Contracts
   Pension plans, **19·**46
   Profit-sharing plans, **19·**46
Guaranteed Bonds, **14·**26–28
Guaranteed Stock, **13·**23
Guarantors, Bankruptcy actions, **22·**27
Guardians
   Fees and commissions, **6·**20
   Of an incompetent, **6·**7
   Of a minor, **6·**7

Hedging, **23·**23–28
   Anticipating requirements, **23·**27
   Balances, **23·**27
   Basis gains and losses, **23·**25–26
   Buying cotton on call, **23·**27–28
      Mechanics of transaction, **23·**28
   Dealers, **23·**24
   Definition, **23·**23
   Excess working capital, **16·**2
   Foreign exchange transactions, **3·**9–10
   Importers, **23·**24
   Insurance and, **23·**26
   Limitations, **23·**25–26
   Manufacturers, **23·**24–25
   Placing a hedge, **23·**26
   Problems in, **23·**26–28
   Processors, **23·**23–24

Hedging (*Continued*)
Producers, 23·24
Shifting a hedge, 23·26–27
Tax status, 23·25
Theory and practice, 23·23
Types of, 23·25
Versus speculation, 23·25
Hepburn Act of 1906, 8·3
Holder in Due Course
Negotiable instruments, 24·14–15
Rights of, 24·17
Holding Companies, 20·34–46
Acquisition of stock control, 20·36–37
Purchase for cash, 20·36
Through exchange of stock, 20·36–37
Advantages and disadvantages, 20·37–39
Changes in corporate structure, 21·22
Creation of subsidiaries by parent company, 20·39–41
Dealings between parent and subsidiary, 20·37
Definition, 20·35
Holding-operating companies, 20·35
Legal restrictions, 20·35–36
Maintaining corporate existence after transfer of assets, 20·39
Majority interest, 20·34
Parent-subsidiary relationship, 20·39–41
Abuse, 20·41
Deep Rock Doctrine, 20·42
Instrumentality rule, 20·41–42
Public utility, 20·42–43
Acquisition of securities and properties, 20·44
Federal Power Act, 20·45
Government regulation, 20·43–45
"Grandfather" clause, 20·44
Periodic reports and accounts, 20·45
Registration of, 20·43
Regulation of, 20·43–45
New security issues, 20·43–44
Simplification and integration, 20·44
Supervision of intercompany loans, dividends, security transactions, 20·44–45
"Upstream" loans, 20·43
Use of Massachusetts Trust, 20·45
Regulation, 20·45–46
Trusts as combination device, 20·36
Types of, 20·35
With one subsidiary, 20·35
Home Loan Bank System, 4·15
Housing and Home Finance Agency, 2·37
Hypothecation Agreements, 10·38

Income
Capitalization analysis, 26·26
Cash income vs. profit, 16·24
Combined statement of income and retained earnings, 8·26
Deferred, 8·20
In income statement, 8·9
Insurance against loss of, 25·21
Losses directly affecting, 25·4–5
Net, 17·72
Net operating, 17·72
Income Bonds, 14·28–29
Income Statement, 8·7–13
Analysis, 8·7–13
Charges to surplus, 8·12–13
Comparative analysis, 8·42–44
Contents, 8·7–8
Cost of goods sold, 8·9–10
Depletion, 8·11–12
Depreciation policies, 8·10–11
Effects of price changes, 8·9–10

Income Statement (*Continued*)
Federal incomes taxes, 8·12
Form of, 8·8
Inventory valuation, 8·9
Nonoperating items, 8·12
Nonrecurring items, 8·13
Other operating expenses, 8·12
Railroads, 7·24
Ratios, 8·35–36
Net profit margin, 8·35
Number of times fixed charges earned, 8·35–36
Operating ratio, 8·35
Sales or revenues, 8·9
Installment sales and deferred income, 8·9
Use by management, 15·24
Income Taxes (See "Taxes")
Incompetent Persons
Guardians of, 6·7
Trusts for, 6·10–11
Incorporation Process, 12·19
State of incorporation, 12·16–18
Indemnification, Of corporate executives, 12·30
Indentures
After-acquired clause, 20·14
Bond, 14·7–17
Debt readjustments, 21·15
Trust, 14·8
Trust Indenture Act of 1939, 14·9–10
Indexes, Profitability, 17·46
Indorsements
Blank, 24·11
By infant or corporation, 24·13
Checks, 24·38–39
Conditional, 24·11–12
"For deposit," 24·12
Forged, 24·13–14
Negotiable instruments, 24·11–14
Method of, 24·13
Qualified, 24·11, 24·12
Restrictive, 24·11
Special, 24·11
Stock certificates, 13·3
Striking out, 24·14
Indorsers
Bankruptcy actions, 22·27
Liabilities of, 24·19–20
Industrial Banking, 2·41
Savings departments, 4·5
Industrial Engineering Studies, 15·19
Industrial Securities
Analysis of, 7·10–14
Cash flow, 7·12
Nature of industry, 7·10–11
Prospective earnings, 7·11–12
Industries, Wasting Asset, 7·13
Information Analysis, Use of computers, 15·4
Insider Trading, 10·50–51
Insolvency (See also "Bankruptcy")
Assessment of stockholders, 13·5–6
Definition, 22·2
Installment Paper, 5·34, 16·14
Installment Sales
Accounts receivable financing, 16·14–15
Effective rates of interest, 2·41
In income statement, 8·9
Institute of Life Insurance, 4·39
Institutional Investors, 9·6
Life insurance companies, 4·37–39
Sales and leaseback arrangements, 26·27
Security purchases, 9·6
Types of, 9·6
Institutional Securities Corp., 4·10–11
"In Store" quotation, 23·35
Obligations of sellers and buyers, 23·35

Insurance
 Against physical damage to property, 25·14–21
 "All-Risk" policies, 25·12
 Apportionment clause, 25·14
 Automobile, 25·20, 25·29
 Availability of, 25·8–9
 Bank deposits, 2·19, 5·6–9
 Builders'-risk contracts, 25·19
 Business coverages, 25·15–16
 Business interruption insurance, 25·21
 Business uses of life insurance, 25·31–36
  Programs for employees, 25·34–36
  Provision for loss of key men and business continuation, 25·31
 Co-insurance clause, 25·13
 Commercial coverage, 25·11–14
 Companies, 4·34–39, 25·37–42
  Admitted insurers, 25·37
  Claims services, 25·39
  Distribution channels, 25·38–49
   American Agency System, 25·38–39
   Direct distribution, 25·38
   Indirect distribution, 25·38–39
  Financial soundness, 25·40–42
  Government regulation, 25·40
  Government securities held by, 11·12
  Insurance brokers, 25·39
  Intercompany organizations, 25·37
  Investments of, 9·6
   In state and local issues, 11·28–29
  Loss prevention services, 25·40
  Scope of underwriting authority, 25·38
  Selecting, 25·37–42
  Stocks, 7·15–16
  Types of, 25·37
 Comprehensive policies, 25·12
 Cost of commercial vs. self-insurance, 25·9–10
 Crime, 25·22–24
  Burglary, 25·23
  Business coverages, 25·23–24
  Characteristic of coverages, 25·23
  Definitions, 25·22–23
  Financial institution coverages, 25·24
  Robbery, 25·23
  Theft and larceny, 25·22
 Endowment, 4·35
 Extended coverage endorsement, 25·14–15
 Extra expense, 25·21
 Fidelity and surety bonding and, 25·24–26
 Fire and allied lines, 25·14–15
  Additional extended coverage, 25·15
  Extended coverage endorsement, 25·14–15
 Fixed capital assets, 17·7–8
 Floater policies, 25·12, 25·19
 General cover, 25·12
 Government regulation, 25·11
 Group, 25·35
 Hedging and, 23·26
 Inland marine policies, 25·17–18
  "Nationwide Definition," 25·18, 25·19
 Jewelers' block policy, 25·15
 Key man, 25·31–34
 Leasehold interest, 25·22
 Liability, 25·26–31
  Acts of agents, 25·28–29
  Automobile owners and operators, 25·29
  Bailment, 25·29
  Business, 25·30
  Business uses, 25·31–36
  Employer liability, 25·27
  Imposed by contracts, 25·29–30
  Liability of landlords and tenants, 25·27–28
  Negligence and, 25·26–27
  Personal, 25·30

Insurance (*Continued*)
 Liability (*Continued*)
  Product liability, 25·28
  Professional, 25·28, 25·30
  Protection provided by, 25·30–41
 Life (See "Life Insurance")
 Loss of income policies, 25·21
 Manufacturers' output policy, 25·15–16
 Marine policies, 25·16–19
  Coverage, 25·16
  Inland, 25·17–18
  Losses, 25·17
 Mercantile block policy, 25·15
 Mortgage, 26·13–14
 Mortgagee clause, 25·14
 Multiple location policies, 25·12
 Ocean marine policies, 25·16–19
 Old Age and Survivors and Disability Insurance (OASDI), 19·51
 Package policies, 25·12
 Pension plans, 25·35
 Policies, 25·11–12
  Against consequential losses, 25·21–22
  Important clauses, 25·13–14
  Standardization of, 25·11–12
  Types of, 25·12–13
 Pro rata distribution clause, 25·13
 Pro rata liability clause, 25·13
 Profits, 25·22
 Programs for employees, 25·34–36
  Salary continuation or deferred compensation plans, 25·35
  Split dollar plans, 25·34–35
 Purchasing, 25·8–10
 Rents and rental value, 25·21–22
 Replacement cost clause, 25·13–14
 Reserves for, 18·11
 Savings and loan, 4·15–16
 Schedule policies, 25·12
 Self-, 25·7–8
 Steam boiler and machinery, 25·20
 Subrogation clause, 25·14
 Temperature damage, 25·22
 Term, 4·35
 Transportation policies, 25·18–19
Intangible Assets, 17·1
 Balance sheet treatment, 8·18–19
 Definition, 8·18
 Valuation of, 8·18–19, 20·28
 Writing off, 21·5
Intangible Fixed Assets, 17·2
Inter-American Development Bank, 3·32
 Fund for Special Operations, 3·32
Intercorporate Readjustments, 21·22–24
 Methods, 21·23–24
Interest
 Anticipation rates, 27·10–12
  Tables, 27·11
 Bonds, 7·4–5
  After maturity, 24·41
  1867–1967, 1·2
  Payment of, 14·7
  Quality of, 1·3
 Brokers' charges, 10·34–35
 Compound, 24·40, 27·20–29
  Arithmetical solution, 27·21
  Definitions, 27·20–21
  Of present value, 27·25
  Finding the compound amount, 27·21–25
  Finding present value by logs, 27·28
  Finding present value from tables, 27·25–27
  Other converse cases, 27·28–29
  Solution by formula, 27·21
  Tables, 27·22–23

Interest (*Continued*)
  Computation of, 27·1–12, 27·20–29
    Merchant's Rule, 24·42, 27·15
    Under partial payment plans, 27·15
    United States rule, 24·42, 27·16
  Computing elapsed time in days, 27·2
  Contractual and implied, 24·40–41
  Convertible bonds, 14·32
  Debt readjustments, 21·15
  Definitions, 24·40, 27·1
    Principal, 27·1
    Rate, 27·1
    Time, 27·1
  Equalization tax, 10·56–57
  Exact, 27·1, 27·7–12
    Anticipation rates, 27·10–12
    On government securities, 27·9–10
    Tables, 27·8–9
  Lawful, 24·40
  Level of, 1·1
    Long cycles and short cycles, 1·1
    Measuring supply and demand of funds, 1·6–8
  Merchantile Rule, 24·42, 27·15
  Method of calculating depreciation. 17·30
  Method of determining, 1·1–5
  Money markets and, 1·1–30
  Negotiable instruments, 24·8, 24·40–42
    After maturity, 24·41
    Contractual and implied, 24·40–41
    Definition, 24·40
    Lawful interest, 24·40
    Stopping of, 24·41–42
    Transfer without, 24·14
  On bank deposits, 5·5–6
  On borrowed funds, 17·50–51
  On installment credit, 2·41
  On Treasury obligations, 11·4
  Ordinary, 27·1, 27·4–6
    Basic formula, 27·4
    Breaking up the time element, 27·4–5
    Odd interest rates, 27·5–6
    One-day rule, 27·6
    Short-cut methods, 27·4
  Payment of, Income bonds, 14·28
  Payment of, Pledged securities, 14·22
  Pegging, 1·1
  Promissory notes, 24·40
  Role of credit control, 1·3, 1·5
  Role of Treasury debt management, 1·5
  Short-term or long-term rates, 1·2
  Simple, 27·1
  Stopping of, 24·41–42
  Structure, 1·1–3
    Changes in, 1·2–3
    Quality of bonds, 1·3
  Tables, 27·2–3
  Types of, 27·1–3
  "United States Rule," 24·42, 27·16
  When interest starts, 24·41
Interlocking Directorates, 20·45, 20·47
Internal Revenue Service
  Approval of pension plans, 19·4–5
  Depreciation regulation, 17·32–33
  On purchase of assets, 20·9
International Bank for Reconstruction and Development, 3·28–29
International Banking, 3·1–30
  Agencies and branches of foreign banks, 3·15
  Balance of payments, 3·1–2
  Financing of foreign trade, 3·15–27
  Foreign branches and affiliates, 3·15–17
    Edge Act corporations, 3·15–16
    Role of the Federal Reserve Banks, 3·16
  Foreign exchange, 3·4–13

International Banking (*Continued*)
  International departments of banks, 3·13–15
    Cables, 3·15
    Commercial credit division, 3·14
    Foreign exchange traders, 3·14
    Foreign tellers, 3·14
    New accounts section, 3·13–14
    Operations of, 3·13
    Travel section, 3·14
  Payments transactions, 3·1–2
  U. S. government and intn'l agencies, 3·30–32
International Dealings in Securities, 10·56–58
International Development Association (IDA), 3·32
International Finance Corporation (IFC), 3·32
International Financial Markets, 3·12–13
  Euro-Dollar Market, 3·12
  Multiple-Currency Bonds, 3·12
  Hard-Currency Bonds, 3·12–13
International Monetary Fund (IMF), 2·28, 3·3, 3·28–29
International Monetary Settlements, 2·5–6
International Monetary System, 3·2–4
  Role of Gold, 3·4
Interstate Commerce Act, 7·21
Interstate Commerce Commission, 7·21
  Competitive bidding required, 9·13
  Depreciation regulation, 17·33
  Financial information published by, 8·6
  Railroad reorganizations and, 22·9
  Regulation of financial reporting, 8·3
Intestate, 6·6
Inventories, 16·7–9
  Adjusting to economic conditions, 15·34
  As working capital, 16·7–9
  Balance sheet treatment, 8·16–17
  Control, 16·7
  Determination of cost, 8·17
  Financing, 15·34, 16·15–16
    Field warehousing, 16·15
    Loans on pledge of commodities, 16·15–16
  Insurance coverage, 25·12
  Investment in, 16·7
  Loans, 2·35–36
  Ratio to net working capital, 8·33–34
  Reserves for future declines, 18·11
  Size of, 16·7
  Systems for controlling, 16·8
    Budgetary control, 16·8
    Min-Max system, 16·8
    Order cycling, 16·8
    Perpetual inventory control, 16·8
    Statistical, 16·8
    Turnover rates, 16·8
    Two-bin, 16·8
  Turnover of, 16·10
  Use of computers, 15·4
  Valuation, 8·9, 16·8–9
    Average cost, 16·9
    Cost or market, whichever is lower, 16·9
    Effects of price changes, 8·9–10
    FIFO method, 8·10, 16·9
    In income statement, 8·9
    LIFO method, 8·10, 16·9
    Methods of, 8·10
    Revaluation allowances, 16·9
    Specific costs, 16·8
Investigations
  Of financial proposals, 9·13–14
  Securities, 9·46
Investment Advisers
  Licensing, 9·44
  Registration of, 9·46–47
  Uniform Securities Act, 9·45–47

GENERAL INDEX

G·23

Investment Advisers Act of 1940, 4·33–34, 10·32
Investment Analysis, 8·6 (See also "Security Analysis")
Investment Banking, 9·8–27
  Accounting and record-keeping, 9·26–27
  As managers of portfolios, 9·27
  Bankers, 9·10
    Retailers, 9·10
    Wholesalers, 9·10
  Bond readjustments, 21·16–17
  Internal organization, 9·10–11
  International security trading, 10·57
  Investment trusts, 9·27
  "Letter of intent," 9·13–14
  Market stabilization, 9·24–25
    Legal restriction on, 9·25
    S.E.C. rules, 9·25–26
  Miscellaneous activities, 9·27
  Nature of, 9·8
  Private placements, 14·42
  Public offerings, 9·22–24
    Issues of small enterprises, 9·2–4
  Purchasing new issues, 9·11–19
    Commercial banks, 9·12
    Competitive bidding, 9·13
    Direct application for, 9·12–13
    Finders, 9·11–12
    Investigation of financial proposals, 9·13–14
    Policies, 9·11
    Pre-existing relations with issuers, 9·11–19
    Purchase group, 9·16–17
    Sources of new financing proposals, 9·11–13
    Traveling representatives, 9·12
    Underwriting contract, 9·14–16
  Responsibilities to issuer and investor, 9·9–10
  Role of Securities Act of 1933, 9·9
  Sale of new issues, 9·19–24
    Opening and closing the books, 9·23
    Price cutting, 9·23–24
    Public offering, 9·22–24
    Selling group, 9·20–21
      Agreement, 9·21–22
  Sales department, 9·19
  Security salesmen, 9·24
  Spreading the risk, 9·16–17
  Statistical and advisory activities, 9·26
  Trading department, 9·26
  Underwriting, 9·14–16
    Stand-by, 9·8
Investment Companies, 4·19–34
  Accounting problems, 4·27–30
  Annual reports, 4·27–30
  Characteristics of, 4·20
  Classification of, 4·22–23
  Common trust funds, 4·25–26
  Companies issuing face amount installment certificates, 4·27
  Extent of managerial discretion, 4·22
  Growth of assets, 4·23
  Investment Company Act, 4·31–33
  Investment counsel, 4·33–34
  Investment profits, 4·20–22
  Management, 5·23–25
    Closed-end vs. open-end, 4·24
    Diversified and nondiversified companies, 4·25
    Investment policy, 4·24–25
    Leverage, 4·28
    Open-end funds, 4·25
  Nature and purpose, 4·19–20
  Periodic payment plans, 4·26–27
  Regulation, 4·31–33
  Stock analysis, 7·16

Investment Companies (*Continued*)
  Taxes, 4·30–31
    State taxes, 4·31
  Unit or fixed trusts, 4·26
Investment Company Act of 1940, 4·19, 4·27, 4·31–33
Investment Company Institute, 4·33
Investment Services, 8·6–7, 10·32
  Bond ratings, 7·5–6
Investment Tax Credit, Capital expenditures, 17·11–12
Investment Trusts, 9·27
  Real estate, 12·9
Investment Value, Method of valuation, 20·26
Investments (See also "Securities")
  Alternative proposals, 17·40
  Analysis, 8·6
  Balance sheet treatment, 8·17–18
  Banks, 5·21–27
    Eligible for purchase, 5·21–22
    Investment department, 5·26
    Portfolio policy, 5·24–25
    Preference for government obligation, 5·22–23
    Profits from sale of, 5·25–26
    Real estate mortgages, 5·26–27
    Tax switching, 5·26
    Valuation of, 5·23–24
  Base, 15·14–15
    Inclusion of leases, 15·15
  Characteristics of, 7·1–2
  Classes of, 7·1
  Counsel, 4·33–34
  Decisions, 17·40–41, 17·49
    Comparison of two opportunities, 17·77
    Risk and uncertainty, 17·75–77
  Definition, 7·1
  Direct vs. indirect, 4·1
  Dollar cost averaging, 7·2
  Equity, 7·1
    Security analysis, 7·14
  Estimating profitability of, 17·22–23
    Accounting or average return method, 17·22, 17·37
    Discounted cash-flow method, 17·23, 17·38–40
    Payback, 17·22, 17·36–37
  Evaluating proposals, 17·36–37
    Accounting or average rate of return method, 17·22, 17·37
    Discounted cash flow, 17·23, 17·38–40
    Disposal value, 17·41
    Excess present value method, 17·40
    Incremental costs and savings, 17·41
    Payback or payout period, 17·22, 17·36–37
    Sunk costs and depreciation, 17·40–41
    Time-adjusted methods, 17·38–40
  Financial reporting services, 8·6
  Financial statement analysis, 8·30
  Fixed income, 7·1
    Security analysis, 7·14
  Funds
    Factors influencing the demand, 9·1
    Need for, 9·1
  Government obligations, 11·6–11
  In foreign securities, 10·56–57
  In subsidiaries, analysis of, 8·16–17, 8·24
  Legal restrictions, 2·21, 7·3
  Liquidity, 7·3
  Management, 6·15–17
  Marketability, 7·3
  Mutual savings banks, 4·5–10
  Of life insurance companies, 4·37–39
  Of savings, 9·2
  Of surplus cash, 16·4–6

Investments (*Continued*)
  Pension plans, 19·30–31
    State and local plans, 19·52–53
  Principles, 7·1–4
  Profit-sharing plans, 19·45–46
  Ranking projects, 17·46–47
  Rate of return on, 15·13–15
    As gauge of performance, 15·13–15
    Components of, 15·15–16
    Determining earnings, 15·14
    Investment base, 15·14–15
  Ratios of return on, 8·38
  Regulatory legislation, 2·21
  Replacement, 17·6
  Retirement plans for self-employed individuals, 19·49
  Return on, 7·2–3
  Safety of, 7·1–2
    Diversification, 7·2
    Forms of safety sought, 7·2
    Inflation hedge, 7·2
    Timing hazard, 7·2
  Savings and loan associations, 4·14–15
  Security analysis, 7·1–24 (See also "Security Analysis")
  Selling securities, 9·1–52
  Small business investment companies, 9·5
  Speculation differs from, 10·29
  Supervisory services, 6·19
    Fees, 6·21
  Tax status, 7·3
  Trusts, 6·13–17
    Absence of express power to sell, 6·14
    Duties of a trustee, 6·14–15
    Management of, 6·15–17
      Fees and commissions, 6·21
    Officers' investment committee, 6·15–16
    Powers of trustees, 6·13–14
    Prudent Man Rule, 6·14
    Resignation of a trustee, 6·15
    Restrictions on investment powers, 6·14
    Reviewing department, 6·16
    Securities analysis department, 6·16–17
    Types of, 6·14
Investors, 9·7
  As buyers of securities, 9·7
  In state and local issues, 11·28–29
  Life insurance companies, 4·37–39
  Responsibilities of investment banker to, 9·8–9
Invoices, Anticipation rates and percentages, 27·10–12
"Iron Reserve," 16·5
Issuers of Securities
  Definition, 9·28
  Responsibilities of investment banker to, 9·8–9
  Summary prospectus, 9·33
Issues, Securities (See also "Investment Banking")
  Purchase of new, 9·11–19
  Sale of, 9·19–24

Jewelers' Insurance Policy, 25·15
Joint Accounts, 5·11–12
  Joint tenants, 5·11–12
  Tenants in common, 5·11
Joint Bonds, 14·29
Joint Stock Companies, 12·10
  Advantages and disadvantages, 12·10
  Method of formation, 12·10
  Tax status, 12·10
Joint Tenants, 5·11–12
Joint Ventures, Promoters, 12·14

Key Men
  Insurance on life of, 25·31–34
  Provision for loss of, 25·31
  Losses from death or disability of, 25·5

Labor Unions, Pension plans, 19·53
Land
  As fixed capital assets, 17·1
  Balance sheet treatment, 8·18, 17·1
  Development financing, 26·15
  Trusts, 26·17
  Valuation of, 8·18
Landlords, Liabilities of, 25·27–28
Last-In First-Out (LIFO), Method of inventory valuation, 8·10, 16·9
Leases and Leasing, 14·42–44
  Advantages, 14·43
  Agreements, 20·31–32
    Difficulties in drafting equitable, 20·34
    Philadelphia plan, 14·24
  Alternative to borrowing, 14·42
  Combination by lease, 20·31–34
  Deductibility of interest, 26·17
  Disadvantages, 14·43
  Equipment, 14·44
  Financial statement treatment, 17·67
  Financing buildings through, 14·42–44
  Form of rental, 20·34
    Guaranty of rental, 20·34
  Gross, 26·18–19
  Inclusion in investment base, 15·15
  Industrial, 20·33
  Lease reporting and the cost of capital, 17·66–67
  Leasehold interest insurance, 25·22
  Leasehold mortgages, 26·15
  Leasing as junior financing, 14·44
  Long-term, 26·17–20
    Net leases, 26·17–18
    Ninety-nine-year, 26·17–18
    Twenty-one-year, 26·18
  Mergers to end, 20·34
  Railroad, 20·33
  Sale-and-leaseback financing, 14·43
  Status of lessor corporation, 20·32–33
  Statutes governing, 20·33
  Tax treatment, 20·31, 21·23
  Typical provisions, 26·19
  Used to spread risks, 25·10
  Variable rent, 26·19–20
Legal Reserve Requirements, 1·20, 2·17, 2·30
Legal Restrictions
  Arrearages on preferred stock, 21·11–12
  Assignments, 21·19–20
  Consolidations and mergers, 20·17–19
  Debt readjustments, 21·15
  Dividends, 18·18–23
  Preferred stock recapitalizations, 21·9
  Reorganization plans, 22·10–11
Legal Tender, 2·4
Lending Institutions, 2·33–41
Letter of Comment, Registration statements, 9·36
Letter of Hypothecation and General Assurance, 3·26
"Letter of Intent," 9·13
Letters of Credit
  Assignable, 3·25
  Authority to purchase, 3·25–26
  Commercial, 3·21–23
  Confirmed and unconfirmed, 3·25
  Documents attached to draft, 3·26
  Handled by international departments of banks, 3·14

GENERAL INDEX

Letters of Credit (*Continued*)
  Import and export, 3·23–24
  Revocable and irrevocable, 3·24–25
  Revolving, 3·25
  Traveler's, 3·26–28
Leverage
  Management investment companies, 4·24
  Real estate investments, 26·23–24
LIFO (Last-in first-out method of inventory valuation), 8·10, 16·9
Liabilities
  Automobile owners and operators, 25·29
  Bailment, 25·29
  Balance sheet treatment, 8·13–14, 8·19–20
  Bank, deposits as, 5·9
  Board of directors, 12·29–30
  Business trusts, 12·8
  Business ventures, 12·2
  Classification of, 8·13–14
  Contingent, 8·20–21
  Current, 8·19–20, 16·1
    Deferred revenue or income, 8·20
    Ratio to owner's equity, 8·33
  Definition, 8·13–14
  Employer, 25·27
  For acts of agents, 25·28–29
  Imposed by a contract, 25·29–30
  Long-term, 8·20
  Miscellaneous, 25·30
  Negotiable instruments, 24·18–20
  Of a fiduciary, 6·17–18
  Of landlords and tenants, 25·27–28
  Of licensees, 25·27
  Of stockholders, 13·1
  Product, 25·28
  Professional, 25·28
  Reserves, 18·7
Licensees, Liabilities of, 25·27
Life Insurance, 4·34–39
  Business uses, 25·31–36
  Endowment, 4·35
  Premiums and dividends, 4·36
  Savings aspects, 4·34–35, 4·37
  Settlements of policies, 4·36–37
  Term insurance, 4·35
  Trusts, 6·9
    Funded, 6·9
    Partially funded, 6·9
    Unfunded, 6·9
  Whole life insurance, 4·35
Life Insurance Companies, 2·36
  Investments held by, 4·37–39
  Mortgages held by, 26·6–7
  Stocks, 7·15–16
Life Insurance Company Income Tax Act of 1959, 4·39
Limited Orders, 10·14–15
Line of Credit, 5·33–34
  Compensating balance, 5·33
Liquidations
  Of futures contracts, 23·18–20
  Reorganizations and, 22·2
  Voluntary, 21·25–26
    Liquidating agency, 21·26
    Procedures, 21·25–26
    To avoid insolvency, 21·25
  Wasting asset industries, 21·25
Listing Securities, 10·9–11
Living Trusts, 6·8–10
Lloyds Association, 25·37
Loans, 5·27–34
  Accommodation paper, 5·31
  Balloon maturity, 5·32
  Bank, 5·27–34

Loans (*Continued*)
  Bank (*Continued*)
    For working capital, 16·14
    Trends in, 2·25–26
    Types of, 5·28–29
    Use of, 5·28
  Banker's acceptances, 5·31
  Brokers', 1·10–11, 10·38–39
    Hypothecation agreement, 10·38
    Restrictions on broker borrowing, 10·38–39
  Call, 10·38
  Cash forecasts and, 15·34
  Collateral, 10·38
  Commercial banks, 2·10
  Compared with investment funds, 9·1
  Computing bank discount, 27·12–18
  Construction, 26·14
  Consumer, 5·34
  Credit analysis, 5·32–33
  Definition, 27·12–13
  Discounts differ from, 5·28–29
  Field warehouse, 5·30, 16·15
  Finding the number of payments to amortize, 27·43–44
  For working capital, 16·13–14
  Hypothecation agreement, 10·38
  Inventory, 2·35
  Line of credit, 5·33–34
  Mortgages, 2·35–38
  Notes, 27·13
  Of bonds, 10·41
  On commodities, 16·15–16
  On stock, 10·23
  Payment of, 15·34–35
  Principles and forms of borrowing, 14·1–5
    Debt financing, 14·1–2
    Debt vs. equity capital, 14·1
    Types of borrowing, 14·2–3
  Rates, 17·48–49
  Regulatory legislation, 2·21, 10·33–34
  Savings and loan associations, 4·14–15
  Secured, 5·29–30
  Security, 5·30–31
  Single-name vs. two-name paper, 5·31
  Term, 5·31–32, 14·3, 16·12
    By banks, 5·34
  To business, 2·34–35
  To corporations, 24·43–44
  To employees, 16·6
  To officers, 16·6
  "Upstream," 20·43
Logarithms, 27·54–56
  Characteristics of, 27·55
  Definition and uses, 27·54–55
  Finding the anti-log, 27·58
  Finding the log of a number, 27·55–57
  Interpolation, 27·57
  Log tables, 27·55, 27·56, 27·59–62
  Using logs to solve problems, 27·58–63
    Successive calculations, 27·65
    To divide numbers, 27·58, 27·63
    To find a root, 27·64
    To multiply numbers, 27·58
    To raise to a power, 27·63
London Money Market, 1·28–29
Losses
  Assumption of risk and loss, 25·7
  Benefits of loss control, 25·6–7
  Control of risk and loss, 25·6–7
  Directly affecting income, 25·4–5
  Due to dishonesty or other criminal acts, 25·5–6
  From death or disability of key personnel, 25·5

GENERAL INDEX

Losses (*Continued*)
  Insurance policies
    Consequential losses, 25·21–22
    Loss of income, 25·21
    Methods of loss reduction, 25·7
    Of property values, 25·3–4
    Self-insurance, 25·7–8
McFadden Act of 1927, 2·13
Machinery, Insurance, 25·20
Mahaffie Act, 21·17, 22·10
Mail Transfers, Foreign exchange, 3·7–8
Maintenance, Depreciation vs., 17·25–26
Managed Monetary Systems, 2·3–4
Management
  Financial statement analysis, 8·31
  Profit as tool of, 15·9
  Use of direct costing, 15·24
  Uses of ratios, 8·40
Management Investment Companies, 4·23–25
Management Shares, 13·23–24
Manipulation
  Commodity trading, 23·11
  Federal regulation, 10·52–53
  Of securities, 10·30
Manufacturers, Working capital ratios, 16·20–21
Margin Requirements, 1·11, 10·32–35
  Brokers' interest charges, 10·34–35
  Commodity trading, 23·17–18
  Customers', 10·33
  Deposited against short sales, 10·23
  Federal control, 10·33–34, 10·53–54
  Margin call, 10·33
  Opening a margin account, 10·33
  Purchase of securities, 10·32–33
  Relations between broker and customer, 10·34
  S.E.C. regulations, 10·33–34, 10·53–54
Marine Insurance Policies, 25·16–19
"Market Offerings," 10·53
Market Orders, 10·14
"Market-Out" Clause, Underwriting contracts, 9·15–16
Market Stabilization, 9·24–25
Market Value, 20·26
  Average cost of capital, 17·64–66
  Method of valuation, 20·26
Market Yields, Actual versus, 17·67–68
Markets
  Acceptance, 1·11–12
  Commercial paper, 1·12–13
  Commodity trading (See "Commodity Trading")
  Comparison approach, valuation method, 26·26
  Federal funds, 1·13
  Foreign exchange, 3·5–13
  Money, 1·1–30
  Over-the-counter, 10·41–46
  Securities, 10·1–58 (See also "Securities Markets")
  Government, 11·11–17
Marshall Plan, 2·29
Massachusetts Trusts, 12·8, 20·45
"Matched Orders," 10·52
Materials, Purchases of, 15·35
Mathematical Methods and Tables, 27·1–65
  Annuities, 27·30–45
  Bank discount, 27·12–18
  Bond valuation, 27·45–54
  Chain discounts, 27·18–20
  Interest, 27·1–12
    Compound, 27·20–29
    Exact, 27·7–12
    Ordinary, 27·4–6
    Types of, 27·1–3

Mathematical Methods and Tables (*Continued*)
  Logarithms, 27·54–65
  Tables
    Annuity valuation, 27·32–33
      Periodic payment required to amortize $1 and interest, 27·36–37
      Present value of annuity of $1 at end of each period, 27·40–41
    Compound interest, 27·22–23, 27·26–27
    Of logarithms, 27·56, 27·59–62
Medical Benefits, For retired employees, 19·25
Meetings
  Boards of directors, 12·32–33
  Stockholders', 12·23–27
Member Bank Call Reports, 1·11
Merchandise Turnover, In statement analysis, 8·36–37
Merchant's Rule, For computing interest, 24·42, 27·15
Mergers (See also "Consolidations")
  Advantages and disadvantages, 20·22–23
  Collateral trust bonds, 14·23
  Definition, 18·5, 20·21
  Effect on surplus, 20·29
  Financial and accounting factors, 20·24–31
  Power to merge, 20·22
  Procedures, 20·22
  Rights of creditors, 20·20–21
  State laws, 20·18
  Terms of, 20·23
  To end leases, 20·34
  Trend of, 20·7–8
Min-Max Inventory Control System, 16·8
Minority Interests
  Stockholders' meetings, 12·26–27
  Subsidiaries, 8·24
Minors, Guardians of, 6·7
Model Business Corporation Act, 12·18
Monetary Policy, 2·28–33
  Dollar drain, 2·29
  Exchange stabilization, 2·28–29
  Federal Reserve policy, 2·28–33
  Fiscal policy and, 2·33
  Limitations of, 2·33
  Money supply and the price level, 2·29
  Trade and exchange controls, 2·28
Monetary Systems, 2·2–4, 2·9–10
  Managed, 2·3–4
  Types of, 2·2–3
Money, 2·1–5
  Bank credit, 1·7–8
  Commodity, 2·3
  Credit and, 2·1–5
  Currency in circulation, 2·8–9
  Definition of, 2·1–2
  Early monetary history, 2·6
  Federal Reserve currency, 2·6–7
  Gold standard, 2·7
  Increased use of demand deposits as, 5·9–10
  International monetary settlements, 2·5
  Markets, 1·1–30 (See also "Money Markets")
  Monetary standards and systems, 2·2–4
  Negotiable instruments payable in, 24·4
  Present monetary system, 2·9–10
  Price level and supply of, 2·29
  Role of, 2·1
  Role of credit, 2·4
  Silver operations, 2·7–8
  Standard, 2·3
  Token, 2·4
  Types of, 2·3–4
  United States supply, 2·6–10
  Value of, 2·5
  Velocity of turnover, 2·29

GENERAL INDEX

Money Markets, 1·1–30
  Acceptance market, 1·11–12
  Affected by prices and bank credit, 1·27
  Broker's loans, 1·10–11
  Commercial paper market, 1·12–13
  Definition, 1·8
  Economic basis, 1·9
  Effect of business cycle on, 1·26–27
  Effect of prices and yields of government securities on, 11·17–19
  Federal funds market, 1·13
  Foreign, 1·27–30
  Government securities and, 11·17–19
  Individual, 1·10–14
  Influence of Federal Reserve policies, 11·19
  Influence on bond prices, 11·19
  Interest rates and, 1·1–30
  International, 1·27–28
  Interpretation of banking statistics, 1·14–25
    Federal Reserve Statement, 1·14–19
    Statement of weekly reporting member banks, 1·21–25
  London, 1·28–29
  Negotiable certificates of time deposit, 1·13–14, 2·26–27
  New York, 1·9–10
    Balances with domestic banks, 1·25
    Causes of movement of funds, 1·25
    Market for credit instruments, 1·9
    Principal lenders and borrowers, 1·9–10
    Relation to foreign money centers, 1·27
    Relation to the interior, 1·25
  Short-term government securities, 1·10
  Supply and demand, 11·18
  Treasury-Federal Reserve accord, 11·19
  Treasury financing and, 1·25–27
Monthly Investment Plan (M.I.P.), 4·26
Moody's Investors Service, 8·6
  Rating systems, 7·6
Mortgage Companies, 26·8
Mortgages
  After-acquired property clauses, 20·21
  As bank investments, 5·26–27
  As security for loans, 5·30
  Bonds, 14·17–21
  Chattel, 2·41
  Closed, 14·18
  Construction loans, 26·14
  Conventional loans, 26·13–14
  Debt by type of lender, 26·3
  Debt outstanding (1957–63), 26·2
  Equipment mortgage plan, 14·24
  Federal agencies handling, 2·37
  F.H.A. loans, 7·7, 26·8, 26·13
  Financing
    By commercial banks, 26·4–6
    By life insurance companies, 26·6–7
    By mortgage companies, 26·8
    By mutual savings banks, 26·6
    By nonfiduciary organizations, 26·7–11
    By real estate investment corporations, 26·9–10
    By real estate investment trusts, 26·10
    By savings and loan associations, 26·1–4
    By savings and loan holding companies, 26·10
    Federal National Mortgage Association, 26·8–9
    Pension and endowment funds, 26·10–11
  Foreclosures, 22·5
  Held by commercial banks, 26·4–6
  Home mortgage business, 2·36
  Insurance, 26·13–14
  Land development financing, 26·15
  Leasehold, 26·15

Mortgages (*Continued*)
  Liens, 26·13
  Loan repayment plans, 26·12–13
    Amortized loans, 26·12
    Balloon payment, 26·12
    Partial amortization loans, 26·12
    Straight-term loans, 26·12
  Loans, 2·35–38, 26·1
    For non-real estate purposes, 2·37–38
  Notes and, 26·12
  Open-end, 26·15–16
  Package, 26·16
  Purchase money, 26·13
  Real estate, 7·6–8
    As bank investments, 5·26–27
    As security for loans, 5·30
    Insured and guaranteed, 7·7
    Security analysis, 7·6–7
  Releases of mortgaged property, 14·15–16
  Second and third, 26·13
  Share collateral, 26·16
  Special features, 26·14–16
  Treatment in consolidations and mergers, 20·21
  Trust deed and, 26·14
  Types of, 2·36–37
  V.A. loans, 2·37, 5·27, 7·7, 26·8, 26·13
Municipal Bonds, 11·24–29
  Investment factors, 11·27–28
  Investors in, 11·28–29
  Marketing of, 11·28
  Methods of repayment, 11·29
    Serial method, 11·29
  Obligations of public housing authorities, 11·27
  Purpose of borrowing, 11·24–25
  Revenue bonds, 11·27
  Special assessment bonds, 11·27
  Tax districts, 11·27
  Tax status, 11·25
Mutual Business Organizations, 12·10–12
  Cooperatives, 12·11
  Professional corporations and associations, 12·12
  Types of, 12·10–11
Mutual Funds, 4·22 (See also "Investment Companies")
  Analysis of stock, 7·16
Mutual Savings Banks, 2·36, 4·4–10

National Association of Credit Management, 21·22
National Association of Insurance Commissioners, 25·11
National Association of Investment Companies, 4·33
National Association of Securities Dealers, Inc., 4·33, 9·21, 10·44–46, 10·54, 10·56
  Activities, 10·45–46
  Rules of fair practice, 10·45
National Bank Act of 1863, 2·12
National Banking Act of 1864, 5·6
National Banking System, 2·6
National Credit Office, 8·7
National Debt, 11·1–6
  Budget policy of government and, 11·4–5
  Certainty of payment, 11·3–4
  Composition, 11·2–3
    Length of debt maturity, 11·2–3
    Treasury obligations, 11·2
    Types of obligations, 11·2
  Cost of, 11·4
    Interest rate, 11·4
  Debt management, 11·5–6
    Objectives, 11·5
  Distribution, 11·3

National Debt (*Continued*)
  Evolution of, 11·1
  Magnitude of, 11·1–2
  Public and private debt compared, 11·1–2
  Role of Treasury, 1·5, 1·26, 2·28, 11·5–6, 11·20–21
National Monetary Commission, 2·13
National Quotation Bureau, Inc., 10·43
National Stock Exchanges, 10·2–3
Natural Gas Industry, 7·21
Negligence
  Culpable, and defenses, 25·26–27
  Definition, 25·26
  Form of tort, 25·26
  Liability and, 25·26–27
Negotiable Certificates of Time Deposit, 1·13–14, 2·26–27
Negotiable Instruments, 24·1–44
  Banker's acceptances, 24·36
  Bills of exchange or draft, 24·2, 24·30–35
  Certificates of deposit, 1·13–14, 2·26–27, 24·3
  Characteristics of, 24·1–2
  Checks, 24·3, 24·36–40
  Classification of, 24·2–3
  Date of, 24·7
    Ante-dated and post-dated, 24·7
    Insertion of date, 24·7
  Defective title, 24·15–16
  Delivery, 24·10–14
    Conditional, 24·10–11
    Stolen instrument, 24·10
  Discharge of, 24·28–30
    Accommodation note, 24·29
    Person secondarily liable, 24·29
    Renunciation of rights by holder, 24·29–30
    Right of party who discharges, 24·29
  Governing law, 24·1
    Codification movement, 24·1
  Holder for value, 24·15
  Holder in due course, 24·14–15
    Rights of, 24·17
  Indorsements, 24·11–14
    By infant or corporation, 24·13
    Forged, 24·13–14
    Kinds of, 24·11–12
    Method of, 24·13
    Striking out, 24·14
    Transfer without, 24·14
    When prior party may negotiate, 24·14
  Interest, 24·8, 24·40–42
    After maturity, 24·41
    Contractual and implied, 24·40–41
    Definition, 24·40
    Lawful interest, 24·40
    Mercantile Rule, 24·42, 27·15
    Stopping of, 24·41–42
    "United States Rule," 24·42, 27·16
  Liabilities of parties, 24·18–20
    Of acceptor, 24·18
    Of accommodation party, 24·20
    Of drawer, 24·18
    Of guarantor, 24·18–19
    Of indorser, 24·19–20
    Of maker, 24·18
    Of person signing as agent, 24·20–21
    Person signing in trade or assumed name, 24·21
    Signature by corporate officers, 24·21
  Negotiability, 24·3–10
    Alteration of instrument, 24·8–9
    Ambiguous construction, 24·8
    Blanks in the instrument, 24·7–8
    Collateral security, 24·6
    Consideration, 24·9

Negotiable Instruments (*Continued*)
  Negotiability (*Continued*)
    "Determinable future time," 24·5
    Discounts and foreign money, 24·4
    Forged signatures, 24·7
    General requirements, 24·3
    Instruments issued in violation of law, 24·10
    Money, 24·4
    Omissions not affecting, 24·6–7
    "Payable on demand," 24·4
    "Payable to bearer," 24·6
    "Payable to order," 24·5–6
    Provisions not affecting, 24·6
    Signature by agent, 24·7
    "Sum certain," 24·4
    Unconditional promise to pay, 24·3–4
    "Writing and signature," 24·3
  Negotiation, 24·10
  Notice of dishonor, 24·25–26
    Protest, 24·27–28
    Time for sending, 24·26
    Waiver of notice, 24·26–27
    When dispensed with, 24·27
  Origin, 24·1
  Payment in due course, 24·25
  Presentment for payment, 24·22–25
    Definition, 24·22
    Requirements, 24·23–24
    Rights of party, 24·24–25
    Time of, 24·24
    Warranties on, 24·22
    When dispensed with, 24·23
    When necessary, 24·22
  Promissory notes, 24·2 (See also "Promissory Notes")
  Rights, liabilities, and warrants, 24·14–22
  Sale of, 24·43
  Scrip certificates, for fractional shares, 13·31
  Subject to original defenses, 24·17–18
  Time deposit, certificates of, 1·13–14, 2·26–27, 24·3
  Trade acceptances, 24·35–36
  Uniform Commercial Code, 24·1
  Uniform Negotiable Instruments Act, 24·1
  Usury, 24·42–44
  Waiver of notice, 24·26–27
  Waiver of protest, 24·27
  Warranties, 24·21–22
    On presentment and transfer, 24·22
  "With interest" added, 24·8
Net Profit Margin, 8·35
New Deal, Banking system, 2·24
New Jersey, Professional Service Corporation Act, 12·12
New York
  Business Corporation Law, 20·20–21
    Capital stock reductions, 21·7
    Common stock recapitalizations, 21·2
    Corporate dissolutions, 21·28
    On consolidations, 20·18–19
  Civil Practice Act and Rules, 12·4
  Foreign exchange market, 3·5
  Free Banking Act of 1838, 2·12
  General Business Law, usurious contracts, 24·44
  Negotiable Instrument Law, 24·37–40
  Restrictions on dividends, 18·19–20
  Savings bank law, 4·6–8
  Transfer taxes, 10·17
New York Commodity Clearing Corp., 23·21–22
New York Cotton Exchange, 23·7
New York Money Market, 1·9–10
New York Stock Exchange, 10·5–13
  Board of Governors, 10·5–6
  Bond brokers and dealers, 10·9

GENERAL INDEX

New York Stock Exchange (*Continued*)
  Bond room, 10·12
  Bond trading, 10·39–41
  Brokerage commissions on stocks, 10·16–17
  Brokerage houses, 10·35–39 (See also "Brokerage Houses")
  Commission houses, 10·7
  Examination of member firms, 10·39
    "Questionnaire," 10·39
  Financial report requirements, 8·1–2
  Floor traders, 10·7–8
  Listing securities, 10·9–11
    Accounting standards, 10·9
    Application, 10·9
    Delisting and withdrawal of registration, 10·10–11
    Department of Stock List, 10·9
    Disclosure requirements, 10·9
    Distribution statement, 10·9
    Listing statements, 10·9–10
    Motives for listing, 10·10
    Policy, 10·10
  Membership, 10·7
    Types of members, 10·7–8
  Methods of trading, 10·12
    Admittance to floor, 10·12
    Auction process, 10·12
  Objectives, 10·5
  Odd-lot dealers, 10·8
  Organization, 10·5
  President, 10·6–7
  Public relations department, 10·12
  Quotations, ticker service, 10·13
  Securing a seat, 10·7
    Price of a seat, 10·7
  Securities trading, 10·13–32 (See also "Securities Trading")
  Settlement of transactions, 10·27–29
  Specialists, 10·8
  Stock Clearing Corporation, 10·12
  Stock posts, 10·12
  Ticker tape system, 10·12–13
    Symbols, 10·13
  Trading facilities, 10·12
  Trading room, 10·12
  Trading securities, 10·13–32
    Odd-lot, 10·14
    Short selling, 10·14
  "Two-dollar" brokers, 10·7
  Unlisted trading, 10·11–12
    Privileges, 10·11–12
  Wire houses, 10·7
No-Par Value Stock, 13·7–10
"No Recourse" Clause, Trust indentures, 14·16
Nonnotification Financing, 16·14
North American Securities Administrators, 9·50
Notes
  Equipment, 14·23
  Promissory, 27·13
    Interest-bearing and noninterest bearing, 27·13
  Treasury, 11·7
Notes Receivable, 16·6–7 (See also "Receivables")
  Balance sheet treatment, 8·16–17
Notice of Dishonor, 24·25–26
  Waiver of notice, 24·26–27

Obsolescence
  Of capital assets, 17·9–10, 17·25
  Of equipment, 17·6–7
Odd-Lot Trading, 10·14, 10·25
  Dealers, 10·8

Offerings of Securities, 10·1
  Public, 9·22–24
  Special offering plan, 10·21
Office Buildings, Financing, 26·29–30
  Breakdown of expenses, 26·29–30
  Competitive, 26·28–29
  Professional buildings, 26·29–30
  Sales and leaseback arrangements, 26·27–28
  Speculative, 26·29
Officers, Corporate, 12·33–36 (See also "Board of Directors")
  Loans to, 16·6
Oil Royalties, Sale of, 10·55–56
Old Age and Survivors and Disability Insurance (OASDI), 19·51
Open-End Companies, 4·24
Open-End Funds, 4·25
Open-End Mortgages, 26·15–16
Open Interest Figures, 23·29–30
  Delivery cycles, 23·30
  Reports, 23·30
Open-Market Operations, 1·20, 2·12, 2·13, 2·15, 2·26, 2·30, 11·15
Operating Expenses, In income statement, 8·12
Operating Ratio, 8·35
Operating Reports, Form, 15·12
Operations
  Costs
    Depreciation, 17·27
    Effect of capital expenditures on, 17·4–12
Option Warrants, 9·7, 10·18–19, 13·29–30
Options or Privileges, 10·25–27
  Purpose of privileges, 10·27
  Puts and calls, 10·26
  Real estate finance, 26·16–17
  To purchase assets, 20·9
Orders
  Brokers, 10·14–15
  Futures trading, 23·15–16
  Securities trading, 10·14–16
    Limited, 10·14–15
    Market, 10·14
    "Matched," 10·52
    Stop-loss, 10·15
    Stopping stock, 10·15
Organizations, Business, 12·1–36
  Corporate, 12·12–36 (See also "Corporations")
  Partnerships, 12·3–6
  Proprietorships, individual, 12·3
Over-the-Counter Market, 10·2, 10·3, 10·41–46
  Bid and asked quotations, 10·3
  Classes of securities traded, 10·42
  Clearing transactions, 10·43–44
  Functions and importance, 10·41–42
  Method of trading, 10·42–44
    National Quotation Bureau, Inc., 10·43
    Negotiation, 10·42–44
  National Association of Securities Dealers 10·44–46
  Railroad equipment trust certificates, 10·44
  Self-regulation, 10·44–46
  Unlisted bond market, 10·44
Owners' Equity
  Capital stock, 13·1
  Ratio of current liabilities to, 8·33
  Ratio of fixed assets to, 8·33
  Ratio to total assets, 8·34
  Turnover of, 8·37

Par Value Stock, 13·4–6
Participating Bonds, 14·30
Participating Preferred Stock, 13·20

Partnerships, 12·3-6
  Advantages and disadvantages, **12·5**
  Agreement, **12·5**
  Business continuation and key man insurance, **25·32**
  Capital contribution of a partner, **24·43**
  Checking accounts, **5·11**
  General, **12·3-4**
  In bankruptcy, **22·33-34**
  Liability, **12·4-5, 12·6**
  Limited, **12·5-6**
    Advantages, **12·6**
    Liability, **12·6**
    Statutory requirements, **12·6**
    Tax treatment, **12·6**
  Management, **12·4**
  Sharing of profits and losses, **12·4**
  Syndicates, **12·6-8**
Patent Pools, 20·46
"Payable on Demand," Negotiable instruments, **24·4**
"Payable to Bearer," Negotiable instruments, **24·6**
"Payable to Order," Negotiable instruments, **24·5-6**
Payback Method, For evaluating investments, **17·22, 17·36-37**
Payrolls, Prepared by banks, **5·5**
Pension Plans, 19·1-36
  Benefits, **19·21-29, 19·34-36**
  Death, **19·26-27**
  Disability, **19·25**
  Earnings base, **19·23**
  Earnings increase to covered level, **19·23**
  Fixed, **19·34-36**
  For severed employees, **19·25-26**
  Integration with Federal benefits, **19·22-23**
  Medical, for retired employees, **19·25**
  On earnings covered by Social Security, **19·21-22**
  Past service pensions, **19·24**
  Percentage of pay per year of service formula, **19·21**
  Social Security benefits, **19·22**
  Combination plans, **19·16-17**
  Deferred-distribution profit-sharing plans, **19·39-40**
  Deferred group annuities, **19·6, 19·12**
    Advantages and disadvantages, **19·11-12**
    Employee preference, **19·12**
    Registration as a securities issue, **19·12**
  Definition, **19·1**
  Deposit-administration group annuity, **19·6**
    Advantages and disadvantages, **19·12-13**
    Employer contributions, **19·28-29**
  Disability, **19·10**
  Disclosure and bonding requirement, **19·34**
  Employee contributions, **19·29-30**
    Providing for, **19·29-30**
    Ratio to benefits, **19·30**
  Employer contributions, **19·27-29**
  Federal Civil Service System, **19·51**
  Financing funded, **19·5-17**
    Advantages and disadvantages of each method, **19·7-17**
    Effect of eligibility on, **19·18-19**
    Method of funding, **19·5**
  For corporate executives, **12·36**
  For self-employed individuals, **19·48-50**
  Government and union, **19·51-53**
  Group annuity plans
    Employer contributions, **19·28**
    Termination of, **19·32**

Pension Plans (*Continued*)
  Group permanent retirement income, **19·7, 19·16**
    Employer contributions, **19·29**
  Individual policy plans
    Employer contributions, **19·29**
    Termination, **19·32**
  Individual retirement income policies, **19·7**
    Advantages and disadvantages, **19·13-16**
  Investments of, **9·6, 19·30-31**
  Labor unions, **19·53**
  Membership eligibility, **19·17-19**
  Money purchase, **19·34-35**
  Mortgage financing by, **26·10-11**
  Necessity for, **19·1-3**
  Pension committee, **19·32-33**
  Provisions, **19·17-34**
    Benefit payments, **19·21-29**
    Maximum age limitations, **19·18**
    Membership eligibility, **19·17-19**
    Minimum age requirement, **19·17**
    Retirement, **19·19-21**
      Deferred, **19·20-21**
      Early, **19·20**
      Women, **19·20**
    Years of service requirement, **19·17**
  Retirement plans for self-employed, **19·48-50**
  Sale-and-leaseback contracts, **26·11**
  Self-administered plans, **19·5-6**
    Advantages and disadvantages, **19·7-8**
    Comparative cost, **19·11**
    Coverage of pensioners already retired, **19·10**
    Disability pensions, **19·10**
    Employer contributions, **19·27**
    Flexibility of contributions, **19·7-8**
    No fixed commitment, **19·9**
    Pension committee, **19·32-33**
    Permanence of plan, **19·9-10**
    Termination of, **19·31-32**
  State and local, **19·51-52**
    Administration, **19·52**
    Investments, **19·52-53**
  Tax aspects, **19·3-5**
    Deductibility of contribution, **19·4-5**
    Internal Revenue Service approval, **19·4-5**
    Requirements for qualification, **19·4**
  Termination of, **19·31-32**
  Tax penalty, **19·32**
  Trustees, **19·33-34**
  Trusts, **6·10**
  Types of, **19·1-5**
  Variable annuities, **19·36**
PERT Cost (Program Evaluation and Review Technique), **15.4**
Petitions
  Arrangements under Chapter XI, **22·17**
  To reorganize, **22·3-4**
  Voluntary bankruptcy, **22·20-21**
Petroleum Industry, Analysis of, **7·14, 10·55-56**
Philadelphia Plan, Of equipment obligations, **14·24**
Plants and Equipment
  Balance sheet treatment, **8·18**
  Branch, **20·8**
  Reserves for expansion, **18·10**
  Valuation of, **20·27-28**
    Effect on production costs, **20·28**
Pledged Securities, 14·22-23
  Payment of principal, **14·22**
Pool Operations, Prevention of, **10·30**
Pooling of Interests, Distinction between purchase and, **20·29**
Portfolios, Security, 9·27
Postal Savings, 4·12

Power of Attorney, 13·15
Pre-emptive Rights, 9·7, 17·56-57
  Option warrants and, 13·30
Preferred Stock, 13·19-22
  Arrearages, 21·10-14
    Examples of settlements, 21·13-14
    Legal factors, 21·11-12
    Meeting the problem of dissent, 21·12-13
    Methods of clearing up, 21·12-14
  Cost of, 17·53-54
  Interest of shareholders in capital stock reductions, 21·6-7
  Of selling company, 20·15-16
  Recapitalizations and readjustments, 21·9-14
    Elimination of burdensome charter provisions, 21·10
    Exchange for a lower dividend issue, 21·10
    Exchange for other securities, 21·10
    Legal restrictions, 21·9
    Purposes of, 21·9-11
    To clear up arrearages on cumulative, 21·10-11
  S.E.C. requirements, 8·21
  Security analysis, 7·7-8
Premiums
  Bonds, 27·45
  Sale of securities, 17·51
Presentment for Acceptance
  Bills of exchange, 24·31-32
  Negotiable instruments, 24·22-25
Prices and Pricing
  Bank credit and, 1·27
  Commodity trading
    Bid and asked prices, 23·33
    Effect on working capital needs, 16·12
    Fluctuations, 23·16-17
    Spot trading, 23·32-33
  Dow theory of stock prices, 10·31
  Effects of changes, in income statements, 8·9-10
  Forecasts of selling, 15·31
  Government bonds, 11·17-24
  Indices of security, 10·30-31
  Influence on money market, 1·26-27
  Level of
    Impact on depreciation, 17·27-28
    Interaction of major factors affecting, 2·5
    Money supply and, 2·29
  New security issues, 9·23-24
Private Placements, 14·3, 14·41-42
  Principal advantages, 14·41-42
  Services of investment bankers, 14·42
  Use of, 14·41
Privileges
  Subscription, 14·32-33
  Warrants, bond, 4·34-35
Pro-forma Statements, 15·25-26
Probability, Laws of, 17·75, 25·2-3
Production
  Costs, 15·31-32
  Depreciation based on, 17·30-31
  Effect of plant valuation on costs of, 20·28
Products, Liability insurance, 25·28
Professional Buildings, 26·29-30
Professional Corporations, 12·12
Profit and Loss Statement, 8·7 (See also "Income Statement")
  For financial planning, 15·2-3
  Forecasts, 15·27
Profit Planning, 15·1, 15·8-25
  Break-even analysis, 15·20-22
  Concepts of profit, 15·8-9
  Cost-volume-profit relationships, 15·17-18
  Decomposing costs, 15·18-19
  Direct costing, 15·23-25

Profit and Loss Statement (*Continued*)
  Flexible budgeting, 15·22-23
  Objectives, 15·9-10
    Measuring results against, 15·11-13
  Operating reports, 15·12
  Rate of return, 15·13-15
    As gauge of performance, 15·13-15
    Components of, 15·15-16
    To evaluate divisions, 15·16-17
  Scope of, 15·10-11
  Tool of management, 15·9
Profit Ratio, In statement analysis, 8·35-36
Profit-Sharing Plans, 19·36-48
  Administrative committee, 19·47
  Deferred-distribution, 19·38-40
    Compared with pension plans, 19·39-40
    Death benefits, 19·44
    Definition, 19·38
    Disability pension benefits, 19·43
    Eligibility for membership, 19·41-42
    Employee contribution, 19·45
    Formula, 19·40-41
    Investments, 19·45-46
    Method of allocation, 19·41
    Provisions, 19·40-48
    Retirement benefits, 19·42-43
    Termination of service, 19·43-44
  Immediate-distribution, 19·36-38
    Relation to basic compensation, 19·37
    Scope and nature, 19·37
    Tax status, 19·38
  Investments, 9·6, 19·45-46
    Full disclosure requirements, 19·45-46
    Group annuity contracts, 19·46
    Individual policies, 19·46
  Retirement plans for self-employed, 19·48-50
  Tax status, 19·48
  Termination of, 19·46-47
  Trustees, 19·47-48
Profitability Index, 17·46
Profits
  Break-even charts, 15·20
  Cash income vs., 16·24
  Concepts of, 15·8-9
  Depreciation based on, 17·31
  Insurance, 25·22
  Investment companies, 4·20-22
  Measuring, 15·8-9
  Net profit margin, 8·35
  Number of times fixed charges earned, 8·35-36
  Test, dividends, 18·21
  Undivided, 18·3
  Variation of, analysis, 8·43
Program Evaluation and Review Technique (PERT), 15·4
Projections
  Balance sheet, 15·26-29
  Financial statements, 8·44
  Retained earnings, 15·29-30
Promissory Notes, 1·12-13, 14·5, 24·2
  Bank discount, 27·12-18
  Bills of exchange treated as, 24·30
  Due date, 27·13-14
  Interest-bearing, 27·13
  Noninterest-bearing, 27·13
Promotions, 12·13-15
  Joint ventures, 12·14
  Legal status, 12·14-15
  Of corporate enterprises, 12·13-15
  Raising capital, 12·16
Property
  Balance sheet treatment, 8·18
  Damage, 25·4
  Dividends, 18·14, 18·17

Property (*Continued*)
  Fixed asset turnover, 17·10–11
  Losses, 25·3–4
  Nature of rights, 26·22
  Prospective earning power, 22·11
  Rents and rental value insurance, 25·21–22
  Sale of, 24·43–44
    Bankruptcy, 22·35–36
    Title to, trustees in bankruptcy, 22·31
    Valuation of, reorganization plans, 22·11
Proprietorships, Individual, 12·3
  Business continuation and key man insurance, 25·32
  Buy-and-sell agreements, 25·32
Prospectus, 8·5
  Accountant's certificate, 9·38
  Age of information, 9·38
  Communication not deemed, 9·33–34
  Exempted securities, 9·38–42
  Final, 9·34
  Preliminary, 9·22, 9·31–32
  Preparation of, 9·38
  Provisions of Securities Act of 1933, 9·28, 9·38
  "Red Herring," 9·31
  Statutory, 9·22
  Summary, 9·22, 9·32–33
Protest
  Negotiable instruments, 24·27–28
  Notice of, 24·27–28
Proxies, 10·50–51, 13·15–17
  Battles, 18·26
  Form, 13·16
  Power of attorney, 13·15
  S.E.C. regulations, 10·50–51, 13·16–17
  Solicitation of, 12·24, 13·16–17
Prudent Man Rule, 7·13
Public Debt (See "National Debt")
Public Offerings, 9·22–24
  Announcing the offer, 9·22–23
  Direct, 9·4
  Issues of small enterprises, 9·2–4
  Opening and closing the books, 9·23
  Price cutting, 9·23–24
  Small business investment companies, 19·5–6
Public Utility Companies, 7·16–21
  Analysis of company, 7·18–20
  Capitalization, 7·19–20
  Character of plant, 7·19
  Classes of, 7·20–21
  Competition, 7·19
  Demand for service, 7·18
  Distinctive features, 7·16
  Earning power, 7·20
  Electric light and power, 7·21
  Franchises, 7·16–17
  Government regulation, 7·18
  Holding companies, 20·42–43
    Regulation of, 20·43–45
    S.E.C. regulations, 20·43–45
  Load factor, 7·19
  Natural gas, 7·21
  Operation ratio, 7·20
  Rates, 7·17
  Regulation of holding companies, 20·43–45
    Acquisition of securities and properties, 20·44
    Federal Power Act, 20·45
    Intercompany loans, dividends, 20·44–45
    Interstate electric companies, 20·45
    New security issues, 20·43–44
    Periodic reports and accounts, 20·45
    Registration of, 20·43
    Simplification and integration, 20·44
    Use of Massachusetts Trust, 20·45

Public Utility Companies (*Continued*)
  Regulatory factors, 7·18–19, 20·43–45
  Securities, 7·16–21
  Telephone and telegraph companies, 7·21
  Types of, 7·16
  "Upstream loans," 20·43
  Valuation, 7·17–18
Public Utility Holding Company Act of 1935, 7·21, 20·43, 21·12
  Debt readjustments, 21·17
  Intercorporate readjustments, 21·24
Purchase Group, Underwriting, 9·16–17
  Contract, 9·18
Purchase of Assets, 20·8–17
  Advantages and disadvantages, 20·16–17
  Approval of directors, 20·10
  Approval of stockholders, 20·10
  Authorization of stock for expansion, 20·11–12
  Dissolution of selling company, 20·11
  Distinction between pooling of interests and, 20·29
  Legal aspects, 20·12–13
    Mortgage liens of the selling company, 20·14
    Right of appraisal, 20·13
    Rights of creditors, 20·13–14
  Necessity for stockholder consent, 20·9, 20·12
  Obligations of seller, 20·14
  Options, 20·9
  Paying off dissenting stockholders, 20·11
    Right of appraisal, 20·13
  Position of purchasing company, 20·11–12
  Position of selling company, 20·12
  Preferred stock of selling company, 20·15–16
  Preliminary negotiations, 20·10
  Procedure, 20·9–10
  Provisions regarding consideration, 20·15
  Subjects of sale, 20·14–15
  Tax advantages, 20·9
  Transfer of assets and consideration, 20·11
  Voluntary reorganizations, 20·8
  When used, 20·8–9
Purchase Warrants, 13·29–30
Put and Call Brokers and Dealers Assn., 10·26
Puts and Calls, 10·26

Quasi-Dividends, 18·16
Quasi-Reorganizations, 18·4, 18·7
Quick Assets Ratio, 8·32
Quorums
  Directors' meetings, 12·32–33
  Stockholders' meetings, 12·26
Quotations, Stock Market
  Bonds, 10·39–40
  Government obligations, 11·14
  Rates of foreign exchange, 3·6–7
  Stock subscription rights, 13·28
  Ticker tape service, 10·12–13

Railroad Retirement Act of 1935, 19·51
Railroads
  Analysis ratios, 7·23
  Equipment trust certificates, 10·44, 22·10
  Financial statements, 7·24
  Government regulation, 7·21–22, 8·3
  Holding companies, 20·46
  Leases, 20·33
  Operating expenses, 7·22–23
  Rates, 7·22
  Readjustments, 22·10
  Reorganization, 22·9–10
    Capital funds, 14·29
    Use of income bonds, 14·29
  Securities, 7·21–24
  Traffic, 7·22

GENERAL INDEX

Rate of Return on Investments, 15·13–15
  Components of, **15·**15–16
  Gauge of performance, **15·**13–15
  Investment base, **15·**14–15
    Inclusion of leases, **15·**15
  Used to evaluate divisions, **15·**16–17
Rates
  Public utility, **7·**17
  Railroad, **7·**22
  Rediscount, **11·**18
Ratings
  Bond issues, **7·**5–6
  Of securities, **10·**32
Ratio Analysis
  "Acid Test," **8·**32–34, **16·**19
  Average collection period, **16·**19
  Balance sheet, **8·**32–34
    Current liabilities to owners' equity, **8·**33
    Current ratio, **8·**32
    Fixed assets to funded debt, **8·**35
    Fixed assets to owners' equity, **8·**33
    Funded debt to net working capital, **8·**33
    Funded debt to total capitalization, **8·**34–35
    Inventory to net working capital, **8·**33–34
    Owners' equity to total assets, **8·**34
  Bank stocks, **7·**15
  Current assets to current debt, **16·**19
  Current debt to inventory, **16·**19
  Current debt to tangible net worth, **16·**19
  Dividend payout, **18·**26
  Financial statements, **8·**31–39
    Significant ratios, **8·**31–32
  Income statement, **8·**35–36
    Net profit margin, **8·**35
    Number of times fixed charges earned, **8·**35–36
    Operating ratio, **8·**35
  Industrial securities, **7·**13–14
  Interstatement, **8·**36–38
  Inventory to net working capital, **16·**19
  Liquidity, **16·**19
  Merchandise turnover, **8·**36–37
  Net sales to inventory, **16·**19
  Operating, **7·**20, **8·**31–39
  Per share, **8·**38–39
  Price-earnings, **7·**8–10
  Proper use of, **8·**39–40
    Standards for comparison, **8·**39
  Public utility companies, **7·**20
  "Quick assets," **16·**19
  Railroads, **7·**23
  Receivables turnover, **8·**36
  Return on investment, **8·**38
  Security analysis, **7·**8–10
  Selective uses of, **8·**39–40
  Turnover of net working capital, **8·**38, **16·**19
  Turnover of owners' equity, **8·**37
  Working capital, **8·**38, **16·**18–23
Raw Materials, Inventories, **16·**7
Readjustments, 21·14–24
  Bond, **21·**16–17
  Debt, **21·**14–22
    Circumstances necessitating, **21·**14
    Compositions, **21·**17–18
    Extension of maturities, **21·**14–15
    Legal aspects, **21·**15–16
    Mechanics of, **21·**16
    Reduction of interest rate, **21·**15
    Types of, **21·**14–15
    Under special legislation, **21·**17
  Definition, **21·**1–2
  Intercorporate, **21·**22–24
    Methods, **21·**23–24
    Under Public Utility Holding Company Act, **21·**24

Readjustments (*Continued*)
  Preferred stock, **21·**9–14
  Railroads, **22·**10
"Real Bills" Doctrine, 2·26
Real Estate
  Appraisals, **26·**25–26
  Escrow accounts, **26·**17
  Financing, **26·**1–32
    By commercial banks, **26·**4–6
    By Federal National Mortgage Association, **26·**8–9
    By individuals, **26·**11
    By mortgage companies, **26·**8
    By mutual savings banks, **26·**6
    By pension and endowment funds, **26·**10–11
    By real estate investment corporations, **26·**9–10
    By real estate investment trusts, **26·**10
    By savings and loan holding companies, **26·**10
    By state and community development commissions, **26·**11
    By syndicates, **12·**7, **26·**11
    Construction loans, **26·**14
    Instruments, **26·**12–16
    Land developments, **26·**15
    Land trusts, **26·**17
    Leasehold mortgages, **26·**14
    Office buildings, **26·**28–29
    Professional buildings, **26·**29–30
    Sales and leasebacks, **26·**26–28
    Selected projects, **26·**26–32
    Shopping centers, **26·**29–32
    Sources of, **26·**1–11
      Financial institutions, **26·**1–7
    Trust deeds, **26·**14
  Instruments, financing, **26·**12–16
    Notes and mortgages, **26·**12–13
    Trust deeds, **26·**14
  Investment analysis, **26·**20–26
    Depreciation and tax factors, **26·**24–25
    Fee ownership, **26·**22
    Financing arrangements, **26·**23–25
    Influence of leverage, **26·**23–24
    Market trends, **26·**22
    Nature of property rights, **26·**22
    Rating of realty investment, **26·**21
    Risk characteristics, **26·**20
    Type of property, **26·**22
  Investment trusts, **4·**26, **12·**9, **26·**10
    Tax status, **12·**9
  Land trust, **26·**17
  Leases, **26·**17–20 (See also "Leases and Leasing")
  Mortgages, **5·**26–27, **5·**30, **7·**6–8 (See also "Mortgages")
  Options, **26·**16–17
  Sales and leaseback arrangements, **26·**26–28
  Syndicates, **12·**7, **26·**11
  Valuation, **26·**25–26
    Cost of replacement approach, **26·**26
    Income capitalization analysis, **26·**26
    Market comparison approach, **26·**26
Real Estate Investment Corporations, 26·9–10
Real Estate Investment Trusts, 26·10
Recapitalizations, 18·4, 21·1–14
  Changes in capital structure, **21·**1–2
  Common stock, **21·**2–8
    Capital account reductions, **21·**4–7
    Changes in number of shares, **21·**3–4
    Changes in par or stated value, **21·**4
    Legal requirements, **21·**2
    Reverse splits or share consolidations, **21·**3–4
    Stock split ups and stock dividends, **21·**3

GENERAL INDEX

Recapitalizations (*Continued*)
Definition, 21·1-2
Preferred stock, 21·9-14
Legal restrictions, 21·9
Receivables (See also "Accounts Receivable")
As working capital, 16·6-7
Turnover of, 8·36, 16·6, 16·10
Receivers
Arrangements under Chapter XI, 22·18
Certificates, 14·30
In bankruptcy, 22·24-25
Trust companies as, 6·23
Reconstruction Finance Corporation, 5·8
Records
Investment banking houses, 9·26-27
Losses due to destruction of, 25·5
Red Herring Prospectus, 9·31
Redeemable Preferred Stock, 13·21-22
Rediscount Rate, 11·18
Referees
Arrangements under Chapter XI, 22·18
Bankruptcy, 22·25-26
Refunding of Bonds, 14·39-40
Registered Representatives, 10·35, 10·46
Registrars
Stock transfers, 13·3-4
Trust companies as, 6·23-24
Registration Statement, 9·26
Accountant's certificate, 9·38
Accounting requirements, 10·49
Amendment of, 9·36-37
Civil liabilities, 9·43
Confidential treatment, 9·35-36, 10·48-49
"Delaying amendments," 9·36
Delisting, 10·49
Effective date, 9·36
Exempted securities, 9·38-42
Filing fee, 9·35, 10·17-18
Financial statements, 9·38, 10·49-50
Information required, 10·48
Letter of comment, 9·36
Posteffective amendments, 9·37
Posteffective period, 9·34-35
Prefiling period, 9·31
Preparation of prospectus, 9·38
Price amendment, 9·36
Private offerings, 9·40-41
Procedure for filing, 9·35-38, 10·47-48
"S" series, 9·35
Securities Exchange Act, 9·28, 10·46-49
Small business investment companies public offerings, 9·5-6
Transactions by dealers, 9·41
Waiting period, 9·31
Acceleration of, 9·32
Withdrawal of, 9·37-38, 10·49
Regulation T, Securities Exchange Act, 10·34
Regulation U, Securities Exchange Act, 10·34
Regulatory Legislation (See "Government Regulation")
Remainderman, Trusts, 6·8
Rents and Rentals
Insurance, 25·21-22
Leased property, 20·34
Reorganizations
Arrangements under Chapter XI, 22·17-18
Bankruptcy Act of 1938, 22·3
Chapter X, 22·3-9
Compensations and allowances, 22·8
Definition, 21·1-2
Arrangements, 22·1
Equity reorganizations, 22·1-2
Insolvency, 22·2
Tax vs. financial, 22·1

Reorganizations (*Continued*)
Dissenters, 22·3
Equity, 22·1-2
Examiners, 22·6
Formal legal, 18·4
Hearings, 22·8
History of procedures, 22·2
Informal accounting, 18·4
Legal limitations, 22·10-11
Paid-in surplus resulting from, 18·4-5
Petitions, 22·3-4
Appraisal of, 22·4
Contents, 22·4
Filing, 22·3-4
Plans, 22·10-14
Acceptance by creditors, 22·7
Approval by court, 22·7
Confirmed by court, 22·7-8
Effect of confirmation, 22·8
Elimination of burdensome maturities, 22·12
Facilitating future financing, 22·13
"Fair and equitable," 22·10-11
Final decree, 22·8
Formulation and approval of, 22·6-7
Hearings on, 22·6
Objectives of, 22·11-12
Presentation of, 22·13-14
Provisions for working capital, 22·12-13
Reduction of fixed charges, 22·12
S.E.C. report, 22·6-7
Statutory requirements, 22·6-7
Submission to security holders, 22·7-8
Use of income bonds, 14·29
Valuation of property, 22·11
Preparation for, 22·11
Protective committees, 22·14-17
Authorization, 22·14-16
Deposit agreement, 22·16
Expenses, 22·16
Formation of, 22·14
Statutory control, 22·16-17
Quasi-reorganization, 18·4, 18·7
Railroads, 22·9-10
Recapitalizations and readjustments, 21·1-28
Representation of security holders, 22·8-9
Trust companies as agents, 6·24
Trustees, 6·24
Appointment, 22·5
Certificates, 22·11
Investigations by, 22·5
Statement and notice to creditors and stockholders, 22·5
Voluntary, 20·8
Repairs, Relation to depreciation, 17·25
Replacements
Capital assets, 17·24-25
Clause, insurance policies, 25·13-14
Unequal lives, 17·43
Report of the Commission on Money and Credit, 2·23-24
Reports
Annual, 8·1-4, 8·4-5
Financial, 8·1-44 (See also "Financial Reports")
Investment companies, 4·27-30
Open interest, commodity trading, 23·30
Operating, 15·12
Quarterly and other interim, 8·5
Statements by corporate executives, 8·5
Reproduction Cost, Method of valuation, 20·27
Repurchase Agreements, 16·5
Reserves
Creating general, 21·6
Definition, 18·7

Reserves (*Continued*)
  For bonded indebtedness, **18**·9–10
  For contingencies, **18**·10
  For future inventory declines, **18**·11
  For insurance, **18**·11
  For plant expansion, **18**·10
  For Treasury stock, **18**·9
  Liability, **18**·7
  Recent trends in terminology, **18**·7–8
  Relationship between funds and, **18**·8
  Secret, **18**·2
  Sinking fund, **18**·9–10
  Surplus, **18**·7 (See also "Retained Earnings")
    Accounting for, **18**·8–9
    Nature of, **18**·8–9
    Purposes and types of, **18**·9–11
  Valuation, **18**·7
Retail Industry, Factors influencing, **7**·14
Retailers, Working capital ratios, **16**·23
Retained Earnings, **18**·6–7
  Administration of, **18**·6
  Balance sheet treatment, **8**·22
  Charges to, **18**·6
  Combined statement of income and, **8**·26
  Cost of, **17**·59–61
    Disagreement as to need for tax adjustment, **17**·60–61
    Selecting the tax rate, **17**·60
  Dating of, **18**·5
  Deficits, **18**·6–7
  Distinction between paid-in surplus and, **18**·3
  Forecasts, **15**·29–30
  Reserves, **18**·7–11
  Sources of, **18**·6
  Statement of, **8**·25
Retirement Funds, Investments in state and local issues, **11**·28–29
Retirement of Bonded Debt, **14**·35–37
  Amortization through sinking fund, **14**·36
  Call feature, **14**·35–36
Retirement Plans for Self-Employed Individuals, **19**·48–50
  Contributions and deductions, **19**·50
  Death benefits, **19**·50
  Definition, **19**·48
  Investments, **19**·49
  Lump sum payments, **19**·50
  Permissible benefits, **19**·49
  Required coverage, **19**·48–49
  Tax status, **19**·49–50
Retirement Provisions
  Pension plans, **19**·19–21
  Profit-sharing plans, **19**·42–43
Retirement Trusts, **6**·8–9
Revenue Act of 1962, **17**·11, **20**·41
Revenue Act of 1964, **17**·12
Revenue Bonds, **11**·27
Revenues
  Analysis of, **8**·9
  Deferred, **8**·20
  In income statement, **8**·9
Rewarding Trusts, **6**·11
Right of Set-off, Bank deposits, **5**·9
Rights
  Pre-emptive, **9**·7, **13**·30, **17**·56–57
  Stock selling ex-rights, **10**·18
  Subscription, **10**·18
  Trading in, **10**·18–19
Risks, **17**·75–77, **25**·1–11
  Areas of risk, **25**·3–5
  Bailments, **25**·10
  Construction contracts, **25**·10
  Control of risk and loss, **25**·1–2, **25**·6–7
    Benefits of loss control, **25**·6–7

Risks (*Continued*)
  Dealing with risk, **25**·6–11
    Assumption of risk and loss, **25**·7
    Available alternatives, **25**·6
    Other risk transfer devices, **25**·10–11
    Purchasing commercial insurance, **25**·8–10
    Self-insurance, **25**·7–8
  Definition, **17**·75, **25**·2
  Diffusion of, commodity exchanges, **23**·9
  Financial, **17**·72
  Investment decisions, **17**·76–77
  Liability to public and employees, **25**·5
  Losses directly affecting income, **25**·4–5
    Business interruption, **25**·4
    Due to destruction of records, **25**·5
    Rental agreements, **25**·5
  Losses due to dishonesty or other criminal acts, **25**·5–6
  Losses from death or disability of key personnel, **25**·5
  Losses of property values, **25**·3–4
    Indirect and direct, **25**·3–4
  Nature of business risks, **25**·1–3
  Objective of, **25**·1
  Probability, laws of, **25**·2–3
  Real estate investments, **26**·20
  Role and duties of risk manager, **25**·1–2
  Role of economists, **25**·2
  Sales contracts, **25**·10–11
  Static risks, **25**·2
  Suretyship, **25**·11
  Surveys and analysis, **25**·2–3
  Use of leased property, **25**·10
Robert Morris Associates, **8**·7
Robinson-Patman Act, **17**·33
Rule Against Perpetuities, **6**·11

Sales
  Analysis of, in income statements, **8**·9
  Contracts, **20**·15, **25**·10–11
    Long-term, **20**·47
  Depreciation based on, **17**·31
  Expansions and, **15**·31
  Goodwill, **20**·14
  In income statement, **8**·9
  Of negotiable instruments, **24**·43
  Of new security issues, **9**·19–24
  Of property, **24**·43–44
  Of stock, **13**·24–25
  Short, **10**·22–24
  Terms of sale, **16**·6–7, **16**·10–11
Sales and Leaseback Arrangements, **26**·26–28
  Financial institutions and endowment funds, **26**·27
  Financing, **14**·43
  Held by pension funds, **26**·11
  Illustration of, **26**·27–28
Sales Finance Companies, **2**·39–40, **16**·14
Salesmen, Securities, **9**·24
Sanctions, Security Act of 1933, **9**·42–43
Savings
  Contractual, **1**·6–7
  Deposit-type, **1**·6
  Direct vs. indirect investment of, **4**·1
  Factors influencing disposition of, **9**·2
  Institutions, **4**·1–39 (See also "Savings Institutions")
  Investment of, **9**·2
  Postal, **4**·12
  Purposes of, **4**·1–3
  Supply of capital and, **9**·2
Savings and Loan Associations, **2**·35–36, **4**·12–16
  Characteristics, **4**·12
  Federal Home Loan Bank system, **4**·15

Savings and Loan Associations (*Continued*)
  Federally chartered, 26·1–4
  Government securities held by, 11·12
  Insurance, 4·15–16
  Loans and investments, 4·14–15, 9·6
  Mortgage loans, 26·1–4
  Operations, 4·13
  State-chartered, 26·4
  Taxes, 4·17–18
  Types of accounts, 4·13–14
Savings and Loan Holding Companies
  Mortgage financing, 26·10
  Stocks of, 7·16
Savings Banks, 4·3–12
  Function of, 4·3
  Government securities held by, 11·12
  Institutional Securities Corporation, 4·10–11
  Investments of, 9·6
  Life insurance and annuities sold by, 4·5
  Mutual savings banks, 4·3–10
    Investments, 4·5–10
    Management and ownership, 4·4
    Savings accounts, 4·5
    Special accounts and services, 4·5
  New York State law, 4·6–8
  Savings Banks Trust Company, 4·10
  Savings departments of commercial banks, 4·11–12
  Taxes, 4·17–18
  Types of savings banks, 4·3–4
Savings Banks Trust Company, 4·10
Savings Bonds, 11·8–9 (See also "Government Obligations")
  Treasury program, 11·20
Savings Deposits, 5·4
Savings Institutions, 4·1–39
  Credit unions, 4·16–17
  Direct vs. indirect investment, 4·1
  Investment companies, 4·19–34
  Life insurance companies, 4·34–39
  Postal savings, 4·12
  Purposes of the saver, 4·1–3
  Role of, 4·1–3
  Savings and loan associations, 4·12–16
  Services and characteristics, 4·3
  Trust companies and departments, 4·19
  Types of, 4·1
SBIC (see "Small Business Investment Companies")
Scrap Value, 17·41
Scrip Certificates
  Dividends, 18·14
  For fractional shares, 13·31
Seasonal Variations, Working capital needs, 16·11
Secondary Distributions, 9·8, 10·21
Securities (See also "Investments," "Stocks")
  Agents, 6·23–24
  Analysis, 7·1–24 (See also "Security Analysis")
  Arbitrage, 10·58
  Balance sheet treatment, 8·16, 8·17–18
  Bank purchase eligibility, 5·21–27
  Bid and asked quotations, 10·2
  Blue sky laws, 9·43–52
  Bonds (See "Bonds")
  Brokers (See "Brokers and Dealers")
  Bulls and bears, 10·22
  Buyers, 9·6–9
    Customers, 9·8
    Employees, 9·8
    Individual, 9·6–8
    Institutional, 9·6
    Investors and speculators, 9·7
    Special groups, 9·7–8

Securities (*Continued*)
  Buyers (*Continued*)
    Stockholders, 9·7
    Suppliers, 9·8
  Classification of, 10·1
  Clearing process, 10·28
  Convertible, 17·58
  Corporate, 10·1
  Definition, 10·1
  Delivery of, 10·28–29
  Determining bases of share exchange, in combination of corporations, 20·30–31
  Discount, 17·51
  Distribution, 9·8, 9·29, 10·22
    Foreign issues, 10·57–58
    Primary, 9·8
    Secondary, 9·8, 10·21
  Ex-dividend or ex-rights, 10·18
  Exempted from Securities Act, 9·38–42
  Financial, 7·14–16
  Fiscal agents, 6·23
  Government obligations (See "Government Obligations")
  Government regulation of trading, 10·46–56
  Indices of prices, 10·30–31
  Industrial, 7·10–14
  International dealings in, 10·56–58
  Investigations of, 9·46
  Investment of surplus cash in, 16·5
  Investment services and ratings, 10·32
  Liquidity, 10·4
  Listing on New York Stock Exchange, 10·9–11
    Statements, 10·9–10
  Margins, 10·32–33
  Marketability of, 10·3–4
  Markets (See "Securities Markets")
  New issues
    Purchase of, 9·11–19
    Sale of, 9·19–24
  Per share ratios, 8·38–39
  Pledged, 14·22–23
  Portfolio management, 9·27
  Premiums, 17·51
  Prices, 9·18, 10·52–54
    Price-cutting, new issues, 9·23–24
  Private offerings, 9·40–41
    Issues of small enterprises, 9·4
  Prospectus, 9·22, 9·28, 9·31–34, 9·38
  Public offering, 9·22–24
    Announcing the offer, 9·22–23
    Direct, 9·4
    Issues of small enterprises, 9·2–4
    Opening and closing the books, 9·23
    Price cutting, 9·23–24
  Public utilities, 7·16–21
  Purchasing new issues, 9·11–19
  Puts and calls, 10·26
  Railroad, 7·21–24
  Ratings by investment services, 10·32
  Registrars, 6·23–24
  Registration of, 9·30–38, 10·47–49
    Fees, 10·17–18
    Procedure, 10·47–48
    Uniform Securities Act, 9·47–48
  Registration statements (See "Registration Statements")
  Regulation of credit, 10·33–34
  Salesmen, 9·24
    Licensing, 9·24
    Standards for, 9·24
  Securities Exchange Act (See "Securities Exchange Act of 1934")
  Selling, 9·1–52
    Costs incurred, 17·51

GENERAL INDEX   G·37

Securities (*Continued*)
  Selling (*Continued*)
    For a controlling person, 9·42
    Investment banking, 9·8–27 (See also "Investment Banking")
    Problem, 9·19
    Sales organization, 9·19–20
    Selling group, 9·20–21
      Agreement, 9·21–22
  Services, 10·32
  Shiftability, 10·4
  Short selling, 10·14, 10·22–24
  Speculation, 10·29–32
  Stocks (See "Stocks")
  Stockholders, 9·7–8 (See also "Stockholders")
  Stop orders, 9·42–43
  Subscription agents, 6·24
  "Switching," 9·23, 9·26
  Tax exempt, 10·1
  "Tombstone ads," 9·22–23
  Trading, 10·13–32 (See also "Securities Trading")
  Transfer agents, 6·23
  Transfer taxes, 10·17
  Types of, 9·7–8
  Uniform Securities Act, 9·45–50
  Unlisted trading, 10·11–12
  Valuation of marketable, 8·16
Securities Act of 1933, 9·27–43
  Antifraud provisions, 9·28
  Communication not deemed a prospectus, 9·33–34
  Disclosure principle, 9·27–28
  "Distribution" explained, 9·29
  Exempted securities, 9·38–42
  Exempted transactions, 9·39–40
    Brokers' transactions, 9·41–42
    Private offerings, 9·40–41
    Sales for a controlling person, 9·42
    Transactions by dealers, 9·41
  Fraud outlawed, 9·28
  General description, 9·28
  Investment banking business and, 9·9
  1954 amendments, 9·34
  Persons and transactions covered, 9·28–30
    Controlling persons, 9·30
    "Issuer," "dealer," and "underwriter" defined, 9·28–29
    Purchase for distribution or "investment," 9·29–30
  Posteffective period, 9·34–35
  Prefiling period, 9·31
  Preliminary prospectus, 9·31–32
  Prohibitions and required acts, 9·30–35
  Prospectus, 9·28
    Final, 9·34
    Preliminary, 9·31–32
    Preparation of, 9·38
    Summary, 9·32–33
  Registration procedure, 9·35–38
    Amendments, 9·36–37
    Confidential treatment, 9·35–36
    Withdrawal of statement, 9·37–38
  Registration statement, 9·28
  Regulation A, 9·39
  Regulation E, 9·39
  Sanctions, 9·42–43
    Civil liabilities, 9·43
    Injunctions and criminal proceedings, 9·42–43
    Stop orders, 9·42
  "Tombstone ads," 9·33–34
  Waiting period, 9·31
    Acceleration of, 9·32

Securities and Exchange Commission (S.E.C.)
  Accounting requirements, 8·2–3
  Authority over financial reporting, 8·2–3
  Market stabilization rules, 9·25–26
  Power to alter rules and practices of exchanges, 10·51–52
  Proxies, 13·16–17
  Public utility regulations, 7·18
  Registration of utility holding companies, 20·43–44
  Regulation A, 9·39
  Regulation E, 9·39
  Regulation of brokers and dealers, 10·54–56
  Regulation S-X, 10·50
  Report of the Special Study of Securities Markets (1963), 9·17
  Report to Congress on the Special Study of Securities Markets (1963), 9·24
  Trust Indenture Act administered by, 14·11
Securities Dealers, National Association of, 10·44–46
Securities Exchanges Act of 1934, 10·46–56
  Administration of, 10·47·56
    Accounting requirements and standards, 10·49–50
    Ownership reports and insider trading, 10·50
    Proxies, disclosure of policies, 10·50–51
    Registration of securities, 10·47–49
    Regulation of brokers and dealers, 10·54–56
    Regulation of trading, 10·51–54
      Control of short selling, 10·53
      Daily statistics of trading, 10·54
      Fair and orderly markets, 10·51
      Margin regulation, 10·53–54
      Power to alter rules and practices of exchanges, 10·51–52
      Prohibition of price manipulation, 10·52–53
      Registration and reorganization of the Exchanges, 10·51
      Stabilizing security prices, 10·53
  Chief provisions, 10·46–47
  Objectives, 10·46
  Ownership reports and insider trading, 10·50
  Regulation T, 10·34
  Regulation U, 10·34
Securities Exchanges, 10·1, 10·2 (See also "Securities Trading" and "Stock Exchanges")
Securities Markets, 10·1–58
  Auction vs. negotiated, 10·1–3
  Bid and asked quotations, 10·2
  Bond trading, 10·39–41
  Breadth of, 10·4
  Brokerage houses, 10·35–39
  Brokers and dealers, 10·4–5
    Distinction between roles, 10·4–5
  Closeness of, 10·4
  "Conditioning," 9·31
  Continuity of, 10·4
  Federal regulation, 10·46–56, 10·51–54
  Functions of, 10·1
  Government securities, 11·11–17
  Indicators, 10·30–32
  Marketability of securities, 10·3–4
  National stock exchanges, 10·2–3
  Nature of, 10·1
  New York Stock Exchange, 10·5–13 (See also "New York Stock Exchange")
  Organization and functions, 10·1–5
  Over-the-counter, 10·2, 10·3, 10·41–46
  Security exchanges, 10·2
  Stabilization, 9·24–25, 10·4, 10·30
    Legal restrictions, 9·25–26
  State and local issues, 11·28
  Trading on exchanges, 10·13–32

GENERAL INDEX

Securities Markets (*Continued*)
Trading on margin, **10·32-35**
Securities Trading, 10·13-32
Bond trading, **10·39-41**
Brokerage commissions on stocks, **10·16-17**
Brokerage houses, **10·35-39** (See also "Brokerage Houses")
Charting price movements, **10·31**
Confirmation of purchase, **10·16**
Corners and manipulation, **10·24**
Dow theory of stock price movements, **10·31**
Execution of orders, **10·15-16**
Federal regulation, **10·46-56**
International, **10·56-58**
   Arbitrage, **10·58**
   Distribution of blocks of foreign issues, **10·57-58**
   Interest equalization tax, **10·56-57**
   Investment in foreign securities, **10·56-57**
   Markets for foreign equities, **10·58**
   Organization dealing in, **10·57**
Large blocks of securities, **10·20-22**
   Exchange distribution, **10·22**
   Specialist block purchase or sale, **10·22**
Margin transactions, **10·32-35**
   Customers' margin requirements, **10·33**
   Interest charges, **10·34-35**
   Opening a margin account, **10·33**
   Relations between broker and customer, **10·34**
   S.E.C. regulations, **10·33-34, 10·53-54**
Market indicators, **10·30-32**
   Security services and ratings, **10·32**
   Stock market charts and tape readers, **10·32**
Multiple, **10·52**
Odd-lot trading, **10·25**
Options or privileges, **10·25-27**
   Puts, calls, and straddles, **10·25-26**
Orders, **10·16**
   Confirmation of, **10·16**
   Limited, **10·14-15**
   Market orders, **10·15**
   Stop-loss, **10·15**
   Stopping stock, **10·15**
   Use of private leased wire system, **10·15**
Over-the-counter markets, **10·41-46**
Ownership reports and insider trading, **10·50**
Privileges, **10·25-27**
   Purpose of, **10·27**
Registration fees, **10·17-18**
Restrictions imposed by Securities Exchange Act, **10·20, 10·53-54**
Rights and stock purchase warrants, **10·18-19**
Secondary distributions, **10·21**
Selling ex-dividend or ex-rights, **10·18**
Settlement of transactions, **10·27-29**
   Clearance and settlement of the money values, **10·28**
   Clearing process, **10·28**
   Comparison of transactions, **10·28**
   Consequences of failure to deliver, **10·29**
   Date of, **10·16**
   Security clearance, **10·28**
   What constitutes good delivery, **10·28-29**
Short sales, **10·22-23**
   Corners and manipulation, **10·24**
   Economic effects, **10·23-24**
   Federal regulation, **10·24-25**
   Loaning rates, **10·23**
   Margins deposited against, **10·23**
   Operation of, **10·22-23**
Special offering plans, **10·21**
Speculation, **10·29-30**
   Advantages and disadvantages, **10·29-30**
   Investment differs from, **10·29**

Securities Trading (*Continued*)
Speculation (*Continued*)
   Manipulation, **10·30**
   Tape readers, **10·32**
   Transaction date, **10·16**
   Transactions, **10·13-14**
   Transfer taxes, **10·17-18**
   Unlisted stocks, **10·11-12**
   When-issued trading, **10·19-20**
      Limitations imposed by S.E.C. **10·20**
      Permissible transactions, **10·19-20**
Security Analysis, 7·1-24
Automobile industry, **7·14**
Bonds, **7·4-8**
Chemical and drug stocks, **7·14**
Common stock, **7·8-10**
Departments in banks, **6·16-17**
Earnings per share, **7·8**
Financial securities, **7·14-16**
   Bank stocks, **7·15**
   Finance companies, **7·16**
   Insurance stocks, **7·15-16**
Financial statements, **7·13**
Function of, **7·4**
Industrial securities, **7·10-14**
   Accounting peculiarities, **7·12-13**
   Capital structure, **7·13**
   Dividend prospects, **7·13**
   Industry analysis, **7·14**
   Nature of industry, **7·10-11**
   Prospective earnings, **7·11-12**
   Ratio analysis, **7·13-14**
   Working capital position, **7·12**
Investments, **7·1-4**
   Characteristics of, **7·1-2**
   Definition, **7·1**
   Diversification, **7·2**
   Legal, **7·3**
   Liquidity, **7·3**
   Marketability, **7·3**
   Return on, **7·2-3**
   Safety, **7·1-2**
   Tax status, **7·3**
   Timing hazard, **7·2**
Objectives, **7·8**
Petroleum industry, **7·14**
Preferred stocks, **7·7-8**
Price-earnings ratios, **7·8-10**
Procedures, **7·10**
Public utility securities, **7·16-20**
   Analysis of company, **7·18-20**
   Classes of, **7·20-21**
   Commission regulation, **7·18**
   Franchises, **7·16-17**
   Rates, **7·17**
   Types of enterprises, **7·16**
   Valuation, **7·17-18**
Railroad securities, **7·21-24**
   Analysis ratios, **7·23**
   Financial statements, **7·24**
   Legal and economic factors, **7·21-22**
   Operating expenses, **7·22-23**
   Railroad rates, **7·22**
   Railroad traffic, **7·22**
Real estate mortgages, **7·6-7**
Retail stocks, **7·14**
Tobacco stocks, **7·14**
Security Dealers
Definition, **9·28-29**
Government obligations, **11·12-13**
Licensing, **9·44**
Transactions exempted from Security Act of 1933, **9·41**
Security Salesmen, 9·24

GENERAL INDEX

Self-Dealing, By directors, 12·33
Self-Employed Individuals Tax Retirement Act of 1962, 19·48
Self-Insurance, 25·7–8
  Conditions necessary for, 25·8
  Cost of commercial insurance vs., 25·9–10
Selling Group, To distribute new issues, 9·20–21
  Abuses, 9·23–24
  Agreement, 9·21–22
  Formation of, 9·21
  Selection of members, 9·20
  Types of, 9·21
Serial Bonds, 14·37–38
Service Charges, Checking accounts, 5·19
Services
  Bank, 5·4–5, 5·15, 5·20–21
  Commercial credit, 8·6–7
  Investment, 8·6–7
Settlement Date, Securities transactions, 10·16
Shareholders (See also "Stockholders")
  Notification of, 18·28
Shares
  Donated, 13·4
  Founders', 13·23–24
  Fractional, 13·30–31
  Management, 13·23–24
Sheltering Trusts, 6·10
Shopping Centers, 26·29–32
  Development and financing, 26·30–31
  Investment analysis, 26·31–32
  Investment criteria, 26·31
Short Sales, 10·22–24
  Commodity exchanges, 23·9–10
  Corners and manipulation, 10·24
  Economic effects of, 10·23–24
  Federal regulation, 10·24–25, 10·53
  Futures trading, 23·15
  Loaning rates, 10·23
  Margins deposited against, 10·23
  Operation of, 10·22–23
  Sale against the box, 10·22
Sight Drafts, 3·8–9 (See also "Bills of Exchange")
Signatures
  By agents, 24·7
  Forged, 24·7
  Negotiable instruments, 24·3, 24·7, 24·20–21
Silver, As money, 2·7
Sinking Funds, 14·4, 14·13
  Acquisition of bonds for, 14·37
  Calculations, 27·34–38
    Finding amount of installments, 27·34–35
    Finding the number of payments, 27·35–38
    Schedule of fund installments, 27·38
  Comparison of serial bonds and, 14·38
  Dangers of excessive charges, 14·37
  Deposit of bonds in lieu of cash payments, 14·37
  For amortization of bonds, 14·36
  For bond retirement, 14·36–38
  For redeemable preferred stock, 13·22
  Reserve, 18·9–10
  Trust companies fiscal agent for, 6·23
  Types of, 14·36–37
Small Business Administration (S.B.A.), 9·4, 16·13
Small Business Investment Act of 1958, 9·4
Small Business Investment Companies (S.B.I.C.), 9·4–6
  Capital, 9·5
  Exempted securities, 9·39
  Permissible investments, 9·5
  Public offerings, 9·3–4
    Exempt from registration, 9·5–6
  Tax treatment, 9·4

Small Businesses
  Capital expenditures, 17·4
  Debt readjustments, 21·17
  Financing, 16·13
  Provision for loss of key men, 25·31
  Raising capital for, 9·2–4
  Public offerings through an investment banker, 9·3–4
  Voluntary chains, 20·48
Social Progress Trust Fund, 3·32
Social Security, 19·51
  Pension benefit payments and, 19·21–22
Sole Proprietorships, 12·3
Special Drawing Rights, I.M.F., 3·3
Specialists, Brokers, 10·8
  Block purchase or sale, 10·22
Speculation
  Commodity trading, 23·11, 23·31–32
  Hedging versus, 23·25
  In foreign exchange, 3·10–11
  In securities, 9·7, 9·17, 10·29–32
    Advantages and disadvantages, 10·29–30
    Investment differs from, 10·29
Spendthrift Trusts, 6·10
Spin-Offs, Split-Offs, and **Split-Ups of Stock,** 21·23
Spot Commodity Markets, 23·32–34
Spread
  Security trading, 10·26
  Underwriters, 9·18–19
Stabilization, Security market, 9·24–2(
Stand-by Underwriting, 9·19
Standard and Poor's Corporation, 8·6
  Bond rating systems, 7·6
Standards, For ratio analysis, 8·39
State and Municipal Bonds
  Investors in, 11·28–29
  Marketing of, 11·28
Statement of Financial Position (See "Balance Sheets")
Statement of Operations, 8·7 (See also "Income Statement")
States
  Blue sky laws, 9·43–44
  Bonds, 11·24–29
  Investments in government securities, 11·12
  Of incorporation, 12·16–17
  Pension plans, 19·51–52
  Real estate financing, 26·11
  Regulations governing consolidations, 20·18–19
Statistics
  Banking, 1·14–25
  Cost, analysis of, 15·19
Steam Boiler Insurance, 25·20
Stock Clearing Corporation, 10·12, 10·28
Stock Exchanges (See also "Securities Trading")
  Bond trading, 10·39–41
  Federal regulation, 10·51–54
  New York, 10·5–13 (See also "New York Stock Exchange")
  Questionnaires, 10·39
  Securities trading, 10·13–32 (See also "Securities Trading")
  Settlement procedure, 10·27–29
  Ticker service, 10·12–13
  Trading facilities, 10·12
Stock Purchase Warrants, 10·18–19
Stock Ticker, 10·12–13
Stockholders, 9·7–8
  As buyers of securities, 9·7
  Assessment in the event of insolvency, 13·5–6
  Consent of
    Consolidations, 20·17, 20·19

Stockholders (*Continued*)
  Consent of (*Continued*)
    Purchase of assets, 20·9, 20·12
  Equity account, 18·1
  Liability of, 13·1
  Meetings, 12·23–27
    Annual meetings, 12·23–24
    Consent meetings, 12·25
    Consent without a meeting, 12·26
    Procedures, 12·24
    Protection of minority interests, 12·26–27
    Quorums, 12·26
    Special, 12·24–25
    Voting, 12·26
  Minority, 12·26–27
    Corporate dissolutions, 21·28
    Protection afforded, by courts, 20·41
  Pre-emptive right, 9·7, 13·24–25
  Purchase of assets, 20·10
    Paying off dissenting, 20·11
  Relationship to corporation, 13·1
  Reorganizations
    Plan submitted to, 22·7–8
    Trustee's statement and notice to, 22·5
  Rights, 13·1, 20·20
    Subscription, 13·24–26
  Use of ratios, 8·40
  Voting by, 13·13–14
Stocks (See also "Bonds" and "Securities")
  Agents, 6·23–24
  Authorized, 13·10–12
    Changes of, 13·11–12
    For expansion purposes, 20·11–12
    Reservation of, 13·11
  Automobiles, 7·14
  Bank, 7·15
  Bonus, 13·28
    Consideration for, 13·28
    Definition and uses, 13·28
  Brokerage commissions on, 10·16–17
  Capital (See "Capital Stock")
  Certificates, 13·1–3
    Endorsement, 13·3
    Negotiability of, 13·2–3
  Chemical and drug, 7·14
  Common, 13·22–23, 16·12
    Avoidance of dilution, 17·55
    Bonus, 9·7
    Capital account reductions, 21·4–7
    Changes in par or stated value, 21·4
    Computation of cost, 17·55–56
    Cost of, 17·54
    Determination of price per share, 17·55
    Direct sale to public, 17·54–56
    Dividend rights, 13·23
    Indirect sale, through convertible securities, 17·58
    Recapitalizations, 21·2–8
      Changes in number of shares, 21·3–4
      Legal requirements, 21·2
    Sale, under pre-emptive rights, 17·56–57
    Security analysis, 7·8–10
    Subscription warrant, 13·27
    Voting and nonvoting, 13·23
  Convertible, 13·22
  Corporate, 13·1–31
  Deferred, 13·23
  Delaware statute, 13·7
  Delisting, 13·23
  Dividends, 7·9, 18·12–14, 21·3 (See also "Dividends")
    Effect on taxes, 18·24–25
  Donated shares, 13·4
  Dow theory of price movements, 10·31

Stocks (*Continued*)
  Earnings per share, 7·8
  Ex-dividend or ex-rights, 10·18
  Founders' shares, 13·23–24
  Fractional shares, 13·30–31
    Method of disposing of, 13·31
    Reasons for, 13·31
    Use of negotiable scrip certificates, 13·31
  Full-paid, 13·12
  "Growth image," 7·13
  Guaranteed, 13·23
  Held in a street name, 13·17
  Institutional demand, 7·9
  Insurance, 7·15–16
  Investor demand, 7·9
  Issued, 13·12
  Mutual stock ownership, 20·47–48
  No-par value, 13·7–10
    Advantages and disadvantages, 13·9–10
    Balance sheet treatment, 13·8–9
      Objectionable methods, 13·9
    Form of certificate, 13·10
    Reasons for adoption, 13·7
    Stated value, 13·7
  Oil, 7·14
  Option warrants, 9·7, 13·29
    Duration of, 13·29–30
    Exercise of, 13·30
    Pre-emptive rights and, 13·30
  Other classes, 13·22–24
  Owners' equity, 13·1
  Par value, 13·4–6
    Changes in, 21·4
    Form of certificate, 13·6
    "Full-Paid and Nonassessable," 13·5–6
    Laws, 13·6
    Significance of, 13·4–6
    Tax status, 13·6
    True value, 13·7
    Use of, 13·4
    Valuation of property or services as payment for stock, 13·5
  Part-paid, 13·12
  Pledged, voting, 14·22–23
  Pre-emptive rights, 13·24, 17·56–57
    Option warrants and, 13·30
  Preferred, 13·19–22, 16·12
    Asset preference, 13·20–21
    Balance sheet treatment, 8·21
    Callable, 13·21–22
    Classes of, 13·20
    Classification of, 13·19
    Convertible, 9·7, 13·22
    Cumulative, 13·19–20
    Definition, 13·19
    Dividend preference, 13·19–20
    Nonvoting, 13·24
    Participating, 13·20
    Protective provisions, 13·21
    Redeemable, 13·21–22
    Security analysis, 7·7–8
    Voting power, 13·21
  Price-earnings ratio, 7·8–10
    Quality of reported earnings, 7·9
    Trend of earnings per share, 7·8–9
  Price indices, 10·30–32
  Pricing of issues, 9·18
  Proxies, 10·50–51, 13·15–17
  S.E.C. regulations, 10·50–51, 13·16–17
  Purchase warrants, 13·29–30
    Detachable and nondetachable, 13·29
    Duration of option, 13·29–30
    Exercise of the option, 13·30
    Nature of, 13·29

Stocks (*Continued*)
  Quality of management, **7**·10
  Reclassification, **21**·7-9
  Retail, **7**·14
  Reverse splits, **21**·3-4
  Rights
    Pre-emptive rights, **13**·24-25
    Subscription, **13**·24-28
  Sale of, **13**·24-25
    Pre-emptive rights, **13**·24
    To customers, **13**·25
    To employees, **13**·25
    To general public, **13**·25
    To stockholders, **13**·24-25
  Scrip certificates, **13**·31
  Security analysis (See also "Security Analysis")
    Common stock, **7**·8-10
    Preferred stock, **7**·7-8
  Share consolidation, **21**·3-4
  Shares, **13**·1
    Book value, **13**·1
    Market value, **13**·1
  Spin-offs, **21**·23
  Split-offs, **21**·23
  Split-ups, **21**·3, **21**·23
  Splits, **18**·12
  Stockholders, **13**·1 (See also "Stockholders")
  Subscriptions, **13**·18
    Form, **13**·18
    Legal status, **13**·18
    Privileged, **17**·57
    Rights, **13**·25-28
      Action by board of directors, **13**·25-26
      Action by stockholders, **13**·26
      Form of warrant, **13**·27
      Letter to stockholders, **13**·26
      Market quotations, **13**·28
      Subscription warrants, **13**·26
      Value, **13**·26-28
  Terms and definition, **13**·10-13
  Tobacco, **7**·14
  Transfer agents, **6**·23, **13**·3
  Transfer procedures, **13**·3-4
    Registrar, **13**·3-4
  Treasury, **13**·12-13, **18**·9
    Methods of acquisition, **13**·13
      By donation, **13**·13
      By purchase, **13**·13
    Reasons for acquisition, **13**·13
  Types of, **9**·7
  Unissued, **13**·12
  Voting power, **13**·13-18
    By stockholders, **13**·13-14
    Contingent voting, **13**·15
    Cumulative voting, **13**·14-15
    Proxies, **13**·15-17
    Voting trusts, **13**·17-18
  Warrants
    Option, **13**·29
    Purchase, **13**·29-30
    Stock subscription, **13**·26
Stop-Loss Orders
  Commodity trading, **23**·15
  Securities, **10**·15
Stop Orders, **9**·42-43
Stop-Payment Orders, Checks, **5**·15
"Straddle," Security trading, **10**·26
Straight-Line Depreciation Method, **17**·28-29
Street Name, Stocks held in, **10**·14, **13**·17
"Strip" or "Strap," Security trading, **10**·26
Subchapter S Corporations, **12**·3, **12**·5
Subscriptions
  Agent, corporate, **6**·24

Subscriptions (*Continued*)
  Form, **13**·18
  Legal status, **13**·18
  Privileged, **17**·57
  Rights, **13**·25-28
    Action by board of directors, **13**·25-26
    Action by stockholders, **13**·26
    Convertible bonds, **14**·32-33
    Letter to stockholders, **13**·26
    Market quotations, **13**·28
    Value of, **13**·26-28
    Warrants, **13**·26
      Form, **13**·27
  Stock, **13**·18
Subsidiaries, Corporate
  Abuse of parent-subsidiary relations, **20**·41
    Protection afforded minority stockholders, **20**·41
  Consolidated statements, **8**·22-25
  Creation by parent company, **20**·39-41
  Dealings between parent and, **20**·37
  Deep Rock Doctrine, **20**·42
  Fiduciary relationship, **20**·41
  Financing capital requirements, **20**·37
  Foreign, **8**·23, **20**·40-41
  Holding companies with one subsidiary, **20**·35
  Indebtedness of, **8**·16-17
  Instrumentality rule, **20**·41-42
  Intercompany items and transactions, **8**·25
  Intercorporate readjustments, **20**·40
  Investment in, **8**·16-17, **8**·24
  Jointly owned, **20**·48
  Minority interests, **8**·24
  Organized for legal reasons, **20**·39
  Sale of assets, collateral trust bonds, **14**·23
  To facilitate management and operations, **20** 40
  To limit parent company's liability, **20**·40
  To secure goodwill, **20**·40
Substitution Cost, Method of valuation, **20**·27
Sum-of-the-Years-Digits Method, **17**·30
  Excess present value solutions, **17**·43-45
Sunk Costs, Depreciation and, **17**·40-41
Sureties, Bankruptcy actions, **22**·27
Surety Bonds, **25**·25-26
Suretyship, **25**·11
Surplus
  Capital, **18**·1
  Capital assets, **17**·7
  Classification of, **18**·1-2
  Defined, **18**·1
  Discovery, **18**·2
  Donated, **18**·2
  Earned, **18**·1-2 (See also "Retained Earnings")
    Elimination of deficit, **21**·5
  Effect of merger or consolidation on, **20**·29
  Improper techniques, **18**·2-3
  In income statement, **8**·12-13
  Nature of, **18**·1-3
  Overstatement of, **18**·2-3
  Paid-in, **8**·21, **18**·3-5
    Distinguished from legal capital and undivided profits, **18**·3
    From business combinations, **18**·5
    From donations, **18**·3-4
    From reacquisition of capital stock, **18**·4
    From recapitalization, **18**·4
    From reorganizations, **18**·4-5
    From sale of stock, **18**·3
    Sources of, **18**·3-5
  Reserves
    Accounting for, **18**·8-9
    Nature of, **18**·8-9
    Purposes and types of, **18**·9-11
  Revaluation, **18**·5-6

Surplus (*Continued*)
  Terminology, 18·2
  Decline in use of term, 18·2
  Understatement of, 18·2–3
Surplus Test, Dividends, 18·20–21
Switching
  Customers, security, 9·23, 9·26
  Liquidation of futures contracts, 23·20
Syndicates, 12·6–8
  Agreements, 12·7
  Real estate, 12·7–8, 26·11
    Federal and state regulation of public offerings, 12·7
    Forms of organization, 12·7

Tables
  Annuity valuation, 27·32–33
    Periodic payment required to amortize $1 and interest, 27·36–37
    Present value of annuity of $1 at end of each period, 27·40–41
  Bond valuation, 27·48–49
  Compound interest, 27·22–23, 27·26–27
  Logarithms, 27·56, 27·59–62
Tangible Assets, Writing down values, 21·5
Tangible Fixed Assets, 17·2
Tape Readers, 10·32
Tax-Anticipation Issues, 11·10, 16·5
Taxes
  Accruals as source of working capital, 16·16
  Banks and mutual thrift institutions, 4·17–19, 5·26
  Bond transactions, 10·41
  Business combinations, 20·7
  Business trusts, 12·9
  Capital budget and, 17·41–46
  Capital gains, 17·60
  Corporation, 12·17–18
  Cost of retained earnings and, 17·60
  Depletion allowances, 8·12
  Dividends, 18·13, 18·23–27
  Federal credit unions, 4·17
  Franchise, 20·30
  Hedging, 23·25
  In income statement, 8·12
  Interest equalization, 10·56–57
  Investment companies, 4·30–31
  Investment tax credit, 17·11–12
  Investments, 5·26, 7·3
  Leased property, 20·31
  Limited partnerships, 12·6
  Of various business organizations, 12·1–2
  On excess working capital, 16·6
  Par value stock, 13·6
  Pension plans, 19·3–5
    Early termination, 19·32
  Profit-sharing plans, 19·38, 19·48
  Purchase of assets, 20·9
  Real estate investment trusts, 12·9, 26·10
  Real estate investments, 26·24–25
  Retirement plans for self-employed, 19·49–50
  State and municipal bonds, 11·24–29
  Surplus cash, 16·6
  Surtax on undistributed earnings, 18·23–24
  Transfer, 10·17
    Bond transactions, 10·41
    Treasury obligations, 11·10
Telephone and Telegraph Companies, 7·21
Temperature Damage Insurance, 25·22
Tenants
  In common, 5·11
  Liabilities of, 25·27–28
Tennessee Valley Authority, Obligations of, 11·8

Term Loans, 14·40–41, 16·12
  By banks, 5·34
  Characteristics, 14·40–41
  Purposes and terms, 14·41
Terminal Bonds, 14·21
Termination, Profit-sharing plans, 19·43–44, 19·46–47
Terminology
  Reserves, 18·7–8
  Surplus, 18·2
Terms
  Of purchase, 16·10
  Of sale, 16·6, 16·10–11
Ticker Tape System, 10·12–13
  Bond quotations, 10·40
Time Bills, 3·10
Time Deposits in Banks, 5·3–4, 16·4–5
Time Drafts, 3·9
  For foreign exchange, 3·7–8
Timing, Capital expenditures, 17·9
Tobacco Industry, Financial analysis, 7·14
"Tombstone Ads"
  Of securities, 9·22–23
  Securities Act of 1933, 9·33–34
Trade Acceptances, 24·35–36
Trade Association, 20·46–47
  Source of financial data, 8·6
Trade Terms, 23·33–35
  "C.A.F. (named destination)," 23·34
  Cash commodity transactions, 23·33–35
  "Delivered (named destination)," 23·34
  "F.A.S. (named port)," 23·33
  "F.O.B. (named point)," 23·33
  ". . . Freight equalized," 23·34
  "In store," 23·35
Transfer of stock, 13·3–4
  Procedure, 13·3–4
  Registrar, 13·3–4
  Taxes, 10·17, 10·41
  Transfer agent, 6·23, 13·3
Transfers, Mail, 3·7–8
Transportation Insurance Policies, 25·18–19
Travelers' Checks, 3·28
Traveler's Letter of Credit, 3·26–28
Treasurer of Corporation, 12·34–35
  Duties of, 15·35–36
Treasury
  "Accord" with Federal Reserve, 2·32
  Bonds, 11·7, 14·30, 16·5
    Investment Series A, 11·9
    Investment Series B-1975–80, 11·9–10
    REA series, 11·10
  Budget policy, 11·4–5
  Certificates, 1·10
  Competitive bidding required, 9·13
  Debt management policies, 1·5, 1·26, 2·28, 11·5–6
    Effect on bond market, 11·20–21
    Objectives, 11·5–6
  Financing program, 2·31, 11·4, 11·10–11
    Advance refundings, 1·26, 11·11, 11·21
    Coupon obligations, 11·10–11
    Effect on money market, 1·25–27
    Exchange offerings, 11·11
    Tax-anticipation issues, 11·10
    Treasury bill auctions, 11·10
  "Floating debt," 11·2–3
  Notes, 5·23, 11·7, 16·5
  Obligations, 11·2
    Foreign series and foreign currency series, 11·10
    Interest rate, 11·4
    Over-the-counter market, 10·3
    Tax status, 11·10

Treasury (*Continued*)
  Obligations (*Continued*)
    Treasury bonds, 11·7
    Treasury notes, 5·23, 11·7, 16·5
    Types of, 11·2
  Policies
    Advance refunding operations, 1·26, 11·11, 11·21
    Deficit financing, 11·21
    Effect on price of government securities, 11·20–21
    "Restricted" issues, 11·20–21
    Savings bond program, 11·20
Treasury Bills, 1·10, 5·23, 11·7, 16·5
  Auctions, 11·10
Treasury Securities
  Pegging the rates on, 11·18
  Rediscount rate, 11·18
Treasury Stock, 13·12–13, 18·9
  Pre-emptive rights, 13·24
Trust Companies, 4·19, 6·1–24
  Agency function, 6·23–24
    Depositary under voting trust agreements, 6·24
    Fiscal agents, 6·23
    For corporations in process of reorganization, consolidation, or mergers, 6·24
    Registrars, 6·23–24
    Subscription agents, 6·24
    Transfer agents, 6·23
  Agency services, 6·18–19
  As fiduciaries, 6·1, 6·21–22
  As fiscal agent, 6·23
  As receiver or trustee, 6·23
  As savings institutions, 4·19
  Corporate agency functions, 6·22–24
  Corporate trust business, 6·21–24
  Corporate trust functions, 6·22
  Custodial accounts, 6·19
  Escrow accounts, 6·19
  Functions and services, 4·19
  Individual co-trustee for corporate bonds, 6·22–23
  Investment management organization, 6·15–17
  Investment powers, 6·13–14
  Investments of, 9·6
  Personal agency functions, 6·18–19
  Personal trust business, 6·2–21
  Reviewing departments, 6·16
  Securities analysis departments, 6·16–17
  Services provided by, 6·18–19
    Agency accounts, 6·19
      With investment service, 6·19
    Custodial accounts, 6·19
    Escrow accounts, 6·19
    Safekeeping accounts, 6·19
  Trust department management, 6·4
  Trustee for bondholders under indenture, 6·22
Trust Deeds, 12·8, 26·14
Trust Indenture Act of 1939, 6·22, 14·9–11
Trustees
  Accountability of, 6·17–18
  Bankruptcy, 22·30–32
  Bonds, 14·8–9, 14·10
    Remedies of, 14·13–14
  Breach of trust, 6·17, 6·18
  Certificates, 14·30
  Corporate, 14·8–9
  Fees and commissions, 6·20–21
  For bondholders under indenture, 6·22
  Investment duties, 6·14–15
  Investment powers, 6·13–14
  Legal investments, 7·3
  Pension plans, 19·33–34

Trustees (*Continued*)
  Profit-sharing plans, 19·47–48
  Prudent man rule, 7·13
  Reorganizations, 22·5–6
  Trust companies as, 6·23
Trusts
  Agency functions
    For corporations, 6·23–24
    Personal trust business, 6·4
  Agents, definition, 6·2
  Agreements, 6·8
  As combination device, 20·36
  Assets
    Accumulation of income, 6·12–13
    Care of, 6·12–13
    Collection of, 6·11–12
  Assignees, 6·7
  Beneficiaries, 6·8, 6·12
  Breach of, 6·17, 6·18
  Business, 12·8–9
  Charitable, 6·11
  Common law, 12·8
  Common trust funds, 4·25–26
  Corporate, 6·21–24
  Corporate fiduciaries, 6·1–4
    Advantages of, 6·3–4
    Banks and trust companies, 6·21–22
    Establishment and growth of, 6·1
    Personal trust business vs., 6·2–3
  Creation of, 6·8
    By agreement or deed of trust, 6·8
    In wills, 6·8
  Deed of trust, 6·8, 14·8
  Definition, 6·1–2
  Duration of, 6·11
  Equipment, 14·23
  Escrow accounts, 6·19
  Express, 6·8, 12·8
  Fiduciaries, 6·1–4
    Corporate vs. personal trust business, 6·2–3
    Definitions, 6·1–2
    Evolution of corporate, 6·2–3
  Fiduciary functions for corporations, 6·21–23
    Corporate agency functions, 6·22
    Corporate trust functions, 6·22
    Individual co-trustee for corporate bonds, 6·22–23
  For emergencies, 6·11
  For incompetent persons, 6·10–11
  Functions of executor, 6·5–6
    Administration, 6·5
    Preparation of inventory, 6·5
    Probating will, 6·5
  Implied, 6·8
  In contemplation of death, 6·9–10
  Income, provisions affecting, 6·13
  Indentures, 14·8
  Instrument provisions, 6·13–15
  Inter vivos, 6·8
  Investment, 9·27
    Absence of express power to sell, 6·14
    Duties of trustees, 6·14–15
    Management of, 6·15–17
    Powers of trustees, 6·13–14
    Prudent man rule, 6·14
    Restrictions on powers, 6·14
    Types of, 6·14
  Irrevocable, 19·47
  Land, 26·17
  Legal concept, 6·7–8
  Liabilities of a fiduciary, 6·17–18
    Accountability of trustees, 6·17–18
    Breaches of trust, 6·17, 6·18
    Dealing with self, 6·18

Trusts (*Continued*)
  Life insurance, 6·9
    Funded, 6·9
    Partially funded, 6·9
    Unfunded, 6·9
  Living, 6·8-10
    In contemplation of death, 6·9-10
    Types of, 6·8-10
  Management of trust investments, 6·15-17
    Officers' investment committee, 6·15
    Reviewing department, 6·16
  Massachusetts, 12·8, 20·45
  Pension and profit-sharing, 6·10
  Personal, 6·7-11
    Fees, 6·20-21
    Operation, 6·11-13
  Personal agency functions, 6·18-19
    Range of, 6·18
    Service provided by trust companies, 6·18-19
  Personal trust business, 6·2-3, 6·4-7
    Functions of department, 6·4
    Functions of executor, 6·5-6
    Guardian of an incompetent, 6·7
    Guardian of a minor, 6·7
    Special types of, 6·10-11
    Work of administrator, 6·6-7
  Provisions, 6·13-15
    Affecting income and principal payments, 6·13
    Investment, 6·13-14
    Nature of, 6·13
  Real estate investment, 4·26, 12·9, 26·10
    Tax advantage, 26·10
  Receipts, 5·29, 16·5
  Remainderman, 6·8
  Retirement, 6·8-9
  Revocable and irrevocable, 6·10
  Rewarding, 6·11
  Rule Against Perpetuities, 6·11
  Rule Against Restraints on Alienation, 6·11
  Settlors, 6·8
  Shares, 12·8
  Sheltering, 6·10
  Spendthrift, 6·10
  Termination of, 6·15
  Testamentary, 6·8
  Testators, 6·8
  Trust business, 6·2
    Corporate vs. personal, 6·2-3
  Trust department management, 6·4
  Trustees
    For bondholders under indenture, 6·22
    Investment duties, 6·14-15
    Investment powers, 6·13-14
    Resignation, 6·15
  Unit or fixed, 4·26
  Voluntary, 6·8
  Voting, 13·17-18, 21·21
Turnover
  Accounts receivable, 16·10
  Bank deposits, 1·23
  Fixed asset, 17·10-11
  Inventories, 16·8, 16·10
  Merchandise, 8·36-37
  Of fixed capital, 17·10-11
  Of fixed property, 17·10
  Of net working capital, 8·38
  Owners' equity, 8·37
  Ratios, in statement analysis, 8·36-38
  Receivables, 8·36, 16·6, 16·10

U-Shaped Cost of Capital Curve, 17·73
Uncertainty and Risk, Definition, 17·75-76

Underwriting
  Compensation of underwriters, 9·18-19
  Contracts, 9·14-16
    Authorization, 9·14-15
    "Market-out" clause, 9·15-16
    Summary of, 9·16
    Types of commitments, 9·15
  Controlling persons, 9·30
  Financial proposals
    Investigation of, 9·13-14
    Sources of, 9·11-13
  Finder's fee, 9·12
  Letter of intent, 9·13
  Pricing of issues, 9·18-19
  Purchase group, 9·16-17
    Contract, 9·18
    Increasing the distributing power, 9·17
    Size and duration, 9·17
    Spreading the risk, 9·16-17
  Purchases for distribution or "investment," 9·29-30
  Sale of new issues, 9·20-21
  Securities Act of 1933, 9·27-43
  Selling group, 9·20-21
  Sources of new financing proposals, 9·11-13
  Stand-by, 9·8, 9·19
  Summary prospectus prepared by, 9·32-33
  Underwriters, definition, 9·29
Uniform Commercial Code, 13·2, 24·1
Uniform Limited Partnership Act, 12·6
Uniform Negotiable Instruments Act, 24·1
Uniform Partnership Act, 12·4
Uniform Securities Act, 9·45-50
  Antifraud provisions, 9·45
  Exemptions, 9·50-52
    Types of transactions, 9·51-52
  Investment advisory activities, 9·45-46
  Registration of broker-dealers, agents, and investment advisers, 9·46-47
  Registration of securities, 9·47-48
    By coordination, 9·48-49
    By notification, 9·48
    By qualification, 9·49-50
    Fees for, 9·49-50
Uniform Small Loan Act, 2·40
Uniform Stock Transfer Act, 13·2
Unions (See "Labor Unions")
United States
  Department of Commerce, 1·8
  Department of Treasury (See "Treasury")
  Government obligations (See "Government Obligations")
  Rule for computing interest, 24·42, 27·16
  Savings Bonds, 11·8-9
Unlisted Trading on Exchanges, 10·11-12
Usury, 24·42-44
  Criminal liability, 24·44
  Definition, 24·42-43
  Exceptions to the general rule, 24·43
  New York State Rule, 24·44
  Transactions not classified as usurious, 24·43-44
  When contract is void, 24·44
  When interest is forfeited, 24·44
Utility Companies (See "Public Utility Companies")

V.A. Loans, 2·37, 5·27, 7·7, 26·8, 26·13
Valuation
  Bank investments, 5·23-24
  Bonds, 27·45-54
  Business, cost of capital and, 17·70-73
  Capital assets, 17·24
  Consolidations and mergers, 20·24-27

Valuation (*Continued*)
  Consolidations and mergers (*Continued*)
    Accounting analysis, **20·**24
    Based on capitalized earning power, **20·**25
    Economic analysis, **20·**24
    Engineering analysis, **20·**24
    Goodwill or going concern value, **20·**26
    Market value, **20·**26
    Nonbalance sheet factors, **20·**24–25
  Fixed tangible assets, **17·**2, **17·**4
  Inventories, **8·**9, **16·**8–9
  Methods of, **20·**26–27
    Book value, **20·**26–27
    Cost less depreciation, **20·**27
    Investment value, **20·**26
    Market value, **20·**26
    Reproduction cost, **20·**27
    Substitution cost, **20·**27
  Of current assets, **20·**28
  Of funded debt, **8·**20
  Of intangible assets, **20·**28
  Of land, **8·**18
  Of marketable securities, balance sheet, **8·**6
  Of wasting assets, **17·**34–35
  Property
    Based on prospective earning power, **22·**11
    Reorganization plans, **22·**11
  Real estate, **26·**25–26
    Cost of replacement approach, **26·**26
    Income capitalization analysis, **26·**26
    Market comparison approach, **26·**26
  Reserves, **18·**7
  Stock dividends, **18·**13
  Stock subscription rights, **13·**26–28
Veterans Administration Guaranteed Mortgages, **2·**37, **5·**27, **7·**7, **26·**8, **26·**13
Volume
  Cost-volume-profit relationship, **15·**17–18
  Choosing measure of volume, **15·**19
Voluntary Associations, **12·**8
Voting
  Bonds, **14·**30
  By stockholders, **13·**13–18
  Cumulative, **13·**14–15
  Pledged stock, **14·**22–23
  Preferred stock, **13·**21
  Stock
    Common, **13·**23
    Contingent voting, **13·**15
    Cumulative voting, **13·**14–15
    Proxies, **13·**15–17
  Stockholders' meetings, **12·**26–27

Wage Earners' Plans, **22·**38–39
  Confirmation by courts, **22·**29
  Instituting the proceeding, **22·**38–39
  Petition and presentation of plan, **22·**39
Warehouse Receipts, **16·**15, **23·**16
  As collateral, **5·**30
Warranties, Negotiable instruments, **24·**21–22
Warrants
  Convertible bonds with, **14·**34–35
  Form for, **13·**27
  Option, **9·**7, **10·**18–19
  Stock purchase, **10·**18, **13·**29–30
  Stock subscription, **13·**26
"Wash Sales," **10·**52
Wasting Assets
  Depletion of, **8·**11–12, **17·**33–36
  Industries, voluntary liquidations, **21·**25
Webb-Pomerene Act Associations, **20·**46
Welfare and Pension Plans Disclosure Act, **19·**34

Welfare Plans
  Disclosure and bonding requirements, **19·**34
  Pension plans (See "Pension Plans")
When-Issued Trading, **10·**19–20
Wholesalers, Working capital ratios, **16·**22
Wills
  Functions of executor, **6·**5–6
  Intestate, **6·**6
  Probating, **6·**5
  Trusts created in, **6·**8
Wire Houses, **10·**7
Women, Retirement age, **19·**20
Working Capital, **16·**1–33
  Advantage of large contingency funds, **16·**2–3
  Analysis, **16·**16–23
    Ratios, **16·**18–23
    Statement of variation, **16·**16–18
  As investment analysis factor, **8·**30
  Budget, **16·**18
  Business expansion needs, **20·**3
  Circular flow of, **16·**3–4
  Cycle, **16·**3
  Definition of, **16·**1
  Effect of depreciation on, **17·**26
  Effect of dividend distributions upon, **18·**25–26
  Excess, **16·**2–3
  Expansion requirements of, **16·**11
  Factors affecting need for, **16·**9–12
    Commodity price changes, **16·**12
    Cyclical and secular changes, **16·**11–12
    Expansion of business, **16·**11
    Inherent hazards and contingencies, **16·**11
    Nature of business, **16·**9–10
    Period of manufacture and cost of product, **16·**10
    Seasonal variations, **16·**11
    Terms of purchase, **16·**10
    Terms of sale, **16·**10–11
    Turnover of accounts receivable, **16·**10
    Turnover of inventories, **16·**10
  Flow, **18·**26
  Inventories, **16·**7–10
  Management of, **15·**1
  Method of cash forecasting, **16·**31
  Nature of, **16·**1–4
  Net, **16·**1
    Turnover, **8·**38, **16·**19
  Plan for reorganization and, **22·**12–13
  Position, **7·**12
  Ratios, **16·**18–23
    Manufacturers, 1951–62, **16·**20–21
    Retailers, 1951–62, **16·**23
    Wholesalers, 1951–62, **16·**22
  Receivables, **16·**6–7
  Requirements, **16·**9–12
    For expansion, **15·**32
  Sources of, **16·**12–16
    Accounts receivable financing, **16·**14–15
    Bank loans, **16·**14
    Deferred payment of taxes, **16·**16
    Depreciation, **16·**16
    Financing small businesses, **16·**13
    Inventory financing, **16·**15–16
    Permanent, **16·**12–13
    Short-term borrowing, **16·**17
    Variable, **16·**13–14
  Sum needed for, **16·**12
  Turnover of net, **8·**38, **16·**19
  Types of, **16·**1–2
    Variable, **16·**1
Workmen's Compensation Laws, **25·**5
World Bank, **3·**31

LIST OF SECTIONS

Numerical

	SECTION
Interest Rates and Money Markets	1
Banking and Lending Institutions	2
International Banking	3
Savings Institutions	4
Banking Services and Procedures	5
Corporate Fiduciaries, Trusts, and Agencies	6
Security Analysis	7
Financial Reports	8
Selling Securities	9
Securities Markets	10
Government Obligations	11
Forms of Business Organization	12
Corporate Stock	13
Long-Term and Intermediate-Term Borrowing	14
Financial Planning	15
Current Asset Planning	16
Capital Asset Planning	17
Corporate Surpluses, Reserves, and Dividends	18
Pension and Profit-Sharing Plans	19
Corporate Expansion, Combination, and Cooperation	20
Recapitalizations and Readjustments	21
Reorganizations and Bankruptcy	22
Commodity Trading	23
Negotiable Instruments	24
Risk Management and Insurance	25
Real Estate Finance	26
Mathematics of Finance	27